W9-BWY-354

Brooks - Cork Library

Discarded
SSCC

Brooks - Cork Library
Shelton State
Community College

REAL ESTATE PERSPECTIVES

An Introduction to Real Estate

Third Edition

JOHN B. CORGEL, PH.D.
Cornell University

HALBERT C. SMITH, DBA, MAI, CRE
University of Florida

DAVID C. LING, PH.D.
University of Florida

Irwin
McGraw-Hill

Boston, Massachusetts   Burr Ridge, Illinois   Dubuque, Iowa
Madison, Wisconsin   New York, New York   San Francisco, California   St. Louis, Missouri

i

Brooks - Cork Library
Shelton State
Community College

Irwin/McGraw-Hill

A Division of The McGraw-Hill Companies

REAL ESTATE PERSPECTIVES: AN INTRODUCTION TO REAL ESTATE

Copyright © 1998 by The McGraw-Hill Companies, Inc. All rights reserved. Previous editions © 1987 and 1992 by Richard D. Irwin, a Times Mirror Higher Education Group, Inc., company. Printed in the United States of America. Except as permitted under the United States Copyright Act of 1976, no part of this publication may be reproduced or distributed in any form or by any means, or stored in a data base or retrieval system, without the prior written permission of the publisher.

This book is printed on acid-free paper.

1 2 3 4 5 7 8 9 0 DOC/DOC 9 0 9 8 7

ISBN 0-256-15245-4

Vice president and Editorial director: *Michael W. Junior*
Publisher: *Gary Burke*
Developmental editor: *Martin Quinn*
Senior marketing manager: *Katie Rose Matthews*
Project manager: *Karen J. Nelson*
Production supervisor: *Scott Hamilton*
Senior designer: *Crispin Prebys*
Designer: *Lucy Lesiak*
Compositor: *Shepard Poorman Communications*
Typeface: *10/12 Times Roman*
Printer: *R. R. Donnelley & Sons Company*

Library of Congress Cataloging-in-Publication Data

Corgel, John B.
    Real estate perspectives : an introduction to real estate / John
  B. Corgel, Halbert C. Smith, David C. Ling -- 3rd ed.
        p.   cm.
    Smith's name appears first on earlier editions.
    Includes index.
    ISBN 0-256-15245-4
    1. Real estate business.   2. Real Property   I. Smith, Halbert
  C., 1934– .   II. Ling, David C.   III. Title.
  HD1375.C628   1998
  333.33--dc21   97-25721

http://www.mhcollege.com

To our families for their patience and understanding during the preparation of this book

JBC
HCS
DCL

PREFACE

REAL ESTATE DECISION MAKING

Real estate is a fascinating field of study and an important component of a nation's income and wealth. It is also a complex field. The ability to make informed decisions regarding the construction, acquisition, use, and disposition of real estate usually requires the application of sophisticated analytical tools. Decisions based on back-of-the-envelope calculations are not adequate for estimating the risk and return of real estate investments and portfolios in increasingly sophisticated real estate markets.

This book is written for those seeking a clear presentation of the numerous investment decisions involved in real estate, such as whether and how to lease, buy, sell, or mortgage a property; how to analyze and predict the forces in the market that determine real estate values; whether and when to renovate, rehabilitate, or demolish a building; and when and how to divest (sell, trade, or abandon) a property. Our objective is to provide a decision-making framework that offers students an intuitive understanding of the material and, thus, the ability to analyze a broad range of real estate problems and decisions. The third edition of *Real Estate Perspectives* stands at the forefront of the trend toward greater use of information technology and quantitative decision-making tools.

As the title suggests, the text is organized according to four perspectives: Investment, Market, Mortgage Finance, and Legal. These perspectives are the predominant viewpoints real estate professional consider when analyzing and implementing important decisions. An overview of each perspective is provided in Chapter 1.

VALUE: THE UNIFYING THEME

Whether person enters the business of real estate in a direct way (e.g., development, ownership, and investment management), becomes involved in real estate service businesses (e.g., brokerage, property management, appraisal), or simply owns a home, he or she must make decisions continually about committing funds to real estate. The process followed and methods implemented for reaching these investment decisions through the process of determining their value represents the unifying theme of *Real Estate Perspectives.* Thus, in a departure from previous editions, we have moved the Investment Perspective—previously labeled the Financial Perspective—to the front of the book. Our view is that students best understand and appreciate the importance of the complex economic, social, and legal processes that affect real estate markets after they have developed an understanding of how real estate valuation and investment decisions are made.

The basic concepts developed in the Investment Perspective are used throughout the remainder of the book. This change allows for a more integrated framework for the study of real estate because all other concepts and principles of real estate analysis can be built around the valuation decision—other factors such as legal considerations, financing requirements and alternatives, and local market conditions are considered primarily in the context of how they affect the value and the rate of return on real estate. For example, real estate students and investors study growth management law and local land use regulations because they know that these rules and regulations may affect the future income-producing ability, and therefore the value, of a property. Also, the "imperfections" in real estate markets—such as the lack of adequate data, the large economic size of parcels, and the immobility of land and structures—are important primarily because of their potential effect on property rents and values.

ORGANIZATION

The four parts or perspectives of this book may be treated as four distinct modules. The order in which the parts occur in a course may be determined by the instructor, although we recommend that the Investment Perspective be covered first. This organization offers the instructor a great deal of flexibility. Not only can the remaining parts be arranged to suit the needs of the course, but after the first chapter in the part is covered, the chapters within each part can be reordered to achieve maximum educational efficiency. Some instructors may prefer to begin with Chapter 20, Real Property Rights, as an introduction to the legal foundation of investment decisions.

INTEGRATION OF GLOBAL CAPITAL MARKETS

A global capital market or portfolio viewpoint on real estate investment decisions has been integrated throughout the text to promote an understanding of the total investment process and how the process is applied to real estate. In recent years, real estate markets have become much more integrated with the general capital markets. Investors compare the risk and return available from a real estate investment with the risk and return of alternative real estate and non–real estate investments (common stocks, corporate bonds, Treasury securities, etc.), resulting in a decision process that considers a portfolio of investment alternatives. In addition, changes in capital markets, such as increases in interest rates, are quickly reflected in property values. Although tenants and landlords interact in decidedly local markets to determine rental rates, property values are increasingly being determined by the risks and returns available in national and international capital markets. Understanding the link between real estate markets and the rest of the capital markets is critical for real estate market participants.

INTENDED AUDIENCE

This text is designed and developed explicitly for a first undergraduate course in real estate, often titled Principles of Real Estate. This course usually is taught in a business school or college of architecture. The text is suitable for an introductory course in graduate real estate programs as well. The typical student will not have previously taken a course in real estate or finance, and no previous knowledge of either is assumed. Because these courses may be either part of a sequence or elective, the text is intended for majors and nonmajors alike. In terms of background or prerequisites, the book is nearly self-contained. Some familiarity with basic economics and business principles is helpful, but even these are reviewed in each part. As a result, students with different backgrounds will find the text very accessible.

PEDAGOGICAL FEATURES

- **Learning Objectives.** Each chapter begins with a set of specific learning objectives. These objectives closely align with the main ideas of the chapter. Questions at the end of the chapter support these learning objectives, reinforcing student learning of key chapter concepts.
- **Real-World Emphasis and Real Estate Focus Boxes.** A real-world focus is integrated throughout the third edition, as indicated by the List of Selected Real-World Examples immediately following the Table of Contents. This real-world flavor is also reinforced by the Real Estate Focus boxes found throughout the book. Every chapter contains two or more specific interest features that appear in a boxed format near a related concept or institutional detail in the text. Some of these Real Estate Focus boxes discuss specific property deals, others contain memorable quotes about real estate from famous people, and others tell distinctive international stories. They provide students with a real-world appreciation of chapter materials.
- *New!* **Calculator Keystrokes.** The modern financial calculator serves as a handheld, preprogrammed computer. Many of the standard financial calculations needed to analyze real estate situations can be performed with these calculators in the classroom. We present the keystrokes needed for solving these problems with financial calculators throughout the text to assist students with acquiring financial analysis skills.

- *New!* **EXCEL Tutorial.** Real estate analyses of a highly specific or advanced nature often cannot be performed with preprogrammed calculators. Solutions to these problems may be found by spreadsheet programming. Most of these problems and their solutions are beyond the scope of this book; however, we provide specific references to EXCEL applications and include a tutorial for using EXCEL in the appendix to Chapter 2 to assist students in getting started.

END-OF-CHAPTER FEATURES

- **Summary.** Every chapter ends with a concise, but thorough, summary of the important ideas—helping students review the key points and providing closure to the chapter.
- **Key Terms with Page References and Glossary.** At the end of each chapter, we present a list of key terms that students should know as part of their real estate education. Convenient page references enable students to easily look up any terms during chapter review. Also, the end-of-text Glossary includes the definitions for each key term, providing a handy resource for student mastery of key concepts.
- **Test Yourself Questions.** This end-of-chapter section includes a set of useful multiple choice questions (approximately 10 per chapter), with answers included in Appendix A. Test Yourself enables students to test themselves on the chapter content and receive instant reinforcement regarding their understanding of the material.
- *New!* **Problems for Thought and Solution.** The end-of-chapter material also includes several (approximately five) discussion-style questions entitled Problems for Thought and Solution. These questions are designed to be thought provoking and therefore provide excellent opportunities for class presentation and discussion.
- *New!* **Internet Exercises and Appendix B.** New to this edition, we introduce problems at the end of selected chapters that require Internet searches to perform the problem analysis. The use of this modern information technology is encouraged and necessary to compete in the modern real estate world. Also, Appendix B, Real Estate-Related Internet Information Sources, includes a number of Internet resources for instructor and student exploration, sorted by chapter and topic.
- **Case Problems.** In an effort to teach key concepts in the context of realistic situations, we include case problems (usually two per chapter). As with the Problems for Thought and Solution, these cases offer instructors and students valuable opportunities to build upon key real estate concepts through class discussion.

· **Additional Readings.** Because students and instructors frequently require sources for additional information about chapter topics, we present an annotated list of books, journal articles, and periodicals for further reference.

ANCILLARY FEATURES

Prepared by Dean Gatzlaff at Florida State University, the supplementary package has been completely enhanced for the third edition. Dean's success in teaching from *Real Estate Perspectives* and close collaboration with the author team ensure a well-thought-out and fully integrated package for both instructor and student.

INSTRUCTOR SUPPORT

· **Instructor's Manual/Test Bank.** Each chapter includes a list of Teaching Objectives, detailed Lecture Notes, and suggested solutions to end-of-chapter problems for Thought and Solution, Internet Exercises, and Case Problems. In addition, a Lab Problem and suggested solution is provided for each part of the text. The Test Bank offers multiple choice and true-false questions for each chapter.

· *New!* **PowerPoint Presentation System.** A series of 10 to 15 slides has been produced for each chapter, providing an overview of the fundamental material for class presentation. The slides have been developed to follow both the text and the detailed lecture notes provided in the Instructor's Manual.

STUDENT SUPPORT

· *New!* **Student Study Guide.** This valuable study resource includes chapter Learning Objectives, glossary of Key Terms, a summary of the Lecture Notes found in the Instructor's Manual, Lab Problems (included in the Instructor's Manual), and additional test questions similar to those included in the Test Bank. Space is provided on each page of the Student Study Guide to facilitate note taking and hands-on application.

· *New!* **Self-Study Software.** This Windows-based program provides students with an electronic study guide, complete with glossary terms and the test questions included in the Student Study Guide. This study tool enables students to determine which topics in the book they need to review again and reinforces the concepts learned.

· *New!* **Ready Notes.** This innovative student supplement provides students with a note-taking system that contains a reduced copy of every slide included in the PowerPoint Presentation System. There is room to take notes next to each slide, providing students with a more complete and organized method for recording lecture notes.

ACKNOWLEDGMENTS

We take this opportunity to thank all who helped us prepare the third edition of *Real Estate Perspectives.* Their comments and suggestions were invaluable to the development of the material.

Paul K. Asabere, Temple University
David Barker, University of Iowa
Donald Bleich, California State University–Northridge
Charles Delaney, Baylor University
Andrew Do, San Diego State University
Dean Gatzlaff, Florida State University
Tom G. Geurts, California State University–San Bernardino
Paul Goebel, Texas Tech University
William C. Handorf, George Washington University
Forrest Huffman, Temple University
John R. Knight, University of the Pacific
Ronald C. Rogers, University of South Carolina
Craig Stanley, California State University–Sacramento
Brenda Stuart, Kent State University
Ron Throupe, Washington State University
John C. Wolfe, Jr., University of Kentucky

This revision has also benefited from the work of the following individuals, who provided detailed comments on preliminary drafts of one or more chapters:

Michael Giliberto, J. P. Morgan
Wayne Archer, University of Florida
John Bovay, CPA, Gainesville, Florida
Gary McGill, University of Florida
Andy Naranjo, University of Florida
Tim Riddiough, MIT
Mike Ryngaert, University of Florida
Marc Smith, University of Florida
Greg Smersh, University of Florida
Dave Harrison, University of Florida

In addition to providing comments on numerous chapters, Dave Harrison, University of Florida, also helped with the development of Online Exercises, Real Estate Focus boxes, and end-of-chapter problems and solutions, as well as offering a critical eye to check the accuracy of the entire text.

We also would like to thank Dean Gatzlaff, Florida State University, for authoring the ancillary package, including the Instructor's Manual/Test Bank, PowerPoint Presentation System, Student Study Guide, Self-Study Software, and Ready Notes. We are confident that users of the book will find these ancillary materials to be first rate.

Finally, we are grateful to the talented staff at Irwin/McGraw-Hill who worked on this revision: Gina M. Huck, Senior Sponsoring Editor; Martin O. Quinn, Development Editor; Jane T. Ducham, Senior Development Editor; Katie Rose Matthews, Marketing Manager; Crispin Prebys, Senior Designer; Karen Nelson, Project Manager; Dina Genovese, Production Supervisor; and Mike Junior, Editorial Director. A special debt of gratitude goes to Gina Huck, who devoted substantial energy to this revision. We have benefited immensely from her commitment to the book.

Reader comments have helped to improve past editions. We welcome any comments and suggestions that may enhance the book. Please send them to us either via Irwin/McGraw-Hill, c/o Editorial, or at our addresses noted below:

John (Jack) B. Corgel, Ph.D.
School of Hotel Administration
Cornell University
Ithaca, New York 14853
Phone (607)255–4305 Fax (607)255–4179   E-mail: jc81@cornell.edu

Halbert C. Smith, DBA, CRE, MAI
Warrington College of Business Administration
Department of Finance, Insurance, and Real Estate
University of Florida
P.O. Box 117168
Gainesville, FL 32611–7168
Phone (352)392–9249 Fax (352)392–0301   E-mail: hsmith@dale.cba.ufl.edu

David C. Ling, Ph.D.
Warrington College of Business Administration
Department of Finance, Insurance, and Real Estate
University of Florida
P.O. Box 117168
Gainesville, FL 32611–7168
Phone (352)392–9307   Fax (352) 392–0301   E-mail: ling@dale.cba.ufl.edu

JBC
HCS
DCL

ABOUT THE AUTHORS

JOHN (JACK) B. CORGEL

Professor Jack Corgel has been a member of the Cornell Hotel School faculty since 1989. He served as the first Director of the Center of Hospitality Research from 1992 to 1994. After receiving undergraduate and Ph.D. (1979) degrees from the University of Georgia in real estate and corporate finance, he taught at the University of Florida, Georgia State University, and the University of Connecticut. During the academic year 1985–1986, he was a visiting scholar at the Federal Home Loan Bank Board in Washington, DC. He is a Fellow of the Homer Hoyt Institute.

Professor Corgel has published over 50 articles in academic and professional journals, mainly on the subjects of real estate finance, investment, valuation, and hospitality real estate. He has published articles in the most prestigious journals in real estate (*Real Estate Economics*), urban economics (*Journal of Urban Economics*), insurance (*Journal of Risk and Insurance*), business law (*Journal of the American Business Law Association*), and Hospitality (*International Journal of Hospitality Management*). In addition, he has written for nearly every national journal read by real estate and hospitality industry professionals.

Professor Corgel devotes considerable time to the development of real estate price indexes and return indexes. He helped create the first rate of return index for lodging property investment called the *Lodging Property Index*. His other research interests include REIT valuation, the value of franchising, real estate price dispersion, and return unsmoothing models.

HALBERT C. SMITH

Halbert C. Smith is a professor in the Department of Finance, Insurance, and Real Estate in the Warrington College of Business Administration and the Graduate School of Business at the University of Florida. He has also served as Chairman of the Department and was the founding Director of the Real Estate Research Center. He received his BS degree from Purdue University, his MBA from Indiana University, and his DBA from the University of Illinois. Smith has served on the faculties of several U.S. universities, and in 1995 was named a Fellow of the International Center for Economic Research in Turin, Italy. Also he has served as a Visiting Professor at the Bocconi Graduate School of Business in Milan and at the Polytechnic University of Turin in the Faculty of Architecture.

Professor Smith is also a director and officer of the Homer Hoyt Institute and affiliated organizations. He was a founding member of the American Real Estate and Urban Economics Association, and in 1970 he served as President of AREUEA. In the early 1970s he served as Chief Economist of the Federal Home Loan Bank Board in Washington, DC, and later served on the boards of directors of several financial institutions. He is Editor-in-Chief of *Real Estate Issues* and has served on the editorial boards of several other academic and professional journals. He is a Fellow of the American Real Estate Society and serves as a member of several committees and the Board of Directors of the Counselors of Real Estate.

Professor Smith is the author of numerous articles in professional and academic journals and several other books dealing with real estate subjects. He was the first recipient (1985) of the George Bloom Award of the American Real Estate and Urban Economics Association for "outstanding contributions to real estate research and analysis and to the work of AREUEA," and in 1990 he received the Alfred E. Reinman, Jr., Distinguished Service Award of the Society of Real Estate Appraisers "for outstanding contributions to the growth and development of the appraisal profession." Dr. Smith also is an honorary member of the Associazione Italiana Consulenti Immobilari (Italian Association of Real Estate Counselors).

DAVID C. LING

Professor Ling is the William D. Hussey Professor of Real Estate and the Director of the Real Estate Research Center in the Warrington College of Business Administration and Graduate School of Business at the University of Florida. His publications have been in the areas of real estate investments, mortgage markets, housing markets, home ownership, and tax policy.

Professor Ling serves on numerous editorial boards including the *Journal of Housing Economics, Real Estate Economics, The Journal of Real Estate Research,* and *Real Estate Finance.* He has provided research and consulting services to several state and national organizations including the Federal National Mortgage Association, the National Association of Home Builders, the National Association of Realtors, and the Florida Association of Realtors. Professor Ling is a Fellow of the Homer Hoyt Institute and board member of the Real Estate Research Institute.

Professor Ling received an MBA (1977) in finance and a Ph.D. (1984) in real estate and finance from The Ohio State University. Prior to moving to the University of Florida in 1989, Ling was a professor of real estate at Southern Methodist University and a visiting economist at the National Association of Home Builders (1984).

CONTENTS IN BRIEF

1 Real Estate Perspectives   2

PART I

INVESTMENT PERSPECTIVE   22

    2 Basic Valuation Concepts   24
       Appendix 2a: Applying Time Value of Money
           Concepts to Real Estate   57
       Appendix 2b: Solving Time Value of Money
           Problems Using Excel   61
    3 Investment Decision Making   72
    4 Federal Income Taxation   106
    5 Forms of Ownership   146
    6 Property Types   172
    7 Risk and Real Estate Investment   190
    8 Management of the Space and Assets   224

PART II

MARKET PERSPECTIVE   260

    9 Real Estate Markets   262
   10 Land Use, Planning, Zoning, and Environmental
       Hazards   294
   11 Market and Feasibility Analysis   324
   12 Introduction to Development   354
   13 Valuation by the Sales Comparison and Cost
       Approaches   374
   14 Valuation by Income Capitalization   410

PART III

MORTGAGE FINANCE PERSPECTIVE   438

   15 Creation of Mortgages   440
   16 Residential Mortgage Types and Borrower
       Decisions   468
   17 Sources of Funds for Residential
       Mortgages   504
   18 Commercial Property Financing   534
   19 Mortgage-Backed Securities   572

P A R T   I V

L E G A L   P E R S P E C T I V E   612

20 Real Property Rights   614
21 Real Property Taxation   640
22 Transfer of Real Property Rights   662
23 Real Estate Brokerage and Listing
Contracts   688
24 Contracts for Sale and Closing   720

APPENDIX A Answers to Test Yourself Questions   756
APPENDIX B Real Estate–Related Internet Information Sources   757

GLOSSARY   G–1
INDEX   I–1

CONTENTS

1 Real Estate Perspectives: An Introduction to Real Estate 2

THE VALUE OF SPACE 3

THE DISCIPLINE OF REAL ESTATE 5
Classical Land Economics 5
The Neoclassical Tradition Is Still Followed Today 5
Ideas about Property Rights and Contracts 9
Financial Economics 9
The Institutions 10

REAL ESTATE IN THE WORLD ECONOMY 11
The Relative Wealth of Real Estate 11

Investments to Improve Land 12
Who Owns America? 13

REAL ESTATE DEFINED 16
The Importance of Value 16

REAL ESTATE PERSPECTIVES: AN OVERVIEW OF THE BOOK 17
Investment Perspective 17
Market Perspective 18
Mortgage Finance Perspective 19
Legal Perspective 19

PART I

INVESTMENT PERSPECTIVE

2 Basic Valuation Concepts 24

VALUE: THE CENTRAL IDEA 25

SOME BASIC CONCEPTS 26
What Is Real Estate Valuation? 26
The Trade-Off between Return and Risk 27
How Are Decisions Made? 27

TIME VALUE OF MONEY 28
Definitions 28
Equations, Tables, Calculators, and Spreadsheets 30

Six Time-Value-of-Money Operations 35
Loan Amortization 43

INVESTMENT ANALYSIS 46
Present-Value Measures 46
Yield Measures 48

CAPITALIZATION RATE INTRODUCED 52

APPENDIX 2a *Applying Time-Value-of-Money Concepts to Real Estate* 57

APPENDIX 2b *Solving Time-Value-of-Money Problems Using EXCEL* 61

3 Investment Decision Making 70

INVESTMENT DECISIONS 71

REAL ESTATE INVESTMENT ANALYSIS 72
Investment Strategies 72

CHARACTERISTICS OF INCOME PROPERTY INVESTMENTS 74
Property Type 74
Rental Income 75
Purchasers as Investors 75
Geographic Scope 75

FORECASTING CASH FLOWS FROM OPERATIONS 76
Potential Gross Income 76
Effective Gross Income 78
Operating Expenses 79
Net Operating Income 79
The Treatment of Nonrecurring Expenses 80
Evaluating the Cash Flow Estimates 81

FORECASTING CASH PROCEEDS FROM SALE 81

MEASURING VALUE AND RETURNS 82
Valuation Using Discounted Cash Flow Models 82
Valuation Using Simple Income Capitalization 87
Why Discount Rates Determine Capitalization Rates 88

THE EFFECTS OF MORTGAGE FINANCING ON CASH FLOWS, VALUES, AND RETURNS 88
Effect of Debt on Projected Cash Flows 88
Why Do Investors Borrow? 90

OTHER INVESTMENT CRITERIA 92
Profitability Ratios 92
Multipliers 93
Financial Ratios 94
Limitations of Ratio Analysis 96
Varying the Assumptions 98

4 Federal Income Taxation 106

INTRODUCTION 107
Objectives and Implementation of U.S. Tax Law 108

FOUR CLASSES OF REAL PROPERTY 108

FORMS OF OWNERSHIP 110

INCOME SUBJECT TO TAXATION 111
Types of Income 111

TAX RATES 112
Marginal versus Average Tax Rates 113
Generalized Income Tax Calculation 115
Example Using Federal Tax Forms 116

SIGNIFICANCE OF PASSIVE ACTIVITY LOSS RESTRICTIONS 120

FORECASTING TAXABLE INCOME FROM OPERATIONS 122
Cash Calculation versus Tax Calculation 123
Costs of Mortgage Financing 123
Depreciation Deductions 124
Tax Credits 128
Suburban Office Building Example 129
What Is Tax Shelter? 130

FORECASTING TAXABLE INCOME FROM SALE 132
Outright Sale 132
Suburban Office Building Example 133
Net Benefits of Tax Depreciation 134
Effect of Taxes on Values and Returns 135
Ordinary versus Capital Gain Income 136

METHODS OF DEFERRING TAXES ON DISPOSITION 138
Installment Sale 138
Like-Kind Exchanges 138

5 Forms of Ownership 146

INTRODUCTION 147

SOLE OWNERSHIP 147

C CORPORATION 148

S CORPORATION 149

GENERAL PARTNERSHIP 150

LIMITED PARTNERSHIPS 151

REAL ESTATE INVESTMENT TRUST 151

LIMITED LIABILITY COMPANY 152

COMPARING OWNERSHIP FORMS 153

A CLOSER LOOK AT LIMITED PARTNERSHIP SYNDICATIONS 154
Types of Real Estate Syndicates 155
Historical and Current Business Environment 156
The Role of the Syndicator 158
Regulation 159

A CLOSER LOOK AT REAL ESTATE INVESTMENT TRUSTS 159

SOURCES OF COMMERCIAL REAL ESTATE EQUITY CAPITAL 161
Private Real Estate Markets 161
Public Real Estate Markets 165

THE RETURN PERFORMANCE OF PUBLIC AND PRIVATE REAL ESTATE 165
Appraisal-Based Index of Historical Unsecuritized Returns 165
REIT-Based Index of Historical Securitized Returns 166
Historical Returns 167

6 Property Types 172

INTRODUCTION 173

RESIDENTIAL RENTAL PROPERTY 173
Some Definitions 173
The Demand for Rental Housing 174
Investment Prospects 175

OFFICE BUILDINGS 176

INDUSTRIAL PROPERTIES 180

SHOPPING CENTERS AND OTHER REAL ESTATE ESTABLISHMENTS 181

OTHER TYPES OF REAL ESTATE 185
Hospitality Properties 185
Undeveloped Land 185
Senior Housing and Continuing Care Facilities 187

7 Risk and Real Estate Investment 190

INTRODUCTION 191

THE CONCEPT OF VARIABILITY 192

SPECIFICATION OF RISK PREFERENCES 195

MEASURING PROJECT-SPECIFIC RISK 197
Variance and Standard Deviation 197
Coefficient of Variation 199
The Use of Subjective Probabilities 200

RISK MANAGEMENT 201
Avoiding Risky Projects 201
Insurance and Hedging 201
Diversification as a Risk-Management Tool 202

THE PORTFOLIO CONCEPT OF RISK 203
Diversifiable Portfolio Risk 203
Covariance and Correlation 205
Examples of Diversifiable Risk 207
Basic Real Estate Diversification Strategies 208
Nondiversifiable Risk 209

CHOOSING AN OPTIMAL PORTFOLIO 209
Why Are So Many Investors Not Well-Diversified? 211

HOW RISKY IS REAL ESTATE? 212
Historical Returns, Risk, and Correlations 212

ACCOUNTING FOR RISK IN VALUATION DECISIONS 215
Risk-Adjusted Discount Rate 215

Quantifying Required Risk Premiums with Asset-Pricing
    Models   217
Sensitivity Analysis   218

8   Management of Space and Assets   224

THE IMPORTANCE OF REAL ESTATE MANAGEMENT   225
Management Responsibilities and Relationships   226

THE VALUE PERSPECTIVE OF MANAGEMENT   228
Creating Cash Flow   229
Maintaining Cash Flow   232
Cash Flow Risk   235

CONTRACTS INVOLVED IN MANAGING SPACE AND ASSETS   236
Management Contracts: Separating Ownership and
    Management   237
The Nature of Leases   240
Residential Leases   242
Commercial Property Leases   246
Specific Lease Contracts   249
Lease Economics: A Value Perspective   250

SPECIAL TOPIC: CORPORATE REAL ESTATE MANAGEMENT   252
Sale-and-Leaseback Decisions   253
The Lease versus Own Decision   254

PART   II

MARKET PERSPECTIVE

9   Real Estate Markets   262

LOCATION MAKES MARKETS "IMPERFECT, IMPERFECT, IMPERFECT"   263
No Arbitrage!   265
Location Theory   266
Residential Location Decisions   268
Commercial and Industrial Firm Location Decisions   269

HOW THE SPACE MARKET OPERATES   272
Funcations of the Space Market   272
Supply and Demand Model with Vacancy   274
Natural Vacancy   274
Factors Influencing Supply and Demand   275
Rents   275

SPACE AND ASSET MARKET INTERACTION   278
The Economic Fundamentals Matter!   279
Government Influences   279

Do the Individuals Matter?   281
The Psychology of Real Estate Markets   283

THE ASSET MARKET   284
Who Participates?   285
Asset Price and Values   286
Replacement Cost and Values   287
"Noisy" Prices   287
Interaction with the Securitized Market   288

10   Land Use, Planning, Zoning, and Environmental Hazards   294

DETERMINING LAND USE   295
The Market Solution   296
Externalities   297

PRIVATE RESTRICTIONS   297

PUBLIC PLANNING FOR LAND-USE CONTROL 300
Development of a Comprehensive Plan 300
Innovation and Flexibility in Comprehensive Planning 303
Implementation and Review of the Comprehensive Plan 304

PUBLIC ZONING FOR LAND-USE CONTROL 304
Purpose of Zoning 304
Legality of Zoning 305
Zoning Administration 308

INCONSISTENCIES WITH PRIVATE MARKET OUTCOMES 310
Impact on Property Values 310
Transferable Development Rights 310
Growth Management 313

ENVIRONMENTAL HAZARDS 314
Governmental Regulation 314
Types of Hazardous Materials 315
Implications for Real Estate Investors 317

11 Market and Feasibility Analysis 324

IMPORTANCE OF MARKET AND FEASIBILITY ANALYSIS 325

TYPES OF MARKET AND FEASABILITY STUDIES 327
General Market Studies 328
Site-Specific Market Studies 331
Feasibility Studies 335

THE PROCESS OF MARKET ANALYSIS 337
Step 1: Define the Problem 337
Step 2: Evaluate Project Constraints 337
Step 3: Delineate the Market Area or Areas 338
Step 4: Estimate Demand for the Project 338
Step 5: Establish Supply Conditions in the Market 344
Step 6: Correlate Supply and Demand and Make Recommendations 345

GEOGRAPHIC INFORMATION SYSTEMS 346

12 Introduction to Development 354

THE CREATION OF REAL ESTATE 355
Development and Construction Businesses 355
Relationships with Consumers and the Public 356
Formation of Development Teams 357

THE DEVELOPMENT PROCESS 360
First Stage: The Idea 360
Second Stage: The Site 361
Third Stage: Feasibility 361
Fourth Stage: The Contracts and Approvals 362
Fifth Stage: The Improvements 363
Sixth Stage: On to the Next Project 365

ECONOMIC FEASIBILITY: A VALUE PERSPECTIVE 365
Market Equilibrium and Disequilibrium 365
Economic Feasibility of an Office Building Development 366

13 Valuation by the Sales Comparison and Cost Approaches 374

ROLE OF THE SALES COMPARISON AND COST APPROACHES 375

TRADITIONAL SALES COMPARISON APPROACH 376
Adjustments 376
Subject Property Compared to Each Comparable Property 382
Types of Adjustments 382
Sequence of Adjustments 382
Reconciliation 384

MULTIPLE REGRESSION MODELS 384

COST APPROACH 388
Cost 389
Accrued Depreciation 389

GROSS RENT MULTIPLIER 393

APPLICABILITY OF THE APPROACHES 395

CASE PROBLEM *Single-Family Residential
Appraisal* 399

14 Valuation by Income Capitalization 410

**INCOME CAPITALIZATION RELATED TO
THE DCF MODEL** 411

FUNDAMENTAL EQUATION 412

INCOME 412
Reserve for Replacements and Other Nonrecurring
  Expenses 413

CAPITALIZATION RATES 414
Overall Capitalization Rate 415
Several Methods, But Only One R_o 420

DISCOUNT RATES 421

**SEPARATE BUILDING AND LAND
VALUATION** 422
Estimating *g* for Buildings 422
Estimating a Building's Depreciation Rate 423
Estimating *g* for Sites 425
Allocating NOI between Building and Site 426

OTHER APPROACHES 427
Gross Income Multiplier 427
Cost Approach 428

RECONCILIATION 428

THE APPRAISAL PROFESSION 429

**REGULATION OF THE APPRAISAL
PROFESSION** 430

**PROFESSIONAL ORGANIZATIONS AND
DESIGNATIONS** 431

APPRAISAL AS A CAREER 432

P A R T   I I I

MORTGAGE FINANCE PERSPECTIVE

15 Creation of Mortgages 440

MORTGAGES 441
International Perspectives of Mortgage Finance 442
The Story of a Mortgage 444
Mortgage Theory 445

CAPITAL FLOW TO MORTGAGES 448
The Four Quadrants of Real Estate Finance 448
Integration of Capital and Mortgage Markets 449

**MORTGAGE BORROWER AND LENDER
RELATIONSHIPS** 449
Extensions of the Simple Mortgage Contract 450
Single-Family Residential Mortgages 453
Income-Property Mortgages 455

**CLAUSES FOUND IN MORTGAGE
DOCUMENTS** 456
Requirements of a Valid and Enforceable Mortgage 457
Common Mortgage Clauses 457
Residential Mortgage Documents 458
Important Clauses in Various Income-Property
  Mortgages 460

**ADJUSTMENTS IN BORROWER AND LENDER
RELATIONSHIPS** 461
Satisfactory Payment in Full 461
Default and Foreclosure 461
Assumption and "Subject to" Transactions 463
Recasting the Mortgage 463
Sale of the Mortgage 463

16 Residential Mortgage Types and Borrower Decisions 468

INTRODUCTION 469
Primary versus Secondary Mortgage Market 470

CONVENTIONAL FIXED-PAYMENT MORTGAGE LOANS 471
Fixed-Payment, Fully Amortizing Mortgages 472
Alternative Amortization Schedules 474

ADJUSTABLE RATE MORTGAGES 476
ARM Mechanics 477
Rate Caps and Other Options 479

PRIVATE MORTGAGE INSURANCE 481

OTHER MORTGAGE TYPES AND USES 482
Purchase Money Mortgages 482
Interest Rate Buydowns and Concessions 483
Package Mortgages 484
Reverse Annuity Mortgages 484
Graduated Payment Mortgages 487
Home Equity Loans 487

THE BORROWER'S MORTGAGE LOAN DECISIONS 489
Mortgage Choice 490
Loan Size 494
The Refinancing Decision 495
The Default Decision 497

17 Sources of Funds for Residential Mortgages 504

INTRODUCTION 505

THE MARKET FOR RESIDENTIAL FINANCING 506

DEPOSITORY LENDERS IN THE PRIMARY MARKET 506
Savings Institutions 507
Commercial Banks 509

NONDEPOSITORY LENDERS IN THE PRIMARY MARKET 510
Mortgage Bankers 511
Mortgage Brokers 514
Other Nongovernment-Sponsored Lenders in the Primary Market 515

GOVERNMENT-SPONSORED MORTGAGE PROGRAMS 515
FHA-Insured Loans 516
VA-Guaranteed Loans 518

THE SECONDARY MARKET FOR RESIDENTIAL MORTGAGES 518

PURCHASERS OF RESIDENTIAL MORTGAGES IN THE SECONDARY MARKET 519
Federal National Mortgage Association 519
Federal Home Loan Mortgage Corporation 521
The Importance of Fannie Mae and Freddie Mac 521
Government National Mortgage Association 522
Life Insurance Companies 523
Other Secondary Market Purchasers 523

THE LENDER'S MORTGAGE LOAN DECISIONS 524
Affordability Ratios 525
The Effects of Federal Programs and Regulations 527

18 Commercial Property Financing 534

INTRODUCTION 535

SOURCES OF FINANCING FOR COMMERCIAL PROPERTIES 536

LOAN DOCUMENTS AND PROVISIONS 538
The Note 538
The Mortgage 539

COMMON TYPES OF PERMANENT MORTGAGES 539
Balloon Mortgages 539
Common Loan Provisions 540
Floating-Rate Loans 541
Installment Sale Financing 541

PERMANENT MORTGAGES WITH EQUITY PARTICIPATION 542
Participation Mortgages 542
Joint Ventures 545
Sale-Leasebacks 545
Convertible Mortgages 546

THE BORROWER'S DECISION-MAKING PROCESS 546
Loan Size 548
Financial Risk 548
Increased Variability of Equity Returns from Leverage 548
Choosing among Alternative Financing Structures 551
The Prepayment and Default Decisions 554

REQUESTING A PERMANENT LOAN 554
Loan Submissions Package 554
Channels of Submissions 557

THE LENDER'S DECISION-MAKING PROCESS 557
The Property and Borrower 558
Maximum Loan Amount 559
The Economic Justification 560

ACQUISITION, DEVELOPMENT, AND CONSTRUCTION FINANCING 560
Land Purchase and Development Financing 561
Construction Financing 562
Sequence of Financing 564

19 Mortgage-Backed Securities 572

INTRODUCTION 573

MORTGAGE SECURITIZATION 573
The Importance of Securitization 574
Securitization and Secondary Markets 574

VALUING INDIVIDUAL MORTGAGES IN THE SECONDARY MARKET 575
Yield-to-Maturity 575
Expected Yield 577
Realized Yield 578
How Are Mortgage Investment Decisions Made? 579

PASSTHROUGH SECURITIES 580
Passthrough Example 582
Agency Passthroughs 584
Conventional Passthroughs 587

SEQUENTIAL PAY STRUCTURES 588
Sequential Pay Example 590
Other Responses to Prepayment Risk 590

VALUING MORTGAGE-BACKED SECURITIES 592

THE COMMERCIAL MORTGAGE-BACKED SECURITIES MARKET 594
Sources of Public Debt for Commercial-Property Investment 594
Brief History of CMBSs 594
Differences between Residential MBSs and CMBSs 595

HOW COMMERCIAL MORTGAGE SECURITIZATION OCCURS 596
Portfolio Refinancing 597
Conduit Arrangements 598
Direct Lending by Investment Banks 598

THE ROLE OF THE RATING AGENCIES 599
Agencies that Rate CMBS Issues 599
Qualitative Review 602
Quantitative Review 602
Credit Enhancement 602

THE SECURITIES 603
Structuring CMBS Issues 604
Valuation: The Price and Yield Relationship 604

PART IV

LEGAL PERSPECTIVE

20 Real Property Rights 614

INTRODUCTION TO REAL PROPERTY RIGHTS 615
Physical Property Rights to Real Estate 616
Real versus Personal Property Rights: The Problem of Fixtures 617
Legal Property Rights of Real Estate Ownership 619
Property Rights: A Value Perspective 620

ESTATES IN REAL ESTATE 621
Freehold Estates 621
Nonfreehold Estates 625

PROPERTY RIGHTS AMONG CO-OWNERS: CONCURRENT ESTATES 626
Direct Co-Ownership Forms 626
Indirect Co-Ownership Forms 629

PUBLIC AND PRIVATE LIMITS ON PROPERTY RIGHTS 631
Government's Role in Determining Property Rights 631
Private Contracts and Other Methods of Limiting Property Rights 633

21 Real Property Taxation 640

NATURE OF THE TAX ON REAL PROPERTY 641

A BRIEF HISTORY OF THE PROPERTY TAX IN THE UNITED STATES 643

MECHANICS OF THE PROPERTY TAX 644
Determining a Jurisdiction's Budget and Tax Rate 644
Tax-Exempt Properties 646

Homestead and Other Exemptions 646
Calculating Tax Liability 647
The Effective Tax Rate 647
Evaluating the Tax on an Individual Property 648
Special Assessments 648
Nonpayment of Taxes 649

CRITERIA FOR EVALUATING THE PROPERTY TAX 650
Efficiency of the Property Tax 651
Potential Disadvantages of the Property Tax 651
Fairness, or Equity, of the Property Tax 653

22 Transfer of Real Property Rights 662

THE IMPORTANCE OF REAL PROPERTY TRANSFER 663

EVIDENCE AND CONVEYANCE OF OWNERSHIP 663
Titles 664
Evidence of Good Title 665
Deeds in Private Grants of Title 667
Public Grants of Title to Real Estate 669
Devise and Descent 669
Foreclosure 670
Adverse Possession and Prescription 670
Title from Nature 671

CONTRACTS FOR TRANSFER OF REAL PROPERTY RIGHTS 671
Validity and Enforceability of Contracts 671
General Categories of Contracts 672
Contract Law: A Value Perspective 672
The Four Basic Contracts 673

PROPER DESCRIPTIONS OF REAL PROPERTY 674

Surveys   675
Metes and Bounds   675
Recorded Plat Map   677
Government Survey System   679

23   Real Estate Brokerage and Listing Contracts   688

BROKERAGE: THE BEST-KNOWN TYPE OF REAL ESTATE BUSINESS   689
Real Estate Brokers as Market Facilitators   689
Economic Rationale for Employing a Broker   690

LAW OF AGENCY   691
Types of Agents   692
Fiduciary Responsibilities   692
Real Estate Agents   693
Transaction Brokers   693
Salespersons as Subagents   694

LICENSING OF REAL ESTATE BROKERS AND SALESPERSONS   695
Brokerage Licensing Administration   695
How to Obtain a Real Estate License   696
License Law Infractions   697

CERTIFICATION OF REAL ESTATE OCCUPATIONS   698

THE MARKETING FUNCTION   698
Market Segmentation and Specialization   698
Service   699
Commercial Brokerage   699
Residential Brokerage   700
International Aspects of Brokerage   701

LISTING CONTRACTS   702

TYPES OF LISTING CONTRACTS   703
Open Listing   703
Net Listing   704
Exclusive Agency Listing   704
Exclusive Right of Sale Listing   705

LISTING CONTRACT PROVISIONS   705
Protective Provisions for Property Owners   707

Protective Provisions for the Broker   707
Termination   709
Splitting the Commission   710

CHOOSING A REAL ESTATE BROKER   710

LISTING SITUATION—EXAMPLE   711

24   Contracts for Sale and Closing   720

THE MOST IMPORTANT DOCUMENT IN REAL ESTATE   721

RIGHTS AND OBLIGATIONS OF SELLERS AND BUYERS   722
Rights and Obligations of Sellers   722
Rights and Obligations of Buyers   723

REQUIREMENTS OF A CONTRACT FOR SALE   723
The Parties Must Be Competent to Act   724
The Parties Must Have Lawful Intent   724
There Must Be an Offer and an Acceptance   724
There Must Be Consideration   725
There Must Be No Defects to Mutual Asset   725
The Contract for Sale of Real Estate Must Be in Writing   726
The Property Must Be Properly Described   726

TITLE   727
Legal Title   727
Equitable Title   727

THE FORM OF THE CONTRACT FOR SALE   728
Simple Contract   728
Standard Form Contracts   729
Components of a Form Contract   730
Estimated Closing Expense Statements   735

CONTINUING SAGA OF A SALE   735

CONTRACTS WITH CONTINGENCIES   738

ASSIGNMENT   738

REMEDIES FOR NONPERFORMANCE 740
Remedies for a Seller 740
Remedies for a Buyer 740
Escrow 741

CLOSING 741
Steps Before Closing 741
Steps at Closing 743
Prorations 743
Buyers' Expenses 744
Sellers' Expenses 745

CLOSING AND CLOSING STATEMENTS 745
Role of the Brokers 746
Role of the Lender 747
Real Estate Settlement Procedures Act 747
Preparation of Closing Statements 748

A P P E N D I X A

Answers to Test Yourself Questions 756

A P P E N D I X B

Real Estate–Related Internet Information Sources 757

GLOSSARY G-1

INDEX I-1

LIST OF SELECTED
REAL-WORLD EXAMPLES

1 Real Estate Perspectives

Advertisement, "Space Available," Exhibit 1–1   4

Graduate Degree Programs in the United States, Real Estate Focus 1–1   7

Real Estate Relative to Worldwide Wealth in 1991, Exhibit 1–3   12

Construction Activity in the United States by Property Type from 1985 through 1995, Exhibit 1–4   13

Salary Information for Real Estate Positions, Real Estate Focus 1–2   14

Donald Trump on Investment, Real Estate Focus 1–3   17

2 Basic Valuation Concepts

How Investment Decisions Are Made   29

Using Table Factors and Calculators: 31

   Future Value of a Lump Sum Investment   31

   Future Value of an Annuity   31

   Required Sinking Fund Amount   31

   Present Value of a Future Lump Sum Payment   31

   Present Value of an Annuity   31

   Required Periodic Mortgage Payment   31

Loan Amortization Schedule   44

Net Present Value of Two Investment Opportunities   48

Internal Rate of Return on Two Investment Opportunities   49

Effective Borrowing Cost of a Mortgage   51

Tutorial on Time-Value-of-Money Concepts, Appendix A   57

Solving Time-Value-of-Money Problems Using EXCEL, Appendix B   61

3 Investment Decision Making

The Investment Objectives of Prudential Property Investment Separate Account   73

Suburban Office Building Example of Discounted Cash Flow Analysis, ongoing throughout chapter   82

Using Net Present Value to Make Acquisition Decision   85

Using the Internal Rate of Return to Make Acquisition Decision   86

The Effects of Mortgage Financing on Cash Flows, Values, and Returns, ongoing Suburban Office Building example   88

Using Profitability Ratios, Multipliers, and Financial Ratios in the Decision-Making Process, ongoing Suburban Office Building example   92

4 Federal Income Taxation

Tax Rate Schedules for Single and Married Taxpayers   113

Federal Income Tax Calculations for Ms. Judy Long   117

Forecasting Taxable Income from Operations, ongoing Suburban Office Building example   129

Forecasting Taxable Income from Property Sales, ongoing Suburban Office Building example   133

Effects of Income Taxes on Value and Returns, ongoing Suburban Office Building example   135

5 Forms of Ownership

Creating Value through Strategic Real Estate Plans, Real Estate Focus 5–1   149

Real Estate Partnerships Begin Comeback, Real Estate Focus 5–2   157

The Development of Information Standards Is Attracting
  Capital to Real Estate Markets, Real Estate Focus 5-3   163
Sales of U.S. Real Estate by Japanese Investors in the 1990s,
  Real Estate Focus 5-4   164
Historical Returns on Private Real Estate   165
Historical Returns on REITs   166

6   Property Types

GM Hunts for Cheap Office Space, Real Estate
  Focus 6-1   178
Trends in Industrial Warehouse Design, Real Estate
  Focus 6-2   180
Characteristics of Shopping Centers   183
Malls Add Fun and Games to Attract Shoppers, Real Estate
  Focus 6-3   184
The Legendary Waldorf-Astoria Hotel, Real Estate
  Focus 6-4   186

7   Risk and Real Estate Investment

Diversification   202
Mean and Standard Deviation of Shopping Center
  Investment   206
Geographic Diversification   208
Portfolio Return and Risk   210
Historical Returns on Real Estate, Stocks, and Bonds   213
Required Rates of Return on Real Estate   217
Sensitivity Analysis   219

8   Management of the Space and Assets

Asset Management Decision Making for Two Chicago Retail
  Centers   226
The Top 10 Property Managers in the United States, 1994,
  Exhibit 8-3   229
A Real Estate Company's (Landmarks Group) Thematic
  Image, Real Estate Focus 8-1   233
Property Losses due to the Great Chicago Flood, 1993   236
Poor Risk Management at the Stouffers-Westchester Hotel
  Fire, 1980   236

Drug testing as a Requirement for Apartment Rental, Real
  Estate Focus 8-3   249
Land Lease for the Empire State Building   250
A Lease-versus-Own Decision   254

9   Real Estate Markets

Donald Trump on the Importance of Location, Real Estate
  Focus 9-1   265
Locations of United States Cities   271
Real Estate Market Changes during the 1996 Olympics in
  Atlanta   273
Overview of the Emerging Real Estate Market in China, Real
  Estate Focus 9-3   280
Real Estate Auctions, Real Estate Focus 9-4   285
The Relationship between Market Prices and Replacement
  Costs of Lodging Properties from 1986 through 1994,
  Exhibit 9-11   288

10   Land Use, Planning, Zoning, and Environmental Hazards

Private Restrictions, Exhibit 10-1   298
Court Decision Upholding the Right of Communities to
  Control Land Use through Police Power, Real Estate
  Focus 10-1   302
Landmark Case on the Legality of Land-Use Control and
  Zoning Regulations, Real Estate Focus 10-2   305
Two Cases Indicating a Shift toward Protection of Property
  Rights, Real Estate Focus 10-3   307
Typical Provisions of Growth Management Laws   313
Types of Environmental Hazards   315

11   Market and Feasibility Analysis

A Major Error of Market Analysis—Euro Disney, Real Estate
  Focus 11-1   326
Problems that Can Occur When an Owner-Developer Ignores
  the Findings of Market Analysis, Real Estate
  Focus 11-2   327

The Housing Element in the Comprehensive Plan for
Jacksonville, Florida, Exhibit 11–2   330

Conversion of a New York Landmark into a New Highest and
Best Use, Real Estate Focus 11–3   334

Feasibility Analysis for Residential Lots on a 40-Acre Site,
Exhibit 11–7   336

Location Quotients for Seattle, Washington,
Exhibit 11–9   341

Geographic Information Systems Analysis for Columbia, SC,
Exhibit 11–12   347

12   Introduction to Real Estate Development

Donald Trump on the Development Business, Real Estate
Focus 12–1   356

A Current Development Concept that Comes from an Old
Idea, Real Estate Focus 12–2   363

Development Projects Completed by the Famous Developer
John Portman, Real Estate Focus 12–3   364

Degree Programs that Concentrate on Real Estate
Development, Real Estate Focus 12–4   369

13   Valuation by the Sales Comparison and Cost Approaches

Multiple Regression Analysis for the Estimation of Apartment
Rents in Louisville, Kentucky,
Exhibits 13–10 and 13–11   387 and 388

Application of the Traditional Approaches to the Appraisal of
a Residential Property, Case Problem   399

14   Valuation by Income Capitalization

Capitalization Rates from 1981–1997, Real Estate
Focus 14–1   416

Relationship between Risk and Discount Rates,
Exhibit 14–4   422

Typical Economic Lives of Income Properties,
Exhibit 14–5   424

Typical Units of Comparison Used in Valuing Income
Properties, Real Estate Focus 14–2   428

Professional Appraisal Organizations and the Designations
They Award, Exhibit 14–10   431

General Requirements for Obtaining the MAI and SRA
Professional Appraisal Designations   431

15   Creation of Mortgages

Schoolchildren on Real Estate Finance, Real Estate
Focus 15–1   442

Land Ownership Systems in Countries around the
World   442

The Emergence of Mortgages and a Mortgage Market in
Russia, Real Estate Focus 15–2   443

The Integration of the Mortgage Market and Capital Markets
in the United States from the 1970s through the 1990s,
Exhibit 15–4   449

16   Residential Mortgage Types and Borrower Decisions

Comparison of 15- and 30-Year Mortgages   473

Freddie Mac's Loan Purchases by Type   474

Calculating Payment Changes on ARMS   480

Valuing Interest Rate Buydowns   483

Payments and Amortization Schedule of RAMs   485

New Mortgage Program Requires no Home Equity, Real
Estate Focus, 16–3   488

Effective Borrowing Costs   492

Choosing between an ARM and FPM   494

New Program that Prequalifies Borrowers, Real Estate
Focus 16–5   495

Calculating the Benefit of Refinancing   496

17   Sources of Funds for Residential Mortgages

Mortgage Debt Outstanding by Type   506

The Savings and Loan Debacle   507

Residential Mortgage Originations by Source   509

Hedging Pipeline Risk with Forward Commitments   513

Calculating Down Payments on FHA Loans   517

Holders of Outstanding Mortgage Debt   520

Automated Mortgage Underwriting, Real Estate
Focus 17–2   526

The Federal Government's Drive to Eliminate Discrimination
in Mortgage Lending, Real Estate Focus 17–3   528

18   Commercial Property Financing

Who Originates and Holds Commercial Mortgages   537

Average Rates on Balloon Mortgages   540

Participation Mortgage, ongoing Gatorwood Apartments
example   543

Typical Loan Terms on Commercial Mortgages   547

Metropolitan Structures Defaults on Several Loans, Real
Estate Focus 18–1   549

Sears Defaults on Sears Tower Mortgage, Real Estate
Focus 18–2   554

Underwriting a Commercial Loan, ongoing Gatorwood
Apartments example   554

Construction of World's Tallest Building Halted by Default,
Real Estate Focus 18–3   561

19   Mortgage-Backed Securities

Passthrough MBS Example   582

Recent Returns on Ginnie Mae Mutual Funds, Real Estate
Focus 19–1   585

Sequential Pay MBS Example   590

CMBS Issue Volume during the 1990s, Exhibit 19–11   595

Nomura Capital's Direct Lending Program, Real Estate
Focus 19–2   600

Duff & Phelps Scale to Rate CMBS, Exhibit 19–15   601

Duff & Phelps Rating Requirements for Hotel Mortgages,
Exhibit 19–16   603

Structure of a CMBS Issue from Nomura Capital,
Exhibit 19–17   604

20   Real Property Rights

How Water Rights Are Defined in the United States, Real
Estate Focus 20–1   617

Definition of Oil and Mineral Rights in the United
States   617

Air Rights in a Development in Washington DC,
Exhibit 20–2   618

Ownership Restrictions Imposed on Aliens in the United
States, Real Estate Focus 20–2, International   620

Community Property States in the United States   627

21   Real Estate Taxation

An Overview of Real Estate Taxation in Other Countries;
Real Estate Focus 21–1, International   642

Use of the Property Tax as a Tool of National Economic
Policy, Real Estate Focus 21–2, International   643

How to Determine a Community's Budget and Tax
Rate   644

How to Calculate a Property Owner's Tax Liability   648

How to Determine Whether a Property Owner's Tax Liability
Is Fair   650

The Property Tax as a Tool of Economic Policy in Japan,
Real Estate Focus 21–4   650

How to Appeal Property Tax Assessments, Real Estate
Focus 21–5   655

22   Transfer of Real Property Rights

REDI and Other Companies that Compile Data on Real
Estate Transactions from Public Records, Real Estate
Focus 22–1   665

Land Title Registration Systems around the World, Real
Estate Focus 22–2 International   666

Land Acquired by Adverse Possession, Real Estate
Focus 22–3   670

A Residential Property Survey, Exhibit 22–2   676

An Encroachment Shown in a Residential Property Survey,
Exhibit 22–3   677

How the Government Rectangular Survey System Works, Exhibits 22–5 through 22–8   680–682

23   Real Estate Brokerage and Listing Contracts

The Law of Agency, see particularly Exhibit 23–3   694

Obtaining a Real Estate License   695

The National Association of Realtors, Its Various Institutes, Societies, and Councils, and Their Certification Programs for Certain Real Estate Specialties   698

Some Major U.S. Properties Owned by Foreigners, Real Estate Focus 23–2   701

Sample Listing Contracts, Exhibit 23–6 and Exhibit 23–8   706 and 712

Actual Listing Situation Example   711

24   Contracts for Sale and Closing

A Real-World Dispute Arising Out of a Contract for the Sale and Purchase of a Property, Real Estate Focus 24–1   729

Anatomy of a Real Estate Transaction   735

A Completed Contract for Purchase and Sale of Real Estate Exhibit 24–2   731

Completed Statements of Buyers' and Sellers' Estimated Closing Costs, Exhibits 24–3 and 24–4   736 and 737

Actual Court Cases on Real Estate Contracts, Real Estate Focus 24–2   739

Anatomy of the Closing of a Real Estate Transaction   741

Composite Closing Statement, Exhibit 24–5   744

Cash Reconciliation Statement, Exhibit 24–6,   746

The Real Estate Settlement Procedures Act (RESPA),   747

Prorationing Expenses between Buyers and Sellers, Exhibit 24–7   749

C H A P T E R

REAL ESTATE PERSPECTIVES

THE VALUE OF SPACE

**THE DISCIPLINE OF
REAL ESTATE**
Classical Land Economics
The Neoclassical Tradition Is Still
    Followed Today
Ideas about Property Rights and Contracts
Financial Economics
The Institutions

**REAL ESTATE IN THE WORLD
ECONOMY**
The Relative Wealth of Real Estate
Investments to Improve Land
Who Owns America?

REAL ESTATE DEFINED
The Importance of Value

***REAL ESTATE PERSPECTIVES:*
AN OVERVIEW OF THE BOOK**
Investment Perspective
Market Perspective
Mortgage Finance Perspective
Legal Perspective

SUMMARY

KEY TERMS

**PROBLEMS FOR THOUGHT
AND SOLUTION**

ADDITIONAL READINGS

LEARNING OBJECTIVES

After reading this chapter students will be able to:

1. Explain the economic history of thought about humans and space in the context of the current study of real estate.

2. Discuss the dimensions of real estate wealth and investment in the world and U.S. economies relative to other real and financial assets.

3. Identify the property types and principal owners of real estate in the United States.

4. Define the term *real estate.*

5. Explain why the investment perspective, which emphasizes value, dominates other real estate perspectives.

INTRODUCTION

As the first edition of this book was being prepared during the early 1980s, the authors agreed that the best way to think about the study of real estate is from alternative points of view, or perspectives. Much of our current understanding of real estate, after all, comes from the contributions of those in fields such as law, economics, and finance. When choosing a title for the book, one of the authors (Dr. Smith) suggested that the book simply be called *Real Estate Perspectives.*

The first chapter of *Real Estate Perspectives* carries the title of the book. It introduces readers to the study of real estate by presenting the various perspectives from which people have viewed, and continue to view, real estate. The chapter discusses the different conceptual foundations for real estate analysis and the importance of real estate in the world economy. Also, it describes the organization of the book into its four parts, called *perspectives,* and introduces the unifying theme of *value,* which is fully developed in the first part—the *Investment Perspective.* The chapter provides the "big picture" of real estate studies to help readers develop a context for learning the specifics in subsequent chapters.

THE VALUE OF SPACE

The study of real estate derives from an elementary fact of life: the existence of space on this planet. Students of real estate behave as social scientists with a special interest in the relationship between humans and space. Former Prime Minister of Great Britain Winston Churchill observed, "We shape our buildings and then our buildings shape us." Mr. Churchill never sought to become a wealthy real estate developer and investor, although he might have been the Donald Trump of his time because he understood the two-way interaction between humans and space.

Successful real estate businesspersons capitalize on their knowledge and intuition about the goods and services humans desire to satisfy their needs for space. Space is a product, and many services in the real estate business accompany the provision of space (see Exhibit 1–1). The human need for space has two aspects: the desire for the right quantity, such as acres of land and square footage of building area, and the desire for the right quality of space, the most important determinant of which is the location. The value of space and the value of services associated with providing space follow from how individuals relate to space from both quantity and quality dimensions.

Individuals also must consider other humans as they satisfy their desire for space. If society places limitations on individuals' relationships to space through imposition of use controls to protect the well-being of all individuals, then the values differ from those in a society that couldn't care less about the well-being of all individuals. The *property rights* granted by societies to use space have as much to do with creating value as the *demand and supply fundamentals* of quantity and quality of space. These principles form the conceptual basis for the *investment perspective* of real estate, which emphasizes value and therefore dominates other perspectives.

EXHIBIT 1-1
SPACE AVAILABLE

Chapter 1 establishes a context for the serious study of real estate—the study of human relationships with space. The chapter begins with a brief history of the real estate discipline. The next section considers the role and influence of real estate on the economies of the United States and other nations around the globe. In the final section, we elaborate on the central theme of *Real Estate Perspectives:* value gives meaning to real estate and knowledge of value and value determination, creation, enhancement, and maintenance serve as primary objectives in human relationships with space.

THE DISCIPLINE OF REAL ESTATE

Opinions vary about whether real estate is a legitimate academic discipline, whether business and architecture schools at universities ought to teach real estate, and even whether the study of real estate can be taken seriously.[1] In the historical summary presented below, we avoid these normative issues in favor of descriptions of how the study of real estate evolved and where it is today. One fact is undeniable—*economics* provides the academic foundation for the study of real estate and the analysis of real estate problems.

CLASSICAL LAND ECONOMICS[2]

Prior to the publication of Adam Smith's *The Wealth of Nations* in 1776, thoughtful people recognized that the value of something derives from its utility, or usefulness to people, and its scarcity. Smith (Adam not Halbert) pondered one of the great questions in economics— how does society allocate resources to the goods and services it produces?—and concluded that land, labor, and capital combine to form useful products. The *natural price* of these products reflects the cost of production.

Early in the next century, classical economists developed a theory of rent (the payment for space) and value by introducing the idea that the cost of land takes different forms: value in use, value in exchange (price), and intrinsic value. The classical economic notions that (a) costs of production determine prices and values and (b) payments for the same land take different forms persist until today.

Challenges to the classical views about the value and cost of production relationship came later in the 18th century from economists who believed that factors of production add value according to their marginal contribution to people's wealth. Specifically, the value of land derives from the demand (utility) for land and not as a residual payment. This thinking set up the classical economic debate about value—is value primarily driven by cost of production on the supplier side or by demand on the utility-maximizing consumer side?

THE NEOCLASSICAL TRADITION IS STILL FOLLOWED TODAY

Alfred Marshall, a British economist who worked during the late 1800s and early 1900s, helped to resolve the classical debate about the determinants of value. As demonstrated in Exhibit 1–2, Marshall argued that value results from the intersection of supply (cost) and demand (utility). He used the analogy of the blades of scissors to make this point. The idea of demand and supply interaction sheds light on the question of whether different payments might apply to the same good. In a perfect market, Marshall contended,

---

[1] Readings on these questions appear at the end of the chapter.

[2] This discussion is an adaptation of selections from Appraisal Institute, *The Appraisal of Real Estate,* 10th ed. (Chicago: Appraisal Institute, 1992), Chapters 2 and 4.

EXHIBIT 1-2

THE DEMAND AND SUPPLY SCISSORS

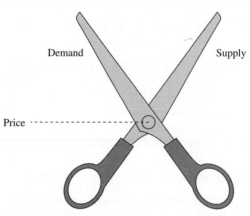

the price (value in exchange), value (intrinsic value), and production cost of a good are equal. In imperfect market settings they differ.[3]

The synthesis of classical ideas carries forward to current thinking about prices and other economic outcomes. How often have you heard someone explain an event in the world as the result of "supply and demand forces"? Later in this book we present specific ideas about values and explore the intricacies of the valuation models used in current practice that have distinctive neoclassical flavors.

Beginning in the mid-1950s a new branch of economics emerged that focuses on urban problems, especially housing issues. Urban and housing economists extend the basic ideas of the early classical and neoclassical economists in complex models designed to better understand and predict how humans relate to space.[4] Their interest in the use of space in cities distinguishes these economists from others.

In recent decades, financial economics has provided an additional foundation for real estate studies. Financial economics provides ways to systematically analyze and measure demand and supply interactions by studying the contracts people negotiate to rent or buy space (i.e., leases and sale contracts) that produces cash flows. The emphasis on cash flow measurement and analysis to capture demand and supply interactions makes this tradition distinctive and powerful.

Real Estate Perspectives is a descendant of a long academic line of real estate textbooks that began with publication of Ernest Fisher's *Principles of Real Estate* in 1923, Richard Ely's (with Morehouse) *Elements of Land Economics* in 1924, and Fredrick Babcock's *The Appraisal of Real Estate* in 1924. This book and real estate as a field of study are deeply rooted in the land economics traditions started at the University of

---

[3] Conditions for perfect and imperfect real estate markets appear in Chapter 9 of this text.

[4] A popular text that documents the knowledge in this area of economics is by Mills and Hamilton (see the additional reading list at the end of this chapter).

REAL ESTATE FOCUS 1-1

A Real Estate Graduate Degree: The Next Step?

Passing a first course in real estate does not necessarily lead to visions of graduate school in real estate. Nevertheless if such visions do appear, the Urban Land Institute publishes a book titled *The Directory of Real Estate Development and Related Education Programs* (Washington, DC, 1994), which contains useful information about these programs. The following list comes from this book:[a]

DBA: Doctorate of Business Administration
Cleveland State University (Department of Finance)

Grad Dip. RE: Graduate Diploma in Real Estate
University of New South Wales

Grad Dip. Val: Graduate Diploma in Valuation
University of New South Wales

MA: Master of Arts
University of California, Los Angeles
University of Florida
University of Nebraska at Omaha
University of Newcastle Upon Tyne
The Ohio State University

MAURP: Master of Arts in Urban and Regional Planning
University of Florida

MBA: Master of Business Administration
The American University
University of British Columbia
California State University, Sacramento
University of California at Berkeley
University of California, Los Angeles
University of Cincinnati
Cleveland State University (Department of Finance)
Columbia University (Graduate School of Business)
University of Connecticut
University of Denver
DePaul University
The George Washington University
Georgia State University
University of Florida
University of Georgia
Indiana University
University of Michigan

University of North Carolina at Chapel Hill
University of North Texas
The Ohio State University
Penn State University
University of Pennsylvania
University of Quebec
Saint Cloud State University
San Diego State University
University of Southern California (School of Business Administration)
Southern Methodist University
Texas A&M University (Finance Department)
University of Texas at Austin
Virginia Commonwealth University
York University

MBA/JD: Master of Business Administration/ Jurum Doctor
University of California, Los Angeles

MDesS: Master in Design Studies
Harvard University

MM: Master of Management
Northwestern University

MP: Master of Planning
University of Virginia

Mphil: Master of Philosophy
University of Reading

MPL: Master of Planning
University of Southern California (School of Urban and Regional Planning)

MRE: Master of Real Estate
University of Amsterdam
University of New South Wales

MRECM: Master of Real Estate and Construction Management
University of Denver

MRED: Master of Real Estate Development
University of Southern California (School of Urban and Regional Planning)

Continued

REAL ESTATE FOCUS 1-1— *Concluded*

A Real Estate Graduate Degree: The Next Step?

MRP: Master of Regional Planning
University of North Carolina at Chapel Hill

MS: Master of Science
University of Illinois at Urbana-Champaign
The Johns Hopkins University
New York University
Penn State University
San Diego State University
University of Southern California (School of Business Administration)
Texas A&M University (Real Estate Center and Department of Agricultural Economics)
Texas A&M University (Finance Department)
University of Wisconsin at Madison

MSB: Master of Science in Business
Virginia Commonwealth University

MSc: Master of Science
University of British Columbia
Heriot-Watt University

MSc LM: Master of Science in Land Management
University of Reading

MSc RE: Master of Science in Real Estate
University of Reading

MSc ULA: Master of Science in Urban Land Appraisal
University of Reading

MSLD: Master of Science in Land Development
Texas A&M University (Department of Landscape Architecture and Urban Planning)

MS/MArch: Master of Science/Master of Architecture
University of Illinois at Urbana-Champaign

MSRE: Master of Science in Real Estate
Georgia State University

MSRED: Master of Science in Real Estate Development

Columbia University (Graduate School of Architecture, Planning, and Preservation)
Massachusetts Institute of Technology

MUP: Master of Urban Planning
Hunter College (CUNY)

MUPDD: Master of Urban Planning, Design, and Development
Cleveland State University (Department of Urban Studies)

MURP: Master of Urban and Regional Planning
Michigan State University

PhD: Doctor of Philosophy
University of British Columbia
University of California at Berkeley
University of California, Los Angeles
University of Connecticut
Georgia State University
University of Florida
University of Georgia
University of Illinois at Urbana-Champaign
Michigan State University
University of North Carolina at Chapel Hill
University of North Texas
The Ohio State University
Penn State University
University of Southern California (School of Business Administration)
University of Southern California (School of Urban and Regional Planning)
Texas A&M University (Finance Department)
University of Texas at Austin
University of Wisconsin at Madison

Real Estate Management
European Business School

---

[a] Also, Cornell University now offers a Master of Professional Studies degree in real estate.

Wisconsin, the University of California at Berkeley, and other universities during the first half of the 1900s. *Real Estate Perspectives* also embodies the financial economics tradition because a great deal of space in the book is devoted to cash flow measurement and analysis. Both traditions extend to academic programs today in real estate, urban and housing economics, and planning.

IDEAS ABOUT PROPERTY RIGHTS AND CONTRACTS

The fundamentals of demand, such as population growth, and supply, such as interest rate changes, explain a great deal about individual and market behavior in valuing space. Notwithstanding, much is unexplained by these fundamentals because of the existence of institutional arrangements designed to protect the welfare of all humans from the actions of individuals and promote fairness in the allocation of space. Countries and the state and local jurisdictions in the United States have unique institutional approaches for handling human relationships with space. These institutional structures range from laws and administrative regulations imposed by government, to standards of practice recommended by professional organizations, to cultural mores. Do these institutions matter in setting the values for space and space-related services? Yes! The unique set of institutional arrangements that continue to develop around the world results in people paying different amounts for space.

The grandparents of all rules governing human relations with space are property and contract laws. Societies, through laws, establish environments for ownership, exchange, and conflict resolution. The lawful rights available to owners of real estate determine the market values of property. What good is it to own property if owners face fines and imprisonment whenever they use it? Property laws define the fundamental rights of ownership, land use controls introduced by societies modify property rights, and contract laws facilitate the transfer of rights to those who value them the most.

Contracts have another important function. They act as the record of market exchanges. The signing of a lease, for example, constitutes an entry in the hypothetical book of market transactions in which a tenant on the demand side and a landlord on the supply side come together as the "blades of the scissors" to determine a payment for the use of space—**rent**. Contracts for sale of property indicate the same kind of interaction for determining payments for ownership of space—the prices of properties.

The study of property rights, land use controls, and contracts may seem tedious. Many terms and concepts must be mastered. But having this knowledge is crucial to understanding real estate markets, and for those less interested in following markets, this knowledge enlightens the intellectually curious about the nature and dynamics of the environment of humans and space.

FINANCIAL ECONOMICS

Neoclassical economics provides two approaches to the study of humans and space. Both approaches rely on the premise that people acquire and exchange the spaces in their lives because these actions enhance their welfare, where economic welfare means wealth.

Increasing wealth underlies investment decisions involving space regardless of whether we look back in time at transactions that occurred, as in one approach, or forward in time to transaction opportunities, as in the other approach. Financial economics blends the two approaches into unified formulas for understanding investment decisions, complete with methods for reaching these decisions. The forward-looking perspective dominates the methods for investment analysis and valuation in financial economics, although the formulas need historical information to run properly.[5]

From the 1960s to the 1990s, increasing numbers of real estate investment and valuation decisions resulted from applications of techniques designed by financial economists for use in corporation finance. Some real estate experts, however, feel that these financial models are inappropriate or overextended for understanding human and space relationships. They argue that real estate, because of its fixed location and indivisibility, violates basic assumptions underlying finance models. Nevertheless, those who face increasingly complex real estate decisions today look first to advancements in financial economics for ideas and tools. *Real Estate Perspectives* contains a thorough treatment of modern financial analysis customized to real estate. The two-legged pants of neoclassical financial economics do not fit perfectly on real estate, but real estate analysis would be nearly bare without finance models.

THE INSTITUTIONS[6]

Neoclassical economics yields many important insights for incorporating the fundamentals of demand, such as incomes, and supply, such as costs, into valuation and other human and space decisions. But neoclassical economics is silent about the role of institutions in these decisions. What are "the institutions"? The term *institutions* refers to arrangements members of society make to support fundamental economic and social activities. Each day, for example, millions of shares of corporate common stock move from the portfolios of sellers to the portfolios of buyers. This fundamental economic activity of allocating capital to and from companies occurs because society sets up institutional arrangements in the form of organized exchanges, such as the New York Stock Exchange, to facilitate stock transfers.

The real estate field has an abundant supply of unique and interesting institutions, including zoning, mortgages, and time-share ownership, which are discussed in this book. Accordingly, *Real Estate Perspectives* informs about the specialized institutions in the field. Institutions do matter in the real estate business! Knowing institutional details often means the difference between profit and loss because institutional arrangements sometimes affect the levels of rents and property values.

A larger issue surrounding institutions involves whether they represent *the* conceptual foundation of real estate. If the arrangements society makes that affect real estate are

---

[5] The text by Richard Brealey and Stewart Myers cited at the end of this chapter provides an excellent treatment of the relevant concepts and methods in financial economics.

[6] The recent writings of Robert Merton motivated this section. See, for example, "Influence of Mathematical Models in Finance on Practice: Past, Present, and Future," *Financial Practice and Education* 5 (Spring/Summer 1995), pp. 7–15.

the anchor of the field, then we must study them carefully because institutional change coming from outside the business often occurs in unexpected and shocking ways. If, by contrast, institutions do not anchor the business, then change occurs internally because of fundamental economic needs. Stated differently, the focus of the study of real estate can be either the details of the relevant and existing institutions or the economics of the business and the responsive evolution of institutional arrangements. Although *Real Estate Perspectives* describes the institutions in real estate, their roles, and their evolution, this book emphasizes the fundamental economics of the real estate business.

REAL ESTATE IN THE WORLD ECONOMY

We concentrate briefly in this section on real estate as a real asset. **Real assets**, such as gold and real estate, take the form of useful things, for example jewelry and homes. They also take the form of investments that change in value due to changes in supply and demand. **Financial assets**, such as stocks and bonds, only take the form of investments. This type of asset originates and prospers based on the efforts of humans making productive use of real assets.

Real estate, the real asset, provides the space humans need and costs money to physically produce. It exists because humans put their money and effort into transforming vacant land into useful space. The wealth of real estate represents all previous contributions humans made to improve land and the prevailing demand and supply conditions in the asset market that affect current wealth levels. During each period, new contributions, investments, add to the level of wealth. Consequently, the accumulated stock of wealth and the flow of investment in real estate compared to other assets indicate the relative importance of human and space relationships in the economy.

Now we concentrate on real estate as a financial asset. Leases allow for the use of real estate for limited periods of time. Mortgages allow the owners of real estate to borrow money using real estate as collateral. Both leases and mortgages grant rights to document holders to the incomes from real estate, but they do not allow holders of the documents to indefinitely control the physical space for human use. Creation of leases and mortgages results in creation of real estate financial assets. Patterns in the creation of the real estate financial assets represent another indicator of the importance of real estate in the economy.

Finally, we concentrate on the ownership of real estate. Identifying the owners of land yields important information about the political environment of societies. Information about who controls real estate serves as an indicator of economic power. Ownership patterns differ markedly across nations. In some countries, government owns most of the real estate. Even in the United States, where private property ownership earns great respect, the public owns most of the land in some states (e.g., Alaska, Oregon).

THE RELATIVE WEALTH OF REAL ESTATE

Experts regularly debate the amount of value attributable to real estate. Estimates vary widely because of the difficulty in obtaining reliable information, especially outside the developed nations of the world. One set of global wealth estimates from Ibbotson

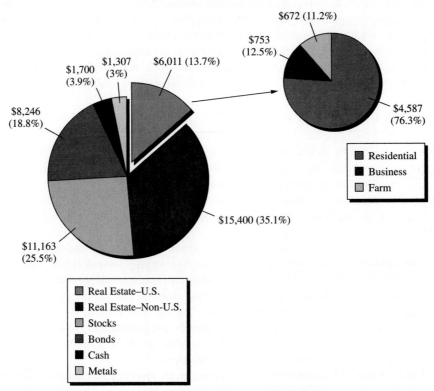

SOURCE: Ibbotson Associates Encorr Software, Chicago, IL. Used with permission. All rights reserved.

Associates places the value of the world's assets at nearly $44 trillion in 1991. As Exhibit 1–3 shows, real estate outside the United States comprises 35.1 percent of the world's wealth and U.S. real estate equals 13.7 percent. Thus, real estate constitutes nearly one-half of the wealth in the world.

The United States takes pride in having a well-housed population. Approximately three-quarters of the wealth of real estate in this country accrues to residential property, which includes single-family homes and apartment properties.

INVESTMENTS TO IMPROVE LAND

Exhibit 1–4 charts the pattern of building construction activity in the United States during the 10-year period 1985 through 1995. The graph reveals that the well-documented slow-down in real estate investment lasted only for a brief period during the late 1980s and

EXHIBIT 1-4

CONSTRUCTION ACTIVITY IN THE UNITED STATES, 1985-1995
(billions of 1992 constant dollars)

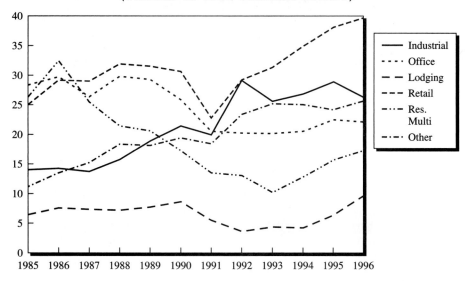

SOURCE: U.S. Department of Commerce, *Current Construction Reports, Value of Construction Put in Place* (Washington, DC, March 1997).

early 1990s. Since 1991, new investment in single-family homes (not shown in Exhibit 1–4) has increased at a healthy pace. The pace of investment in business and multifamily structures remained sluggish until 1993 when a general upward trend returned. The most dramatic increases in investment have occurred in retail and multifamily real estate.

Building construction and production of items that go into buildings represent a substantial portion of the nation's business activity each year. In 1995, gross private domestic investment, which includes expenditures in the United States for buildings, machinery, and equipment was about $1 trillion. Investment in buildings constitutes about one-half of this total and ranges from 5 to 7 percent of gross domestic product.

WHO OWNS AMERICA?

Ownership of real estate signifies the rights granted to members of society for use of real estate in the personal and commercial parts of their lives. To obtain these rights owners often give up some rights to others who lend them money. Lenders obtain contingent ownership of real estate. That is, lenders only become the kind of owners that occupy properties when the equity owners fail to make payments on mortgage loans. Therefore, a full examination of the question—who owns America's real estate?—must consider both owners: the equity owners and the lenders who have mortgage holdings.

REAL ESTATE FOCUS 1-2

A Real Estate Career = $

How much money can you expect to make if you select a career in real estate? A glance at the list of the world's richest people suggests that the amount of money someone can make in real estate is limitless. Five of the world's 29 multibillionaires ($5 billion or more) identified by *Forbes* (July 17, 1995) accumulated their fortunes in real estate. If entrepreneurial activities scare you, then choose a "regular job," and as the table below indicates, regular jobs in the real estate business pay handsomely! Notice that total compensation includes base salary plus incentive bonuses. Incentive pay constitutes a growing share of total compensation, which continues to increase faster than the rate of inflation.[a]

[a] See Carl Bruno, "Trends in Management Compensation," *Real Estate Finance Journal* 11 (Summer 1995), pp. 60–66.

REAL ESTATE COMPENSATION SURVEY 1997, SELECTED POSITIONS

Position	1996 Base Salary Range[1]			Average Bonus Percent Salary[2]
	High	**Median**	**Low**	
Chief Operating Officer	$239,100	$185,000	$130,900	48.6
Regional Executive	$182,200	$135,000	$87,800	46.0
MIS Executive/IT Director	$98,600	$75,000	$51,400	17.8
Director of Research	$118,600	$92,500	$66,400	18.5
Portfolio Executive	$124,800	$93,000	$61,200	37.7
Financial Executive/CFO	$175,000	$136,500	$98,000	39.0
Finance Director	$121,900	$89,000	$56,100	30.3
Financial Analyst	$61,500	$48,500	$35,500	13.3
Asset Manager, Office	$102,000	$81,700	$61,400	31.5
Asset Manager, Retail	$94,300	$75,000	$55,700	28.2
Asset Manager, Industrial	$90,200	$75,000	$59,800	24.9
Asset Manager, Multifamily	$85,500	$70,000	$54,500	30.1
Property Manager, Office	$72,900	$60,000	$47,100	18.3
Property Manager, Retail	$74,200	$55,000	$35,800	19.0
Property Manager, Industrial	$63,000	$55,000	$47,000	20.0
Propety Manager, Multifamily	$58,500	$50,000	$41,500	12.6
On-Site Manager, Office	$55,900	$44,900	$34,000	9.6
On-Site Manager, Retail	$65,800	$52,800	$39,700	11.6
On-Site Manager, Industrial	$48,300	$40,000	$31,700	7.3
On-Site Manager, Multifamily	$35,100	$30,000	$24,900	11.3
Development Executive/Partner	$145,600	$121,000	$96,400	33.9
Project Manager	$82,700	$69,800	$56,800	19.2
Land Engineer	$81,500	$75,300	$69,200	25.5
Construction Executive	$125,800	$102,000	$78,200	22.5
Leasing Executive	$135,400	$100,000	$64,600	51.0
Leasing Representative	$77,500	$55,300	$33,100	54.5
Leasing-M/R Analyst	$59,800	$44,300	$28,700	19.4
Acquisitions Executive	$168,600	$130,000	$91,400	43.0
Acquisitions Associate	$83,000	$65,000	$47,000	22.8
Acquisitions-M/R Analyst	$56,400	$47,000	$37,600	13.6

SOURCE: CEL & Associates, Inc., 1997 National Real Estate Compensation Survey. Published in *Urban Land* (May 1997).

[1] Quartiles: High = 75th percentile, Median = 50th percentile, Low = 25th percentile. Numbers are rounded to the nearest hundred.

[2] Bonus earned in 1996, paid either in 1996 or 1997.

E X H I B I T   1 - 5

WHO OWNS AMERICA? (billions of dollars)

	Commercial Real Estate	Owner-Occupied Homes
Total value of private and public real estate[a]	$3,989	$6,800
Owner's equity value	$3,008 (75.4%)	$3,804 (55.9%)
Corporate	743	
Value of mortgages	$981 (24.6%)	$2,996 (44.1%)
Unsecuritized	961	1,695
Securitized	20[b]	1,301

SOURCE: Mike Miles, John Roberts, Donna Machi, and Robert Hopkins, "Sizing the Investment Markets: A Look at the Major Components of Public and Private Markets," *Real Estate Finance* 11 (Spring 1994), pp. 39–49.

[a] Note that the total value of U.S. real estate differs from the estimate in Exhibit 1–3. The estimate in that exhibit does not include public real estate and was made three years earlier.

[b] Estimated from other sources.

The table in Exhibit 1–5 provides a rough indication of the dimensions of the ownership rights of equity owners and lenders. While not a complete picture, the following observations emerge from these data:

- Homeowners and mortgage lenders on homes jointly own the majority of America.

- Homeowners carry more debt on their homes than do commercial real estate owners.

- Corporate owners control a large share of all commercial real estate in the United States.

- Unsecuritized commercial mortgages—mortgages held in the portfolios of lenders—far exceed securitized commercial mortgages—mortgages sold to investors in securities markets—yet the trend toward more securitization continues.

- About equal amounts of unsecuritized and securitized residential mortgages exist.

So, who owns America? Individuals who have homes and small commercial properties and their lender partners do. Nevertheless, the trend continues toward greater institutional and corporate ownership of commercial properties and increased holdings of all types of mortgages through mortgage-backed securities largely held by pension funds.

The copyrighted material is reprinted with permission from "The Journal," a publication of The Institutional Investor, Inc. 488 Madison Avenue, New York, New York 10022.

E X H I B I T   1 - 6

VALUE PERSPECTIVE OF REAL ESTATE

	implies		implies	
Real estate (Real property)	→	Lawful actions involving rights granted by society in land	→	Monetary value

---

REAL ESTATE DEFINED

Ask 100 people to define the term *real estate* and expect many different answers. People bring a variety of perspectives to discussions about real estate. To most, real estate conjures up ideas of the physical combination of land and buildings. To others, real estate means either a type of investment or a type of business.

According to old English common law, the term *real* stems from the notion that real actions serve as alternative remedies to payments in money for rectifying injustices.[7] For example, someone borrows $5,000 to buy a parcel of land then fails to make any loan payments. Instead of trying to recover the money loaned, the lender simply takes a lawful real action to repossess the land.

The term *estate* means a collection of rights. Thus, **real estate** correctly refers to collections of rights associated with real actions. Because **real property** refers to these same rights, the two terms are commonly used interchangeably in practice, and occasionally in this text.

THE IMPORTANCE OF VALUE

Monetary value bridges the gap between the somewhat abstract definition of real estate given above and how the world normally interprets human relationships with space (e.g., rents for use of space and prices for ownership of assets), hence the importance of the value perspective of real estate. As pictured through the conceptual diagram in Exhibit 1–6, actions involving the exercise of rights granted by society in land become more meaningful when considered in terms of money. If society grants no rights for use of land or no lawful actions exist, then real estate has zero monetary value. Examining this logic in reverse, we recognize that valuation of real estate by owners, appraisers, and government proceeds only after consideration of the possible rights and actions associated with the land.

Real Estate Perspectives emphasizes the private market and public (government) actions in real estate from the four perspectives around which the book is organized, as discussed in the next section. The integrating concept is value. Value gives meaning to real estate and knowledge of value, including value determination, creation, enhancement, and maintenance, serves as a primary objective in human interactions with space.

---

[7] Some of the insights in this and the following paragraph come from Peter F. Colwell and Joseph W. Trefzger, "The Economics of Real Estate Principles," *Illinois Real Estate Letter* (Summer/Fall 1994), pp. 5–10.

REAL ESTATE FOCUS 1-3

Donald Trump's Personal Investment Perspective

". . . experience taught me a few things. One is to listen to your gut, no matter how good something sounds on paper. The second is you're generally better off sticking with what you know. And the third is that some- times your best investments are the ones you don't make."

SOURCE: Donald Trump, *The Art of the Deal* (New York: Random House, 1978), p. 21.

REAL ESTATE PERSPECTIVES: AN OVERVIEW OF THE BOOK

The third edition of *Real Estate Perspectives* retains the same general organizational structure as the first two editions, namely that real estate is viewed from four perspectives: investment, market, mortgage finance, and legal. These perspectives represent the predominant viewpoints professionals consider when analyzing and implementing real estate decisions.

INVESTMENT PERSPECTIVE

Real estate decision making centers on investment valuation. Potential investors wish to pay prices low enough to obtain adequate returns on their investments, while sellers wish to obtain prices high enough to justify disposing of property. Each transaction involving the ownership or use of real estate involves similar investment calculations, whether the real estate is an owner-occupied home, an investment property, a lease arrangement, a share in a limited partnership, or some other form of ownership.

In addition to the decision to purchase and sell real estate, investment decisions recur during the period of ownership. For example, owners must repeatedly determine how much to spend on property maintenance and repair. Owners also must decide about whether to rehabilitate, modernize, and expand spaces or to convert properties to other uses. Even the decision to abandon real estate involves an investment decision.

Chapters 2 and 3 introduce the modern valuation and investment decision framework. This framework has three components: forecasting cash flows from operating real estate, forecasting cash proceeds from the sale of real estate at the end of the holding period, and converting cash flow estimates into present values. Chapter 4 considers the pervasive effects of federal income tax law on real estate decisions and values, while Chapter 5 describes the forms of ownership for real estate investors. The coverage of this material is more detailed than in previous editions of *Real Estate Perspectives*, in keeping with the increased trend toward securitization of real estate ownership as evidenced by the rapid growth of real estate investment trusts.

The defining characteristics of each major property type, such as apartments, retail centers, and office buildings, appear in Chapter 6. In Chapter 7, we investigate the effects

INVESTMENT VALUE: AN INTEGRATING FRAMEWORK

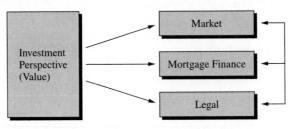

of risk on rates of return, property values, and portfolio decisions. Chapter 8 covers real estate management decisions and the important role of management in maximizing investment returns and property values.

As suggested by Exhibit 1–7, the basic concepts developed in the investment perspective apply throughout the remainder of the book. This allows for an integrated framework for the study of real estate because all other concepts and principles of real estate analysis surround the investment decision. Other factors such as legal considerations, financing requirements and alternatives, and local market conditions are considered primarily in the context of how they affect the rate of return and investment value.

MARKET PERSPECTIVE

In this perspective, real estate is viewed as an economic good. Like other economic goods exchanged in markets, people buy, lease, use, rehabilitate, and sell real estate to maximize their wealth.

While the investment perspective concentrates on real estate decisions from the view of the individual decision maker, this section views real estate from a broader market perspective. The individual decisions of market participants become observable as market outcomes. Movements in market rents and prices reflect the collective decisions involved in the investment perspective. Thus, understanding how individual real estate decisions are made helps in predicting how real estate markets will behave.

Chapter 9 explains the motivating forces behind market behaviors in the space market where investors trade the rights to occupy space and in the asset market where investors trade the rights to own the space. The 10th chapter in this edition of *Real Estate Perspectives* describes how governments, through enactment of land use, zoning, and environmental regulations, limit the rights of real estate market participants for the public's benefit. Chapter 11 addresses the issue of how market analysts obtain and process relevant data for predicting real estate market movements. This applied approach to market analysis differs from traditional textbook treatments that rely on theories of urban economics and geography rather than the practice of market analysis. The economics and feasibility of the design, development, and construction that create the physical real estate are covered in Chapter 12.

Chapters 13 and 14 discuss residential appraisal of market value and estimation of market values for income properties, respectively. Chapter 14 builds on material presented in the investment perspective, specifically the underlying value concepts and risk and return relationships. Chapters 13 and 14 also build directly on the discussion and analysis of real estate markets contained in Chapters 9 and 11. The idea here is that appraisers of market value are primarily in the business of providing detailed market analysis to their clients.

MORTGAGE FINANCE PERSPECTIVE

The use of mortgage financing instruments to transfer money and credit for the purposes of developing and acquiring real estate is pervasive. Chapters 15 through 19 are devoted to real estate finance issues such as the laws governing mortgage contracts, the lending institutions that supply mortgage money, the types of residential and commercial mortgage instrument choices, the borrower's mortgage loan decisions, the lender's mortgage loan processing decisions, the influence of government programs and policies, how mortgages are valued in the secondary market, and how mortgage securitization continues to revolutionize the financing of real estate

LEGAL PERSPECTIVE

Real estate ownership and transfers of ownership must meet the requirements of property law and contract law. These ground rules and institutional arrangements for carrying them out are presented in the legal perspective. Chapter 20 discusses real property rights, while Chapter 21 describes local restrictions on property ownership created by the property tax. Chapter 22 highlights the importance of transferable property rights and the contracts, methods, and institutions used in the conveyance of these rights. Real estate brokerage and listing contracts are presented in Chapter 23. This material is updated to reflect the new emphasis on buyer agents, dual agency, and nonagency relationships. Chapter 24 covers the contracts and institutional arrangements associated with the sale of real estate, providing a comprehensive picture of the process for successfully completing transactions.

It is important to stress that legal concepts are fundamental to the creation and protection of property values. Rational people will only invest in property if they do not fear confiscation by government or unauthorized use by neighbors. Investors must be the exclusive beneficiaries of increases in property values, and they must be free to transfer their ownership interests to those who will put properties to their most valuable use.

SUMMARY

Chapter 1 of *Real Estate Perspectives* establishes a context for the serious study of real estate—the study of human relationships with space. *Real estate* means the physical combination of land and buildings to some and a type of investment or business to others, but the term originates from English common law meaning real actions involving rights to land. We state that interpretations of real estate in the world stress the value consequences of actions taken by those interacting with space. Hence, value serves as the main theme of this book.

Rooted in economics, real estate studies emerged during the first half of the 20th century. Real estate analysis today relies on ideas about property rights, understanding the role of institutions, and the tools and advancements in economics and corporate finance.

Real estate comprises a major portion of the world's wealth and investment. Homeowners and home mortgage lenders still hold the dominant ownership positions in U.S. real estate, although corporations and pension funds continue to increase their investments in properties and real estate securities.

KEY TERMS

Financial asset 11	Real estate 16	Rent 9
Real asset 11	Real property 16	

PROBLEMS FOR THOUGHT AND SOLUTION

1. What is the distinguishing idea underlying a neoclassical economic analysis of human relationships with space?

2. What would happen to the value of the undeveloped land you own if suddenly the law changes so that all currently undeveloped land must remain undeveloped and in its natural state now and forever?

3. Who actually owns America's real estate?

4. Give a brief history of recent (since 1985) real estate investment activity in the United States and provide some predictions for the future.

5. Why is investment value such an important concept in real estate—so important that it emerges as the central theme of this text?

ADDITIONAL READINGS

Brealey, Richard A., and Stewart C. Myers. *Principles of Corporate Finance,* 5th ed. New York: McGraw-Hill, 1996.
A textbook used widely in universities for teaching financial economic concepts and methods.

Mills, Edwin S., and Bruce W. Hamilton. *Urban Economics.* New York: Harper Collins College, 1994.
A textbook that contains the important concepts in urban economics.

Diaz, Julian III. "Science, Engineering, and the Discipline of Real Estate." *Journal of Real Estate*

Literature 1 (July 1993), pp. 183–95.
An article that explores the development of real estate as a field of study.

Nourse, Hugh O. "A Note on the Origin of Real Estate in Collegiate Schools of Business," *Journal of Real Estate Research* 10, no. 2 (1995), pp. 227–34.
An article that summarizes the history of real estate curriculum in business schools and discusses the early textbooks used in courses.

To stay current with the real estate business, the following journals and newsletters are recommended:

National Real Estate Investor (monthly), Communication Channels, Inc., Atlanta.

Mortgage and Real Estate Executive Report (biweekly), Warren, Gorham, and Lamont, Inc., Boston.

Commercial Property News (biweekly), Miller Freeman Publications, New York.

Journal of Property Management (bimonthly), Institute of Real Estate Management, Chicago.

International Real Estate Journal (bimonthly), International Real Estate Institute, Scottsdale, Arizona.

Real Estate Forum (monthly), Real Estate Forum, Inc., New York.

Urban Land (quarterly), Urban Land Institute, Washington, DC.

The following publications contain up-to-date information about current laws, including tax laws, affecting real estate:

Real Estate Law Report (monthly), Warren, Gorham, and Lamont, Inc., Boston.

Journal of Real Estate Taxation (quarterly), Warren, Gorham, and Lamont, Inc., Boston.

To follow the rapidly changing techniques in real estate financial economics, see the following publications:

Real Estate Review (quarterly), Warren, Gorham, and Lamont, Inc., Boston.

Real Estate Finance (quarterly), Institutional Investor, Inc., New York.

Real Estate Finance Journal (quarterly), Warren, Gorham, and Lamont, Inc., Boston.

Real Estate Issues (quarterly), Counselors of Real Estate, Chicago.

PART

I

INVESTMENT
PERSPECTIVE

2
Basic Valuation Concepts

3
Investment Decision Making

4
Federal Income Taxation

5
Forms of Ownership

6
Property Types

7
Risk and Real Estate Investment

8
Management of the Space and Assets

The Investment Perspective of real estate provides the foundation for what most real estate educators agree is the core of real estate studies today. The common core is the concept of value and the elements of investment decision making.

The Investment Perspective begins with an important chapter (2) presenting the theory and concepts underlying real estate value. Chapter 3, titled *"Investment Decision Making,"* demonstrates how investors determine the merits of virtually any kind of real estate investment opportunity. This general framework for making investment decisions is extended in Chapter 4 to include the effects of income and capital gain taxes on decision making.

Investment decisions vary in many interesting ways depending on the type of investor involved and the type of property under consideration. So in Chapters 5 and 6, the characteristics of alternative ownership forms such as individual, partnership, and corporate, and different property types, such as apartments, retail centers, office buildings, and hotels are defined. The initial concern of investors in real estate is their return on investment relative to alternative investments, but as discussed in Chapter 7, the risk of cash flow and property value declines weighs heavily on the minds of investors when making investment decisions. Finally, Chapter 8 describes how real estate, once acquired, is professionally managed, including day-to-day operations and the decisions to renovate, lease, and sell.

From this foundation we build to specific applications in the Market Perspective, such as those found in the real estate development chapter (12) and the two appraisal chapters (13 and 14). The concept of value and investment decision making also provides the essential foundation for applications in the Mortgage Finance Perspective, especially in the chapters covering residential mortgage instruments (17), income property finance (18), and secondary mortgage markets (19).

2
C H A P T E R

Basic Valuation Concepts

VALUE: THE CENTRAL IDEA

SOME BASIC CONCEPTS
What Is Real Estate Valuation?
The Trade-Off between Return and Risk
How Are Decisions Made?

TIME VALUE OF MONEY
Definitions
Equations, Tables, Calculators,
    and Spreadsheets
Six Time-Value-of-Money Operations
Loan Amortization

INVESTMENT ANALYSIS
Present-Value Measures
Yield Measures

**CAPITALIZATION RATE
INTRODUCED**

SUMMARY

KEY TERMS

TEST YOURSELF

**PROBLEMS FOR THOUGHT
AND SOLUTION**

INTERNET EXERCISES

CASE PROBLEMS

ADDITIONAL READINGS

**APPENDIX 2a: APPLYING
TIME-VALUE-OF-MONEY
CONCEPTS TO REAL ESTATE**

**APPENDIX 2b: SOLVING TIME-
VALUE-OF-MONEY PROBLEMS
USING EXCEL**

After reading this chapter, students will be able to:

1. Perform time-value-of-money calculations using each of the six basic operations.

2. Solve basic present value and yield problems.

3. Calculate the effective cost of a mortgage loan.

4. Explain and use the decision rules for net present value and internal rate of return.

R eal estate decision making centers on investment valuation. The investment decision involves more than just whether to buy a property, because investment decisions recur during the period of ownership. For example, owners must repeatedly determine how much to spend on property maintenance and repair. Decisions also must be made periodically about rehabilitation, modernization, expansion, conversion of the property to another use, or demolition of the existing improvements. Even the decision to abandon real estate involves an investment decision.

Each of these decisions involves comparing uncertain future benefits to the cost of the investment. The costs and benefits frequently assume the form of cash flows to the equity investor. This chapter examines how the timing of cash flows affects the value and rates of return on real estate investments and, thus, the decision-making process. Time-value-of-money concepts serve as the cornerstone of most investment analysis techniques described in this and other business texts (e.g., accounting and finance).

This chapter focuses on the underlying concepts of valuation. The chapters that follow show how investment analysis provides quantitative information in specific real estate decision-making settings (e.g., property acquisition, residential mortgage finance, income property appraisal, etc.). The chapter begins with some basic concepts such as the definition of value and the trade-off between risk and return. The chapter then moves to time-value-of-money concepts. Finally, it presents the main investment decision-making techniques used in real estate.

VALUE: THE CENTRAL IDEA

Real estate is a complex real asset consisting of land and structures. The ownership of real estate provides certain property rights, including the right to use and the right to sell the property. In general, the value of a parcel of real estate is the present worth of the expected future benefits associated with ownership of the property rights. Any limitations on these rights reduce the value of the parcel. The valuation of property rights fundamentally influences real estate appraisal, investment, and finance.

Real estate appraisers estimate the values of real property rights. Their task often involves estimating **market value**—the price a typical buyer would pay should the property be placed on the market.

Real estate investors seeking to make investments need to know the value of real property rights so they do not bid too much for these rights. The valuation problem in real estate investment analysis is estimating the price a particular investor should pay for a property, given that investor's unique tax situation, financing opportunities, and expectations regarding future market conditions. This personalized estimate of value, which we will call **investment value**, differs from market value in that the concern is with what a particular investor would be willing to pay, rather than with what a typical investor might pay for the property.

Mortgage lenders provide a third perspective on value. They obtain property rights through the mortgage contract in the form of a legal claim against the borrower (the note) and the property (the mortgage) and receive the promised mortgage payment each period. The payment typically includes interest on the loan and a partial repayment, or **amortization**, of the principal. The borrower makes a mortgage payment each period to satisfy the claim of the lender. These claims have value, and because mortgages are frequently bought and sold in secondary markets, their valuation is a major concern in mortgage finance.

SOME BASIC CONCEPTS

This section defines the investment decision, discusses the importance of risk in the decision-making process, and presents a simple illustration of the process.

WHAT IS REAL ESTATE VALUATION?

Real estate investors earn returns on their investment from two sources. First, they may receive cash flows from the operation of the property. Cash flow is the property's income, such as money received from renting space or units, in excess of all of the property's expenses, such as maintenance and property taxes. Second, investors in real estate may benefit from appreciation in the value of real property over time.

Many investors also cite tax shelter benefits as a motivation for investing in real estate. In the context of the above classification system, these benefits can be thought of as simply a special type of cash inflow. To understand the intuition behind this result, one must first recognize that all incremental cash flows affect valuation and, second, that reducing cash outflows, such as taxes, is equivalent to increasing cash inflows.

Real estate valuation concerns the problem of estimating these future cash inflows and outflows and converting them into an estimate of present value. A property's valuation depends on expectations regarding the

1. Magnitude of the expected cash flows.
2. Timing of the expected cash flows.
3. Riskiness of the expected cash flows.

Clearly, the magnitude of the cash flows is important because value is positively related to the total amount of cash flows expected to be received over the life of the investment. The timing of the future cash flows also is important because investing requires the sacrifice of cash at purchase in exchange for uncertain future cash flows. When investors walk away from the settlement table after purchasing property, their balance of cash (or other securities such as stocks and bonds) has been reduced by the required down payment on the property. Why will investors sacrifice assets in order to acquire property? They endure the sacrifice because they expect the benefits from future cash flows to exceed the burden of the down payment. Clearly, the timing of these future cash flows matters. For example, if investors must wait, say, 20 years for a series of annual cash flows to begin, they would surely value them less than if the same series of cash flows were to begin immediately after the acquisition of the property. To induce investors to wait for investment benefits, there must be compensation in the form of a reduced purchase price. That is, future cash flows must be "discounted" for time before they can be compared to current cash inflows and outflows.

THE TRADE-OFF BETWEEN RETURN AND RISK

The components of return in a real estate investment—periodic cash flow from operations and price appreciation—usually vary with time. Either of these return components could be up one period and down the next. This fact, more than anything else, complicates real estate decisions: All decisions are based on expected cash flows, but what actually happens is seldom, *if ever*, exactly what the investor expected. Risk is the possibility that actual outcomes will vary from what was expected when the property was purchased. Thus, while risk is usually associated with "downside" movements in cash flows and returns, the "upside" potential also enters into the measurement of risk. Because most investors are risk averse, the basic relationship between risk and return is positive: The more risk investors bear when undertaking an investment, the greater rate of return they should expect (require), although the higher risk also means there is a greater likelihood of loss. When valuing real estate, accounting for risk and the way in which investors respond to it introduces an important complication. In fact, some analysts argue that real estate analysis *is* risk analysis![1]

HOW ARE DECISIONS MADE?

To illustrate how real estate investment decisions are made, consider the following example. Suppose the seller of a small office building asks $700,000 for the property. A potential investor estimates that the property is worth $740,000 (investment value). The lender to whom the investor is applying for a loan engages the services of a real estate appraiser to estimate the market value of the property, and the appraiser estimates a typical investor would pay $680,000 (market value) for the property.

---

[1] See Austin J. Jaffe and C. F. Sirmans, *Fundamentals of Real Estate Investment*, 3rd ed. (Upper Saddle River, NJ: Prentice Hall, 1995).

What should the investor do? In this case the investor should attempt to purchase the property at the appraiser's estimated market value. If the true market value of the property is indeed $680,000, this strategy will increase the investor's wealth by $60,000 (investment value minus market value). The investor should not be anxious to pay more than market value—even though he values the acquisition more than a typical investor—because future resale prices will likely be at or near market value. If the investor pays (his unique) investment value, there will be no net benefit. The problem is exactly how investors should calculate investment value and market value.

TIME VALUE OF MONEY

This section begins with some definitions, and then discusses and applies the six basic time-value-of-money operations. An understanding of these operations provides the necessary preparation for the study of real estate investment analysis.

DEFINITIONS

Money is an economic good. Like other economic goods, such as televisions and automobiles, people prefer to have more money than less money (that is, magnitudes matter) and they prefer to have it *now rather than later*. If money is received later, for example next week instead of today, it isn't worth as much to those receiving it, and an adjustment is required. This adjustment is called **interest**. The interest that is lost from not having the money to invest must be deducted. Understanding how to compensate for money received at different times is the essence of the time-value-of-money problem. The adjustment procedures should reflect the preferences of people for money received at different times in the future.

Assume an investor has $100 to invest and desires a 10 percent return on investment; that is, $10 in income from the investment.

$$\text{Rate of return} = \text{Income from the investment/Value of the investment}$$

$$0.10 = X/\$100$$

$$X = \$10$$

The investor considers three plans that may be purchased, each covering 10 years. These plans are as follows:

Plan A: The investor receives $10 at the end of the first year, plus the original $100, and no other returns during the remaining nine years.

Plan B: The investor receives $1 at the end of each year for 10 years, plus the original $100 at the end of 10 years.

Plan C: The investor receives $10 at the end of the 10th year of the plan, plus the original $100, and no other returns.

Each plan returns the investor's $100, plus $10 of interest. Which plan should the investor adopt? A more challenging question is why should the investor choose Plan A?

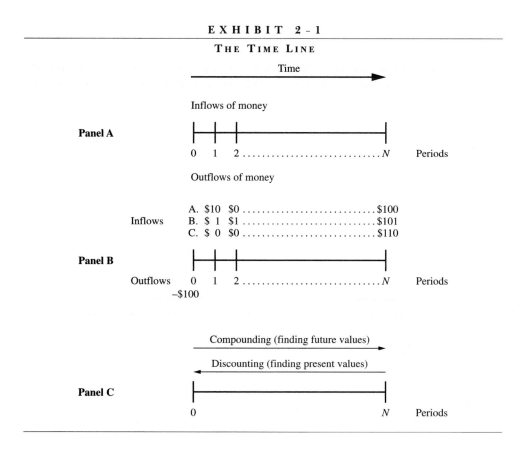

<EXHIBIT 2-1>

EXHIBIT 2 - 1

THE TIME LINE

The answer lies in the fact that money can be put to one of two possible uses when it is received. First, the investor may spend the money, for example, by taking a friend to a movie. Second, the investor may invest the money. With Plan A, the investor has the greatest opportunity to spend the money or to earn interest on the money throughout the 10-year period by reinvesting the $10 received at the end of year 1. The $10 invested for nine years will accumulate more interest than 10 yearly investments of $1 each. Therefore, investors who plan to reinvest their returns prefer earlier returns to later returns because of the opportunity to earn interest. Investors who consume their money returns have the same time preferences for early returns. Would you want to wait 10 years to take your friend to a movie?

The time line. The ability to visualize graphically the time pattern of money returns is helpful in working with time-value-of-money concepts. Panel A of Exhibit 2–1 presents a time line, which is simply an aid for visualizing the time pattern of money returns. The line is broken into periods, beginning on the left with the present period, period 0, and ending on the right with the terminal period, period N. Annual time periods are typically used, but sometimes monthly periods are appropriate (e.g., when analyzing mortgage payments).

All money *inflows* are placed on top of the line, and all *outflows* of money (e.g., the period 0 investment) go beneath the line, corresponding to the period in which they occur. The inflows and outflows from the investment decision involving the three alternative plans are shown in Panel B of Exhibit 2–1. Note that the $100 investment is located beneath the line at period 0, and the three sets of inflows are located on top of the line beginning at the end of period 1. All future inflows and outflows are assumed to occur at the end of the period in which they are received or paid, respectively.

Terminology. The following are common terms used in applying time-value-of-money concepts:

Present value (PV)—the value of money in period 0. "Taking the present value of inflows" means converting future money returns to what they would be worth now (i.e., in period 0).

Future value (FV)—the value of money in some period beyond period 0. "Taking the future value of money" means converting money received in the current period (or some prior period) to what it would be worth in the future.

Lump sum—a one-time receipt or expenditure occurring in a given period. In Panel B of Exhibit 2–1, the $10 received under Plan A is an example of a lump sum, as is the $110 received in the 10th period under Plan C.

Ordinary annuity (A)—a common amount of money received in every period (i.e., a series of equal lump sums). The series of $1 annual cash flows under Plan B is an example of an annuity.

Compounding—calculation of future values, as shown in Panel C of Exhibit 2–1.

Discounting—calculation of present values, as shown in Panel C of Exhibit 2–1.

EQUATIONS, TABLES, CALCULATORS, AND SPREADSHEETS

Various mathematical equations aid in making the critical adjustments for differences in cash flow amounts during different periods. These equations either put interest in (compounding) or take interest out (discounting) of money flows, depending on the desired adjustment. It is not necessary, however, that these equations be solved for each adjustment. Instead, the analyst may refer to a set of interest tables, operate a financial calculator, or use a personal computer.

Time-value-of-money adjustments, as applied in real estate investment analysis, traditionally have been accomplished using six mathematical operations. Exhibit 2–2 lists these operations and their associated mathematical equations. In the equations for monthly adjustments, the annual interest rate is divided by 12 ($m = 12$) to obtain the monthly interest rate, and the number of years (n) is multiplied by 12 to obtain the total number of monthly periods.

EXHIBIT 2-2

EQUATIONS FOR TIME-VALUE-OF-MONEY ADJUSTMENTS

Operation	Symbols	Equation for Annual Adjustment (n = number of years) (r = annual interest rate)	Equation for Monthly Adjustment ($m = 12$) (r = annual interest rate)
1. Future value of a lump sum	FV	$(1+r)^n$	$(1+r/m)^{nm}$
2. Future value of annuity	FV_a	$\dfrac{(1+r)^n-1}{r}$	$\dfrac{(1+r/m)^{nm}-1}{r/m}$
3. Sinking fund payment	A	$\dfrac{r}{(1+r)^n-1}$	$\dfrac{r/m}{(1+r/m)^{nm}-1}$
4. Present value of a lump sum	PV	$\dfrac{1}{(1+r)^n}$	$\dfrac{1}{(1+r/m)^{nm}}$
5. Present value of annuity	PV_a	$\dfrac{1-[1/(1+r)^n]}{r}$	$\dfrac{1-[1/(1+r/m)^{nm}]}{r/m}$
6. Mortgage constant	R_m	$\dfrac{r}{1-[1/(1+r)^n]}$	$\dfrac{r/m}{1-[1/(1+r/m)^{nm}]}$

Exhibit 2–3 includes examples of interest tables for real estate applications used in making time-value-of-money adjustments. The tables are categorized according to interest rates and periods. Panel A of Exhibit 2–3 is a 10 percent, annual table, while Panel B is a 10 percent, monthly table. Note that the effective (or realized) interest rate is 10 percent in the annual table and 0.833 percent, or 10 percent divided by 12 months, in the monthly table. Periods are shown on the extreme left and right margins of the tables. All cash flows are assumed to occur at the end of each period.

The six columns in the table in Exhibit 2–3 correspond to the six operations needed to make time-value-of-money adjustments. The tables were developed to relieve financial analysts of having to solve one of the equations in Exhibit 2–2 each time they needed to make an adjustment to cash inflows or outflows. Instead, analysts simply turned to the appropriate table, selected on the basis of interest rate and annual or monthly period requirements, and, for a given operation (i.e., one of the six columns) and number of periods, read the factor inside the table for the desired adjustment. These table factors are solutions to the equations shown in Exhibit 2–2. Before the advent of handheld calculators, interest tables were a time-saving device for making time-value-of-money adjustments. We use interest tables in this chapter to illustrate time-value-of-money calculations be-cause they are a useful learning tool. It is doubtful, however, that one would use them to solve real-world financial problems because they provide information for a limited number of interest rates and time periods. Today, most time-value-of-money calculations are made using either a handheld calculator or a personal computer.

Through the manipulation of the financial functions of handheld calculators, any problem that may be solved with the equations or interest tables may be solved with a

EXHIBIT 2 - 3

ANNUAL AND MONTHLY INTEREST TABLES FOR REAL ESTATE APPLICATIONS

10.00% annual interest rate

Years	1 Amount of $1 at Compound Interest	2 Accumulation of $1 per Period	3 Sinking Fund Factor	4 Present Value Reversion of $1	5 Present Value Ordinary Annuity $1 per Period	6 Installment to Amortize $1	Years
1	1.100000	1.000000	1.000000	0.909091	0.909091	1.100000	1
2	1.210000	2.100000	0.476190	0.826446	1.735537	0.576190	2
3	1.331000	3.310000	0.302115	0.751315	2.486852	0.402115	3
4	1.464100	4.641000	0.215471	0.683013	3.169865	0.315471	4
5	1.610510	6.105100	0.163797	0.620921	3.790787	0.263797	5
6	1.771561	7.715610	0.129607	0.564474	4.355261	0.229607	6
7	1.948717	9.487171	0.105405	0.513158	4.868419	0.205405	7
8	2.143589	11.435888	0.087444	0.466507	5.334926	0.187444	8
9	2.357948	13.579477	0.073641	0424098	5.759024	0.173641	9
10	2.593742	15.937425	0.062745	0.385543	6.144567	0.162745	10
11	2.853117	18.531167	0.053963	0.350494	6.495061	0.153963	11
12	3.138428	21.384284	0.046763	0.318631	6.813692	0.146763	12
13	3.452271	24.522712	0.040779	0.289664	7.103356	0.140779	13
14	3.797498	27.974983	0.035746	0.263331	7.366687	0.135746	14
15	4.177248	31.772482	0.031474	0.239392	7.606080	0.131474	15
16	4.594973	35.949730	0.027817	0.217629	7.823709	0.127817	16
17	5.054470	40.544703	0.024664	0.197845	8.021553	0.124664	17
18	5.559917	45.599173	0.021930	0.179859	8.201412	0.121930	18
19	6.115909	51.159090	0.019547	0.163508	8.364920	0.119547	19
20	6.727500	57.274999	0.017460	0.148644	8.513564	0.117460	20
21	7.400250	64.002499	0.015624	0.135131	8.648694	0.115624	21
22	8.140275	71.402749	0.014005	0.122846	8.771540	0.114005	22
23	8.954302	79.543024	0.012572	0.111678	8.883218	0.112572	23
24	9.849733	88.497327	0.011300	0.101526	8.984744	0.111300	24
25	10.834706	98.347059	0.010168	0.092296	9.077040	0.110168	25
26	11.918177	109.181765	0.009159	0.083905	9.160945	0.109159	26
27	13.109994	121.099942	0.008258	0.076278	9.237223	0.108258	27
28	14.420994	134.209936	0.007451	0.069343	9.306567	0.107451	28
29	15.863093	148.630930	0.006728	0.063039	9.369606	0.106728	29
30	17.449402	164.494023	0.006079	0.057309	9.426914	0.106079	30
31	19.194342	181.943425	0.005496	0.052099	9.479013	0.105496	31
32	21.113777	201.137767	0.004972	0.047362	9.526376	0.104972	32
33	23.225154	222.251544	0.004499	0.043057	9.569432	0.104499	33
34	25.547670	245.476699	0.004074	0.039143	9.608575	0.104074	34
35	28.102437	271.024368	0.003690	0.035584	9.644159	0.103690	35

EXHIBIT 2-3 (continued)

ANNUAL AND MONTHLY INTEREST TABLES FOR REAL ESTATE APPLICATIONS

10.00% annual interest rate

	1 Amount of $1 at Compound Interest	2 Accumulation of $1 per Period	3 Sinking Fund Factor	4 Present Value Reversion of $1	5 Present Value Ordinary Annuity $1 per Period	6 Installment to Amortize $1	
36	30.912681	299.126805	0.003343	0.032349	9.676508	0.103343	36
37	34.003949	330.039486	0.003030	0.029408	9.705917	0.103030	37
38	37.404343	364.043434	0.002747	0.026735	9.732651	0.102747	38
39	41.144778	401.447778	0.002491	0.024304	9.756956	0.102491	39
40	45.259256	442.592556	0.002259	0.022095	9.779051	0.102259	40
41	49.785181	487.851811	0.002050	0.020086	9.799137	0.102050	41
42	54.763699	537.636992	0.001860	0.018260	9.817397	0.101860	42
43	60.240069	592.400692	0.001688	0.016600	9.833998	0.101688	43
44	66.264076	652.640761	0.001532	0.015091	9.849089	0.101532	44
45	72.890484	718.904837	0.001391	0.013719	9.862808	0.101391	45
46	80.179532	791.795321	0.001263	0.012472	9.875280	0.101263	46
47	88.197485	871.974853	0.001147	0.011338	9.886618	0.101147	47
48	97.017234	960.172338	0.001041	0.010307	9.896926	0.101041	48
49	106.718957	1057.189572	0.000946	0.009370	9.906296	0.100946	49
50	117.390853	1163.908529	0.000859	0.008519	9.914814	0.100859	50

10.00% annual interest rate · · · · · · · · · · · · · · · 0.8333% monthly effective interest rate

Months							Months
1	1.008333	1.000000	1.000000	0.991736	0.991736	1.008333	1
2	1.016736	2.008333	0.497925	0.983539	1.975275	0.506259	2
3	1.025209	3.025069	0.330571	0.975411	2.950686	0.338904	3
4	1.033752	4.050278	0.246897	0.967350	3.918036	0.255230	4
5	1.042367	5.084031	0.196694	0.959355	4.877391	0.205028	5
6	1.051053	6.126398	0.163228	0.951427	5.828817	0.171561	6
7	1.059812	7.177451	0.139325	0.943563	6.772381	0.147659	7
8	1.068644	8.237263	0.121400	0.935765	7.708146	0.129733	8
9	1.077549	9.305907	0.107459	0.928032	8.636178	0.115792	9
10	1.086529	10.383456	0.096307	0.920362	9.556540	0.104640	10
11	1.095583	11.469985	0.087184	0.912756	10.469296	0.095517	11
12	1.104713	12.565568	0.079583	0.905212	11.374508	0.087916	12
Years							Years
1	1.104713	12.565568	0.079583	0.905212	11.374508	0.087916	1
2	1.220391	26.446915	0.037812	0.819410	21.670855	0.046145	2
3	1.348182	41.781821	0.023934	0.741740	30.991236	0.032267	3
4	1.489354	58.722492	0.017029	0.671432	39.428160	0.025363	4
5	1.645309	77.437072	0.012914	0.607789	47.065369	0.021247	5

E X H I B I T   2 - 3   (c o n c l u d e d)

ANNUAL AND MONTHLY INTEREST TABLES FOR REAL ESTATE APPLICATIONS

10.00% annual interest rate   0.8333% monthly effective interest rate

	1 Amount of $1 at Compound Interest	2 Accumulation of $1 per Period	3 Sinking Fund Factor	4 Present Value Reversion of $1	5 Present Value Ordinary Annuity $1 per Period	6 Installment to Amortize $1	
6	1.817594	98.111314	0.010193	0.550178	53.978665	0.018526	6
7	2.007920	120.950418	0.008268	0.498028	60.236667	0.016601	7
8	2.218176	146.181076	0.006841	0.450821	65.901488	0.015174	8
9	2.450448	174.053713	0.005745	0.408089	71.029355	0.014079	9
10	2.707041	204.844979	0.004882	0.369407	75.671163	0.013215	10
11	2.990504	238.860493	0.004187	0.334392	79.872986	0.012520	11
12	3.303649	276.437876	0.003617	0.302696	83.676528	0.011951	12
13	3.649584	317.950102	0.003145	0.274004	87.119542	0.011478	13
14	4.031743	363.809201	0.002749	0.248032	90.236201	0.011082	14
15	4.453920	414.470346	0.002413	0.224521	93.057439	0.010746	15
16	4.920303	470.436376	0.002126	0.203240	95.611259	0.010459	16
17	5.435523	532.262780	0.001879	0.183975	97.923008	0.010212	17
18	6.004693	600.563216	0.001665	0.166536	100.015633	0.009998	18
19	6.633463	676.015601	0.001479	0.150751	101.909902	0.009813	19
20	7.328074	759.368836	0.001317	0.136462	103.624619	0.009650	20
21	8.095419	851.450244	0.001174	0.123527	105.176801	0.009508	21
22	8.943115	953.173779	0.001049	0.111818	106.581856	0.009382	22
23	9.879576	1065.549097	0.000938	0.101219	107.853730	0.009272	23
24	10.914097	1189.691580	0.000841	0.091625	109.005045	0.009174	24
25	12.056945	1326.833403	0.000754	0.082940	110.047230	0.009087	25
26	13.319465	1478.335767	0.000676	0.075078	110.990629	0.009010	26
27	14.714187	1645.702407	0.000608	0.067962	111.844605	0.008941	27
28	16.254954	1830.594523	0.000546	0.061520	112.617635	0.008880	28
29	17.957060	2034.847258	0.000491	0.055688	113.317392	0.008825	29
30	19.837399	2260.487925	0.000442	0.050410	113.950820	0.008776	30
31	21.914634	2509.756117	0.000398	0.045632	114.524207	0.008732	31
32	24.209383	2785.125947	0.000359	0.041306	115.043244	0.008692	32
33	26.744422	3089.330596	0.000324	0.037391	115.513083	0.008657	33
34	29.544912	3425.389447	0.000292	0.033847	115.938387	0.008625	34
35	32.638650	3796.638052	0.000263	0.030639	116.323377	0.008597	35
36	36.056344	4206.761236	0.000238	0.027734	116.671876	0.008571	36
37	39.831914	4659.829677	0.000215	0.025105	116.987340	0.008548	37
38	44.002836	5160.340305	0.000194	0.022726	117.272903	0.008527	38
39	48.610508	5713.260935	0.000175	0.020572	117.531398	0.008508	39
40	53.700663	6324.079581	0.000158	0.018622	117.765391	0.008491	40

calculator—and usually much faster and more accurately. Financial calculators, which have the necessary formulas preprogrammed into their computational algorithms, are merely a more efficient device for making time-value-of-money adjustments than are equations or interest tables. Although financial calculators vary, all have five basic keys (or registers):

> *N*—the number of compounding (or discounting) periods.
>
> *I*—the periodic (usually monthly or annual) interest rate.
>
> *PV*—the lump sum amount invested in period 0 or the discounted value of future cash flows at period 0.
>
> *PMT*—the periodic level payment or receipt (annuity).
>
> *FV*—the lump sum cash flow or the future value of an investment.

The key to solving time-value-of-money problems is knowing what, if anything, to enter into each of these five registers. In the problems that follow, and throughout the text, the basic keystrokes needed to solve a problem are identified without specifying the exact sequence of keystrokes necessary to solve the problem on a particular calculator.

Spreadsheet programs such as EXCEL and LOTUS 1-2-3 have significantly increased the use of personal computers in the analysis of real estate decisions. Appendix B discusses how to solve time-value-of-money problems using an EXCEL spreadsheet.

SIX TIME-VALUE-OF-MONEY OPERATIONS

The six time-value-of-money operations presented in this section are mathematically grounded in the equations in Exhibit 2–2 and correspond to the six columns of the interest tables in Exhibit 2–3. Some of these traditional operations are more important for real estate decision making than others, especially Operations 4 through 6.

Operations 1 and 2. Operations 1 and 2 are used for calculating future values resulting from the compounding of interest. Compound interest means the investor earns interest on the principal amount invested plus interest on any previous interest earned.

Suppose that Astute Investor deposits $1,000 today in an interest-bearing account at a local bank. The account pays 10 percent compounded annually, and Astute expects to withdraw the principal plus compound interest at the end of five years. Operation 1 is used to determine how much Astute will accumulate by the end of the fifth year. Panel A of Exhibit 2–4 provides a time-line demonstration of the cash flows for this problem.

To solve the problem, the present value (*PV*) amount of $1,000 is converted to a future value (*FV*) occurring at the end of five years. The conversion is made by multiplying the *PV* by the Column 1 (from Exhibit 2–3, Panel A) table factor (*TF*) for the specific interest rate and given period of time. Because the interest rate is 10 percent and the period is five years, the equation for conversion is

EXHIBIT 2-4

TIME-LINE DEMONSTRATION FOR OPERATIONS 1 AND 2
(example problems)

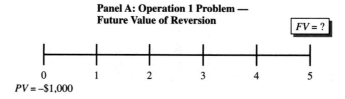

Panel A: Operation 1 Problem —
Future Value of Reversion

FV = ?

0   1   2   3   4   5
PV = –$1,000

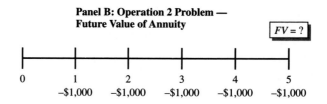

Panel B: Operation 2 Problem —
Future Value of Annuity

FV = ?

0   1   2   3   4   5
    –$1,000 –$1,000 –$1,000 –$1,000 –$1,000

$$FV = PV \times TF \text{ (Column 1, 10 percent, five years)}$$
$$= \$1,000 \times 1.610510$$
$$= \$1,610.51$$

The corresponding calculator keystrokes are

$N = 5$	$I = 10\%$	$PV = 0$	$PMT = -1,000$	$FV = ?$

The question mark in the future value register indicates that *FV* is the unknown. The $1,000 lump sum investment is entered as a negative number, consistent with the fact that it is an outflow from the perspective of the investor. These two procedures are identical to solving the equation for the future value of a lump sum investment. The Column 1 *TF* is the solution to the Exhibit 2–2 equation at 10 percent for five years, and the *FV* key on the calculator is programmed to solve the same equation. Solving using a calculator requires the user to enter *N, I,* and *PV* (the "knowns"); pressing the *FV* key (the "unknown") produces the $1,610.51 solution.

Note that if any four of the five required inputs are known, the fifth can be determined. For example, assume the future value of $1,610.51 is known and that *I,* the annual interest rate, is unknown. Entering $1,610.51 in the *FV* register (along with *N* = 5, *PV* = −$1,000, and *PMT* = 0) and pressing the *I* key will produce the answer of 10 percent.

Now assume Astute Investor plans to deposit $1,000 at the end of *each* year in a 10 percent, annually compounded account and wants to know how much these deposits will be worth at the end of five years. As shown in Panel B of Exhibit 2–4, the deposit flows (payments) are an annuity (*A*). Therefore, solving this problem involves finding the future value of the annuity. Column 2 *TF*s are used to convert the $1,000 annuity (i.e., cash flows occurring at the end of each period) to future values. The conversion equation and calculator keystrokes are

$$FV_a = A \times TF \text{ (Column 2, 10 percent, five years)}$$

$$= \$1,000 \times 6.105100$$

$$= \$6,105.10$$

$N = 5$	$I = 10\%$	$PV = 0$	$PMT = -1,000$	$FV = ?$

Future value is again the unknown. Note that when finding the future value of a series of level payments (deposits), the level deposit amount is entered as a negative number in the *PMT* register and the *PV* register contains a zero amount (or is empty). This tells the calculator that the amount will be deposited *every* year for N years. When finding the future value of a lump sum (Operation 1), the one-time deposit is entered in the *PV* register—the *PMT* register contains a zero or is empty.

Finally, assume that Astute Investor also is considering making monthly deposits of $83.33 ($1,000/12) for five years. *N* in this case is 60 (5 × 12) and *I*, the monthly interest rate, is equal to 0.83333 percent (10 percent/12). The Column 2 *TF* comes from the monthly interest rate table and is equal to 77.437072. The conversion equation is

$$FV_a = A \times TF \text{ (Column 2, 10 percent/12, 60 months)}$$

$$= \$83.33 \times 77.437072$$

$$= \$6,452.83$$

The corresponding keystrokes are

$N = 60$	$I = 10\%/12$	$PV = 0$	$PMT = -83.33$	$FV = ?$

Whether payments are made monthly or annually, Astute Investor would deposit a total of $1,000 per year. However, if payments of $83.33 are made monthly, Astute will accumulate $6,452.83 at the end of five years versus $6,105.10 with annual deposits. Why is there a $347.73 difference in future values if total principal payments over the five-year period are the same with both strategies? The difference is due to compound interest. Interest earned in any period is a function of the periodic interest rate (yearly, monthly, etc.) *and* the amount on deposit at the beginning of the period. When interest is compounded monthly instead of annually, the average principal balance in any year is higher—allowing the investor to earn more "interest on interest."

Operation 3.   The third column of the interest tables is called the **sinking fund factor**. It is used to find an annuity payment, given that the future value is known. Therefore, the sinking fund problem is the mirror image of the previous problem.

Suppose Astute Investor desires to buy some jewelry for a daughter when she graduates from college five years from now. Astute estimates the jewelry may be purchased

EXHIBIT 2-5

TIME-LINE DEMONSTRATION—SINKING FUND EXAMPLE

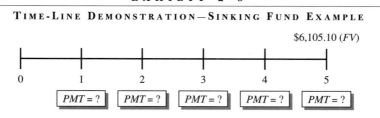

for $6,105.10 in five years and wants to save an equal amount in each of the next five years so that, with compound interest at 10 percent annually, $6,105.10 is available at the end of the fifth year. The cash flows for this problem are shown on the time line in Exhibit 2–5.

The conversion equation for this problem is similar to previous equations except that now the objective is to solve for *PMT*, the annuity amount. The conversion equation and the calculator keystrokes are

$$A = FV \times TF \text{ (Column 3, 10 percent, five years)}$$
$$= \$6,105.10 \times 0.163797$$
$$= \$1,000.00$$

$N = 5$	$I = 10\%$	$PV = 0$	$PMT = ?$	$FV = 6{,}105.10$

The calculator produces a result of −$1,000. The negative result means Astute must pay out (i.e., put aside) $1,000 per year to obtain the $6,105.10 in five years. The table factor, known as the sinking fund factor, is from the third column, fifth row, of the 10 percent annual interest rate table in Exhibit 2–3, Panel A. Because this problem is the mirror image of the previous future value of an annuity problem, the annuity investment is $1,000.

Column 3 has several important applications for real estate analysis. Suppose the owner of an apartment complex estimates that $50,000 will be required to replace carpets and appliances at the end of their useful lives in seven years. The owner wants to set aside an equal amount at the end of each of the next seven years from rental income so that, with compound interest of 10 percent, the deposits will grow to exactly $50,000. Using the same conversion equation with $TF = 0.105405$ or using calculator keystrokes to solve the problem, the answer is −$5,270.27. Thus, the apartment complex owner should set aside $5,270.27 in an interest-bearing account each year to replace the appliances and carpets. Such accounts are commonly known as "reserve for replacement" accounts.

Operations 4 and 5. Operations 4 and 5 are used to convert future dollar amounts to present values. The concept underlying these operations is important for investment analysis because converting future dollar amounts to present values is the cornerstone of

EXHIBIT 2-6

TIME-LINE DEMONSTRATION FOR OPERATIONS 4 AND 5
(example problems)

Panel A: Operation 4 — Present Value of Reversion

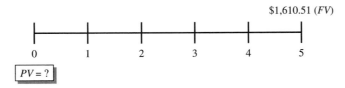

Panel B: Operation 5 — Present Value of Annuity

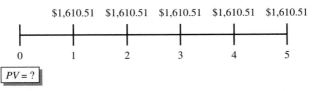

valuation. Operation 4 is used to calculate the present value of future lump sum receipts. Consequently, it is useful for discounting future cash flows, positive or negative, back to the present.

Assume Astute Investor has been offered an investment opportunity that provides $1,610.51 at the end of five years, as shown in Panel A of Exhibit 2–6, and is able to earn 10 percent on other investments (i.e., 10 percent is the required rate of return on investments of this type). How much can Astute pay today for this $1,610.51 future lump sum receipt and still earn 10 percent?

This problem calls for the conversion of a future amount to a present value. The conversion equation is

$$PV = FV \times TF \text{ (Column 4, 10 percent, five years.)}$$

$$= \$1,610.51 \times 0.620921$$

$$= \$1,000.00$$

Astute should be willing to pay up to $1,000 today for the right to receive $1,610.51 in five years if Astute can earn 10 percent on similar investments. The corresponding keystrokes are

$N = 5$	$I = 10\%$	$PV = ?$	$PMT = 0$	$FV = 1,610.51$

The calculator produces a result of −$1,000. Present values are shown as negative amounts because calculators require a matching of inflows (+) with outflows (−) to perform calculations.

Another interpretation of this result is that Astute is exactly indifferent between having $1,000 today and having the right to receive $1,610.51 five years from today. How can this be? Why doesn't Astute prefer the larger amount?

Present value as a point of indifference. To understand why Astute is indifferent between having $1,000 today and having the right to receive $1,610.51 five years from today, recall the future value of a lump sum problem depicted in Panel A of Exhibit 2–4. If Astute invests a lump sum of $1,000 at 10 percent he will accumulate $1,610.51 at the end of five years. Thus, Astute can either (1) purchase (today, for $1,000) the right to receive $1,610.51 at the end of five years or (2) invest the $1,000 elsewhere at 10 percent. The second option also will yield $1,610.51 in five years; thus, Astute has a "take it or leave it" attitude toward the first option because he can replicate the $1,610.51 payoff on his own by simply investing the $1,000 at 10 percent. The present value of the $1,000 is the only value that makes Astute indifferent between the two options, assuming a 10 percent required rate of return.

What if Astute could purchase the right to receive $1,610.51 in five years for $900 today? Would he be happy to undertake this investment? Given that we know Astute is indifferent to the investment opportunity if the asking price is $1,000, clearly he would be happy to invest at a price of $900. Why? If Astute were to invest the $900 at 10 percent, he would accumulate $1,449.46 at the end of five years. Because Astute cannot replicate the $1,610.51 payoff by investing $900 in an alternative investment, he would be happy to pay $900 today for the investment. By paying $900 today for an investment worth $1,000 to him, Astute's wealth would increase by $100.

Why would Astute not be willing to pay more than $1,000—say $1,100—for the right to receive $1,610.51 in five years? If Astute were to invest the $1,100 at 10 percent, he would accumulate $1,771.56 at the end of five years. That is, he could do better with an alternative investment. In fact, Astute should reject the investment at any price greater than $1,000 because he could more than replicate the $1,610.51 payoff on his own.

Operation 4 can be used to find the present value of multiple lump sums. For example, in the above problem, there may have been an additional lump sum of $2,000 at the end of year 7 in addition to the $1,610.51 at the end of year 5. The value of this additional lump sum is $1,026.32 and was found by entering $2,000 as *FV*, 7 as *N*, 10 as the interest rate, and then solving for *PV*. The result of this operation is added to the previous result (i.e., $1,000) to obtain a total value of $2,026.32 for the investment opportunity. Once cash flow amounts are "brought back" to period 0, they may be added or subtracted.

Now suppose that the same investor is confronted with an opportunity to receive $1,610.51 at the end of *every* year for five years, as shown in Exhibit 2–6, Panel B. The investor requiring a 10 percent return needs to know the maximum amount to pay for this annuity and still earn his required 10 percent return. Two options are available for converting the annuity to a present value. One is to apply Operation 4 five times, once for each year, then sum the results. The less time-consuming option is to use Operation 5. The conversion equation and the calculator keystrokes are

$$PV_a = A \times TF \text{ (Column 5, 10 percent, 5 years)}$$
$$= \$1,610.51 \times 3.790787$$
$$= \$6,105.10$$

N = 5	I = 10%	PV = ?	PMT = 1,610.51	FV = 0

Note that because the cash flows will be received *every* year over the five-year period, the annuity amount is entered into the *PMT* register. There is no lump sum (*FV*) amount.

An income property example. The following example demonstrates that the expected cash flows from income-producing properties typically come from two sources:

1. Cash flow from operations.
2. Cash flow from the subsequent sale of the property.

Both cash flow components must be considered when estimating either the market value or the investment value of a property.

Consider a small office building investment that is expected to produce \$10,000 in income from operations each year for five years. The expected sale of the property at the end of the fifth year will generate an additional (lump sum) net cash flow of \$100,000. The equation to convert these future cash flows into a present value is

$$PV = A \times TF \text{ (Column 5, 10 percent, five years)} +$$
$$FV \times TF \text{ (Column 4, 10 percent, five years)}$$
$$= \$10,000 \times 3.790787 + \$100,000 \times 0.620921$$
$$= \$37,908 + \$62,092$$
$$= \$100,000$$

The first term on the right-hand side of the conversion equation represents the valuation of the annual operating income (i.e., the annuity), while the second term represents the valuation of the lump sum sale proceeds. The present value of both components can be determined with the following keystrokes:

N = 5	I = 10%	PV = ?	PMT = 10,000	FV = 100,000

Note that the \$10,000 annuity is entered into the *PMT* register and the lump sum sale proceeds are entered in the *FV* register.

Typically, the annual cash flows from operations are not expected to be constant. Thus, one must apply Operation 4 multiple times, once for each year, then sum the results. If the annual cash flows are separately valued, the lump sum proceeds in year 5 (*FV*) would be \$110,000.

Operation 6. Operation 6 is used to calculate mortgage payments. The table factor for this operation is called a mortgage constant. From the interest tables, the factor is obtained by adding the sinking fund factor (Column 3) to the interest rate (e.g., 10 percent). The result is the number found in Column 6 of the interest tables.

Assume Astute Investor is considering the purchase of a $120,000 home. In addition to making a cash down payment, Astute expects to obtain mortgage debt financing. Astute can afford to make monthly payments of $877.57 and is searching for the largest possible mortgage loan.

To potential lenders (mortgage bankers, commercial banks, etc.), a mortgage loan is an investment with a cash outflow equal to the amount of money loaned to the borrower. The expected income on the lender's mortgage investment is the periodic (usually monthly) payment that the borrower promises to make in exchange for obtaining the loan. The lender typically makes the loan proceeds available to the borrower at "closing," which is when the borrower-buyer (Astute) and the seller get together to exchange ownership of the property. Before passing ownership (title to the property) to Astute, the seller requires payment of $120,000 at closing. Astute must borrow an amount equal to $120,000, minus the cash down payment.

If Astute desires to make monthly payments of $877.57 for 30 years (360 months), what is the maximum amount that a lender who requires a 10 percent annual return would be willing to lend? To answer this question, the lender must first determine the present value of the promised payments. The conversion equation using Operation 5 and Panel B of Exhibit 2–3 is

$$PV_a = A \times TF \text{ (Column 5, 0.8333 percent, 360 months)}$$

$$= \$877.57 \times 113.950820$$

$$= \$100,000$$

The corresponding keystrokes are

$N = 360$	$I = 10\%/12$	$PV = ?$	$PMT = -877.57$	$FV = 0$

The maximum amount the lender should be willing to lend is $100,000, the present value of the promised payments.

Would the lender be happy to lend $95,000 at closing if Astute promises to pay $877.57 monthly for 30 years? Yes, because at closing the lender would effectively write a check to Astute for $95,000, and in exchange, the lender would receive a (legal) promise from Astute that has a present value of $100,000, given a 10 percent (annual) rate of return. The lender's wealth would therefore increase $5,000 ($100,000 − $95,000) by closing the loan with Astute.

Mortgage borrowers do not typically walk into a lender's office and state the amount of monthly payments they wish to make. Rather, the borrower applies for a particular loan amount. For example, assume Astute decides to borrow $100,000 at 10 percent annual interest for 30 years. What would be the monthly payment? To answer this question, the following conversion equation can be solved for A, the level mortgage payment:

$$\$100{,}000 = A \times TF \text{ (Column 5, 10 percent/12, 360 months)}$$
$$A = \$100{,}000 \times 1/113.950820$$
$$= \$100{,}000 \times 0.0087757$$
$$= \$877.57$$

The inverse of the annuity table factor ($1/113.950820 = 0.0087757$) is the monthly "mortgage constant," that is, the monthly payment per $1 loan amount. The annual mortgage constant (assuming monthly payments) is 10.53 (0.0087757×12). The table factors in Column 6 of Exhibit 2–3 are, in fact, mortgage constants that can be multiplied by any loan amount to determine the periodic payment.

Mortgage payments are typically referred to as **debt service,** as in payment to service the outstanding debt. The conversion equation for finding the monthly debt service (DS), given a loan amount (LA) and mortgage constant (R_m), is

$$DS = LA \times R_m$$
$$= \$100{,}000 \times TF \text{ (Column 6, 0.833 percent, 360 months)}$$
$$= \$100{,}000 \times 0.0087757$$
$$= \$877.57$$

The corresponding keystrokes are

$N = 360$	$I = 10\%/12$	$PV = 100{,}000$	$PMT = ?$	$FV = 0$

Because the loan amount is entered into the PV register as a positive number (inflow to the borrower), the calculator produces a payment of $-\$877.57$ (i.e., an outflow).

LOAN AMORTIZATION

The mortgage constant has as its components an interest rate *on* the unpaid principal balance and a rate for return *of* principal. Each time a debt-service payment is made, the lender receives interest and part of the loan's principal amount back. This gradual return of the amount loaned is known as amortization of principal. The rate at which the principal is returned is a function of the number of periods of the loan and the interest rate. The rate of principal amortization is a sinking fund factor. The interest rate is stated in the loan contract as the mortgage interest rate; thus the mortgage constant (R_m) is equal to the mortgage interest rate (I) plus the corresponding sinking fund factor, which is based on the mortgage interest rate and the term of the loan.

The breakdown of the fixed mortgage payment between interest and return of principal is given in the **loan amortization schedule.** For our example of a $100,000 mortgage at 10 percent interest for 30 years with monthly payments, the (partial) amortization schedule is shown in Exhibit 2–7. At period 0 (that is, the present), the amount outstanding on the loan is $100,000. With a monthly interest rate of 0.83333 percent (10 percent/12),

EXHIBIT 2-7

AMORTIZATION SCHEDULE

Assumptions:
$100,000 loan at 10% interest to be amortized monthly for 30 years.
Monthly DS = $877.57

Month	Interest Payment	Principal Reduction	Remaining Loan Balance
0			$100,000.00
1	$833.33	$ 44.24	99,955.76
12	829.10	48.47	99,444.12
24	824.03	53.54	98,830.04
36	818.42	59.15	98,151.65
48	812.23	65.34	97,402.22
60	805.39	72.18	96,574.32
120	758.81	118.77	90,938.02
150	725.23	152.34	86,875.52
180	682.17	195.41	81,664.56
210	626.93	250.65	74,980.49
240	556.07	321.50	66,406.86
270	465.18	412.39	55,409.50
300	348.60	528.97	41,303.23
330	199.06	678.51	23,209.17
360	7.25	870.32	0.00

the borrower owes $833.33 in interest (0.0083333 × $100,000) for the first month. The total debt service is $877.57, as previously calculated; thus the amount of the payment going to reduce principal is $44.24 ($877.57 − $833.33). At the end of month 1, after the first payment, the amount outstanding is $99,955.76 ($100,000 − $44.24). Following the same procedure for month 12, we can calculate the interest payment as $829.10 (0.0083333 × $99,492.59) and the principal payment of $48.47 ($877.57 − $829.10). The amount outstanding at the end of month 12 is $99,444.12. The procedure is repeated for each month of the mortgage maturity.

Occasionally, mortgage loans do not require that the principal be amortized over time. Thus, the payment on these **interest-only loans** consists entirely of interest. For example, assume the same terms as above, except that the $100,000 mortgage is interest-only. In this case, the total payment would equal $833.33 each month, and the principal balance would remain $100,000 over the life of the loan.

It is helpful to notice some important relationships in the loan amortization schedule. Exhibit 2–8 graphically illustrates the points. First, the debt service (payment) remains constant throughout the life of the loan. Second, the portion of the payment that goes toward the reduction of principal increases every month. As a result, the remaining principal balance declines (at an increasing rate) until a zero balance is reached at the end of the 30-year loan term. Third, the interest payment decreases each month. This occurs

E X H I B I T   2 - 8

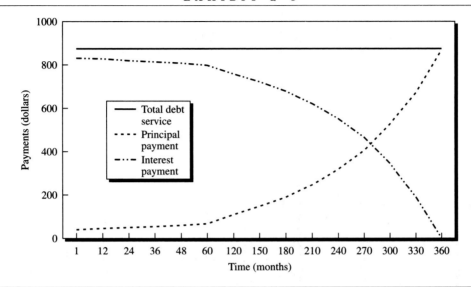

because interest payments due at the end of the month depend on the remaining principal balance at the beginning of the month. A declining principal therefore implies declining interest payments. In the early life of the loan, most of the debt service is interest with very little principal. This relationship reverses in the later years of the loan.

Calculating the remaining loan balance. Another common problem in dealing with mortgages is finding the amount outstanding at some point before the end of the loan term (at which point the amount outstanding equals zero). For example, if the borrower sells the house to relocate, the borrower and lender must determine the unpaid principal balance at that time. The unpaid balance at any point in time can be taken from the amortization schedule if one has already been constructed. However, most analysts will find it easier to use the amortization function that is built into most calculators.

There is, however, a time-value-of-money technique for determining the unpaid principal balance at any point in time in case your calculator does not have an amortization function (or in case you have yet to learn how to use it). The solution technique is simple: The unpaid balance at any time is equal to the present value of the remaining mortgage payments, when the discount rate is equal to the contract interest rate. Consider the $100,000, 10 percent, 30-year loan with monthly payments introduced above. Recall that the monthly debt service payment is $877.57. The remaining mortgage principal balance at the end of the fourth year, RMB_{48}, immediately after making the 48th payment, is $97,402.04. The conversion equation and corresponding keystrokes are

$$RMB_{48} = PV_a = A \times TF \text{ (Column 5, 10 percent/12, 312 months)}$$
$$= \$877.57 \times 110.990629$$
$$= \$97,402.04$$

$N = 312$	$I = 10\%/12$	$PV = ?$	$PMT = 877.57$	$FV = 0$

Why 312 months? Because there are 312 monthly payments remaining on a 30-year loan after four years.

INVESTMENT ANALYSIS

The purpose of investment analysis is to provide quantitative information to real estate decision makers. Quantitative information may take a variety of forms reflecting results from any or all of the intermediate steps in the investment analysis. The emphasis here is not with a particular type of real estate problem; solutions to real estate investment, appraisal, and finance problems are developed more fully in subsequent chapters. Rather, this section is concerned with the measures used in real estate investment analysis. These measures fall into two related categories: present-value measures and yield measures.

PRESENT-VALUE MEASURES

Many of the decisions and recommendations in real estate investment, appraisal, and finance follow from determinations as to how much real property rights are worth today. The present values of real property rights are found by converting future incomes generated from controlling these rights to values in the present. These conversions are simply direct applications of time-value-of-money concepts.

Take the case of a pension fund manager (someone who invests money for pension funds) who wants to purchase an apartment building for the pension fund's portfolio during 1998. Two properties are available to the manager, Cedar Ridge and Oak Glen. The manager asks the real estate acquisitions staff to estimate the expected incomes for each property during the next five years, and also asks them to estimate the proceeds from the sale of each complex at the end of the fifth year (2003). Exhibit 2–9 shows these estimates, together with a time-line display of the expected inflows of money.[2]

To find the present values of the benefits of the two properties, the cash flows from operations and the sale proceeds are multiplied by the appropriate Column 4 factors from the interest tables. Alternatively, a calculator or computer may be used. The pension fund manager estimates that the required rate of return (discount rate) for the fund is 10 percent.

---

[2] Analyses of this kind most frequently use a 10-year time horizon. A five-year period is used here for simplicity.

E X H I B I T   2 - 9

FUTURE INCOMES FROM TWO ALTERNATIVE APARTMENT INVESTMENT OPPORTUNITIES

| | Cedar Ridge | | Oak Glen | |
| | Estimated Cash Flows from | Estimated Sale | Estimated Cash Flows from | Estimated Sale |
Year	Operations	Proceeds	Operations	Proceeds
1999	$45,000		$40,000	
2000	$45,000		$40,000	
2001	$45,000		$40,000	
2002	$45,000		$40,000	
2003	$45,000	$425,000	$40,000	$450,000

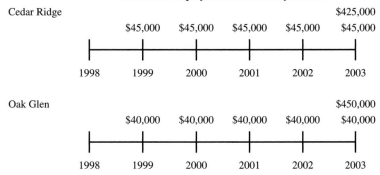

Time-Line Displays of Future Money Inflows

These conversions are found in Exhibit 2–10. The present value of the returns from the Cedar Ridge investment opportunity is $434,477, while the present value of the Oak Glen alternative is $431,047.

Cedar Ridge apparently is a better investment for the pension fund because of its higher present value. However, one important consideration has been omitted—the asking price of each property.

Net present value.   The **net present value** (*NPV*) is defined as the difference between the present value of the cash inflows (*PV$_{in}$*) and the present value of the cash outflows (*PV$_{out}$*). In symbols,

$$NPV = PV_{in} - PV_{out}$$

If, for example, the asking prices are $450,000 for Cedar Ridge and $420,000 for Oak Glen, then the present values for the cash outflows for these two investments are $450,000 and $420,000, respectively. The *NPV*s of the two opportunities are

$$NPV \text{ (Cedar Ridge)} = \$434,477 - \$450,000 = -\$15,523$$

$$NPV \text{ (Oak Glen)}\quad = \$431,047 - \$420,000 = \$11,047$$

EXHIBIT 2-10

PRESENT VALUE CALCULATIONS FOR ALTERNATIVE APARTMENT INVESTMENT OPPORTUNITIES

Cedar Ridge

Year	Cash Flows and Sale Proceeds	Column 4 Table Factor (10%)	Present Value
1999	$ 45,000	0.909091	$ 40,909
2000	45,000	0.826446	37,190
2001	45,000	0.751315	33,809
2002	45,000	0.683013	30,736
2003	470,000	0.620921	291,833
			434,477

Oak Glen

Year	Cash Flows and Sale Proceeds	Column 4 Table Factor (10%)	Present Value
1999	$ 40,000	0.909091	$ 36,364
2000	40,000	0.826446	33,058
2001	40,000	0.751315	30,053
2002	40,000	0.683013	27,321
2003	490,000	0.620921	304,251
			431,047

The *NPV* simply compares the costs (PV_{out}) with the benefits (PV_{in}) of investment opportunities. This measure is interpreted using the following very simple, but very important, decision rule: If the *NPV* is greater than zero, the property should be purchased, assuming the investor has adequate resources; if the *NPV* is negative, the investment should be rejected. If the *NPV* equals zero, the investor is indifferent. A positive *NPV* means the investor expects to earn a return greater than her required rate of return for such an investment.

Now that the asking price has been incorporated into the analysis, a different picture emerges concerning the pension fund's investment in the two apartment properties. Although the Cedar Ridge cash flows from annual operations and from the sale of the property have a higher present value, the cost of the property is sufficiently high to make the *NPV* negative. Oak Glen is the only acceptable property because of its positive *NPV*. If both properties had been acceptable because of positive *NPV*s, the property with the highest *NPV* would be chosen if only one could be purchased.

YIELD MEASURES

Often it is awkward to express measures of returns or costs in dollar terms. For example, if the pension fund manager in the previous example were to inform the fund's policy

EXHIBIT 2-11

CALCULATION OF IRR FOR CEDAR RIDGE APARTMENT
INVESTMENT OPPORTUNITY

Year	Cash Flows and Sale Proceeds	Column 4 Table Factor (10%)	Present Value	Column $ Table Factor (9%)	Present Value
1999	$ 45,000	0.909091	$ 40,909	0.917341	$ 41,284
2000	45,000	0.826446	37,190	0.841680	37,876
2001	45,000	0.751315	33,809	0.772183	34,748
2002	45,000	0.683013	30,736	0.708425	31,879
2003	470,000	0.620921	291,833	0.649931	305,468
			$434,477		$451,255

NPV (Asking Price = $450,000)   −$15,523 $1,255

IRR (exact) = 9.07%

Calculator Keystrokes

N = 5	I = ?	PV = −450,000	PMT = 45,000	FV = 425,000

board that the Oak Glen investment is expected to provide an *NPV* of $11,047, it would be difficult for policy makers to evaluate how well this investment compares to other investment opportunities such as stocks, bonds, and other real estate investments. If, however, the pension fund portfolio has an overall yield of 10 percent, and the Cedar Ridge property is expected to yield 12 percent, then policy makers are able to make comparisons to other real estate investment opportunities and certain stocks and bonds. Yield measures are an alternative way of providing quantitative information to decision makers. They are important for performing real estate investment analysis, for evaluating the cost of borrowing in a mortgage contract, and for analyzing various other real estate problems. Several applications of yield measurements are demonstrated in the following section.

Internal rate of return. The most popular yield measure is the **internal rate of return** (*IRR*). Although certain technical problems are associated with its use, the internal rate of return continues to be the standard, comprehensive measure of effective returns and costs in real estate and other business fields, such as corporate finance. The *IRR* also is called the **yield to maturity, effective yield,** or **effective cost.**

Perhaps the clearest way to view the *IRR* is in its relationship to *NPV*. The *IRR* is the rate of return that equates PV_{in} to PV_{out}. Thus, it is the rate of return that results in *NPV* equaling zero. Recall from the analysis of Cedar Ridge and Oak Glen that the incomes and sales proceeds were discounted at the required rate of return of 10 percent. In neither case was 10 percent the *IRR*, because the *NPV* was nonzero for both properties. To find the *IRR*, other rates must be tried in the process of discounting the cash flows to find the rate that makes *NPV* equal zero.

Exhibit 2–11 presents the results of calculating the *IRR* on the Cedar Ridge investment by a trial-and-error method. As determined earlier, the *NPV* using a 10 percent discount rate is −$15,523. This means that to drive the *NPV* toward zero (i.e., to make the present value of the inflows equal to $450,000), a lower discount rate must be applied to the projected cash flows because the lower the rate, the higher the present value. At 9 percent, the *NPV* is a slightly positive $1,255. This means the *IRR* lies between 9 and 10 percent, because at some rate between 9 and 10 percent (probably very close to 9 percent), *NPV* is zero. Using the calculator keystrokes shown at the bottom of Exhibit 2–11, the *IRR* is calculated as 9.07 percent.

The decision rule for the *IRR* is consistent with that for the *NPV*: If the *IRR* is greater than or equal to the investor's required rate of return, the investment should be accepted; otherwise it should be rejected. When the *IRR* is equal to the required rate, the investor is earning exactly the required rate of return (and the *NPV* = 0) and is therefore indifferent between accepting and rejecting the project.

The *IRR* can be calculated with most calculators using the system of cash flow (*CF*) keys. These keys, which allow the user to specify the precise pattern of cash inflows and outflows over time, can be used to obtain summary measures of return, such as *IRR* and *NPV*. Although the method of solution varies across calculators, these keys greatly simplify the computational process when the inflows (or outflows) are different each period.

Lender yield/effective cost of borrowing. Applications of yield measures abound in the area of mortgage finance. When a mortgage lender makes a loan, it is an investment in expectation of a return. The investment (PV_{out}) is the loan amount, while the present value of the money inflows (PV_{in}) is the present value of the debt-service payments and any other payments to be received by the lender. The lender's yield is the *IRR* that equates the loan amount with the present value of the payments to be received by the lender.

The mirror image of the lender's yield is the borrower's effective cost of borrowing. Lender yield and effective cost of borrowing are found using the same calculation. The only difference is that the cash flows on the time lines are reversed; that is, inflows to the borrower are outflows to the lender.

Suppose a mortgage lender offers a borrower the following two options:

1. A $100,000 loan with terms of 11 percent, 30 years, and annual payments.
2. A $100,000 loan with terms of 10 percent, 30 years, and annual payments, with the requirement that the borrower must make a one-time $4,000 payment of interest when the loan is taken out.

Which is the least costly option for the borrower and, therefore, the least profitable for the lender? The annual mortgage payment (*DS*) for each loan is calculated as follows:

$$\text{Option 1: } DS = LA \times R_m$$

$$= \$100,000 \times TF \text{ (Column 6, 11 percent, 30 years)}$$

$$= \$100,000 \times 0.115025$$

$$= \$11,502.50$$

E X H I B I T   2 - 1 2

**TIME-LINE PRESENTATION FOR LENDER YIELD/EFFECTIVE COST
OF BORROWING EXAMPLE**

Option 1

Lender perspective

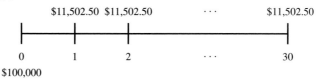

Borrower perspective

Option 2

Lender perspective

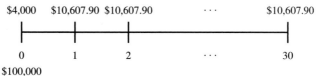

Borrower perspective

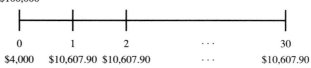

Option 2: $DS = LA \times R_m$

         $= \$100{,}000 \times TF$ (Column 6, 10 percent, 30 years)

         $= \$100{,}000 \times 0.106079$

         $= \$10{,}607.90$

Therefore, in exchange for a $4,000 payment when the loan is taken out, the borrower will save $894.60 ($11,502.50 − $10,607.90) in payments each year. To judge whether the borrower should accept the second option, consider the lender yield and the effective cost of borrowing. Exhibit 2–12 shows time-line presentations of the lender and borrower perspectives on these two options.

The yield measures are easy to calculate for Option 1. Both the lender yield and the effective cost of borrowing are 11 percent because the present value of an $11,502.50 annuity over 30 years at 11 percent is $100,000 (remember Column 5 is the reciprocal of Column 6). In fact, the effective cost of borrowing will always equal the stated (or contract) interest rate when there are *no up-front financing costs.* For Option 2, however, the payment is based on $100,000, but the actual net loan proceeds equal $96,000 ($100,000 − $4,000). Thus, the lender yield and effective cost of borrowing must be calculated by finding the rate that equates the present value of the $10,607.90 annuity payment to $96,000—the lender's net outflow.

Because the present value of the $10,607.90 annuity discounted at 10 percent is $100,000, a higher discount rate is required to drive the present value down to $96,000. A discount rate of 11 percent is a logical choice because Option 1 yields/costs 11 percent. This calculation is

$$PV_a = A \times TF \text{ (Column 5, 11 percent, 30 years)}$$

$$= \$10,607.90 \times 8.693762$$

$$= \$92,222.56$$

Because $92,222.56 is below $96,000, the yield/cost of this loan is below 11 percent. Therefore, the borrower should choose Option 2. Using calculator keystrokes,

$N = 30$	$I = ?$	$PV = 96,000$	$PMT = -10,607.90$	$FV = 0$

The exact lender yield/effective cost of borrowing is 10.50 percent.

Finding the lender yield and effective cost of borrowing involves exactly the same procedures as finding the *IRR*. In the above example, the rate was narrowed to between 10 and 11 percent by trial and error, just as when calculating the *IRR* by trial and error.

While other financial analysis tools exist, the *PV*, *NPV*, and *IRR* are probably the most important for supplying quantitative information to real estate decision makers. They are merely summary measures reflecting the results of many important intermediate steps studied in subsequent chapters.

CAPITALIZATION RATE INTRODUCED

The *IRR* is a comprehensive measure of return because it takes into account the quantity and timing of *all* cash flows that are expected to be received over the life of the investment. However, other measures of yield or return can be calculated for an income property. For example, the capitalization ("cap") rate on an acquired property, *R*, is defined as

$$R = CF/AP$$

where *CF* is the expected cash flow in year 1 and *AP* is the acquisition price. For the Cedar Ridge investment opportunity,

$$R = \$45,000/\$450,000$$
$$= 10.00\%$$

The **capitalization rate** is a measure of the current relationship between a property's income stream and price. It is not an overall measure of return because it ignores future cash flows from operations and expected appreciation (or depreciation) in the value of the property. It is analogous to the "dividend yield" on a common stock, defined as the projected dividends in the current year divided by the current stock price. All else the same, investors prefer stocks (income properties) with the highest dividend yield (cap rate). Given this relationship, and the widespread use of capitalization rates within the real estate industry, one may be tempted to rely on such measures for investment decisions. It is important to recognize, however, that the cap rate is not adequate as a final measure of investment desirability because properties can vary greatly with respect to future cash flows and appreciation. Investors should base decisions on measures such as *IRR* and *NPV* that consider all future cash flows.[3]

SUMMARY

Quantitative evaluations of real estate today involve heavy use of financial analysis techniques, such as valuation theory, time-value-of-money concepts, and specialized analytical procedures as they apply to real estate.

Valuation of property rights is the cornerstone of financial analysis, the general framework for analyzing problems in real estate appraisal, finance, and investment. Investment analysis involves the use of time-value-of-money concepts to provide quantitative information for solving problems and making decisions in appraisal, investment, and finance. An estimate of value is an example of the type of quantitative information real estate decision makers need. In addition to estimates of value, mortgage lenders are interested in their yields on mortgages, and borrowers are concerned with the effective cost of mortgage borrowing. Similarly, real estate investors are interested in knowing the rate of return on their investment.

Time-value-of-money concepts are the cornerstones of most financial analysis techniques. There are six traditional time-value-of-money operations:

(1) finding the future value of a lump sum investment, (2) finding the future value of an annuity, (3) finding the sinking fund factor, (4) finding the present value of a future lump sum payment, (5) finding the present value of an annuity, and (6) finding mortgage constants. Time-value-of-money problems may be solved with interest tables, financial calculators, or computers.

Students should be warned here about overreliance on the quantitative information—the "numbers"—provided by financial analysis techniques. As discussed in Chapter 9, real estate markets are imperfect. This suggests that qualitative information, in the form of appraiser, lender, and investor interpretations and judgment, plays a significant role in real estate decision making. Therefore, quantitative information from investment analysis should be viewed as merely one important input into the real estate decision-making process. Judgment and interpretations also are important inputs. Moreover, as a general rule, investment analysis techniques tend to become less reliable as markets become less perfect or competitive.

---

[3] Capitalization rates are discussed further in Chapters 3 and 14.

KEY TERMS

Amortization 26
Capitalization rate 53
Debt service 43
Effective cost 49
Effective yield 49

Interest 28
Interest-only loan 44
Internal rate of return 49
Investment value 26
Loan amortization schedule 43

Market value 26
Net present value 47
Sinking fund
   factor 37
Yield to maturity 49

TEST YOURSELF

Answer the following multiple choice questions:

1. How much will a $50 deposit made today be worth in 20 years if the compound rate of interest is 10 percent?
   a. $150.00.
   b. $286.37.
   c. $309.59.
   d. $336.37.
   e. $2,863.75.

2. How much would you pay for the right to receive $80 at the end of 10 years if you can earn 15 percent interest?
   a. $19.15.
   b. $19.77.
   c. $38.48.
   d. $38.82.
   e. $70.65.

3. How much would you pay to receive $50 in one year and $60 in the second year if you can earn 15 percent interest?
   a. $88.85.
   b. $89.41.
   c. $98.43.
   d. $107.91.
   e. $110.00.

4. What amount invested each year at 10 percent annually will grow to $10,000 at the end of five years?
   a. $1,489.07.
   b. $1,637.97.
   c. $1,723.57.

   d. $1,809.75.
   e. $2,000.00.

5. How much would you pay for the right to receive nothing a year for the next 10 years and $300 a year for the following 10 years if you can earn 15 percent interest?
   a. $372.17.
   b. $427.99.
   c. $546.25.
   d. $600.88.
   e. $1,505.63.

6. What is the present value of $500 received at the end of each of the next three years and $1,000 received at the end of the fourth year, assuming a required rate of return of 15 percent?
   a. $900.51.
   b. $1,035.59.
   c. $1,713.37.
   d. $1,784.36.
   e. $2,049.06.

7. What is the required mortgage constant for a 10 percent, 25-year loan?
   a. 0.092296.
   b. 0.096307.
   c. 0.108347.
   d. 0.109159.
   e. 0.110168.

8. Using the mortgage constant computed in the previous problem, what is the annual payment for a $75,000 loan?
   a. $6,922.20.

b. $7,223.03.

c. $8,126.03.

d. $8,186.93.

e. $8,262.60.

9. If an income-producing property is priced at $5,000 and has the following income stream

Year	After-Tax Cash Flow
1	$1,000
2	−2,000
3	3,000
4	3,000

would an investor with a required rate of return of 15 percent be wise to invest at the current price?

a. No, because the project has a net present value of −$1,139.15.

b. No, because the project has a net present value of −$1,954.91.

c. Yes, because the project has a net present value of $1,069.66.

d. Yes, because the project has a net present value of $1,954.91.

e. An investor would be indifferent between purchasing and not purchasing the above property at the stated price.

10. If you owned a property that you expect will require a new $2,500 roof at the end of five years from today, how much would you set aside in equal installments from income each year to be assured of having the necessary capital? You can reinvest your capital at 10 percent annual interest.

a. $294.56.

b. $310.46.

c. $372.27.

d. $409.49.

e. $500.00

PROBLEMS FOR THOUGHT AND SOLUTION

1. Dr. Bob Jackson owns a parcel of land that a local farmer has offered to rent for the next 10 years. The farmer has offered to pay $20,000 today or an annuity of $3,200 at the end of each of the next 10 years. Which payment method should Dr. Jackson accept if his required rate of return is 10 percent?

2. You are able to buy a mortgage note for $1,000 that gives you the right to receive $438 in each of the next three years. What is the yield on this loan?

3. A friend wants to borrow $635 and agrees to return $1,000 at the end of the fourth year from today. What is the yield or effective cost of borrowing?

4. Calculate the *IRR*s for the following investment opportunities:

	Project 1		Project 2
Year	Cash Flow	Year	Cash Flow
0	−$10,000	0	−$10,000
1	1,000	1	1,000
2	2,000	2	12,000
3	12,000	3	1,800

5. C. Colbert bought an apartment house with $60,000 cash and a mortgage loan of $100,000. The loan was made at an interest rate of 10.5 percent and requires annual payments for 25 years. What are the payments on this loan?

6. How much would you pay for an investment that provides $1,000 at the end of the first year if your required rate of return is 10 percent? Now compute how much you would pay at 8 percent and 12 percent rates of return.

7. Your grandmother gives you $10,000 to be invested in one of three opportunities: real estate, bonds, or zero coupon bonds. If you invest the entire $10,000 in one of these opportunities with incomes shown below, which investment offers the highest rate of return?

Investment	Year 1	Year 2	Year 3	Year 4	Year 5
Real estate	$1,300	$1,300	$1,300	$1,300	$9,000
Bond	$1,000	$1,000	$1,000	$1,000	$11,000
Zero coupon	$0	$0	$0	$0	$18,000

8. Big Hearted Bank offers you a mortgage loan of $50,000. The repayment schedule will be four payments of $15,000, but the first payment is deducted from the loan amount when you receive the money today. What is the effective cost of borrowing on this loan if the remaining payments must be made at the end of the next three years?

9. Calculate the present value of the incomes given below assuming interest rates of 8 percent and 20 percent.

Year	Income
1	$3,000
2	4,000
3	6,000
4	1,000

INTERNET EXERCISES

Time-value-of-money operations are one of the most important tools used by real estate investors. While these functions may be performed with handheld financial calculators or spreadsheets, the Internet offers many easy-to-use and fairly powerful programs to assist in completing these operations. For example, the Good Neighbor Reinvestment Mortgage Assistance Loan Program, commonly known as Ginger Mae, offers an online rate calculator. The calculator can be used to compare the difference in monthly payments for loans with different maturities or interest rates.

1. Go to the Ginger Mae home page at

   http://www.gingermae.com/

   and activate the rate calculator. Estimate the monthly payments on a $100,000 loan with 10 percent (annual) interest assuming loan terms of 15 and 30 years. How much will your monthly payments increase if you choose the 15-year loan over the 30-year mortgage?

2. Using the Ginger Mae rate calculator, estimate the monthly payments on a 30-year, $100,000 loan assuming interest rates of 8 percent, 10 percent, and 12 percent. How much higher will your monthly payments be if the interest rate is 10 percent instead of 8 percent? How much higher will your monthly payments be if the interest rate is 12 percent instead of 8 percent?

CASE PROBLEMS

1. Upon graduating from college, Vince Krugman landed a job as a naturalist at the local wildlife sanctuary. Having been an animal lover his entire life, Vince finds the job extremely fulfilling in every aspect but salary. Nonetheless, with a wedding planned for later in the year, Vince decided he's tired of living in overcrowded, noisy apartment complexes and wants to find a starter home where he and his fiancée, Sally Robinson, can begin their life together. Having been a scientist his entire life, Vince knows little about financial matters, so he's asked you to help him out. The first thing he tells

you is that he and Sally have decided that they can spend $4,000 per year on house payments. He also mentions that he stopped by the bank a few days ago and was told he could get a 30-year loan at 10 percent interest. Wanting to find the best possible (most expensive) house within their price range, Vince first asks you how much money they can borrow on these terms from the bank. He then tells you a local finance company offered to loan him $35,000 in return for his promise to pay $4,000 per year for 30 years. Should he borrow from the finance company or the bank, and how much more (less) money can he borrow if he uses the bank?

2. Having heard about the excellent advice you gave their son and future daughter-in-law, John and Eileen Krugman have dropped by seeking your advice. John and Eileen have five years left until retirement, at which time they would like to cash out their investment portfolio and travel the world.

Recently, their life has been turned upside down, as first their son announced he was getting married, and then they learned John was getting transferred and they must find a new place to live. They have recently met with both a real estate agent and the local mortgage banker in the town they must move to. During those conversations they were informed that they could receive a $50,000 mortgage with monthly amortization taken out at 15 percent for 30 years. Uncertain as to whether they should buy a new home, or simply rent a small condo for the next five years, the Krugmans want your answers to the following questions. First, if they sell the home at the end of five years when they retire, what will the mortgage balance be at that time? Second, how much principal amortization will they achieve over the five-year period? Finally, how much interest will they pay over the five-year period?

ADDITIONAL READINGS

The following books contain expanded examples and discussion of time-value-of-money concepts:

Crowe, Robert M. *Time and Money: Using Time Value Analysis in Financial Planning*. Homewood, IL: Dow Jones–Irwin, 1987.

Goebel, Paul R., and Norman G. Miller. *The Complete Guide for Mortgage Mathematics*. Englewood Cliffs, NJ: Prentice Hall, 1991.

Gaines, George, Jr., and David S. Coleman. *Real Estate Math*. Chicago: Real Estate Education Company, 1990.

CHAPTER 2: APPENDIX 2a

Applying Time-Value-of-Money Concepts to Real Estate

OPERATION 1: FUTURE VALUE OF A LUMP SUM

How much will $1 be worth at some future time if invested at a given interest rate?

Example: If you deposit $1 today at 10 percent interest, it will be worth approximately $2.59 10 years from now.

N = 10	I = 10%	PV = 1	PMT = 0	FV = ?

Example: If you purchase a parcel of land today for $25,000, and you expect it to appreciate 10 percent per year in value, how much will your land be worth 10 years from now?

N = 10	I = 10%	PV = 25,000	PMT = 0	FV = ?

The previous setup produces the correct answer of $64,843.56.

Problem: You purchase a piece of real estate today for $15,000. You expect to hold the property for eight years and then sell it. You believe the property will increase in value approximately 15 percent per year. How much should you be able to sell the property for in eight years?
Answer: $45,885.34

OPERATION 2: FUTURE VALUE OF ANNUITY

How much will a series of $1 payments invested each period at a given interest rate be worth at some future time?

Example: If you deposit $1 at the end of each of the next 10 years, and these deposits earn interest at 10 percent, the series of deposits will be worth approximately $15.94 at the end of the 10th year.

N = 10	I = 10%	PV = 0	PMT = 1	FV = ?

Example: If you deposit $50 per month in a savings and loan association at 10 percent interest, how much will you have in your account at the end of the 12th year?

N = 144	I = 10%/12	PV = 0	PMT = 50	FV = ?

Future value = $13,821.89

Problem: You purchase a parcel of land for $50,000. How much will you have to sell the property for in 15 years to earn a return on both your $50,000 outlay and expected annual payments of $1,000 for taxes and insurance? These funds could be invested at comparable risk to earn a 10 percent return.
Answer: $240,634.89

OPERATION 3: SINKING FUND FACTOR

How much must be deposited each period at a given interest rate to accumulate $1 at some future time?

Example: If you deposit $0.062745 (a little over 6 cents) each year for 10 years at 10 percent interest, you will have $1 at the end of the 10th year.

N = 10	I = 10%	PV = 0	PMT = 0.062745	FV = ?

Example: If you wish to accumulate $10,000 in a bank account in eight years, and the account will draw 15 percent compounded monthly, you must deposit $54.45 each month for eight years.

N = 96	I = 15%/12	PV = 0	PMT = ?	FV = 10,000

Monthly payment = $54.45

Problem: You purchase a building (exclusive of land) for $50,000, which is expected to depreciate to zero over the next 50 years. If amounts to cover each year's depreciation are taken from the building's income and invested at 10 percent, how much must the annual amounts allocated for depreciation be?
Answer: $42.96

OPERATION 4: PRESENT VALUE OF A LUMP SUM

How much is $1, due at some time in the future, worth today when discounted at a given interest rate?

Example: If someone owes you $1, which is due in five years and can be discounted at 10 percent, it is worth approximately 62 cents today.

N = 5	I = 10%	PV = ?	PMT = 0	FV = 1

Example: If your parents purchased an endowment policy of $10,000 for you and the policy will mature in 12 years, how much is it worth today, discounted at 15 percent?

N = 12	I = 15%	PV = ?	PMT = 0	FV = 10,000

Present value = $1,869.07

Problem: You own a remainder estate in a property, which means you may obtain title and possession at a future time. If the property is expected to be worth $50,000 in 15 years when your remainder interest will ripen, what is the present value of your interest, discounted at 10 percent?
Answer: $11,969.60

Problem: You want to buy a house for which the owner is asking $62,500. The only problem is that the house is leased to someone else with five years remaining on the lease. However, you like the house and believe it will be a good investment. How much should you pay for the house today if you could strike a bargain with the owner under which she would continue receiving all rental payments until the end of the leasehold, at which time you would obtain title and possession of the property? You believe the property will be worth the same in five years as it is worth today and that this future value should be discounted at a 10 percent annual rate.
Answer: $38,807.58

OPERATION 5: PRESENT VALUE OF ANNUITY

How much is $1 per period for a given length of time worth today when discounted at a given interest rate?

Example: If someone pays you $1 per year for 20 years, the value of the series of future payments discounted at 10 percent is approximately $8.51.

| $N = 20$ | $I = 10\%$ | $PV = ?$ | $PMT = 1$ | $FV = 0$ |

Example: If you are at retirement age and one of your benefit options is to accept an annual annuity of $7,500 for 15 years, you could take an equivalent lump-sum settlement of $57,045.60 if the annuity is discounted at 10 percent.

| $N = 15$ | $I = 10\%$ | $PV = ?$ | $PMT = 7,500$ | $FV = 0$ |

Present value = $57,045.60

Problem:
a. What price should you pay for the right to receive the annual income of $10,000 for 20 years from a piece of real estate if the series of income payments is discounted at 10 percent? (Assume the property will be worth zero at the end of the 20-year period; therefore, there is no value to your right to sell or continue owning the real estate beyond 20 years.)
   Answer: $85,135.64
b. If the property in part *a* is forecast to be worth $50,000 at the end of the 20-year period, what should you pay for it?
   Answer: $92,567.82

OPERATION 6: CAPITALIZATION RATE AND MORTGAGE CONSTANT

How much must be paid each period to pay back (amortize) a debt of $1, including interest at a given rate?

Example:

a. If you borrow $1 for five years and agree to repay the debt annually with interest at a rate of 10 percent, you must pay a little over 26 cents each year.

$N = 5$	$I = 10\%$	$PV = 1$	$PMT = ?$	$FV = 0$

Yearly payment = $0.263797

b. If you agreed to amortize the loan above in monthly installments, your payments would be a little over 2 cents each month.

$N = 60$	$I = 10\%/12$	$PV = 1$	$PMT = ?$	$FV = 0$

Monthly payment = $0.021247

c. The annual total of your monthly payments would be a little over 25 cents. $12 \times 0.021247 = \$0.254964$.

Problem:

a. You want to purchase a house having a price of $80,000. The real estate salesperson believes you could obtain an 80 percent monthly payment loan for 29 years at a 15 percent interest rate. How much would your monthly payments be?
Answer: $810.75

b. What percentage of the original loan amount is your monthly payment? (Note: This percentage is termed a monthly loan constant.)
Answer: 1.2668 percent

c. What percentage of the original loan amount is the annual total amount of your monthly payments? (Note: This percentage is termed an annual constant for a monthly payment loan.)
Answer: 15.20 percent

CHAPTER 2: APPENDIX 2b

Solving Time-Value-of-Money Problems Using EXCEL

Solving time-value-of-money problems can be accomplished quickly and accurately with the aid of computer spreadsheet packages such as EXCEL or LOTUS 1-2-3. The following EXCEL-based examples are designed to guide you through the process of solving the six basic time-value functions introduced in this chapter.

THE BASIC LAYOUT

After opening EXCEL, you should see a grid of cells with each column labeled alphabetically and each row labeled numerically. A cell is identified as the intersection of a column and a row, such as B4.

	A	B	C
1			
2			
3			
4			
5			
6			

Above this grid is a series of pull-down menus, which can be activated by clicking on the desired menu title (FILE, EDIT, VIEW, INSERT, FORMAT, TOOLS, DATA, WINDOW, or HELP), and a set of tool-bars containing pictorial shortcut keys known as icons. These icons are designed to simplify the processing and formatting of information contained within your spreadsheet. Throughout the following examples, we will provide instructions using both the pull-down menus and shortcut icons.

GETTING STARTED

Recall from the chapter that each time-value-of-money operation employs the same five pieces of information: number of periods entailed (N), periodic interest rate (I), present value (PV), periodic payment (PMT), and future value (FV). Given any four of these inputs, you should be able to solve for the fifth, unknown quantity. Because all time-value operations incorporate this same set of information, one easy way to solve many problems quickly is to develop a spreadsheet template that incorporates this information. Enter each of the five input labels in column A as shown.

	A	B	C
1	Number of periods (N) =		
2	Periodic rate (I) =		
3	Present value (PV) =		
4	Periodic payment (PMT) =		
5	Future value (FV) =		
6			

Values for each of these components then may be entered in column B and referenced in formulas to solve for the unknown factor. The primary advantage of using this method is the ability to alter one or more of the inputs and let the computer automatically recalculate the new solution. This spreadsheet template now can be used to solve six problems that were previously solved in the chapter using interest tables and calculators.

OPERATION 1: FUTURE VALUE OF A LUMP SUM

Suppose that Astute Investor deposits $1,000 today in an interest-bearing account at a local bank. The account pays 10 percent compounded annually, and Astute expects to withdraw the principal plus compound interest at the end of five years. Operation 1 is used to determine how much Astute will accumulate by the end of the fifth year.

To solve the problem, the present value (PV) amount of $1,000 must be converted to a future value (FV) occurring at the end of five years. To do this, enter the given information into the input section of your time-value template as shown.

	A	B	C
1	Number of periods (N) =	5	
2	Periodic rate (I) =	10%	
3	Present value (PV) =	−1,000	
4	Periodic payment (PMT) =	0	
5	Future value (FV) =		
6			
7	Future value =	$1,610.51	

The future value answer is $1,610.51. This cell is shaded to indicate that it is a solution rather than an input assumption. To replicate this answer, first move the cursor to cell B7. This is the cell where the answer is to be displayed. To calculate the future value, activate the INSERT pull-down menu and select the Function option. Alternatively, clicking the function wizard icon

produces the same result. A menu of available options should now appear, and you should select the financial function category and the *FV* (Future Value) function name. Click the Next> button to continue. A window should appear guiding you through the calculation. Specifically, for this example, at the *rate* prompt enter B2 specifying the cell containing the requested information. Similarly, at the *nper* prompt enter B1, at the *pmt* prompt enter B4, and at the *pv* prompt enter B3. The *type* prompt allows you to specify when the cash flows occur: 1 indicates that they occur at the beginning of each period, while 0 signifies that they occur at the end of each period. For this example, enter 0. Click on the Finish button to close the function wizard. The future value of $1,610.51 should now be displayed in cell B7.

OPERATION 2: FUTURE VALUE OF A SERIES OF LEVEL PAYMENTS

Now assume Astute Investor plans to deposit $1,000 at the end of each year in a 10 percent, annually compounded account and wants to know how much these deposits will be worth at the end of five years.

To solve the problem, the future value (*FV*) of the annual annuity payment must be calculated. To do this, first clear all information from your spreadsheet template except the input section labels. Then, enter the new assumption information into the input section of your time-value template as shown.

	A	B	C
1	Number of periods (*N*) =	5	
2	Periodic rate (*I*) =	10%	
3	Present value (*PV*) =	0	
4	Periodic payment (*PMT*) =	−1,000	
5	Future value (*FV*) =		
6			
7	Future value of annuity =	$6,105.10	

The future value of the annuity solution in cell B7 is $6,105.10 and is calculated as follows. First, move the cursor to cell B7 where your new answer is to be displayed. To calculate the future value, activate the INSERT pull-down menu and select the Function option (or activate the function wizard icon). You should once again select the financial function category, the *FV* (Future Value) function name, and click the Next> button to continue. As before, a window should appear guiding you through the calculation. For this example, enter B2 at the *rate* prompt, B1 at the *nper* prompt, B4 at the *pmt* prompt, B3 at the *pv* prompt, and 0 at the *type* prompt. Click on the Finish button to close the function wizard. The future value of $6,105.10 should now be displayed in cell B7.

OPERATION 3: THE SINKING FUND FACTOR

Suppose Astute Investor desires to buy some jewelry for a daughter when she graduates from college five years from now. Astute estimates the jewelry may be purchased for $6,105.10 in five years and wants to save an equal amount in each of the next five years so that with compound interest at 10 percent annually, $6,105.10 is available at the end of the fifth year.

The Financial Category of EXCEL's function wizard can again be used to easily solve for the required annual contribution/payment. First, clear all information from your time-value template except the input section labels. Then enter the new information provided into the input section of your spreadsheet as shown.

	A	B	C
1	Number of periods (*N*) =	5	
2	Periodic rate (*I*) =	10%	
3	Present value (*PV*) =	0	
4	Periodic payment (*PMT*) =		
5	Future value (*FV*) =	$6,105.10	
6			
7	Required annual pymt. =	($1,000.00)	

The annual payment of $1,000 in cell B7, shaded to indicate that it is a solution rather than an input, is calculated as follows. First, move the cursor to cell B7 where your new answer is to be displayed. Activate the function wizard and select the financial function category. This time, however, select *PMT* (Payment) from the list of available function names. Click on Next> to continue. An input window should again appear guiding you through the calculation. Specifically, at the *rate* prompt enter B2, at the *nper* prompt enter B1, at the *pv* prompt enter B3, at the *fv* prompt enter B5, and at the *type* prompt enter 0. Click on the Finish button to close the function wizard. The required annual payment necessary to meet Astute Investor's five-year savings goal is a $1,000 outflow and should now be displayed in cell B7.

OPERATION 4: PRESENT VALUE OF A LUMP SUM

Assume Astute Investor has been offered an investment opportunity that will provide a $1,610.51 payment at the end of five years. If Astute is able to earn 10 percent on other investments (i.e., 10 percent is the required rate of return on investments of this type), how much can Astute pay today for this $1,610.51 future lump sum receipt and still earn 10 percent?

   This problem calls for the conversion of a future amount to a present value. Once again, clear your spreadsheet of all information except the input section labels and enter the new information provided as shown.

	A	B	C
1	Number of periods (N) =	5	
2	Periodic rate (I) =	10%	
3	Present value (PV) =		
4	Periodic payment (PMT) =	0	
5	Future value (FV) =	$1,610.51	
6			
7	Present value =	($1,000)	

The present value of the future $1,610.51 lump sum cash flow is $1,000. To produce this solution, move the cursor to cell B7. Activate the function wizard, select the financial function category, and choose the *PV* (Present Value) function name. Click on Next> to continue. At the *rate* prompt enter B2, at the *nper* prompt enter B1, at the *pmt* prompt enter B4, at the *fv* prompt enter B5, and at the *type* prompt enter 0. Click on the Finish button to close the function wizard. The present value of the lump sum payment, equal to $1,000, should now be displayed in cell B7. It is calculated as a negative number because the future value amount is entered as a positive number.

OPERATION 5: PRESENT VALUE OF A SERIES OF LEVEL PAYMENTS

Suppose Astute Investor is confronted with an opportunity to receive $1,610.51 at the end of every year for five years. Astute, who requires a 10 percent return, needs to know the maximum amount he can pay for this annuity and still earn his required 10 percent return.

This problem requires the conversion of a series of future payments to a present value. The spreadsheet solution is accomplished in a manner very similar to that employed by Operation 4. First, clear your time-value template of old and extraneous information and enter the new data as shown.

	A	B	C
1	Number of periods (*N*) =	5	
2	Periodic rate (*I*) =	10%	
3	Present value (*PV*) =		
4	Periodic payment (*PMT*) =	$1,610.51	
5	Future value (*FV*) =	0	
6			
7	Present value of annuity =	($6,105.10)	

The present value of an annuity of $1,610.51 per year is $6,105.10. To calculate, position the cursor in cell B7, activate the function wizard, select the financial function category, and highlight the *PV* (Present Value) function name, click on the Next> button to continue, and fill in the appropriate references in the space provided (i.e., *rate* = B2, *nper* = B1, *pmt* = B4, *fv* = B5, and *type* = 0). Click on the Finish button to close the function wizard. The present value solution of $6,105.10 should now be displayed in cell B7.

OPERATION 6: CALCULATING MORTGAGE PAYMENTS

Assume Astute Investor is considering the purchase of a $120,000 home. To finance the purchase, Astute plans to make a $20,000 down payment and obtain mortgage debt financing for the remaining $100,000 obligation. If Astute decides to borrow $100,000 at 10 percent annual interest for 30 years, what would be the monthly payment?

Astute's monthly debt service can once again be calculated quickly and accurately using EXCEL. Clear the previous input assumptions and enter the new information provided, as shown.

	A	B	C
1	Number of periods (*N*) =	360	
2	Periodic rate (*I*) =	0.83%	
3	Present value (*PV*) =	$100,000	
4	Periodic payment (*PMT*) =		
5	Future value (*FV*) =	0	
6			
7	Monthly payment =	($877.57)	

Note that when entering the data, monthly compounding increases the number of periods (30 × 12) and decreases the periodic rate (10%/12) relative to annual compounding. The calculated monthly payment is $877.57. To calculate, move the cursor to cell B7, activate the function wizard, select the financial function category, highlight the *PMT* (Periodic Payment) function name, click on the Next> button to continue, enter the requested cell references (*rate* = B2, *nper* = B1, *pv* = B3, *fv* = B5, and *type* = 0), and click on the Finish button to close the function wizard and view your results. The required monthly payment of $877.57 should now be displayed in cell B7.

CONCLUSION

Spreadsheet users should be aware the examples provided in this appendix barely scratch the surface of computing power available within these packages. As you become more familiar with EXCEL, we encourage you to investigate the wide range of computing options available within the software.

3

C H A P T E R

INVESTMENT DECISION MAKING

INVESTMENT DECISIONS

REAL ESTATE INVESTMENT ANALYSIS
Investment Strategy

CHARACTERISTICS OF INCOME PROPERTY INVESTMENTS
Property Type
Rental Income
Purchasers as Investors
Geographic Scope

FORECASTING CASH FLOWS FROM OPERATIONS
Potential Gross Income
Effective Gross Income
Operating Expenses
Net Operating Income
The Treatment of Nonrecurring Expenses
Evaluating the Cash Flow Estimates

FORECASTING CASH PROCEEDS FROM SALE

MEASURING VALUE AND RETURNS
Valuation Using Discounted Cash Flow Models

Valuation Using Direct Capitalization
Why Discount Rates Determine
    Cap Rates

THE EFFECTS OF MORTGAGE FINANCING ON CASH FLOWS, VALUES, AND RETURNS
Effect of Debt on Projected Cash Flows
Why Do Investors Borrow?

OTHER INVESTMENT CRITERIA
Profitability Ratios
Multipliers
Financial Ratios
Limitations of Ratio Analysis

VARYING THE ASSUMPTIONS

SUMMARY

KEY TERMS

TEST YOURSELF

PROBLEMS FOR THOUGHT AND SOLUTION

CASE PROBLEMS

ADDITIONAL READINGS

After reading this chapter, students will be able to:

1. Identify the basic types and characteristics of property investments.

2. Reconstruct operating statements for potential investments as well as interpret the results.

3. Forecast annual cash flows, net of expenses, from renting and operating an income property.

4. Forecast cash flows from the eventual sale of the property.

5. Calculate the net present value and internal rate of return on a proposed investment.

6. Calculate and interpret basic financial ratios which apply to real estate investment decisions.

7. Understand and explain why investors borrow money and what effect leverage has on the investment decision.

INVESTMENT DECISIONS

Many individuals, businesses, and institutions invest some portion of the money they receive, net of expenses. Real estate is among the investment options for these funds. Other options include stocks; corporate bonds; local, state, and U.S. government securities; tangibles such as gold, art, and antiques; savings accounts; certificates of deposit; individual retirement accounts; and commercial paper. Investors will commit some of their scarce investment dollars to real estate acquisitions only if the benefits equal or exceed the benefits associated with these other investment options.

This chapter presents the conceptual and analytical framework for making real estate investment decisions. The framework has four basic components: forecasting cash flows from the operation of the property net of expenses; forecasting cash proceeds from the eventual sale of the property; converting future cash flow streams into present value; and applying decision-making criteria to compare the expected benefits and costs. This presentation answers a very important question about real estate investment: How should investors reach real estate investment decisions?

The emphasis in real estate investment decision making is on real property rights—specifically, the extent of the rights received in exchange for invested funds. In accordance with the concept that the value of real estate is equal to the present value of its future income, the benefits of acquiring real estate are the incomes these investments generate. The magnitude, duration, and variability of the cash flows generated by the real estate underlie the value of the benefits investors obtain from the property rights they acquire.

may differ from those of other investors. The objective of analyzing real estate investments, therefore, is to compare the values of all property rights in real estate investment opportunities against sellers' asking prices. The total value of the set of property rights to be acquired is the investment value of the real estate; if this value is greater than the acquisition price, then investors are on solid financial ground to proceed with the investment. The emphasis of the chapter is on income-producing properties; owner-occupied housing is highlighted in subsequent chapters.

REAL ESTATE INVESTMENT ANALYSIS

This section addresses the question of how real estate investment decisions are made during the acquisition phase of a real estate ownership cycle. Although these processes and procedures pertain to investing through direct purchase and ownership, they also apply generally to other methods and types of investments, such as the indirect purchase of real estate by the acquisition of stock in a company that, in turn, purchases the real estate.

INVESTMENT STRATEGY

Formation of an investment strategy is the starting point for investment analysis. The investment strategy establishes a plan that guides investors. Do investors actually prepare strategies for investment, or is this only a step found in textbooks? The answer is that it is both. Most institutional real estate investors (pension funds, life insurance companies, etc.) follow a written, formal investment strategy. Although many individual investors probably do not follow explicit, preestablished investment strategies, individual investors implicitly know their investment objectives and the general course they plan to follow.

Although there is no statistical evidence to support the claim, many believe the number and severity of investment errors are reduced by following a strategy and by applying a systematic framework to analyze potential investments. Limiting such errors is critical in real estate for two reasons: (1) there is usually much money at risk, and (2) the investor's reputation or track record is crucial for obtaining financing and dealing with potential tenants.

The investment strategy may be separated into three components: investment philosophy, investment objectives, and investment policies.

Investment philosophy. An **investment philosophy** outlines the relationship investors would like to have with real estate investments—mainly whether they will be *active* or *passive* investors. Active investment implies direct equity participation in which investors take active roles in finding, buying, managing, and selling the real estate. A passive investor, by contrast, might elect to invest in real estate through a real estate investment trust (REIT) or partnership syndication, leaving the acquisition and property management to others—for a fee.

The investment philosophy of individual, corporate, and institutional investors reflects their preferences for risk and return. Some investors are highly risk averse and unwilling to invest in risky projects, such as new developments, even though high returns are possible.[1] The degree of risk aversion may be related to the investor's wealth or to some institutional consideration.[2] Recognition of the investor's risk preferences is an important prerequisite to establishing investment objectives and policies.

Investment objectives. **Investment objectives** should follow from investment philosophies, as well as from other individual factors (e.g., tax status). The objective of preservation of capital, for example, follows from a philosophy of avoiding high risk. The objective of obtaining substantial tax benefits from real estate investments results from the investor's tax status. Thus, objectives may be viewed as general guidelines for choosing specific properties.

The following statement of the objectives of the Prudential Property Investment Separate Account (PRISA), one of the largest commingled real estate funds,[3] includes the specific objectives of earning current income, benefiting from appreciation, and diversifying across property types and locations:

The objective of PRISA is to obtain an attractive rate of current income from the property investments that offer prospects of long-term growth, in order to enhance the resources of participating pension plans to provide benefit payments. To fulfill that objective, Prudential invests PRISA funds primarily in the purchase of income-producing real property, including office and industrial buildings, shopping centers, other retail stores, apartments, hotels, and motels. Suitable diversification is maintained as to type of property and location. Particular attention is given to properties that are located in growth areas, may be leased on the basis of permitting suitable rent revisions, and are considered to have good appreciation potential.[4]

Investment policies. **Investment policies** create a profile of investments that satisfy investor objectives and are consistent with the investor's philosophy. Investment policies may include financial criteria, such as "property value appreciation of at least 5 percent," and nonfinancial criteria, such as "the age of the buildings must not exceed 10 years."

Investment policies also may include special considerations, such as investing only in small properties (e.g., "Apartment properties should have no more than 50 units" and "Office buildings should be no more than 50,000 square feet"). Once the set of policies is drawn up, investors have a profile of desired investments.

The investment strategy serves as a preliminary screening device. Any potential property investment that is inconsistent with investor policies, objectives, or philosophy

---

[1] New development projects are inherently more risky than existing property investments because there is no historical track record to consider.

[2] Pension fund managers, for example, can be held personally liable for their actions under the Employee Retirement Income Security Act (ERISA) of 1974.

[3] PRISA, managed by Prudential Life Insurance Company, combines investable funds from several pension funds (mostly corporate) to buy real estate.

[4] *A New Dimension in Pension Funding: PRISA—The Prudential Property Investment Separate Account,* 1970.

is rejected. Potential property investments that are found to be generally consistent with the investment strategy are evaluated further.

CHARACTERISTICS OF INCOME PROPERTY INVESTMENTS

Income property investments can be characterized by property type (apartment, office, etc.), by the type of rental income they produce, and by the geographic scope of the market.

PROPERTY TYPE

It is evident that many different types of real estate exist—for example, shopping centers, office buildings, industrial buildings, and apartments. Within each category, substantial variations can exist in quality, age, and size. For example, large regional shopping malls are easily distinguished from local strip shopping centers. However, the general characteristics of each property type can help focus an investor's search efforts and increase the probability of finding an investment that is consistent with the investor's goals and objectives.

The variety of possible property types is displayed in Exhibit 3–1. Investors entering the property selection process should understand that it is not possible to become an expert in all types of real estate. Indeed, most investors and advisers concentrate their efforts on a limited number of property types. However, the basic analytical framework for making real estate investment decisions presented in this chapter is directly applicable to all property types. Details on specific property types are presented in Chapter 6.

EXHIBIT 3-1

TYPES OF INCOME PROPERTY

Following is a partial list of the types of income properties. No official classification system for properties exists, so readers may think of some types of properties not listed here. Nevertheless, this list should provide some idea of the range and diversity of income-producing properties.

Apartments	Recreational properties
Hotels and motels	Rental houses
Restaurants	Commercial properties (freestanding)
Warehouses	Shopping centers
Service stations	Office buildings
Automobile repair shops	Farms, orchards, and groves
Automobile dealerships	Mixed-use properties
Parking lots and garages	Specialty properties
Hospitals	Resorts
Nursing homes	Grain elevators
Continuing-care retirement centers	Lumber yards
Senior assisted living properties	Amusement parks

RENTAL INCOME

Income-producing properties generate income either for owners who use the properties themselves or for owners who lease the properties. For owner-users, the income is usually reflected in the income of a business or profession. For example, owners may operate a store, a medical office, or a dental office in a property they own. They measure the amount of income the property generates by the rent they could obtain by leasing the property on the open market. In effect, the income an owner-occupied income property generates is implicit; an explicit rent (i.e., actual payment in money) is not specified.

Leased income properties generate explicit rent. Rent is specified in the lease contract; thus, it is called **contract rent**. This rent may or may not be equal to the rent that could be obtained by renting the property on the open market—the **market rent**. The lease contract may call for fixed rentals or for some growth in rental rates that is not necessarily as large as the growth in market rentals. Investors primarily consider contract rent if the potential investment property is leased long-term to a financially reliable tenant. Investors primarily consider market rent if the property is leased on a short-term basis or if they believe a longer-term tenant may break the lease or otherwise be unable to pay the promised contract rent.

PURCHASERS AS INVESTORS

In contrast to purchasers of single-family homes, purchasers of income properties usually have different motivations and objectives. They purchase such properties primarily to receive (1) periodic income and (2) appreciation. While home buyers also may seek the income-tax advantages and protection from inflation of home ownership, these objectives are usually secondary to shelter and amenities (e.g., swimming pool, good neighborhood, and scenic site).

GEOGRAPHIC SCOPE

While housing markets are local, investment markets for many income properties are regional, national, or international. When they seek financial benefits, some investors are little concerned about whether the properties are located across town or across the country. Many real estate investors are large firms or wealthy persons who employ asset and property managers in the markets where their properties are located. Many large office buildings, shopping centers, and other income properties in the United States are owned partially or wholly by foreign investors from around the world. Similarly, U.S. individual investors and firms own income properties around the world.

Most income properties, however, tend to be purchased by local investors. Small apartment buildings, shopping centers, commercial buildings, and office buildings are not usually of interest to institutional investors, yet they may offer substantial benefits to local investors who may be better able to evaluate them than distant investors. Also, personal management and supervision make the ownership of such properties feasible for many small investors.

FORECASTING CASH FLOWS FROM OPERATIONS

A primary objective in cash flow forecasting is estimating net operating income (NOI), which is calculated by deducting all expenses associated with operating and maintaining the property from the property's rental income. Net operating income excludes debt financing expenses, personal expenses, and other nonproperty expenses. In other words, NOI focuses on the income produced by the property after operating expenses but before debt service and the payment of income taxes. These latter expenses are personal and unique to each owner and not related to the property's basic income-producing ability. Net operating income therefore is a very important indicator of property performance.

In estimating expected NOI, investors and other market participants rely on (1) the experience of similar properties in the market and (2) the historic experience of the subject property. The current owners may not be renting the subject property at the going market rate, and its current expenses may differ from market averages. Thus, potential investors must evaluate all income and expense items in terms of current market conditions. Investors in existing properties typically start by placing these items in a **reconstructed operating statement** format, as shown in Exhibit 3–2. This format includes some types of income and expense, but excludes others usually included in accounting statements or reported for income tax purposes.

To show how the investor forecasts the cash flows from operations, suppose an investor is considering the purchase of a small suburban office building. The basic assumptions for this potential investment are shown in Exhibit 3–3.

POTENTIAL GROSS INCOME

The starting point in estimating NOI is to forecast **potential gross income**. PGI is the total annual income the property would produce if it were fully rented and had no collection losses (in other words, if tenants always pay the full rent on time). Potential gross income is the estimated rent per unit (or per square foot) for each year multiplied by the number of units (or square feet) available for rent. Investors forecast PGI by examining the terms of the existing lease(s) and the present tenant(s), if any. From this examination

EXHIBIT 3-2

RECONSTRUCTED OPERATING STATEMENT

	Potential gross income (PGI)
−	Vacancy and collection (VC)
+	Miscellaneous income (MI)
=	Effective gross income (EGI)
−	Fixed Operating Expenses (OE)
−	Variable Operating Expenses (OE)
=	Net operating income (NOI)

EXHIBIT 3 - 3

INPUT ASSUMPTIONS FOR SUBURBAN OFFICE BUILDING EXAMPLE

Input	Assumption
Number of units	18 total units: 8 on first floor and 10 on second floor
Asking price	$885,000
Projected increase in value	3% per year
Contract rents	12 units at $900 per month and 6 units at $700 per month
Projected rental increases	3% per year
Vacancy and collection losses	10% per year
Operating expenses	45% of effective gross income
Holding period	5 years
Selling expenses	5% of sale price
Financing:	
Loan-to-value ratio	75% of acquisition price
Interest rate	9 percent
Maturity	30 years with monthly payments
Up-front financing costs	3% of loan amount

investors decide whether to forecast PGI based on contract rents or market rents. If the property is under a long-term lease to a financially reliable tenant, the basis for PGI is primarily contract rent. Otherwise, the basis should be market rent.

Example. The Suburban Office Building has eight first-floor units with long-term leases, renting for $900 per month. The second floor contains 10 units, 4 of which rent for $900 per month and 6 for $700, all under short-term leases. Therefore, potential gross income in the first year of operations is estimated to be $180,000, calculated as follows:

First floor:		
8 units × $900 × 12 months	=	$ 86,400
Second floor:		
4 units × $900 × 12 months	=	$ 43,200
6 units × $700 × 12 months	=	$ 50,400
Potential Gross Income (PGI)	=	$180,000

This presentation of projected contract rents in year 1 also is known as the property's *rent roll.*

The analyst should gather rental data on similar properties to judge whether the contract rents are equal to market rents. For example, to determine the market rents for the second-floor units of the Suburban Office Building, the analyst would obtain data on second-floor units in similar buildings. If comparable rents are as shown in Exhibit 3–4, the analyst might conclude the monthly market rent for the second-floor units is about the average of the three comparables or $1.08 (or $12.96 per year) per square foot. Thus, market rents for the second floor units are estimated as

EXHIBIT 3 - 4

MARKET RENTS FOR COMPARABLE SECOND FLOOR UNITS

| | Comparables | | | Subject |
	1	2	3	Property
Rent/month	$900	$1,080	$990	?
Square feet per unit	900	910	940	950
Rent per square foot	$1.00	$1.19	$1.05	?

$$\$1.08 \times 950 \text{ sq. ft.} \times 10 \text{ units} = \$10,260 \text{ per month}$$
$$\$10,260 \times 12 \qquad = \$123,120 \text{ per year}$$

In this case, market rents for the second floor are estimated to be $29,520 ($123,120 − $93,600) more than current contract rents. This suggests that there is ample room for upward adjustments to rental rates when current leases expire.

EFFECTIVE GROSS INCOME

It is unlikely that the Suburban Office Building would be completely occupied year round or that all rents would be collected. Therefore, the second step in estimating NOI is for investors to forecast vacancy and collection (VC) losses. Again, investors should forecast these losses on the basis of (1) the historical experience of the subject property and (2) the experiences of competing properties. The normal range for VC losses is 5 to 15 percent of PGI, although vacancies well in excess of 15 percent have occurred in overbuilt markets. The expected VC loss is subtracted from PGI.

In addition to basic rental income, there may be miscellaneous income from sources such as garage rentals, parking fees, laundry machines, and vending machines. The miscellaneous income would be added to PGI.[5] The net effect of the vacancy allowance and miscellaneous income results in **effective gross income** (EGI).

Example.   Assuming contract rents, VC losses of 10 percent, and no other income, the EGI for the Suburban Office Building is

PGI	$180,000	
− VC	18,000	(0.10 × 180,000)
= EGI	$162,000	

---

[5] It is common in office leases and some retail leases to include a provision that protects investors from increases in operating expenses over the term of the lease. "Expense stops" place an upper limit on the amount of operating expenses that investors must pay. Operating expenses in excess of the "stop" amount are paid by the tenant. These payments from the tenant are typically displayed as "expense reimbursement revenue" and are added in, along with miscellaneous income, in the calculation of effective gross income.

E X H I B I T   3 - 5

S U B U R B A N   O F F I C E   B U I L D I N G   R E C O N S T R U C T E D   O P E R A T I N G   S T A T E M E N T

Potential gross income (PGI)			$180,000
Less: Vacancy and collection losses (VC)			18,000
Effective gross income (EGI)			$162,000
Less: Operating expenses (OE)			
Fixed expenses			
Real estate taxes	$15,900		
Insurance	12,000	$27,900	
Variable expenses			
Utilities	$13,900		
Garbage collection	1,000		
Supplies	4,000		
Repairs	6,000		
Maintenance	12,000		
Management	8,100	$45,000	
Total expenses			$ 72,900
Net operating income (NOI)			$ 89,100

OPERATING EXPENSES

The expenses typical owners incur in operating their property are termed **operating expenses** (OE). They are divided into two categories: fixed and variable expenses. Fixed expenses do not vary with the level of operation (i.e., occupancy) of the property. The most common fixed expenses are real property taxes and property insurance—owners must pay them whether the property is vacant or totally occupied.

Variable expenses, as the name implies, vary with the level of operation of the property; they are higher for a higher level of occupancy and lower for a lower level. They include items such as utilities, garbage and trash removal, maintenance, repairs, supplies, and management.

NET OPERATING INCOME

Investors obtain the final estimate of NOI for the first year of operations by subtracting all operating expenses from EGI. With assumed operating expenses for the Suburban Office Building, Exhibit 3–5 shows NOI in a reconstructed operating statement. In the example, total operating expenses in the first year are estimated at $72,900, or 45 percent of EGI, which in turn makes NOI equal to $89,100 in year 1. Net operating income, thus, is the amount of money left after paying the expenses of operation, but before paying the mortgage payment and income taxes.

Assuming the investor expects to hold the property for five years before selling, NOI in years 2 through 5 also must be estimated. Exhibit 3–6 contains these estimates. Given the assumptions in Exhibit 3–3—PGI increasing 3 percent per year, 10 percent vacancy and collection losses, and operating expenses at 45 percent of EGI—NOI is

EXHIBIT 3 - 6

SUBURBAN OFFICE BUILDING: NET OPERATING INCOME

		1	2	3	4	5
	PGI	$180,000	$185,400	$190,962	$196,691	$202,592
−	VC	18,000	18,540	19,096	19,669	20,259
=	EGI	162,000	166,860	171,866	177,022	182,332
−	OE	72,900	75,087	77,340	79,660	82,050
=	NOI	$ 89,100	$ 91,773	$ 94,526	$ 97,362	$100,282

expected to increase from $89,100 in year 1 to $100,282 in year 5. This projected stream of NOI is the fundamental determinant of property value. In an analogy to the stock market, NOI is the property's annual "dividend" and must be sufficient to provide the investor with an acceptable rate of return.

THE TREATMENT OF NONRECURRING EXPENSES

Many major components of income properties such as roofs and flooring wear out faster than the building itself; thus owners may replace them several times during the building's expected economic life. In addition, investors typically expect to incur "retenanting" expenses when leases expire and the vacant space must again be made ready for occupancy. These tenant improvements may be relatively minor. To release an apartment, for example, owners may simply apply a fresh coat of paint and clean the carpet. However, in some situations these expenditures can be quite large. As an example, the releasing of office space often requires that substantial changes be made to the space, such as removing or adding walls, raising ceilings, and altering electrical capacity. In fact, many office leases provide a new tenant with an "improvement allowance." This lease provision obligates the landlord to incur a prespecified dollar amount of expenditures to improve the space to the tenant's specifications.

When new leases are signed on some types of properties, the leasing agents are usually entitled to leasing commissions that typically range from 2 to 4 percent of the face value of the lease (monthly rent times number of months). Investors often make explicit estimates of these future leasing commissions in their discounted cash flow forecasts.

Nonrecurring expenses such as roof replacements, tenant improvements, and leasing commissions are commonly referred to as *leasing and capital costs* in cash flow projections. These expenditures are treated as "below-line" costs; that is, they are subtracted *from* NOI in the year in which they are expected to be incurred. Net operating income minus leasing and capital costs is defined as **cash flow before debt service and income tax**. For simplicity, leasing and capital costs will not be explicitly considered in the example problems that follow.

EVALUATING THE CASH FLOW ESTIMATES

Investors should consider some important questions when reconstructing the operating statement and projecting the future level of rents, vacancies, and operating expenses. The answers to these questions assist in the evaluation of the completeness and accuracy of the operating statement and the reasonableness of future projections.

Are the sources of income and expenses appropriate? Investors should include only those sources of income and expenses that relate directly and entirely to the income-producing ability of the property. Operating expenses do not include financing costs and federal income taxes because these expenses are specific to the investor. Estimates of operating expenses also exclude capital expenditures and business-related expenses that are not directly attributable to the operation of the property—for example, the unnecessary "business" lunches and club memberships deducted by the current owner. Tax depreciation (discussed in Chapter 4) also is excluded from operating expenses.

Have the trends for each revenue and expense item been considered? This question is important in evaluating the revenue and expense forecasts. Investors should avoid considering only short-term or current events to the detriment of long-term trends. For example, current vacancy rates may be high, although average rates for the past 20 years have been somewhat lower. Thus, current market conditions could easily bias a forecast of future vacancy rates.

What have been the experiences of comparable properties regarding each revenue and expense item? Considering the experience of the subject property only, regardless of its current status, is often too narrow a perspective. Whenever possible, investors should obtain information about revenue and expense items for comparable properties. As an example, property tax trends for frequently reassessed comparable properties may be better for forecasting the future property taxes of the subject property than its own past property tax trends. Obtaining this information on comparable properties requires that investors develop and maintain relationships with various market participants such as appraisers, brokers, lenders, and other investors.

FORECASTING CASH PROCEEDS FROM SALE

The second major source of cash flow comes from the disposition (typically, the sale) of the property. The sale is when the property "reverts" back to the owner; hence sales are frequently referred to as **reversions**. Because income properties are usually held for a limited time period, the cash flows from sale must be forecast in addition to the cash flows from annual operations. The general form of the cash flow from sale is

$$
\begin{array}{rl}
 & \text{Expected selling price (SP)} \\
- & \underline{\text{Selling expenses (SE)}} \\
= & \text{Net sale proceeds (NSP)}
\end{array}
$$

The expected selling price (SP) of the property must be estimated first. This is usually done by assuming some growth rate in the value of property over time or by assuming some constant relationship between NOI and value. In our Suburban Office Building example, the value of the property is expected to increase 3 percent per year from the initial value of $885,000. Thus, the value at the end of five years is expected to be $1,025,958.

Net selling price (NSP) is obtained by subtracting **selling expenses** (SE) from the expected selling price. Selling expenses include brokerage fees, lawyer's fees, and other costs associated with the sale of the property that represent cash outflows. Selling expenses in our example are expected to be 5 percent of the sale price, or $51,298. When deducted from the estimated selling price, this leaves an expected NSP of $974,660.

$$
\begin{array}{rlll}
 & \text{SP} & \$1,025,958 & [885,000 \times (1.05)^5] \\
- & \text{SE} & \underline{51,298} & [1,025,958 \times 0.05] \\
= & \text{NSP} & \$\ \ 974,660 &
\end{array}
$$

MEASURING VALUE AND RETURNS

To this point we have discussed the estimation of future cash flows—both from operations and the expected future sale of the property. The next step in the valuation and decision-making process is to apply a decision criterion to the projected cash flows. The focus is on valuation models that require the estimation of cash inflows and outflows over the expected holding period, although a somewhat less complicated valuation model—simple income capitalization—also is discussed.

VALUATION USING DISCOUNTED CASH FLOW MODELS

The term **discounted cash flow** (DCF) **analysis** refers to the process and procedures for estimating NOIs, NSP, and the discount rate, and then using these inputs to generate meaningful summary information for investors. Although the NOIs and NSP may be estimated directly by making assumptions about future events, the estimation of the appropriate discount rate for a real estate investment is often more subjective and indirect. The discount rate is the investor's required rate of return and is determined by the riskiness of the project's NOIs and NSP, investor preference for risk, and the risk-free (or base) rate of return. The latter is typically measured as the rate of return available on a risk-free government security of comparable maturity.[6]

---

[6] Determining the appropriate discount rate for income property investments is discussed in more detail in Chapter 7.

Discounted cash flow analysis has become the main financial analysis tool to evaluate the merits of real estate investments. Although much of the effort in discounted cash flow analysis goes toward the estimation of the NOIs, NSP, and discount rate, the following summary measures of value and return are the bottom-line concerns of investors: investment value, net present value, and the internal rate of return on equity.

The net present value method. Investors are keenly interested in the investment values of properties because they reflect their individualized inputs and because investment values may be compared directly to asking prices or the development costs of properties. Investment values are the present values of the investor's interests in, or claims against, income from the properties. In equation form, investment value can be written as

$$IV = \sum_{t=1}^{n} \frac{NOI_t}{(1+y)^t} + \frac{NSP_n}{(1+y)^n} \tag{3–1}$$

where y is the investor's required discount rate on cash flows net of operating expenses, but before debt service payments and income taxes are deducted.[7] The traditional, although subjective, approach to estimating the appropriate discount rate is to begin with a risk-free rate (e.g., the current interest rate on a U.S. Treasury security), and then add risk premiums for expected risks of the real estate investment. (See a more detailed discussion in Chapter 7.) More objective approaches are difficult to implement because data from which risk premiums may be estimated are either nonexistent or too costly to acquire.

If investment value is greater than or equal to the acquisition price (or development cost) of the property, the investor should invest. The decision rule can therefore be stated as

If IV ≥ AP, accept

If IV < AP, reject

This is exactly the same as saying that the property should be acquired if the NPV is zero or positive—as discussed in Chapter 2—because NPV = IV − AP. The decision rule is straightforward and is one of the main reasons discounted cash flow analysis is so well accepted in current practice by real estate investors.

To illustrate the calculation of NPV, consider again our Suburban Office Building example. The acquisition price of this investment is $885,000. In exchange for the acquisition price, the investor would acquire a set of property rights, and these rights are expected to produce the stream of NOI shown previously in Exhibit 3–6, as well as net sale proceeds in five years of $974,660. These cash flows are summarized in Exhibit 3–7.

The present value of the cash flows in Exhibit 3–7, excluding the initial investment, are calculated using the concepts developed in Chapter 2. The present value factors (PVFs) equal the present value of the right to receive a lump sum payment of $1 at the end of each

---

[7] Investment value is often calculated using the cash flows that investors expect to receive net of mortgage payments and federal income taxes. These effects are discussed later in this chapter and in Chapter 4.

EXHIBIT 3-7

OPERATING CASH FLOWS FROM SUBURBAN OFFICE BUILDING EXAMPLE

Year	Initial Investment	Net Operating Income	Net Sale Proceeds	PV Factor @ 12 %	Present Value
0	($885,000)			1.000000	($885,000)
1		$ 89,100		0.892857	79,554
2		91,773		0.797194	73,161
3		94,526		0.711780	67,282
4		97,362		0.635518	61,875
5		100,283	$974,660	0.567427	609,952
				Net present value	$6,823

year, given a 12 percent discount rate.[8] Multiplying the expected cash flows by the PVFs results in present value. Summing these present values yields an investment value of $891,823 and an NPV of $6,823.[9] Note that equation (3–1) is simply an algebraic representation of the calculations performed in Exhibit 3–7.

Using our first investment decision rule, the investment would be accepted because the investment value exceeds the acquisition price. Using the NPV method, we can state the decision rule as follows:

If NPV ≥ 0, accept

If NPV < 0, reject

To further analyze the NPV method, the NPVs at different discount rates can be calculated using either the format demonstrated in Exhibit 3–7 or a handheld calculator. These results are displayed in Exhibit 3–8. Spreadsheet programs, such as EXCEL or LOTUS 1-2-3, are ideally suited to solving problems using the format displayed in Exhibit 3–7.

Note that as the required rate of return increases, the NPV goes down. Also note that when the cash flows are discounted at 12.2062 percent, the NPV equals zero. At discount rates less than 12.2062 percent the NPV is positive, indicating an accept decision. When the discount rate is greater than 12.2062 percent, NPV is negative, indicating a reject decision. The rate at which NPV is exactly equal to zero is called the **internal rate of return**.

The internal rate of return method.   The rate of return on the investment is an essential concern of investors. The internal rate of return on equity (IRR) is the discount rate that makes the present value of the cash flows equal to the asking price. In equation form, the IRR is the rate that makes the present value of the cash flows equal to the acquisition price. The equation is written as

---

[8] For example, the present value factor of 0.797194 for year 2 can be calculated with the following keystrokes: $N = 2$, $I = 12\%$, $PV = ?$, $PMT = 0$, and $FV = 1$.

[9] Most financial calculators allow the user to solve for the present value of a stream of uneven cash flows by using the cash flow (CF) key. In this example, $-885,000$ would be entered as CF_0, 89,100 as CF_1, 91,773 as CF_2, and 94,526, 97,362, and 1,074,942 (100,282 + 974,660) as CF_3, CF_4, and CF_5, respectively.

E X H I B I T 3 - 8

NET PRESENT VALUES AT DIFFERENT DISCOUNT RATES

Required Rate of Return (y)	Net Present Value
8.00 %	$154,370
10.00	76,819
11.00	40,934
12.00	6,823
12.2062	0
13.00	(25,618)
14.00	(56,486)
16.00	(113,862)
18.00	($165,965)

$$AP = \sum_{t=1}^{n} \frac{NOI_t}{(1+r)^t} + \frac{NSP_n}{(1+r)^n}$$

where AP is the acquisition price (cash outflow) and r is the internal rate of return. As discussed in Chapter 2, the only method for calculating the IRR in the absence of a calculator or spreadsheet program is trial and error. Returning to our example, we know the asking price of the Suburban Office Building is $885,000.

Suppose we select 11 percent as the discount rate. At this rate the present value of the cash inflows is $925,934. However, the asking price is $885,000—thus the IRR is not equal to 11 percent. But is the IRR higher or lower than 11 percent? To answer this question, note that the PV at 11 percent produces an IV that is $40,934 greater than the acquisition price. To lower the present value of the cash flows in the direction of $885,000, we must increase the discount rate. With a 12 percent discount rate, the PV of the cash inflows is $891,823, still in excess of the $885,000 asking price. However, at 13 percent, the present value of the cash flows equals $859,382 and the NPV is equal to ($25,618). Thus, a 13 percent discount rate is too high. This indicates that the discount rate that makes the NPV equal to zero, the IRR, is somewhere between 12 and 13 percent. As shown in Exhibit 3–9, the discount rate that exactly solves the IRR equation is 12.2062 percent.[10]

Should the project be accepted or rejected? Because investors require a 12 percent rate of return and expect to earn approximately 12.2 percent, the project should be accepted. The decision rule for the internal rate of return method is, therefore,

If $r \geq y$, accept

If $r < y$, reject

where r is the calculated *IRR* (or the expected rate) and y is the required discount rate.

---

[10] Financial calculators also allow the user to solve for the internal rate of return of a stream of uneven cash flows by using the cash flow (CF) key. In this example, $-885,000$ would be entered as CF_0, 89,100 as CF_1, 91,773 as CF_2, and 94,526, 97,362, and 1,074,942 ($100,282 + 974,600$) as CF_3, CF_4, and CF_5, respectively. Then solve for I. The calculations that appear in Exhibit 3–9 were actually performed with a spreadsheet program.

EXHIBIT 3-9

COMPUTATION OF INTERNAL RATE OF RETURN FOR SUBURBAN OFFICE BUILDING EXAMPLE

Year	Cash Flows	Present Values			
		11%	12%	12.2062%	13%
0	($885,000)	($885,000)	($885,000)	($885,000)	($885,000)
1	89,100	80,270	79,554	79,407	78,850
2	91,773	74,485	73,161	72,892	71,872
3	94,526	69,117	67,282	66,911	65,511
4	97,362	64,135	61,875	61,422	59,714
5	1,074,943*	637,926	609,952	604,368	583,436
Net present value		$40,934	$6,823	$0	($25,618)

* The cash flow in year 5 is the sum of NOI in year 5 and the estimated net selling price.

Comparing NPV and IRR. With NPV we selected a discount rate (and solved for value); with IRR we are solving for a "correct" discount rate. Note that both NPV and IRR come from the same discounted cash flow equation. Therefore, we would expect that decisions using the two DCF methods would be fairly consistent and, to a large extent, this is true. In fact, both NPV and IRR produce the same accept/reject signal with respect to a particular investment opportunity—if a project's NPV is greater than zero, the IRR will exceed the required rate of return (y).

However, the IRR has some inherent assumptions that make its use as an investment criterion problematic in some situations. For example, the IRR method does not discount cash flows at the investor's required rate of return (y). This is significant because both NPV and IRR (implicitly) assume that the cash flows from an investment will be reinvested. With the NPV method, cash flows are implicitly assumed to be reinvested at the investor's required rate of return. However, with the IRR method, it is implicitly assumed that cash flows are reinvested at the IRR, not at the actual rate the investor is able to earn on reinvested cash flows.

A related problem with the use of the IRR as a decision criterion is that it will not necessarily result in wealth maximization for the investor. In particular, the IRR may produce a different ranking than NPV of alternative investment opportunities. If all positive NPV investments cannot be purchased by the investor—perhaps because of limited financial resources—the use of IRR instead of NPV may lead to the selection of a project with a lower NPV than one of the rejected projects.

An additional difficulty with the IRR decision criterion is that multiple solutions are possible for investments where the sign (+ or −) of the cash flows changes more than once over the expected holding period. That is, more than one discount rate may equate the present value of future cash flows with the initial investment. In most of the example problems used in this book, an initial cash outflow (−) is followed by a series of cash inflows (+) from operations and sale of the property. It is possible, however, that the net cash flow from operations could be negative in some future year(s)—perhaps due to large renovation expenses. This additional "sign flip" could result in multiple IRRs. This is problematic because investors may not be aware that multiple IRR solutions to their investment problems exist, and it is not clear which IRR investors would choose even if they did know that there were multiple solutions to the problem.[11]

For all these reasons, the use of NPV is preferable to IRR for making decisions in most situations. However, the IRR is widely used for making comparisons across different investment opportunities.

VALUATION USING DIRECT CAPITALIZATION

The value of an income property over an n-year holding period has been shown to be

$$IV = \sum_{t=1}^{n} \frac{NOI_t}{(1+y)^t} + \frac{NSP_n}{(1+y)^n}$$

This valuation procedure requires the explicit forecast of NOI for each year of the expected holding period, as well as the expected NSP in year n. However, if NOI is assumed to grow forever at a constant annual rate equal to g, it can be shown that this fundamental valuation equation reduces to

$$V_t = \frac{NOI_{t+1}}{y - g}$$

Estimating value by dividing NOI in year 1 by $(y - g)$ is called *direct capitalization,* and it is widely used by real estate appraisers to estimate the market value of income properties. The investor's required rate of return, y, minus the expected growth rate in NOI, g, can be referred to as R, a *capitalization rate.* Note that $R = (y - g)$ is a rate that can be used to convert first-year NOI into an estimate of current value. However, unlike y, R is *not* a discount rate that can be applied to future cash flows.

To further explore the relationship between discount rates and capitalization rates, we can rearrange the above expression to produce

$$y = \frac{NOI_{t+1}}{V_t} + g$$

NOI divided by value (or acquisition price) is equal to the property's current yield, or capitalization rate. Thus,

$$y = R + g$$

This formulation clearly shows that the investor's required holding period return must be obtained from two sources:

1. The property's periodic dividend (i.e., NOI).
2. Appreciation (or depreciation) in the value of the property.

---

[11] For more discussion of the potential problems associated with using the IRR as an investment decision-making criterion, see Stephen A. Ross, Randolph W. Westerfield, and Bradford D. Jordan, *Fundamentals of Corporate Finance* (Homewood, IL: Richard D. Irwin, 1995).

If a larger portion of y—the required yield—is expected to be obtained from price appreciation, then a smaller portion of y must be provided in the form of current yield (i.e., cap rates can be lower). That helps explain why cap rates often vary across property types and across markets—expected appreciation can be very different.

WHY DISCOUNT RATES DETERMINE CAP RATES

Although the relationship between multiperiod discount rates, capitalization rates, and expected price appreciation can be written as $y = R + g$, it is important to recognize which way causality runs. In competitive capital markets, y is a function of returns available on competing investments of similar risk—including stocks, bonds, and other financial assets. Thus, capitalization rates are a function of holding period returns on other assets and the expected appreciation of the subject property; that is, $R = y - g$. This direct relationship between real estate discount rates and rates of return available on other capital and financial assets has increased dramatically in recent years.

The point is that y, in conjunction with expected appreciation and current rental income, determines the maximum amount investors are willing to bid for a property, which in turn determines actual transaction prices, and thus R. Therefore, cap rates do not determine values; cap rates *react* to changes in cash flow projections and/or changes in required returns on competing investment alternatives. Note that this *integration* of real estate markets with general capital markets can cause a variation in local real estate values and therefore in observed cap rates if, for example, yields on risky corporate bonds were to change.

THE EFFECTS OF MORTGAGE FINANCING ON CASH FLOWS, VALUES, AND RETURNS

Every real estate investment involves the use of money, of which there are two sources: equity and debt. An investor can use all equity or all debt, or some combination of the two. To this point we have considered only income property investments purchased with 100 percent equity (or "self") financing. However, most investors make at least some use of debt financing when acquiring real estate. The purpose of this section is to consider the effects of debt financing on cash flows, values, rates of return, and risk.

EFFECT OF DEBT ON PROJECTED CASH FLOWS

The use of mortgage debt affects the investors' required cash inflow at acquisition, the investors' net cash flows from operations, and the net cash flows from the eventual sale of the property. This section discusses these cash flow effects.

Effect on initial investment. In the absence of borrowed funds, investors must self-finance an amount equal to the acquisition price of the property. When a mortgage loan is obtained, the cash down payment required at closing, E, can be found as follows:

EXHIBIT 3-10

GENERAL FORM FOR ESTIMATING BEFORE-TAX CASH FLOWS FROM OPERATIONS

	Potential gross income (PGI)
−	Vacancy and collection (VC)
+	Miscellaneous income (MI)
=	Effective gross income (EGI)
−	Fixed operating expenses
−	Variable operating expenses
=	Net operating income (NOI)*
−	Nonrecurring expenses
=	Cash flow before debt service and income taxes
−	Debt service (DS)
=	Before-tax cash flow (BTCF)

* Assumes no reserves for replacement.

$$E = \text{Acquisition Price} - \text{Net Loan Proceeds}$$

where the net loan proceeds equal the face (or stated) amount of the loan, minus up-front financing costs paid to the lender. Up-front financing costs include any charges or fees the borrower pays to obtain the mortgage financing. Examples include discount points, loan origination fees, and costs associated with having the property surveyed or appraised. Assume the $885,000 acquisition price of the Suburban Office Building is to be financed with 75 percent debt. Up-front financing costs will equal 3 percent of the $663,750 (0.75 × $885,000) loan amount, or $19,913. Thus,

$$E = \$885,000 - (\$663,750 - \$19,913) = \$241,163$$

Effect on cash flows from operations. Before-tax cash flow from annual operations (BTCF) is defined as NOI minus mortgage payments (debt service). The general form for estimating BTCF is shown in Exhibit 3–10.

BTCF is the amount of money left over from property operations each year after paying all operating expenses and nonrecurring expenses, and servicing the mortgage debt. This *residual amount* also is referred to as the equity investor's (before-tax) *dividend*.

Consider again the Suburban Office Building example. Seventy-five percent of the $885,000 purchase price can be borrowed with a 30-year, 9 percent annual interest rate mortgage. Up-front financing costs will equal 3 percent of the loan amount and payments will be made monthly. These loan terms produce a loan amount equal to $663,750, monthly payments of $5,341, and annual payments of $64,088.[12] Projected

---

[12] The keystrokes for this calculation are $N = 360$; $PV = -663,750$; $PMT = ?$; $FV = 0$; and $I = 9/12$. This series of keystrokes produces a monthly payment of $5,340.68.

BTCF in year 1 thus is equal to $25,012. Estimates of the BTCFs for the entire five-year holding period are displayed in Exhibit 3–11.

Effect on cash flow from sale. Most mortgage loans require that the remaining mortgage balance be paid in full to the lender when the property is sold. The before-tax equity reversion (BTER) is defined as the net selling price minus the remaining mortgage balance (RMB) at the time of sale. In other words, the BTER is the amount of money investors net from the sale of the property, after paying all sale expenses, including the remaining mortgage balance, but before paying income taxes due on sale. The general form of the BTER is displayed in Exhibit 3–12.

The remaining mortgage balance at the end of year 5 on the Suburban Office Building loan is $636,404. Thus, the estimated BTER in year 5 is $338,256. A summary of this calculation is provided in Exhibit 3–13.

It is clear that the use of mortgage debt reduces the investors' required cash outflow at acquisition and, all else the same, reduced investment costs increase expected returns and net present values. However, mortgage debt also decreases the net (of debt service) cash flows from operations and the net cash flows from a subsequent sale of the property. When will debt financing increase the expected return on equity? When the reduction in the initial equity investment, E, exceeds the reduction in the present value of the BTCFs and the BTER. The use of 75 percent leverage increases the NPV of the Suburban Office Building from $6,823 to $58,524 and the IRR from 12.2 to 17.9 percent.

WHY DO INVESTORS BORROW?

There are two basic reasons why investors borrow funds—use **financial leverage**—for real estate investment. The first reason is limited financial resources. If an investor desires to purchase real estate but does not have sufficient assets to pay cash for the property, then borrowing is the only alternative. The price the investor (borrower) must pay is the interest rate on the borrowed funds.

The second reason for the use of mortgage financing is that it alters the expected risk and return of real estate investments. In particular, the use of leverage amplifies the rate of return investors earn on their invested equity. This *magnification* of equity returns is known as positive or negative financial leverage, and it may induce investors to at least partially debt finance (i.e., use "other people's money") even if they have sufficient resources to avoid borrowing.

Effect of debt on NPV and IRR. The before- and after-debt NPV and IRR associated with the Suburban Office Building are summarized below.

Cash Flows	NPV	IRR
Before-debt	$ 6,823	12.2%
After-debt	$58,524	17.9%

In this case the investment is expected to benefit from positive financial leverage—both the calculated NPV and IRR are significantly increased by the use of borrowed funds.

E X H I B I T   3 - 1 1

SUBURBAN OFFICE BUILDING: BEFORE-TAX CASH FLOW FROM OPERATIONS

		1	2	3	4	5
	PGI	$180,000	$185,400	$190,962	$196,691	$202,592
−	VC	18,000	18,540	19,096	19,669	20,259
=	EGI	162,000	166,860	171,866	177,022	182,332
−	OE	72,900	75,087	77,340	79,660	82,050
=	NOI	89,100	91,773	94,526	97,362	100,283
−	DS	64,088	64,088	64,088	64,088	64,088
=	BTCF	$ 25,012	$ 27,685	$ 30,438	$ 33,274	$ 36,195

E X H I B I T   3 - 1 2

GENERAL FORM OF THE CALCULATION OF BEFORE-TAX EQUITY REVERSION

	Expected selling price (SP)
−	Selling expenses (SE)
=	Net sale proceeds (NSP)
−	Remaining mortgage balance (RMB)
=	Before-tax equity reversion (BTER)

E X H I B I T   3 - 1 3

	SP	$1,025,958
−	SE	$ 51,298
=	NSP	$ 974,660
−	RMB	$ 636,404
=	BTER	$ 338,256

When will the use of financial leverage increase NPV relative to the NPV with no debt? When the cost of borrowing is less than the required rate of return. The effective borrowing cost for the Suburban Office Building is 9.77 percent, including the effect of up-front financing costs.[13] However, if the investor's required rate of return remains 12 percent, the investor has an incentive to substitute debt financing for equity financing because the cost of equity financing exceeds the cost of borrowed funds. Put differently, if the investor can borrow an additional dollar at an effective rate of 9.77 percent, then an

---

[13] The keystrokes for this calculation are $N = 60$; $PV = 643,838$; $PMT = -5,340.68$; $FV = 0$; and $I = ?$, where $643,838 equals the net loan proceeds ($663,750 − $19,912).

additional dollar can be left invested in other assets (of similar risk) that are expected to earn 12 percent.

It should be stressed, however, that financial leverage increases the riskiness of the equity investment by increasing the risk of default and by making the *realized* return on equity more sensitive to changes in rental rates and expense levels. Thus, investor required rates of return should increase as the amount of leverage increases. As a result, the decision to substitute more debt financing for equity financing is more complicated than suggested by the above discussion because the increase in *expected* return from the use of debt may not be large enough to offset the corresponding increase in risk and required return.

In most DCF analyses of income property, the assumed discount rate exceeds the cost of mortgage debt, leading to the conclusion that positive financial leverage exists. The risk to the equity investor associated with the use of borrowed funds is discussed more completely in Chapter 18.

OTHER INVESTMENT CRITERIA

In addition to calculating the investment value, net present value, or the internal rate of return, an investor may find it desirable to analyze a number of ratios. In fact, before the introduction of discounted cash flow analysis, real estate investment decisions were based on ratio analysis. It is still frequently used in conjunction with discounted cash flow analysis to make real estate investment decisions. These ratios—or *rules of thumb*—can be grouped into three categories: profitability ratios, multipliers, and financial ratios.

PROFITABILITY RATIOS

The ultimate determination of an investment's desirability is its capacity to produce income in relation to the capital required to obtain that income. Two frequently used profitability ratios are discussed in this section: the capitalization rate and the equity dividend rate.

Capitalization rate. The **capitalization rate**—also known as the overall rate of return—was introduced in Chapter 2 and now is defined as

$$R = \frac{\text{Net Operating Income}}{\text{Acquisition Price}}$$

where R indicates the (first year) return on the total investment—that is, the return on funds supplied by both equity investors *and* lenders. As such, it measures the overall income-producing ability of the property. To illustrate, consider the Suburban Office Building, which had an acquisition price of $885,000 and estimated first-year NOI of $89,100. The capitalization rate therefore is

$$R = \frac{\$89,100}{\$885,000} = 0.1007, \text{ or } 10.07\%$$

Is 10.1 percent an acceptable overall rate of return? This question can only be addressed by comparisons with cap rates on similar properties in the market area.

Equity Dividend Rate. Because most property investments involve the use of mortgage funds, and because the cost of mortgage debt may differ among investment opportunities, the usefulness of the capitalization rate—which ignores the effects of debt financing—is limited. Another widely used rate of return measure—the **equity dividend rate** (EDR)—is defined as

$$EDR = \frac{\text{Before-Tax Cash Flow}}{\text{Initial Equity Investment}}$$

The equity dividend rate shows investors what percentage of their equity investment will be returned to them in cash before income taxes for one year. Note that the difference between the EDR and R is that the effects of debt financing have been subtracted from both the numerator and the denominator of the EDR. Thus, the cash flow in the numerator measures the amount received by the equity investor after paying all operating expenses *and* after servicing the debt. This "residual" cash flow is then compared to the equity investors' initial cash investment. For this reason, the EDR also is referred to as the investor "cash-on-cash" return.

The EDR for the Suburban Office Building is

$$EDR = \frac{\$25,012}{\$241,163} = 0.1037, \text{ or } 10.37\%$$

The estimated EDR of 10.37 percent can be compared to the EDR of similar properties to determine its relative magnitude.

Although the EDR is useful in distinguishing among investments with different financing structures, it considers only the return in the first year of operations. However, standard procedures require that all cash flows over the expected holding period be incorporated into the analysis.

MULTIPLIERS

Two multipliers are frequently used—the net income multiplier and the (effective) gross income multiplier. The net income multiplier, NIM, is defined as

$$NIM = \frac{\text{Acquisition Price}}{\text{Net Operating Income}}$$

Recall that the overall cap rate is equal to NOI divided by the acquisition price. The NIM is, therefore, simply the reciprocal of the cap rate—properties with a relatively high cap rate (overall yield) sell for a lower multiple of NOI.

The gross income multiplier, GIM, is defined as

$$GIM = \frac{\text{Acquisition Price}}{\text{Effective Gross Income}}$$

The GIM is used more frequently than the NIM; however, it must be used with great care. To compare gross income multipliers, the properties should be traded in the same market and should be equivalent in expense patterns, risk, location, physical attributes, time, and terms of sale.[14]

For the Suburban Office Building, the NIM and GIM are calculated as follows:

$$NIM = \frac{\$885,000}{\$89,100} = 9.9$$

$$GIM = \frac{\$885,000}{\$162,000} = 5.5$$

The multipliers can be used to obtain a quick estimate as to whether a property is priced reasonably in relation to its gross or net income. While multipliers vary greatly, the range for annual gross income multipliers is normally between 4 and 8. Net income multipliers for office properties usually range between 5 and 12. The multipliers for the Suburban Office Building are within the realm of reasonable expectation for an office property. However, appropriate multipliers for comparison purposes should be estimated from actual transactions of similar properties in the same market area.

FINANCIAL RATIOS

Investors and lenders commonly analyze potential investments using a variety of ratios. These ratios deal with the income-producing capacity of the property to meet operating and financial obligations. Many of these ratios are helpful to lenders in assessing the risk of lending to investors on particular projects. In fact, income property lenders typically require that borrowers include estimates of these ratios in the loan application package submitted to lenders. Lenders are concerned with whether properties will generate sufficient income to service the debt and, eventually, ensure that the loan principal will be repaid. Several widely used ratios that are useful for this purpose are discussed below.

Operating expense ratio. This ratio expresses operating expenses as a percentage of EGI; thus the **operating expense ratio** (OER) is

$$OER = \frac{\text{Operating Expenses}}{\text{Effective Gross Income}}$$

The greater the OER, the larger the portion of effective rental income consumed by operating expenses. Knowledgeable market participants are aware of typical operating expense ratios; thus this ratio may provide information to investors and lenders. For example, if the OER of a property is higher than average, it may signal that expenses are out of control or, perhaps, that rents are too low. However, investors should not simply

---

[14] Note that the GIM is sometimes calculated using potential, instead of effective, gross income.

seek properties with low OERs; as discussed earlier, ratios are most useful as preliminary screening devices.

For the Suburban Office Building, OER in year 1 is calculated as

$$\text{OER} = \frac{\$72{,}900}{\$162{,}000} = 0.45, \text{ or } 45\%$$

Break-even ratio. The **break-even ratio** (BER), frequently called the default ratio, measures the ability of an income property to cover its obligations and is defined as

$$\text{BER} = \frac{\text{Operating Expenses} + \text{Debt Service}}{\text{Potential Gross Income}}$$

The lower the break-even ratio, the greater the decline in gross revenue—or the increase in operating expenses—can be before investors experience negative cash flow from operations. For our example, the break-even ratio is

$$\text{BER} = \frac{\$72{,}900 + \$64{,}088}{\$180{,}000} = 0.76, \text{ or } 76\%$$

Thus, operating and financial obligations represent about 76 percent of PGI in year 1.

The investment analysts should compute the operating and break-even ratios for all properties that will require investors to incur operating expenses and financing charges. A relatively efficient property will exhibit a low operating ratio. Investors should be aware that operating ratios are affected significantly by lease terms that require tenants to pay all or a portion of expenses such as utilities or property taxes. The break-even ratio provides an indication of the tolerance for vacancy of the property. The margin of safety between cash inflows and cash outflows is the difference between 100 percent and the break-even ratio. For the example property, both ratios are reasonable. Operating expense ratios typically range from 25 to 50 percent, while the break-even ratio typically varies between 60 and 80 percent.

Loan-to-value ratio. This ratio measures the percentage of value encumbered by debt. The higher the ratio, the less protection the lender has from loss of capital in the event of default and foreclosure. If property values decline after the origination of the mortgage, the **loan-to-value ratio** (LTV) may increase even though scheduled principal amortization is reducing the remaining mortgage balance. To protect their capital in the event that property values do fall, lenders generally require that the initial LTV not exceed 75 to 80 percent. In addition, legal requirements are usually imposed on the maximum loan to value ratios that institutional lenders can incur. In equation form,

$$\text{LTV} = \frac{\text{Mortgage Balance}}{\text{Property Value}}$$

For our example property, the initial LTV is

$$LTV = \frac{\$663,750}{\$885,000} = 0.75, \text{ or } 75\%$$

Debt coverage ratio. The **debt coverage ratio** (DCR) shows the extent to which NOI can decline before it is insufficient to service the debt. It therefore provides an indication of the safety associated with the use of borrowed funds and is defined as

$$DCR = \frac{NOI}{DS}$$

For the example property,

$$DCR = \frac{\$89,100}{\$64,088} = 1.39$$

The debt coverage ratio provides an indication of safety from legal default in the event rental revenues fall and the mortgage payment is in jeopardy; normally, lenders require this ratio to be at least 1.2. The loan-to-value ratio and the debt service coverage ratio are measures of the financial risk associated with the investment and should be computed for every investment using borrowed funds.

The common ratios used in the analysis of real estate investments are summarized in Exhibit 3–14.

LIMITATIONS OF RATIO ANALYSIS

There are two basic arguments for using ratios instead of discounted cash flow methods. First, ratios are much easier to calculate and more widely understood than NPV and IRR. Second, because discounted cash flow analysis requires estimation of BTCFs and the BTER, often many years in the future, some believe the numbers can be easily manipulated to achieve any result the analyst desires.

The basic shortcoming of multipliers and single period rate of return measures is that they do not consider future cash flows. For example, the estimated NIM of 9.9 for the Suburban Office Building may be low relative to similar properties. But does this necessarily imply that the current asking price is too low and that the property should be purchased? Perhaps the investor should consider alternative explanations for the apparently low multiplier. For example, it is possible that the property has not been well maintained by the current owner. This deferred maintenance would have to be taken care of shortly after purchase if the property is going to be competitive in the office rental market. Given that potential investors anticipate substantial expenditures subsequent to the purchase, investors are willing to pay less today for each dollar of current NOI.

Another possible explanation for a relatively low NIM (high cap rate) is that the property may be located in an office market that is declining relative to most office markets in the area. As a result, potential investors are forecasting less growth in rental rates than in other markets. Given lower growth rates in rents, investors are, again, going to bid less today for each dollar of current NOI—thereby lowering the NIM. Note that lower multipliers imply higher current yields, that is, capitalization rates. If investors expect less

EXHIBIT 3-14

COMMON RATIOS USED IN REAL ESTATE INVESTMENT ANALYSIS

Ratio	Form	Use	Comment
Overall cap rate (R)	$\dfrac{NOI}{\text{Acquisition Price}}$	To indicate the rate of return on total investment (both lender and equity position)	The capitalization rate or overall rate is more commonly applied in appraisals
Equity dividend rate (EDR)	$\dfrac{BTCF}{\text{Initial Equity Investment}}$	To indicate the investor's one-period rate of return	This ratio accounts only for the income benefits; it ignores tax and appreciation advantages
Net income multiplier (NIM)	$\dfrac{\text{Acquisition Price}}{NOI}$	To indicate the relationship between NOI and total investment	A quick method of comparing the income to total investment of one property to others sold in the market
Gross income multiplier (GIM)	$\dfrac{\text{Acquisition Price}}{EGI}$	To indicate the relationship between gross income and total investment	A quick method of comparing the income to total investment of one property to others sold in the market
Operating expense ratio (OER)	$\dfrac{OE}{EGI}$	To indicate the tolerance for vacancy of the property	Normal range is 25–50 percent of EGI
Default or break-even ratio (BER)	$\dfrac{OE + DS}{PGI}$		The higher the ratio, the greater the probability of negative cash flow
Loan-to-value ratio (LTV)	$\dfrac{\text{Mortgage Balance}}{\text{Acquisition Price}}$	Limited by lenders to protect their capital from default and foreclosure losses	Maximum allowable on income property usually 75 percent–80 percent
Debt coverage ratio (DCR)	$\dfrac{NOI}{DS}$	Used by lenders to see how much NOI can decline before it will not cover debt service	Lenders usually seek a 1.20 to 1.30 coverage ratio but may vary their requirements

growth in rental income and, therefore, appreciation in a particular market, they must be compensated in the form of a higher current yield. However, differences in maintenance expenditures and rental growth rates are ignored if investment decisions are based solely on comparisons of NIM or capitalization rates.

Although ratios have their place in real estate investment analysis, there are serious problems associated with the use of multipliers and single-period measures of return performance. These ratios are usually intended to provide information about a specific aspect of the real estate investment. They are single-period, before-tax measures and are void of formal decision rules. Their strength comes in isolating specific aspects of a property or investment and facilitating *comparisons* with similar investment opportunities. For example, an operating ratio of 70 percent says nothing about the acceptability of the investment, but when compared with similar properties having 40 percent operating ratios, it illuminates an undesirable feature and perhaps an opportunity associated with the investment.

The quantitative analysis, then, should be a combination of discounted cash flow analysis and ratio analysis. These methods require considerable data, many assumptions, and much judgment.

VARYING THE ASSUMPTIONS

Estimates of potential gross income from operations, vacancy rates, and operating expenses are presumably based upon market experiences of comparable properties, as well the subject property, but changes in local market conditions, inflation, and other factors cause variations over the holding period. The assumptions involved in calculating mortgage payments may also be variable because these expenses are usually dependent upon the specific investor's financial position and capacity, not just the project or property being considered for purchase. For example, investors may have the option of obtaining a 70 percent, 25-year, 8 percent loan or a 75 percent, 20-year, 8.5 percent loan.

Different variable input assumptions will cause the investment value or the IRR of properties to change. Or, given a certain acquisition price, the rate of return on the investor's equity will change with differing assumptions about rental growth, expense levels, financing terms, and price appreciation. When considering a proposed investment, investors should usually calculate several investment values or rates of return using a variety of different input assumptions.

Although investment values and rates of return can be determined by hand calculation, the computations are greatly facilitated by the use of personal computers, especially when a variety of input assumptions are considered. The use of spreadsheet programs such as EXCEL and LOTUS 1-2-3 allow investors to quickly calculate the effect of a changed variable assumption on cash flows, values, and rates of return. Numerous spreadsheet programs that facilitate the valuation and investment decision-making process are available for investors to purchase, or the analyst may custom design a spreadsheet. For complex analyses involving numerous leases, properties, or both, sophisticated PC-based programs such as ARGUS, PRO-JECT, and DYNALEASE can be purchased—although the cost of these programs far exceeds the modest price (if any) of most spreadsheet software.

SUMMARY

Investment is one of the most interesting and important areas of study in the field of real estate. Whether the student is considering a career in a corporation or institution that invests in real estate, or is seeking knowledge for personal investment reasons, several questions must be answered to make better-informed real estate investment decisions.

This chapter presents the conceptual and analytical framework for making real estate investment decisions. The framework has four basic components:

forecasting cash flows from the operation of the property net of expenses; forecasting cash proceeds from the eventual sale of the property; converting future cash flow streams into present values; and applying a decision-making criterion to compare the expected costs and benefits.

The question addressed in this chapter is how real estate investment opportunities are analyzed. This analysis requires knowledge of the financial system, time-value-of-money operations, and real estate principles, such as the importance of location. The process of answering the question of how real estate investments should be analyzed begins with the development of a formal investment strategy. This strategy screens out incompatible opportunities. It also helps investors avoid costly mistakes.

Our perspective is that of the investor in real estate who has a unique set of holding period and financing requirements, and expectations about the future that may differ from those of other investors. The objective of analyzing real estate investments, therefore, is to compare the values of all property rights in real estate investment opportunities against the sellers' asking prices. The total value of the set of property rights to be acquired is the investment value of the real estate; if this value is greater than the asking price, then equity investors are on solid financial ground to proceed with the investment. Other important factors that are difficult to quantify may steer investors away from real estate investments.

A case study (Suburban Office Building) described the decision framework for analyzing a specific investment. Much attention has been paid to the quantitative analysis of real estate investments. This chapter presents the accepted procedures for such an analysis. Real estate investment analysis involves discounted cash flow techniques, specifically IRR and NPV, and performance ratios, including the operating ratio, debt coverage ratio, and break-even ratio. The authors recommend discounted cash flow techniques because they are multiperiod in nature, consider all sources of return, and lead to useful decision rules. Performance ratios provide additional information.

KEY TERMS

Break-even ratio 95
Capitalization rate 92
Cash flow before debt service
  and income taxes 80
Contract rent 75
Debt coverage ratio 96
Discounted cash flow analysis 82
Effective gross income 78

Equity dividend rate 93
Financial leverage 90
Internal rate of return 84
Investment objectives 73
Investment philosophy 72
Investment policies 73
Loan-to-value ratio 95
Market rent 75

Net selling price 82
Operating expense ratio 94
Operating expenses 79
Potential gross income 76
Reconstructed operating
  statement 76
Reversion 81
Selling expenses 82

TEST YOURSELF

Answer the following multiple choice questions:

1. Income multipliers

  a. Are useful as a preliminary analysis tool to weed out obviously unacceptable investment opportunities.

  b. Are adequate as the sole indication of a property's investment worth.

  c. Relate the property's price or value to after-tax cash flow.

  d. None of the above.

2. The overall capitalization rate
  a. Is the reciprocal of the net income multiplier.
  b. Incorporates the effect of mortgage financing.
  c. Considers the risk associated with an investment opportunity.
  d. All of the above are true.

3. The operating expense ratio
  a. Highlights the relationship between net operating income and operating expenses.
  b. Shows the percentage of potential gross income consumed by operating expenses.
  c. Expresses operating expense as a percent or decimal fraction of effective gross income.
  d. Is the reciprocal of the break-even ratio.

4. The break-even ratio
  a. Is sometimes called the default ratio.
  b. Relates net operating income to operating expenses.
  c. Indicates the relationship between gross income and operating expenses.
  d. Expresses the extent to which net operating income can decline before becoming insufficient to meet the debt service obligation.

5. The equity dividend rate
  a. Incorporates income tax considerations.
  b. Expresses before-tax cash flow as a percent of the required equity cash outlay.
  c. Expresses before-tax cash flow as a percent of the property's value or price.
  d. Expresses net operating income as a percent of the required equity cash outlay.

6. A real estate investment is available at an initial cash outlay of $10,000 and is expected to yield cash flows of $3,343.81 per year for five years. The internal rate of return is approximately
  a. 2 percent.   *c.* 23 percent.
  b. 20 percent.   *d.* 17 percent.

7. The net present value is equal to
  a. The present value of expected future cash flows, plus the initial cash outlay.
  b. The present value of expected future cash flows, less the initial cash outlay.
  c. The sum of expected future cash flows, less initial cash outlay.
  d. None of the above.

8. Present value
  a. In excess of zero means a project is expected to yield a rate of return in excess of the discount rate employed.
  b. Is the value now of all net benefits that are expected to accrue in the future.
  c. Will always equal zero when the discount rate is the internal rate of return.
  d. Will always equal a project's purchase price when the discount rate is the internal rate of return.

9. The internal rate of return equation incorporates
  a. Future cash outflows and inflows, but not initial cash flows.
  b. Future cash outflows and inflows, and initial cash outflow, but not initial cash inflow.
  c. Initial cash outflow and inflow, and future cash inflows, but not future cash outflows.
  d. Initial cash outflow and inflow, and future cash outflow and inflow.

10. The purchase price that will yield an investor the lowest acceptable rate of return
  a. Is the property's investment value to that investor.
  b. Is the property's net present value.
  c. Is the present value of anticipated future cash flows.
  d. Is computed using the risk-free discount rate.

PROBLEMS FOR THOUGHT AND SOLUTION

Use the following information to answer questions 1–3.

You are considering the purchase of an office building for $1.5 million today. Your expectations include these: first-year gross potential income of $340,000; vacancy and collection losses equal to 15 percent of gross potential income; operating expenses equal to 45 percent of effective gross income. You expect to sell the property five years after it is purchased. You estimate that the market value of the property will increase 4 percent per year after it is purchased and you expect to incur selling expenses equal to 6 percent of the estimated future selling price.

1. What is estimated net operating income (NOI) for the *first* year of operations?

2. What is the estimated overall rate of return for the *first* year of operations?

3. What dollar amount will you net from the sale of the property at the end of year 5?

4. A retail shopping center is purchased for $2.1 million in 1996. During the next four years, the property appreciates at 4 percent per year. At the time of purchase, the property is financed at a 75 percent loan-to-value ratio for 30 years at 8 percent with monthly amortization. At the end of year 4, the property is sold with 8 percent selling expenses. What is the before-tax equity reversion?

5. An office building is purchased with the following projected cash flows:

   - NOI is expected to be $130,000 in year 1 with 5 percent annual increases.
   - The purchase price of the property is $720,000.
   - 100 percent equity financing is used to purchase the property.
   - The property is sold at the end of year 4 for $860,000 with selling costs of 4 percent.
   - The before-tax required rate of return is 14 percent.

   a. Calculate the before-tax internal rate of return (IRR).

   b. Calculate the before-tax net present value (NPV).

6. With a purchase price of $350,000, a warehouse provides for an initial before-tax cash flow of $30,000, which grows by 6 percent per year. If the before-tax equity reversion after four years equals $90,000, and an initial equity investment of $175,000 is required, what is the IRR on the project? If the before-tax required rate of return on the project is 10 percent, should the project be undertaken?

7. You are considering the acquisition of an office building. The purchase price is $775,000. Seventy-five percent of the purchase price can be borrowed with a 30-year, 7.5 percent mortgage. Payments will be made *annually*. Up-front financing costs will total 3 percent of the loan amount. The expected before-tax cash flows from operations, assuming a five-year holding period, are as follows:

Year	NOI
1	$48,492
2	53,768
3	59,282
4	65,043
5	71,058

The before-tax cash flow from the sale of the property is expected to be $295,050. What is the net present value of this investment assuming a 12 percent required before-tax rate of return? What is the before-tax internal rate of return?

Use the following information to answer questions 8–11:

You are considering the purchase of an apartment project for $1.4 million today. Your expectations include these: first-year gross potential income $230,000; vacancy and collection losses equal to 7 percent of gross potential income; and operating expenses equal to 30 percent of effective gross income. You can obtain a standard fixed-rate mortgage for 80 percent of the purchase price at 10 percent (annual) interest for 30 years. Payments will be made *monthly*.

8. What is the total amount of debt service for the first year of operations?

9. How much mortgage interest will be paid during the first year?

10. Calculate the expected net operating income for the first year.

11. After servicing the mortgage debt, how much income from the property in the first year will be available to pay federal income taxes?

CASE PROBLEMS

1. An investment opportunity having a market price of $100,000 is available. You could obtain a $75,000, 25-year mortgage loan requiring equal monthly payments with interest at 9.5 percent. The following operating results are expected during the first year:

Effective gross income	$25,000
Less operating expenses	$13,000
NOI	$12,000

For the first year only, determine the
a. Gross income multiplier
b. Operating expense ratio
c. Debt coverage ratio
d. Break-even ratio
e. Overall rate
f. Equity dividend rate

2. You are considering the purchase of a quadruplex apartment. Effective gross income during the first year of operations is expected to be $33,600 ($700 per month per unit). First-year operating expenses are expected to be $13,440 (at 40 percent of EGI). The purchase price of the quadruplex is $200,000. The acquisition will be financed with $60,000 in equity and a $140,000 standard fixed-rate mortgage. The interest rate on the debt financing is 8 percent and the loan term is 30 years. Assume, for simplicity, that payments will be made *annually* and that there are no up-front financing costs.
a. What is the (overall) capitalization rate?
b. What is the (effective) gross income multiplier?
c. What is the equity dividend rate (the before-tax return on equity)?
d. What is the debt service coverage ratio?
e. Assume the lender requires a minimum debt coverage ratio of 1.2. What is the largest loan that you could obtain if you decided that you wanted to borrow more than $140,000?

3. You are considering the purchase of an apartment complex. The following assumptions are made:

- The purchase price is $1 million.
- Potential gross income (PGI) for the first year of operations is projected to be $171,000.
- PGI is expected to increase 4 percent per year.
- No vacancies are expected.
- Operating expenses are estimated at 35 percent of effective gross income.
- The market value of the investment is expected to increase 4 percent per year.
- Selling expenses will be 4 percent.
- The holding period is four years.
- The appropriate rate of return to discount projected NOIs and the projected NSP is 12 percent.
- The after-debt required rate of return is 14 percent.
- 70 percent of the purchase price can be borrowed with a 30-year, monthly payment mortgage.
- The annual interest rate on the mortgage will be 11.5 percent.
- Financing costs will equal 2 percent of the loan amount.
- There are no prepayment penalties.

a. Calculate net operating income (NOI) for each of the four years.
b. Calculate the net selling price from the sale of the property.
c. Calculate the net present value of this investment (assuming no mortgage debt). Should you purchase? Why?

d. Calculate the internal rate of return of this investment (assuming no debt). Should you purchase? Why?

e. Calculate the monthly mortgage payment. What is the total per year?

f. Calculate the loan balance at the end of years 1, 2, 3, and 4. (Note: the unpaid mortgage balance at any time is equal to the present value of the remaining payments, discounted at the contract [face] rate of interest).

g. Calculate the amount of principal reduction achieved during each of the four years.

h. Calculate the total interest paid during each of the four years. (Remember that debt service equals principal plus interest.)

i. Calculate the (after-debt) required initial equity investment.

j. Calculate the before-tax cash flows (BTCF) for each of the four years.

k. Calculate the before-tax equity reversion (BTER) from the sale of the property.

l. Calculate the (after-debt) net present value of this investment. Should you purchase? Why?

m. Calculate the (after-debt) internal rate of return of this investment. (assuming no debt and no taxes). Should you purchase? Why?

n. Calculate, for the first year of operations, the
   1. Overall (cap) rate of return.
   2. (After-debt) return on equity.
   3. Gross income multiplier.
   4. Debt coverage ratio.

4. Shown in the table is the actual three-year operating statement of a two-story store and apartment building.

	3 Years	2 Years	Last Year
Income (actual)			
Store rentals	$21,600	$22,400	$24,000
Apartment rentals	16,500	17,900	17,700
Effective gross income	$38,100	$40,300	$41,700
Expenses:			
Taxes, real estate	$ 5,200	$ 5,200	$ 5,400
Insurance	1,300	50	150
Utilities	2,500	2,900	2,800
Custodian	1,800	2,000	2,100
Supplies	116	190	125
Repairs	616	8,000	3,100
Miscellaneous	1,000	1,100	900
Total expenses	$12,532	$19,440	$14,575
Net operating income	$25,568	$20,860	$27,125

In addition, you have the following information:

Insurance premiums on the various policies are paid for a three-year period and come due at various times.

Utilities are expected to be the average of the last three years plus 5 percent.

Many major repairs were made two years ago, and expensive repairs should not be needed for another 10 years.

Prepare a reconstructed operating statement for this year using the information given and your common sense as a guide. Be sure to explain your choices. Use percentages in your analysis where appropriate.

ADDITIONAL READINGS

The following books contain multiple chapters on real estate discounted cash flow analysis and investment decision making:

Brueggeman, William B., and Jeffrey D. Fisher. *Real Estate Finance and Investments*, 10th ed. Homewood, IL: Irwin, 1997.

Greer, Gaylon E. *Investment Analysis for Real Estate Decisions*, 3rd ed. Chicago: Dearborn Financial Publishing, 1997.

Jaffe, Austin J., and C. F. Sirmans. *Fundamentals of Real Estate Investment*, 3rd ed. Englewood Cliffs, NJ: Prentice Hall, 1995.

The following periodic journals contain numerous articles on real estate investment decision making:

Real Estate Issues, published three times annually by the Counselors of Real Estate, Chicago, IL.

Real Estate Finance, published quarterly by Institutional Investor, Inc., New York, NY.

The following article contains a summary of Internet/ Web resources and their implications for real estate investment:

Miller, Norman G. "Web Implications and Resources for Real Estate Finance," *Real Estate Finance* 13, no. 3 (Fall 1996), pp. 74–83.

4

C H A P T E R

FEDERAL INCOME
TAXATION

INTRODUCTION
Objectives and Implementation of United
States Tax Law

**FOUR CLASSES OF REAL
PROPERTY**

FORMS OF OWNERSHIP

**INCOME SUBJECT TO
TAXATION**
Types of Income

TAX RATES
Marginal versus Average Tax Rates

**GENERALIZED INCOME TAX
CALCULATION**

**EXAMPLE USING FEDERAL
TAX FORMS**

**SIGNIFICANCE OF PASSIVE
ACTIVITY LOSS
RESTRICTIONS**

**FORECASTING TAXABLE
INCOME FROM OPERATIONS**
Cash Calculation versus Tax Calculation
Operating Expenses versus Capital
Improvements

Costs of Mortgage Financing
Depreciation Deductions
Tax Credits
Suburban Office Building Example
What Is Tax Shelter?

**FORECASTING TAXABLE
INCOME FROM SALE**
Outright Sale
Suburban Office Building Example
Net Benefits of Tax Depreciation
Effect of Taxes on Values and Returns
Ordinary versus Capital Gain Income

**METHODS OF DEFERRING
TAXES ON DISPOSITION**
Installment Sale
Like-Kind Exchanges

SUMMARY

KEY TERMS

TEST YOURSELF

**PROBLEMS FOR THOUGHT
AND SOLUTION**

CASE PROBLEMS

ADDITIONAL READINGS

LEARNING OBJECTIVES

After reading this chapter, students will be able to:

1. Incorporate income tax considerations into a discounted cash flow analysis.

2. Distinguish between active, passive, and portfolio income, and explain the tax treatment of each classification.

3. Explain the federal income tax treatment of mortgage financing and depreciation.

4. Discuss the differential tax treatment of ordinary versus capital gain income and ordinary versus capital assets.

5. Explain the primary methods employed to defer, reduce, and/or eliminate tax liabilities.

INTRODUCTION

The ownership of income property produces cash flows from operations and cash flow from the eventual sale of the property. Both of these cash flow components are subject to federal income taxation. In a sense, investors have a *residual* claim on the property's cash flows—they receive only that which is left over after the federal government collects its (fair?) share of the cash flows. Consequently, the measure of value most relevant to investors is the present value of the **after-tax cash flows** from operations and sale. Although investors are not expected to be income tax experts—tax accountants and attorneys are readily available—wise investors should not make a commitment to purchase income property without investigating the income tax implications.

Chapter 3 introduced discounted cash flow (DCF) analysis of income-producing real estate. This chapter extends DCF analysis to include the effects of federal income taxes. Our discussion focuses on the major provisions of the U.S. tax code that affect real estate investments. The chapter first identifies and discusses the importance of the classifications of real estate for tax purposes. It then presents the ownership forms, such as sole proprietorship, partnership, and so on, that can be used to acquire income property. A general discussion of the U.S. tax system and how it treats real estate is followed by an analysis of how specific federal income tax provisions affect income property during both the operation phase and the disposition stage.[1]

Because federal income tax laws affecting real estate are extensive and complex, only abbreviated explanations of the most relevant issues are presented here. This information should be considered a starting point for learning about the tax consequences of

---

[1] This chapter focuses on federal tax policies and provisions. State income taxes may affect after-tax cash flows and returns from real estate investments. However, state income tax provisions often parallel federal provisions. Moreover, several states have no individual income tax (e.g., Florida and Texas).

owning real estate. The concepts and issues are presented from the perspective of individual noncorporate taxpayers. Tax law applicable to corporations frequently differs significantly from that which applies to individuals and partnerships.

OBJECTIVES AND IMPLEMENTATION OF UNITED STATES TAX LAW

The most obvious objective of U.S. tax law is to raise revenues efficiently and equitably for the operations of the federal government. Another objective has led to favorable tax laws for real estate investment: the promotion of economically and socially desirable activities. Stimulating real estate investment has been viewed as economically desirable because the construction industry is the largest employer of U.S. workers. Moreover, construction creates a demand for products and services for a vast number of other industries, such as the lumber, appliance, carpeting, and real estate service (e.g., brokerage, appraisal, and property management) industries. Congress also designed the tax laws to promote certain socially desirable real estate–related activities such as the construction and rehabilitation of housing for low-income households and the rehabilitation of nonresidential historic structures.

All this is not to suggest that everything in the tax code has a strong economic or social rationale. Many tax provisions that apply to real estate are the result of competing political interests, and provisions favoring real estate are more likely to be passed by Congress when the influence of real estate lobbyists is particularly strong.

Tax legislation is combined into a single immense section of the federal statutory law called the Internal Revenue Code. Congress frequently revises this code, and some of these revisions have been extensive. In particular, the Tax Reform Act of 1986 reversed the trend toward increasing tax benefits for real estate investors by eliminating or modifying some of the most favorable real estate provisions that were enacted in previous years, particularly 1981. Consequently, the emphasis in real estate investments in recent years has been more on cash flow and property value appreciation and less on tax benefits.

The U.S. Department of Treasury issues regulations and rulings interpreting the Internal Revenue Code. The Treasury Department also created the Internal Revenue Service (IRS) to collect federal taxes and to clarify and interpret regulations.

FOUR CLASSES OF REAL PROPERTY

For purposes of federal income taxes, real estate is classified into four categories:

1. Real estate held as a **personal residence**.
2. Real estate held for sale to others—**dealer property**.
3. Real estate held for use in a trade or business—**trade or business property**.
4. Real estate held as an investment for the production of income—**investment property**.

REAL ESTATE FOCUS 4-1

Federal Income Tax Law

Federal income tax law is found in a bulky document known as the Internal Revenue Code, frequently referred to as the Code. Approximately 18 pages of the Code are devoted to explaining what income is taxable. This is followed by more than 3,000 pages of exceptions, amplifications, and attempts at clarification. The Treasury Department has supplemented the Code with over 5,000 pages of regulations in a generally vain attempt to make its provisions more comprehensible. The Internal Revenue Service has published voluminous material devoted to clarifying the Treasury Department regulations. All this is overshadowed by a massive library of court decisions in settlement of disputes between tax collector and taxpayers.

SOURCE: Gaylon E. Greer and Michael D. Farrell, *Investment Analysis for Real Estate Decisions* (Chicago: Dearborn Financial Publishing, 1992), p. 151.

The primary importance of these classifications is that they determine whether the real estate investment can be depreciated for federal income tax purposes. **Tax depreciation**, if permitted, allows investors to reduce the amount of taxable income they report from the investment by an amount that is intended to reflect the wear and tear that income properties experience over time. Depreciation "write-offs" reduce taxable income and income tax liabilities, thereby increasing the net cash flows investors receive.

Principal residences are properties used as taxpayers' homes and cannot be depreciated for income tax purposes. Income-producing real estate may be classified for tax purposes as dealer, trade or business, or investment property. Real property held for resale by a dealer is not depreciable for tax purposes because such property is viewed as inventory—not as a long-term investment. Generally speaking, Congress allows depreciation deductions only on assets held as investments rather than those held for immediate resale. Thus, investors prefer not to have property classified as dealer property. An example of an individual or firm that would typically be classified as a dealer is a home builder who, in the normal course of business, constructs homes for sale to home buyers. It is important to remember that the dealer versus investor classification is *investment specific* not *taxpayer specific*. Thus, a taxpayer could be a dealer with respect to one activity (e.g., home building) but an investor with respect to one or more other activities (e.g., investing in small apartment buildings).

An income property investment that is not classified as dealer property is either trade or business property or investment property, and generally both can be depreciated for tax purposes. Consider the operator of a restaurant who owns the building in which the restaurant is located as well as the restaurant business. In this case, the owner acquired the building with the intent to operate, modify, or do whatever is necessary to the structure to maximize the income from his restaurant business. For tax purposes, this real estate investment would be classified as trade or business property.

What about a taxpayer who owns an apartment complex? Although this activity would seem to be an **investment activity**, this investment also would be classified as a trade or business property. In fact, most income-producing real estate is included in this category with the apparent rationale that income property investors are actively engaged in the "business" of providing rental space to tenants.[2] Although this seems to accurately depict individual owners of small rental properties who are often actively involved in operating the property, what about taxpayers who employ property managers to take care of the day-to-day operations? What about taxpayers who acquire their real estate by purchasing an interest in a partnership that, in turn, purchases the income properties? Despite the possible lack of active management, the IRS considers the taxpayers involved in these investments to be operators of a trade or business activity, perhaps if for no other reason than they bear the responsibility for employing the property manager.

How does the tax treatment of trade or business property differ from investment property? Under both classifications, owners may deduct all operating expenses as well as an allowance for depreciation. However, on the sale of a trade or business property (held for more than one year), the investor is allowed to treat the gain or loss as a Section 1231 transaction. The primary importance of this treatment is that net losses from the sale of Section 1231 assets are fully deductible in the year in which they are incurred. In contrast, losses on the sale of assets deemed to be held for investment (e.g., stocks, bonds, etc.) may *not* be fully deductible when incurred because of restrictions on the deductibility of losses on capital assets. (Capital gains and losses are discussed in more detail below.)[3]

Most income property investments are classified as held for use in a trade or business. The tax treatment associated with this category of real estate is the primary focus of this chapter.

FORMS OF OWNERSHIP

A major decision involving the form of ownership is required when an investment in real estate is made. The two major classifications of organization forms are corporate and noncorporate. If real estate is being acquired by a single investor, it may be held in his or her name as a sole proprietorship. Alternatively, the individual investor may choose to have the property held in the form of a corporation with all the stock owned by the individual. When more than one person will own the real estate, it may be held in a corporation or in a noncorporate organization such as a partnership (general or limited). If the real estate will be held by 100 or more investors, a real estate investment trust (REIT) is an additional alternative.

The selection of the appropriate ownership form for investing in real estate is largely driven by federal income tax considerations and the ability of some or all of the investors to avoid personal liability for the debts and obligations of the entity. Additional considerations such as the ability to access debt and equity capital, the avoidance of management

---

[2] An exception to this rule are investments in unimproved land that are subject to a ground lease.

[3] In addition to differences in tax treatment on sale, limitations on investment interest expenses may affect the amount of deductible mortgage interest on investment property. No such limitations are associated with the deduction of mortgage interest on trade or business property.

responsibility, and the ability of investors to dispose of their interest in the entity also affect the decision.

Because corporations are a separate taxable entity, rental income from the properties, net of deductible expenses, is first taxed at the corporate level. Any after-tax profits distributed to the investor(s) by the corporation in the form of dividends are then subject to tax at the personal level. This double taxation of the rental income has made the corporate ownership form less desirable for real estate investments than alternative ownership forms such as sole proprietorships, limited partnerships, and REITs, which can generally avoid double taxation. This chapter, therefore, focuses attention on the consequences associated with using these unincorporated ownership forms to purchase income property. Alternative ownership forms, and their advantages and disadvantages relative to sole proprietorships and limited partnerships, are discussed in detail in Chapter 5.

INCOME SUBJECT TO TAXATION

In Chapter 3 we discussed how to calculate the equity investor's expected cash flows from annual operations (BTCFs) and from the eventual sale of the property (BTER). These two cash flow components must be of sufficient magnitude to provide investors with an acceptable return on their invested equity capital. These two sources of investor income, however, are potentially subject to taxation at the state and federal level.

TYPES OF INCOME

For many years, different sources of income have been taxed differently under the federal tax code. For example, until 1981 **unearned** (nonlabor) **income** was subject to a far higher maximum tax rate than was **earned income**, also called labor income. Capital gains also have generally been taxed less heavily than other income. Capital gains result from the sale of capital assets or assets that are treated as capital assets for income tax purposes.

Just prior to the passage of the 1986 tax legislation, income subject to taxation under the IRC was divided into two general categories: ordinary income and capital gains. The 1986 legislation established the following three types of income subject to federal taxation: active income, portfolio income, and passive income. These three sources may be taxed at ordinary income tax rates or, in some cases, at (lower) capital gain rates.

Active income. Income earned from salaries, wages, commissions, fees, and bonuses is classified as **active income**. This income will be taxed at ordinary income tax rates and is the income that many real estate investors have attempted to *shelter* with tax losses from income property investments.[4]

Portfolio income. Income from investments in securities is classified as **portfolio income** and includes interest and dividend income on investments such as stocks and

---

[4] Prior to 1986, active income was generally referred to as *earned income*.

bonds. Dividends from the ownership of a REIT or any other real estate corporation are classified as portfolio income, as is interest on a mortgage or mortgage-backed security. Also, gains from the sale of financial securities, such as stocks and bonds, are considered portfolio income.[5]

Passive activity income. The 1986 act introduced a new income class, passive income, and put restrictions on the deductibility of losses from passive activities. **Passive income** is defined to include income generated from trade and business activities in which the taxpayer does not "materially" participate *and* income generated from certain rental activities such as rental real estate.[6] Thus, *all* income property investments are classified as passive investments for the purpose of the passive activity loss rules—regardless of how material is the investor's participation. For example, owners of small apartment buildings that frequently find themselves doing "light" plumbing repair in the middle of the night probably do not think of themselves as "passive" investors. Nevertheless, in the context of *this* section of the tax code, their rental real estate activities are deemed to be passive in the eyes of the IRS and are therefore subject to *passive activity loss restrictions*. Unfortunately, this passive label is confusing because, in a *different* section of the code discussed above, virtually all income property investments are classified for depreciation purposes as trade or business properties—presumably because such investors are actively engaged in the business of providing rental space to tenants. Confused? Well, so are many tax accountants and tax attorneys. And there is more! For example, as discussed later in the chapter, some taxpayers with adjusted gross incomes less than $100,000 are not subject to the passive activity loss rules.

TAX RATES

To estimate the tax implications of a real estate investment, we must consider the tax rates individuals face, as well as the amount of taxable income the investment generates. Effective with the 1993 tax year, there are five statutory tax rates for individuals ranging from 15 percent to 39.6 percent.[7] Exhibit 4–1 shows these tax rates and associated ranges of taxable income for single taxpayers with no dependents in 1996. The corresponding tax rate schedule for married taxpayers (filing jointly with their spouse) is displayed in Exhibit 4–2. All taxable income of single taxpayers below $24,000 is taxed at a 15 percent rate. Thus a taxpayer with taxable income of exactly $24,000 would have a $3,600 ($24,000 ×

---

[5] Prior to 1986, portfolio income was generally referred to as *unearned income*.

[6] Material participation is defined, albeit not strictly, by an examination of the particular business as to its operations, and then the decision is made as to whether the taxpayer's participation is material. Material participation may be defined in several ways, such as 500 hours of work per year.

[7] The Tax Act of 1993 abandoned the lower tax rates enacted in 1986 for high-income households by raising the rate from 21 percent to 36 percent on 1996 taxable income above $147,700 on a joint return ($121,300 for single taxpayers). In addition, the top statutory rate of 39.6 percent is more than 40 percent higher than the 28 percent top rate that existed prior to the 1993 Tax Act.

E X H I B I T   4 - 1

E X H I B I T   4 - 1

SINGLE TAXPAYERS: 1996 TAX RATE SCHEDULE

If Taxable Income Is Over	But Not Over	Your Tax Liability Is	Of the Amount Over
$ 0	$ 24,000	15%	$ 0
24,000	58,150	$ 3,600 + 28%	24,000
58,150	121,300	13,162 + 31%	58,150
121,300	263,750	32,738 + 36%	121,300
263,750	—	84,020 + 39.6%	263,750

E X H I B I T   4 - 2

MARRIED TAXPAYERS: 1996 TAX RATE SCHEDULE

If Taxable Income Is Over	But Not Over	Your Tax Liability Is	Of the Amount Over
$ 0	$ 40,100	15%	$ 0
40,100	96,900	$ 6,015 + 28%	40,100
96,900	147,700	21,919 + 31%	96,900
147,700	263,750	37,667 + 36%	147,700
263,750	—	79,445 + 39.6%	263,750

0.15) federal income tax liability. If taxable income exceeds $24,000, but is less than $58,150, taxes due would equal $3,600, plus 28 percent of the amount over $24,000. For example, assume a single taxpayer has taxable income of $50,000. From Exhibit 4–1, taxes due would be calculated as follows:

$$\text{Taxes due} = \$3,600 + [0.28 \times (\$50,000 - \$24,000)]$$
$$= \$3,600 + [0.28 \times \$26,000]$$
$$= \$10,880$$

The income ranges to which the five rates apply are indexed to inflation. Thus, if general inflation in the United States economy averaged 3 percent per year from 1996 to 1999, the 15 percent rate would apply to taxable income of up to $26,225 [$24,000 $\times$ (1.03)^3] in 1999 for a single taxpayer.

MARGINAL VERSUS AVERAGE TAX RATES

The tax rate that corresponds to a particular range of taxable income is referred to as a *marginal* tax rate because it is the rate that applies to a marginal (or additional) dollar of taxable income or loss. The marginal tax rate for a single taxpayer with $50,000 in taxable

REAL ESTATE FOCUS 4-2

Does the Same Tax Rate Apply to Both Positive and Negative Taxable Income?

What if the apartment building investment in the example below produced negative taxable income from operations instead of the expected $5,000? If tax losses on income property investments are deductible without limit against all types of income, then 28 percent is the investor's marginal tax rate on taxable losses as well as gains. That is, the tax treatment of income property is *symmetric* when losses are fully deductible.

However, passive activity loss restrictions cause the tax treatment of income property to be *asymmetric*. If rental income is sufficient to produce positive taxable income, the U.S. Treasury fully "shares" in the investor's good fortune by taxing the rental income at the investor's marginal rate. However, under the passive activity loss (PAL) restrictions, the Treasury may not fully share in the losses that occur if low rental income or large deductions produce negative taxable income. This complicates the estimation of the appropriate marginal tax rate to apply to rental cash flows because the marginal tax rate on losses may be zero in some situations.

---

income is 28 percent because that is the rate paid on the last dollar of taxable income and is the rate that would be paid on an additional dollar.

The average (or effective) rate of tax paid on the $50,000 is calculated as follows:

$$\text{Average tax rate} = \frac{\text{Total tax}}{\text{Taxable income}} = \frac{\$10,880}{\$50,000} = 0.2176, \text{ or approximately } 22\%$$

The average rate of 22 percent is lower than the 28 percent marginal rate because taxable income below $24,000 is subject to the lower 15 percent rate. When increments to taxable income are taxed at progressively higher rates, average rates will be equal to or below marginal rates.

When forecasting the tax consequences of an income property investment, should the investor use the expected average rate or the expected marginal rate? For investment decisions, taxpayers should compare the required initial investment to the net after-tax benefit from *adding* the asset to their portfolio. That is, real estate investment analysis is an *incremental* analysis. For example, assume the taxpayer's $50,000 of taxable income discussed above is generated by a combination of salary income, dividend income, and income from a rental house. Furthermore, assume the taxpayer is considering the acquisition of a small apartment building that is expected to produce $5,000 in taxable income from operations. As shown in Exhibit 4–1, all the additional $5,000 would be taxed at a 28 percent rate. Thus, the appropriate rate for this taxpayer to use when evaluating potential real estate (or any other) acquisitions is 28 percent.[8]

---

[8] If the expected taxable income from an investment will span several tax brackets, then the calculation of the marginal rate is slightly more complicated, but the concept is the same. In effect, the marginal rate for a proposed investment would be a weighted average (or blend) of the rates applied to the additional taxable income.

E X H I B I T   4 - 3

GENERAL TAX FORMULA FOR INDIVIDUALS

	Salaries
+	Business income (Schedule C)
±	Capital gains or losses (limited to $3,000)
+	Interest income
+	Dividend income
±	Rents, royalties, and partnerships
±	Adjustments
=	Adjusted gross income (AGI)
−	Itemized personal (or standard) deduction(s)
−	Personal exemptions
=	Federal taxable income

GENERALIZED INCOME TAX CALCULATION

Most noncorporate taxpayers compute taxable income using the general tax formula shown in Exhibit 4–3. First, adjusted gross income (AGI), which includes all the taxpayer's income, is calculated. Examples listed in Exhibit 4–3 include wages and salary, business income, capital gains or losses, interest and dividend income, and rents, royalties, and partnership income. A taxpayer would report as business income the net profit (or loss) from the operation of a business. The interest on securities such as taxable government bonds, corporate bonds, and mortgages is reported as interest income. Dividends on stock investments, including dividends from real estate operating companies and real estate investment trusts, would be reported as dividend income. Income received from the use of intangible property (e.g., patents, copyrights, and formulas) and rents from an income-producing property would be included as income from rental real estate, royalties, and partnerships—as would income received from an interest in a partnership that, in turn, invested in income property.[9] Thus, the income and expenses associated with owning rental property, either in the form of a sole proprietorship or partnership, are included as income from rental real estate, royalties, and partnerships.

From AGI, the taxpayer deducts certain personal expenditures as well as personal and dependency exemptions to calculate taxable income. As a general rule, personal expenditures are disallowed in arriving at taxable income. However, the IRS does allow specific expenses to be deducted. Such expenditures include state and local income taxes, charitable contributions, limited medical expenses, interest on a home mortgage, and property taxes on a personal residence.

---

[9] A partnership is not a separate taxable entity. Rather, the partnership merely files an informational return, which provides the data that each partner requires in order to report his or her distributive share of the partnership's income and deductions.

In lieu of itemizing allowable personal expenditures, taxpayers may take (claim) the **standard deduction**. The standard deduction is a specified amount set by Congress, with the amount depending on the filing status of the taxpayer. In 1996, a taxpayer who was married and filed a joint return (with his or her spouse) could claim a $6,700 standard deduction. Single taxpayers and household heads were entitled to standard deductions of $4,000 and $5,900, respectively. Taxpayers take the standard deduction if it exceeds the sum of their itemized deductions.

In calculating federal taxable income, the taxpayer also is allowed a personal exemption and an exemption for his or her spouse (if filing jointly) and each dependent (typically a child). The personal exemption frees a specified amount of income from tax and was $2,550 in 1996. Thus a single taxpayer with two dependent children could exclude an additional $7,650 (3 × $2,550) from taxation. Both the standard deduction and the personal exemption are indexed for inflation. A taxpayer's tax liability is determined by multiplying federal taxable income times the applicable tax rate.[10]

EXAMPLE USING FEDERAL TAX FORMS

To demonstrate the importance of these basic tax concepts, consider the partial 1996 tax return of Ms. Judy Long. Exhibit 4–4 is Ms. Long's federal form 1040, which summarizes all tax calculations. Ms. Long is a single mother of two; thus, filing as head of household, she is allowed three personal exemptions. Her wage income for 1996 totaled $100,000. Several mutual bond funds and certificates of deposit produced $4,000 in interest income, and her common stocks paid $2,000 in total dividends. The sale of a rental property generated a $20,000 long-term capital gain (line 13). The $4,272 loss on line 17 (rental real estate, royalties, partnerships, etc.) resulted from the operation of her rental property. Note that this loss is fully offset against other income, thereby reducing taxable income by $4,272, to $121,728.

From where does this $4,272 loss come? It flows from Schedule E of the 1040 (Exhibit 4–5), where Ms. Long details the income and expenses associated with the ownership of her rental house. During 1996, Ms. Long received $11,492 in rental income. Deductible expenses totaled $11,869, including hazard insurance ($480), maintenance ($400), repairs ($820), and the $1,140 paid to the local property management firm Ms. Long had contracted with for property management services. Mortgage interest of $5,982 and property taxes of $3,047 are also deductible. Rents received minus deductible expenses equal −$377. This latter amount is not exactly equal to before-tax cash flow (BTCF) because it ignores the principal amortization portion of the monthly mortgage payments. Principal amortization is a cash outflow but is not deductible for tax purposes because it represents a return of funds to the lender, not an expense. If, for example, principal repayments totaled $500 during 1996, then BTCF would equal −$877 (−$377 − $500).

---

[10] Although 39.6 percent is the maximum statutory rate, some high-income households may actually pay (effective) rates of up to 42.24 percent. This is due to changes such as limiting allowable itemized deductions and the phasing out of personal exemptions if AGI exceeds a threshold amount.

E X H I B I T 4 - 4

Form **1040** Department of the Treasury—Internal Revenue Service
U.S. Individual Income Tax Return (L) **1996** IRS Use Only—Do not write or staple in this space.

For the year Jan. 1–Dec. 31, 1996, or other tax year beginning _____ , 1996, ending _____ , 19 ___ OMB No. 1545-0074

Label
(See page 11.)

L A B E L   H E R E

Your first name and initial *JUDY C.*   Last name *LONG*   Your social security number *327:14:2237*

If a joint return, spouse's first name and initial   Last name   Spouse's social security number

Use the IRS label. Otherwise, please print or type.

Home address (number and street). If you have a P.O. box, see page 11. *2212 NW 83 ST.*   Apt. no.

For help finding line instructions, see pages 2 and 3 in the booklet.

City, town or post office, state, and ZIP code. If you have a foreign address, see page 11. *GATORVILLE, FL 32608*

Presidential Election Campaign (See page 11.)

	Yes	No	Note: Checking "Yes" will not change your tax or reduce your refund.
Do you want $3 to go to this fund?			
If a joint return, does your spouse want $3 to go to this fund?			

Filing Status

Check only one box.

1 ☐ Single
2 ☐ Married filing joint return (even if only one had income)
3 ☐ Married filing separate return. Enter spouse's social security no. above and full name here. ▶ _____
4 ☒ Head of household (with qualifying person). (See instructions.) If the qualifying person is a child but not your dependent, enter this child's name here. ▶ _____
5 ☐ Qualifying widow(er) with dependent child (year spouse died ▶ 19 ___). (See instructions.)

Exemptions

6a ☐ **Yourself.** If your parent (or someone else) can claim you as a dependent on his or her tax return, **do not** check box 6a.

b ☐ **Spouse**

c **Dependents:**		(2) Dependent's social security number. If born in Dec. 1996, see inst.	(3) Dependent's relationship to you	(4) No. of months lived in your home in 1996
(1) First name	Last name			
MILLY LONG			*DAUGHTER*	*12*
BILLY LONG			*SON*	*12*

If more than six dependents, see the instructions for line 6c.

No. of boxes checked on lines 6a and 6b *1*

No. of your children on line 6c who:
• lived with you *2*
• did not live with you due to divorce or separation (see instructions) _____
Dependents on 6c not entered above _____
Add numbers entered on lines above ▶ *3*

d Total number of exemptions claimed

Income

Attach Copy B of your Forms W-2, W-2G, and 1099-R here.

If you did not get a W-2, see the instructions for line 7.

Enclose, but do not attach, any payment. Also, please enclose Form 1040-V (see the instructions for line 62).

7	Wages, salaries, tips, etc. Attach Form(s) W-2	7 *100,000*
8a	Taxable interest. Attach Schedule B if over $400	8a *4,000*
b	Tax-exempt interest. DO NOT include on line 8a 8b	
9	Dividend income. Attach Schedule B if over $400	9 *2,000*
10	Taxable refunds, credits, or offsets of state and local income taxes (see instructions)	10
11	Alimony received	11
12	Business income or (loss). Attach Schedule C or C-EZ	12
13	Capital gain or (loss). If required, attach Schedule D	13 *20,000*
14	Other gains or (losses). Attach Form 4797	14
15a	Total IRA distributions . . 15a ___ b Taxable amount (see inst.)	15b
16a	Total pensions and annuities 16a ___ b Taxable amount (see inst.)	16b
17	Rental real estate, royalties, partnerships, S corporations, trusts, etc. Attach Schedule E	17 *(4,272)*
18	Farm income or (loss). Attach Schedule F	18
19	Unemployment compensation	19
20a	Social security benefits . 20a ___ b Taxable amount (see inst.)	20b
21	Other income. List type and amount—see instructions _____	21
22	Add the amounts in the far right column for lines 7 through 21. This is your **total income** ▶	22 *121,728*

Adjusted Gross Income

If line 31 is under $28,495 (under $9,500 if a child did not live with you), see the instructions for line 54.

23a	Your IRA deduction (see instructions) 23a	
b	Spouse's IRA deduction (see instructions) 23b	
24	Moving expenses. Attach Form 3903 or 3903-F 24	
25	One-half of self-employment tax. Attach Schedule SE 25	
26	Self-employed health insurance deduction (see inst.) 26	
27	Keogh & self-employed SEP plans. If SEP, check ▶ ☐ 27	
28	Penalty on early withdrawal of savings 28	
29	Alimony paid. Recipient's SSN ▶ _____ 29	
30	Add lines 23a through 29	30
31	Subtract line 30 from line 22. This is your **adjusted gross income** ▶	31 *121,728*

For Privacy Act and Paperwork Reduction Act Notice, see page 7.   Cat. No. 12600W   Form **1040** (1996)

EXHIBIT 4-4 (cont.)

Form 1040 (1996)   Page **2**

Tax Compu- tation	32	Amount from line 31 (adjusted gross income)		32	*121,728*
	33a	Check if: ☐ **You** were 65 or older, ☐ Blind; ☐ **Spouse** was 65 or older, ☐ Blind. Add the number of boxes checked above and enter the total here . . . . ▶ 33a			
	b	If you are married filing separately and your spouse itemizes deductions or you were a dual-status alien, see instructions and check here . . . . . ▶ 33b ☐			
	34	Enter the larger of your: { **Itemized deductions** from Schedule A, line 28, **OR** **Standard deduction** shown below for your filing status. **But see the** instructions if you checked any box on line 33a or b **or** someone can claim you as a dependent. • Single—$4,000 • Married filing jointly or Qualifying widow(er)—$6,700 • Head of household—$5,900 • Married filing separately—$3,350 }		34	*12,200*
	35	Subtract line 34 from line 32		35	*109,528*
If you want the IRS to figure your tax, see the instructions for line 37.	36	If line 32 is $88,475 or less, multiply $2,550 by the total number of exemptions claimed on line 6d. If line 32 is over $88,475, see the worksheet in the inst. for the amount to enter .		36	*7,650*
	37	**Taxable income.** Subtract line 36 from line 35. If line 36 is more than line 35, enter -0-		37	*101,878*
	38	**Tax.** See instructions. Check if total includes any tax from a ☐ Form(s) 8814 b ☐ Form 4972 . . . . ▶		38	*24,911*
Credits	39	Credit for child and dependent care expenses. Attach Form 2441	39		
	40	Credit for the elderly or the disabled. Attach Schedule R .	40		
	41	Foreign tax credit. Attach Form 1116	41		
	42	Other. Check if from a ☐ Form 3800 b ☐ Form 8396 c ☐ Form 8801 d ☐ Form (specify) _____	42		
	43	Add lines 39 through 42		43	
	44	Subtract line 43 from line 38. If line 43 is more than line 38, enter -0-. . . . . ▶		44	*24,911*
Other Taxes	45	Self-employment tax. Attach Schedule SE		45	
	46	Alternative minimum tax. Attach Form 6251		46	
	47	Social security and Medicare tax on tip income not reported to employer. Attach Form 4137 .		47	
	48	Tax on qualified retirement plans, including IRAs. If required, attach Form 5329		48	
	49	Advance earned income credit payments from Form(s) W-2		49	
	50	Household employment taxes. Attach Schedule H.		50	
	51	Add lines 44 through 50. This is your **total tax** . . . . ▶		51	*24,911*
Payments	52	Federal income tax withheld from Forms W-2 and 1099 . .	52		
	53	1996 estimated tax payments and amount applied from 1995 return .	53		
	54	**Earned income credit.** Attach Schedule EIC if you have a qualifying child. Nontaxable earned income: amount ▶ _____ and type ▶	54		
Attach Forms W-2, W-2G, and 1099-R on the front.	55	Amount paid with Form 4868 (request for extension) . . .	55		
	56	Excess social security and RRTA tax withheld (see inst.) . .	56		
	57	Other payments. Check if from a ☐ Form 2439 b ☐ Form 4136	57		
	58	Add lines 52 through 57. These are your **total payments** . . . . ▶		58	
Refund Have it sent directly to your bank account! See inst. and fill in 60b, c, and d.	59	If line 58 is more than line 51, subtract line 51 from line 58. This is the amount you **OVERPAID**		59	
	60a	Amount of line 59 you want **REFUNDED TO YOU.** . . . . ▶		60a	
	▶ b	Routing number ☐☐☐☐☐☐☐☐☐ c Type: ☐ Checking ☐ Savings			
	▶ d	Account number ☐☐☐☐☐☐☐☐☐☐☐☐☐☐☐☐☐			
	61	Amount of line 59 you want **APPLIED TO YOUR 1997 ESTIMATED TAX** ▶	61		
Amount You Owe	62	If line 51 is more than line 58, subtract line 58 from line 51. This is the **AMOUNT YOU OWE.** For details on how to pay and use **Form 1040-V**, see instructions . . . . ▶		62	
	63	Estimated tax penalty. Also include on line 62	63		

Sign Here Keep a copy of this return for your records.	Under penalties of perjury, I declare that I have examined this return and accompanying schedules and statements, and to the best of my knowledge and belief, they are true, correct, and complete. Declaration of preparer (other than taxpayer) is based on all information of which preparer has any knowledge.		
	▶ Your signature	Date	Your occupation
	▶ Spouse's signature. If a joint return, BOTH must sign.	Date	Spouse's occupation

Paid Preparer's Use Only	Preparer's ▶ signature	Date	Check if self-employed ☐	Preparer's social security no.
	Firm's name (or yours if self-employed) and address ▶		EIN	
			ZIP code	

✪ *Printed on recycled paper*   *U.S. Government Printing Office: 1996 — 407-058

EXHIBIT 4-5

SCHEDULE E (Form 1040)	Supplemental Income and Loss	OMB No. 1545-0074
Department of the Treasury Internal Revenue Service (M)	(From rental real estate, royalties, partnerships, S corporations, estates, trusts, REMICs, etc.) ▶ Attach to Form 1040 or Form 1041. ▶ See Instructions for Schedule E (Form 1040).	19**96** Attachment Sequence No. **13**

Name(s) shown on return	Your social security number
JUDY C. LONG	327 14 2237

Part I   Income or Loss From Rental Real Estate and Royalties   Note: *Report income and expenses from your business of renting personal property on **Schedule C** or **C-EZ** (see page E-1). Report farm rental income or loss from **Form 4835** on page 2, line 39.*

1	Show the kind and location of each rental real estate property:	2	For each rental real estate property listed on line 1, did you or your family use it for personal purposes for more than the greater of 14 days or 10% of the total days rented at fair rental value during the tax year? (See page E-1.)		Yes	No
A	DETACHED SINGLE-FAMILY HOME 2212 SHADOW BEND DR. DALLAS, TEXAS			A		✓
B	....			B		
C	....			C		

	Income:		Properties			Totals (Add columns A, B, and C)	
			A	B	C		
3	Rents received	3	11,492			3	
4	Royalties received	4				4	
	Expenses:						
5	Advertising	5					
6	Auto and travel (see page E-2) .	6					
7	Cleaning and maintenance . . .	7	400				
8	Commissions	8					
9	Insurance	9	480				
10	Legal and other professional fees	10					
11	Management fees	11	1,140				
12	Mortgage interest paid to banks, etc. (see page E-2)	12	5,982			12	
13	Other interest	13					
14	Repairs	14	820				
15	Supplies	15					
16	Taxes	16	3,047				
17	Utilities	17					
18	Other (list) ▶	18					
19	Add lines 5 through 18	19	11,869			19	
20	Depreciation expense or depletion (see page E-2)	20	3,895			20	
21	Total expenses. Add lines 19 and 20	21	15,764				
22	Income or (loss) from rental real estate or royalty properties. Subtract line 21 from line 3 (rents) or line 4 (royalties). If the result is a (loss), see page E-2 to find out if you must file **Form 6198** . . .	22	(4,272)				
23	Deductible rental real estate loss. **Caution:** *Your rental real estate loss on line 22 may be limited. See page E-3 to find out if you must file **Form 8582**. Real estate professionals must complete line 42 on page 2*	23	(4,272)	)(	)(	)	
24	**Income.** Add positive amounts shown on line 22. **Do not** include any losses					24	
25	**Losses.** Add royalty losses from line 22 and rental real estate losses from line 23. Enter the total losses here .					25	(4,272))
26	Total rental real estate and royalty income or (loss). Combine lines 24 and 25. Enter the result here. If Parts II, III, IV, and line 39 on page 2 do not apply to you, also enter this amount on Form 1040, line 17. Otherwise, include this amount in the total on line 40 on page 2					26	(4,272)

For Paperwork Reduction Act Notice, see Form 1040 instructions.   Cat. No. 11344L   Schedule E (Form 1040) 1996

A fundamental concept developed in this chapter is that BTCF does *not* equal taxable income—in fact, taxable income is usually less than BTCF because the investor is allowed a tax depreciation deduction, even though there is no corresponding cash outflow. Thus, depreciation reduces *taxable* income, but not BTCF. In our example, Ms. Long is allowed a $3,895 deduction for depreciation, thereby increasing the loss reported for tax purposes to $4,272. This loss reduces the amount of other income, which would have been taxed, by $4,272. If the income within this **tax shelter** would have been taxed at 31 percent, the tax loss reported on Ms. Long's rental activity saved her $1,324 (0.31 × $4,272) in federal income taxes in 1996. Although the property produced negative before-tax cash flow (−$877), the tax savings of $1,324 resulted in an *after-tax* cash flow from operations of $447 (−$877 + $1,324).[11]

SIGNIFICANCE OF PASSIVE ACTIVITY LOSS RESTRICTIONS

For individuals and partnerships, tax losses from passive activities can be used to offset positive taxable income from other passive activities, but *not* other active or portfolio income (such as wages, interest, and dividends). Losses that cannot be used in a particular year can be "banked" and used to offset passive income in future years. Also, cumulative losses are allowed in full at the time of sale of the property if a gain or loss is recognized for tax purposes. It is significant that PAL restrictions apply even if the losses are caused by decreases in market rental rates, increases in vacancy rates, or both. That is, even *real* losses—that is, situations in which BTCF is negative—are *not* deductible.

Several important exceptions exist to passive activity loss restrictions. First, regular corporations are not subject to the rule. Second, taxpayers who actively manage residential rental investments may deduct up to $25,000 in passive losses against nonpassive income if their adjusted gross income (without regard to the losses) is less than $100,000.[12] "Active" management requires that a taxpayer have a 10 percent interest in the property (and not be a limited partner) and be involved in the management of the property on a

---

[11] Lines 22 and 23 on Schedule E warn the taxpayer that if the rental activity produces a taxable loss, the taxpayer may be required to file Form 6198 and/or Form 8582 to determine whether all or part of the taxable loss will be disallowed in the current year. These forms pertain to the so-called at-risk limitations (Form 6198) and passive activity loss restrictions (Form 8582) that are discussed later in the chapter.

[12] This amount is phased out at $1 for every $2 of income above $100,000. Thus, a taxpayer with adjusted gross income of $120,000 could deduct up to $15,000 [$25,000 − (0.5 × $20,000)] of passive losses against active or portfolio income. Two related rationales for the small landlord provision have been provided. The first is based on the uncertainty regarding the true nature of the income from actively managed properties. With active management, some of the income is earned and thus should be treated like other earned income. The second rationale reflects the difficulties of real estate diversification for small investors attempting to use their management and maintenance skills. Diversification (by geographic area and property type) becomes particularly important when passive losses are deductible only against positive taxable income from passive activities. Without diversification, large losses can more easily occur. While stock and bond mutual funds allow small investors to diversify easily, real estate diversification for small owners is difficult.

"substantial and continual basis." The threshold for active participation is lower than for material participation.[13]

In our example, Ms. Long reported a loss for tax purposes from her real estate rental activities of $4,272. This loss sheltered other income that would have been taxed at a 31 percent rate, producing tax savings of $1,324 (0.31 × $4,272) in 1996. However, before flowing the entire $4,272 loss forward from Schedule E to the top page of the 1040, Ms. Long (or her tax preparer) had to make sure (by completing Form 8582) the $4,272 loss reported on Schedule E was not limited by PAL restrictions. Had the $4,272 loss been limited, the amount transferred to the top page of the 1040 would have been less than the amount of negative taxable income associated with the operation of the property in 1996.[14]

---

[13] Passive activity loss restrictions were further eased for some investors by the Omnibus Budget Reduction Reconciliation Act of 1993. This act relaxed the "automatically passive" status of rental real estate and introduced once again the opportunity to shelter salary or other income with rental losses. The act targets this relaxation to those in the "real estate property business," which includes nearly every type of real estate operation, including development and construction, acquisition, conversion, rental, operation, management, leasing and brokerage. To be eligible for a waiver of the "automatically passive" rule you must: (1) materially participate in the real property businesses; (2) spend more than half of your time for the year in those real property businesses; and (3) spend over 750 hours in total in these real property businesses. From an industry perspective, this relief measure provides a more evenhanded treatment of rental real estate than did the prior law.

[14] As indicated on line 22 of Schedule E, Ms. Long also must determine whether she must file Form 6198. Completion of this form may reveal that some or all of the loss from her rental real estate is disallowed because the loss exceeds the amount the taxpayer has at risk. If so, the loss reported on line 22 will be less than the loss reported on line 21 of Schedule E. At-risk rules limit the cumulated deductible losses on an investment to the amount at risk. The apparent rationale for these rules is to not allow investors to claim losses for tax purposes that exceed the amount they have invested or "at risk" in the property. However, the at-risk basis includes not only the investor's initial equity contribution, but also the amount of mortgage debt secured by the property. Thus, the at-risk basis is generally equal to the acquisition price of the property (equity plus debt). While it is certainly possible that cumulative tax losses may exceed the investor's equity contribution, it is unlikely that such losses will exceed the sum of equity and debt. Therefore, most taxpayers will not find their losses from rental activity limited by the at-risk rules. However, it is the taxpayer's responsibility to determine whether this is so. Ms. Long has determined that the $4,272 loss does not exceed her at-risk basis in the property. Strictly speaking, the at-risk basis of a limited partner at any point in time is equal to the initial equity contribution, plus *nonrecourse* mortgage debt, plus (minus) any positive (negative) taxable income from the property that the taxpayer has already reported, less any (before-tax) cash flow received from operations. Nonrecourse mortgage debt is debt the investor is not personally liable to repay in the event that the borrower ceases to make timely payments; the lender forces a sale of the property to recover capital; and the foreclosure sale proceeds are less than the unpaid mortgage balance. The at-risk basis of an S-corporation shareholder is not increased by the mortgage debt obligations of the corporation. Tax basis is covered in more detail in Chapter 5.

The alternative minimum tax (AMT) also may affect the tax consequences of real estate investments, although its effect is likely to be small relative to passive activity loss restrictions. Individuals must pay the higher of their regular tax liability or their minimum tax liability. The latter is 26 percent of their AMT taxable income up to $175,000 ($87,500 for single taxpayers), and 28 percent thereafter. AMT income is equal to regular taxable income, plus specified tax preferences, less a $40,000 exemption for married taxpayers ($30,000 for singles or individual filers). The exemption is reduced 25 cents for each dollar by which the AMT tax base exceeds $150,000. Tax depreciation in excess of the amount that would have been taken had 40-year straight-line depreciation been used is an AMT preference item; thus, technically, all income property investors must figure their AMT. Moreover, if investors are paying the AMT instead of their regular tax liability, then their marginal tax rate is the AMT rate, not their "regular" marginal rate.

FORECASTING TAXABLE INCOME FROM OPERATIONS

Recall that in Chapter 3 we discussed at length how to calculate net operating income (NOI) from rental property. The calculation of NOI involved deducting from gross rental income the expenses associated with keeping the property operating and competitive in its market area. These operating expenses include property taxes, management, utilities, maintenance, and insurance. From NOI, the mortgage payment is then deducted, resulting in the property's estimated before-tax cash flow (BTCF) from operations.

In addition to before-tax cash flow, the ownership of income-producing real estate also generates taxable income. This section discusses the calculation of taxable income (TI), the tax liability (TAX), and the after-tax cash flow (ATCF) from operating income property. We will see that taxable income (TI) differs from BTCF for several reasons. First, when calculating taxable income, the tax code allows investors to deduct an allowance for depreciation from NOI. This deduction is not a cash expense. Second, only the interest portion of the loan payment, not the total payment, is deductible from NOI for tax purposes. In addition, the investor may deduct (amortize) a portion of any financing costs (discount points, origination fees, etc.) that were incurred when the loan was obtained. The general forms for calculating the annual tax liability and the after-tax cash flow from operations are displayed side-by-side in Exhibit 4-6.[15]

In the calculation of BTCF, debt service (DS) is split into its two components: interest (INT) and principal amortization (PA). The amount of deductible interest in a given taxable year is equal to total interest paid to the lender(s) in that year. The separation of loan payments into interest and principal is discussed in detail in Chapter 2. The calculation of depreciation deductions and amortized financing costs are discussed in the following sections.

EXHIBIT 4-6

	Taxable Liability from Operations	vs.	After-Tax Cash Flow
	Net operating income (NOI)		Net operating income (NOI)
−	Depreciation (DEP)		
−	Interest expense (INT)		− Interest expense (INT)
−	Amortized financing costs (AFC)		− Principal amortization (PA)
=	Taxable income (TI)		= Before-tax cash flow (BTCF)
×	Tax rate (TR)		− Tax liability (TAX)
=	Tax liability (TAX)		= After-tax cash flow (ATCF)

---

[15] For simplicity, the effects of nonrecurring expenses such as leasing commissions and tenant improvements on taxable income are ignored in this example.

CASH CALCULATION VERSUS TAX CALCULATION

As shown in Exhibit 4–6, two calculations are required to estimate after-tax cash flows. The cash calculation involves a sequence of adjustments to the NOI the investment is expected to generate. One of these adjustments is for income taxes. A separate tax calculation is made to estimate the tax effects. The sole purpose of the tax calculation is to estimate the expected income tax liability of the real estate investment in a given year. This requires an estimate of the income subject to taxation. This taxable income is usually different (i.e., lower) than the actual (or before-tax) cash flow generated by the property. As Exhibit 4–6 indicates, the difference between taxable income and before-tax cash flow is that principal amortization (PA) is subtracted from net operating income to find before-tax cash flow, and depreciation (DEP) and amortized financing costs (AFC), both noncash expenses, are subtracted from NOI to find taxable income.

OPERATING EXPENSES VERSUS CAPITAL IMPROVEMENTS

The expenses of operating and maintaining income property investments are cash outflows that reduce net cash flows from operations. Operating expenses are generally deductible for income tax purposes in the year that they are paid.

However, certain expenses may be cash outflows but may not be deductible in the tax calculation. For example, investors sometimes set aside money each year to accumulate a fund for the eventual replacement of personal property such as kitchen equipment and lobby or reception furniture. These **replacement reserves** are not tax deductible even if the money is set aside in a separate account.

A distinction also must be made between the classification of tax deductible operating expenses and capital expenditures—the latter are not fully deductible when incurred. Operating expenses are defined for tax purposes as expenditures made to operate the property and keep it in good repair—they do not fundamentally alter the value of the property. A capital expenditure, on the other hand, increases the value (or useful life) of the property and is therefore not immediately deductible. Rather, the capital expenditure is added to the tax basis of the property and "recovered" through annual depreciation deductions (or when the property is sold), as explained below.

Generally, investors prefer to have expenditures classified for tax purposes as operating expenses rather than capital expenditures because the former are immediately deductible whereas the latter are deducted or recovered over 27 to 40 years. Tax benefits, like other cash flow benefits, have higher present values when they are received sooner rather than later.

COSTS OF MORTGAGE FINANCING

The use of mortgage debt to help finance an income property investment has four essential tax consequences. First, the "price" the investor pays for borrowing, that is, the interest, is generally deductible in the year it is paid.[16] Repayment of principal is not a tax-deductible expense. Second, mortgage debt is included as part of the depreciable basis. This means that the annual depreciation deduction is not affected by the mix of debt and equity financing that is used because the entire acquisition price (minus the land) is deductible. Third, mortgage funds are not taxable as income; thus, the loan proceeds the borrower receives when the property is acquired are not taxable. In addition, a borrower may subsequently take out a second mortgage, or refinance the first mortgage, without incurring taxable income.

Finally, up-front financing costs are not fully deductible in the year in which they are paid, as they are for personal residences. Instead, these costs must be amortized over the life of the loan. For example, if up-front financing costs on a 30-year loan total $3,000, the investor may deduct $100 per year when calculating taxable income from operations. If the loan is prepaid before the end of year 30 (perhaps because the property is sold), the remaining up-front financing costs are fully deductible in the year in which the loan obligation is extinguished. If our example loan was prepaid in year 5, then $2,600 [$3,000 − (4 × $100)] could be deducted in year 5.

DEPRECIATION DEDUCTIONS

A logical conclusion about the tax benefits from real estate investment is that they largely come from depreciation, the noncash expense item in the tax calculation. The size of the depreciation deduction is prescribed by law and the IRS and depends on three factors: the amount of the depreciable base or "cost basis," the allowable cost recovery period of the asset, and the allowable method of depreciation.

Depreciable basis. Properties held for use in trade or business or as investments are depreciable. Land, however, is not depreciable because it does not wear out over time. Regulations require that when nondepreciable and depreciable properties, such as land and buildings or improvements, are acquired together for a lump sum, the acquisition cost must be allocated on the basis of the respective values of the land and buildings or other improvements on the land; that is, the **depreciable basis** must be clear. Depreciation deductions can be maximized by allocating as much of the cost of acquiring property as possible to the depreciable buildings and improvements and as little as possible to the nondepreciable land. The IRS does not state how the respective values are to be determined. Perhaps the most accurate and defensible method (to the IRS) is to have an independent real estate appraiser separately estimate the value of the land and buildings. The values of the land and improvements also may be deduced from the values placed on the

---

[16] The distinction discussed earlier between investment property and trade or business property is important because the interest paid on a mortgage may not be fully deductible if the property is held for "investment purposes."

land and buildings by the local property tax assessor. As a general rule, the value of the improvements constitutes 70 to 90 percent of the total value of the property.[17]

Cost recovery period. The conceptual reason for the allowance of tax depreciation deductions is that income properties depreciate or "wear out" as the improvements age—the roof shingles become less water resistant, the heating and air conditioning system is less effective, the wood framing is more susceptible to water and infestation, and so on. As a result, the services and amenities provided by the property will be less valuable to the occupants, in real terms, at the end of a year than at the beginning of that year because of this wear and tear. By allowing tax depreciation, Congress is permitting investors to deduct an estimate of this wear and tear as a legitimate expense associated with generating the rental income.

Students may be quick to point out that in most real estate markets and in most time periods, properties typically increase in nominal value. If properties are increasing in nominal value, isn't this evidence that the properties are *not* wearing out? And if the properties are not wearing out, why should investors be allowed to take a deduction that is, in theory, meant to approximate this aging? The answers to these questions are found in the distinction between nominal price appreciation and real appreciation. Observable increases in nominal property values may reflect an improvement in the location value of the property (due to changes in supply and demand), or the increases may reflect the amount of general inflation that has occurred in the economy (usually as measured by the consumer price index). Nevertheless, the remaining economic life of the property is decreasing over time and this "loss" of economic life should be considered a legitimate cost of providing leasable space to tenants. In a sense, the depreciation allowance is meant to provide for the replacement of the asset (recovery of initial capital costs) by the end of its economic life.

For many years, the Treasury Department attempted to set and enforce realistic economic-life standards for real estate (i.e., how long property would last in service). Beginning with the Economic Recovery Tax Act of 1981 (ERTA), Congress created a different system that prescribes depreciation lives without direct reference to how long the property would be in service, now known as **cost recovery periods**. However, the post-ERTA cost recovery periods were far too short, relative to the actual economic lives of income property, and this worked to the advantage of real estate investors because the shorter the depreciation life, the larger the depreciation allowances.

The Tax Reform Act of 1986 and subsequent legislation have significantly altered the tax treatment associated with rental real estate. Residential income property (e.g., apartments) purchased after May 13, 1993, may be depreciated over no less than 27½

---

[17] In most cases, the distinction between depreciable improvements and nondepreciable land is obvious. However, the treatment of improvements to the land such as grading, filling, roads, and landscaping is less clear. If the work on the land must be replaced or removed when the building is replaced, these land preparation costs are depreciable.

years.[18] Nonresidential property (e.g., shopping centers and office buildings) may be depreciated over no less than 39 years.[19]

Method.   Over the years, two basic methods of depreciating real estate have been allowed: the straight-line method and a variety of accelerated methods. Currently, only the straight-line method is permitted for the depreciation of newly acquired or developed real estate. Straight-line depreciation is less generous to investors than accelerated methods—assuming the same cost recovery period—because accelerated methods result in greater depreciation allowances in the early years of the depreciation schedule than does straight-line depreciation.

The actual depreciation allowance for a given year is found by multiplying the depreciable basis by the appropriate depreciation rate. This rate is a function of the cost recovery period and the method. With a 27½-year recovery period and the straight-line method, the depreciation rate is

$$\text{Straight-line rate} = \frac{1}{\text{recovery period}} = \frac{1}{27.5} = 0.03636, \text{ or } 3.636\%$$

If the depreciable basis is $100,000, the depreciation allowance is $3,636 (0.03636 × $100,000). With a 39-year recovery period, the rate is 0.02564 (i.e., 1/39) and the depreciation allowance, assuming a $100,000 basis, is $2,564.

The actual computation of the depreciation allowance is complicated slightly by a tax rule known as the midmonth convention. Regardless of the actual date of purchase, the tax law assumes the purchase occurred on the 15th of the month (i.e., midmonth). For example, if an apartment property is purchased January 10, the depreciation rate in the first year is

$$11.5 \text{ (months)}/12 \text{ (months)} \times 0.036363 = 0.03485$$

If the purchase is on April 15, the first-year rate is

$$8.5 \text{ (months)}/12 \text{ (months)} \times 0.0363636 = 0.02576$$

After the first year of ownership, the depreciation rate is the straight-line rate (i.e., either 0.03636 or 0.02564).

Despite the midmonth convention, the allowable depreciation deduction is easily calculated. Once the depreciable basis is determined, the investor simply refers to the

---

[18] An income property is considered a residential property for income tax purposes if at least 80 percent of the gross rental income is derived from the leasing of living space. What about a downtown apartment building that has retail space on the first floor? So long as the rental income from the retail tenants does not exceed 20 percent of total rental income, the property is considered residential and may be depreciated over the shorter 27½-year recovery period.

[19] From 1986 until 1993, nonresidential income property could be depreciated (straight-line) over 31½ years. Just prior to 1986, both residential and nonresidential property could be depreciated over 19 years using 175 percent declining balance depreciation. For real property placed in service after March 15, 1984, and before May 9, 1985, the recovery period was 18 years. A 15-year recovery period was available for property placed in service before March 16, 1984, and after 1980. These more generous cost recovery methods and periods may continue to be used so long as the property is owned by the same investor(s).

E X H I B I T   4 - 7

C O S T   R E C O V E R Y   T A B L E   F O R   R E S I D E N T I A L   I N C O M E   P R O P E R T Y

If Recovery Year Is	And the Month in the First Recovery Year the Property Is Placed in Service Is											
	1	**2**	**3**	**4**	**5**	**6**	**7**	**8**	**9**	**10**	**11**	**12**
1	3.485	3.182	2.879	2.576	2.273	1.970	1.667	1.364	1.061	0.758	0.455	0.152
2	3.636	3.636	3.636	3.636	3.636	3.636	3.636	3.636	3.636	3.636	3.636	3.636
3	3.636	3.636	3.636	3.636	3.636	3.636	3.636	3.636	3.636	3.636	3.636	3.636
4	3.636	3.636	3.636	3.636	3.636	3.636	3.636	3.636	3.636	3.636	3.636	3.636
5	3.636	3.636	3.636	3.636	3.636	3.636	3.636	3.636	3.636	3.636	3.636	3.636
10	3.637	3.637	3.637	3.637	3.637	3.637	3.636	3.636	3.636	3.636	3.636	3.636
15	3.636	3.636	3.636	3.636	3.636	3.636	3.637	3.637	3.637	3.637	3.637	3.637
20	3.637	3.637	3.637	3.637	3.637	3.637	3.636	3.636	3.636	3.636	3.636	3.636
25	3.636	3.636	3.636	3.636	3.636	3.636	3.637	3.637	3.637	3.637	3.637	3.637
29	0.000	0.000	0.000	0.000	0.000	0.000	0.152	0.455	0.758	1.061	1.364	1.667

appropriate IRS table to calculate the percentage of the original depreciable basis that is deductible in any given year. The midmonth convention is built into these tables. An abbreviated cost recovery table for residential property is displayed in Exhibit 4–7. Only one column of percentages is used, depending on the month the property was placed in service. Each year the investor multiplies the original depreciable basis by the appropriate percentage to determine the cost recovery deduction for that year.

Prior to 1986, 175 percent declining balance depreciation was available on income property. The accelerated depreciation rate in the first year using 175 percent declining balance depreciation and a 19-year recovery period is

$$175\% \text{ declining balance rate} = 1.75 \times \frac{1}{\text{recovery period}} = 1.75 \times \frac{1}{19} = 0.09211$$

Thus, if the depreciable basis is $100,000, the accelerated allowance is $9,211, leaving an unrecovered depreciable basis of $90,789 ($100,000 − $9,211). The accelerated rate of 0.09211 is applied to the remaining unrecovered basis to determine the depreciation allowance in a given year, although the IRS supplies taxpayers with depreciation tables similar to Exhibit 4–7 to simplify the calculations. Note that the accelerated deduction of $9,211 (which was available prior to 1987) is $6,647 greater than the $2,564 first-year deduction allowed with 39-year straight-line depreciation.

Example.   On September 21, 1995, Mr. Smith purchased an apartment building for $800,000. Of this amount, $700,000 is allocated to the value of the depreciable improvements. Because September is the ninth month of the year, Mr. Smith uses column 9 in Exhibit 4–7. For year 1, the percentage is 1.061. Therefore, Mr. Smith is allowed a deduction of $7,427 (0.01061 × $700,000). In years 2 through 28, the deduction will be 3.636 or 3.637 percent of $700,000. In year 29, if he has not yet disposed of the property, his cost recovery deduction will be $5,306 (0.00758 × $700,000). The 0.758 percent in year 29 is equal to the percent of the original depreciable basis not depreciated in years 1 through 28.

Substantial improvements. Under current tax rules, **substantial improvements** to a property made in the years after purchase are treated as a separate building. Thus, total depreciation would equal the deduction on the improvements, plus the deduction on the original depreciable basis, which may still be calculated using an "old" method of depreciation if the property was acquired prior to a change in depreciation tax law.

Personal property. When investors purchase income property, they also often purchase furniture and fixtures ("personal property") in addition to the land and improvements (the "real property"). For example, hotel acquisitions typically include beds, tables, lobby furniture, and other items. An apartment building may include window air conditioners and movable refrigerators. Generally, **personal property** is any tangible property not permanently attached to the building structure. The distinction between real and personal property is important for tax purposes because personal property (1) may be depreciated over shorter periods than real property and (2) may be depreciated using accelerated methods. For example, items such as carpeting and draperies may be depreciated over 3 years, office equipment and fixtures over 7 years, and landscaping and sidewalks over 15 years. The 3- and 7-year life assets are allowed 200 percent declining balance depreciation, while the 15-year property is allowed 150 percent declining balance. With, for example, 200 percent declining balance depreciation, the accelerated depreciation rate is obtained by multiplying the straight-line rate by 2. This differential treatment of personal property relative to real property creates an incentive to allocate as much of the purchase prices of property as possible to personal assets that may be depreciated over shorter lives. As a general rule, the allocation of the purchase price is based on each component's fair market value at the time of the sale. Depreciation schedules for various categories of personal property are published by the IRS.

TAX CREDITS

The law allows taxpayers to take tax credits—allowances that are deductible directly from the taxes otherwise owed by the taxpayer—for rehabilitation of older and historic structures and for construction and rehabilitation of low-income housing. These tax credits exist because policy makers apparently believe the private market will not provide for the rehabilitation of older and historic structures and will underproduce housing units for low-income households without tax incentives to developers.

The rehabilitation investment tax credit may be used by real estate investors with passive income who supply funds for the rehabilitation of *older* structures. This tax credit may be taken at one of two levels:

1. A 10 percent tax credit may be taken on qualified rehabilitation expenditures on nonresidential structures that were first placed in service before 1986.

2. A 20 percent tax credit may be taken for rehabilitation expenditures on nonresidential structures or residential structures that are rental properties, so long as the property is on the National Register of Historic Places or nominated for placement.[20]

As an example, suppose a developer buys a National Register property for $200,000 and spends $500,000 in 1998 on repairs and restoration approved by the Department of the Interior. The developer's 1998 tax credit is $100,000 (0.20 × $500,000). The $100,000 credit may only be applied to the portion of the developer's tax liability that results from passive income in 1998. The rehabilitation investment tax credit is a subsidy feature of the tax code designed to encourage investment in the preservation of still-useful and historically significant structures. The historic-property tax credit (20 percent) regulations are highly restrictive with respect to the use of materials, construction methods, and building redesign to preserve the historic character of the structures. Thus, redevelopers of nonresidential properties may opt for the 10 percent tax credit because of the less restrictive redevelopment provisions.

Low-income housing. The 1986 tax legislation replaced all previous **low-income housing** tax incentives with a new system that entitles taxpayers who either construct or rehabilitate low-income housing units to benefit from tax credits. The value of these tax credits is determined by several rules, but it can be as much as 70 percent of the investment in low-income housing over 10 years. Unlike tax credits for rehabilitating older property, low-income housing credits may be applied to the taxes from active and portfolio income regardless of whether or not developers materially participate in management. In order to qualify as low-income housing, the project must set aside a certain number of units for lower income households. The project must also meet a rent restriction, special rules for existing housing, state credit authorization, and certification.

SUBURBAN OFFICE BUILDING EXAMPLE

In order to add the income tax effects to the discounted cash flow analysis of the Suburban Office Building that was last discussed in Chapter 3, assume the following: 80 percent of the $885,000 acquisition price is allocable to the building; the investor's marginal federal income tax rate is 28 percent; and the investor requires a 12 percent after-tax return on equity.

As was shown in Exhibit 4–6, two calculations are required to estimate after-tax cash flows from operations. One of these adjustments is for income taxes, which requires a separate calculation. The sole purpose of the tax calculation is to estimate the expected income tax liability of the real estate investment in a given year. This requires an estimate of the income subject to taxation. Following the general format displayed in Exhibit 4–6, taxable income for the first year of operations is displayed in Exhibit 4–8.

---

[20] The National Register of Historic Places is a list of properties, areas, and districts that are unique or have some historic significance. The register is maintained by the U.S. Department of Interior. Placement on the register is made through nomination by a local historic properties committee.

EXHIBIT 4-8

SUBURBAN OFFICE BUILDING: TAXABLE LIABILITY FROM OPERATIONS IN YEAR 1

	Net operating income (NOI)	$89,100
−	Depreciation (DEP)	18,154
−	Interest expense (INT)	59,553
−	Amortized financing costs (AFC)	664
=	Taxable income (TI)	10,729
×	Tax rate (TR)	0.28
=	Tax liability (TAX)	$3,004

Taxable income is estimated at $10,729. Recall from Chapter 3 (Exhibit 3–11) that estimated BTCF in year 1 is $25,012; thus, taxable income is $14,283 less than the (before-tax) cash flow generated by the property. The difference between taxable income and before-tax cash flow is that principal amortization (PA) is subtracted from net operating income to find before-tax cash flow, while depreciation (DEP) and amortized financing costs (AFC) are subtracted from NOI to find taxable income. Five-year projections of taxable income and tax liability from operations are reported in Exhibit 4–9. After-tax cash flows (ATCFs) from operations are displayed in Exhibit 4–10.

WHAT IS TAX SHELTER?

During the early years of the holding period, principal amortization is usually smaller than depreciation (and amortized financing costs). This means taxable income from operations is less than the actual cash being received (i.e., before-tax cash flow). This result is called a **partial tax shelter** because part of the cash received from operations is sheltered from income tax.

Sometimes in real estate investments, mortgage interest and depreciation are so large that taxable income is negative. Negative taxable income creates a **deep tax shelter**. Investors may be able to use negative taxable income from real estate investments to offset positive taxable income from other sources, such as salary, bonds, and other real estate investments.

Negative taxable income from an income property investment is a legitimate part of the return on investment and must be included in the discounted cash flow analysis. Suppose a property in its first year of operation is expected to generate $20,000 in before-tax cash flow. Also assume the tax calculation yields a negative taxable income of $30,000, and the investor's marginal tax rate is 28 percent. The after-tax cash flow is shown in Exhibit 4–11.

Because taxable income is negative when multiplied by the tax rate, the result (TAX) is also negative. When the negative value for the tax is included in the calculation of after-tax cash flow, it becomes positive (that is, subtracting a negative is equivalent to adding). Therefore, after-tax cash flow is comprised of two components: cash flow and tax effect. In this case, the tax effect is positive due to the tax savings generated.

EXHIBIT 4-9

EXPECTED TAXES FROM OPERATIONS

		1	2	3	4	5
	NOI	$89,100	$91,773	$94,526	$97,362	$100,283
−	INT	59,553	59,128	58,663	58,154	57,597
−	DEP	18,154	18,154	18,154	18,154	18,154
−	AFC	664	664	664	664	17,256*
=	TI	10,729	13,827	17,046	20,391	7,276
×	TR	0.28	0.28	0.28	0.28	0.28
=	TAX	$ 3,004	$ 3,872	$ 4,773	$ 5,709	$ 2,037

* Unamortized up-front financing costs = $19,912 − 4($664) = $17,256

EXHIBIT 4-10

EXPECTED CASH FLOW FROM OPERATIONS

		1	2	3	4	5
	PGI	$180,000	$185,400	$190,962	$196,691	$202,592
−	VC	18,000	18,540	19,096	19,669	20,259
=	EGI	162,000	166,860	171,866	177,022	182,332
−	OE	72,900	75,087	77,340	79,660	82,050
=	NOI	89,100	91,773	94,526	97,362	100,283
−	DS	64,088	64,088	64,088	64,088	64,088
=	BTCF	25,012	27,685	30,438	33,274	35,195
−	TAX	3,004	3,872	4,773	5,709	2,037
=	ATCF	$ 22,008	$ 23,813	$ 25,665	$ 27,564	$ 34,158

EXHIBIT 4-11

	Taxable Liability	vs.	After-Tax Cash Flow	
=	TI	($30,000)	= BTCF	$20,000
×	TR	0.28	− TAX	($8,400)
=	TAX	($8,400)	= ATCF	$28,400

It could be argued that taxable income on a particular project is either positive or zero—if allowable deductions exceed rental income the **excess deductions** are wasted. However, if the investor can use the excess deductions from the project to offset income from other sources, that is, if passive activity loss restrictions are not fully binding, the excess deductions are not wasted because they produce additional tax savings. Thus, if the investor has $30,000 in negative taxable income from a real estate investment, then

EXHIBIT 4-12

Calculating Taxes Due on Sale	vs.	Calculating Cash Flow From Sale
Gross sales price (GSP)		Gross sales price (GSP)
− Selling expenses (SE)		− Selling expenses (SE)
= Net sale proceeds (NSP)		= Net sale proceeds (NSP)
− Adjusted basis (AB)		− Remaining mortgage balance (RMB)
= Taxable gain (TG)		= Before-tax equity reversion (BTER)
× Tax rate (TR_{cg})		− Taxes due on sale (TDS)
= Taxes due on sale (TDS)		= After-tax equity reversion (ATER)

$30,000 of other positive taxable income may be sheltered; for a 28 percent–bracket taxpayer, $8,400 is saved in taxes. Note that the additional $8,400 in tax savings only occur if the property is purchased by the taxpayer, in which case the savings are directly attributable to the investment.

FORECASTING TAXABLE INCOME FROM SALE

The previous sections discuss the calculation of taxes from operations. This section focuses on the tax liability associated with the disposition of the property. Some interesting and beneficial treatments of gains from the sale of real estate are available to sellers of either trade or business or investment properties. The treatment of gains from property dispositions fall into two general categories: (1) "outright" sale treatment in which realized gains are fully recognized for tax purposes in the year of sale and (2) tax-deferred arrangements, including installment sales and like-kind exchanges, in which the proceeds and realized taxable gain are not fully recognized until a later year, if ever.[21] As a rule, taxpayers prefer to pay taxes later rather than sooner. The calculation of taxable gains from outright sales is discussed first. Installment sales and like-kind exchanges are then briefly considered.

OUTRIGHT SALE

When sellers of income properties receive the full sale price in cash or its equivalent, the sale is usually treated as an outright sale. This means the realized gain must be recognized for tax purposes in the year of sale and the associated tax liability must be paid. The general form for the calculations of taxable gains and cash flow from sale is shown in Exhibit 4–12.

---

[21] For example, if the gain is deferred until the taxpayer's death, the gain will escape income taxation. Keep in mind, however, that death is not a popular tax planning strategy.

The starting point in calculating taxes due on sale (TDS) is the gross selling price, which is equal to any cash or other property received as payment for the property.[22] Expenses directly associated with marketing and selling the property, such as brokerage, legal, and recording fees, may then be deducted to establish the net sale proceeds (NSP), which is sometimes referred to as the amount realized.

For tax purposes, the total taxable gain on the sale or other disposition of the property is the NSP minus the adjusted basis (AB). The adjusted basis, in turn, is equal to the original acquisition price of the property, including land and acquisition fees, *minus* the total amount of tax depreciation that has been taken since the property was placed in service. The adjusted basis is sometimes referred to as the book (or depreciated) value of the building. Any excess of the NSP over the adjusted basis results in a taxable gain, and any deficit results in a taxable loss. The total taxable gain is then multiplied by the capital gain tax rate, TR_{cg}, to determine TDS. The after-tax equity reversion (ATER) is equal to BTER minus TDS. Capital gains, ordinary gains, and their associated tax rates are discussed below.

The difference displayed in Exhibit 4–12 between the IRS's definition of a taxable gain and the (before-tax) cash flow received from sale (BTER) should be stressed. Similar to taxable income from operations, the taxable gain from sale is not equal to the BTER (unless the adjusted basis is equal to the unpaid mortgage balance). Thus, multiplying the BTER by the capital gain tax rate to determine TDS is incorrect.

SUBURBAN OFFICE BUILDING EXAMPLE

For the Suburban Office Building, the market value of the property is expected to increase to $1,025,958 at the end of the five-year holding period. Selling expenses—all assumed to be deductible for tax purposes—are 5 percent of the sale price, or $51,298. The remaining mortgage balance (RMB) in year 5 will be $636,404; thus the BTER is expected to be $338,256. The adjusted tax basis of the property (including land), after the fifth year of depreciation is deducted, is

$$AB = \text{original acquisition price} - \text{total depreciation}$$
$$= \$885,000 - 5(\$18,154)$$
$$= \$794,230$$

Assuming the entire gain is taxed at TR_{cg}, TDS and the ATER are $50,520 and $287,736, respectively. These calculations are summarized in Exhibit 4–13.

Exhibit 4–14 graphically displays the tax consequences associated with the sale of our example property. The total taxable gain of $180,430 is equal to NSP − AB (A − C). The portion of TDS attributable to appreciation in the value of the property is $89,660 (A − B), while the portion due to tax depreciation is $90,770 (B − C). What would be

---

[22] The gross selling price also includes any liabilities against the property assumed by the buyer. For example, as partial payment, the buyer may assume responsibility for the seller's unpaid mortgage balance. This "loan relief" is valuable to the seller and is therefore treated for tax purposes as being equivalent to cash.

EXHIBIT 4-13

SUBURBAN OFFICE BUILDING EXAMPLE

	Taxes Due on Sale		vs.	Cash Flow from Sale	
	GSP	$1,025,958		GSP	$1,025,958
−	SE	51,298		− SE	51,298
=	NSP	974,660		= NSP	974,660
−	AB	794,230		− RMB	636,404
=	TG	180,430		= BTER	338,256
×	TR_{cg}	0.28		− TDS	50,520
=	TDS	$50,520		= ATER	$287,736

EXHIBIT 4-14

COMPONENTS OF TAXABLE GAIN ON SALE

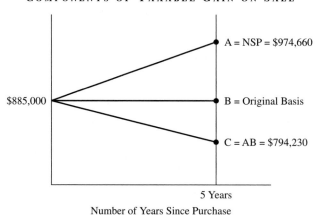

the taxable gain if NSP were equal to $885,000, the original acquisition price? One might be tempted to conclude that no taxes would be due on sale if the investor purchased the property for $885,000 and then netted the same amount from the sale five years later. However, a taxable gain of $90,770 ($885,000 − $794,230) would still be reported, an amount equal to total tax depreciation over the five years.

NET BENEFITS OF TAX DEPRECIATION

As discussed previously, tax depreciation typically results in either a partial (TI < BTCF) or deep (TI < 0) tax shelter. This tax-sheltering ability, perhaps constrained by passive activity loss restrictions, reduces the annual tax liability of investors who own income property. However, tax depreciation reduces the adjusted basis of the property, which results in a larger taxable gain when (if) the property is sold. The *net* benefit of tax depreciation is reduced by the present value of the increased taxes due on sale.

Consider, for example, the Suburban Office Building that is expected to generate an annual deduction of $18,154. If this shelters $18,154 in rental income from the property that would have been taxed at a 28 percent rate, the deduction will save the taxpayer $5,083 in taxes (0.28 × $18,154) every year for five years, or $25,416 (0.28 × $90,770) over five years.

However, when the property is sold, TG will be $90,770 larger, and TDS will be $25,416 greater, than if the property had not been depreciated. The net benefit of depreciation over the five-year period, assuming a 12 percent discount rate, is therefore

$$\text{Net Benefit of Depreciation} = \sum_{y=1}^{5} \frac{0.28(\$18,154)}{(1.12)^y} - \frac{0.28(\$90,770)}{(1.12)^5}$$

$$= \$18,324 - \$14,421 = \$3,903$$

The present value of the annual tax savings is $18,324. The present value of the increased taxes due on sale is $14,421. The net present value of deferring $90,770 in taxable income over five years is therefore $3,903.

This calculation demonstrates that the primary tax advantage of depreciation is that it provides **deferral benefits**. Income that would have been taxed at ordinary rates—$18,154 per year in our example—is, effectively, not taxed until the property is sold. In a sense, the IRS "loans" the investor the $25,416 (0.28 × $18,154 × 5) over the five-year period, and it is not repaid until the property is sold. Note that this amounts to an interest-free loan from the IRS. Also note that if the capital gains tax rate is less than the ordinary rate (at which the taxpayer deducts annual depreciation), the interest rate on the loan will be negative because the investor will "pay back" in the year of sale an amount smaller than what was "borrowed" during the operating years.

EFFECT OF TAXES ON VALUES AND RETURNS

The after-tax cash flows from the Suburban Office Building are summarized in Exhibit 4–15. The initial equity investment is equal to

$$E = \$885,000 - (\$663,750 - \$19,912) = \$241,162$$

where $663,750 (0.75 × $885,000) is the face amount of the loan and $19,912 is the amount of the up-front financing costs (0.03 × $663,750). Assuming a 12 percent required return on equity, the present value of the ATCFs and the ATER is $257,069, yielding an NPV of $15,907 and an IRR of 13.7 percent. The project should therefore be accepted.[23]

Exhibit 4–16 summarizes the effects of mortgage debt financing and income taxes on the NPV and IRR associated with our office building example. Note that taxes reduce NPV and IRR, although both are greater than on a before-debt, before-tax basis. These summary results seem to suggest that the benefits of debt financing more than offset the

---

[23] The NPV and IRR also can be solved for using the cash flow (CF) keys of a financial calculator.

EXHIBIT 4 - 1 5

OPERATING CASH FLOWS FROM SUBURBAN OFFICE BUILDING EXAMPLE

Year	Initial Investment	ATCFs	ATER	PV Factor @ 12%	Present Value
0	($241,162)			1.000000	($241,162)
1		$22,008		0.892857	19,650
2		23,813		0.797194	18,983
3		25,665		0.711780	18,268
4		27,564		0.635518	17,517
5		34,158	$287,736	0.567427	182,651
				Net present value	$15,907
				Internal rate of return	13.7%

EXHIBIT 4 - 1 6

EFFECT OF DEBT AND TAXES ON NPV AND IRR: SUBURBAN OFFICE BUILDING EXAMPLE

	NPV	IRR
Before-debt, before-tax	$ 6,823	12.2%
After-debt, before-tax	58,524	17.9
After-debt, after-tax	15,907	13.7

negative effect of taxes. However, recall from Chapter 3 that the use of debt financing increases the riskiness of the investor's return. Thus, it is generally inappropriate to apply the same discount rate to the three different cash flow streams (with and without debt, etc.), as we have done in the office building example for the sake of illustration. The effects of debt financing on risk and required returns are discussed in more detail in Chapter 18.

ORDINARY VERSUS CAPITAL GAIN INCOME

All recognized gains and losses must eventually be classified as either capital or ordinary. The distinction is important because net capital gains, under the tax rules in place in 1997, are subject to a maximum 28 percent rate. Because the maximum tax rate on ordinary income is 39.6 percent, taxpayers may benefit by having a gain classified as a long-term capital gain (LTCG) instead of ordinary income.[24]

---

[24] A preferential tax rate on capital gains was included in the tax law from 1921 to 1987, when it was eliminated by the Tax Reform Act of 1986. A modest preferential rate was reintroduced in 1991 because capital gains were subject to a maximum rate of 28 percent, while ordinary income could be taxed at a rate as high as 31 percent. The 1993 Tax Act significantly increased the possible differential by increasing the maximum ordinary rate to 39.6 percent, while keeping the maximum capital gain tax rate at 28 percent.

Definition of a capital asset. For the most part, an asset held for investment purposes is a **capital asset**. Examples include stocks, bonds, mortgages, and vacant land. Real property held for use in trade or business is not, technically speaking, a capital asset. Recall that virtually all income property is classified as trade or business property. As previously discussed, real estate held as trade or business property is referred to as a Section 1231 asset if it is held by the taxpayer more than one year.

Tax treatment for capital assets. Once it is determined that a capital (not a Section 1231) gain or loss has been realized, it is necessary to classify the gains and losses as either short-term or long-term. To be classified as a long-term capital gain (LTCG) or long-term capital loss (LTCL), the asset must be held for more than a year. If the asset is held for a year or less, the gain or loss is classified as a short-term capital gain (STCG) or a short-term capital loss (STCL).

To compute the capital gain tax liability, investors must first determine all STCGs, STCLs, LTCGs, and LTCLs. These gains and losses are then aggregated. If the aggregation results in a net LTCG, the gain is taxed at capital gain tax rates. If the aggregation produces a net STCG, it is taxed at ordinary tax rates. Finally, if the aggregation results in a net short- or long-term loss, only $3,000 of losses may be deducted in full against ordinary income in any one year. In short, long-term capital gains are fully taxed at preferential capital gain tax rates. However, investors have a limited ability to deduct losses on capital assets against ordinary income because of the $3,000 limitation.

Tax treatment for Section 1231 assets. Investors may have a variety of Section 1231 assets, including various rental properties, that produce gains and losses when sold. At the end of the tax year, Section 1231 gains are netted against Section 1231 losses. Aggregate Section 1231 gains are treated as capital gains; aggregate losses on these investment activities are treated as ordinary losses that are deductible, *without limit*, against ordinary income.[25]

For example, assume Gary receives $87,000 in salary income and has $20,000 of Section 1231 gains and $30,000 of Section 1231 losses in the current year. Gary has no other income, losses, or deductions affecting his AGI. The net Section 1231 loss of $10,000 is treated as an ordinary loss; thus, Gary's AGI is $77,000 ($87,000 salary minus $10,000 of ordinary loss). This example illustrates one important advantage of income property being classified as a Section 1231 asset. Because the net Section 1231 loss is treated as ordinary, it is fully deductible in the current year. If the $20,000 in gains and the $30,000 in losses were treated as capital gains and losses, Gary would have a $10,000 net long-term capital loss, of which only $3,000 would be deductible against Gary's salary and other active and portfolio income for the current year.

---

[25] An exception to this rule requires that net 1231 gains be treated as ordinary income to the extent that the taxpayer deducted net 1231 losses during the previous five years. See Lawrence C. Phillips and John L. Kramer, *Federal Taxation 1996* (Upper Saddle River, NJ: Prentice Hall, 1995), pp. 13-2–13-9.

METHODS OF DEFERRING TAXES ON DISPOSITION

The potentially large amount of taxes due on the sale of income property can be a significant deterrent to ordinary sales. Although taxes on gains generally cannot be *eliminated*, two methods—installments sales and like-kind exchanges—can be used in certain situations to *defer* the payment of capital gain taxes.

INSTALLMENT SALE

One of the most popular methods for deferring taxes due on the sale of income property is the use of an installment sale. Under this method, the seller allows the buyer to pay the purchase price over a number of years. In effect, the seller collects a down payment and then "loans" the buyer the remainder of the purchase price. The buyer then makes periodic payments to the seller (lender) which consist of both interest and principal amortization. Because the seller receives the sale proceeds (the principal on the installment loan) over a number of years, the IRS allows the seller to pay the taxable gain over a number of years. Essentially, the timing of capital gain tax payments is matched with the receipt of the principal on the installment sale loan. The obvious benefit to investors is that they are not liable for all taxes on capital gains in the year of the sale, as with ordinary sales. Spreading the recognition of the gain over several years reduces the present value of the tax payments.

Installment sale reporting offers the investor an opportunity to do considerable tax planning, as well as to defer payment of capital gain taxes. Suppose an investor plans to retire from salaried employment in five years but thinks the time to sell a particular property is now. Perhaps an installment sale arrangement could be structured so that the investor receives most of the sale proceeds after retirement, when the investor will be in a lower tax bracket. This strategy not only defers the payment of taxes from sale, it also lowers the total tax on capital gains.

Is there a disadvantage to installment sales? Presumably, if the seller were to "cash out" of the property with an ordinary sale, the entire net-of-tax sale proceeds could be immediately reinvested in other assets. However, with an installment sale, the seller also must wait to receive the remainder of the sale proceeds from the buyer. If the interest rate on the installment loan is at least equal to the rate at which sale proceeds could be invested, the use of an installment sale is clearly beneficial—taxes are deferred and the seller earns at least his or her opportunity cost on the installment loan.

LIKE-KIND EXCHANGES

The second major option for deferring capital gains taxes is the like-kind exchange. Under Section 1031 of the Internal Revenue Code, owners of real estate, under certain circumstances, may exchange their properties for other properties and avoid paying taxes at the time of the transaction. The primary motivation for a like-kind exchange is to alter property ownership status, yet postpone some or all capital gains taxes.[26] Additionally, an exchange may be the best way to market property in a difficult market setting.

To enter into a like-kind exchange, the following requirements must be met:

1. The properties in an exchange must be trade or business or investment properties. This means dealer properties and principal residences cannot be included in the tax-deferred part of exchanges. Trade or business property may be exchanged for investment property and vice versa.
2. The properties in an exchange must be *like-kind* properties. To satisfy this requirement real estate cannot be exchanged for personal property such as mortgages, bonds, stocks, farm animals, and so on. However, apartment buildings can be exchanged for office buildings, office buildings for shopping centers, shopping centers for industrial warehouses, and the like.
3. Any cash or personal property (i.e., nonlike-kind property) used to equalize the positions of the exchangers must be identified as *boot*. The receipt of boot makes the exchange taxable, in part.

Boot is present in most real estate exchanges because the values of two (or more) properties in exchanges are seldom equal. Thus, after it is determined that the exchange qualifies under the first two requirements of Section 1031, partial capital gain tax liabilities must be calculated for each of the exchanging parties. Generally, the tax liability in an exchange is closely related to the tax on the boot received.

SUMMARY

The U.S. income tax system is designed to raise revenues in an equitable manner and to promote socially and economically desirable activities. One of these activities is the production of improvements on land for housing (a socially desirable activity) and another is the production of income-producing real estate (an economically desirable activity).

Federal income taxes affect real estate decisions in all of the three major phases of the ownership cycle—origination, operation, and disposition. The principal decision to be made during the origination phase involves the selection of a form of ownership that offers both tax and nontax advantages (e.g., avoidance of personal liability).

Tax shelter benefits from the ownership of real estate are realized during the operation phase, mainly through allowances for depreciation. Depreciation deductions, as a noncash expense, result in lower taxable incomes, thus saving taxes. Sometimes taxable income is negative, which allows certain investors to offset other positive taxable income (this is called a deep tax shelter). Current depreciation rules prescribe a 27½-year cost recovery period for residential property and a 39-year recovery period for commercial property. But current tax rules regarding passive activity losses may limit investors from fully utilizing the tax shelter benefits of depreciable real estate.

For projects involving the rehabilitation of older nonresidential structures, tax credits may be taken. If the property has historical significance, 20 percent of all qualifying rehabilitation expenditures may be taken as a tax credit, subject to passive activity loss limits.

---

[26] Like-kind exchanges postpone, but do not eliminate, capital gain taxes because the investor's tax basis in the old property becomes the starting tax basis in the new property.

Tax credits are available to all who invest in low-income housing.

Real estate investors have three basic options for tax treatment when they sell property—ordinary sale treatment, installment sale treatment, and like-kind exchange. With ordinary sale treatment, investors generally receive all of the sale price in the year of the sale and must pay any tax liability from capital gains in that year. Installment sale treatment allows investors to pay taxes when partial payments of the sale price are received in keeping with the installment sale agreement between the buyer and seller. Finally, real estate investors may exchange their properties for other real estate and defer all or some of the capital gain tax liability, so long as the exchanged properties are in trade or business use or held as investments.

KEY TERMS

Active income 111
After-tax cash flows 107
Capital asset 137
Cost recovery period 125
Dealer property 108
Deep tax shelter 130
Deferral benefits 135
Depreciable basis 124
Earned income 111

Excess deductions 131
Investment activity 109
Investment property 108
Low-income housing 129
Partial tax shelter 130
Passive income 112
Personal property 128
Personal residence 108

Portfolio income 111
Replacement reserves 123
Standard deduction 116
Substantial improvements 128
Tax depreciation 109
Tax shelter 120
Trade or business property 108
Unearned income 111

TEST YOURSELF

Answer the following multiple choice questions:

1. According to the 1986 Tax Reform Act, taxable income from the rental of actively managed depreciable real estate is classified as
   a. Active income.
   b. Passive income.
   c. Portfolio income.
   d. Passive income if taxable income is negative; active income if taxable income is positive.

2. Which of the following forms of ownership involve both limited *and* unlimited liability?
   a. Limited partnership.
   b. Corporation.
   c. General partnership.
   d. Sole proprietorship.
   e. None of the above.

3. Under current federal income tax law, what is the shortest cost recovery period available to investors purchasing residential income property?
   a. 15 years.
   b. 19 years.
   c. 31.5 years.
   d. 39 years.
   e. None of the above.

4. The rate of tax paid on the next (or last) dollar of taxable income is the investor's
   a. Marginal tax rate.
   b. Effective tax rate.
   c. Average tax rate.
   d. None of the above.

5. Which of the following is not required in order for a taxpayer to take a depreciation deduction on a real estate investment?

  a. The improvements must have a finite life.
  b. Ownership must be intended to generate income.
  c. The taxpayer must have contributed at least 20 percent of the initial cash (equity) down payment.
  d. The real estate must be held for use in trade or business *or* as an investment.
  e. None of the above.

6. If an investor is a "dealer" with respect to certain real estate, then that real estate is classified (by the IRS) as being held
  a. As a personal residence.
  b. For sale to consumers.
  c. For use in trade or business.
  d. As an investment.
  e. None of the above.

7. Even if the total tax deductions do not exceed net operating income, a portion of the before-tax cash flow comes to the investor tax free so long as the depreciation deduction exceeds
  a. Net operating income.
  b. Principal reduction (repayment).
  c. Mortgage interest.
  d. Effective gross income.
  e. None of the above.

8. A major drawback of a corporation is that
  a. The flow-through method of accounting is not available to corporations.
  b. Shareholders have limited liability.

  c. Corporations do not allow shareholders to participate in management decisions.
  d. None of the above.

9. The adjusted basis is
  a. Purchase price minus all expenses incurred during the holding period.
  b. Purchase price less recovery allowances.
  c. Purchase price adjusted for capital improvements and cost recovery allowances.
  d. Purchase price minus all expenses, plus all income received during the holding period.

10. When a property is sold for less than its remaining book value, its depreciation is
  a. Estimated correctly.
  b. Underestimated.
  c. Overestimated.
  d. Approved by the IRS.

11. A substantial improvement is:
  a. Treated like a separate building.
  b. Added to the adjusted basis.
  c. Depreciated like personal property.
  d. Amortized over five years.

12. Residential property must have _____ of its rental income from the lease of units occupied by tenants as housing.
  a. 20 percent.
  b. 50 percent.
  c. 80 percent.
  d. 75 percent.

PROBLEMS FOR THOUGHT AND SOLUTION

1. Why do investors generally care whether the IRS classifies cash expenditures as operating expenses rather than capital expenditures?

2. How are the discount "points" associated with financing an income property handled for tax purposes?

Use the following information to answer questions 3–5:

Five years ago you purchased a small apartment complex for $1 million. You borrowed $700,000 at 12 percent for 25 years with annual payments. The original depreciable basis was $750,000 and you have used 27½-year straight-line depreciation over the five-year holding period. If you sell the property today for $1,270,000 . . .

3. What will be the tax liability from sale? Assume

6 percent selling costs and a 33 percent marginal tax bracket.

4. What will be the after-tax equity reversion (cash flow) from sale?

5. Over the entire five-year holding period, how much were your taxes reduced by the annual depreciation deductions?

6. What are the four classifications of real estate holdings for tax purposes? Which classifications of property can be depreciated for tax purposes?

7. Give three definitions of *tax shelter*.

Use the following information to answer questions 8–10:

You have just purchased an apartment complex that has a $100,000 depreciable basis. You are in the 28 percent marginal tax bracket. All taxable gains (both ordinary and capital) on the future sale of the property will be taxed at your 28 percent ordinary rate. 10 percent is the rate at which you discount future tax bene-fits (and costs) from depreciation deductions. Assume you would depreciate the property on a straight-line basis over 28 (*not* 27½) years.

8. What is your annual deprecation deduction?

9. If you never sold the property, what would be the present value of the annual tax savings from depreciation?

10. If you sold the property at the end of five years, what would be the *net* (of capital gain taxes) value of the depreciation deductions?

11. Black Acres Apartment, Inc., needs to compute taxable income (TI) for the preceding year and wants you to assist. The effective gross income (EGI) was $52,500; operating expenses were $21,000, of which $2,000 was put into a fund for future replacement of stoves and refrigerators; debt service was $26,662, of which $25,126 was interest; and depreciation was $17,000. Compute the taxable income from operations.

CASE PROBLEMS

1. You are considering the purchase of a small apartment complex. The purchase price (including acquisition costs) is $1 million. Gross potential income in the first year is estimated at $175,000 and vacancy and collection losses are estimated to be 12 percent of gross potential income. Operating expenses are expected to be $38,000 in year 1. The investor will obtain a $700,000 loan at 12 percent annual interest with annual payments for 25 years. Additional financing expenses will equal $25,000. Assume that 25 percent of the purchase price is payment for land and that the building will be depreciated over 27½ years using straight-line depreciation. Your marginal tax bracket is 33 percent.

    a. Calculate the mortgage payment, the interest deduction, the depreciation deduction, and the amortized financing costs for the first year of operations.

    b. What will be your net equity investment at "time zero"?

    c. Estimate the after-tax cash flows from the first year of operations. Be sure to set up a "tax" table and a "cash" table.

2. Compute the after-tax cash flow from the sale of the following nonresidential property: The purchase price is $450,000. The investor will obtain a $360,000 loan. There will be no financing costs. The investor expects the market value of the property to increase to $472,500 over the anticipated two-year holding period. Selling costs are expected to be 6 percent of the estimated sales price. The investor is in the 28 percent marginal tax bracket. Assume that the balance of the loan at the time of sale will be $354,276. Also assume that 15 percent of the purchase price represents the value of the land, and that improvements (the building) are depreciated over $31\frac{1}{2}$ years using straight-line depreciation. (This property was purchased prior to 1993 when the cost recovery period for nonresidential property was $31\frac{1}{2}$ years.)

a. Compute the annual depreciation deduction.

b. Compute the adjusted basis at the time of sale (after two years).

c. Compute the tax liability from sale.

d. Compute the after-tax cash flow (equity reversion) from sale.

3. A real estate investor is considering the purchase of an office building. The following assumptions are made:

- The purchase price is $775,000.
- The project is a two-story office building containing a total of 34,000 leasable square feet.
- Gross rents are expected to be $10 per square foot per year.
- The vacancy rate is expected to be 15 percent of potential gross income per year.
- Operating expenses are estimated at 45 percent of effective gross income.
- 75 percent of the purchase price will be financed with a 20-year, monthly amortized mortgage at an interest rate of 15 percent. There will be no financing costs.
- Of the total acquisition price, 75 percent represents depreciable improvements.
- The investor is in the 28 percent marginal tax bracket.

Answer the following questions for the first year of operations:

a. What is the equity (cash) down payment required at "time zero"?

b. What is the annual tax depreciation deduction?

c. What is the total amount of debt service?

d. What is the estimated net operating income?

4. A real estate investor is considering purchasing a warehouse. Analysis has resulted in the following facts:

- The asking price is $450,000.
- There are 10,000 square feet of leasable area.
- The expected rent is $5 per square foot per year; rents are expected to increase 5 percent per year. Since the property is leased to an AAA-grade tenant for 25 more years, no vacancy factor is deducted.
- The tenant will pay all operating expenses except property taxes and insurance. These two expenses will equal 20 percent of the effective gross income (EGI) each year.
- The investor can borrow 80 percent of the total cost for 20 years at an interest rate of 12 percent with monthly payments and financing costs of 3 percent of the amount borrowed.
- Eighty-five percent of the total cost is depreciable over the useful life of 39 years using the straight-line method.
- The investor expects to sell the investment at the end of year 5 for 5 percent more than the original purchase price. Selling expenses are assumed to be 6 percent.
- The investor is in the 33 percent tax bracket.

Compute the after-tax cash flows and after-tax equity reversion for the holding period.

5. The property to be analyzed is a two-story, multitenant office building containing 10,000 square feet of rentable space. The building is situated on a 25,000-square foot site that is partially landscaped and contains 35 parking spaces. The property is being offered for $500,000. An investor in the 28 percent marginal tax bracket is considering acquisition.

Multitenant office buildings are sometimes leased on a gross rental basis. In this case, the property owner pays all operating expenses. All leases contain real estate tax stops, which require tenants to pay property taxes above a stipulated base amount. Income from the building is $10.51 per square foot of gross rentable area, for a total of $105,100 per annum before vacancy losses. Office buildings in the area experience a vacancy rate slightly greater than 7 percent of potential gross income.

Table 1 contains income and expense information for the property (first year pro forma). Expenses were estimated after studying the building's operating history and that of comparable buildings in the area.

A loan of $375,000 is available at 12.5 percent interest with a 30-year amortization schedule and annual payments.

The investor will use the straight-line depreciation method over a 31½-year period. The expected purchase price of $500,000 is allocated 85 percent to building and 15 percent to the land. This allocation is supported by the local tax assessor's records.

Rental income is expected to grow by 8 percent per year. Expenses, except real estate taxes, which are subject to an expense stop at $15,800 (total), are expected to grow by 4 percent per year.

The capitalization rate, based on the first-year relationship between NOI and value (asking price), is applied to expected net operating income in year 2 to determine the future sales price. Selling expenses are 7 percent of the sale price. All passive activity losses (PAL) from the investment will be used to shelter income from passive income generators (PIGs), of which the investor has a "barn full." These are the important questions:

a. Assuming a two-year holding period, should the investor make this investment given a required rate of return of 14 percent? Defend your answer with quantitative evidence from the analysis you perform.

b. Discuss the implications of your findings with respect to the contributions of cash flow, tax effect, and property appreciation.

TABLE 1

RECONSTRUCTED   INCOME   AND   EXPENSE
STATEMENT (FIRST YEAR PRO FORMA)

Potential gross income		$105,100
Less: Vacancy at 7.04%		7,400
Effective gross income		$ 97,700
Less: Operating expenses		
Electricity	$2,000	
Water	400	
Sewer fees	30	
Heating fuel	7,600	
Payroll/contract cleaning	3,600	
Cleaning supplies	700	
Janitorial payroll	4,300	
Janitorial supplies	400	
Heating/air-conditioning	2,100	
Electrical repairs	400	
Plumbing repairs	500	
Exterior repairs	400	
Roof repairs	400	
Parking lot repairs	200	
Decorating (tenant)	1,800	
Decorating (public)	400	
Miscellaneous repairs	1,100	
Management fees	4,500	
Other administrative fees	1,000	
Landscaping maintenance	400	
Trash removal	600	
Window washing	200	
Snow removal	2,200	
Miscellaneous services	500	
Total operating expenses		35,730
Real estate taxes		15,800
Net operating income		$ 46,170

ADDITIONAL READINGS

Entire textbooks are written on the subject of real estate taxation. Examples include these:

Manolakas, Thomas G., and Paul E. Anderson. *Tax Factors in Real Estate Operations*. Upper Saddle River, NJ: Prentice Hall, 1990.

Weiss, Robert M., and Robert E. Dallman. *Tax Planning for Real Estate Transactions*. Upper Saddle River, NJ: Prentice Hall, 1983.

Faggen, Ivan, et al. *Federal Taxes Affecting Real Estate*. New York: Matthew Bender, 1990.

Most textbooks on real estate investment have one or more chapters on real estate taxation. Examples include these:

Jaffe, Austin J., and C. F. Sirmans. *Fundamentals of Real Estate Investment*, 3rd ed. Upper Saddle River, NJ: Prentice Hall, 1995.

Greer, Gaylon E. *Investment Analysis for Real Estate Decisions*, 3rd ed. Chicago: Dearborn Financial Publishing, 1997.

Brueggeman, William B., and Jeffrey D. Fisher. *Real Estate Finance and Investment*, 3rd ed. Homewood, IL: Irwin, 1997.

Pyhrr, Stephen, et al. *Real Estate Investment*. New York: John Wiley & Sons, 1989.

Numerous textbooks about the taxation of individuals serve as comprehensive reference texts. Examples include these:

Phillips, Lawrence C., and John L. Kramer. *Federal Income Taxation*. Englewood Cliffs, NJ: Prentice Hall, 1995.

Willis, Eugene, et al. *West's Federal Taxation: Comprehensive Volume*. St. Paul, MN: West, 1995.

C H A P T E R

FORMS OF OWNERSHIP

CHAPTER OUTLINE

INTRODUCTION

SOLE OWNERSHIP

C CORPORATION

S CORPORATION

GENERAL PARTNERSHIP

LIMITED PARTNERSHIPS

REAL ESTATE INVESTMENT TRUST

LIMITED LIABILITY COMPANY

COMPARING OWNERSHIP FORMS

A CLOSER LOOK AT LIMITED PARTNERSHIP SYNDICATIONS
Types of Real Estate Syndication
History and Current Business Environment
The Role of the Syndicator
Regulation

A CLOSER LOOK AT REAL ESTATE INVESTMENT TRUSTS

SOURCES OF COMMERCIAL REAL ESTATE EQUITY CAPITAL
Private Real Estate Markets
Public Real Estate Markets

THE RETURN PERFORMANCE OF PUBLIC AND PRIVATE REAL ESTATE
Appraisal-Based Index of Historical Unsecuritized Returns
REIT-Based Index of Historical Securitized Returns
Historical Returns

SUMMARY

KEY TERMS

TEST YOURSELF

PROBLEMS FOR THOUGHT AND SOLUTION

INTERNET EXERCISE

ADDITIONAL READINGS

1. Identify various real estate ownership structures and explain the advantages and disadvantages of each.

2. Discuss the role limited partnership syndications and real estate investment trusts play in real estate markets.

3. Explain the major differences between public and private equity markets as a source of real estate capital and comment on the relative significance of each funding alternative.

INTRODUCTION

One of the critical decisions real estate investors must make is the form of business organization to be used in purchasing and holding the real estate. For individual investors, the options include a sole proprietorship, C corporation, S corporation, or limited liability company. Multiple investors must choose between a corporate ownership form, a general or limited partnership, or a limited liability company. If the real estate will be held by 100 or more investors, a real estate investment trust (REIT) is an additional alternative.

The choice of ownership form is driven largely by federal income tax rules and the ability of some or all of the investors to avoid personal liability for the debts and obligations of the entity. Additional objectives such as the ability to access debt and additional equity capital, the avoidance of management responsibility, and the ability of investors to dispose of their interest in the organization also affect the decision.

We first discuss and compare the alternative ownership forms. Subsequent sections provide a more detailed look at the two most important ownership structures: real estate limited partnerships and real estate investment trusts.

SOLE OWNERSHIP

Individuals who own modest real estate portfolios may simply choose to hold the properties in their own name. With a **sole proprietorship**, all cash flow and income tax consequences of real estate ownership "flow through" directly to the individual's income tax return (Form 1040, Schedule E), thereby avoiding the taxation of income at the entity level. Tax deductible losses on income properties may be used to offset positive taxable income from other sources (wages, dividends, etc.), subject to passive activity loss restrictions (as discussed in Chapter 4). Ms. Judy Long, whose partial income tax return was displayed and discussed in Chapter 4, held her rental house in the form of a sole proprietorship.

The major advantages of owning real estate as a sole proprietorship are that it is simple and inexpensive—no legal or accounting fees are required to establish a separate entity. A major disadvantage is that a sole proprietor is subject to unlimited liability from the business of owning and renting property. This includes liability from contractual obligations associated with the property, including mortgage debt, as well as obligations arising from tort actions brought against the individual. Where feasible, insurance may reduce these exposures. However, there is still the risk that the sole proprietor will be sued for something not covered by insurance or sued for more than the insurance coverage.

C CORPORATION

A **C corporation** must file articles of incorporation in the state in which it is formed. Once created, a C corporation must hold board meetings and receive shareholder approval for major corporate decisions. C corporations constitute a legal and taxable entity that is separate from the shareholders. Thus, the C corporation earns income and incurs tax liabilities. Income taxes are paid on net corporate income, and C corporations have their own tax rate structure and rules. Dividends from a C corporation are not deductible by the corporation and are taxable to the shareholders. Thus, one of the major disadvantages of using a C corporation to hold income-producing real estate is that the income from the underlying property or properties will be taxed twice. C corporation income is subject to tax at rates as high as 35 percent and individuals can be subject to rates as high as 39.6 percent. Thus, the effective double tax rate on income from properties can be as high as 60.74 percent.[1]

A C corporation provides limited liability for its shareholders for obligations of the corporation. This limited liability includes liability from contractual obligations as well as obligations arising from tort actions brought against the corporation.

Tax losses of a C corporation do *not* flow through to its shareholders. Instead, these losses can be carried back 3 years and forward 15 years. Carrying forward losses for use against future positive taxable income reduces the present value of the associated tax savings, unless the negative effects of deferral are offset by increases in the tax rate at which future losses are deducted. C corporations are not generally a desirable structure for owning income property because there are alternative ownership forms that provide limited liability but avoid double taxation and allow current use of losses.

Although C corporations are not typically used if the primary business of the entity is to invest in income-producing real estate, many corporations do own a significant amount of real estate (GM, Microsoft, Burger King, etc.). Moreover, these corporations are gradually recognizing the importance of real estate as a strategic asset, and they are beginning to take a more proactive approach to its management (see Real Estate Focus 5–1).

---

[1] This is calculated as $[1 - (1 - 0.35) \times (1 - 0.396)] = 0.6074$. Beginning in 1993, a 35 percent tax rate applies to corporate taxable income in excess of $10 million. The maximum tax rate on corporate capital gains is also 35 percent. Regular C corporations are not subject to passive activity loss restrictions.

REAL ESTATE FOCUS 5-1

More Companies Create Value through Strategic Real Estate Plans

In recent years, a number of companies including Chevron Corp., Dole Food Co., Exxon, Pacific Gas & Electric Co., Pacific Telesis Group, Prudential Insurance, Sears Roebuck, Sun Oil, US West, and Westinghouse Electric Corp. have decided to sell or spin off billions of dollars of corporate real estate assets. Such sales are expected to accelerate in coming years. Companies are selling assets that no longer are needed for their operations because of corporate restructurings, downsizings, or relocations.

Although the current market value of corporate real estate can be significant relative to book value, it historically has been an overlooked and underutilized asset on corporate balance sheets. But as companies have gradually realized the importance of real estate as a strategic asset, they are beginning to take a proactive approach to its management. Many corporations, with the help of outside consultants, are developing strategic real estate plans.

While such plans may differ in their particulars, companies generally have common goals. Among them are to increase shareholder value, optimize returns on existing real estate assets as well as any assets acquired in the future, move highly leveraged real estate off the balance sheet, realize tax-deductible losses, increase liquidity, raise capital for various corporate purposes (including growth and expansion), and redeploy corporate resources from real estate to core businesses.

SOURCE: Barry Barovick and Stephen Duffy, *Real Estate Newsline*, 13, no. 2 (February/March 1996), E & Y Kenneth Leventhal Real Estate Group.

S CORPORATION

An **S corporation** is created in the same manner as a regular C corporation. An S election is a federal tax election that must be made with the unanimous consent of the shareholders. An S corporation possesses the same limited liability benefits for its shareholders as do C corporations. However, although an S corporation is a separate legal entity, it is not a separate taxable entity. Taxable income and losses flow through to each stockholder and are reported on their individual tax returns. Thus, the income produced by the holdings of an S corporation is not taxed twice. However, this flow-through of taxable income may cause cash flow problems for shareholders if the S corporation does not also distribute cash.[2]

A major drawback of S corporations for some investor groups is that they must not have more than 75 shareholders.[3] Another potential limitation is that S corporation

---

[2] Although losses of an S corporation flow through to its shareholders, the ability of the shareholders to utilize these losses is subject to several limitations. First, shareholders cannot utilize losses that are in excess of the amount they have invested, their at-risk basis. The at-risk basis is generally equal to the amount paid for the stock, minus (plus) allocated tax losses (gains), minus cash distributions received. Note that the debts and liabilities of the S corporation do *not* increase the shareholder's at-risk basis in the stock. Thus, if the S corporation takes out a mortgage on property it owns, no part of the mortgage is included in the amount the individual shareholders have at risk. This could significantly limit the amount of tax deductions that can be used by shareholders. Shareholder loans to the S corporation do increase the shareholder's basis.

[3] For more detail on S corporation requirements, see Chapter 17 in Thomas G. Manolakas and Paul E. Anderson, *Tax Factors in Real Estate Decisions* (Upper Saddle River, NJ: Prentice Hall, 1990).

investors are subject to passive activity loss restrictions if they do not materially participate in the management of the corporation. A taxpayer materially participates only if she is involved on a regular, continuous, and substantial basis in the operation of the activity.[4] If the shareholder does not materially participate in the trade or business of the S corporation, the shareholder's interest in the S corporation is considered (for tax purposes) to be a passive activity. In such a case, the investor's share of the S corporation's tax losses can only be offset against other passive income of the investor. (See the discussion of passive activity loss rules in Chapter 4.) Finally, the S corporation's income or loss must be allocated to each shareholder in proportion to his or her ownership of the corporation. Allocation of these items based on some other criteria—that is, "special" allocations—is not allowed.

GENERAL PARTNERSHIP

General partnerships are formed according to state law, must have their own taxpayer identification number, and must file an informational federal income tax return with the IRS. General partnerships are treated as conduits for tax purposes; taxable income and losses flow through to the partners who pay the tax. Thus, double taxation does not exist. A partner's share of income, losses, and cash flow is determined by the partnership agreement and may vary from item to item. In particular, if certain conditions are met, a partnership can allocate income and deductions in a manner different than each partner's interest in the partnership. Tax losses from a general partnership are subject to passive activity loss restrictions, regardless of the level at which the taxpayer participates in the activities of the partnership. As with the S corporation, flow-through taxation may cause cash flow problems at the partner level if there is no corresponding cash distribution from the partnership.[5]

A major disadvantage of a general partnership is that none of the partners has limited liability. In fact, general partners are liable for *all* debts of the partnership. This includes contractual debts and debts arising from tort actions against the partnership. General partners are also jointly and severally liable for wrongful acts committed by other partners in the course of the partnership's business. Therefore, the personal assets of the general partners are subject to the claims of the partnership's creditors. For this reason, real estate general partnerships are fairly uncommon and those that do exist tend to have only a few partners.

---

[4] For more detail on material participation, see Chapter 8 in Lawrence C. Phillips and John L. Kramer, *Federal Taxation* (Upper Saddle River, NJ: Prentice Hall, 1995).

[5] The utilization of losses for general partners is very similar to the tax treatment of S corporation losses. However, unlike S corporations, each partner's share of the debts and liabilities of the partnership *do* increase the at-risk basis of the partner's interest in the partnership. As a result, a partner may be able to deduct more tax losses than a comparable S corporation shareholder.

LIMITED PARTNERSHIPS

A **limited partnership** is created and taxed in the same way as a general partnership. However, a limited partnership allows some of the investing partners to avoid personal liability for more than the amount of their investment. A limited partnership must have at least one "general" partner and one "limited" partner. The former assumes unlimited liability for the debts of the partnership; the latter places at risk only the amount of the equity investment. Moreover, the responsibility for the management of the partnership rests with the general partner(s) who is frequently a knowledgeable real estate builder or investor. Note that the general partner can be a corporation, which creates limited liability for the owner(s) of the corporation acting as the general partner. Limited partnerships can be small, private partnerships or large, publicly traded partnerships. With regard to distributions and double taxation, limited partnerships are similar to general partnerships—double taxation does not exist.[6]

The flow-through feature of a limited partnership coupled with limited liability for the limited partners largely explain why the limited partnership form of ownership has been, by far, the preferred ownership form of income property investors. However, the Internal Revenue Service does not allow an organization of individuals to call themselves a partnership—and avoid double taxation—if the organization acts (looks and smells) like a corporation. Thus, an organization that has more corporate characteristics than noncorporate characteristics will be classified by the IRS as a corporation for tax purposes. Therefore, care must be taken in the limited partnership agreement to distinguish the organization from a corporation. This is usually accomplished by specifying a date for the termination of the partnership (corporations have continual life), restricting in some way the transferability of partnership interests (corporations have free transferability of shares); or subjecting one or more partners to unlimited liability (all shareholders in a corporation have limited liability). Note that the criterion of unlimited liability is automatically accomplished with a limited partnership because the general partner(s) is subject to unlimited liability.

REAL ESTATE INVESTMENT TRUST

In 1960, Congress passed the Real Estate Investment Trust Act, which authorized the corporate form of ownership for real estate, but with no taxation at the entity level if specific requirements are satisfied. A REIT raises equity through the sale of shares to the public. REITs also borrow funds, usually from commercial banks. With these funds, REITs either acquire properties or mortgages. REITs can be small and privately held or large and publicly traded on a major stock exchange. Investors in publicly traded REITs can sell their shares readily and receive returns from the appreciation in stock value.

---

[6] The ability of limited and general partners in a limited partnership to utilize losses is identical to the treatment afforded participants in a general partnership.

REITs have been described as mutual funds for real estate in that they afford the same advantages to investors: diversification and liquidity. Diversification comes from the large portfolios that a REIT can own. Liquidity is achieved because shares of stock are generally more easily disposed of than the underlying properties, especially if the shares are traded on a stock exchange. Some REIT shares can be purchased for as little as $1, much less than the minimum equity contribution required for a partnership interest. Relative to limited partnerships, shareholders may have more control over the management decisions of the REIT because the trustees must be elected by the stockholders.

REIT shareholders receive the same limited liability protection as shareholders in C corporations. With regard to distributions and double taxation, REITs are similar to S corporations. However, unlike an S corporation, the tax losses of a REIT do not flow through to shareholders. Moreover, REITs must meet a long list of restrictive conditions on an ongoing basis in order to avoid taxation at the entity level. For example, at least 100 investors must own a REIT's shares and, to ensure diversified ownership, five or fewer investors cannot own more than 50 percent of the REIT's shares. A REIT must distribute at least 95 percent of its taxable income to shareholders in the form of dividends, which significantly limits the ability of a REIT to retain earnings for future investment. Fully 75 percent of the value of a REIT's assets must consist of real estate assets, cash, and government securities. Real estate mortgages and mortgage-backed securities are considered real estate for the purposes of this test. At least 75 percent of the REIT's gross income must be derived from real estate assets. These last two requirements ensure that the REIT invests primarily in real estate. In addition, not more than 30 percent of the REIT's gross income can be derived from the sale of real property held for less than four years and no more than five properties can be sold in any one year.[7]

LIMITED LIABILITY COMPANY

The emergence of this form of business entity has changed the analysis of ownership form selection. Most states have adopted limited liability company (LLC) legislation and the IRS has ruled on their classification status. If the LLC lacks at least two of the four standard corporate characteristics, the IRS has ruled that the LLC should be taxed as a partnership. However, an LLC can still provide liability protection to the owner-members.

In general, the owners of an LLC are not personally liable for obligations of the LLC beyond their investment, nor are they personally liable for the mistakes committed by other members or employees of the LLC. However, individual members are generally personally liable for their own negligence or wrongful acts.[8]

---

[7] For more detail on REIT requirements, see Chapter 21 in Thomas G. Manolakas and Paul E. Anderson, *Tax Factors in Real Estate Decisions* (Upper Saddle River, NJ: Prentice Hall, 1990) and Peter M. Fass, Michael E. Shaff, and Donald B. Ziff, *Real Estate Investment Trusts Handbook* (New York: Clark, Boardman, Callaghan, 1996).

[8] There is uncertainty regarding the limited liability of LLC members that conduct business in states that do not recognize an LLC.

E X H I B I T 5 - 1

OWNERSHIP FORM COMPARISON SUMMARY

Investor Objective	Sole Ownership	C Corporation	S Corporation	General Partnership	Limited Partnership	REITs	Limited Liability Company
Avoid double taxation	Yes	No	Yes	Yes	Yes	Yes[1]	Yes
Pass-through tax losses	Yes	No	Yes[2]	Yes[2]	Yes[2]	No	Yes[2]
Limited liability	No	Yes	Yes	No	Yes[3]	Yes	Yes
Avoidance of management responsibility	No	Yes	Yes	No	Yes[4]	Yes	Yes
Ease of transfer of interest[5]	Yes	Yes	Yes	No	No	Yes	Yes
Flexibility in allocating tax losses	No	No	No	No	Yes	No	No

[1]Provided they meet a long list of restrictive conditions on an ongoing basis.

[2]Investors cannot utilize losses that are in excess of the amount they have at risk. S corporation shareholders cannot include their share of any corporation mortgage debt in the calculation of their basis.

[3]The general partner(s) is subject to unlimited liability.

[4]The general partner manages the operations of a limited partnership.

[5]Sole proprietorships and corporate forms allow ownership interests to be freely transferred; however, the actual liquidity of corporate shares depends on the size of the firm and whether the shares are traded on a major exchange.

With regard to distributions and double taxation, LLCs are similar to general and limited partnerships. The same limitations on the utilization of losses that apply to a partner in a general or limited partnership also apply to a member of an LLC.

COMPARING OWNERSHIP FORMS

Exhibit 5–1 summarizes the ability of alternative ownership forms to meet the various objectives of investors. For individual owners, sole proprietorships are not necessarily preferred because of unlimited liability, even though they are the least expensive and simplest alternative. Individuals also can choose to form a C or S corporation, although the latter usually dominate because they avoid double taxation and allow the pass-through of tax losses (to the extent of the shareholder's tax basis). As between sole ownership and S corporations, investors gain limited liability by choosing to use an S corporation instead of owning the real estate directly; however, there are more initial and ongoing costs associated with an S corporation.

For groups of investors, the choice of ownership form is first constrained by the desired size of the group. With 75 or fewer investors, the organization will typically choose between an S corporation and a limited partnership; the general partnership alternative is usually inferior to a limited partnership because of the exposure of all partners to unlimited liability. As between an S corporation and a limited partnership, the latter has traditionally been the dominant choice for several reasons. First, prior to 1983,

S corporations were not allowed to receive more than 20 percent of their gross revenue from income property rents—a restriction that precluded their use for organizations primarily interested in investing in rental real estate. Second, unlike limited partnerships, an investor's share of the debts and liabilities of the S corporation does *not* increase the basis of the shareholder's interest in the corporation. This restriction could limit the amount of tax losses that shareholders are able to deduct against other sources of income in any year.

The use of S corporations by small investor groups has been increasing in recent years. Besides the 1983 tax law change, this increased use can largely be attributed to the Tax Reform Act of 1986, which significantly reduced the tax benefits associated with income property investments. In particular, TRA 1986 eliminated accelerated depreciation and lengthened allowable cost recovery periods—thereby significantly reducing allowable depreciation deductions and the probability that tax losses will occur. In addition, TRA 1986 introduced passive activity loss restrictions that limit the ability of noncorporate investors to offset any income property tax losses against salary and portfolio income. Moreover, the legislation reduced federal income tax rates, thereby reducing the after-tax value of any tax losses that do occur (and that are not deferred by passive activity loss restrictions). These tax changes greatly reduced the *relative* tax advantage of limited partnerships over S corporations.

Investor groups of more than 100 usually must choose between organizing as a limited partnership or a REIT. These two alternatives have numerous similarities. Both allow passive investors to exchange the responsibility for day-to-day management for limited liability, and both can avoid the double taxation of rental income. Prior to 1986 when tax considerations played a more important role, REITs were disadvantaged relative to limited partnerships because of their inability to pass through tax losses to investors. The substantial tax changes in 1986 that increased the relative attractiveness of S corporations for small investor groups also increased the attractiveness of the REIT ownership structure relative to limited partnerships. These tax changes are somewhat responsible for the dramatic growth in REITs during the early 1990s and for the significant decline of public limited partnerships.

A CLOSER LOOK AT LIMITED PARTNERSHIP SYNDICATIONS

A **syndicate** is defined as a group of persons or legal entities who come together to carry out a particular activity. A real estate syndicate, therefore, is a group organized to develop a parcel of land, buy an office building, purchase an entire portfolio of properties, make mortgage loans, or perform other real estate activities. Real estate syndicates traditionally have organized as limited partnerships. The real estate syndicator, therefore, is the general partner in a limited partnership, and the other members are limited partners. The limited partners in real estate syndicates cannot participate in the syndicate's business activities beyond their initial investment of funds, or they lose their limited-partnership status for tax purposes. The syndicator organizes such groups and manages the activities they are organized to carry out. Much of the syndicator's work is raising money. The other members of the real estate syndicate are usually money partners or investors. Syndicators generally enhance the productivity of real estate because without their efforts and organizational skills, fewer new development projects would be initiated, fewer existing property transactions would occur, and fewer mortgage loans would be made. However, as discussed below, syndicators contributed to the massive overbuilding that occurred in many real estate markets during the 1980s. This overbuilding greatly reduced the efficiency of some real estate. In fact, some property that was developed would have produced higher returns had it remained farmland.

From the perspective of the limited partners, substantial costs may offset the benefits of investing in real estate through limited-partnership syndications. The sponsor of the syndication—the general partner(s)—and professionals hired by the syndicator—lawyers, accountants, and real estate acquisition personnel—normally charge substantial fees to limited partners for services to create and manage the partnership. Because of these fees, sometimes less than 80 cents of every dollar contributed by investors is actually invested in properties.

TYPES OF REAL ESTATE SYNDICATION

Real estate syndications can be classified in several ways; for example, they are often described as either *public offerings* or *private offerings*. This classification refers to the manner in which the syndication is structured for purposes of state and federal securities regulations. In general, public offerings are larger than private offerings both in terms of the money raised from real estate investors and in terms of the number of investors in the syndicate. Public offerings typically require a minimum equity investment of $5,000, whereas private offerings usually require a significantly larger equity investment. Public offerings, unlike private offerings, involve general solicitation (e.g., investment bankers and personal financial planners calling potential investors on the phone) and advertising the offering in the media. For a private offering, syndicators, who are often local developers, typically act as their own brokers and attempt to market the investment opportunity to a selected few (wealthy) investors. Large public offerings must be fully registered with federal and state securities regulators, whereas smaller private placements can be exempt from full registration and costly disclosure regulations.

Another way to classify real estate syndications is by the amount of the syndicate's business activity that has been carried out at the time the offering is made to investors. A *fully specified fund* is an offering in which the syndicator has either acquired or developed all of the properties (or mortgage loans), or has purchased an option that grants the syndicator the right, but not the obligation, to acquire the properties. The offering *prospectus* is the document presented to potential investors in the syndication. It describes various aspects of the offering and usually contains information on the operating performance of properties acquired. Thus the future returns from the fully specified fund can be estimated by potential investors. Private offerings are likely to be fully specified. In fact, private offerings typically involve just one property or project.

Prospectuses for other types of offerings describe funds in which only a portion of the money available to invest has been used to purchase rights to real estate. This type of syndication is known as a *partially specified fund*. Finally, some syndication offering documents provide investors with only a description of the type and nature of the real estate investments that will be made. These *unspecified* or *"blind" funds* are the most difficult for investors to analyze and have come under the closest scrutiny from securities regulators. Public offerings are usually unspecified or only partially specified when initially sold to investors. Real estate syndicates also are classified somewhat more informally as leveraged offerings (which use mortgage loans as well as investor funds to purchase real estate) or unleveraged offerings.

HISTORY AND CURRENT BUSINESS ENVIRONMENT

The origins of modern real estate syndicates are the raw land syndicates that were organized in California during the 1960s. Syndication of real estate spread to many different property types and situations in the early 1970s, but it was limited primarily to California. A real estate syndication explosion occurred during the early 1980s. Sales of *public* real estate syndication offerings in 1977 were less than $500 million. By 1979, revenues had grown to about $750 million. In 1981, sales were approximately $1.75 billion; they topped $8 billion in both 1985 and 1986, and were approximately $7 billion in 1987.[9]

What caused this explosive growth during the early 1980s? Most observers agree that two factors were at work. First, rapid inflation, rising real incomes of white collar workers, and more working women during the late 1970s pushed many households into the maximum federal income tax brackets. Second, the Economic Recovery Tax Act of 1981, which created the accelerated capital cost recovery system (see Chapter 4), greatly enhanced the tax shelter benefits of real estate. Therefore, more taxpayers needed tax shelter, and real estate syndicates provided a means of accessing the newly created tax benefits of real estate.[10]

What has happened to the sales of public limited partnerships since 1987? In 1989 sales fell to $3 billion and by 1990 sales had decreased to $879 million. Sales in 1994 and 1995 were $396 million and $355 million, respectively.

What caused the enormous decline of the public real estate syndication business after 1987? The first blow was the passage of TRA 1986, which substantially reduced the tax benefits associated with income property investments, as discussed earlier. The second major disturbance in commercial real estate markets in the 1980s has been referred to as a *lender frenzy*. This term refers to the financing of income-producing real estate construction to the point of extraordinary excess supply in the middle of the decade, and the continuing financing of it to maintain the excess supply throughout the remainder of the decade and into the 1990s. It has been estimated that $80 to $100 billion in excess com-

---

[9] These data are compiled by Robert A. Stranger & Co., Shrewsbury, New Jersey.

[10] The major change under ERTA was in lowering the number of years over which a taxpayer could depreciate real estate from an average of 50 years before 1981 to 15 years. The shorter the depreciable life, the larger the depreciation allowance in each year of the investment, and therefore the greater the tax shelter.

REAL ESTATE FOCUS 5-2

Real Estate Partnerships Begin Comeback

While 1994 was a lousy year for many types of investments, there were some significant price increases in one battered group of securities: old real estate limited partnerships. Average resale prices of partnerships that own apartment buildings more than doubled last year in the informal, low-volume secondary market, a new survey shows. Average prices for some other types of real-estate partnerships rose 20 percent to 40 percent, according to the survey by Dallas research firm Partnership Profiles Inc.

Resale prices are still generally far below what investors paid when the partnerships were originally sold. But the price increases were still good news for long-suffering partnership holders. "The market is telling you things are improving," says Glen Bigelow, a New York investment manager who buys old real estate partnerships for private investment pools. The old partnerships "are not a black hole forever," he says.

Investors hold billions of dollars of limited partnerships that make them part owners of apartment and office buildings, shopping centers, and a wide range of other business ventures, from cable-television systems to oil-drilling operations. Many partnerships have performed dismally and dragged on for years longer than expected. Most partnerships were never designed to be traded, and only a small minority of them change hands in the secondary market.

Spencer Jefferies, president of Partnership Profiles, says the price increases reflect an improvement in real estate market conditions and the fact that many partnerships increased or resumed the payment of distributions to investors. In addition, "there are a lot more people that are coming into the secondary market" as buyers, including some affluent retirees and real estate professionals looking to profit from a real estate recovery, he says.

Even with the rise in resale prices, though, partnership investors who don't have an urgent need for cash should generally hang on to their securities, partnership specialists say. At current levels, prices are still almost always below the value of the underlying assets, as estimated by partnership managers and independent appraisal firms. Such seeming discounts have helped spur buying interest in old real estate partnerships. Another big draw has been income. Current (cash-on-cash) yields have drifted down during the past year, though, as prices have climbed.

SOURCE: *The Wall Street Journal*, January 13, 1995.

---

mercial real estate was constructed.[11] This excess supply of space pushed up vacancies and dramatically reduced rental rates. Many lending institutions contributed to the lending frenzy, most notably savings and loan associations. However, commercial banks, foreign investors, pension funds, and life insurance companies continued to pour money into commercial real estate after 1986, even though vacancy rates were at extraordinary levels.[12]

Although the public market for real estate limited partnerships has been moribund the past several years, there have been significant signs of improvement (see Real Estate Focus 5–2). Moreover, the private limited partnership market is still the most

---

[11] See Patric H. Hendershott and Edward J. Kane, "Causes and Consequences of the 1980s Commercial Construction Boom," *Journal of Applied Corporate Finance* (May 1992), pp. 61–70.

[12] The lender frenzy is discussed in detail by James R. Follain, Patric H. Hendershott, and David C. Ling, "Real Estate Markets since 1980: What Role Have Taxes Changes Played," *National Tax Journal* (September 1992), pp. 253–66.

EXHIBIT 5-2

SYNDICATION PROCESS: THE ROLE OF THE SYNDICATOR

Origination Phase	→	Operation Phase	→	Completion Phase
The syndicator		The syndicator		The syndicator
Develops the concept		Manages the		Prepares the properties
for the syndication		syndication		for sale
Organizes the legal		Manages the property		Sells the property
entity (e.g., limited		(frequently)		(frequently)
partnership)				Dissolves the
Has the offering				syndication or
memorandums				resyndicates
drafted				
Markets the ownership				
interests to investors				
Acquires the real estate				

important source of equity capital for small and medium-size investments. In addition, REITs that do not have enough retained earnings to take advantage of expansion or acquisition opportunities may consider "de-REITing" and becoming limited partnerships.

THE ROLE OF THE SYNDICATOR

Who are real estate syndicators (general partners) and exactly what do they do? Because the risks and returns from real estate syndications are difficult for investors to evaluate, the success of an offering often depends on the reputation and track record of the syndicator. Today's private syndicator is a businessperson who usually is well known in the local business community. Typically, the private syndicator has a background in real estate, most often brokerage or development. Public syndicators, in contrast, have been large national firms in which syndication is one of several real estate–related services the firm offers.

Syndicators organize, manage, and control the syndicate from origination through completion (e.g., a 10-year period). As shown in Exhibit 5–2, the syndicator's role in the syndication process is most important during origination. Much of the syndicator's work in this phase involves coordination with lawyers on the preparation of the offering documents, with accountants to set up the syndicate's accounting system, and with real estate brokers to acquire the property or properties. These activities may be done in-house or with the aid of outside professionals. Real estate brokerage, for example, is typically handled in-house whereas legal counsel typically comes from outside law firms.[13]

During the operations phase, the syndicator manages the syndicate and, frequently, the property. Managing the syndicate involves making sure investors receive their cash distributions and statements of tax losses, typically on a quarterly basis. Many syn-

---

[13] If it is a public offering, the syndicator may also work with marketing agents (e.g., a financial services firm like Merrill Lynch) to market the syndication shares to investors.

dicators, especially larger ones, have an in-house property-management division. Finally, the completion phase involves the sale of the property or properties and dissolution of the syndicate. The syndicator either performs these activities or *resyndicates* the property, which involves a sale to another group of investors that the syndicator has organized.

REGULATION

Real estate syndications are heavily regulated by state and federal governments. Government regulation is usually rationalized by the argument that markets will fail and innocent consumers will be hurt without the intervention of a disinterested third party. The general argument for regulating limited-partnerships syndications is that investors require information to make rational investment decisions; therefore, without government regulation requiring syndicators to *disclose* and *disseminate information*, the market would not operate efficiently. Stricter regulation that prohibits certain sponsors from operating has been justified on the grounds that it is needed to protect the public against unscrupulous syndicators.

A CLOSER LOOK AT REAL ESTATE INVESTMENT TRUSTS

Equity REITs invest in and operate income-producing properties, whereas **mortgage REITs** purchase mortgage obligations (typically commercial) and thus become, effectively, real estate lenders. **Hybrid REITs** invest a significant percentage of their assets in both properties and mortgages. **Finite-life REITs** are established to purchase and operate properties for a prespecified number of years, at which time the REIT disposes of its assets and distributes the proceeds to the shareholders. The lack of active management of the portfolio after acquisition and the prespecified dissolution date ensure that finite-life REITs operate purely as investment conduits. As a result, the perceived quality of the management team is not as important as with **infinite-life REITs**, which operate as going concerns.

REITs are either open- or closed-ended. **Closed-end REITs** do not offer shares of stock to the public after the initial stock is sold and the assets of the REIT are purchased. This protects the shareholders from the subsequent issue of additional shares, which could potentially dilute their equity interest. **Open-end REITs** are able to sell new shares to raise capital for the acquisition of additional assets (properties or mortgages) or other uses. This ability to issue additional equity can enhance the ability of the REIT management to make timely property acquisitions, especially given the REIT's limited ability to finance acquisitions with retained earning because they are required to pay out 95 percent of taxable income in dividends. Most REITs are equity, infinite life, and open-ended.

The REIT Act of 1960 envisaged a conservative investment vehicle with pass-through features that would encourage long-term investment in real estate by individual, taxable investors. In fact, prior to the Tax Reform Act of 1986, REITs were generally precluded from managing their own properties. The expectations of the REIT Act of

1960 were largely realized. Pre-1990 REITs were largely passive investment vehicles that owned diverse portfolios of properties. Most REITs arranged for both portfolio and property management through an external advisor and management did not participate extensively in stock ownership. REIT portfolios were typically static and perhaps best described as "diversification plays." Additionally, the conventional strategy of diversifying risk across property types and geographical location created little or no economies of scale or specialized expertise in managing the portfolio. As a pass-through vehicle, REITs could be expected to trade on the yield of the underlying real estate assets, less a liquidity discount. Many pre-1990 REITs were also finite-life REITs, which limited their growth potential because they were slated for liquidation at some prespecified terminal date.

After 1991, the REIT initial public offering (IPO) market exploded with 113 new issues coming to market by August of 1996 that raised well over $18 billion in equity capital.[14] Secondary equity offerings and unsecured debt offerings by REITs also increased significantly. The conventional explanation in the financial press for the 1992–1994 surge in REIT offerings is that the general rise in stock prices in the early 1990s lowered dividend yields on equities. Simultaneously, the fall in interest rates in 1992–1993 produced relatively low yields on fixed-income investments. However, the severe real estate recession of the late 1980s and early 1990s lowered real estate prices and increased the cash flow/price ratio (the dividend yield) on real estate, thereby increasing the relative attractiveness of real estate securities as "yield plays." In addition, the severity of the real estate recession produced a flood of foreclosures and bankruptcies, and contributed significantly to the failure of numerous financial institutions and to the weakening of the many life insurance companies that had been active real estate lenders. The evaporation of these traditional financing sources sent the industry in search of alternative sources of capital.

The post-1990s equity REITs differ from their predecessors in their organization, business plans, and ownership structure. Most of the recent REIT IPOs are fully integrated operating companies that can be characterized as "management plays" rather than as passive conduits for investors' capital. Their managements usually have substantial equity positions in the company, and all are infinite-life REITs. Property management is either done internally or by management that works solely for the benefit of the REIT shareholders. Property investments are focused by property type and geographic market because this specialization allows shareholders to benefit more fully from the specific expertise of the management. In fact, many REIT operating companies sell at premiums over the underlying yield, largely in anticipation of growth in earnings through development, refinancing, or restructuring. Many preexisting REITs also have begun to manage their portfolios more actively and to reposition themselves as property specialists.

In addition to more active management, the new REITs have attracted significantly more institutional investors than their predecessors. This increased institutional involvement has been attributed to the growing acceptance of REITs among pension fund investors as viable alternatives to direct investments in real estate and to the prospects of greater liquidity in the REIT market.

---

[14] The source for this information is the National Association of Real Estate Investment Trusts, *REIT Watch* (August 1996).

A final development that has contributed to the proliferation of new REIT issues in the 1990s is the evolution of the umbrella partnership REIT, or UPREIT structure. As an UPREIT, the REIT is a managing partner and typically majority owner in a single large umbrella partnership that, in turn, owns all or part of individual property partnerships. Owners transferring their individual partnership interests into the umbrella partnership can receive umbrella partnership units or REIT shares in return for their partnership interests—without triggering a taxable sale. The UPREIT structure has played a critical role in bridging the private and public real estate markets by deferring a potential capital gain tax penalty associated with the conversion of partnership ownership of real estate to public REIT ownership.[15]

SOURCES OF COMMERCIAL REAL ESTATE EQUITY CAPITAL

This section assesses the value of commercial real estate in the United States and discusses additional sources of real estate equity capital such as pension funds, life insurance companies, and joint ventures.

The value of commercial real estate in 1994 was estimated to be approximately $4 trillion in Chapter 1 (see Exhibit 1–5). Approximately $1 trillion of this total represented the value of commercial mortgages and $800 billion represented the value of real estate owned by industrial and service corporations. Thus, the value of equity positions in commercial real estate is approximately $2.2 trillion. The sources of this equity capital are summarized in Exhibit 5–3.[16]

PRIVATE REAL ESTATE MARKETS

Private market investors have the option to purchase properties directly. Purchasing individual properties directly in the private market gives the investor complete control of the asset: who leases it, who manages it, how much debt financing is used, and when it is sold.

Another investment alternative in the private markets is to purchase an interest in a pooled investment, such as a private REIT, commingled fund (discussed below), limited partnership, S corporation, or limited liability corporation. With pooled investments, the investor receives the income, appreciation, and tax benefits that are produced by direct investments. In addition, the investor receives the benefits associated with investing in portfolios of properties: diversification; economies of scale in the acquisition, management, and disposition of properties; the ability to obtain debt financing at the portfolio level; and the expertise of the management team assembled by the corporation's board of directors, general partner, or pension fund advisory firm. In exchange for these benefits, the investors relinquish management control to the active manager, as well as some fee(s).

---

[15] The UPREIT structure also may make many of the 1990s REITs more difficult to value because of additional uncertainty about conflicts of interest in the management of UPREIT properties. Additionally, the complex organizational structure can make interpretation of accounting statements more difficult.

[16] Sources of commercial mortgage debt are discussed in Chapters 18 and 19.

EXHIBIT 5 - 3

SOURCES OF COMMERCIAL REAL ESTATE EQUITY CAPITAL
VALUES AS OF JUNE 1995

Private Markets	**Public Markets**
Size: $2.2 trillion	*Size:* $60 billion
Direct Equity Investments:	Publicly traded REITs
Sole proprietors	Real estate operating companies
Pension funds	Partnerships: public placements
Life insurers	
Offshore investors	
Joint ventures	
Savings associations	
Commercial banks	
Pooled Equity Investments:	
Private REITs	
Commingled funds	
Partnerships: private placements	
S corporations	
Limited liability corporations	
Opportunity funds	

It is therefore important that management's interests are closely aligned with those of the investors. This at least partially explains the trend toward self-managed REITs in the 1990s, where the compensation of the management team is more directly related to the return performance of the REIT.

Pension funds. Because of their large and expanding pool of assets, **pension funds** have long been recognized as a major source of real estate equity capital. However, for a number of reasons, many pension funds have been reluctant to become equity investors in commercial real estate. One reason is that pension funds are tax exempt and therefore unable to take advantage of any tax benefits associated with income property. Second, the trustees of pension funds are required to be conservative in their investment decisions in order to protect the funds that working individuals are accumulating for retirement. Real estate has often been viewed by pension funds as too risky and difficult to manage. Moreover, real estate markets are characterized by a lack of information necessary for quantitative investment analysis.

Despite these drawbacks and their lack of real estate experience, pension funds have become a dominant participant in commercial real estate equity markets in recent years. The 1995 value of pension fund–owned real estate has been estimated at $75 billion to $100 billion.[17] Pension funds also are pushing to increase the sophistication of real estate investment decision making. Their influence is helping to increase the supply of market

---

[17] See Glenn R. Mueller, Keith R. Pauley, and William K. Morrill, Jr., "A Primer for Private and Public Equity Choices in a Real Estate Portfolio Management Context," *Real Estate Finance* (Spring 1995), pp. 12–21.

REAL ESTATE FOCUS 5-3

Development of Information Standards Could Help Attract More Capital to Real Estate Markets

As an asset class, real estate is beginning to attract more investment by pension funds and other institutional investors, but it has yet to achieve comparable stature with the larger and more established markets for equity and fixed-income investments. In the perception of investors, the real estate market has lacked consistent standards for compiling, measuring, and disclosing information comparable to those that govern public trading in stocks and bonds.

Real estate has traditionally been an entrepreneurial business, with properties bought and sold in private markets. Information has not been consistently reported and property valuations have been based on appraisals that lag current market conditions. Because of such ambiguities, investors have been uncertain as to the true value of their prospective investments, and the overall liquidity of these investments has been impaired.

The gradual shift of real estate ownership from entrepreneurs to institutions, and the linking of real estate financing with the capital markets, have heightened the need for information standards. With definitive standards to guide them, institutional investors could more readily analyze individual properties and portfolios as well as REITs and mortgage-backed securities; they could also compare the performance of real estate with other asset classes. This could give investors a higher comfort level and help to attract investment capital to real estate. Moreover, real estate companies and plan sponsors could more easily access the capital markets and reduce their capital costs.

Anticipating the need for guidelines, the National Council of Real Estate Investment Fiduciaries (NCREIF), the Pension Real Estate Association (PREA), and the National Association of Real Estate Investment Managers (NAREIM) created a task force in 1994 and compiled a recommended set of information standards.

Over the long term, the creation of consistent information guidelines for the real estate industry will bring more liquidity and more capital to the institutional real estate market. Equally important, the standards will enable institutional investors to increase their allocation to the real estate asset class.

SOURCE: Jack Haly and David Duncan, *Real Estate Newsline*, 13, no. 1 (January 1996), E&Y Kenneth Leventhal Real Estate Group.

---

level and property level information that is available to all investors (see Real Estate Focus 5-3).

Pension funds must decide whether to make their real estate investments directly or to pursue their investment strategy by investing in REITs and/or commingled real estate funds. If the pension fund chooses to make direct investments, it must then decide whether to set up an in-house staff to make and oversee investments or to employ a pension fund advisory firm to handle its real estate investments.

Commingled real estate funds are offered by major banks, life insurance companies, and real estate firms to pension funds for investment in real estate. Because many pension funds do not have the expertise for real estate investment, commingled fund managers collect contributions from various pension funds and "commingle" them to purchase properties. About one-half of the $75 billion pension funds allocated to real estate in 1989 was placed with managers of commingled funds. The balance was invested directly in real estate, usually through local real estate companies. Liquidity has been a problem. Some pension fund investors who intended to move money out of certain

REAL ESTATE FOCUS 5-4

Japanese Seek to Sell More U.S. Real Estate

In 1994 a Japanese bank was seeking buyers for a $200 million package of 10 troubled U.S. properties and distressed loans, including loans on the Ritz-Carlton Huntington Hotel in Pasadena, California, and L'Auberge Del Mar Resort & Spa in Del Mar, California. In early 1994, Nippon Credit Bank Ltd. sold loans and equity in 16 Howard Johnson Motor Lodges, which carried a face value of $72 million, to an American investment group for just $19 million.

The Japanese owners, who poured more than $70 billion into U.S. real estate between 1986 and 1994, were striving to complete the real estate sales quietly, according to American advisers and buyers, due to embarrassment over their losses. Many invested at the top of the market, and many of the properties they bought had dropped in value by at least 30 percent. The sales were concentrated in California and Hawaii, where Japanese institutions made about two-thirds of their real estate investments. Many were anxious to unload hotels and resorts, which are costlier to maintain than office buildings.

Meanwhile, a growing number of American real estate investors were eager to take advantage of the Japanese selling spree. In April of 1994, Bedrock Partners, a Los Angeles investment group, bought that city's Checkers Hotel from Sumitomo Bank Ltd. for about $13 million. Sumitomo also sold a pool of loans with an original face value of about $50 million. An investment fund managed by Boston-based Aldrich, Eastman & Waltch paid Shimizu Construction Co. $72 million, or about 50 percent of replacement cost, for the Camelback Esplanade, an office, hotel, and retail complex in Phoenix.

Japanese investors and lenders also sold at a loss such trophy properties as the Hyatt Regency Waikoloa in Hawaii, the Galleria in Scottsdale, Arizona, and the Doral Telluride ski resort in Colorado.

SOURCE: *The Wall Street Journal*, June 10, 1994.

---

commingled real estate funds have had to wait long periods for their redemption request to be satisfied. This at least partially explains the dramatic increase in the ownership of REITs by pension funds.

Joint ventures. In a **joint venture,** a lender and a developer-investor form a business partnership to develop or purchase a specific real estate property or properties. A joint venture is generally treated as a general partnership for income tax purposes, and the duration of the investment activity is limited by time. Joint ventures are usually formed for projects that require large amounts of capital, supplied by an institutional lender, and specialized expertise, which is provided by the developer. Many savings and loan associations and commercial banks were active as joint venture partners during the 1980s—often with disastrous results.

Other direct equity investors. Life insurers have traditionally been a major player in equity markets. In recent years, however, they have been net sellers of ownership positions in commercial real estate, due, at least in part, to the severe real estate recession of the late 1980s and early 1990s that dampened their enthusiasm for real estate. Foreign investors also have grabbed headlines for their active participation in United States real estate markets. After pouring more than $70 billion into U.S. real estate during the 1980s, Japanese investors became active sellers in the 1990s. (See Real Estate Focus 5–4.)

Pooled investments. The bulk of U.S. commercial real estate not owned by institutional investors (pension funds and the like) is owned by private REITs, partnerships (private placements), S corporations, and, increasingly, limited liability companies.

PUBLIC REAL ESTATE MARKETS

The **public market** for commercial real estate consists of publicly traded REITs, public limited partnerships, and real estate operating companies (REOCs). This later category consists of large, publicly traded construction and development firms—primarily large home builders. REITs are now more broadly accepted as an industry group by mutual funds and other institutional investors, especially pension funds. Public REITs provide most of the benefits and risks of a private REIT, in addition to improved liquidity and greater access to public debt and equity markets—which increase the financial flexibility of the REIT. As with private REITs, these benefits are associated with the loss of control over the individual properties.

With a total market capitalization approaching $80 billion at the end of 1996, REITs held less than 3 percent of the total commercial property inventory. However, although the shift from private ownership to public ownership of commercial real estate is still in its early stages, the revolution is moving rapidly.[18]

THE RETURN PERFORMANCE OF PUBLIC AND PRIVATE REAL ESTATE

To obtain evidence on the relative return performance of real estate, two publicly available sources of real estate performance data can be analyzed: (1) the National Council of Real Estate Investment Fiduciaries (NCREIF) Classic Property Index, which measures returns on a large portfolio of *privately held*, institutional-quality real estate, and (2) the National Association of Real Estate Investment Trusts (NAREIT) Index, which measures returns on a large portfolio of *publicly held* real estate. An introduction to, and description of, each index follows.

APPRAISAL-BASED INDEX OF HISTORICAL UNSECURITIZED RETURNS

The NCREIF organization publishes a quarterly index of value-weighted real estate returns.[19] The **NCREIF Classic Property Index** (NCPI) measures the historical performance of income properties held by (or for) pension funds and profit-sharing plans. The NCPI includes both income (NOI) and capital (value appreciation or depreciation)

---

[18] For more on the shift from private to public ownership of commercial real estate, see Michael L. Evans, "The Big Switch: Public Capital Replaces Private Debt," *Real Estate Issues* (August 1994), pp. 5–8, and the Urban Land Institute, "The REIT Renaissance: The Corporatization of Income-Producing Real Estate," *ULI Special Report*, 1995.

[19] *Value-weighted* means that the return on each property used to construct the index is weighted by the property's market value as a percentage of the total market value of the properties that comprise the index.

components which are combined to generate quarterly total returns. The NCPI is calculated on an all-cash, unleveraged basis, before management fees are deducted, and is standardized with a value of 100 representing the fourth quarter of 1977.

Properties included in the index may be wholly owned or joint ventures, but they must be existing, investment-grade, income-producing properties held by fiduciaries on behalf of tax-exempt institutions. Development projects and agricultural properties are specifically excluded. In order to eliminate the effects of mortgage indebtedness on valuation, only unlevered properties are included in the NCPI.[20] The universe of properties upon which the index is based changes each quarter as new members join NCREIF and existing members alter their holdings through sales and acquisitions. At the end of second quarter 1995, there were 1,784 properties in the NCPI, with a combined market value of $26.7 billion. The properties in the NCPI are also used to calculate 37 subindexes, including separate indexes for the five major property types: apartment, office, retail, R&D/office, and warehouse. Separate indexes also are calculated for various geographic regions and subregions of the United States, both by property type and in the aggregate.

One potential weakness with using NCREIF data is that the quarterly increase or decrease in the market value of each property is determined by an appraisal of the property, unless the property happens to sell during the quarter, in which case the transaction price is used. This methodology for determining the quarterly change in property value has received substantial criticism—empirical evidence suggests that using appraisal estimates rather than transaction prices may smooth the indicated changes in value and therefore bias estimates of the return volatility downward.[21] Nonetheless, the NCREIF Classic Property Index remains a primary source for information on the risk-return characteristics of income-producing property.

REIT-BASED INDEX OF HISTORICAL SECURITIZED RETURNS

An alternative source of historic real estate return information is the National Association of Real Estate Investment Trusts (NAREIT) Index. The **NAREIT index** is a value-weighted index that tracks the total return (income plus capital) pattern of all exchange-listed REITs on a monthly basis.[22]

---

[20] Beginning in 1996, NCREIF began publishing a separate index, the NCREIF Property Index (NPI) that contains all equity acquisitions as well as debt-financed properties that have been "unlevered." An unlevered property return is one in which NCREIF has made an attempt to remove the effects of financial leverage on the property's return.

[21] For more on the effect of appraisal-based returns on return volatility, see David M. Geltner, "Smoothing in Appraisal-Based Returns," *Journal of Real Estate Finance and Economics* 4 (1991), pp. 327–45, and Jeffrey D. Fisher, David M. Geltner, and R. Brian Webb, "Value Indices of Commercial Real Estate: A Comparison of Index Construction Methods, *Journal of Real Estate Finance and Economics* 9 (1994), pp. 137–64. Geltner (1991) also shows that such appraisal smoothing may bias the mean return.

[22] *Exchange-listed* means the shares are traded on the New York Stock Exchange, the American Stock Exchange, or over the counter on the National Association of Securities Dealers Automated Quotation (NASDAQ) system.

The NAREIT organization groups all qualified REITs into three main categories for reporting purposes. First, an Equity REITs Index is calculated for those REITs whose primary assets are direct property investments. Second, a Mortgage Index is reported, based on the performance of those companies whose primary assets are mortgages, mortgage-backed securities, or both. Third, a Hybrid Index is calculated for those firms that hold a mixture of direct property and mortgage investments. Detailed information regarding the return performance of specific property types (apartments, warehouses, etc.) also is available. NAREIT, which was established on December 31, 1971, covered, as of November 1996, 211 publicly traded REITs with a total market capitalization of $79.9 billion.[23] Equity REITs account for nearly 88 percent of this total market value, with mortgage and hybrid REITs splitting the remaining 12 percent fairly evenly. In the analysis presented below, we use the Equity REIT Index to measure real estate returns.[24]

It is important to realize that NAREIT return data are based on publicly traded securities. To the extent that these security prices represent factors not inherently attributable to the underlying property (such as the stock market's opinion of the REIT manager's ability), observed performance patterns may not be representative of the true risk and expected returns associated with investing in the underlying real estate.

HISTORICAL RETURNS

The NCREIF and NAREIT indexes described above provide useful information on the historical returns. Exhibit 5–4 presents the mean return of four different asset classes over three different time periods. In addition to the NCREIF Classic Property Index and the NAREIT indexes, the stock and bond data are derived from the S&P 500 Index and Lehman Brothers G/C Index respectively. The S&P 500 is a value-weighted index of 500 stocks that account for over 80 percent of the total market capitalization of all firms listed on the New York Stock Exchange (NYSE), while the Lehman Index is comprised of both corporate bonds and U.S. Treasury securities.

Exhibit 5–4 reveals that equity REITs, unlike direct property investments, have return characteristics similar to those associated with stocks. For example, the average annual return on stocks (as measured by the S&P 500) from the first quarter of 1978 through the second quarter of 1995 was 16.2 percent. The corresponding return on equity REITs was 15.7 percent. Direct property investments (as measured by the NCPI) appear to exhibit a lower average return than stocks and equity REITs.[25] In fact, the estimated

---

[23] The market capitalization of a stock is equal to the number of publicly traded shares times the current market price of the stock.

[24] Other measures of REIT return performance are available—for example, the Wilshire Real Estate Securities Index and the Lehman Brothers Equity REIT Index. For a detailed description of these two indexes and more information on the NAREIT indexes, see S. Michael Giliberto, "Real Estate Stock Indices," *Commercial Real Estate Quarterly* (August 1994), Lehman Brothers.

[25] The NCPI returns have been "unsmoothed" using the statistical technique developed by Geltner (1989) and Fisher, Geltner, and Webb (1994). This technique attempts to adjust for the appraisal-induced smoothing of value changes that are inherent in the NCPI.

EXHIBIT 5-4

AVERAGE RETURN: REAL ESTATE VERSUS OTHER ASSETS

	1990(1)–1995(2)	1985(1)–1995(2)	1978(1)–1995(2)
NCPI*	7.7%	7.3%	12.8%
NAREIT	11.6	11.6	15.7
Stocks	12.3	16.9	16.2
Bonds	9.3	10.7	10.4

*The NCPI returns have been "unsmoothed" to adjust for the appraisal-induced smoothing of value changes that is inherent in the NCPI. The technique used follows Jeffrey D. Fisher, David M. Geltner, and R. Brian Webb, "Value Indices of Commercial Real Estate: A Comparison of Index Construction Methods," *Journal of Real Estate Finance and Economics* 9 (1994), pp. 137–64.

NCREIF returns seem to match bond returns more closely than stocks. It should also be evident from Exhibit 5–4 that the returns of all four asset classes were not stable over time. The relative risk of these alternative investments is discussed in Chapter 7.

SUMMARY

In this chapter, we considered the various forms of ownership that can be used to channel investment funds into real estate. These include sole proprietorships, corporations (regular "C" and "S"), partnerships (general and limited), real estate investment trusts (REITs), and limited liability corporations. Special attention is given to the prominent roles played by limited partnerships and REITs. The choice of ownership form is largely driven by federal income tax rules and the desire of some investors to avoid personal liability for the debts and obligations of the entity. Additional investor considerations include the amount of management responsibility, the ability of the chosen ownership form to facilitate the acquisition of mortgage debt and additional equity capital, as well as the liquidity of the investment. For groups of 75 investors or fewer, limited partnerships and S corporations are the dominant form of ownership. Investor groups of more than 100 usually choose between organizing as a limited partnership or a REIT, and the use of REITs has grown dramatically during the 1990s.

More than $2.2 trillion of equity capital is invested in U.S. commercial real estate. In addition to sole proprietorships, corporations, partnerships, and REITs, pension funds, life insurance companies, and foreign investors own a sizable portion of U.S. commercial real estate. Despite their historical reluctance to invest in commercial real estate, pension funds have become an increasingly important source of equity capital. Pension funds and life insurance companies, often referred to as institutional investors, have also pushed to increase the sophistication of real estate investment decision making. The gradual shift of commercial real estate ownership from entrepreneurs to institutions, and the linking of real estate debt and equity financing with other assets in the capital markets (i.e., stocks and bonds), have heightened the need for consistently reported information on property level incomes and valuations. The creation of consistent information guidelines for the commercial real estate industry will help attract even more investment capital and accelerate the shift from private ownership to public ownership of commercial real estate.

KEY TERMS

C corporation 148
Closed-end REITs 159
Commingled real estate funds 163
Equity REITs 159
Finite-life REITs 159
General partnerships 150
Hybrid REITs 159

Infinite-life REITs 159
Joint venture 164
Limited partnership 151
Mortgage REITs 159
NAREIT index 166
NCREIF Classic Property Index 165
Open-end REITs 159

Pension funds 162
Private market 161
Public market 165
S corporation 149
Sole proprietorship 147
Syndicate 154

TEST YOURSELF

Answer the following multiple choice questions:

1. Investor groups of more than 100 that must choose an ownership form typically choose between
   a. An S corporation and limited partnership.
   b. A limited partnership and REIT.
   c. A REIT and C corporation.
   d. A REIT and general partnership.

2. Double taxation is most likely to occur if the income-producing properties are held in the form of a(n)
   a. S corporation.
   b. Limited partnership.
   c. C corporation.
   d. Real estate investment trust.
   e. Limited liability company.

3. Which of the following ownership forms is the *least* able to flow through tax losses to investors?
   a. S corporation.
   b. Real estate investment trust.
   c. Limited partnership.
   d. Limited liability corporation.

4. With regard to double taxation, distributions, and the treatment of the losses, general partnerships are *most* like
   a. S corporations.
   b. C corporations.

   c. Limited partnerships.
   d. Real estate investment trusts.

5. Special allocations of income or loss are available if the form of ownership is a(n)
   a. S corporation.
   b. Real estate investment trust.
   c. Limited partnership.
   d. C corporation.

6. Real estate syndicates traditionally have been legally organized as
   a. S corporations.
   b. C corporations.
   c. Limited partnerships.
   d. Real estate investment trusts.

7. A real estate investment trust, generally,
   a. Must have fewer than 100 shareholders.
   b. Can only invest directly in income-producing properties.
   c. Can pass tax losses through to shareholders.
   d. None of the above.

8. Which of the following forms of ownership involve both limited *and* unlimited liability?
   a. Limited partnerships.
   b. Corporation.
   c. General partnership.
   d. Sole partnership.
   e. None of the above.

9. Which statement is *false* concerning the limited partnership form of ownership?
   a. The general partner has nearly complete control and is liable for debts and actions of the partnership.
   b. The limited partners have no management control and are not liable except to the amount of their investment.
   c. The limited partners cannot enjoy tax deduction benefits but the general partners can.
   d. The partnership is not a taxable entity.
   e. None of the above.

10. Which statement is *false* concerning private real estate offerings?
   a. They typically require a larger minimum investment than public offerings.
   b. The underlying properties are usually fully specified.
   c. They usually involve general solicitation and advertising in the media.
   d. They can be exempt from full registration with the SEC and costly disclosure regulations.

PROBLEMS FOR THOUGHT AND SOLUTION

1. Is there any limitation on the amount of tax losses that investors in an S corporation can deduct?

2. In a general partnership, for what debt are each of the general partners liable?

3. What are the major restrictions that a REIT must meet on an ongoing basis in order to avoid taxation at the entity level?

4. With respect to limited partnership syndications, distinguish among fully specified funds, partially specified funds, and blind funds.

5. What caused the enormous decline in the public real estate syndication business after 1987?

6. Compare the tax advantages and disadvantages of holding income-producing property in the form of a REIT to the tax advantages and disadvantages of holding property in the form of a real estate limited partnership. Does either form of ownership dominate *from a tax perspective*? Has the relative attractiveness of these two ownership forms been affected by the Tax Reform Act of 1986? Explain why or why not.

7. Briefly describe a commingled fund. Who are the investors in these funds and why do these investors use commingled funds for their purchases?

INTERNET EXERCISE

Real estate investment trusts have become a popular vehicle for real estate investment during the 1990s. Investors can now monitor the performance of REITs, as well as non-REIT stocks and bonds, using the National Association of Real Estate Investment Trusts (NAREIT) REITWatch utility on the World Wide Web.

1. Go to the NAREIT home page:

   http://www.nareit.com/

and download the latest REIT performance report. In 500 words or less, analyze the recent performance of REITs and compare their returns to those realized on portfolios of stocks and bonds. Have REITs outperformed stocks and bonds over the last 12 months? Have equity, mortgage, or hybrid REITs exhibited the strongest recent performance?

ADDITIONAL READINGS

The following textbooks contain additional information on real estate ownership forms:

Manolakas, Thomas G., and Paul E. Anderson. *Tax Factors in Real Estate Operations*. Upper Saddle River, NJ: Prentice Hall, 1990.

Weiss, Robert M., and Robert E. Dallman. *Tax Planning for Real Estate Transactions*. Upper Saddle River, NJ: Prentice Hall, 1983.

Faggen, Ivan, et al. *Federal Taxes Affecting Real Estate*. New York: Matthew Bender, 1990.

Phillips, Lawrence C., and John L. Kramer. *Federal Income Taxation*. Upper Saddle River, NJ: Prentice Hall, 1995.

Willis, Eugene, et al. *West's Federal Taxation: Comprehensive Volume*. St. Paul, MN: West, 1995.

The following textbooks contain additional material on real estate investment trusts and limited partnerships:

Greer, Gaylon E. *Investment Analysis for Real Estate Decisions*, 3rd ed. Chicago: Dearborn Financial Publishing, 1997.

Brueggeman, William B., and Jeffrey D. Fisher. *Real Estate Finance and Investment*, 10th ed. Burr Ridge, IL: Irwin, 1997.

Ford, Deborah Ann. *Fundamentals of Real Estate Investment for Decision Makers*. St. Paul, MN: West, 1994.

6

C H A P T E R

PROPERTY TYPES

INTRODUCTION

RESIDENTIAL RENTAL PROPERTY
Some Definitions
The Demand for Rental Housing
Investment Prospects

OFFICE BUILDINGS

INDUSTRIAL PROPERTIES

SHOPPING CENTERS AND OTHER RETAIL ESTABLISHMENTS

OTHER TYPES OF REAL ESTATE
Hospitality Properties
Undeveloped Land
Senior Assisted Living and Continuing Care
    Retirement Communities

SUMMARY

KEY TERMS

TEST YOURSELF

PROBLEMS FOR THOUGHT AND SOLUTION

INTERNET EXERCISE

ADDITIONAL READINGS

After reading this chapter, students will be able to:

1. List several advantages and disadvantages of investing in apartments, office properties, industrial properties, shopping centers, hospitality properties, undeveloped land, and senior assisted living/continuing care retirement communities.

2. Describe the differences between Class A, B, and C office buildings

3. Discuss the major demographic trends likely to affect the rental housing market over the next 20 years.

4. Describe the differences between neighborhood, community, regional, super-regional, and specialty shopping centers.

INTRODUCTION

Many different types of real estate exist, including office buildings, apartments, industrial buildings, shopping centers, and undeveloped land. Properties within each category can vary greatly in quality, age, size, and other characteristics. For example, the office building category includes both high-rise structures located in central business districts and one-story doctors' offices located in rural areas. Industrial buildings can range from large production plants to mini-storage facilities. Moreover, potential returns and the degree of risk also vary significantly with property types. A well-located office building leased to high quality tenants on a long-term basis has risk and return characteristics that are very different from investments in raw land at the urban fringe. In order to make acquisition decisions that are consistent with their investment philosophies and objectives, investors must be aware of the advantages and disadvantages of the various property types.

This chapter presents an introductory discussion of the most common types of property. *Residential* rental properties include apartment buildings of various sizes, single-family homes, duplexes, triplexes, fourplexes, government-assisted housing, and housing for the elderly. The term *commercial property* encompasses all nonresidential real estate, including office buildings, shopping centers, industrial and warehouse buildings, and hospitality properties such as hotels and motels. After the discussion of residential rental properties, sections on office properties, industrial properties, shopping centers, and other types of real estate such as hospitality properties, undeveloped land, and senior assisted living and continuing care retirement communities follow.

RESIDENTIAL RENTAL PROPERTY
SOME DEFINITIONS

The majority of residential rental units are contained in multifamily structures; that is, apartment buildings that contain five or more housing units. Multifamily structures are often classified by developmental density and architectural style. **High-rise apartment buildings** are popular in more major city centers where the price of land is at a premium and the intensive use of land is a necessity. Buildings classified as high-rise have at least 10 to 15 stories. Larger structures may have a variety of recreational amenities, a continuously staffed front desk or all-night attendants, and retail establishments such as convenience stores and newsstands.[1]

Mid-rise apartments range in height from four to nine stories and are found in both cities and suburbs. Mid-rise apartment buildings in city centers may provide underground parking or no parking at all, whereas their suburban counterparts usually have parking available. Inside, a common hallway provides access to each unit on a floor. Some buildings provide a wide range of amenities, as well as on-site management and service personnel.

Garden apartments have a relatively low density of development and thus are often located in suburban and nonurban areas where land is comparatively less expensive. These complexes may consist of numerous low-rise buildings, including a separate building containing a management office and clubhouse. The demand for on-site exercise facilities has increased significantly in recent years. Large garden complexes are also likely to have spacious lawns, extensive landscaping, and numerous outdoor amenities including swimming pools and tennis courts.

Condominium complexes typically contain units with adjoining walls but with separate entrances and patios to each unit and ample parking. Units may be occupied by the owner or leased to a tenant. The condominium arrangement provides the owner-investor with individual ownership of the unit and joint ownership of the common areas, parking area, and recreational facilities. Generally, management control of the complex rests with an owners' association, which has responsibility for maintenance, taxes, insurance, water and sewage, and common-area facilities. The owner is responsible for the interior of the unit, including the interior walls. Owner-occupied condominiums have served as a bridge from rental to the ownership of single-family detached homes for many families, especially during periods of high interest rates when ownership becomes less affordable.

THE DEMAND FOR RENTAL HOUSING

Like all economic goods, prices and rates of return on various types of rental housing depend on the demand for, and the supply of, units. The demand for rental housing is influenced by changes in population, household incomes, and household tastes.

The most important influence on rental housing demand in a local area is population. However, sheer changes in population alone do not explain changes in the demand for housing. For example, housing demand is more affected by the change in the number of *households* than by the change in the number of *people*. In states with high divorce rates, such as California, divorce, which creates two households from one, is a major contributor to the demand for housing. Conversely, numerous recent articles document the growing

---

[1] In a few large metropolitan areas such as New York City, units in many high-rise apartment buildings are privately owned, although they are still typically referred to as *apartments*.

acceptance among adult children of moving back in with Mom and Dad for extended periods of time, thereby reducing the demand for housing.

In addition to household formations, the demand for rental housing is extremely sensitive to the proportion of households that own versus rent. General demographic characteristics such as age, sex, and occupation are also important determinants of rental housing demand. For example, many analysts argue that the demand for rental housing is, and will be, negatively affected by the aging of the baby boom generation. As more and more boomers cross into middle age—prime home buying years—the demand for rental housing, all else the same, has fallen. Moreover, as the boomers are replaced by the much smaller Generation X, the prime renter-age category of 18–34 years old will shrink even further—from about 70 million persons in 1990 to 63.5 million in the year 2000. These negative age-cohort effects on rental housing may be offset somewhat by increases in groups that tend to favor apartments over single-family owner-occupied housing: single persons, recent immigrants, and nontraditional families (cohabitants). In addition, senior rental housing is predicted to be one of the great growth areas over the next two decades. It is important to point out, however, that many of these demographic trends, such as the aging of the baby boomers, can be (and were) predicted with some degree of accuracy. Thus, their anticipated effects on the demand for housing are already reflected in current prices. Price adjustments due to these factors occur only when expected demographic trends are altered.

The second major factor affecting rental housing demand is income. Households tend to consume more housing as their incomes increase. Thus, future housing demand is directly linked to changes in household incomes. Forecasting income changes in a particular market requires an understanding of local business cycles, the regional and national business cycles, and employment trends. (These issues are further discussed in Chapters 9 and 11.)

The final major determinant of rental housing demand, and certainly the least quantifiable, is taste or lifestyle. Will households spend more of their discretionary income on housing or will increases in leisure pursuits and vacations consume a larger proportion of household incomes? Will the current trend toward more and larger bathrooms continue, or will renters in coming years decide that larger kitchens are a priority? Are larger, well-equipped exercise facilities in, and tennis courts out? Are upscale apartments with single-family features (an extra bedroom, garage parking) in, and condominiums out? The answers to these and many related questions will have a significant effect on rental property values over time.

INVESTMENT PROSPECTS

The demand for quality housing has continued to be strong over the past few decades. Also, the demand for rental housing is usually not severely affected by short-run downturns in the general economy, so vacancy rates in residential properties are generally lower than those for other types of rental property. For example, the National Council of Real Estate Investment Fiduciaries (NCREIF) reports that during the severe real estate recession of the late 1980s and early 1990s, the average investment-grade multifamily structure declined in value just 14 percent from the peak of the multifamily market in 1985. In contrast, industrial and office properties declined, on average, 40 percent and 54 percent, respectively. Moreover, the short-term lease contracts that normally exist between landlords (investors) and tenants in residential rental properties allow landlords to frequently adjust rents to market levels when the leases expire. This is especially important during periods of high inflation or rapidly increasing demand for rental housing. Finally, residential real estate affords small investors many opportunities to invest by taking direct equity positions in modest, local structures. Although the returns on residential rental properties tend to be somewhat less risky than other property types, this does not imply that they are generally better investments. Why? Investors typically must pay a higher price for less risky cash flows, all else the same, and this reduces their expected return.

A major drawback of investing directly in residential rental property is the heavy property management burden. Unlike commercial property, rental housing is in use 24 hours a day. This continuous use tends to increase the demand for maintenance, repairs, and other services. In addition, tenant turnover can be rapid because leases are relatively short. All of the above reasons imply large commitments of time for investors who decide to manage their own properties, or a substantial commitment of funds (usually 5 to 8 percent of effective gross income) by investors who use professional property managers.

OFFICE BUILDINGS

The office building as it is known today started with the introduction of "skyscrapers" in the late 19th century. The concentration of skyscrapers within a city became known as the central business district (CBD). During the latter part of the 20th century, we have witnessed the development of multiple business districts within cities and in the suburbs. The high price of land and increasing congestion of the CBD have fueled the growth of multi-nodal metropolitan areas. This decentralization of the urban landscape is often referred to as **urban sprawl**.

While there is no definitive standard for classifying office buildings, the real estate profession commonly refers to office buildings in the following way:

- *Class A.* These buildings usually command the highest rents because they are most prestigious in their tenancy, location, and overall desirability. They are usually newer structures located in the CBD, and are typically owned by institutional investors such as insurance companies, real estate investment trusts, and pension funds. Class A properties also have been a prime target of foreign investors in recent years.
- *Class B.* The rents in these buildings are usually less than in Class A buildings because of a less desirable location; fewer amenities; less impressive lobbies, elevators, or appearance; or a relatively inefficient layout of the leasable space.
- *Class C.* These buildings, which were usually once Class A or B, are older and reasonably well maintained but are below current standards for one or more reasons. Rents are set to match the rent-paying ability of lower-income tenants.

The two most important determinants of an office property's classification are age and obsolescence. However, older buildings can be classified as Class A structures if they accommodate the current needs of potential tenants. If the space cannot be improved and updated, the class of the building is likely to decline. For example, many office buildings—even relatively new ones—cannot be easily retrofitted to accommodate technological advances in computer networks and telecommunications.

According to the Institute of Real Estate Management (IREM), there are 12 fundamental criteria for classifying office buildings: location, ease of access, prestige, appearance, lobby, elevators, corridors, office interiors, tenant services, mechanical systems, management, and tenant mix.[2] Most of these factors are interdependent; for example, highly prestigious buildings are likely to have attractive appearances, an impressive lobby, and quality tenants. The prestige of a building is also a function of its location. For suburban buildings, access to major highways and linkages with places such as restaurants, high-income residential areas, and shopping facilities are extremely important.[3]

The demand for office space is directly related to the level of office employment, which, in turn, is related to the demand for services supplied by the occupants of office buildings. Increases in the number and size of service employers such as doctors, lawyers, accountants, real estate firms, commercial banks, mortgage banks, and environmental consulting firms translate into expanded demand for office space. The demand for the services supplied by the occupants of office space is affected by population changes; local, regional, and national economic factors; and changes in the tastes of companies and households.

The growth of the service sector of the U.S. economy during the 1970s and 1980s created a tremendous demand for office space. High-rise office buildings in downtown areas, low-rise buildings in suburban office parks, and office condominiums proliferated in many urban areas. However, similar to its effect on residential properties, the severe real estate recession of the late 1980s and early 1990s brought new office construction to a virtual standstill as office property values fell well below construction costs in most markets.

As investments, office buildings have some distinct characteristics. For example, long-term leases, when signed with quality corporate tenants, are relatively secure. Also, most office leases today are indexed for inflation and sometimes for property expenses (e.g., property taxes). Furthermore, office space is increasingly subject to "net leases" that shift much of the operating risk directly to tenants.[4] Another characteristic has been the strong demand for office space in many major urban areas, which has been fueled by a conversion of the U.S. employment base from manufacturing to service jobs.

The disadvantages of office-property investments are related to the unique characteristics of office buildings. Office-property investments may be riskier than residential rental property because of the higher degree of expertise required to manage and lease

---

[2] See *Principles of Real Estate Management* (Chicago: Institute of Real Estate Management, 1991).

[3] For a more detailed discussion of these criteria, see Chapter 10 in ibid.

[4] See Chapter 8 for more detail on typical office lease terms.

REAL ESTATE FOCUS 6-1

GM Leads Office Bargain-Hunters Downtown

The jewel of Detroit's skyline, the Renaissance Center, opened in 1976 at a cost of $357 million. It would take at least $750 million to replace it today. So what is the sprawling, five-tower office-and-hotel complex worth to a buyer? $73 million is what General Motors Corp. agreed to pay in a deal completed in October of 1996.

The nosedive in Renaissance Center's value reflects the fate of many big office complexes built in the 1970s and early '80s. Outdated but not obsolete, they are finally finding buyers after a long slump in the downtown market—albeit at fire-sale prices. The reason: Rents and construction costs in booming suburban markets now approach or even exceed downtown levels. Meanwhile, quality-of-life improvements in some cities have made them attractive again to deal-hungry investors flush with capital.

For Detroit, GM's purchase could mean that Renaissance Center will finally realize its promise and spur a genuine downtown revival. The relocation of GM's headquarters to the riverfront complex is expected to encourage other businesses to locate downtown, boost property values, and perhaps even jolt a moribund con-

struction market that has seen just three major office buildings erected downtown in the last 20 years.

GM plans eventually to be the sole occupant of Renaissance Center's office space, and as such its deal is unusual. Few companies have GM's resources, space needs, or close ties to a city, but a lot of other companies are bargain-hunting downtown. "The irony is that downtowns have to compete on price at all," says Robert Bach, national director of market analysis with the real estate firm Grub & Ellis Co. in Los Angeles. "When these buildings were built in the '70s and '80s they were the cream of the crop." But the vogue for vast office complexes has passed. Today, corporate landlords want office space without the added costs and upkeep on public plazas and retail shops. "The Renaissance Center's sense of scale is out of whack" with today's more modest needs for space, says Jeffrey Shell, a senior managing director with Cushman & Wakefield in Southfield, Michigan.

SOURCE: *The Wall Street Journal*, October 1996.

office space. Management and leasing errors by inexperienced agents often have devastating effects on the cash flows from office buildings. Because prestige is important to the success of office developments, leasing to lower-quality tenants, for example, places a building in a lower quality category in the eyes of the market. In addition, significant releasing costs (including tenant improvements and leasing commissions) are often required to make the space ready for new tenants when vacated by the current tenant. Even worse, rapidly changing technology and tenant tastes can quickly cause office buildings to become outdated—if not obsolete. (See Real Estate Focus 6–1.)

Several challenges are facing the office sector as we approach the turn of the century. First, many corporations have begun downsizing their employee staffs. This is especially evident in industries such as commercial banking and insurance. Moreover, corporations are not only cutting staff, they are taking every opportunity to reduce the amount of space used by each (retained) employee. This pervasive trend is in contrast to recent decades when employers tended to *increase* the amount of working space provided per employee. The reduction in space per employee is consistent with the much publicized increase in office telecommuting, that is, working from the home, vacation spot, or even car, via fax machines, computer modems, and cellular phones. Another trend expected to reduce the

---

E X H I B I T   6 - 1

CHANGING OFFICE SUPPLY AND DEMAND FACTORS

- **Factors Affecting Supply and Demand in the Year 2000**

  New technologies—the virtual office, E-mail, telecommuting
  Cost-containment—reengineering of corporate America, outsourcing
  Office sharing—hoteling and work-at-home patterns
  Changing management practices—decentralized decision making, resource flexibility
  Demographic forces—two-worker families, aging of baby boomers, labor-force mobility
  Employee satisfaction—health consciousness, child care, colleague interaction
  Exterior office environment—security, access, amenities
  Interior office environment—air quality, comfort, security
  Globalization—multinational companies, overseas influences

- **Corporate/Entrepreneurial Responses to Changes in Demand**

  Changing norms for space per employee by tenant type and activity
  Office of the future—accommodating new technologies
  Energy efficiency and ergonomics—how do office space users apply these principles?
  The production function of the service firm—land, labor, and capital (office space costs relative to other costs of doing business and relative to historic occupancy costs)

- **Impact on Future Office Investment Performance**

  Net effects on office demand (absorption, rents)
  Regional variations (sunbelt versus north, older versus newer cities)
  Supply response (renovation of older offices, advantages of new construction)
  Effect on investor demand (pricing, capital flows)
  Implications for asset management
  Implications for investment and exit strategies

SOURCE: *Investment Strategy Annual* (Chicago: LaSalle Advisors, 1996).

demand for space per employee is **hoteling**—having salespersons, the auditing staff of accounting firms, and other office personnel who are frequently out of the office share the use of unreserved space when they need to be in the office.

Second, the explosive employment growth of the late 1970s and early 1980s fueled by baby boomers and women entering the workforce is subsiding, providing for considerably less absorption of office space. In the downtown office sector, the best-performing markets will feature 24-hour environments with strong residential, retail, and cultural districts close to the CBD. Big losers may be eight-hour business districts in cities beset by poverty, crime, the lack of significant residential communities, and poor mass transportation. The challenge for the developers of new office space is to install systems that can handle future technological changes and reduce retrofitting costs.[5] A summary of changing office supply and demand factors, and the likely responses to those factors, is presented in Exhibit 6–1.

---

[5] Many of these office market trends are discussed in *Emerging Trends in Real Estate* (Chicago: Equitable Real Estate Investment Management, Inc., and Real Estate Research Corporation, October 1995 and October 1996).

R E A L E S T A T E F O C U S 6 - 2

Trends in Industrial Warehouse Design

Investors are concentrating on "higher cube" boxes, with clear space of up to 30 feet, and on "flat-flat" floors that can accommodate picking systems, which enable access to higher storage stacks. Warehouses have evolved from storage facilities into logistically advanced distribution-processing centers with goods "through put" rather than inventoried. Frequently, shipments are trucked in from the factory, delivered to one loading dock, where they're bar coded and moved inside, and then are divided and quickly reloaded onto trucks waiting at the other end of the building.

Major shippers place an increasing premium on accurately timed deliveries and pickups along the hub-and-spoke points in their distribution networks. Bigger-cube warehouses are more efficient, allowing more cargo to be packed into the facility and providing space for larger truck-turning radiuses. They should have fiber optic cabling and sufficient power sources to run inventory tracking systems, as well as high-pressure early-detection sprinkler systems. But the logistics process will become increasingly high-tech, and adaptation to ever greater demands for speed and reliability will be an ongoing process.

SOURCE: *Emerging Trends in Real Estate* (Chicago: Equitable Real Estate Investment Management, Inc., and Real Estate Research Corporation, 1997).

INDUSTRIAL PROPERTIES

Industrial properties range from large plants and factories to small warehouses. Plants and factories are special use properties and are not easily converted to other uses. Thus, they are relatively risky and are usually avoided by investors, except those who specialize in the specific production processes employed at the plant (i.e., the companies that use the facilities).

The most popular type of industrial property investment, especially for institutional real estate investors, is the **warehouse**, which provides space for the temporary storage of goods. Business operators frequently choose to lease, rather than own, their required storage space. Leasing is a frequent choice because of income tax considerations and because leasing frees up capital to invest in other aspects of the business. Many industrial tenants prefer to lease space on a long-term basis with net leases (where most or all of the operating expenses are paid by the tenants). Thus, warehouses provide investors with relatively low-risk, long-term investments that often fit the investment objectives of conservative investors, such as pension funds.

Warehouses are relatively simple to construct, have a long economic life, and require little management effort compared to other income-producing properties. Generally, warehouse buildings—with their open space for storage—are the most resilient of the major property types to functional obsolescence. However, the growing length and width of trucks require distribution warehouses that can accommodate them. This need has rendered many warehouses partially, if not completely, obsolete. Real Estate Focus 6–2 discusses additional trends in the design of warehouse properties.

The demand for industrial space is derived from consumer demand for products by the industrial sector. For example, increases in consumer demand for bottled beverages increases the demand by bottlers for storage space. Increases in the number and size of industrial firms such as computer chip manufacturers, beer producers, grocery stores, and furniture makers translate into expanded demand for warehouse space. As in other sectors of the economy, the demand for the services supplied by the users of warehouse space are affected by population changes; local, regional, and national economic factors; and changes in the tastes of companies and households.

Recently, special-use properties, such as miniwarehouses and research and development buildings, have become popular with noninstitutional investors. Miniwarehouses are located close to businesses and apartment units that have little space available for storage. In many areas, occupancy rates in miniwarehouses have been extremely high. Research and development buildings can be extremely risky because a property specially designed for the needs of one tenant may not be suitable for the next tenant; thus, substantial costs may be involved in readying the property for re-leasing.

In recent years, much of the development of light industrial and research and development use has occurred in **industrial parks**. These sites resemble residential subdivisions and offer a controlled environment with buildings designed to accommodate a wide variety of tenant needs. Limited partnerships, discussed in Chapter 5, develop and manage many of these facilities.

SHOPPING CENTERS AND OTHER RETAIL ESTABLISHMENTS

Retail establishments are found in a variety of forms. The simplest is a freestanding retail outlet (e.g., a fast-food outlet). Many retail establishments today, however, are found in shopping centers. Shopping centers, more than freestanding establishments, are popular with individual investors and institutions that invest in income-producing properties.

Before discussing the advantages and disadvantages of shopping-center investments, consider the various types of shopping centers:

1. **Neighborhood or "strip" center.** This type of center is located for the convenience of a close-by resident population. It contains retail establishments offering mostly convenience goods (e.g., groceries and drugs) and services (e.g., barber shop and dry cleaning). These centers are usually "anchored" by a large chain grocery store or drugstore. The gross leasable area of the anchor(s) and nonanchored tenant space is approximately 50,000 square feet, but it may be as large as 150,000 square feet. The trade area of a shopping center is the geographic area from which it draws its customers. A strip center's trade area is typically within a 5- to 10-minute drive of the center. Such a center can usually succeed in a trade area with a population of 1,000 to 2,500 if it is well located.

2. **Community center.** This is a larger version of a neighborhood center. This type of center is often anchored by a discount department store and may include outlets such as clothing stores, banks, furniture stores, video rental stores, fast food operations, and professional offices (e.g., dentists). The gross leasable area (GLA) is usually three times that of a neighborhood center. A community center's trade area is usually within a 10- to 15-minute drive of the center. Most of these centers are early generation malls.

3. **Regional and super-regional centers.** Regional centers usually have at least two anchor tenants that are major department stores (e.g., Sears) and at least 200,000 square feet of gross leasable area devoted to nonanchor tenants. Major tenants are national chains or well-established local businesses that have high credit ratings and significant net worth. These retailers draw people from a much larger area than the neighborhood or community centers. Minor tenants are located between the anchor tenants to capture customers. Often regional centers contain several stores of one type (for example, three to five shoe stores). Many include small fast-food outlets arranged in food courts. Regional centers usually serve a population of 150,000 to 300,000. In recent years, through expansion of regional centers and through new development, super-regional centers have emerged. These centers may have as many as five or six major tenants and hundreds of minor tenants in over a million square feet of space.

4. **Specialty shopping centers.** These centers are characterized by a dominant theme or image. Many in downtown areas are located in a rehabilitated historic structure and area. Two variations of specialty shopping centers have increased in importance in recent years. **Outlet centers** sell name-brand goods at lower prices by eliminating the wholesale distributer. Retailers at **off-price centers** are able to offer large discounts on name-brand merchandise that consists of factory overruns, seconds and discontinued items, and overstocks from other stores.

The increased development of **power centers** is an important retail trend. Power centers have gross leasable areas ranging from 250,000 to 750,000 square feet. The dominating feature of a power center is the high ratio of anchors to ancillary tenants. Typically, power centers contain three or more giants in hard goods retailing (toys, electronics, home furnishings, etc.). Home Depot and Wal-Mart are two prominent retailers that frequently locate their stores in power centers. The characteristics of the various shopping center types are summarized in Exhibit 6–2.

The retail tenant's primary concerns are the availability of adequate space for its business, the volume of consumer traffic generated by the center, and the visibility of the tenant's location within the center. Additional challenges are presented by the special requirements of some tenants. For example, furniture and appliance stores require loading

E X H I B I T   6 - 2

CHARACTERISTICS OF SHOPPING CENTERS

Type	Leading Tenant (basis for classification)	Typical Gross Leasable Area (GLA) (square feet)	General GLA Range (square feet)	Usual Minimum Site Area (acres)	Minimum Patron Support Required
Neighborhood	Supermarket or drugstore	50,000	30,000–150,000	3	1,000–2,500 people
Community	Variety, discount, or junior department store	150,000	100,000–300,000	10 or more	40,000–150,000 people
Regional	One or more full-line (sometimes freestanding) department stores of at least 100,000 square feet GLA	400,000	300,000–750,000	30–50 or more	150,000 or more people
Super-regional	Three or more full-line (sometimes freestanding) department stores of at least 100,000 square feet GLA	1 million	1 million– 2 million	85 or more	1 million or more people in primary-tertiary trade area

SOURCE: Urban Land Institute, *Shopping Center Development Handbook,* 2nd ed. (Washington, DC: ULI, 1985).

docks, food service providers have garbage disposal problems, and supermarkets need an abundance of close-by short-term parking.[6]

Shopping-center investment is probably the most complex of income property investments. The market for shopping centers is dynamic. On the demand side, the growth of an urban area and national economic events can quickly alter market characteristics (e.g., family income and population density). On the supply side, competition for market areas is intense. Smaller centers are generally riskier than larger ones because they are more susceptible to competition from new strip centers and retail areas. One implication of these changing conditions is that the owners and managers of the center must be constantly aware of whether the tenant mix of the center is properly serving the market. Shopping center developers and investors base their decisions on a demographic profile of the area that quantifies the number of people who are likely customers, the discretionary incomes of these customers, and their retail expenditures. Developers of new centers are aware that they must attract customers away from other shopping centers.

The ownership arrangements and lease contracts between owners or managers and tenants are generally quite complicated. For example, hours of operation, types of goods sold, common promotions, freight handling, and share of common areas maintenance (CAM) expenditures must be negotiated. Nonanchor tenants often make flat or indexed rental payments plus an additional payment based on some percentage of their gross sales. As the sales volume of the tenant increases through inflation and growth in retail demand in the area, the investor's cash flows should increase accordingly. These arrangements are termed **percentage leases,** and they allow the owner(s) to share in the tenant's ability to

---

[6] For more detail on the requirements of retail tenants, see Chapter 10 in *Principles of Real Estate Management* (Chicago: Institute of Real Estate Management, 1991).

REAL ESTATE FOCUS 6-3

Malls Add Fun and Games to Attract Shoppers

Shoppers who wander onto the fourth floor of the new Circle Center mall in Indianapolis are unwittingly taking part in an experiment that could reshape the American mall. There's nowhere up there to shop. Teenagers wearing space-age wrap-around goggles lob "virtual" grenades at one another. A young girl gapes as her father is hoisted horizontally in a sling, pokes his head into goggles, then clumsily smashes his virtual hang glider off the walls of a canyon (also virtual). An airline steward disappears into "Virtual World" for a death-race through mining tunnels on Mars.

After spending a few dollars on these flashy games, the mall visitor can head for a nine-screen cinema or one of seven theme restaurants and bars. Together, they are the prototype for Simon Property Group Inc.'s push into mall entertainment.

"People don't have to go to Orlando to be entertained," proclaims David Simon, president and chief executive of the Indianapolis-based mall-development company. "Companies are figuring out ways to make it portable. And what better place to locate than in a mall?"

There is little doubt that malls need to distinguish themselves in the crowded retail landscape. At the average mall, consumers are making shorter visits and visiting fewer stores than in the past; spending levels have plateaued. Experts attribute this to increasing competition from discounters, as well as a decline in leisure time in two-income families.

But some large mall owners remain dubious about the whole entertainment-center idea. Houston-based Hines Interest, which has installed ice-skating rinks at two of its malls, remains wary. "We continue to look at these high-tech entertainment formats, and we continue to be concerned when we go somewhere and see that the customers are overwhelmingly male teenagers," explains Don McCrory, who runs Hines's retail division.

SOURCE: *The Wall Street Journal*, January 23, 1996.

---

generate sales volume. Tenants also typically share in paying the center's operating expenses. Lease clauses providing for adequate rent and operating-expense sharing are a source of risk to investors.[7]

Several important issues and trends may have a significant effect on the viability of some shopping center investments. First, the United States is overstored. Since 1972 the amount of retail space per capita has almost tripled to 20 square feet. Second, homogeneous mass-marketing approaches are becoming increasingly ineffective. Racially, culturally, and economically, the United States is diversifying as minority populations grow and the middle class shrinks. Successful chain stores must modify their product mix across stores to fit submarket demographic profiles. Third, the eroding purchasing power and increased consumer debt burden of the typical household may have far-reaching effects on shopping center returns. Another uncertainty is the impact of electronic shopping (through the Internet or cable TV) on retail establishments. Trips to malls are down as time-pressed consumers are shopping closer to home. Also, as suburban crime becomes a more pressing issue, the safety and security of a shopping center will increase in importance.[8]

---

[7] Retail leases are discussed in detail in Chapter 8.

[8] These important issues and trends are discussed in *Emerging Trends in Real Estate* (Chicago: Equitable Real Estate Investment Management, Inc., and Real Estate Research Corporation, October 1995 and October 1996).

OTHER TYPES OF REAL ESTATE

Although residential, office, industrial, and retail are the most common uses of real property, there are numerous other uses for space such as hospitality properties, continuing care (nursing home) facilities, and even undeveloped land.

HOSPITALITY PROPERTIES

Hotels are establishments that provide transient lodging for the public as well as meals and entertainment. Motels are establishments located on or near a highway that are designed to serve the motor traveler. Hotels and motels serve several distinct markets including the traveler (transient market) and the visitor or conventioneer (destination market). Convention hotels cater to meetings of businesses and other organizations and are often located in the downtown areas of major cities. Resort hotels are located near entertainment and vacation-related activities.

The markets for hospitality properties are highly susceptible to changes in general economic conditions and, because there are no leases in hospitality properties, these types of investments may be riskier than other income-property investments, although with high risk comes the opportunity for high returns. Also, because these properties are not subject to long-term leases, they are more flexible and less vulnerable to unexpected increases in inflation. Hospitality space is usually valued on a per-room basis. For example, major hotels sell for $80,000 to $90,000 per rentable room.

The success of a hospitality investment is largely driven by its location and how well the services offered by the hotel match the needs in a particular market. Income projections are complicated because many of the income and expense items fluctuate widely with changes in seasonal demands. Therefore seasonally adjusted averages should be used as inputs into the discounted cash flow valuation model for hospitality properties.

The success of hospitality property investments is highly dependent on management. A hotel is a service business. Thus, managers should be versed in all aspects of this type of business, not just in collecting room rents and providing maintenance. Because cash flows are dependent on the management of the hospitality business, the ownership of hospitality properties by passive third-party investors is much less common than with the other major property types. As a result, properties often are owned by one of the national corporate chains. Properties that are owned by third-party investors are typically run by management chains. When the chain works under contract for a percentage fee, the cost of management is treated as a normal operating expense by the owner. In an alternative arrangement, institutional (third-party) investors may lease the property to specialized operators. In this case, the investors have an ownership interest in a property that produces lease payments that are net of all operating expenses.

UNDEVELOPED LAND

Undeveloped, or "raw," land is one of the riskier real estate investment opportunities. Investors in raw land are speculating that urban growth will produce increasing demands

REAL ESTATE FOCUS 6 - 4

Property Profile: The Legendary Waldorf-Astoria

The Waldorf-Astoria Hotel opened on New York City's Park Avenue during the Great Depression in 1931. At that time, it was the largest hotel in the world, with 1,852 rooms. From the onset, the Waldorf established itself as an elitist hotel. Until the early 1980s, the Waldorf's management refused to advertise, relying solely on its clientele's references as a means of attracting new customers.

In the more difficult and competitive times of the present, the Waldorf has managed to maintain its aura of elegance and distinction. Even in its attempt to serve the convention business, management insists that the Waldorf is not a "convention" hotel. It continues to provide customers with extravagant services. For example, if a guest informs the hotel's management that relatives are arriving that day for their first visit to New York, the hotel dispatches its limousine to pick up the relatives and sends them a dozen roses and a box of candy. Management considers these services as vital to overturn the notion that "when you turn off the lights and the bed is comfortable, all hotels are the same."

The Waldorf remains the standard setter and innovator of the upper end of the hotel industry, just as it has since 1931. The Waldorf-Astoria is much more than simply another improvement on land—it is a truly unique *business*.

SOURCE: *U.S. News and World Report,* February 13, 1984.

for conversion of undeveloped land to apartments, shopping centers, and other uses. The returns investors receive from investments in undeveloped land depend entirely on land value increases because undeveloped land does not generate income—unless minerals are extracted or the land is put to some agricultural use. Sufficient increases in value may come soon, they may come years from now, or they may never come. Forecasting urban growth, much less its timing and direction, is a very inexact science. Moreover, the increasing public scrutiny being given to all types of real estate development has dramatically increased the legal, political, and environmental risks associated with land development. At a minimum, the land investor must be environmentally sensitive and well informed about locations that may have restrictions on their future development. Examples include officially designated wetlands, areas with endangered species, upland habitats, and areas with underground toxic waste. Environmental issues are discussed in more detail in Chapter 10.

There also are unavoidable carrying costs in land investment. These costs include property taxes, interest payments if the properties are partially debt financed, and the opportunity cost of the invested equity. In addition, the income tax features of these investments are not favorable. Land cannot be depreciated for tax purposes, and there are limitations on interest deductibility. Lack of liquidity is also a feature of raw land. However, because of the relatively high risks, higher returns should be expected on raw land investments.

The success of undeveloped land investments depends on good location in relation to the pattern of growth and the following other considerations:

1. Access to major highways.
2. Proximity to political jurisdictions that provide public services, such as police and fire protection.
3. Proximity to utility service districts for the provision of water, sewer, gas, electricity, and telephone services.
4. Favorable topography (i.e., lack of slopes) and soil.
5. Favorable political climate for rezoning requests.

Raw, or undeveloped, land is not the same as developable land. Before construction of the improvements to the land can begin, a great deal of infrastructure must be in place. For example, the land must be cleared and graded and streets, sidewalks, and utilities must be put in place. Increasingly, some of the land must also be set aside for greenways and community areas.

SENIOR ASSISTED LIVING AND CONTINUING CARE RETIREMENT COMMUNITIES

More than one out of every five Americans will be 65 or older by 2030. Thus, a major growth sector in urban land use over the next two decades will be senior housing and continuing care (nursing home) facilities. Elderly parents are increasingly unlikely to live at the homes of their adult children. Relatively healthy seniors not yet in need of nursing home facilities are seeking alternatives. Many analysts project that these seniors will increasingly demand housing with apartment-style units in a community setting with food services, planned activities, and attached medical-nursing home facilities. As with hospitality properties, the success of senior assisted living projects is highly dependent on management because of the large number of services provided on-site. As a result, the ownership of these properties by small, owner-operators or by passive third-party investors is likely to be much less common than with the other major property types.

SUMMARY

A major question of concern to real estate investors is what alternative investment opportunities are available in real estate. We have examined this issue from two perspectives. In this chapter, we considered the various types of real properties that can serve as investments, including residential income properties, office buildings, industrial buildings, shopping centers, and hospitality properties. In Chapter 5 we considered the various forms of ownership that can be used to channel investment funds into real estate. The choice of investment mode—the combination of property type and ownership form selected by the individual investor, business, or institution—is a complex decision that has a pronounced effect on the expected return and risk of the investor's asset portfolio. Thus, it is important that property type and ownership form selections be consistent with the investment strategy and objectives of the investor.

KEY TERMS

Community center 182
Condominium
  complexes 174
Garden apartments 174
High-rise apartment
  buildings 173
Hoteling 179

Industrial parks 181
Mid-rise apartments 174
Neighborhood or "strip" center 181
Off-price centers 182
Outlet centers 182
Percentage leases 183

Power centers 182
Regional and super-regional
  centers 182
Specialty shopping centers 182
Urban sprawl 176
Warehouse 180

TEST YOURSELF

Answer the following multiple choice questions:

1. Which of the following is probably the most complex investment?
   a. Regional shopping center.
   b. Industrial warehouse.
   c. Single-tenant office building.
   d. Garden-style apartment complexes.

2. Which of the following statements about neighborhood (strip) centers is *not* true?
   a. They are usually anchored by a large chain grocery store or drugstore.
   b. The gross leasable area is usually about 50,000 square feet.
   c. They are usually anchored by at least two major department stores.
   d. Their trade area is typically within a 5- to 10-minute drive of the center.

3. Which of the following is the dominating feature of a power center?
   a. It is usually anchored by at least two major department stores.
   b. It sells name-brand goods at lower prices by eliminating the wholesale distributor.
   c. It is usually anchored by a large chain grocery store or drugstore.
   d. It has a high ratio of anchor tenants to smaller (auxiliary) tenants.

4. Garden-style apartments
   a. Are typically found in downtown areas.
   b. Have a relatively low density of development.

   c. Usually include retail establishments such as convenience stores and newsstands.
   d. Often have underground parking.

5. Which of the following property types is likely to have the heaviest property management burden?
   a. Apartment complex.
   b. Industrial warehouse.
   c. Single-tenant office building.
   d. Retail power center.

6. Which of the following is *not* a typical advantage of office building investments?
   a. Long-term leases reduce the cost of frequently re-leasing space.
   b. Most leases are indexed for inflation.
   c. Most leases tie the total rent payments to the sales of the tenant's business.
   d. All of the above are advantages of office building investments.

7. Rental housing demand is most influenced by
   a. Changes in population.
   b. Changes in the number of households.
   c. The cost of condominium ownership.
   d. The local business cycle.

8. What trend is the most responsible for making many existing office buildings obsolete?
   a. The growth of the U.S. service sector over the last several decades.
   b. Technological advances in computer networks and telecommunications

c. The increasing use of net leases.

d. The acceleration of urban sprawl.

9. Which property type is generally most resilient to functional obsolescence?

   a. Apartment complex.

   b. Industrial warehouse.

   c. Single-tenant office building.

   d. Retail power center.

e. Neighborhood shopping center.

10. Which property type is probably least affected by unexpected increases in inflation?

    a. Apartment complex.

    b. Industrial warehouse.

    c. Single-tenant office building.

    d. Hotels.

    e. Neighborhood shopping center.

PROBLEMS FOR THOUGHT AND SOLUTION

1. Many analysts argue that the demand for rental housing is, and will be, negatively affected by the aging of the baby boom population. Why? Are there any demographic or sociological trends that may offset, completely or partially, the negative baby boom effect?

2. Some property types, such as industrial warehouses, are perceived to be less risky investments than alternative property types. Does this mean that warehouses are superior investments? Explain why or why not.

3. Compare neighborhood, community, and regional shopping centers on the basis of (1) leading tenant, (2) typical size, and (3) minimum required patron support.

4. Discuss some of the important issues and trends that investors in regional malls should consider in their acquisition and disposition decisions.

INTERNET EXERCISE

Real estate investment trusts often specialize in a particular type of property such as health care facilities or office buildings. The National Association of Real Estate Investment Trusts (NAREIT) REITWatch utility can be used to monitor the performance of each REIT sector, and thus, insight can be gained into the underlying strength of each market segment.

1. Go to the NAREIT home page:

   http://www.nareit.com/

and download the latest REIT segmented performance report. Briefly assess the performance of each REIT property type sector. Which property types had the highest returns? Which had the lowest? Finally, compare the segmented returns to those realized on the S&P 500. Which sectors realized similar returns over the most recent reporting period?

ADDITIONAL READINGS

Detailed information on the various property types is contained in

Principles of Real Estate Management. Chicago: Institute of Real Estate Management, 1991.

Pyhrr, Stephen; James R. Cooper; Larry E. Wofford; Steven D. Kapplin; and Paul D. Lapides. *Real Es-*

tate Investment: Strategy, Analysis, and Decisions, chapters 21–27. New York: John Wiley & Sons, 1989.

John McMahan. *Property Development*, chapters 7–11. New York: McGraw-Hill Publishing Company, 1989.

C H A P T E R

RISK AND REAL ESTATE INVESTMENT

INTRODUCTION

THE CONCEPT OF VARIABILITY

SPECIFICATION OF RISK PREFERENCES

MEASURING PROJECT-SPECIFIC RISK
Variance and Standard Deviation
Coefficient of Variation
The Use of Subjective Probabilities

RISK MANAGEMENT
Avoiding Risky Projects
Insurance and Hedging
Diversification as a Risk-Management Tool

THE PORTFOLIO CONCEPT OF RISK
Diversifiable Portfolio Risk
Covariance and Correlation
Examples of Diversifiable Risk
Basic Real Estate Diversification Strategies
Nondiversifiable Risk

CHOOSING AN OPTIMAL PORTFOLIO
Why Are So Many Investors Not Well-Diversified?

HOW RISKY IS REAL ESTATE?
Historical Returns, Risk, and Correlations

ACCOUNTING FOR RISK IN VALUATION DECISIONS
Risk-Adjusted Discount Rate
Quantifying Required Risk Premiums with Asset Pricing Models
Sensitivity Analysis

SUMMARY

KEY TERMS

TEST YOURSELF

PROBLEMS FOR THOUGHT AND SOLUTION

CASE PROBLEMS

ADDITIONAL READINGS

After reading this chapter, students will be able to:

1. Calculate and interpret basic measures of risk for both individual assets and portfolios of assets.

2. Identify the problems with, and limitations of, traditional sources of real estate risk and return data, and use this information to address the question "How risky is real estate?"

3. Incorporate information regarding project riskiness into the investment decision-making process.

4. Describe sensitivity analysis.

INTRODUCTION

The goal of most investors is to maximize their wealth by making intelligent investment decisions. Investors contribute assets to business ventures from which they expect to receive returns *on* their investment in addition to the eventual return *of* the investment. By committing the use of their assets to a particular acquisition, investors take the chance of losing some or all of their assets, or losing the opportunity to invest in other ventures with more favorable outcomes. In order to attract investor funds, investment projects must offer some anticipated compensation in proportion to the amount of risk investors will be undertaking; the greater the risk, the greater must be the potential compensation. Therefore, it becomes extremely important to quantify and measure risk when valuing an investment project.

How risky is real estate investment? Although real estate investors in the United States and other countries have accumulated a great deal of wealth over the years, the severe real estate recession of the late 1980s and early 1990s provides recent evidence that real estate investments may entail substantial risks. The National Council of Real Estate Investment Fiduciaries (NCREIF) reports that the values of large, high quality office buildings fell 53 percent, on average, from 1985 to 1994. The average decline for smaller, less desirable office properties was even larger. Industrial warehouses experienced a 40 percent value decline over the same time period. Apartment investors, on average, suffered the smallest capital losses during the real estate recession—apartment values declined 14 percent from 1988 to 1994. Note that these declines are measured in nominal terms and *real* declines in values (adjusted for inflation) were even larger.

The severity of the real estate recession produced a flood of foreclosures and bankruptcies, and contributed significantly to the failure of numerous financial institutions and to the weakening of the many life insurance companies that were active real estate lenders. Although surveys in the mid-1990s revealed that investors expected real estate acquisitions to provide "solid" returns through the remainder of the 1990s, only a few of these same investors foresaw the length and severity of the recent real estate recession. Thus, it is clear that considerable risk is associated with real estate investments.

This chapter discusses the sources and measurement of real estate risk, as well as how to account for risk in the valuation of real estate. In addition to the riskiness of individual properties, risk is also viewed from a portfolio context. With the proper consideration and incorporation of risk, the decision on the investment of funds in a particular real estate venture reduces to a single question: Do the expected returns from this investment compensate the investor for the risks taken, given the investor's overall investment strategy and preference for risk?

THE CONCEPT OF VARIABILITY

Investment risk can be defined as the possibility that future cash flows—and therefore returns and values—will be different from what was expected when the investment was undertaken. Because *risk* refers to the probability of earning a return greater or less than the expected return, **probability distributions** provide the foundation for risk measurement. A probability distribution defines the likelihood of certain events occurring. Probability distributions may be determined after long and rigorous tests, or they may be based on quite logical theorems; for example, the probability of a fair coin coming up heads is one-half. In contrast, **subjective probability distributions** represent an opinion or guess as to the likelihood of particular events occurring. For example, economists may state that there is a 50 percent chance that the national economy will experience average growth over the next five years, a 20 percent chance that there will be either a mild boom or a mild recession, and a 5 percent chance that the economy will experience either a strong boom or a deep recession. These possible states of the economy and their associated probabilities are shown in Exhibit 7–1. Notice that the sum of the probabilities in a distribution must be 100 percent.

Assume three investment alternatives are being considered:

EXHIBIT 7-1

RETURN ESTIMATES ON THREE ALTERNATIVE INVESTMENTS

		Rate of Return if State of Economy Occurs		
State of the Economy	Probability	T-Bonds	Office Building	Shopping Center
Deep recession	0.05	7.0%	3.0%	5.0%
Mild recession	0.20	7.0	5.5	8.5
Average economy	0.50	7.0	7.0	11.0
Mild boom	0.20	7.0	8.5	13.5
Strong boom	0.05	7.0	11.0	17.0
Expected return $E(R)$		7.0%	7.0%	11.0%

1. A U.S. Treasury zero-coupon bond with a remaining maturity of five years that offers a 7 percent annual rate of return if held for the entire five years.[1]
2. A small office building that is expected to yield a 7 percent annual return if purchased today and sold at the end of five years.
3. A neighborhood shopping center that is expected to produce an 11 percent annual return if held for five years.

The rate of return on the zero-coupon Treasury bond is known with certainty—it will yield 7 percent per year regardless of the state of the economy. Thus, the zero-coupon bond has no risk.[2] However, the actual, or realized rates of return on the two income property investments will not be known until the end of the five-year holding period. Because their rate-of-return outcomes are not known with certainty, these investment alternatives are defined as risky.

Probability distributions may be either *discrete* or *continuous*. A discrete probability distribution has a finite number of outcomes; thus, Exhibit 7–1 contains a discrete probability distribution with five possible outcomes. Each outcome, or state of the economy, has a corresponding probability. For example, the probability of the Treasury bond providing a 7 percent return is 1.00, and the probability of the office investment producing an 11 percent return is 0.05.

By multiplying each possible outcome by its probability of occurrence, and then summing these products, we can determine a weighted average of outcomes. The weights are the probabilities, and the weighted average is defined as the **expected value**. The outcomes in the example are annual rates of return. The expected rate of return, $E(R)$, is expressed in equation form as follows:

$$\text{Expected rate of return} = E(R) = \sum_{i=1}^{n} o_i \, p_i \qquad (7\text{–}1)$$

Here o_i is the ith possible outcome (state of the economy), p_i is the probability that the ith outcome will occur, and n is the number of possible outcomes. Using Equation 7–1, the expected rate of return on the office building investment is equal to

$$
\begin{aligned}
E(R) &= o_1(p_1) + o_2(p_2) + o_3(p_3) + o_4(p_4) + o_5(p_5) \\
&= 3.0\%(0.05) + 5.5\%(0.20) + 7.0\%(0.50) + 8.5\%(0.20) + 11.0\%(0.05) \\
&= 7.0\%
\end{aligned}
$$

---

[1] A zero-coupon bond does not pay periodic interest (or principal) to the investor. Instead, "zeros" provide a single cash flow to investors on the maturity date of the bond, and that cash flow is the redemption price (face value) of the bond. Without periodic payments, the zero-coupon bond must provide all its return in the form of price appreciation; that is, a redemption price at the maturity of the bond that is higher than the initial purchase price.

[2] Treasury bonds that do pay periodic interest are subject to reinvestment risk, which is the risk that interest rates will fall and the periodic payments will have to be reinvested at lower rates. For zero-coupon bonds, no portion of the total return is dependent upon the interest rate at which interim cash flows are reinvested. Thus, a zero-coupon bond has zero reinvestment risk if held to maturity. Note that the zero-coupon Treasury bond return is riskless in the sense that a *nominal* return of 7 percent is assured. However, the *real* return on a zero-coupon bond is risky because it will depend on the rate of general inflation over the investment holding period.

EXHIBIT 7 - 2

PROBABILITY DISTRIBUTIONS

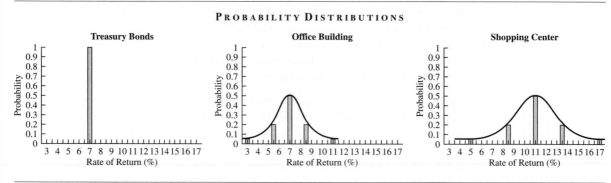

The expected rate of return on the neighborhood shopping center is 11 percent and is calculated similarly.[3]

Future economic conditions may actually be better, in between, or more severe than the five discrete probabilities indicate. Therefore, consideration of an unlimited number of possible outcomes is often a more complete approach. This situation is represented by a continuous probability distribution. Both discrete and continuous probability distributions can be expressed graphically. The bar graphs in Exhibit 7–2 represent the discrete probability distributions of Exhibit 7–1. The range of possible discrete returns for the office building investment is from 3 to 11 percent. Note that the height of each bar represents the probability of occurrence, and the assumed distribution of rates of return for the office investment is *symmetric* around the 7 percent expected return (i.e., equal on both sides of the expected value). The range of possible returns for the shopping center is from 5 to 17 percent. The graph for the Treasury bond investment shows the returns represented by a single spike; that is, there is no chance that the actual return will be different from 7 percent.

Continuous distributions depicting the three investments that are consistent with the discrete distribution also are contained in Exhibit 7–2. The continuous probability distribution for the Treasury bond investment lies on top of the discrete distribution. For the office building and shopping center, the area under the probability curve represents the probability of occurrence. Therefore, the probability that investors will earn less than a 5 percent return on the shopping center investment is quite low, as the area under the curve to the left of 5 percent is quite small. Conversely, the probability that the realized return will be between 5 and 17 percent is considerably greater.

At this point, the problem is to decide which of these investments, if any, investors should choose. The relative attractiveness of the alternatives ultimately depends on investor attitudes toward risk.

---

[3] The expected value or mean is not the only statistic available for describing the central value of a probability distribution or the central value of an actual sample from a distribution. The median is the outcome that lies exactly in the middle of the possible or realized outcomes. That is, it is the outcome that exceeds half of the outcomes and is exceeded by the other half. The mode is the outcome with the highest probability of occurrence.

EXHIBIT 7-3

ATTITUDES TOWARD RISK

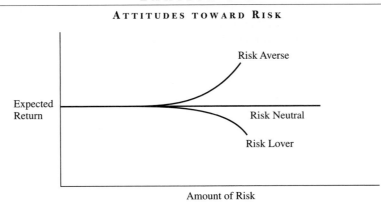

SPECIFICATION OF RISK PREFERENCES

Consider first the comparison between the Treasury bond and the office building, both of which are *expected* to produce a 7 percent annual return over the projected five-year holding period. Assume a full or partial interest in either investment can be purchased for $30,000. Which do you prefer?[4]

A critical element of each investor's investment strategy is a determination of the investor's preferences for risk. Risk preferences cannot be ignored in the development of investment philosophy, objectives, and policies. As Exhibit 7–3 shows, three general states of the relation between risk and return exist. *Risk-loving* investors are willing to accept lower returns for taking on greater risks. This response to risk is quite uncommon. The *risk-neutral* investor requires the same return regardless of the risk incurred. Again, most investors do not behave in this manner. *Risk-averse* investors must be rewarded—in the form of a higher expected return—for assuming more risk. Thus, to attract risk-averse investors, expected returns must increase as the level of investment risk increases.

Virtually all investors are risk averse and would therefore choose the T-bond over the office building. Why? Because although both investments are *expected* to produce a 7 percent return, the actual (or realized) return on the office building could vary greatly from 7 percent. Most investors would avoid the office building and its more volatile (less predictable) cash flows and returns if a riskless Treasury bond investment offering the same return with no risk were available. In fact, in order to sell the office building, the current owner would likely be forced to reduce the asking price because doing so would increase its expected rate of return relative to the Treasury bond—perhaps enough to convince investors to forsake the certain 7 percent return in exchange for undertaking the risky office building investment.[5]

[4] A full interest would be obtained if the investor became the sole owner of the asset. A partial interest would be obtained if the investor shared ownership of the asset with other investors (e.g., a partnership).

[5] Recall that if the expected future cash flows from an investment alternative are held constant, a reduction in the purchase price will increase the expected return (yield).

We will assume in this book that investors are risk averse; that is, rational investors require an expectation of higher return to be induced to accept a riskier investment, holding all else constant. Investors often misunderstand this positive relationship between risk and return. It does not *guarantee* a higher return for undertaking a riskier investment. In fact, there is some probability that investors will *realize* lower returns on the riskier investments than on the less risky alternatives. Compensation for accepting riskier investments comes in the form of a higher *expected* rates of return at the time of purchase.[6]

What about a partial interest in the neighborhood shopping center that also can be purchased for $30,000, and is currently priced to yield an 11 percent rate of return? Relative to the Treasury bond (which dominates the office building for risk-averse investors), the shopping center investment holds out the expectation of a higher return. However, the range of possible returns is from 5 to 17 percent. Thus, the higher expected return would be purchased at a cost. Whether or not the increased *expected* return of 4 percent per year would be sufficient to induce the investor to forsake the safe Treasury bond investment in exchange for the risky shopping center would depend on investor attitudes toward risk. Also it depends, as we shall see, on the relationship between the variability of the shopping center's returns and the variability of other assets currently owned.

Because most investors are risk averse, the key question in formulating an investment strategy is "How risk averse is this particular investor?" Exhibit 7–4 presents the risk-return functions for two investors. Aunt Jane is a retired schoolteacher on a fixed income, with limited investment capital from her life's savings. She is highly risk averse because a low rate of return on the $30,000 would seriously affect her lifestyle. In contrast, Ms. Jones is a successful young professional with a steady and growing salary and some accumulated investment capital. If a slumping economy were to generate a low return on a $30,000 office building or shopping center investment, Ms. Jones would be sad, but it would not seriously affect her current lifestyle. She will therefore likely accept lower returns than Aunt Jane for the same level of risk and is willing to take on far greater levels of risk.[7]

Specifying risk preference is entirely subjective—there are no easily applied objective measures of risk aversion. Using their best judgment, analysts identify investors' degree of risk aversion and then attempt to find investment opportunities with risk and

---

[6] Gamblers who "invest" at casinos and in lotteries may appear to be risk lovers; that is, they appear willing to accept *lower* rates of return in exchange for higher risk. A typical explanation given for this behavior is that gambling produces entertainment benefits or returns for these individuals, as well as potential monetary returns. If the entertainment value, or thrill, increases with the level of risk, engaging in gambling does not necessarily indicate that the individual is a risk lover.

[7] Intuitively, the reason most investors are risk averse is that their marginal utility or satisfaction from additional dollars of spendable income declines as the extra income increases. That is, most individuals are characterized by a diminishing marginal utility of income (or wealth). For example, if the return on Aunt Jane's savings were to increase $10,000 per year as the result of undertaking a risky investment, Aunt Jane would surely be more satisfied with her lifestyle. However, a decrease of $10,000 in investment earnings could prove disastrous, perhaps requiring the sale of her home. Thus, if a $10,000 increase or decrease were equally likely, Aunt Jane is likely to avoid the investment because an additional $10,000 in income would add less to her lifestyle than losing $10,000 would hurt.

EXHIBIT 7-4

INVESTOR RISK PREFERENCES

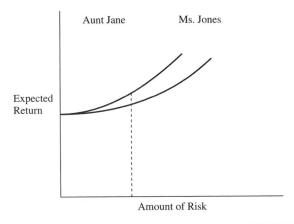

return characteristics that are consistent with the overall investment strategy. For individual investors, the degree of risk aversion is usually related to their age and wealth, as it is in the cases of Aunt Jane and Ms. Jones. Among institutional investors, the degree of risk aversion is often related to the importance of preserving capital and the extent to which investment managers are personally liable for their actions. For example, life insurance companies place a high premium on preserving capital because they *must* pay claims, and managers of pension fund investments are legally personally liable for their actions as investment managers.

MEASURING PROJECT-SPECIFIC RISK

The concepts of discrete probability distributions and expected values (or rates of return) can be used to quantify risk. We know that risk is present when the estimated distribution of cash flows or returns has more than one possible outcome, but how should risk be measured and quantified? The remainder of this chapter is devoted to answering this question. In this section the riskiness of an investment is held in isolation. Later, we analyze the riskiness of assets held in a portfolio.

VARIANCE AND STANDARD DEVIATION

Variance is a measure of the dispersion of a distribution around its expected value. The larger the variance, the greater the dispersion. The variance of a distribution is calculated as

E X H I B I T   7 - 5

VARIANCE OF RETURN ON OFFICE BUILDING INVESTMENT

State of the Economy	Probability	Outcome	Deviation From Expected Return	Deviation Squared	Squared Deviation Times Probability
Deep recession	0.05	3.0%	−4.0%	16.00	0.80
Mild recession	0.20	5.5	−1.5	2.25	0.45
Average economy	0.50	7.0	0.0	0.00	0.00
Mild boom	0.20	8.5	1.5	2.25	0.45
Strong boom	0.05	11.0	4.0	16.00	0.80
Expected return (outcome)	=	7.0%		Variance =	2.50

$$Variance = \sigma^2 = \sum_{i=1}^{n} (o_i - E(R))^2 p_i \qquad (7\text{--}2)$$

where

σ_2 = variance

o_i = outcome (return, cash flow, etc.) for each state of the economy

$E(R)$ = expected outcome (value)

p_i = probability of the ith state occurring

Equation 7–2 shows that the variance is the sum of the squared deviations from the expected value, weighted by each deviation's probability of occurrence.

To illustrate, we calculate the variance of the rate of return on the office building investment from Exhibit 7–1. The expected rate of return on this investment is 7 percent. Using Equation 7–2, the variance of the return is calculated as 2.50. These calculations are summarized in Exhibit 7–5.

Variance is measured by differences in percentage returns. However, the return percentages are squared. Because it is difficult to interpret a squared percentage, another measure, the **standard deviation**, is more frequently used as a measure of dispersion, or risk. The standard deviation is simply the square root of the variance, and is written as σ. Thus, the standard deviation of the office building investment is

$$Standard\ deviation = \sigma = \sqrt{\sigma^2} = \sqrt{2.50} = 1.58\%$$

One standard deviation is the distance of 1.58 percent in either direction from the office building's 7 percent expected return; two standard deviations are double that distance. The standard deviation comes from a discrete probability distribution with only five possible outcomes. If instead we assume that the 1.58 percent standard deviation came from a distribution of returns that is continuous and approximately normal, additional interpretations of the standard deviation are possible. For example, we can state that 68.3 percent of

EXHIBIT 7 - 6

RETURN AND RISK MEASURES FOR EXHIBIT 7-1
INVESTMENT ALTERNATIVES

Expected Return or Risk Measure	Investment Alternatives		
	Treasury Bond	Office Building	Shopping Center
Expected return	7.00%	7.00%	11.00%
Variance	0.00	2.50	6.10
Standard deviation	0.00	1.58	2.47
Coefficient of variation	0.00	0.23	0.22

the outcomes will fall between plus and minus one standard deviation of the expected value and that 95.4 percent of the outcomes will fall between plus and minus two standard deviations of the expected value. Adding and subtracting the 1.58 percent standard deviation of return on the office building from the 7 percent expected return results in 8.58 percent and 5.42 percent, respectively. Thus, 68.3 percent of the actual five-year returns will fall between 5.42 and 8.58 percent. Once the mean and standard deviation are established, it is possible to determine the probability of occurrence of values or returns over any desired interval within the distribution. For example, investors can determine the probability that the actual return will be less than 5 percent, greater than 12 percent, or between 8 and 11 percent.[8]

Exhibit 7–6 contains the expected rates of return and standard deviations of the three investment alternatives, along with their coefficients of variation, discussed in the next section. The Treasury bond investment has a zero standard deviation because there will be no dispersion between the actual return and the expected 7 percent return. This lack of dispersion is displayed graphically in Exhibit 7–2. The shopping center has the largest standard deviation of the three alternatives.

COEFFICIENT OF VARIATION

Investments with higher expected returns generally have larger standard deviations than investments with smaller expected returns. For example, the expected return on the neighborhood shopping center is 11 percent, versus 7 percent on the office building. The corresponding standard deviations are 2.47 and 1.58 percent. Is the community shopping

---

[8] Determining the probability of occurrence over a specific interval within the distribution is accomplished by converting distances from the expected value into the number of standard deviations from the expected value. These standardized distances are contained in a reference table, sometimes called a table of Z-values. Such a table shows the portion of the area under the normal distribution lying to the left or right of various specific values. For an extended discussion, see Gaylon E. Greer, *Investment Analysis for Real Estate Decisions*, 3rd ed. (Chicago: Dearborn Financial Publishing, 1997). Discussion of this issue also can be found in college textbooks on introductory statistics.

center more risky? In an absolute sense, yes. However, to interpret properly the relative riskiness of two investments, it is sometimes useful to go one step further and to calculate the **coefficient of variation**, which is the standard deviation of the return divided by the expected return. For the office building investment,

$$Coefficient\ of\ variation = \frac{standard\ deviation}{expected\ return} = \frac{1.58\%}{7.0\%} = 0.23, \text{ or } 23\% \qquad (7\text{--}3)$$

The coefficient of variation is a measure of *risk per unit of return*. Thus, by dividing the standard deviation by the size of the expected return, the coefficient of variation provides a *relative* (or scaled) measure of riskiness that can be useful when comparing the attractiveness of alternative investments. Investments with lower risk per unit of return are generally preferred to investments with higher risk per unit of return. For example, the coefficient of variation on the shopping center is (2.47 percent/11.0 percent) $\times$ 100 = 22 percent, slightly lower than the office building. Although the dispersion of possible returns is much larger for the shopping center, the dispersion relative to the level of expected return is nearly identical to that of the office building.

THE USE OF SUBJECTIVE PROBABILITIES

The challenge in analyzing real estate investment risk lies in the measurement of risks. The ideal process would be to collect data from recent periods on the returns for the property under evaluation (often referred to as the *subject property*). The analyst then would calculate the historical mean and standard deviation of returns as a first measure of the property's risk. Even if past returns were not available for the subject property—for example, if it were a new development—data on returns from comparable properties could be gathered. This approach is essentially the way risk analysis is done for stock and bond investments.

Unfortunately, data on past returns for subject properties and comparables are not usually available. Unlike stocks and bonds, one cannot simply leaf through back issues of the *Wall Street Journal* to obtain past data on returns from shopping centers in Kansas or office buildings in Tampa, for example. Moreover, real estate markets are not nearly as active as securities markets, and therefore data on recent sales are not readily available.

These data constraints mandate that the analysis of real estate investment risks follow alternative—and not altogether satisfactory—courses. One course involves the use of subjective probabilities. This is the course that we have used thus far in examples of future, or *ex ante*, risk and return measures. Analysts may believe that the assignment of probabilities in this manner is too subjective to be of much use in some situations. However, the use of subjective probabilities is the only way in many cases to quantify the risk of real estate investments; the unwise alternative is to do no risk analysis at all.

This discussion of subjective probability distributions illustrates an important point. Real estate investors generally face two sources of risk: (1) the risk associated with uncertain outcomes, given a known probability distribution, and (2) the additional risk that results from the fact that the assumed distribution may itself be incorrect. Even if historical data on the properties of interest are available, the data may not accurately reflect *current* expectations about future returns and risk. Therefore, this second source of risk is quite important.

RISK MANAGEMENT

Thus far we have concentrated on defining and measuring the riskiness of income property investments (as manifested in the expected variability of holding period returns). We also have argued that most investors are risk averse in that, other things being equal, they prefer assets with higher potential mean returns—given comparable levels of risk—and avoid assets with more volatile (higher standard deviations of returns) cash flows and returns. This section discusses the primary tools investors may employ to reduce the variability of their investment returns: (1) avoiding risky projects, (2) using insurance to transfer risk to others, and (3) diversification.

AVOIDING RISKY PROJECTS

One way to reduce the variability of investment returns is to invest in less risky projects or securities—for example, certificates of deposits (CDs) and U.S. Treasury securities. Unfortunately, this low-risk strategy tends to reduce the chances of achieving larger returns because expected returns in a competitive market tend to increase or decrease along with the risk associated with the investment. Should investment opportunities appear that are priced to yield a return in excess of what market participants require on similar investments of comparable risk, investors in search of positive Net Present Value (NPV) projects will quickly enter the market—driving prices *up* and expected returns *down* until they are commensurate with the level of perceived risk. This suggests that the availability of positive NPV investments in a particular market is *negatively* related to how well functioning and competitive the market is. Put differently, the persistent search by well-informed investors competing for positive NPV projects tends to reduce the likelihood that such opportunities will exist. These same competitive market forces also provide discipline for sellers of income properties and other securities. If market participants perceive that a property is overpriced, lack of interest from informed investors in its acquisition will typically force sellers to reduce the asking prices until the expected returns are comparable to other investment alternatives of similar risk.

INSURANCE AND HEDGING

Losses from fire, flood, and other natural hazards have the potential to devastate investment returns. Indeed, if unprotected, the destruction of the real estate could produce investment returns that are severely negative. Although the prediction of fire and casualty losses is virtually impossible for a *particular* property, it is possible to predict with a reasonable degree of accuracy the percentage of homes that will experience, say, fire damage in any particular year. Predictability based on statistical averages from large numbers is the foundation of the insurance industry. For large insurance firms with many policyholders in diverse locations, the degree of risk associated with providing the insurance is quite small. As a result, real estate investors can, and should, transfer many risks to insurance companies in exchange for a certain insurance premium.

Viewed as an individual investment, buying hazard insurance has a very uncertain and volatile payoff: If the house burns down, the payoff or "return" is enormous; if no fire occurs, the payoff will equal zero. However, viewed from a portfolio perspective, the insurance is a risk-reducing investment because it will provide a positive payoff if the investment in the house, which is often a significant component of household portfolios, performs poorly (i.e., suffers damage). Insurance is a form of hedging, defined as a strategy of investing in an asset with an expected return pattern that wholly or partially offsets your exposure to a particular source of risk. Many vehicles exist in financial markets for hedging risk.

In short, insurance and other forms of hedging provide a mechanism for real estate investors to replace *uncertainty* with *certainty*. This transfer of risk is rational in many situations because very few individuals or firms (presumably only the largest and most wealthy) are in a position to self-insure against catastrophic losses.

DIVERSIFICATION AS A RISK-MANAGEMENT TOOL

Investors can further reduce the variability of investment returns by the use of **diversification**. The intuition behind the concept of diversification is illustrated by the maxim "Don't put all your eggs in one basket." As an example, consider the following two "investment" alternatives:

(1) Flip a fair coin once: If heads, you win $10,000; if tails, you lose $9,500.
(2) Flip a fair coin 100 times: If heads, you win $100; if tails, you lose $95.

The expected values of the two alternatives, EV_1 and EV_2, are equal to

$$EV_1 = [(0.50)(\$10,000) + (0.50)(-\$9,500)] = \$250$$
$$EV_2 = [(0.50)(\$100) + (0.50)(-\$95)] \times 100 = [\$2.50] \times 100 = \$250$$

Both investments have an expected value or payoff of $250. However, the first alternative is extremely risky in that the actual outcome will be either a positive $10,000 or a negative $9,500. Thus, the actual outcome will vary greatly from the expected outcome of $250. With the second alternative, the investor is, in essence, purchasing a partial interest in 100 different coin flips. This "portfolio" of coin flips will produce a payoff much closer to the $250 expected value. Assuming identical purchase prices, risk-averse investors would choose the second alternative because it allows for a significant reduction in investment risk *without* sacrificing expected return.

THE PORTFOLIO CONCEPT OF RISK

Preceding sections presented what is commonly referred to as the **mean-variance** approach to comparing investment alternatives. Mean-variance analysis portrays investors as weighing the advantages of expected benefits from alternative courses of action against the disadvantages of the particular risks that apply. More specifically, mean-variance analysis explicitly recognizes that the expected variability, as well as the expected amount, of future cash flows is fundamental to the determination of market values in a competitive market. Other things equal, mean-variance investors are assumed to prefer assets with higher mean returns (given comparable levels of risk) and to avoid assets whose cash flows and returns are expected to be more volatile (less predictable) than assets with the same expected return. With this approach, the standard deviation of the investment's cash flows or rate of return, or perhaps the coefficient of variation, is used as the measure of risk when making comparisons among investments.[9]

The portfolio concept of risk states that investments should be accepted or rejected on the basis of their effect on the risk and return of the entire portfolio of assets. Most investors do not invest in only one asset, but rather in many assets. These portfolios can consist of diverse investments stemming from different financial markets and submarkets. A portfolio may include numerous different stocks, a combination of stocks and bonds, several income property investments, gold, or combinations of these and other investment alternatives. Combining assets into portfolios reduces risk because those assets that experience less than expected returns will be offset to some degree by assets whose returns are greater than expected. Because of this interaction, the standard deviation of the return on a portfolio is usually less than the average standard deviation of individual investments. Thus, it is rational for investors to hold portfolios of assets rather than single assets in an attempt to decrease risk, perhaps without reducing expected returns. Mean-variance analysis still applies at the portfolio level. However, investors are now concerned with the expected return and variance of their portfolios, rather than the risk-return characteristics of individual assets.

DIVERSIFIABLE PORTFOLIO RISK

The literature of finance categorizes risk as either **diversifiable** or **nondiversifiable**. Diversifiable risk, also called **unsystematic risk**, can be eliminated from a portfolio by holding securities and other investments with returns that are less than perfectly **correlated**. Perfectly correlated returns always move exactly together when market conditions change; perfectly negatively correlated returns always move exactly opposite. If one asset in the

---

[9] There is some controversy over the mean-variance approach. The assumption that investor utility or satisfaction depends only on the mean return and the variance of the return can be justified by assuming that returns from investments are normally distributed, or that higher and higher amounts of income increase the investor's utility, but at a decreasing rate. Available empirical evidence suggests that the first of these assumptions may not be true, whereas the latter assumption leads to many theoretically undesirable properties. In spite of these potential shortcomings, the mean-variance approach is widely used in practice.

E X H I B I T   7 - 7

HISTORICAL RETURNS AND RISK

Year	Stock	Shopping Center	Equally Weighted Portfolio
1992	14%	−10%	2.0%
1993	−10	8	−1.0
1994	23	12	17.5
1995	−5	17	6.0
1996	8	−5	1.5
1997	12	15	13.5
Mean return	7.00%	6.17%	6.58%
Standard deviation	12.36%	11.13%	7.37%

E X H I B I T   7 - 8

HISTORICAL STANDARD DEVIATION OF STOCK RETURN

Year	Realized Return	Actual Average	Squared Deviations
1992	14%	7.0%	49.0
1993	−10	−17.0	289.0
1994	23	16.0	256.0
1995	−5	−12.0	144.0
1996	8	1.0	1.0
1997	12	5.0	25.0
Average return	7.0%	Sum of squared deviations	764.0

$$Variance = \sigma^2 = \frac{total\ of\ squared\ deviations}{n-1} = \frac{764}{5} = 152.8$$

$$Standard\ deviation = \sigma = \sqrt{\sigma^2} = \sqrt{152.8} = 12.36\%$$

portfolio reacts negatively to a market downturn, losses may be offset through holding another asset that reacts positively.

To further illustrate the concept of diversification, consider the realized rates of return reported in Exhibit 7–7 for two investments: a common stock and a shopping center. In 1990, the stock produced a positive 14 percent return; the income property, a negative 10 percent. Over the six-year holding period from 1992 through 1997, the stock and shopping center produced average annual returns of 7 percent and 6.17 percent, respectively. The average return on a portfolio invested 50 percent in each of the two assets was 6.58 percent. The historical standard deviation of the annual stock return was 12.36 percent. The procedure for calculating this standard deviation is displayed in Exhibit 7–8.

The procedures used in Exhibit 7–8 are standard for calculating the mean, variance, and standard deviation of returns from sample data. Computer spreadsheet programs and most financial calculators also can be used to perform these calculations more quickly. The procedures are similar to those used for calculating expected returns and risk measures using subjective probabilities (see Exhibit 7–5). The major difference is that each time period (in this case year) receives an equal weight when using historical data. The standard deviation for the shopping center investment over the same time period was 7.11 percent.

Inspection of Exhibit 7–7 shows that, if held separately, the two assets produced fairly volatile returns. However, when combined in a portfolio, the return volatility decreased to 7.37 percent, significantly less than the volatility of either asset separately held.

The reason the combination of the stock and shopping center resulted in a significant reduction in risk at the portfolio level is that their returns tended to move somewhat countercyclically to one another over the sample period. When the stock's return falls, the return on the shopping center often increases, and vice versa. In statistical terms, the returns were negatively correlated over the sample period.

COVARIANCE AND CORRELATION

Covariance (COV) is an absolute measure of the tendency of an asset's return to vary with that of another asset over time. The covariance between the stock and shopping center returns was -29.6 during the sample period. This indicates that the returns on the two assets tended to move in opposite directions. The calculation of the covariance for our example is contained in Exhibit 7–9. Essentially, the covariance of historical returns is calculated for two assets by first finding the deviation of each asset's return in each period from the average return over the sample period. The annual deviations on the first asset are then multiplied by the corresponding annual deviation on the second asset. These annual products (of deviations) are then summed over the sample period. The summed deviations are then divided by the number of periods (months, years, etc.) in the sample. The result is the covariance of the returns on the two assets. Covariances are more easily calculated with spreadsheets and calculators.

Covariance statistics can take on values ranging from minus infinity to positive infinity, making it difficult to know when a covariance is "large" or "small." Therefore, a related statistic, the **correlation coefficient** (ρ), is often used to measure the degree of co-movement between two variables. The correlation coefficient is calculated as

$$Correlation\ coefficient = \rho_{AB} = \frac{COV_{AB}}{\sigma_A \sigma_B} \tag{7–4}$$

The correlation coefficient standardizes the covariance by dividing the covariance by the product of the individual standard deviations. This provides a *relative* measure of co-movement. The sign of the correlation coefficient is the same as the covariance, so a positive sign indicates that the two variables move together; a negative sign means they move in opposite directions. If ρ_{AB} is close to zero, the variables move independently of one another. In addition, the correlation coefficient only ranges from -1.0 to $+1.0$,

---

E X H I B I T   7 - 9

COMPUTATION OF COVARIANCE OF RETURNS FOR STOCK AND SHOPPING CENTER

	Stock			Shopping Center			
Year	Realized Return	Actual Average	Squared Deviations	Realized Return	Actual Average	Squared Deviations	(Stock deviation) × (Center deviation)
1992	14%	7.0%	49.0	−10%	−16.17%	261.3	−113.2
1993	−10	−17.0	289.0	8	1.83	3.3	−31.1
1994	23	16.0	256.6	12	5.83	34.0	93.3
1995	−5	−12.0	144.0	17	10.83	117.3	−130.0
1996	8	1.0	1.0	−5	−11.17	124.6	−11.2
1997	12	5.0	25.0	15	8.83	78.0	44.2
Sum	42.0%		764.0	37%		618.8	−148.0

$$Mean\ return\ on\ stock = \frac{sum\ of\ returns}{number\ of\ periods} = \frac{42.0}{6} = 7.00\%$$

$$Stock\ return\ variance = \sigma_A^2 = \frac{squared\ deviations}{n-1} = \frac{764.0}{5} = 152.8$$

$$Stock\ standard\ deviation = \sqrt{\sigma_A^2} = \sqrt{152.8} = 12.36\%$$

$$Mean\ return\ on\ shopping\ center = \frac{37}{6} = 6.17\%$$

$$Shopping\ center\ return\ variance = \sigma_B^2 = \frac{squared\ deviation}{n-1} = \frac{618.83}{5} = 123.8$$

$$Shopping\ center\ standard\ deviation = \sqrt{\sigma_B^2} = \sqrt{123.8} = 11.13\%$$

$$Covariance = COV_{AB} = \frac{sum\ of\ stock\ deviations\ times\ shopping\ center\ deviations}{n-1} = \frac{-148.0}{5} = -29.6$$

---

making it much easier to interpret the extent to which the two variables are related than using the covariance. In our example,

$$\rho_{AB} = \frac{COV_{AB}}{\sigma_A \sigma_B} = \frac{-29.6}{(12.4)(11.1)} = -0.22$$

The correlation coefficient of −0.22 indicates a negative correlation between the returns on the common stock and shopping center over the sample period.[10]

It should be clear that if the returns on two assets are highly *negatively* correlated, then the variance of a portfolio consisting of the two assets will be less than the variance of the return on either asset held in isolation. It should be stressed, however, that negative

---

[10] There are statistical tests that allow the analyst to determine whether the correlation between two series is significant in a statistical sense. For a discussion of correlation and related statistics, see any standard college textbook on elementary statistics.

correlation is not required to achieve risk reduction at the portfolio level. All that is required to achieve some reduction in the riskiness of the portfolio is for the correlation to be less than +1.0 between the returns on an asset and the returns on assets already held in the portfolio. However, the potential for risk reduction at the portfolio level is much greater as the correlation moves further away from +1.0.

EXAMPLES OF DIVERSIFIABLE RISK

Diversifiable or *unsystematic risk* is the term used to describe the risk due to the unrealized return expectations of a particular property. Some of this risk is property or site specific; for example, poor management of an apartment complex may lead to higher operating expense levels, decreased occupancy, or both. In addition, the relative attractiveness of the property's location may change due to new real estate development or road construction in the immediate area. For example, increased vacancies could result from an inconsistent land use on an adjacent parcel (e.g., a noisy factory next to an office building). The value of a property also may be affected by changes in its environment or the sudden awareness that the existing environment is hazardous or potentially hazardous. For example, developers and investors have become increasingly concerned about the existence of toxic waste buried on a site or an adjacent property. Environmental problems can cause significant losses because investors may be subject to cleanup costs that far exceed the value of properties. In addition, real estate values are often affected by property tax laws, zoning, and other restrictions imposed by local governments. Legislative risk results from the uncertainty surrounding future changes in these laws and regulations.

In addition to property- or site-specific risks, the returns on real estate investments also may vary as a result of changes in the local, regional, or national economy. However, economic, social, and political changes typically do not affect all cities and regions equally. For example, real estate markets in small public university towns can be significantly affected by sudden changes in the budget of the state that provides the majority of the university's funding. Cities such as Houston and Denver, whose economies had traditionally been linked to the fortunes of the oil industry, suffered high commercial and residential vacancy rates when the price of oil collapsed in 1985. Local real estate markets less dependent on the oil industry were less directly affected. In some cases, national or regional changes or "shocks" create growth and prosperity in one region, while having a negative effect elsewhere. A classic example of this has been the shift in U.S. industrial growth from the Midwest to the South and Southwest.

Poor management, deteriorating local market conditions, changes in traffic patterns, and the discovery of environmental hazards, as well as other unanticipated changes, likely affect some properties in some locations throughout the United States and the world. However, it is unlikely that all properties will experience unexpected problems or advantages at the same time. Diversification reduces the risk of large variations in portfolio returns due to the performance of an individual investment.

BASIC REAL ESTATE DIVERSIFICATION STRATEGIES

The examples of diversifiable risk discussed above suggest two basic diversification strategies for investors seeking to hold an efficient portfolio of real estate: (1) investing in different property types and (2) investing in different geographical areas. An additional diversification strategy is to combine investments in public (i.e., securitized) and private (i.e., unsecuritized) real estate markets.

Property type diversification. Property types are discussed in detail in Chapter 6. The demand by potential tenants for the various types of leasable space is a **derived demand**. For example, a decrease in the demand for industrial goods causes a decrease in the demand for industrial space. Similarly, the demand for office space is derived from the demand for the services provided by the tenants of office buildings, such as law and accounting firms, banks, insurance companies, real estate brokerage firms, and mortgage banks. The demand for retail space in a market is directly related to the population in the trade area and to the disposable income of the population. The demand for apartment units fluctuates with the number of households in a given market that typically rent their living space—for example, single households under the age of 30.

General economic trends will likely alter the demand for all types of space; for example, the general U.S. recession from 1989 to 1992 had an adverse effect on the return performance of all property types. However, if the demand (and supply) for various property types is not driven by the same economic forces, or if the various property types respond differently to changes in the local, regional, or national economy, investors can reduce portfolio risk by holding ownership interests in several or all of the above property categories.

Geographic diversification. Another popular method of diversifying is geographically. Although national economic trends can have a significant effect on real estate markets, local market conditions are often more important than national economic trends. In fact, it is often argued that real estate markets are decidedly local. To the extent that this is true, a portfolio of geographically diverse properties may provide better risk-return characteristics than a geographically concentrated real estate portfolio. For example, when the economies of Dallas, Houston, Denver, and other cities in the so-called oil extraction states were rocked by falling oil prices in the mid-1980s, all real estate values were negatively affected, not just office buildings that suffered directly from the demise of numerous oil and oil related companies that were prime demanders of office space. The across-the-board decline in real estate values in these areas produced low or negative returns for virtually all investors. However, the losses were especially significant for those investors with real estate portfolios concentrated in these areas, including small local investors who had purchased small rental properties and institutional investors that had large investment holdings in these areas.

Combining public and private market investments. As discussed in Chapter 6, the dramatic growth in securitized real estate markets in recent years provides investors with expanded opportunities to purchase interests in real estate that can be exchanged in public markets. The most prominent example is the growth in the market value of REITs that are traded on major stock exchanges. Recent evidence suggests that the performance of public market and property investments have differed, often significantly, over the last 20 years. This evidence suggests that investors may obtain additional diversification benefits by holding a portion of their real estate investments in the form of publicly traded real estate securities, primarily REITs.[11]

NONDIVERSIFIABLE RISK

What happens when more stocks, bonds, and real estate are added to a portfolio? In general, the riskiness of a portfolio will fall as the number of assets increases. Moreover, the extent to which portfolio risk declines depends on the degree of correlation between the returns on the asset that is added and the returns on assets already included in the portfolio. The smaller the correlation, the greater is the risk reduction achieved by adding the asset.

It is difficult to find assets whose expected returns are negatively correlated—most assets tend to do well when the national economy is strong and less well when the national economy is weak. Thus, although diversification can eliminate much of the risk from a portfolio of assets, unanticipated events or "shocks" that affect all, or most, assets will inevitably produce variations in portfolio returns over time—even in large, well-diversified portfolios. Thus, even extensive diversification cannot eliminate risk. Nondiversifiable risk is frequently referred to as systematic risk or market risk.

CHOOSING AN OPTIMAL PORTFOLIO

The above discussion of diversification strongly suggests that consideration of just the mean return and standard deviation of return for individual investments will not ensure that an optimal portfolio is selected. In fact, according to mean-variance portfolio theory, rational investors base their assessment of an investment's risk (and hence its price) on its contribution to portfolio risk and return. Specifically, investors judge investment alternatives on the basis of their portfolio "efficiency." An investment is efficient in a portfolio context if its acquisition

- Increases the expected return on a portfolio without increasing portfolio risk, or
- Decreases the riskiness of the portfolio without sacrificing the portfolio's expected rate of return.

---

[11] For more on the proper role of publicly traded real estate securities in a mixed-asset portfolio, see David J. Hartzell, Charles H. Wurtzebach, and David E. Watkins, "Combining Publicly Traded Real Estate Securities with Privately Held Portfolios," *Real Estate Finance* 12 (Fall 1995), pp. 26–40, and Glenn R. Mueller, Keith R. Pauley, and William K. Morrill, Jr., "A Primer for Private and Public Equity Choices in a Real Estate Portfolio Management Context," *Real Estate Finance* 12 (Spring 1995), pp. 12–21.

E X H I B I T   7 - 1 0

PORTFOLIO RETURN AND RISK UNDER DIFFERENT COMBINATIONS

Proportion of Portfolio in Stock	Proportion of Portfolio in Shopping Center	Portfolio Return $E(R_p)$	Standard Deviation of Return (σ_p)
0.00	1.00	6.17%	11.13%
0.20	0.80	6.33	8.71
0.40	0.60	6.50	7.40
0.50	0.50	6.58	7.37
0.60	0.40	6.67	7.78
0.80	0.20	6.83	9.66
1.00	0.00	7.00	12.36

Assume $E(R_p)$ is the expected rate of return on the portfolio; w_A and w_B are the fractions of the portfolio invested in assets A and B; $E(R_A)$ and $E(R_B)$ are the expected returns on the two assets, and ρ_{AB} is the correlation coefficient for assets A and B. Then, σ_p, the standard deviation of the two asset portfolios is

$$E(R_p) = (w_A)E(R_A) + (w_B)E(R_B)$$

$$\sigma_p = \sqrt{w_A^2\sigma_A^2 + w_B^2\sigma_B^2 + 2w_Aw_B\rho_{AB}\sigma_A\sigma_B}$$

Much research has shown that a portfolio can be fully diversified in the sense that its unsystematic risk is eliminated by choosing perhaps as few as 15 or 20 assets at random.[12] This type of diversification is often termed *naive diversification*.

The objective of portfolio risk management is to develop an *efficient* portfolio by eliminating diversifiable risk. This is achieved by including assets with varying return correlations in the portfolio. The degree of correlation and the effect this correlation will have on a portfolio can be estimated to help investors choose the optimal collection of assets. Assets can be selected on the basis of their relative riskiness as well as at random. For example, an asset that is quite risky can be combined in a portfolio with a risk-free asset to reduce the overall risk of the portfolio. This so-called *efficient* or *smart diversification* makes it possible to reduce the unsystematic risk in a portfolio to zero with fewer assets under a smart diversification strategy than under a naive strategy.

The expected return and standard deviation for portfolios consisting of various combinations of the stock and shopping center are displayed in Exhibit 7–10. Note that if the percentage of the portfolio allocated to the stock had been zero over the sample period, the average return on the portfolio, R_p, and the portfolio standard deviation would have equaled 6.17 percent and 11.13 percent, respectively—the average return and standard deviation for the shopping center. With 20 percent invested in the stock, the average return on the portfolio increases to 6.33 percent *and* the portfolio standard deviation falls to 8.71 percent. With 40 percent of the portfolio invested in the stock, the average return on the portfolio increases slightly to 6.50 percent and the portfolio standard deviation falls still further to 7.40 percent. For proportions greater than approximately 0.50, the return on

---

[12] The basis for modern portfolio theory is generally credited to Harry Markowitz, "Portfolio Selection," *Journal of Finance* 7, no. 1 (March 1952), pp. 77–91.

the portfolio continues to increase. However, the standard deviation of the portfolio also increases over this range. That is, for proportions greater than about 0.50, the typical positive relationship holds between risk and return.

What is especially significant about the above example is that for stock proportions less than 0.50, investors could have enhanced the return on their portfolio *and* reduced the volatility of the portfolio return by allocating a larger percentage of the portfolio to the stock. Does this result violate the assertion made earlier in the chapter that increases in expected returns can only be purchased in competitive markets by undertaking more risk? No, the result merely demonstrates the power of efficient diversification. By choosing low or negatively correlated assets, investors can construct portfolios that reduce risk without sacrificing return. Indeed, the example above demonstrates that diversification may increase the return on the portfolio, at least over some combinations of the two assets. Although estimation of the risk and return on multiple asset portfolios is beyond the scope of this text, the intuition of the two-asset example is directly applicable to the multiple asset case.

WHY ARE SO MANY INVESTORS NOT WELL-DIVERSIFIED?

Despite the widespread use of modern portfolio theory by many market participants, especially pension funds and other institutional investors, some investors clearly behave in a manner that appears inconsistent with portfolio theory. For example, many home-owning households are very poorly diversified with a large percentage of their wealth invested in their home. Many readers also can point to individuals, perhaps even parents or other relatives, that have pursued a narrowly focused investment strategy such as investing almost exclusively in local rental houses, small apartments, or some other asset. Are these home owners and investors irrational? Perhaps. However, numerous other factors and considerations can constrain or push households to hold undiversified investment portfolios. For example, many households place a great deal of value on housing and home ownership and thus are willing to allocate a significant portion of their monthly income to housing payments. From a pure mean-variance portfolio perspective, their chosen portfolios can look inefficient because they contain few or no stocks, bonds, or other assets. However, this perspective probably understates the satisfaction, and therefore the return, these households receive from owning and consuming housing. Moreover, many households have invested, or are investing, heavily in human capital, such as education, work experience, and the like.

What about the numerous investors who allocate a significant portion of their wealth, and perhaps time, to investments in local rental properties? Perhaps their desire to actively manage their rental properties precludes them from diversifying geographically. In addition, their limited resources may not allow them to be active purchasers of more expensive properties such as office buildings and shopping centers. Diversification by property type is therefore problematic. Why not mix more stocks, bonds, and other assets into their rental housing portfolio? Perhaps they consider themselves experts at acquiring, managing, and disposing of rental homes and they want to apply this perceived comparative advantage to as many rental homes as possible. Or, perhaps they truly expect returns on their real estate portfolio to far exceed returns on a **mixed-asset portfolio**, that is, one that contains a variety of assets. If their expected returns are high enough, it may be rational for them to "load up" on local real estate because the benefits are expected to offset the increased costs associated with their risky, undiversified portfolio.

In short, the use of mean-variance theory and techniques continues to grow rapidly, especially among institutional investors. Moreover, apparent irrational investment behavior, especially by local, less wealthy investors, may actually result from wealth constraints, the perceived advantages of owning and operating a particular property type, or an emphasis on investing in a particular geographic market. Holding an undiversified portfolio also can be rational if the investor truly believes the return prospects outweigh the increased risks of pursuing such a strategy.

HOW RISKY IS REAL ESTATE?

To evaluate the performance of an asset class, such as real estate, it is important to be able to measure both the potential risk and expected return associated with holding the asset. From a technical standpoint, portfolio models require past data on returns because the measurement of portfolio risk and diversification relies on the calculation of historical means and variances as well as covariances among the returns from the different assets in the portfolio. For stocks and bonds, this measurement objective represents little problem because an abundance of historic performance data is available. Unfortunately, return information for real estate is much harder to come by, and is often less accurate than the information available on traditional stock and bond alternatives. If the real estate is held by a *publicly traded* corporation, for example, by a REIT that is traded on one of the major stock exchanges, accurate historical return data are generally available. However, as we mentioned earlier in conjunction with estimating standard deviations for project-in-isolation risk analysis, past data on returns for *privately held* real estate assets are usually not available. Only large institutions with a large number of properties already in their portfolios can readily use portfolio models for real estate investment analysis. Even then, institutions must have the properties in their portfolio appraised, usually on a quarterly basis, to obtain an estimate of the increase in value.

HISTORICAL RETURNS, RISK, AND CORRELATIONS

The NCREIF and NAREIT indexes described in detail in Chapter 5 provide useful information on the absolute level of risk and expected return associated with real estate. What may be more important to potential investors, however, is the riskiness of real estate relative to other assets. Exhibit 7–11 presents the mean return and standard deviation of four different asset classes over three different time periods. Return and volatility measures for a portfolio consisting of an equal fraction of each of the assets also are included.

EXHIBIT   7 - 1 1

AVERAGE RETURN AND STANDARD DEVIATION: REAL ESTATE VERSUS OTHER ASSETS

	1990(1)–1995(2)		1985(1)–1995(2)		1978(1)–1995(2)	
	Average	**Standard Deviation**	**Average**	**Standard Deviation**	**Average**	**Standard Deviation**
NCPI	7.7%	9.1%	7.3%	7.1%	12.8%	7.6%
NAREIT	11.6	16.2	11.6	13.8	15.7	13.9
Stocks	12.3	11.9	16.9	15.3	16.2	14.8
Bonds	9.3	5.6	10.7	6.0	10.4	8.4
Equally weighted portfolio	10.2	7.6	11.6	7.4	13.7	7.8

* The NCPI returns have been "unsmoothed" to adjust for the appraisal-induced smoothing of value changes that is inherent in the NCPI. The technique used follows Jeffrey D. Fisher, David Geltner, and Brian Webb, "Value Indices of Commercial Real Estate: A Comparison of Index Construction Methods," *Journal of Real Estate Finance and Economics* 9 (1994), pp. 137–164.

The NCREIF Classic Property Index (NCPI) measures the performance of properties held by pension funds. The NAREIT Index tracks the total return of publicly traded REITs. The stock and bond data are derived from the S&P 500 Index and Lehman Brothers G/C Index, respectively.[13]

Exhibit 7–11 suggests that equity REITs, unlike direct property investments, have risk and return characteristics similar to those associated with stocks.[14] However, direct property investments—as measured by the NCPI—appear to exhibit both a lower average return and standard deviation than stocks and equity REITs. In fact, the volatility of the NCPI seems to match the volatility of bonds more closely than stocks.

Turning to an examination of the equally weighted portfolio (25 percent NCPI, 25 percent NAREIT, 25 percent stocks, and 25 percent bonds), we find diversification would have resulted in a higher return with virtually no increase in risk, as compared to investing in just real estate (NCPI). In fact, from the first quarter of 1990 through the second quarter of 1995, the portfolio would have dominated exclusive real estate investment because the return was higher and the standard deviation was lower.

These significant diversification benefits can be explained by examining the return correlations presented in Exhibit 7–12, which shows that NCPI is virtually uncorrelated

---

[13] The S&P 500 is a value-weighted index of 500 stocks that account for over 80 percent of the total market capitalization of all firms listed on the New York Stock Exchange (NYSE), while the Lehman Index is comprised of both corporate bonds and U.S. Treasury securities.

[14] Several authors have argued that the volatility of REITs overstates the "true" volatility of the underlying properties held by REITs because REIT returns tend to be highly correlated with the general stock market. For more discussion, see Joseph Gyourko and Donald B. Keim, "What Does the Stock Market Tell Us about Real Estate Returns," *Journal of the American Real Estate and Urban Economics Association* 20, no. 3 (1992), pp. 457–85, and S. Michael Giliberto, "Equity Real Estate Trusts and Real Estate Returns," *The Journal of Real Estate Research* 5, no. 2 (1990), pp. 259–65.

EXHIBIT 7-12

RETURN CORRELATIONS OVER DIFFERENT TIME PERIODS

Panel A: 1990(1)–1995(2)

	NCPI	NAREIT	Stocks	Bonds
NCPI	1.000	0.136	0.002	−0.261
NAREIT		1.000	0.628	0.381
Stocks			1.000	0.614
Bonds				1.000

Panel B: 1985(1)–1995(2)

	NCPI	NAREIT	Stocks	Bonds
NCPI	1.000	0.082	−0.018	−0.164
NAREIT		1.000	0.630	0.346
Stocks			1.000	0.276
Bonds				1.000

Panel C: 1978(1)–1995(2)

	NCPI	NAREIT	Stocks	Bonds
NCPI	1.000	0.090	−0.072	−0.239
NAREIT		1.000	0.680	0.404
Stocks			1.000	0.383
Bonds				1.000

with stocks and is negatively correlated with bonds over all three time periods. This relationship leads to the diversification benefits quantified above because investors in the equally weighted portfolios are likely to experience quarters with poor real estate performance corresponding to quarters of strong returns to other portfolio assets. In effect, diversification allows investors to insulate themselves from potential losses by reducing the volatility of the overall cash flows they receive.[15]

As with mean returns and standard deviations, correlations are not constant over time. However, a close inspection of Exhibit 7–12 reveals that although the relevant correlations are not constant over time, they are at least relatively stable and consistent.

---

[15] For more on the historical risk and return characteristics of income-producing real estate, see Emily J. Norman, G. Stacy Sirmans, and John D. Benjamin, "The Historical Environment of Real Estate Returns," *The Journal of Real Estate Portfolio Management* 1, no. 1 (1995), pp. 1–24.

ACCOUNTING FOR RISK IN VALUATION DECISIONS

Real estate investment analysis using the discounted cash-flow (DCF) methodology requires specification of three major items: the cash flows in each period, the reversion when the property is sold, and the discount rate. We described the techniques for estimating cash flows and reversions in Chapters 3 and 4. What remains to be specified is the required discount rate, and this is of critical importance because present values are extremely sensitive to changes in the required discount rate. The most frequently used technique for explicitly incorporating risk into a DCF analysis is to *risk adjust* the discount rate that is (1) used to convert future cash flows into present value and (2) used as the minimum required rate of return in an IRR analysis. This section discusses the specification of the risk-adjusted discount rate. A subsequent section discusses sensitivity analysis, a commonly used technique for quantifying the riskiness of cash flow and rate of return projections.

RISK-ADJUSTED DISCOUNT RATE

With a *risk-adjusted* discount-rate approach, investors first estimate future cash flows, then make judgments about the riskiness of the cash flows. For example, if an investor expects to hold the asset for five years, the investor's *minimum* discount rate (opportunity cost) is the rate of return currently available on risk-free five-year Treasury securities. The investor then adds a risk premium to the risk-free rate that reflects the perceived riskiness of the property's cash flow estimates. Algebraically, the required rate of return can be expressed as

$$E(R_j) = R_f + RP_j \qquad (7\text{--}5)$$

where $E(R_j)$ is the expected or required rate of return on the *j*th investment, R_f is the current return available on risk-free Treasury securities of comparable maturities, and RP_j is the required risk premium.

As an example, assume potential investors in downtown Chicago office buildings are currently requiring a 12 percent annual rate of return on their expected 10-year investments. Also assume that Treasury bonds with remaining maturities of 10 years are currently priced to yield 6 percent per year. The 12 percent expected annual rate of return is therefore composed of a 6 percent compensation for time, as measured by the risk-free rate, and a 6 percent risk premium.[16]

Can the required risk premium be determined by considering only the riskiness of the investment being evaluated, perhaps as measured by the standard deviation of its

---

[16]Some analysts believe return premiums also should be added for nonmarketability because real estate, in comparison to other investments, is less liquid. This practice is not generally followed. However, some analysts believe that illiquidity will become an important part of standard valuation. See Zvi Bodie, Alex Kane, and Alan J. Marcus, *Investments*, 2nd ed. (Burr Ridge, IL: Irwin, 1994) for a discussion of how illiquidity can be incorporated into a valuation model.

expected return? If investors have the ability to diversify away the unsystematic risk of their portfolios, the answer is no. In analyzing the riskiness of the next investment opportunity, they should be interested only in the amount of systematic risk the new investment would bring to their portfolio. The unsystematic risk is of no concern because it can be eliminated through diversification. In fact, in a competitive market, investors should not expect to be compensated for bearing unsystematic risk because properties will be priced to yield a return that is just sufficient to provide the typical (that is, well-diversified) investor with an adequate rate of return. Investors seeking additional compensation for bearing unsystematic risk, in the form of a reduced price and larger RP_j, are likely to be outbid by well-diversified investors.

The consideration of systematic risk requires considerable information because the investor needs data on the correlation between returns on the asset in question and the returns on her current portfolio. This determination of acceptable investment projects in a portfolio context is not unlike many shopping decisions people face in everyday life. For example, consumers do not select neckties solely because of how attractive they appear as they hang on the department store rack. The shopper must consider how the necktie will look with certain combinations of pants, shirts, and sports jackets. An *efficient* necktie acquisition is one that can be worn with numerous existing combinations. In short, a particular tie may catch the shopper's eye, but if it does not work well with the shopper's current wardrobe, the tie has little value. Similar analogues apply to buying a sofa or a new music CD, adding a basketball player to an existing team, or choosing a wife or husband.[17]

Abstracting discount rates from the market. Investors struggling to determine their required rate of return on a potential investment frequently find themselves asking the following question: "What rate of return are other investors requiring on similar investments?" Although attitudes toward risk—and therefore required risk premiums—vary across investors, the ability to abstract this information from other investors is very useful in calibrating the investor's risk premiums and required rates of return. In fact, most real estate investors rely heavily on such information in determining their required rate of return.

The Real Estate Research Corporation (RERC) surveys the *before-tax* return expectations of a representative sample of large institutional real estate investors. Published quarterly in the *Real Estate Report*, this survey provides insights into the required returns and risk adjustments used by the largest investors when making acquisitions. As such, this and other surveys (formal and informal) provide valuable information to individual investors.

A portion of a table from an issue of the *Real Estate Report* is reproduced in Exhibit 7–13. The mean required return for third-quarter 1996 investments in all property types was 11.6 percent. The spread over 10-year Treasury returns was 4.8 percentage points, or 480 basis points (one basis point equals 0.01 percent). It is important to empha-

---

[17] However, when making a proposal of marriage, it is probably not advisable to dwell on the "diversification benefits" that your intended would bring to your "portfolio."

EXHIBIT 7-13

REQUIRED RATES OF RETURNS ON INVESTMENT-GRADE PROPERTIES
VERSUS COMPARABLE TREASURY SECURITIES: 1992-1996

	3Q92	3Q93	3Q94	3Q95	3Q96
Required R.E. return	12.2%	12.1%	11.7%	11.5%	11.6%
Return on 10-year Treasuries	6.4	5.4	7.5	6.1	6.8
Spread over Treasuries	5.8	6.7	4.2	5.1	4.8

SOURCE: Real Estate Research Corporation. This survey was conducted in July, August, and September of 1996 and reflects required returns for third-quarter 1996 investments. Treasury bond returns are for the last month of the respective quarter.

size that these required returns are for large, investment grade (i.e., *relatively* low risk) properties. Generally, properties that are less than investment grade are more risky due to their smaller size, advanced age, location in a small or transient market, or some combination of these and other shortcomings.

QUANTIFYING REQUIRED RISK PREMIUMS WITH ASSET-PRICING MODELS

A major problem with the traditional risk-adjusted discount-rate approach to real estate valuation is that the specification of the risk premium is, in the end, highly subjective, relying heavily upon the analyst's judgment. This subjectivity of the discount-rate specification is perceived by many to be a weakness of the discounted cash-flow model. At a minimum, it has frequently left investors wondering whether more objective quantitative models for specifying the discount rate are available.

Modern asset-pricing models, developed initially for the valuation of stocks, are able to quantify the relationship between systematic risk and required rates of return. A **single-factor model** for asset pricing classifies sources of investment risk into two categories: (1) systematic (or macroeconomic) factors and (2) property-specific (microeconomic) factors that are diversifiable and therefore fall out of the model. The most widely used version of the single-factor model assumes that the macroeconomic risk factors can be represented by a single index of stock market returns, such as the Standard & Poor's 500. The systematic risk of an individual asset is then measured by determining the sensitivity of the individual asset's return to changes in the macroeconomic risk factor (stock market index). If the covariance between returns on the asset and the macroeconomy is zero, the asset bears no systematic risk because changes in the macroeconomy do not affect returns on the individual asset. Because the return on most assets positively covaries, at least to some extent, with changes in the macroeconomy, systematic risk cannot be diversified away.

In most empirical applications of the single-factor model, the historical risk of an asset is measured by the covariance between the returns on the asset and the returns on the stock market index that is used as a proxy for systematic risk. This covariance (divided by the variance of the stock market index) is referred to as the investment's beta coefficient, or β_j.[18] The market risk premium, *MRP*, can be measured as the difference between the return on the broad-based stock return index, minus the risk-free rate. The risk premium on the asset being evaluated, RP_j, is calculated as

$$RP_j = \beta_j \times MRP \qquad\qquad (7\text{--}6)$$

With this formulation, RP_j will be determined by the premium earned by all investors for bearing systematic (macroeconomic) risk, *MRP*, times the sensitivity or exposure of the *j*th investment to systematic risk. If $\beta_j = 0$, RP_j will equal zero and the discount rate will equal the risk-free rate. An investment whose return has historically moved one-for-one with the proxy for macroeconomic risk will have a beta equal to one and, therefore, an RP_j equal to the *MRP*. The intuition here is that if an investment is equally as volatile as the macroeconomy (stock market), determined by a $\beta_j = 1$, then the required risk premium on the asset, RP_j, should equal the risk premium on the market.[19]

Multifactor asset-pricing models assume that there are several sources of risk, that large subsets of assets respond to fluctuations in these factors, and that the influence of these risk factors on asset returns cannot be diversified away. That is, these variables or risk factors have been shown to have a systematic effect on asset returns. Thus, investors should expect compensation in the form of an increased expected return for bearing the risk associated with these factors.[20]

SENSITIVITY ANALYSIS

Many of the input variables that determine the after-tax cash flows on an income property cannot be forecasted with certainty over the asset's expected holding period. The standard approach, however, is for investors to use their best guesses, that is, point estimates, for each of the variables for each year of the holding period. For example, if gross rental income in year 1 is estimated at $100,000, and the investor assumes that income will grow 3 percent per year, then the investor assumes gross rental income will be $103,000 in year 2. However, the investor realizes that rental income in year 2 will not be *exactly* equal to $103,000; in fact, the issue of concern to the investor is *how much different* income will be from the $103,000 point estimate. Also we know that other key variable assumptions

---

[18] Beta can be determined statistically by regressing the historical returns of the asset being valued on the historical returns of the stock market index (the proxy for changes in returns due to macroeconomic fluctuations). In the single-factor model, the dependent variable is the actual return on the specific investment over a large number of periods. The independent variable is the actual return on the stock market portfolio. Historical betas for many stocks, including most publicly traded REITs, are listed in several major financial publications (for example, *Value Line*) and are also published by such institutions as Merrill Lynch, the Wharton School, and Wells Fargo Bank. Betas for other investments must be calculated by the investor.

[19] The single-factor model is an empirical application of the capital asset pricing model (CAPM). Development of the CAPM is jointly credited to William Sharpe, John Lintner, and Jan Mossin. See William E. Sharpe, "Capital Asset Prices: A Theory of Market Equilibrium Under Conditions of Risk," *Journal of Finance* 19 (September 1964), pp. 425–42; John Lintner, "The Valuation of Risky Assets and the Selection of Risky Investments in Stock Portfolios and Capital Budgets," *Review of Economics and Statistics* 47 (1965), pp. 13–37; and Jan Mossin, "Equilibrium in a Capital Market," *Econometrica* 34 (1966), pp. 867–87.

[20] For further discussion of single and multifactor pricing models, see Zvi Bodie, Alex Kane, and Alan J. Marcus, *Investments,* 2nd ed. (Burr Ridge, IL: Irwin, 1994), pp. 768–83.

E X H I B I T   7 - 1 4

THE SENSITIVITY OF IRR TO CHANGES IN GROWTH RATES, VACANCIES, AND OPERATING EXPENSES

Growth in Rents and Prices	IRR	Constant Vacancy Rate	IRR	Operating Expenses (% of EGI)	IRR
−1%	2.6%	17%	11.7%	55%	9.0%
1	8.5	13	12.8	50	11.3
3	13.7	10	13.7	45	13.7
5	18.4	7	14.6	40	16.1
7	22.7	3	15.7	35	18.4

such as operating expense levels and future selling prices will not be exactly realized. Intuitively, then, we know that many of the variables in a DCF analysis are subject to some type of probability distribution. Sensitivity analysis is a technique that indicates exactly how much the NPV or IRR of an investment will change in response to a given change in a single input variable.

Sensitivity analysis begins with the expected values (best guesses) for each variable input. This is often referred to as the *base case* solution. To illustrate, recall the input assumptions for the Suburban Office Building in Exhibit 3–3. These base case assumptions, along with an assumed tax rate of 28 percent and a depreciable basis equal to 80 percent of the purchase price, produced the after-tax cash flows from operations (ATCFs) and the after-tax equity reversion (ATER) shown in Exhibits 4–10 and 4–13. The resulting base case, after-debt, after-tax, NPV and IRR of $15,907 and 13.7 percent, respectively, are shown in Exhibit 4–16.

Now we ask a series of "what-if" questions: "What if gross rental income does not increase at the assumed 3 percent annual rate?" "What if operating expenses consume more than 45 percent of gross income?" "What if vacancy rates are higher than the assumed 10 percent level?" Sensitivity analysis can provide the investor with answers to questions such as these.

Exhibit 7–14 shows the sensitivity of the IRR on the Suburban Office Building to variations in these three key input variables. If we are correct about the range of possible outcomes for these variables, variation in the vacancy rate from the assumed 10 percent level will not have a significant effect on the realized IRR, assuming all other input variables are forecasted with complete accuracy. Even if vacancy rates are 17 percent in each year of the five-year holding period, the IRR falls from 13.7 percent to 11.7 percent. However, the estimated IRR is very sensitive to assumptions about the growth rate in rents and resale prices. For example, if rents and prices increase 1 percent rather than 3 percent per year, the IRR will be 8.5 percent instead of 13.7 percent. On the other hand, growth in excess of 3 percent per year will significantly improve the return performance of the Suburban Office Building. The IRR also is fairly sensitive to variations in operating expense levels. For example, if operating expenses consume 55 percent rather than 45 percent of effective gross income, the IRR will fall to 9 percent. Note that computer spreadsheet models are ideally suited for performing sensitivity analysis because such models automatically recalculate IRR and NPV when a variable input is changed.

Although sensitivity analysis is probably the most widely used risk analysis technique, it is not without limitations. Consider the results of the sensitivity analysis presented in Exhibit 7–14. We learned that the IRR would fall to 2.6 percent if rents and resale prices decrease 1 percent per year and would increase to 22.7 percent if 7 percent growth occurs. Thus, we learn that IRRs of 2.6 and 22.7 are *possible*. The analysis, however, does not tell us what is *probable*. For example, a 22.7 percent IRR will occur if annual growth rates equal 7 percent. However, we do not know the probability that 7 percent growth will occur.[21]

Overly conservative cash flow forecasts. DCF analysis requires that the analyst's "best guess" of future cash flows, such as effective gross income and future selling prices, be "plugged into" the DCF equation. If the analyst is relatively uncertain about these "point estimates" of expected future cash flows, the appropriate approach is to "penalize" the uncertain cash flows by using a higher discount rate than would be used with a similar, but less risky, property. In short, an internally consistent application of DCF requires that adjustments for properties perceived to be relatively risky be made in the discount rate, *not* by incorporating overly conservative or "worst-case" cash flow forecasts.

SUMMARY

The term *risk* is synonymous with *variability*. Thus the more variable the returns on an asset such as a real estate investment, the more risky the asset and the lower is its value, all else being the same. Risk in real estate investments can be divided into two broad categories. Systematic risk is the variation in returns caused by general market conditions; unsystematic risk is the variation caused by property-specific sources such as property management. In the traditional method for specifying discount rates known as the risk-adjusted discount-rate approach, risk premiums for systematic and unsystematic risk are subjectively added to a risk-free rate to account for the expected variation in cash flows and returns. These risk premiums are included in the required discount rate to compensate the investor for taking on the systematic and unsystematic risks of the investment.

---

[21] Modified versions of the basic DCF model have been developed that allow the analyst to specify probability distributions, rather than point estimates, on key input variables such as inflation and gross rental income for each year of the expected holding period. The use of probability distributions instead of point estimates for the multiperiod cash inflow and outflows is known as *simulation*. The specification of probability distributions determines both the range of values that certain variables can obtain in any year (minimum to maximum) *and* the likelihood of occurrence of each value within the range. Simulation is not as well understood as sensitivity analysis, but is a potentially powerful tool for the analysis of real estate investment risk. Numerous simulation programs are available for use with popular spreadsheet programs such as LOTUS 1-2-3 and Microsoft Excel. Prominent examples include @RISK and CRYSTAL BALL. The availability and ease of use of these spreadsheet "add-on" simulation programs is starting to produce wider use and acceptance of simulation.

The incorporation of risk analysis into the overall decision-making process for real estate investments includes the specification of investor risk preferences, identification of major investment risks, and risk management. The most crucial of these elements is risk management because it involves measurement of risk. Risk measurement is guided by two alternative perspectives—project-in-isolation risk analysis and portfolio risk analysis.

Project-in-isolation risk analysis focuses on measuring the riskiness of one investment at a time. Since past data are rarely available to calculate the standard deviations of real estate returns, the analysis of risk depends on the use of subjective probability techniques. These techniques allow the analyst to estimate means and standard deviations of returns and thus to interpret the riskiness of an investment. Sensitivity analysis is a popular form of project-in-isolation risk analysis that looks at the effects on returns of changes in one input.

The portfolio concept of risk considers the riskiness of various assets taken together and is a more encompassing framework for risk analysis. Two implications arise from the portfolio concept. First, it allows for virtual elimination of unsystematic risk through asset diversification (naive diversification) and may lead to a lowering of systematic risk (smart diversification). Second, it allows analysts to estimate discount rates objectively through the use of asset pricing models. This extension is of great importance because the subjective specification of discount rates is perhaps a major shortcoming of real estate investment analysis using discounted cash-flow methods.

KEY TERMS

Coefficient of variation 200
Correlated 203
Correlation coefficient 205
Covariance 205
Derived demand 208
Diversifiable 203

Diversification 202
Expected value 193
Mean-variance 203
Mixed-asset portfolio 212
Nondiversifiable 203
Probability distributions 192

Single-factor model 217
Standard deviation 198
Subjective probability
    distributions 192
Unsystematic risk 203
Variance 197

TEST YOURSELF

Answer the following multiple choice questions:

1. Most investors are
   a. Risk averse.
   b. Risk neutral.
   c. Risk lovers.
   d. None of the above.

2. The coefficient of variation
   a. Provides an absolute measure of risk.
   b. Provides a relative measure of risk.
   c. Is affected by the correlation of asset returns on cash flows.
   d. Both a and c.

   e. Both b and c.

3. When the returns on an asset are more volatile than the returns on the market portfolio (index), the beta of the asset is
   a. Greater than zero but less than one.
   b. Greater than one.
   c. Less than one.
   d. Less than zero.
   e. None of the above.

4. What type of risk can be eliminated from a portfolio of real estate holdings if the various holdings have returns that are less than perfectly correlated?

a. Unsystematic (diversifiable) risk.
b. Systematic risk.
c. Beta risk.
d. Security risk.

5. Combining assets in a portfolio so that the risk of the portfolio is less than the sum of the risks of each individual asset is called
a. Subjective probability analysis.
b. Risk measurements.
c. Risk aversion.
d. Diversification.
e. Capital asset pricing.

6. Risk management includes all of the following except
a. Transferring risks.

b. Measuring risks.
c. Diversification.
d. Purchasing insurance.
e. Risk management includes all of the above.

7. The availability of positive NPV investments in a particular market is _____ related to how competitive the market is and how well it functions.
a. Positively.
b. Negatively.
c. Not.

8. If the calculated covariance between two assets is positive, the correlation coefficient
a. Is always positive.
b. Is always negative.
c. Could be positive or negative.

PROBLEMS FOR THOUGHT AND SOLUTION

1. The positive relationship between risk and return is often misunderstood. Does it mean you are guaranteed a higher return when you undertake a riskier investment? Explain.

2. List some examples of diversifiable risk that are site specific.

3. Discuss and explain how sensitivity analysis works. Why would you consider doing sensitivity analysis on a proposed investment?

4. What are the primary tools that investors can employ to reduce the variability of returns on their real estate investments?

5. Distinguish between systematic and unsystematic risk. List some examples of each.

6. Explain the difference between naive diversification and efficient diversification.

7. In a competitive market, what type of risk can investors expect to be compensated for in the form of a higher expected return?

8. What is an investment's beta coefficient?

9. Distinguish between single-factor asset-pricing models and multifactor asset-pricing models.

10. Define environmental risk and include several examples.

CASE PROBLEMS

1. Consider the following two investments:

Investment A		Investment B	
Return	Probability	Return	Probability
3%	0.10	4%	0.05
5	0.20	5	0.25
8	0.40	6	0.40
10	0.20	7	0.25
12	0.10	8	0.05

a. Calculate the expected return on each investment.
b. Calculate the variance and standard deviation of each.
c. Calculate the coefficient of variation for each investment. When may it be useful to calculate?
d. Which investment do you prefer, using the mean-variance rule?

2. You are considering the purchase of a small residential rental property for $200,000 in equity. You feel there are three possible scenarios for future cash flows and appreciation:

> **Pessimistic**—The after-tax cash flow (ATCF) will be $20,000 in the first year, then decrease 3 percent per year over a six-year holding period. The after-tax proceeds from sale (ATER) will be $180,000.
>
> **Most likely**—The ATCF from operations will be $20,000 per year for the next six years and the ATER will be $200,000.
>
> **Optimistic**—The ATCF from operations will be $20,000 in the first year and then increase 4 percent over the six-year holding period. The ATER at the end of year 6 will be $230,000.

You believe there is a 25 percent probability that the pessimistic scenario will occur, a 50 percent probability for the most likely scenario, and a 25 percent probability for the optimistic scenario.

a. Compute the IRR for each scenario.

b. Compute the expected IRR.

c. Compute the variance and standard deviations of the IRRs.

3. Consider the following historical returns on two investments:

REALIZED RETURN

Year	Investment A	Investment B
1991	3%	−7%
1992	10	−1
1993	−2	10
1994	−6	3
1995	15	12

Calculate the following:

a. Mean return on investment A.

b. Variance of return on investment A.

c. Standard deviation of return on investment A.

d. Mean return on investment B.

e. Variance of return on investment B.

f. Standard deviation of return on investment B.

g. Covariance of the returns on A and B.

h. Correlation coefficient between A and B.

i. Standard deviation of return on a portfolio that consisted of 50 percent A and 50 percent B.

ADDITIONAL READINGS

Most textbooks on real estate investment have one or more chapters on risk and real estate investment. Examples include these:

Jaffe, Austin J., and C. F. Sirmans. *Fundamentals of Real Estate Investment.* Upper Saddle River, NJ: Prentice Hall, 1995.

Greer, Gaylon E. *Investment Analysis for Real Estate Decisions*, 3rd ed. Chicago: Dearborn Financial Publishing, 1997.

Brueggeman, William B., and Jeffrey D. Fisher. *Real Estate Finance and Investment*, 10th ed. Burr Ridge, IL: Irwin, 1997.

Pyhrr, Stephen, et al. *Real Estate Investment.* New York: John Wiley & Sons, 1989.

Many corporate finance and investment textbooks treat risk in more detail than this chapter. See, for example, these books:

Bodie, Zvi; Alex Kane; and Alan J. Marcus. *Investments*, 3rd ed. Burr Ridge, IL: Irwin, 1996.

Ross, Stephen A.; Randolph W. Westerfield; and Jeffrey F. Jaffe. *Corporate Finance*, 4th ed. Burr Ridge, IL: Irwin, 1996.

C H A P T E R

MANAGEMENT OF THE SPACE AND ASSETS

THE IMPORTANCE OF REAL ESTATE MANAGEMENT
  Management Responsibilities and
    Relationships

THE VALUE PERSPECTIVE OF MANAGEMENT
  Creating Cash Flow
  Maintaining Cash Flow
  Cash Flow Risk

CONTRACTS INVOLVED IN MANAGING SPACE AND ASSETS
  Management Contracts: Separating
    Ownership and Management
  The Nature of Leases
  Residential Leases
  Commercial Property Leases

Specific Lease Contracts
Lease Economics: *A Value Perspective*

SPECIAL TOPIC: CORPORATE REAL ESTATE MANAGEMENT
  Sale-and-Leaseback Decisions
  The Lease versus Own Decision

SUMMARY

KEY TERMS

TEST YOURSELF

PROBLEMS FOR THOUGHT AND SOLUTION

CASE PROBLEMS

ADDITIONAL READINGS

After reading this chapter, students will be able to:

1. Explain the role and importance of property, asset, and portfolio management to real estate owners.

2. Discuss how real estate management affects cash flows and values.

3. Discuss the details of agency problems in real estate management.

4. List the requirements of a lease to judge its validity.

5. Identify typical provisions in residential, commercial property, and ground leases.

6. Value leasehold interests.

7. Perform the financial analysis required for decisions made by corporate real estate managers.

THE IMPORTANCE OF REAL ESTATE MANAGEMENT

Direct investment in properties requires far more management than investment in corporate stocks, bonds, and real estate securities. Properties need maintenance, repair, and periodic renovation; rents must be collected, expenses paid, and new users found when the users of space leave. These responsibilities overlay investment management activities that come with ownership of any asset, such as buying, selling, and forming portfolios. Owners sometimes choose *active* roles in all aspects of forming their real estate portfolios and managing their real estate investments. Some owners elect to handle the management of investments themselves, then hire firms to manage the property, whereas other owners take *passive* roles in property *and* investment management.

As noted in Chapter 1, ownership of commercial real estate in the United States becomes more and more concentrated in institutions and corporations each year. Significant trends of the past few years—securitization of real estate, lender possession of real estate through foreclosure, and the enormous flow of investment capital to pension and mutual funds—have led to greater institutional ownership of real estate during recent years. Institutions, especially pension funds, and corporations normally take passive routes to their involvement in real estate by hiring outside managers, whereas individual owners more often choose active involvement in management. Outside managers continue to grow in number as demand grows for their services. Many development companies moved into real estate management and now generate revenues by serving as outside

EXHIBIT 8 - 1

REAL ESTATE MANAGEMENT FOR A CHICAGO RETAIL PROPERTY

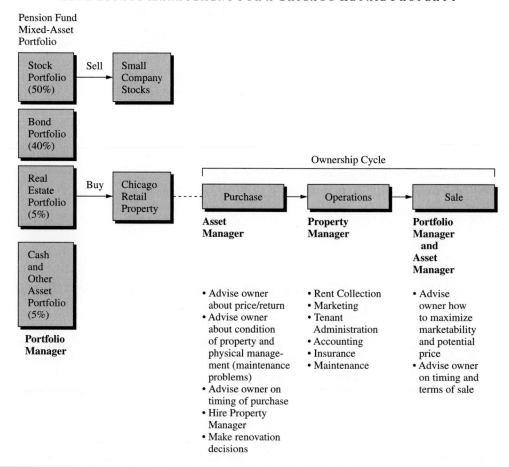

managers. Today, real estate management comes in three flavors: portfolio, asset, and property management.

MANAGEMENT RESPONSIBILITIES AND RELATIONSHIPS

Exhibit 8–1 outlines the responsibilities and relationships among the three types of managers employed by passive owners of real estate. Generally, **portfolio managers** advise owners of investment portfolios about the kinds of investments needed to fulfill portfolio objectives for return and risk, as discussed in Chapter 7. **Asset managers** analyze investment opportunities, assist in acquiring assets, assure that assets remain productive during ownership, and assist in asset sales. **Property managers** oversee the day-to-day activities of real estate, such as rent collection, physical maintenance, and space user relations. This unique division of labor in real estate management occurs because of the unsecuritized, real asset characteristics of real estate. Unlike stocks and bonds, real estate investment and ownership entails detailed knowledge in a variety of specialized subjects, such as location analysis, environmental regulation, and building engineering.

The United States pension fund portrayed in Exhibit 8–1 currently maintains an investment portfolio comprised of 50 percent stocks, 40 percent bonds, 5 percent real estate, and 5 percent cash and other assets. The portfolio manager, the money management unit of a life insurance company hired by the pension fund as a consultant, advises the pension to divest of some of its stock in small companies and increase its real estate holdings. An examination of the pension's real estate portfolio reveals an imbalance that indicates the need for a large (over $10 million) retail shopping center in a major midwestern metropolitan area, such as Chicago.

Portfolio management.   Portfolio managers view assets in a larger context than only one asset. For real estate investments, managers are concerned about the return and risk of a single property investment opportunity and how they affect the performance of both the entire mixed-asset portfolio and the component real estate portfolio. The techniques of portfolio analysis suggested in Chapter 7 assist portfolio managers in monitoring the performance of the existing portfolio and discovering inconsistencies with the performance objectives of owners. As shown in Exhibit 8–1, the responsibilities of portfolio managers begin and end with recommendations for asset dispositions and acquisitions; however, in many situations portfolio management and real estate asset management occur within the same firm.[1]

Asset management.   Exhibit 8–2 shows some of the top 10 asset managers in the United States real estate during 1996. What responsibilities do these firms handle for their client owners? As shown in Exhibit 8–1, the asset manager's first task involves working with real estate brokers and owners to find potential retail property investments that satisfy the scale and location objectives established by the portfolio manager. The asset manager, a subsidiary of the same life insurance company performing the portfolio management, advises the pension fund investment committee on the purchase price, physical condition, and terms of purchase for each potential investment. Two retail centers for sale in Chicago satisfy the portfolio requirements. The recommendation: purchase The Big Shoulders Mall for $9.5 million (asking price, $10 million), either require as a condition of sale that the seller repair all cracks in the parking areas or adjust the sale price at closing for these

---

[1] See books by Hudson-Wilson and Wurtzebach, and Pagliari listed at the end of this chapter for additional information.

EXHIBIT 8 - 2

TOP 10 ASSET MANAGERS

Company	Location of Headquarters	Millions of Square Feet of Office Space Under Management
Equitable Real Estate Investment Mgt., Inc.	Atlanta	99
Heitman/JMB Advisory Corp.	Chicago	66
Hines	Houston	63
Lincoln Property Company	Dallas	37
Jones Land Wooten USA	New York	23
Paragon Group and Affiliates	Dallas	16
Aldrich, Eastman, and Waltch	Boston	15
The RREEF Funds	San Francisco	14
M S Management Services	Chicago	14
Koll	Newport Beach, CA	10

SOURCE: *Real Estate Forum*, "Annual Directory of Top Asset Managers" (March 1996), pp. 45–53.

repairs, and attempt to complete the purchase before the end-of-year holiday season. In addition, the asset manager recommends hiring Sandburg Property Management of Chicago to handle day-to-day management. A detailed plan of capital improvements prepared by the asset manager and Sandburg gives the pension fund an idea about upcoming expenditures to keep the center financially viable. At the end of the holding period, perhaps 10 years in the future, the asset manager will advise the pension fund about marketing the property and terms of the sale.

Property management. Exhibit 8–3 shows the top 10 property management firms. What exactly do these firms and the hundreds of smaller firms like Sandburg do to earn fees? Property managers carry responsibility for all aspects of the physical space in accordance with the asset manager's plan. In the agreement between the asset manager and Sandburg, Sandburg's responsibilities include marketing and leasing, maintenance and repairs, tenant relations, insurance, accounting, human resource management, and providing timely information to the asset manager about events affecting the property.

THE VALUE PERSPECTIVE OF MANAGEMENT

Real estate owners want it all! They want the highest possible cash flows from their properties this year and they want cash flows to continually increase so that they reach the highest possible levels during future years. If this occurs, owners achieve maximum returns on investment and maximize the values of their properties. The goals of owners also should represent the goals of real estate managers, although as discussed later in this

EXHIBIT 8-3

TOP 10 PROPERTY MANAGERS

Rank (1996) and Company	Location of Headquarters	Millions of Square Feet Managed for a Fee
Colliers International Property Consultants, Inc.	Boston	360
Insignia Financial Group, Inc.	Greenville	330.23
Trammell Crow Co.	Dallas	226
Heitman Properties, Ltd.	Chicago	186.36
New America Management	Dallas	183
Koll, The Real Estate Services, Co.	Newport Beach, CA	172
LaSalle Partners, Ltd.	Chicago	154.9
Compass Mgmt. & Leasing, Inc.	Atlanta	148
CB Commercial Real Estate Group Inc.	Los Angeles	125.15
Cushman & Wakefield Inc.	New York	110
PM Realty Group	Houston	110
Lincoln Property Co.	Dallas	80

SOURCE: *Commercial Property News,* August 1, 1996, pp. 21, 23.

chapter, goals sometimes diverge. If the goals of owners and managers align, then managers narrowly define their jobs as creating cash flow, maintaining cash flow, and managing variations in cash flow to enhance the value of properties. In this way, they adopt a *value perspective* of real estate management.

CREATING CASH FLOW

Creating cash flow means creating value, and creating value dominates the other goals of management in any business. Creating cash flow through management of real estate occurs in many ways. Most importantly, managers must know the specific objectives on which to focus, they must know the market possibilities, and they must anticipate and evaluate the effects of change.

What objectives? Reduced to a simple definition, cash flow results from the difference between income and expenses. Accordingly, should managers devote their attention to income generation or expense control? Although managers tend to first concentrate on easily corrected problems, such as out-of-control expense, the potential returns from focusing on income generation often exceed those from controlling expenses, as the following example demonstrates.

Panel A in Exhibit 8–4 presents a cash flow statement for a 250-unit apartment property that currently provides its owners with $500,000 cash flow before debt service payments, or net operating income (NOI). The owners feel that management should

---

EXHIBIT 8 - 4

CREATING CASH FLOW IN AN APARTMENT PROPERTY

Panel A: Initial Conditions

Potential gross income	$1,250,000	
Less: Vacancy (20%)	250,000	
Effective gross income		1,000,000
Less: Controllable expenses	350,000	
Less: Uncontrollable expenses	150,000	
Net operating income (NOI)		$500,000

Panel B: Focus on Expense Control

Potential gross income	$1,250,000	
Less: Vacancy (20%)	250,000	
Effective gross income		1,000,000
Less: Controllable expenses	**315,000**	
Less: Uncontrollable expenses	150,000	
NOI		$535,000

Panel C: Focus on Income Generation

Potential gross income	$1,250,000	
Less: Vacancy (14.4%)	**180,000**	
Effective gross income		1,070,000
Less: Controllable expenses	350,000	
Less: Uncontrollable expenses	150,000	
NOI		$570,000

---

increase NOI by 10 to 15 percent. Management immediately embarks on a cost-cutting campaign that results in a 10 percent reduction in controllable expenses, as shown in Panel B. This approach only increases NOI by 7 percent, to $535,000. After firing management, the owners learn from an audit that if management has spent the same amount of time reducing vacancy through aggressive marketing, vacancy loss would likely decline to $180,000 (14.4 percent) and NOI would increase to $570,000, a 14 percent gain, as shown in Panel C.

Knowing the market.   The results from the previous example happen in markets in which lowering vacancy occurs without lowering rent. Under more typical market conditions, does lowering rent so that vacancy loss equals zero provide owners with the greatest cash flow? Beginning economics students learn that total revenues of the firm equal the prices of goods sold multiplied by the quantity of goods sold. If the good is space, then total cash flow comes from multiplying the amount of rent charged by the amount of space rented. Logic dictates that maximum cash flow occurs when all space becomes occupied and the occupants pay the highest rent the market will bear. Should asset and property managers follow this rule?

EXHIBIT   8 - 5

CREATING CASH FLOW THROUGH RENT AND OCCUPANCY MANAGEMENT

Panel A

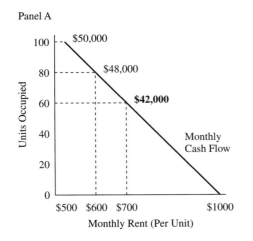

Panel B

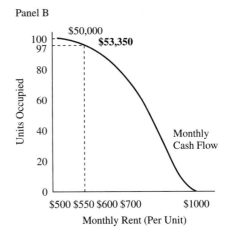

The Compartments Apartments REIT owns a 100-unit complex in Washington, DC. Finding the current monthly cash flow of $42,000 (60 occupied units at $700 monthly rent) unsatisfactory, Compartments hires Salvation Property Management to boost cash flow through rent and occupancy management. As shown in Exhibit 8–5, Panel A, Salvation recommends lowering the rent to $500, thus increasing the complex to full occupancy and monthly cash flow to $50,000. If a relationship exists as in Panel B, then maximum cash flow of $53,350 occurs at $550 rent with 97 occupied units, and Salvation erred.

The relationship between rent and occupancy varies from market to market and over time. Professional property managers usually have sufficient day-to-day experience in the market to judge the effect of changes in rents on the occupancy of properties.

Property renovation and repositioning.   Real estate managers encounter a multitude of opportunities to create cash flow by responding to changes in market conditions through making physical and other alterations to properties. Some common responses include major renovations of apartment properties, adjusting the tenant mix of retail centers, and changing the franchise affiliations of hotels. Major changes to properties designed to create cash flow should not be confused with minor changes intended to maintain cash flow, as discussed in the next section.

Any change costs money. Successful changes bring in more money than they cost. Therefore, the management's recommendations to owners about property renovations and repositioning follow from applications of the tools of financial analysis developed in Chapters 2 and 3. In the example that follows, we demonstrate an approach to a renovation decision using relatively simple financial analysis tools. A more complete analysis appears in real estate finance text.[2]

The Middle Center, a successful retail mall in the Midwest, generates $200,000 each year in income for its owners before debt payments (NOI). Income growth will slow from 2 percent annually to 1 percent unless the owners invest $500,000 to renovate the property. After renovation, income growth should increase by 3 percent annually. Core Management, the asset manager, performed the following analysis to convince the owners that renovation makes economic sense:

Value of Middle *without* renovation

Current NOI	$200,000
Growth rate of NOI	1%
Current capitalization rate	10%
Value $200,000/(.10–.01)	$2,222,222

Value of Middle *with* renovation

Current NOI	$200,000
Growth rate of NOI	3%
Current capitalization rate	10%
Value $200,000/(.10–.03)	$2,857,143

Value change due to renovation	$634,921 ($2,857,143–$2,222,222)
Cost of renovation	500,000
Net change in owner wealth	$134,921

MAINTAINING CASH FLOW

Although properties differ, general management principles apply to all real estate. Successful real estate managers understand that maintenance of cash flow depends on marketing the space, establishing good relations with space users, and efficient administration. These responsibilities primarily rest with the property management firm.

Marketing rental space. Even though rental of commercial space differs in many respects from rental of residential space, marketing both requires the same steps: analysis of effective demand at various rent levels, the skillful use of selling techniques, credit and financial analysis of prospective tenants, and economic analysis of the profitability from potential tenants. Often, the most likely tenants occupy nearby buildings. **Concentric marketing,** which involves promotions to neighboring space users, represents one component of comprehensive marketing programs designed to maintain cash flow. Other components include general advertising, publicity, and sales promotion.

Often commercial property management gives too little thought to naming properties and creating a thematic image around which to gear promotional activities. A **thematic image** capitalizes on the property name and unique architectural style or relies on logo types, signs, and colors in the promotional materials and activities designed to lure prospective clients to the site (see Real Estate Focus 8–1).

---

[2] See William B. Brueggeman and Jeffrey D. Fisher, *Real Estate Finance and Investments* (Burr Ridge, IL: Richard D. Irwin, 1997), 10th ed., pp. 483–86.

REAL ESTATE FOCUS 8-1

A Real Estate Company's Thematic Image

The logo of the Landmarks Group, a crystal bouquet, represents an expanding and upward-looking source of light. All advertising, promotional materials, and communications utilize the logo to tie together members of the group and to represent the group to the outside world.

At Tampa Bay Park, We Make Our Mark By Helping Other Companies Make Theirs.

The Landmarks Group

After selecting a thematic image, management implements a promotional program that emphasizes the theme. Signs and advertising brochures anchor these programs, which usually require a budget of 3 to 5 percent of effective gross income. Property managers sometimes use direct-mail advertising. Candidate lists come, for example, from photographing the directories in the lobbies of other buildings in the market area. Some experts believe that one half of those who sign leases do so because they received a favorable impression when viewing the property. If true, the best advertisement becomes a well-maintained property.

Marketing managers gain an advantage by learning the names of decision makers in the firm with space needs and their favorite activities or sports. For example, the pictures and artifacts in a person's office tell a great deal about their interests. By discussing the activity or capitalizing on it in other ways, managers develop invaluable personal rapport.

Showing property represents a key step in property merchandising. Professional property managers instruct resident managers and leasing agents on proper showing techniques. Highlighting building features and amenities, stressing the quality of tenants, and avoiding superfluous remarks characterize professional space presentations.

Relations with space users. Space users, the foundation of cash flow, represent the owners' greatest asset. A well-developed, customer-oriented policy toward tenants to assure steady cash flow consists of a tenant selection policy, an ongoing tenant relations program, and a rent collection program. Professional tenant administration seeks to reduce vacancies and tenant turnover, produce a compatible group of tenants, and lower rent-collection expenses. Some general guidelines for evaluating the quality of prospective tenants include the following:

- *Creditworthiness*—Before selecting any tenant, property managers should obtain credit reports. These reports, available today from several companies at reasonable cost, reflect directly on the tenants' capacity to pay. Employment levels, sales volume, and other income characteristics of tenants may require substantiation using these reports.
- *Tenant compatibility*—Selection of new tenants should depend on compatibility with existing tenants. Retail and commercial prospects should be considered only if they complement businesses already occupying space.
- *Permanence potential*—By carefully evaluating the staying power of prospects, lower vacancy rates and other administrative costs result. Apartment applications reveal frequency of moves and job changes. Bank references and testimonials from business associates provide similar information on commercial and industrial prospects.

Dissatisfied tenants present serious problems. In most cases, a poor relationship between the landlord and tenants stems from misunderstandings. In addition to a written statement covering the fundamental points of the original agreement between the two parties, managers should explain rent-collection policies, review the operating regulations of the property, discuss the methods of enforcing them, and make certain tenants understand maintenance policies and the division of responsibilities between the owner and tenant. These policies and procedures ideally appear in tenant brochures.

Rent collection on a monthly basis remains a nearly universal practice, usually on the first day of each month. In a well-run real estate management office, more than 75 percent of all rents due come in on the first day of each month. Tenants pay their rent as promptly as the efficiency, effectiveness, and reasonableness of the collection policy permits. If property managers do not act immediately in situations of delinquency, tenants lose a sense of responsibility. Procedures for taking action against tenants who fail to meet their rental obligations forestall problems. Actions usually entail sending reminder notices to delinquents and initiating legal action, called *eviction,* to remove tenants, who do not respond.[3]

Administration. Property managers prepare annual budgets that include all anticipated income and expense items. Monthly operating statements include all operating in-

---

[3] State laws govern how eviction occurs.

come from sources such as unit rents, parking, swimming pool, washing machines, dryers, and vending machines. Operating statements also include all operating expenses and debt service. They allow owners to review the cash flow performance and the percentage of the budget spent to date, thus providing budgetary control as well as cash control. A maintenance program provides the services and repairs necessary to preserve investments while satisfying and providing for the well-being of tenants. A complete maintenance program incorporates four types of maintenance activities:

1. *Physical integrity*—Property managers bear responsibility for assuring that each element of the physical structure functions as it should. These structural elements require attention: walks, driveways, parking areas, foundations, exterior walls, stairways, roofs, interior walls, and gutters.
2. *Functional performance*—Managers carry major responsibilities to assure the functioning of the property's mechanical equipment. This equipment usually demands maintenance attention: heating, ventilating, and air-conditioning (HVAC) systems; plumbing; electrical systems; elevators; locks and security systems; laundries; storage areas; and swimming pools and other recreational amenities.
3. *Housekeeping and cleanliness*—The readiness and capability of the separate cleaning and maintenance staffs in responding to tenant requests for service affect a building's reputation.
4. *Merchandising*—Because investment properties succeed on the marketing of the space, certain maintenance operations occur solely for merchandising reasons. Items such as a carpeted lobby, well-landscaped grounds, and the use of color inside and outside buildings may not create greater functionality, but may increase marketability.

CASH FLOW RISK

A former football coach of the University of Texas once said "When a team passes the football three things can happen (completion, incompletion, and interception), and two of them are bad!" The real estate manager seeking to increase cash flow essentially "passes on every play." Outright interruptions and declines in cash flow occur for a multitude of reasons other than adverse changes in market conditions. Some of these reasons include fires, natural disasters, environmental problems, legal actions, power outages, computer malfunctions, vandalism, and even events occurring at neighboring properties. At the expense of overextending football analogies, owners and managers of real estate implement three defensive alignments against attacks on cash flow: portfolio management, contracting, and risk management.

• *Portfolio management*—As discussed in Chapter 7, certain diversifiable risks nearly vanish if owners assemble portfolios of assets possessing different cash flow patterns. In the real estate portfolio, diversification usually occurs by owning several properties of different types and locations. Take, for example, events at neighboring properties. An event, such as the adjacent property's manager allowing garbage to pile up for several months, will negatively influence cash flow as tenants leave. However, events such as the development of a rose garden on the adjacent property will positively affect cash flow as tenants find their space more pleasant. With enough properties in a portfolio, the positive influences cancel out negative influences on cash flow.

- *Contracting*—Owners find some protection from financial claims by tenants when disruptive events occur through insertion of clauses in their lease contracts with tenants that protect owners against legal actions. Nevertheless, the compensation and protection insurance policies and leases provide may not offset the total loss experienced by owners when disaster strikes. The losses incurred by the owners of downtown properties from the "Great Chicago Flood" on April 13, 1993, for example, far exceeded the financial protection afforded by their insurance and lease contracts.[4] Sometimes, however, owners become fully compensated for losses of the physical property due to disaster with replacement cost insurance.

- *Risk management*— Insurance contracts transfer risk from property owners to insurance companies. In the practice of modern risk management, risk transfer constitutes only one part of a risk-management program. The other major part is risk abatement. In 1980, a deadly and destructive fire struck the Stouffers-Westchester Hotel north of New York City, and 26 persons died. Investigators discovered, among other things, that several combustible items (e.g., coat racks) were placed near the only exit from the affected meeting rooms. Once the fire struck these items, people were unable to reach the exit. Inspections by management might have corrected this practice and saved lives. Regular property inspections designed to uncover sources of risk represent the most important element of risk-abatement programs.

CONTRACTS INVOLVED IN MANAGING SPACE AND ASSETS

Exhibit 8–6 shows the various contracts typically structured by the owners and managers of commercial real estate. Passive owners of large properties contract with portfolio managers and asset managers jointly or separately, and asset managers contract with property managers. Owners of smaller properties often contract directly with property managers. Asset and property managers generally work together to sign tenants to lease contracts. Finally, property managers initiate contracts with suppliers of the products and services needed to run properties. In this section, we investigate some of the many details about management contracts and leases.

---

[4] For an interesting account of the effects of this disaster, see Micheal F. Csar "Damming the Risk," *Real Estate Finance Journal* (Summer 1993), pp. 56–61.

EXHIBIT 8-6

CONTRACTS IN REAL ESTATE MANAGEMENT

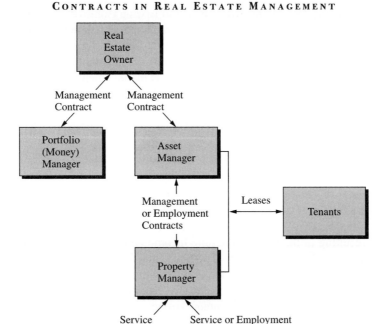

MANAGEMENT CONTRACTS: SEPARATING OWNERSHIP AND MANAGEMENT

The existence of management contracts means that owners of real estate give up a certain amount of control of their properties to managers. More formally, management contracts establish *agency relationships* between the parties in which managers have *fiduciary responsibilities* to owners. The agency relationship and fiduciary responsibility simply mean that managers must act in the best interest of owners, and not in their own best interest to the detriment of owners. Could management ever act in its own best interest at the expense of owners? Certainly, agency problems have gained considerable notoriety in corporation finance as shareholders (owners) attempt to forestall the self-interested behavior of top management.[5] Violation of fiduciary responsibilities constitutes violation of the

---

[5] See Stephen A. Ross, Randolph W. Westerfield, and Bradford D. Jordan, *Fundamentals of Corporate Finance* (Burr Ridge, IL: Richard D. Irwin, 1995), pp. 10–14.

Laws of Agency in each state. The brokerage contract between sellers of property and real estate brokers also establishes agency relationships. Details about the Laws of Agency appear in Chapter 23, "Real Estate Brokerage and Listing Contracts."

Management contracts contain many provisions that describe the responsibilities of managers and the limits of their authority. Property managers, for example, usually maintain broad control over the routine leasing activities in apartment properties. For leasing of office space, the responsibility often lies with asset management and may require owner approval due to the monetary amount and length of office leases. Management contracts frequently restrict management's ability to borrow funds in the names of the owners or properties, change accounting policies, determine timing of payments to owners, and commit owners to the sale of properties.[6]

Compensation and incentives to reduce agency problems. The agency problem reduces to a question of whether management gets more money and other benefits than it is entitled to, called *perk extraction,* or does less than called for in the contract, called *shirking.* The management contract should contain incentives for managers to work hard for owners, resulting in the highest possible income and asset value. Management compensation arrangements serve as the most powerful tool for creating the correct incentives.

Property managers usually receive compensation based on property income, but which income—potential gross income, effective gross income, net operating income, or before-tax cash flow?[7] The literature contains strong conceptual arguments and statistical findings for basing fees on NOI and not on rent collected (EGI), as traditionally done in the industry.[8] In Exhibit 8–4, we showed that property management should focus attention first on lowering vacancy, then on lowering expenses. Exhibit 8–7 shows the same example with a 3 percent management fee on EGI and a 6 percent fee on NOI. Both the owner and manager remain better off if the manager focuses on rent collections *if* the manager keeps expenses at the same level (Panel C). However, if the manager spends an extra $50,000 on advertising as shown in Panel D, then the manager's compensation does not change if fees are based on EGI, but the owner becomes worse off. Herein lies the essence of the real estate management agency problem. The lesson is that setting income-based management fees as a percentage of EGI does not create incentives for managers to control operating expenses while attempting to boost rental income. Basing fees on NOI creates the correct incentives, although the incentives of the owner and manager never become perfectly aligned.

Portfolio and asset managers typically receive compensation based on asset values—approximately .5 to 1.5 percent of the value of assets under management. Although the

---

[6] For a detailed discussion of management contracts, see Tanis Reid and Robert A. Maniscalco, "Commercial Property Management Contracts: A Primer," *Real Estate Review* 22 (Spring 1991), pp. 91–96.

[7] Other less common compensation arrangements include flat fees and fees based on square footage under management.

[8] Austin J. Jaffe, "A Reexamination of the Problem of Management Fee Assessment," *Journal of Property Management* (January-February 1979), pp. 39–47 and Sidney B. Rosenberg and John B. Corgel, "Agency Costs in Apartment Property Management Contracts," *American Real Estate and Urban Economics Journal* 18 (Summer 1990), pp. 184–202.

EXHIBIT   8 - 7

**CREATING CASH FLOW IN AN APARTMENT PROPERTY
INCLUDING MANAGEMENT FEES**

			Management Fee
Panel A: Initial Conditions			
Potential gross income	$1,250,000		
Less: Vacancy (20%)	250,000		
Effective gross income		1,000,000	$30,000 (3%)
Less: Controllable expenses	350,000		
Less: Uncontrollable expenses	150,000		
Net operating income (NOI)		$500,000	30,000 (6%)
Panel B: Focus on Expense Control			
Potential gross income	$1,250,000		
Less: Vacancy (20%)	250,000		
Effective gross income		1,000,000	30,000
Less: Controllable expenses	315,000		
Less: Uncontrollable expenses	150,000		
NOI		$535,000	32,100
Panel C: Focus on Income Generation			
Potential gross income	$1,250,000		
Less: Vacancy (14.4%)	180,000		
Effective gross income		1,070,000	32,100
Less: Controllable expenses	350,000		
Less: Uncontrollable expenses	150,000		
NOI		$570,000	34,200
Panel D: Focus on Income Generation *but at the Expense of Expenses*			
Potential gross income	$1,250,000		
Less: Vacancy (14.4%)	180,000		
Effective gross income		1,070,000	32,100
Less: Controllable expenses	**400,000**		
Less: Uncontrollable expenses	150,000		
NOI		$520,000	31,200

---

same kinds of agency problems inherent in income-based fees do not exist, value-based compensation presents a different set of problems. Because of the infrequency of real estate sales, appraisals determine the values for compensation purposes. The duration between appraisals, how much management contributes to value changes, managers not selling properties at appropriate times because of losing fees, and who pays for appraisals emerge as some of the issues with value-based compensation.[9]

---

[9] In addition, Stephen E. Roulac, "How to Structure Real Estate Investment Management," *Journal of Portfolio Management* (Fall 1981), pp. 32–35 argues that certain activities under the responsibility of portfolio and asset managers, such as acquiring properties, require greater effort and expertise than operating responsibilities and thus should have higher percentage fees. A similar argument by Kenneth A. Shearer, "Computing Management Fees," *Journal of Property Management* (September-October 1993), pp. 50–51 suggests that management fees should relate more closely to the cost of providing the management instead of being based on income, value, square footage, or some other property measure.

EXHIBIT 8-8

THE LEASE CONTRACT

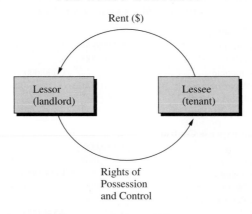

Rent ($)

Lessor (landlord)

Lessee (tenant)

Rights of
Possession
and Control

THE NATURE OF LEASES

A lease creates a contractual relationship between the owners of real estate and the users of space. The lease specifies the rights and obligations of owners and users and legally divides the bundle of rights in real estate into two interests called the **leased fee estate** of owners and the **leasehold estate** of users. Chapter 20 discusses these estates in greater detail. As shown in Exhibit 8–8, owners, also known as lessors and landlords, obtain rights through leases to collect rent for set terms and regain control of properties at the end of the terms in the same condition, except for reasonable wear and tear. The users, also known as lessees and tenants, obtain rights to use properties for the lease terms.

While leases usually appear as written documents, state laws specify which circumstances require written leases. Generally, only leases of more than one year must be written to be enforceable in court. Also, the courts can interpret leases as either contracts or conveyances because they convey a major right of property ownership—the exclusive right of occupancy and use— from owners to tenants. The practical significance of this decision lies in the legal remedies available in case of disputes. If defined as contracts, the legal remedies for violations include the rights to sue for damages or specific performance, as well as the right to abrogate leases. If regarded as conveyances, the remedy for either party becomes only termination of leases and return of property to lessors. Courts in different states vary considerably in their interpretations of leases, but the modern trend is to regard leases more as contracts than as conveyances.

For violations, such as an apartment owner failing to maintain the property in a habitable condition, the lessee's most efficient remedy involves moving and not paying the rent. Conditions under which tenants in residential leases may withhold rent or make repairs and alterations with rent money follow from state landlord-tenant laws and court rulings. On the other side, if a tenant fails to pay the rent, the owner can, through the legal procedures in each state, have the tenant evicted. **Eviction** terminates the rights of the lessee to the property.[10]

Rights and obligations of owners and tenants.   Leases create rights and obligations for both lessors and lessees. For residential leases, the obligations of lessors extend beyond lease contracts as the result of court rulings and state statutes. Any lease gives lessors the right to rent and to receive properties back at the end of leases, which is termed **reversion.** Residential lessors' obligations, as mentioned above, include keeping the property in a safe and habitable condition. Other rights that cannot be waived in residential leases include privacy from unreasonable entry by lessors and cancellation of leases in case fire or other hazards destroy properties.

"Safe and habitable condition" definitions in local housing codes and state landlord-tenant laws assist the courts in determining violations of tenants' rights. In some cases, tenants have successfully withheld rents from landlords, if they place the rents in a trust or escrow account until landlords remedy the unsafe or uninhabitable conditions. In other instances, especially in emergencies, tenants may legally use rent payments to make repairs.

Unreasonable entry by the lessors also becomes a matter of judgment. Clearly, frequent entry, such as more than once a month, or entry at inconvenient times, such as during the night, for nonemergency reasons constitutes harassment. Leases often permit entry during the last month of a lease to show the property to prospective tenants and for routine maintenance. Even under these provisions, entries must occur at reasonable times and in acceptable frequencies.

Most residential leases contain provisions regarding the tenant's obligations in the event of property destruction. Tenants do not need to pay for services not received. If lessors provide equally acceptable substitute quarters during property restoration, lessees must continue paying rent. In the absence of such arrangements, however, lease cancellation occurs.

Valid and enforceable leases.   The requirements of valid leases resemble the requirements of valid contracts and property conveyance, such as deeds discussed in Chapter 22. If the required elements appear in the lease, then it is valid. For enforcement by the courts, other factors may be considered. The length of most residential leases equals one or two pages, whereas many commercial leases consist of 50 pages or more of complex provisions. Nevertheless valid and enforceable leases regardless of property type usually contain the following elements:

- *Names of lessors and lessees*—Names should appear and both parties
   should sign the document.

---

[10] For a discussion and economic analysis of residential landlord-tenant relations see Warner Z. Hirsch, *Law and Economics* (New York: Academic Press, 1979), chap. 3.

- *Description of property*—The lease must contain a description of the property adequate for easy identification. Acceptable types of descriptions include street addresses and recorded plats in urban areas and government rectangular survey system and metes and bounds in rural areas.[11]
- *Consideration*—On the lessor's side, giving up the use of the property constitutes valuable consideration. On the lessee's side, the promise to pay rent defines the consideration.
- *Legality of objective*—Issues arise about the lessors' responsibility and liability when lessees use the property illegally. For example, do the lessors have any responsibility if they lease their property to tenants who process and store illegal drugs? Generally, the answer depends on whether the lessors knew or should have known about the illegal operation. If lessees use the property in a manner that does not conform to the zoning laws, the lease remains valid. Lessees and the local government may dispute the permitted use of the property, but such a dispute does not affect the lessors' right to lease the property and collect rent.
- *Offer and acceptance*—Offer and acceptance indicates a meeting of the minds between the lessors and lessees. Statements to the effect that the lessors agree to lease property for a specified period and that the lessees agree to lease the property and pay a certain amount of rent periodically are adequate to meet this requirement.
- *Written Form*—In most states, leases for longer than one year must be in writing.

RESIDENTIAL LEASES

The very short and simple residential lease that follows becomes valid and enforceable once signed:

I, Wilson W. Wilson, do hereby agree to lease my property at 1 One Run from January 1, 1998, through December 31, 1998, to Lee L. and Leah L. Lee, who do hereby agree to pay rent in the amount of $10,000 on the first day of each month.
Wilson W. Wilson, Lessor   Lee L. Lee, Lessee   Leah L. Lee, Lessee

_____   _____   _____

Nevertheless, most leases contain additional provisions that create various rights and obligations of both lessors and lessees. This section discusses some of the additional provisions typically included in residential leases.

Possession and use of property.   Leases should identify the periods during which lessees may occupy the properties, particularly the beginning date. Specifying the exact

---

[11] See Chapter 22 for details about the various ways to describe real estate.

REAL ESTATE FOCUS 8-2

Is Drug Testing Good (and legal) Apartment Management?

Summerwood Commons, a 167-unit apartment complex in Euclid, Ohio (10 miles east of Cleveland) was a condemned haven for drug users before undergoing a major renovation and change in management during 1994. Applicants for apartments in the reopened property were asked to fill out standard forms seeking information about prior residence and creditworthiness. The application included an additional question—Would you undergo a drug test as a condition for residence in this complex? Hundreds of applicants agreed to the test stating that they just wanted a safe place to live.

Some believe that testing is a good and legal management strategy, especially because the complex is owned by a private corporation controlled by four Presbyterian churches. Others contend that for a variety of reasons, not including errors in testing and civil rights, this residency requirement violates Fair Housing Laws designed to eliminate discrimination. It has been unlawful for decades to deny housing to persons with handicaps. "Persons afflicted with the disease of chemical dependency fall within that definition," says Avery Friedman, a fair-housing attorney in Cleveland.

SOURCE: Associated Press, August 3, 1994.

---

period avoids the possibility of creating tenancies at will, a problem covered in Chapter 20. In these instances, the frequency of rental payments—month to month, quarter to quarter, and so on—determines the lease term.

Unless restricted by leases, the lessees may use properties in any legal manner. Often, however, lessors want to limit property usage. For example, they may limit the property to residential use or to occupancy by no more than three persons. Or they may exclude pets. Lessees should read use restrictions carefully before signing a lease.

Maintenance and repairs. Lessors of agricultural, commercial, and industrial properties usually have no obligation to maintain and repair those properties, unless required by the lease document to do so. Even lessors of detached, single-family homes usually have no such obligation. In these situations, lessees make needed repairs and maintenance to return the property to the lessors in the same general condition it was in at the beginning of the lease. This rule, however, does not apply to the leasing of multiunit apartment buildings. In recent years, court decisions and state statutes have imposed an obligation on lessors of apartments in multiunit structures to maintain the properties in a safe and habitable condition in accordance with community housing codes.

Leases usually identify the obligations of each party for maintenance and repairs. If lessees abuse a property or do not meet the lease requirements for maintenance and repairs, lessors can pursue the legal remedy of eviction. Lessors also can sue for damages or retain all or a portion of a security deposit as liquidated damages. If lessors fail to maintain a property in a safe and habitable condition or to live up to the obligations created in leases, lessees may (1) declare leases voided and move out, (2) continue to occupy properties and pay rent but sue lessors for damages, or (3) continue occupancy, but reduce rent payments proportionally to the deteriorated condition. Obviously, any of these remedies may result in disagreements with and counteractions by the lessors.

Lessors' right of entry. Lessors usually have no right of entry to agricultural, commercial, industrial, or detached single-family properties. As pointed out above, lessees have complete responsibility for maintenance and repairs, and leases grant them exclusive right of occupancy and use. The only exceptions involve rights of entry by lessors to collect rent and to prevent waste—lessees' physical abuse of a property or damage that may result from not making repairs. For example, if a water pipe breaks, the lessor could enter the property to fix the pipe and repair any resulting damage.

Lessees' right to assign and sublet. Unless prohibited or limited by leases, lessees have full rights to assign or sublet their leasehold. An **assignment** transfers the lessees' rights to new lessees, who buy the original lessees' total collection of rights. Nevertheless, if the new lessees do not live up to the provisions of the lease, such as paying rent, the lessors can sue the *original* lessees as well as the new lessees. The original tenants remain liable under lease assignments unless released from future obligations by landlords.

A **sublet** involves the sale of part of the lessees' rights. It could involve partitioning of space, with the new lessees occupying part of the original lessees' space. It could involve a sublease of the entire property for a portion of the original lessees' term, for example, 5 years out of the original 10-year term. In either situation, the original lessees also become lessors and the parties now have a **sandwich leasehold,** as demonstrated in Exhibit 8–9.

In a subleasehold, the original lessees remain completely liable for rental payments and other lease provisions to the lessors. In many cases, lessors do not even know about subleaseholds. In lease assignments, the new tenants become primarily liable for rent and other lease provisions. Lessors can go back to the original lessees only after attempting and failing to obtain satisfaction from the new tenants. Consequently, in the lease document, most lessors attempt to limit the right of lessees to assign or sublet.

Many leases state that lessees cannot assign or sublet the property without the lessor's written permission. The lessors could then check the potential assignees' or sublettors' credit history and rental experience in previous apartments. Protection for lessees comes from clauses stating that lessors must have valid reasons for refusing permission to assign or sublet. Failure to grant permission would have to result from poor credit ratings, a history of delinquent rental payments, or a record of destructive behavior in prior apartments.

Landlord-tenant laws. Most states have enacted **landlord-tenant laws** to address the many issues that arise between residential lessors and lessees. These laws have been enacted because state legislatures feel that neither contract law nor common law adequately describes the relationships between owners or managers of large buildings and apartment dwellers. Landlord-tenant laws vary from state to state, but usually cover appli-

EXHIBIT 8-9

SANDWICH LEASEHOLD

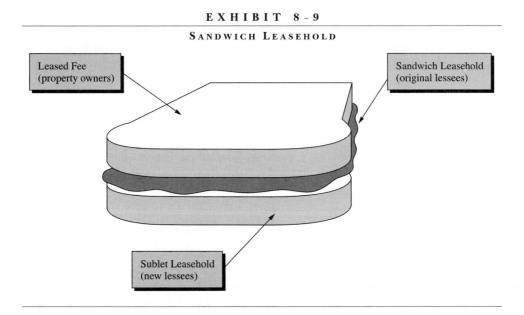

cation fees, security deposits, advance rents, defects, landlords' right of entry, maintenance and repairs, and rule changes. Apartment buildings with four or fewer units are
usually exempt from such laws. Landlord-tenant laws do not extend to commercial property leases under the theory that office, retail, and industrial tenants can protect themselves
against questionable landlord practices. Some of the common types of landlord-tenant
laws include the following:

1. *Fees and deposits*—Landlord-tenant laws state that landlords may charge
   reasonable application fees to cover the costs of checking prospective tenants' references and creditworthiness. Landlords may require tenants to
   pay security deposits to cover any breach of the lease. The laws generally
   allow such deposits, but limit their amount and govern their handling,
   accounting, and return policies on termination of leases.
2. *Advance rent*—Landlords often require tenants to pay the final month's
   rent or more in advance. This protects them if tenants move and refuse to
   pay the last period rent. Generally, treatment of advance rents under the
   law resembles treatment of security deposits.
3. *Defects*—Tenants receive an inspection sheet on which to note defects
   when they enter properties. This protects both parties later if claims arise
   against security deposits. Tenants should prepare such a list if they do not
   receive one from the landlord.
4. *Maintenance and repairs*—Laws require landlords to maintain properties
   in safe and habitable conditions. Going beyond the common law minimum

standards, however, the laws specify some of the components of habitable condition. For example, landlords must (1) provide hot and cold running water and sufficient heat to meet seasonal needs, (2) keep common areas clean and provide waste receptacles, (3) maintain in safe and working order all plumbing, electrical, heating, air-conditioning, and other major equipment and appliances, and (4) maintain the property in conformity with all applicable housing, zoning, and fire codes.

5. *Right of entry*—The laws give landlords the rights of entry to inspect for maintenance and repairs, protect against waste, and show apartments according to lease provisions. Landlords, for example, cannot enter apartments to watch television with tenants on their couches unless invited by tenants.

COMMERCIAL PROPERTY LEASES

Tenants legally occupy space for many types of businesses—offices, small stores, restaurants, specialty shops, department stores, fast-food outlets, service stations, and manufacturing plants, among others—using commercial leases. Even leases on small commercial properties involve longer and more complex documentation than residential leases. Most commercial leases have terms of 3 to 50 years or longer. Thus, they need to cover a wide range of possible circumstances and happenings that are less likely to occur during shorter-term residential lease periods.

Commercial leases create business relationships between lessors and lessees. Lease documents contain rent formulas and determine which parties pay which expenses and what happens when expenses increase.

The following classification system for commercial leases, whose components are not mutually exclusive, applies: (1) classification by the extent to which the lessor pays operating expenses, (2) classification on the basis of rental payments and timing, and (3) classification by the terms of leases.

Lessors' payment of expenses. Lessors may pay all, some, or none of the operating expenses. In a **gross lease,** lessors pay all operating expenses. From lessors' viewpoints, gross lease rental payments must cover the payment for space and operating expenses, as it does in residential properties. In a **net lease,** the most common type in commercial properties, lessees pay some or all of the operating expenses. When lessees pay operating expenses, the lease becomes a **net** or **net-net** lease. The first "net" provision usually obligates lessees to pay property taxes, while the second "net" obligates them to pay insurance premiums. When the lessees pay all operating expenses, including repairs and maintenance, the lease becomes an **absolutely net, net-net-net lease, or triple-net** lease.

The extent to which lessors and lessees share the payment of operating expenses depends on the relative bargaining power of both parties and on market conditions for the type of property involved. Today, most commercial leases require lessees to pay all or some operating expenses. Leases on small- and medium-size properties particularly tend to involve a sharing of expenses between lessors and lessees. Some leases involve a compromise—they contain **expense stop** clauses, **escalator** clauses, and **pass-through** clauses that require lessors or lessees to pay operating expenses up to a given amount, a specified portion of the expenses, or a specified portion of any increase.

For example, an office lease states that the tenant pays $20 per square foot per year in rent, the landlord pays operating expenses up to $3 per square foot (a stop provision), and the lease becomes triple net above the $3 per square foot expense level. Alternatively, the lease could state that the tenant makes a gross lease payment of $25 per square foot, but all increases in property taxes and insurance become the responsibility of the tenant (a pass-through provision).

Basis for rent payment and timing. A lease may require a fixed amount of rent, a variable amount based on a percentage of the lessees' gross sales receipts, an amount subject to periodic renegotiation, or an amount determined by an index. Following is a list of the common forms of leases based on rental:

1. *Fixed rental*—Leases can specify fixed rental payments or change payments by set amounts or percentages at given dates. In these **step** leases, the amount of rent is determined at the beginning of the lease agreement.
2. *Percentage rental*—Gross sales of the lessees' business provide the basis for percentage leases. Under this system, common in retail property leases, lessors share in the space user's profits and the risk. Typically, an amount must be paid regardless of the gross receipts, the **base rent,** plus a percentage of gross receipts, the **percentage** or **overage rent.**
3. *Renegotiation rental*—A renegotiation provision sometimes appears in commercial leases to determine rent. A percentage of the property's market value or a relationship to the rental on other competing properties in the market serves as basis for initial rent. At periodic intervals, such as every two years, lessors and lessees agree to renegotiate rental payments based on a reappraisal of the property's value or of market rents.
4. *Indexed rental*—Sometimes commercial lease rentals become tied to an index, usually the consumer price index. As the index moves up or down, rent adjusts up or down by a specified amount or percentage.

Whereas residential leases and some commercial leases require payments at the beginning of the periods, most retail leases call for payments at the end of the period so the period's gross receipts can be determined. Variations require payment of base rental at the beginning of a period, and overage rental at the end of the period. A variety of rental payment frequencies appear in leases, including monthly, quarterly, semiannual, or annual schedules, although most commercial leases call for monthly payments—the same as residential leases.

Term of leases. Lease classifications also depend on the length of the term, for example, short-term and long-term. While the distinctions become somewhat arbitrary and subjective, short-term leases usually cover 3 to 5 years or less. A more meaningful classification makes short-term leases 3 years or less, medium-term leases 3 to 10 years, and long-term leases 10 years or longer.

Important considerations for lessors.   Commercial lessors have the same concerns as residential lessors. They want reliable lessees who pay rent on time, take care of the property, cooperate in allowing reasonable access for inspections, and use the property compatibly with other uses in the area. Yet commercial lessors have additional considerations and may need to investigate potential lessees more intensively.

The creditworthiness of commercial lessees usually depends on their ability to operate a business profitably. Thus, commercial lessors usually analyze the need for the lessees' businesses in the community and lessees' ability to operate businesses. Lessors often analyze tenants' business history and managerial abilities. Additionally, lessors analyze lessees' management structure, financial strength through credit reports and financial statements, and competitive market position.

Certain types of firms have good compatibility with each other, whereas others detract from each other. For example, dress shops and shoe stores help attract customers to each other, but a mortuary could repel customers of retail stores. Reputation and prestige also affect surrounding businesses and, ultimately, property values. Highly regarded tenants contribute to the desirability of an office building or a shopping center.

Many tenants require specialized space or equipment. For example, physicians and dentists require small rooms and specialized plumbing. Usually, lessees provide any special equipment, but they expect lessors to install items regarded as part of the real estate, including plumbing, electrical service, sinks, stoves, and cabinets.

Important considerations for lessees.   Commercial lessees have concerns similar to those of lessors. They want properties that are compatible for their uses, well located for their businesses, and well maintained, and that enable them to operate their businesses profitably. The property's location and physical characteristics should meet the lessees' needs. Commercial establishments rely on traffic and access appropriate to their use. A good location for a shoe store, for example, might not be good for a physician's office. The physical characteristics of the site and building must be considered. Is the size and type of space appropriate? Is there ample parking? Is the building in good repair and well maintained?

Most businesses seek growth. Will the property accommodate expansion? For the firm that expects to expand, the lease should give the lessee the right to occupy additional space, after a specified notice period, at market rental rates. If additional space is not available, the lease should provide for cancellation, after reasonable notice.

While lessees cannot expect one-sided terms, they can negotiate. Negotiating techniques and skill represent powerful tools in determining commercial lease provisions. Tenants serve themselves well by becoming aware of the art of negotiation.[12]

---

[12] An enormous literature exists on the general topic of negotiation, and the literature on real estate negotiation continues to grow. See Martin I. Zankel, "Principles of Negotiation," *Real Estate Review* 21 (Fall 1991), pp. 39–47. Other examples of lease negotiation articles include: Robert T Tunis, "Protecting

REAL ESTATE FOCUS 8-3 International

The Effect of a Country's Laws on Rents

Lease contracts contain provisions that establish the rules for tenants' temporary use and possession of landlords' properties. Other rules come from the laws of the country or state having jurisdiction over real estate. In the United States, the rights of tenants in residential leases are protected by state landlord-tenant laws, as discussed in this chapter. For commercial property leases, contract laws and public policy provide a general set of rules, but landlords and tenants largely remain free from restrictions on setting provisions, such as the terms of leases and rent adjustments.

In some European countries and other parts of the world, laws exist to protect tenants in commercial property leases from exploitation by landlords. For example, many European countries set the terms of leases by law (e.g., nine years in France) and allow tenants to break

their leases at short intervals (e.g., every three years in France). The laws in other countries allow commercial tenants to remain in properties for extended periods of time, and most countries limit by law adjustment of rent over time.

Countries that grant these liberal rights to tenants grant them valuable options such as the option to cancel leases and the option to stay on at below-market rent. These options cannot be destroyed by the lease contracts signed by landlords and tenants. The lesson from this story is that landlords and tenants planning to do business in a foreign country need to carefully study the country's lease laws. Also, real estate analysts who make rent comparisons across countries must make adjustments to observed rents for the options created by law.

SPECIFIC LEASE CONTRACTS

Shopping center leases. The complexity of shopping center leases generally exceeds that of many other lease structures because of the trilateral relationship between a particular tenant, owners, and the other tenants in the center.[13] The center's owner and management want compatible tenants who will contribute to the effectiveness of the entire center. Consequently, carefully crafted lease provisions and tenants' association rules govern these relationships, and membership in a tenants' association and agreement to abide by its rules are important clauses in such leases. Other important clauses in shopping center leases govern signs and displays, business hours, cancellation, the level of merchandise inventory, utilities, fixtures, relocation, and tenant improvements.

Ground leases. Leases for vacant land or for the land portion of an improved parcel of real estate are termed **ground** or **land leases.** They run for long terms, ranging from 20 to 99 years or longer, and usually call for absolutely net rental payments to the landowners. In addition to property taxes and maintenance expenses, lessees usually agree to

Tenant Interests in Lease Negotiations," *Real Estate Review* 20 (Spring 1990), pp. 41–44; Lance S. Davidson, "Leasing Commercial Real Estate Issues and Negotiating," *Real Estate Review* 18 (Spring 1988), pp. 69–73, Kenneth A. Posner, "Effective Rent as a Measure of Tenant Negotiation Leverage," *Real Estate Review* 23 (Fall 1993), pp. 25–29, and John de Clef Pineiro, "Negotiating Built-Out Allowances," *Real Estate Review* 24 (Winter 1994), pp. 67–71.

[13] See, for example, David W. Barron, " The Small-Store Tenant's Guide to Shopping Center Leases," *Real Estate Review* (Winter 1995), pp. 29–36.

pay for any construction costs, insurance expenses, property assessments, and liability awards to injured parties. In short, land lessors bear no expenses and liabilities for the property and simply receive a periodic rent—ground rent. Owners use ground leases when they have no desire to operate a property or construct buildings but want a steady, secure income from the property, want to preserve ownership rights for themselves or future generations, and want some control over the use of their property.

Ground leases convey the rights of occupancy and use to lessees who expect to use properties for almost any purpose, from single-family residential to large commercial and industrial uses. Single-family homes occupy leased land in areas where land costs are extremely high—notably Hawaii—and many prominent commercial and industrial buildings rest on leased land. The Empire State Building in New York City, for example, occupies leased land, although currently the same owner controls both the building and land. Also, in New York City, Rockefeller Center occupies land leased for 99 years from Columbia University.

Ground lessees usually construct buildings on the land. In fact, many ground leases *require* lessees to construct buildings so that the land will support higher lease payments. In addition to a long stream of periodic lease payments, lessors obtain the entire property—land and buildings—at the termination of the lease.

Whether lessors pay for the value of buildings, or any part thereof, at the termination of the lease becomes a matter for lease negotiation. Many ground leases, particularly longer-term leases of 50 to 99 years, require no such payment, whereas shorter-term leases sometimes require lessors to pay the current market value of the buildings at the end of the lease term based on one or more appraisers' estimates of the value. Occasionally, the lease specifies a predetermined amount.

Lessees generally have the right to borrow on a mortgage against their leasehold interest to construct buildings. The lease also reflects the requirement of most lenders for the right to assign or sublet the property if the lessees default on either the mortgage or the lease agreement. Lenders insist that lessors notify them of any default so they can remedy the default and either operate the property or assign or sublet the leasehold.

Lessors in ground leases do not give up their right to sell their leased fee interest. Any purchasers take title to the property subject to the leases, provided the lessees gave adequate public notice by recording the lease or by physically possessing the property.

Through ground leases, lessees occupy and use properties without the capital outlay required to purchase land. They often expect to have no use for the properties at termination of the lease and thus place no premium on ownership rights. Lessees construct buildings specifically designed for their use. They also receive favorable income tax treatment through the deductibility of lease payments, interest on a leasehold mortgage, and depreciation allowances.

LEASE ECONOMICS: A VALUE PERSPECTIVE

As discussed in Chapter 20, a *fee simple* interest refers to landlords' ownership interests without consideration of leases. If leases exist, then fee simple interests become *leased fee* interests and tenants maintain the *leasehold interests*. If rents in lease contracts equal rents

EXHIBIT 8-10

RENT PATTERNS FOR THE DEAL AND RENTAL LEASE

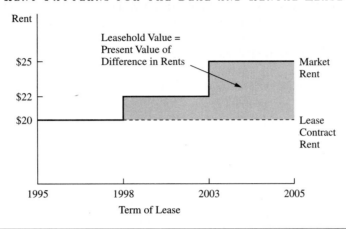

in the market, then the values of fee simple interests equal the values of leased fee interests. However if market rents *exceed* lease contract rents, then tenants possess valuable leaseholds. The following equation emphasizes this point:

$$\text{Value of the leasehold} = \text{Value of the fee simple} - \text{Value of the leased fee}$$

In words, the tenant's claim on the space has value if the market value of the property exceeds the value of the property when considering the "drag" on its value from the below-market rent leases.

Why is this relationship important? Just as trades occur between buyers and sellers of real estate (fee simple and leased fee interests), control of leaseholds changes hands in real estate markets. Trades occur because, for example, a company wants the space controlled by another company or a landlord wants to "buy out" the lease of an existing tenant to help sell the property. In addition, tenants with valuable leaseholds, those with below-market rents, may assign or sublet the space at market rents and keep the difference between the rent they pay and the rent they collect under the sandwich leasehold. Finally, tenants with valuable leaseholds may borrow against that value from banks (i.e., perhaps 50 percent) under **leasehold mortgages.** Regardless of the reasons for leasehold transactions, the value of leaseholds emerges as the critical input for transactions.

For example, Joe Deal entered into what he felt was a good deal three years ago in 1995 when he signed an annual payment lease for 5,000 square feet of office space in his building at $20 per square foot per year with Dr. Gilbert Rental, a faith healer. The lease allows the tenant to freely assign the lease (that is, sell the leasehold). Currently in December of 1998, professional office space of comparable quality rents for $22 and should rise to $25 by the end of the Dr. Rental lease term in 2005. Because Dr. Rental has lost money and faith in faith healing, he decides to assign the space to an aspiring fortune-teller. A graphic of the actual and assumed rental patterns and the leasehold valuation appears in Exhibit 8–10. The value of the leasehold is reached as follows:

Valuation of the leasehold:[14]

$$\text{Value of fee simple} = \text{PV annuity ($25 $\times$ 5000 s.f.), 10\%, 7 years} - \text{PV annuity}$$
$$(\$3 \times 5000), 10\%, 5 \text{ years}$$
$$= \$608,552 - \$56,862$$
$$= \$551,690$$
$$\text{Value of leased fee} = \text{PV annuity ($20 $\times$ 5000 s.f.), 10\%, 7 years}$$
$$= \$486,842$$
$$\text{Value of leasehold} = \$551,690 - \$486,842$$
$$= \$64,848$$

Dr. Rental sold the leasehold to the fortune-teller on January 1, 1999, for $64,848. The analyst who performed the valuation selected a 10 percent discount rate because it matches the rate at which the fortune-teller can borrow money. The rates used to value leases align with borrowing rate because leasing is an alternative to borrowing.[15]

Suppose in the example above that Deal had granted in the original lease an option allowing Dr. Rental to renew the lease for two additional years at the initial rent. This option gives even more value to the leasehold than $64,848 because it extends the period over which the tenant pays below-market rent. Pricing the options created in leases using option-pricing models from corporate finance represents the frontier of lease economics.[16] Aren't you glad we will not go any further with this topic?

SPECIAL TOPIC: CORPORATE REAL ESTATE ASSET MANAGEMENT

As with most topics found in *Real Estate Perspectives,* we cannot give adequate coverage to real estate management in a single chapter. This section of the chapter highlights a special topic in real estate management that could not be omitted: corporate real estate asset management.

As noted in Chapter 1, corporations represent the largest owners of commercial real estate in the United States, and for any particular company, real estate constitutes from 25 percent to 40 percent of the value assets on its balance sheet. It remains surprising therefore that corporate asset management and facilities management gained recognition only in the past 15 years as specialized career paths and fields of study in real estate. What is corporate real estate management? Simply stated, corporate asset managers strive to add to the values of shares of stock in their companies by the wise deployment of the real estate needed for current business purposes and the other real estate on the books.

---

[14] Payments assumed at end of year, although most leases call for payments at the beginning of the period.

[15] See James S. Schallheim, *Lease or Buy?* (Boston: Harvard Business School Press, 1994) for an excellent treatment of this concept.

[16] See Stephen M. Schwab, "Asset Management: A Guide to Valuing Options," *Journal of Property Management* 60 (July-August 1995), pp. 52–53.

Corporations have three types of real estate on their balance sheets:

1. Real estate used in the production of revenues from the goods and services in their main lines of business, including office buildings, retail outlets, and warehouses.
2. Real estate not currently used—perhaps acquired as part of a large property transaction, company acquisition, or merger.
3. Real estate used in real estate businesses that companies conduct aside from their main-line businesses.

For each type of real estate, asset managers face a multitude of questions and decisions. First, should the company venture into the real estate business, in which it rents space to others, trades properties, or develops properties for profit? Many large corporations entered the real estate business by establishing subsidiaries during the 1980s, but nearly all divested or shrunk these businesses as the returns dwindled. Second, should the company retain ownership of surplus real estate in anticipation of future opportunity? The downsizing trend of recent years removed most surplus real estate from corporate balance sheets. Finally, should the company buy to own or build to own the real estate needed for its core businesses, or instead lease the properties needed, including sale and the leaseback of properties currently owned? The role of corporate asset managers today centers on these types of decisions and managing the portfolios of leases created from decisions to lease property.[17]

SALE-AND-LEASEBACK DECISIONS

During the past three decades, many corporations, such as IBM and Time, sold properties they owned for office and other purposes to institutional investors and in the same transaction became tenants in the buildings. These transactions, called **sale-and-leaseback** or sale-leaseback deals, bring the following benefits to the corporation and the investor:[18]

The benefits to the corporation include

- Low cost of funds for investment in main-line business projects. The money that comes from selling buildings may be less expensive than borrowing, all things considered.
- Favorable impact on earnings. The operating cost of owning often exceeds that of leasing.
- Maintaining control without ownership problems. Because leaseback transactions involve long-term leases with many renewal options, corporations retain total control without the problems of ownership.

---

[17] The term *outsourcing* refers to corporations contracting with a professional real estate management firm to manage their real estate.

[18] Chip Conley, "The Explosion in Leveraged Sale-Leasebacks," *Real Estate Review* (Fall 1984), pp. 56–60.

The benefits to the investor include

- Rental security. The corporate tenants in the space provide good rental security. High-quality tenants attract other high-quality tenants.
- Tax savings. Investors obtain depreciation deductions.
- Low management responsibilities. The corporations typically sign triple-net leases.
- Appreciation. Through appreciated value, investors benefit from the major corporate presence.

The decision to sell a corporate building and lease it back requires careful measurement of the net cash flows from leasing versus owning the property, including the proceeds from the sale. Typically, the corporation receives a large cash flow in the year of sale and incurs some additional rental costs during the period of occupancy. The net present value of these two cash streams determines if the shares of stock in the company increase as the result of the transaction.

THE LEASE VERSUS OWN DECISION

Many of the considerations and the financial analysis of corporate decisions to lease versus buy additional space for operations closely resemble sale-and-leaseback decisions. If we accept the idea that leasing constitutes an alternative form of financing, then it does not matter if leasing helps finance the expansion of space needed for operations or it helps finance some other corporate endeavor, such as the development of a new product line.

The Corsmithling Companies, a manufacturer of natural fertilizer, two years ago leased a 100,000-square-foot plant and warehouse in Cleveland for five years with a five-year renewal option.[19] Renovation work to make the space suitable for the company's operations cost $2 million. Recent sales growth to a current level of $100 million means that now the renovated warehouse no longer provides adequate space for operations. Corsmithling's strategic planning team produced two options for rectifying the crowded conditions at the plant:

1. *Lease* another 100,000 square feet in a nearby and recently renovated property at favorable terms: a three-year lease with two three-year options to renew at the initial rent. This alternative will support growth in sales up to $500 million.
2. *Buy and build* a 200,000-square-foot facility on a 20-acre parcel in Akron at a total cost of $11 million for land, building, and improvements. The new plant will support sales of up to $600 million and only covers three acres; thus, 17 acres exist for future needs. The president of the company prefers to own rather than lease and to have the entire workforce in one location despite the disruptive move to Akron.

Exhibits 8–11 and 8–12 present information on the two alternatives, including a first-year return on investment.

---

[19] The numbers for this example come from Christopher A. Manning, "The Economics of Real Estate Decisions," *Harvard Business Review* (November-December 1986), pp. 12–22.

EXHIBIT 8-11

CORSMITHLING DECISION: INCREASE IN FIRST-YEAR CASH FLOW

Change in First-Year Operations	Lease Alternative	Akron Buy-and-Build Alternative
Increase in first-year sales revenue	$20,000,000	$20,000,000
Increase in first-year costs		
Lease or mortgage interest expense	500,000	700,000
	(lease payment)	(mortgage)
Labor costs	6,000,000	5,000,000
Materials costs	6,600,000	6,900,000
Energy costs	400,000	600,000
Transportation costs	500,000	1,000,000
Other operating costs	5,000,000	3,800,000
Total cost increases	$19,000,000	$18,000,000
Change in first-year cash flow	$1,000,000	$2,000,000

EXHIBIT 8-12

CORSMITHLING DECISION: CAPITAL INVESTMENT AND RETURN

Capital Investment	Lease Alternative	Akron Buy-and-Build Alternative
Land, new building, and parking lot	$0	$ 8,000,000
Cost of new plant improvements	$1,500,000*	3,500,000
Training, loss of productivity in transition, miscellaneous costs	500,000	1,600,000
Employee relation costs	0	500,000
Total plant expansion cost	2,000,000	13,600,000
Less available financing	0	8,000,000**
Total additional investment required	2,000,000	5,600,000
Change in first-year operating profits (from Exhibit 8–11)	1,000,000	2,000,000
First-year return on investment	50%	37.5%

  * Savings by not having to write off improvements from renovation.

 ** Amount of mortgage financing available.

The first-year financial analysis reveals that Corsmithling should remain in Cleveland and lease additional space because the return of 50 percent exceeds the return of 37.5 percent from the buy-and-build alternative. Because both alternatives yield impressive returns, management could decide to please the president by making the move to Akron and rely on increasing real estate values to boost returns over the longer term of eight years. An eight-year analysis, treating the $2 million and $5 million as outflows for the two alternatives, $1 million and $2 million as constant inflows for the alternatives, and assuming that the Akron property becomes worth $10 million at the end of eight years, gives internal rates of return of 47.8 percent for the lease alternative and 38.2 percent for the Akron alternative. The Akron property would have to increase to over $36 million by the end of the eighth year to financially equate the returns on the two alternatives.

SUMMARY

The field of real estate management includes portfolio managers who track the cash flow patterns of many assets to properly combine them, asset managers who advise owners about critical actions involving specific properties, and property managers who handle day-to-day management responsibilities. All real estate managers follow strategies designed to increase the size and reduce the variation of cash flow (the *value perspective*) for owners.

Two important contracts tie the owners, managers, and space users together: management contracts and leases. Properly constructed management contracts have compensation provisions to align the incentives of owners and managers. Lease contracts separate the rights of occupancy and use of real estate from the other rights of ownership. Residential leases include a number of provisions only limited by state or local landlord-tenant laws.

Commercial and ground leases involve lengthier, more complex documents than residential leases. In addition to term and rental payments, they usually cover matters such as use of the property, operating expenses, fixtures and tenant's fixtures, renewal and expansion, assignment and subletting, security for rent payments, liability to third parties, abandonment, and subordination of the lease to mortgage financing. Ground leases constitute long-term conveyances of the use and occupancy rights of land. They give lessees time to construct buildings in order to use the property most efficiently and provide lessors with stable, secure income.

Because corporations own considerable real estate for their main businesses and sometimes other purposes, corporations often hire inside real estate managers as well as "outsourcing" this work to independent management companies. Corporate real estate management involves analysis for decisions regarding actions such as sale-and-leaseback of property, renovation, and building versus leasing. All these actions potentially affect the prices of company shares.

KEY TERMS

Asset manager 226
Assignment 244
Base rent 247
Concentric marketing 232
Eviction 234
Expense stop clauses 247
Gross lease 246
Ground (land) lease 249

Landlord-tenant laws 244
Leased fee estate 240
Leasehold estate 240
Leasehold mortgage 251
Net lease 246
Pass-through clauses 247
Percentage rent 247

Portfolio manager 226
Property manager 226
Reversion 242
Sale-and-leaseback 253
Sandwich leasehold 244
Sublet 244
Thematic image 232

TEST YOURSELF

Answer the following **multiple choice** questions.

1. A management agreement establishes an agency relationship between
   a. The owner of the property and a tenant.
   b. The owner of the property and a property manager.
   c. The property manager and a tenant.
   d. The owner of the property, the property manager, and a tenant.
   e. The owner of the property and local government.

2. A promotional program for marketing rental space should be related to
   a. The property's thematic image.
   b. Market conditions for rental space.
   c. The budget for promotional activities.
   d. The type of space available.
   e. All of the above.

3. The system for compensating property managers would probably provide more incentive for controlling expenses if compensation were based on
   a. Potential gross income.
   b. Hours worked.
   c. Net operating income.
   d. Effective gross income.
   e. Minimizing wages.

4. In most states, residential landlord-tenant laws have been enacted to
   a. Protect tenants from landlords.
   b. Protect landlords from tenants.
   c. Govern landlord-tenant relationships in apartment buildings having four or fewer units.
   d. Establish standard provisions in residential leases.
   e. Allow landlords to charge more rent.

5. Lessors who want to make sure their rents increase at least as fast as inflation would key their increases to which method?
   a. Percentage of rental based on gross receipts.
   b. Fixed rental.
   c. Renegotiation rental at two-year intervals.
   d. A general index of inflation.
   e. A general index of construction costs.

6. The terms of ground leases are usually
   a. Less than five years.
   b. Five to 10 years.
   c. 10 to 12 years
   d. Less than 20 years.
   e. 20 to 99 years.

7. Rental payments on ground leases are usually
   a. Gross.
   b. Absolutely net.
   c. Partially net.
   d. Negotiable.
   e. Held in escrow.

8. A sandwich leasehold is
   a. A lease on a small restaurant.
   b. The assignment of a lessee's rights to a new lessee.
   c. The interest of a lessee who sublets part of the lessee's rights to a sublessee.
   d. A lease by an owner to two or more parties.
   e. A reverse lease from the lessee back to the owner.

9. Current NOI for a 10-year-old retail center equals $50,000. After a $300,000 renovation, NOI should climb to $75,000. If the market capitalization rate equal 12 percent, what is the value of the center after renovation?
   a. $625,000.
   b. $500,000.
   c. $350,000.
   d. $600,000.
   e. None of the above.

10. Using the results from the previous question, should the owner spend $300,000 to renovate?
    a. Yes.
    b. No.
    c. Not enough information given to make a decision.
    d. Ask someone else.

PROBLEMS FOR THOUGHT AND SOLUTION

1. Explain the difference between the right to assign a lease and the right to sublet.

2. How do asset and property managers decide whether they should concentrate on increasing effective gross income or reducing controllable expenses?

3. Can management usually maximize effective gross income by setting rent so that vacancy equals zero?

4. Explain the role of the corporate real estate manager.

5. Why do agency problems exist in real estate management contracts and how can they be resolved most effectively?

CASE PROBLEMS

1. You recently accepted the position of resident manager of a 20-unit apartment building near the campus of a major university. The building is approximately 20 years old, and although well located relative to the university, it has experienced above-normal vacancy rates during the past two to three years. The owner has asked you to determine why the vacancy rate has been high and what actions could be taken to achieve a lower vacancy rate of 2 to 3 percent.

In surveying rents of competing properties, you find they are in line with your property's rents. Also, you find that their vacancy rates have been above the community average. On further investigation, you find that newer, more modern apartments on the periphery of the city are absorbing a high proportion of new tenants. These units provide dishwashers, microwave ovens, ceiling fans, swimming pools, and exercise rooms. Their rents are about $100 per month higher than your units.

Your building appears worn. The carpeting is soiled and dark, the walls are drab, and the interior furnishings are dated and worn. The units provide none of the amenities of the newer complexes (no pool, exercise room, microwaves, dishwashers, or ceiling fans).

What types of analyses would you undertake to solve the vacancy dilemma?

What types of recommendations might you make to the owner?

2. The Dumb Corporation leases 20,000 feet of warehouse space from Realty Investors Foresight for $8 per foot triple net with an expense stop of $1 per foot. The lease runs from 1990 through June 30, 2010. It requires the rent, paid monthly, to be adjusted on July 1 of each year. The amount of the adjustment is calculated as a direct percentage of the change in the consumer price index (CPI) from the years before the current year. For example, the adjustment to be made on July 1, 1996, reflects the change in the CPI between 1994 and 1995. The lease requires adjustments to the annual rent, which is then divided by 12 to obtain the monthly rent for the year July 1 through June 30. In 1990, the monthly rent was $13,333 ($160,000 per year). Shown below is the CPI from 1989 to 1995. Expenses have been $2 per foot from 1990 through 1995, but are expected to increase to $2.50 in 1996. Calculate the adjustments and the annual rent and expenses for 1991 through 1996.

Year	CPI	Annual rent with CPI Adjustment
1989	4.65%	
1990	6.11	
1991	3.06	
1992	2.90	
1993	2.75	
1994	2.67	
1995	2.72	
1996	2.85	

ADDITIONAL READINGS

The following books contain chapters written by recognized authorities on real estate portfolio management about the important topics and issues in the field:

Hudson-Wilson, Susan, and Charles H. Wurtzebach. *Managing Real Estate Portfolios.* Burr Ridge, IL: Richard D. Irwin, 1994.

Pagliari, Joseph L. Jr. *The Handbook of Real Estate Portfolio Management.* Homewood, IL: Richard D. Irwin, 1995.

The following newsletter reports on advancements in the asset management business:

Real Estate Workouts & Asset Management (monthly). Warren, Gorham, and Lamount, Inc., Boston.

This book contains insights about real estate management:

Alexander, Alan A., and Richard F. Muhlebach, *Managing and Leasing Commercial Properties.* New York: John Wiley and Sons, 1990.

Real Estate Review publishes many articles each year on commercial property management. One example is a useful article on selecting a property manager:

Pacetti, Eileen, and Joseph S. Rabianski. "Selecting a Property Management Firm." *Real Estate Review* (Summer 1993), pp. 70–74.

The *Journal of Property Management* is devoted to informing the real estate management industry about advancements in the field. Frequently, articles appear about computer software, including useful reviews such as this one:

Morey, Scott, and Don Giudice. "Survey of Property Management and Accounting Software." *Journal of Property Management* (May-June 1995), pp. 58–65.

Three professional organizations—Building Owners and Managers Association International (BOMA), the Institute of Real Estate Management (IREM), and the International Council of Shopping Centers (ICSC)—publish books and brochures dealing primarily with technical aspects of property management. Examples are listed below, along with the addresses of the organizations, so interested readers can obtain additional information.

From the International Council of Shopping Centers, 665 Fifth Avenue, New York, New York 10022:
The ICSC Guide to Operating Shopping Centers the Smart Way.
Advanced Shopping Center Management.

From the Building Owners and Managers Association International, 1250 Eye Street, N.W., Washington, D.C. 20005:
BOMA Experience Exchange Report for Office Buildings.
Office Building Lease Manual.
Leasing Concepts.
A Guide to Commercial Property Management.

From the Institute of Real Estate Management, 430 North Michigan Avenue, Chicago, Illinois 60610-9025:
Principles of Real Estate Management, 13th ed. Chicago: IREM, 1991.
Kelley, Edward N., CPM. *Practical Apartment Management,* 3rd ed. Chicago: IREM, 1990.
Income/Expense Analysis: Conventional Apartments. Chicago: IREM, annual.
Income/Expense Analysis: Federally Assisted Apartments. Chicago: IREM, annual.

P A R T

II

THE MARKET
PERSPECTIVE

9.
Real Estate Markets

10.
*Land Use, Planning, Zoning,
and Environmental*

11.
Market and Feasibility Analysis

12.
Introduction to Development

13.
*Valuation by the Sales Comparison and
Cost Approaches*

14.
Valuation by Income Capitalization

This part of *Real Estate Perspectives* views real estate from a Market Perspective. If investors understand how real estate markets behave, they are better able to put scarce real estate to its most economically and socially productive use. No single real estate market exists; instead the real estate market takes many varied forms. The current convention is to think of real estate as two different types of economic goods: space and assets. Trading of the rights to use space occurs in the rental (space) market, in which owners rent spaces to tenants. Owners also buy and sell these collections of spaces in the property asset markets. Generally, the two markets react similarly to changing market conditions and government policies, but important differences also occur. Another way to think about real estate markets is to consider how new spaces and assets are developed in markets dominated by existing properties. In this part of the text, we truly view the market from a variety of perspectives.

The Market Perspective begins with a chapter that explains the operations of real estate markets (Chapter 9). This chapter also identifies how location defines real estate markets and market opportunities. Government has a large role in real estate markets through the regulation of land use and environmental hazards, as described in Chapter 10. Chapter 11 presents the process of actually analyzing markets and project feasibility, considering government regulation along with the economic, physical, and financial opportunities for and constraints on investment. Chapter 12 extends this discussion, introducing students to the steps in real estate development.

The two chapters on market valuation and appraisal (13 and 14) complete the Market Perspective. As *value* is the unifying conceptual theme for this text, valuations lead most real world decisions involving real estate. These chapters demonstrate how professional appraisers apply various approaches to estimate the market values of real estate.

9
C H A P T E R

REAL ESTATE MARKETS

LOCATION MAKES MARKETS "IMPERFECT, IMPERFECT, IMPERFECT"
No Arbitrage!
Location Theory
Residential Location Decisions
Commercial and Industrial Firm Location
  Decisions

HOW THE SPACE MARKET OPERATES
Functions of the Space Market
Supply and Demand Model with Vacancy
Natural Vacancy
Factors Influencing Supply and Demand
Rents

SPACE AND ASSET MARKET INTERACTION
The Economic Fundamentals Matter!

Government Influences
Do the Individuals Matter?
The Psychology of Real Estate Markets

THE ASSET MARKET
Who Participates?
Asset Price and Values
Replacement Cost and Values
"Noisy" Prices
Interaction with Securitized Market

SUMMARY

KEY TERMS

TEST YOURSELF

PROBLEMS FOR THOUGHT AND SOLUTION

CASE PROBLEMS

ADDITIONAL READINGS

After reading this chapter, students will be able to:

1. Explain the implications of fixed location on the behavior of real estate markets and how firms, households, and cities find desirable locations.

2. Analyze the strength of a rental (space) market by examining the relationship between the actual vacancy rate and the long-run vacancy rate.

3. Identify the determinants of apartment, retail, and office rents and asset prices.

4. Explain how competition in the capital asset market influences discount rates for real estate.

5. Analyze a real estate asset market to determine whether prices and development will increase in the future by examining the relationship between asset values and their replacement costs.

6. Identify fundamental economic factors that influence movements in real estate markets and prices from personal, governmental, and psychological factors.

LOCATION MAKES MARKETS "IMPERFECT, IMPERFECT, IMPERFECT"

The title to this first section of Chapter 9 pokes fun at the answer to *the* most famous real estate question—What are the three most important things about real estate? (The answer usually given is "location, location, location.") The title makes the point that imperfections in real estate markets derive largely, although not exclusively, from location characteristics. Why should we study this "stuff"? Some excellent opportunities to make money in real estate come from understanding why people and businesses locate where they do, and then taking advantage of information about locations.

The nature of a market reflects the character of the good or service traded in that market. In addition to the lags in putting real estate into service and the high costs of adjusting the space and changing the users, real estate markets operate differently from some other markets because every property differs substantially from every other property in at least one essential respect—its location. Each property possesses a **location monopoly,** meaning that the property trades in its own market and the owner retains some control over the price. Because of differences in property locations, real estate defies the label of a homogeneous product. *Product homogeneity*, when each unit of the product is identical to all other units—stands as one condition for a perfect competitive market. Other conditions include these:

1. *Free markets.* A perfectly competitive market operates without external control, such as from governments.

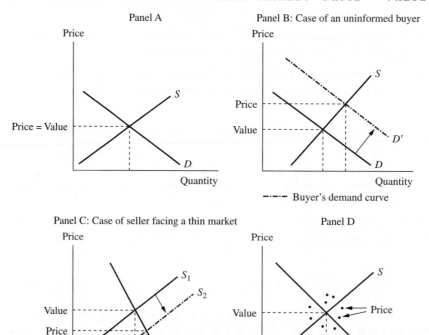

EXHIBIT 9 - 1

IN A PERFECTLY COMPETITIVE ASSET MARKET — PRICE = VALUE

2. *Perfect knowledge*. All market participants possess perfect knowledge about all competing goods and their prices and share the same expectations for the future.
3. *Size and control*. Many buyers and sellers operate in the market and no individual buyer or seller gains enough power to influence prices.
4. *Mobility and divisibility*. Participants can divide products into smaller units for sale. Also, product mobility exists, such that excess demand conditions, wherever they occur, vanish as suppliers freely move products to satisfy those conditions.

As demonstrated in Exhibit 9–1, Panel A, the transaction price equals the value in perfectly competitive market trading. The price occurs at the intersection of the lines that represent the demand and supply fundamentals, the same point at which the appraiser estimates the market value. Market imperfections cause prices to deviate from the market values. The buyer in Panel B, Mr. Legroc, makes a bid on a property with a restaurant that

REAL ESTATE FOCUS 9-1

Donald Trump on Locations.

"Perhaps the most misunderstood concept in real estate is that the key to success is location, location, location. Usually that's said by people who don't know what they're talking about."

SOURCE: Donald Trump, *The Art of the Deal* (New York: Random House, 1987), p. 38.

---

exceeds the bid he would have made had he known that the university located nearby just announced a sizable cutback in enrollment and staff. This transaction results in a one-time increase in the price for the property (not aggregate demand), and thus the price moves above the value based on the fundamentals. Because Mr. Legroc stands as the only buyer or seller without perfect information about the location, all subsequent transactions in the immediate area occur at prices that equal values.

Now consider the plight of Ms. Lah who, because of a job transfer, needs to sell her condominium. Unfortunately, few buyers exist in this small condominium market so she either must wait many months to sell at the market value or offer the property at a discount, which she does. As shown in Panel C, the actions of Ms. Lah temporarily increase the supply of condominiums at a price below their value.

Panel D in Exhibit 9–1 shows how prices in an imperfect market occur near the market value. How long and by how much transaction prices differ from market values represent two important questions for making money in real estate.

NO ARBITRAGE!

Even if conditions become unfavorable at a location, owners cannot move properties to more advantageous markets or locations. Because of fixed locations, real estate also becomes more susceptible to problems at adjacent properties. The fixed location of real estate significantly raises the **information costs** of market participants. Not only must they acquire information about national and regional market factors, such as interest rates and population migration patterns, they must have all available information about local markets and site-specific factors of the subject, adjacent, and competing properties.

The term **arbitrage** defines the act of buying assets at one price and simultaneously selling them at higher prices without taking on additional risk. We know from the previous discussion that arbitrage opportunities stemming from moving properties in total or in part to better locations or local markets defy the laws of physical and economic reality. But how about arbitrage based on other real estate market idiosyncrasies, including misinformation about locations, seller impatience, bargaining experience, and market psychology?

Imperfect, but not inefficient, markets.   Real estate markets can present observant investors with situations in which property values exceed their posted asking prices. To make money by acting on these opportunities, observant investors must follow two rules. The first rule, not totally within their control, requires that they act on opportunities immediately and ahead of all other observant investors. The second rule requires that investors cannot spend so much money on the transactions that all the money made from buying low and selling high vanishes because of transaction costs, such as brokerage and attorney fees. Many students of real estate markets have pondered the limitations of these rules, as discussed in a review by Dean Gatzlaff and Dogan Tirtiroglu.[1]

The first rule begs the question of real estate market efficiency. **Efficient markets** have many observant investors as participants who use information about prices of previous transactions, other publicly available information, and sometimes private information to remove, through arbitrage, any differences between prices and values. Studies of housing and commercial property markets find a great deal of efficiency in the real estate markets. These results suggest that investors not only must observe opportunities, they must possess incredible speed or access to private information to capitalize on the imperfections of real estate markets. Some studies find substantial arbitrage opportunities, but equally large transaction costs that wipe out gains from taking actions on those opportunities—in these instances the second rule becomes a serious constraint.

LOCATION THEORY

Given the lack of arbitrage opportunities and the results of market efficiency tests, does it make sense to continue the study of real estate markets, especially the theory of location decisions? Yes, for several reasons:

1. While arbitrage can yield large short-term gains, most people make money in real estate by adopting a long-term view. Long-term gains result from knowing the fundamentals of the market and delivering the product successfully, as in any business.
2. Real estate markets are prone to distortions from the sudden entry of government and the uninformed participant. Properties at better locations occupy positions in the market that allow owners to make the most and lose the least from these unexpected and sudden changes.
3. One never wants to be among the uninformed!

Classical location theory. The classical view of land values of the early 1800s applies to an agrarian economy. The English economist and social philosopher David Ricardo argued that land rents, the bids made for the use of land, although related to location, derive from the *fertility* of the land for agricultural production. The most fertile land commands the highest rent.

Later, a German economist, von Thunen, expanded the theory of land rent based on location advantage. Von Thunen argued that rent results from *accessibility* of land to market centers. Good access creates value because it results in lower transportation costs

---

[1] Dean H. Gatzlaff and Dogan Tirtiroglu, "Real Estate Market Efficiency: Issues and Evidence," *Journal of Real Estate Literature* 3 (July 1995), pp. 157–89.

E X H I B I T 9 - 2

E X H I B I T 9 - 2

B I D - R E N T C U R V E I N A N A G R I C U L T U R A L E C O N O M Y

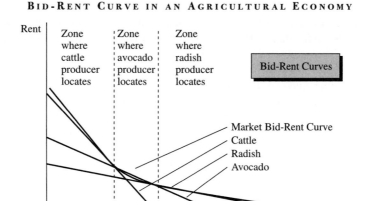

for producers taking their products to the market. Therefore, the arrangement of land uses around a market center arises from the bids for locations made by producers. Producers with the greatest transportation costs per unit of distance to the center make the highest bids for close-in locations because they stand to save the most in transportation costs.

Exhibit 9–2 presents the bid-rent curve in one direction from a market center for three agricultural producers. All economic activity is assumed to occur at the market center, all land possesses equal productivity, and each producer produces only one commodity. The first producer raises cattle, which have extremely high transportation costs. This producer's steep bid-rent line indicates relatively high bids for locations close to the center. The other producers grow avocados and radishes, respectively. The less steep slopes of their bid-rent functions indicate a willingness to accept locations farther from the center because of their lower transportation costs. The bids along the market bid-rent curve present a pattern of agricultural land uses in which the cattle producer secures the location closest to the center, and the others settle for locations farther out.

Classical location theory explains location decisions on the basis of the relationship between transportation costs and the productivity of land. It explains market behavior when these two factors are the only factors under consideration.

Neoclassical location theory: capital and land substitution. During the latter part of the 20th century, Alonso and other economists extended von Thunen's ideas to an urban spatial economy.[2] In the simplest version of this theory, the single market center becomes

[2] For an extended discussion of classical and early neoclassical location theory, see William Alonso, *Location and Land Use* (Cambridge, MA: Harvard University Press, 1964).

the city's central business district instead of the agricultural market center. Uses of land include office buildings, apartment complexes, industrial plants, and residences rather than farming. Bidding, still based strongly on the need to avoid transportation costs but not on agricultural productivity, determines the allocation of land to different uses. The presence of buildings also adds another dimension to location decisions.

The neoclassical view of location decisions recognizes land as a factor of production, along with labor and capital, and the value of each input comes from its contribution to the value of the final product or service. This means producers add factors of production based on their relative economic contributions to the good or service offered to the market. The cost of any factor to producers depends on the demand and supply of that factor, hence the neoclassical economics foundation.

To some extent, the factors of production become *substitutes* for one another as some factors become expensive relative to others. Using robots to manufacture automobiles, for example, involves substituting cheap capital for high-cost labor. When energy prices increase dramatically, the cost of operating capital becomes expensive relative to other inputs, which results in the substitution of cheaper labor for expensive-to-operate capital.

The concept of **factor substitution** maintains a pivotal role in land-use decisions. As the price of land becomes excessive in terms of what the market demands at the location, capital improvements to land substitute for land. This explains why multistory buildings appear in and around central business districts, shopping centers, and other important centers in major cities.

High rents occur in and around central locations because producers make high bids for central locations to avoid transportation costs. Not every producer, however, can readily substitute capital for land. Some production processes, such as assembly line automobile manufacturing, cannot change from horizontal to vertical directions. Thus, land-use patterns also result from the ability of producers to effectively substitute capital for land. In summary, two economic principles have a pervasive influence on the determination of land uses:

1. The pattern of transportation costs in the city and the need or desire of firms and individuals to avoid such costs.
2. Capital and land substitution and the ability or desire of firms and individuals to substitute buildings for land.

RESIDENTIAL LOCATION DECISIONS

Theorists recognized that the same economic factors that affect location decisions of firms—the need to avoid transportation costs and the need for quantities of land—also influence the location decisions of individual households.[3] Thus, the same two fundamental principles underlie the household location decision.

---

[3] See the following important book: Richard F. Muth, *Cities and Housing* (Chicago: University of Chicago Press, 1969).

1. Households, like firms, seek to avoid transportation costs and thus have incentives to locate as close to economic centers as possible. Transportation costs of wage earners involve both the actual outlays for travel and the cost of forgone wages due to time lost during travel. Transportation costs, therefore, *increase* with distance from a center.
2. Households demand different quantities of land. Because businesses and households bid for central locations, the price of land *decreases* with distance from the economic centers of cities.

The trade-off facing each household involves how far from the center the household should purchase or rent housing, given that transportation costs increase and land prices decline with distance. At the equilibrium location, households spend the desired amount on commuting costs while satisfying their desire for land and housing.

Trade-off models of household location decisions also give insights about urban policy questions, such as population density and future area growth. By examining what would happen to household equilibrium locations if, for example, the local government issued tax exempt bonds to spur new housing construction or changed the fare structure of the mass transportation system, local planners can judge how policies will affect future land use. These models predict that policies to increase the cost of housing relative to other goods will lead to outward expansion of the city. Policies to lower the cost of transportation, such as an expansion of the highway system, also will lead to outward expansion.

COMMERCIAL AND INDUSTRIAL FIRM LOCATION DECISIONS

Transportation costs and land requirements largely determine the locations of commercial and industrial firms. In addition to minimizing their own transportation costs, firms seek to reduce transportation costs for their customers, employees, and materials suppliers. Good location linkages with customers and suppliers minimize costs.

Two types of linkages dominate the location decisions of commercial and industrial firms. **Input linkage** refers to the location relationship between a firm and its suppliers of services and production materials. **Output linkage** refers to the location relationship between firms and their customers. Assume a hypothetical automobile manufacturer seeks a location for a plant in a Third World country. As shown in Exhibit 9–3, the raw materials (input) for the manufacturing process come from the northeastern and north-central regions of the country. A concentration of skilled labor (input) for the company's production resides in the main university city in the north-central region of the country. The main markets (output) for automobiles are found in the equatorial cities of the southern and western regions. Thus, with transportation costs equal in all directions, the center of the country emerges as the logical location for the plant. This location establishes optimal input and output linkages—it minimizes transportation costs from and to the input and product markets.

The plant's location changes if the assumption of equal transportation costs in all directions is changed. If, for example, the transportation system remains underdeveloped

EXHIBIT 9-3

INPUT AND OUTPUT LINKAGES FOR AN AUTO MANUFACTURING FIRM

Hypothetical Third World Country

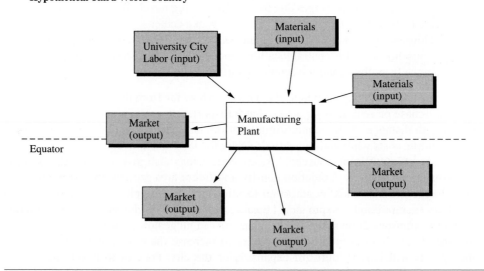

in the northern region relative to the southern region, higher transportation costs exist to and from the north, and the optimal location of the plant moves somewhat north of the central location.

The type of manufacturing operation also influences location decisions because it dictates the transportation costs of the input and output linkages. Some firms add weight to their products during production, for example, a soft-drink bottling company that adds water. Firms that add weight seek locations close to the market to avoid the relatively higher transportation costs of moving heavy or bulky product to customers. Other firms' production processes lead to lost weight, such as steel plants that require large amounts of iron ore, coke, and limestone to make a relatively small amount of steel. For this type of plant, the optimal location is near the source of materials.

Many commercial firms, such as retail, hotel, and restaurant operations, seek locations that provide optimal linkages to their customers. As in the cases of firms that add or detract weight, the type of goods commercial firms sell strongly influences their location decisions. If a product or service has a *high density of demand,* meaning that frequent purchases occur as with convenient groceries, the establishment needs a relatively small surrounding trade area to be profitable. Such an outlet may locate almost anywhere with a nearby resident population, little competition, and appropriate zoning.

An establishment selling goods with a *low density of demand,* meaning infrequently purchased items such as antique books, requires a relatively large trade area to do business. Such establishments must locate centrally in relation to the population to minimize the transportation costs of their widely dispersed customers.

E X H I B I T   9 - 4

LOCATION OF FIRMS AT BREAKS IN TRANSPORTATION

Panel A

| Materials | Break in Transportation | Plant | Market |

Panel B

| Materials | Plant | Break in Transportation | Market |

* Denotes terminal costs—unloading and loading product.

The location of cities.[4] Have you ever wondered why major cities originally located where they did? Access to cheap water transportation helps explain the location of major port cities such as New York, Boston, San Francisco, and San Diego. But what about Atlanta, Denver, and Dallas? Most city locations grew out of the desire of firms to avoid transportation costs.

Apart from a few resort communities, American cities started from industrial bases. Through their location decisions, industrial firms seek to avoid transportation costs to and from sources of materials and markets. Industrial firms also seek to avoid the *terminal* costs associated with transferring materials or products from one mode of transportation to another. These points of transfer, called **breaks in transportation** occur along the coastline and other less obvious places.

Exhibit 9–4 illustrates a firm's location decision given a break in transportation between the source of materials and the market. Assume the same transportation costs in all directions and that the firm engages in neither a weight-gaining nor weight-losing business. Locating the plant on a site somewhere other than at the break in transportation, as in Panel A, means the firm faces two sets of terminal costs: one at the break in transportation and one at the plant location. The logical decision then becomes to locate the plant *at* the break in transportation, as in Panel B, to avoid one set of terminal costs.

Many large American cities appear on the map along the Atlantic and Pacific coasts largely because industrial firms sought to avoid additional terminal costs. Denver also appears on the map at a break in transportation; before the development of modern transportation systems, crossing the Rocky Mountains required a change in transportation

[4] From Richard F. Muth, *Urban Economic Problems* (New York: Harper & Row, 1975), chap. 2.

modes. Atlanta was called Terminus because for many years the city operated at the end of railroad systems in the southeastern United States. Dallas has a similar railroad heritage.

The benefits and costs associated with transportation have a major impact on the location of cities. Although the theory of "terminal (or transportation) costs avoidance" does not completely explain the location of all cities, it does provide an economic rationale for the location of many cities. Cities develop from the economic location decisions of firms and households. They also prosper as the result of the surrounding physical environment, as in the cases of Fort Lauderdale, Florida, and Vail, Colorado, and even from regulatory circumstances, such as Las Vegas, Nevada.

HOW THE SPACE MARKET OPERATES

The decisions that determine who owns land and how much land becomes allocated to various private uses including farms, homes, offices, manufacturing plants, stores, hotels, golf courses, tennis courts, and used-car lots take place in real estate markets, given the limits placed by government through land use controls. The *market* means an environment in which buyers and sellers come together to exchange and determine the prices of goods and services. This environment might take the physical form of a marketplace in a city, an electronic computer network, or the offices of dealers and brokers. Real estate transactions do not occur in a single, universal market. The real estate market consists of two markets: the market for *physical* space—the **space market**—presented in this section, and the market for *financial* assets—the **asset market**—discussed in the final section of this chapter.

The same economic principles of supply and demand that determine economic outcomes for other products and services govern the amount of space produced and the prices of improved real estate. The unique characteristics of real estate, the most important being its fixed location and the time lags to create or remove space in response to changes in demand, also affect how real estate markets operate. This section presents a simple model of real estate market operations and explains how market participants react to changes in demand and supply.

FUNCTIONS OF THE SPACE MARKET

In general, the space markets perform the following three functions, each through the price mechanism:

1. Allocate existing space among those who demand space.
2. Expand or contract space to meet changing conditions.
3. Determine new uses for land.

To demonstrate the functions of real estate markets, consider the case of Atlanta prior to the 1996 Olympics. This event produced dramatic short- and long-term effects on

E X H I B I T   9 - 5

FUNCTIONS OF THE SPACE MARKET: THE CASE ATLANTA DURING THE OLYMPICS

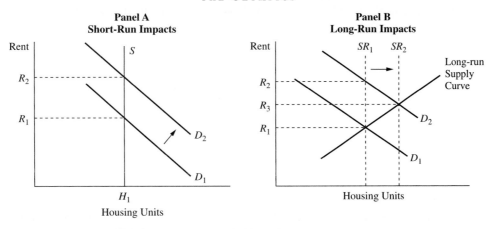

Panel A
Short-Run Impacts

Panel B
Long-Run Impacts

the city's rental housing market, as shown in Exhibit 9–5. Panel A shows the perfectly vertical position of the short-run supply curve for rental housing. This curve means that, even though demand increases from D_1 to D_2, apartment developers and existing property owners who can convert their spaces to rental use do not have the ability first to add to the supply of rental units and then easily reverse their actions when the Olympics end. The increase in demand from the influx of visitors to the area, therefore, causes rents for existing properties to increase from R_1 to R_2. Rent increases result in a reallocation of space in the market. Tenants who cannot afford the higher rent during the Olympics move to lower-quality rental housing, and visitors who can afford higher rents occupy the space. The space market works in this way to carry out its first function: to allocate existing space among those who demand space.

As shown in Panel B, the supply line for rental housing in Atlanta becomes more horizontal in the long run. During the months preceding the Olympics, existing space begins to expand and to become more fully utilized to meet the increase in demand from temporary residents. Bedrooms appear in the basements and attics of single-family homes in the area, for example. Rents begin to come down from R_2 to R_3 as the short-run supply of space increases from SR_1 to SR_2. The space market now works to carry out its second function: to expand or contract space to meet changing conditions.

Eventually, building and permanent conversion of new rental units commences to accommodate the migration of households attracted to Atlanta for permanent residency resulting from the Olympics. This conversion of agricultural land to urban use represents the third function of the space market: determination of new uses for land. The long-run supply curve in Panel B indicates this outcome.

SUPPLY AND DEMAND MODEL WITH VACANCY

The model of demand and supply in the space market starts with a simple equation, $V_a = S - D$. The letters V_a stand for the amount of vacant space in the markets for commercial real estate such as offices, shopping centers, and apartments. Also, it could stand for the number of unsold units of real estate, such as single-family homes and condominiums. The letter S symbolizes the supply of rental space (or number of units) available and that will soon appear, and D represents the amount of space (or number of units) currently rented.

Vacancy rarely equals zero. In "good" markets, the supply of real estate generally exceeds demand by some amount because of vacancy due to tenant turnover. In "bad" markets, the supply far exceeds demand because not enough space users seek the available space. The inventory of vacant space, V_a, varies over time, from geographic market to geographic market, and from property type to property type.

To illustrate how landlords behave, suppose an office building landlord has 200,000 square feet of space to rent, and the current rent is $15 per square foot per year. If demand declines or remains unchanged in the near future, the landlord will aggressively, but probably unsuccessfully, try to sign 5- to 10-year leases at the $15 rent. However, if demand is expected to accelerate, the landlord may voluntarily hold some space in inventory to capture potentially higher rents in the near future.

NATURAL VACANCY

The level of vacancy defined as V_a represents the *actual* or observed amount of vacant space in the market at a point in time. The actual vacancy rate equals the amount of vacant space as a percent of all available space. Assume the amount of vacant space in an office market equals 2 million square feet. This translates into a vacancy rate of 10 percent given that the total amount of available office space equals 20 million square feet (2 million square feet/20 million square feet = 10 percent). In the long run, supply and demand forces come into balance, and an equilibrium or **natural vacancy** (V_n) rate results. Suppose the natural vacancy rate in the same office market stands at 12 percent. Thus, the *difference* between the actual vacancy rate and the natural vacancy rate becomes a key indicator of space market strength.

Exhibit 9–6 presents several market scenarios and the appropriate reactions of office market developers to differences between the actual and the natural vacancy rates. The poorest development scenario is Number 3, in which the actual vacancy rate is twice the natural vacancy rate. If scenario Number 5 occurs, developers will react positively because natural vacancy well exceeds actual vacancy.

How do we find V_n to make use of this key indicator of space market strength? While no proven estimation techniques exist, one simple approach involves taking the average of actual vacancy over many years, making sure to include one or more complete real estate cycles. In several studies, statistical analyses of the long-term relationship between V_a and

EXHIBIT 9-6

EVALUATION OF SPACE MARKET STRENGTH IN AN OFFICE MARKET

Scenario	Actual Vacancy Rate		Natural Vacancy Rate	Result	Developer Reaction
1.	12%	=	12%	The market is *equilibrium*.	Development occurs at a normal pace.
2.	15	>	12	The market is *somewhat overbuilt*.	Development occurs at a slower than normal pace.
3.	24	>	12	The market is *substantially overbuilt*.	Development stops.
4.	10	<	12	Demand is strong relative to existing supply.	Development occurs at a faster than normal pace.
5.	6	<	12	The market is *substantially underbuilt*. Demand is very strong.	Development occurs at a rapid pace.

rent have led to estimates of V_n for apartment markets in major U.S. cities.[5] These studies rely on the relationship between rents and vacancy discussed later in this section.

FACTORS INFLUENCING SUPPLY AND DEMAND

The real estate investors and developers who become the best forecasters of future vacancy, and therefore future supply and demand conditions, tend to be the most financially successful. The first step in making accurate supply and demand forecasts involves identifying the *factors* that affect the supply and demand of units for sale and for rent.

Generally, demand for improved real estate stems from the number of participants in the market, their incomes and wealth, the prices of substitute properties, and credit conditions, such as interest rates. The determinants of supply include the prices of factors of production—land, labor, and materials, the number of developers in the market, developers' expectations about the future, and credit conditions. Detailed lists of important supply and demand factors for housing, retail, and office markets appear in Exhibit 9–7. These factors may be overridden by government policies affecting land use both domestically and internationally.

RENTS

The definition of rent takes many forms beyond the notion of a simple payment for space. *Contract* or *stated rent* means the payment for space under a gross lease. **Net contract rent** means payment for space under a net lease. **Net effective rent** equals contract or net

---

[5] See, for example, Stuart A. Gabriel and Frank E. Nothaft, "Rental Housing Markets and the Natural Vacancy Rate," *American Real Estate and Urban Economics Association Journal* (Winter 1988), pp. 419–29 and James D. Shilling, C. F. Sirmans, and John B. Corgel, "Price Adjustment Process for Rental Office Space," *Journal of Urban Economics* 22 (1987), pp. 90–100.

E X H I B I T   9 - 7

D E M A N D   A N D   S U P P L Y   F A C T O R S   F O R
V A R I O U S   P R O P E R T Y   T Y P E S

Market	Demand Factors	Supply Factors
Housing	New household formations	Prices of factors of production used in the construction process
	Age composition of new households	Productivity of factors of production and technology
	Household income	
	Mortgage credit conditions	The numbers of builders in the market
	Prices of substitute units	Builders' expectations about sales in the future
	Ownership costs	
	Expectations about the future	Demolitions
	Seasonality	Credit conditions
Retail	Number of consumers	Prices of factors of production
	Consumer income	Productivity of factors of production
	Consumer tastes and preferences	Number of developers
	Prices of substitute products	Developer expectations
	Credit conditions and payment plans	Demolitions
		Conversions
		Credit conditions
Office	Number of local firms	(Similar to retail market supply factors)
	Type of business of local firms	
	Number of local firms expanding or upgrading	
	Number of new firms entering the local market	
	Number of local firms ceasing business or leaving local market	
	Office space square feet per employee	

SOURCE: Neil Carn et al., *Real Estate Market Analysis*, (Englewood Cliffs, N.J.: Prentice Hall, 1988).

contract rent minus the financial equivalent of concessions granted to tenants to induce them to sign leases, such as few months of free rent, free parking, and liberal tenant-finish allowances.[6] It is important to note that when performing an analysis of rents, one should not compare contract rent with effective rent. Effective rent is generally recognized as the best measure of the true cost of occupied space.

From the discussion earlier in this chapter, we know that distance from important centers of economic activities—retail centers, universities, and airports, for example—and key fundamentals—such as the income level of people in the area, the size of the space, and age of improvements—explain much about the level of rents for properties. Nevertheless, these factors do not totally explain rent levels. Many studies attempt to find the *other* factors that contribute to rent setting so landlords can provide features that the market demands, and sometimes to answer public policy questions.

---

[6] When a tenant signs a lease, the landlord usually provides a certain amount of money per square foot, the *tenant finish allowance,* so the tenant can design and decorate the space to suit his or her needs and tastes.

REAL ESTATE FOCUS 9-2

Trends in the External Environment that Will Affect Real Estate Markets

For several decades Anthony Downs has served as one of the leading experts on trends in housing and commercial real estate markets. Working as a Senior Fellow at the Brookings Institute and consultant to Salomon Brothers in 1994, Downs prepared a document that presents his thoughts about significant trends that will affect the direction of real estate markets from 1995 through 2020. In this document, *Key Trends in the External Environment of Commercial Real Properties* (New York: Salomon Brothers, July 1994), Downs identifies the following key trends:

· **Population growth**. From 1995 through 2020 the U.S. population will increase by 60 million people, about the same number added during the period of rapid growth of real estate markets from 1969 through 1994. Downs expects that the growth in demand for space from the enlarged population will create outstanding development opportunities beginning in 2000.

· **Information technology**. The continuing advancements in information technology will accelerate trends already under way in the economy and real estate markets. Some of these trends include decentraliza-

tion of firms and households to more remote locations, movements of workers from lower productivity to higher productivity industries, and changes from large to smaller production units. Many questions remain about the extent to which people will substitute personal interactions at work, school, and shopping for working, learning, and ordering goods and services through computer networks. Downs expects that the need for personal interaction will persist so that businesses, such as well-run shopping malls, will survive the changes in information technology.

· **Racial and ethnic composition of the population**. Charts from the report presented below show a decided shift in the composition of the U.S. population from 1995 through 2020. The percentage of non-Hispanic whites will decline in favor of higher percentages of Hispanics and Asians. By 2020, 45 percent of U.S. children will come from minority households. Downs predicts that because of these trends levels of education and real incomes will fall. Real estate markets must respond with access to educational institutions and low-cost housing opportunities.

ETHNIC COMPOSITION OF THE U.S. POPULATION, 1995 AND 2020

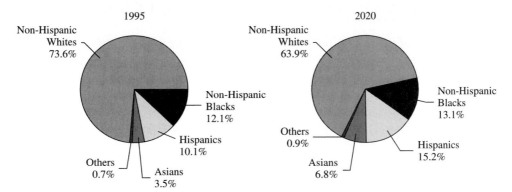

SOURCE: U.S. Census Middle Projections.

Apartment rent. An extensive review of apartment rent studies by John Benjamin and Stacy Sirmans uncovered several less well acknowledged factors that consistently influence rent levels.[7] The question of whether apartment complexes should include luxury amenities often plagues landlords. Holding all other factors constant, 11 out of 11 studies found a significant positive effect on rent from luxury amenities. The issue remains as to whether the additional rent justifies the cost of these amenities. Similar findings occurred when studies focused on features, such as including utilities in the rent, allowing pets, granting rental concessions, and providing good security. Surprisingly, a higher quality neighborhood equated to higher rents in only 50 percent of the studies surveyed.

Retail rent. Studies of rents in shopping centers focus on their unique market orientation and rental structure. One study, for example, confirmed the direct tradeoff between the base rent and the percentage rent paid on the basis of tenant sales.[8] As the percentage rent obligation increases, the base rent payment declines. Another study found that shopping center rents vary significantly with building configuration and tenant location within the center, and that they demonstrated considerable sensitivity to changing economic conditions in the local area.[9]

Office rent. The rents for office space also exhibit a great deal of sensitivity to local market demand and supply conditions. John F. McDonald estimates that if the local office vacancy rate declines by 1 percent, say from 19 percent to 18 percent, then landlords have the opportunity to charge nearly $1 more per square foot of rent, say from $20 per square foot to nearly $21.[10] As with other property types, office rents vary significantly with location and building quality. Other important factors that have a positive effect on rents include the height of the offices (i.e., higher floors) in the building, the number of services provided by the landlord, and whether the building was specially built for the tenant.[11]

SPACE AND ASSET MARKET INTERACTION

Characteristics of the market for physical space include the amount of observable space on the supply side and the derived demand for goods and services on the demand side. The demand for retail space in shopping malls for computer games, for example, derives

---

[7] John D. Benjamin and G. Stacy Sirmans, "Apartment Rent: Rent Control and Other Determinants," *Journal of Property Research* 11 (Spring 1994), pp. 27–50.

[8] John D. Benjamin, Glenn W. Boyle, and C. F. Sirmans, "Retail Leasing: The Determinants of Shopping Center Rents," *American Real Estate and Urban Economics Association Journal* 18 (Fall 1990), pp. 302–12.

[9] C. F. Sirmans and Krisandra A. Guidry, "The Determinants of Shopping Center Rents," *Journal of Real Estate Research* 8 (Winter 1993), pp. 107–14.

[10] John F. McDonald, "Vacancy Rates and Effective Rents in Chicago's Office Market," *Illinois Real Estate Letter* (Summer/Fall 1993), pp. 8–9.

[11] See, for example, John L. Glasscock, Shirin Jahanian, and C. F. Sirmans, "An Analysis of Office Market Rents: Some Empirical Evidence," *Journal of the American Real Estate and Urban Economics Association* 18 (Spring 1990), pp. 105–19, and William C. Wheaton and Raymond G. Torto, "Office Rent Indices and Their Behavior Over Time," *Journal of Urban Economics* 35 (March 1994), pp. 121–39.

from popular demand for playing computer games. Leasing of physical spaces creates cash flows to landlords during the period of tenant use. When real estate sells in the asset market, buyers receive the rights to cash flows that the spaces generate. Rents reflect the prices of space and **sale prices** reflect the values of assets and the right to collect rents.

Both space and asset markets require segmentation for analysis purposes. Property type represents one important segmentation. Buyer and seller behavior in establishing prices of homes in a Chicago suburb, for example, adjusts to the entry of a new regional shopping center nearby. Nevertheless, buyers and sellers do not examine sales of shopping centers for information about possible selling prices for homes; they observe the sales of other homes in the area. The other major segmentation, by geographic area, occurs because of the highly localized nature of real estate due to its fixed location. Changes in the market for homes in Hawaii, for example, do not influence home buyer behavior in Maine. On the other hand, the space and asset markets for other types of property, such as large industrial plants and luxury hotels, have regional, national, or international participants on the demand side.

THE ECONOMIC FUNDAMENTALS MATTER!

In Chapters 2 through 8, which give an investment perspective, the values of properties depended on their income potential and how investors perceive the riskiness of the incomes. Income results from rents minus expenses; thus, if expenses do not vary substantially across properties, increases in rents and reductions in vacancies primarily affect values positively. What causes rents to increase and vacancies to decline in the space market? These changes occur because some locations and other property characteristics become relatively more attractive on the demand side or more scarce on the supply side. Values also increase because some component of the discount rate declines, such as the general level of interest rates or the market's perception of the riskiness of rents. Remember these two important points:

1. Events in the space market that determine rents and variations in rents are fundamentally linked to values in the asset market.
2. Events in the capital markets that affect interest rates and the relative attractiveness of all types of assets as investments affect real estate asset values.

We define the **economic fundamentals** as the characteristics of national, regional and local markets (as listed in Exhibit 9–7); of property locations; and of the capital improvements at those locations that make one property command higher and more stable rent and consistently lower vacancy than other properties. What else besides these economic fundamentals matters to the determination of rents and asset sale prices?

GOVERNMENT INFLUENCES

If only the economic fundamentals matter, then anyone interested in knowing about real estate markets would simply build statistical models that capture the fundamental determinants of supply and demand and then use the models to predict market movements.

REAL ESTATE FOCUS 9-3, INTERNATIONAL

The New Real Estate Market in China

Before 1987, the real estate industry in the People's Republic of China added only 3 to 4 percent of GNP, which falls short of levels in most Eastern European socialist economies. Recently, property prices in China have accelerated at a rapid pace and government reforms place China in the real estate world spotlight. In 1995, the Law of the People's Republic of China on Urban Real Property Administration went into effect. The law does many things to promote the creation of a private real estate market, including title registration, establishment of property development companies, legalization of mortgages, and legal recognition of leases. The question of property rights, such as prohibiting trespass, eviction, and foreclosure, remains open.

The law specifically addresses real estate speculation, an issue facing many nations attempting the transformation from socialist to market economies. While investment follows economic fundamentals, speculation follows market trading psychology. Governments attempt to limit speculation in favor of investment to promote productive use of societal resources and to restrict wealth redistribution based on nonfundamentally driven motives. Under the law in China, for example, the government grants long-term development rights to a development company. If development does not commence within one year, the government assesses the company an "idle land" fee of 20 percent. Also, the law assesses large gains from property sales with taxes of 30 to 60 percent.*

*See Lim Lan Yuan, "Implications of China's New Property Law on Real Estate Investments," *Real Estate Finance* (Fall 1995), pp. 96–101.

Certainly the fundamentals of the supply and demand for space play a large role in determining space market rents and asset market sale prices, but many times other factors, such as interest rates and the actions of governments, lead to unusual and unpredictable outcomes.

During the early 1980s, for example, prices in the real estate asset market were increasing at the same time that vacancies in the space market were increasing. This unusual result was explained by Patrick Corcoran who argued that federal government tax policy and policies toward financial institutions artificially lowered the cost of development.[12] Developers therefore could create and sell assets with less regard for the economic fundamentals of demand in the space market.

Another potential distortion of real estate markets comes from local land use control and zoning. Chapter 10 contains details about the structure and administration of these laws, but the question here centers on their real estate market effects. If governments impose controls on the use of someone's land to protect the welfare of all citizens, then one expects that the value of the land declines by virtue of the rights of use taken away. Given that land use designations change and regulations do not apply in the same way to all properties, the potential exists for substantial market distortion from this nonfundamental source. But what if local planners, as students of the real estate markets, engage in the political process of assigning uses to land with both the market and the public welfare in mind—they "follow the market." In that case, land use assignment by public planners

---

[12] Patrick J. Corcoran, "Explaining the Commercial Real Estate Market," *Journal of Portfolio Management* (Spring 1987), pp. 15–21.

turns out not to differ substantially from development of land predicted from the economic fundamentals. The issue of how local land use controls influence values remains the subject of considerable debate among real estate market experts. A review of the literature on this topic reveals very little evidence that local land use and zoning laws negatively influence property values.[13] The results of these studies, however, do not prove conclusively that planners follow the market.

DO THE INDIVIDUALS MATTER?

If only the fundamentals matter, then the people involved in property transactions have no direct effect on rents and values—properties rent and sell for the same prices regardless of the individuals on either side because everyone faces the same demand and supply fundamentals. If the people matter in addition to the fundamentals, then the analysis of the terms in contracts between people for exchanging property rights, such as leases and contracts for sale, offers opportunities to learn about the levels and movements of rents and property values.

To consider this issue further, let us assume that P stands for the transaction price of an apartment property in Chicago sold by an individual to an insurance company— $P = \$5$ million. Let V stand for the true, but unknown, value of the property based strictly on the fundamentals. If only the fundamentals matter, then $P = V = \$5$ million. If special circumstances specific to the individual or the insurance company become part of the transaction, then P + or − Error $\neq V = \$5$ million. This means that we cannot trust P as an accurate measure of the true value of the property because the people in the transaction created a distortion—the error. A small distortion would not necessitate an adjustment to P by an appraiser so that it accurately reflects V; only a large distortion would necessitate an adjustment.

How do these distortions occur? Information problems represent one source of error. Suppose the individual selling the property lives in Washington, DC, and has little information about real estate market conditions in Chicago. By contrast, the insurance company sends a small army of bright real estate analysts to Chicago to study the market. In this instance, $P < V$ because the insurance company was more knowledgeable and would never buy at $P > V$, whereas the individual might sell at $P < V$. We discussed these information problems, along with other imperfections in real estate markets, earlier in this chapter.

Bargaining power and negotiating experience also may play roles in causing P to vary from V. An insurance company that engages regularly in transactions could "outfox" an individual who infrequently trades property. Finally, impatience creates distortions. The individual might need to sell the property quickly, thus allowing the property to go to the insurance company at $P < V$.[14]

---

[13] J. M. Pogodzinski and Tim R. Sass, "Measuring the Effects of Municipal Zoning Regulations: A Survey," *Urban Studies* 28, no. 4 (1991), pp. 597–621.

[14] For a presentation of the theory of price formation (why P does not equal V), see Daniel C. Quan and John M. Quigley, "Price Formation and the Appraisal Function in Real Estate Markets," *Journal of Real Estate Finance and Economics* 4 (1991), pp. 127–46.

E X H I B I T   9 - 8

POSSIBLE PRICE FROM THE BUYER AND SELLER GAME

Trading Region
("True" value, offer, counteroffer, and
final transaction prices fall within this region)

Minimum	Maximum
Seller will	Buyer will
accept	pay
(reservation	(reservation
price)	price)

Exhibit 9–8 shows a price continuum along which all possible Ps occur. At the left end lies the minimum price that the seller will accept and at the right end lies the maximum price the buyer will pay. Between these **reservation prices** lies the region that includes V, P, and the error that equates them. If the buyer's reservation price lies to the left of the seller's reservation price, then a transaction will not occur, in theory.

Empirical findings.   Studies in financial economics support the conclusion that the market values of securities move in reaction to the presence of tax and leverage *clienteles*— investors with special interests in avoiding taxes and taking on debt. Brian Maris and Fayez Elayan review this literature and find in their study a tax-induced clientele willing to pay more for equity REITs.[15] Only a few studies address the question of whether people make a difference to the values of unsecuritized real estate. During the 1980s, some real estate market observers believed that limited partnership syndications overpaid for properties intended to deliver maximum tax benefits to limited partners. However, holding other factors constant, William Beaton and C. F. Sirmans found that the prices paid for apartments in one study area were statistically equal across organizational forms of buyers.[16] Recently, findings from a study of lodging property transactions between 1985 and 1992 by John B. Corgel and Jan deRoos confirm that some buyers, individuals and foreign, consistently overpaid for properties, and certain sellers, financial institutions and the Resolution Trust Corporation, accepted too little for properties.[17] Definitive answers to questions about the influences of people on rents and property prices will come from additional studies of the types mentioned in this section. However, many studies support the contention that the economic fundamentals dominate in the space and asset markets.

---

[15] Brian A. Maris and Fayez A. Elayan, "A Test for Tax-Induced Clienteles in Real Estate Investment Trusts," *Journal of Real Estate Research* (Summer 1991), pp. 169–89.

[16] William Beaton and C. F. Sirmans, "Do Syndications Pay More for Real Estate?" *Journal of the American Real Estate and Urban Economics Association* (Summer 1986), pp. 206–15.

[17] John B. Corgel and Jan A. deRoos, "Buying High and Selling Low in the Lodging-Property Market," *Cornell Hotel and Restaurant Administration Quarterly* (December 1994), pp. 33–38.

THE PSYCHOLOGY OF REAL ESTATE MARKETS

Now we consider the effects on rents and prices of people acting *irrationally and collectively*. Do people rely on rumors and behave like stampeding cattle, while ignoring the economic fundamentals, when buying real estate? Such irrational buyer behavior underlies a phenomenon known as a **speculative bubble**. A bubble exists in the price of an asset if its price becomes high just because people think it will go higher in the future.[18] Studies of real estate prices in the United States and Japan confirm the existence of speculative bubbles during the 1980s. Karl Case and Robert Shiller interviewed hundreds of homeowners in several United States cities and found that some unknown factor apart from the demand and supply fundamentals caused dramatic increases in home prices.[19] The increases induced potential home buyers to purchase houses just before prices rose even higher, and this increase in demand accelerated the pace of price increases. Kyung-Hwan Kim and Seoung Hwan Suh performed a statistical study of land and housing prices in Japan and Korea and found evidence of a price bubble in Japan, but not in Korea.[20]

Cycles. We may never know for sure what caused the nonfundamentally driven increase in real estate prices during the 1980s. Perhaps it was a rational response to government policy to promote investment in real estate, irrational herd instinct on the part of buyers, or both effects contributed to the wild price increases. Historically, real estate markets have always followed long and deep cyclical patterns. Exhibit 9–9 comes from an article by Steven Grenadier about the persistence of real estate cycles.[21] The graph shows the long and radical decline of office market vacancy rates prior to the dramatic increase in vacancy during the 1980s. High vacancy rates persist through the mid-1990s. Does this mean that the United States office market will experience a long and steady decline in vacancy during the late 1990s and early 2000s?

Explanations for the boom-and-bust cycles of real estate markets focus on (1) the long length of the construction period for most properties, (2) mortgage lenders' unwillingness to stop lending when markets become overbuilt, and (3) lenders' failure to initiate loans when development becomes justified by the fundamentals. Grenadier's three-stage model of the development process emphasizes the option characteristics of leasing, construction, and raw land purchase. Simulations of the model confirm that properties that take longer to build do operate in markets characterized by more overbuilding and shortage. A developer who starts a project in a sound market may finish the project in a weak market two or three years later. In addition, the model results indicate that the high costs of changing tenants, the high costs of altering the space of existing buildings given changes in demand, and the high costs of changing the space plans given changes in demand during

---

[18] See Joseph E. Stiglitz, "Symposium on Bubbles," *Journal of Economic Perspectives* 4 (1990), pp. 13–18.

[19] Karl E. Case and Robert J. Shiller, "The Behavior of Home Buyers in Boom and Post-Boom Markets," *New England Economic Review* (November/December 1988), pp. 29–46.

[20] Kyung-Hwan Kim and Seoung Hwan Suh, "Speculation and Price Bubbles in the Korea and Japanese Real Estate Markets," *Journal of Real Estate Finance and Economics* 6 (January 1993), pp. 73–87.

[21] Steven R. Grenadier, "The Persistence of Real Estate Cycles," *Journal of Real Estate Finance and Economics* 10 (March 1995), pp. 95–119.

EXHIBIT 9-9

VACANCY RATES FOR THE U.S. OFFICE MARKET, 1972-1990

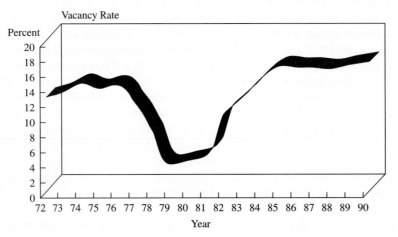

SOURCE: Coldwell Banker and Building Owners and Managers Association, from Grenadier (1995).

construction contribute to the persistence of high vacancy during weak markets and low vacancy during periods of strong demand. Rents and vacancy react very slowly to changing fundamentals due to endemic costs associated with altering the space and its usage.

THE ASSET MARKET

The term *asset market* is synonymous with the *financial asset market* and the *capital asset market*, in which the suppliers of capital invest their money in assets. Capital comes in two forms: equity capital, such as the money from individual investors who own properties, and debt capital, such as the money from banks that grant loans. Decisions about how to allocate capital depend on return and risk relationships among alternative investment opportunities, as discussed in Chapter 7. Real estate appears attractive to individual investors and banks compared to bonds, for example, if the returns on real estate exceed the returns on bonds with the same risk. As noted in Chapter 1, capital assets come in two forms: financial assets and real assets. Real estate, both through investment in the real asset and creation of associated financial assets such as mortgages, competes directly with other assets for capital in this market.

Most assets continue to trade in **unsecuritized markets**, which means among other things that property-level prices do not appear among the stock and bond listings in financial newspapers, such as *The Wall Street Journal*. Corporations that only hold real estate and recently many REITs have appeared to form a **securitized market** for real estate. While small compared to the unsecuritized real estate markets, the securitized

REAL ESTATE FOCUS 9-4

Can Sellers Obtain Higher Prices by Auctioning Their Properties?

The overwhelming majority of real estate sales occurs with the aid of brokers as *negotiated posted-offer* transactions. This means that sellers publicly or privately list the prices of their properties so that potential buyers can make bids with the knowledge of the prices sellers hope to obtain. Then, buyers and sellers haggle over the final price and terms. Do sellers "leave money on the table" by following this convention? Would sellers of real estate receive higher offers in the market if they did not reveal the prices they hoped to obtain, and instead auctioned their properties?

These questions came to the forefront a few years ago when the Resolution Trust Corporation (RTC) was charged with selling real estate and mortgages obtained by the federal government when it closed failed savings and loan associations. The RTC selected an auction approach to selling many of these assets. As in the case of the RTC, most property auctions occur in troubled times, when many properties are for sale and sellers need money from quick sales of their properties to cover financial positions elsewhere. Studies confirm auction discounts up to 25 percent from negotiated prices, depending on a variety of circumstances.*

During good markets it seems possible that auctions will yield higher prices than negotiated sales. Kenneth Lusht found a slight auction premium in a study of Australian house transactions during the 1980s and George Gau and Daniel Quan argue that auctions bring out buyers who find it costly to search the market and then haggle over price; thus, they tend to pay more at auctions to avoid these costs.**

---

* For a review of these studies and an excellent treatment of the subject of auctions, see Daniel C. Quan, "Real Estate Auctions: A Survey of Theory and Evidence," *Journal of Real Estate Finance and Economics* 9 (July 1994), pp. 23–49.

** See the article cited above for a lengthier discussion and the locations of these studies.

---

market segment for assets represents a growing and extremely important segment. Its importance lies in the public, and almost continuous, availability of price information about real estate.

WHO PARTICIPATES?

The participants in the United States commercial real estate asset market, as discussed in Chapter 5, include a wide array of domestic and international individuals and institutions. On the equity ownership side, corporations and partnerships maintain the largest positions. However, many of these entities consist of small organizations formed by individuals. On the debt side, participation mostly comes from major financial institutions and investment banks. Securitized interests represent the fastest-growing segments on both sides of the real estate asset market. Real Estate Investment Trusts purchased vast amounts of property with equity capital in recent years. Mortgage lending supported by investment banks led to the creation of many billions of dollars of commercial mortgage-backed securities during the mid-1990s.

ASSET PRICES AND VALUES

If we assume for the moment a competitive asset market, such that the true values of real estate assets equal the prices observed from transactions, then $V = P =$ the present value of future incomes at the current discount rate, where V stands for value and P stands for the transaction price. A literal interpretation of this equation means that real estate prices and values depend on the current level of income, the future prospects for income growth, and the discount rate. Because of the fundamental linkage between the space market and asset market, and from the discussion of the determinants of rents in the previous section of this chapter, we know that prices and values vary according to the physical characteristics of properties, their locations, and the economic conditions of the market environments—the economic fundamentals! The incomes capture the influences of these fundamentals.

Prices and values also vary according to conditions in the capital markets. The discount rate incorporates these conditions. In Chapter 7 we defined the discount rate as $E(R_j) = R_f + RP_j$. The term R_j represents the required return on investment, the discount rate R_f represents the current return on Treasury securities of comparable maturity, and RP_j is the required risk premium.

The R_f applies uniformly to all capital assets so its movements do not affect real estate asset markets differently than other asset markets. The risk premium, RP_j, thus becomes the key determinant of real estate prices for two reasons. First, this rate reflects the volatility of current and future cash flows in the space market in the eyes of the suppliers of capital. Second, the risk premium often exceeds the risk free rate. It would not be uncommon in the mid-1990s to observe a discount rate for real estate equal to 16 percent, the R_f equal to 6 percent, and the risk premium equal to 10 percent.

Suppose Investor Bob encounters a real estate investment opportunity for which the expected return equals 16 percent, given an asking price of $1 million and his estimates of operating cash flows and proceeds from a sale in seven years. If the prices of corporate stocks of similar risk produce a return of 18 percent, then Bob allocates his capital to stocks.

Now suppose Bob learns that, because of recent lease renegotiation, the incomes from the real estate investment will be considerably more stable and less likely to produce losses than initially expected, such that the revised risk premium becomes 8 percent rather than 10 percent. Under the revised scenario the price of $1 million becomes justified and real estate appears relatively more attractive than stocks of comparable risk and return.

Prices and values depend heavily on expectation of income growth and the continuing reevaluation of the riskiness of one asset versus another. The important points to remember from this section are these:

1. The prices paid for real estate assets relate directly to the rental income generated by the property. Rental income varies with the economic fundamentals of the property, especially the physical characteristics, location characteristics, and local economic conditions.
2. Real estate prices and values move in accordance with the perceptions of capital suppliers about the variability of rental income relative to compet-

ing investment opportunities. Expectations of variability become embedded in the discount rate through the risk premium.

REPLACEMENT COST AND VALUES

Nobel Prize winning economist James Tobin maintained that the market value of a firm should equal the replacement cost of its assets.[22] He defined the equilibrium condition as $Q = 1$, where Q is the market value divided by replacement cost. We borrow this concept to better understand when real estate becomes too expensive and too cheap. In equation form,

$$Q \text{ (real estate)} = \text{Price or Value/Replacement Cost}$$

In equilibrium, transaction prices and values equal replacement cost; therefore $Q = 1$.

The replacement cost of properties includes the cost of land and the cost of labor, materials, and services to put buildings in operation. Replacement cost also includes the profit of developers. When transaction prices of properties exceed replacement cost, $Q > 1$, developers seize the opportunity to develop competing properties and sell them for more than total development costs, including normal developer profit. When $Q < 1$, prices of existing properties appear cheap relative to their replacement cost. Development then slows or stops and investors begin taking positions in existing properties in anticipation of upward movements of prices toward their replacement cost. Exhibit 9–10 provides a graphical demonstration of this important concept.

During the late 1980s and early 1990s prices fell to levels well below replacement cost. As shown in Exhibit 9–11, which tracks Q in the lodging property market from 1986 through 1994, Q reached a low of .39 in 1992 and began moving up toward 1.0, as it was in 1986 and as theory would predict.[23] Savvy investors who bought operating properties during this period when their price were low relative to replacement cost earned exceptional returns with the recovery of prices.

"NOISY" PRICES

Earlier in this section we assumed that the transaction prices of properties equal their true values. This assumption has been the subject of a long-standing and continuing debate about whether transaction prices have too much "noise" to serve as trustworthy indicators of real estate values. What does the term **noisy prices** mean in this context? As discussed at the beginning of the chapter, transaction prices sometimes deviate from what they should be based on the fundamentals because of disturbing influences from the buyers and sellers in transactions and other factors that induce dramatic movements in prices,

---

[22] For more information on Tobin's Q without going back to Tobin's original work, see Steven B. Perfect and Kenneth W. Wiles, "Alternative Constructions of Tobin's Q: An Empirical Comparison," *Journal of Empirical Finance* 1 (1994), pp. 313–41.

[23] See John B. Corgel, "Capital Flow to Lodging Real Estate," *Real Estate Finance* (January 1996), pp. 13–19.

EXHIBIT 9 - 10

ASSET MARKET EQUILIBRIUM CONDITIONS

Equilibrium
Normal development

Market Price ⚖ Replacement Cost

Upward Pressure on Prices
Slow development
Buy existing properties

Price ⚖ Cost

Downward Pressure on Prices
Rapid development

Price ⚖ Cost

EXHIBIT 9 - 11

PATHS OF LODGING PROPERTY Q

Q

1.6
1.4
1.2
1.0
.8 (1.0)   (.72)   (.65)   (.57)   (.57)   (.52)   (.47)   (.49)
.6   (.39)
.4
.2

	1986	1987	1988	1989	1990	1991	1992	1993	1994
Luxury	1.0	1.40	.69	.64	1.07	.96	.46	.30	.38
Mid Price	.90	.56	.65	.57	.57	.43	.30	.45	.47
Economy	.81	.54	.49	.51	.50	.46	.35	.44	.53

DATA SOURCE: Hospitality Valuation Services International

such as government regulation and market psychology. These deviations are referred to as *noise*. The critical question remains—are prices too noisy?

A large literature exists on this question, but no firm answer has emerged. Some studies find excessive volatility in real estate prices whereas others show that real estate prices move in concert with fundamental indicators.

INTERACTION WITH SECURITIZED MARKET

During the past decade in the United States and in many other developed nations, the real estate asset market evolved into two markets: the traditional property market and a securitized market. In the United States, over 100 new REITs appeared during the 1993 through

1995 period and now many publicly traded corporations, such as Host Marriott, operate exclusively as real estate investment companies. In other countries, investors have broadened opportunities to publicly trade securities backed by real estate owned by companies and property trusts.[24]

Although still small in comparison to the market in which individual properties trade, the existence and growth of a real estate securities market revolutionized how we think about and study real estate markets. Specifically, real estate securities trade almost continuously; thus, capital market participants observe the prices of real estate each day. Prices of securitized real estate on March 16th, for example, incorporate all information that became available on March 16th that could influence rent levels, volatility, and growth. Incorporation of information occurs far more frequently and quickly in securitized markets in than unsecuritized asset markets due to the greater frequency and volume of trading.[25]

Do the prices of real estate securities contain information about market movements that would not appear until later in the prices of properties? Could the savvy investor study the behavior of prices in the securitized market and then successfully use that information to make money by buying and selling in the property market? These questions provide justification for studies in **price discovery**. Richard Barkham and David Geltner's studies of the securitized and unsecuritized markets in the United States and England led them to conclude that the important information about movements in real estate fundamentals shows up first in security prices and not until a year later in property prices.[26] While no trading rules were explored in this research, the results indicate that opportunities exist to profit in the property market by analyzing the behavior of prices in the securities market.

SUMMARY

Traditional thinking about real estate markets recognizes the local nature of these markets and that each property type operates in a unique economic environment. Events during the 1980s provided insights into the operations of real estate markets. Now instead of viewing the retail market in Denver, for example, as one market, we consider it two markets: the market for retail space and the market for retail assets or properties.

The events of the 1980s also provided insights about how fundamental factors, such as physical property characteristics, location characteristics, and local economic conditions, influence rents in the space market and prices in the asset market. These fundamentals *are* the primary determinants of rents and prices. They also tie the two markets together. This chapter explains how the markets operate in response to the fundamentals. Also, it examines the evidence on how

---

[24] See Chapter 5 for more information.

[25] Securitization is discussed in more detail in Chapter 19.

[26] Richard Barkham and David Geltner, "Price Discovery in American and British Property Markets," *Real Estate Economics* 23 (Spring 1995), pp. 21–44.

nonfundamental factors such as the irrational behavior of individual market participants, certain government actions, and market psychology influence rents and prices.

The stock phrase about the three things someone needs to know about real estate comes under scrutiny in this chapter. We take a careful look at what location means to real estate markets and conclude that the fixed location of properties limits arbitrage. This imperfection, while serious, may not limit the development of real estate markets as participants find ways to acquire information more cheaply and introduce trading innovations for the claims against the asset. The rapidly growing market in real estate securities provides evidence of this kind of innovation.

Rent constitutes the price of space in the space market. Rent levels and changes therefore yield important information about the strength of the space market. The current vacancy rate is another indicator, especially when viewed relative to the long-run vacancy in the market. The market reaches equilibrium when the current vacancy equals the long-run vacancy. When the current vacancy does not equal the long-run vacancy, market participants have an indication of the future direction of rents and they begin development activity to create new space.

Sale price constitutes the price of the asset in the asset market. The relationship between replacement cost and asset prices is the key indicator of strength in this market. In equilibrium, asset prices equal replacement costs. When they are not equal, market participants have an indication of the future direction of asset prices and they begin development activity to add to the number of properties.

In this chapter, we have attempted to assemble much of the available knowledge about real estate markets. The stock of knowledge, however, changes dramatically each year.

KEY TERMS

Arbitrage 265
Asset market 272
Breaks in transportation 271
Economic fundamentals 279
Efficient markets 266
Factor substitution 268
Information costs 265

Input linkage 269
Location monopoly 263
Natural vacancy 274
Net contract rent 275
Net effective rent 275
Noisy prices 287
Output linkage 269

Price discovery 289
Reservation price 282
Sale price 279
Securitized market 284
Space market 272
Speculative bubble 283
Unsecuritized market 284

TEST YOURSELF

Answer the following multiple choice questions:

1. The optimal location for a soft-drink bottling plant is
   a. Near the source of raw materials (other than water).
   b. Midway between the sources of raw materials and customers.
   c. Near the markets for the product.
   d. At the edge of a mountain range.
   e. It doesn't matter; the plant could be located anywhere.

2. Which is *not* a function of real estate markets?
   a. To allocate existing space.
   b. To expand or contract space to meet changing conditions.
   c. To determine land uses.
   d. To delineate market boundaries.
   e. All of the above.

3. Which characteristic of real estate is primarily responsible for the imperfect nature of real estate markets?
   a. Government.
   b. Fixed location.
   c. Market psychology.
   d. Speculative bubbles.
   e. Diversity of demand.

4. If $Q = 1.2$, what is the condition of the asset market?
   a. The market is weak and prices will rise.
   b. The market price is high and developers have an excellent opportunity to build.
   c. This indicator has nothing to do with strength in the asset market.
   d. Prices should rise dramatically in the future.
   e. Replacement costs are too high.

5. Speculative bubbles
   a. Result from irrational and collective behavior in the asset market.
   b. Regularly occur in real estate markets.
   c. Occur in the space market but not in the asset market.
   d. Occur when $Q > 1$.
   e. Sometimes happen in the bath tub.

6. What is the difference between net contract rent and net effective rent?
   a. Net contract rent is the base rent and net effective rent is based on a percentage of tenant revenues.
   b. Net contract rent is what is actually paid after deducting rental concessions.
   c. Payment of net effective rent becomes effective at the beginning of the lease term; net contract rent payments begin later.
   d. Net effective rent has been adjusted for rental concessions.
   e. The two terms have the same meaning.

7. What are the consequences of the fixed location of real estate?
   a. The property cannot be moved to take advantage of better market opportunities elsewhere.
   b. The property cannot be moved to avoid a negative influence on value from usage of adjacent property.
   c. Market participants must invest more in information about the asset because of all the factors that can affect values at a location.
   d. Answers a, b, and c are all correct.
   e. None of the above.

8. Transaction prices of real estate assets
   a. Equal the buyers' reservation prices.
   b. Equal the sellers' reservation prices.
   c. Fall exactly in the middle between the buyers' and sellers' reservation prices.
   d. Are set by real estate brokers based on their perceptions of buyers' reservation prices.
   e. Fall somewhere between the reservation prices of buyers and sellers depending on the bargaining skill of the people.

9. Why do some firms spend more money than others on rent to secure locations close to important economic centers?
   a. Mainly to gain greater prestige.
   b. To avoid transportation costs to the center.
   c. To have better access to commercial services.
   d. Only firms with substantial wealth can afford central locations.
   e. All of the above are correct answers.

10. Real estate markets have been characterized by periods of dramatic overbuilding and shortage. Why have these boom-and bust cycles occurred?
    a. The cost of changing tenants is very high.
    b. The costs of altering existing space is very high.
    c. Construction periods are very long.
    d. Changing plans during construction is very costly.
    e. All of the above are correct answers.

PROBLEMS FOR THOUGHT AND SOLUTION

1. Describe how discount rates for real estate are influenced by activities in the capital markets.

2. Describe how discount rates for real estate are influenced by changes in the economy.

3. How is the long-run or natural vacancy rate determined and what purpose does it serve?

4. Is there any distortion from asset prices based strictly on the fundamentals created by the people involved in transactions?

5. The existence of a securitized real estate market provides an opportunity for price discovery in the property asset market. What does price discovery mean and why is it important?

CASE PROBLEMS

1. A manager of a large commingled fund that invests pension fund money in real estate has hired your consulting firm for advice about which metropolitan markets currently offer the best prospects for high returns from rent increases on office property investment. As part of your analysis, you compute long-run vacancy rates, current vacancy rates, and vacancy rates for one year in the future for five metropolitan areas as shown below.

Area	Current Vacancy	Vacancy Forecast (one year from now)	Natural Vacancy
Detroit	8%	9%	10%
Atlanta	13	20	15
Cleveland	8	6	7
Denver	15	15	20
Salt Lake City	10	12	15

Which two metropolitan areas offer the best potential?

Give reasons for your selections.

2. Your first job after college is with a REIT that hired you to help liquidate its apartment portfolio to enable the company to concentrate more on retail property investments. Seven years ago the REIT acquired two apartment properties at the same location in Los Angeles. The two properties were at one time operated as one property. They were divided five years ago by a fence to facilitate an attractive refinancing opportunity. During discussions about pricing the properties for sale, your boss states that the two properties will ultimately sell for exactly the same price. After all, the properties are virtually indistinguishable from one another. You then call your boss a naive idiot for believing that the properties will sell for the same price. The properties, you claim, could sell for substantially different prices. You had better defend yourself with convincing arguments and perhaps a graphic demonstration. Your boss is a little upset!

ADDITIONAL READINGS

The following book contains a thorough treatment of real estate markets from an urban economics perspective:

DiPasquale, Denise, and William C. Wheaton. *Urban Economics and Real Estate Markets*. Englewood Cliffs, NJ: Prentice Hall, 1996.

A less rigorous treatment appears in

McKenzie, Dennis J., and Richard M. Betts. *Essentials of Real Estate Economics*. Upper Saddle River, NJ: Prentice Hall, 1996.

An excellent review of traditional thinking about real estate markets is

Ratcliff, Richard U. *Real Estate Analysis.* New York: McGraw-Hill, 1961, Chapter 10.

Two strong syntheses of location theory are

Hirsch, Werner Z. *Urban Economics.* New York: Macmillan, 1984, Chapter 3.

Mills, Edwin S., and Bruce W. Hamilton. *Urban Economics.* New York: Harper Collins College Publishers, 1994, Chapter 5.

A good practical overview of real estate and capital markets is found in

American Institute of Real Estate Appraisers. *The Appraisal of Real Estate*, 11th ed. Chicago: AIREA, 1996, Chapters 4 and 6.

Data on real estate prices and rents in various geographical markets can be obtained from many sources today. Two good sources are

National Real Estate Index, published by Koll, Emeryville, California.

Existing Home Sales, published by the National Association of Realtors.

10

CHAPTER

LAND USE, PLANNING, ZONING, AND ENVIRONMENTAL HAZARDS

DETERMINING LAND USE
The Market Solution
Externalities

PRIVATE RESTRICTIONS

PUBLIC PLANNING FOR LAND-USE CONTROL
Development of a Comprehensive Plan
Innovation and Flexibility in
    Comprehensive Planning
Implementation and Review of the
    Comprehensive Plan

PUBLIC ZONING FOR LAND-USE CONTROL
Purpose of Zoning
Legality of Zoning
Zoning Administration

INCONSISTENCIES WITH PRIVATE MARKET OUTCOMES
Impact on Property Values

Transferable Development Rights
Growth Management

ENVIRONMENTAL HAZARDS
Governmental Regulation
Types of Hazardous Materials
Implications for Real Estate Investors

SUMMARY

KEY TERMS

TEST YOURSELF

PROBLEMS FOR THOUGHT AND SOLUTION

INTERNET EXERCISES

CASE PROBLEMS

ADDITIONAL READINGS

After reading this chapter, students will be able to:

1. Write brief definitions of planning and zoning that emphasize the difference between the two functions.

2. Explain how economic principles determine the use of individual parcels of real estate.

3. Cite two reasons why the market system may not operate to maximize the net social benefits of land use.

4. Identify two bases for legal attacks on zoning.

5. Identify the principal provisions typically contained in state growth management legislation.

6. Explain how a system of transferable development rights works.

7. Identify the major types of environmental hazards and the steps real estate investors should take to protect themselves.

DETERMINING LAND USE

In a private enterprise economy, individuals, businesses, and institutions own much of the nation's property. They make decisions about how land is used, usually with the objective of maximizing the individual owner's wealth or rate of return. In the absence of legal limitations, they may give little or no concern to how a particular land use will affect neighboring owners or the larger community.

Recognizing the impact that land uses may have on a neighborhood and community, local governments typically regulate how land may be used through **zoning**. Acceptable land uses are specified for various areas, or zones. A general, or comprehensive, plan for the community determines the acceptable land uses.

Chapter 9 noted that real estate markets perform the important functions of allocating existing space among those who demand space, expanding or contracting space to meet changing needs, and determining land uses. This third function of land-use determination operates primarily through two economic principles:

1. As transportation costs increase, the values of parcels of land tend to decrease relative to similar parcels with lower transportation costs.
2. As land prices increase, capital investment (i.e., improvements) on individual parcels of land is intensified, in effect substituting capital for additional land.

The operation of these economic principles of real estate markets helps determine how individual parcels of real estate are used. Land uses are usually identified in relatively broad categories such as single-family residential, multifamily residential, retail strip, shopping center, office, light-industrial, and heavy-industrial uses. Similar land uses tend to occupy similar locations and thus form patterns of land uses. For example, single-family residential uses tend to occupy large sections of an urban area. Similarly, retail, office, and industrial uses tend to be grouped in the same or similar geographic areas. This occurs because economic principles have similar effects on similar users of real estate. If one manufacturing firm finds economic advantage in terms of transportation cost savings and capital requirements at one location, other manufacturing firms may find a similar advantage at adjacent or similar sites. This tendency for similar land uses to agglomerate has been termed *economic zoning*.

Although market forces tend to produce groups or patterns of land uses, economic advantage also may accrue to competing and inharmonious land uses. Such uses, if not precluded by private or public restrictions, may obtain a monopoly position and enable their owners to profit at the expense of long-run social benefits. For example, a convenience store located in the center of a high-class residential subdivision would undoubtedly generate a great deal of business. Such a use, however, might lower the attractiveness of the subdivision to the extent that lowered land values would more than offset the value of the commercial use. Furthermore, the same motivation would lead other commercial firms to purchase other sites for commercial use to capture at least a portion of the potential business. This eventually could destroy the uniform nature of the subdivision and reduce residential land values greatly.

THE MARKET SOLUTION

Economic theory suggests that, in the absence of transaction costs, market participants tend to *negotiate away* the economic disadvantage of land-use decisions that lower net social benefits. In the convenience store example, the residential owners, recognizing that their property values would be reduced by a convenience store, would try to purchase the rights of the commercial firm to construct and operate the store.

Transaction costs, however, inhibit this process. Such costs include the cost of gathering information about property values, attorneys' fees, and the participants' time and effort in the negotiations. The market solution also assumes that both parties could measure and agree on the impact of the inharmonious use on both the user and the neighboring property owners.

Another problem arises in the market solution. The adverse influence may affect several or many parties, but some affected parties may not participate in the negotiations. Some property owners, for example, may not agree with the majority that the convenience store is a detriment to the neighborhood. Or, even if they do agree, they may not be willing to bear their fair share of the costs of purchasing the convenience store's rights, to spend the time and effort in the negotiations, to hire attorneys, or to forgo the convenience of shopping at the store (even if they agree that it is detrimental to property values). This unwillingness of some parties to participate in a common course of action is known as the *free-rider problem*. The result is to inhibit market processes from negotiating solutions to externally imposed negative influences.

EXTERNALITIES

Externally imposed influences, positive or negative, are termed *externalities*. They are particularly important in real estate analysis because of fixity of location; properties cannot be moved to escape negative externalities. There are many examples of potential *negative externalities:* A factory may spew smoke and dirt on neighboring properties; a supermarket may generate odors that are wafted to adjacent properties; occupants of a house may keep an unmowed and littered yard that detracts from the neighborhood; and college fraternity members may throw wild parties, producing unwanted noise for neighbors.

Positive externalities also may be important influences on property values. Residents who maintain attractive yards and keep their houses painted, for example, enhance the values of neighboring properties. Similarly, owners of office buildings, shopping centers, or even industrial properties who maintain their properties attractively contribute to property values in the general area. Both public and private facilities may provide positive externalities. Public parks, swimming pools, and other recreational facilities may have an important positive effect on area properties.

While positive externalities have the opposite effects on property values as negative externalities, they do not offset each other. A negative externality is usually more capable of destroying property values than a positive externality is capable of enhancing values. For example, it is unlikely that a public park on one side of a single-family residence could offset the adverse effect of a garbage dump on the other side. Builders or buyers can probably find other sites adjacent to the park, but not adjacent to the garbage dump, thus placing the site subject to the negative influence at a disadvantage. Property owners thus attempt to protect their property values from negative externalities by two means: *private restrictions* and *public restrictions*.

PRIVATE RESTRICTIONS

Landowners can create various restrictions on land use. These restrictions generally take the form of **restrictive covenants** and **easements** in deeds or subdivision plats as discussed in Chapter 20. The limitations typically include matters such as architectural style, size, and quality of improvements; the purpose for which the improvements may be used; outbuildings; external attachments such as vapor stacks, TV antennas, porches, and other protrusions; sheltering of automobiles and animals; and activities that might create nuisances such as burning, operating a business, or creating noise. Owners create private restrictions by recording them in the platting documents for a new subdivision, by including them in deeds given to purchasers of land, or both. For example, Exhibit 10–1 contains the deed restrictions for Oak Crest Estates. Any purchasers of property in the subdivision are subject to the restrictions, which any owner of property in the subdivision can enforce through a court action seeking injunctive relief.

Commercial easements are usually created in the same way: Owner-developers reserve the right for utility companies to install and maintain utility lines across individual

E X H I B I T 1 0 - 1

DECLARATION OF RESTRICTIONS, OAK CREST ESTATES

This indenture entered into this 23rd day of May, A.D. 1967, by Fletcher Land & Cattle Co., a Florida corporation, as the owner of the fee simple title to the following described real property, situate, lying and being in Alachua County, Florida:

Lots, parcels or tracts of land, being serially numbered from One (1) to Fifty-three (53), both inclusive, known as OAK CREST ESTATES, as same are identified, surveyed, and set apart on the survey plat of Harris H. Green, Registered Land Surveyor, under date of March 10, 1966, as per Plat Book "G", page 45, of the Public Records of Alachua County, Florida.

and such owner being desirous of selling and conveying various and sundry lots, parcels, or tracts of lands, surveyed as aforesaid, and to provide for restrictions and covenants to run with the title of each of said lots for the joint and mutual benefit of this owner and its several respective grantees, successors in title, and their respective heirs and assigns;

IT IS, THEREUPON, BY THESE PRESENTS, hereby stipulated, covenanted, and agreed by and between the undersigned owner of the above described lands, and its several and respective grantees and successors in title, each of whom, by the acceptance of the delivery of a deed of conveyance from said undersigned owner, hereafter, to any lot, tract, or portion of the lands above described and referred to herein and on said survey plat of OAK CREST ESTATES, as aforesaid hereby agree and obligate themselves to comply with and abide by each and every of the following restrictions, conditions and covenants hereafter set forth, as follows:

1. The following restrictive covenants shall run with the title of each of the lots or parcels in said survey plat and be binding upon all parties, firms, corporations and any other persons claiming title thereto until January 1, 2010 A.D.

2. Each of said lots or parcels shall constitute and remain a single home site and none of them shall be sold in part, or resubdivided by these owners or any of their successors in title.

3. Each lot or home site herein referred to shall be used for residential purposes only and no commercial enterprises shall be conducted thereon; and there shall be constructed thereon only one building for residential use, exactly as hereafter provided, which shall contain a minimum of One Thousand Five Hundred square feet of ground floor space for living area, exclusive of garage, car ports or porches attached thereto; except that there may be constructed on each of said lots or home sites a single service building for use as a pump house or tool storage building, provided that such second allowed building shall be constructed at a location no closer than 100 feet from the front lot lines, or 20 feet from the rear lot lines. For the purpose of determining the front lot lines of the various building sites herein referred to same shall be and are hereby specified as the lines of such lots contiguous to and facing east on the street area designated as N.W. 91st Terrace; those facing north and facing south on the street area designated as N.W. 9th Avenue, N.W. 10th Place (including the cul-de-sac area) and N.W. 11th Place (including the cul-de-sac area); also those lots facing east and west on the street area designated as N.W. 94th Street.

4. No residence or building shall be placed upon any of the lots in such subdivision except in conformity with the setback and side lot provision as fixed by the zoning regulations of Alachua County, Florida, provided that no such residence or building shall be constructed closer than 25 feet from the front lot lines or 15 feet from the side lot lines.

E X H I B I T   1 0 - 1   (c o n c l u d e d)

5. Each home shall be designed and planned as a single-family dwelling unit and there shall be no apartment buildings, duplexes, or temporary residences of any kind whatsoever, constructed upon either of said lots other than a single-family dwelling unit.

6. No house trailers, temporary construction, or dwellings may be moved to either of said lots from other sites; no dwelling having tin roofs shall be placed, erected, or constructed upon either of said lots.

7. No detached garage or other outbuildings shall be constructed upon any of the lots in such subdivision excepting only one additional building for use as a pump house, for the storage of tools and equipment as herein provided.

8. Except for unforeseen circumstances beyond the control of the owner, no residence shall remain uncompleted for more than nine months from the start of construction.

9. No poultry, cattle, horses, or swine shall be kept, housed, or maintained upon either of the lots in said subdivision.

10. Before commencing the construction of any improvements to be placed upon any of the lots or parcels contained in said survey plat, adequate plans and specifications therefor shall be submitted to and approved by an officer or director of Fletcher Land & Cattle Co., a Florida corporation, provided that approval shall not be unreasonably withheld or refused. All plans so submitted shall require, and all residences constructed in accordance therewith shall be so designed and constructed that the interior of all garages, car ports, or outbuildings shall be so constructed and placed that the interior thereof shall not be visible from the street area or areas upon which the residence served thereby is built; it shall be further required that the front elevation and each of the side elevations of all residences to be constructed in this subdivision shall be of identical materials, except where the front elevation contains only a portion of brick or concrete block or other masonry materials.

11. Any of the owners of either of the lots in said subdivision who shall be hereafter guilty of violating any one or more of the foregoing restrictive covenants shall be required to respond in damages to anyone or all other owners of lots in said subdivision and, in addition, be required to remove and correct such violation, and in addition to such damages and such action shall pay to any party or parties who shall successfully conclude a suit for the purpose of obtaining damages and the removal of such violation a reasonable fee for the services of their attorneys in that behalf, together with any and all other costs lawfully taxed in such proceedings.

12. All persons, firms and corporations who may hereafter succeed to the title, or acquire any lien or interest against or in the above described real property and improvements situated thereon, do hereby jointly and severally agree to keep and maintain the said improvements in a good state of repair and to properly care for and maintain all lawns and shrubbery in a neat and attractive condition.

properties. The easements are identified and recorded in the subdivision plat, and they bind all future purchasers by references in deeds to restrictions and easements of record. Utility easements usually enhance values by providing access to essential public services; however, they can also be negative influences. Utility easements have been discovered under buildings, gardens, patios, and other inconvenient places. Needless to say, the value of such improvements is impaired if they must be totally or partially destroyed to service the utility.

Restrictive covenants and easements are generally effective devices for controlling land uses and dealing with nuisances within subdivisions. Nevertheless, they carry two important drawbacks for controlling land uses within most political jurisdictions: enforcement procedure and geographic scope. With respect to the first, owners in a subdivision carry the responsibility of enforcement. They must take the initiative by instituting court action to stop any violations of the restrictive covenants. If violations occur and owners are unaware of the private restrictions or lack the motivation or resources to institute court action, the violations may continue.

The second drawback—limited geographic scope—obviously renders private restrictions ineffective as a device to control land uses beyond the boundaries of the subdivision. In a few cases in which a single developer creates an entire community, this drawback does not apply. Examples are new towns and communities such as Columbia, Maryland; Reston, Virginia; and Palm Coast, Florida. These communities have an extensive list of restrictive covenants that owners agree to abide by when they purchase properties. Since the restrictive covenants apply to the entire community, the private restrictions have the force of public controls.

PUBLIC PLANNING FOR LAND-USE CONTROL

Public land-use planning and zoning involves the development of guidelines and criteria for the determination and control of future land uses in a community or geographic area. Public land-use planning and zoning is carried on by cities, counties, and regional planning agencies, usually through a planning commission of elected or appointed officials. The theory of public planning is that the separation of land uses enhances property values by controlling negative externalities. Residential areas are protected from commercial and industrial uses, and these uses are protected from the intrusion of residential uses. Thus, the negative impacts of these uses on each other are minimized.

The authority to control land uses is vested in cities and counties by the states through the police power. City or county governments often appoint members of planning commissions. The planning commissions usually serve in an advisory capacity to the elected bodies that appoint them; all major plans and decisions are subject to the elected body's discretion. In order to carry out its work, the planning commission employs a staff of professional planners. A typical planning organizational structure is shown in Exhibit 10–2. The planning commission and staff normally have several functions. These include developing a comprehensive plan, recommending action on rezoning, approving site plans, and controlling commercial signs.

DEVELOPMENT OF A COMPREHENSIVE PLAN

A **comprehensive plan** is a general guide to a community's future growth and development. It involves projecting a community's future population growth, its requirements for water and other natural resources, its physical characteristics (e.g., existing development and soil conditions), its need for public services (e.g., schools and utilities), its need for

EXHIBIT 10-2

TYPICAL PLANNING ORGANIZATION

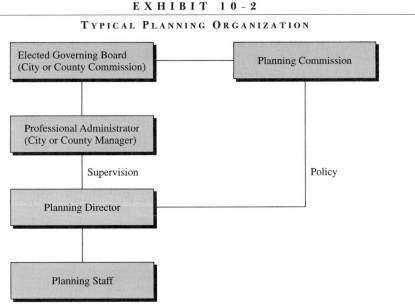

various types of land use (e.g., single-family residential and office), financial resources, and political constraints. Thus, a comprehensive plan attempts to guide future growth and development to accommodate the various needs of the community.

Objectives.   In preparing and maintaining a comprehensive plan, a planning commission must identify *objectives* based on community *goals*. Although such goals are by necessity general in nature, they provide direction to the planning process. Goals may not be stated explicitly but may be implied from decisions made in public hearings and by elected governing bodies. For example, decisions regarding expansion of a utility or transportation system, subdivision approvals, and rezoning requests may indicate whether a community favors or wishes to limit growth. Such decisions also may indicate the types of growth that are favored or discouraged. Zoning regulations and utility-expansion decisions, for example, may indicate clearly that certain types of industries are favored (e.g., computer companies), while others are not (e.g., industrial plants).

Similarly, communities can direct and regulate the volume of residential growth. An aggressive utility-expansion policy will encourage residential development at the urban fringe, whereas a limited expansion policy or one that requires developers to pay special fees will have the opposite effect (see Real Estate Focus 10–1). The building permit process that builders and developers must follow also can be streamlined or onerous. Onerous processes will encourage builders and developers to prefer other communities or areas.

REAL ESTATE FOCUS 10-1

Limits on Growth through Local Land-Use Controls: The Case of Petaluma, California

During the past two decades, several communities in the United States have instituted provisions in their land-use and zoning regulations to limit growth. These communities include Ramapo, New York; Boca Raton, Florida; and Boulder, Colorado. One of the most interesting court cases involving limits on growth occurred in Petaluma, California. This rapidly growing community south of San Francisco instituted a number of provisions to control its growth during the early 1970s. One of these measures placed a cap on the number of housing units that could be provided in the city in any year (approximately 6 percent of the total stock, or about 500 units).

The Construction Industry Association of Sonoma County (builders) challenged the regulation, asserting it violated the constitutional right to travel. The Federal District Court agreed with the builders and struck down the regulation. The Court of Appeals overturned the ruling, thus allowing the plan to stand as a legitimate use of the city's police power. The U.S. Supreme Court refused to hear the case, so the Court of Appeals' ruling stands.

The higher courts have universally upheld the right of a community to use the police power to control land use. The Petaluma case is one example.

SOURCE: *Construction Industry Association of Sonoma County* v. *City of Petaluma*, 275 F. Supp. 574 (1974); *Construction Industry Association of Sonoma County* v. *City of Petaluma*, 522 F. 2nd 897 (9th cir. 1975).

Governing boards identify specific *policies* to guide the planning effort. For example, a city commission may state that the community should attempt to rejuvenate commercial activity in the central business district or that it should avoid six-lane streets. The comprehensive plan must then be formulated with these goals in mind. Sometimes the goals are contradictory. A goal to develop an adequate street system for a community's expected traffic growth, for example, may conflict with the desire of residents not to have streets widened to accommodate additional traffic.

Existing and future conditions. Also in the early phases of the public planning process, the planning staff takes an *inventory* of the existing conditions in the community and forecasts *future growth*. The inventory of existing conditions, which provides the base on which forecasts are made, includes items such as total population, total employment, household income, household size, number of miles of highways, topography, retail sales, and water usage. Several key measures, such as total population, are forecast to establish future conditions in, say, 2005, 2010, and 2015. The comprehensive plan, therefore, shows where and how the expected growth should be accommodated. For example, the plan will outline districts for new residential, commercial, and industrial development and describe how additional water resources will be allocated to these districts.

Alternative approaches. After identifying objectives and forecasting future growth, planners must consider ways of accommodating both. Planners would have to identify and evaluate the advantages and disadvantages of each possibility. The evaluation process considers matters such as existing land-use patterns and plans for the provision of utilities, community facilities, transportation, and housing. Similar evaluations are required for alternative plans for residential, retail, industrial, and office development. Explicitly or implicitly, this evaluation involves a direct trade-off between the overall costs and benefits to the community of a particular alternative, compared to the costs and benefits of another.

Political process. Selection of a final comprehensive plan is usually a lengthy process. The governing board must adopt the plan, which usually requires significant public input through public meetings. Politics normally plays an important role in the process. A united stand by a large number of voters against the designation of a street as a major traffic artery or of a particular area as a commercial development, for example, may provide enough political pressure for a governing body to change that portion of a plan.

INNOVATION AND FLEXIBILITY IN COMPREHENSIVE PLANNING

A comprehensive plan usually must undergo continued scrutiny and thus needs to be sufficiently *flexible* to accommodate periodic modifications. Ideally, a comprehensive plan should guide, yet be consistent with, market forces and activity. When market forces are inconsistent with a plan, pressures will mount to change the plan. Yet repeated modifications will cause loss of confidence in the plan. It can also be rendered ineffective through legal actions and political pressures. In such cases, the planning process usually begins again.

To provide adequate flexibility, modern plans allow for nontraditional development and encourage an overall, or composite, approach by developers. Plans may encourage the use of such innovations as **planned unit developments** (PUDs), in which variances from traditional requirements for such matters as setback lines (distance of buildings from lot lines) and minimum areas per lot are allowed in exchange for larger areas of open space, public facilities, and attractive layouts and designs.

PUDs often integrate residential and commercial developments, which traditionally have been separated to eliminate externalities. Condominiums, attached single-family houses, and zero-lot-line layouts (in which houses are built up to the lot line on one side) add flexibility to traditional residential development. Additionally, some modern comprehensive plans are formulated with a *point system*. In these plans, new developments must accumulate a specified minimum number of points, which may be obtained by a variety of layouts and designs. For example, points would be awarded for open space, recreational facilities, streets, curbs, sewers, adequate private restrictions, and a demonstration that the existing infrastructure can accommodate the additional residents.

Finally, some communities use *performance standards* to allow facilities such as computer plants to locate in commercial districts. These standards are based on the extent to which operations impose negative externalities on surrounding parcels. Performance standards, like PUD regulations, represent attempts to reduce the emphasis on the traditional land-use and zoning theory that strict separation of land uses is required to control externalities. Economists have argued that such strict separation is inefficient. The benefits of controlling externalities in many cases are insufficient to justify the costs imposed on society by separating land uses. For example, if all of the employment centers are on one side of the community and all residential areas are on the other, large public expenditures for roads and public transportation will be required.

IMPLEMENTATION AND REVIEW OF THE COMPREHENSIVE PLAN

A comprehensive plan is usually general in nature. It identifies land uses in categories such as single-family residential, commercial, and industrial. These categories must be subdivided further by types, sizes, and permitted activities. For example, a residential district might be divided into R-1, where only half-acre lots for single-family homes are allowed, and R-2, where apartments are allowed. A commercial district might be divided into BP (business and professional), BR (retail sales and services), and BH (highway-oriented business services). Dividing the comprehensive plan's general land-use categories into more specific districts or zones is accomplished in the zoning ordinance. Since the characteristics of zones are defined rather precisely, the intent of the comprehensive plan can be enforced. Zoning, therefore, is usually the principal device for carrying out the comprehensive plan.

After formulation and implementation of a comprehensive plan, the plan must be monitored continually. Few plans stand the test of time without modification, and comprehensive plans especially are buffeted by many sources. Conflicts inevitably arise among developers, builders, environmentalists, and public interest groups.

PUBLIC ZONING FOR LAND-USE CONTROL

From the previous description, recall that *zoning* was defined as the regulation of land uses, population densities, and building types and sizes by ordering the uses of land according to special districts or zones. Such systems usually contain 10 to 15 broad categories of land use, with a number of subcategories in each broad category. For example, in the residential category may be subcategories for single-family detached, single-family attached, multifamily up to four or eight units, multifamily high rise, and so on. The zoning categories also may limit building heights and sizes and the number of unrelated occupants living in the same unit. The number of unrelated occupants, as well as various other requirements, such as adequate plumbing facilities in dwelling units, is for many communities governed by a separate set of regulations known as the *housing code*.

PURPOSE OF ZONING

Zoning is intended to control negative externalities through the implementation of the comprehensive plan. High transaction costs in the real estate market, however, make an

REAL ESTATE FOCUS 10-2

The Landmark Decision on the Legality of Land-Use Control and Zoning Regulations

The Ambler Realty Company intended to sell the 68-acre tract of land it owned in the village of Euclid, Ohio, to an industrial developer. However, in 1922, Euclid enacted a land-use/zoning ordinance that set aside part of this tract for residential development. Ambler Realty sued Euclid, claiming the ordinance resulted in a "taking" of Ambler's property without payment of just compensation, as prescribed by the United States Constitution.

The District Court agreed with Ambler Realty, but in a landmark decision the U.S. Supreme Court ruled that Euclid was not taking any part of the tract for a public purpose and that this ordinance was a legitimate use of the village's police power to control land uses.

This Supreme Court ruling has withstood the test of time in that it has served as an important precedent in virtually all subsequent disputes involving inverse condemnation. The ruling legitimized both land-use control as a police power exercise and the separation of land uses into districts and zones for land-use control.

SOURCE: *Village of Euclid, Ohio* v. *Ambler Realty Co.* 272 U.S. 365, 47 S. Ct. 1/4, 71 L. Ed. 303 (1926).

---

efficient market solution impossible. These costs consist of the time and effort required to assess property value impacts, the inaccuracies of those assessments and lack of agreement about the impacts, legal fees, capital costs, and free-rider costs. Since an efficient market solution cannot occur, negative externalities arise and result in reduced property values. Thus, zoning attempts to reduce or limit negative externalities through public or community action, with the objective of enhancing and preserving property values.

LEGALITY OF ZONING

As discussed in Chapter 20, real property refers to the exclusive right of owners to use and dispose of real estate (the tangible good) as they desire. Property rights, however, are not total and absolute; they are subject to the inherent constraints imposed by governments: taxation, police power, eminent domain, and escheat. Zoning is an exercise of police power—the right of a government to enact and enforce laws to protect the health and welfare of its citizens. Since zoning may greatly limit the use of property, some citizens may not agree that zoning protects their health and welfare. Increasingly numerous and severe land-use regulations have led some observers to contend that land is becoming more of a public resource than private property. For this reason, both zoning laws in general and their specific applications have been attacked on both constitutional and applied grounds. Indeed, zoning laws have been attacked in courts as confiscation of property without compensation—an act prohibited by the U.S. Constitution (see Real Estate Focus 10–2)!

Although some zoning laws have been declared unconstitutional, most have met constitutional tests, and zoning as a general practice has been legally acceptable in the United States for over 50 years. Almost all cities of any size have zoning laws, as do many counties. Some states require cities and counties to engage in comprehensive planning, which normally results in zoning as an implementing device. For example, several states have enacted growth management legislation that requires local jurisdictions to have comprehensive plans that meet state requirements.

The general thrust of court decisions on zoning laws is that zoning is constitutional and will be upheld when zoning ordinances are reasonable, are based on a comprehensive plan, and provide for all types of housing. Courts have overturned zoning ordinances that do not provide for low- and moderate-income housing on the grounds that they are *exclusionary*—they exclude certain types of people from living in the community. Similarly, zoning ordinances that have attempted to impose large minimum lot sizes (*e.g.*, two acres) and thus to limit population have been overturned on the grounds that they are arbitrary and exclusionary.

The taking issue. The question of whether zoning laws or other types of regulation that limit property rights and values require the property owners to be compensated is known as *the taking issue*. This terminology stems from the phrase in the United States Constitution: "... nor shall private property be *taken* for public use without just compensation." The philosophy that has guided court decisions for many years was stated by Justice Oliver Wendell Holmes in 1922 in a famous U.S. Supreme Court decision, *Pennsylvania Coal Company v. Mahon*. He wrote, "The general rule at least is, that while property may be regulated to a certain extent, if regulation goes too far it will be recognized as a taking" (260 U.S. at 415).

Nevertheless, a 1987 study pointed out that the limitation of property rights by zoning laws must be severe and flagrant before the courts grant compensation to property owners. The authors concluded that in *eminent domain takings*, compensation is almost always expected and required; yet courts usually have *refused* to grant compensation to owners whose rights have been limited or taken by *zoning laws*.[1] Two more recent decisions by the U.S. Supreme Court (June 1992 and June 1994), however, may shift the legal doctrine more toward the side of property owners. (See Real Estate Focus 10–3.)

Inverse condemnation. A number of zoning ordinances have been challenged in lawsuits for **inverse condemnation**. Inverse condemnation is a legal action for just compensation taken by a landowner against government for a partial taking. As pointed out above, most of these actions have been unsuccessful as the example in Real Estate Focus 10–2 shows; however, a few have succeeded when allowable use intensities were reduced. The lowering of land-use density is known as *downzoning*. Downzoning generally has been upheld on the grounds that property values in general, including the value of the affected parcel, may be preserved or enhanced by lowered use intensities. However, when landowners have shown that a community intended to buy land, but instead downzoned it, the courts have ruled against downzoning on the basis that the community had already recognized the value of the land. The downzoning was simply a way to avoid the cost of purchasing the land.

---

[1] Jerry T. Ferguson and Robert H. Plattner, "Can Property Owners Get Compensation for 'Takings' by Zoning Laws?" *Real Estate Review* 16, no. 4 (Winter 1987), pp 72–75.

REAL ESTATE FOCUS 10-3

Two Cases Indicating a Shift toward Protection of Property Rights

(1) *LUCAS* v. *SOUTH CAROLINA COASTAL COUNCIL*

This case reasserted the principle that property owners are entitled to just compensation if the value of their property is destroyed by laws that are enacted subsequent to their purchase of the property, even if the laws have the objective of preventing harmful or noxious uses of the property. The facts of the case are that Mr. Lucas bought two lots zoned for single-family residential use on the Isle of Palms near Charleston, South Carolina. He intended to build single-family homes on the sites, such as those on the adjacent parcels. At that time, Lucas's lots were not subject to the state's coastal zone building permit requirements. In 1988, however, the state legislature enacted the Beachfront Management Act, which had the effect of barring Lucas from erecting any permanent habitable structures on the parcels. He filed suit against the enforcing state agency, contending that even though the act may have been a lawful exercise of the state's police power, the ban on construction deprived him of all "economically viable" use of his property and therefore effected a "taking" that required the payment of just compensation. The state trial court agreed with him and entered an award of more than $1.2 million.

The state Supreme Court, however, reversed the trial court, saying that it was bound to accept the legislature's "uncontested findings" that new construction in the coastal zone threatened a valuable public resource. The court said that when a regulation is designed to prevent "harmful or noxious uses" of property akin to public nuisances, no compensation is owing under the Takings Clause, regardless of the regulation's effect on a property's value.

The U.S. Supreme Court reversed the South Carolina Supreme Court decision saying that ". . . the question must turn, in accord with this court's "takings" jurisprudence, on citizens' historic understandings regarding the content of, and the state's power over the "bundle of rights" that they acquire when they take title to property. Because it is not consistent with the historical compact embodied in the Takings Clause that title to real estate is held subject to the state's subsequent decision to eliminate all economically beneficial use, a regulation having that effect cannot be newly decreed and sustained, without compensation being paid the owner."

SOURCE: *Lucas v. South Carolina Coastal Council*, No. 505 U.S. 1003; 112 S. Ct. 2886 (1992).

(2) *DOLAN* v. *CITY OF TIGARD*

The U.S. Supreme Court may have significantly shifted doctrine in the takings issue with its decision in *Dolan* v. *City of Tigard* in June 1994. In this case the Court decided that conditions imposed by the city on the development of Ms. Dolan's property were not sufficiently related to the public interest to be constitutional. In order to demolish an old building and construct a new building on her property, Ms. Dolan had been required to dedicate a portion of her land lying within the 100-year flood plain for improvement of a storm water drainage system, and, in addition, to dedicate a 15-foot strip of land along the flood plain for a pedestrian-bicycle pathway. The U.S. Supreme Court ruled that the test used by the Oregon courts of "reasonably related" was not sufficiently strict and, instead, said that the test should be one of "rough proportionality." That is, the requirement for the dedication of land must be roughly proportional to the objective of the regulation under which the requirement was made and to the public interest. Based on this decision, it appears that local governments and other jurisdictions will be considerably more constrained in their imposition of requirements on owners and developers of property than they have been in the past.

SOURCE: Donald C. Guy and James E. Holloway, "Real Estate Development and the Takings Clause: *Dolan v. City of Tigard*," *Real Estate Issues* 20, No. 2 (August 1995), pp. 20–24.

ZONING ADMINISTRATION

Often property owners seek to have the zoning classification of their property changed. A developer, for example, may want to construct a residential subdivision on land currently zoned for agriculture, or an apartment building owner may wish to increase the size of the project to accommodate more units. The planning and zoning commission and staff normally review all such *rezoning requests*.

In considering rezoning requests, the following criteria are used:
1. Will the new zoning be consistent with the comprehensive plan?
2. Should the comprehensive plan be modified?
3. What effect will the new zoning have on surrounding land uses and on the larger community?

A request for rezoning that is consistent with the comprehensive plan is much easier to justify than one that varies from the comprehensive plan. If the request is inconsistent, the question becomes whether the comprehensive plan should be modified. If the rezoning request is reasonable, realistic, and consistent with current and expected development patterns, the plan should be modified to accommodate the changed zoning.

Finally, if either of the first two criteria justifies the request, its impact on surrounding land uses and the community should be evaluated. Will the change lead to more intensive use of other parcels? What effect will these changes have on neighboring property values? Will the change stimulate other rezoning requests?

Unlike a rezoning request that involves a proposal to change the zoning classification of a parcel, a **variance** request usually involves a minor change in the rules in an existing zone. Consider the situation presented in Exhibit 10–3. The Martin family has purchased a lot in a residential subdivision and plans to build a home with a pool and a detached garage on the lot. The local zoning regulation states that for property zoned R-1, any improvements must be set back 50 feet from the road. Since the owners are planning a garage that violates the setback regulation, they must obtain a zoning variance. Thus, the variance would involve only an adjustment in the setback requirement in this case, not a change in the R-1 classification.

Planning and zoning commissions also are charged with the responsibility of reviewing and approving site plans for large projects such as shopping centers, apartment complexes, and office developments. A **site plan** is a map of a project on its site. It identifies the building arrangement on the site and normally includes several views, or *elevations*, for the planned development. Matters such as parking, traffic circulation, ingress and egress, and landscaping also are specified.

The planning commission also approves residential subdivision plats. It considers the design of the subdivision, adequacy of streets, drainage and other utilities, and compliance with the city's *subdivision ordinance*. After approval, the plat can be recorded and the developer can proceed. The subdivision ordinance establishes a specific set of controls for the development of residential subdivisions in the community. In the past, some communities experienced a poor quality of subdivision development, which imposed costs on

E X H I B I T   1 0 - 3

V A R I A N C E   R E Q U E S T :   M A R T I N   R E S I D E N C E

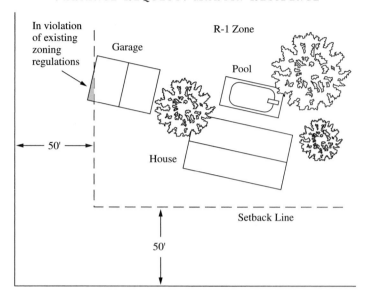

the entire community. The county or city, for example, usually takes over the maintenance of streets and gutters in a subdivision shortly after completion of the development. If poor-quality materials and designs are permitted, taxpayers in the community will soon bear a heavy financial burden to maintain these improvements to the land. Therefore, to ensure high-quality subdivision development, the subdivision ordinance sets forth engineering standards (*e.g.*, the type of pavement that must be used for streets).

The planning staff reviews site plans both from the point of view of the developer's efficient utilization of the site and also with regard to the public's concerns. For example, ingress and egress may be planned at an undesirable location in terms of safety or convenience. The commission would require the developer to change this before granting approval. Or the commission might require a vegetation buffer between the development and adjacent properties to make the new project less objectionable to its neighbors. Usually approval of the site plan is required before a developer is granted a building permit. The authority to review and approve these plans helps ensure the wise and efficient use of land.

Many communities have enacted *sign ordinances* that limit the size, location, and lighting of signs in commercial districts and shopping centers. The planning and zoning commission's function usually is similar to that of site-plan approval. It reviews proposed signs to ensure they comply with all relevant ordinances and regulations. Approval of a proposed sign allows the applicant to proceed with its construction.

INCONSISTENCIES WITH PRIVATE MARKET OUTCOMES

IMPACT ON PROPERTY VALUES

Inherently, planning and zoning substitute nonmarket for market decisions. This substitution may either enhance or degrade property values. To the extent that planning and zoning protect areas from inconsistent or undesirable land uses (such as a bar in the middle of a residential neighborhood), property values are protected and enhanced. But when the comprehensive plan and zoning provide too much land for one purpose and not enough for another, property values may be hurt. The plan may cause utilities to be extended in one direction where development does not occur, but not to areas where development would otherwise occur. By limiting densities, zoning may contribute to *urban sprawl*; by allowing high densities, zoning may contribute to *congestion* and other negative externalities. Such results may have a negative impact on property values and lead to legal actions claiming unfair and capricious zoning decisions and inverse condemnation of property rights. Moreover, systems of land-use control limit the property development rights (sometimes unfairly) of certain property owners in favor of the public welfare. Some local governments have attempted to mitigate these problems by instituting transferable development rights (TDR) systems.

TRANSFERABLE DEVELOPMENT RIGHTS

A relatively new method of regulating land uses is through the use of **transferable development rights** (TDRs). With this method the right to develop some properties to their maximum potential is taken away or reduced, but the development rights given up may be sold to the owners of other properties. Development rights of some property owners are reduced, but the owners have a means of obtaining compensation for their lost rights. Thus, those who receive the rights pay the owners of rights taken or reduced. (See Real Estate Focus 10–4.)

For this method to work, there must be a *sending* area of development rights and a *receiving* area, in which property owners are eligible to purchase the rights. By purchasing development rights, property owners in the receiving area are allowed to develop their properties beyond the limit allowed by zoning. The allowable additional density is known as a *bonus maximum.*

The TDR system protects and preserves threatened areas or properties by limiting further development. TDR programs have been implemented in New York, Chicago, Denver, and San Francisco primarily to preserve historic districts and landmarks; in Montgomery and Calvert Counties, Maryland, and the Pinelands of New Jersey primarily to preserve agricultural land and open space; in Palm Beach and Dade Counties, Florida, to preserve environmentally sensitive areas; and in Hollywood, Florida, to preserve access

REAL ESTATE FOCUS 10-4

TDRs from Grand Central Station

Although the Penn Central Transportation Co., Inc., owner of Grand Central Terminal in New York City, wanted to construct a 56-story office building above the terminal, the application was rejected by the New York City Landmarks Preservation Commission—the station is a historic landmark, and its character would be substantially changed. Penn Central sued the city. The litigation took nearly 10 years and was decided by the U.S. Supreme Court in 1972 in favor of the city.

Penn Central then decided to sell a portion of its development rights. The Philip Morris Corporation had planned to build its world headquarters on a small (20,000 square-foot) lot on 42nd Street across from the terminal but needed more space than zoning allowed. Thus, in 1978, Philip Morris purchased development rights from Penn Central that allowed construction of approximately 75,000 additional square feet of floor space for $2,240,000. This price was about double the market value of land in the area, but it allowed Philip Morris to construct an additional three and one-half floors in the building.

---

to the beachfront.[2] As Exhibit 10–4 shows, the intensity of use allowed under normal zoning is reduced in the sending areas and increased in the receiving areas. In urban areas, the intensity of use can be specified in terms of numbers of floors or floor-area ratios (square feet per floor lot size), while in rural areas intensity can be specified in terms of the number of structures or units per acre.

The use of TDRs is not a substitute for zoning but instead is a complementary tool for land-use regulation. Although courts might find that zoning laws that attempt to differentiate among small areas and types of structures are discriminatory, TDRs provide compensation to landowners whose development rights are restricted. They also rely more on market forces in determining the value of development rights than do condemnation proceedings in which a landowner's rights are simply taken with compensation established by a court.

There are, however, some problems with TDRs. Unless demand is matched with the supply of TDRs, they cannot be sold immediately to private recipients. To remedy this difficulty, some plans have established a TDR "bank," in which TDRs are deposited after being purchased by the jurisdiction or a private institution, such as a commercial bank. They are then available for purchase when the demand increases. Such a bank requires capital and leads to further problems of determining which TDRs to buy and sell, the value of the TDRs, and the tax liability for the TDRs. The Chicago TDR plan failed because of a lack of demand for the TDRs.

Another problem with TDR plans is they usually apply to only a few properties having historic, environmental, or recreational significance. For example, in the Palm

---

[2] David E. Levy, *Transferable Development Rights*, unpublished master's thesis, Graduate School, University of Florida, 1985.

EXHIBIT 10-4

OPERATION OF TDR SYSTEMS

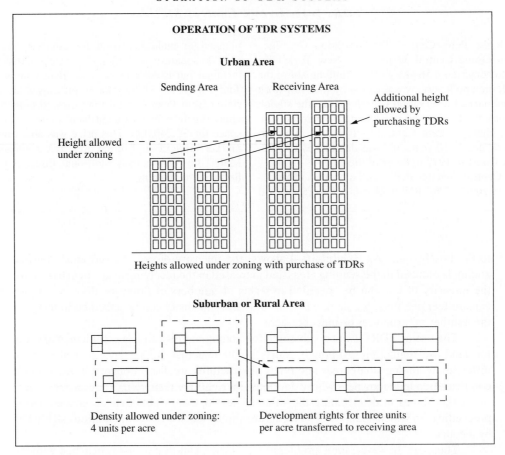

OPERATION OF TDR SYSTEMS

Urban Area

Sending Area   Receiving Area

Additional height allowed by purchasing TDRs

Height allowed under zoning

Heights allowed under zoning with purchase of TDRs

Suburban or Rural Area

Density allowed under zoning: 4 units per acre

Development rights for three units per acre transferred to receiving area

Beach plan, development rights may be transferred only from properties in "reserve" or "conservation" areas in the unincorporated portion of the county. The TDRs may be used only as bonuses in planned unit developments (PUDs) within the urban service area of the unincorporated portion of the county. Only one transaction has occurred there, and relatively few transactions have occurred in other plans.

Thus, TDRs appear to be a viable tool for land-use regulation in conjunction with zoning, but their use seems limited to a few socially significant properties in small areas in which there is strong development demand. Variations of the basic concept may be devised that will extend the usefulness of TDRs to larger areas; however, it seems likely that greater flexibility could be built into traditional zoning to accomplish the same objectives.

GROWTH MANAGEMENT

Many communities and some states have attempted to "manage" growth, particularly those communities and states experiencing rapid growth. Rapid growth produces problems and difficulties in meeting the needs of both existing and new populations. For example, new housing areas may not have adequate infrastructure—roads, sewers, utilities, and fire and police protection. Older areas may experience increased traffic, an increased burden on social services, and higher taxes to help pay for new infrastructure.

Growth management laws at the state level usually require local jurisdictions to plan for and meet certain requirements. Typically these laws include provisions that require

1. Local jurisdictions (counties and cities) to have acceptable comprehensive plans. Such plans typically must be submitted to a state agency to judge acceptability.
2. Proposals for large-scale developments to be accompanied by **economic and environmental impact statements** (studies) that analyze the project's impact on surrounding areas. They usually must show that existing infrastructure will handle the added burdens or demonstrate how the burdens will be accommodated. They must also show that the environment will not be significantly degraded and that existing schools, fire and police protection, and social services are adequate to handle the new population or that the new development will include provision of these services.
3. Further development at the local level to be prohibited unless adequate infrastructure, schools, police and fire protection, and social services are in place when development commences (termed the **concurrency** requirement).
4. Local governments to include an **affordable housing allocation** in their comprehensive plans. This type of requirement means that local governments must encourage or mandate a "reasonable and fair" component of new housing construction for lower-income families.

Additionally, state laws may *permit* local communities to use the following techniques to manage growth and new development:

1. Establish **urban service areas**. For these areas boundaries are delineated around a community within which the local government plans to provide public services and facilities and beyond which urban development is discouraged or prohibited. Boundaries are usually designed to accommodate growth for 10 to 20 years with the intended result being that the community can provide more efficient services and that rural land and natural resources will be protected from development.
2. Establish **extraterritorial jurisdiction**. Some states give local governments powers to plan and control urban development outside their boundaries until annexation can occur.
3. Establish **growth limits**. The annual number of residential building permits is limited on the basis of objective criteria for determining the "best"

development proposals. The best proposals may be judged on the basis of a **point system**, in which the community planners award points according to the degree to which projects meet stated standards and criteria. For example, points may be awarded for adequacy of storm and sanitary sewers; adequacy of streets; provision of sidewalks, common areas, or playgrounds; and preservation of the natural environment.

4. Imposition of growth moratoriums. A **growth moratorium** is a temporary prohibition of development because of an immediate need to forestall a public health, safety, or welfare problem. Such problems may include the lack of sewage treatment capacity or intense traffic congestion. A moratorium is typically imposed for one to three years in order to allow time for the problem to be resolved.

Additionally, some states award tax advantages to firms that agree to develop businesses or industrial facilities in areas considered less desirable, for example in interior areas rather than along a seacoast. Such plans have not been widely adapted or implemented, however, since they lead inevitably to charges of favoritism and discrimination against firms already in the less favorable areas. Also, it is difficult to determine whether a firm would build in the more favorable areas without the tax break. In reality firms might prefer the less favorable areas without the tax break.

ENVIRONMENTAL HAZARDS

GOVERNMENTAL REGULATION

State and federal control of land uses has increased greatly over the past 20 years. This increase has occurred because of the awareness of environmental hazards. For example, a partial list of federal environmental control laws includes the Clean Air Act, the Clean Water Act, the Resource Conservation and Recovery Act, the Toxic Substances Control Act, the Safe Drinking Water Control Act, the Comprehensive Environmental Response Compensation and Liability Act, and the Occupational Safety and Health Act. Environmental hazards are regulated by federal, state, and local agencies such as the federal Environmental Protection Agency (EPA), the U.S. Department of Housing and Urban Development, state Environmental Protection Agencies (EPAs), local departments of environmental quality, local building and fire departments, and property lenders and loan insurers.

The scope and intensity of environmental regulation means property owners are subject to huge dollar amounts of potential liability if environmental hazards are found on their properties. For example, under the "Superfund" legislation (Comprehensive Environmental Response Compensation and Liability Act of 1980 and subsequent amendments), property owners must clean up many kinds of toxic wastes if they knew or had any reason to know the property was contaminated when they purchased it. Lenders who foreclose also may be subject to this cleanup requirement. Furthermore, some courts have required owners to clean up toxic wastes on their properties, even if they were *unaware* of its existence when they bought the property.

REAL ESTATE FOCUS 10-5

What Can Happen to a Property's Value When It Becomes Contaminated

The Shadyside Apartment complex consisted of 32 apartment units, with enough land to construct 40 additional units. In 1987 residents in neighboring homes began to notice gasoline odors in their basements. After considerable investigation by health authorities and a local pipeline company, it was discovered that one of the pipelines had developed a leak. About 100,000 gallons of gasoline had escaped, with most of it settling in a geological basin under the apartment buildings.

The pipeline company, working with the EPA, took immediate steps to recover the gasoline and to purify the water table upon which the gasoline was floating. Over a period of about two years 60 percent of the product was recovered; however, the EPA indicated that pumping, monitoring, and aeration would have to continue for at least 10 years.

Many residents moved out of the apartments, rents had to be lowered, and the complex took on a seedy appearance. Meanwhile, the gasoline floating on the water contaminated several nearby water company wells, requiring permanent shutdown and the need to draw water from other sources. This closure raised the water table under the apartments, resulting in continual flooding and ruining all interior finishes. Maintenance costs increased dramatically.

Two appraisals of the apartment project were made—one considered the property just before the gasoline leak occurred, while the second appraisal considered the full impact of the leak and concluded that the total loss in value to the property was about two-thirds of the before-value. The loss in value shown by the appraisals, together with the increased costs and lack of marketability of the property resulted in an out-of-court settlement in which the owner was paid the full before-value of the property and was able to keep the property.

SOURCE: Robert W. Hall, "The Causes of Loss in Value: A Case Study of a Contaminated Property," *Real Estate Issues* 19, no. 1 (April 1994), pp.23–27.

TYPES OF HAZARDOUS MATERIALS

Several types of hazardous materials are often present in properties, and these materials are a major concern of property owners, prospective buyers, lenders, and the public (See Real Estate Focus 10–5). These hazardous materials are sometimes termed **toxic waste**, or **sludge**.[3] Toxic waste includes the following materials, substances, and gases: asbestos, fiberglass, lead paint, polychlorinated biphenyls (PCBs), leaking underground storage tanks (LUSTs), and radon.

Asbestos and fiberglass. Asbestos has been a major problem in buildings constructed before the early 1970s. It was the primary material used for insulation and was considered ideal until its health hazards were discovered. It crumbles when subjected to physical pressure (this characteristic is termed *friable*) and releases tiny fibers into the air. These fibers are inhaled into the lungs and reduce breathing capacity.

Other forms of asbestos, such as vinyl asbestos tile (often used in kitchens and bathrooms) and jacketed asbestos insulation around hot-water tanks and pipes (if sealed airtight) do not present this problem. Asbestos in the tile is fused, or glued, into an inert, safe mass; and the airtight jacketing prevents fibers from being released into the air.

[3] David A. Smith, "Investor Topics: Investor Protection against Environmental Risks," *Real Estate Review* 19, no. 2 (Summer 1989), pp. 14–19.

Nevertheless, asbestos in all forms (but especially as building insulation) has caused a virtual panic. High concentrations of airborne fibers over a long time can produce malignancies and functional impairment of the lungs. Asbestos removal programs for public buildings (especially schools) and some private buildings have been undertaken. The cost of removal is very expensive and sometimes exceeds the value of the building. The EPA estimates that the cost over 30 years to comply with federal asbestos removal mandates will be $53 billion.

More recently, however, several studies have suggested asbestos is not as big a problem as originally believed. They have shown that the airborne concentrations of asbestos fibers in most buildings are not sufficiently high to cause health impairment. In fact, the only time serious health risks are created is when asbestos is ripped out of walls, and thus released into the air. But removal has been the required solution. It seems likely that reevaluation of the asbestos problem will result in less-stringent removal requirements and greater reliance on *sealing, encapsulation*, and *fusion* of the asbestos where it exists.

Fiberglass is widely used to replace asbestos for insulation. However, it has some of the same characteristics as asbestos and may have similar, harmful effects. Real estate investors should be aware of potential problems with this product.

PCBs and LUSTs. Polychlorinated biphenyls (PCBs) typically were used in electrical equipment, such as transformers, capacitors, and fluorescent lights. When broken, these types of equipment release PCBs into the ground or air, and exposure to PCBs can cause cancer and other health problems. Fortunately, PCB-producing components are relatively easy to identify and remove. Nevertheless, the existence or discovery of large PCB contaminations can be a matter of concern and liability for real estate investors (see Real Estate Focus 10–6.)

Leaking underground storage tanks (LUSTs) are potentially a huge problem for real estate investors. While the underground tanks in service stations are the largest source of such sludge, many others exist as well. Septic tanks and oil tanks of abandoned houses are but two examples. Many industrial firms have stored fuel or buried wastes in underground receptacles, and these sites are often unmapped and forgotten.

Lead paint and radon. Lead paint has ceased to be a major problem in most parts of the country because its dangers have been known for about 25 years, and it is no longer used. Also, it is relatively easily removed or covered up. Still, however, it is a problem in some old rooming houses, primarily in large cities. Occupants and owners of these types of houses should take steps to have any potential problem remedied.

Radon is a naturally occurring radioactive gas that is formed by the breakdown of uranium. Radon is found in soils containing uranium, granite, shale, and phosphate. These rocks and soils are common and are constantly generating radon. Radon gas is "slippery," meaning it is not chemically bound or attracted to other materials. Thus, it flows easily between the air spaces in soil as it is released during radioactive decay. Radon has a half-life of 3.8 days. As radon decays, it produces products that are "sticky," that is, attach themselves to objects such as walls in a home or dust particles that can be inhaled into the

REAL ESTATE FOCUS 10-6

Long Haul

Pipeline companies first added polychlorinated biphenyls, or PCBs, to lubricating oils as a safety measure to prevent flash fires in extremely hot compressors. Unfortunately, the exceptional stability that makes PCBs a fire retardant also means they don't break down in the environment. At Texas Eastern, PCBs leaked through motor seals and down the pipeline, ultimately contaminating at least 49 sites. By the 1970s, the potentially adverse health effects of exposure to PCBs had become an issue. The EPA banned their manufacture in 1979. But the oil—and the PCBs—must still be removed from the old pit. To that end, Texas Eastern plans to drill half a dozen groundwater monitoring wells at $20,000 each to help determine the extent of the contamination. It expects many more wells will be needed to fully map the location of the PCBs.

Then there's the matter of removing the contaminated soil. Special trucks will be needed to cart it to the nearest hazardous waste dump, more than 100 miles away. That can cost $500 per cubic yard, and the Gladeville pit may contain 500 cubic yards of soil by one estimate.

No wonder, then, that the broader, systemwide cleanup will take time, money, and more money. Already, Texas Eastern has 29 people working on the project full-time, and 200 mapping wells have been dug at contaminated sites along its pipeline. The company still estimates that it will take $400 million to clean up all the PCBs. And the job won't be completed anytime soon: Texas Eastern says it will be 10 years before all the contaminated soil is located and carried away.

SOURCE: "Poison Pills: In the Take-Over Game, Hidden Waste Dumps Haunt Buyer and Seller," *The Wall Street Journal*, April 3, 1990.

---

lungs. These products have even shorter half-lives that can be in terms of minutes. As these products decay, they release small bursts of energy that can damage lung tissue.

If radon gas accumulates in sufficient quantities in a building, the chances of contracting lung cancer are increased significantly. The U.S. Environmental Protection Agency reports that 5,000 to 20,000 lung cancer deaths a year in the United States may be attributable to radon.

Screening tests are available to determine whether radon accumulates in buildings in sufficient concentrations to cause health problems. Corrective actions should be taken in buildings where radon buildup occurs. These actions include sealing cracks in floors and foundations, venting gases from the soil beneath and around a building, and increasing ventilation inside the building. In a few areas, radon can be so pervasive as to make any building occupancy hazardous.

IMPLICATIONS FOR REAL ESTATE INVESTORS

Purchasers, owners, and lenders must be aware of potential environmental hazards on real estate. To protect themselves, both legally and economically, prospective buyers and lenders should require environmental risk assessments from qualified environmental consultants. Also, buyers of new properties should require confirmation from the developer that there are no toxic wastes that could be harmful to the property. The Federal Home Loan

Mortgage Corporation and the Federal National Mortgage Association now require environmental assessments before they will purchase a loan.

Three types of environmental value assessments may be needed. A *Phase I EVA* is based largely on a sampling of air and water sources, a search of property records, and a visual inspection of the property. It seeks to determine whether there is a reasonable basis to suspect the presence of an environmental risk and whether there are environmental restrictions on the use of the property.

A *Phase II EVA* involves extensive testing; it is required when a Phase I report reveals the presence of significant amounts of toxic waste. It seeks to determine to a reasonable degree of scientific certainty whether the suspected environmental risk is or is not present.

A *Phase III EVA* has the following objectives. If the Phase II EVA has demonstrated the presence of an environmental risk, this assessment seeks to (1) quantify its type and extent, (2) develop an acceptable remediation plan, (3) develop budget estimates for the remediation plan, and (4) identify any restrictions on use or incremental operating costs required to prevent or minimize future environmental liabilities.[4]

These reports, together with written representation from the developer or current owner, comprise a set of documentary protections for investors. They are particularly necessary because liability insurance to cover toxic wastes cannot be purchased. The risk can only be minimized or shifted to the seller through documentary provisions.

SUMMARY

Planning and zoning are devices to control land use. Communities use these tools because the land uses that might otherwise result are sometimes detrimental to long-term property values and community standards. Decisions made in a market that is inefficient due to high transaction costs produce these undesirable land uses. These costs include information gathering, legal fees, negotiating time, and the free-rider problem.

Planning is the process of developing guidelines for controlling growth and development. A community's comprehensive plan, while providing constraining bounds to development, must also be flexible to accommodate changing conditions. A comprehensive plan therefore must be broad in scope, long-range in outlook, and flexible in application. Zoning assigns specific permitted uses to individual parcels of land to carry out the comprehensive plan.

An appointed commission assisted by a professional staff typically carries out planning and zoning. A community's elected governing body (city council or city commission) has the final authority over planning and zoning matters. Typically, it delegates to planning commissions the final authority in variance requests, approval of site plans, and sign control.

Individual property owners may control the future use of property through restrictions in deeds or recorded plats. These restrictions bind subsequent owners, so long as the restrictions do not violate public policy. Private restrictions and easements, however, are not effective devices for wide-scale land-use control. Enforcement is limited to affected property own-

---

[4] Albert R. Wilson, "The Environmental Opinion: Basis for an Impaired Value Opinion," *Appraisal Journal*, LXII, no. 3 (July 1994), pp. 410–23.

ers, and application is limited to an individual parcel, tract, or subdivision.

Lawsuits have attacked zoning from a variety of standpoints. However, the courts have upheld its constitutionality and ruled that specific applications are valid when they are reasonable, nonexclusionary, and comprehensive. Courts have overturned specific applications that were arbitrary, did not provide for low-income housing (and thus were discriminatory against low-income groups), or resulted in the confiscation of property rights without compensation. Decisions by the U.S. Supreme Court in the cases of *Lucas* v. *South Carolina Coastal Council* and *Dolan* v. *City of Tigard* seem to provide added protection for owners whose property values are destroyed by subsequent legislation or whose property is taken by public zoning and regulation.

Transferable development rights (TDRs) have gained limited use in large cities and other urbanized areas. The TDR system limits development of some properties, but allows the owners of those properties to sell the development rights to owners of other properties, who are then allowed to develop beyond the intensity permitted by zoning. While the use of TDRs may be effective in guiding development in areas of intensive growth, the system has important drawbacks that will likely limit its more widespread adoption.

States and local jurisdictions experiencing rapid growth have adopted a wide variety of measures to manage such growth. Some states have adopted laws requiring cities and counties to develop comprehensive plans, require economic and environmental impact statements in large development proposals, prohibit new development unless concurrency provisions are met, and require an allocation of affordable housing in new residential developments. Additionally, some states have given local communities the right to establish urban service areas, plan and control urban development outside their boundaries, limit new developments on the basis of objective criteria, and impose development moratoriums.

Environmental hazards have become an important land-use problem in recent years. Asbestos, fiberglass, PCBs, LUSTs, lead paint, and radon gas are some of the most common forms of toxic wastes, or sludge. Real estate investors face huge potential financial liabilities from these hazards because owners (and lenders that foreclose) can be required to clean them up. Investors should protect themselves by having environmental inspections and by requiring written statements from developers and owners certifying that no hazards exist and that if toxic wastes are found, the developers or former owners will bear the costs of cleanup and other losses.

KEY TERMS

Affordable housing allocation 313
Comprehensive plan 300
Concurrency 313
Easements 297
Economic and environmental
  impact statements 313
Extraterritorial jurisdiction 313
Growth limits 313
Growth moratorium 314

Inverse condemnation 306
Leaking underground storage
  tanks (LUSTs) 316
Planned unit developments 303
Point system 314
Polychlorinated biphenyls
  (PCBs) 316
Radon 316
Restrictive covenants 297

Site plan 308
Sludge 315
Toxic waste 315
Transferable development
  rights 310
Urban service area 313
Variance 308
Zoning 295

TEST YOURSELF

Answer the following multiple choice questions.

1. Zoning is an exercise of which type of general limitation on property rights?
   a. Eminent domain.
   b. Taxation.
   c. Police power.
   d. Escheat.
   e. All of the above.

2. A comprehensive plan usually deals with which of the following elements?
   a. Land uses.
   b. Population.
   c. Public services.
   d. Natural resources.
   e. All of the above.

3. The reasons(s) a market solution is claimed not to be adequate for land-use control is (are)
   I. The effects of transaction costs.
   II. The contention that markets are too efficient.
   III. Lack of full participation by affected parties.
   IV. Inequity of market decisions.
   a. I.
   b. II.
   c. I and II.
   d. III and IV.
   e. I and III.

4. In cities, the authority for approving site plans for large projects usually rests with the
   a. City council or commission.
   b. Mayor or city manager.
   c. Planning board or commission.
   d. Planning board or commission staff.
   e. Zoning review board.

5. Downzoning generally has been upheld by the courts *except* when it has been shown that
   a. Property values would be affected.
   b. The community intended to buy the land.

   c. The downzoning was not in accordance with the comprehensive plan.
   d. Public rights would be reduced.
   e. The public objected.

6. Who normally pays to clean up sludge on a property?
   a. The current property owner.
   b. A former property owner.
   c. The federal government.
   d. The lender.
   e. The state government.

7. Radon gas is
   a. A naturally occurring result of geologic activity.
   b. A relatively recent phenomenon caused by the earth's warming.
   c. Important only in the western United States.
   d. Controllable by soil treatment.
   e. Regarded as a nuisance but not a health hazard.

8. Transferable development rights (TDRs)
   a. Are replacing zoning as a tool of land-use control.
   b. Can be applied to most properties in most situations.
   c. Can be used in suburban areas but not in central cities.
   d. Are limited as a tool of land-use control to a few socially significant properties in small areas where there is strong development demand.
   e. Are a viable land-use control tool only for skyscrapers.

9. Sludge includes
   a. Sewage waste only.
   b. Sewage waste and naturally occurring gases.
   c. Asbestos, lead paint, and fiberglass.

  d. PCBs and LUSTs.

  e. Any type of hazardous materials or gases.

10. The assessment of environmental hazards on a property is important to

  a. Owners.

  b. Lenders.

  c. Prospective buyers.

  d. Secondary mortgage market agencies.

  e. All of the above.

PROBLEMS FOR THOUGHT AND SOLUTION

1. Assume that you own a small apartment building close to a major commercial street and a service station. You learn that there has been a major leak of underground storage tanks from the service station, and the gasoline has spread onto and below the surface of your property. Identify at least five sources of value loss to your property from the contamination.

2. A local businessman has applied for a permit to construct a bar that will feature "adult dancing" in a commercially zoned area across the street from your residential subdivision. As an owner of a $120,000 house within the subdivision would you favor or oppose this development? What effect do you think it could have on the value of your property? If you were opposed, how could you fight approval of the permit?

3. A medium-size city has proposed to build a "greenway" through the center of the city along a creek. The city wants to clear a strip about 50 feet wide and construct a paved path for bicycles and foot traffic (walkers and joggers). Proponents claim that it would be a highly desirable recreational facility for the community, while a very vocal and insistent group of opponents claims that it would degrade the environment and open properties along the creek to undesirable users and influences.

   Identify some specific positive and negative aspects of the proposal. Would you be in favor of the proposal, if you lived in the city? Would it make a difference if you lived along the creek?

4. The main argument traditionally advanced in favor of zoning is that it protects property values. Do you believe this contention? If so, how does zoning protect property values? If you do not believe the contention, why not?

5. Do you believe that the owners of properties contaminated by events that occur on another property (gasoline leakage or spills, for example) should be responsible for cleaning up their properties? Why or why not? If not, who should pay for the cleanup?

INTERNET EXERCISES

1. On the World Wide Web go to

   <http://www.greenbelt.org/gba/ugbs.html>

   a. What are urban growth boundaries?

   b. How are they used?

2. On the World Wide Web go to

   <http://www.arch.buffalo.edu/pairc>

Peruse the resources available at this site and choose a topic of interest to you such as planning, zoning, growth management, or environmental protection. Find information about this topic by using the links to the site and write a short report (one page) about what you find.

CASE PROBLEMS

1. One of the authors of this book, together with four other parties, bought some land for speculation about 10 years ago. It is located in the path of city growth and is near several shopping centers and residential developments. The land was divided into 25 lots of 1 to 1 1/2 acres each and was zoned BR (retail sales and services).

This zoning category includes a variety of personal and professional services, financial institutions, retail stores, restaurants, bars, and motels. Mini-warehouses are not mentioned in this category, but they were included in the comprehensive plan for the area. Three of the lots were sold for construction of mini-warehouses.

After eight years, all of the lots had been sold except two lots adjacent to the mini-warehouses. The owner of the mini-warehouses decided to buy the two remaining lots to expand her operations. The price of the lots was $100,000 each, which was agreeable to the buyer, who signed a contract of purchase and then applied for a building permit.

The application was rejected on the grounds that the comprehensive plan had been changed, and mini-warehouses were no longer mentioned in the plan for this area. The buyer withdrew her offer (based on a contingency for obtaining all relevant permits), and no other offers have been forthcoming. The lots have been appraised for $70,000 each, excluding the possibility of mini-warehouse use.

  a. Should the owners of the two lots be compensated by the county for the loss of property rights and value?

  b. Based on the trend of court decisions in cases of partial takings, what is the probability of a successful inverse condemnation lawsuit?

2. In the late 1980s, a large life insurance company paid $10 million for a 10-story office building in Denver to serve as its regional headquarters. No inspection for environmental hazards was made. Four years later, EPA inspectors discovered there were large amounts of asbestos insulation in the walls and ceilings. The company was ordered to have the insulation removed.

The company obtained estimates of $2 million to have the material removed and learned the building would have to be vacated while the work was performed. Management decided to sell the building and buy or construct another one for its regional operations.

Real estate values had not increased in Denver during this period, and buyers had become very wary of buildings containing asbestos. Real estate professionals advised the company that buyers would probably discount offers at least 10 percent from the amount that would otherwise be considered market value.

  a. What price could the company expect to receive for the building?

  b. What types of costs would the company incur to overcome the asbestos problem?

ADDITIONAL READINGS

The following text is an excellent introduction to the field of urban planning:

Catanese, Anthony J., and James C. Snyder. *Urban Planning*, 2nd ed. New York: McGraw-Hill, 1988.

This article makes the same point as Real Estate Focus 10–3:

Epstein, Paul C. "Dedications and Exactions: The Supreme Court Levels the Playing Field." *Appraisal Journal* LXIII, no. 4 (October 1995), pp. 453–56.

The author of this article contends that environmental liability, combined with constrained capital availability for new development projects, will introduce new standards of development evaluation and serve to constrain the pace of new development:

Roulac, Stephen E. "Environmental Due Diligence Information Requirements and Decision Criteria." *Journal of Real Estate Research* 8, no. 1 (Winter 1993), pp. 139–47.

The author of the following article presents appraisal methodology and case studies dealing with the valuation of contaminated properties:

Patchin, Peter J. "Contaminated Properties and the Sales Comparison Approach." *Appraisal Journal* LXII, no. 3 (July 1994), pp. 402–9.

This article includes an overview of environmental hazards facing real estate investors. It also deals with physical solutions to these hazards and to legal and documentary protection:

Smith, David A. "Investor Topics: Investor Protection against Environmental Risks." *Real Estate Review* 19, no. 2 (Summer 1989), pp. 14–19.

This article reports on a study of regulatory policies, often achieved through zoning ordinances, used by state and local governments to encourage or mandate the production of affordable housing units. The authors conclude that these programs have been effective, but by themselves are inadequate to meet the needs for affordable housing:

Smith, Marc T.; Charles J. Delaney; and Thomas Liou. "Inclusionary Housing Programs: Issues and Outcomes." *Real Estate Law Journal* 25, no. 2 (Fall 1996), pp. 155–71.

11
C H A P T E R

MARKET AND FEASIBILITY ANALYSIS

IMPORTANCE OF MARKET AND FEASIBILITY ANALYSIS

TYPES OF MARKET AND FEASIBILITY STUDIES
General Market Studies
Site-Specific Market Studies
Feasibility Studies

THE PROCESS OF MARKET ANALYSIS
Step 1: Define the Problem
Step 2: Evaluate Project Constraints
Step 3: Delineate the Market Area or Areas
Step 4: Estimate Demand for the Project
Step 5: Establish Supply Conditions in the Market
Step 6: Correlate Supply and Demand and Make Recommendations

GEOGRAPHIC INFORMATION SYSTEMS

SUMMARY

KEY TERMS

TEST YOURSELF

PROBLEMS FOR THOUGHT AND SOLUTION

INTERNET EXERCISE

CASE PROBLEMS

ADDITIONAL READINGS

After reading this chapter, students will be able to:

1. Name three different types of market studies.

2. Explain how market analysis fits into the real estate development process.

3. Perform two types of highest and best use studies, given data on costs, income, and expenses.

4. Determine whether different market studies are general or site-specific.

5. Outline the steps to perform a feasibility study.

6. Estimate demand for houses in a specified price range for a specified forecast period, given population data and forecasts, data on household formation, and data on income characteristics of the population.

IMPORTANCE OF MARKET STUDIES AND FEASIBILITY ANALYSIS

Market studies and feasibility analysis are important to the efficient and profitable use of real estate for several reasons. First, real estate markets are imperfect, especially with respect to locational differences. For this reason, specialized knowledge is required of developers, builders, buyers, lenders, and other market participants that only market studies provide.

Second, market and feasibility analyses are important tools in the financial analysis of real estate investments. A market study is a critical first step for determining project feasibility, since the information provided by market studies helps determine whether investors will invest or buy into a particular market. After that decision is made, investors, developers, and buyers must decide in which projects to put their money and effort. The type of information market studies provide includes the expected rents and occupancy rates in future periods for rental properties, such as office buildings and shopping centers, or the expected levels of sales and prices for salable properties, such as residential and office condominiums.

Third, because many market studies are undertaken for land development and new construction ventures, they are a principal source of information for the preparation of design-related questions, such as the number of bedrooms that buyers of residential condominiums are demanding in today's market, and which amenities (such as recreation facilities) purchasers of office condominiums consider desirable.

Finally, mortgage lenders usually require market and feasibility studies for large commercial property deals. An analysis of the market, all types of constraints, and financing information normally must be included in the package of information known as the *loan submission package*. These packages are supplied to lenders by borrowers wishing to secure construction and long-term mortgage financing.

REAL ESTATE FOCUS 11-1

Euro Disney—Major Errors of Market Analysis

After successfully developing large theme parks in California, Florida, and Japan, the Walt Disney Company believed it could capitalize on the huge European market by constructing a major theme park just east of Paris. While some French people objected to the importation of American culture into France, the French government encouraged the project because of the potentially huge positive economic impact in terms of jobs and additional taxes. Nevertheless, major errors were made in the analysis (or lack thereof) of the European market, and for the first two years of operation after its opening in 1992, Euro Disney was in danger of failure. The errors of market analysis cost Disney and other investors well over $1 billion! What were the most important of these errors?

Probably the biggest error was an assumption (unsupported by market analysis) that the demand for Disney recreation was inelastic—that is, Disney could set very high (monopolistic) prices, and the Europeans would pay them. For example, park admission was set at $42.25, and a room in the main hotel cost $340 per night—prices above those at the American theme parks. While the number of visitors was almost as high as projected, they avoided the Disney hotel by staying in other cheaper hotels nearby or in Paris and commuting. They also stayed on average only two days instead of the four-day average stay in Florida, probably also a reflection of the severe recession then gripping Europe. And they spent less on meals in the park, in part at least because of the initial policy of not serving alcoholic beverages.

Since Europeans are used to drinking wine with meals, they did not want to have an expensive meal without the wine. (This policy was subsequently changed.)

The Euro Disney park was realized only after long and intense negotiations with the French government, labor unions, contractors, and suppliers. Apparently Disney executives succeeded in alienating many of these people with an attitude that "we know best." Thus, when the park's success was in jeopardy, many officials and others were not as helpful as they might otherwise have been. And the consortium of banks that provided much of the project's capital was stringent in renegotiating terms of the loans to help bail Disney out. While the banks agreed to put up another $500 million, they required that Disney contribute another $750 million. Also, a member of the Saudi Arabian royal family agreed to invest $500 million in return for a 24 percent stake in Euro Disney.

While it appears that Euro Disney has made a turnaround and can now be considered "successful" in terms of its current operations, it went through almost three years of difficult times and near bankruptcy because of an arrogant attitude that "we know best, and we can determine the market." Euro Disney proved on an international scale how wrong such an attitude can be.

For more details about the Euro Disney debacle, see Robert F. Hartley, *Marketing Mistakes,* 6th ed. (New York: John Wiley and Sons, 1996), Chapter 9, pp. 113–28.

Unfortunately, builders, developers, and owners wishing to expand often pay too little attention to market studies and feasibility analysis. Many failures of real estate projects, small and large, can be traced to missing or inadequate market and feasibility analyses. Owners, builders, and developers often believe that they "know" the market based on their own past experiences. Often, however, market conditions change, or a new project is sufficiently different from a previous project that the same elements for success do not exist. (See Real Estate Focus 11–1.) Sometimes a developer of a new project simply wants to cut costs and believes that the market or feasibility study is the easiest place to save money. And occasionally, a developer ignores good advice after employing a market analyst who makes a conclusion that the developer does not want to hear (see Real Estate Focus 11–2).

REAL ESTATE FOCUS 11-2

Ignoring the Findings of Market Analysis

Safeway Developers, a developer of small apartment and retail properties in Columbus, Ohio, was owned by Art Bohannan. Bohannan bought a small tract of land along the west side of a major four-lane highway extending from the outskirts to downtown Columbus. The site was large enough to accommodate only five or six stores, but the developer believed it would be successful because of its location along the highway. He planned to rent the spaces to a barber shop, a pizza carry-out, a dry cleaner-laundry, a delicatessen, and a restaurant. He was able to obtain a loan commitment of 75 percent of the cost of the land and construction of the building. He then hired Ben Thomas, MAI, a local appraiser and market analyst to do an "appraisal" for him.

Thomas told him he could do an appraisal, but asked if he had had a feasibility study performed in order to determine the likelihood of success of the proposed development. Bohannan said "No, I've done enough of these small strip centers to know that this will succeed." Nevertheless, Bohannan agreed to Thomas's suggestion that he first do a feasibility study, and then if it turned out favorably, he could do the appraisal, using much of the market analysis performed for the feasibility study for the appraisal.

The conclusion of the feasibility study was that the strip center would not be successful as configured by Bohannan for the following reasons:

1. All of the establishments in the center, except the restaurant, would sell convenience goods—that is, goods for which people do not make special trips.

2. The center would be located on the wrong side of the road for people going home to stop to pick up convenience goods, and the only nearby residential area was across the major, divided four-lane highway.

3. The population within a 5- to 10-minute drive was not sufficient to support the convenience stores, given other competitive locations.

4. A nice sit-down restaurant should do well, as people will travel a considerable distance and overcome significant barriers to find a good restaurant.

5. Instead of the convenience stores, Thomas suggested that Bohannan reconfigure the center and find a major shopping goods type of tenant (for example, a furniture store, or a lawn and garden supply store) for the remainder of the space.

Bohannan did not believe Thomas's conclusions (and besides, he would have to change the specific set of plans he had submitted to the bank and obtain new permits from the city). Therefore, he decided to build the center as originally planned. Within six months all of the convenience stores had abandoned the center and only the restaurant was doing well. Within one year Bohannan sold the center for approximately 60 percent of its total cost.

TYPES OF MARKET AND FEASIBILITY STUDIES

Market studies fall into two broad categories, as shown in Exhibit 11–1. **General market studies** determine the potential for a particular type of development in a large geographic area, without reference to any specific parcel of land, whereas *site-specific market studies*, as the name implies, pertain to only one site or tract of land. A site-specific market study usually relates to the value, proposed use, change in use, and feasibility of a project at a given site. A **feasibility study** is broader in scope than a market study. It includes a market study (or studies), but it also analyzes the financial and investment aspects of a proposed project.

EXHIBIT 11-1

TYPES OF MARKET AND FEASIBILITY STUDIES

Category	Objectives
1. General market studies	a. To determine general real estate needs in a community.
	b. To determine market potential for a particular type of development in a metropolitan area.
2. Site-specific market studies	
a. Highest and best study	a. To determine how best to use a use particular site or property.
b. Predetermined use study	b. To determine whether market demand and supply will support a particular use of a site.
c. Marketability study	c. To determine how best to market a project and over what time period.
3. Feasibility study	To determine whether a proposed project will be successful in terms of a client's objectives, which may include social and psychological goals, as well as financial and investment objectives. Usually an IRR or NPV is specified as an investment objective. A market study is included as a component of a feasibility study.

GENERAL MARKET STUDIES

City planning departments and Chambers of Commerce often undertake (or hire consultants) to do market studies concerning the future need for real estate in the city. Typically, these studies seek to answer such questions as these:

1. How much will the population increase (decrease) in the next several years? What will be the characteristics (income, age, education) of the population?
2. What types of real estate will be needed to accommodate the population? How many new single-family residences can be sold? At what price levels? Where? How many should be detached and how many attached (apartments and condominiums)?
3. How much and what types of commercial and industrial real estate will be needed? Where?
4. What new public infrastructure will be needed to support the population and new real estate?

Private companies may also do general market studies or have them done. For example, a shopping center developer who has developed retail centers successfully in the eastern United States may wish to consider opportunities in Texas. General market studies could be undertaken to discover the potential for new shopping center developments in cities such as Houston, Dallas, and Austin. The objective would be to select the city or cities with the greatest market potential.

Exhibit 11–2 contains a summary of the results of a "housing element" market study to estimate the number of new housing units needed in Jacksonville, Florida, during the next 13 years. Note that it starts with an historical analysis and forecast of population, household population, household size, and total households. It then analyzes and forecasts the number of dwelling units, replacement units, and total units needed. The purpose, of course, is to see the pattern of what has happened and what is likely to happen in the future if these same trends continue.

Next, the supply of housing is analyzed, and the number of new owner-occupied and renter-occupied housing units required to meet the increasing population and number of new households is forecast. Note that the number of housing units must be large enough to accommodate also a "normal" level of vacancies and the replacement of housing units demolished or otherwise removed from the supply of available housing. Finally, the number of new housing units needed is divided between single-family detached and multifamily units, based on past trends in this ratio. Since the historic ratio between privately financed housing and housing requiring some public assistance has been 75 percent private to 25 percent public, the analysts believe this ratio will hold until 2010.

The purpose of such a general housing market study is to provide planning information for city policy makers regarding infrastructure needs and for builders and developers in formulating plans to develop and sell new housing. For any particular builder or developer, the number of new housing units needed would have to be broken down further by type, price class, and location. Builders or developers also would have to determine how many and what types of units they could sell in the market in view of the demand and the number that would likely be provided by other builders and developers.

Another type of general market study is termed *gap analysis*. Gap analysis involves the search for gaps—that is, undersupplies—of categories and specific types of properties in a community. A gap is a difference between a normal demand and supply relationship and the current situation in a community. For example, if the normal supply of lawn and garden stores is two for each 50,000 in population, and in your city of 250,000 there are only five, there may be an opportunity to provide additional lawn and garden stores.

The apparent existence of a gap, of course, does not guarantee that a real gap exists. For example, if the gap is based on the normal ratio of lawn and garden stores in suburbs or in medium-size cities, the same ratio probably does not apply to the center city areas of large metropolitan areas such as New York or Chicago, where many people live in apartments or condominiums without lawns or gardens.

The example shown in Exhibit 11–3 shows an analysis of hotel rooms in three cities of similar size. The preliminary analysis indicates that there *may* be a gap for hotel rooms in Baton Rouge, since its ratio of hotel rooms per 1,000 employees is lower than for the other two cities. An analyst must exercise caution, however, before making a recommendation based on this analysis. The character of the cities and conditions within them may differ considerably. For example, Baton Rouge may not draw as many conventions and meetings as Des Moines and Columbia, thus requiring a lower ratio of hotel rooms. Or the economies of Columbia and Baton Rouge may not be growing as fast as that of Des Moines, thus requiring lower ratios. Finally, Des Moines and Columbia may be more industrialized than Baton Rouge, requiring more hotel rooms for visiting businessmen.

EXHIBIT 11-2

HOUSING ELEMENT FOR COMPREHENSIVE PLAN 2010
JACKSONVILLE, FLORIDA

Population and Household Trends and Forecast

Year	Total Population	Household Population*	Average HH Size	Total Households
1990	654,047	636,504	2.56	248,635
1995	694,446	676,367	2.50	270,547
2000	727,404	708,999	2.46	288,210
2005	754,785	736,254	2.43	302,985
2010	780,533	761,476	2.43	313,364

* The difference between total population and household population represents the number of persons living in group housing (e.g., dormitories, prisons, and nursing homes).

Housing Demand

Year	Total Dwelling Units*	Replacement Units	% of Total Units	New Units Needed*	Total New Units Needed*
1990	270,726	3,053	1.13	25,314	28,367
1995	294,036	3,373	1.14	23,208	26,681
2000	314,148	3,670	1.17	20,112	23,782
2005	331,490	3,917	1.18	17,342	21,259
2010	343,326	4,133	1.20	11,836	15,969

*New units needed is the difference between the total dwelling units at each time period minus the number at the previous time period. Total new units needed is the sum of new units needed plus replacement units. Replacement units are those needed for demolitions and other slippage from the inventory of usable units. The difference between total households and total dwelling units equals the number of vacancies plus the number of group housing units.

Required Housing Supply

Year	Owner Occupied	Renter Occupied	Vacant	Total	Average HH Size
1990	160,236	88,563	21,929	270,728	2.561
1995	173,803	96,062	24,170	294,036	2.509
2000	185,430	102,488	26,163	314,081	2.465
2005	195,484	108,045	28,016	331,545	2.428
2010	202,187	111,750	29,389	343,326	2.428

Single-Family Detached Units Needed

Year	Owner Occupied	Renter Occupied	Vacant
1990	151,811	28,734	11,524
1995	164,871	31,256	12,717
2000	176,087	33,330	13,780
2005	185,809	35,170	14,770
2010	192,321	36,402	15,506

E X H I B I T   1 1 - 2   C o n c l u d e d

Multifamily Units Needed

Year	Owner Occupied	Renter Occupied	Vacant
1990	7,449	59,737	9,577
1995	8,090	64,979	10,569
2000	8,641	69,291	11,452
2005	9,117	73,115	12,274
2010	9,439	75,670	12,885

SOURCE: Housing Element, *Comprehensive Plan 2000* (Jacksonville, FL: Jacksonville Planning Department)

E X H I B I T   1 1 - 3

H O T E L   R O O M   A N A L Y S I S

City	Total Employment	First Class Hotel Rooms	First Class Hotel Rooms per 1,000 Employees
Des Moines	180,000	920	5.11
Columbia, S.C.	220,000	1,010	4.59
Baton Rouge	200,000	820	3.91

Thus, the gap shown in Exhibit 11–3 indicates a *potential* opportunity; further analysis is required to know whether the gap can be explained by other factors or whether the gap represents a real opportunity.

S I T E - S P E C I F I C   M A R K E T   S T U D I E S

These studies are performed after specific parcels of land have been identified for development or redevelopment. The use of the land (*e.g.*, residential condominium, office park, or retail center) may or may not have been predetermined. If the study is to determine the use of the land, it is called a *highest and best use study*. Such a study may pertain to a vacant site (or one that will be made vacant) or to an existing property (with improvement).

Highest and best use of a vacant site. Owners (or potential buyers) of sites seek to maximize the value of the site by constructing improvements that provide the highest use (and thus the highest value) to the site. Thus, they often need a study to determine which use among several possible uses will maximize the site's value. Determination of the **highest and best use of a vacant site** also is used in appraisal to estimate the value of sites separately from any improvements.

EXHIBIT 11-4

HIGHEST AND BEST USE ANALYSIS OF A SITE AS THOUGH VACANT

	Use		
	Apartment Building	**Office Building**	**Retail Building**
Cost of construction	$1,000,000	$900,000	$800,000
Effective gross income	250,000	200,000	180,000
Operating expenses	120,000	80,000	69,000
Net operating income	130,000	120,000	111,000
Income to building at 12 percent (cost × .12)	120,000	108,000	96,000
Income to site	10,000	12,000	15,000
Indicated site value at 10 percent (income to site/.10)	$100,000	$120,000	$150,000

The principle that a site's value is determined by its *potential* highest and best use holds true even for sites having existing buildings on them. Many sites with older buildings, for example, regularly sell for many times the value of the buildings, because the buildings can be demolished and new highest and best use buildings constructed. The type of analysis employed to determine highest and best use of a site is shown in Exhibit 11–4. Suppose that a site could reasonably be expected to be used for an apartment building, an office building, or a retail building. The analyst estimates the cost of constructing each type of building and then estimates the income and expenses that would be incurred for the three logical alternative uses. The net operating income is obtained by deducting the operating expenses from the effective gross income for each alternative.

Next, an allowance for a return on the capital invested in each building is subtracted from the net operating income (NOI) in order to determine how much of the NOI should be allocated to the site. The reason for subtracting a return on the building is that we are considering alternative uses for the site, and the decision as to which building should be constructed depends on the income remaining for the site after a market return is provided for the capital invested in the building. In this example, we assume that the market return on all three buildings is 12 percent.

As one can see from these estimates, the site's highest and best use would be the retail building. It produces the highest site income, after deducting the return on the capital invested in the building for all three alternative uses. Note that the highest and best use is not necessarily the most costly building or the building producing the highest gross income or even the highest net operating income. Rather, the relationships among these variables determine the highest and best use; it is the use that maximizes the income (return) to the site and hence its value.

Highest and best use of a property as improved. An improved property's highest and best use is determined by comparing rates of return on logical, competing types of *occupancies*. An analysis of the **highest and best use of a property as improved** is

E X H I B I T   1 1 - 5

HIGHEST AND BEST USE ANALYSIS OF A PROPERTY AS IMPROVED

	Use		
	Offices	**Small Stores**	**Demolish and Construct New Retail Building**
Capital required	$120,000	$100,000	$825,000
Effective gross income	19,000	17,100	180,000
Operating expenses	3,000	1,000	69,000
Net operating income	16,000	16,100	111,000
Rate of return on required capital	13.3%	16.1%	13.5%

shown in Exhibit 11–5. Suppose the property analyzed above contains a building, and the owner has asked a real estate analyst to determine the type of tenants who would produce the highest return on the investment in the property. Two alternative uses of the existing building are offices and small stores. Another alternative that must be considered, because the building is more than 25 years old, is to demolish the existing building and construct a new building. This consideration does not suggest that many buildings 25 years old are ripe for demolition, only that the possibility must be considered. Furthermore, 25 years is only a rule of thumb; in fact, it is not unusual for buildings less than 25 years old to be demolished to make way for higher and better uses. Of course, most buildings last much longer, and it is usually not feasible to demolish them until much later in their useful lives. Exhibit 11–5 shows the three alternatives, with their associated capital, income, and expense requirements.

As shown by this analysis, the highest and best use of the property as improved would be for small stores. It produces the highest return on invested capital. Note that demolition of the existing building is not warranted at this time. If it were, the investor would construct the highest and best use as though vacant. The cost of this building plus demolition cost of the existing building ($800,000 + $25,000) are shown as the third alternative in Exhibit 11–5. Highest and best use analysis of the site as though vacant is also required in an appraisal in which the value of the site must be valued separately from the value of the building. (We will see in Chapter 13 that the cost approach to estimating the value of a property requires such a separate estimate.)

Predetermined use studies. Site-specific studies, in which the use of the land has been predetermined, are often needed by developers of new projects. The conceptual scheme for land development in Exhibit 11–6 places the market study between the land acquisition and planning phase (Phase 1) and the final analytical phase (Phase 3), in which preliminary architectural plans are prepared and the financial analysis is performed. The market study has two functions. First, it is a screening mechanism for determining whether developmental constraints, such as severe zoning or access problems, preclude or hinder projects.

REAL ESTATE FOCUS 11-3

New Highest and Best Use for a New York Landmark

Among Donald Trump's major current projects is the transformation of the Gulf and Western Building from offices into apartments and condominiums. In partnership with General Electric Investments (GEI), which is financing the joint venture, and the Galbreath Co., Trump intends to gut the 700,000 square foot tower down to its steel frame and build a 60-story super luxury apartment-condominium project equivalent in height to the existing 44-story office building. In 1993 Mr. Trump approached GEI's chief executive officer, Dale Frey, and floated the idea of the building's transformation. "It's what I consider to be the finest site anywhere in New York and perhaps the world," Trump said in explaining his proposal. "It sits at the corner of Central Park West and Central Park South, and, with the exception of that building, there is no such address." The project commenced in June 1995 and was expected to take two years at a cost of $200 million.

EXHIBIT 11-6

CONCEPTUAL SCHEME FOR LAND DEVELOPMENT

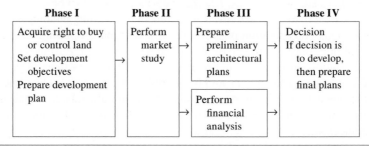

Second, the market study provides essential inputs for preliminary architectural and development plans and for the financial analysis. The real estate market study should answer the following six fundamental questions:[1]

1. *Are there any constraints on the development of the project?* Severe problems with zoning, utilities, access, environmental protection, community relations, or soil and topography can lead to an early decision to abort projects. Even if these considerations are not found to be severe constraints on development, information gathered on their possible effects may be useful in preparing cost estimates for the financial calculations.

2. *How large will the market be in future periods and what proportion can be attracted to the subject site?* This question involves the quantity of space—the number of units that can be sold (as in a residential condominium) or the number of square feet that can be leased (as in an office

---

[1] Vincent G. Barrett, "Appraisal Should Be Market Study: Techniques of Analysis," *Appraisal Journal* 47 (October 1979), pp. 538–55.

building)—and the timing of the sales or leases. The interaction between quantity and time in the sale or lease of property is called the **absorption rate**. If, for example, the market for residential condominiums is sufficiently strong that developers sell 10 of a possible 50 units in the first three months of marketing, the initial quarterly absorption rate is 20 percent (10/50 units). If the remaining units are sold in the next five quarters, the overall absorption rate is 15.67 percent per quarter (100%/6 quarters).

3. *How much may be charged in the market?* This relates to the prices when the units are to be sold or to rents when they are to be leased.

4. *What types of units are demanded in the market?* For residential developments, type refers to building styles, such as garden or high rise. For shopping centers, this question refers to the types of retail outlets that might be appropriate for the center (such as drug store or fashion garments).

5. *What sizes should the units be?* For both residential and commercial developments, size refers to the square footage required for each unit.

6. *What amenities or special facilities should be provided?* To market residential condominiums effectively, for example, it is often necessary to incorporate tennis courts, workout rooms, and swimming pools in the development plan. In hotel developments, it may be essential to include meeting or convention facilities.

Marketability studies. Marketability studies are undertaken to determine how best to market a project and over what time period. Such studies are often done for existing properties and seek to answer questions such as what image the property has in the market. To what types of buyers (renters) does it appeal? Can modest changes be made that will result in a substantially upgraded market niche? How can a favorable market image be created? How should it be marketed—by brokers or by a private sales force, for example? What type of advertising is needed? How long will it take to sell (or rent) the properties or units? What prices can be attained in the market?

A marketability study often is included in a predetermined use market study. In such a situation, although the property will be new, most of the same questions must be answered. It should result in a marketing plan that will lead to a forecast absorption rate and sellout period.

FEASIBILITY STUDIES

In concept, feasibility analysis is more comprehensive than market analysis. In any particular case a market analysis could be much more thorough and detailed than a feasibility study. A feasibility study, however, includes consideration of costs and financing, which a market study does not. The objective of a feasibility study is to determine whether a proposed project will meet the objectives of the developer or investor. Usually there are qualitative as well as quantitative objectives, such as those stated for the developer in the following example. A feasibility study usually involves both market analysis *and* forecasts

EXHIBIT 11-7

FEASIBILITY ANALYSIS FOR RESIDENTIAL LOTS ON A 40-ACRE SITE

	Year 1	Year 2	Year 3
Lot sales (from projections of market study)	$450,000	$2,000,000	$3,000,000
Less: Development costs			
Land preparation	150,000	50,000	
Sanitary and storm sewers	200,000	100,000	
Curbs and gutters	200,000	100,000	
Streets	250,000	150,000	
Water	100,000		
Electricity and lighting	180,000		
Recreational facility	500,000		
Legal fees and permits	40,000	10,000	10,000
Overhead	45,000	200,000	300,000
Less: Marketing costs	7,500	30,000	40,000
Less: Financing costs (interest)	240,000	240,000	240,000
Less: Loan repayment			2,000,000
Total outflows	1,912,500	880,000	2,590,000
NET INFLOW (OUTFLOW)	$-1,462,500	$1,120,000	$ 410,000

IRR = 3.63%
NPV @ 15.0% = -$155,277

Note: All sales, costs, and expenses are assumed to occur at the end of each year.

of development and financing costs. Typically, these result in a forecast of the internal rate of return (IRR), net present value (NPV), or both for the project, since most developer-investors have specific objectives for these measures.

Example.   Exhibit 11–7 contains sales projections for a three-year period that resulted from a market study for a proposed residential development. A 40-acre tract of land could be purchased for $1.1 million and developed into 100 residential lots that would sell for between $40,000 and $75,000 each. The feasibility analyst further estimated the development, marketing, overhead, and financing costs associated with the project. The developer could obtain a land acquisition and development loan of $2 million at an interest rate of 12 percent for the development period. Proceeds from the loan would be used to pay for the land, with the remainder being used to fund development costs. The developer's stated objectives are to provide attractive sites for builders of middle to middle-upper priced houses. Sites that posed environmental or other unusual development problems, and any project that produces less than 15 percent return would not be considered. The feasibility analyst's conclusions were that this site could meet the developer's first two objectives. The remaining question was whether it could meet the investment objective.

Given an estimated IRR of only 3.6 percent and an NPV of approximately -$155,277 at 15 percent, the project would be judged *not* feasible. The analyst reached this conclusion only after considering all possible constraints that might affect the project.

In other words, the zoning was appropriate, the land was physically capable of supporting the project, there were no other legal or environmental problems, and there were no social problems (such as organized resistance by neighbors or environmentalists).

If the land developer were also a home builder, characteristics, costs, and prices of the homes would have to be included in the analysis. As pointed out previously, results of the market analysis would be used to help determine home styles, features, sizes, layouts, and the like. The costs would have to be detailed and reliable. And the likelihood of increasing costs and expenses during the absorption period would need to be carefully analyzed. Sellout of the homes would have to be projected for the absorption period, with ranges provided for the possibility of shorter and longer absorption periods than forecast. The principles of feasibility analysis, as illustrated in the land development example of Exhibit 11–7, however, would be the same.

THE PROCESS OF MARKET ANALYSIS

The step-by-step process of developing a real estate market study has three phases. The initial phase, which includes the first two steps described below, considers all project constraints and defines the market area for the study. The next phase involves collecting and processing demand and supply data. The final phase correlates supply and demand data and conclusions from the study.

STEP 1: DEFINE THE PROBLEM

Definition of the problem is a prerequisite to any investigative study or research project. For a site-specific market study in which the use is predetermined, the problem involves finding answers to the six fundamental questions presented above. Once this need is recognized, the market analyst sets forth a plan for examining the questions. The plan may take the form of a general proposal to a client or an actual plan of work (time and budget) that considers work items for subsequent steps.

STEP 2: EVALUATE PROJECT CONSTRAINTS

Although demand and supply conditions may appear favorable for development in a particular market, any of several factors may cause a project to be aborted or unduly delayed. The sooner these factors are identified and evaluated the better. The following factors should be considered at this point:

1. Zoning problems (e.g., obtaining a zoning change to allow for development at the desired density).
2. Utility problems (e.g., obtaining cooperation of a municipality for extending services to the site).
3. Parking problems (e.g., inadequate space for both employee and customer parking).

4. Negative community reactions (e.g., organized opposition by neighborhood residents).
5. Access problems (e.g., inability to secure enough curb cuts for the driveways needed).
6. Environmental problems (e.g., toxic waste from a former user of the site).
7. Topographic or soil problems (e.g., severe slopes or poor soil drainage).

STEP 3: DELINEATE THE MARKET AREA OR AREAS

The geographic limits of the **market area** are determined in general by the density of demand (potential buyers per square mile) for the products or services to be offered at the site. Therefore, the market area for residential condominiums, because they are purchased infrequently, would be much larger than the market area for convenience groceries. Establishing precise market area boundaries involves considerable judgment. Precision is often sacrificed as a matter of convenience. Political jurisdictions or census tracts, for example, are sometimes chosen in the specification of market areas to facilitate collecting supply and demand data. As a general rule, the lower the density of demand for the commodity to be offered at the site, the less precision is required in setting market area boundaries.

Travel time and distance are also critical factors. One method for setting the boundaries of a market area for residential developments relies heavily on travel time. It begins by defining the market or *competitive area* as the area within which dwelling units are substitutable for one another.[2] As shown in Exhibit 11–8, the market area is determined by (1) finding the major employment centers within, say, 10 minutes driving time from the subject site and (2) defining a geographic area that has boundaries indicated by a 10-minute drive in all directions from each employment center. Any residential development with similar units for sale and located in this area would be viewed as a competitor that may draw customers away from the subject development. The boundaries of this market should be adjusted for the presence of physical barriers, such as swamp areas and flood plains, and for demographic characteristics, such as a high concentration of apartments. Also, the critical travel time (e.g., 10 minutes or 15 minutes) depends on the size of the urban area and the capacity of the highway network.

STEP 4: ESTIMATE DEMAND FOR THE PROJECT

Estimation of **derived demand** is the most crucial step in preparing a market study. The demand for real estate is derived from consumers' demands for the goods and services supplied at particular locations. For example, the demand for a retail outlet that sells personal computers in a shopping center is derived from the local demand for the outlet's product—personal computers. Similarly, the demand for residential condominiums is derived from the local demand for the type of housing service a condominium provides. These housing services might include low maintenance responsibility for owners, ameni-

---

[2] See John McMahan, *Property Development* (New York: McGraw-Hill, 1989), pp. 134–36.

EXHIBIT 11-8

MARKET AREA DETERMINATION FOR A PROPOSED RESIDENTIAL DEVELOPMENT

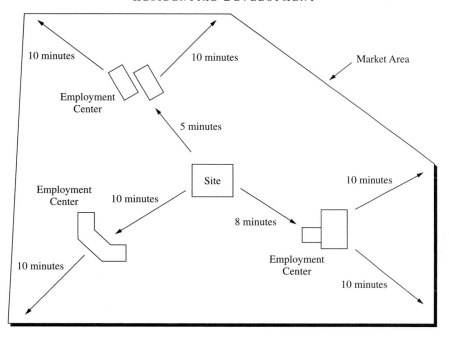

ties such as a pool and tennis courts, and smaller living space than is usually found in traditional single-family detached homes.

Regardless of the type of property for which future demand is being estimated, analysis of growth trends and patterns is essential. Forecasts should begin with carefully done projections or extrapolations of past trends of population growth and decline. Then, judgment determines whether projections need to be adjusted upward or downward because of local economic events expected to occur in the future (e.g., a company has announced plans to build a new plant in the city next year).

Applied demand analysis. As a practical matter, the demand for real estate is related not only to the number of potential purchasers of goods and services but also to their incomes and employment characteristics, other demographic factors (such as household size), prices, taxes, interest rates, and expectations. Before introducing a model that considers these factors in estimating demand for a particular project, data requirements must be discussed. Although data for demand analyses may come from several sources, these data may be broadly classified into two categories.

Primary data are obtained directly from face-to-face or telephone interviews and written questionnaires. These data are important for establishing buyer or renter attitudes, opinions, and preferences at one point in time. Because of the tremendous expense of collecting primary data, there is seldom a time series of interview studies available from which trends in buyer or renter behavior may be determined.

Secondary data come from published sources such as U.S. Census Bureau reports, local planning commission documents, and traffic counts from state departments of transportation. Because these data are collected and tabulated by others, they are usually less expensive to acquire than primary data. Thus, market analysts attempt to substitute secondary for primary data whenever possible. One advantage of secondary data is that trends in consumer behavior may be examined. Their major disadvantage is that they are usually aggregated and therefore do not yield individualized information on buyer or renter attitudes, opinions, and preferences that may come from primary data. If their resources were unlimited, market analysts would prefer to have substantial amounts of primary data collected in the same way for several prior time periods.

Estimating future employment and population. A traditional approach for estimating future local area employment is **economic base analysis** (EBA). This method divides employment into two categories, **basic employment** and **nonbasic employment**, and it is based on the assumption that changes in basic employment drive changes in total employment. Population changes are then projected on the basis of the historic relationship between total employment and population.

Basic employment consists of jobs in industries that sell goods or services mainly outside the local area, called *export industries*, whereas nonbasic employment consists of jobs in industries that sell goods and services consumed within the local area, called *service industries*. The ratio of an expected change in basic employment to the change in total employment is usually around 1.0, or somewhat lower. That is, a change in basic employment of 100 will result in 90 additional employees in nonbasic employment, if the ratio is 0.9. The resulting change in total employment will be 190, and if the historic ratio of employment to population is 1 to 3, total population will increase by 570 persons.

Location quotients are a tool for helping decide which industries are basic and which are not. The quotients are ratios between the percentage of a particular type of employment in a community and the percentage of that type of employment in the entire nation. Thus, the formula for a location quotient is

$$LQ = \frac{\% \text{ of employment in industry X in community Y}}{\% \text{ of employment in industry X in the United States}}$$

When the $LQ > 1$, the community is producing excess output for exporting, so the industry is regarded as part of the community's economic base. When the $LQ <$ or $= 1$ the community is not producing excess product for export, and that industry is not regarded as part of the community's economic base. As an example, consider the location quotient for manufacturing in Seattle:

$$LQ = \frac{16.65\%}{14.20\%} = 1.17$$

EXHIBIT   11-9

SELECTED LOCATION QUOTIENTS FOR SEATTLE

Industry Type	Location Quotient
Agriculture, mining, and other	.49
Construction	1.11
Manufacturing	1.17
Transportation, communications, and public utilities	1.16
Wholesale trade	1.19
Retail trade	.98
Finance, insurance, and real estate	1.14
Services	.99
Government	.79

Therefore, manufacturing is considered part of the economic base of Seattle. This result is not surprising when one realizes that the world's largest manufacturer of airplanes (the Boeing Company) is located there. Location quotients for major industry categories for Seattle are shown in Exhibit 11–9.

While the logic of economic base analysis is enticing, there are obviously potential problems with its use in forecasting population. The ratios of basic to nonbasic employment, and of employment to population increases may (and do) change gradually over time. The changes in these ratios cannot be detected by EBA except after the fact. Also, the problem of forecasting changes in basic employment, the key variable, is hazardous at best. For example, an EBA-based forecast of population growth of Evansville, Indiana, proved to be totally incorrect when a major industry, Servel Corporation, decided to leave—an event unforeseen in the EBA.

Population projections and forecasts also are available to market analysts directly from local planning agencies or chambers of commerce. While data from these sources are usually reliable, professional analysts also should make their own forecasts, in order to check their thinking and to determine the reliability of the secondary sources. This can be done from EBA, by using the *simple linear projection technique* as follows, or by using more sophisticated methods for projecting population. Often, simple techniques are as accurate as more complicated techniques. The simple linear technique can be demonstrated using the data from Exhibit 11–10. It is based on the equation for a straight line, $Y = a + bx$, where Y is population, a is the Y axis intercept, b is the slope of the line (that is, $\Delta Y/\Delta X$), and x is the number of annual changes.

Example.   Using data from Exhibit 11–10, the population for the year 2000 can be projected. First, calculate b from the past data as

$$b = \Delta Y/\Delta X$$

$$= 160,000 - 145,000/4 \text{ (annual changes)}$$

$$= 3,750$$

EXHIBIT 11-10

POPULATION DATA FOR DEMONSTRATING PROJECTION TECHNIQUE

Period	Year	Population	Percent
1	1995	145,000	—
2	1996	150,000	0.034
3	1997	153,000	0.020
4	1998	155,000	0.013
5	1999	160,000	0.032

Because a is 145,000, the beginning period population, the equation for Period 6 (2000) population becomes

$$Y = 145,000 + 3,750 \times 5 \text{ (annual changes)}$$
$$= 163,750$$

Other projection techniques include nonlinear projection, weighted-average projection, moving-average projection, and ratio projection.[3]

Residential condominium example. As shown by the tree diagram in Exhibit 11–11, the potential demand for new residential condominiums comes from two sources: new households and internal mobility. A third potential source is the demand for condominiums as investments, but investment demand is not considered important for this project.

The first step in estimating demand from new households for the next period is to project, then forecast, population. The *projection* is based on either an EBA, a simple linear model, or a more advanced technique. The *forecast* is obtained by modifying the projection according to the judgment of the analyst. To obtain the number of households, the forecast population for the next period is divided by the appropriate person-per-household ratio. This ratio has declined in the United States from slightly over four persons per household in the late 1700s to less than 2.5 today. However, these ratios remain fairly stable over the relatively short span of a normal forecasting period. A reliable estimate of the next-period ratio of persons per household should be available from recently published demographic data for the area. Most new households result from immigration.

Not every new household can afford a new condominium unit. Thus, an affordability analysis is performed to segment the total number of new households into those households that can afford new condominium units and those that cannot. Two pieces of information are needed for the affordability analysis. First, the expected financing conditions for the next period must be specified, including the mortgage interest rate, loan-to-value

---

[3] For a more detailed discussion of population projection techniques, see Michael Greenberg, Donald A. Krueckeberg, and Connie Michaelson, *Local Population and Employment Projection Techniques* (New Brunswick, N.J.: Rutgers University, Center for Public Policy Research, 1984).

A CONCEPTUAL APPROACH FOR MARKET ANALYSIS: RESIDENTIAL CONDOMINIUM EXAMPLE

Potential Sources of Sales

1. New Households (each period)

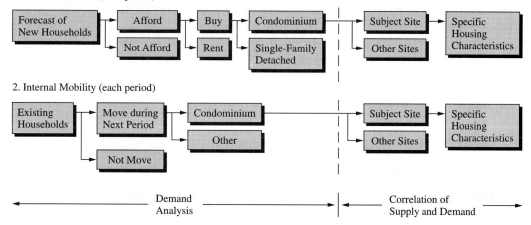

2. Internal Mobility (each period)

ratio (percentage down payment required), and term.[4] Second, the analyst must estimate the incomes of new households moving into the area. Several techniques are available for making such estimates; however, new households are usually assumed to have approximately the same incomes as existing households. With these data, one may estimate the number of households that are able to afford the mortgage payments on a new condominium unit in the expected price range of units in the property.

A certain proportion of the households that are able to afford to purchase units will choose to rent instead. The most accurate method for determining this proportion is to collect primary data on current buy-versus-rent behavior; also, secondary data on rent-versus-buy ratios are usually available from local planning departments and chambers of commerce.

The final segmentation performed for this part of the demand analysis is to find the proportion of buyers that will purchase condominium units and the proportion that will purchase single-family detached houses. Again, the most accurate estimates come from primary data (such as interviews with new households to determine current buyer behavior), but it is easier to assume that the current distribution of condominiums versus single-family detached houses will persist into the next period.

Once the expected number of households that will purchase condominiums is estimated, sales to the specific site must be allocated. This is a crucial step. Allocation of demand to the site and specification of housing characteristics, such as the number of

---

[4] See Chapters 16 and 17 for details on residential financing.

bedrooms and the amenities, depend on competitive (supply) conditions in the market. Discussion of these steps is deferred to the later discussion of correlating demand and supply.

Internal mobility (that is, the number of households moving within the same market area) is the second potential source of residential condominium sales. To estimate internal mobility, the number of existing households must be segmented into those that expect to move during the next period and those that do not. As with segmenting the new household portion of the market, the best approach is to survey households.[5] This survey queries existing households on moving plans. Alternatively, real estate brokers may provide accurate estimates of the proportion of households that move during a given period. The remaining steps in the analysis of demand from internal mobility are identical to those for estimating new household demand, as shown in Exhibit 11–11.

STEP 5: ESTABLISH SUPPLY CONDITIONS IN THE MARKET

The supply of competing units in the market is estimated by consulting two sources of information: (1) building permits and (2) existing and recently completed projects of competitors. The compilation of data on competitors' projects is known as the *competitive market survey*.

Because real estate developers must obtain building permits from local governments before beginning construction, it is possible to project supply additions that will occur soon. A number of methods are available for projecting housing starts from housing permits. For most market studies on commercial properties, reliable estimates of additional supply are developed simply by having good building permit data and knowing (1) the probability that the permitted project will be completed (usually in excess of 90 percent) and (2) the average length of construction period for the type of development planned.

Although the analysis of building permits provides information on the number of units and the amount of square footage to be added to the existing supply, such an analysis does not reveal much information about market acceptance, amenities, pricing, and other current market characteristics. These additional data, however, are often obtainable on existing and recently completed projects. The following information about competing properties may be obtained from a competitive market survey:

1. Number and type of units (e.g., 10 one-bedroom, 30 two-bedroom, *etc.*).
2. Size (square footage) of the units (*e.g.*, one-bedroom, 900 square feet).
3. Rents or sale prices.
4. Acreage and density per acre (e.g., 15 acres, 12 units per acre).
5. Number of units rented or sold and the amount of time required. Information about market absorption is difficult to obtain for some competitive properties, especially rental properties.

---

[5] See Joseph Rabianski and James D. Vernor, "The Use of Questionnaires in Marketability Research," in *Readings in Market Research for Real Estate*, ed. James D. Vernor (Chicago: American Institute of Real Estate Appraisers, 1985).

6. Number of units remaining on the market.
7. Amenities offered and parking provided.

STEP 6: CORRELATE SUPPLY AND DEMAND AND MAKE RECOMMENDATIONS

The final step in the market analysis should be directed toward answering the six questions posed earlier. The segmentation of total demand for condominiums between the subject site and other sites is the direct result of correlating supply and demand. Correlation, therefore, answers Question 2—how large will the market be in future periods and what proportion can be attracted to the subject site? This is the same as asking what will be the excess demand for this type of property at this particular site.

The proportional allocation of future market demand to the site is called the **capture rate**. Assigning a capture rate to the subject property is more judgmental than scientific. The analyst, after identifying total market demand during the next period, incorporates the information about building permits and the competitive market survey to develop such estimates.

Determining future sales depends on how competitive the project will be. The critical determination of potential sales, therefore, is the result of analyzing building permit activity and making judgments as to how well the subject property will compete against other projects.

The competitive market survey data are essential for answering the four remaining questions regarding prices (or rents), types of units, sizes of units, and amenities. One assumption is that the combination of prices, types, sizes, and amenities that has been successful in the recent past will likely be successful in the future. Because consumer behavior constantly changes, market analysts should augment their findings from competitive market surveys with primary data to assess evolving market trends.

Final recommendations from the market analysis will be used both in the financial analysis component of the feasibility study and in the development of preliminary architectural plans. For the financial analysis, the analyst needs the following information from the market analysis:

1. The number of units of each type expected to be sold over the absorption period.
2. The prices of the units expected to be sold.

To prepare preliminary architectural plans, the architect requires the following information from the market analysis:

1. The number of units of each type expected to be sold over the absorption period.
2. The style of the structures and units.
3. The sizes of the units.
4. The amenities required for the project.

Thus, if the market analysis is designed and implemented to answer the six fundamental questions, the process will proceed smoothly toward yielding answers to the larger questions of whether to develop the real estate for the proposed use and what features to include if the real estate is to be developed.

GEOGRAPHIC INFORMATION SYSTEMS (GIS)

Geographic information systems (GIS) are gaining widespread use among professional real estate market analysts. These systems use sophisticated computer programs that map real estate information in many different ways. By visualizing the data an analyst can see spatial relationships between many variables such as location and property values, customers and stores, and population characteristics and sales. Such observations are typically not possible with tables and charts. GIS is a tool that requires considerable technical knowledge and often large amounts of data. Therefore, its use has not developed as quickly as its usefulness would indicate, but it now appears ready for a major takeoff, buttressed by the availability of powerful desktop computers, reasonably priced software, the growing availability of census data in various GIS formats, and data from local public GIS systems in many counties.

GIS is a computerized system of information for an area (such as a state, county, or metropolitan area or subarea) that contains data on many types of demographic, economic, transportation, and property characteristics. A GIS consists of different "layers" that can be turned on or off and manipulated with regard to size, color, symbols, and other characteristics to create maps. Layers are of three types: polygon, line, and point. For example, polygon layers, such as census tracts, can contain data on the age, occupation, income, and other characteristics of the people living within each tract. Line layers, such as highways or streets, are often necessary to indicate location on a map; they may also contain data on address ranges or traffic counts. Point layers are often used for various types of property (such as residential, vacant commercial, restaurants, offices, and so on) and may contain data on square footage, assessed value, or other attributes.

Using GIS a real estate analyst may, for example, identify potential sites within a metropolitan area for the development of new apartments, a shopping center, or any other common use. For any site, the analyst can then query the system for data on population and household characteristics, data on individual existing establishments, or statistics (counts and averages) on the characteristics of existing establishments within various zones surrounding the site, for example, within a two-mile radius or specified trade area. Many companies have researched the demographic and economic characteristics necessary for a successful site and have established site criteria for their specific business use.

As an example, suppose that a major grocery chain is considering a site for a shopping center (with a grocery store and other retail uses) in Columbia, S.C. Exhibit 11–12 shows a GIS map of the metropolitan area with the selected site, Dentsville Square Shopping Center. The map depicts highways, population density by census tract, and existing grocery stores in the Columbia area. By selecting any given grocery store, detailed data can be available about its size, owner, and volume of business. Additionally, the GIS can be used to calculate detailed information for a market area (such as a two-mile or five-mile radius) around Dentsville Square. This information might include num-

EXHIBIT 11-12

POPULATION DENSITY AND GROCERY STORES
(COLUMBIA, SOUTH CAROLINA)

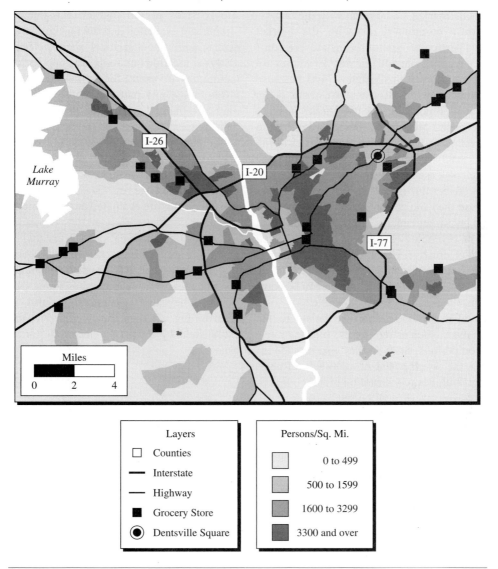

Layers		Persons/Sq. Mi.	
☐ Counties			0 to 499
— Interstate			500 to 1599
— Highway			1600 to 3299
■ Grocery Store			3300 and over
◉ Dentsville Square			

ber of persons, number of households, median household income, estimated annual retail expenditures, daily traffic counts, number of other grocery stores, and the total and vacant square footage of other retail properties. Thus, by having a GIS program and the appropriate data, an analyst can quickly and easily determine whether the site meets basic criteria and should be investigated further.

SUMMARY

Market studies are of two types: general and site-specific. General market studies deal with the real estate needs of a community or with the market potential for a particular type of real estate in a community. Three types of site-specific market studies are useful in different situations. Highest and best use studies determine how best to use a vacant site or an existing property. Predetermined use studies analyze whether a proposed project will be absorbed by the market in given price levels and characteristics of the property. Marketability studies result in a marketing program to sell or lease units over a given time period.

Feasibility studies are broader in scope than market studies because they include market studies and also financial and investment analysis. They also may deal with social and psychological goals of the client, such as social good or prestige. Usually one of the products of a feasibility analysis is an estimate of the IRR or NPV that the project will produce, which can be compared with the client's investment objective.

Market studies provide important inputs to the feasibility analysis, such as rent levels, vacancy rates, and absorption periods. Such studies also provide information for the development of architectural plans in conjunction with new construction projects.

Market studies must deal with both the demand and supply sides of the market. Possible project constraints are evaluated and the market area or areas are determined. Specific tools such as economic base analysis, location quotients, and population projection techniques are useful for estimating demand. Income levels, household patterns, and social characteristics may be obtained from both primary and secondary data sources.

To answer the remaining questions about a property, market studies develop estimates of future supply conditions from data on building permits and the competitive market survey. Finally, supply and demand considerations are evaluated and recommendations are prepared.

Geographic information systems are becoming important tools in the market analyst's toolbox. These systems are powerful methods for visualizing and analyzing areas and specific sites for a variety of purposes. They are particularly useful for quickly determining whether a particular site meets criteria established by a firm for locations for its stores or branches.

KEY TERMS

Absorption rate 335
Basic employment 340
Capture rate 345
Derived demand 338
Economic base analysis 340
Feasibility study 327

General market studies 327
Geographic information systems 346
Highest and best use of a property as improved 332
Highest and best use of a vacant site 331

Location quotient 340
Market area 338
Marketability studies 335
Nonbasic employment 340
Primary data 339
Secondary data 340

TEST YOURSELF

Answer the following multiple choice questions:

1. A developer has a parcel of land near a metropolitan rail transit station. What type of study does the developer need to indicate the market potential for this parcel?

   a. General market study.

b. Site-specific study in which the use is predetermined.
c. Financial analysis.
d. Highest and best use study.
e. Real estate appraisal.

2. In the conceptual scheme for the development of a parcel of land, what role does the market study play?
a. It provides essential information for the financial analysis.
b. It provides essential information for the preliminary architectural plans.
c. It helps the developer obtain mortgage financing.
d. It evaluates possible constraints.
e. All of the above.

3. Which is *not* one of the fundamental questions a market study should answer?
a. What type of financing is being offered in the market?
b. What size of units are purchasers or renters demanding?
c. What amenities are typical in the market?
d. What prices or rents are being asked in the market?
e. What architectural styles are being demanded in the market?

4. The specific purpose of economic base analysis is to
a. Project population.
b. Reduce the problem of estimating employment growth to one variable, basic employment.
c. Forecast household size.
d. Extrapolate past levels of basic employment.
e. Separate the effects of basic and nonbasic employment growth on population change to obtain a better understanding of how urban areas grow.

5. For analyzing current and future supply in the market, analysts rely on
a. Competitive market surveys and building permit data.
b. Primary data.

c. Secondary data with primary data.
d. Construction cost estimates.
e. All of the above.

6. The highest and best use of a vacant site is the specific improvement that will
a. Maximize total property value.
b. Minimize total property value.
c. Maximize the rate of return to the total property.
d. Maximize site value.
e. Maximize the flexibility of the site's use.

7. The type of study used to decide whether to demolish an existing building and construct a new one is a
a. Feasibility study.
b. Highest and best use of the property as improved study.
c. Marketability study.
d. Highest and best use of the site as though vacant study.
e. General market study.

8. The objective of a feasibility study is to
a. Estimate the IRR that a project will realize.
b. Estimate the NPV that a project will realize.
c. Estimate both the IRR and NPV that a project will realize.
d. Conclude whether a project will meet the investor's objectives.
e. Conclude whether the forecast IRR and NPV will be acceptable.

9. If a developer wishes to develop a plan to lease offices in an existing building, she should request (or be counseled that she needs) which type of study?
a. General market study.
b. Existing use study.
c. Marketability study.
d. Feasibility study.
e. Site-specific market study.

10. According to economic base analysis, what is the driving factor in causing cities to grow in population?

a. Basic employment.

b. Nonbasic employment.

c. Growth in total employment.

d. Growth in nonbasic employment.

e. Growth in basic employment.

PROBLEMS FOR THOUGHT AND SOLUTION

1. Ronald Frump, a local real estate tycoon, has asked you to analyze one of his properties. It consists of a one-acre site and a 25-year-old warehouse. Specifically, he wants to know whether the existing building should be torn down and a new one constructed, and if so, what type and size of building should be constructed. You consider the zoning and other constraints to the type of property that could be created and decide the following three alternatives are the most likely buildings for the site:

	1 100,000 sq. ft. Warehouse	2 150,000 sq. ft. Warehouse	3 100,000 sq. ft. Light Manufacturing Building
Cost to construct	$2,000,000	$3,000,000	$2,500,000
Effective gross income	500,000	600,000	500,000
Operating expenses	200,000	200,000	150,000
NOI	300,000	400,000	350,000
Return to building (12.5%)	250,000	375,000	312,500
Return to site	?	?	?

If the site were vacant (or is made vacant), which building should be constructed, and what would be the value of the site, using a capitalization rate of 11 percent?

2. In analyzing the highest and best use of the Frump property as improved, you decide the existing building could be converted to light manufacturing use for a cost of $50,000. Demolition of the existing building would cost $25,000.

	Existing Use	Light Manufacturing Use	Demolish and Construct New Building
Cost to acquire	$1,000,000	$1,000,000	$1,000,000
Cost to demolish	-0-	-0-	25,000
Capital expenditure	-0-	50,000	2,500,000
Effective gross income	100,000	150,000	500,000
Operating expenses	15,000	30,000	150,000
NOI	$85,000	$120,000	$350,000

Which alternative is the highest and best use of the property as improved and what return does it provide?

3. Why do community agencies, such as chambers of commerce and city planning departments, often do an economic base study (or have one done for them)?

4. Explain why the highest and best use of a site as though vacant is always one of the alternatives in a study of the property's highest and best use as improved.

5. Identify at least five locational attributes that are important to the location of a fast-food restaurant.

INTERNET EXERCISE

Calculate location quotients for the major industrial categories listed in Exhibit 11–9 for *your* county. On the World Wide Web go to (http://www.census.gov). Select Subjects A–Z; then select "United States Economic Profile" and "County and State Economic Profiles." From the data provided about the number of employees in each category, you can quickly and easily calculate location quotients. After calculating the location quotients, identify which categories of employment are basic and which are nonbasic for your county. Then briefly describe the economic base of your county.

CASE PROBLEMS

1. Mr. Henry J. Cobman, the president of Curley's, one of the nation's major fast-food chains, has hired Larry Fine to perform a market study of a corner site that is currently improved with an abandoned service station. Larry completes a market study of this site for a Curley's restaurant with the following recommendations:

   a. The future market for the restaurant is sufficiently large to support a Curley's restaurant at the subject site.

   b. Curley's should build a restaurant using the standard design, size, and configuration established by the Curley's company. A children's playground also should be included.

   Shortly thereafter, Mr. Cobman discovered that an underground gasoline tank from the service station had ruptured, resulting in environmental contamination of the site. This problem prohibited Curley's from obtaining a building permit, and Mr. Cobman is threatening to sue Larry for not uncovering facts about this environmental problem.

   In your opinion, was Larry responsible for reporting to Mr. Cobman about this problem?

   Defend your answer.

2. Perfect Population Projections Inc. (PPP) has entered into a contract with the city of Popular, Pennsylvania, to project the future population of the city. Popular has become a popular place in recent years as indicated by the following data:

Year	Population	Total Employment	Basic Employment	Nonbasic Employment
1995	50,000	25,000	6,250	18,750
1996	53,000	26,500	6,625	19,875
1997	57,000	28,500	7,125	21,375
1998	65,000	32,500	8,125	24,375
1999	70,000	35,000	8,750	26,250
2000	?	?	9,000 (estimated from surveys)	?

   The contract states that PPP must project Popular's population for the year 2000 using both a simple linear method and an economic base analysis. The ratio of population to total employment is 2.0833.

   Your help is needed!

ADDITIONAL READINGS

Books on real estate market analysis include these:

Carn, Neil, Joseph Rabianski, Ronald Racster, and Maury Seldin. *Real Estate Market Analysis: Techniques and Applications.* Upper Saddle River, N.J.: Prentice Hall and National Association of Realtors, Commercial-Investment Council, 1988.

Clapp, John M. *Handbook for Real Estate Market Analysis.* Upper Saddle River, N.J.: Prentice-Hall, 1987.

More in-depth treatment of highest and best use analysis can be found in these books:

Appraisal Institute. *The Appraisal of Real Estate,* 11th ed. Chicago: Appraisal Institute, 1997, Chapter 12.

Smith, Halbert C., Linda Crawford Root, and Jerry D. Belloit. *Real Estate Appraisal,* 3rd ed. Scottsdale, AZ: Gorsuch Scarisbrick, 1995, Chapter 4. Also, Chapter 7 in this book deals with market analysis for appraisals.

The following article cautions real estate market analysts on the use of population projections from various publicly available sources:

Clark, Dave. "Proprietary Demographic Projections Are Unreliable." *Real Estate Review* 18 (Fall 1988), pp. 59–64.

This article is a position paper adopted by the Joint Valuation/Research Subcommittees of the National Council of Real Estate Investment Fiduciaries (NCREIF) on the role, purpose, and procedures for market analysis in appraisals:

Wincott, D. Richard, and Glenn R. Mueller. "Market Analysis in the Appraisal Process." *Appraisal Journal,* LXIII, no. 1 (January 1995), pp. 27–32.

The following article presents a structure for market analysis. It also suggests nine specific improvements to the customary practice of real estate market analysis.

Malizia, Emil E. and Robin A. Howarth, "Clarifying the Structure and Advancing the Practice of Real Estate Market Analysis." *Appraisal Journal,* LXIII, no. 1 (January 1995), pp. 60–68.

Would you like to know what fundamental changes are taking place in the U.S. economy that are altering real estate values and that will determine the relative success of various types of real estate in the future? If so, read this article:

Rabin, Sol L. "Institutional Real Estate Investors Confront the Frayed-Collar Economy." *Real Estate Issues,* 20, no. 3 (December 1995), pp. 1–7.

12

C H A P T E R

INTRODUCTION TO DEVELOPMENT

THE CREATION OF REAL ESTATE
Development and Construction Businesses
Relationships with Consumers and the Public
Formation of Development Teams

THE DEVELOPMENT PROCESS
First Stage: The Idea
Second Stage: The Site
Third Stage: Feasibility
Fourth Stage: The Contracts and Approvals
Fifth Stage: The Improvements
Sixth Stage: On to the Next Project

ECONOMIC FEASIBILITY: A VALUE PERSPECTIVE
Market Equilibrium and Disequilibrium
Economic Feasibility of an Office Building
    Development

SUMMARY

KEY TERMS

TEST YOURSELF

PROBLEMS FOR THOUGHT AND SOLUTION

INTERNET EXERCISES

CASE PROBLEMS

ADDITIONAL READINGS

LEARNING OBJECTIVES

After reading this chapter, students will be able to:

1. Discuss issues specific to the development and construction businesses.

2. Identify the members of development teams and describe their roles and relationships.

3. Present the sequence of steps in a typical development project.

4. Evaluate the economic feasibility of a simple development project.

5. Formulate successful strategies for constructing land improvements.

THE CREATION OF REAL ESTATE

Development of land and construction of improvements on land represent the two necessary activities for creation of the real estate people use for residential and commercial purposes. *Land development* is the process of changing raw land to a developed state. This process includes acquisition of land, installation of **improvements to land** such as streets and utilities, and securing zoning changes from local governments. Construction of **improvements on the land** is the process of bringing developed land to an improved condition in which land and buildings are ready for occupancy. Development and construction extend to significant alterations of existing properties, for example, renovation of retail centers and repositioning hotels.

The term **developer** describes a person or firm that both develops land and constructs improvements on developed parcels (See Real Estate Focus 12–1). Strictly defined, developers only develop land and **builders** construct buildings. This division of labor exists mainly in the production of residential subdivisions. Developers acquire large parcels of land, obtain zoning approval, subdivide parcels into lots, add improvements to land, and sell developed lots either to builders who construct houses or to individuals who hire builders to construct custom houses.[1] For income-producing property, land development and construction usually occur in one long step by a single individual or firm—the developer.

DEVELOPMENT AND CONSTRUCTION BUSINESSES

Developers (and builders) are in business to make money. Development provides the opportunity to make (lose) enormous amounts of money. The accomplishment of producing permanent improvements on land also provides much satisfaction for many people. From an economic perspective, they accomplish the goal of making money from development by combining their entrepreneurial talent with proper amounts of land, labor, materials,

---

[1] During 1995, 40 percent of the nearly one and one-half million houses constructed in the United States were custom-built houses according to the National Association of Homebuilders.

REAL ESTATE FOCUS 12-1

Donald Trump on the Nature of Real Estate Development

One of Marci's problems was that he tried to apply the principles of bridge building to a residential development. When you build a bridge, under contract to the government, you calculate the costs and sign the contract for a set amount. All you need to do to earn a profit is to bring the project in on budget. In developing real estate it's a whole different ball game. You can budget costs, but you can't truly project revenues, because you're always at the mercy of the market. The variables include how much you get per unit, how long it takes to sell out, and what your carrying costs are along the way. The less you commit to spend up front, the less you're at risk later.

SOURCE: Donald Trump, *The Art of the Deal* (New York: Random House, 1987), p. 217.

and financial capital to produce real estate. From a business perspective, they accomplish their goals by acting as managers who plan, organize, and control the process of development and construction through the marketing and sale phase. From the central perspective of this text—the value perspective—developers make money by completing projects for which the values exceed the total costs of development and construction. This means developers produce new streams of cash flows at locations, often where no cash flows existed before.

Chapter 12 presents considerable institutional detail about the business of development and construction. More importantly, this chapter provides a value perspective of real estate development and construction that serves as a conceptual foundation for understanding why real estate is created.

RELATIONSHIPS WITH CONSUMERS AND THE PUBLIC

Land development and construction fundamentally alter the bundle of physical and legal property rights in land discussed in Chapter 20. These alterations occur in direct response to the needs of residential and commercial property consumers. The economic feasibility of projects therefore depends on developers' careful reading of consumer preferences and on successful marketing efforts to consumers.

Because of fixed locations, alteration of property rights in one parcel to meet consumer needs often changes the property rights, and thus the cash flows, of nearby parcels. As described in Chapter 10, governments establish intricate regulatory controls such as zoning, building codes, and housing codes to protect property owners and the public from the actions of developers. Violations of these regulations may extinguish the rights government grants to developers to create real estate.

So developers play a delicate game in pursuit of their goal of making money. On offense, developers aggressively advance projects to obtain returns on their investments of money and time. On defense, developers guard against losses that may result from violations of the public trust. Good relations with public agencies take on added importance because of the need for infrastructure. The term **infrastructure** refers to publicly

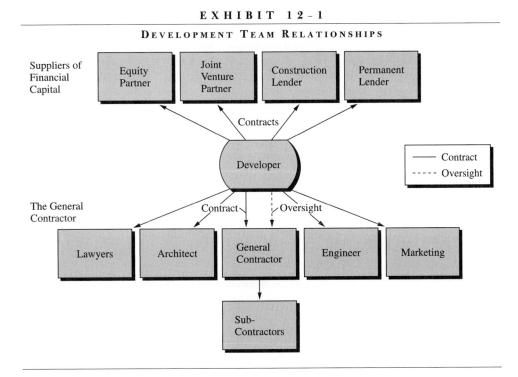

EXHIBIT 12-1

DEVELOPMENT TEAM RELATIONSHIPS

provided products, such as highways and utilities, and services, such as police and fire protection. As one developer stated, "There are two things you need in development—financing and sewage."

FORMATION OF DEVELOPMENT TEAMS

From a business perspective, developers function both as entrepreneurs, who commit time and money for uncertain returns, and managers, who assemble and administer the resources necessary to ensure project success. Exhibit 12–1 shows various business relationships involving a developer and others. These relationships fall into two categories: those with **development team** members who supply services, materials, and labor directly to create the physical real estate and those with suppliers of financial capital.

Suppliers of financial capital. Development and construction projects, like other real estate investments, have a financial capital structure usually comprised of part equity and part debt. Developers may contribute some money, but partners or stockholders provide most of the equity capital for projects. In Chapter 5, we present the ways in which equity investment occurs to help finance real estate. Individuals, operating through partnerships, and securities investors, operating through ownership of REIT shares, make equity investments in existing property and development ventures. These decisions depend on near-term return and risk tradeoffs and on their long-term investment objectives.

Joint venture arrangements represent another way of raising equity (and debt) capital. In **equity joint ventures**, "money" partners supply all funds necessary to advance projects, while developers supply ideas and the managerial skills to complete projects. Money partners include pension funds and life insurance companies seeking newly developed properties for their portfolios or corporations that require space for their operations at new locations. Developers in these arrangements are sometimes referred to as **fee developers** because their compensation largely comes in the form of fees and not from the operation and sales of properties. In **mortgage joint ventures**, lenders receive mortgage payments and portions of cash flows after debt service payments and some of the proceeds from property sales. Developers receive a small share of cash flow, some or all of the tax benefits, and fee compensation for development and construction services rendered.[2]

Successful developers maintain especially good relations with construction lenders (e.g., banks) and permanent lenders (e.g., life insurance companies) because these debt capital providers usually contribute 60 to 70 percent of the financial capital for development projects. Debt financing for development comes from a variety of sources. Traditional bank and life insurance company mortgage financing produces most of the debt capital, although development project financing can come from corporate borrowing and possibly through investment bankers who participate in the creation of mortgages and then issue mortgage-backed securities. In Chapter 18, we provide a detailed discussion of mortgage financing for income-property development. Chapter 19 outlines the process followed in the creation of commercial mortgage-backed securities.

The general contractor. The bottom section of Exhibit 12–1 shows the relationship between developers and suppliers of labor, services, and materials. The relationship between developers and lawyers begins with the acquisition of rights to develop land and continues through the signing of leases or sales contracts at the end of projects. In between, the involvement of lawyers includes preparing partnership agreements; reviewing and modifying loan contracts; and preparing employment contracts with architects, engineers, and contractors.

Architects, landscape architects, and engineers provide essential services during the early phases of the project. Architects translate the ideas of developers into architectural renderings and plans. Engineers work with architects to ensure that architectural plans result in structurally sound buildings. The relationships among architects, engineers, and developers continue throughout the project. Architects and engineers often serve as the developers' agents on technical matters in their dealings with the general contractor.

Builders often retain outside marketing agents to lease or sell the completed space if this expertise does not exist within their own company. Medium-size and large development companies usually maintain a marketing department within the firm. This depart-

---

[2] A discussion of joint ventures also appears in Chapter 18.

EXHIBIT 12-2

THE CONSTRUCTION MANAGER AND THE DEVELOPER

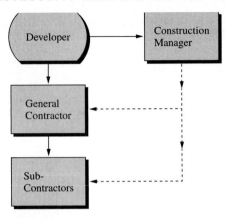

ment sometimes becomes a profit center. Marketing activity occurs well before the completion of the project so that as much space as possible becomes presold or preleased. For rental properties, the amount of money developers receive from lenders at the time of completion often depends on the amount of preleased space. Thus, project success can often depend heavily on developers having relationships with effective marketing agents.

Exhibit 12–1 also presents a typical relationship between developers and suppliers of labor and materials.[3] When in-house expertise in land preparation and construction is not available, developers enter into contractual relationships with **general contractors**. General contractors bear the responsibility for the physical implementation of projects. Usually, **subcontractors** assemble labor and materials to complete specific tasks in the project such as plumbing, painting, and electrical. General contractors hire and supervise subcontractors. Developers do not contract directly with subcontractors. This set of relationships between contractors and developers exists for relatively uncomplicated construction projects during which the potential for conflicts between developers and contractors remains low.

The construction manager. Hiring a **construction manager** represents a slightly different approach to completing construction, as shown in Exhibit 12–2. Some developers prefer to work directly with contractors to maintain strict control over the introduction of labor and materials to their projects. For complicated projects, developers and the general contractor often become involved in a steady stream of conflicts over minor details and sometimes over major issues. Many developers prefer not to be burdened with the day-to-day oversight of project construction. Thus, developers contract with construction management firms to serve as the agent of the developer in an oversight capacity. Agents

---

[3] Sometimes development firms do business within large companies that include construction companies.

EXHIBIT 12-3

TYPICAL STAGES IN DEVELOPMENT AND CONSTRUCTION

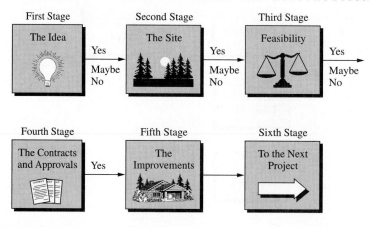

must act in the best interests of principals; thus, the contract between developers and construction management firms allows developers to focus on marketing and other important aspects of projects rather than resolving problems related to construction.

THE DEVELOPMENT PROCESS

Real estate development and construction projects should proceed according to a logical sequence of events. However, the process followed in the real world by developers may not resemble our textbook example. The process outlined in this section and graphically displayed in Exhibit 12–3, therefore, is a normative (what should be) representation of the steps involved in taking undeveloped parcels of land to their fully developed states. This section also discusses how the development team members interact in development projects. Because of the unique nature of each development project, a great deal of innovation and creativity occurs throughout the process of successful real estate development.

FIRST STAGE: THE IDEA

Every real estate development project begins with an idea. The idea embodies developers' preconceptions about projects—their sizes, locations, and the types of tenants or buyers who will ultimately use the space (See Real Estate Focus 12–2). It also embodies intuition about key issues, such as the financial structuring and preliminary feasibility of the project. For example, a developer envisions a project to build a medium-size office building near an airport. The developer believes an equity joint venture with a pension fund constitutes the best way to finance the project because mortgage lenders now seem reluctant to lend money for office developments.

Although many real estate professionals conceive of sound development concepts, developers have the initiative to advance their concepts to implementation. Therefore, moving to the next stage in the process—in which the development concept becomes refined—involves a crucial step. It requires developers to take specific actions and make definite commitments to projects.

SECOND STAGE: THE SITE

The most important activities during the second stage are site selection, site analysis, and acquisition of development rights. The concept sets the initial parameters for site location. For the airport office building, the location parameters suggest two alternative sites near an emerging office center in the vicinity of the airport. The analysis of the sites includes investigations into legal ownership, current zoning (and opportunities for rezoning), soil conditions, topography, visibility, and access.

For projects to advance further, developers must contact property owners to acquire development rights. The most popular arrangements for acquiring development rights include **option contracts**, **contracts for sale with contingencies**, **binders**, and **letters of intent**. Option contracts and contracts for sale with contingencies tie up properties for specified periods in return for the payments of fees—the option price or an earnest-money deposit with contingency contracts. Binders require deposits in exchange for rights of first refusal. Letters of intent do not secure properties. Owners may sell properties while developers are studying market feasibility or trying to obtain financing. Letters of intent are more risky for this reason, but less costly because of the absence of earnest-money deposits. Exhibit 12–4 reviews the characteristics of the contracts for acquiring rights prior to development.

Several other crucial activities begin during this stage. These include determining the availability of general contractors and initial discussions with prospective tenants, lenders, and investors.

THIRD STAGE: FEASIBILITY

Unavailability of an acceptable site stands as an obvious reason to halt progress on projects. However if site selection, site analysis, and acquisition activities proceed smoothly, then projects advance to the feasibility stage.

As suggested in the previous section of this chapter, developers sometimes pass judgment on the feasibility of projects in advance of the preparation of market and financial feasibility studies. Preliminary investigative work by developers and preparation of formal studies, typically performed by consultants (as discussed in Chapter 11), represent two of the most crucial elements of this stage. Information from the market analysis component

EXHIBIT 12-4

REVIEW OF CONTRACTS FOR ACQUIRING DEVELOPMENT RIGHTS

Contract	Action	Security of Development Rights	Expense
Option	Developer buys right to purchase property at set price over specific period	Excellent— property owner cannot sell to others	High— 1 to 3 percent of property price
Contract for sale with contingencies	Developer makes offer contingent upon certain events occurring	Excellent if property owner has difficulty selling and accepts offer, but cannot be successful in active markets	Low— only an earnest money deposit
Binder	Developer buys a right of first refusal from property owner	Good but does not prevent property owner from selling to others	Low to medium depending on obligation to developer
Letter of intent	Developer issues letter demonstrating intent to buy property from owner	Poor but developer may obtain free right of first refusal	Zero

of the feasibility study helps architects make preliminary drawings and engineers develop cost estimates. The feasibility study, architectural drawings, and cost estimates, along with an appraisal, comprise a major portion of the loan submission package submitted to construction and permanent lenders. A negative feasibility study or unavailability of favorable financing means the project recycles to an earlier stage or terminates. With all of these essential elements in place, developers can commit to completing their projects.

FOURTH STAGE: THE CONTRACTS AND APPROVALS

The decision to commit to projects means signing formal contracts with members of the development team and others. At this stage, developers obtain commitments from lenders, sign contracts with the general contractor and construction manager, sign leases with major tenants, and enter into partnership agreements with equity partners. The process of securing approvals from public agencies occurs concurrently with contract negotiations. This process represents one of the most important activities during the development process—if zoning approval, building permits, and in some areas, multiple environmental and

REAL ESTATE FOCUS 12-2

Development Concepts May Not Involve New Ideas!

As noted above, real estate development begins with a concept or idea. The concept does not need to be new—an old concept may emerge. The Anaheim Plaza renovation provides a case in point.

The first suburban shopping centers built during the 1950s consisted of a line of retail stores with a large parking area in front. Later, the concept of the shopping mall became popular, with a central building surrounded by parking. During the 1970s, Anaheim Plaza was renovated from a 1950s-style center to a mall (see exhibit). As shopping preferences changed, the mall lost its appeal and in 1994 it was bulldozed. In its place a "power center" was built that consists of a collection of large national retailers.

Interestingly, this "new" power center concept strongly resembles the straight-line shopping center concept of the 1950s in its physical configuration (see exhibit)!

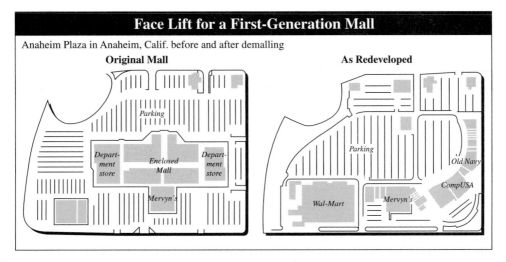

Face Lift for a First-Generation Mall

Anaheim Plaza in Anaheim, Calif. before and after demalling

Original Mall   **As Redeveloped**

SOURCE: *The Wall Street Journal*, April 16, 1996, p. B-1.

utility agency approvals are not granted, the project cannot legally proceed to the next stage. With contracts signed and all approvals granted, developers stand ready to initiate the physical development and construction of real estate.

FIFTH STAGE: THE IMPROVEMENTS

Two major concerns emerge when adding the improvements to land and improvements on land. First, developers must make certain the project proceeds in a timely manner. Every month, interest accrues on the growing unpaid balance of the development or construction loan. Thus, to ensure timely progress, developers work closely during this period with the general contractor, construction manager, engineer, and architect.

REAL ESTATE FOCUS 12-3, INTERNATIONAL

An International Real Estate Developer—John Portman

John Portman is an architect by trade, having received his degree in architecture from the Georgia Institute of Technology in the 1950s. This explains why many of his properties are characterized by a unique architectural style featuring dramatic atrium designs. He is also noted for providing attractive space for pedestrian movement at street level in his properties.

Portman ventured overseas during the oil crisis of the mid-1970s. He completed projects in Europe, the Mid-east, and the Far East, including China. The ability of his firm to blend familiar styles from the United States with cultural characteristics of the countries in which he is building has made Portman one of the most successful international developers from the United States.

IMPORTANT PORTMAN DEVELOPMENT PROJECTS

Domestic

Renaissance Center (Detroit, 1976)—controversial downtown, mixed-use development.
Westin Peachtree Plaza Hotel (Atlanta, 1976)—tallest hotel in the southern United States.
Embarcadero Center (San Francisco, 1981)—renowned mixed-use development.
Marriott Marquis (New York, 1985)—cornerstone of Times Square redevelopment.

International

International Trade Mart (Brussels, 1975)—1.5 million square feet developed with money from U.S. and European investors.
Ho Chung Marina (Hong Kong, 1981)—marina with 238 houses, shopping, and recreational facilities.
Pavilion Inter-Continental Hotel (Singapore 1982)—deluxe, 504-room hotel.
Landmark City (Jakarta, 1985)—four apartment towers, 624-room hotel, and retail space.
Tomorrow Square (Shanghai, expected completion in 1999)—55-story office building.

Marketing represents the second major concern. Actually, leasing activities for rental properties and sales activities for salable properties, such as residential condominiums, begin before the project management stage. The marketing group needs to prelease or presell as much of the *product* as possible. Successful leasing agents pay special attention to the needs of potential tenants by offering the best possible money allowances for finishing the interior space (for amenities such as carpets and wall covering). Successful sales agents pay special attention to the mortgage financing needs of potential buyers. The work of the marketing force continues at an active pace during actual development and construction, and immediately thereafter.

The marketing effort becomes a high priority for developers because the success of projects ultimately depends on the timing and the absorption of the project into the market. Developers often lack large reserves of funds, and projects commonly experience cost overruns. This problem suggests that early lease signings and sales preclude the need for expensive additional capital (such as short-term borrowing without collateral). Perhaps more important, permanent-loan commitments for rental properties contain rental-achievement clauses that restrict the amount of funds available to repay construction loans unless preleasing reaches a prescribed level (e.g., 60 percent) near the end of construction. With properties listed for sale, marketing also plays an important role because financing contracts may limit developers from earning much money on the sale of, for example, the first 80 percent of the properties. Often, developers earn their required rates of return and excess returns from the proceeds of sales on, for example the last 20 percent of the properties sold.

SIXTH STAGE: ON TO THE NEXT PROJECT

Technically, project completion occurs when all of the physical elements of the improvements are in place and local building code enforcement officials issue the required **certificate of occupancy (CO)**. Issuance of the CO occurs when the structure becomes habitable in the opinion of the local building inspector, even though certain interior improvements may not be in place at that time (e.g., carpets). These events officially end the relationships between developers and most members of the development team. Also, the relationship between developers and construction lenders ends because the permanent loan closes at this stage. The equity owners (e.g., partnership) take control of property operations, which often involves hiring property and asset management, at this point, or sales occur.

The marketing group remains very active during the completion stage. Preopening advertising and promotion occur prior to any opening events. Because developers focus almost exclusively on the business of developing real estate and constructing land improvements, they begin looking forward to the next project or to the completion of another ongoing project at this stage (See Real Estate Focus 12–3).

ECONOMIC FEASIBILITY: A VALUE PERSPECTIVE

In Chapter 11, we explain the meaning of *feasibility* in the real estate business and the institutional goals of feasibility studies. Next we explore the concept of feasibility again in the context of the market value of specific development opportunities. This perspective of feasibility coincides with the central theme of *Real Estate Perspectives*—the value perspective.

MARKET EQUILIBRIUM AND DISEQUILIBRIUM

Developers create real estate for the same profit motive that drives any producer to manufacture its products. If, for example, it costs $1.00 to produce a tube of toothpaste and the tube sells in stores for $1.69, then the manufacturing firm earns a profit on its toothpaste business. The cost of manufacturing toothpaste varies only slightly over time and from firm to firm. Also, the pricing of toothpaste remains within a fairly narrow range. While the principle of maximizing the difference between unit cost and unit sale price is the same in the development business, the costs and pricing of real estate have much more uncertainty than those of toothpaste.

As noted in Chapter 9, real estate markets operate imperfectly because location uniquely defines the character of each property. Thus, no perfect substitutes exist for a given property. Further, we noted that real estate markets experience cycles leading to underproduction of real estate, and subsequently, overbuilding. These outcomes result, in part, from the sheer time it takes to complete projects. A developer may begin a project in a very healthy market, but two years into the project the market may have weakened considerably.

When the demand by tenants for a particular kind of space equals available supply (that is, the space market reaches equilibrium), the market rewards developers with "normal" returns on their investments of money and time—they earn the required risk-adjusted rate of return. In disequilibrium, developers stand to make either extraordinary returns or suffer extraordinary losses. The following equilibrium conditions guide developers in their decisions about pursuing projects even before the completion of formal feasibility studies:

1. Current vacancy rate equals the long-run or natural vacancy rate.
2. Gross rent per square foot on occupied space equals expenses per square foot, including operating expenses, economic depreciation, real debt, financing costs, and a normal dividend return to equity owners.
3. Total cost of development, which includes developer profit of approximately 5 percent, equals the value of the developed property (i.e., $Q = 1$).

Favorable conditions for development exist in disequilibrium when some or all of these conditions are not equalities, but instead carry positive signs. If, for example, the natural vacancy rate equals 12 percent and the current vacancy rate equals 6 percent; gross rent per square foot equals $20 and all expenses equal $15 per square foot; and most importantly, the full cost to develop a property equals $10 million and the sale price upon completion of construction equals $14 million, then developers have a strong economic incentive to commit to the development. Development projects have **economic feasibility** whenever the present market value of the developed property equals or exceeds the present value of all project costs.

ECONOMIC FEASIBILITY OF AN OFFICE BUILDING DEVELOPMENT

The CSL Integrated Concept Group specializes in the development of small office buildings at airport locations. After an analysis of the market, the company decides to purchase an option on a parcel of land near an airport in a medium-size city. The analysis indicated that the current vacancy rate of 7 percent in the airport area stands well below the natural vacancy rate of 12 percent. Also, the rent of $18.95 per square foot on a triple-net basis for new office space in the area exceeds that needed to cover all expenses by a comfortable margin.

The option cost of $20,000 represents about 1 percent of the total land purchase price. Upon completion, CSL plans to sell the property to one of the pension funds that purchased properties of this type from CSL in the past. These investors pay the market value of leased-up property. Plans call for a five-story, 100,000-square-foot building, with 95,000 net rentable square feet, designed for multiple-tenant occupancy.

EXHIBIT 12-5

DEVELOPMENT COST OF CSL'S AIRPORT OFFICE BUILDING

Land		$1,951,600
Hard costs		
Site work	147,000	
Building shell	4,900,000	
Tenant finish	1,288,000	
Landscape and sprinkler system	224,000	
Utilities	67,900	
Off-site construction	30,800	
Total hard costs		6,657,700
Soft costs		
Government permits and fees	13,300	
Architect and engineering fees	268,100	
Surveying	8,400	
Legal and accounting fees	70,000	
Appraisal	14,000	
Promotion and advertising	63,000	
Leasing commissions	287,000	
Construction interest	742,000	
Construction loan closing costs	52,500	
Construction loan points	106,400	
Permanent loan closing costs	49,000	
Permanent loan points	212,800	
Development fee	280,000	
Operating expenses during lease-up	2,730,000	
Contingency	575,400	
Total soft costs		5,471,900
Total construction cost		14,081,200
Less: NOI during lease-up		2,055,900
Development cost to stabilization		$12,025,300

The option on the land gives CSL the opportunity to determine the economic feasibility of the project prior to commissioning a consultant to perform a formal feasibility study. Preliminary analysis indicates that the site offers enough potential to justify the purchase of the option. Determining the economic feasibility of the project involves two steps: estimating the cost of the project and estimating the market value at lease-up.

Cost estimation.   The proposed office building will take two years to complete and another year to reach full lease-up. During that time, CSL will incur a wide variety of costs associated with this development. In addition to the cost of land, development ventures such as this involve **hard** (sometimes referred to as direct) **costs** and **soft** (sometimes referred to as indirect) **costs**. Exhibit 12–5 contains estimates of the development costs of the project, which amount to about $12 million net of the income received from operating the building until lease-up and sale.

EXHIBIT 1 2 - 6

MARKET VALUE OF CSL'S AIRPORT OFFICE BUILDING

Gross rental income (95,000 sq. ft. @ $18.95)	$1,800,250
Less: Vacancy and collection allowance (5%)	90,013
Effective gross income	1,710,237
Less: Operating expenses for common areas ($3.75 sq. ft)	356,250
Net operating income	$1,353,987
Indicated sale price at 11% cap rate	$12,308,973
Q-Ratio ($12,308,972/$12,025,300)	1.0236

In the category of hard costs, site work involves clearing the land of vegetation and leveling the land for construction; the building shell item refers to the cost of erecting the main structure: tenant finish is an allowance given to tenants to furnish their spaces; the landscaping and sprinkler system item covers all costs outside the shell, including the parking area; utilities refers to the costs of all underground systems on the site; and off-site construction involves extending transportation and utilities to the site. These costs represent expenditures on labor and materials related directly to producing the improvements to and on the land.

The soft costs include fees for government and professional services, such as legal services; expenses related to construction and permanent financing; development company overhead and building expenses during lease-up; a contingency; and CSL's development fee.

Market value estimation. Exhibit 12–6 indicates that the project's $12,308,972 market value, and thus the expected sale price to a pension fund, slightly exceeds the development cost (Q = 1.0236). This estimate comes from the application of a simple income capitalization valuation method discussed in Chapter 14, but relies on a conservative capitalization rate of 11 percent in this market for this type of property.

Developer rate of return. The Q-ratio indicates that the project is a "thin" deal if CSL is depending heavily on the sale proceeds to earn a reasonable return on investment. Lenders require that CSL contribute the land as equity in the project and they will lend the balance of the cost to develop. Contribution of land, sometimes held for some time prior to development, often substitutes for cash down payments in the financing of development projects. This means that CSL's contribution amounts to the equivalent of $2 million, and the lender supplies all of the money needed to construct the improvements. As shown in Exhibit 12–7, the company will earn its development fee at the end of construction and then receive its investment in land back plus the difference between the sale price and cost with the sale of the property. The internal rate of return on the three-year investment equals 9.2 percent.

REAL ESTATE FOCUS 12-4

How to Become a Real Estate Developer

Being a developer is one of the most fascinating occupations in the real estate business and one that offers greater economic returns and notoriety than perhaps any other career in the industry. Many prominent and flamboyant personalities, such as Donald Trump, earned their reputations from real estate development. Also, several owners of professional sports teams, such as the DeBartolo family of Youngstown, Ohio, who own the San Francisco 49ers, made or enhanced their fortunes by developing real estate.

Credibility, or a good track record, is essential for success in the real estate development business because most of the money for development comes from others. Aspiring young developers are still able to enter the business on their own despite the emergence in recent decades of large regional and national development companies. Small, local developers usually obtain experience and training either in real estate brokerage, in which they learn the local market dynamics, or in construction and home building.

Young people also enter this business along corporate tracks. They typically bring to the corporation some real estate experience and considerable real estate and business education. One survey found that large national real estate companies prefer MBA graduates (often with minors in real estate) from top national and regional schools.* Smaller companies do not exhibit such a strong preference for MBAs. Many major United States universities offer specialized master's degrees in real estate, with an emphasis on development. Massachusetts Institute of Technology, the University of Southern California, and the University of North Carolina, to name a few, have structured interdisciplinary programs with a strong development flavor. These degrees are popular alternatives to an MBA. A list of the major universities in the United States that offer degrees in real estate appears in Chapter 1.

* Mark Kroll and Charles Smith, "Real Estate Development and the MBA Degree," *Journal of Real Estate Development* (Winter 1988), pp. 30–34.

EXHIBIT 12-7

CSL's RATE OF RETURN ON THE AIRPORT OFFICE PROJECT

Period	Cash Outflow	Cash Inflow
0 (closing)	$1,951,600	$0
1	0	0
2 (end construction)	0	280,000 (Development Fee)
3 (sale)	0	$2,235,272
IRR = 9.2%		

Risks and the decision to proceed. An experienced development company will carefully weigh the rate of return against the risks. As CSL's management knows, many things can go wrong during the next three years to jeopardize its return including poor weather, labor problems, interest rate increases, and local market changes that slow lease-up. Given these high risks and the low rate of return, CSL management decides to forfeit the $20,000 land option price and not pursue the project any further.

SUMMARY

Developers (broadly defined to include builders) are businesspeople. See Real Estate Focus 12–4. They bring together labor, capital, land, and their own entrepreneurial skills to produce improvements to and on land. To successfully complete projects, developers must perform as competent managers and must rely on other business disciplines, especially marketing.

Successful developers establish good relationships with consumers; the public, including agencies responsible for providing infrastructure; and members of the development team, including engineers, architects, the marketing force, contractors, and construction managers. Relationships with the public become especially delicate during development because of the serious conflicts that often occur between public regulators, consumers, and developers over issues such as rezoning.

Following a well-designed process for the completion of development and construction projects represents another important element of success. This begins with ideas or concepts for the improvement of parcels of land. Developers refine and advance these ideas to decision points regarding whether to proceed. This involves the acquisition of development rights to the parcel and project feasibility studies. Once committed to projects, the developers' role becomes one of negotiating contracts and managing projects efficiently.

Determining the right time to proceed with development requires a basic understanding of real estate market equilibrium concepts. The potentially most profitable time to develop occurs when the long-run vacancy rate in the target market well exceeds the current vacancy rate, rents cover all expenses, and the Q-ratio exceeds one. As demonstrated in the chapter example, developers sometimes must turn their backs on potentially viable projects, including forfeiture of option payments for land, when the values of the projects do not meet expectations.

KEY TERMS

Binder 361
Builder 355
Certificate of occupancy 365
Construction manager 359
Contract for sale with
  contingencies 361
Developer 355

Development team 357
Economic feasibility 366
Equity joint venture 358
Fee developer 358
General contractor 359
Hard costs 367
Improvements to land 355

Improvements on the land 355
Infrastructure 356
Letter of intent 361
Mortgage joint venture 358
Option contract 361
Soft costs 367
Subcontractors 359

TEST YOURSELF

Answer the following multiple choice questions:

1. All of the following are members of the development team except
   a. Lawyers.
   b. Engineers.
   c. Zoning board.
   d. General contractor.
   e. Construction manager.

2. The role of the architect in the development process is
   a. To translate the ideas of developers into plans and renderings.

b. To advise developers on technical matters pertaining to the development and construction of projects.

c. To work closely with engineers to see that the plans are followed during development and construction.

d. All of the above.

e. None of the above.

3. During the concept-refinement stage of the development process
   a. The feasibility study is prepared.
   b. Development rights are acquired.
   c. The site is purchased.
   d. The bank loan is obtained.
   e. All of the above.

4. Time is a critical factor during the project management stage of construction mostly because
   a. Weather conditions always change.
   b. Labor strikes are likely for longer projects.
   c. Interest costs are based on unpaid balances of loans that grow during development.
   d. Developers typically get bored with their projects.
   e. Building permits usually expire.

5. In the market for new single-family homes, developers typically
   a. Provide all the money for development and construction.
   b. Take on both development and construction activities.
   c. Are responsible for development work but not the construction of homes.
   d. Work for owners of land to develop and construct homes.
   e. Have several days off each week.

6. The main objective of the marketing group in real estate development is
   a. To have advertising brochures printed.
   b. To secure financing from lenders.
   c. To assist general contractors with construction work.

d. To prelease or presell as much space as possible.

e. To bring coffee and doughnuts to developers in the morning.

7. Certificates of occupancy are issued by
   a. The local museum director.
   b. The local planning and zoning commission.
   c. The local building inspector.
   d. The local chamber of commerce.
   e. The local police.

8. For a development project to be feasible
   a. The market value of the project must exceed the construction loan amount.
   b. The construction loan amount must exceed the cost of development.
   c. The cost of development must exceed the market value of the project.
   d. A feasibility study must say so.
   e. None of the above answers are correct.

9. Which of the following approaches to tying up property rights prior to development provides the most protection to developers against loss of property to another buyer?
   a. Contract for sale with contingencies.
   b. Binder.
   c. Letter of intent.
   d. Option contract.
   e. All of the above provide the same protection.

10. An equity joint venture involves a relationship between a developer and a "money partner" to supply a new property asset for the money partner. Which of the following investors is a typical money partner in equity joint ventures?
    a. Pension fund.
    b. Life insurance company.
    c. Corporation.
    d. All of the above.
    e. None of the above.

PROBLEMS FOR THOUGHT AND SOLUTION

1. Under what conditions would a developer contract with a construction manager instead of dealing directly with a general contractor?

2. What are the advantages and disadvantages of using a letter of intent to tie up property rights versus other types of preliminary contracts?

3. Discuss why developers who establish poor relationships with the public have more difficulty completing projects than developers who have good relations with the public, including public agencies.

4. A development project is economically feasible if the market value of the operating property exceeds the cost of development. When might a developer *not* advance an economically feasible project?

5. Why do many development companies perform development services for others for the fee income instead of developing properties with their own money to operate or sell?

INTERNET EXERCISE

The Opportunity Development Company has been successful in the past with development projects for clients who qualify for property tax reductions authorized by states seeking to encourage growth within their borders. Opportunity now has a client who wishes to build its corporate offices in a state in the western United States that has an aggressive property tax reduction program. Opportunity has no development experience in the western part of the United States. They have hired you as a consultant to research state programs of this type. Go online and find the relevant information. (Hint: try **www.pikenet.com** and search under area development.)

CASE PROBLEMS

1. The Corgel, Smith, and Ling Development Company has successfully developed three apartment complexes on land owned by Smith before its formation in 1997. Corgel thought it was time for the company to attempt different types of projects. Ling identified a potential site along a major highway near two of the company's apartment projects. Since many young adults reside in these apartments, the developers thought the site should be developed as a sports bar with accompanying recreation facilities (e.g., a beach volleyball court). The company decided the next step was to have a market study performed by Reliable Feasibility. Reliable, which completed the study in four weeks for $10,000, reported a strong demand for a sports bar in the area. The company then contacted the owner of the parcel to negotiate a contract for sale. The owner informed them that the site was sold to a national restaurant chain during the previous week.

   a. In what way did the company go wrong (and squander $10,000 plus lost time)?

   b. What could they have done to make this a successful deal?

2. The Perspectives Development Company is involved in negotiations with a land owner for a parcel that Perspectives hopes to develop as an apartment complex. Perspectives estimates the following development costs for the project:

Land	To be determined
Hard costs	$40 million
Soft costs (including developer fee of $1 million)	$20 million

An appraisal indicates that the property will be worth $70 million following completion and lease up.

a. What is the maximum offer Perspective should make to the land owner?

b. What is *q* if Perspectives pays the price determined in *a*?

c. What is Perspectives' rate of return if the land is the company's equity in the deal and the property is sold upon completion and lease-up for market value?

ADDITIONAL READINGS

Two general works on real estate development are

Peiser, Richard B., with Dean Schwanke. *Professional Real Estate Development*. Washington, D.C.: Dearborn Financial Publishing, and Urban Land Institute, 1992.

Miles, Mike E., Richard L. Haney, and Gayle Berens. *Real Estate Development: Principles and Process*. Washington, D.C.: Urban Land Institute, 1996.

A collection of readings on development theory and practice is found in

Urban Land Institute. *Classic Readings in Real Estate Development*. Jay M. Stein, ed. Washington D.C.: ULI, 1996.

An excellent book on house construction, design, and systems is

Harrison, Henry S. *Houses: The Illustrated Guide to Construction, Design, and Systems*. Chicago: Real Estate Education Company, 1992.

Real estate development principles for specific property types are discussed in the Community Builders Handbook Series of the Urban Land Institute (1090 Vermont Avenue, NW, Washington, DC 20005). The handbooks include these titles:

Casazza, John, and Frank H. Spink, Jr. *Shopping Center Development Handbook*, 2nd ed. Washington, DC: Urban Land Institute, Community Builders Handbook Series, 1983.

Lochmoeller, Donald C., et al. *Industrial Development Handbook*. Washington, DC: Urban Land Institute, Community Builders Handbook Series, 1975.

O'Mara, W. Paul, and John A. Casazza. *Office Development Handbook*. Washington, DC: Urban Land Institute, Community Builders Handbook Series, 1982.

Bookout, Lloyd W., Jr., and Kenneth Leventhal & Company. *Residential Development Handbook*. Washington, DC: Urban Land Institute, Community Builders Handbook Series, 1990.

Schwanko, Dean. *Mixed-Use Development Handbook*. Washington, DC: Urban Land Institute, Community Builders Handbook Series, 1987.

An inside view of the operations and management of successful development companies is presented in

Suchman, Diane R. *Managing a Development Company*. Washington, DC: Urban Land Institute, 1987.

For information about real estate development educational programs, see

Directory of Real Estate Development and Related Educational Programs. Washington, DC: Urban Land Institute, 1995.

Articles on current real estate development issues are found in

Real Estate Finance (Institutional Investor, Inc., 488 Madison Ave., New York, NY 10022).

Real Estate Review (New York University School of Continuing Education, the Real Estate Institute, 11 West 42nd Street, New York, New York 10036).

13
C H A P T E R

VALUATION BY THE SALES COMPARISON AND COST APPROACHES

ROLE OF THE SALES COMPARISON AND COST APPROACHES

TRADITIONAL SALES COMPARISON APPROACH
  Adjustments
  Subject Property Compared to Each
    Comparable Property
  Types of Adjustments
  Sequence of Adjustments
  Reconciliation

MULTIPLE REGRESSION MODELS

COST APPROACH
  Cost
  Accrued Depreciation

GROSS RENT MULTIPLIER

APPLICABILITY OF THE APPROACHES

SUMMARY

KEY TERMS

TEST YOURSELF

PROBLEMS FOR THOUGHT AND SOLUTION

INTERNET EXERCISE

ADDITIONAL READINGS

CASE STUDY: Single-Family Residential Appraisal

After reading this chapter, students will be able to:

1. Explain why the sales comparison and cost approaches are important methods of appraisal.

2. Make adjustments in the proper sequence in the sales comparison approach.

3. Calculate a rate of change of the sale prices, given two sales of the same property over time.

4. Interpret the results of a multiple regression analysis.

5. Calculate the main types of accrued depreciation in the cost approach.

6. Estimate a property's value by gross rent multiplier (GRM) analysis, given prices, rents, and information on comparable properties.

7. Reconcile three or more final adjusted sale prices in the sales comparison approach into an indicated value, or two or more indicated values into a final estimate of value.

ROLE OF THE SALES COMPARISON AND COST APPROACHES

As Chapter 2 emphasizes, the market value of a parcel of real estate is the key concept in making investment decisions. We now arrive at the point in this book (Chapters 13 and 14) where we describe and demonstrate the methods of estimating real estate values. The two general methods (or approaches) presented in this chapter provide a means for estimating a property's **market value** without directly considering the property's income-producing potential. In fact, these two approaches are often used to estimate the values of nonincome-producing properties, such as one- to four-family homes, vacant land, and public properties. Nevertheless, these two approaches are also often used, together with the income capitalization approach, to appraise income-producing properties.

When used in the appraisal of income-producing properties, these approaches are often accorded less weight in the final value conclusion than the income capitalization approach because the estimation process is less direct. Instead of measuring the value of the income-producing potential directly, they measure it *indirectly* by estimating the prices that *investors* are likely to pay for a property by comparing the property with similar properties that sold recently and by estimating the cost of replicating the property (including site), less any reduction in market value from today's costs.

The use of these two approaches in estimating the values of one- to four-family residential properties is an important economic function and has kept many real estate appraisers employed. The role of appraisers in performing this function is changing, but the question of value of some 75 million homes in the United States will continue to be important, both to the people who own them and to society in general. While the

EXHIBIT 13-1

STEPS IN THE SALES COMPARISON APPROACH

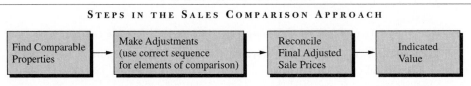

traditional sales comparison and cost approaches will undoubtedly continue to be used for large, unique properties, multiple regression models will likely replace the traditional sales comparison and cost approaches for the vast majority of standard single-family homes. Nevertheless, the concepts involved in the traditional sales comparison and cost approaches are important in the valuation process, and these approaches will continue to be used both for the appraisal of income-producing properties and large, unique single-family properties. We present both the traditional approaches and multiple regression models in this chapter.

TRADITIONAL SALES COMPARISON APPROACH

The sales comparison approach is a general method for appraising all types of properties by comparing a property being appraised (subject property) with similar properties that have sold recently. Ideally, no adjustments would be needed if the comparable properties were exactly like the subject property and the transactional details were the same. The real estate market, however, is imperfect; no two properties are exactly alike, and the motivational and financing aspects of transactions vary greatly. Therefore, appraisers must make adjustments by additions and subtractions to and from the sale prices of comparable properties. All the adjustments result in a final adjusted sale price for each comparable property. Then the appraiser reconciles the **final adjusted sale prices** into an **indicated value** from the sales comparison approach. Exhibit 13–1 shows these steps.

ADJUSTMENTS

Appraisers must consider eight types of **adjustments** divided into two categories in following the sales comparison approach. If the subject property is *better* than the comparable property with respect to any of these items, the comparable property's sale price would be adjusted *upward*, and vice versa if the subject property is inferior to the comparable property. The eight types of adjustments are

1. Transactional characteristics.
   a. Conditions of sale.
   b. Financing terms.
   c. Market conditions.

2. Property characteristics.
   a. Location.
   b. Physical characteristics.
   c. Legal characteristics.
   d. Use.
   e. Nonrealty items (personal property).

The first three, labeled *transactional characteristics*, concern the nature and terms of the transactions; they recognize that matters other than the physical nature and location of a property help determine value. The five **property characteristics** concern the differences between the properties—they recognize that the locational, physical, and legal differences between properties, plus the ways in which the properties are used and the presence or absence of personal property, help determine differences in values. Each of these types of adjustments is explained in greater depth.

Conditions of sale.   The transaction price of comparable properties may not reflect relative equality in bargaining power between buyers and sellers. Or personal relationships may cause a transaction price to be lower than market value, such as when a parent "sells" real estate to a son or daughter. Appraisers must be aware of these factors and check each comparable property transaction to ensure that it truly was an **arm's-length bargain** between buyers and sellers who have relatively equal bargaining power. If any nonarm's-length bargaining occurred in the transaction, the appraiser should reject the property as a comparable because market-derived adjustments for such conditions are impossible to obtain. For example, how can an appraiser know how much to adjust a comparable transaction for a sale from a father to his daughter?

Financing terms.   Occasionally, properties are sold with nonmarket financing. For example, an owner may grant a below-market interest rate to a buyer or a buyer may assume an existing loan at a below-market interest rate, although this is becoming rare because most institutional lenders have **due-on-sale clauses** in their mortgages that require sellers to pay off a loan upon sale of the property. While nonmarket financing occurs most frequently during periods of high interest rates, the possibility of nonmarket financing must always be considered, and transaction prices of comparable properties must be adjusted accordingly when such financing occurs.

Favorable financing terms can cause buyers to pay a somewhat higher price to get lower mortgage payments (see Exhibit 13–2). The price differential between a property having normal market financing and the same property having more favorable financing can be estimated (at least conceptually) by comparing similar properties, some with favorable financing and others without favorable financing. Another method that has been shown to be reliable is to discount the monthly difference in mortgage payments for a period of five years (recognition period) and use 50 percent of this amount as the adjustment.[1] Thus, if the market interest rate were 12.0 percent for a 30-year, monthly amortized

---

[1] For a more detailed explanation of this method, see Halbert C. Smith and John B. Corgel, "Adjusting for Nonmarket Financing: A Quick and Easy Method," *Appraisal Journal* 52, no. 1 (January 1984), pp. 75–83.

EXHIBIT 13 - 2

PROPERTY SOLD WITH AND WITHOUT FAVORABLE FINANCING

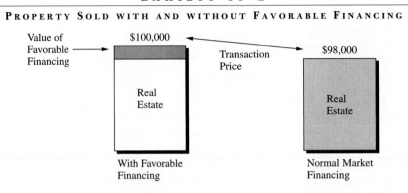

$100,000 mortgage, and the buyer could obtain a similar loan from the seller or someone else at an interest rate of 10 percent, the difference in monthly mortgage payments would be $1,028.61 − $877.57 = $151.04. This amount would be discounted monthly for five years at the borrower's opportunity cost rate (say 10 percent) to a present value of $7,108.75. This amount would then be multiplied by 50 percent to obtain $3,554.38, the amount of the adjustment. The selling price of the comparable property would then be adjusted downward by $3,554.38, since the buyer was willing to pay this much more to obtain the lower interest rate. For example, if the selling price of the property were $130,000, the price adjusted for financing would be $130,000 − $3,554 = $126,446.

Why use only five years as the recognition period? Because buyers do not recognize such theoretical financial advantages for longer than five years. Why use only 50 percent of the present value of the difference in mortgage payments? Because buyers and sellers typically have equal bargaining power (in an arm's-length market transaction) and tend to split the financial advantage.

Market conditions. The transaction prices of comparable properties are historic: They may have occurred yesterday, last month, or several months ago. The older they are, the greater the likelihood the market has changed since then; the same comparable property probably would not sell at the date of the appraisal for the same price as a month or several months before. Changes in **market conditions** result from inflation or deflation, increased or decreased demand, and/or increased or decreased supply.

Appraisers must be sensitive to changes in market conditions. They can estimate the amount of such changes by tracking sales of properties over time. For example, consider three properties in the same neighborhood that all sold today and at some time during the past 18 months. Exhibit 13–3 shows the monthly compound rates of increase in the market prices of these properties and the mean of these rates, which is about .0049 (.49 percent per month). Appraisers could then use this rate to adjust the normal sale prices of comparable properties for the number of months since they were sold. The result is the **market-adjusted normal sale price.** For example, if a comparable property sold 10 months ago

EXHIBIT 13-3

SEQUENTIAL ANALYSIS OF MARKET TRANSACTIONS

Property	Date of Previous Sale	Price at Previous Sale	Price Today	Compound Monthly Rate of Increase
A	6 mos. ago	$82,500	$85,000	.0050 ($412.50)
B	12 mos. ago	$91,000	$97,500	.0058 ($527.80)
C	18 mos. ago	$88,600	$95,000	.0039 ($345.54)
			$\overline{X}$ (mean) =	.0049

EXHIBIT 13-4

LINKAGES FOR A TYPICAL RESIDENTIAL PROPERTY

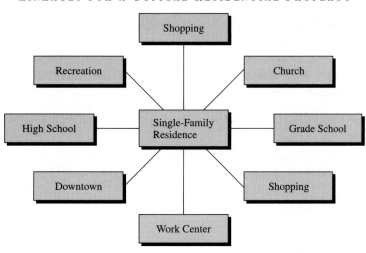

for $100,000, and no prior adjustments are required, its market-adjusted normal sale price would equal $100,000 + $100,000 × (.0049 × 10) = $104,900.

Location.   Location involves the time-distance relationships between a property and all other potential origins and destinations of people coming to and going from the property. These relationships are termed *linkages*. Exhibit 13–4 shows linkages for a typical residential property.

A location adjustment is appropriate only when a comparable property has a set of linkages significantly different from those of the subject property, such as when a comparable is in a different neighborhood. Thus, an appraiser derives location adjustments by

E X H I B I T   1 3 - 5

PAIRED SALES ANALYSIS FOR LOCATION ADJUSTMENT

Pair	Property	Neighborhood	Recent Sale Price	Difference	Difference as a Percentage of B
1st	A	Convenient Acres	$85,000		
	B	Far-Out Hills	83,000	$2,000	2.41
2nd	A	Convenient Acres	94,300		
	B	Far-Out Hills	90,000	4,300	4.78
3rd	A	Convenient Acres	87,750		
	B	Far-Out Hills	84,800	2,950	3.48
				$\bar{X}$ (mean) =	3.56

comparing the prices of similar properties, some of which are in the subject property's neighborhood and some in the comparable property's neighborhood. The general method of comparison is known as *paired sales analysis* as seen in Exhibit 13–5, which shows the prices of three pairs of very similar properties. One property in each pair is in the subject property's neighborhood (Convenient Acres), while the other property is in the comparable property's neighborhood (Far-Out Hills). As calculated in Exhibit 13–5, houses in Convenient Acres sell for an average of 3.56 percent more than similar houses in Far-Out Hills. Thus, a Far-Out Hills comparable property's market-adjusted normal sale price should be increased by about 3.56 percent when appraising a subject property in Convenient Acres. In other words, home buyers appear to be willing to pay about 3.5 percent more for the better location of Convenient Acres compared with Far-Out Hills.

This analysis assumes that the paired properties are highly similar in all respects except location, or that adjustments have already been made to their sale prices to reflect any dissimilar property characteristics. It also assumes that the neighborhoods are similar in other respects (such as upkeep and attractiveness) or that sale prices have been adjusted to reflect dissimilar neighborhood characteristics.

Physical characteristics. Adjustments for physical characteristics cover all the ways a comparable property differs physically from the subject property. These include differences such as lot size, size of the structure, floor plan, architectural style, condition, type of construction, quality of construction, materials, and the presence or absence of various features such as garage, fireplace, built-in appliances, bookshelves, second or third bathroom, carpet, swimming pool, or patio. Again, appraisers use the paired sales technique to estimate the value difference these considerations cause. Appraisers compare the sale prices of pairs of recently sold properties that are highly similar except for a particular physical characteristic. The difference in sale prices for each pair is then a good indication of the value of the feature.

As an example, paired sales analysis can be used to determine how much value a swimming pool adds to properties by noting the differences in sale prices of two pairs of properties. In Exhibit 13–6, Properties A have a swimming pool, whereas Properties B do not. Thus, in this market, swimming pools appear to add about 5.2 percent in value to

EXHIBIT 13-6

PAIRED SALES ANALYSIS FOR PHYSICAL CHARACTERISTIC ADJUSTMENT

Pair	Property	Recent Sale Price	Difference	Differences as a Percentage of Homes W/O
1st	A (with)	$115,000		
	B (w/o)	110,000	$5,000	4.5
2nd	A (with)	137,500		
	B (w/o)	130,000	7,500	5.8
				$\overline{\times} = 5.2$

homes. The market-adjusted normal sale price of comparable properties not having a pool should be increased by this percentage if a subject property has a pool.

Legal characteristics. Potentially, an adjustment must be made if the legal estate, or rights, of a comparable property differ from those of the subject property. For example, the rights to be conveyed from seller to buyer for the subject property may be a fee simple estate, while one of the comparables that sold was a leasehold estate. Other things being equal, the fee simple estate would be worth more, and a positive adjustment would have to be made to the comparable to reflect the greater rights in the subject property. In reality, however, the value of the adjustment is almost impossible to measure from the market. Therefore, in most cases a property, although physically and locationally similar, should not be considered a comparable if the legal estates are different. In other words, a comparable property having a different legal estate than the subject property *should be eliminated as a comparable.* (Note: Legal estates are discussed in more detail in Chapter 20.)

Use. Two properties can be physically and locationally alike, but their **uses** may differ, requiring either an adjustment or elimination of the property as a comparable. For example, an appraiser may be appraising an older single-family residence near the center of a medium-size city. One of the comparables is a similar house next door. The only problem is that the comparable property is used for law offices, whereas the subject is still used for single-family occupancy. Although both properties may be zoned for offices and have the same legal estate, the value of the subject property depends on its anticipated use. If the appraiser believes that it will continue to be used for single-family purposes because there is little demand for offices in the area, he cannot use the law offices as a legitimate comparable. If, however, he expects the subject property to be converted to office use, he could use the law offices as a comparable. Note that the decision depends on *anticipated* use of the subject, not historic or current use.

Nonrealty items. Sometimes either the subject property or one of the comparables will contain items of personal property such as furniture, equipment, rugs, automobiles, fireplace equipment, TVs, and the like. The price of the comparable must therefore be adjusted to reflect either the presence or lack of these **nonrealty items**. Remember, it is the current market value of these items that must be adjusted, not their original cost or today's replacement cost.

SUBJECT PROPERTY COMPARED TO EACH COMPARABLE PROPERTY

When making adjustments, *the subject property is always stated as superior or inferior to a comparable property.* For example, if the subject property's location is 10 percent superior to that of the comparable property, it should be stated that, "The location of the subject property is 10 percent better than the location of Comparable X." Thus, if the comparable property sold for $100,000, the location adjustment is $10,000 and is added to the comparable property's price. It would be improper to state that the comparable property is inferior to the subject property by some amount or percentage because the value of the subject property is not known.

TYPES OF ADJUSTMENTS

Appraisers use two types of adjustments: dollars and percentages. If the dollar difference is known, the appraiser simply adds it to or subtracts it from the comparable property's price. Some adjustments (such as, financing and physical characteristics) are usually made in dollars, whereas adjustments for market conditions and location are typically made in terms of percentages. For example, the appraiser might say that one location may be regarded as about 10 percent better than another or that market conditions have resulted in value increases of about 8 percent in the past year.

SEQUENCE OF ADJUSTMENTS

Appraisers should make adjustments in a definite *sequence*, as Exhibit 13–7 shows. Note that prices are calculated after adjustments 2, 3, and 8. Adjustments 1 and 2 are applied to the *transaction price*, adjustment 3 to the **normal sale price**, and adjustments 4 to 8 to the market-adjusted normal sale price. Although the sequence makes no difference for dollar adjustments, it does make a difference for percentage adjustments. The percentage is multiplied by the next previous price in the sequence, rather than the actual transaction price. The purpose of the sequence is to adjust the comparable property's price, first to reflect the price it would have sold for under normal market terms when it actually sold, and then for any changes in market conditions since the actual transaction. When appraisers obtain a price that reflects normal terms in today's market, they can apply adjustments for differences in property characteristics. They should *not* apply them, however, to the transaction price, because that price is not applicable in the current market.

   Example. Exhibit 13–8 summarizes the sales comparison approach with an example in which the market value of a single-family residence is estimated from three comparable sales. Note that the adjustments are made in the recommended sequence. All of the transactions for the comparable properties were arm's-length, so no adjustment was necessary for conditions of sale. The price of Comparable No. 3 was adjusted downward by

EXHIBIT 13-7

SEQUENCE OF ADJUSTMENTS

Transaction Price
  Conditions of sale
  Financing terms

Normal Sale Price
  Market conditions

Market-Adjusted Normal Sale Price
  Location
  Physical characteristics
  Legal characteristics
  Use
  Nonrealty items

Final Adjusted Sale Price

EXHIBIT 13-8

SALES COMPARISON APPROACH ADJUSTMENT GRID

Element of Comparison	Comparable Sale No. 1	Comparable Sale No. 2	Comparable Sale No. 3	Subject Property
Price	$114,000	$117,000	$123,000	?
Conditions of sale	Arm's-length	Arm's length	Arm's length	N/A
Financing terms	Market	Market	Below market $150 lower monthly payments −$3,530	N/A
Normal Sale Price	$114,000	$117,000	$119,470	N/A
Market conditions	Equal	+.43%	Equal	Today
Market-Adjusted Normal Sale Price	$114,000	$117,500	$119,470	N/A
Physical Characteristics				
Bedrooms/baths	4/1 1/2 +$1,000	Equal	4/3 −$1,800	4/2
Landscaping	Equal	Equal	Inferior +$500	Above average
Living area	$2,300	$2,200 +$2,500	$2,300	$2,300
Maintenance	Equal	Excellent −1,000	Equal	Above average
Garage	1-car +$2,000	Equal	Equal	2-car
Legal Characteristics	Same	Same	Same	Fee simple
Use	Same	Same	Same	Single fam.
Nonrealty Items	None	Drapes −$1,000	None	None
Final Adjusted Sale Price	**$117,000**	**$118,000**	**$118,170**	

$3,530 to reflect the favorable financing obtained by the buyer of this property. The $150 per month difference in mortgage payments was discounted for five years (monthly) at the borrower's opportunity cost rate of 10 percent, and this amount was divided in half to reflect the probability that the buyer and seller split this financial advantage. The normal sale price for each comparable is then calculated.

Only Comparable No. 2 required an adjustment for market conditions because it sold five months ago, whereas Nos. 1 and 3 sold recently, and no changes occurred in the market since their sales. After this adjustment, the result is the market-adjusted normal sale price.

The individual adjustments for various differences in physical characteristics, legal characteristics, use, and nonrealty items are shown next. Note that the legal characteristics and use are the same for the subject property and all comparables. If there were differences between the subject and a comparable, the comparable should in most cases not be considered comparable and should not be used. The final adjusted sale prices reflect the various adjustments to each comparable property.

RECONCILIATION

The final step in obtaining an indicated value of the subject property from the sales comparison approach is to reconcile the final adjusted sale prices. In this step appraisers consider which, if any, of the comparable properties' adjusted sale prices are better indications of the subject property's value than the others. More complete data, fewer and smaller adjustments, and more recent transactions probably would cause them to consider the adjusted sale prices for some comparables better indicators of value than others. On the other hand, if the data are about equally complete, the adjustments are about the same, and the transactions are of about equal vintage, appraisers would weight all adjusted sale prices equally. In this case, the indicated value would be the mean, or average, of the adjusted sale prices.

In reconciling the *final adjusted sale prices* in Exhibit 13–8, however, the appraiser weighted Comparable B more heavily (40 percent) than the other two (30 percent each). This is because he believed that Comparable B was more similar to the subject property and that fewer adjustments were required. As shown in Exhibit 13–9, reconciliation is a weighted averaging process. The weighted average price is then rounded to obtain the *indicated value* from the sales comparison approach.

MULTIPLE REGRESSION MODELS

While the technological tools for using **multiple regression analysis** (MRA) for the appraisal of one- to four-family residences have been available for many years, the availability of adequate data has been a major constraint. This constraint can be overcome with the use of the enormous data banks of the Federal National Mortgage Association (Fannie Mae) and the Federal Home Loan Mortgage Corporation (Freddie Mac). The data on millions of transactions in which these secondary mortgage market organizations are

---

EXHIBIT 13-9

RECONCILIATION

Comparable A:	30% × $117,000	=	$35,100
Comparable B:	40% × 118,000	=	47,200
Comparable C:	30% × 118,170	+	35,451

Indicated Value (sales comparison approach) **$117,751**, rounded to

$117,800

---

involved are now stored in digital form and will be available online to lenders and appraisers. The models and procedures that will govern the application of these data sources are now largely developed and will undoubtedly lead to major changes both in the scope of the residential appraisal function and in the way that residential appraisals (and appraisals of other property types, as well) are conducted. Although the vast majority of appraisals of one- to four-family residences are done because they are required for a home buyer to obtain a loan from a lending institution, many of these appraisals may not be required in the future (see Real Estate Focus 13–1), or, if they are required, they will be done by computerized multiple regression analysis.

Multiple regression analysis, however, is useful for appraising other types of properties in addition to one- to four-family residences. In general, it can be employed whenever relatively large numbers of transactions of similar properties can be found. Typically data from at least 40 or 50 transactions must be available to make MRA a viable method. In many communities such data may be available for apartments, offices, and other types of commercial buildings (e.g., retail buildings). Furthermore, appraisers can build their own data banks for these types of properties; they need not rely on large external data banks such as those of Freddie Mac or Fannie Mae.

The method takes the usual form of a multiple regression equation as follows:

$$Y = \alpha + \beta_1 X_1 + \beta_2 X_2 + \beta_3 X_3 + \ldots + \beta_n X_n + \epsilon$$

where Y = **dependent variable** (price or rent)

α = constant

β = coefficients

X = **independent variables** (value-determining characteristics)

ϵ = residual variance in prices unexplained by independent variables

Example. The market rental rate for units in an apartment complex in Louisville, Kentucky, was estimated using MRA analysis.[2] Data for 42 observations (apartment complexes) were originally collected, but only 36 were used in the final model. The final

---

[2] This example is adapted from Halbert C. Smith, Linda Crawford Root, and Jerry D. Belloit, *Real Estate Appraisal*, 3rd ed. (Scottsdale, AZ: Gorsuch Scarisbrick, 1995), Appendix B, pp. 328–333.

REAL ESTATE FOCUS 13-1

Residential Appraisers: The Next Extinct Species?*

The Federal Home Loan Mortgage Corporation (Freddie Mac) and the Federal National Mortgage Association (Fannie Mae) have initiated new automated underwriting services, with the objective of greatly reducing the time for home loan approvals. The Freddie Mac system is called "Loan Prospector," and the Fannie Mae system is called "Desktop Underwriter." The systems allow lenders to fill out application forms on laptop computers in the borrower's home. The information is sent to the lender's office computer by modem and then to Freddie Mac or Fannie Mae, which rate the risk of the loan by comparing it to statistical models of previously issued loans. The lender then receives a credit evaluation within a few minutes and a *collateral assessment* within two to three days. Loans are then classified by Fannie Mae or Freddie Mac as "accepted," "referred,"

or "caution." For the majority of loans—those classified as "accepted"—the average settlement time for a loan will be reduced from about 45 days to about 5 days. For other loans, additional steps, one of which could be an appraisal, are taken to determine the safety of the loan. Obviously, the settlement time for these loans will be longer, but the agencies expect the average time for all loans to be less than 10 days. Loan origination fees are expected to be cut by 20 to 50 percent. One of the major costs that will be reduced, of course, will be appraisal fees.

---

* In the appraisal profession *residential appraisers* are defined to be appraisers who are specially qualified or who specialize in the appraisal of one- to four-family residences. Appraisers who appraise larger residential properties (apartments) are considered to be *commercial appraisers.*

---

explanatory equation (obtained after adjustments to two prior models) contained the independent variables shown in Exhibit 13–10 and the summary statistics:

The R^2 **statistic** measures how well the model fits the data. It compares the observed rent of each property with the estimated rent that is computed by the regression model, showing that the model in this case can explain 88.5 percent (.885) of the differences between the computed and observed rents. This is a high R^2 and is a good result, provided the other summary statistics are within acceptable ranges.

The **standard error** statistic measures the likely amount of error in an estimate using the model. Thus, for an estimate of market rent of $450 (the average rent in this market), the standard error is expected to be $12.93, or about 2.9 percent (12.93/$450). The standard error can be used to establish a confidence interval around an estimated rent, as demonstrated for the rental estimate in Exhibit 13–11.

The degrees of freedom represent the computational "leg room" afforded by the number of observations. Each observation in the sample provides one degree of freedom, but one degree of freedom is lost for each variable and for each statistic calculated (the mean and standard deviation). In this example 17 degrees of freedom remain from the 36 observations after subtracting one degree each for the mean, standard deviation, and 17 variables. Ideally, the residual degrees of freedom should be at least 30; thus, this result casts some doubt on the applicability of regression analysis in this case.

The summary F **value** provides a measure of the predictive ability of the model. It should equal at least 3, and in this case is quite high at over 80. The t statistics for the individual variables are calculated by dividing the coefficient for each variable by its

EXHIBIT 13-10

MULTIPLE REGRESSION ANALYSIS FOR APARTMENT RENTS

Variable	Variable Name	β	t
X_1	Dishwasher	5.08	6.63
X_2	Tennis court	4.36	6.64
X_3	Sauna	12.40	24.49
X_4	Yearly leases only	−11.00	12.52
X_5	Interaction factor 1*	−6.40	13.96
X_6	Interaction factor 2*	−7.30	8.26
X_7	Extra utilities	22.10	6.05
X_8	Poor neighborhood	−17.00	19.50
X_9	Utilities provided	4.02	6.20
X_{10}	Furnished unit	24.70	73.44
X_{11}	Baths per bedroom	3.15	3.16
X_{12}	Square feet per bedroom	1.47	7.57
X_{13}	Location	−3.30	7.70
X_{14}	Efficiency	−57.00	26.83
X_{15}	Two-bedroom apt.	48.70	282.25
X_{16}	Three-bedroom apt.	104.27	450.59
X_{17}	Four-bedroom apt.	164.92	435.58

* Note: Interaction factor No.1 calculates the value increase of the combined presence of a dishwasher, tennis court, and sauna. Interaction factor No. 2 calculates the value increase resulting from the presence of two of these.

R^2 = 0.88520
Standard error   = 12.93
Degrees of freedom = 17
F-statistic   = 80.78
Constant   = 134.68

standard error. The result gives a measure of the significance of each variable, and usually should equal 2.0 or higher. Since the model shown above is the final run of three, all of the variables appear to be highly significant.

The **constant** is the base value that represents all positive and negative factors that are not explained by the equation and to which the coefficients, or adjustment factors, are added. The **β coefficients** represent the marginal contribution of their respective variables to the predicted value (market rent).

Exhibit 13–11 shows the application of the final model to the estimation of the market rent for the one-bedroom apartment units in the subject property. Rental rates for the other types of units can then be calculated using the amounts added or subtracted by the coefficient for the appropriate variable.

We can use the **standard error** (SE) to give us an approximation of the variability of rents for apartments of this type.[3] For one-bedroom apartments, therefore, we can say that approximately 68 percent will have rents ranging from $425.03 to $450.89 (one SE), approximately 95 percent of these apartments will have rents ranging from $412.10 to $463.82 (two SEs), and over 99 percent of the apartments will have rents ranging from

---

[3] The standard error of the forecast (not calculated here) gives a slightly more precise confidence interval, particularly for estimates farther from the mean.

EXHIBIT 13-11

APPLICATION OF MRA MODEL TO SUBJECT ONE-BEDROOM APARTMENTS

Variable Number	Variable Name	β	Number of Units	Contribution to Rent
X_1	Dishwasher	5.08	1	5.08
X_2	Tennis court	4.36	1	4.36
X_3	Sauna	12.40	0	0.00
X_4	Yearly leases only	−11.14	1	−11.14
X_5	Interaction factor 1	−6.48	0	0.00
X_6	Interaction factor 2	−7.38	1	−7.38
X_7	Extra utilities	22.10	0	0.00
X_8	Poor neighborhood	−17.48	0	0.00
X_9	Utilities provided	4.02	1	4.02
X_{10}	Furnished unit	24.74	1	24.74
X_{11}	Baths per bedroom	3.15	1	3.15
X_{12}	Square feet/bedroom	1.47	300	441.00
X_{13}	Location inconvenience	3.36	7.70	−25.87
X_{14}	Efficiency apartment	−57.27	0	
X_{15}	Two-bedroom apt.	48.77	0	
X_{16}	Three-bedroom apt.	104.27	0	
X_{17}	Four-bedroom apt.	164.92	0	
Total				$437.96

Indicated rent for one-bedroom unit	$437.96
Indicated rent for efficiency unit	$437.96 - 57.27 = 380.69$
Indicated rent for two-bedroom unit	$437.96 + 48.77 = 486.73$
Indicated rent for three-bedroom unit	$437.96 + 104.27 = 542.23$
Indicated rent for four-bedroom unit	$437.96 + 164.92 = 602.88$

$399.17 to $476.75 (three SEs). Thus, a major advantage of using MRA is that it provides a basis for establishing a confidence interval around the predicted value.

COST APPROACH

The basic idea of this approach is that the value of a *new* building tends to equal the cost of reproducing it today. For a building that is *not* new the appraiser can identify and measure reductions in the value from today's reproduction cost. Reductions in value from today's reproduction cost are termed *accrued depreciation*. After the appraiser has estimated the building's value by subtracting all elements of accrued depreciation from the building's cost, the site value is estimated separately and added to the building value. This relationship is shown by the following expression:

$$V_o = (\text{Reproduction cost} - \text{Accrued depreciation}) + \text{Site value}$$

Exhibit 13–12 shows the steps in the cost approach. Each element of the approach is considered below in greater depth.

EXHIBIT 13-12

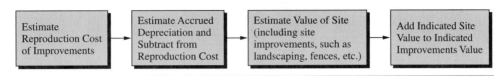

COST

Estimating a building's cost can be a long and detailed task. If appraisers attempt to add up the individual costs of all materials, parts, components, assemblies, labor, and overhead of even a small house, they easily could take several hours or days.[4] Appraisers, however, do not need such a detailed estimate and therefore often rely on alternative methods of obtaining the cost estimates, even though this may cause a loss of some accuracy. Thus, appraisers tend to rely on builders' cost figures, to maintain comparative cost data on a square-foot or cubic-foot basis for various types of houses, and to use cost estimating services. The appraisers' resulting cost figures would not be useful for building contractors but are accurate enough for appraisals.

For appraisal purposes, there are two possible types of cost: **reproduction cost** and **replacement cost**. The reproduction cost of a building is the cost to construct the building today, replicating it in exact detail. This includes any outdated functional aspects of the building such as poor room arrangement, better-than-necessary fixtures, or inadequate equipment. It also includes the cost of any outmoded materials such as surface wiring, steel window frames, and steel plumbing.

In contrast, replacement cost is the money required to construct a building of *equal utility*.[5] This includes the use of modern construction techniques, materials, and design and represents the cost of a building for which some or all outdated aspects are eliminated.

Appraisers principally use reproduction cost, since it represents the building as it actually exists except for accrued depreciation. When using replacement cost, appraisers must keep track of any functional obsolescence that is removed from the cost figure so that it is not wrongly subtracted as accrued depreciation. Also, appraisers may be criticized because replacement cost represents only a hypothetical building, not the actual appraised building. This analysis and discussion assumes that reproduction cost is used in the cost approach.

ACCRUED DEPRECIATION

Buildings can lose value for three reasons: The physical materials and components wear out; the building becomes functionally less usable and desirable compared with newer

---

[4] Such a detailed cost estimation procedure is called the *quantity survey method*.

[5] The term *utility* means satisfaction. Therefore, a building of equal utility is a building that provides satisfaction equal to that of the building being appraised if it were new.

EXHIBIT 13-13

ELEMENTS AND EXAMPLES OF ACCRUED DEPRECIATION

Elements of Accrued Depreciation	Typical Examples
1. Physical deterioration	
a. Short-lived	
(1) Curable	Completely worn-out items such as paint, roofing, floor cover, appliances, HVAC, and interior decoration
(2) Incurable	Partially worn-out items such as paint, roofing, floor cover, appliances, HVAC, and interior decoration
b. Long-lived (always incurable)	The building itself—foundation, walls, roof structure, windows, doors, floors, stairs
2. Functional obsolescence	
a. Curable	Absence of a bathroom, outdated fixtures, too few electrical outlets, lack of bookcases, too-high ceilings, lack of insulation
b. Incurable	Architectural design, floor plan, electrical system, plumbing
3. External obsolescence (always incurable)	Introduction of a nonconforming use in neighborhood; transition from higher to lower uses; odors; unpleasant sights

Note: HVAC stands for heating, ventilating, and air-conditioning.

buildings; and external forces reduce the building's usefulness within its surroundings. Thus, the three major elements of accrued depreciation that must be estimated are **physical deterioration, functional obsolescence** and **external obsolescence**. Exhibit 13–13 shows how these elements are further divided.

Physical deterioration. This category of accrued depreciation is divided into *short-lived* and *long-lived* components. Short-lived components last a shorter time than the building itself lasts and must be replaced one or more times during a building's economic life. Long-lived components consist of the main parts of the building itself—foundation, walls, roof, and the like. The short-lived components are further divided into *curable* and *incurable* elements. Curable elements are those whose cost of replacement will be no greater than the value added by replacing them. For example, if a house needs painting, the value of that house usually will be increased by at least the cost of the paint job.

Incurable elements are those whose cost exceeds the value added when they are fixed or replaced. For example, if a house does not need painting but is painted anyway, the value increase will be less than the cost of the paint job. Similarly, if the roofing or furnace are only partially worn out but are replaced, the value increase will be less than their cost. Nevertheless, the building with incurable elements is worth less than it would be if the incurable elements were new. Thus, the appraiser must estimate the value loss due to partial wearing out of the short-lived components and include it in accrued depreciation.

Similarly, the long-lived components of a building gradually wear out. Appraisers must estimate value loss due to the partial deterioration of the structural components and include it in accrued depreciation. They do this by multiplying the ratio of effective age of the building to its total economic life by the building's reproduction cost minus the reproduction cost of the short-lived items, as represented by the following equation:

LLPD = (Effective age/Economic life) × (RC of building − RC of short-lived items)

where

LLPD	= Long-lived physical deterioration
Effective age	= Physical age adjusted for better-than-average or worse-than-average maintenance
Economic life	= Total useful life of building, during which it will produce positive net operating income
RC of building	= Reproduction cost of entire building
Short-lived items	= RC of all components of the building that have shorter economic lives than the building itself (e.g., electrical system, plumbing system, furnace, water heater, roof)

Example. The total reproduction cost of a building is $500,000, the effective age of the building is 10 years, its total economic life is 60 years, reproduction cost of the short-lived curable items is $20,000, and reproduction cost of the short-lived incurable items is $100,000. The long-lived physical deterioration would be calculated as follows:

$$LLPD = (10/60) \times [\$500,000 - (\$20,000 + \$100,000)]$$
$$= .1667 \times \$380,000$$
$$= \$63,346$$

Functional obsolescence. The usefulness and desirability of existing buildings are compared with those of new buildings, which compete for potential buyers. Newer building materials, construction techniques, and designs, coupled with changing consumer tastes and preferences, generally make older buildings less desirable and thus less valuable than newer buildings. Also, some buildings contain materials and features that are more expensive than buyers are willing to pay for, and appraisers must count the excess costs contained in such buildings' reproduction costs as functional obsolescence. Examples are gold-plated faucets and swimming pools on small residential properties.

Note that functional obsolescence is a different type of accrued depreciation from physical deterioration. An old-fashioned bathtub, for example, may be in excellent physical condition but probably would not contribute as much value to a house as a less costly, more modern tub.

As with physical deterioration, appraisers also divide functional obsolescence into curable and incurable elements. As the examples in Exhibit 13-13 suggest, items causing *curable* functional obsolescence generally are those that can be corrected without major modification of the structure. For example, a half bath may be added in an existing clothes closet or similar available space; old fixtures or appliances can be replaced; electrical outlets can be added; ceilings can be lowered; or insulation can be added without major alteration of the structure.

Appraisers calculate the amount of curable functional obsolescence (CFO) by two procedures:

1. CFO = Cost of installing item in existing structure − Cost of Installing item if building were new
2. CFO = Cost of replacing item − Remaining value of existing item

The first procedure is used to estimate the functional obsolescence due to the absence of items the appraiser considers functionally appropriate or necessary in a structure being built today (e.g., a second bathroom). Note that the depreciation figure obtained is the *excess* cost of retrofitting the items in the existing building, as compared with the cost of their installation in a building being built today. The excess is the cost of tearing out and modifying the existing structure to accommodate the item, which would not be incurred in a new structure.

The second procedure is used to estimate the functional obsolescence resulting from items that are partially obsolete but that still have some value. For example, if the bath fixtures are outdated but still usable, the functional obsolescence is the difference between the cost of replacing them and the value remaining in the old fixtures.

Incurable functional obsolescence (IFO) is related to the structural characteristics of the building—floor plan, architectural design, or major system(s)—that would require major remodeling or rehabilitation of the structure. Appraisers estimate the amount of such functional obsolescence by capitalizing the rent loss or increased expense resulting from the unfavorable condition:

$$IFO = \text{Rent loss (increased expense)} \times \text{Gross rent multiplier}[6]$$

Example. A house with a poor floor plan produces $20 per month less rent than a house having a more desirable floor plan. If the appropriate monthly gross rent multiplier is 100, the accrued depreciation would be

$$IFO = \$20 \times 100$$
$$= \$2,000$$

External obsolescence. This is a loss of a *building's* value through influences outside of the property. It is always incurable, since the building would have to be moved to cure it. Noxious odors, unpleasant sights, and increased traffic due to more intensive uses (such as commercial or industrial) introduced into a residential neighborhood are examples of this type of accrued depreciation. Since the value of only the building is being estimated at this point, appraisers must allocate the total amount of external obsolescence between building and site on the basis of the approximate ratio of building value to total property value. The formula for **external obsolescence (EO)** thus is:

$$EO = \text{Rent loss} \times GRM \times (\text{Building value/Property value})$$

---

[6] GRMs are discussed in the next section.

Example. A single-family house is located on a major street that is becoming increasingly commercial. The property next door has just been rezoned for a small shopping center, increasing the likelihood of more traffic, noise, trash, and odors. The owners find they must reduce the rent by $50 per month to attract tenants. The appropriate GRM for the area is 100, and houses typically represent about 80 percent of total property value. Thus, the amount of accrued depreciation to the building caused by external obsolescence would be

$$EO = \$50 \times 100 \times .80$$
$$= \$4,000$$

GROSS RENT MULTIPLIER

Appraisers sometimes use a variant of the income capitalization approach, known as **gross rent multiplier** (GRM) analysis, to appraise small, income-producing residential properties. While income capitalization uses *net* operating income, GRM analysis uses *gross* income. A crucial assumption, therefore, is that expenses for comparable small residential properties are approximately equal.

Another key assumption of GRM analysis is that the subject property is either a rental property or *could be* a rental property; that is, it is similar to other properties that are rented. Appraisers thus can estimate gross rental rates from other similar properties in the market. They may make adjustments to account for differences between the comparable properties and the subject property. For example, if a comparable property's gross rent includes utilities, but the subject property's does not, the expected monthly utility bill would be subtracted from the comparable's rent to obtain an adjusted gross rent. After obtaining adjusted gross rents from several comparable properties, the appraiser can impute a reconciled indicated gross rent to the subject property.

Appraisers then obtain a gross rent multiplier from several comparable properties that have sold recently. The formula for a GRM is

$$GRM = \text{Sale price/Monthly gross rent}$$

No adjustments are made either to the sale price or to the monthly gross rent, since any adjustment would have to be made proportionately to both numerator and denominator in the equation. For example, a higher gross rent due to an extra bedroom also would result in a proportionately higher sale price. After obtaining GRMs for the comparables, appraisers derive a single, reconciled GRM and multiply it by the indicated rent for the subject property; thus, the estimated value of the property (V_o) would be

$$V_o = GRM \times \text{Indicated monthly rent}$$

Exhibit 13–14 shows the steps in GRM analysis, and Exhibit 13–15 shows an example of the use of GRM analysis in appraising a small rental house.

EXHIBIT 13-14

STEPS IN GROSS RENT MULTIPLIER ANALYSIS

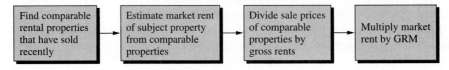

EXHIBIT 13-15

APPRAISAL BY GRM ANALYSIS

An appraiser is appraising a small rental house. Five comparable rentals are found that have the monthly rents and recent sales prices below.

Comparable No.	Price	Rent	GRM
1	$49,550	$450	110.11
2	44,820	415	108.00
3	42,500	380	111.84
4	42,950	385	111.56
5	44,000	400	110.00

The appraiser concludes from this analysis that the appropriate GRM should be 110.0. The appraiser also finds five rental properties quite similar to the subject property, which provide a good basis for estimating market rent. There are some differences between the comparable properties and the subject property. Currently, it is renting for $350 per month, but the appraiser believes this rental may not reflect the current market. The elements of comparison are identified and assigned the following value differences:

Item	Comparables 1	2	3	4	5	Subject
Rent	$405	$425	$440	$465	$470	?
Bathrooms	1	2 (−$20)	2 (−$20)	2 (−$20)	1	1
Garage size	Carport (+$10)	One-car	One-car	Two-car (−$15)	One-car	One-car
Basement	Unfinished	Unfinished	Unfinished	Finished (−$15)	Unfinished	Unfinished
Utilities payment	Tenant	Tenant	Tenant	Tenant	Owner (−$55)	Tenant
Adjusted rent	$415	$405	$420	$415	$415	

The appraiser concludes that the indicated market rent is $415.00 per month. This figure is then multiplied by the indicated gross rent multiplier of 110.0.

$$415.00 \times 110.0 = \$45,650, \text{ or } \underline{\underline{\$45,700}} \text{ in round numbers.}$$

The indicated house value from gross rent multiplier analysis is thus $45,700.

APPLICABILITY OF THE APPROACHES

The sales comparison approach is applicable to almost all one- to four-family residential properties and to many larger, income-producing properties. Whenever recent sales of similar properties can be found, appraisers can make reasonable adjustments to the sale prices to reflect the characteristics of the subject property. This approach has the additional advantage of being easily understood by buyers and sellers. They usually can follow the procedures and check the data to determine whether they agree with the appraiser's value estimate.

Multiple regression analysis is applicable to the direct value-estimation process for one- to four-family residences and for the estimation of rents and values of larger, income-producing properties. The principal limitation on use of multiple regression analysis is usually the availability of adequate data on similar properties.

The cost approach is applicable to most properties less than 15 years old, and is perhaps most appropriate for tract houses less than 15 years old. Such homes usually have a good record of costs, and depreciation is not so extensive that it cannot be measured. For structures older than 15 years, depreciation becomes large and increasingly difficult to estimate. The cost approach is less applicable for larger, more customized single-family homes and large income-producing properties. Both costs and depreciation are difficult to estimate and are less accurate.

The cost portion of the cost approach (in which reproduction cost is estimated) is also useful in analyzing the feasibility of proposed income-producing properties. If all other conditions are met, and the present value of the forecast cash flows is equal to or greater than the estimated cost, construction of the new property would be feasible.

Gross rent multiplier analysis is applicable to the appraisal of rental houses and small apartment houses having up to about 16 units. It requires recent sales of similar properties from which GRMs can be calculated. Appraisers can use the same comparables, or others that have not necessarily sold recently, as a basis for deriving market rent. They can use this approach only when there are several comparable properties that have similar rental and expense patterns in the market.

SUMMARY

Appraisal is the process of estimating the values of parcels of real estate. The process involves the systematic comparison of the sale prices of a subject property and several comparable properties. Professional appraisers use three general methods, or approaches: sales comparison, cost, and income capitalization (the topic of Chapter 14). Multiple regression analysis can be used directly as a variant of the sales comparison approach or as a component of one of the other approaches (such as estimating market rents to be capitalized in the income capitalization approach).

Appraising one- to four-family residential properties has been an important activity for many appraisers, and the most applicable method for these appraisals has been the traditional sales comparison approach. However, the appraisal of small residential properties is becoming increasingly computerized, and the traditional sales comparison approach is being replaced by multiple regression analysis. Nevertheless, the sales comparison approach will continue to be important in the appraisal of income-producing properties and some residential properties. The approach involves the analysis of the eight elements of comparison: conditions of sale, financing terms, market conditions, physical characteristics, location, legal characteristics, use, and nonrealty items. Appraisers adjust the sale price of each comparable property to reflect differences between it and the subject property for each element. They follow a sequence of adjustments calculated either as percentages or dollar amounts.

In the cost approach the appraiser subtracts the building's accrued depreciation from its current repro-duction cost. Three types of accrued depreciation may exist: physical deterioration, functional obsolescence, and external obsolescence. Reproduction cost of the building minus accrued depreciation equals the building's indicated value. The estimated site value is then added to obtain the indicated property value by the cost approach.

For the appraisal of one- to four-family rental residences and small apartment buildings, gross rent multiplier analysis is often appropriate. In this method an estimate of the gross income for the subject property is multiplied by a monthly gross rent multiplier, obtained by dividing recent sale prices of similar properties by their gross incomes.

KEY TERMS

Adjustments 376
Arm's-length bargaining 377
β coefficient 387
Constant 387
Dependent variable 385
Due-on-sale clause 377
F value 386
External obsolescence 390
Final adjusted sale price 376

Functional obsolescence 390
Gross rent multiplier 393
Independent variable 385
Indicated value 376
Market conditions 378
Market-adjusted normal
  sale price 378
Market value 375
Multiple regression analysis 384

Nonrealty items 381
Normal sale price 382
Physical deterioration 390
Property characteristics 377
R^2 statistic 386
Replacement cost 389
Reproduction cost 389
Standard error 386
Use 381

TEST YOURSELF

Answer the following multiple choice questions:

1. The final price for each comparable property reached after all adjustments have been made is termed the
   a. Final estimate of value.
   b. Final adjusted sale price.
   c. Market value.
   d. Indicated value.
   e. Replacement value.

2. The final price from each appraisal approach is termed the

   a. Final estimate of value.
   b. Final adjusted sale price.
   c. Market value.
   d. Indicated value.
   e. Replacement value.

3. The final price after reconciliation of the answers obtained from two or more approaches is termed the
   a. Final estimate of value.
   b. Final adjusted sale price.
   c. Market value.

d. Indicated value.

e. Replacement value.

4. A new house in good condition that has a poor floor plan would suffer from which type of accrued depreciation?

a. Short-lived curable physical deterioration.

b. Long-lived incurable physical deterioration.

c. Curable functional obsolescence.

d. Incurable functional obsolescence.

e. External obsolescence.

5. To reflect a change in market conditions between the date on which a comparable property sold and the date of appraisal of a subject property, which type of adjustment is made?

a. Conditions of sale.

b. Market conditions.

c. Location.

d. Financing terms.

e. Unit.

6. You have appraised a single-family residence using all three approaches to value. The indicated values are, respectively, sales comparison approach, $89,800; cost approach, $92,400; and gross rent multiplier analysis, $87,500. You decide the sales comparison approach is most reliable and should be weighted 50 percent. The cost approach is next in reliability, and it should be weighted 40 percent. GRM analysis should be weighted 10 percent. What is your final estimate of value (rounded to the nearest $100)?

a. $91,000.

b. $89,900.

c. $90,200.

d. $90,600.

e. $90,900.

7. In appraising a single-family home, you find a comparable property very similar to the subject property. One important difference, however, concerns the financing. The comparable property sold one month ago for $120,000 and was financed by the seller, who took back an 80 percent, 30-year mortgage at 9.5 percent interest. If current market financing terms are 80 percent,

30-year mortgages at 13 percent interest, by how much (and in which direction) should you adjust the sale price of the comparable property? The monthly payments on the market financing would be approximately $1,062, while the monthly payments on the financing provided by the seller are approximately $807 (Note: Assume the borrower's opportunity cost rate is 10%).

a. Add $6,000.

b. Subtract $6,000.

c. Subtract $12,000.

d. Add $12,000.

e. None of the above.

8. You find two properties that have sold twice within the last two years. Property A sold 22 months ago for $98,500; it sold last week for $108,000. Property B sold 20 months ago for $105,000; it sold two weeks ago for $113,500. What is the average monthly *compound* rate of change in sale prices?

a. .0081.

b. .0050.

c. .0041.

d. .0063.

e. .0391.

9. A comparable property sold 10 months ago for $100,000. This sale price is adjusted to a normal sale price of $98,500. Using the adjustment for market conditions calculated in Problem 8, what would be the market-adjusted normal sale price of the comparable property?

a. $104,100.

b. $95,462.

c. $95,900.

d. $102,539.

e. $98,480.

10. A comparable property sold six months ago for $150,000. The adjustments for the various elements of comparison have been calculated as follows:

> Location: −5 percent
> Market conditions: +8 percent
> Physical characteristics: +$12,500

Financing terms: −$2,600
Conditions of sale: -0-
Legal characteristics: -0-
Use: -0-
Nonrealty items: −$3,000

What is the comparable property's final adjusted sale price?
a. $160,732.
b. $164,400.
c. $169,600.
d. $162,500.
e. $163,232.

PROBLEM FOR THOUGHT AND SOLUTION

You have performed a multiple regression analysis in order to estimate the value of a single-family home. You have collected data on 43 properties for five independent variables and their prices. A summary of the regression output follows.

Dependent variable:	Price/$1,000
Constant:	9.16
R^2:	0.890
Standard error:	8.74

MULTIPLE REGRESSION OUTPUT SUMMARY

Variable Number	Variable Name	β Coefficient	Std. Error
X_1	Square feet livable area/100	0.664	0.16
X_2	Effective age (years)	−1.68	0.64
X_3	Quality of location (rank)	4.38	0.94
X_4	Quality of construction (rank)	3.68	1.62
X_5	Lot size (Square feet/100)	2.84	2.04

a. Which variable appears to have the least explanatory power? Why?
b. Explain the meaning of the constant, R^2, and standard error.
c. Calculate the estimated value of the property under appraisal. It contains 2000 square feet of livable area, has an effective age of 10 years, has a location ranking of 4, a quality-of-construction ranking of 3, and a lot size of 12,500 square feet.
d. What would be the 95 percent confidence interval?

INTERNET EXERCISE

Find out who hires appraisers, what types of career opportunities are available to appraisers, and capabilities and skills that appraisers should have. Also determine which universities have specialized graduate programs emphasizing appraisal. On the World Wide Web go to (http://www.appraisalinstitute.org). Select "Careers" to pursue the answers to these questions.

Also, from the Yellow Pages of your telephone book look under "Real Estate Appraisers" to find the name of two appraisers in your area who hold MAI or SRA designations. Then from the home page of the "Appraisal Institute" select "Find an Apraiser." Enter the information about each appraiser's name and address to obtain more information about the person's background and specialties.

ADDITIONAL READINGS

The following books are widely used general appraisal texts covering the sales comparison and cost approaches:

Appraisal Institute. *The Appraisal of Real Estate*, 11th ed. Chicago: American Institute of Real Estate Appraisers, 1996.

Lusht, Kenneth L. *Real Estate Valuation: Principles and Applications*. Burr Ridge, IL: Richard D. Irwin, 1997.

Smith, Halbert C., Linda Crawford Root, and Jerry D. Belloit. *Real Estate Appraisal*, 3rd ed. Scottsdale, AZ: Gorsuch Scarisbrick, 1995.

The following journal is devoted to real estate appraisal. Each issue contains 10 to 15 articles on a variety of current topics in the appraisal profession:

The Appraisal Journal (quarterly), Appraisal Institute, 875 North Michigan Avenue, Chicago, IL 60611.

The following special issue of the *Journal of Real Estate Research* is devoted to articles reporting on research in real estate appraisal:

Grissom, Terry V., and Halbert C. Smith, ed. *Journal of Real Estate Research* 5, no. 1 (Spring 1991).

The following article discusses the application of linear regression analysis to economic variables in the sales comparison and income capitalization approaches:

Kincheloe, Stephen C. "Linear Regression Analysis of Economic Variables in the Sales Comparison and Income Approaches." *The Appraisal Journal* LXI, no. 4 (October 1993), pp. 576–85.

APPRAISAL CASE PROBLEM

Single-Family Residential Appraisal

This case problem contains the heart of a narrative single-family residential appraisal. Most of the analysis has been completed for all three major approaches with each significant adjustment justified from market data. Students should complete the final step(s) to each approach and then reconcile the indicated values into a final estimate of value.

THE SUBJECT PROPERTY

The property to be appraised is a small, single-family house in Gainesville, Florida. The property rights involved are those of a fee simple absolute estate. The structure is approximately 23 years old and is of concrete-block construction. Quality of construction and current condition are average. The house contains 974 square feet of finished area, including a living room, dining area, kitchen, three bedrooms, and one bathroom. There is also a 45-square-foot entry porch, a 31-square-foot patio, and a 71-square-foot outside utility room.

The house has central heating and a gas water heater, but no air-conditioning. Utility services are average and adequate. There are no apparent major structural defects.

The site measures 76 feet by 107 feet and covers 8,132 square feet. The surrounding neighborhood comprises similar single-family properties, most of which appear average in appeal and marketability.

"Highest and best use of the site as though vacant" would be a new single-family house. It would contain approximately 1,100 square feet, with the additional area used for a half bath and slightly larger rooms. It would also have air-conditioning, and all physical deterioration would be eliminated.

"Highest and best use of the property as improved" is continued single-family residential occupancy. Neither the zoning nor the type of structure would accommodate any other kind of occupancy. The structure appears to have approximately 30 years of economic life remaining. The date of value is August 15, 1996.

SALES COMPARISON APPROACH

The sales comparison approach involves three similar homes located within four blocks of the subject property (see Exhibits CP–1 through CP–4). The three comparables were similar to the subject property with respect to construction quality, age, condition, and the number of bedrooms and bathrooms. Market-derived adjustments for the differences in gross living area and for air-conditioning were made. The appraiser used paired sales analysis to determine the sizes of the adjustments.

Comparable property No. 1 is three blocks south of the subject property in Highland Court Manor. It sold in May 1996 for $38,000. It is a concrete block home with approximately 962 square feet of floor space and no central air-conditioning.

Comparable property No. 2 is four blocks east of the subject property and has no central air-conditioning. It has approximately 1,078 square feet and sold for $39,900 in January 1996.

Comparable property No. 3 is a concrete block home with central air-conditioning four blocks south of the subject property in Highland Court Manor. It sold for $41,000 in July 1996 and has approximately 1,052 square feet.

MARKET ANALYSIS FOR ADJUSTMENTS

Comparables No. 2 and 3 are very similar homes. They have no significant differences except for central air-conditioning and gross living area. The appraiser adjusted comparable No. 3 plus $400 for its smaller size and minus $1,600 for its central air-conditioning. The adjusted value of comparable No. 3 is $39,800, or only $100 less than the actual sale price of comparable No. 2. This insignificant difference indicates no adjustment for market conditions is required.

Comparables No. 1 and 2 are very similar homes. There are no significant differences except for gross living area; comparable No. 2 has 116 square feet more. Comparable No. 2 sold for $1,900 more than comparable No. 1:

EXHIBIT CP-1

SALES COMPARISON APPROACH ADJUSTMENT GRID

Property	Address
Comparable sale No. 1	2602 N.E. 11 Street
	Gainesville, FL 32601
Comparable sale No. 2	2924 N.E. 15 Street
	Gainesville, FL 32601
Comparable sale No. 3	2322 N.E. 11 Street
	Gainesville, FL 32601
Subject property	3024 N.E. 10 Street
	Gainesville, FL 32601

	Comparable Sale No. 1	Comparable Sale No. 2	Comparable Sale No. 3	Subject Property
Price	$38,000	$39,900	$41,000	?
Financing	Market	Market	Market	N/A
Conditions of sale	Normal	Normal	Normal	No sale
Normal sale price	$38,000	$39,900	$41,000	_____
Market conditions*	Equal	Equal	Equal	Today
Market-adjusted normal sale price	$38,000	$39,900	$41,000	_____
Physical:				
Bedroom/bath	_____	_____	_____	3/1
Landscaping	_____	_____	_____	Average
Living area†	_____	−$1,644	−$1,248	974 sq. ft.
Air-conditioning‡	_____	_____	−$1,600	None
Carport	_____	_____	_____	Carport
Maintenance	_____	_____	_____	Average
Final adjusted sale price	_____	_____	_____	?

Range of value = _____

    × (mean) = _____

* See market conditions adjustment (Exhibit CP–2).

† See gross living area adjustment (Exhibit CP–3).

‡ See air-conditioning adjustment (Exhbit CP–4).

Comparable No. 2	$39,900.00	1,078 sq. ft.
Comparable No. 1	− 38,000.00	− 962 sq. ft.
	$ 1,900.00	116 sq. ft.

$$\frac{\$1,900.00}{116 \text{ sq. ft.}} = \frac{\$16.37 \text{ per square foot}}{\text{or } \$16.00/\text{sq. ft. rounded off.}}$$

Comparables No. 1 and 3 are very similar homes. There are no significant differences except for gross living area and air-conditioning. The appraiser adjusted the difference in gross living area at $16 per square foot, after which the adjusted sale price of comparable No. 3 was $39,600.

EXHIBIT CP-2

MARKET CONDITIONS ADJUSTMENT

Property	Address
Comparable sale No. 2	2924 N.E. 15 Street Gainesville, FL 32601
Comparable sale No. 3	2322 N.E. 11 Street Gainesville, FL 32601

	Comparable Sale No. 2	Comparable Sale No. 3
Price	$39,900	$41,000
Living area		+ 400*
Central A/C		− 1,600†
Adjusted sale price	$39,900	$39,800

*1,078 sq. ft. (Comp. No. 2) − 1,052 sq. ft. (Comp. No. 3) = 26 sq. ft., 26 sq. ft. × 16.00 = $400.00 rounded.

†See air-conditioning adjustment.

EXHIBIT CP-3

GROSS LIVING AREA ADJUSTMENT

Property	Address
Comparable sale No. 1	2602 N.E. 11 Street Gainesville, FL 32601
Comparable sale No. 2	2924 N.E. 15 Street Gainesville, FL 32601

	Comparable Sale No. 1	Comparable Sale No. 2
Price	$38,000	$39,900
Living area	962 sq. ft.	1,078 sq. ft.

To be completed by students:

Calculate the final adjusted sale price for each comparable property and reconcile these prices into an indicated value for the sales comparison approach. In the reconciliation process, assume that all three comparables are considered equally valid and therefore that equal weights should be assigned to them. Round the indicated value to the nearest $100.

EXHIBIT CP-4

AIR-CONDITIONING ADJUSTMENT

Property	Address
Comparable sale No. 1	2602 N.E. 11 Street Gainesville, FL 32601
Comparable sale No. 3	2322 N.E. 11 Street Gainesville, FL 32601

	Comparable Sale No. 1	Comparable Sale No. 3
Price	$38,000	$41,000
Living area		− 1,400
GLA-adjusted price	$38,000	$39,600
Comparable No. 3	$39,600.00	
Comparable No. 1	− 38,000.00	
Price paid for A/C	$1,600.00*	

*This implies the market values air-conditioning at approximately $1,600.00.

GROSS RENT MULTIPLIER ANALYSIS

Although the property is not rented today, it is highly possible the property will be rented in the future. Therefore, the appraiser derives a gross rent multiplier and market rent for the subject property. He found the market rent of the subject property by comparing three rented homes located within 12 blocks of the subject property. He made adjustments for differences in gross living area, air-conditioning, and carports. Then he multiplied the estimated market rate by the appropriate gross rent multiplier to get the estimated value of the subject property (see Exhibits CP–5 and CP–6).

Comparable rental No. 1 is six blocks east of the subject property in Carol Estates and has monthly rent of $325. The structure has 973 square feet and includes three bedrooms and one bath, central air-conditioning, and a carport. The home is of concrete block construction.

Comparable rental No. 2 is 12 blocks south, in Carol Estates, and rents for $325. The three-bedroom, one-bath home has 1,236 square feet of living area but has neither central air-conditioning nor a carport.

Comparable rental No. 3 is four blocks east of the subject property in Highland Court Manor; it rents for $325. No. 3 has 1,052 square feet of living area, central air-conditioning, and a carport.

The three properties in this analysis are all within four blocks of the subject property. All three are of concrete block construction and contain three bedrooms and one bathroom. Two properties have a one-car carport, while comparable No. 2 has none.

EXHIBIT CP-5

DERIVATION OF GROSS RENT MULTIPLIER

Property	Address
Sale and rental No. 1	2602 N.E. 11 Street Gainesville, FL 32601
Sale and rental No. 2	2924 N.E. 15 Street Gainesville, FL 32601
Sale and rental No. 3	2322 N.E. 11 Street Gainesville, FL 32601

	Sale/Rental No. 1	Sale/Rental No. 2	Sale/Rental No. 3
Sale price	$38,000	$39,900	$41,000
Monthly rent	310	325	325
GRM*	?	?	?

All properties appear to be equally comparable.

*GRM = Sale Price/Monthly Rent.

EXHIBIT CP-6

INDICATED MONTHLY MARKET RENT

Property	Address
Comparable rental No. 1	1619 N.E. 31 Avenue Gainesville, FL
Comparable rental No. 2	1441 N.E. 18 Avenue Gainesville, FL
Comparable rental No. 3	2322 N.E. 11 Street Gainesville, FL
Subject property	3024 N.E. 10 Street Gainesville, FL

	Comparable Rental No. 1	Comparable Rental No. 2	Comparable Rental No. 3	Subject Property
Monthly rent	$325	$325	$325	?
Market condition	9/90	9/90	9/90	
Physical:				
Bedroom/bath	_____	_____	_____	3/1
Landscaping	_____	_____	_____	Average
Living area	_____	−$34	−$10	974 sq. ft.
Air-conditioning	−$13	_____	−$13	None
Carport	_____	+$10	_____	Carport
Maintenance	_____	_____	_____	Average
Adjusted monthly market rent	?	?	?	?

All three rental comparables are small concrete-block homes located within 12 blocks of the subject property. All three have three bedrooms and one bathroom and are equally weighted.

Adjustments were made as follows:

1. The appraiser based adjustments for central air-conditioning on the $1,600 value determined by paired sales analysis in Exhibit CP–4. He divided $1,600 by the gross rent multiplier to determine the adjustment ($1,600/124 = $13.00).
2. The appraiser made adjustments for size by multiplying the differences in square feet between Comparables 2 and 3 and Comparable 1 by the $16 cost per square foot, and then dividing this amount by the gross rent multiplier.

Comparable No. 2

$$(1{,}236 \text{ sq. ft.} - 974 \text{ sq. ft.}) \times 16.00/124 = \$33.81, \text{ or } \$34$$

Comparable No. 3

$$(1{,}052 \text{ sq. ft.} - 974 \text{ sq. ft.}) \times 16.00/124 = \$10.06, \text{ or } \$10$$

To be completed by students:

Determine the appropriate market rental and GRM for the subject property and calculate the indicated value for the subject property. Round this number to the nearest $100.

COST APPROACH

Using the cost approach, the appraiser can derive the market value of a subject property by estimating the reproduction cost of a building, subtracting accrued depreciation (including physical deterioration, functional obsolescence, and external obsolescence), and adding the market value of the site.

REPRODUCTION COST

The appraiser used Marshall & Swift's *Residential Cost Handbook* and its accompanying procedures to obtain the reproduction costs of the subject property—what it would cost if it were built today. He used rates for a one-story concrete-block house of average construction quality.

Category	Area	Cost/Sq. Ft.	Cost
Living area	974 sq. ft.	$35.00	$34,090
Open porch	45 sq. ft.	8.00	360
Patio/walks	31 sq. ft.	6.45	200

Utility room	71 sq. ft.	$16.00	1,136
Carport	205 sq. ft.	$8.00	1,640
Site improvements			
Driveway			500
Total estimated reproduction cost			$37,926

SOURCE: *Residential Cost Handbook* (Los Angeles: Marshall and Swift Company, 1996).

ACCRUED DEPRECIATION

The appraiser estimated the amounts of various elements of accrued depreciation by the observed-condition-breakdown method. He observed each item and estimated the extent to which the item suffered from deterioration or obsolescence. Then he multiplied the appropriate ratios by the replacement costs of the items.

The subject property has no central air-conditioning system. This is a feature that today's market for homes demands in the subject neighborhood. The rent loss due to lack of central air-conditioning is $13; the appraiser multiplies this by the gross rent multiplier of 124 to obtain the incurable functional obsolescence of $1,600.00 ($13 × 124).

External obsolescence stems from forces outside the property that have a negative effect on the property value. As a result of these forces, the property structure is worth less than it would be at a different location. The appraiser believes no external obsolescence exists for the subject property.

SITE VALUATION

Comparable site No. 1 in Highland Estates (Lot 15) is one block west of the subject property in northeast Gainesville. The site sold for $8,500 in March 1996. The topography is level, and the lot size is 143.30 by 76.90 feet. The utilities (electric, sewer, and water) are provided.

Comparable site No. 2 in Palmetto Woods No. 3 (Lot 16) is two miles west of the subject property in northwest Gainesville. It sold for $10,800 in July 1996. The site is level, and the lot size is 86.00 by 100.14 feet. Electric, sewer, and water are all provided.

Comparable site No. 3 in Palmetto Woods No. 3 (Lot 6) is also two miles west of the subject property. It sold for $11,000 in June 1996, and the lot measures 80.00 by 118.56 feet. The site is level; electric, sewer, and water are provided.

The adjustments, summarized in Exhibit CP–8, were as follows.

MARKET CONDITIONS ADJUSTMENT

The appraiser made no adjustment for market conditions. Exhibit CP–2 contains the justification for this.

LOCATIONAL ADJUSTMENTS

Comparable sites No. 2 and 3 are in the Palmetto Woods subdivision. The average value of the homes in the subject neighborhood is $40,000, whereas the average value in

E X H I B I T   C P - 7

A C C R U E D   D E P R E C I A T I O N

Physical Deterioration

						Totals
Curable short-lived						
General cleanup		$100				
Replace broken window		20				
Total						
Incurable short-lived						$120

Item	Cost	Life	Age	SFF at 10%	Accrued Depreciation	
Hot water heater	$ 150	15	7	.031474	$ 33.05	
Roofing	1,560	15	7	.031474	343.70	
Floor covering	1,440	15	7	.031474	317.26	
Electrical fixtures	300	20	7	.017460	36.67	
Plumbing fixtures	1,165	30	7	.006079	49.57	
Appliances	600	15	7	.031474	132.19	
Gas furnace	820	20	7	.017460	100.22	
Total	$6,035				$1,012.66 or	$1,013

Incurable long-lived		
Total reproduction cost	$37,926	
Curable deterioration	−120	
Total cost new of incurable short-lived items	−6,035	
Cost to be depreciated	$31,771	

$$\frac{\text{Effective age}}{\text{Economic life}} = \frac{7}{50} = .14$$

Total = .14 × $31,771		4,448
Total physical deterioration		$5,581

Functional Obsolescence

Curable: None		
Total	$ -0-	
Incurable	$1,600	
Total	$1,600	
Total functional obsolescence		$1,600

External Obsolescence

Total external obsolescence	-0-
Total accrued depreciation	$7,181

EXHIBIT CP-8

SITE SALES ADJUSTMENTS

	Comparable Site No. 1	Comparable Site No. 2	Comparable Site No. 3	Subject Property
Price	$8,500	$10,800	$11,000	?
Market conditions	3/96	7/96	6/96	
Location	_____	−$2,700	−$2,700	
Size/shape	_____	_____	_____	
Topography	_____	_____	_____	
Utilities	_____	_____	_____	
Final adjusted sale price	$8,500	$8,100	$8,300	

Palmetto Woods is $53,000. Because homes in Palmetto Woods average 33 percent (or $13,000) more than those in the subject neighborhood, the appraiser made a 25 percent downward adjustment.

$$\$53,000 - 40,000/\$53,000 = .25$$

(Note that an upward adjustment of $13,000 from $40,000 would be 33 percent.)

The above three sales range from $8,100 to $8,500. Comparable site No. 1 was located only one block west of the subject property. The appraiser gave comparable site No. 1 the most weight because of its similar location. Comparable sites Nos. 2 and 3 supported the indication of comparable site No. 1.

Comparable site No. 1	70 percent × 8,500 =	$5,950
Comparable site No. 2	15 percent × 8,100 =	$1,215
Comparable site No. 3	15 percent × 8,300 =	$1,245
Indicated site value		$8,410, or $8,400

To be completed by students:

Summarize the results of the cost approach analysis and determine an indicated value for this approach.

RECONCILIATION OF THE VALUE INDICATIONS TO A FINAL VALUE ESTIMATE

To be completed by students:

Reconcile the three indicated values into a final estimate of value. Develop a rationale for the weight to be assigned to each indicated value and multiply that weight by the indicated value. Finally, sum the weighted values to obtain a final estimate of value. Round this number to the nearest $100.

	Weight	Indicated Value	Weighted Value
Sales comparison approach	___ percent	_____	_____
GRM analysis	___ percent	_____	_____
Cost approach	___ percent	_____	_____
Final estimate of value	100%		_____

14

C H A P T E R

VALUATION BY INCOME CAPITALIZATION

INCOME CAPITALIZATION RELATED TO THE DCF MODEL

FUNDAMENTAL EQUATION

INCOME
Reserve for Replacements and Other
Nonrecurring Expenses

CAPITALIZATION RATES
Overall Capitalization Rate
Several Methods, But Only One R_o

DISCOUNT RATES

SEPARATE BUILDING AND LAND VALUATION
Estimating g for Buildings
Estimating a Building's Depreciation Rate
Estimating g for Sites
Allocating NOI between Building and Site

OTHER APPROACHES
Gross Income Multiplier
Cost Approach

RECONCILIATION

THE APPRAISAL PROFESSION

REGULATION OF THE APPRAISAL PROFESSION

PROFESSIONAL ORGANIZATIONS AND DESIGNATIONS

APPRAISAL AS A CAREER

SUMMARY

KEY TERMS

TEST YOURSELF

PROBLEMS FOR THOUGHT AND SOLUTION

CASE PROBLEMS

ADDITIONAL READINGS

After reading this chapter, students will be able to:

1. Estimate NOI in a reconstructed operating statement, given income and expense data for a property.

2. Identify the two main components of capitalization rates.

3. Calculate overall capitalization rates by market extraction, simple mortgage-equity analysis, and CAPM analysis, given appropriate data.

4. Calculate the effective net growth rate for a depreciating building, given appropriate data.

5. Estimate a property's market value by direct capitalization, using an overall rate.

INCOME CAPITALIZATION RELATED TO THE DCF MODEL

The valuation (or appraisal) of real estate is often a key step in making decisions about whether to buy, sell, lend, borrow, or renovate properties. As explained in Chapter 2, the value of any property depends on the benefits it can provide to an owner. In the case of income-producing real estate, the benefits are incomes that are expected over the future life of the property. The income and expenses for each future year may be forecast, and the net incomes or cash flows can then be discounted to obtain an estimate of the property's value. Recall that the discounted cash flow model explains the decision-making process of investors in income-producing real estate.

Appraisers sometimes use the discounted cash flow model when valuing income-producing properties. However, appraisers often find other methods that rely on recent transactions to be more useful for valuation purposes. Direct capitalization (discussed later in this chapter) and the sales comparison approach (discussed in Chapter 13), for example, rely on the decisions of investors who have recently purchased similar properties. If appraisers know the prices paid for similar properties and the annual net incomes they are expected to produce, they can calculate a **capitalization rate** and divide it into the forecast net income of the subject property.

For example, an appraiser finds five recent sales of comparable properties. For each property she divides the annual net income by the sale price and finds that the average of the capitalization rates is 10 percent. She then estimates the net operating income (NOI) of the subject property to be $100,000. Dividing the $100,000 by 10 percent produces a value estimate of the subject property of $1 million ($100,000/0.10 = $1,000,000). The appraiser did not have to estimate the future cash flows because the investors who purchased the comparable properties had *already done so.* The value estimate produced by this short-cut method, which relies on prices paid by similar investors for similar properties, is often *more* reliable for the purpose of estimating a property's market value because there are fewer forecasts and judgments to be made. In effect, the appraiser relies on decisions already made in the market to help "read" the market.

FUNDAMENTAL EQUATION

The example above illustrates the use of the income capitalization equation presented in Chapter 3:

$$V = I/R \qquad (14\text{--}1)$$

for which

$$V = \text{value}$$
$$I = \text{income}$$
$$R = \text{capitalization rate}$$

As with any equation having three variables, if any two are known, the third can be calculated. Thus, after rearrangement, appraisers can use the formula to estimate R if V and I are known:

$$R = I/V \qquad (14\text{--}2)$$

and they can use it to estimate I if R and V are known:

$$I = R \times V \qquad (14\text{--}3)$$

A capitalization rate is a percentage ratio of annual income to the value or sale price of a property. Recall that R is equal to investors' required before-tax yield (y) minus the expected growth rate (g) of income and value. Although there are several ways of estimating capitalization rates and various methods of applying them to a property's income, the basic concept of a capitalization rate remains the same: the ratio of one year's income to the price or value of a property. This chapter presents the basic methods of capitalization rate estimation and application, which are adequate for the appraisal of almost all types of income-producing properties. The numerator and denominator of the basic formula are discussed next.

INCOME

In appraisals, the income that appraisers capitalize is a specific type: **net operating income**. Recall from Chapter 3 that NOI is calculated by deducting all expenses and allowances from the property's effective gross income. NOI excludes financing expenses, personal expenses, and other nonproperty expenses. In other words, it focuses on the income produced by the property before debt service and income taxes are paid. These expenses are personal and unique to each owner and not related to the property's income-

---

EXHIBIT 14-1

SUBURBAN OFFICE BUILDING RECONSTRUCTED OPERATING STATEMENT

Potential gross income			$180,000
Vacancy and collection losses			18,000
Effective gross income			$162,000
Less: Operating expenses			
Fixed			
Real estate taxes	$15,900		
Insurance	12,000	$27,900	
Variable			
Utilities	$13,900		
Garbage collection	1,000		
Supplies	4,000		
Repairs	6,000		
Maintenance	12,000		
Management	8,100	45,000	
Reserve for replacements and			
other nonrecurring expenses		2,500	
Total expenses			$ 75,400
Net operating income			$ 86,600

---

producing ability. In estimating expected NOI, appraisers rely on (1) the experience of similar properties in the market and (2) the historic experience of the subject property, if it is an existing property. The owners may not rent the subject property at the going market rate, and its expenses may differ from market averages.

Thus, appraisers must evaluate all income and expense items in terms of other similar properties in the same market. They place these items of income and expense in a reconstructed operating statement as shown in Exhibit 14–1. This format includes some types of income and expenses but excludes others that usually are included in accounting statements or reported for income tax purposes. Furthermore, appraisers forecast income and expenses for the current year, rather than using estimates for a previous or future year. Information for the comparable properties also must be reformulated to be consistent with the reconstructed operating statement of the subject property.

RESERVE FOR REPLACEMENTS AND OTHER NONRECURRING EXPENSES

Appraisers usually include another type of expense (an allowance) in a reconstructed operating statement. This allowance is known as a **reserve for replacements and other nonrecurring expenses**, and it is estimated by annualizing all the costs of periodically replacing the parts of a building that wear out faster than the building itself and other nonrecurring expenses such as leasing commissions, tenant improvements, and retenanting expenses. Examples of building components that wear out faster than the building itself are items such as the roof, electrical system, wall coverings, floor coverings, plumbing system, kitchen equipment, heating and air conditioning systems, and painting or other interior and exterior decoration. Thus, with a reserve for replacements and other non-recurring expenses of $2,500, included in the reconstructed operating statement in Exhibit 14–1, the NOI would be $86,600.

The reserve for replacements and other nonrecurring expenses is calculated by multiplying the cost of each item to be replaced or nonrecurring expense by a sinking fund factor at the appropriate discount rate for the expected life of the item. For example, if the cost of replacing a roof is expected to be $3,000, its expected life is 15 years, and the discount rate (y) is 11.0 percent, the annual amount would be $3,000 \times 0.029065 =$ $87.20.[1] In other words, if an owner each year put $87.20 into an account or an investment yielding 11.0 percent, she would have $3,000 at the end of 15 years. Or, if the owner of a large office building expects a major tenant to leave after five years and the re-leasing of the space will require $50,000 to raise the ceilings, increase electrical capacity, and otherwise make the space ready for a new tenant, with an 11 percent discount rate, $8,029 would have to be set aside each year to accumulate the $50,000 over five years.[2]

The curious reader may be wondering why a reserve for replacements and other nonrecurring expenses is used in a reconstructed operating statement for appraisal purposes but not for investment decision-making or investment analysis purposes. The answer is that it reflects the difference between using discounted cash flow (DCF) analysis for investment decision making and analysis and using direct capitalization for valuation. In direct capitalization only one year's NOI is capitalized into value; thus, the first year NOI must be adjusted to reflect the present value of future nonrecurring expenses. In DCF analysis the expenditure for each replacement or nonrecurring expense is included in the DCF statement in the year that it is expected, and each year's cash flow is then discounted to a present value. For example, in a DCF analysis the expected $3,000 cost of replacing the roof at the end of 15 years would be included as a deduction from income in year 15, or the proportionate value loss could be treated as a reduction in the projected sale price if the expected holding period is shorter than 15 years. The present values are then summed to obtain the value of the property.

CAPITALIZATION RATES

The denominator (R) of the basic formula $V = I/R$ is the general symbol for a capitalization rate. However, whenever a specific property, or a component of or interest in the property, is being appraised, the symbol is modified to reflect the property, component, or interest. For example, an entire property (the fee simple interest)[3] may be the subject of an appraisal, or only the site, the building, or some other legal or financial interest. Therefore, the income to that particular component or interest must be estimated, and the

---

[1]The calculator keystrokes are N = 15, I = 11%, PV = 0, PMT = ?, FV = 3,000.
[2]The calculator keystrokes are N = 5, I = 11%, PV = 0, PMT = ?, FV = 50,000.
[3]Legal estates are discussed in Chapter 20.

E X H I B I T   1 4 - 2

CAPITALIZATION RATES

Symbol	Type of Capitalization Rate	Income to Which Applied
R	General Symbol	Income
R_o	Overall capitalization rate	NOI (entire property)
R_B	Building capitalization rate	Building income (I_B)
R_L	Land capitalization rate	Land income (I_L)
R_e	Equity capitalization rate (also equity dividend rate)	Equity income (before tax cash flow—BTCF)
R_m	Mortgage capitalization rate (also mortgage constant)	Debt income (annual debt service—ADS)
R_{LF}	Leased fee capitalization rate	Leased fee income (I_{LF})
R_{LH}	Leasehold capitalization rate	Leasehold income (I_{LH})

appropriate capitalization rate must be used. These rates and their symbols are listed in Exhibit 14–2. In all cases, appraisers divide the capitalization rate into the income from the property or component to obtain value.

OVERALL CAPITALIZATION RATE

General formula. Recall from Chapter 3 that a capitalization rate (R) is comprised of a discount rate and a growth rate: $R = y - g$. For the fee simple (complete) interest in a specific property, the R becomes R_o, (**overall capitalization rate**), and the formula would therefore be

$$R_o = y_o - g \tag{14–4}$$

where

R_o = Overall capitalization rate

y_o = Discount rate, or yield for the overall property

g = Forecast compound annual growth rate of the NOI and property value for the remaining economic life or holding period

Although g is termed a "growth" rate, it could be negative as well as positive. That is, a property's NOI and property value could decline as well as increase. If the property's expected growth rate is negative, the sign in the formula changes from minus to plus. Thus, the formula for negative growth becomes

$$R_o = y_o - (-g) \tag{14–5}$$
$$R_o = y_o + g \tag{14–6}$$

Therefore, in cases in which *appreciation* is expected in a property's NOI and market value, the sign in the formula is negative ($-$); in cases in which **depreciation** is expected in a property's NOI and market value, the sign in the formula is positive ($+$). A negative

REAL ESTATE FOCUS 14-1

Capitalization Rates: How Stable Are They?

Analysts typically believe that real estate capitalization rates are relatively stable over time. After all, if incomes to properties rise or fall, prices should tend to increase or decrease proportionately, leaving the capitalization rate unchanged. Nevertheless, as can be seen in the graph below, the median capitalization rate declined during the 1980s from about 10.5 percent to about 7.5 percent, then rose during the early 1990s to about 9.5 percent in 1993–94, and then fell to about 9.2 percent in 1995–97.

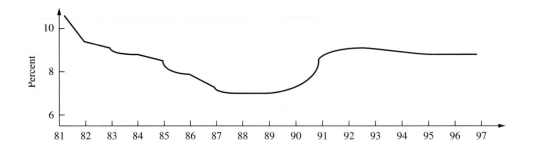

Richard B. Gold contends in an article entitled "The Nine Percent Solution" that there are two components to the cap rate: a core rate with an equilibrium level of 9.0 percent and a transitory rate that varies over the course of the real estate cycle.* The tendency, however, is for cap rates to return to their core level equilibrium during "normal" market periods. Consider these questions regarding the stability of capitalization rates:

1. Describe the general nature of the real estate cycle from the early 1980s to the mid-1990s. What would cause the transitory portion of the cap rate to rise and fall over the real estate cycle, as Gold contends?

2. When capitalization rates fall and property incomes remain unchanged, what would this trend indicate about the *prices* investors paid? What does it say about the yields investors are demanding?

3. When capitalization rates fall and prices decline (as they did in the late 1980s), what does this trend say about the *incomes* to real estate?

———

*Richard B. Gold, "The Nine Percent Solution," *Real Estate Issues* 21, no. 2 (August 1996), pp. 23–26.

SOURCE of capitalization rate data: Real Estate Research Corporation, *Quarterly Real Estate Investment Summary* 25, no. 3 (1996).

---

sign produces a lower R_o and higher value, reflecting the expected appreciation, while a positive sign produces a higher R_o and lower value, reflecting the expected depreciation.

The overall capitalization rate R_o is perhaps the most widely used and useful type of all capitalization rates. It is simply the percentage ratio of the NOI produced by properties to their selling prices.

Example. The appraiser obtains a discount rate (y_o) of 11.0 percent for the Suburban Office Building. He expects the property's NOI and market value to grow by 2.5 percent per year over the 10-year holding period:

EXHIBIT 14-3

DIRECT MARKET EXTRACTION OF R_o

Office Building	Forecast NOI	Price	R_o (NOI/price)
A	$40,000	$512,800	0.078
B	57,000	647,700	0.088
C	50,000	588,200	0.085
D	36,000	395,600	0.091
E	45,000	562,500	0.080

$\bar{x}$ (mean) = 0.0844

$$R_o = .11 - 0.025$$
$$= 0.085$$

The value of the Suburban Office Building, using this R_o, would be

$$V_o = NOI/R_o \qquad (14\text{--}7)$$
$$= \$86,600/0.085$$
$$= \$1,018,824, \text{ say } \$1,018,800$$

Direct market extraction. As shown in Exhibit 14–3, the most straightforward method for estimating an R_o is by *direct market extraction*. In evaluating the Suburban Office Building, the appraiser found five comparable properties that sold recently and calculated their R_os.

The average (mean) of the five R_os is 0.0844. Thus, the appropriate indicated R_o appears to be about 8.4 percent (0.084). Dividing this rate into the property's NOI produces the following indication of market value:

$$V_o = NOI/R_o$$
$$= \$86,600/0.085$$
$$= \$1,030,952, \text{ say } \$1,031,000$$

The reciprocal of R_o is 1/0.085, or 11.76. Thus, another way of looking at the relationship between income and value is to say that office buildings similar to the subject property sell for about 11.76 times their forecast first-year NOIs. The process of directly dividing NOI by an R_o is called **direct capitalization.**

Simple mortgage equity analysis. Overall rates (R_os) are the most important and widely used capitalization rates. When adequate, reliable market data are available, appraisers prefer to estimate overall rates directly from recent transactions of similar income properties. Often, however, estimates of NOI for the comparable properties may not be reliable, and the sale prices may reflect special considerations such as favorable financing or unusual income tax advantages. Thus, appraisers often must rely on other methods for estimating R_os. Perhaps the most useful such method derives from **mortgage equity analysis.**

Mortgage equity analysis recognizes that R_os include rates of return and capital recovery rates for both the equity portion and the debt (mortgage) portion of an investment. As in the separate valuations of land and buildings, the asset is divided into two parts: its debt and equity components. Appraisers weight the capitalization rates for the two parts by the proportion of each part of the total. They then add the two weighted rates to obtain the R_o. Thus, if they can obtain market terms for mortgage financing (from which they can derive an R_m) and equity dividend rates (R_e), they can calculate an R_o as the weighted average of R_m and R_e:

$$R_o = mR_m + (1 - m) R_e \qquad (14\text{--}8)$$

where

R_o = overall capitalization rate
m = **loan-to-value** (or mortgage) **ratio**
R_m = mortgage capitalization rate (mortgage constant)
$(1 - m)$ = equity-to-value ratio
R_e = equity capitalization rate (equity dividend rate)

Equity dividend rates (R_e) are obtained by dividing before-tax cash flow (BTCF) by the value (or amount) of the equity (V_e):

$$R_e = \text{BTCF}/V_e \qquad (14\text{--}9)$$

where

BTCF = before-tax cash flow (NOI − ADS)
V_e = value of the equity (sale price − mortgage balance)

Example. An investor could obtain mortgage financing at 75 percent of value for the Suburban Office Building carrying a 9.5 percent interest rate (y_m) for 25 years, with monthly payments. The R_m (or annual mortgage constant) for this loan is 0.104844 (0.008737, which is the monthly mortgage constant, × 12). Equity dividend rates for three similar properties that sold recently are shown in Exhibit 14–4.

Thus, an R_e of 0.0426 is chosen, and R_o is calculated as follows:

$$R_o = 0.75 (0.104844) + 0.25 (0.0426)$$
$$= 0.078633 + 0.010650$$
$$= 0.089283$$

The overall capitalization rate of 0.089283 is a weighted average of the annual cost of debt and the annual cost of equity, as measured by equity yields on similar properties.

The value of the property using this R_o would be

$$V_o = \text{NOI}/R_o$$
$$= \$86,600/0.089283$$
$$= \$969,949, \text{ say } \$969,900$$

EXHIBIT 14-4

EQUITY DIVIDEND RATES

	Comparable		
	A	B	C
BTCF	$ 9,500	$ 7,800	$ 8,250
V_e	225,118	190,244	185,393
R_e (BTCF/V_e)	0.0422	0.0410	0.0445
	$\bar{x}$ (mean) = 0.04257		

Single-factor asset pricing model. With the flowering of real estate investment trusts and their listing on the large securities exchanges, it is now possible to estimate a discount rate for real estate from the securities market. A growth rate then must be added to the discount rate to obtain an overall capitalization rate.

As discussed in Chapter 7, in a single-factor asset pricing model, the cost of equity capital is the sum of a risk-free return plus a premium for the risk associated with investment in the equity. It is represented by the following equation:

$$y = R_f + B(\text{MRP}) \tag{14-10}$$

where

$$y = \text{opportunity cost of capital}$$
$$R_f = \text{risk-free rate of return}$$
$$B = \text{beta of the subject property}$$
$$\text{MRP} = \text{market risk premium}$$

The risk-free rate of return is usually measured by the return on U.S. Treasury bonds that have a similar maturity to that of a typical investment in real estate, typically assumed to be about 10 years. Recall that betas measure the covariance between the returns on the asset being valued and the returns on the stock market index that is being used as a proxy for systematic risk. Betas are determined statistically by regressing the historical returns of the asset being valued on the historical returns of the stock market index. Because return data for privately held, infrequently traded properties are not available, betas are often obtained for publicly traded real estate investment trusts (REITs) and used as a proxy for the beta of the asset being valued. The market risk premium can be measured as the return on the Standard & Poor's 500 stocks minus the risk-free rate.

Example. The recent 10-year Treasury bond rate was reported to be 6.65 percent. A large publicly traded REIT specializing in suburban office buildings was reported to have a beta of 0.65, and the MRP was recently reported to be 11.07 percent. These numbers are used in Equation 14–10 as shown below:

$$y_E = 0.0665 + 0.65 \, (\, 0.1107)$$
$$= 0.138455$$

This is the REIT's estimated cost of equity capital, which must then be combined with the REIT's cost of debt capital to obtain a blended cost of capital. Assume that the REIT has a debt-to-equity ratio of 1 to 1 and a debt beta of 0.30, and that the market risk premium for debt is 0.0335. Thus, the debt cost of capital for the REIT is as follows:

$$y_D = .0665 + .30 \, (0.0335)$$
$$= 0.076550$$

Based on the REIT's debt-to-equity ratio, these two rates are then weighted 50 percent each to produce a blended rate as follows:

$$y_o = .5 \, (0.138455) + .5(0.076550)$$
$$= 0.107503$$

This blended rate is an estimate of the appropriate rate at which to discount the property's NOI. It would then be used in the basic formula to obtain an R_o as follows:

$$R_o = y_o - g$$
$$= 0.107503 - 0.025$$
$$= 0.082503$$

Using this R_o to capitalize NOI produces an indicated value of the property as follows:

$$V_o = NOI/R_o$$
$$= \$86,600/0.082503$$
$$= \$1,049,659, \text{ say } \$1,049,700$$

SEVERAL METHODS, BUT ONLY ONE R_o

The preceding sections show four methods for estimating R_o for a particular property in a given market: the general formula, market extraction, simple mortgage equity analysis, and single-factor asset pricing model. The questions that naturally arise are, "Which one is correct?" or "Which should I use?" All are correct, of course; they are simply different methods of analyzing market data to estimate a property's value. Even so, the methods will not produce the same numerical results. Markets are not totally efficient, and different methods of analysis will not yield the same conclusions. Nevertheless, if accurate, reliable data are available for the various methods, the resulting R_os should be quite close.

The choice of method(s) depends on data availability and reliability. The preferred method *if* good price, income, and expense data are available for at least three (and preferably more) comparable properties is direct market extraction of R_o. Remember, however, that observed transaction prices should not reflect any nonmarket considerations such as unusual financing or other concessions. Also, income and expense data must be placed in a reconstructed operating statement format and income and expenses for the comparable properties estimated to reflect the *same* period as the subject property's NOI. In other words, direct market extraction requires the same availability, reliability, and consistency of data and analysis for the comparable properties as for the subject property.

Mortgage equity analysis and the general formula are substitute methods for deriving R_o. They are often used because appraisers cannot obtain accurate, reliable data for direct market extraction. Often, however, they are able to obtain typical mortgage financing data and equity dividend rates on comparable properties. In these situations, one of the mortgage equity methods is preferable to direct market extraction.

The single-factor asset pricing model is probably the least reliable because it uses data that are not directly derived from the local market and do not take into consideration factors concerning the specific property. Therefore, it should usually be used as a check on the reasonableness of the other methods.

DISCOUNT RATES

Discount rates are the largest component of most capitalization rates. As noted above, they represent the multiperiod rate of return, or required yield, on invested capital. The symbol for a multiperiod discount rate (yield) is y, and the symbols for the yield associated with properties or their components are as follows:

$$y = \text{general symbol for ROI, or yield}$$
$$y_o = \text{overall yield on an entire property}$$
$$y_B = \text{yield on a building}$$
$$y_L = \text{yield on land}$$
$$y_m = \text{yield on a mortgage (interest rate)}$$
$$y_e = \text{yield on equity}$$
$$y_{LF} = \text{yield on a leased fee}$$
$$y_{LH} = \text{yield on a leasehold}$$

The distinction between multiperiod yields (discount rates) and profitability ratios was discussed in Chapter 3 but bears repeating here. Profitability ratios such as the overall capitalization rate (R_o) and the **equity dividend** (capitalization) **rate** (R_e) explicitly consider the income or cash flow return for only one year. Future incomes or cash flows, including forecast appreciation or depreciation, are considered implicitly to the extent they were considered in the expectations of investors in the comparable properties from which the R_o or the y_o was extracted. Multiperiod yields, on the other hand, explicitly incorporate all of the forecast cash inflows and outflows over the expected holding period.

Appraisers can estimate yield rates by extracting yields on comparable properties and reconciling them to represent the yield of a subject property. Before-tax yields on land and buildings, given varying levels of risk, generally fall in the ranges shown in Exhibit 14–5.

EXHIBIT 14-5

RISK AND DISCOUNT RATES

Risk Level	Land	Buildings
Low	6–8	7–10
Medium	8–11	10–13
High	11–14	13–17
Speculative	14 up	17 up

SEPARATE BUILDING AND SITE VALUATION

Sometimes appraisers must estimate the values of buildings and sites separately. Calculation of property taxes, for example, requires this separation. Also, the cost approach, as we saw in Chapter 13, requires a separate site value, and investors sometimes purchase either the site or the building separate from the other. In these cases separate capitalization rates for the site and buildings must be estimated, and they must be applied to (divided into) the portion of the NOI appropriate to the site or building. In both cases of valuation, that is, of the building and of the site, the discount rate portion of the capitalization rate remains the same; however, the growth rate portion of the capitalization rates varies between building and site.

ESTIMATING g FOR BUILDINGS

Because in *real* terms (not counting inflation) almost all buildings depreciate (lose value) over time, the expected real growth rate for buildings is usually negative.[4] However, g is usually estimated in *nominal* terms, that is, including expectations of future inflation (or deflation), because discount rates almost always include investors' expectations about future inflation. Thus, in estimating an appropriate growth rate (g_B) for a building, an appraiser must consider both the real rate of expected depreciation over the building's remaining economic life (REL) and the rate of expected inflation. The estimate for g_B is the net result of these two forecasts.

For example, if the expected rate of inflation is 3 percent, and the building is expected to depreciate in real terms at the rate of 1 percent per year, g_B for the building would be 3 percent $-$ 1 percent $=$ 2 percent. In other words, the income and market value of the building would be expected to grow in *nominal* terms at a net rate of 2 percent per year. Thus, we can see that g_B will normally be lower than the growth rate both for the site under the building (g_S) and for the total property (both land and building).

---

[4]There may be relatively brief periods in which changes in supply do not keep pace with demand shifts, and in these rare and brief periods the increase in market value of some buildings may outstrip their real depreciation rates. Also, the values of architecturally unique buildings, such as the Guggenheim Museum in New York City, may keep up with inflation, but even these buildings must occasionally be modernized or rehabilitated. These costs must be deducted from the building's values in judging whether their values have kept pace with inflation.

In estimating investors' expectations of future inflation, appraisers may rely on surveys of investment expectations performed by some private firms and universities, they may conduct their own surveys, or they may calculate the implicit expectation from recent similar transactions. For example, if an appraiser knows that the sale price of a building that sold recently (not including the site) was based on a discount rate (y_B) of 10 percent and a building capitalization rate (R_B) of 8.5 percent, she could estimate the remaining economic life of the building, calculate the real depreciation rate, and subtract that rate from the growth rate for the building (g_B). The difference would be the expected inflation rate.

Example.
$$y_B = 0.10$$
$$g_B = y_B - R_B$$
$$= 0.100 - 0.085$$
$$= \underline{0.015}$$
$$\text{REL} = 50 \text{ years}$$
$$\text{SFF}_{10\%,\ 50\ \text{yrs.}} = 0.000859$$

Real rate of
$$\text{depreciation} = 1.00 \times 0.000859$$
$$= 0.000859, \text{ or about } 0.086 \text{ percent per year}$$

Inflation rate in
$$\text{discount rate} = g_B - \text{real depreciation rate}$$
$$= 0.015 - 0.000859$$
$$= 0.014, \text{ or about } 1.4 \text{ percent}$$

ESTIMATING A BUILDING'S DEPRECIATION RATE

The real rate of depreciation for a building is based on its remaining economic (or useful) life. Generally buildings have economic lives in the ranges shown in Exhibit 14–6. To estimate a building's remaining economic life, appraisers must first estimate its total economic life. For example, if the building is an apartment building of average construction quality and well located, they might estimate its total economic life as 50 years. Appraisers then estimate the building's *effective age*, or chronological (actual) age adjusted up or down for worse than average or better than average maintenance. Suppose the apartment building being appraised is actually 15 years old but has been maintained in much better than average condition. An appraiser might estimate its effective age as 10 years. Its remaining economic life for appraisal purposes therefore would be 50 years − 10 years = 40 years. Note that *average* maintenance is assumed for the remaining term, since the future owners and future quality of maintenance are unknown.

Example. A building is expected to have a remaining economic life of 40 years; that is, it will depreciate during this time and will have no value at the end of the period. The appropriate discount rate is 11.0 percent, which contains a rate of expected inflation of 2.5 percent. The formula for the net growth rate of the building (g_B) is

$$g_B = I_R - (\text{Dep} \times \text{SFF}) \tag{14–11}$$

EXHIBIT 1 4 - 6

TYPICAL ECONOMIC LIVES OF INCOME PROPERTIES

Type of Property	Economic Life (years)
Hotels and motels	30–40
Apartments	40–60
Warehouses	50–75
Banks	40–50
Offices	20–60
Stores	30–50
Shopping centers	15–30
Restaurants	10–20
Garages and repair shops	40–60
Specialty properties	15–75

where

g_B = net growth rate for the building

I_R = expected rate of inflation contained in the discount rate

Dep = total real percentage loss in building value and income over its remaining economic life or the holding period

SFF = annual sinking fund factor for the building's remaining economic life or holding period at the discount rate

Thus, in this example, g_B would be

$$g_B = 0.025 - (100\% \times 0.001719)^5$$
$$= 0.025 - 0.001719$$
$$= 0.023281, \text{ or about } 2.3\%$$

The building capitalization rate would therefore be

$$R_B = y_B - g_B \qquad\qquad (14\text{--}12)$$
$$= 0.11 - 0.023$$
$$= 0.087, \text{ or } 8.7\%$$

Note that g_B is subtracted from y_B in this case to reflect a positive net growth rate.

Example. A building is expected to experience real depreciation of about 40 percent over a 10-year holding period. The appropriate discount rate is 11 percent, and investors' expectations for future inflation are about 2 percent per year. The building growth rate (g_B) would be

$$g_B = 0.02 - (0.40 \times 0.059801)$$
$$= 0.02 - 0.024$$
$$= -0.004, \text{ or about } -0.4\%$$

___
[5]The keystrokes to calculate the SFF are: N = 40, I = 11%, PV = 0, PMT = ? and FV = 1.

The building capitalization rate would be

$$R_B = y_B - (-g_B)$$
$$= 0.11 + 0.004$$
$$= 0.114, \text{ or } 11.4\%$$

Note that g_B is added to y_B in this case to reflect a negative net growth rate.

ESTIMATING g FOR SITES

After having obtained estimates of g and g_B, we can calculate an estimate of the site's growth rate (g_S) using the following equation. It calculates the (g_S) that causes the weighted average of the g_B and the g_S to equal the overall growth rate (g):

$$g_S = [g - (B \times g_B)]/S \tag{14–13}$$

where

g_s = growth rate for the site
g = overall growth rate
B = building percentage of total property value
g_B = growth rate for the building
S = site percentage of total property value

Example. Assume the appropriate discount rate for the Suburban Office Building is 11 percent, and the overall growth rate is estimated to be 3 percent. Based on assessed values, we estimate the building to comprise approximately 80 percent and the site approximately 20 percent of the total property value. The expected inflation rate contained in the discount rate is 2.5 percent, and the remaining economic life of the building is 40 years. The growth rate for the building is therefore

$$g_B = I_R - (\text{Dep} \times \text{SFF})$$
$$= 0.025 - (100\% \times 0.001719)$$
$$= 0.023281, \text{ or about } 2.33\%$$

And the growth rate for the site is calculated as follows:

$$g_S = [3.0 - (0.8 \times 2.33)]/0.2$$
$$= 5.68\%$$

The capitalization rate for the building (R_B) would therefore be

$$R_B = y_o - g_B$$
$$= 0.11 - 0.0233$$
$$= 0.0867, \text{ or } 8.67\%$$

And the capitalization rate for the site (R_S) would be

$$R_S = 0.11 - 0.0568$$
$$= 0.0532, \text{ or } 5.32\%$$

ALLOCATING NOI BETWEEN BUILDING AND SITE

To estimate separate values of the site and building, a portion of the NOI must be allocated to each. This requires that the site value (V_S) be estimated separately by the sales comparison approach and its income I_S calculated as the product of R_S and V_S. That is, $I_S = R_S \times V_S$.

Continuing with the example, assume that the site value has been estimated by the sales comparison approach as \$349,600. The income to the site would be $0.0532 \times \$349,600 = \$18,599$, say \$18,600, and the income to the building would be

$$I_B = \text{NOI} - I_S$$
$$= \$86,600 - \$18,600$$
$$= \$68,000$$

The indicated value of the building (V_B) would be

$$V_B = I_B/R_B \qquad\qquad (14\text{--}14)$$
$$= \$68,000/0.0867$$
$$= \$784,314, \text{ say } \$784,300$$

The indicated value of the property would therefore be

$$V_o = V_B + V_S \qquad\qquad (14\text{--}15)$$
$$= \$784,300 + \$349,600$$
$$= \$1,133,900$$

Can the process be applied in reverse? That is, can the value of the building be estimated first, its income calculated, and the difference between it and NOI be allocated to the site? The answer is: very rarely—only when the building is the highest and best use of the site as though vacant. The reason that this procedure cannot be used when the building is not the highest and best use of the site as though vacant is that any other building would have a lower value, thus producing a lower NOI that would not result in the correct site value. For example, suppose that in the preceding example the highest and best use building would have a value of \$1,000,000 and the property produced NOI of \$120,000. The income to the building would be $0.0867 \times \$1,000,000 = \$86,700$, and the site income would be $\$120,000 - \$86,700 = \$33,300$. The indicated site value would be $\$33,300/0.0532 = \$625,940$.

If the site value had been estimated by the reverse process in the preceding example, its indicated value would be

$$V_S = I_S/R_S \qquad\qquad (14\text{--}16)$$
$$= \$18,600/0.0532$$
$$= \$349,624, \text{ say } \$349,600$$

This site value is clearly incorrect because it is lower than the value indicated under its highest and best use. A rule of thumb to remember in real estate valuation is that the value of a site is never penalized because of the building on it. The value of a site is always determined by its highest and best use.

EXHIBIT 14-7

GIM ANALYSIS FOR SUBURBAN OFFICE BUILDING

	Comparable		
	A	B	C
Effective gross income	$92,500	$88,300	$94,700
Sale price	$573,500	$573,950	$681,840
GIM (sale price/EGI)	6.2	6.5	7.2

$\bar{x}$ (mean) = 6.6

EXHIBIT 14-8

APPRAISAL OF SUBURBAN OFFICE BUILDING COST APPROACH

Reproduction cost			$1,205,000
Less: Accrued depreciation			
Physical deterioration			
Curable		$20,400	
Incurable			
Short-lived	$ 45,000		
Long-lived	238,800	283,800	
Total physical		$304,200	
Functional obsolescence			
Curable		35,000	
Incurable		165,400	
Total functional		200,400	
External obsolescence			-0-
Total accrued depreciation			504,600
Indicated building value			700,400
Plus site value			349,600
Indicated property value			$1,050,000

OTHER APPROACHES

The sales comparison and cost approaches also are often used in the appraisal of income-producing properties, particularly small, relatively new properties for which relevant data are readily available. While these approaches are presented in chapter 13, their application to the Suburban Office Building is shown in summary form in Exhibits 14–7 and 14–8.

GROSS INCOME MULTIPLIER

Gross income multiplier (GIM) analysis is considered an application of the sales comparison approach for the valuation of income properties. In GIM analysis applied to income properties, appraisers compare sale prices of comparable properties on a unit basis: the dollar. Thus, the sale prices of comparable properties might be $6 or $7 for

REAL ESTATE FOCUS 14-2

Typical Units of Comparison Used in Appraising Income Properties

Property Type	Unit(s) of Comparison
Rental housing	Square feet of living area
Rental stores	Square feet of gross leasable area
Office buildings	Square feet of net leasable area
Industrial buildings	Square feet of gross building area
Apartment buildings	Rooms; dwelling units
Hotels and motels	Rooms
Hospitals and nursing homes	Beds
Restaurants, bars, and theaters	Seats
Factories	Finished units per day
Farms	Bushels per acre
Orchards and groves	Pounds per acre
Mines	Tons of ore per day

every dollar of *annual effective* gross income, as Exhibit 14–7 shows. The appropriate GIM for the Suburban Office Building appears to be about 6.6, and the property's indicated value would thus be $162,000 × 6.6 = $1,069,200.

Appraisers may also use other units of comparison to compare sale prices. Units of comparison adjust for size differences, and appraisers use them when properties are similar except for size. For example, if two apartment properties are similar except that one contains 200 units and the other 300, they could be compared on a price-per-apartment basis. If the 200-unit property sold for $10 million—a price of $50,000 per unit—it would indicate that the 300-unit property should sell for about $15 million. Real Estate Focus 14–2 shows typical units of comparison that appraisers use for various types of income properties.

COST APPROACH

Exhibit 14–8 shows the estimation of the value of the Suburban Office Building by the **cost approach**. Appraisers usually place less reliance on this approach for income properties because of the difficulties in measuring costs and depreciation. Income is the most important characteristic for which these properties are purchased, and the greatest reliance is thus placed on the approach that converts income to present value. The cost approach is used primarily as a check on the other approaches.

RECONCILIATION

Exhibit 14–9 summarizes the various indications of market value for the Suburban Office Building obtained in this chapter. Appraisers obtain a final estimate of value by **reconciliation** of these indications into a final estimate of value. Experience, logic, and judgment

EXHIBIT 14-9

SUBURBAN OFFICE BUILDING SUMMARY OF VALUE INDICATIONS

Approach	Indicated V_o
Income capitalization	
R_os derived by	
General formula	$1,018,800
Direct market extraction	1,031,000
Simple M/E analysis	969,900
Single factor asset pricing model	1,049,700
Separate building and site valuation	1,133,900
GIM analysis	1,069,200
Cost approach	1,050,000

serve as the criteria for determining the weight assigned to the indicated value from each approach. The range of indications for the Suburban Office Building is $164,000 ($1,133,900 − $969,900); the mean is $1,046,071. In most income property appraisals, however, appraisers would not estimate R_o by four different methods, but rather would use the one or two best methods, determined by the availability and reliability of data. Nevertheless, in the Suburban Office Building example, R_o has been estimated by four methods that produce value indications that are reasonably close. The appraiser might average them to obtain an indicated value using R_o. The average (mean) of these four indications is $1,017,350, and that figure is weighted 60 percent in the final reconciliation.

The value indication produced by the separate valuation of building and land ($1,133,900) is the highest of all the methods used. This method, however, is probably the most unreliable because it requires the analyst to estimate separate effective growth rates for the building and site based on the building's expected rate of depreciation. For this reason, it is weighted only 10 percent.

The value indication generated by GIM analysis is weighted 20 percent because it converts income into a present value. The cost approach is less applicable to the appraisal of an income property than the other methods; it is therefore weighted only 10 percent. The final estimate of value, $1,042,600, is the weighted average of all of the value indications, as Exhibit 14–10 shows.

THE APPRAISAL PROFESSION

Appraisal is a much-needed function in real estate. Property values are not readily apparent, and decision makers often must have professional help and advice because of the complexity of real estate investment. The process of evaluating real estate may be contrasted with that for evaluating the prices of stocks traded on the New York Stock Exchange. In that market, many transactions occur each minute, and prices are known almost instantaneously. Each share of a company's stock is like every other share. Unlike stocks, no two properties are exactly alike, and transactions of similar properties may be

EXHIBIT 14-10

SUBURBAN OFFICE BUILDING RECONCILIATION OF VALUE INDICATIONS

Value Indication	Amount	Weight	Weighted Amount
Direct capitalization	$1,017,350	.60	$610,410
Building plus site	1,133,900	.10	113,390
GIM analysis	1,069,200	.20	213,840
Cost approach	1,050,000	.10	105,000
FINAL ESTIMATE OF VALUE			$1,042,640
		say	$1,042,600

infrequent, resulting in a scarcity of price data. Appraisers often must make detailed and systematic adjustments among several dissimilar properties to estimate values.

Estimates of value are important because they determine the prices owners ask for their properties and potential buyers are willing to pay. Most people are unwilling to sell a possession, especially their most valuable possession—real estate—for less than it is worth; most buyers do not want to pay *more* than it is worth.

Similarly, real estate investors, particularly investors in large properties, realize they do not have the knowledge and resources to consider and analyze all of the various impacts of their decisions. Even if they are able, they usually want objective viewpoints of knowledgeable outsiders—professionals whose egos are not involved in the decision and who have track records of estimating values reliably.

REGULATION OF THE APPRAISAL PROFESSION

Responsibility for regulating the appraisal profession is shared by the federal government and the states. The real estate in most "federally regulated transactions"—including loans made by federally regulated or insured lenders and transactions with the federal government or its agencies—must be appraised by a state-licensed or **certified appraiser**. There are some exceptions to the requirement, the principal one being for residential properties below $250,000. A *licensed* appraiser may be used for any "noncomplex" appraisal of one- to four-family properties of less than $1 million. However, lenders making loans on residential properties valued at $1 million or more and on most commercial properties must use only state-*certified* appraisers. Appraisal standards must conform to the **Uniform Standards of Professional Appraisal Practice** (USPAP) of the Appraisal Standards Board of the **Appraisal Foundation**, the public organization charged with establishing standards for appraisals and appraisal reports minimum qualifications for licensed and certified appraisers.

The state role in regulating appraisers involves administering the certification and licensing process. This includes providing educational programs, examinations, and disciplinary actions. The Appraisal Subcommittee of the Federal Financial Institutions Examination Council (FFIEC) oversees and monitors the regulatory agencies, the states, and the Appraisal Foundation to ensure compliance with federal law and regulations.

E X H I B I T   1 4 - 1 1

APPRAISAL ORGANIZATIONS AND DESIGNATIONS

Appraisal Organization	Professional Designation	Indication of Skills
Appraisal Institute*	MAI (Member, Appraisal Institute)	Competence to appraise and evaluate all types of real estate.
	SRA (Senior Residential Appraiser)	Competence to appraise one- to four-family residential properties. Does not cover other types of properties.
Appraisal Institute of Canada	AACI (Accredited Appraiser Canadian Institute)	Competence to appraise all real estate.
American Society of Appraisers	ASA (Member, ASA)	Competence to appraise property in the field of the member's specialty.
National Association of Independent Fee Appraisers	IFA (Member, IFA) IFAS (Senior Member, IFA) IFAC (Appraiser-Counselor Member)	All indicate general competence to appraise property.
International Association of Assessing Officers	CPE (Certified Personalty Evaluator)	Competence to assess personal property.
	AAE (Accredited Assessment Evaluator)	Competence to assess property.
	CAE (Certified Assessment Evaluator)	
National Association of Review Appraisers	CRA (Certified Review Appraiser)	Experience in reviewing appraisals.
American Society of Farm Managers and Rural Appraisers	AFM (Accredited Farm Manager) ARA (Accredited Rural Appraiser)	Competence to manage farms.
National Association of Real Estate Appraisers	CREA (Certified Real Estate Appraiser)	Competence to appraise real estate.
National Association of Master Appraisers	MSA (Master Senior Appraiser) MFLA (Master Farm and Land Appraiser) MRA (Master Residential Appraiser)	Competence to appraise real estate. Competence to appraise rural properties. Competence to appraise residential properties.

*On January 1, 1991, two organizations (the American Institute of Real Estate Appraisers and the Society of Real Estate Appraisers) merged to form the Appraisal Institute. Three designations of the former organizations (RM, SRPA, and SREA) are still held by some members, but the designations are no longer being awarded.

PROFESSIONAL ORGANIZATIONS AND DESIGNATIONS

There are a number of professional appraisal organizations that provide educational programs, political involvement, and professional designations for their members. (See Exhibit 14–11.) The Appraisal Institute is the largest and best known of these, having some 20,000 members and candidates out of an estimated 200,000 appraisers nationwide.

The MAI designation of the Appraisal Institute indicates competence to appraise and evaluate all types of real estate. Candidates for this designation must complete a graduate level program in one of several approved universities or complete a series of required courses sponsored by the organization. Additionally, candidates must meet certain experience requirements, and they must prepare a *demonstration appraisal report* that shows their ability to perform a complete and well-documented appraisal on an income-producing property. Finally, MAI candidates must pass a lengthy and thorough comprehensive examination.

The Appraisal Institute also awards the residential appraisal designation SRA (senior residential appraiser). This designation indicates competency to appraise one- to four-family residences. Since the educational, experience, and testing requirements for this designation do not include income-producing properties, it can be attained in less time than the MAI designation. Typically, it takes beginning appraisers a minimum of five years to attain the MAI designation and approximately one-half that time to attain the SRA designation.

APPRAISAL AS A CAREER

Appraisal is one of the easiest and best routes of entry to the real estate field. Appraisal firms typically employ recent college graduates in beginning positions. While some background in real estate is desirable, appraisers expect to educate new employees, at least in the procedures used by the firm. Those entering the field typically begin by serving as research assistants, then do portions of appraisals, then perform complete appraisals under the supervision of senior appraisers, and finally take responsibility for complete appraisal jobs.

The ideal background for someone entering the appraisal profession is an undergraduate degree in business administration, with a major in real estate, including one or two appraisal courses, or some other major such as finance with several real estate courses, including appraisal. Some appraisal firms today require, or express a preference for, someone having a master's degree with a major in real estate. The graduates of specialized master's degree programs in appraisal have an ideal educational background for appraisal, and demand for these students is high.

Appraisers must be *analytically* inclined. They should be well trained in such basic disciplines as economics, accounting, statistics, finance, building construction, and urban planning. They also should know the English language well and be able to write thorough, convincing, and grammatically correct appraisal reports. They should be independent in nature and have a sure sense of professional and ethical standards. Perhaps most importantly, they should enjoy doing field research and "digging out" information that is often difficult to find. As in other real estate fields, appraisers must be able to work with people. They receive diverse, often conflicting, and unreasonable demands from clients. They must be able to turn such requests to their advantage by convincing clients of the desirability of using their firms, even if some requests cannot be met, and establishing a base for more assignments. To prevent potential conflicts with clients, an appraiser's fees are not linked to the property value estimate or other conclusion. Client, employee, and professional relationships are all important elements in the appraisal profession.

SUMMARY

Income capitalization is a short-cut method to the multiperiod discounted cash flow model for estimating market value. For appraisal purposes, income capitalization can provide more reliable results in many cases than DCF analysis, because it relies on the analysis and price decisions already made by investors in the market. Prices and income data on similar income-producing properties are used to estimate an appropriate net operating income and capitalization rate for the subject property. The appraiser's main tasks are to (1) find information on comparable properties that have sold recently, (2) analyze reconstructed operating statements of comparable properties in order to develop a reconstructed operating statement for the subject property, (3) determine that the prices of the comparable properties represented arm's-length market conditions, (4) find an overall capitalization rate from the comparable sales, and (5) divide the cap rate into the market NOI of the subject property.

Interests other than the complete (fee simple) property rights also may be valued by income capitalization. Sometimes sites and buildings, leased fee estates and leaseholds, and equity and debt interests must be valued separately. In all of these cases appropriate cap-

italization rates and incomes must be estimated. The capitalization rate is then divided into the income to obtain an estimate of value.

Overall capitalization rates can be estimated by several methods. Direct market extraction from recent sales is the preferred method when adequate, reliable data are available. Other methods rely on debt and equity cap rates or yields and the separate valuation of land and building. Conceptually, any capitalization rate contains two major components: a discount rate and a growth rate.

The estimation of values is critical to real estate activity, and therefore the appraisal profession performs a vital social function. The profession is regulated by the federal and state governments, and, in addition, there are a number of organizations that serve the professional needs of their members. Although entrance requirements have increased in recent years, it is still a relatively easy profession to enter and one in which college graduates can find beginning jobs. It also serves as the door to other fields in real estate, such as property management, investment management, counseling, brokerage, and development.

KEY TERMS

Appraisal Foundation 430
Capitalization rate 411
Certified appraiser 430
Cost approach 428
Depreciation 415
Direct capitalization 417
Discount rate 421

Equity dividend rate 421
Gross income multiplier 427
Loan-to-value ratio 418
Mortgage equity analysis 417
Net operating income 412
Overall capitalization rate 415

Reconciliation 428
Reserve for replacements and other nonrecurring expenses 413
Single-factor asset pricing model 419
Uniform Standards of Professional Appraisal Practice 430

TEST YOURSELF

Answer the following multiple choice questions.

1. Which of the following expenses is not an operating expense?
   a. Utility.
   b. Reserve for replacements and other nonrecurring expenses.
   c. Management.
   d. Mortgage payment.
   e. Advertising.

2. To estimate the value of the equity portion of a real estate investment, an appraiser divides the equity income (BTCF) by which of the following?
   a. Equity yield rate (y_e).
   b. Equity dividend rate (R_e).
   c. Overall capitalization rate (R_o).
   d. Mortgage constant (R_m).
   e. Discount rate (y_o).

3. An overall capitalization rate (R_o) is divided into which type of income or cash flow to obtain an indicated value?
   a. Net operating income (NOI).
   b. Effective gross income (EGI).
   c. Before-tax cash flow (BTCF).
   d. After-tax cash flow (ATCF).
   e. Potential gross income (PGI).

4. Which of the following types of properties probably would not be appropriate for income capitalization?
   a. Apartment building.
   b. Shopping center.
   c. Farm.
   d. Warehouse.
   e. Public school.

5. Reserves for replacement and other nonrecurring expenses are allowances that reflect
   a. The annual depreciation of the building.
   b. The annual depreciation of the long-lived components of the building.
   c. The annual depreciation or appreciation of the entire property.
   d. The annual depreciation of the short-lived components of the building and expenses that occur only occasionally.
   e. The depreciation or appreciation of the land.

6. What overall capitalization rate is indicated by the following characteristics of equity and debt in a transaction?

$$m = .80$$
$$R_M = .123432$$
$$R_E = .1400$$

   a. 14.00 percent.
   b. 12.00 percent.
   c. 12.67 percent.
   d. 13.25 percent.
   e. 12.50 percent.

7. An appraiser estimates that a property will produce NOI of $25,000, the y_o is 11 percent, and the growth rate is 2.0 percent. What is the total property value (unrounded)?
   a. $277,778.
   b. $227,273.
   c. $323,762.
   d. $243,762.
   e. $231,580.

8. An apartment property sold recently for $625,000. It produces NOI of about $60,000, indicating an R_o of 9.60 percent. If the y_o is 11.6 percent, the building constitutes approximately 80 percent of the total property value, and the building has a remaining economic life of 50 years, what net growth rate is applicable to the building?
   a. 2.00 percent.
   b. 1.95 percent.
   c. 1.56 percent.
   d. 1.00 percent.
   e. 1.75 percent.

9. The organization that establishes standards of appraisal practice and qualifications for apprais-

ers to be licensed and/or certified in the various states is the

a. Appraisal Institute.

b. Appraisal Qualifications Board.

c. Appraisal Foundation.

d. Appraisal Subcommittee.

e. Appraisal Standards Board.

10. The entity(ies) that license and certify appraisers is (are) the

a. Appraisal Foundation.

b. Appraisal Institute.

c. Appraisal Standards Board.

d. States.

e. Both a and b.

PROBLEMS FOR THOUGHT AND SOLUTION

1. The typical mortgage available in the market for apartment properties carries an interest rate of 10 percent, is amortized monthly for 25 years, and could be obtained for 80 percent of value. What would be the indicated R_o by simple mortgage equity analysis, if equity dividend rates (R_es) are running about 12.5 percent?

2. You are asked to appraise a vacant parcel of land. Your analysis shows that if apartments were constructed, the portion of the NOI attributable to the land would be $30,000 per year. If offices were constructed, the portion attributable to land would be $25,000, and the portion contributed by a small neighborhood shopping center would be $27,500. All of these uses would be legal. If the appropriate R_L is .105 (10.5 percent), what is the value of the site?

3. Data for five comparable income properties that sold recently are shown in the accompanying table.

Property	NOI	Sale Price	Overall Rate
A	$57,800	$566,600	.1020
B	49,200	496,900	.0990
C	63,000	630,000	.1000
D	56,000	538,500	.1040
E	58,500	600,000	.0975

What is the indicated overall rate (R_O)?

4. A site has been appraised at $300,000. The income to the building on the site (I_B) has been estimated to be $87,500. The building has a remaining economic life of 40 years, the appropriate discount rate is 9.5 percent, and the effective net growth rate for the building is 2.5 percent. What is the value of the building?

5. Given the facts of Problem 4, what is the value of the entire property (V_o), rounded to the nearest $500?

CASE PROBLEMS

1. Given the following owner's income and expense estimates for an apartment property, formulate a reconstructed operating statement. The building consists of 10 units that could rent for $550 per month each.

OWNER'S INCOME STATEMENT

Rental income (last year)		$60,600
Less: Expenses		
Power	$2,200	
Heat	1,700	
Janitor	4,600	
Water	3,700	
Maintenance	4,800	
Reserves	2,800	
Management	3,000	
Depreciation	5,000	
Mortgage payments	6,300	34,100
Net income		$26,500

Estimating vacancy and collection losses at 5 percent of potential gross income, reconstruct the operating statement to obtain an estimate of NOI. Remember, there may be items in the owner's statement that should not be included in the reconstructed operating statement.

2. Using the NOI obtained in Case Problem 1 and an R_o of 11.0 percent, calculate the property's indicated value. Round your final answer to the nearest $500.

ADDITIONAL READINGS

The following text focuses on income capitalization:

Fisher, Jeffrey E., and Robert S. Martin. *Income Property Valuation*. Chicago: Dearborn Financial Publishing, 1994.

The following general texts contain chapters on income capitalization:

Appraisal Institute. *The Appraisal of Real Estate*, 11th ed. Chicago: AI, 1996.

Lusht, Kenneth L. *Real Estate Valuation: Principles and Applications*. Burr Ridge, IL: Richard D. Irwin, 1997.

Smith, Halbert C., Linda Crawford Root, and Jerry D. Belloit. *Real Estate Appraisal*, 3rd ed. Scottsdale, AZ: Gorsuch, Scarisbrick, 1995.

The following article develops a model for estimating the reserves for replacement in the appraisal of apartment properties:

Outhred, David R. "Reserves for Replacement in Apartment Properties." *Appraisal Journal* LXIII, no. 1 (January 1995), pp. 69–80.

This article discusses a number of conceptual and applied problems in the appraisal process:

Smith, Halbert C. "Inconsistencies in Appraisal Theory and Practice." *Journal of Real Estate Research* 1, no. 1 (Fall 1986), pp. 1–17.

The author of this article contends that the IRR does not equal the capitalization rate plus a growth rate because it neglects property appreciation, rental step-ups, and below-line costs.

Eppli, "The Theory, Assumptions, and Limitations of Direct Capitalization." *Appraisal Journal* LXI, no.3 (July 1993), pp. 419–25.

The following article discusses the process of analyzing the relationships between capitalization rates and discount rates in order to judge their consistency and reliability:

Wincott, Richard D., Kevin A. Hoover, and Terry V. Grissom. "Capitalization Rates, Discount Rates, and Reasonableness." *Real Estate Issues* 21, no. 2 (August 1996), pp. 11–15.

The following articles deal with the estimation of discount rates and their application in DCF analysis:

Kelly, Hugh F. "Recent Evidence on Investor Preferences and Yield Requirements." *Real Estate Issues* 21, no. 2 (August 1996), pp. 1–6.

Riggs, Kenneth P. Jr. "Pricing Risk: Choosing a Discount Rate," *Real Estate Issues* 21, no. 2 (August 1996), pp. 16–22.

The author of this article compares and contrasts direct capitalization with DCF analysis:

Martin, W. B. "Direct Capitalization or DCF Analysis?" *Appraisal Journal* LXI, no.3 (July 1993), pp. 390–93.

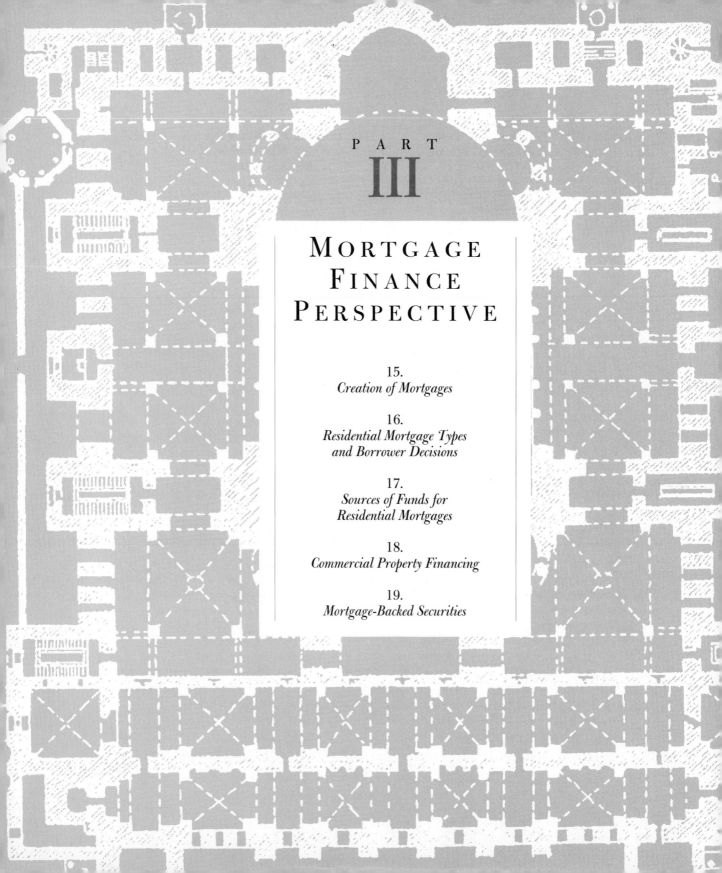

PART III

MORTGAGE FINANCE PERSPECTIVE

15.
Creation of Mortgages

16.
*Residential Mortgage Types
and Borrower Decisions*

17.
*Sources of Funds for
Residential Mortgages*

18.
Commercial Property Financing

19.
Mortgage-Backed Securities

Mortgages, loans secured by real estate, have a role in nearly all transactions involving single-family homes and many income-property transactions. Mortgages are used either because real estate purchases require more up-front money than most buyers have or because buyers find it economically advantageous to borrow. This *financing decision* follows directly from the decision to invest in real estate and depends on the same value concepts as the investment decision.

The Mortgage Finance Perspective begins with Chapter 15, which covers basic mortgage theory and many of the legal aspects of how mortgages are created. The chapter also presents a general discussion of how investment capital flows to the mortgage market. Specific details of the types of mortgages offered to home buyers and how home buyers make decisions about mortgage financing appear in Chapter 16. Chapter 17 presents the lender side of the single-family mortgage story. This chapter discusses how lenders raise funds for loans and how they decide to whom to lend money. The important role of government and government-related agencies in this process also is detailed in this chapter.

Commercial property mortgage finance differs in many interesting ways from single-family mortgage finance. In Chapter 18, we describe the behavior of commercial property lenders and borrowers, and the types of mortgages used in commercial property mortgage finance. Finally, the fascinating and ever-changing world of mortgage-backed securities is described in Chapter 19. Nearly one half of all single-family mortgages and a growing percentage of all commercial property mortgages are sold in the public capital markets as securities. We feel that students of real estate should be familiar with the development of public sources of mortgage financing for real estate.

15
C H A P T E R

CREATION OF MORTGAGES

CHAPTER OUTLINE

MORTGAGES
   International Perspectives of Mortgage
     Finance
   The Story of a Mortgage
   Mortgage Theory

**CAPITAL FLOW TO
MORTGAGES**
   The Four Quadrants of Real Estate
     Finance
   Integration of Capital and Mortgage
     Markets

**MORTGAGE BORROWER AND
LENDER RELATIONSHIPS**
   Extensions of the Simple Mortgage
     Contract
   Single-Family Residential Mortgages
   Income-Property Mortgages

**CLAUSES FOUND IN
MORTGAGE DOCUMENTS**
   Requirements of a Valid and Enforceable
     Mortgage

   Common Mortgage Clauses
   Residential Mortgage Documents
   Important Clauses in Various Income-
     Property Mortgages

**ADJUSTMENTS IN BORROWER
AND LENDER RELATIONSHIPS**
   Satisfactory Payment in Full
   Default and Foreclosure
   Assumption and "Subject to" Transactions
   Recasting the Mortgage
   Sale of the Mortgage

SUMMARY

KEY TERMS

TEST YOURSELF

**PROBLEMS FOR THOUGHT
AND SOLUTION**

INTERNET EXERCISE

CASE PROBLEMS

ADDITIONAL READINGS

After reading this chapter, students will be able to:

1. Describe the ways in which state laws define security interests in mortgage contracts.

2. Discuss how decisions are made in the capital markets to allocate funds to mortgages.

3. Distinguish between the institutional arrangements for residential and commercial property mortgages.

4. Identify the major clauses in mortgage contracts.

5. Distinguish between valid, invalid, enforceable, and unenforceable mortgage contracts.

6. Describe the process of mortgage default and foreclosure.

MORTGAGES

Since arriving at the university to teach real estate 20 years ago, Professor Legroc, his wife, and their 10 children have resided in an apartment. Professor Legroc saved as much as he could during this time and now has $40,000 for the purchase of a home. Because he has been so busy writing textbooks, he has not kept track of the prices of houses near the university (he must live near the university because he cannot afford a car). He discovers that $40,000 represents only 20 percent of the amount needed to purchase a house. Professor Legroc informs his family not to worry because they can borrow the remainder of the money they need from the bank. The bank simply requires some signed legal documents that give the bank the right to take the house away from the Legroc family if they stop making payments to repay the loan from the bank. These legal documents constitute a mortgage.

Mortgages occupy the central place in the real estate finance systems of developed countries throughout the world. Because the acquisition cost of real estate generally exceeds the amount of equity capital available to investors, mortgages represent one of the three basic contracts found in most transactions transferring real property rights (along with the listing contract and the contract for sale). The **mortgage** is a special form of debt contract created between borrowers, who *pledge real estate as the security for loans,* and lenders who operate businesses that originate mortgages. Loans secured by automobiles, farm animals, and other types of personal or intangible property do not qualify as mortgage loans because they do not involve real estate as the loan security!

The study of mortgage contracts generally falls within the larger domain of real estate finance, which encompasses three areas;

1. Legal contracts between mortgage lenders and borrowers.

R E A L   E S T A T E   F O C U S   1 5 - 1

In Their Own Words

School children when asked to define real estate financing:

"Real estate financing is even more important than it sounds."

"Most real estate financing more or less involves some money."

SOURCE: Bob Williams, "Kids Say the Darndest Things," *Skylines*, March 1989.

---

2. Financial aspects of mortgage lending, specifically the evaluation of mortgage terms and deal structuring.
3. Institutional arrangements for mortgage lending, including the characteristics and regulation of mortgage lenders.

Although substantial interaction exists among these three areas—especially between mortgage contract provisions and the financial aspects of mortgages—we defer discussion of financial and specific institutional matters until Chapters 16–19. This chapter, as part of the Mortgage Finance Perspective, focuses on rules governing the contractual relationships between mortgage lenders and borrowers and provides an overview of how and why debt capital flows through the financial system. The overview serves as a foundation for the study of specific institutional arrangements in the creation of mortgages.

The laws governing mortgage contracts differ markedly in the nations of the world and among states in the United States. The clauses in mortgage contracts also differ, depending on whether loans are for single-family residential property or for income property (e.g., hotels, office buildings, and shopping centers) and whether loans are for new development and construction ventures or for acquisition of existing properties. This chapter highlights differences in mortgage laws among jurisdictions and describes how contract provisions vary according to the type of property being mortgaged.

INTERNATIONAL PERSPECTIVES OF MORTGAGE FINANCE

The system that supplies mortgage money in each nation follows from both the country's political environment and its traditions. In free-market economies, mortgage money flows freely for real estate investment. The government's role in such economies is limited to helping markets operate efficiently and fairly. In more centrally controlled economies, government has a far more active role.

In the United States, **equity** financing comes directly from individuals and institutions that collect money from individuals, mainly banks, pension funds, and life insurance companies.[1] Highly advanced mortgage markets also exist for financing residential and

---

[1]See Chapter 5 for a detailed discussion of the sources of equity capital for real estate.

REAL ESTATE FOCUS 15-2, INTERNATIONAL

Creation of Russian Mortgages

Despite formidable obstacles, not the least of which include the lack of a history of private property ownership and an absence of mortgage law that allows lenders to foreclose on delinquent borrowers, a primary residential mortgage market is beginning to develop in Russia.

Because of a strong current and potential demand for home ownership, some lenders recently began accepting applications for loans with real estate pledged as the collateral. To limit their risk in this precarious lending environment, lenders require some of the following provisions in lending contracts:

1. Relatively quick repayment—a long-term for a loan means 10 years and many loans last for only one year with the opportunity for a roll over.

2. Down payments of 30 to 40 percent.

3. That the borrower be an employee of the lender.

4. A separate realty company to own the property, from which the borrower leases the property until repayment.

Many other problems, such as the lack of borrower credit history and a societal distaste for foreclosure, mean that establishment of a well-organized and competitive mortgage market will not occur until well into the 21st century. Nevertheless, some Russian households are now homeowners as the result of mortgage financing.

SOURCE: Neela Banerjee and Gabreila Teodorescu, "Russians Become Homey With Mortgages," *The Wall Street Journal,* September 27, 1995, p. A12.

income property investments. **Financial intermediaries,** such as banks and life insurance companies, and partnerships between mortgage companies and Wall Street investment banking firms help to make the U.S. real estate financing system the most advanced in the world. Governments support this system for financing single-family residential property by guaranteeing certain loans and securities backed by mortgages. Governments also intervene to promote fairness in residential mortgage lending.[2] Several developed nations including Canada, Germany, Switzerland, and Belgium also have sophisticated private mortgage markets, although these markets do not yet rival those in the United States.

Real estate investment in other free-world countries, such as England, Japan, Portugal, and India, occurs without highly competitive private mortgage markets. Banks originate mortgage loans for income properties in these countries, but often as a secondary means of financing and without competitive pricing of loan terms. Income property investment in these nations usually occurs with equity capital from traditional institutions (e.g., life insurance companies and banks) and trading companies. Residential finance takes place with substantially more direct government support (that is, subsidies) than in the United States.

Investors in the United States, Canada, France, Belgium, Spain, and several other European and Pacific Rim countries use securities markets to raise mortgage money for

[2]The term *equity* is sometimes used in place of the word *fairness.* This usage should not be confused with the use of the term *equity* when describing the money contributed by investors from their own sources (that is, money not borrowed).

real estate investment. This means that money comes through channels originating with the sale of bond-like securities called **mortgage-backed securities** (MBS) to investors without the aid of financial intermediaries or substantial involvement of government. As discussed in Chapter 19, the United States maintains a strong leadership position in the innovation and growth of securitized mortgage financing.

In parts of the world in which the political system severely limits private ownership of land, real estate financing exists almost entirely as a government-supported activity. In Russia, parts of Eastern Europe, China, parts of Africa, and parts of Central America, governments own and finance the development of most of the land.

Competitive mortgage lending and borrowing happen in a limited number of nations in the world, but in the nations where mortgage contracts exist, they play an important role in real estate investment. The mortgage markets in the United States evolved faster and more completely than anywhere else in the world because strong mortgage and contract laws exist in every state to protect the integrity of the borrower and lender relationship. These laws grant lenders broad powers and rights to foreclose on borrowers who fail to uphold the provisions of mortgage contracts. The peoples of many countries remain unwilling to grant such powers and rights to lenders.

THE STORY OF A MORTGAGE

Exhibit 15–1 maps the life of a mortgage. It shows that the birth of a mortgage occurs as the result of a contract negotiated between a lender and a borrower in the **primary mortgage market**. Money that flows to the lender from two sources enables the lender to participate in the creation of a mortgage. Deposits, including certificates of deposit sold by banks, insurance policy premiums, and contributions into pension accounts, represent one of the two sources of mortgage money. The second source comes from the sale of the mortgage to investors in the **secondary mortgage market**.

The mortgage contract facilitates an exchange between the lender, who gives money, and the borrower, who gives legal documents (identified as the mortgage and note in Exhibit 15–1) to the lender. As discussed in the next section, these documents empower the lender to take actions to recover the money if the borrower fails to repay the loan. The mortgage, now defined as these legal documents, resides for some part of its life or for its entire life in the portfolio of the lender. If the lender decides to sell the mortgage in the secondary market, then the mortgage will only reside in the portfolio for a few months.

Firms known as **conduits** assist in various ways with the movement of the mortgage from the lender's portfolio through the secondary market, and ultimately, into the investment portfolios of investors (e.g., pension fund or mutual fund). In the creation of many income-property mortgages, conduits take the form of a partnership between a mortgage company, which acts as the originator of the mortgage, and an investment banking firm, which provides the money. In the single-family mortgage finance system, conduits buy mortgages directly from originating lenders, as shown in Exhibit 15–1.[3]

[3]The Federal National Mortgage Association (Fannie Mae) and the Federal Home Loan Mortgage Corporation (Freddie Mac) are the public conduits of this type in the United States. Chapter 19 contains details about these organizations.

EXHIBIT 15-1

THE LIFE OF A MORTGAGE

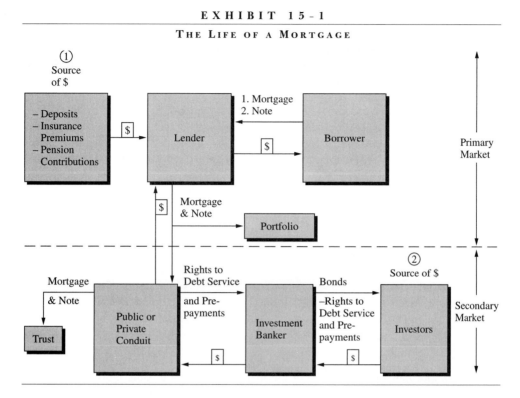

The conduit and the investment banker (or only the investment banker) combine the mortgage with other similar mortgages into a *pool* and transform the mortgage into mortgage-backed securities. During this securitization process, the legal documents move to a trust and usually remain there until the full repayment of the mortgage debt. Also, Securities and Exchange Commission approval and a credit rating by a rating agency, such as Standard & Poors, are often obtained. Following securitization, the investment banker sells the securities to the investor. The investor buys *rights* to receive payments of interest, principal, and prepayment of the debt from all the mortgages in the pool in relation to what they initially invest. The investor may hold the securities or sell them to another investor through a securities broker, as discussed in Chapter 19.

MORTGAGE THEORY

The relationship between the parties in a simple mortgage contract illustrated in the primary market portion of Exhibit 15–1 shows that the mortgage lender promises to lend the money if the borrower promises to give the lender two legal documents: a mortgage and a note. Mortgages are legal documents giving lenders *contingent* claims against real estate. The contingency becomes reality when borrowers default on their loans, usually by not making payments in accordance with the provisions of the contract. In the case of borrower default, lenders exercise the claim against the property through a procedure known as **foreclosure** to force public sales of the properties. Properties, therefore, serve as security for mortgage loans. Recording of mortgages, usually at county courthouses following the closing of the transaction, evidences the pledge of the property as security for loans.

The note provides another form of security for the loan. In some states, this **promissory note** is called a *bond,* but there is no substantive difference between this instrument and a note. Borrowers, on issuing promissory notes, make personal promises to repay loans. Lenders may enforce these personal promises upon default, if the expected proceeds from sales of properties will not cover outstanding balances of loans.[4] In some states, a separate court action called a **deficiency judgment** can be filed against borrowers if the proceeds from foreclosure sales fail to fully repay lenders.[5] This right exists regardless of whether the mortgage documents contain a note or not. Finally, mortgage documents containing notes with specific language about borrowers' promises to repay loans, as are typically used in single-family residential financing, establish **recourse financing.** The absence of promissory language in the mortgage documents, as in many income-property mortgages, indicates no recourse against borrowers' personal assets. This condition is usually referred to as **nonrecourse financing.** However as just noted, the courts may issue deficiency judgments against borrowers in situations when lenders are not fully repaid from the foreclosure sales of properties.

Title and lien theories. One of the major differences in state mortgage law concerns the type of security interest lenders obtain in mortgage agreements. Historically, when landowners sought to borrow money from lenders, the actual title to real property was deeded by borrowers to lenders, who received interest payments in the form of the profits generated by farming or otherwise using the land during the period the loan principal was outstanding. Title reverted to borrowers only after full repayment of loan balances. Subsequently, legislatures and the courts substantially modified this practice. Today, mortgage interest payments flow independently of the profits from land, and states follow modern theories of mortgage security that allow borrowers to retain title to the real estate pledged as security for loans.

Under current state laws, mortgages given by borrowers (mortgagors) bestow on lenders (mortgagees) either a title to or a lien against property. In so-called **title-theory** states, lenders, as in earlier times, technically receive title to property in mortgage contracts.[6] Yet, the law and the courts in these states modify the property rights given to

---

[4]Lenders seldom exercise their rights to collect from borrowers, but instead seek repayment by foreclosing on the property.

[5]The theory behind the deficiency judgment is that borrowers' responsibilities under mortgage contracts do not end with the foreclosure sale. Deficiency judgments, however, are difficult to obtain, especially in cases involving defaults by owners of owner-occupied homes, because courts tend to favor borrowers over lenders.

[6]In some title-theory states, the mortgage instrument carries a name other than a mortgage. In Georgia, for example, the instrument that transfers title to the lender in a mortgage contract is called a security deed. In some other title-theory states, it is called a mortgage deed.

E X H I B I T   1 5 - 2

MORTGAGE CONTRACT WITH A DEED OF TRUST

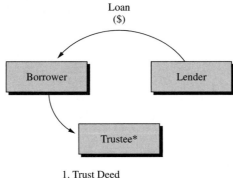

Loan
($)

Borrower   Lender

Trustee*

1. Trust Deed
2. Promissory Note
   (technical conveyance)

*The trustee may be the agent of the lender.

lenders in mortgage contracts so that they can exercise these rights only if borrowers default. In practice, mortgage contracts in title-theory states carry **power-of-sale clauses** that allow lenders, upon borrower default, to cut short the foreclosure process. Thus, the title-theory arrangement, compared to the lien theory arrangement, often saves time and money for lenders who can bypass certain foreclosure procedures.

In **lien-theory** states lenders do not receive titles, but instead, get security interests that grant them the right to bring formal foreclosure actions to force sales of property in the event of borrower default. Foreclosure actions, discussed later in this chapter, may take months after borrowers have had reasonable time to pay overdue installments.

Deeds-of-trust.   A variation of title theory (in some states lien theory) occurs in states that use either **deeds of trust** or trust deeds instead of mortgages.[7] In these states, third-party trustees (e.g., a trust company or bank) receive titles to properties via trust deeds issued by borrowers. Exhibit 15–2 shows this relationship. The trust deed closely resembles a mortgage including a power-of-sale clause. In case of borrower default, lenders inform trustees, and trustees then take action to force the sale of properties. These actions may involve either initiating public notices of foreclosure or initiating lawsuits to foreclose.

---

[7]The following states use deeds of trust: Alaska, California, Colorado, District of Columbia, Mississippi, Missouri, Montana, Nebraska, Nevada, New Mexico, North Carolina, Oregon, South Carolina, Tennessee, Texas, Virginia, Washington, and West Virginia.

EXHIBIT 15-3

CAPITAL FLOW MATRIX FOR REAL ESTATE
(EXAMPLES OF MONEY SOURCES IN EACH QUADRANT)

	Private	Public
Equity	Individuals' pension funds	Equity REITs, real estate corporations
Debt (mortgages)	Banks, insurance companies	Mortgage-backed securities, mortgage REITs

CAPITAL FLOW TO MORTGAGES

The creation of mortgage contracts occurs in an important segment of the economy called the financial markets. Financial markets consist of various segments including; (1) money markets in which suppliers and demanders of short-term securities (i.e., maturity of one year and less) interact and (2) **capital markets** in which suppliers and demanders of long-term securities interact. Mortgages fall in the domain of the capital markets. More or less money flows from investors to fund mortgages in the capital markets depending on whether the supply and demand conditions favor mortgages relative to other security investment opportunities, such as government securities and corporate bonds.

THE FOUR QUADRANTS OF REAL ESTATE FINANCE

Money for real estate investment comes from four sources in the capital markets—two equity sources and two debt, or mortgage, sources. As shown in Exhibit 15–3, the capital flow matrix includes the following quadrants:

1. Private equity—money invested directly in properties by those who take ownership of the properties (e.g., individuals and pension funds).
2. Private debt—mortgage money provided by financial intermediaries (e.g., banks and insurance companies) that collect money from individual depositors and others for direct property lending.
3. Public equity—money invested in shares issued and traded in securities markets of firms that take ownership of properties (e.g., equity REITs and real estate corporations).
4. Public debt—money invested in shares issued and traded in securities markets of pools of mortgage loans (e.g., mortgage-backed securities and mortgage REITs).

Dramatic change occurred within each of the two mortgage quadrants during the past decade, especially in the creation of income-property mortgages. Subsequent chapters in the Mortgage Finance Perspective provide substantial detail and trace developments in both quadrants.

E X H I B I T   1 5 - 4

MORTGAGE RATES VERSUS T-BOND RATES

SOURCE: See footnote no. 8, Goebel and Ma (1993)

INTEGRATION OF CAPITAL AND MORTGAGE MARKETS

Are mortgage markets really a part of the capital markets? Because mortgages create liens on specific assets traded in a separate market (i.e., the property market), changes in yield spreads may not result from capital market pricing, but instead, from external influences. Recent studies however show that residential mortgage and the capital markets became well integrated during the late 1980s.[8] As shown in Exhibit 15–4, mortgage rates and Treasury bonds began following a nearly identical pattern during the late 1980s with about a 100 basis point yield spread—the difference due largely to prepayment risk.

MORTGAGE BORROWER AND LENDER RELATIONSHIPS

The top part of Exhibit 15–1 (showing the primary mortgage market) presented earlier in this chapter illustrates one of the many types of contractual relationships between lenders and borrowers in the primary mortgage market. This section builds on this simple mortgage contract concept by extending the scope of borrower and lender relationships through discussions of junior mortgages, third-parties replacement of borrowers in the mortgage contracts, contractual relationships that fall outside the limits of traditional mortgage contracts, and financing relationships commonly formed in single-family and income-property transactions.

---

[8]See, for example, Paul R. Gobel and Christopher K. Ma, "The Integration of Mortgage Markets and Capital Markets," *Journal of the American Real Estate and Urban Economic Association,* 21 (1993), pp. 511–538.

EXTENSIONS OF THE SIMPLE MORTGAGE CONTRACT

Suppose the mortgage contract relationship has the following characteristics:

1. The lender is a bank.
2. The borrower has not pledged the property to any other lender as security for another loan and plans to own the property until the loan repayment. Thus, the contract constitutes a **first mortgage**. This means that in the case of default by the borrower, the bank stands first in line to collect the unpaid balance at the foreclosure sale.[9]
3. The transaction occurs in a lien-theory state.
4. The mortgage contract is silent on what happens to the borrower-lender relationship if the property sells.[10]

To extend the concept of this simple mortgage contract, we simply vary one or more of the assumptions.

Junior mortgage. Suppose the borrower contacts a mortgage company to request an additional loan and pledges the same real property as security for this new loan. The mortgage company considers the market value of the property and the remaining balance of the first mortgage loan. Because the market value exceeds the balance of the first mortgage loan by a significant amount, and the borrower maintains a good credit standing, the mortgage company grants the loan.

The borrower and the mortgage company created a **junior mortgage**—in this case, a second mortgage—by their action. Consequently, in the case of default, the mortgage company stands in line behind the bank for repayment from the proceeds of a foreclosure sale, as discussed later in this chapter. Junior mortgages therefore have greater risk of losses due to default than first mortgages on the same property and thus include more restrictive and less attractive terms, including shorter terms to maturity and higher interest rates. The last section of this chapter contains some additional implications of junior mortgages in foreclosure actions.

State mortgage laws provide no restrictions on the number of junior mortgages on a particular property. As many junior mortgages can exist on a property as lenders will lend money.

Wrap-around mortgage. Suppose a new person enters the scene, the buyer, who offers to buy the property from the borrower but does not have enough cash to make a down payment. The borrower agrees to provide financing to the buyer, and, because the mortgage loan with the bank has such an attractive interest rate, the borrower decides to

---

[9]This assumes that no superior liens exist, such as property tax liens and mechanic's liens (i.e., those placed on the property by suppliers of labor or materials).

[10]Usually, these contracts contain specific language about how relationships are affected by property sales. Most residential mortgages contain a clause, discussed later in this chapter, that makes the loan due in the event of property sale. Income-property mortgages also contain language about what happens to the mortgage relationship when the property sells.

keep the original loan. The mortgage contract between the borrower and the buyer is a **wrap-around mortgage.**

Under the wrap-around mortgage contract, the buyer obtains all property rights by making one large payment per month to the borrower for the two loans—the original loan from the bank and the additional financing for the buyer's down payment, now *wrapped* together. The borrower keeps part of this payment and sends the usual payment to the bank each month. In the event of default and foreclosure, the borrower retains a second-mortgage position behind the bank, whose position remains unaffected by the wrap-around loan.

Wrap-around financing occurs regularly in commercial property transactions, but less often in residential property deals because of the presence of due-on-sale clauses discussed later in this chapter. It takes many forms.[11] Regardless of its form, creative financing contracts of this type need careful crafting to protect the buyer from foreclosure loss if the original borrower defaults on the first mortgage loan. The buyer, for example, should be allowed to make payments to the first mortgage lender for the defaulting borrower and continue to credit those payments to the outstanding balance of the wrap-around loan.

Assumption of an existing mortgage. Suppose the buyer does not require financing from the borrower, but instead plans to take over payments on the loan with the bank. Whether the buyer may replace the borrower in the original mortgage contract without the permission of the bank depends on whether the contract permits this type of adjustment.

The buyer may enter the contract either **subject to the mortgage** or by **assumption of the mortgage** (more common). If the buyer takes title to the property subject to the existing mortgage, the buyer does not take on personal liability for repayment of the mortgage in case of default. That is, the promissory note between the borrower and the bank remains in effect, and the borrower remains personally liable in the event of a default by the buyer. The mortgage part of this contract, however, is redrafted—reflecting the change in the name of the borrower—so that the buyer's property becomes security for the loan. Potentially, both names may appear on the note, that is, the borrower and the buyer become co-liable.

If the buyer takes title to the property by assuming the existing mortgage, both the mortgage and the note change, and only the buyer becomes personally liable in case of default provided that the seller is relieved of liability by the lender. Sometimes the seller also retains liability.

Purchase money mortgage. Suppose the buyer obtains first mortgage financing from the borrower, and thus the bank never became a party to the agreement. The owner, therefore, takes the role of both the seller of the property and the first mortgage lender to the buyer. Such an agreement is known as a **purchase money mortgage**[12].

---

[11]In deed-of-trust states this arrangement is referred to as an *all-inclusive deed of trust.*

[12]Purchase money mortgages are also discussed in Chapter 18.

E X H I B I T   1 5 - 5

PURCHASE MONEY MORTGAGE AND LAND CONTRACT

Panel A: Purchase Money Mortgage
(with separate contract for sale)

Panel B: Land Contract
(financing contract and contract for sale are merged)

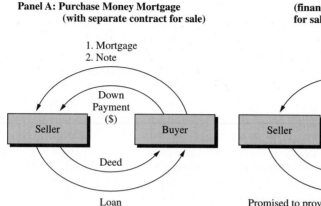

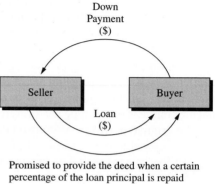

A standard purchase money mortgage arrangement appears in Exhibit 15–5, Panel A. The seller receives a down payment and gives the deed to the property under the contract for sale.[13] The seller also receives the mortgage documents for providing a loan to the buyer. The seller, therefore, acquires a first mortgage and follows normal legal procedures of foreclosure in case of default.

Land contract. Assume the borrower, now the seller of the property, provides *all* financing needed by the buyer (the down payment equals zero or a very small amount). As shown in Exhibit 15–5, Panel B, the seller receives a small down payment and gives a loan to the buyer for the balance of the purchase price. However, *no* mortgage is created as in the case of a purchase money mortgage. In these **land contracts**, sellers retain titles to properties, usually until some percentage (e.g., 50 percent) of the loan becomes repaid.[14] Should the buyer miss a payment, the seller has the right to reclaim possession of the property almost immediately.

Land contracts have a long history as instruments for transferring rights to real estate, especially in rural areas where the parties know one another and deals occur with relatively small down payments (e.g., the sale of farmland). Land contracts appear only occasionally in transactions involving urban real estate.

---

[13]Refer to Chapters 22 and 24 for discussions of deeds and contracts for sale, respectively.

[14]Once this point is reached, land contracts often convert to purchase money mortgages.

SINGLE-FAMILY RESIDENTIAL MORTGAGES

Mortgage lender and borrower relationships differ between single-family residential and income properties for several reasons. Most important, single-family residential mortgages exhibit a highly standardized form so that they may freely trade in a secondary mortgage market. The secondary mortgage market encourages standardization of the mortgage contract to make mortgages more easily tradable. Income-property mortgage contracts, by contrast, remain less standardized despite advancements in securitization of these mortgages. The environment for creation of income-property mortgages exhibits more creativity and sophistication than the primary market for single-family mortgages, leading to a wider array of contract clauses. Finally, the security for repayment of income-property mortgages follows from the ability of the property to generate income from commercial usage versus household income.

Existing properties. New property developments have different mortgage financing arrangements than existing, operating properties because of the greater risk of new developments. Because new developments do not have operating histories, they become more risky to finance.[15] Existing properties have track records, and their collateral values are more easily assessed.

Contracts between borrowers and lenders for financing existing single-family homes fall into three general categories (details about the financial characteristics of these mortgages appear in Chapters 16 and 17):

1. Conventional mortgages—the conventional mortgage loan arrangement represents a straightforward loan agreement in which the borrower gives a note and a mortgage in exchange for the loan from an institutional lender without direct government support.[16]
2. Government-supported mortgages—government acts as a third party in the creation of some residential mortgage contracts. Government sells insurance policies against borrower default, as in the case of Federal Housing Administration (FHA) loan programs. The government guarantees loans against default for certain borrowers, as in the case of Veteran Administration (VA) loan programs. And, in some instances, government supplies subsidies to help borrowers buy their own homes, as in the case of loans subsidized through state housing finance authorities.
3. Owner (seller) financing—owner financing traditionally represents a small portion of residential financing in the United States. However, during

---

[15]The risk lies in the possibility the developer (borrower) will fail some time before the completion of the project, and the lender will be forced to take over. The value at completion may not exceed the cost to construct. Lenders are not in business to complete partially developed real estate.

[16]On average, conventional loans comprise about 90 percent of all residential loans from institutional lenders, while government- supported loans make up much of the balance during periods of low and moderate interest rates.

E X H I B I T   1 5 - 6

FINANCING RELATIONSHIPS FOR CONSTRUCTION ON SINGLE-FAMILY HOMES

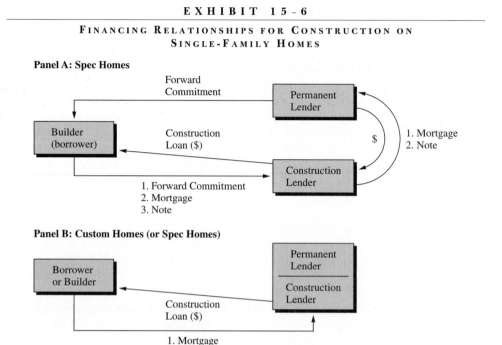

Panel A: Spec Homes

Forward Commitment

Permanent Lender

Builder (borrower)

Construction Loan ($)

$

1. Mortgage
2. Note

Construction Lender

1. Forward Commitment
2. Mortgage
3. Note

Panel B: Custom Homes (or Spec Homes)

Borrower or Builder

Permanent Lender

Construction Lender

Construction Loan ($)

1. Mortgage
2. Note

periods of extremely high interest rates, contracts between buyers and sellers can account for a large percentage of all residential loan contracts. These contracts are mostly purchase money mortgages and mortgage assumptions with second mortgages.

Construction financing. Because of the inherent risks in construction and development financing, builders of single-family homes often enter into contractual relationships for two loans, sometimes with two different lenders. The **construction loan** finances the development of the site and construction of the improvements during the construction period. The **permanent loan** extends for a long term as a normal first mortgage loan for existing property.

Exhibit 15–6 shows the relationships between builders of single-family residential properties and lenders for two types of residential construction activities. The first, in which some builders specialize, involves the construction of *spec* (speculation) homes. Builders in this business develop residential lots, build houses (usually of similar style, size, and quality), and sell the houses on the open market. The second business involves custom homes. Builders in this market work for the owners of lots to build houses according to the owners' specifications. Some builders perform a hybrid of spec and custom home building by selling lots on the open market, but with a condition of the sale that they receive contracts to build custom homes.

Panel A of Exhibit 15–6 presents a common financing arrangement for the construction of spec homes. This arrangement involves an agreement among the builder, the construction lender, and the permanent lender in which the permanent lender agrees to pay off the construction lender upon completion of the project.

Initially, builders prepare plans and studies for presentation to permanent lenders, such as banks and savings and loan associations. If the permanent lender likes the deal, the lender issues a **forward** (or "takeout") **commitment** to the builder. Builders face no obligation to *take down* (use) the funds committed, although they usually do or forfeit the commitment fee (e.g., 1 percent of the loan amount).

Builders often need forward commitments to secure construction financing from construction lenders, such as commercial banks, that issue **covered construction loans**. Sometimes construction lenders grant loans without permanent loan commitments called **open-end**, or uncovered **construction loans**. Forward commitments constitute promises by permanent lenders to pay off construction loans upon completion of construction and, therefore, function as security for construction loans. Construction lenders also have the additional security provided by the mortgage on the land, any notes signed by borrowers, and possibly letters of credit obtained by borrowers from banks. Once construction ends, permanent lenders pay off construction lenders, mortgage documentation transfers to permanent lenders, and builders begin paying back permanent lenders, often as a result of the sale of houses.

For custom homes and certain spec home ventures, two loans result, often from only one lender. This relationship appears in Exhibit 15–6, Panel B. When construction ends, construction loans convert to permanent loans, and owners make payments to lenders as in any mortgage loan arrangement.

Short-term construction loans require considerable monitoring and carry substantial risk. Long-term permanent loans carry less risk. The comparative risks of construction and permanent lending help explain the dual-loan structure even when only one lender is involved.

INCOME-PROPERTY MORTGAGES

As with contracts for single-family residential financing, mortgages differ for existing income-property transactions relative to new development and construction.

Existing properties. The contractual relationships between borrowers and lenders for the financing of existing income properties often become highly complex, but usually they begin with the simple mortgage contract. Perhaps the most common extensions in mortgage contracts for existing income properties involve the introduction of clauses that alter the stream of payments from the borrower to the lender. Features such as partial amortization, income and equity participation, and various prepayment penalty clauses can be included in income-property mortgage contracts. We discuss these features in Chapter 18.

Construction financing.   The financing model for construction of income properties resembles that for spec home construction. The forward commitments in these financing arrangements contain specific targets for the timing of construction completion, for the timing of taking down the money, and for rental achievement. For example, builders sometimes must have 70 percent of the space rented by the month following the completion of construction for the permanent lender to lend the full value of the forward commitment. If only 60 percent of the space becomes rented, permanent lenders will pay out only, say, 80 percent of the construction loan. This means builders need short-term financing to pay off the balance of the construction loan. Most lenders pay out a base amount of the forward commitment, the *floor,* upon the completion of construction, but the full amount, the *ceiling*, flows with rental achievement.

CLAUSES FOUND IN MORTGAGE DOCUMENTS

The term *mortgage documentation* refers to the legal instruments that constitute the mortgage contract. In the typical single-family residential mortgage contract, the mortgage documentation contains the promissory note and the mortgage. For income-property mortgages, the documentation may include the forward commitment letter, the lender and developer partnership agreement, and a letter of credit, in addition to the note and mortgage(s). This section begins by presenting the requirements for valid and enforceable mortgage contracts and some standard clauses found in most mortgage and related documents. Subsequently, we present the clauses in the note and mortgage of a standard single-family residential loan agreement, and finally, several of the clauses that often appear in construction loan mortgages and forward commitments.

REQUIREMENTS OF A VALID AND ENFORCEABLE MORTGAGE

As for other contracts, valid mortgage contracts must have an offer and acceptance, competent parties, legal objectives, and consideration. Also, as in valid and enforceable real estate contracts for sale discussed in Chapter 24, mortgage contracts should be in writing, and the property being mortgaged should be properly described. Beyond these requirements, valid and enforceable mortgage contracts should

1. Identify the set of property rights (e.g., leasehold or fee simple) being mortgaged.
2. Include words of conveyance (in title theory states) (e.g., "Grantor hereby grants, bargains, sells, and conveys to Grantee . . .").
3. Include the signature of the mortgagor (and sometimes the mortgagor's spouse).

4. Be delivered to the mortgagee and recorded.
5. Contain a reference to the note, because a mortgage is not valid unless an actual debt exists.

The final requirement highlights an important point about the relationship between the mortgage and the note. Because mortgages usually become recorded in the public record (normally in the county clerk's office following the closing), whereas notes, as personal pledges to repay debts, remain unrecorded, the financial terms of the loan appear in notes but not in mortgages. This protects the privacy of the contract. Thus, notes usually evidence the debt and contain the essential details for repayment of the debt, such as interest rate and loan maturity.

COMMON MORTGAGE CLAUSES

Although it is difficult to describe all of the clauses found in mortgage contracts, the discussions that follow address some of the more common provisions.

Acceleration clause. As a result of the **acceleration clause,** which usually appears in the note, the holder of the note obtains the right to all remaining payments on the loan should the borrower default. This clause avoids the technicality of having to bring a separate lawsuit for each remaining payment when borrowers default on the payment currently due. Thus, the payments become accelerated for the purpose of bringing foreclosure action.

Prepayment and late payment clause. The note may contain a **prepayment clause** that imposes a penalty on borrowers for making early payments on the amount borrowed. Lenders include these clauses to avoid having to reinvest funds unexpectedly. How strictly lenders enforce prepayment penalties depends on the prevailing interest rate and whether it stands above or below the contract rate. Prepayment penalties rarely appear in residential mortgage contracts. They frequently become an important point of negotiation in income property contracts. **Yield maintenance**, which sometimes involve complex financial calculations, plays an important role in determining prepayment penalties in income property mortgages. Some income property mortgages include lock-out provisions that prevent borrowers from prepaying during a set period. Chapter 18 contains additional information about yield maintenance and lock out. Lenders also may include late payment penalty clauses to discourage borrowers from paying after the due date each month (e.g., a $20 penalty may be assessed if payment is received after the 15th day of the month).

Due-on-sale clause. Found in most residential and many commercial mortgages today, this is an acceleration clause that is enforceable upon the sale of the property. Thus, if the property transfers to a new owner, the new owner may *not* automatically assume the mortgage under the prevailing terms. These clauses protect lenders against properties being transferred to persons of higher security risk. More recently, due-on-sale clauses have been used to prevent low-interest-rate loans from being assumed at lower than current interest rates.[17]

Insurance clause.   Lenders usually insist that borrowers carry hazard and fire insurance on the mortgaged property to protect their investments. Frequently, lenders insist on collecting the premium for this insurance along with the payment of interest and principal—a practice known as **escrowing**.[18] Residential mortgage lenders also escrow property tax payments.[19] Escrowing protects lenders against borrowers neglecting to make such payments. These clauses appear in the mortgage.

Interest escalation and adjustment clause.   The note in some mortgage contracts contains a clause that allows lenders to make changes in the interest rate. An escalation clause, sometimes found in land development and construction loans, gives lenders the right to increase, but not decrease, the rate of interest (e.g., changes are tied to upward movements in the prime rate). Interest adjustment clauses, common in residential mortgages, allow the adjustments in the interest rate strictly in accordance with the movement, up or down, of some interest-rate index.

RESIDENTIAL MORTGAGE DOCUMENTS

The note used in standard residential contracts is a fairly short and simple instrument. The standard mortgage note contains the following information:

1. The date the note is executed.
2. The name of the mortgagor and mortgagee.
3. An acceleration clause.
4. The terms of the debt including the interest rate, manner of payment (i.e., type of amortization), frequency of payment (usually monthly), and maturity date.
5. Prepayment penalty.
6. Escalation clause on delinquent payments.

The standard residential mortgage form extends somewhat longer than the note. The clauses in the mortgage fall into two categories: *uniform* clauses, or covenants that

---

[17]A public debate over the enforceability of due-on-sale clauses by lenders was settled in favor of lenders in a 1982 U.S. Supreme Court case and as the result of passage of the Garn-St Germain Depository Act of 1982.

[18]An escrow account is set up by the lender to make the insurance payments to the insurance company when they are due.

[19]Thus, the term *PITI* describes the total mortgage payment (e.g., monthly) to the lender, where P is principal, I is interest, T is taxes(1/12 of annual amount), and the second I is insurance (1/12 of annual amount).

apply in all states, and *nonuniform* clauses that conform to the laws of a particular state.[20] The uniform covenants in these documents require the following:

1. Borrowers will pay principal and interest in accordance with the note.
2. Lenders will escrow insurance and taxes.
3. Payments will be applied first to taxes and insurance, then to interest, and then to principal.
4. Borrowers will give lenders notice of all liens affecting the property.
5. Borrowers will maintain hazard insurance.
6. Borrowers will maintain the property in good repair.
7. If borrowers break any covenants, lenders can take necessary action to protect their security interest in the property.
8. Lenders may enter the property for inspection by giving reasonable notice.
9. In the event of condemnation of the property, lenders are to be paid first.
10. Any changes in the original terms of the contract do not release borrowers from the contract in general.
11. Any lack of action by lenders should not be considered abandonment of the contract or debt.
12. All remedies in the contract can be exercised by lenders concurrently or successively.
13. Successors to lenders (new holders of the mortgage) are bound by the contract with the borrower.
14. If any part of the mortgage contract conflicts with state law, the remainder of the contract remains in effect.
15. Borrowers shall be given a copy of the mortgage.
16. A due-on-sale clause will be included.

Because nonuniform covenants in mortgages comply with state law, readers should examine a copy of the standard mortgage or trust-deed document used in their state. Some typical nonuniform mortgage covenants include these:

1. Specific acceleration remedies may be available to lenders on borrower default. These include power-of-sale provisions giving lenders or trustees (in trust-deed states) certain powers to expedite foreclosure sales.
2. Assignment of rents to lenders may be an additional security for loans (i.e., a lender may collect any rents from the property on default).
3. Advances of additional funds to borrowers may be made under the same contract.
4. Borrowers are released from contracts on satisfying the terms of the contracts.
5. Borrower waives all dower, homestead, and redemption (statutory) rights under the contract.

---

[20]The term *covenant* means promise.

The standard trust deed for residential lending resembles the standard mortgage both in appearance and in its covenants. Some notable differences between trust deeds and mortgages include the following:

1. Three parties are named in the contract instead of two (a trustee also is named).
2. Lenders are given nonpossessionary security interests, whereas trustees are given possessionary security interest.
3. Trustees are given the power of sale.
4. Provisions are made for an alternate trustee.

IMPORTANT CLAUSES IN VARIOUS INCOME-PROPERTY MORTGAGES

Mortgage contracts for most income-property lending do not follow a standardized form and can get quite complex. As the secondary market for income properties matures, increased standardization will occur for permanent loans. The provisions of construction and development loans will remain fairly unique to each contract.

Construction loans and real estate development loans have many similarities because both provide borrowers with funds for improvements on land. From the viewpoint of lenders, the flow of funds to borrowers for construction and development should be "slow out and fast in." Under the advance clause in these contracts, borrowers draw funds from lenders when needed to complete the next phase of the project ("slow out"). Usually, borrowers must show reasonable progress toward completing prior phases to obtain *draws*. As discussed above, repayment of construction historically has occurred at the end of construction with permanent loan funds, either from the same lender or another lender ("fast in"). Repayment of land development loans may occur in a lump sum with completion of development or with the sale of individual lots.[21]

ADJUSTMENTS IN BORROWER AND LENDER RELATIONSHIPS

During long-term relationships between borrowers and lenders in mortgage contracts, events often occur that require adjustments to, and termination of, mortgage contracts before their maturity dates. When selling mortgaged property, for example, borrowers may repay the outstanding loan balances early. In other situations, borrowers may default on payments, forcing lenders to take legal action to recover the remaining balances of loans. A third party, as another example, may assume the loan in conjunction with a sale

---

[21]Also see Chapter 18.

of the property. Borrowers and lenders sometimes renegotiate the terms of original mortgage contracts, and lenders often sell mortgages to investors. This section discusses the reasons for these adjustments and termination of mortgage contracts and examines some of their consequences.

SATISFACTORY PAYMENT IN FULL

Full repayment terminates mortgage contracts. Lenders return notes to borrowers marked "paid" and execute a legal document called a *release* that eliminates the mortgage lien. Recording of the release occurs so the public record shows the removal of the lien. Even if full repayment of the mortgage debt occurs before the maturity date (i.e., prepayment), the borrower may fully satisfy the terms of mortgages, although sometimes with prepayment penalties.

DEFAULT AND FORECLOSURE

Exhibit 15–7 presents the sequence of events surrounding a typical mortgage default and property foreclosure. A mortgage goes into default when the borrower fails to meet some obligation in the mortgage contract. Mortgage defaults usually result from failure to make timely payments of principal and interest but also can result from nonpayment of property taxes and insurance premiums. A technical default, although rare, happens when, for example, the borrower fails to adequately maintain the property. **Delinquency**, resulting from failure to make timely payments, is determined by dates specified in mortgage contracts. For example, monthly payments due on the first day of the month become delinquent on the 15th day of the month. **Default** is defined as prolonged delinquency.

Courts in all states establish a legal right of delinquent borrowers called the **equity right of redemption**. This important right gives borrowers a certain period to make up overdue payments (i.e., to redeem their equity in the property). While the courts set the exact period, it typically lasts two to three months.

Lenders exercise their right to force the sale of properties to gain repayment of mortgage debts by filing foreclosure suits against the properties of delinquent borrowers in states that follow **judicial foreclosure** rules or by publishing public notice in newspapers of their intent to foreclose in states that follow **nonjudicial foreclosure** rules. Generally, states that follow judicial foreclosure procedures are lien-theory states and states that follow non judicial foreclosure procedures are title-theory and deed-of-trust states. In these states, mortgage instruments contain **power-of-sale clauses** that allow foreclosure without going to court.

A foreclosure suit constitutes a motion before the court to end the borrower's equity right of redemption and sets the date for the sale of the property. The courts often seek alternative solutions by attempting to find ways to reestablish good relations between borrowers and lenders. However, without the possibility of a solution, the time, date, and

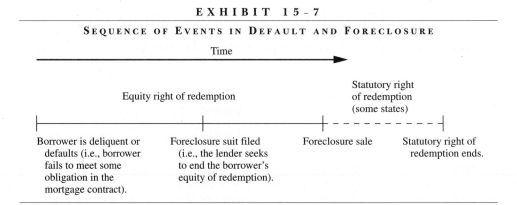

E X H I B I T   1 5 - 7

SEQUENCE OF EVENTS IN DEFAULT AND FORECLOSURE

location of the sale are set (e.g., two weeks from the current date, 12 noon at the county courthouse).[22]

Public foreclosure sales offer properties to the highest bidders. Frequently, the first mortgage lender becomes the highest bidder because the lender needs to protect its interest in the property and needs to come up with the least cash to buy the property. For example, assume a lender lends $40,000 to a borrower for a property purchased for $50,000. Later, the value of the property declines to $39,000 and the borrower defaults and leaves a remaining balance of $39,700 for the property. Any bidder other than the lender would have to pay more than that amount *in cash* to outbid the first-mortgage lender.

In some states, borrowers' rights in a mortgage contract do not end with foreclosure sales. The law in some states sets a period of **statutory redemption** (e.g., one year) that gives borrowers the right to regain full ownership in foreclosed property simply by buying properties back from purchasers for the price paid at foreclosure sales (plus interest). Purchasers of foreclosed property obtain certificates of sale immediately and sheriff's deeds at the end of the period of statutory redemption.

Sometimes borrowers and lenders agree that the time-consuming, expensive, and potentially damaging process of foreclosure does not serve the best interests of both parties. To cure the default in these instances, borrowers issue **deeds-in-lieu of foreclosure**, which means they turn the keys to properties over to lenders and forfeit any claims they have to the properties.

---

[22]Lenders have two incentives to have the foreclosure proceeding completed within the shortest possible time. First, they want to prevent borrowers from letting properties deteriorate. Second, they want to minimize the costs of foreclosure, in terms of both legal fees and lost interest.

REAL ESTATE FOCUS 15-3

Solving the Deferred Maintenance Problem in the Mortgage Contract

Why do mortgage lenders worry about the maintenance of the borrower's property? In most instances lenders have more money invested than borrowers. If the borrower defaults and the property was not well maintained, which often happens in conjunction with default, then the lender takes over a renovation problem.

Mortgage contracts now include stricter clauses than they did in the 1980s to protect against this problem because lenders took over many properties having deferred maintenance in recent years. Lenders have always insisted on receivership and rental assignment clauses to allow a third party to run the mortgaged property when the lender successfully obtains a technical default decree from a court. By the time a technical default becomes recognized, the property probably already has substantial deferred maintenance.

Mortgage contracts now contain clauses that require borrowers to establish accounts that receive deposits each period from the property cash flow to pay for routine maintenance. These accounts may be part of or in addition to capital reserve accounts established for major expenditures on properties.

ASSUMPTION AND ''SUBJECT TO'' TRANSACTIONS

Situations may arise in the lives of mortgages in which sales of properties do not mark the end of the original mortgage contracts. A mortgage contract, for example, may not include a due-on-sale clause, as with FHA and VA loans, so the buyer of the property can "step into" the original mortgage contract in place of the seller and original borrower. These mortgage assumptions and "subject to" transactions were discussed earlier in this chapter.

RECASTING THE MORTGAGE

The initial terms of the relationship between mortgage lenders and borrowers sometimes change over time. For example, the two parties may agree to recast the mortgage instead of a foreclosure action. In such cases, lenders agree to add delinquent interest and other costs to the principal owed if borrowers agree to pay over longer periods of time or at slightly higher rates of interest. Recasting can occur without changing public records.

SALE OF THE MORTGAGE

Mortgages, especially single-family residential mortgages, trade as securities in active secondary markets. This means mortgage lenders sell mortgage documents (and thus the rights to receive future payments) to third parties. Because the original lenders often continue to service mortgages by collecting payments, borrowers may not know that their mortgages have been sold.[23] Thus, from the perspectives of most borrowers, mortgage sales have no effect on mortgage contract relationships.

SUMMARY

Because the purchase of real estate requires substantial funds, buyers enter into mortgage contracts with lenders to obtain some portion of the money needed. The basic mortgage contract consists of two legal documents: the note, which contains the financial terms of the contract and the personal pledge of borrowers to repay the debt, and the mortgage, which gives lenders legal claims against properties. Depending on state law, the security interest takes two different forms: specific liens, title to properties to lenders with restricted rights, or titles with restricted rights that become vested in trustees.

Extension and modification of the simple mortgage contract occurs in a variety of ways. Such arrangements include junior mortgages, wrap-around mortgages, mortgage assumptions, purchase money mortgages, and land contracts. These and other contract structures serve as the basis for many of the financing contracts found today in the single-family and income-property markets. Mortgage agreements differ not only by property type but also by whether the properties exist and operate now or will be developed with the mortgage money.

Clauses constitute the building blocks of the mortgage contracts. These clauses take a fairly universal and straightforward form in single-family mortgage contracts, but they can become quite diverse and complex in income-property contracts.

The relationship between mortgage lenders and borrowers often changes or ends as the result of events that occur during the lives of mortgage contracts. The default and foreclosure process represents the most legally, financially, and emotionally troublesome of these events. This process, culminating in sales of properties, usually results in financial losses for both parties.

KEY TERMS

Acceleration clause 457
Assumption of the mortgage 451
Capital markets 448
Conduits 444
Construction loan 454
Covered construction loan 455
Deeds-in-lieu of foreclosure 463
Deeds of trust 447
Default 461
Deficiency judgment 446
Delinquency 461
Equity 442
Equity of redemption 461
Escrowing 458

Financial intermediaries 443
First mortgage 450
Foreclosure 446
Forward commitment 455
Judicial foreclosure 461
Junior mortgage 450
Land contract 452
Lien theory 447
Mortgage 441
Mortgage assumption 000
Mortgage-backed securities 444
Nonjudicial foreclosure 461
Nonrecourse financing 446

Open-end construction loan 455
Permanent loan 454
Power-of-sale clause 447
Prepayment clause 457
Primary mortgage market 444
Promissory note 446
Purchase money mortgage 451
Recourse financing 446
Statutory redemption 462
Subject to the mortgage 451
Title theory 446
Wrap-around mortgage 451
Yield maintenance 458

---

[23]Lenders frequently sell the right to service mortgages—the servicing contract. The mortgage servicer receives a small fee from the interest payment.

TEST YOURSELF

Answer the following multiple choice questions:

1. In states in which trust deeds are used, the trustee can be a
   a. Bank (other than the lender).
   b. Savings and loan (other than the lender).
   c. Lawyer.
   d. Trust company.
   e. All of the above.

2. A mortgage loan between the buyer and seller of the property in which the buyer gets title to the property in exchange for a first mortgage is a(n)
   a. Wrap-around mortgage.
   b. Land contract.
   c. Adjustable rate mortgage.
   d. Purchase money mortgage.
   e. FHA mortgage.

3. To make sure that insurance and property taxes are paid on time, lenders include
   a. Income and equity participation features.
   b. Subordination clauses.
   c. Rental-achievement clauses.
   d. Yield-enhancement clauses.
   e. Escrow clauses.

4. When lenders sell mortgages to third parties,
   a. They must have the permission of the borrower.
   b. Borrowers frequently don't know the mortgage has been sold.
   c. The mortgage must be a first mortgage.
   d. The mortgage must be in foreclosure.
   e. They are breaking the law.

5. Due-on-sale clauses
   a. Are found in most conventional residential mortgages.
   b. Are not found in FHA and VA mortgages.
   c. Are fully enforceable by lenders.
   d. Apply when the property is sold but not when a default occurs.
   e. All of the above.

6. The clause in certain mortgage contracts that allows lenders or trustees to bring foreclosure action without formal court proceedings is the
   a. Subordination clause.
   b. Equity of redemption clause.
   c. Due-on-sale clause.
   d. Foreclosure clause.
   e. Power of sale clause.

7. The forward commitment
   a. Is given by the permanent lender.
   b. Is given by the construction lender.
   c. Is binding on the borrower as well as the lender.
   d. Cannot be taken down for six months in most cases.
   e. Is prohibited in some states.

8. When a mortgage is assumed
   a. The new borrower cannot take over the mortgage for 90 days.
   b. The new borrower signs a note with the lender, and the old note is no longer in effect.
   c. The old note remains in effect.
   d. The mortgage often does not contain a due on sale clause.
   e. The new borrower comes under rules of strict foreclosure in most states.

9. Mortgage money is raised in the capital market and not the money market because
   a. Real estate is highly capital intensive.
   b. Mortgages are typically long-term loans and the capital markets allocate funds for long-term investment.
   c. The money market cannot handle the demand for mortgage financing.
   d. The capital markets determine capitalization rates that help determine mortgage rates.
   e. All of these answers are correct.

10. Construction loans differ from permanent loans in that for construction loans
    a. The term is shorter.

b. The money goes out from the lender slowly and comes in fast.

c. Repayment is covered by a forward commitment.

d. The nature of the collateral makes them more risky.

e. All of these answers are correct.

PROBLEMS FOR THOUGHT AND SOLUTION

1. Why does the United States have the most highly developed mortgage markets in the world?

2. What conditions must be present for funds to flow in the capital markets to debt finance real estate via mortgages?

3. Why do due-on-sale clauses appear in most residential mortgages?

4. Explain how a wrap-around mortgage works.

5. Describe the foreclosure process and what happens to borrowers' ownership rights in a lien theory state that allows statutory redemption.

INTERNET EXERCISE

Perspectives Mortgage is considering the origination of mortgage loans in Arizona, a state in which it has not operated in the past. The president of Perspectives calls your firm, which frequently serves as consultants to Perspectives, for a quick answer to the question—is Arizona a judicial or non judicial foreclosure state? Go online and get this information in five minutes! (Hint: try **www.ired.com**)

CASE PROBLEMS

1. The Riskaruin Mortgage Company was purchased recently by Careless Insurance Company to originate mortgage loans. Riskaruin expects that many of the mortgage loans it originates will go into default. Thus, it wants to set up business in a state with foreclosure laws favorable to lenders. How would you advise them to proceed? What legal provisions should they be looking for?

2. Your friend, Al Waysright, says that when you buy a home after graduating from college, you should definitely assume the seller's mortgage if the rate is lower than the current market rate. Al plans to assume a mortgage when he buys a home. He sees no problems with this approach because his dad is rich and, therefore, the bank will certainly allow him to take over the seller's mortgage. How would you respond to this know-it-all friend?

ADDITIONAL READINGS

These books contain chapters with detailed discussions of mortgage laws and contracts:

McLoughlin, Daniel P. *Principles of Real Estate Law*. New York: McGraw-Hill, 1992.

Gibson, Frank, James Karp, and Elliot Klayman. *Real Estate Law*. Chicago: Dearborn Financial Publishing, 1992.

Brueggeman, William B., and Jeffrey D. Fisher. *Real Estate Finance and Investments*. Burr Ridge: Richard D. Irwin, 1997.

Dennis, Marshall W. *Residential Mortgage Lending*. Englewood Cliffs, N.J.: Prentice- Hall, 1992.

An excellent article about mortgage foreclosure laws among the states is:

Durham, James Geoffrey. "In Defense of Strict Foreclosure. A Legal and Economic Analysis of Mortgage Foreclosure." *South Carolina Law Review* (Spring 1985), pp. 461–510.

The following real estate periodicals regularly contain useful articles about mortgage creation:

Commercial Property News.
Mortgage and Real Estate Executives Report.
National Real Estate Investor.
Real Estate Finance.
Real Estate Finance Journal.
Real Estate Review.

16
C H A P T E R

RESIDENTIAL MORTGAGE TYPES AND BORROWER DECISIONS

INTRODUCTION
Primary Versus Secondary Mortgage
Market

CONVENTIONAL FIXED-PAYMENT MORTGAGE LOANS
Fixed-Payment, Fully Amortizing
Mortgages
Alternative Amortization Schedules

ADJUSTABLE RATE MORTGAGES
ARM Mechanics
Rate Caps and Other Options

PRIVATE MORTGAGE INSURANCE

OTHER MORTGAGE TYPES AND USES
Purchase Money Mortgages
Interest Rate Buydowns and Concessions
Package Mortgages
Reverse Annuity Mortgages
Graduated Payment Mortgages
Home Equity Loans

THE BORROWER'S MORTGAGE LOAN DECISIONS
Mortgage Choice
Loan Size
The Refinancing Decision
The Default Decision

SUMMARY

KEY TERMS

TEST YOURSELF

PROBLEMS FOR THOUGHT AND SOLUTION

INTERNET EXERCISE

CASE PROBLEMS

ADDITIONAL READINGS

After reading this chapter, students will be able to:

1. Distinguish between the primary mortgage market and the secondary mortgage market.

2. Explain several alternatives to a fully amortizing loan.

3. Explain the mechanics of adjustable rate mortgages including the calculation of revised monthly payments and the advantages and disadvantages of interest rate caps.

4. Discuss the role and importance of private mortgage insurance in the residential mortgage market.

5. Calculate the value of an interest rate buydown, given the normal monthly payments, the payments with the buydown, and the appropriate interest (discount) rate.

6. Calculate the effective borrowing cost of a mortgage, given the elements of the loan (maturity, amortization, contract interest rate, amount, up-front financing costs).

7. Quantify the benefits of refinancing an existing fixed-rate loan when mortgage interest rates decline.

INTRODUCTION

Because a home is the largest single purchase most households ever make, they usually do not have enough accumulated wealth to pay cash. Typically, they prefer to borrow most of the funds, rather than wait many years before saving the full amount. Therefore, a system of mortgage lending has developed in which people with excess funds lend them to people who need funds to buy houses. With mortgage credit available, households can purchase homes now and then pay for them over 10, 20, or 30 years, plus interest.

Although some people, such as wealthy families and older couples who have saved most of their lives, may have accumulated enough wealth to pay cash for a home, many still choose to borrow at least a portion of the purchase price. This is because the interest rates and terms of borrowing on home loans tend to be favorable relative to rates and terms on credit cards, car loans, and other consumer debt. In addition, households can then use the funds freed by the borrowing to invest in other assets and, they hope, earn a rate of return that is greater than the cost of the mortgage funds. As discussed in Chapter 3, such use of funds is referred to as *positive financial leverage.* Moreover, the use of borrowed funds allows households to better diversify their portfolio of investments. If home purchasers were required to pay all cash, many household portfolios would be even more overweighted in housing than they are currently. For these reasons—lack of funds, the possibility of positive financial leverage, and a better diversified portfolio—most home buyers borrow at least a portion of the needed funds.[1]

The first part of this chapter introduces the various types of residential loans commonly available to home owners in the residential mortgage market. In addition to selecting a mortgage type, home owners also must choose the number of up-front discount points to pay and their desired loan-to-value ratio (LTVR). After obtaining the mortgage funds, borrowers usually have the option to prepay the mortgage, as well as the option to default. These numerous borrower decisions are analyzed in the second part of the chapter.[2]

The many types of available residential loans can be thought of as the **mortgage menu**. What determines the items on a lender's mortgage menu? Similar to restaurant food and other consumer products, lenders in the highly competitive residential mortgage market offer only those mortgage products for which there is consumer demand and on which they can expect to earn a reasonable profit. Residential lenders across the United States have added hundreds of different products to their mortgage menus, especially during the last 20 years. The majority of these mortgage items have been dropped, either because borrowers did not "order" them or because lenders could not adequately profit by offering them. For example, U.S. housing economists have long argued that payments on residential mortgages should be tied (indexed) to inflation. However, despite the sound economic rational for indexed mortgages and the willingness of numerous lenders to originate them, they have never caught on and have been dropped from lenders' mortgage menus.

PRIMARY VERSUS SECONDARY MORTGAGE MARKET

The market for home mortgage loans can be divided functionally into the **primary mortgage market** and the **secondary mortgage market**. The primary market is the loan origination market, where borrowers and lenders negotiate mortgage terms. Numerous institutions supply money to borrowers in the primary mortgage market, including savings and loan associations, commercial banks, credit unions, and mortgage banking companies. Financial institutions fund their loan originations with deposits from savers, while mortgage banking companies typically borrow on a short-term basis from commercial banks to fund their home mortgage originations. These direct sources of home mortgage funds are discussed in detail in Chapter 17.

Mortgage originators can either hold the loans in their portfolios or sell them in the secondary mortgage market. The largest purchasers of residential mortgages in the secondary mortgage market are the **Federal National Mortgage Association**, "Fannie Mae," and the **Federal Home Loan Mortgage Corporation**, "Freddie Mac." These

---

[1] Although most home buyers make extensive use of mortgage debt to purchase a home, more than 50 percent of all owning households own their home free and clear. Because such a large percentage of households make no use of mortgage debt, the average loan-to-current-market value ratio in the United States is only about 33 percent. See David C. Ling and Gary A. McGill, "Measuring the Size and Distributional Effects of Homeowner Tax Preferences," *Journal of Housing Research 3,* no. 2 (1992), pp. 273–302.

[2] The commercial mortgage market is discussed in Chapter 18.

government sponsored enterprises (GSEs), also discussed in Chapter 17, were created by acts of Congress to promote an active secondary market for home mortgages by purchasing mortgages from local originators.

Originating lenders who wish to dispose of their mortgages also can use them as collateral for issuing mortgage backed securities (MBSs). Although MBSs are considered in detail in Chapter 19, we provide a brief description here because it helps clarify the operation of the primary mortgage market.

Residential MBSs are created by pooling a group of similar mortgages. The owner then uses the mortgage pool as collateral for the issuance of a new security—the MBS. For example, a mortgage banker assembles a $100 million pool of 8.5 percent, 30-year, fixed payment mortgages. The mortgage banker then sells an undivided interest, or participation, in the mortgage pool to hundreds of investors who are promised an 8 percent rate of interest on their invested capital. The issuer continues to service the underlying mortgages, collecting payments from borrowers and "passing through" (1) any principal repayments and (2) 8 percent interest on any outstanding principal that the issuer of the MBS has not returned to the investors. The difference between the 8.5 percent rate on the underlying mortgages and the 8.0 percent rate paid to investors is kept by the issuer. This "spread" must cover the issuer's issuance and servicing costs and provide a reasonable rate of return. When a mortgage is used as collateral for the issuance of an MBS, the underlying mortgage is said to be "securitized." Agencies and private companies that pool mortgages and sell MBSs are called **conduits**.

Fannie Mae, Freddie Mac, and other MBS issuers are frequent purchasers of home loans in the secondary market. Life insurance companies, pension funds, individual (retail) investors, mutual funds, and foreign investors are typical purchasers of MBSs. In addition, savings institutions and commercial banks are increasingly likely to sell the loans they originate to issuers of MBSs, while simultaneously purchasing MBSs in the secondary market.[3] The existence of a well-functioning secondary market makes the primary mortgage market more efficient. If mortgage originators are able to sell their mortgage investments quickly, either outright or by issuing MBSs, they obtain funds to originate more loans in the primary market.

CONVENTIONAL FIXED-PAYMENT MORTGAGE LOANS

Mortgage loans that do not enjoy government backing in the form of FHA insurance or a Veterans Administration (VA) guarantee (both discussed in Chapter 17) are termed **conventional mortgages**. They are the dominant type of loan originated by most financial institutions, accounting for approximately 85 percent of all single-family home mortgage loans, on average, during the 1985 through 1994 time period. Local financial institutions generally prefer to make conventional loans because they can more easily tailor the loans

---

[3]Reasons why financial institutions may prefer to hold mortgage-backed securities instead of whole loans are discussed in Chapter 17.

to fit the needs of the community and individual borrowers. Also, government-backed loans require more paperwork, are governed by more regulations, and have higher administrative costs.

A **conforming conventional loan** is one that meets the standards required for purchase in the secondary market by Fannie Mae or Freddie Mac. Both of these secondary market agencies are subject to government oversight, even though they are privately owned. Congress sets the maximum size of home mortgage loans that the GSEs are allowed to purchase from originating lenders in the secondary market, which Fannie Mae and Freddie Mac primarily use as collateral for the issuance of MBSs. To conform to the underwriting standards of the GSEs, the loan must not exceed a certain percentage of the property's value, monthly payments on the loan must not exceed a certain percentage of the borrower's income, and, as of January 1996, the loan must not exceed $207,000 on single-family homes.[4] Loans that do not satisfy one or more of these underwriting standards are termed **nonconforming conventional loans,** with nonconforming loans that exceed $207,000 called **jumbo loans.** Because conforming loans can be more readily bought and sold in the secondary mortgage market (i.e., they are more liquid), they carry a lower contract interest rate than otherwise comparable nonconforming loans. Over the last several years, this interest rate advantage has averaged approximately 0.40 percentage points. On a $90,000 loan, this translates into monthly payment savings of $26, assuming the contract interest rate on a conforming mortgage is 9 percent.

FIXED-PAYMENT, FULLY AMORTIZED MORTGAGES

Technically, conventional single-family mortgages can take any form negotiated between a borrower and a lender. Historically, however, the most common form has been a fixed-rate, level-payment, fully amortized mortgage. Fully amortizing mortgages are paid off completely by periodic (usually monthly) payments. At maturity, the loan balance is zero. The mechanics of these mortgages were discussed in Chapter 2, including the patterns of principal repayments and mortgage balances over time. A majority of single-family residential loans are of this type, as are many loans for income-producing properties. As the loan is amortized, the owner's equity interest grows, so long as the property value does not decline. When fully amortizing loans call for equal periodic payments they are known as **fixed-payment mortgages** (FPMs). Before adjustable rate mortgages were introduced, the dominance of FPMs in the home loan market was unchallenged. With adjustable rate mortgages (discussed later), monthly payments can change as interest rates vary, although the loans remain fully amortizing.

15-Year mortgages. The most common loan term on an FPM is 30 years. However, **15-year mortgages** continue to increase in popularity, and 40-year mortgages are available from some lenders. With a 15-year loan, the borrower pays substantially less interest over the life of the loan when compared to a 30-year loan. For example, consider a $90,000

---

[4]As of January 1996, limits on two-, three-, and four-family properties are $264,700, $320,050, and $397,800, respectively.

EXHIBIT 16-1

TOTAL INTEREST PAID ON 9 PERCENT FPM OF $90,000

	30-Year	15-Year
Monthly payment	$ 724.16	$ 912.84
Total payments (loan term × monthly payment)	260,698	164,311
Minus: Principal amortization	90,000	90,000
Equals: Total interest	$170,698	$74,311

FPM with an annual interest rate of 9 percent. With 30-year amortization, the monthly payment is $724.16; with 15-year amortization, the payment is $912.84. As calculated in Exhibit 16–1, total interest paid over the life of the 30-year and 15-year mortgages would be $170,698 and $74,311, respectively.

At first glance, the 15-year mortgage would seem to provide an interest savings—over a 30-year time period—equal to $96,387 ($170,698 − $74,311). The *present value* of this $96,387 in interest savings over the 30-year period equals $18,603. This calculation, however, ignores the higher payments required on the 15-year loan. Because the borrower's monthly payment is $188.68 higher with a 15-year mortgage, the borrower is saving (or consuming) $188.68 less each month. If the $188.68 in foregone savings could be invested in other assets that are expected to earn, say, a 9 percent return, then the future value of the foregone savings would equal $71,397.60 at the end of 15 years.[5] Thus, the extra payment of $188.68 would result in the borrower having $71,397.60 less wealth available at the end of 15-years. The present value of this foregone wealth accumulation is $18,602.60.[6]

Note that the present value of the forgone savings (due to the higher 15-year payments) is equal to the present value of the reduction in interest payments. Thus, in this example, there is no benefit (in terms of household wealth) to using the 15-year mortgage. Why is the calculated present value of the foregone savings *exactly* equal to the present value of the reduction in interest payments? Because the example assumes that the contract interest rate—the cost of debt—is equal to the interest rate that could be earned on the foregone savings—the opportunity cost of equity.

What then is the most important consideration when choosing between a 15-year and 30-year FPM? If borrowers feel that the mortgage interest rate is greater than the rate of return they could earn on their investments, and *if* the borrowers can afford the higher payment, then strong consideration should be given to the 15-year mortgage. However, even if borrowers can afford to make the higher monthly payment, they should probably choose the 30-year mortgage if they feel that their opportunity cost of equity is greater than the cost of debt.

The above example assumes the contract rate is the same on both the 15-year and 30-year FPM. However, the contract rate of 15-year FPMs is typically about one-half of a

---

[5]The calculator keystrokes are: N = 180, I = 9 percent/12, PV = 0, PMT = 188.68, and FV = ?.

[6]The calculator keystrokes are N = 180, I = 9 percent/12, PV = ?, PMT = 0, and FV = 71,397.60.

EXHIBIT 16-2

FREDDIE MAC'S SINGLE-FAMILY LOAN PURCHASES
(BY PRODUCT AND YEAR)

Loan Product	1993		1994		1995	
	Dollars in Billions	Percent of Total	Dollars in Billions	Percent of Total	Dollars in Billions	Percent of Total
30-year fixed-rate	$115.4	50	$ 70.6	57	$58.2	60
15-year fixed-rate	68.5	30	25.5	21	13.8	14
ARMs	21.2	9	17.3	14	21.0	22
Balloons (fixed-rate)	24.4	11	10.0	8	3.9	4
Total	$229.5	100	$123.4	100	$96.9	100

SOURCE: Freddie Mac

percent (50 basis points) lower than the rate on an otherwise comparable 30-year FPM. This interest rate differential increases the relative attractiveness of the 15-year mortgage.

It also is important to point out that the opportunity cost of equity and the cost of mortgage debt should be adjusted for risk. The *expected* rate of return on alternative investments, such as stocks, may exceed the mortgage rate, but this does not necessarily imply home owners should increase their use of mortgage debt in order to buy more stocks because their returns are more variable than the cost of fixed-rate mortgage debt. Therefore, the expected return on stocks must be greater than the cost of mortgage debt by an amount large enough to compensate for the risk differential. Put differently, if the alternative asset has less predictable cash flows than the mortgage, the expected return on the alternative asset must be adjusted downward before comparing it to the cost of the mortgage debt.

How popular are 15-year mortgages? Based on the mortgages Freddie Mac purchases in the secondary market, 30 percent of total originations were 15-year mortgages in 1993, 21 percent in 1994, and 14 percent in 1995 (see Exhibit 16–2). Among home owners who are refinancing (not shown), versus those using the mortgage to acquire the property, the 15-year mortgage has been at least as popular as the 30-year mortgage in the 1990s. For example, 43 percent of refinancing borrowers selected a 15-year mortgage in 1993, while 41 percent selected a 30-year mortgage.

ALTERNATIVE AMORTIZATION SCHEDULES

Numerous alternatives to a fully amortizing loan are available. For example, borrowers may choose to pay only interest over the life of the loan, and to then pay off the loan completely in one repayment of principal at maturity. Alternatively, they may partially amortize the loan and then pay a large lump-sum payment at maturity. In addition, borrowers may select, say, a 30-year fully amortizing loan, and then make additional payments to reduce principal more quickly than scheduled. These alternative patterns of amortization identify loans as **interest-only loans**, **partially amortized mortgages**, or **early payment mortgages**, respectively.

Interest-only (straight-term) mortgages. Interest-only mortgages are repaid in full with one payment on maturity of the loan. During the life of the loan, however, borrowers make interest payments periodically (e.g., monthly). For example, assume the borrower and lender agree to a $90,000, 30-year, interest-only loan at 9 percent. The monthly payment is $675.00 (0.09/12 × $90,000). If the loan were to be fully amortized over 30 years, the monthly payment would equal $724.16. The $49.16 difference is principal amortization. Unlike the amortizing mortgage, the loan balance on the interest-only loan would remain constant at $90,000.

Although such loans are used infrequently to finance single-family homes, they are used quite often in land transactions. Typically, developers purchase land with interest-only loans, expecting to be able to repay the loans after the development and sale of lots. During development, they pay only interest.

Partially amortizing mortgages. Partially amortizing mortgage loans require periodic payments of principal, as well as interest, but they are not paid off completely over the loan term. A balance remains on these loans at maturity that must be repaid in one relatively large lump sum. The remaining balance is called a balloon and is satisfied with a **balloon payment**. For example, assume the $90,000, 9 percent loan would be amortized over 30 years, but the loan term is 7 years. The monthly payment is, again, $724.16. However, the remaining mortgage balance at the end of year 7 would equal $84,276. The borrower at that time must either (1) negotiate a new $84,276 loan with the original lender at current rates, (2) negotiate a loan with a new lender and use the proceeds to pay off the original lender, or (3) sell the property and use the sale proceeds to pay off the original lender.

Partially amortized loans are not often used to finance home purchases, except in cases where the seller of the home is providing some or all of the mortgage financing (that is, in "seller-financed" deals). Seller financing occurs frequently during periods of high interest rates, when buyers are less able to obtain adequate and affordable financing from traditional lenders. The partial amortization lowers the borrower's payments, as compared with full amortization over the same period. For example, if the $90,000, 9 percent loan were fully amortized over the seven-year loan term, the monthly payment would increase from $724.16 to $1,448.02.

Early payment mortgages. An early payment mortgage is a regular mortgage on which the borrower is allowed, but *not* required, to repay ahead of schedule. For example, if a borrower makes each scheduled monthly payment of principal and interest, and then adds the next month's scheduled principal reduction, the effective term of the loan will be cut approximately in half, and therefore the borrower will save a large portion of the total interest cost.

Consider a 30-year 10 percent loan of $80,000 with monthly payments of $702.06. For the first month, the interest is $666.67 (0.10/12 × $80,000) and the *scheduled* principal repayment is $35.39; for the second month, interest is $666.37 and the scheduled principal repayment is $35.69; and for the third month, interest is $666.09 and principal repayment is $35.98. Assume the borrower pays the normal payment of $702.06 in the first month, plus the second month's principal repayment of $35.69 ($702.06 + 35.69 = 737.75). In the second month, the borrower pays the $702.06 plus the third month's principal repayment of $35.98 ($702.06 + $35.98 = $738.04). Because the principal repayments increase every month, the borrower will need to pay higher total amounts each month. However, by so doing, the mortgage will be paid off in approximately 15 years rather than 30 years.

It is important to remember that borrowers do not have the *right* to pay down the balance of the loan more quickly than what is called for in the promissory note unless an early repayment clause is included in the contract. Virtually all home mortgages contain this clause. Thus, most 15-year and 30-year mortgages can, effectively, be turned into early payment mortgages if the borrower so chooses.

Nevertheless, it may not be financially wise for a borrower to pay ahead on a loan. The primary decision criterion is the same one used to evaluate the desirability of a 15-year loan relative to a 30-year loan. If borrowers can invest the additional amounts (the next month's principal repayment) at a higher risk adjusted return than the 10 percent interest rate on the loan, they would be ahead financially to do so. Often, however, the relatively small amounts cannot be invested at a higher risk-adjusted return than the mortgage interest rate, and therefore, many home buyers are often well advised to pay off their mortgages faster than scheduled.

ADJUSTABLE RATE MORTGAGES

Fixed-payment mortgages serve lenders and borrowers well when mortgage interest rates are both relatively low and stable. However, during the late 1970s and early 1980s, inflation and interest rates on FPMs increased dramatically to average 14.4 percent from 1979 through 1982. Beginning in the mid-1970s, mortgage rates also became more volatile (that is, less predictable). This increase in the level and volatility of mortgage rates caused two major problems. First, the higher required monthly payments on an FPM made housing less affordable. Second, the increased volatility of mortgage rates made lenders nervous. Why? Recall that S&Ls and other depository institutions were in the business of making long-term FPMs using short-term deposits and savings. Suppose the average cost of their short-term deposit liabilities was 9 percent. If lenders were to originate FPMs at 11 percent, they could hope to earn a 2 percent spread on their mortgage investments. However, if the interest rate paid to depositors were to increase suddenly, say to 11 percent, the average cost of deposit liabilities would quickly increase to 11 percent. *New* mortgages would be made at higher rates, perhaps 13 percent. However, the 9 percent mortgages they previously made would remain outstanding, thereby reducing the average spread (profit) on their mortgage investments. When interest rates, both short term and long term, accelerated in the late 1970s and early 1980s, the average spread that many FPM lenders were earning on their fixed-rate mortgage investments actually became *negative*. This negative spread contributed significantly to the eventual failure of many S&Ls. Funding long-term FPMs with short-term deposits and savings creates a **maturity imbalance problem** for S&Ls because their assets (mortgages) are long term whereas their liabilities (savings

REAL ESTATE FOCUS 16-1

An ARM and a Leg?

Shirley Wynn of Miami wrote to Coral Gables Federal Savings and Loan to tell the bank that it made a mistake in computing the interest due on her mortgage, overcharging her $1,464 in the course of three years. The bank apologized and refunded the overpayment. Wynn was one of the lucky ones. According to a congressional review and a study by a former federal auditor, John Geddes, thousands of others across the nation with adjustable rate mortgages may have been overcharged. Basing his estimate on an examination of 7,000 loan accounts, Geddes says a third of the outstanding ARM loans have been miscalculated. Overpayments could total $8 billion.

The main problem seems to be errors by deficient computer programs and poorly trained employees. As many borrowers were charged too little as too much. Mortgage lenders say Geddes needs more data before drawing such sweeping conclusions, but his efforts have already brought change. Lenders are more carefully scrutinizing their procedures, federal examiners are auditing loan portfolios, and some consumers have filed class-action lawsuits.

SOURCE: "Mortgages: An ARM and a Leg?" *Time*, December 24, 1990.

---

deposits and CDs) are short term. To address the maturity imbalance problem and to avoid or reduce their exposure to the interest rate risk associated with making FPMs, many lenders began searching for alternatives to the FPM. The most popular alternative mortgage in the home loan market is the **adjustable rate mortgages** (ARM).

ARM MECHANICS

The interest rate on ARMs must be tied to a published index of interest rates that is beyond the control of the lender. Examples of such indexes are (1) the average cost of funds of S&Ls, (2) the national average mortgage rate for the purchase of existing homes, and (3) the monthly average on U.S. Treasury securities with maturities of one, two, three, or five years. At predetermined intervals, lenders must decrease interest rates on ARMs as the index declines, and they may increase them as the index rises. They also must give notice of interest rate changes to borrowers at least 30 days in advance, and they may not charge a prepayment penalty if the borrowers decide to pay off their loans.

Lenders may establish their own ARM plans within these regulations and guidelines. However, administrative costs, competition, and secondary market requirements limit most lenders' flexibility. Frequent adjustments are costly and may result in a loss of goodwill with borrowers if competitors limit the frequency and magnitude of adjustments. In fact, lenders may place interest rate caps on ARMs that limit the amount the interest rate can change at any one time or that limit the total interest rate increase over the life of the loan to a maximum number of percentage points (usually 5 or 6 percentage points). Secondary market purchasers of ARMs have limited the rate and payment adjustments for mortgages they will acquire. As Real Estate Focus 16–1 demonstrates, it is important for borrowers to know how the payments on their ARM loans are calculated.

E X H I B I T   1 6 - 3

MORTGAGE RATES AND ARM SHARE OF CONVENTIONAL ORIGINATIONS

	Average Rate— 30-Year Mortgages	Average Rate— 1-Year ARMs	30-Year Rate − 1-Year Rate	ARM Percent
1985	12.4%	10.0%	2.4%	51%
1986	10.2	8.4	1.8	30
1987	10.2	7.8	2.4	43
1988	10.3	7.9	2.4	58
1989	10.3	8.8	1.5	38
1990	10.1	8.4	1.8	28
1991	9.3	7.1	2.2	23
1992	8.4	5.6	2.8	20
1993	7.3	4.6	2.7	20
1994	8.4	5.3	3.0	39
1995	7.9	6.1	1.9	33

When the ARM market first began to develop in the early 1980s in response to high and volatile interest rates, lenders and borrowers experimented with numerous ARM designs. In fact, between 400 and 500 different types of ARM products were being offered in early 1984.[7] Over time, the terms of ARMs have become more uniform. Currently, the most popular is a one-year adjustable ARM based on 30-year amortization. The initial contract rate remains in effect for one year. Contract interest rates and payments are adjusted annually based on the index of one-year U.S. Treasury obligations on the payment adjustment date, *plus* a **margin** of 2 to 3 percentage points. The margin is determined by the lender, and is not subject to regulation. The margin remains fixed for the life of the loan. Thus, changes in the ARM interest rate result from movements in the yield on one-year Treasury securities (the index), not changes in the margin. One-year ARMs are typically available with and without interest rate caps that limit interest rate adjustments. Lenders are attracted to ARMs because they reduce their exposure to interest rate risk. Many borrowers choose ARMs because the initial rate is often lower than rates on FPMs.[8]

Exhibit 16–3 displays the ARM share of conventional originations from 1985 through 1995. Over this time period, the ARM share has varied from 20 to 51 percent, and it has been highly positively correlated with both the *level* of rates on 30-year FPMs and with *changes* in the difference between 30-year rates and ARM rates. The ARM share of the jumbo market is typically more than double that of the conforming market.

Example. Consider a $100,000 ARM with a 30-year amortization schedule. The adjustment interval is one year and the interest rate on the payment adjustment date will

---

[7]Jack M. Guttentag, "Recent Changes in the Primary Mortgage Market," *Housing Finance Review* (July 1984), pgs. 221–55.

[8]According to a 1995 Freddie Mac survey of ARM lenders, more than 75 percent of lenders also offered both "3/1" ARMs and "5/1" ARMs in addition to one-year ARMS. The former is fixed for three years and then adjusts annually and the latter is fixed for five years before it begins to adjust annually.

equal the interest rate on one-year Treasury securities, plus a margin of 2.75 percentage points. Also assume that the current rate on one-year Treasury securities is 3.30 percent—which would seem to imply a 6.05 percent interest rate (3.30 + 2.75). However, the first-year contract interest rate is 4.5 percent.

The monthly payment in year 1 is $506.69 and the remaining mortgage balance at the end of year 1 is $98,387.[9] If the interest rate on one-year Treasury securities is still 3.30 percent at the end of year 1, the contract interest rate in year 2 will equal the one-year Treasury rate plus the margin, or

$$= 3.30\% + 2.75\%$$
$$= 6.05\%$$

Thus, the monthly payment in year 2 will equal $600.35.

Note that even though the Treasury index rate remained unchanged at 3.30 percent, the contract rate increased 1.55 percentage points to 6.05 percent on the first payment adjustment date. The initial interest rate, in this case 4.50 percent, is sometimes referred to as a **teaser rate** if it is less than the index rate plus the margin at the time the mortgage is originated.

RATE CAPS AND OTHER OPTIONS

Two types of interest rate caps are typically available on ARMS. **Adjustment rate caps** (or rate caps) limit the amount that the contract interest rate can increase or decrease at each payment adjustment (anniversary) date. Adjustments rate caps, if they are included, are usually 1 or 2 percentage points. **Life-of-loan caps** establish a ceiling that the contract rate may never exceed and are stated as a number of percentage points over the initial contract rate. For example, if the initial interest rate is 4.5 percent, and the life-of-loan cap is 5 percentage points, the contract interest rate on the loan may never exceed 9.5 percent. Loans with caps frequently have both annual and life-of-loan caps. A loan with a 2 percent annual cap and a 6 percent life-of-loan cap is frequently referred to as a "2/6" rate cap.

Assume our one-year, 4.5 percent ARM also has a 2 percent adjustment rate cap and a 6 percent life-of-loan cap. If the yield on one-year Treasury securities at the end of year 1 is 4.30 percent, the contract rate in year 2 would be 7.05 percent in the absence of caps (4.30 + 2.75), but 6.50 percent in the presence of 2 percent annual rate caps. Another example of calculating ARM payments is presented in Exhibit 16–4.

It may appear that borrowers always prefer smaller (tighter) adjustment caps that limit the amount that the contract rate can increase in any given year or over the life of the loan. However, what benefits the borrower works to the detriment of the lender. If short-term interest rates rise by, say, 3 percentage points over the year, but the existence of 1 percent rate caps limits the interest rate increase to 100 basis points, the present value of the remaining payments on the loan decreases. This decrease benefits the borrower because the loan is a liability—and reductions in liabilities increase net worth. However,

[9]The calculation of mortgage payments and remaining loan balances was discussed in detail in Chapter 2.

EXHIBIT 16-4

CALCULATING CHANGES IN ARM INTEREST RATES AND PAYMENTS

Assumptions:

Loan amount:	$70,000
Annual rate cap:	1%
Life-of-loan cap:	5%
Margin:	2.75%
First year contract rate:	6.00%
1-year Treasury rate at end of year 1:	3.75%
1-year Treasury rate at end of year 2:	5.50%
Loan term in years:	30

Calculations:

Initial monthly payment	$= \$419.69$
Loan balance end-of-year 1	$= \$69,140$
Year 2 contract rate	$= \$3.75\% + 2.75\% = 6.5\%$
Year 2 monthly payment	$= \$441.95$
Loan balance end-of-year 2	$= \$68,306$
Year 3 contract rate—no caps	$= 5.50\% + 2.75\% = 8.25\%$
Year 3 contract rate—with 1% caps	$= 6.5\% + 1.0\% = 7.5\%$
Year 3 payment (based on 7.0% rate)	$= \$68,506 \times MC_{(7.00\%/12,336)} = \$486.93$

---

the mortgage loan is a lender asset, and potential changes in asset values are not passively accepted by rational lenders and other mortgage investors who are averse to interest rate risk.

How do lenders balance the pricing of ARMs with rate caps relative to ARMs without such caps? They must increase the *expected* return on the ARM with caps in some fashion. Thus, borrowers who choose ARMs with rate caps can expect a higher initial contract rate, a higher margin, more up-front financing costs, or some combination of the three.

It should be apparent that ARMs contain a wide variety of features and provisions. When comparing a particular ARM to a fixed-payment mortgage or to other ARMs, the borrower should calculate the payments and effective borrowing cost (EBC) of the ARM under several different assumptions about changes in the index interest rate—including the calculation of the payments and EBC assuming the contract rate increases the maximum amount allowed by rate caps, if they are included. This suggests that ARM wrestling requires the consideration and comparison of all of the following:

- Initial interest rates.
- Margins.
- Adjustment rate caps.
- Life-of-loan caps.
- Discount points.
- Other up-front financing costs.

PRIVATE MORTGAGE INSURANCE

Many lenders require **private mortgage insurance** (PMI) for conventional loans over 80 percent of the security property's value. Private mortgage insurance companies provide such insurance, which usually covers the top 20 percent of loans. In other words, if a borrower defaults and the property is foreclosed and sold for less than the amount of the loan, the PMI will reimburse the lender for a loss up to 20 percent of the loan amount. Thus, the net effect of PMI from the lender's perspective is to reduce default risk.[10]

As an example, assume a borrower purchased a $100,000 home with 5 percent cash and a $95,000 loan. The initial LTVR is quite high (95 percent), so mortgage insurance is required in the amount of $19,000—20 percent of the loan. Suppose the borrower defaults after the loan has been paid down to $94,000. Suppose further the market value of the property falls to $90,000. The lender then looks to the mortgage insurer for compensation for the impending $4,000 loss.

Mortgage insurance companies have generally followed a practice of reimbursing the lender in full should a foreclosure become necessary. In this example, this option provides a zero net loss for the lender and a $4,000 loss for the insurance company. The outcomes of this option are summarized as follows:

Lender's position:	
Payment from insurer	$94,000
Loss of mortgage asset	(94,000)
Net profit	$0
Insurance company position:	
Takes ownership of property	$90,000
Pays remaining balance to lender	(94,000)
Net loss	($4,000)[11]

About 15 companies currently provide PMI. These companies operate by collecting insurance premiums from borrowers, which are then pooled and used to pay claims to lenders when a mortgage default occurs. The insurance companies must aggressively market their products to the thousands of originators of single-family home mortgage loans.[12] In turn, the loan originators must meet the requirements of the insurance company

---

[10]Another type of mortgage insurance that borrowers may obtain provides for the continuing payment of the mortgage after the death of the insured person. This special form of life insurance enables the survivors of the deceased to continue living in the house.

[11]The above discussion ignores the transaction costs that the insurer would incur in the process of taking title to the property and subsequently selling it in the open market. These costs increase the net loss associated with taking title to the property. A second option available to the insurer is to simply reimburse the lender for the amount of the loan actually covered by the policy. Unless the property has fallen precipitously in value, the better alternative for the insurer is to pay the lender the amount of the remaining mortgage balance, take title to the property, and sell it for its current market value. However, if property values in a residential market have declined significantly, lenders are likely to limit their losses to the amount contained in the insurance contract.

[12]In addition to primary residences, PMI is available for second homes, multifamily properties, and some mobile homes and commercial properties.

to become an agent. Once approved, originating lender-agents obtain the necessary qualifying information from a loan applicant for submission to the underwriters of the insurance company. Insurance companies must respond quickly, often within 24 hours, in order to provide competitive service to their agents.

Premiums on PMI can be paid by the borrower in a lump sum at the time of origination or in monthly installments that are, effectively, added to the mortgage interest rate. For example, a one-time premium equal to 2.5 percent of the loan amount may be required at closing. For our example, this would mean a premium payment at closing of $2,375 (0.025 $\times$ $95,000). Alternatively, a monthly premium payment equal to, say, 0.0833 percent (1 percent annually) of the remaining loan balance may be included in the monthly mortgage payment and passed on by the lender to the insurance company. Thus, the first month's premium in our example would be $79.17 (0.000833 $\times$ $95,000). The premium would decline as the balance of the loan is amortized. Because the probability of borrower default is directly tied to the initial (and subsequent) LTVRs, the cost of PMI is positively related to the initial LTVR.

Cancellation of PMI coverage may be allowed if the borrower has a record of timely payments and the remaining loan balance is less than 80 percent of the *current* market value of the home. A new appraisal, paid for by the borrower, is typically required as proof of the increase in the value of the property.

OTHER MORTGAGE TYPES AND USES

Mortgages on real property can be used in different ways to accomplish different functions in a transaction. Mortgages identified by the function they play in achieving certain objectives include purchase money mortgages, buydown and other below-market rate mortgages, package mortgages, and reverse annuity mortgages.

PURCHASE MONEY MORTGAGES

Whenever a seller lends all or part of the purchase price of a property to the purchaser, and the loan is secured by a mortgage on the property, the mortgage is termed a **purchase money mortgage** (PMM). Such mortgages, briefly discussed in Chapter 15, often are used in transactions involving single-family homes. Their primary functions are to provide purchasers with higher loan-to-value ratios than they are able, or willing, to obtain from a traditional mortgage lender, to provide purchasers with a lower cost of financing than what is generally available, or to provide both.

Suppose the Browns want to sell their home for $100,000. The Greens want to buy it but can pay only $10,000 in cash. They can borrow $80,000 with a first mortgage from Third Federal Savings and Loan, but they are still short $10,000. The Browns agree to lend them $10,000, with a second mortgage—a PMM. In effect, the Browns are "taking paper" in lieu of $10,000 in cash at closing. The second mortgage will have a position inferior to the first mortgage in the event of default.

E X H I B I T   1 6 - 5

VALUING INTEREST RATE BUYDOWNS

$ 724.16	Monthly payment at 9 percent annual rate
− 568.86	Monthly payment at 6.5 percent annual rate
$ 155.30	Monthly difference
$5,590.80	Total savings over three years
$4,883.69	Present value of monthly savings at 9 percent*

*Calculator keystrokes: N = 36, I = 9%/12, PV = ?, PMT = 155.30, and FV = 0.

Purchase money mortgages are used to finance other types of real estate as well. Landowners often partially finance the sale of large tracts for development with a PMM. They take cash for a portion of the sale price but finance the remainder themselves. The PMM is paid off from the proceeds of lots as they are developed and sold. The landowner, in effect, is a partner of the developer.

INTEREST RATE BUYDOWNS AND CONCESSIONS

During periods of high interest rates and low demand, home sellers often offer purchase money mortgages to potential buyers at below-market interest rates. In similar environments, home builders often buy down the interest rate on the first one to five years of loans to purchasers of homes in the new development. The builder accomplishes this by entering into an agreement with a local lender who originates the loans. The builder agrees to pay the lender a lump sum for every loan issued to purchasers of homes in the builder's new development. To entice the lender to originate the mortgages, the lump sum payment must adequately compensate the lender for the lower payments in the initial years.

Buydowns enable builders to advertise a much lower interest rate for the first few years and still maintain "list" prices. Buydowns, as well as purchase money mortgages offered by sellers at below market rates, attract some potential buyers who would otherwise be repelled by the interest rate. Builder buydowns may enable some buyers to qualify for a loan—based on the first few years' mortgage payments—who otherwise would not qualify. Sometimes total mortgage payments are drastically reduced by builder buydowns and below market rate seller financing. Assume, for example, that the current market rate of interest on a 30-year FPM is 9 percent and that the builder/seller is willing to buy down the rate on a $90,000 mortgage to 6.5 percent for three years. As detailed in Exhibit 16–5, the interest rate buydown reduces the monthly payment by $155 for three years, which has a present value of $4,884 (when discounted at 9 percent). Rational lenders will require a lump sum payment of at least $4,884 from the builder at closing.

Builders often advertise other sales incentives such as "free" swimming pools, furniture, bonds, or vacations. The advertising of buydowns and other sales incentives has been an effective marketing device for builders and other sellers in many areas; however, such plans have some important hazards for home loan borrowers.

Payment shock.   The first hazard of obtaining a loan with a temporarily reduced interest rate is payment shock. Many borrowers seem unaware of, or unconcerned about, future payment increases after the buydown period or other special financing expires. These borrowers are not prepared when the payments later increase drastically, and often find themselves unable, or unwilling, to make the payments. Some may attempt to sell their homes, while others may default and willingly allow the lender to foreclose and obtain title to the property. Many PMMs have short (3- to 10-year) maturities and are either interest-only or partially amortized with a balloon payment due at maturity. When the PMM matures at the end of 3 to 10 years, the borrower is forced to satisfy the balloon by selling liquid assets (stocks, MBSs, etc.), by obtaining a second mortgage from a more expensive traditional source, by refinancing into a larger mortgage and using the proceeds to pay off both the PMM and the first mortgage (if one exists), or by selling the house to satisfy the PMM obligation. All of these strategies may increase the cost of debt financing at the maturity of the PMM.

Inflated prices.   The second hazard of buydowns and other below-market rate financing is the likelihood that the property cannot be sold for as much as the owners paid. High interest rates dampen demand and keep prices down. To cover the cost of offering below-market interest rates, builders and sellers attempt to increase the sale prices of the homes. In fact, potential buyers should assume that the value of buydowns and other below-market financing incentives is added to the price of the home. Thus, the value of favorable financing should be *subtracted* from a home's price to estimate its resale value without the below–market rate financing. If the builder's selling price of the home in our example is $100,000, then a reasonable estimate of market value is $95,116 ($100,000 − $4,884).

PACKAGE MORTGAGES

Package mortgages provide additional funds for home buyers. The mortgage includes home-related items of personal property such as a range, dishwasher, refrigerator, and furnishings. When these items are included in the mortgage, the lender can lend a larger amount, and the home buyer can amortize the equipment over a much longer period, usually at a lower rate, than if the items were financed by a consumer loan.

REVERSE ANNUITY MORTGAGES

Reverse annuity mortgages (RAMs) provide additional monthly income to home owners who have a sizable equity in their homes. Such home owners are usually older persons who have paid off a substantial portion of their mortgages and have realized appreciation in the value of homes. Often retired, these home owners typically require additional monthly income to cover their living expenses, but for many reasons, they are not willing to sell their homes in order to invest the proceeds in income-producing assets. They often are, in a sense, "cash poor" in that a large percentage of their accumulated wealth is in housing equity. Their substantial investment in housing produces valuable housing

EXHIBIT 16-6
REVERSE ANNUITY MORTGAGE[1]

Year	Beginning Balance	Payment	Interest	Ending Balance
1	$ 0	$4,707	$ 0[2]	$ 4,607[3]
2	4,607	4,607	415	9,629
3	9,629	4,607	867	15,104
4	15,104	4,607	1,359	21,070
5	21,070	4,607	1,896	27,574
6	27,574	4,607	2,482	34,663
7	34,663	4,607	3,120	42,390
8	42,390	4,607	3,815	50,813
9	50,813	4,607	4,573	59,993
10	59,993	4,607	5,399	70,000

[1]$70,000, 9 percent, 10-year loan
[2]9 percent of beginning balance
[3]Beginning balance, plus payment, plus interest

services, but not the cash income they need to support their lifestyle. Essentially, a RAM allows the home owner to liquidate a portion of their housing equity without having to sell the house and moves.

In a RAM, a lender agrees to pay the home owner a monthly payment, or annuity, and to be repaid from the home owner's equity when he or she sells the home or obtains other financing to pay off the RAM. A fixed-term RAM provides a fixed payment for a certain period of time, usually 10 years. For example, consider a household that owns a $100,000 home free and clear of mortgage debt. The RAM lender agrees to a $70,000 RAM for 10 years at 9 percent. For simplicity, assume payments are made *annually* to the homeowner. The annual payment on this RAM would $4,607.41. The calculator key-strokes are:

$N = 10$	$I = 9\%$	$PV = 0$	$PMT = ?$	$FV = 70,000$

The annual payment, accrued interest, and accumulated loan balance are displayed in Exhibit 16–6.

Note that the disbursement and loan payment pattern on a RAM are not at all like a typical mortgage where the borrower receives the entire loan proceeds at closing and then immediately begins to make monthly payments of interest and, usually, principal. With a RAM, the loan proceeds are distributed to the borrower in small periodic amounts. Interest on the loan disbursements begins to accumulate immediately. However, no payments of any kind are made on the loan until the borrowers, or their heirs, pay off the loan with proceeds from the sale of the house (or other assets from the borrower's estate).

If the property is sold or the homeowner dies prior to the end of the 10-year term, the accumulated loan balance can be paid off with the sale proceeds. If the owner is still living, the loan balance must still be paid to the lender, and this may force a sale of the

REAL ESTATE FOCUS 16-2

A Reverse Mortgage

Starting in 1996, the Federal National Mortgage Association in Washington began offering a reverse mortgage program to lenders across the country. The interest rate is adjustable, based on the one-month certificate of deposit index. It is adjusted monthly and carries a 12-point adjustment cap. To apply, homeowners must be at least 62 years old. Homeowners can set it up as a line of credit to be drawn as needed, or they can elect to receive monthly payments.

In the past, few investors were willing to buy a reverse mortgage in the secondary mortgage market. Without that option, lenders were forced to carry the loan at the local level instead of selling it to investors. As a result, many lenders were not interested in reverse mortgages. The Federal Housing Administration offers reverse mortgages, but the terms are very restrictive. Fannie Mae's reverse mortgage program, called Home Keepers, provides a secondary mortgage market for lenders.

The downside of reverse mortgages is felt mainly by the heirs. "The ultimate consequence is that—like the bumper stickers you see on recreational vehicles say— you're out spending your kids' inheritance," said Michael Noel, vice president of special programs at Pinnacle Financial Corp. in Orlando. "You are essentially spending the equity in your home that would otherwise pass to your heirs." In other words, when you die, your house is sold and the proceeds are used to pay off the reverse mortgage loan. Anything left over goes to the heirs. But if the home value is less than the loan amount, the heirs do not have to make up the difference—it is essentially forgiven, according to Fannie Mae. That is another reason lenders were reluctant to offer reverse mortgages before Fannie Mae was willing to buy them on the secondary market.

SOURCE: Suzie Schottlekotte and Martha McKenzie, "A Reverse Mortgage," NYT Regional Newspapers, February 1996.

house—and likely produce a great deal of negative publicity for the lender. To address this "mortality risk," several alternatives to the fixed-payment, fixed-term RAM have emerged. In one, the payments to the home owner cease at the end of the loan term, but the owner is allowed to stay in the house as long as she chooses, or as long as she lives. Interest on the unpaid mortgage balance simply continues to accrue at the contract rate. The home owner's heirs then use the sale proceeds or other estate assets to satisfy the outstanding obligation. Other RAM plans include the use of deferred life annuity contracts from life insurance companies to eliminate the mortality risk of RAMs.

One factor that has increased the popularity and availability of RAMs is the FHA Reverse Mortgage Program that Congress created in 1987. Among other things, this program provides mortgage insurance for RAMs originated by FHA-approved lenders. Since the origination of the program, there has been slow but growing acceptance of RAMs among conventional lenders. In 1997, Fannie Mae also began offering a RAM program to lenders across the country (see Real Estate Focus 16–2). Many analysts predict the demand for RAMs will grow as the baby-boom generation continues to age.[13]

---

[13]RAMs have received increased attention in recent years from practitioners and academics, as well as from policy makers. Evidence of this interest is that an entire issue of the *Journal of the American Real Estate and Urban Economics Association* (vol. 22, no. 2, Summer 1994) was recently given over to articles on RAMs.

GRADUATED PAYMENT MORTGAGES

Graduated payment mortgages (GPMs) were originally designed to alleviate the affordability problems that borrowers face with FPMs during periods of high interest rates. The monthly payment on a GPM is smaller in the initial years than on an FPM with the same contract rate. This reduced initial payment addresses the borrower's affordability problem. The monthly payments, however, then gradually increase every year over a 5- to 10-year period. Because the payments on a GPM are lower in the early years, they must be higher than on an FPM in the later years or lenders would have no incentive to originate GPMs.

GPMs have, at times, been very popular with younger households that expect their incomes to increase over time. The reduced initial payments on a GPM may allow the household to purchase a bigger home than could be afforded with an FPM. Although the mortgage payments increase over the first 5 to 10 years of the mortgage, the series of payments may better match household income over time.

It should be pointed out that the monthly payments in the early years of a GPM are generally less than the amount of interest that is accumulating on the outstanding mortgage balance. The shortfalls in interest in these early years are *added* to the remaining loan balance because the lender is, effectively, disbursing an additional "loan" to the borrower each month in which there is a shortfall. This increase in the outstanding loan balance in the early years is called **negative amortization**. An increasing loan balance impedes the borrower's ability to build up equity in the property. This, all else the same, increases the probability of default, which concerns both the borrower and the lender.

HOME EQUITY LOANS

A form of second mortgages, **home equity loans,** became a booming industry in the 1980s. Approximately one in four private houses now carries a home equity mortgage, up from 1 in 15 in 1983. Home equity loans owe their recent popularity to comparatively low interest rates, tax-favored status, and easy availability, not to mention very aggressive marketing by lenders. Although traditionally used to finance home improvements, they have become all-purpose loans.

Types of loans. Banks and savings institutions dominate home equity lending, but they now compete with credit unions, finance companies, brokerage houses, and insurance companies. The loans come in two forms:

1. *Closed-end loans*—a fixed amount is borrowed all at once and repaid in monthly installments over a set period, such as 10 years.
2. *Open-end lines of credit*—money is borrowed as it is needed, drawn against a maximum amount that was established when the account was opened. Interest is paid on the balance due, just as with a credit card. This type of credit often offers a choice of paying down the loan on a pre-arranged schedule or paying only interest for the first several years. The interest rate is usually adjustable. Open-end lenders frequently provide a book of special checks that allows the borrower to tap the line of credit or

REAL ESTATE FOCUS 16-3

New Mortgage Program Requires No Home Equity

A number of lenders are now offering a no-equity home loan. Marketed primarily as a means for debt consolidation, this new breed of second mortgages is breaking the rules of traditional underwriting by allowing homeowners to borrow more than their home's value—up to 125 percent.

The concept is simple: Borrowers shift mounting credit card debts, car loans, and other bills into a single mortgage payment that carries a lower interest rate. Monthly expenses are reduced while debts are repaid more quickly. Part of the loan also can be used to finance home improvements.

No-equity mortgages run anywhere from $10,000 to $100,000 and carried a note rate of between 11 percent and 14 percent in 1997. Although more expensive than home equity loans, which carried variable-rate interest ranging from 8.25 percent to 10.5 percent, that's far be-

low the 17.5 percent to 20 percent rates charged on revolving loan credit lines.

No-equity loans have caught on with homeowners unable to qualify for traditional home equity loans, either because they haven't been in their homes long enough to build up appreciable equity or because their equity stakes have declined due to falling or stagnant housing values. The concept also has gained acceptance in the public bond markets, where investors ultimately purchase these loans.

Critics charge the loans are risky gimmicks that create a class of sustained debtors and that borrowers spend years paying down their debt just to regain positive equity.

SOURCE: Vivian Marino, "New Mortgage Program Requires No Home Equity," *Associated Press*, February 1997.

---

that allows borrowing through a regular checking account. Some banks even allow cash to be drawn at a teller's window or from an automatic teller machine.

How much can one borrow? Equity in a house—its market value minus the unpaid balance owed on existing mortgage debt—is the basis for deciding how much one can borrow against the property. Few financial institutions allow homeowners to extract more than 80 percent of the value of a home, and on a house worth $500,000 or more, the cutoff may be as low as 50 percent. Therefore, if a house is appraised at $200,000 and has a $100,000 mortgage balance, and the lender applies a 75 percent loan-to-value ratio, a homeowner could borrow $150,000, minus the $100,000 existing debt, or an additional $50,000. An alternative type of second mortgages that competes with home equity loans, called the no-equity home loan, allows home owners to borrow up to 125 percent of their home's value (see Real Estate Focus 16–3.)

Interest rates. Most lenders base their adjustable home equity loan rates on the prime rate, which is the rate banks charge their best commercial borrowers. The prime rate published daily by *The Wall Street Journal* is a common benchmark. The rate charged may be 1 or 2 percentage points above that figure. In 1990, for example, when the prime rate was 10 percent, the average home equity loan interest rate was 11.6 percent. Other indexes include the 90-day Treasury bill rate and the average 30-day jumbo ($100,000)

CD rate. Both of these indexes are more responsive to interest trends than the prime rate, and they are therefore more volatile. In addition to interest, many lenders charge a yearly fee of $25 to $45.

Closing costs.   Assorted up-front charges for such items as a property appraisal, attorney's fees, a credit investigation, and title insurance can mount up to $750 or more of closing costs on home equity loans. Competitive pressures, however, lead some lenders to waive all closing costs.

Tax advantages.   Interest on consumer debt, such as loans to finance the acquisition of automobiles, college tuition, and household appliances and electronics, is *not* tax deductible. But interest on home equity loans up to $100,000 is generally 100 percent deductible for federal and many state tax returns. Closing costs, however, generally are not deductible, except for points charged up-front on a closed-end loan.[14]

Guidelines.   Home equity loans can provide an important source of financing under certain circumstances. However, borrowers should follow a few rules, including these:

- Treat the loan as an investment for improving their house, financing an education, or starting a business. It should be used cautiously to consolidate debts whose interest is not tax deductible or to cover emergency expenses.
- Use open-end loans to cover deferred costs such as college tuition and multiphased home improvements. Closed-end loans should be used for refinancings and other lump sums.
- Beware of teaser rates, the kind that ratchet up after a year or two.
- Whenever possible, reject the interest-only option. Schedule installments that will retire the debt in 10 years or less.
- Base the size of the loan on ability to repay, rather than on the amount of equity available. A useful rule is that mortgage and home equity loan payments should not exceed 35 percent of gross monthly income.

THE BORROWER'S MORTGAGE LOAN DECISIONS

Once a household has decided to purchase a particular home, it is faced with a number of financing decisions. First, the buyer must choose a mortgage instrument from the mortgage menu. Possible selections include 15-year and 30-year FPMs and 1-year ARMs. A choice also must be made between the contract interest rate and the number of discount

---

[14]For a discussion of the federal income tax rules that apply to home equity loans, see John L. Kramer and Lawrence C. Phillips, *Federal Income Taxation 1996 (Individuals)* (Upper Saddle River, NJ: Prentice Hall, 1995), pp. 7–25.

points. For example, fixed-rate lenders typically offer a 30-year FPM with no up-front discount points—although they usually charge a one-point loan origination fee and other up-front costs associated with obtaining the mortgage financing. In addition, the lender usually offers to reduce the contract rate in exchange for the payment of up-front discount points.

Households also must choose their desired loan-to-value ratio, although the maximum LTVR is typically limited to some percentage of the acquisition price. The choice of LTVR and mortgage type may be interdependent. For example, if the household chooses an ARM with a significantly lower initial interest rate than what is currently available on an FPM, the household may be able to afford to finance a larger portion of the acquisition price.

The diversity of contracts and LTVRs available in mortgage markets reflects the diversity of borrowers with respect to accumulated wealth, current income, risk aversion, expected holding period, and other characteristics. Borrowers should select the mortgage contract that best fits their particular circumstances.

After the mortgage has been originated, the household usually has the option to prepay the mortgage (in whole or in part) and the option to default. Borrowers typically do not give serious consideration to default unless the value of the property has fallen well below the remaining mortgage balance. Prepayment may be caused by a household's decision to move, by refinancing to obtain a lower interest rate, or by refinancing to obtain a larger mortgage and thereby drawing some of the household's equity out of the property.

We consider next the primary decision criterion by which the various mortgage options should be judged: effective borrowing cost. We then consider the household's initial LTVR decision and the ongoing prepayment and default decisions that borrowers face after mortgage origination.

MORTGAGE CHOICE

When prospective buyers of single-family homes seek financing, they must consider several provisions of the mortgage contract that can affect the cost of both the financing and the property. The contract interest rate is the most obvious component of the cost of debt. In addition, the lender can require the borrower to pay a number of up-front financing costs, including discount points, at the time of loan origination. These charges increase the borrower's cost of debt financing. The following sections discuss the nature of these considerations and demonstrate the procedures for analyzing them.

Up-front financing costs. Lenders charge points for several reasons. The first is that for tax accounting purposes, financial institutions can include up to two points as income in the year the loan is made (any additional point income must be spread over the next 12 years). Financial institutions that are under pressure to generate more income may be eager to charge as many points as possible to increase their current year's income. Lenders also charge discount points to adjust the loan yield upward by relatively small

R E A L   E S T A T E   F O C U S   1 6 - 4

Mortgage Maze

The growth of the secondary market, in which mortgages are packaged into securities and bought and sold, as well as fierce competition among lenders, means that listed rates may appear similar from one bank or broker to another. But old-fashioned homework can still help you beat the averages. "The more research you do, the more stones you turn over, the better you'll do," says Keith Gumbinger, a vice president at HSH Associates, a mortgage-information provider in Butler, NJ.

Here are some experts' strategies for navigating what remains a bewildering and expensive process:

Compare apples with apples. Remember the last time you bought a car? Picking a mortgage isn't all that different. Loans now come with various options and requirements and widely differing rates and associated costs. Some lenders charge up-front origination fees and "points" that lower the loan's interest rate, while others nickel-and-dime customers to death with fees.

Seek out competitive differences. Like car dealers, mortgage lenders vary widely. Savings and loans that hold mortgages in their portfolios may offer slightly lower rates than banks and mortgage brokers, whose loans are sold in the secondary market.

Don't hesitate to haggle. Just about everything, including discount points and origination fees, may be negotiable. Less-obvious costs, such as title-escrow charges, lawyer fees and whether a new survey is required for a refinancing, also may be up for negotiation. "Ninety percent of customers shop interest rates, but they fail to shop closing costs and points and other things that are negotiable."

SOURCE: "Mortgage Maze: How to Cash In on Ever-Lower Rates," *The Wall Street Journal,* November 22, 1996.

---

amounts. On fixed-rate loans, discount points also reduce the borrower's incentive to refinance because contract rates decrease as the number of discount points increases.[15]

In addition to discount points, borrowers usually pay a loan origination fee of between 1 and 2 percent of the loan amount. Other borrower costs typically associated with acquiring mortgage financing include loan application and document preparation fees ($200–$700), the cost of having the property appraised ($150–$300), credit check fee ($35–$75), title charges and mortgage insurance (each 0.5 percent–1.0 percent of the loan amount), charges to transfer the deed and record the mortgage ($40–$200), survey costs ($200–$300), pest inspection ($25–$75), and attorneys' fees. Borrowers must be prepared to pay a loan origination fee and other up-front costs, but they should shop around and compare discount points and other terms, not just contract interest rates (see Real Estate Focus 16–4.)

---

[15]Additional explanations for variations in contract rates and discount points include differences in prospective borrowers and lenders with respect to tax rates, expectations about the borrower's holding period, and expectations about future interest rates. For more discussion, see Charles A. Stone and Anne-Marie Zissu, "Choosing a Discount Point/Contract Rate Combination," *The Journal of Real Estate Finance and Economics* 3, no. 3 (September 1990), pp. 283–92, and T. L. Yang, "Self-Selection in the Fixed-Rate Mortgage Market," *Journal of the American Real Estate and Urban Economics Association* 20, no. 3 (Fall 1992), pp. 359–92.

EXHIBIT 16-7

EFFECTIVE BORROWING COST WITH DIFFERENT NUMBERS OF DISCOUNT POINTS AND YEARS OUTSTANDING*

Discount Points	Number of Years Loan is Outstanding					
	2 Yrs.	4 Yrs.	6 Yrs.	8 Yrs.	10 Yrs.	30 Yrs.
0.00	9.61%	9.11%	8.94%	8.86%	8.81%	8.72%
0.50	9.89	9.26	9.05	8.95	8.89	8.78
1.00	10.18	9.42	9.17	9.05	8.97	8.83
1.50	10.46	9.57	9.28	9.14	9.06	8.89
2.00	10.75	9.73	9.40	9.23	9.14	8.95
2.50	11.04	9.89	9.51	9.33	9.22	9.01

*30-year fixed payment mortgage with contract rate of 8.5 percent and other up-front financing costs of $2,000

To consider the effect of up-front financing costs on the effective (or true) cost of borrowing, consider an 8.50 percent, 30-year, $100,000 FPM, with a monthly payment equal to $768.91. Assume up-front financing costs, excluding discount points but including the origination fee, equal $2,000. Exhibit 16–7 displays the effective borrowing cost for different combinations of discount points and number of years the loan remains outstanding. If there are no discount points and the borrower repays the loan after two years, the effective borrowing cost (EBC) is 9.61 percent. The calculator keystrokes are

$N = 24$	$I = ?$	$PV = \$98,000$	$PMT = -\$768.91$	$FV = -\$98,421$

The EBC of 9.61 percent is greater than the 8.50 percent contract rate because of the $2,000 in total up-front financing costs.

Adding discount points to the $2,000 in other up-front costs increases the EBC because it decreases the net loan proceeds *without* altering the scheduled monthly payment or remaining loan balances. One discount point (equal to $1,000 on a $100,000 loan) decreases the net loan proceeds to $97,000 and increases the EBC to 10.18 percent with a two-year holding period. The payment of 2½ discount points would increase the EBC to 11.04 percent. The effect of up-front financing costs on the EBC decreases as the holding period increases. For example, with 2½ discount points the EBC decreases from 11.04 percent with a two-year holding period to 9.22 percent if the loan remains outstanding for 10 years. As the holding period increases toward 30 years, the EBC will approach, but not equal, the contract interest rate of 8.5 percent.

Note that the effect of discount points on the EBC is more pronounced with shorter holding periods. Thus, borrowers who *expect* they may have to move relatively soon should probably choose to pay few or no discount points and a slightly higher contract interest rate. The higher contract rate will increase their EBC less than the up-front payment of points. Conversely, borrowers who expect to keep the loan outstanding for a long period of time should consider paying discount points to *buy down* the interest rate. Why? The monthly savings from paying the discount points to reduce the contract rate will be greater the longer the loan remains outstanding. Note that because the length of time the loan will be outstanding is uncertain, the effective or true cost of each mortgage option is not known at the time of origination.

Estimating closing costs. The **Real Estate Settlement and Procedures Act** (RESPA) is a federal law that requires lenders (commercial banks, savings and loans, credit unions) to provide information on all costs associated with closing (settling) a residential loan.[16] Whenever a buyer obtains a new first mortgage loan from one of these lenders, the loan is insured by the FHA or guaranteed by the VA, or the loan will be sold to Fannie Mae or Freddie Mac, the lender must provide the applicant with a "good faith" estimate of all closing costs within three business days of the loan application. In addition, the borrower must be permitted to inspect the estimated settlement expenses one business day before closing.

As discussed in more detail in Chapter 24, the estimated closing expenses include both the cost of acquiring legal ownership of the property and the costs of obtaining the mortgage financing, if applicable. For the purposes of estimating effective borrowing costs, only those up-front expenses associated with obtaining the mortgage funds should be included, such as discount points, loan origination fees, credit report, appraisal fee, and the like. In particular, those settlement costs associated with obtaining ownership of the property, such as buyer's title insurance (if required) and attorney fees, should not be included in the EBC calculation. A simple test should be applied to estimated closing expenses: If the expense would be incurred even if no mortgage financing were obtained, it is an expense associated with obtaining ownership and should not be included in the EBC calculation.

The **Truth-in-Lending Act** is a federal law that requires lenders to provide residential borrowers with estimates of the total finance charges and the **annual percentage rate** (APR). The APR is the loan's EBC, assuming the loan is outstanding until maturity. Thus, for the 8.5 percent 30-year FPM discussed above, the APR is the EBC assuming the loan is outstanding for 30 years (last column, Exhibit 16–7).

Comparing mortgage options. Borrowers selecting among different mortgage types should calculate the EBCs of the various options. Consider the choice between the 8.50 percent FPM in Exhibit 16–7 with 1½ discount points and a one-year ARM with a 6.00 percent first year interest rate, a margin of 2.75 percent, no interest rate caps, 1½ discount points, and $2,000 in other up-front financing costs. The first row in Exhibit 16–8 displays the EBCs on the FPM for various holding periods. The second row contains the EBCs of the ARM assuming the yield on one-year Treasury securities (the index rate) is 5 percent at the beginning of years 2 through 10. With a margin of 2.75 percent, this means the contract rate will be 7.75 percent in years 2 through 10. If the index rate remains at 5.0 percent, the ARM is less expensive than the FPM, regardless of the holding period.

However, if the yield on one-year Treasury securities is 6 percent at the beginning of years 2 and 3, 7 percent at the beginning of year 4, and remains at 7 percent in years

---

[16]Commercial loans are not covered by RESPA. Residential mortgage loans are defined as those issued to finance the acquisition of one- to four-family homes, condominiums, and cooperatives.

EXHIBIT 16-8

EFFECTIVE BORROWING COST OF FPM VERSUS ARM*

Mortgage Choice/Interest Rate Scenario	Number of Years Loan is Outstanding				
	2 Yrs.	4 Yrs.	6 Yrs.	8 Yrs.	10 Yrs.
8.5 percent FPM/any interest rate scenario	10.46%	9.57%	9.28%	9.14%	9.06%
1-year ARM, 6.0% initial contract rate, index rate = 5% at the beginning of all 10 years	8.77	8.30	8.15	8.07	8.03
1-year ARM, 6.0% initial contract rate, index rate = 5% at the beginning of year 1; 6% at the beginning of years 2 and 3; 7% at the beginning of years 4–10	9.25	9.24	9.38	9.44	9.48

*Calculations assume 1.5 discount points, other up-front financing costs of $2,000, and a 30-year loan term. The ARMs have a margin of 2.75 percent and no rate caps.

5 through 10, the desirability of the ARM relative to the FPM depends on the period of time the loan is outstanding. For relatively short holding periods (less than six years), the ARM is less expensive than the FPM. For longer periods, however, the FPM is the preferred option. Note that the EBC of the ARM is affected by both the holding period *and* the course of future short-term interest rates—both of which are difficult to predict.

LOAN SIZE

Despite the relative importance of home mortgage debt in U.S. capital markets, little is actually known about how households select their desired amount of mortgage debt. However, several factors appear to be important. First, the use of mortgage debt depends critically on the relative costs of debt and equity financing. Consider a household that has agreed to purchase a home for $100,000. Assume that household currently owns several other assets, including $100,000 in mortgage-backed securities. This household has two basic financing options: (1) sell the $100,000 in MBSs and put its own money into the house or (2) debt finance a portion of the purchase price. If the household chooses the first option, it is, effectively, lending the money to itself. What is the cost of this self-financing? It is the rate of return that the household could have earned on the MBSs if they had not been sold. This foregone rate of return is the household's cost of equity (or self-financing). If the risk-adjusted cost of self-financing is *equal* to the effective borrowing cost of the debt financing, the borrower is indifferent between the two options from a financial perspective. However, if the cost of self-financing is greater than the cost of mortgage debt, the household has an incentive to finance some, if not all, of the purchase with debt.

Although the relative costs of debt and equity capital are important determinants of household mortgage debt, other factors are also important. For example, the use of mortgage debt is constrained by the household's current and expected future income. As discussed in more detail below, lenders require that monthly mortgage payments not exceed a certain percentage of the household's total monthly income. Thus, lack of income may reduce the household's ability to make extensive use of mortgage debt—even if debt is perceived to be the less expensive option. On the other hand, the use of self-financing is

REAL ESTATE FOCUS 16-5

Many Buyers Look for Loans First, Then Houses

Home buyers, increasingly educated in the process of buying a home, are getting prequalified for loans by lenders before they go shopping. Prequalification informs potential home buyers of several important factors before they go to their local real estate agent.

First, buyers find out exactly how much they can afford. Second, prequalification ensures purchasers they will get approval for a mortgage before they find a home. Third, the process helps determine the type of mortgage that's best suited for the potential borrower. Finally, the process gives some buyers a competitive edge over other buyers by giving them "cash buyer" status.

The Mortgage Bankers Association is currently promoting a national awareness campaign entitled "See Your Lender First," which focuses solely on getting potential home buyers prequalified. "Seeing a lender first eliminates the uncertainty and anxiety associated with getting a home loan," said Paul Reid, president of the Mortgage Bankers Association. "Home buyers will be looking at homes that they and their real-estate agent know they can afford." Reid said that with a pre-approved mortgage, a home buyer's negotiating position is stronger because the contract isn't contingent on the buyer getting mortgage approval.

Lenders are seeing an increase in applicants seeking prequalified status as home buyers are responding to the banking trade group's program and the publicity surrounding rising mortgage interest rates. The monthly payment an applicant is qualified for includes principal, interest, taxes, and insurance.

SOURCE: Dow Jones News Service, April 20, 1996.

constrained by the amount of the household's accumulated wealth. Thus, even if the cost of equity financing is perceived to be less expensive than the cost of debt, households may substitute self-financing for debt financing only to the extent of their available nonhousing wealth.

THE REFINANCING DECISION

Because of frequent declines in mortgage interest rates, a large percentage of home mortgage originations in the last decade have been refinancings, including nearly half of all loans made from early 1991 to early 1994. Because of the size of the costs and benefits involved, refinancing is a decision that mortgage borrowers should carefully consider.

In common practice, there is a rule of thumb that is often proposed as a refinancing decision criterion. It is based on the spread between the *existing* contract rate and the rate that is *currently* available. Under the interest rate spread rule, when the current market rate drops to some minimum "spread" below the rate on the existing mortgage loan, the borrower should refinance. The spread most commonly suggested is 1.5 to 2 percent. However, the interest rate spread rule has numerous deficiencies. Among others, it ignores the costs of refinancing, it fails to discount the future benefits of refinancing, and it fails to recognize the effect of the borrower's holding period on the benefits of refinancing.

The most accurate guide to a refinancing decision is net present value. This decision rule compares the discounted value (present value) of future payment reductions to the immediate costs of obtaining a new loan. The costs of refinancing an existing mortgage are large, often ranging from 4 to 9 percent of the new loan amount, and vary depending upon the number of discount points and other fees charged by the lender.

EXHIBIT 16-9

USING INCREMENTAL NPV TO ANALYZE THE REFINANCING DECISION

New loan held to maturity:

Month	No Refinance	Refinance	Difference	PV of Difference
0	$0	($3,000)	($3,000)	($3,000)
1–300	514.31	428.53	85.78	9,440
301–360	0	428.53	(428.53)	(1,672)
				NPV = $4,768

New loan held for 10 years:

Month	No Refinance	Refinance	Difference	PV of Difference
0	$0	($3,000)	($3,000)	($3,000)
1–120	514.31	428.53	85.78	6,491
120	42,853	44,407	(1,554)	(514)
				NPV = $2,977

New loan held for 3 years:

Month	No Refinance	Refinance	Difference	PV of Difference
0	$0	($3,000)	($3,000)	($3,000)
1–36	514.31	428.53	85.78	2,658
36	46,709	47,160	(449)	(333)
				NPV = ($675)

To illustrate the use of NPV as a guide to the refinancing decision, consider the following problem. Five years ago a borrower received a mortgage loan of $50,000. The loan has a contract interest rate of 12 percent and is being amortized with monthly payments of $514.31 over 30 years. The current loan balance is $48,831.61. The mortgage rate currently available is 10 percent and the borrower has found a lender who will refinance the $48,831.61 remaining loan balance at the current rate for 30 years. The new monthly payment would be $428.53. Total up-front financing costs on the new loan, including discount points, would be $3,000. Assume the appropriate discount rate is 10 percent. Should the borrower refinance?

The answer is sensitive to the length of time the new loan will be outstanding. If the new loan is held to maturity, refinancing will lower the borrower's monthly payments by $85.78 for the next 300 months, but increase them by $428.53 in months 301–360. These incremental inflows and outflows are summarized in the top panel of Exhibit 16–9. The present value of the payment savings in months 1–300 is $9,440, while the present value of the additional payments in months 301-360 is equal to $1,672. The NPV of refinancing is therefore $4,768 ($9,440 − $1,672 − $3,000), indicating the borrower should refinance.

The middle panel of Exhibit 16–9 displays the incremental cash flows from refinancing if the new loan will be outstanding for 10 years. In this case, the borrower still incurs up-front costs of $3,000. However, the payment savings are realized for only 10 years, reducing their present value to $6,491. If the borrower refinances, the remaining balance on the new loan will be $1,554 greater than what the balance of the existing mortgage would be 10 years from now (15 years after the origination of the existing mortgage). The present value of this difference in loan balances is $514, and the NPV of refinancing is reduced from $4,768 to $2,977. If the new loan remains outstanding for just three years (bottom panel of Exhibit 16–9), the NPV of refinancing is a *negative* $675. Note that the NPV of refinancing is very sensitive to both the up-front costs *and* the number of months the new loan is expected to be outstanding.[17]

It should be pointed out that this NPV procedure for analyzing the refinancing decision overstates the benefits from a current refinancing because there is a potential benefit from postponing refinancing until rates fall still further. If a borrower prepays now, he or she gives up the option to prepay the existing mortgage later. Thus, the NPV from refinancing must be sufficiently positive to offset this lost option value. The value of waiting to refinance is positively related to expected interest rate volatility. If interest rates are not expected to vary much over the borrower's expected holding period, this lost option value is less significant than if rates are expected to be very volatile.

THE DEFAULT DECISION

Default occurs when the mortgage borrower ceases to make timely payments of principal and interest. When this occurs, the lender must either renegotiate the terms of the mortgage with the borrower or take action to obtain title to the property. Technically, loans also are in default if the borrower fails to perform numerous other contractual obligations such as paying property taxes or maintaining adequate hazard insurance. When a technical default occurs, but the borrower is still making monthly payments, the lender will usually display forbearance—that is, the lender will work with the borrower to cure the problem. However, the lender has the right to initiate foreclosure proceedings.

From the lender's perspective, the degree of default risk is related both to the probability that the market value of the home will fall below the remaining loan balance (plus the costs of foreclosure) and to the risk that the lender will not be able to take possession of the home from the borrower in a timely fashion.

Why do borrowers become delinquent and sometimes default? There are two primary explanations. The first has to do with the borrower's ability to pay. The loss of employment, divorce, and other shocks to the household may hamper the borrower's ability (or willingness) to continue to service the debt. The second explanation centers on the amount of equity in the property. Borrowers with positive equity may not default even if a household shock renders them unable to make payments. To avoid the monetary and psychic costs of default, borrowers with positive equity can sell the property and use the proceeds to satisfy the outstanding loan balance. However, if the value of the home falls

---

[17]For simplicity, the effects of income taxes also were ignored. In general, interest paid on a home mortgage is fully deductible when calculating taxable income. Thus, the payment reduction benefits from refinancing are partially offset by increased taxes. For example, if the homeowner's tax rate on additional income is 28 percent, then the after-tax reduction in the monthly payment is generally 72 percent of the before-tax reduction. For our Exhibit 16–9 example, the after-tax payment reduction would be $61.76 (0.72 × $85.78)

below the value of the outstanding mortgage (negative equity), the borrower has an incentive to default. For example, if the outstanding mortgage balance is $80,000, but the current market value of the house that has been pledged as collateral is $65,000, the borrower has an incentive to default. What would be the payoff from such a strategy? The borrower would lose an asset worth $65,000, but also would be relieved of an $80,000 mortgage liability. Thus, default would produce a $15,000 benefit, ignoring default costs.[18]

Do borrowers immediately default if the value of their home falls below the value of the mortgage? Many homeowners with negative equity continue to make their monthly payments, perhaps because of fear of a bad credit rating, or because the house has more value to them than it would if sold in the open market, or because they expect property values to recover. In addition, as with the option to prepay for interest-related reasons, there is also value in waiting to default. This is because the option to walk away from the mortgage in the future has value, and this value is lost when the mortgage is terminated in the present. However, if house prices decline precipitously, as they did, for example, in many parts of Texas, Oklahoma, and Colorado during the mid- to late-1980s, households are increasingly likely to give the house back to the lender. The empirical evidence also suggests that household shocks, such as divorce and the loss of employment, may trigger a borrower with negative equity, who has been delaying the decision, to default.

SUMMARY

Prospective home buyers are confronted with a number of choices and options when deciding what type of mortgage financing to obtain. Conventional loans (those that do not enjoy some form of government support) are clearly the dominant choice, accounting for roughly 85 percent of all single-family home loans. If these loans conform to standards set by secondary market issuers of mortgage-backed securities (MBSs), they are frequently sold, or pooled and sold. In fact, with the development of elaborate secondary markets for residential mortgage securities, primary lenders may originate and sell the loan virtually simultaneously. Thus, they never actually fund the position. Because of these intricate linkages between primary and secondary mortgage market activities, it is impossible to gain an in-depth understanding of one market without first having a working knowledge of the other.

Conventional versus government guaranteed financing is not the only mortgage choice potential borrowers face. They must also select a payment schedule that matches their risk tolerance and affordability concerns. Thirty-year, fixed-rate mortgages are currently the most popular alternative, while adjustable rate mortgages are gaining ground. Fifteen-year, fixed-rate mortgages still account for a sizable fraction of the market, while innovations such as interest-only loans, partially amortized mortgages, and early payment mortgages are also available.

Home buyers who borrow more than 80 percent of the purchase price are required to purchase private mortgage insurance (PMI). PMI typically insures the lender against default risk of up to 20 percent of the loan amount. If the insured borrower defaults, the insurer will generally reimburse the lender for the remaining loan balance, take title to the property, and

---

[18]As mentioned in Chapter 15, the lender could seek a $15,000 deficiency judgment in court. However, the costs and limitations of pursuing a deficiency judgment mitigate its power.

sell the asset for its current market value. About 15 companies currently provide PMI, which can be paid either as a lump sum or in monthly installments. After the loan has been paid down sufficiently, borrowers are able to cancel their mortgage insurance.

Potential buyers should be aware of many alternative mortgage instruments that can alter the required payment schedule. For example, sellers may issue purchase money mortgages to alleviate buyer affordability problems, or buyers may "buy down" the interest rate to alter the payment schedule. Blanket mortgages, which secure more than one property; reverse annuity mortgages, which allow homeowners to draw equity out of their residence; and package mortgages, which include home-related items such as appliances and furnishings are also available.

Finally, a form of second mortgages, home equity loans, became a booming industry in the 1980s. These tax-favored loans are now carried by approximately 25 percent of private houses. In choosing among home equity loans, borrowers must not only decide how much to borrow, but also whether to use a closed-end loan or an open-end line of credit, and how to realize the lowest interest rates and closing costs. When using home equity financing, borrowers should generally treat the loan as an investment, beware of teaser rates,

reject the interest-only option, and base the loan size on the ability to repay, rather than on the amount of equity available. If these guidelines are followed, second mortgages can provide a useful source of funds for a household.

Borrowers, who should select the appropriate mortgage type based on effective borrowing cost, also face default and refinancing decisions. Basic financial theory indicates that the borrower should refinance when the present value of the payment savings exceeds the costs associated with the refinancing. In actuality, borrowers must time this decision, as a potential cost to refinancing today is the inability to refinance at even lower rates tomorrow. As for default, basic financial theory again indicates that the borrower should default if and when the current market value of the property falls below the value of the outstanding mortgage. In reality, many homeowners with negative equity continue to make their monthly payments, perhaps because of fear of a bad credit rating or because the house has more value to them than it would have if sold in the open market. In addition, there is also value in waiting to default because the option to walk away from the mortgage has value that is lost when the mortgage is terminated.

KEY TERMS

Adjustable rate mortgage 477
Adjustment rate caps 479
Annual percentage rate 493
Balloon payment 475
Buydowns 483
Conduits 471
Conforming conventional
   loan 472
Conventional mortgages 471
Early payment mortgages 474
Federal Home Loan Mortgage
   Corporation 470
Federal National Mortgage
   Association 470

15-Year mortgage 472
Fixed-payment mortgages 472
Government-sponsored
   enterprises 471
Graduated payment mortgage 487
Home equity loans 487
Interest-only loans 474
Jumbo loans 472
Life-of-loan caps 479
Margin 478
Maturity imbalance problem 476
Mortgage menu 470
Negative amortization 487

Nonconforming conventional
   loan 472
Package mortgage 484
Partially amortized mortgages 474
Primary mortgage market 470
Private mortgage insurance 481
Purchase money mortgage 482
Real Estate Settlement and
   Procedures Act 493
Reverse annuity mortgage 484
Secondary mortgage market 470
Teaser rate 479
Truth-in-Lending Act 493

TEST YOURSELF

Answer the following multiple choice questions:

1. The most typical adjustment interval on an adjustable rate mortgage (ARM) is
   - *a.* 6 months.
   - *b.* 1 year.
   - *c.* 3 years.
   - *d.* 10 years.
   - *e.* None of the above.

2. A characteristic of a partially amortized loan is
   - *a.* No loan balance exists at the end of the loan term.
   - *b.* A balloon payment is required at the end of the loan term.
   - *c.* All have adjustable interest rates.
   - *d.* All have a loan term of 15 years.
   - *e.* None of the above.

3. Private mortgage insurance (PMI) is usually required on _____ loans with loan-to-value ratios greater than _____ percent.
   - *a.* Home, 75.
   - *b.* Home, 60.
   - *c.* Income property, 75.
   - *d.* Income property, 80.
   - *e.* None of the above.

4. If a mortgage is to mature (become due) at a certain future time without any reduction in principal, this is
   - *a.* A second mortgage.
   - *b.* An amortized mortgage.
   - *c.* A limited reduction mortgage.
   - *d.* An interest-only mortgage.
   - *e.* An open-end mortgage.

5. The dominant loan type originated by most financial institutions is the
   - *a.* Fixed-payment, fully amortized mortgage.
   - *b.* Adjustable rate mortgage.
   - *c.* Purchase money mortgage.
   - *d.* FHA-insured mortgage.

6. Which of the following statements is true about 15-year and 30-year fixed payment mortgages?
   - *a.* 30-year mortgages are more popular than 15-year mortgages among homeowners who are refinancing.
   - *b.* Borrowers pay more total interest over the life of a 15-year mortgage than on a 30-year loan.
   - *c.* The remaining balance on a 30-year loan declines more quickly than an otherwise comparable 15-year mortgage.
   - *d.* Assuming they can afford the payments on both mortgages, borrowers should chose a 30-year mortgage over an otherwise identical 15-year loan if their risk-adjusted opportunity cost of equity exceeds the mortgage rate.

7. Which of the following mortgage types have the most default risk, assuming the initial loan-to-value ratio, contract interest rate, and all other loan terms are identical?
   - *a.* Interest-only loans.
   - *b.* Early payment loans.
   - *c.* Partially amortized loans.
   - *d.* Purchase money mortgages.

8. A mortgage that is intended to enable older households to "liquify" the equity in their home is the
   - *a.* Graduated payment mortgage (GPM).
   - *b.* Adjustable rate mortgage (ARM).
   - *c.* Purchase money mortgage (PMM).
   - *d.* Reverse annuity mortgage (RAM).

9. Adjustable rate mortgages (ARMs) commonly have all the following *except*
   - *a.* A "teaser" rate.
   - *b.* A margin.
   - *c.* An index.
   - *d.* A periodic interest rate cap.
   - *e.* An inflation index.

10. The Real Estate Settlement and Procedures Act (RESPA) does all except
    - *a.* Require advanced good faith estimates of closing costs.
    - *b.* Require disclosure of the annual percentage rate (APR) on a loan.

c. Require that a home mortgage borrower be permitted to inspect settlement expenses one business day before closing.

d. RESPA does all of the above.

11. Annual percentage rate stems from
 a. The Federal "Truth in Lending Act" of 1968.

b. The Real Estate Settlement Procedures Act of 1974/1977.

c. The Equal Credit Opportunity Act of 1974/1976.

d. State real estate licensing laws.

e. Rules of the Federal Trade Commission.

PROBLEMS FOR THOUGHT AND SOLUTION

1. Calculate the original loan size of a fixed payment mortgage if the monthly payment is $1,146.78, the annual interest rate is 8.0 percent, and the original loan term is 15 years.

2. On an adjustable rate mortgage, do borrowers always prefer smaller (tighter) rate caps that limit the amount the contract interest rate can increase in any given year or over the life of the loan? Explain why or why not.

3. Explain the potential tax advantage associated with home equity loans.

4. Distinguish between conforming and nonconforming residential mortgage loans and explain the importance of the difference.

5. Discuss the role and importance of private mortgage insurance in the residential mortgage market.

6. Consider a $75,000 mortgage loan with an annual interest rate of 8 percent. The loan term is 7 years, but monthly payments will be based on a 30-year amortization schedule. What is the monthly payment? What will be the balloon payment at the end of the loan term?

7. Explain the maturity imbalance problem faced by savings and loan associations that hold fixed payment home mortgages as assets.

8. A mortgage banker is originating a conventional fixed payment mortgage with the following terms:

> Annual interest rate: 9.0 percent
>
> Loan term: 15 years
>
> Payment frequency: monthly
>
> Loan amount: $160,000
>
> Total up-front financing costs: $4,000

a. Calculate the annual percentage rate (APR) for Truth-in-Lending purposes.

b. Do you think the APR accurately reflects the effective borrowing cost? Explain.

9. Give some examples of up-front financing costs associated with residential mortgages. What rule can one apply to determine if a settlement (closing) cost should be included in the calculation of the effective borrowing cost?

CASE PROBLEMS

1. A new home is available from a builder that would normally be financed with an $80,000 loan at 8.5 percent with monthly payments over a 30 year term. The builder is offering potential buyers an $80,000, 30-year, loan that carries a 6.5 percent annual interest rate for 3 years. After 36 monthly payments, the contract rate would increase to 8.5 percent. The builder has worked out an arrangement with First Federal Savings and Loan. First Federal will originate and own the mortgage. If the home is purchased with the interest rate buydown, the builder's selling price is $107,000. If purchased without the buydown, the selling price is $100,000.

a. How much would you expect the builder to have to pay First Federal up-front to buy down the payments on each loan for 3 years?

b. Would you recommend that the buyer make use of the interest rate buydown? Explain.

2. Assume the following for a one-year adjustable rate mortgage loan that is tied to the one-year Treasury rate:

> Loan amount: $150,0000
>
> Annual rate cap: 2%
>
> Life-of-loan cap: 5%
>
> Margin: 2.75%
>
> First-year contract rate: 5.50%
>
> One-year Treasury rate at end of year 1: 5.25%
>
> One-year Treasury rate at end of year 2: 5.50%
>
> Loan term in years: 30

Given these assumptions, calculate the following:

a. Initial monthly payment

b. Loan balance end of year 1

c. Year 2 contract rate

d. Year 2 monthly payment

e. Loan balance end of year 2

f. Year 3 contract rate

g. Year 3 payment

3. Assume an elderly couple owns a $140,000 home that is free and clear of mortgage debt. A reverse annuity mortgage (RAM) lender has agreed to a $100,000 RAM. The loan term is 12 years, the contract interest rate is 9.25 percent, and payments will be made at the end of each month.

a. What is the monthly payment on this RAM?

b. Fill in the following partial loan amortization table:

Month	Beginning Balance	Monthly Payment	Interest	Ending Balance
1				
2				
3				
4				
5				

c. What will be the loan balance at the end of the 12-year term?

d. What portion of the loan balance at the end of year 12 represents principal? What portion represents interest?

4. Assume the following:

> Loan Amount: $100,000
>
> Interest rate: 10 percent annually
>
> Term: 15 years, monthly payments

a. What is the monthly payment?

b. What will be the loan balance at the end of nine years?

c. What is the effective borrowing cost on the loan if the lender charges three points at origination and the loan goes to maturity?

d. What is the effective borrowing cost on the loan if the lender charges three points at origination and the loan is prepaid at the end of year 9?

5. Five years ago you borrowed $100,000 to finance the purchase of a $120,000 home. The interest rate on the old mortgage loan is 10 percent. Payments are being made *monthly* to amortize the loan over 30 years. You have found another lender who will refinance the current outstanding loan balance at 8 percent with monthly payments for 30 years. The new lender will charge two discount points on the loan. Other refinancing costs will equal $3,000. There are no prepayment penalties associated with either loan. You feel the appropriate opportunity cost to apply to this refinancing decision is 8 percent.

a. What is the payment on the old loan?

b. What is the current loan balance on the old loan (five years after origination)?

c. What would be the monthly payment on the new loan?

d. Should you refinance today if the new loan is expected to be outstanding for five years?

INTERNET EXERCISES

For residential mortgage markets, accurate interest rate information is available on-line from the Federal Home Loan Mortgage Corporation, commonly referred to as "Freddie Mac," and from the Federal National Mortgage Association, known as "Fannie Mae." These sites also contain information on the differences between the primary and secondary mortgage market.

1. Go to the Freddie Mac home page:

   http://www.freddiemac.com/

   and download the latest primary mortgage market survey. What was the average interest rate charged on 30-year, fixed-rate residential mortgages last week? What was the average 15-year fixed-rate?

What was the one-year ARM rate? Do these figures represent an increase or a decrease over the previous week's rates?

2. Go to the Freddie Mac home page and download information regarding Freddie Mac's role in the mortgage market. Briefly discusses the role secondary market institutions play and how they increase the efficiency of real estate markets. (Hint: the site has a FAQ link with answers to "Frequently Asked Questions" that may prove beneficial.)

3. Repeat problem 2 using data from Fannie Mae:

   http://www.fanniemae.com/

ADDITIONAL READINGS

Substantial portions of the following books are devoted to residential mortgage financing:

Brueggeman, William B., and Jeffrey D. Fisher. *Real Estate Finance and Investments,* 10th ed. Burr Ridge, IL: Richard D. Irwin, 1997.

Clauretie, Terrence M., and G. Stacy Sirmans. *Real Estate Finance,* 2nd ed., Upper Saddle River, NJ: Prentice Hall, 1996.

Fabozzi, Frank J., and Franco Modigliano. *Mortgage and Mortgage-Backed Securities Markets.* Cambridge: Harvard Business School Press, 1992.

Wiedemer, John P., *Real Estate Finance,* 7th ed. Upper Saddle River, NJ: Prentice Hall, 1995.

For those who wish to learn more about current issues and to stay abreast of the residential mortgage finance field, we recommend the following journals:

Secondary Mortgage Markets (quarterly), Federal Home Loan Mortgage Corporation, Mailstop 288, 8200 Jones Branch Drive, McLean, VA 22102.

Mortgage Banking (quarterly), Mortgage Bankers Association, Washington, DC 20073–0021.

17
CHAPTER

SOURCES OF FUNDS FOR RESIDENTIAL MORTGAGES

INTRODUCTION

THE MARKET FOR RESIDENTIAL FINANCING

DEPOSITORY LENDERS IN THE PRIMARY MARKET
Savings Institutions
Commercial Banks

NONDEPOSITORY LENDERS IN THE PRIMARY MARKET
Mortgage Bankers
Mortgage Brokers
Other Nongovernment-Sponsored Lenders in the Primary Market

GOVERNMENT-SPONSORED MORTGAGE PROGRAMS
FHA-Insured Loans
VA-Guaranteed Loans

THE SECONDARY MARKET FOR RESIDENTIAL MORTGAGES

PURCHASERS OF RESIDENTIAL MORTGAGES IN THE SECONDARY MARKET
Federal National Mortgage Association
Federal Home Loan Mortgage Corporation

The Importance of Fannie Mae and Freddie Mac
Government National Mortgage Association
Life Insurance Companies
Other Secondary Market Purchasers

THE LENDER'S MORTGAGE LOAN DECISIONS
Affordability Ratios
The Effects of Federal Programs and Regulations

SUMMARY

KEY TERMS

TEST YOURSELF

PROBLEMS FOR THOUGHT AND SOLUTION

INTERNET EXERCISE

CASE PROBLEMS

ADDITIONAL READINGS

LEARNING OBJECTIVES

After reading this chapter, students will be able to:

1. Comment on the size of the residential mortgage market in the U.S. capital markets.

2. Name and differentiate between the various nongovernment sources of home mortgage loans.

3. Explain the various activities of mortgage bankers and how they differ from depository institutions such as commercial banks, savings and loan associations, and credit unions.

4. Identify and discuss government sponsored mortgage programs designed to aid home buyers.

5. Distinguish among the primary activities of the Federal National Mortgage Association, the Federal Home Loan Mortgage Corporation, and the Government National Mortgage Association.

6. Discuss the residential lenders' loan underwriting process. Calculate and interpret multiple measures of mortgage affordability and default risk.

INTRODUCTION

This chapter continues our examination of the residential mortgage market. In the preceding chapter, we discussed the most common types of conventional (that is, nongovernment sponsored) mortgage instruments available to homeowners, including fixed-payment mortgages (FPMs) and adjustable rate mortgages (ARMs). We then considered the numerous financing decisions that a household faces after deciding to purchase a home, including the amount of mortgage debt to use, the type of loan to select from the mortgage menu (for example, ARM versus FPM), and the tradeoff between the contract interest rate and the number of up-front discount points. We also considered two decisions that many borrowers face after obtaining mortgage funds: refinancing and default. We did not discuss where and how households obtain home loans.

This chapter first discusses the various sources of these home mortgage funds in the primary market (savings institutions, mortgage bankers, etc.), as well as the most prominent government sponsored programs that operate in the primary market. We then discuss the major purchasers of home loans in the secondary mortgage market. Finally, we outline the typical process residential lenders use when deciding whether to provide mortgage funds to a household.

E X H I B I T   1 7 - 1

**MORTGAGE DEBT OUTSTANDING BY TYPE OF LOAN
(YEAR-END 1995, IN BILLIONS OF DOLLARS)**

Loan Type	Amount	Percent of Total
Residential (1–4 family)	$3,627	77%
Apartment (multifamily)	288	6
Commercial	707	15
Farm	85	2
Total	$4,707	100%

SOURCE: *Federal Reserve Bulletin* (January 1997), Table 1.54, "Mortgage Debt Outstanding."

THE MARKET FOR RESIDENTIAL FINANCING

Mortgage borrowers must compete to borrow funds in the credit markets. They must bid against other individuals, partnerships, corporations, financial institutions, state and local governments, and the U.S. government. Total mortgage debt outstanding at the end of 1995 exceeded $4.7 trillion. Exhibit 17–1 identifies the four major types of mortgage debt. As of year-end 1995, residential (home) mortgage debt exceeded $3.6 trillion and accounted for 77 percent of total outstanding mortgage debt. Loans to fund the acquisition of apartment (multifamily) buildings represented 6 percent of the total, and loans to fund commercial real estate investments (office buildings, shopping centers, etc.) accounted for 15 percent of the total.

How large is the $3.6 trillion in outstanding residential debt? By way of comparison, the accumulated deficit of the U.S. government was approximately $5.0 trillion at the end of 1995. The $3.6 trillion also is 2.7 times as large as the value of all outstanding corporate bonds and 3.4 times as large as the amount of outstanding consumer debt.[1]

DEPOSITORY LENDERS IN THE PRIMARY MARKET

Depository institutions, such as savings and loan associations, savings banks, credit unions, and commercial banks, are major sources of home financing. These institutions also are called **financial intermediaries** because they bring together depositors and mortgage borrowers. They collect the (often small) savings of many individuals, households, and organizations, then lend larger sums to individuals, households, and organizations who need them. Depository lenders are limited in the kinds of loans they can originate, in the percentage of their assets that can be invested in certain types of loans, and in the qualifications that can be accepted for mortgage borrowers and for the property that is

---

[1]The source for these comparisons is the *Federal Reserve Bulletin*, January 1997, Tables 1.54, 1.41, 1.59, and 1.55.

REAL ESTATE FOCUS 17-1

The Savings and Loan Debacle

During the late 1980s and early 1990s, approximately one-half of the nation's S&Ls failed. The story of those failures is a sad story of bad public policy, inadequate regulation, and some (relatively few) incompetent and fraudulent managers. The government (and ultimately all taxpayers) paid the huge costs—up to $500 billion by many estimates—because the government guarantees each account in an S&L up to $100,000.

The bad public policy largely responsible for the mess was the deregulation of financial institutions coupled with a deposit insurance system that did not penalize institutions with risky portfolios of loans and investments. In the early 1980s, Congress authorized S&Ls to expand their activities into new lending and investment areas, but only after they were allowed to raise interest rates paid on deposits. Their earnings became increasingly constrained, and many S&L managers began a reckless search for higher profits. They made large loans on bad real estate projects, began trading in bond options and futures, and made direct investments in risky business ventures. Nevertheless, their deposit insurance premiums (the amount they had to pay periodically to the Federal Savings and Loan Insurance Corporation for insurance of accounts) stayed the same per deposit dollar. This is like a driver with 10 accidents paying the same rate for auto insurance as a safe driver. Even some S&Ls that followed a more traditional, conservative approach failed. Their portfolios of low-yielding mortgages precluded the possibility of making more lucrative loans to offset high deposit rate costs.

At the same time that S&Ls were beginning to become involved in risky loans and investments, regulation and supervision of their activities were reduced. Consequently, some S&L managers, trying desperately to improve their earnings and avoid collapse, not only accepted too much risk but also engaged in outright fraud. While this factor has received a lot of attention, it seems likely to be overplayed. One study showed that S&L losses caused by fraud amounted to only 3 percent of total losses. The vast majority of losses were caused by factors beyond the control of S&L managers.*

*From a study by Ely and Co. and reported in *The Wall Street Journal*, July 20, 1990.

---

pledged as collateral for the loan. A number of different regulatory authorities often have oversight responsibilities for an institution.

SAVINGS INSTITUTIONS

Savings institutions include savings and loan associations, savings banks, and credit unions. During the past several years, **savings and loan associations** (S&Ls), because of government deregulation and competitive pressures, have evolved from highly specialized home mortgage lending institutions to more general financial institutions. Today, in addition to home loans, S&Ls are permitted to make loans on commercial and industrial property, second mortgage loans, consumer loans, and commercial loans. They also offer many other services such as checking accounts, credit cards, financial advice, real estate and stockbrokerage services, safe deposit boxes, and traveler's checks. Looking back, there is little doubt that the expanded activities of many S&Ls—especially the involvement of some in the much riskier commercial real estate market—created some of the substantial losses suffered by many S&Ls in the late 1980s and early 1990s (see Real Estate Focus 17–1).

To cope with massive losses and the closing of many S&Ls (and some commercial banks), Congress passed the Financial Institutions Reform, Recovery, and Enforcement Act (FIRREA) in 1989. FIRREA has affected many aspects of the mortgage lending business, including the portfolio (asset) requirements of regulated lenders, the licensing of real estate appraisers, and the minimum capital requirements of depository institutions.

To become a "Qualified Thrift Lender" an S&L must hold at least 70 percent of its investments in residential mortgage loans or mortgage-backed securities. Core capital (net worth) requirements mandate that S&Ls have equity capital (common stock, retained earnings, and other liquid assets) equal to at least 3 percent of the value of the S&L's assets. In addition, S&Ls must retain as equity capital an amount equal to at least 8 percent of the value of its **risk-weighted assets**. Assets are assigned a risk measure (or weight) by federal regulators of 0 to 200 percent. For example, a home mortgage loan carries a 50 percent weight. If the S&L makes an $80,000 loan, $3,200 in capital is required to support the loan ($0.50 \times 0.08 \times \$80,000$). If the risk weighting (level) is 0 (e.g., government bonds), no additional risk-based capital is required beyond the 3 percent core capital. The purpose of the risk-based capital requirements is to require the owners of financial institutions to have more equity capital at risk if they choose more risky investments.

For all practical purposes, **savings banks** (SBs) are now indistinguishable from S&Ls, but in the past they had wider investment powers than S&Ls. SBs, found primarily in the Northeast, started as depository institutions for working people; hence, these banks have names such as Dime Savings Bank and Bowery Savings Bank. Because their liabilities have historically been longer-term savings accounts, SBs have long favored home mortgage loans as investments. In recent years, SBs have invested more in mortgage-backed securities that are backed by the full faith and credit of the U.S. government. Savings banks, like S&Ls, make all types of real estate loans, as well as consumer loans, commercial loans, and second mortgage loans. They also sell life insurance and provide a wide variety of financial services similar to those offered by S&Ls.

Over 18,000 **credit unions** operate in the United States. Their charters restrict them to serving a group of people who can show a common bond such as employees of a corporation, government unit, labor union, or trade association. Credit unions offer a unique attraction as a depository institution because they pay no income taxes. They are typically small and focus on making small loans to their members for purposes such as buying a car or making home improvements. Credit unions, like savings banks and S&Ls, have the authority to make all types of loans and to offer services such as credit cards and safe-deposit boxes. Unlike S&Ls and SBs, they can pay interest on checking accounts. FIRREA also restructured the regulatory system of savings institutions. Both federal and state governments charter savings banks and S&Ls. At the federal level, the U.S. Treasury Department (Office of Thrift Supervision) charters and, along with the Federal Housing Finance Board (FHFB), regulates SBs and S&Ls. The Savings Association Insurance Fund (SAIF) of the Federal Deposit Insurance Corporation (FDIC) insures deposits up to $100,000 in S&Ls and SBs. Credit unions are chartered and regulated by the National Credit Union Administration Board and their deposits, up to $100,000, are insured by the National Credit Union Share Insurance Fund.

EXHIBIT 17-2

**TOTAL CONVENTIONAL ONE- TO FOUR-FAMILY ORIGINATIONS
(IN BILLIONS, AND PERCENT OF TOTAL BY SOURCE)**

	Total (billions)	Savings Institutions	Commercial Banks	Mortgage Banks	Other[1]
1985	$245.8	46%	21%	31%	2%
1986	411.5	49	25	25	2
1987	399.2	50	28	20	2
1988	383.7	48	25	26	2
1989	394.1	38	30	31	1
1990	376.7	35	36	27	1
1991	499.9	27	30	43	1
1992	818.9	26	28	46	1
1993	895.4	23	29	47	1
1994	625.6	23	31	46	1
1995	561.5	20	26	53	1

[1]Other includes life insurance companies, pension funds, federal credit agencies, and state and local credit agencies.
SOURCE: Federal Home Loan Mortgage Corporation

The diminished, though still important, role of savings institutions in the origination of home mortgages is demonstrated in Exhibit 17–2. In the late 1980s, savings institutions were responsible for approximately 50 percent of conventional one- to four-family originations. This percentage declined to approximately 25 percent in the early 1990s. The reduced importance of S&Ls in the primary market has been offset by an expanded role for mortgage banks and commercial banks (both discussed below).

COMMERCIAL BANKS

Commercial banks (CBs) primarily engage in the business of making short-term loans to businesses for inventory financing and other working capital needs. In addition, large CBs often make term loans (unsecured loans having terms of 5 to 15 years) and mortgage loans to corporations and other businesses. The origination of home mortgage loans is a growing activity for many CBs, which fund these loans with their deposit liabilities. However, similar to S&Ls, CBs are increasingly likely to immediately sell their residential originations in the secondary mortgage market. A few large CBs also are creating their own home mortgage pools from their loan originations and using the mortgage pools as collateral for issuing mortgage-backed securities.

Commercial banks indirectly provide additional funds for the housing market in three ways. First, they buy mortgage-backed securities in the secondary mortgage market, as do savings institutions. Second, they provide short-term funds to mortgage banking companies (as will be discussed below) to enable them to originate mortgage loans and hold them until the mortgage banking company can sell the loans in the secondary mortgage market. This type of financing is termed **warehousing** because the mortgage bankers put up the originated loans as security for the bank financing and the loans are "stored" (at the bank or with a trustee) for a relatively short time. Third, CBs make short-term construction loans that provide funds for the construction of buildings. As explained in Chapter 18, builders must usually pay off construction loans when the buildings are completed.

Commercial banks are either state or federally chartered. National charters are issued by the Comptroller of the Currency. Banks with national charters must belong to the Federal Deposit Insurance Corporation (FDIC), which insures deposits up to $100,000. State-chartered banks can join the FDIC system if they qualify and are willing to subject themselves to federal regulation. The credit policies of commercial banks are supervised by the Federal Reserve System (Fed). The Fed also is responsible for determining the percentage of bank liabilities that must be set aside (reserved) in the form of cash or other highly liquid short-term securities. These reserve requirements affect the solvency of the bank as well as the amount of money commercial banks are able to invest in the economy. In addition, the Fed monitors the compliance of commercial banks with the Truth-in-Lending Act and the Community Reinvestment Act (both discussed below).

NONDEPOSITORY LENDERS IN THE PRIMARY MARKET

The depository lenders discussed in the previous section have historically dominated the home mortgage origination business. Using savings deposits, these institutions funded long-term home mortgage loans and then held the whole loans as investments. That is, they have been **portfolio lenders**. However, as financial institutions in the United States suffered through the 1980s and early 1990s, during which time numerous S&Ls (and some commercial banks) failed, mortgage companies emerged as the dominant source of home mortgage originations. As can be seen in Exhibit 17–2, mortgage companies accounted for over 50 percent of all conventional home mortgage originations in 1995. Their share of the FHA/VA originations market (discussed below) is even larger—it exceeds 80 percent.

Mortgage banking companies vary widely in the scope of their activities. **Mortgage bankers** are full service mortgage companies—they process, close, provide funding, and sell the loans they originate in the secondary mortgage market. They also typically service the loans they have sold (collect monthly payments, etc.). However, some mortgage companies specialize in the details of loan origination. These firms are referred to as **mortgage brokers**. Brokers do not provide the funding (or capital) for the loan, nor do they service the loans after they have been sold. Instead, they serve as an intermediary between those who demand mortgage funds (borrowers) and those who supply the funds (lenders or secondary market investors).

This section first examines the activities and growing importance of mortgage bankers and brokers. We then briefly discuss other primary market lenders such as investment banks and finance companies.

MORTGAGE BANKERS

Mortgage bankers lend funds for home financing. They are not financial intermediaries, however, because they do not accept deposits. Mortgage banking companies use their own equity and borrowed capital to originate loans, but they usually sell the loans immediately to institutional investors and secondary mortgage market participants. Thus, they are not portfolio lenders. In fact, mortgage bankers typically obtain commitments from secondary market investors and conduits to buy a specified dollar amount of loans that meet certain criteria. Because the loans come from various parts of the country and the default risk of each loan cannot easily be evaluated by secondary market investors, the home loans originated by mortgage bankers are usually either insured or conforming loans that meet the requirements of Fannie Mae and Freddie Mac. Such insurance or underwriting standards mitigate much of the default risk of home mortgage loans for lenders, allowing the loans to be more easily sold to investors in the secondary market.

The mortgage banking business is largely owned by parent companies, chiefly commercial banks and insurance companies. Recent years have witnessed substantial concentration in the mortgage banking business, with the largest 25 firms controlling a significant percentage of the business.

Loan commitments and funding.   If the borrower is applying for a fixed payment mortgage, the lender usually offers the applicant several choices on when to "lock in" the contract interest rate. These choices may include the time the loan application is taken, when the lender commits to fund the loan, or when the property is acquired from the seller (at closing).

As mentioned above in the discussion of commercial banks, a major source of financing for mortgage companies is bank lines of credit. Commercial banks make open-end loans (up to a maximum amount) that enable the mortgage companies to originate many home mortgage loans. When the loans are sold to institutional investors or conduits (including Fannie Mae and Freddie Mac), the bank line of credit can be paid down, and the process starts again. In addition to warehousing loans, some large mortgage bankers raise funds to originate mortgages by issuing commercial paper. Commercial paper is a short-term (180–270 days) promise to pay on the part of the mortgage banker that carries a lower interest rate than the prime rate (the rate banks charge their best customers).

Servicing.   In addition to originating loans, most mortgage bankers retain the right to service the loans for the secondary market investors who have purchased them from the mortgage banker. **Loan servicing** includes collecting the monthly payment from the borrower and insuring that the borrower's monthly escrow payments for hazard insurance and property taxes are sufficient to allow the servicer to pay in full the annual insurance premium and property taxes on behalf of the borrower when they are due. Servicers also are responsible for sending out notifications if the borrower is delinquent with his or her payment. Mortgage bankers and other servicers receive a monthly fee for servicing the loan that amounts to 0.25 to 0.50 percent (annually) of the outstanding loan balance. For example, if the outstanding balance of a loan at the beginning of a month is $100,000, and the annual servicing fee is 0.375 percent, then the servicer's fee for that month would be $31.25 (0.00375/12 × $100,000). If the borrower's monthly mortgage payment is $750, the servicer would keep $31.25 and pass $718.75 on to the secondary market investor that owns the mortgage.

Sales of mortgage loans.   Mortgage bankers continually sell their originated loans, pay off the warehouse loans, and start the process over again. However, their fixed-rate commitments to borrowers expose mortgage bankers to risk. For example, assume during a given week that a lender commits to originate and fund a number of 30-year, fixed-payment mortgages. These commitments are added to the originator's **mortgage pipeline**—a term used to describe the lender's approved, but currently unfunded, loan commitments. Also, assume borrowers choose to lock in the contract rate when they receive the commitment and that the rate is 8 percent. The approved borrowers will usually have 45 to 60 days to close ("take down") the loans. If mortgage interest rates decline, some of the borrowers may choose not to close the loan at the end of the 45 or 60 days because, in the meantime, they have obtained a lower rate from another lender. This potential loss of borrowers is called pipeline fallout risk. If interest rates rise after the lender makes the commitment at 8 percent, a larger percentage of loans in the pipeline will close because borrowers will be unable to find a better deal.

However, if rates rise over the commitment period, the contract rate at closing will be less than the current market rate and the mortgage banker will have to sell the newly originated loan at a discount (for *less* than the amount originated). On the other hand, if rates fall over the commitment period, those loans that do close can be sold at a premium in the secondary market. To avoid exposure to interest rate and, therefore, price variations over the loan processing and commitment periods, many mortgage bankers prefer to purchase a **forward commitment** from a secondary market investor with a prespecified future selling price. This commitment obligates the secondary market investor to purchase, and the mortgage banker to sell, a prespecified dollar amount of a certain type of loan. The commitment is for a limited period of time, usually 30 days to six months. The forward commitment also will typically specify the price (and therefore the yield) at which the mortgages will be purchased. For example, the secondary market investor may commit to purchase $20 million of 9 percent fixed-payment mortgages (FPMs) at a price of "99." This means that the investor will pay the mortgage banker $99 per $100 of outstanding mortgage principal for any 9 percent mortgage delivered to the investor during the commitment period. This discounted price and the promised payments on the loans determine the investor's yield on the acquisition.[2] The forward commitment provides assurance to the warehousing lender that the mortgage banker will be able to sell the originated loans and pay off the warehouse loan.[3]

---

[2]As discussed in Chapter 19, the expected yield also depends on the length of time the secondary market investor expects the mortgages to be outstanding.

[3]Despite the risks, some mortgage bankers do originate loans without a forward commitment. The mortgage banker still has the option to negotiate with secondary market investors for the sale of these loans. The sale of loans that have already been made is called an *immediate commitment.* Even though loans sold on an immediate commitment currently exist, industry practice allows the mortgage banker up to 60 days to deliver the mortgages to the investor.

EXHIBIT 17-3

AN EXAMPLE OF HEDGING INTEREST RATE RISK
IN A MORTGAGE PIPELINE

Pieces of the Mortgage Pipeline

Hedged by purchasing forward commitments	Hedged by purchasing standby forward commitments	Portion of pipeline not hedged because mortgage banker is confident these loans will not close.

Mortgage bankers know from experience that many borrowers will not be willing, or able, to take down the loans for which the borrowers have received commitments from lenders. For this reason, mortgage bankers also often purchase **standby forward commitments** from secondary market investors that give them the right, but *not* the obligation, to sell a prespecified dollar amount of a certain loan type to the seller of the standby commitment. If a larger than expected portion of the loans in the mortgage banker's pipeline are taken down by borrowers, perhaps because interest rates have risen, the option to sell the prespecified amount of mortgages granted by the standby commitment is exercised by the mortgage banker. However, if mortgage rates have fallen over the commitment period, and an unexpectedly large amount of pipeline fallout occurs, the mortgage banker does not have to deliver mortgages to the seller of the standby commitment. This protects the mortgage banker from having to deliver mortgages that did not originate during the commitment period.

Exhibit 17–3 depicts a typical strategy mortgage bankers use to protect against changes in interest rates over the commitment period. The three rectangles represent the total number of mortgages of a specific type—for example, 30-year FPMs with 8.5 percent contract rates—on which the mortgage banker has issued commitments to borrowers. The left-hand portion of the pipeline is hedged by obtaining forward commitments. This is the portion of the pipeline the lender is confident will be taken down by borrowers, regardless of changes in interest rates. The right-hand portion of the pipeline represents the loans the lender expects not to be taken down. This portion does not need to be hedged against changes in interest rates and mortgage prices. For the middle portion of the pipeline, the mortgage banker is willing to incur the expense of obtaining a standby forward commitment in order to be protected against interest rate increases, and not have to deliver if this portion of the pipeline is not taken down by borrowers.

Experience and current interest rate expectations dictate the relative size of the three rectangles. If mortgage rates rise unexpectedly over the commitment period, the actual number of loans taken down can exceed the number for which the mortgage banker has purchased forward commitments. If so, the originator then exercises her right to deliver mortgages to the seller of the standby forward commitment. However, if rates fall and pipeline fallout is therefore greater than expected, the mortgage banker will have purchased an expensive standby commitment that was not fully utilized.

Most mortgage bankers use forward or standby forward commitments to sell their pools of originated loans to large investors or conduits in the secondary market (e.g.,

Fannie Mae, Freddie Mac, and investment bankers such as Salomon Brothers), who then use them as collateral for issuing MBSs. However, some of the larger mortgage banks also are active issuers of private MBSs or Ginnie Mae MBSs (discussed in detail in Chapter 19). Mortgage banks that issue MBSs use the loans they originate as collateral. They also purchase loans from other originators to use as collateral for their MBS issues.[4]

Sources of revenue. Mortgage bankers earn revenues from several activities. Like all home loan originators, mortgage bankers normally charge borrowers a nonrefundable application fee of between $50 and $200 at the time of the loan application. Mortgage bankers also charge an origination fee that is payable if and when the loan closes. The origination fee is typically 1 percent of the loan amount and is separate from any discount points that the mortgage banker may require the borrower to pay at closing. The application and loan origination fee cover all or part of the costs mortgage bankers incur in processing the loan application, including the commission earned by the loan representative who takes the loan application and works with the borrower in documenting and processing the required paperwork. In addition to these up-front fees, mortgage bankers earn monthly fees from servicing the mortgages they originate and sell. This has been the most profitable aspect of the mortgage banking business. Mortgage bankers also stand to make (or lose) money when they sell loans into the secondary market without forward commitments or other hedges.

Regulation. Mortgage bankers are not regulated by any specialized government entity. However, as corporations or partnerships they are subject to state laws that apply to these business forms. Moreover, most mortgage bankers seek to acquire and maintain approval as a qualified lender or servicer from Fannie Mae, Freddie Mac, the FHA, and other secondary market investors. As a result, they are subject to periodic audits from these agencies.

MORTGAGE BROKERS

Mortgage lending has become increasingly complex. As a result, the demand for knowledgeable mortgage brokers has increased significantly. As mentioned above, a mortgage broker operates differently than a mortgage banker in that a broker does not actually provide what the borrower ultimately desires: a loan. Instead, a mortgage broker specializes in serving as an intermediary between the borrower (the customer) and the lender (the client). Many mortgage brokers serve as correspondents for large mortgage bankers who desire to do business in an area but do not feel the volume of business justifies the expense of staffing a local office. As compensation, the broker receives a fee for taking the loan application and a portion of the origination fee if and when the loan closes. Many

---

[4]In the absence of forward commitments, some sophisticated mortgage bankers hedge the interest rate risk on their mortgage commitments by purchasing securities, such as futures contracts, whose market prices will increase (decrease) if interest rates rise (decrease), unlike the prices of mortgage securities. By "putting on a hedge" as soon as they agree to fund a pipeline of fixed-rate loans at a given interest rate, the mortgage banker gains protection from unexpected changes in mortgage interest rates.

industry analysts expect the role of mortgage brokers to continue to grow in conjunction with the explosion in information technology. As brokers gain access to instantaneous interest rate quotes from hundreds of mortgage originators, their ability to find the lowest cost option for borrowers will increase the value of their services.

OTHER NONGOVERNMENT-SPONSORED LENDERS IN THE PRIMARY MARKET

The dramatic growth in the secondary mortgage market and the increasing popularity of residential MBSs have encouraged many firms to enter the home mortgage origination business. For example, companies with experience in other types of consumer lending, such as General Motors Acceptance Corporation and AT&T Capital, are now underwriting home loans. Several Wall Street investment banks and finance companies (Household Finance, Household International, etc.) also are originating home loans. The originations provide these firms with the mortgage collateral they need to issue residential MBSs. Even some large real estate brokerage firms and home builders have entered the market. Nevertheless, these other sources still account for less than 1 percent of the residential originations market (see Exhibit 17–2).

GOVERNMENT-SPONSORED MORTGAGE PROGRAMS

The interactions of buyers and sellers in free and competitive markets may not result in a fair distribution of income or of the goods and services that household incomes command. Further, markets with well-identified imperfections, such as many real estate markets, may produce even less equitable distributions because, for example, low-income, poorly educated consumers may have difficulty obtaining the same information as other consumers. Also, discrimination of various forms may contribute to economic inequality. In fact, a general perception persists among many U.S. housing economists and policy makers that an inadequate level of housing production would occur if government policies and programs were not in place to help middle- and lower-middle-income households obtain mortgages and purchase homes. The quest for fairness in housing and mortgage finance markets is viewed as a legitimate and ongoing concern of governments.

A noted economist, Allan Meltzer, once stated that housing policy in the United States has been essentially *mortgage policy*, the purpose of which has been to stimulate housing production by increasing the availability of mortgage credit. The primary approach to increasing the availability of mortgage credit has been to rely on private market participants to supply the funds and manage the risks of our housing finance system. One advantage of this basic approach is that the private sector is more efficient in fund raising and risk management. In addition, this approach allows the government to focus on those areas where the private market is unable to provide solutions to perceived problems.

Some government programs make loans directly to home buyers in the primary market. Examples at the federal level include the Farm Credit System and the Farmers

Home Administration. In addition, state governments issue tax-exempt debt to support loans with below-market interest rates for first-time home buyers. Many state and local housing agencies also offer low-interest loan programs to low and moderate income households. The most prominent government sponsored housing finance programs that operate in the primary market at the national level are the Federal Housing Administration (FHA) default insurance program and the Veterans Administration (VA) program that provides guarantees on loans made by private lenders to qualified veterans.

FHA-INSURED LOANS

The FHA insures loans made by private lenders that meet FHA's property and credit-risk standards. The insurance is paid for by the borrower and protects the FHA-approved lender against loss of capital from borrower default. Unlike conventional mortgage insurance, which protects the lender against some *portion* of the potential loan loss, **FHA mortgage insurance** covers *any* lender loss after foreclosure and conveyance of title to the property to the U.S. Department of Housing and Urban Development (HUD). The FHA borrower pays both an up-front premium equal to 2.20 percent of the loan amount, plus a monthly premium for 5 to 10 years. The up-front premium can be included in the loan amount and therefore paid for over the life of the loan. On a 30-year loan of $80,000 having a 10 percent interest rate, the up-front mortgage insurance premium (MIP) is $1,760 (0.022 × 80,000). Thus, the total amount borrowed would be $81,760, and the amount added to the monthly payments to amortize the MIP would be $15.44.[5] The total monthly payment (including MIP) would be $717.50. The premiums are deposited by FHA into the **Mutual Mortgage Insurance Fund**, which reimburses lenders in case of foreclosure.

In addition to the up-front MIP, FHA borrowers also must pay a 0.5 percent annual premium on the outstanding balance of the loan for 5 to 10 years. The higher the initial LTVR, the longer the monthly premium must be paid. On the $80,000 loan, the annual premium would be 0.005 × $80,000 = $400. This amount is divided by 12 and the result is added to the monthly payments ($400.00/12 = $33.33). This premium decreases each year as the outstanding balance decreases. As with private mortgage insurance, FHA insurance increases the effective borrowing cost of the mortgage.

The FHA has many programs to insure mortgages for various types of properties. Some of the programs, for example, insure loans for low-income housing, nursing homes, cooperative apartments, and condominiums. The most widely used FHA program insures single-family home mortgages and is authorized by Title II Section 203 of the National Housing Act. Thus, these loans are often called **Section 203 loans**. The maximum amount on these loans varies from area to area and is increased each year by the rate of general inflation in the economy. As of January 1, 1996, the limit in low-cost areas was $78,660, while in high-cost parts of the country the limit was $155,240. Within these extremes, other limits often are established on a county-by-county basis.

---

[5]The calculator keystrokes are N = 360, I = 10 percent/12, PV = −1,760, PMT = ?, and FV = 0.

The down payment calculation on FHA loans is a complicated process that depends on whether the seller pays any of the buyer's closing costs, whether the loan amount is above or below $50,000, and whether allowable closing costs are added to the property value or sale price (whichever is lower). The *basic* type of calculation is shown below. To obtain the formulas and actual calculations for a loan, a prospective borrower should consult an FHA lender.

1. For properties costing $50,000 and less, the loan amount is calculated as 97 percent of the acquisition cost, which is equal to the property value *plus* allowable closing costs. (Note: Allowable closing costs do not include points.) For example, on a $39,000 property with allowable closing costs of $1,000, the loan amount would be $38,800 (0.97 × $40,000), which implies a required down payment of $1,200.
2. For properties costing more than $50,000, the loan amount is calculated as 97 percent of the first $25,000, plus 95 percent of the remainder. For example, on a $78,000 property with allowable closing costs of $2,000, the loan amount would be calculated as follows:

$$\$25,000 \times 0.97 = \$24,250$$
$$+ (\$80,000 - \$25,000) \times 0.95 = \underline{\$52,250}$$
$$\text{Loan amount} = \$76,500$$

The required down payment would equal $3,500. The $76,500 loan amount translates into an LTVR of 98.1 percent ($76,500/$78,000).

These down payment calculations assume the seller is not paying any of the buyer's closing costs. If the seller or any other third party pays some or all of the buyer's closing costs, this amount must be subtracted from the amount to be financed. Because FHA-insured loans are made with higher LTVRs, and because the FHA assumes the entire risk of default, premiums charged by the FHA are usually higher than otherwise comparable private mortgage insurance premiums.

Before the FHA was established in 1934, the typical home loan was relatively short term (5 to 15 years) and required principal repayment in full at the end of the term of the loan (that is, loans were nonamortizing). With the decline in incomes during the Great Depression, many people could not repay their mortgage loans and lost their homes through foreclosure. Policy makers reasoned that if the terms for home loans were extended to 20 years, if the principal could be repaid a little at a time (i.e., fully amortized) over the term of the loans, and if a government agency provided insurance against losses, the possibilities for home ownership would be greatly enhanced. First, lenders would be encouraged to again make home mortgage loans because of the insurance feature. Second, more families could afford homes because of the longer maturities of loans. Third, fewer defaults would occur because of the amortization feature. Thus, the FHA was organized to demonstrate the feasibility of home lending with long-term, amortized loans with insurance protection for lenders participating in the program.

VA-GUARANTEED LOANS

The Department of Veterans Affairs (VA) is a government agency whose purpose is to help veterans readjust to civilian life. **VA-guaranteed loans** help veterans obtain home mortgage loans for which they might not otherwise qualify. Usually, the VA guarantees loans originated by private lending institutions to veterans up to a maximum loss of $50,750. Thus, if a veteran defaults, the VA will reimburse the lender for any loss up to this amount after the property has been foreclosed and sold.

The VA will guarantee loans to eligible veterans up to 100 percent of a property's value. However, the VA does charge a funding fee that is a percentage of the loan, with the percentage based on the down payment. As of March 1995, the percentage is 2.0 percent on loans with no down payment, 1.5 percent on loans with a 5 to 9.99 percent down payment, and 1.25 percent on loans with a 10 percent or higher down payment.[6] The funding fee can be added to the loan amount (financed). Closing costs can not be included in the amount of the loan.

The VA also prohibits lenders from charging points (or discounts) to veterans for making a loan. Sellers of properties, however, may be willing to pay points to help veterans obtain loans to buy their properties. In areas where eligible veterans cannot obtain loans from approved VA lenders, the VA can make direct loans to them.

THE SECONDARY MARKET FOR RESIDENTIAL MORTGAGES

The primary market lenders discussed above either hold the individual mortgages in their portfolios, sell the mortgages in the secondary market, or use the mortgages as collateral for the issuance of a mortgage-backed security (MBS). The holders of the mortgage securities, either by origination, by the purchase of loans in the secondary market, or by the purchase of MBSs, represent the ultimate source of mortgage funds for borrowers.

Well-developed private secondary markets exist for most securities, such as stocks and bonds, and for some physical assets. However, the secondary market for residential mortgages before government involvement in the early 1970s was fragmented and poorly developed. The reasons for a weak private secondary mortgage market included the variation in mortgage instruments among states, the differences among properties that serve as collateral for the mortgage, differing appraisal practices, and varying loan standards and underwriting practices of lending institutions (that is, the process and policies for evaluating the risks of mortgage loan default). This lack of standardization made it extremely difficult for potential purchasers in the secondary mortgage market to analyze the risk and return characteristics of mortgage investments, which, in turn, increased the return (or yield) they required on mortgage investments—if they were willing to purchase mortgages at all. The originating lenders then passed on these higher required yields to mortgage borrowers in the form of higher mortgage rates. In addition, mortgage origina-

---

[6]These fees apply only to "regular" veterans who have not before made use of the program. Veterans of the National Guard and the Reserves are not eligible.

tors perceived home loans to be relatively illiquid because they could not be quickly and easily sold in an active secondary market. This lack of liquidity also resulted in fewer loans and higher mortgage interest rates for home buyers.

The lack of a well-functioning secondary market for residential mortgages was addressed by government action through the restructuring of the secondary mortgage market in the early 1970s. Since that time, innovation and growth have characterized the residential mortgage market. More than half of all residential mortgage loans originated in the United States are now sold into the secondary mortgage market and used as collateral for the issuance of MBSs. This securitization of pools of standardized residential mortgages has greatly increased the liquidity and efficiency of the mortgage market. By attracting nontraditional investors, such as pension funds, life insurance companies, and mutual funds, MBSs have brought many new sources of investment capital into the residential mortgage market.

PURCHASERS OF RESIDENTIAL MORTGAGES IN THE SECONDARY MARKET

The largest purchasers of residential mortgages in the secondary market are the Federal National Mortgage Association, "Fannie Mae," and the Federal Home Loan Mortgage Corporation, "Freddie Mac." These government sponsored enterprises (GSEs) also are the largest issuers of residential MBSs, which are written against pools of mortgages purchased from primary market originators. The sale of MBSs and the issuance of other note and bond obligations are the primary sources of the funds used by the GSEs to pursue their activities. In addition to the GSEs, a number of traditional government agencies, such as the FHA, the VA, and the **Government National Mortgage Association** (Ginnie Mae), buy, hold, and insure mortgages and MBSs. The activities of these traditional agencies are funded by federal tax dollars. Any debt obligations they issue are backed by the full faith and credit of the U.S. government. There also are numerous state and local credit agencies that buy and hold residential mortgages. Their activities are financed primarily by the sale of tax-exempt bonds.

FEDERAL NATIONAL MORTGAGE ASSOCIATION

The Federal National Mortgage Association was organized in 1938 to provide a secondary market for FHA-insured mortgages and, later, VA-guaranteed loans. Congress expected it to set an example for private lenders and investors of how to operate in the secondary mortgage market. Fannie Mae became a semiprivate organization in 1968 when it was moved off the U.S. government's budget. At that time, it was authorized to sell one-third of its capital stock to private owners and to have two-thirds of its board of directors elected by the private owners of the company. However, one-third of its board of directors would be appointed by the president of the United States, and it could continue to borrow with government assistance (the importance of which is discussed below). Fannie Mae also continued to be obligated to help attain the national goal of safe and decent housing for

EXHIBIT 17-4

HOLDERS OF OUTSTANDING RESIDENTIAL MORTGAGE DEBT (YEAR-END 1995, IN BILLIONS OF DOLLARS)[1]

Commercial banks	$664	(18%)		
Savings institutions	438	(12%)		
Life insurance companies	7	(< 1%)		
Financial Institutions			$1,109	(30%)
Fannie Mae	$168	(5%)		
Freddie Mac	40	(1%)		
Other federal agencies	67	(2%)		
Total federal agencies			$275	(8%)
MBSs insured by Fannie Mae	$570	(16%)		
MBSs insured by Freddie Mac	512	(14%)		
MBSs insured by Ginnie Mae	461	(13%)		
Private MBS pools	214	(6%)		
Total MBS pools[2]			$1,757	(49%)
Individuals and others[3]			$ 486	(13%)
All holders			$3,627	(100%)

[1] SOURCE: *Federal Reserve Bulletin*, Table 1.54, January 1997

[2] Outstanding balances of MBSs insured or guaranteed by the agency indicated.

[3] Others include mortgage companies, REITs, noninsured pension funds, and credit unions.

low- and moderate-income families. In 1970, Fannie Mae was authorized to purchase conventional mortgages in addition to FHA-insured and VA-guaranteed loans.

Fannie Mae now has well-developed programs for the purchase of both conventional and government-underwritten residential mortgages from mortgage companies, commercial banks, savings and loan associations, and other approved lenders. The majority of these acquired mortgages are combined into packages or mortgage pools, securities are written against the pools, and the securities are then sold to investors (these MBSs are covered in detail in Chapter 19). The agency obtains its funds for the acquisition of mortgage pools by selling stock in the public capital market (its stock is traded on the New York Stock Exchange), by selling MBSs, by obtaining (forward) commitment fees from originating lenders for loan purchases, by earning interest on its mortgage portfolio and other investments, and by issuing government-guaranteed notes and bonds.

At year-end 1995, Fannie Mae held $168 billion in mortgages in its portfolio, or about 5 percent of the $3.6 trillion in outstanding residential mortgages (see Exhibit 17–4). In addition, approximately $570 billion in MBSs issued by Fannie Mae and owned by a wide variety of investors were outstanding. Because the MBS investors are the actual owners of the mortgage pools used as collateral for the MBSs, these mortgages are not listed as Fannie Mae assets. The MBSs issued and insured by Fannie Mae, along with their outright ownership of $168 billion in mortgages, accounted for 21 percent of the outstanding residential mortgage market.

FEDERAL HOME LOAN MORTGAGE CORPORATION

Congress created the Federal Home Loan Mortgage Corporation in 1970. Freddie Mac's purpose, like that of Fannie Mae, is to develop the private secondary mortgage market. It was originally designed to create an active secondary market for mortgages originated by savings and loan associations. The S&Ls had not found Fannie Mae particularly helpful because S&Ls primarily originated conventional loans, and Fannie Mae was not authorized to purchase conventional loans until 1970. Freddie Mac currently buys both government-underwritten and conventional loans from all types of lenders. The majority of these loans are pooled and used as collateral for the issuance of MBSs. Thus, Freddie Mac and Fannie Mae are operationally quite similar. Freddie Mac, however, puts greater emphasis on issuing MBSs; at year-end 1995, Freddie Mac held only $40 billion in mortgages. However, $512 billion in MBSs, or 14 percent of total residential mortgages outstanding, had been issued by Freddie Mac.

THE IMPORTANCE OF FANNIE MAE AND FREDDIE MAC

Today, Fannie Mae and Freddie Mac are two of the country's largest financial intermediaries. When these GSEs purchase loans in the secondary market, the originating lenders, or a firm that has purchased the servicing rights, continues to service the loans, remitting in bulk, to the GSEs, the payments they receive from borrowers.

One of the key functions of the GSEs, and a primary source of income for them, is the forward commitments they make to purchase loans from qualified originators. By issuing (selling) a commitment, the GSE pledges to purchase "qualified" loans from originators over a specified period of time. For example, the GSE may commit to purchase 8 percent, 30-year, fixed-rate mortgages issued by the originator at a fixed price; for example, at par or at some percentage of par (i.e., at a discount or premium). With a fixed price commitment, the GSE bears the interest rate and price risk. If, for example, mortgage rates increase after the commitment is issued, the GSE must still purchase the mortgages at the agreed-upon price—even though the market value of the mortgages has declined. Many argue that it is efficient for the GSEs to assume from originators the interest risk associated with fixed-rate mortgages because their size and market knowledge allow them to more easily absorb, or hedge, their interest rate exposure over the commitment period.

In developing and facilitating the secondary market in mortgages, Fannie Mae and Freddie Mac have developed standardized documents and procedures for loans submitted to them for purchase. Standard forms for notes, mortgages, and appraisals, together with standard underwriting criteria, have brought more conformity to the primary, as well as the secondary, mortgage market because their criteria for qualifying borrowers and properties establish market norms. In fact, many other secondary market investors will only purchase mortgages that meet the underwriting standards of the GSEs. Because of this GSE-induced standardization, investors today are much better able to buy and sell mortgages and MBSs because the risk/return characteristics of these securities are more easily analyzed. Moreover, the GSEs have provided liquidity to mortgage originators at critical times. The increased standardization and liquidity the GSEs provide have greatly improved mortgage market efficiency. The GSEs also have helped increase the flow of investment dollars into the mortgage market as their activities have helped to attract investors who ignored mortgage investments prior to the development of the secondary mortgage market and MBSs.

Finally, it should be noted that the federal government has no direct responsibility for the obligations of the GSEs, and these obligations are not included in the federal budget. However, capital market investors assume the GSEs are supervised closely enough to ensure that they will not default on the debt they issue to help fund their mortgage purchases.[7] Moreover, investors clearly believe the government will step in and pay off the debts of the GSEs, if necessary. Evidence of the close relationship GSEs enjoy with the federal government is that they are able to borrow money in the capital markets at rates only slightly above those paid by the U.S. Treasury. Many private participants in the secondary market have argued that the government's implicit guarantee of GSEs' liabilities should be eliminated because it gives the GSEs an unfair competitive advantage—the implicit guarantees lower the GSEs' cost of obtaining funds. Furthermore, some observers argue that the primary beneficiaries of this guarantee are the private investors who own the publicly traded stock of the GSEs. The proper relationship between the GSEs and the federal government is the topic of an ongoing public policy debate.[8]

GOVERNMENT NATIONAL MORTGAGE ASSOCIATION

The National Housing Act of 1968, which reorganized Fannie Mae, also created the Government National Mortgage Association (Ginnie Mae). The 1968 act charged Ginnie Mae with the obligation to pursue several activities. One role of Ginnie Mae is to subsidize the cost of housing for low-income families. This is accomplished by purchasing below-market mortgages originated by local lenders under various housing programs designed by the FHA. Ginnie Mae buys these below-market-rate loans at par—instead of at a discount—from the originating lenders. Thus, the difference between the loan's par value and discounted value is absorbed by Ginnie Mae, not the originating lender.

Ginnie Mae's most important activity is to guarantee pass-through mortgage-backed securities issued by approved issuers (e.g., mortgage bankers). Ginnie Mae does not buy and sell large numbers of mortgages. Rather, its role under the National Housing Act is to guarantee the timely payment of principal and interest on MBSs issued by private lenders. Ginnie Mae guarantees MBSs backed primarily by pools of FHA-insured and VA-

---

[7]The GSEs are monitored by the Office of Secondary Market Examination and Oversight (OSMEO), whose authority comes from the Federal Housing Enterprise Financial Safety and Soundness Act passed by Congress in 1992. OSMEO seeks to ensure that GSEs have sufficient capital to withstand significant increases in defaults on the mortgages used as collateral for the MBSs they issue.

[8]A recent report by the Department of Housing and Urban Development argues that the vital public purposes of the GSEs could be undermined if they were privatized; that is, if the Federal government's implicit guarantee of their liabilities were removed. See *Privatization of Fannie and Freddie Mac: Desirability and Feasibility* (Washington D.C.: Office of Policy Development and Research, U.S. Department of Housing and Urban Development, 1996).

guaranteed mortgages. These securities carry the full faith and credit of the U.S. government. Ginnie Mae mortgage-backed securities are free of default risk and therefore trade at relatively low yields. This tremendously successful program, discussed in more detail in Chapter 19, has channeled vast sums of investment capital into the residential mortgage market. At year-end 1995, $461 billion in MBSs guaranteed by Ginnie Mae were outstanding, or about 13 percent of the residential mortgage market.

LIFE INSURANCE COMPANIES

Historically, one of the largest sources of funds for commercial mortgages has been the approximately 1,900 life insurance companies. These companies obtain large amounts of investable funds from policyholders. Policy premiums must be held and invested during the time between the policy origination and payout at the time of death. Although life insurance companies (LICs) are not depository institutions, they are heavily regulated by the various states that charter them as well as those states in which they do business.

Although LICs invest mostly in corporate stocks and bonds and government securities, they do make residential mortgage investments. However, they make relatively few loans *directly* to finance single-family homes. In fact, LICs make less than 1 percent of the value of all home loans originated in the primary market. Size is a major problem. Many LICs are extremely large financial institutions with millions of dollars to invest daily. Making loans directly to individual home buyers across the nation would require LICs to establish local office facilities and would put them in direct competition with S&Ls, CBs, and mortgage companies. However, many LICs provide funds for home mortgage finance by purchasing the MBSs issued by Fannie Mae and Freddie Mac, or guaranteed by Ginnie Mae. Life insurance companies also purchase private MBSs that are issued by mortgage companies, commercial banks, Wall Street investment banks, and other nongovernment entities. By purchasing these MBSs in the secondary market, LICs, pension funds, and other investors pump funds *indirectly* into the primary mortgage market. Thus, LICs provide funds for home mortgage loans, although they are not a likely source of direct funding in the primary market.

OTHER SECONDARY MARKET PURCHASERS

In addition to the GSEs, there are a number of federal credit agencies that support the primary and secondary mortgage market. The list includes the Farm Credit System, the Federal Agricultural Mortgage Corporation (Farmer Mac), the Farmers Home Administration (FmHA), the Financing Corporation (FICO), and the Federal Financing Bank (FFB).

State and local housing finance agencies also are a significant source of mortgage financing for first-time home buyers and for those engaged in developing low- and moderate income housing. The key to the success of these state and local programs has been the ability to finance their activities by issuing bonds exempt from federal taxation. Because investors in these bonds do not pay federal taxes on the interest they receive, the bonds can be issued with interest rates only 70 to 80 percent of the rates on typical bonds, which pay interest that is taxable to the investor. During recent years, private companies also have taken on a greater role in the secondary mortgage market. These private companies purchase mortgages for securitization, and the MBSs they issue are rated by commercial rating agencies (see Chapter 19 for more details).

THE LENDER'S MORTGAGE LOAN DECISIONS

The first step for a potential borrower is to apply for a mortgage loan—usually to a financial institution or mortgage company—and pay a mortgage application fee. The residential loan application form contains sections for the applicant to provide information about the property to be financed, personal information, projected income and housing expenses, judgments and other debts, assets, liabilities, and credit references. Using this information, together with other information obtained by the lender (e.g., a credit report and an appraisal of the property's value), the lender attempts to minimize the risk of default by employing loan underwriting standards that will either allow the loan to be sold in the secondary mortgage market, or give the lender confidence the borrower will not default. If the lender decides to fund the loan, a commitment letter will be sent to the applicant. The lender may require the approved applicant to pay a commitment fee. The applicant then has the right, but not the obligation, to require the lender to provide the approved funds by the end of the commitment period (usually 45 to 60 days).

When making a mortgage loan, lenders face two types of risk with respect to the borrower and collateral:

1. The borrower will be unwilling or unable to make the monthly payments required by the debt agreement (the note).
2. The value of the security for the loan (the home) will not be adequate to pay off the remaining loan balance if the borrower defaults and the lender must foreclose on the property.

To avoid these risks, most lenders who originate home loans (savings institutions, commercial banks, and mortgage companies) quickly sell their loans to large institutional mortgage investors (e.g., life insurance companies) or to the secondary market agencies (Fannie Mae and Freddie Mac). Because secondary mortgage market purchasers assume the risks of mortgage investing from the originating lenders, they establish loan underwriting criteria, or standards, that loans they purchase must meet. Even lenders that do not intend to sell their loans into the secondary market will typically follow standard underwriting guidelines so they are able to sell their loans later if they choose.

The following loan underwriting standards are used to judge the acceptability of loans to finance one- to four-family residential properties:

1. *A satisfactory credit record.* The borrowers' credit records must indicate they have paid their debts on time.
2. *A satisfactory employment outlook.* The borrowers must have reasonably stable jobs that are expected to continue. Their employment records should not show a high frequency of moves or periods of unemployment.

3. *Adequate income*. The borrowers must have incomes that are more than sufficient to pay all of their monthly bills, plus the mortgage payments. To make this assessment, lenders employ several payment to income ratios that are identified and discussed in the next section. If the borrowers are employed on a full-time basis with a single employer, there is little problem in verifying the applicant's income. However, if the income of the borrower comes from multiple sources, it becomes more difficult to verify the income and determine whether the income is likely to continue.

4. *Adequate security*. The residential properties that serve as security (collateral) for the loans must have market values that will accommodate the borrowers' requested loan-to-value ratios (e.g., 80 or 90 percent). Additionally, the properties must have a high probability of maintaining their values in the future so that, if the borrowers default several years after the origination of the loans, property values will exceed the remaining loan balances. If property values increase or remain level, the cushion of security for the loans (borrower equity), will increase because the monthly amortization of principal decreases the outstanding loan balances. To implement this standard, lenders require appraisals on all properties that will serve as security for loans.

AFFORDABILITY RATIOS

To implement underwriting standard number 3, lenders use several ratios to judge applicants' qualifications for a loan. The ratios for FHA and VA loans are established by those agencies and must be used by the FHA- and VA-approved lenders. The ratios used for conventional loans are established by the lenders themselves, if the loans will not be sold in the secondary market. If, however, the loans are expected to be sold, the ratios established by the secondary market purchasers must be used.

Most lenders calculate two ratios that measure affordability when qualifying mortgage borrowers. Both ratios consider the borrower's desired monthly payment (principal and interest) and a monthly average of annual property tax payments and hazard (fire) insurance premiums. The industry acronym for principal, interest, taxes, and insurance is *PITI.*

Conventional loans. When underwriting home loans, most lenders use the following two ratios that meet the requirements for purchase by the secondary mortgage market agencies:

$$\frac{\text{Monthly PITI}}{\text{Monthly Gross Income}} \leq 28 \text{ percent}$$

$$\frac{\text{Monthly PITI} + \text{Other Monthly Obligations}}{\text{Monthly Gross Income}} \leq 36 \text{ percent}$$

REAL ESTATE FOCUS 17-2

The Promise of Automated Underwriting

Consumers are already well-acquainted with the blink-of-an-eye responses that technological advances make possible. Most people do not think twice about swiping credit cards through a machine on the gas pump or letting a supermarket check-out scanner tabulate grocery bills. Within a few years, automated underwriting will become so commonplace that home buyers will find it hard to imagine buying a home any other way.

To use an automated underwriting system such as Freddie Mac's Loan Prospector, a lender first enters a borrower's application information into its own computer system. The information then is transmitted to a central computer, which collects additional information on the applicant from credit repositories. The automated underwriting system weighs all information to determine the likelihood that the loan will repay as agreed, based on the way similar mortgages with comparable borrower, property, and loan characteristics have performed in the past.

On the basis of this comprehensive evaluation, automated underwriting systems assess the riskiness of the loan. Loan Prospector, for example, divides loans into three risk categories. Once a risk classification has been made, the automated underwriting system communicates the information to the lender, along with any guidance about where potential problems lie. The process is completed within minutes, enabling the lender to make a faster and more accurate loan decision.

Automated underwriting does not forsake the fundamentals of manual underwriting. As with the traditional approach, automated underwriting evaluates mortgage applications on the basis of collateral, credit reputation and capacity—what the mortgage underwriting industry refers to as the *three Cs*. The value added by automated underwriting lies in its ability to analyze many factors simultaneously.

SOURCE: Peter E. Mahoney and Peter M. Zorn, "The Promise of Automated Underwriting," *Secondary Mortgage Market,* 13, no. 3 (November 1996).

Other monthly obligations would include payments on auto loans and credit cards, alimony and child support payments, other insurance premiums, and other mortgage debt. The first ratio is often referred to as the underwriter's required "housing expense" or "front-end" ratio; the second is called either the "capital obligations" or the "back-end" ratio.[9]

FHA loans. The FHA requires the following two ratios be met for FHA-insured loans:

$$\frac{\text{Monthly PITI}}{\text{Monthly Gross Income}} \leq 29 \text{ percent}$$

$$\frac{\text{Monthly PITI} + \text{Other Monthly Obligations}}{\text{Monthly Gross Income}} \leq 41 \text{ percent}$$

The VA does not employ a front-end ratio when qualifying borrowers; however, it does use the same back-end ratio as the FHA.

---

[9]At the time this was written, it appeared the standard front-end ratio was going to be increased to 33 percent; the back-end ratio to 39 percent.

Pushed by Freddie Mac and Fannie Mae, automated loan underwriting is revolutionizing America's home finance system by improving the process and reducing costs (see Real Estate Focus 17–2).

THE EFFECTS OF FEDERAL PROGRAMS AND REGULATIONS

Recent years have witnessed widespread controversy concerning allegations of racial discrimination in residential mortgage lending. This controversy is part of an ongoing policy debate over whether lower-income and minority neighborhoods receive sufficient mortgage credit. Two pieces of federal legislation are particularly relevant to this debate: the **Home Mortgage Disclosure Act** (HMDA) **of 1975** and the **Community Reinvestment Act** (CRA) **of 1977**.[10] The first discourages lenders from avoiding ("redlining") certain neighborhoods, while the second encourages mortgage originators to actively lend in their community. The CRA also requires financial institutions to evaluate their lending practices. Numerous studies have revealed locational disparities in the volume of mortgage lending activity and in mortgage loan rejection rates across neighborhoods. Mortgage rejection rate disparities and a general concern about housing affordability, "underserved areas," and lending discrimination appear to have been the impetus behind the 1992 passage of the Housing and Community Development and Government Service Enterprise Act. These disparities also are likely to have motivated the recently increased enforcement of CRA, under the Financial Institutions Reform, Recovery and Enforcement Act of 1989, which requires the publication of CRA "grades" by individual financial institutions.[11] The regulatory guidelines and mandates of these legislative initiatives clearly indicate a concern about spatial patterns in mortgage lending outcomes.

Observed mortgage lending disparities across neighborhoods may be efficient; alternatively, they may be attributable to discrimination, information externalities, or both. Whether or not mortgage originators efficiently provide credit to predominantly minority and lower-income neighborhoods has enormous significance for public policy. Arbitrary denial of credit based on race may harm individual households by impeding home ownership, which in turn may also have important effects on education, safety, and job access. Arbitrary denial of credit to low-income or minority neighborhoods (redlining) may lead to disinvestment and economic decline in these neighborhoods.

Disparities in mortgage rejection rates and originations across neighborhoods do not necessarily imply that mortgage originators have been discriminatory toward neighborhoods in their lending practices. Neighborhood risk variables that are correlated with race may explain these disparate outcomes. In fact, most recent studies have not found evidence

---

[10]The Equal Credit Opportunity Act (ECOA) of 1974, which prohibits discrimination in credit transactions on the basis of race, sex, national origin, and the like; and the Fair Housing Act of 1968, which prohibits discrimination in any part of a housing transaction on the basis of these same factors, also are relevant to this discussion but have received substantially less attention from both regulators and the press.

[11]The primary tool that federal financial supervisory agencies have to achieve the purposes of the CRA is their power to approve or disapprove applications for bank charters, deposit insurance, branching, mergers, and the purchase of shares in other regulated financial institutions. The financial sector's view of the impact of the CRA on possible growth limitations through blocked mergers and the like is reflected in the inclusion of lenders' CRA ratings in capital market agency ratings of financial institutions.

REAL ESTATE FOCUS 17-3

The Federal Government's Drive to Curb Bias in Mortgage Lending

The Clinton Administration's campaign to curb racial bias in mortgage lending is stirring up a strong backlash. The case that most upsets lenders is a Justice Department action against Chevy Chase Federal Savings Bank. Justice alleges that the thrift, the largest in the Washington area, ignored mostly black areas of the capital and adjacent Prince Georges County, MD., when seeking business. Among other alleged transgressions, they said its failure to locate branches in those areas was "redlining"—deliberately avoiding minority neighborhoods. Under pressure, Chevy Chase signed an $11 million settlement, which included an agreement to open more branches or loan offices in minority neighborhoods and to offer below-market interest rates to black applicants.

Chevy Chase notes, in its defense, that Justice didn't cite any specific examples of discrimination, and the thrift says its lending isn't biased. Lenders and many other critics say that, in this case, Justice went far beyond normal government scrutiny of whether a given bank rejects minority applications too freely. Bankers complain that the settlement allows Justice to tell them where to do business.

The CRA is also being used to hold up the enormous number of bank mergers and acquisitions that are in process. When the Federal Reserve Board considers proposed consolidations, banks with satisfactory or even excellent ratings, based on their lending records, may nonetheless be challenged by the government and community activists on CRA grounds. The CRA "opens up the regulatory process to blackmail," contends Paul M. Horvitz, a banking economist at the University of Houston. As he sees it, "The community groups know they can cause major delays, and they can use that threat to extort things from banks."

SOURCES: *The Wall Street Journal*, July 26, 1994 and February 7, 1995.

---

of redlining, when the riskiness of the borrower's neighborhood is included in the analysis. Nonetheless, geographic disparities in lending are receiving increased scrutiny and the costs to lenders from failure to comply with federal regulations can be substantial (see Real Estate Focus 17–3).

SUMMARY

Prospective home buyers have a number of choices and options when deciding where to obtain mortgage financing. Depository institutions such as savings and loan associations, savings banks, credit unions, and commercial banks have accounted for over half of all conventional one- to four-family residential mortgage originations over the past decade. Mortgage banking companies account for virtually all of the remaining originations, with only 1 percent of originations coming from other sources, such as government agencies and life insurance companies.

Although government agencies play a minor role in directly funding home loans, governments nevertheless play a very important role in the primary mortgage market. Clearly, the most familiar government housing policy interventions to most Americans are the Federal Housing Administration (FHA) default insurance program and the Department of Veterans Affairs (VA) program that provides guarantees on loans made by private lenders to qualified veterans. The FHA program, which typically insures qualified borrowers using "Section 203" loans, covers any lender loss after foreclosure and conveyance of title to the property to the U.S. Department of Housing and Urban Development (HUD). The insurance requires an up-front fee of 2.20 percent of the loan amount, as well as a monthly premium. VA loan guarantees, on the other hand, insure lending institutions against default up to a maximum of $50,750. While the VA will guarantee 100 percent of the property's value, making zero down payment loans common, a funding fee is charged that is inversely related to the size of the borrower's down payment.

Originators of home loans in the primary market either hold the mortgages in their portfolios, sell them in the secondary market, or use the mortgages as collateral for the issuance of a mortgage-backed security (MBS). More than half of all residential mortgage loans originated in the United States are now sold into the secondary mortgage market. The largest purchasers of residential mortgages in the secondary market are the Federal National Mortgage Association, "Fannie Mae," and the Federal Home Loan Mortgage Corporation, "Freddie Mac." These government sponsored enterprises (GSEs) also are the largest issuers of residential MBSs, which are written against pools of mortgages purchased from primary market originators.

In developing and facilitating the secondary market in residential mortgages, Fannie Mae and Freddie Mac have developed standardized documents and procedures for loans submitted to them for purchase. Standard forms for notes, mortgages, and appraisals, together with standard underwriting criteria, have brought more conformity to the primary, as well as the secondary, mortgage market because their criteria for qualifying borrowers and properties have established market norms. In fact, many other secondary market investors will only purchase mortgages that meet the underwriting standards of the GSEs. Because of this standardization, investors today are much better able to buy and sell mortgages and MBSs because the risk return characteristics of these securities are more easily analyzed. The increased standardization and liquidity provided by the GSEs has greatly improved mortgage market efficiency.

When deciding whether to extend credit, lenders typically examine a borrower's credit record, employment outlook, income stream, and collateral. They then calculate affordability ratios to help determine if the borrower meets their standards. In addition, due to increased awareness and enforcement of civil rights legislation, many lenders have created programs designed to extend credit to low- and moderate-income borrowers, particularly ethnic minorities, who do not meet traditional standards. Failure to comply with these legislative mandates can prove very costly for the lender.

KEY TERMS

Commercial banks 509
Community Reinvestment Act of 1977 527
Credit unions 508
FHA mortgage insurance 516
Financial intermediaries 506
Forward commitment 512
Government National Mortgage Association 519

Home Mortgage Disclosure Act of 1975 527
Loan servicing 511
Mortgage bankers 510
Mortgage brokers 510
Mortgage pipeline 512
Mutual Mortgage Insurance Fund 516
Portfolio lenders 510

Risk-weighted assets 508
Savings and loan associations 507
Savings banks 508
Section 203 loans 516
Standby forward commitment 513
VA-guaranteed loans 518
Warehousing 509

TEST YOURSELF

Answer the following multiple choice questions:

1. When acting as a mortgage broker, mortgage banking companies
   a. Collect monthly payments and forward them to the mortgage investor.
   b. Make short-term purchases of mortgages in order to make a market for long-term investors.
   c. Package a pool of mortgages together and sell a separate security (MBS) based on the underlying pool of mortgages.
   d. None of the above.

2. The Federal Housing Administration (FHA) typically does which of the following?
   a. Loans money directly to borrowers.
   b. Loans money directly to lenders.
   c. Insures loans made by lenders to qualified borrowers.
   d. Guarantees loans made by lenders to qualified borrowers.

3. Which type of financial institution in the primary mortgage market provides the most funds for the residential (owner-occupied) housing market?
   a. Life insurance companies.
   b. Savings and loan associations.
   c. Mutual savings banks.
   d. Credit unions.
   e. Commercial banks.

4. For all except very high loan-to-value conventional home loans the standard payment ratios for underwriting are
   a. 28 percent and 36 percent.
   b. 25 percent and 33 percent.
   c. 29 percent and 41 percent.
   d. 33 percent and 56 percent.
   e. None of these.

5. The numerator of the standard housing expense (front-end) ratio in home loan underwriting includes:

   a. Monthly principal and interest.
   b. Monthly principal, interest, and property taxes.
   c. Monthly principal, interest, property taxes, and hazard insurance.
   d. All of these plus monthly obligations extending 10 months or more.
   e. All of the above (including d) plus estimated monthly maintenance expense.

6. The most profitable activity of residential mortgage bankers is typically
   a. Loan origination.
   b. Loan servicing.
   c. Loan sales in the secondary market.
   d. Loan brokerage activities.
   e. None of the above.

7. FHA borrowers pay an up-front premium equal to _____ that _____ be included in the amount financed, as well as a monthly premium, paid for five to seven years, that is equal to _____.
   a. 5.0 percent of the initial loan amount, can't, 2.2 percent/12 times the remaining loan balance.
   b. 2.2 percent of the initial loan amount, can, 0.50 percent/12 times the remaining loan balance.
   c. 2.2 percent of the initial loan amount, can't, 2.2 percent/12 times the remaining loan balance.
   d. 2.2 percent of the initial loan amount, can, 2.2 percent/12 times the remaining loan balance.
   e. None of the above.

8. Savings banks are now virtually indistinguishable from
   a. Credit unions.
   b. Savings and loan associations.
   c. Commercial banks.

    d. Mortgage banks.

    e. None of the above.

9. The reduced importance of _____ in the primary mortgage market has been largely offset by an expanded role for _____.

    a. Commercial banks, savings and loan associations.

    b. Mortgage banks, commercial banks.

    c. Commercial banks, mortgage banks.

    d. Savings and loans associations, mortgage banks.

10. *Warehousing* refers to

    a. Short-term loans made by mortgage banks to commercial banks.

    b. Short-term loans made by commercial banks to mortgage banks.

    c. Long-term loans made by commercial banks to mortgage banks.

    d. Short-term loans made by commercial banks to finance the construction of industrial warehouses.

    e. None of the above.

PROBLEMS FOR THOUGHT AND SOLUTION

1. What is the primary purpose of the risk-based capital requirements that Congress enacted as part of the Financial Institutions Reform, Recovery, and Enforcement Act (FIRREA)?

2. Explain forward commitments and standby forward commitments. Which part of the mortgage banker's pipeline is often hedged with forward commitments? With standby forward commitments? Why?

3. Describe the basic activities of Fannie Mae in the secondary mortgage market. How are these activities financed?

4. Explain the importance of Fannie Mae and Freddie Mac to the housing finance system in the United States.

5. Describe the activities mortgage bankers often engage in to generate income.

6. Describe the mechanics of warehouse financing, which commercial banks often provide to mortgage banking companies.

INTERNET EXERCISE

Government sponsored mortgage programs play an important role in residential mortgage markets. Programs such as FHA insurance and VA loan guarantees have enabled many borrowers to obtain mortgage loans they would not have qualified for in the absence of assistance. To keep potential applicants aware of eligibility requirements, and changes in those requirements, the Veterans Administration posts a guide to VA home loans on the World Wide Web.

1. Go to the VA HOME LOANS web site:

http://www.va.gov/vas/lgyinfo.htm

and download the latest eligibility requirements for VA loan guarantee program participation. Briefly describe the requirements, including how to obtain a loan, who is eligible, the costs associated with obtaining a guarantee, and any relevant loan size limitations.

CASE PROBLEMS

1. You have just signed a contract to purchase the house of your dreams. The purchase price is $120,000 and you have applied to AmFirst Savings and Loan for a $100,000 first mortgage loan. The interest rate is 8.5 percent and the loan will be amortized with monthly payments over 30 years. Annual property taxes are expected to be $2,000 per year. Hazard insurance will cost $400 per year. Your monthly car payment is $400, which will continue to three years. Your monthly gross income is $5,000.

   Calculate:
   a. The monthly payment of principal and interest (PI).
   b. One-twelfth of annual property tax payments and hazard insurance payments.
   c. Monthly PITI (principal, interest, taxes, and insurance).
   d. The housing expense (front-end) ratio.
   e. The capital obligations (back-end) ratio.

2. The following mortgage is to be originated by an FHA-approved lender to a qualified borrower:

   > Loan amount: $65,000
   >
   > Interest rate: 8.5 percent annual
   >
   > Loan term: 30 years

   a. What is the monthly mortgage payment, excluding mortgage insurance premiums?
   b. What is the up-front FHA mortgage insurance premium?
   c. What is the total amount borrowed assuming the up-front mortgage insurance premium is financed?
   d. What is the total monthly payment in the first year, including the effect of up-front premiums and the effect of the annual premium that must be paid monthly for 5 to 10 years?

ADDITIONAL READINGS

Substantial portions of the following books are devoted to residential mortgage financing:

Brueggeman, William B., and Jeffrey D. Fisher. *Real Estate Finance and Investments*, 10th ed. Homewood, IL: Richard D. Irwin, 1997.

Clauretie, Terrence M., and G. Stacy Sirmans. *Real Estate Finance,* 2nd ed. Englewood Cliffs, NJ: Prentice Hall, 1996.

Fabozzi, Frank J., and Franco Modigliano. *Mortgage and Mortgaged-Backed Securities Markets*. Boston: Harvard Business School Press, 1992.

Wiedemer, John P., *Real Estate Finance,* 7th ed. Englewood Cliffs, NJ: Prentice Hall, 1995.

For those who wish to learn more about current issues and to stay abreast of the field of residential mortgage finance, we recommend the following journals:

Secondary Mortgage Markets (quarterly), Federal Home Loan Mortgage Corporation, Mailstop 288, 8200 Jones Branch Drive, McLean, Virginia 22102.

Mortgage Banking (quarterly), Mortgage Bankers Association, Washington, D.C., 20073–0021.

18
CHAPTER

COMMERCIAL PROPERTY FINANCING

INTRODUCTION

SOURCES OF FINANCING FOR COMMERCIAL PROPERTIES

LOAN DOCUMENTS AND PROVISIONS
The Note
The Mortgage

COMMON TYPES OF PERMANENT MORTGAGES
Balloon Mortgages
Common Loan Provisions
Floating Rate Loans
Installment Sale Financing

PERMANENT MORTGAGES WITH EQUITY PARTICIPATION
Participation Mortgages
Joint Ventures
Sale-Leasebacks
Convertible Mortgages

THE BORROWER'S DECISION-MAKING PROCESS
Loan Size
Financial Risk
Increased Variability of Equity Returns from Leverage
Choosing among Alternative Financing Structures
The Prepayment and Default Decisions

REQUESTING A PERMANENT LOAN
Loan Submission Package
Channels of Submission

THE LENDER'S DECISION-MAKING PROCESS
The Property and Borrower
Maximum Loan Amount
The Economic Justification

ACQUISITION, DEVELOPMENT, AND CONSTRUCTION FINANCING
Land Purchase and Development Financing
Construction Financing
Sequence of Financing

SUMMARY

KEY TERMS

TEST YOURSELF

PROBLEMS FOR THOUGHT AND SOLUTION

CASE PROBLEMS

ADDITIONAL READINGS

After reading this chapter, students will be able to:

1. Identify the most common types of long-term commercial mortgages and the most common provisions contained in these mortgages.

2. Identify and explain four financing structures that allow lenders to share in the successful operation of the properties they finance (equity participation).

3. Define and explain positive and negative financial leverage and the risks to the borrower associated with the use of borrowed funds.

4. Identify and explain the items commonly included in a loan submission package.

5. Identify the characteristics of the loan application that lenders focus on when making their funding decisions.

6. Discuss a typical sequence of financing for a new development.

INTRODUCTION

Most commercial, or income-producing, properties require debt financing when they are purchased, as do single-family residential properties.[1] Although the basic documents used in commercial and residential mortgage markets—the note and the mortgage—are the same, they must be tailored to meet the different property types and situations that arise in financing commercial properties.

This chapter considers the primary sources of debt financing for commercial properties. Although many of the same institutions that originate home loans also finance commercial properties, their roles are different. For example, life insurance companies play a much larger role in this market than in the single-family residential market, whereas the role of mortgage banks is significantly reduced.

We first consider the most common types of long-term (permanent) commercial mortgages. Unlike residential mortgage markets, 25- or 30-year mortgages are found infrequently, as mortgages with 5- to 10-year terms are the most common. In addition, a number of commercial mortgage structures alter the standard borrower-lender relationship in that the lender's yield with these structures varies directly with the cash flows produced by the property that is pledged as collateral.

In addition to choosing a financing structure, commercial investors also must determine the size of the mortgage that is most advantageous to them. Here, investors must carefully consider the cost of available mortgage financing, the cost of equity (or self) financing, and the effect of debt (that is, financial leverage) on risk and return.

---

[1]Recall that the term *commercial properties* includes the various types of rental housing, including apartment buildings.

From the lender's perspective, the underwriting process for commercial loans is more complicated than for residential loans, and it focuses more on the property being used as collateral for the loan. The applicant's willingness and ability to service the debt is not as crucially important as it is with residential loans because commercial mortgages are often nonrecourse; that is, the commercial lender can look only to the property for the timely payment of principal and interest. Prospective borrowers must submit a formal loan submission package to the lender. The size and details of the submission package vary with the size of the loan request, with the type of property being used as collateral (office, apartment, and so on), and on whether the loan proceeds will be used to finance an existing property or a proposed development. Once the loan application and related material are submitted for funding consideration, the lender decides to approve, reject, or renegotiate the loan terms and conditions.

The chapter concludes with a discussion of the various types of short-term mortgage debt often used to finance the development and construction of new properties, including land acquisition loans, land development loans, and construction loans.

SOURCES OF FINANCING FOR COMMERCIAL PROPERTIES

Recall from Chapter 17 that total mortgage debt outstanding at the end of 1995 exceeded $4.7 trillion. Approximately $1 trillion of this total represents loans to finance the acquisition of commercial real estate, including loans on apartment (multifamily) buildings. The first column of Exhibit 18–1 displays the amount of outstanding commercial mortgage debt by holder-investor, as of year-end 1995. Commercial banks are the largest single source of long-term commercial real estate debt, holding 34 percent of the total amount outstanding. Life insurance companies also are a major participant in this market, holding 20 percent of the total outstanding debt. The remaining debt is held by foreign investors (13 percent), savings institutions (9 percent), investors in commercial mortgage-backed securities (8 percent), pension funds (3 percent), and other investors (12 percent). The "other" category consists primarily of federal, state, and local credit agencies that supply mortgage funds for the acquisition of low- and moderate-income rental housing.

Commercial banks, which significantly increased their commercial real estate lending activity during the mid- to late-1980s, retrenched somewhat during the severe real estate recession of the early 1990s. However, commercial banks and life insurance companies continue to dominate the commercial mortgage market. Savings institutions, after the debacle of the 1980s, have become relatively less important as commercial property lenders. Foreign banks, foreign investors, and U.S. pension funds, on the other hand, have gained importance as long-term commercial lenders. As noted in Chapter 5, foreign investors find U.S. real estate to be a relatively attractive, stable outlet for funds, and they have increased their debt, as well as equity, financing of U.S. properties. Pension funds invest vast sums for their participants' future retirement benefits, and many pension funds are gradually increasing the portion of their portfolios that are invested in high-grade com-

EXHIBIT 18-1

ORIGINATIONS AND HOLDINGS OF CONSTRUCTION AND LONG-TERM COMMERCIAL MORTGAGES (END OF YEAR, 1995)

	Long-Term Holdings		Long-Term Originations		Outstanding Construction Loans	
	(billions)	Percent of Total	(billions)	Percent of Total	(billions)	Percent of Total
Total	$981.0	100	$255.9	100	$97.8	100
Savings institutions	92.8	9	13.1	5	17.0	18
Commercial banks	332.8	34	193.6	76	64.8	66
Mortgage bankers	6.8	1	6.1	2	10.0	10
Life insurance companies	195.1	20	35.0	14	0.6	1
Pension funds	30.8	3	5.2	2	0.1	0
Foreign investors[1]	124.6	13	n.a.	n.a.	n.a.	n.a.
Private CMBS investors[2]	83.4	8	0.0	0	0.0	0
Other[3]	114.7	12	2.9	1	5.3	5

[1] Not available.

[2] *CMBS* stands for commercial mortgage-backed securities.

[3] Includes federal credit agencies, state and local credit agencies, and the long-term debt of real estate investment trusts.

SOURCES: Equitable Real Estate Investment Research Real Estate Outlook: 1996, Atlanta, GA and the U.S. Department of Housing and Urban Development, Office of Financial Management

mercial real estate, either directly through equity investments, or indirectly through long-term mortgages.

The market for commercial mortgage-backed securities (CMBSs) is one of the most dynamic and fastest-growing sectors in the capital markets. Whereas residential MBSs are issued against a pool of residential mortgages, CMBSs are backed by a pool of commercial mortgages or, perhaps, a single large commercial loan. Although the value of outstanding commercial mortgages being used as collateral for CMBSs is in the range of $83 billion, or 8 percent of the total outstanding, the size of the market is significant given CMBSs were virtually nonexistent prior to 1990. Many analysts predict that as much as 20 to 25 percent of outstanding commercial mortgages will be securitized by the year 2000. (The CMBS market is discussed in detail in Chapter 19.)

The second column of Exhibit 18–1 contains total 1995 originations. Commercial banks are again the dominant force in this market, responsible for 76 percent of all long-term originations (excluding foreign lenders). Life insurance companies are net purchasers of long-term loans in the commercial secondary mortgage market in that they originate only 14 percent of all loans, but hold 20 percent of the total amount outstanding. Federal, state, and local credit agencies account for less than 1 percent of all commercial originations, but they are major purchasers of loans in the secondary market.

Exhibit 18–1 shows that the construction loan market also is dominated by commercial banks, which hold 66 percent of the outstanding construction loans on commercial properties. The remainder of the construction market is served by savings institutions (18 percent), mortgage bankers (10 percent), and federal, state, and local credit agencies (5 percent).

LOAN DOCUMENTS AND PROVISIONS

Generally, fewer rules and other constraints govern loan terms and lender-borrower relationships for commercial property financing than for single-family residential financing. This creates flexibility and heterogeneity in commercial mortgage contracts. Nevertheless, all is not chaos. Standard provisions are frequently used in financing agreements and the abilities of different property types to generate income to cover debt service can be generalized. In fact, many of the typical provisions in commercial loans are similar to those in residential financing. Lenders use the same basic types of documents, and many of the same standard clauses apply. These documents and provisions are briefly described in the remainder of this section.[2]

THE NOTE

As in residential mortgage financing, the **note** is the document used to create a debt when a loan is made to finance real estate. In residential property financing, the note is usually a relatively simple document. In commercial property financing, however, the note is usually quite lengthy. It contains the terms of the loan and the provisions agreed to by each party. It presents, in detail, the borrower's obligations in various situations. The provisions typically deal with such matters as these:

- Amounts and timing of periodic payments.
- Calculation of payments above the basic level.
- Record keeping.
- Calculation of income.
- Property maintenance.
- Default.
- Penalties.

Because the note is the document that creates personal liability for borrowers, many commercial properties are financed without the use of a note. When a note is used and borrowers have personal liability, the arrangement is known as **recourse financing**. When a note is not used and the borrowers do not have personal liability, the arrangement is known as **nonrecourse financing**. In these cases, the provisions of the debt are contained in the mortgage or a separate contract.

From the perspective of the equity investor, nonrecourse financing can significantly reduce the downside risk associated with investing in commercial real estate. If rents and property values should fall, equity investors can walk away from the property, bearing no

---

[2]Chapter 15 provides more detailed explanations of mortgage loan documents.

personal responsibility to repay the outstanding mortgage balance. Commercial mortgages originated prior to the late 1980s were generally nonrecourse. When nonrecourse financing is coupled with high initial loan-to-value ratios (LTVs), equity investors have limited downside risk, but unlimited upside potential. This situation makes it more likely investors will "gamble" on marginal investments. In fact, nonrecourse financing and high initial LTVs are at least partially to blame for the massive overbuilding that occurred in commercial real estate markets during the 1980s. Since then, commercial lenders have generally reduced maximum allowable LTVs, and are increasingly likely to require borrowers to bear some personal liability for repaying mortgage funds.

THE MORTGAGE

The income property **mortgage** creates security for the lender. As in a residential mortgage, it states the lender can have the property sold to satisfy the debt if the borrower defaults on any of the obligations in the note. The lender must follow foreclosure proceedings, determined by state law, just as in residential foreclosures.

COMMON TYPES OF PERMANENT MORTGAGES

Three main repayment mechanisms are used in the market for long-term (permanent) commercial mortgages: fully amortizing loans, partially amortizing loans, and interest-only loans. Recall that payments on fully and partially amortizing loans contain both interest and principal each period. Payments on interest-only loans, as the name implies, contain no principal repayments, and are therefore nonamortizing. On a fully amortized loan, the principal repayment portion is large enough to reduce (or amortize) the outstanding balance to zero over the term of the loan. On a partially amortized loan, the payments are based on an amortization schedule that is longer than the actual term of the loan. Thus, the outstanding balance is not reduced to zero when the loan matures. This requires the borrower to satisfy the remaining loan balance with a balloon payment.

BALLOON MORTGAGES

The **balloon mortgage** is the most common instrument used to finance commercial property. Payments are typically based on a 25-year or 30-year amortization schedule, but the loan matures in 5, 7, or 10 years. Exhibit 18–2 contains a survey of commercial mortgage rates completed in March 1996. These rates were obtained from the *Barron's/ John B. Levy & Co. National Mortgage Survey* of large institutional lenders nationwide. The average rate on 5-year balloon mortgages with 25- to 30-year amortization was 7.25 percent. Assuming 30-year amortization and a $1 million mortgage results in a monthly payment of $6,821.76 and a remaining loan balance at maturity of $943,788. The borrower must satisfy the $943,788 obligation by either selling the property at the end of the five-year term or by refinancing (perhaps with the original lender) at the then-current interest rate.

EXHIBIT 18-2

AVERAGE MORTGAGE RATES ON BALLOON MORTGAGES IN MARCH 1996

Term of Loan	Average Rate	Points	Amortization
5 years	7.250%	0–1	25–30–year schedule
7 years	7.375	0–1	25–30–year schedule
10 years	7.625	0–1	25–30–year schedule

SOURCE: *Barron's/John B. Levy & Co. National Mortgage Survey,* Richmond, VA, March 31, 1996

The relatively short loan term on a balloon mortgage reduces the lender's inflation and interest rate risk. If interest rates increase after the origination of a balloon mortgage, the value of the remaining payments, and therefore the value of the mortgage, falls less than if the loan could be outstanding the full 25 or 30 years. For example, if interest rates were to rise from 7.25 percent to 7.75 percent immediately after origination of the five-year, 7.25 percent balloon mortgage, its market value would decline from $1 million to $979,828.[3] However, if both the term of the loan and the amortization period were 30 years, the present value of the remaining payments, and therefore the value of the loan, would decline to $952,212.[4] Although reducing the term of the mortgage to 5 years reduces the lender's interest rate risk, the 25- or 30-year amortization schedule does not reduce the *affordability* of the mortgage relative to a standard fixed-payment mortgage.

Contract rates on commercial mortgages are determined by the perceived riskiness of these investments relative to a riskless alternative. The widely used riskless benchmark is the return that is available on a noncallable, nondefaultable, Treasury security with a comparable maturity. Yields on balloon mortgages are typically 125 to 200 basis points greater than yields on Treasury securities with comparable maturities.

COMMON LOAN PROVISIONS

As discussed in Chapter 17, homeowners typically have the right to partially or completely prepay the remaining loan balance on home mortgages. Moreover, no prepayment penalties are associated with early repayments. When paying off the remaining balance, the residential borrower's only obligation is to make a lump sum payment to the lender in an amount equal to the remaining principal balance, which is often referred to as the "par value" of the mortgage. Homeowners frequently prepay mortgages at par when mortgage rates fall below the rate on their existing mortgage.

Most commercial loans do not allow borrowers to freely prepay at par, as they contain either a lock-out provision, a prepayment penalty, or occasionally, both. A **lock-out provision** prohibits prepayment of the mortgage for a period of time after the origination of the mortgage. For example, a commercial mortgage can have a 10-year term, a

---

[3]The calculator keystrokes are N = 60, I = 7.75/12, PV = ?, PMT = 6,821.76, and FV = 943,788.

[4]The calculator keystrokes are N = 360, I = 7.75/12, PV = ?, PMT = 6,821.76, and FV = 0. If the lender did not expect the below-market rate loan to be outstanding the full 30 years, the value decline would be less.

25-year amortization schedule, and a 5-year lock-out period. Some lock-out periods may encompass the entire loan term, rendering the mortgage completely nonprepayable. Lock-out periods reduce the risk that lenders will have to reinvest the remaining loan balance at a lower rate when borrowers prepay mortgages with above-market rates. Thus, lock-out provisions reduce lenders' **reinvestment risk.**

Many commercial mortgages contain **prepayment penalties** instead of, or in addition to, lock-out provisions. These penalties are often expressed as a percentage of the remaining loan balance, say 2 to 4 percent. Prepayment penalties increase the up-front costs of refinancing and, therefore, reduce the benefits. Another common form of prepayment penalties are **yield-maintenance agreements**. With such an agreement, the prepayment penalty borrowers pay depends on how far interest rates have declined since origination. Why? When interest rates decline and borrowers prepay, lenders must reinvest the remaining loan balance at current (lower) rates. Effectively, lenders lose the present value of the difference between the payments on the old mortgage and the payments on a new mortgage at current rates. With a yield-maintenance agreement, the prepayment penalty can be set to approximate this lost present value, or some portion of this lost present value, if the agreement calls for the lender's yield to be maintained for a period of time less than the remaining term of the loan. Note that because the prepayment penalty increases as the spread between the old and new rate widens, the value of the borrower's prepayment option can be effectively eliminated, regardless of how much interest rates decline.

FLOATING RATE LOANS

It is not uncommon for commercial mortgages to have adjustable, or floating, interest rates. The index on a **floating rate mortgage** is typically the prime rate (the rate banks charge their best customers) or the London Interbank Offer Rate (commonly referred to as LIBOR). Floating rate loans decrease the lender's interest rate risk, which tends to reduce the rates on floating rate loans relative to fixed-payment mortgages, all else the same. However, floating rate mortgages can increase the default risk of a mortgage because the borrower may not be able to continue to service the debt if payments increase significantly on the loan.[5]

INSTALLMENT SALE FINANCING

One of the most popular methods of deferring the taxes due on the sale of a commercial property is the **installment sale**. Under this method, the seller allows the buyer to pay the purchase price over a number of years. In effect, the seller collects a down payment and then "loans" the buyer the remainder of the purchase price. The buyer then makes periodic payments to the seller (lender) that consist of both interest and principal amortization. Because the seller receives the sale proceeds (the principal on the installment loan)

---

[5]See Chapter 16 for examples of how to calculate the revised payments on mortgages that have interest rates tied to a market index.

over a number of years, the IRS allows the seller to recognize the taxable gain over a number of years. Essentially, the timing of capital gain tax payments is matched with the receipt of the principal on the installment sale loan. Spreading the recognition of the gain over several years reduces the present value of the tax payments.

Because the installment sale may provide the seller with significant tax benefits, the seller may be willing to offer the buyer a below-market rate of interest. Installment sales are also popular with buyers because the seller often uses underwriting standards that are less strict than those used by traditional third-party lenders. This may allow the borrower to increase the ratio of total debt to total property value, thereby minimizing the borrower's required down payment.

PERMANENT MORTGAGES WITH EQUITY PARTICIPATION

In this section we consider several variations in the standard borrower-lender relationship that allow the lender's yield to vary directly with the cash flows produced by the property that is pledged as collateral.

PARTICIPATION MORTGAGES

Commercial mortgage loans are often structured to give the lender an "equity-like" interest in the property through a "participation" in the property's operating cash flows, a participation in the cash flows from the eventual sale of the property, or both. In exchange for a share in the property's income or appreciation, the lender must offer the borrower a below-market rate of interest. In addition to paying normal interest, **income kickers** (also called *income participations*) require borrowers to pay the lender a specified percentage of the property's gross or net income (or perhaps any income in excess of a predetermined breakeven amount). **Equity kickers** (also called *equity participations*) call for splitting the proceeds from the sale of the property. For example, pension funds have at times favored a loan structure in which they offer permanent financing at a rate 75 to 150 basis points below market in exchange for 25 to 50 percent of both operating cash flows and proceeds from sale. Participations are designed to help protect the lender from unexpected increases in inflation and interest rates and to allow the lender to share in benefits (and costs) that usually accrue only to the equity investors—assuming that property values are positively related to changes in inflation.

Consider the example summarized in Exhibit 18–3. The lender is offering a $10 million fixed-payment mortgage with a 7.625 percent interest rate and, for simplicity, *annual* payments. With a loan term of 10 years and a 30-year amortization schedule, the annual payment is $857,038.[6] If the borrower expects to sell the property at the end of five years and pay off the remaining $9,449,517 loan balance, what is the effective cost of this financing package in the absence of a lender participation? Because there are no up-front

---

[6]The calculator keystrokes are N = 30, I = 7.625, PV = −10,000,000, PMT = ?, and FV = 0.

EXHIBIT 18-3

ASSUMPTIONS FOR A PARTICIPATION LOAN
ON GATORWOOD APARTMENT COMPLEX

Input	Assumption
Number of units	296 units with average monthly rent of $534.91
Purchase price	$13,375,000
Projected increase in gross rents	3% per year
Vacancy and collection losses	10% per year
Operating expenses	$437,500 in year 1, increasing 3.5 percent thereafter
Holding period	5 years
Estimated selling price	Year 6 NOI capitalized at 10%
Selling expenses	5% of sale price
Financing:	
Loan amount	$10,000,000
Interest rate	7.625%
Amortization schedule	30 years, *annual* payments
Loan term	10 years
Up-front financing costs	None
Lender participation	25% of annual BTCF

financing charges, the borrower's before-tax effective borrowing cost (EBC) is equal to 7.625 percent—the contract interest rate.[7] This is also the lender's expected before-tax yield on the mortgage.[8]

If the lender also is to receive 25 percent of the annual before-tax cash flows (BTCFs), the EBC of the loan will be determined by the contract interest rate *and* by the ability of the property to produce income. The holding period cash flows from operations implied by the assumptions in Exhibit 18–3 are contained in Exhibit 18–4. The estimated BTCFs determine the lender's participation each year. For example, in addition to the regular mortgage payment of $857,038, the lender also receives an income participation of $103,866 (0.25 × $415,462) in the first year.

The cash inflows and outflows on the income participation mortgage are summarized in Exhibit 18–5. The 25 percent income participation in the annual BTCFs increases the EBC (and the lender's before-tax yield) from 7.625 to 8.86 percent. Although not shown, a 25 percent equity participation in the before-tax cash flows from sale, in addition to the income participation, would further increase the EBC to 10.68 percent. However, if the EBC on balloon mortgages that are currently available to finance similar properties is approximately 7.625 percent, competitive market pressures will force the lender to reduce the contract rate on the participation mortgage in order to make its EBC competitive with a 7.625 percent fixed-payment mortgage. In this example, if the lender reduced the contract rate to 6.1 percent, the EBC of the participation loan would decline from 8.86 percent

---

[7]The calculator keystrokes are N = 5, I = ?, PV = −10,000,000, PMT = 857,038, and FV = 9,449,517.

[8]Because of different tax situations, the borrower's *after-tax* EBC will not equal the lender's *after-tax* yield. For tax purposes, payments to the lender under a participation are generally deductible as interest from the borrower's taxable income.

E X H I B I T   1 8 - 4

GATORWOOD APARTMENT COMPLEX:
BEFORE-TAX CASH FLOWS FROM ANNUAL OPERATIONS

		1	2	3	4	5
	PGI	$1,900,000	$1,957,000	$2,015,710	$2,076,181	$2,138,467
−	VC	190,000	195,700	201,571	207,618	213,847
=	EGI	1,710,000	1,761,300	1,814,139	1,868,563	1,924,620
−	OE	437,500	452,813	468,661	485,064	502,041
=	NOI	1,272,500	1,308,488	1,345,478	1,383,499	1,422,579
−	DS	857,038	857,038	857,038	857,038	857,038
=	BTCF	$ 415,462	$ 451,450	$ 488,440	$ 526,461	$ 565,541

E X H I B I T   1 8 - 5

EXPECTED CASH FLOWS ON A PARTICIPATION MORTGAGE

Year	Loan Proceeds	Loan Payments	Participation Flows	Total Cash Flows
0	($10,000,000)	$ 857,038[1]	$ 0	($10,000,000)
1		857,038	103,866[3]	960,903
2		857,038	112,862	969,900
3		857,038	122,110	979,148
4		857,038	131,615	988,653
5		$10,306,555[2]	$141,385	$10,447,940
				EBC = 8.86%

[1] $10,000,000 loan at 7.625% with 30-year amortization and annual payments

[2] Fifth-year payment plus remaining principal balance of $9,449,517

[3] 25% participation times $415,462 BTCF

to 7.625 percent, thus making it competitive with the standard fixed-payment balloon mortgage.[9] If the lender is sharing in the sale proceeds as well as the annual income, the contract rate would be reduced still further.

Finally, it is important to note that a participation mortgage is "straight debt" in that the lender remains strictly a creditor. The lender does not obtain an ownership interest in the property as lenders do in joint ventures, which are discussed next. The additional payments the lender receives, whether from operating cash flows or sale proceeds, are classified as **contingent interest**, that is interest contingent on the equity performance of

---

[9]The lender will likely not be forced to reduce the EBC on the participation loan to the EBC available on fixed-rate mortgages. Why? Because the risk to the borrower is reduced by the lender's cash flow participation. This is because total payments on a standard fixed-rate mortgage are less variable than the cash flows from operations. With a participation, the borrower, in effect, "sells" the lender a portion of the equity cash flows in exchange for a reduced payment on the less risky debt. In short, the return on the borrower's equity is less variable with a participation. For the same reasons, the risk to the lender is increased (over a standard loan) by the participation. Thus, the lender will "price" the loan such that the EBC is greater than an otherwise comparable standard loan to compensate the lender for the greater risk.

the property. Participation mortgages have been especially popular during periods of high inflation and interest rates because the below-market interest rate allows the borrower to qualify for a loan with a higher loan-to-value ratio. However, the participation reduces the upside potential of the borrower's return, because the lender will share in any larger-than-expected increases in rents, resale values, or both.

JOINT VENTURES

A **joint venture** produces a borrower-lender relationship that is very similar to a participating mortgage in that the lender expects to receive a portion of the cash flows from operation or sale of the property, or both, as well as a scheduled mortgage payment. However, with a joint venture, the lender actually acquires an ownership interest in the property by supplying a portion of the required equity capital, in addition to supplying the permanent debt financing. Thus, unlike a participating mortgage where the lender has a straight-debt position, lenders actually form a partnership (or a corporation) with the borrower in a joint venture. The joint venture lender's total return will therefore come from two sources: a return on the debt position (the debt service) and a return on the equity position (the cash flow participation).

Most real estate joint ventures involve the construction of new properties, with the lender (often a large life insurance company) providing the majority of the capital. For example, the lender will typically finance 75 to 80 percent of the total development costs, plus provide a significant portion of the required equity. The developer primarily provides the expertise in project selection, development, construction, and management. The developer and lender may split the net income from operation, sale, or both equally, or in any other manner agreed upon. For example, the lender might obtain a specified percentage of gross or net proceeds first, after which any remaining proceeds would be split equally. Obviously, such arrangements require a complex partnership agreement to cover the rights and obligations of each party. The lender is particularly concerned about record keeping, payment of bills, and accurate income accounting.

SALE-LEASEBACKS

Lenders sometimes prefer to take a complete equity position, rather than a debt position. The institution may therefore agree to purchase an existing property or to underwrite all development and construction costs for a proposed new property. This property is then leased back to the user of the property, who becomes a rent-paying tenant (lessee). With sale-leasebacks, the tenants obtain the use of a structure that is presumably well suited to their needs. Because no equity capital is required, the arrangement also allows funds that are not invested in the property to be invested in other assets or in other facets of the owner's business. From the owner's viewpoint, a sale-leaseback also carries the advantages of 100 percent financing and the deductibility of lease payments for tax purposes. However, appreciation in the value of the property accrues to the lender-owner, as do the depreciation deductions for tax purposes. Sale-leaseback agreements often contain an option for the repurchase of the property, after a specified period and on specified terms, by the lessee.

A *land* sale-leaseback is a financing form frequently available from insurance companies. The institution purchases the land, which is subsequently leased back to the owner-tenant. The institution also provides the long-term mortgage for the building. The lender's cash receipts include both debt service on the mortgage note and lease payments on the land. Because the lender has a long-term economic interest in the land, it may gain from any unexpected property price appreciation. In addition, the lender frequently participates in the operating cash flows, proceeds from the sale of the improvements, or both. Although the owner-tenant relinquishes his economic interest in the land, depreciation deductions are retained, which, along with the lease payments on the land and the interest payments on the building mortgage, are generally fully deductible. Because of the benefits the lender receives from the land acquisition and the cash flow participations, the mortgage rate is usually below market.

CONVERTIBLE MORTGAGES

A **convertible mortgage** gives the lender an option to convert the mortgage debt to equity after a specified number of years. The option may allow the lender to purchase a specified percentage of the property by paying the market value of the portion converted. For example, a 60 percent convertibility feature allows the lender to purchase a 60 percent equity position after five years by paying 60 percent of the property's market value at that time. Agreed-on appraisers would determine the market value, and the 60 percent would be paid by writing down (reducing) the loan balance.

THE BORROWER'S DECISION-MAKING PROCESS

Once investors have decided to purchase commercial property, they are faced with a number of decisions. First, they must choose a financing structure. Do they use a standard balloon mortgage or a floating rate loan, or do they pursue more complicated structures such as participations and joint ventures? Investors must also choose their desired amount of debt, although the loan size is typically limited by the income-producing ability and value of the property and by the investor's aversion to the increased risk associated with larger amounts of debt financing.

Exhibit 18–6 contains information on the typical loan terms offered by the dominant commercial lenders during the fourth quarter of 1996. Insurance companies and pension funds offered fixed rate mortgages on high quality (class A) properties with contract rates ranging from 7.5 to 8.15 percent. This rate exceeded the yield on 7- to 10-year Treasury securities by 125 to 175 basis points (1.25 to 1.75 percentage points). Maximum LTVs

---

EXHIBIT 18-6

COMMERCIAL MORTGAGE CAPITAL SOURCES
LENDER REQUIREMENTS, FOURTH QUARTER, 1996[1]

Insurance Companies/Pension Funds
("A" quality real estate)

Rates	7.50–8.15%
Spreads over Treasuries	125–176 bp
Maximum LTV	75%
Minimum debt service coverage	1.20
Loan term	7–10 years

Commercial Banks
("A" quality real estate)

Rates, fixed	7.25–8.15%
Rates, floating	6.60–7.60%
Spreads over Treasuries on fixed-rate loans	125–176 bp
Spreads over LIBOR on floating rate loans	100–200 bp
Maximum LTV	75%
Minimum debt service coverage	1.15–1.20
Loan term	1–10

Conduits
("B" and "C" quality real estate)

Rates	8.20–9.15%
Spreads over Treasuries	200–275 bp
Maximum LTV	75%
Minimum debt service coverage	1.20
Loan term	5–10 years

[1] Represents typical transaction, not full range.

SOURCE: Equitable Real Estate Investment Management, Inc.

---

were 75 percent and first year NOI had to be at least 120 percent of the annual debt service.

In addition to fixed-rate loans, commercial banks offered floating rate mortgages. Spreads over short-term Treasury securities ranged from 125 to 175 basis points (bp), while spreads over the London Interbank Offering Rate (LIBOR) ranged from 100 to 200 basis points. Loans originated or purchased by conduits for use as collateral for commercial MBSs had contract rates ranging from 8.20 to 9.15 percent, and spreads ranging from 200 to 275 basis points. The higher rates and spreads reflect the lower quality of the collateral (class B and C properties) typically associated with commercial loans originated or purchased by conduits.

We next discuss the borrower's choice of loan size, carefully considering the advantages *and* disadvantages of using financial leverage. We then discuss the trade-offs between the various financing structures that borrowers must be aware of when searching for and negotiating a commercial mortgage. The ongoing prepayment and default decisions borrowers face after origination are then considered.

LOAN SIZE

In Chapters 3 and 17 we briefly discussed the two basic reasons why real estate investors and homeowners borrow funds—use financial leverage—for their real estate purposes. The first reason is limited financial resources. If an investor desires to purchase real estate, but does not have sufficient assets to pay cash for the property, then borrowing is the only alternative. The second reason for the use of mortgage financing is that it alters the expected risk and return of real estate investments. In particular, the use of leverage may amplifies the rate of return that investors earn on their invested equity. This *magnification* of equity returns is known as positive (or negative) financial leverage, and may induce investors to at least partially debt finance (use "other people's money") even if they have sufficient resources to avoid borrowing.

The use of financial leverage will increase the estimated IRR of the project when the cost of borrowing is less than the IRR, calculated assuming the property is purchased with 100 percent equity financing. Although the use of leverage may appear to enhance the equity investor's expected return, it should be stressed that financial leverage also increases the riskiness of the equity investment by increasing the risk of default *and* by making the *realized* return on equity more sensitive to changes in rental rates and expense levels. Thus, the increase in *expected* return from the use of debt may not be large enough to offset the corresponding increase in risk.

FINANCIAL RISK

Mortgage lenders have a claim on operating cash flows that is superior to the claims of the equity investor. Therefore, increasing the amount of borrowed funds—and thus the promised mortgage payment—increases the probability that NOI will be insufficient to cover the mortgage payment obligation. The risk that NOI will be less than debt service is often referred to as **financial risk**. Default risk is the risk that borrowers will cease to make timely payments of principal and interest, as per the mortgage agreement. Such behavior could lead to lender foreclosure on the property if not cured by the borrower (see Real Estate Focus 18–1). In typical real estate investments, small amounts of debt financing do not materially affect the probability of mortgage default because there is an adequate cushion (debt coverage ratios are far in excess of 1.0). However, as the amount of leverage increases beyond a critical level, it becomes increasingly likely that debt service will exceed NOI. In such a situation, the borrower will have to draw on money from other sources in order to avoid default.

INCREASED VARIABILITY OF EQUITY RETURNS FROM LEVERAGE

The amount of debt financing affects the amount and the variation (from expectations) of before-tax cash flows available for distribution to the equity investor. More specifically, the expected variability of the return to equity investors increases with the amount of financial leverage. This is because a given amount of variation in NOI will have increasingly larger effects on the equity return as the use of debt increases.

REAL ESTATE FOCUS 18-1

Falling Real Estate Prices Contribute to Numerous Chicago Defaults

In early 1994, Aetna Life Insurance Co. moved to foreclose on the $95 million mortgage on One Illinois Center, the first building erected in Metropolitan Structures' pathbreaking development over the former Illinois Central railyards east of Michigan Avenue. Failure by Metropolitan Structures to pay property taxes precipitated the foreclosure complaint.

The foreclosure was the latest in a series of reversals for Chicago-based Metropolitan Structures that exposed the difficulty of development and ownership in a falling real estate market, even for an owner with strong financial partners. After acquiring the property through foreclosure, Aetna sold it in September 1996 for less than 60 percent of the original loan amount.

In 1993, Metropolitan Structures was on the wrong end of a $625 million foreclosure of two loans on the twin office towers flanking the Chicago Mercantile Exchange. The settlement required the developers to hand over the property to CME Finance NV, their Japanese-backed lender. In 1992, the developer also had to give back Boulevard Towers North, 225 N. Michigan, to Prudential Insurance Co. of America after defaulting on a $78 million mortgage.

SOURCE: Adapted from Tom Andreoli, "Woes at Illinois Center," *Crains Chicago Business* (February 7, 1994). Copyright Crain Communications Inc., Chicago, IL.

To demonstrate the acute sensitivity of equity returns to the use of debt financing, we refer again to the Gatorwood Apartment example discussed earlier in the chapter. Recall that the base case assumptions in Exhibit 18–3—including a $10 million, 7.625 percent, fixed-payment balloon mortgage—produced an effective borrowing cost of 7.625 percent. The before-tax equity reversion (BTER), calculated in Exhibit 18–7, is equal to $4,446,569. This BTER, along with the BTCFs in Exhibit 18–4 and the initial equity investment of $3,375,000, produce a before-tax IRR of 18.52 percent.[10]

We now investigate the sensitivity of cash flows, IRRs, and risk to variations in the initial LTVR and to variations in the assumed annual rate of growth in rents and resale prices. These sensitivities are displayed in Exhibit 18–8. The results in the first column of Exhibit 18–8 were calculated with a spreadsheet assuming a 0 percent LTV. Columns 2 through 4 assume LTVs of 40, 60, and 80 percent, respectively. First, note that estimated NOI is not affected by the assumed LTV. In the absence of financial leverage (column 1), the estimated BTCF equals the NOI of $1,272,500, and the required initial equity investment is equal to $13,375,000—the purchase price of the property. Annual debt service with a 40 percent LTV (7.625 interest for 30 years with annual payments) is $458,515. This results in a BTCF of $813,985 and an equity investment of $8,025,000. The estimated BTCF decreases as the LTV increases, but so does the required equity investment. Note that the equity dividend rate (BTCF/initial equity) increases as the amount of leverage increases. This increase in the equity dividend rate as the LTV increases will occur

---

[10]The calculator keystrokes are N = 5, I = ?, CF_0 = −3,375,000, CF_1 = 415,462, CF_2 = 451,450, CF_3 = 488,440, CF_4 = 526,461, and CF_5 = 5,012,110. The cash flow in year 5 is equal to the BTCF in year 5, $565,541, plus the BTER of $4,446,569.

EXHIBIT 18 – 7

PROCEEDS FROM THE SALE OF GATORWOOD APARTMENTS[1]

	Selling price (SP)	$14,627,459[2]
−	Selling expenses (SE)	731,373
=	Net selling price (NSP)	13,896,086
−	Remaining mortgage balance (RMB)	9,449,517
=	Before-tax equity reversion (BTER)	$ 4,446,569

[1] See Exhibit 18–3 for required assumptions.

[2] Equal to NOI in year 6 ($1,462,746) capitalized at 10%

EXHIBIT 18 – 8

THE EFFECTS OF DEBT FINANCING ON CASH FLOWS, IRRS, AND RISK

Initial loan-to-value ratio	0%	40%	60%	80%
NOI in year 1	$ 1,272,500	$1,272,500	$1,272,500	$1,272,500
− Debt service	—	458,515	683,773	857,038
= BTCF	$ 1,272,500	$ 813,985	$ 584,727	$ 415,462
Initial equity*	$13,375,000	$8,025,000	$5,350,000	$3,375,000
BTCF/initial equity	9.51%	10.14%	10.93%	12.31%
Growth rate in rents and resale prices:				
−1% (5% probability)	5.19%	3.37%	0.81%	−4.81%
1% (20% probability)	7.96	8.18	8.47	8.98
3% (50% probability)	10.64	12.54	14.80	18.52
5% (20% probability)	13.26	16.57	20.33	26.17
8% (5% probability)	17.09	22.16	27.64	35.71
Mean IRR	10.68%	12.50%	14.58%	17.84%
Standard deviation of IRR	2.52	3.98	5.67	8.45
Coefficient of variation	0.24	0.32	0.39	0.47

* The initial equity is equal to the total purchase price minus the loan amount.

whenever the annual mortgage constant (contract interest rate plus principal amortization) is *less* than the overall capitalization rate. The annual mortgage constant (annual payment/loan amount) in this example is equal to 8.57 percent, and the initial cap rate (NOI/price) is 9.51 percent.[11] Thus, increasing leverage increases the estimated equity dividend rate in this example.

The middle section of Exhibit 18–8 displays the calculated IRR for annual growth rates in rents ranging from −1 to 8 percent. The probability of each growth rate scenario is listed in parentheses. With no leverage and a −1 percent decline in rents, the calculated IRR is 5.19 percent. Recall that the use of leverage will increase the estimated IRR if the unlevered IRR exceeds the cost of debt. Because there are no up-front financing costs in

---

[11] The annual mortgage constant can also be determined with the following keystroke sequence: N = 30, I = 7.625, PV = −1, PMT = ?, and FV = 0.

our example, the cost of debt (the EBC) is equal to the contract rate of 7.625 percent. Thus, increasing the LTV will decrease the calculated IRR if gross rents decrease 1 percent per year because 5.19 percent is less than 7.625 percent. With rental growth rates of approximately 1 percent or higher, increasing the use of leverage increases the estimated IRR (because the unlevered IRR for these growth rates is greater than 7.625 percent—the cost of debt).

Although increased leverage increases, in some cases substantially, the estimated IRR when rental growth rates exceed approximately 1 percent per year, this benefit of financial leverage must be weighed against the cost of increased risk. Given the assumed probability distribution of rental growth rates, the mean and standard deviation of the IRR with no leverage are 10.68 percent and 2.52 percent, respectively. With a 40 percent LTV, the *expected* IRR increases to 12.50 percent. However, the standard deviation of the IRR increases to 3.98 percent. Even higher expected returns can be "purchased" with additional leverage—but at the "price" of significantly increased risk.

The use of mortgage debt to help finance the acquisition of real estate is pervasive, and therefore its effect on risk and return should be clearly understood. Many market participants recommend the extensive use of debt. In fact, one of the basic tenants of the numerous "get rich by investing in real estate schemes" is to make maximum use of "other peoples' money." The discussion and example above, however, demonstrates that leverage is a "double-edged sword." Its use enhances returns when the property is performing well. However, if the property performs poorly, the extensive use of debt can make a bad situation worse, although the right to default limits the amount of downside risk when nonrecourse financing is used.

CHOOSING AMONG ALTERNATIVE FINANCING STRUCTURES

In previous sections we discussed a number of debt financing options available on commercial properties including balloon mortgages, floating rate mortgages, installment sale financing, participations, joint ventures, and sale-leasebacks. Moreover, in contrast to residential mortgages, we observed how the terms and provisions of commercial mortgages can vary greatly with each particular loan.

When comparing commercial mortgage structures, it is important to be aware of how borrowers and lenders evaluate the trade-offs between the various loan types and contract provisions. When the borrower must give up something in order to benefit along another dimension of the financing structure, decision making becomes more difficult. For example, when a lender offers a below-market interest rate in exchange for a participation in the property's cash flows, borrowers must decide if the value of the below-market financing exceeds the value of the equity cash flows that are being, effectively, "sold" to the lender. In a land-sale leaseback, borrowers must decide if the present value of the land-lease payments is less than the present value of maintaining ownership of the land.

It is important to recognize that *both* the borrower and the lender can expect to benefit from choosing a financing structure other than a standard balloon mortgage. A "win-win" situation at origination can be created if the borrower and lender place a different value on the cash flows that are sacrificed or gained. This differential valuation could reflect differences in risk preferences, portfolio considerations, or expectations about future changes in rents and values. For example, assume a lender has offered to reduce the contract rate on an office building mortgage by 1 percentage point in exchange for 50 percent of the appreciation in the value of the property. Also, assume that the borrower is *less* optimistic about the potential for future value increases than is the typical borrower or lender in this market and that the lender is *more* optimistic about the prospects for price appreciation. In this case, the borrower expects to benefit from using the participation agreement because the borrower's "cost" of acquiring the below-market interest rate is minimal if the borrower expects little or no appreciation. On the other hand, the lender may consider the "cost" of obtaining the participation—the interest rate reduction—a real "deal" if the lender expects more price appreciation than the typical market participant. In short, both the lender and borrower expect to benefit from negotiating an alternative to the standard balloon mortgage. However, after the mortgage has been originated, one party will turn out to be wrong about future price increases and lose, and one party will be correct and gain from the participation agreement.

To aid in the mortgage selection process, borrowers should calculate the anticipated effective borrowing cost and the internal rate of return on equity of the various options. Unfortunately, however, the selection process is more complicated than merely choosing the financing alternative that is expected to produce the lowest EBC or the highest IRR. These calculations must be adjusted to reflect the relative risk of the financing alternatives. The key question is, How does the borrower compare risks?

Assessing the relative risk of alternative financing structures is simplified to some extent because the property's basic income-producing ability does not vary with the method of financing. However, as discussed above, the method and amount of debt financing does affect the before-tax cash flows from operations and the variability (riskiness) of these flows. For example, the use of a participation mortgage may slightly decrease the borrower's *expected* return on equity. However, the participation also causes the borrower's equity return to be less sensitive to variations in rental income and future sale prices because the lender is now bearing some of this risk. How much lower should the expected (required) return on equity be with participations to compensate for the decreased risk relative to a standard balloon mortgage? That depends directly on the borrower's perception of how variable operating cash flows and sale proceeds are likely to be and on the risk tolerances and preferences of both parties.

Exhibit 18–9 summarizes the spectrum of financing alternatives along several dimensions. With respect to the risk of future price fluctuations, straight debt is the most risky from the borrower's perspective because the lender does not participate or share in future sale proceeds. However, a participation or a joint venture agreement reduces the effects of price fluctuations on the borrower's return because the lender shares in the risk of price changes. Borrowers, effectively, sell off a portion of the benefits of equity ownership in exchange for a lower, *more certain*, mortgage payment. With a land sale-leaseback, borrowers bear the price risk associated with the building(s), while lenders bear the price risk associated with the land. Lenders bear all of the price risk in a "complete" sale-leaseback.

E X H I B I T   1 8 - 9

FINANCING INCOME-PRODUCING PROPERTY
BORROWER PERSPECTIVE

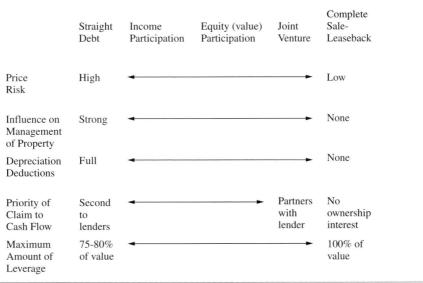

	Straight Debt	Income Participation	Equity (value) Participation	Joint Venture	Complete Sale-Leaseback
Price Risk	High	←		→	Low
Influence on Management of Property	Strong	←		→	None
Depreciation Deductions	Full	←		→	None
Priority of Claim to Cash Flow	Second to lenders	←		→ Partners with lender	No ownership interest
Maximum Amount of Leverage	75–80% of value	←		→	100% of value

Straight debt places full responsibility for the management of the property on the borrower, while participations and joint venture agreements can give lenders an increased say in management decisions. Complete sale-leasebacks, the other extreme, eliminate the borrower's control of the property, although the borrower-tenant may be responsible for the day-to-day operations of the property (maintenance, bill paying, and so on) if the lender-landlord does not hire a property manager. With straight debt and participations, the owner claims 100 percent of the available tax depreciation deductions. However, these deductions are typically shared in a joint venture agreement, and lost completely in a sale-leaseback that involves both the land and improvements. With straight debt, the borrower's claim on the cash flows is second, or "residual," to the lender's.

With participations and joint ventures, borrowers become partners, in whole or in part, with the lender. With land sale-leasebacks, the borrower's cash flow claims are subordinate to both the mortgage and lease payments. With regular or complete sale-leasebacks, the borrower has no claims on the property's cash flows. If straight debt is used, financing is limited to approximately 80 percent or less of the property value. Thus, significant equity contributions are required. Participations and joint ventures may require less borrower equity, whereas both land and regular sale-leasebacks require no borrower equity; they effectively provide for 100 percent financing. As this discussion suggests, the relative costs and benefits of the various financing options are difficult to assess and highly dependent on the specific terms of the agreements.

THE PREPAYMENT AND DEFAULT DECISIONS

As with residential mortgages, the most accurate guide to a commercial mortgage refinancing decision is net present value. This decision rule compares the present value of future payment reductions to the immediate costs of obtaining a new loan. Similar to a residential mortgage, the costs of refinancing an existing commercial mortgage are large and can vary depending upon the number of discount points and other fees charged by the new lender. In addition, the up-front costs of commercial refinancing typically include a prepayment penalty—perhaps in the form of a yield-maintenance agreement. Moreover, lock-out provisions may preclude the borrower from refinancing. For these reasons, the risk to the lender of a prepayment due to a decline in interest rates is small relative to the prepayment risk of residential mortgages.

The signature risk of commercial mortgage lending and investing is default risk. Putting aside transaction costs and other considerations, commercial borrowers would tend to default on their loans if the value of the property were to fall below the value of the remaining mortgage balance. This is especially true if the mortgage is nonrecourse. However, the evidence indicates that commercial borrowers do not default the minute the value of the remaining mortgage balance exceeds the market value of the property. The propensity of commercial borrowers to default also is impeded by the costs of default. Many commercial borrowers with negative equity continue to make monthly payments because they expect the market value of the property to increase. These costs include both direct costs such as penalty fees or any recourse the lender holds to other assets of the borrower, and indirect costs such as greater difficulty or higher cost of obtaining mortgage financing subsequent to the default. Nevertheless, commercial defaults regularly occur (see Real Estate Focus 18–2).

REQUESTING A PERMANENT LOAN

There are three basic steps involved in obtaining debt financing for a commercial property investment. First, the prospective borrower submits a formal loan application. Second, the lender analyzes the information contained in the loan application, as well as other information, and decides whether or not to fund the loan. This process is referred to as the **loan underwriting process**. If the decision is made to fund the loan, a formal commitment is made to the borrower. After both the borrower and lender have satisfied the terms of the agreement, the loan is "closed." This section discusses step 1: the loan application process. The lender's decision-making process is discussed in the next section, while the loan closing process is discussed in detail in Chapter 24.

LOAN SUBMISSION PACKAGE

When seeking a long-term mortgage loan, investors must provide prospective lenders with the relevant information lenders need to assess the profitability and risk of each application. The required information is usually filled in on a number of prepared forms, which

REAL ESTATE FOCUS 18-2

The Building That Ate Chicago

At 110 stories, the Sears Tower dominates Chicago's urban skyline. At 3.6 million square feet, it also carries considerable sway in the Windy City's real estate market. But this prominent structure, America's tallest, is no longer a source of profits for Sears. In 1994, the Sears Tower fell into foreclosure, heaping hundreds of millions of dollars in losses on some of the country's biggest investors.

What prompted the country's biggest retailer to join the rolls of corporate deadbeats? Money—lots of it. The loans were nonrecourse, meaning that in the event of default, the lenders could lay claim only to the building, not to any of Sears' other assets.

In the late 1980s, Sears struck an arrangement with a consortium of lenders to mortgage the building for $850 million, even as real estate markets were collapsing. The lending consortium, which included Metropol-

itan Life and New York Life, as well as the pension funds of Ameritech and AT&T, was put together by Aldrich Eastman & Waltch, a manager of real estate investments for pension funds. In some ways the mortgage offered more advantages to Sears than an outright sale: It allowed the retailer to pull cash out of the building without paying some $150 million in capital gains tax that a sale would trigger.

However, the real estate recession pushed vacancies up and rents down. By late 1993, the value of the Sears tower had fallen to about $400 million, less than half the loan amount. Many observers were certain Sears would avoid the embarrassment of foreclosure. They were wrong.

SOURCE: Adapted from Richard D. Hylton, "The Building That Ate Chicago," *Fortune* (October 4, 1993). Copyright Time Inc.

---

are bound together with other information as a loan submission package. Unlike residential loans, a commercial loan application is not a standardized form because it is designed by lenders to suit their specific requirements. However, pressure to standardize commercial loan documents continues to mount as the secondary market for commercial mortgages and mortgage-backed securities continues to expand.

Relative to residential loans, the underwriting process for commercial loans is more complicated and focuses more on the property being used as collateral for the loan. The primary reason for this difference in emphasis is the anticipated source of funds for loan repayment. Lenders expect that payments on residential loans will come from the personal income of the borrower. Payments on commercial loans are expected to come from income generated by the property. As a result, the commercial loan underwriting process focuses first on the property being pledged as collateral for the loan.

The size and details of the submission package vary with the size of the loan request, the type of property being used as collateral (office, apartment, etc.), and whether the loan proceeds will be used to fund an existing property or a proposed development. However, loan submission packages usually include the following items.

Loan application.   The loan application is the specific document in the package that requests funds. It specifies the amount (or percentage of value) requested, the maturity of the loan, the interest rate, commitment terms, and identity of the borrower(s). It also usually includes the borrower's financial statements, a credit report, a projection of how the loan is to be repaid, and the borrower's experience with similar projects.

Property description.   The property that will secure the loan and its location must be described in considerable detail. Maps and photos of the area are usually included, as are surveys, plot plans, and topographical maps (all discussed in Chapter 22). If the project is a proposed development, additional information such as building plans, renderings, specifications, and data on soil characteristics also are included.

Legal aspects.[12]   Lenders require a precise description of the property and identification of any easements or encroachments. Information about property taxes, special assessments, and deed restrictions must also be included. On new construction, zoning is often a crucial matter, and prospective borrowers usually must demonstrate that proper zoning has been obtained. Other land-use controls and environmental requirements such as flood plain restrictions and water runoff provisions must be discussed, and compliance demonstrated. Environmental impact statements or other reports must be included, as required. These reports are intended to confirm the absence or presence of hazardous materials on the site. The environmental site assessment has become increasingly important in the lender's decision-making process because of recent regulatory changes and because numerous recent court rulings have held lenders liable for clean-up costs on contaminated properties when they foreclose and take title.

Loan applicants also must provide a favorable title opinion or a commitment for title insurance. Lenders want to make certain a long-term mortgage loan will constitute a first lien on the property, and in the case of serious default, the borrower's rights could be foreclosed, the property sold, and the proceeds used to pay off the debt.

Cash flow estimates.   Because the main source of repayment for commercial loans is cash flow from operations, lenders typically require a complete projection of future cash flows from operations, that is, a discounted cash flow analysis. How much weight is placed on the applicant's estimate of the property's future income-producing ability depends on the skills and knowledge of the lender's underwriting staff and the reputation of the loan applicant.

Appraisal report.   Lenders typically require a third-party fee appraisal of the property as an estimate of its market value. Maximum loan amounts are often a percentage of the property's value, and some lenders limit the loan-to-value ratio of their loans. The borrower's appraisal firm must be acceptable to the lender, or the lender will require another appraisal by a firm that is acceptable. Federally regulated lenders must order appraisal reports from an approved appraisal firm. Borrowers cannot shop appraisers to

[12]The legal perspective is discussed in detail in Chapters 20–24.

find the highest value estimate. Although the lender uses all of the information in the submission package in the underwriting process, lenders usually place considerable weight on the estimate of market value contained in the appraisal report. However, lenders also will physically inspect the property.

Feasibility study. Lenders may require a feasibility study for proposed projects, although many believe an appraisal report is sufficient, or they may allow feasibility to be addressed in the appraisal report. A separate feasibility study is preferable for large projects, however, because it addresses issues that appraisals usually do not (see Chapter 11). In-depth market analysis demonstrating the demand for the proposed property, and existing and projected supply shows both the applicant and lenders the probability of success.

CHANNELS OF SUBMISSION

A loan submission package may be presented directly to lenders or may go through a mortgage banker or mortgage broker. Prospective borrowers often submit loan requests directly to savings and loans, mutual savings banks, life insurance companies, or pension funds. Such institutions have commercial property lending units that consider such requests. Informal discussions with loan officers in these firms inform would-be borrowers of the expected items in a loan submission package.

Another channel for loan requests is through mortgage bankers. Many of these firms enjoy close business relationships with large institutional lenders and may have ready access to several such lenders. A business relationship in which a large lender agrees to purchase loans or to consider loan requests from a mortgage banker is termed a **correspondent relationship**. Many mortgage bankers specialize in seeking loan opportunities and in putting together loan submission packages that meet the requirements of large institutional lenders. Mortgage brokers help borrowers and lenders find each other. They may also assist borrowers in assembling loan submission packages.

THE LENDER'S DECISION-MAKING PROCESS

The borrower submits the loan application, the appraisal, and related information to the lender for funding consideration. Usually, one of the lender's loan underwriters is assigned primary responsibility for analyzing the loan, summarizing the application information on internal forms, and making a recommendation to a loan committee to approve, reject, or renegotiate the loan terms and conditions. Lenders use a fairly standard set of criteria when evaluating commercial applications. We first discuss some qualitative issues and standards mortgage lenders consider in evaluating the property and the borrower. We subsequently review the ratios and return measures commonly used in the quantitative analysis of the loan application.

The Property and Borrower

When evaluating the loan application, lenders concentrate on the characteristics of the application that will have the most influence on the performance of the property being used as collateral. In particular, lenders generally consider the following characteristics:[13]

- *Property type.* Commercial mortgages include loans secured by office buildings, shopping centers, industrial and warehouse buildings, and hospitality properties such as hotels and motels. Each of these property types represents an investment in a diverse business with different operating margins, regulatory constraints, and supply and demand fundamentals (see Chapter 6). For example, the most important influence on rental housing demand, and therefore rents, is the current and future population of households in the *local* area. The demand for many hotel and motel rooms, however, is not primarily a function of the local population base. Because the analyses for the different property types are considerably different, some lenders choose to specialize in particular property types.
- *Location.* Local markets have a significant effect on how properties perform. For this reason, lenders often perform the same kinds of market and feasibility analyses investors and appraisers undertake.
- *Tenant quality.* Tenants typically fulfill their lease obligations as long as their business is profitable. However, it is not uncommon for tenants with bankrupt, or even struggling businesses to default on their leases. Lenders are therefore concerned about the number of tenants in each property and their creditworthiness, especially the dominant or "anchor" tenants in office and retail properties.
- *Lease terms.* Cash flow from operations is derived from leases. Therefore, lenders must evaluate important lease terms such as base rental rates, escalation clauses, expense payment provisions, and renewal and cancellation options. The complexity of lease terms varies by loan size and property type.
- *Property management.* Property management can significantly affect the operating performance of a property. Thus, lenders must evaluate the manager's experience and knowledge of the local market.
- *Building quality.* The age, design, and physical appearance of the building can dramatically affect its income-producing ability. In particular, lenders should be concerned about any deferred maintenance or required capital expenditures that may affect the ability of the borrower to service the debt.
- *Environmental concerns.* As previously mentioned, environmental issues and concerns have become increasingly important. Environmental damage or liability can cause a significant loss in the value of the property.

---

[13]For a more detailed discussion of the qualitative factors lenders consider when underwriting loans, see David P. Jacob and Cymbal R. Duncan, "Commercial Mortgage-Backed Securities," *The Handbook of Mortgage-Backed Securities*, 4th ed., ed. Frank J. Fabozzi, (Chicago: 1995) Probus Publishing.

• *Borrower quality*. Although the nonrecourse nature of many commercial loans causes the lender to focus on the property, borrower quality is still an important consideration.

MAXIMUM LOAN AMOUNT

Several factors may determine whether the borrower's requested loan amount is too high. First, some lenders have limits on the size of the loans they can make relative to the value of the property being used as collateral. In any case, lenders usually set their own limits on loan-to-value ratios that vary by property type and, often, by the market in which the property is located. In some cases, especially when interest rates are relatively high, the maximum allowable loan is determined by the debt service coverage ratio or the break-even ratio.

Debt service coverage ratio.   As discussed in Chapter 3, the debt coverage ratio (DCR) shows the extent to which NOI can decline before it is insufficient to service the debt. It therefore provides an indication of the safety associated with the use of borrowed funds. The DCR for our Gatorwood Apartment example, assuming a $10 million loan, is

$$DCR = \frac{NOI}{Debt\ Service} = \frac{\$1,272,500}{\$857,038} = 1.48$$

Because NOI in the first year of operations is expected to be almost half again as large as the prospective mortgage payment, there appears to be sufficient protection against a decline in rental rates and net operating income.

If the lender feels that $1,272,500 is a reasonable estimate of first year NOI, the DCR can be used to calculate the maximum allowable loan given the lender's minimum acceptable DCR. For example, if the lender requires the DCR to be 1.25 or greater, we can obtain the maximum debt service payment by rearranging the DCR formula as follows:

$$Maximum\ Debt\ Service = \frac{NOI}{Minimum\ DCR} = \frac{\$1,272,500}{1.25} = \$1,018,000$$

This maximum annual debt service, together with a 7.625 percent interest rate, annual payments, and a 30-year term, implies a maximum loan of $11,878,124 (88.8 percent LTV).[14] Although the property can support a $11,878,124 loan, the maximum allowable loan will be determined by the lender's maximum allowable LTV if it is less than 88.8 percent, which is very likely.

---

[14]The calculator keystrokes to find the maximum loan amount are: N = 30, I = 7.625, PV = ?, PMT = 1,018,000, and FV = 0. To calculate the maximum LTV, simply divide the maximum loan amount of $11,878,124 by the purchase price (value), given in Exhibit 18–3, of $13,375,000.

Break-even ratio.   A third limit on the loan amount is often the requirement that the break-even ratio not exceed a maximum amount. This ratio indicates the percentage of occupancy required to guarantee sufficient income from a property to meet all cash outlays incurred operating *and* financing the property. Generally, lower ratios are better than higher ratios; they imply that the property can be supported by fewer occupants. The normal range of this ratio is 70 to 90 percent. The break-even ratio in year 1 for our Gatorwood Apartment example assuming a $10 million loan is

$$Break\text{-}Even\ Ratio = \frac{Operating\ Expenses + Debt\ Service}{Efective\ Gross\ Income} = \frac{\$437,500 + \$857,038}{\$1,710,000} = 0.76$$

THE ECONOMIC JUSTIFICATION

If the requested loan amount does not exceed the lender's underwriting guidelines, a decision must be made about whether the entire loan proposal makes sense on economic grounds. In addition to requiring review of the qualitative characteristics of the loan proposal discussed above, this decision requires that the lender check the cash flow and resale projections contained in the appraisal report and in the borrower's submission package. The lender is also aware that if the property produces an adequate return for the borrower, there is little chance the borrower will default on the mortgage. Thus, the lender will typically estimate the capitalization rate and the equity dividend rate, as well as the borrower's expected IRR.

ACQUISITION, DEVELOPMENT, AND CONSTRUCTION FINANCING

The development, construction, and operation of large income properties takes time and different types of effort. The developer may acquire land that must then be made ready (improved) for construction. The improved land may be sold as individual lots, as is typical with new home development, or it may be used as an industrial or office park, or as a site for some other form of income-producing property. Different financing requirements usually are involved in the various phases of a property's life, and lending arrangements have evolved to serve these needs. **Land acquisition loans** finance the purchase of the raw land. **Land development loans** finance the installation of the on-site and off-site improvements to the land—such as sewers, streets, and utilities—that are necessary to ready the land for construction. **Construction loans** are used to finance the costs associated with erecting the building or buildings.

Some lenders may be willing to make acquisition, development, and construction (ADC) loans. In these loans, the same lender advances enough money for the developer to purchase the land and develop it to the point that it is ready for a building to be constructed on it. Then, the lender advances additional funds for construction, with the developed land and partial construction serving as security for the loan. The existence of one lender and one set of loan documents simplifies the financing process and eliminates

REAL ESTATE FOCUS 18-3

Towering Debt Halts Skyscraper

Dreams of a 125-story building that would have been the world's tallest began to fade in August of 1992 when Mellon Bank Corp. of Pittsburgh foreclosed on the land development loan on the proposed site of the project. The developer, Miglin-Beitler Developments, could not find construction financing for the needlelike building that would have soared 15 stories above Sears Tower. In confirming the foreclosure, Mellon Bank said, "The $25 million debt matured and hasn't been paid." Foreclosure actions continued and the bank took control of the property.

Miglin-Beitler announced plans for the $450 million skyscraper in 1989 and began searching worldwide for construction financing. The project had been approved in the zoning process and was ready to go for any developer who wanted to acquire it from Mellon Bank. But there was little chance in the depressed office market of 1992 that anyone would pay anywhere near the $25 million Mellon needed to break even.

SOURCE: Adapted from Jerry C. Davis, "Towering Debt Halts Skyscraper," *Chicago Sun-Times*, August 12, 1992.

potential conflicts of interest between the various lenders. Thus, it would seem to make sense for one lender to finance all stages of the process with one (ADC) loan. However, it is more often the case that the different stages involve loans from different lenders, even though each lender often requires that a detailed set of provisions be met by one or more of the other lenders involved.[15]

Ultimately, the success of land development and construction loans depends on the developer's ability to complete projects with market values in excess of development and construction costs. The developer's failure to create adequate value at any stage of the development process may result in default and foreclosure (see Real Estate Focus 18–3).

The remainder of this section provides an overview of land acquisition, land development, and construction financing. We also briefly discuss a number of loan agreements that provide mortgage financing for the period of time after construction is completed, but before the permanent (long-term) financing is available.

LAND PURCHASE AND DEVELOPMENT FINANCING

Raw land is acquired either by speculators or developers. Speculators generally hope to realize significant price appreciation on the land because of zoning changes, the construction of new roads, changes in local development patterns, or other changes that increase the value of the land. Developers, on the other hand, typically have specific plans for the transformation of the raw land into improved real estate. Both speculators and developers may need to finance the purchase of a land parcel; however, land acquisition loans are probably the most difficult of all mortgage loans to obtain. Undeveloped (raw) land

---

[15]Many ADC loans experienced difficulties and resulted in large losses to savings and loan associations during the latter 1980s. Since then, regulations governing such loans have become much stricter, and most financial institutions have been unwilling to make them.

produces no periodic rental income that can be use to make mortgage and property tax payments. In fact, repayment of the land acquisition loan is usually expected to come from the eventual sale of the land—and the timing and value of future land sales is highly uncertain. This repayment uncertainty makes these loans very risky for lenders.

At the end of 1995, about $17 billion of land acquisition loans from financial institutions were outstanding. Commercial banks held 74 percent of this total, while savings and loan associations held 14 percent. It should be noted that a developer's ability to subsequently obtain a construction loan may be affected by the land acquisition mortgage. The construction loan would be a second lien (which the construction lender is unlikely to accept), or the land purchase mortgage would have to be subordinated to the construction loan (which the land purchase lender is unlikely to accept). Thus, instead of borrowing funds from a third-party lender to purchase land, developers often attempt to have the landowners finance the purchase. The landowners may become partners with the developer (thus taking an equity position in the development), or they may take a land purchase money mortgage from the developer (in lieu of cash) but agree to subordinate the purchase money mortgage when land development, construction financing, or both are needed to proceed with the project. In this way, the seller of the raw land also becomes a lender.

Developers may also secure land for future development with a **land purchase option**. The purchase of such an option from the landowner gives the developer the right, but *not* the obligation, to purchase the land before the expiration date of the option at a predetermined price. If the developer decides not to exercise the option, only the price of the option is lost.

Once the raw land has been purchased, it must be made ready for construction—it must be developed. The land development phase includes the actual site preparation work such as clearing, grading, and the installation of streets and utilities, but also includes obtaining the appropriate zoning and other required permits, as well as the surveying and engineering work that must be completed before a shovel can be turned. Land development loans are also extremely risky and therefore the lender must be convinced that the proceeds from the development loan will create enough additional value to adequately secure the loan. The submission package for a land development loan must therefore include feasibility and market studies, as well as site planning information, surveys, soil reports, financial information on the borrower, and an independent appraisal of developed value.

CONSTRUCTION FINANCING

Construction of the building(s) can begin once the land has been made ready. Construction lenders (such as commercial banks, savings and loans, and insurance companies) almost always require that the loan to finance the construction of new buildings be a first lien on the property. Thus, the developer must already own the land free and clear or must convince the land acquisition and development lenders to subordinate their loan. The land and development lenders may do this in exchange for an equity position in the project. Occasionally, the developer will obtain the land under a long-term lease (50 to 99 years) from the owner. In these cases, the developer usually expects to be the permanent owner of the building.

Construction loans are short-term arrangements that cover the length of the construction period. The interest rate is usually a floating rate set at 2 percent to 5 percent above the prime lending rate. Unlike other mortgage loans where the borrower receives the entire loan proceeds at closing, construction loans allow the developer to obtain funds in "draws" after the completion of specified stages of the building. In this way, the lender is assured that adequate components of the property exist to secure the next draw on the loan in case the borrower defaults. For example, 20 percent of the loan might be payable after the footings, foundation, and floors are in place; 20 percent after the walls and roof are constructed; 20 percent on completion of plumbing and electrical work; and the remaining 40 percent after completion of the entire building. Another method is to advance the developer amounts actually spent during the previous months, audited and verified by the lender.

Interest on the construction loan can be paid to the lender monthly. However, in most cases the interest payments are deferred and added to the outstanding construction loan balance. The construction loan, and accumulated interest, is then paid off with the proceeds from the sale of the property to an investor(s), or by a long-term, permanent mortgage loan.

The primary risk of a construction loan is that the developer will fail to complete the project in a timely manner, or fail to complete it at all. Builders may experience cost overruns, poor weather, strikes, structural or design problems, or difficulties with subcontractors. The builder may simply be badly managed. In addition, failure to pass various building code inspections may delay the ability of tenants to occupy the building (and pay rent). All of these risks are assumed by the construction lender. Thus, construction lenders must have specialized skills in monitoring and controlling the construction process.

Take-out commitments. Construction lenders often have attempted to minimize risk by requiring the developer to obtain a **take-out commitment** before agreeing to provide the funds for construction. These commitments assure (short-term) construction lenders they will not become long-term, or even intermediate-term, lenders. The take-out commitment is issued by a long-term lender, such as an insurance company, who agrees to disburse the permanent loan proceeds when the project has been completed according to the takeout lender's specifications. These specifications often include a requirement that the property be substantially leased-up (maybe 60 to 70 percent) before the permanent loan proceeds are fully disbursed. The contract interest rate is usually determined at the time the loan proceeds are disbursed and is set equal to the rate on a prespecified benchmark security (e.g., the seven-year Treasury bond), plus a predetermined spread. Other terms of the permanent financing (LTV, amortization schedule, etc.) are determined at the time the take-out commitment is issued.

The permanent lender may agree in the take-out commitment to disburse the full amount of the permanent loan when construction of the building(s) is completed. However, it is more typically the case that a specified occupancy rate must be achieved before the developer is able to obtain the full amount of funds specified in the permanent loan contract. Consider the commonly used **floor-to-ceiling commitment.** If occupancy falls short of the specified rate when the building is completed, the permanent lender will not disburse the full amount of the loan proceeds (the ceiling). Rather, lenders will advance a lower loan amount—the floor. The construction lender recognizes that the occupancy rate required to obtain the full amount of the permanent financing may not be achieved, in which case the construction loan may not be paid off. Therefore, the construction lender typically will require the borrower to obtain a second-mortgage commitment—called a **gap** (or bridge) **loan**—from yet another lender to cover the potential difference between the construction loan and the floor amount advanced by the lender. Because of the risk involved if the second mortgage is needed, both the commitment fees and the interest rates on gap loans are high.

Open-ended loan.   Another type of construction loan provides financing for the construction period *without* a take-out commitment from a permanent lender. These speculative or "open-ended" construction loans are extremely risky because the lender is exposed to all the risks associated with construction lending, plus the risk associated with the lease-up period. Given that successful developments will likely rent quickly and find permanent (take-out) lenders, speculative lenders are exposed to a great deal of downside risk with open-ended loans because they are more likely than other construction lenders (who are protected from problems during the lease-up period) to end up with unsuccessful projects. Thus, speculative construction lenders may be forced to foreclose more often or to provide intermediate or, perhaps, long-term financing for undesirable projects. For this reason, speculative loans should be considered only for the construction of properties that are in short supply in the local market. In such conditions, it is more likely that the leased-up property can be sold or a permanent loan can be readily obtained should the borrower decide to retain ownership.

Mini-perm loan.   Rather than separately negotiating a construction loan, a permanent mortgage, and bridge or gap financing, in some cases the developer obtains a single short-term permanent mortgage—or **mini-perm loan**—from an interim lender that provides financing for the construction period, the lease-up period, and for several years beyond the lease-up stage. Developers may be attracted to mini-perms, which enable them to proceed with construction without long-term financing, if they expect to sell the project or refinance into a permanent loan before the term of the mini-perm loan expires. These loans were widely used, and perhaps partially responsible for, the development frenzy that occurred during the 1980s.

SEQUENCE OF FINANCING

Mortgage financing for new income properties is frequently not obtained in the same order that the work on the properties occurs. Landowners and land acquisition lenders usually want some evidence that a land development loan can be obtained to improve the raw land. Land development lenders want to make certain the building(s) will be constructed, so they want to see loan commitments from a construction lender. Construction lenders, in turn, often want to be assured that long-term permanent financing will be

EXHIBIT 18-10

ALTERNATIVE LOAN PACKAGES FOR DEVELOPMENT PROJECTS

	Risky permanent loan	
Construction loan with take-out commitment	Floor amount	Safe permanent loan
	Bridge or gap loan	
Open-ended construction loan		Safe permanent loan
Mini-perm loan	?	Safe permanent loan
Construction period	Lease-up period	Stable operations

available to pay off (or *take out*) the construction loan. Therefore, developers often must work backward through some or all of the financing chain.

For example, if construction lenders in a given market are requiring borrowers to obtain permanent loan commitments, developers must first convince a permanent lender to provide a loan commitment that is contingent on the building being constructed and, typically, leased-up to a predetermined level. With this permanent mortgage commitment in hand, developers can approach construction lenders, who are then willing to consider short-term construction financing. After getting the construction loan commitment, the developer can apply for a development loan, a land purchase loan, or both. In short, each loan commitment demonstrates project feasibility to the next lender in the sequence.

Exhibit 18–10 summarizes a number of loan packages that may be used to finance improvements to income properties over the life cycle. The horizontal axis covers the life cycle of the improved real estate: the construction period, the lease-up period, and the subsequent period of stable operations. The length of the construction and lease-up periods are unknown. For example, extremely successful projects can be fully leased by the end of construction. In such a case, there would be no separate lease-up period after construction.

The first financing package depicted at the top of Exhibit 18–10 is one where a permanent lender has commited to provide long-term financing to the developer upon completion of construction. This structure is relatively rare because it exposes the permanent lender to the substantial economic risks of the lease-up period. The lease-up period is often "the period (moment) of truth" for many commercial development projects because the "build it and they will come" philosophy of many developers has often proven to be a recipe for disaster.

To avoid the risk of the lease-up period, permanent lenders will usually disburse an agreed-upon amount upon completion of construction (the floor), but will usually not provide full funding until the project is adequately leased. The construction lender, however, wants to specialize in the construction phase of property life cycles and therefore is also anxious to avoid the risk of the lease-up period. For these reasons, an interim lender usually steps in to bear the risk of the lease-up period by providing an interim gap loan. The existence of the gap financing assures the construction lender of being taken out when construction is completed. Again, if the property is fully leased upon completion of construction, the full amount of the permanent loan is disbursed by the take-out lender and no gap financing is required.

With an open-ended construction loan, no take-out commitment is required. Thus, the construction lender is exposed to the risks of the lease-up period because it is uncertain when the developer will be able to obtain permanent financing. Finally, mini-perm loans provide financing for the construction and lease-up phases, and for several years beyond.

SUMMARY

Most commercial properties require debt financing tailored to meet the unique aspects of the given situation. While many of the same institutions (commercial banks, life insurers, savings institutions, etc.) that originate home loans also provide commercial property financing, the loan terms are considerably different. For example, commercial mortgages are typically shorter in term, limit or penalize prepayment, and sometimes include cash flow participation clauses. In addition, because both lenders and borrowers within the primary commercial mortgage market tend to be large, relatively sophisticated investors, few constraints are needed, or employed, to protect either party. Finally, unlike residential mortgage financing, commercial property financing has historically been nonrecourse, although the trend in the 1990s has been toward more exposure of borrowers to personal liability.

The three main repayment mechanisms used in the market for long-term (permanent) commercial mortgages are fully amortizing loans, partially amortizing loans, and interest-only loans. Fixed rate, partially amortizing mortgages with balloon payments are the most commonly used structure, although it is not uncommon for commercial mortgages to have adjustable, or floating, interest rates. Fixed-rate commercial mortgages do not typically allow borrowers to freely prepay at par because they contain either a lock-out provision, a prepayment penalty such as a yield-maintenance agreement, or both. Floating rate loans generally are prepayable at par without penalty.

Commercial mortgage loans are occasionally structured to give the lender an "equity-like" interest in the property through a "participation" in the property's annual cash flows, the cash flows from the eventual sale of the property, or both. These contingent interests are frequently referred to as income and equity kickers, respectively. Joint ventures, sale-leaseback agreements, and convertible mortgages are alternative means of providing lenders with an equity stake in the property.

After selecting the appropriate financing structure, investors must next select their desired loan amount. Borrowed funds *magnify* the equity returns to a given project, both positively and negatively. By employing higher loan-to-value ratios—using more financial leverage—investors can increase their expected returns. However, by doing so, they also increase the variability of equity returns and the probability NOI will not be sufficient to cover the mortgage payment obligation. This latter concern is often referred to as *financial risk*. Other decisions facing commercial borrowers subsequent to loan origination include the decision to prepay and the decision to default. In both situations, net present value calculations should guide decision making, remembering of course, that it is important to include all potential costs, such as a diminished credit rating, when selecting the default option.

To obtain debt financing for a commercial property investment, the prospective borrower must first submit a formal loan application package. This loan submission package typically includes items such as the loan application, property description, legal aspects, cash flow estimates, appraisal report, and feasibility study. The package may be presented directly to lenders or through a mortgage banker or mortgage broker. The lender must then evaluate both the property and the borrower to determine if they wish to fund the investment. When evaluating the loan application, lenders pay particular attention to the property type, location, tenant quality, lease terms, property management, building quality, environmental concerns, and borrower quality. When determining the maximum loan amount, lenders also employ the debt coverage and break even ratios. Finally, if the application meets all lender standards, its economic justification is considered. The key question is this: Does this project make good economic sense? If the answer is yes, the application is approved and the loan is closed.

The final section of this chapter focused on acquisition, development, and construction (ADC) financing. The development, construction, and operation of large income properties takes time and different types of efforts. Although some lenders are willing to provide one loan that funds the land acquisition, land development, and construction of the structure, this is not the typical arrangement. More likely, a land acquisition loan finances the purchase of the parcel, a land development loan covers the costs of developing the land to the point where building construction can begin, and a construction loan pays for the construction period of the property life cycle. Permanent (long-term) financing is not employed until the lease-up period is completed and stable operations have commenced. "Gap" loans are relatively expensive, but are often employed as a buffer or intermediate financing device between construction loans and the permanent long-term financing, thus reducing the risk to both construction and permanent project lenders. Mini-perm loans are another option. They provide financing for the construction and lease-up phases and for several years beyond. Finally, when arranging financing for income-producing properties, it is often necessary to work backwards, obtaining commitments from subsequent stage lenders before current construction stages will get funded. Commitments from subsequent lenders, in short, demonstrate project feasibility to the preceding lender.

KEY TERMS

Balloon mortgage 539	Gap loan 564	Mini-perm loan 564
Construction loans 560	Income kickers 542	Mortgage 539
Contingent interest 544	Installment sale 541	Nonrecourse financing 538
Convertible mortgage 546	Joint venture 545	Note 538
Correspondent relationship 557	Land acquisition loans 560	Prepayment penalties 541
Equity kickers 542	Land development loans 560	Recourse financing 538
Financial risk 548	Land purchase option 562	Reinvestment risk 541
Floating-rate mortgage 541	Loan underwriting process 554	Take-out commitment 563
Floor-to-ceiling commitment 563	Lock-out provision 540	Yield-maintenance agreements 541

TEST YOURSELF

Answer the following multiple-choice problems:

1. Using financial leverage on a real estate investment can be for the purpose of all *except*
   a. Greater diversification.
   b. Greater expected return on the leveraged investment.
   c. Being able to acquire the property.
   d. Reduction of financial risk for the leveraged investment.

2. Which of these lenders is most likely to provide a large construction loan today?
   a. Savings and loan.
   b. Credit union.
   c. Commercial bank.
   d. Life insurance company.
   e. REIT.

3. Which of these loans is a life insurance company most likely to invest in?
   a. Single-family home loan.
   b. Small commercial property loan (nonconstruction).
   c. Large office building loan (nonconstruction).
   d. Large construction loan.
   e. Small construction loan.

4. Which of these entities is most likely to specialize in investing in (funding) "permanent" loans on high-quality office buildings?
   a. Commercial bank.
   b. Savings and loan association.
   c. Pension fund.
   d. Mortgage banker.

5. A participation loan is one where the lender receives a below-market contract interest rate, but may
   a. Receive a percentage of operating income.
   b. Pay a prespecified percentage of operating expenses.
   c. Receive a percentage of the future sale price.
   d. Both *a* and *b*.
   e. Both *a* and *c*.

6. Increasing the amount of debt on a property will increase the equity investor's expected IRR if
   a. The initial cap rate exceeds the loan constant.
   b. Before-tax unleveraged IRR exceeds the effective interest rate on debt.
   c. After-tax unleveraged IRR exceeds the after-tax effective interest rate.
   d. Before-tax leveraged return exceeds the effective interest rate.
   e. None of the above.

7. Which of these ratios is an indicator of the financial risk for an income property?
   a. Debt coverage ratio.
   b. Break-even ratio.
   c. Equity dividend rate.
   d. Both *a* and *b*, but not *c*.
   e. All three, *a, b* and *c*.

8. Which of these is a valid motivation for a participation loan?
   a. It lowers the borrower's required debt service.
   b. It gives the lender protection against unexpected inflation.
   c. It provides a mechanism to control the distribution of business risk between lender and borrower.
   d. *a* and *b*, but not *c*.
   e. All three, *a, b* and *c*.

9. Which of these financial firms is most likely to invest in a large, long-term mortgage loan on a shopping center?
   a. Credit union.
   b. Commercial bank.
   c. Savings and loan association.
   d. Life insurance company.
   e. Mortgage banker.

10. Lenders often require a specified rent-up percentage as a condition for granting what type of loan?
    a. Construction loan.
    b. Land development loan.
    c. Long-term permanent loan.

d. Gap loan.

e. Land purchase loan.

11. If the property's NOI is $22,560, operating expenses are $12,250, debt service is $19,987, and gross income is $41,500, the breakeven ratio is approximately equal to

    a. 82.5 percent.

    b. 83.2 percent.

    c. 77.7 percent.

    d. 76.5 percent.

e. None of the above.

12. If the property's NOI is expected to be $22,560, operating expenses are $12,250, and the debt service is expected to be $19,987, the debt coverage ration (DCR) is approximately equal to

    a. 0.89.

    b. 1.13.

    c. 1.84.

    d. 1.74.

    e. None of the above.

PROBLEMS FOR THOUGHT AND SOLUTION

1. Financial leverage, value and return

   a. Define *financial risk*.

   b. When will increasing the loan-to-value ratio at origination increase the calculated IRR on a proposed income-producing property?

   c. Should the investor select the origination LTV that maximizes the calculated IRR? Explain why or why not.

2. Distinguish between recourse and nonrecourse financing. Has the trend in the 1990s been toward more or less recourse loans?

3. Explain lock-out provisions and yield-maintenance agreements. Does the inclusion of one or both of these provisions affect the borrower's cost of debt financing? Explain.

4. Define income and equity kickers. How does their inclusion in the commercial mortgage contract affect the borrower's cost of debt financing? Explain.

5. Distinguish among land acquisition loans, land development loans, and construction loans. How would you rank these three with respect to lender risk?

6. What is the difference between take-out commitments and standby commitments? As a potential borrower, would you be more or less interested in obtaining a standby commitment instead of a take-out commitment if you expected long-term commercial mortgage rates to increase during the construction period?

7. Define gap loans and mini-perm loans.

CASE PROBLEMS

1. You work for Underwater Savings and Loan and you have decided to loan $400,000 to an investor who is going to purchase a small apartment complex. You have offered the investor a standard fixed-rate mortgage loan with an 8 percent interest rate, *annual* payments, and 30-year amortization. Total up-front financing costs will equal 2 percent of the loan amount. The investor-borrower has made a counterproposal. In exchange for a 6 percent interest rate with *annual* payments and 30-year amortization, the borrower offers you 30 percent of his annual net operating income (NOI). You expect NOI will be $20,000 per year. There will be no up-front financing costs on this second option. You expect that whichever loan you agree to originate, it will be outstanding for five years. Assume that you view each loan as being equally risky, and that 8 percent is an appropriate discount rate. Which loan should Underwater originate? Why?

2. You have decided to purchase an industrial warehouse. The purchase price is $1 million and you expect to hold the property for five years. You have narrowed your choice of debt financing packages to the following two alternatives:

   • $700,000 loan, 10 percent interest rate, 30-year term, annual, interest-only payments. That is, the annual payment will *not* include any amortization of principal. No up-front financing costs.
   • $850,000 loan, 10 percent interest rate, 30-year term, annual, interest-only payments. No up-front financing costs.

   What is the difference, in dollars, in the (before-tax) NPV of this industrial warehouse acquisition if you use the second alternative (the $850,000 loan) instead of the first? Assume the appropriate before-tax discount rate is 12 percent.

3. You are considering the purchase of an industrial warehouse. The purchase price is $1 million. You expect to hold the property for five years. You have decided to finance the acquisition with the $700,000 loan, 10 percent interest rate, 30-year term, and annual *interest-only* payments. (That is, the annual payment will not include any amortization of principal.) There are no up-front financing costs. You estimate the following cash flows for the first year of operations:

$$\begin{array}{ll} \$135,000 & \text{Effective gross income} \\ \underline{27,000} & \text{Operating expenses} \\ \$108,000 & \text{NOI} \end{array}$$

   a. Calculate the overall rate of return (or "cap rate").
   b. Calculate the debt coverage ratio.
   c. Calculate the breakeven ratio
   d. What is the largest loan that you can obtain (holding the other terms constant) if the lender requires a debt service coverage ratio of *at least* 1.2?

ADDITIONAL READINGS

Substantial portions of the following books are devoted to commercial mortgage financing:

Brueggeman, William B., and Jeffrey D. Fisher. *Real Estate Finance and Investments*, 10th ed. Burr Ridge, IL: Richard D. Irwin, 1997.

Clauretie, Terrence M., and G. Stacy Sirmans. *Real Estate Finance*, 2nd ed. Upper Saddle River, NJ: Prentice Hall, 1996.

For those who wish to learn more about current issues and to stay abreast of the field of commercial mortgage finance, we recommend the following journals:

Real Estate Finance (quarterly), Institutional Investor, Inc., 488 Madison Avenue, New York, NY 10022. Phone: (212)224–3184.

Commercial Property News (twice monthly), Miller Freeman Inc., a United News & Media Company, One Penn Plaza, New York, NY 10119. Phone: (212)714–1300.

Real Estate Issues (three times annually), The Counselors of Real Estate of the National Association of Realtors, 430 North Michigan Avenue, Chicago, IL 60611. Phone: (312)329–8257.

19

C H A P T E R

MORTGAGE-BACKED SECURITIES

INTRODUCTION

MORTGAGE SECURITIZATION
The Importance of Securitization
Securitization and Secondary Markets

VALUING INDIVIDUAL MORTGAGES IN THE SECONDARY MARKET
Yield-to-Maturity
Expected Yield
Realized Yield
How Are Mortgage Investment Decisions Made?

PASSTHROUGH SECURITIES
Passthrough Example
Agency Passthroughs
Conventional Passthroughs

SEQUENTIAL PAY STRUCTURES
Sequential Pay Example
Other Responses to Prepayment Risk

VALUING MORTGAGE-BACKED SECURITIES

THE COMMERCIAL MORTGAGE-BACKED SECURITIES MARKET
Sources of Public Debt for Commercial-Property Investment
Brief History of CMBSs

Differences between Residential MBSs and CMBSs

HOW COMMERCIAL MORTGAGE SECURITIZATION OCCURS
Portfolio Refinancing
Conduit Arrangements
Direct Lending by Investment Banks

THE ROLE OF THE RATING AGENCIES
Agencies That Rate CMBS Issues
Qualitative Review
Quantitative Review
Credit Enhancement

THE SECURITIES
Structuring CMBS Issues
Valuation: The Price and Yield Relationship

SUMMARY

KEY TERMS

TEST YOURSELF

PROBLEMS FOR THOUGHT AND SOLUTION

CASE PROBLEMS

ADDITIONAL READINGS

After reading this chapter, students will be able to:

1. Discuss how securitization and the secondary mortgage markets increase the flow of investment funds to mortgages.

2. Explain the differences between the yield-to-maturity, expected yield, and realized yield on mortgage-backed securities.

3. Explain the advantages of investing in passthrough mortgage-backed securities relative to investing in individual mortgage loans.

4. Explain the advantages to investors of having sequential-pay collateralized mortgage obligations available instead of only passthrough mortgage-backed securities.

5. Discuss the effects of borrower prepayments on the prices and yields of mortgages and mortgage-backed securities.

6. Discuss how investment risks differ between residential and commercial mortgage-backed securities and how contract terms and the securities rating agencies affect these risks.

INTRODUCTION

Approximately one-half of all residential mortgage loans originated in the United States are sold into the secondary mortgage market and used as collateral for the issuance of mortgage-backed securities (MBSs). Residential MBSs are the largest single form of non-Treasury marketable debt. The amount outstanding approached $1.8 trillion in 1995, roughly 30 percent greater than the value of all outstanding corporate bonds. This securitization of pools of standardized residential mortgages has greatly increased the liquidity and efficiency of the residential market and has attracted many new sources of investment capital.

The development of the commercial mortgage-backed securities (CMBS) market has proceeded more slowly than the residential MBS market. Although the pace of commercial mortgage securitization has accelerated rapidly since 1991, less than 15 percent of outstanding commercial mortgages in the United States served as collateral for CMBSs in 1996.

The purpose of this chapter is to explain how residential and commercial mortgages are securitized and valued in the secondary mortgage market.

MORTGAGE SECURITIZATION

Securitization refers to the process of creating securities from single assets, or more commonly, from collections of assets. Sometimes firms represent the collections of assets and sometimes portfolios of real estate become the collection of assets, such as in the case of equity REITs. The securitization of mortgages falls into the broad category of asset-backed securitization. This category includes assets as diverse as automobile loans and student loans. Usually, asset-backed securitization involves a collection or pool of similar assets, and thus, an issue of mortgage-backed securities emerges from the securitization of a collection of mortgages with similar characteristics.

We may draw an analogy between securitization and baking a cherry pie. Cherries, representing the mortgages, are assembled in a crusted pie plate and placed in the oven. Baking, which represents securitization, transforms the cherries into a more liquid form so that one cherry becomes nearly indistinguishable from another. Mortgage securitization essentially transforms mortgages into more "liquid" bonds.

Each piece of the baked pie represents one mortgage-backed security, and like the piece of pie that includes parts of all of the cherries, investors in a mortgage-backed security obtain rights to the cash flows from all of the mortgages in the collection. As noted later in this chapter, many ways exist to structure the rights to the cash flows from securitized mortgages.

THE IMPORTANCE OF SECURITIZATION

To demonstrate the importance of securitization in the debt financing of real estate, let us contrast how money flows to mortgages in the traditional **financial intermediation** system and as the result of securitization. Financial intermediation involves a gradual process of accumulating money for mortgage lending. A financial institution, for example a commercial bank, collects deposits from individuals who mostly reside within a few miles of the bank. Once enough deposits come into the bank, a mortgage loan is originated for, perhaps, 30 years. If the bank either cannot sell or refuses to sell the mortgage, the bank's money remains invested in that one mortgage loan for many years.

Now assume a lender, such as a mortgage banker, originates the same loan with money borrowed from a commercial bank using a warehouse loan. The mortgage loan becomes part of a package with other similar mortgages that is used as collateral for the issuance of a mortgage-backed security (MBS). The mortgage banker then sells the MBS to a wide variety of institutions, corporations, foreign investors, and mutual funds. Following the sale of the MBS, the mortgage banker repays the commercial bank and borrows more money to originate another loan. The lesson from this comparison—mortgage securitization results in a far greater number of loans for home purchases and real estate investment because the sources of money are far more extensive than in the traditional system of financial intermediation.

SECURITIZATION AND SECONDARY MARKETS

During the 1930s, the U.S. Congress passed laws to protect investors against fraudulent practices by those who raise money through the sale of rights to future cash flows from businesses and assets.[1] These securities laws provide investors with "security" because any business or asset owner must follow a detailed set of procedures for supplying information to investors about the business or asset and its management before the rights to

---

[1]The Securities Act of 1933 and the Securities Exchange Act of 1934.

future cash flows can be legally sold. The Securities and Exchange Commission (SEC) has responsibility for establishing and enforcing these procedures.

Armed with the protection of securities laws, investors in the initial offerings of securities feel safer than without such laws, and they also feel certain that any other investor who might buy the securities from them in the future will feel the same sense of security. Thus, investor security lies at the core of the initial sale of securities, but perhaps more importantly, it lies at the core of trading in the secondary market.

Liquidity further induces potential investors to invest in mortgages and MBSs. The existence of a secondary market means that investors can more easily sell their mortgage holdings when mortgages trade as securities rather than whole loans. If mortgage securities become actively traded, as with most residential mortgage-backed securities, investors also benefit from the ability to determine the market value of their investments each day. This level of liquidity also enables investors to put up mortgage-backed securities as collateral for borrowing money for other purposes.

Securitization forces standardization of mortgage instruments and underwriting practices, which can lower the costs of financing with mortgages. Finally, investors in mortgage-backed securities do not become involved in the business of collecting payments from mortgage borrowers or dealing with delinquency and default. A small fee is embedded in the cost of mortgage securitization to pay the originating lender or a separate company for servicing the underlying mortgages.

Before discussing how residential MBSs are structured and valued, we first analyze how individual home loans are valued in the secondary market. These concepts provide the background and tools required for the analysis of securitized mortgage pools.

VALUING INDIVIDUAL MORTGAGES IN THE SECONDARY MARKET

Recall from Chapter 2 that the value of any investment opportunity is equal to the present (discounted) value of its expected future cash flows. Thus, determining value requires the investor to estimate both the expected cash flows and the required risk-adjusted rate of return. In the absence of borrower default, the cash flows on a mortgage investment consist of (1) the periodic (usually monthly) payment of principal and interest and (2) the remaining mortgage balance, which is paid in a lump sum when the borrower terminates the mortgage. The required return (yield) is determined by investigating the yields currently available on similar investments. By similar, we mean investments with the same cash flow characteristics, risk of default, and expected holding period.

YIELD-TO-MATURITY

Consider a $100,000 standard fixed-rate mortgage with an 8.75 percent annual interest rate, monthly payments, and an original loan term of 30 years. The monthly payment on this mortgage is $786.70. Assume, for simplicity, that the mortgage was originated yesterday, and is today being marketed in the secondary mortgage market. At what price will this mortgage sell?

The answer depends on the return that investors-purchasers in the secondary market are currently requiring and, in almost all cases, on how long potential investors expect the mortgage to remain outstanding. If the yield investors are currently requiring, the **market yield,** is equal to the contract rate of interest, the value of the mortgage will equal the remaining mortgage balance. That is, the market value will equal the **par value** of the mortgage.[2] If the market yield is less than the contract rate of interest, the mortgage will sell for a **premium;** if greater, the mortgage will sell at a **discount** to par value.

For example, if secondary market investors require an 8.50 percent return on mortgage investments of this type, the present value of the remaining cash flows on this 8.75 percent mortgage is equal to $102,313.20—assuming the mortgage is not prepaid by the borrower prior to maturity. The keystrokes for this calculation are

$N = 360$	$I = 8.50\%/12$	$PV = ?$	$PMT = 786.70$	$FV = 0$

With these assumptions, the mortgage would sell for $2,313.20 more than the $100,000 remaining mortgage balance, or par value. This $2,313 premium reflects the difference between discounting the mortgage payments at 8.5 percent and discounting at the contract rate of 8.75 percent. Recall that if the remaining payments were discounted at the contract rate of 8.75 percent, the present value would equal $100,000—the par value. In short, $2,313.20 represents the present value to investors of a mortgage that pays 8.75 percent interest when their current opportunity cost is 8.5 percent.

If mortgage investors require a 9 percent return on mortgage investments of this type, the present value of the remaining cash flows is equal to $97,772.54—assuming again that the mortgage is not prepaid by the borrower prior to maturity. The keystrokes are

$N = 360$	$I = 9.0\%/12$	$PV = ?$	$PMT = 786.70$	$FV = 0$

This $2,227.46 discount from par value reflects the difference between the 9 percent discount rate and the 8.75 percent contract rate. Discounts are necessary on existing mortgages that have below-market contract rates. In essence, the purpose of the discount is to provide potential investors with a yield equal to the current market yield. Because the periodic payments cannot be increased, the seller must provide potential buyers with an expected capital gain to make up the difference between the 9 percent required yield and the 8.75 percent contract rate. Investors will receive $100,000 in principal payments on the example mortgage. By paying $97,772.54 up-front for $100,000 in principal payments over the life of the loan, the potential investor expects to realize a $2,227.46 capital gain on the mortgage investment. Thus, the 9 percent yield required by the market will come from two sources: (1) the 8.75 monthly interest and (2) the $2,227.46 capital gain. Said differently, paying $97,772.54 for $100,000 in principal increases the expected yield 0.25 percentage points to the required 9 percent.

---

[2]In addition to par value, the remaining mortgage balance is sometimes referred to as the "book value" or "face value" of the mortgage.

The premium investors pay when the required market return is *less* than the contract interest rate produces, in essence, a *negative* capital gain. In the example above, the value of the 8.75 percent mortgage when comparable market yields are 8.5 percent is $102,313.20. Thus, investors are willing to pay $102,313.20 up-front for the right to receive $100,000 in subsequent principal payments, in addition to interest, over the life of the loan. In short, investors are willing to incur a capital loss of up to $2,313.20 because the contract interest rate is 0.25 percent greater than the current market rate.

EXPECTED YIELD

The calculation of yield-to-maturity assumes the mortgage will not be terminated prior to the end of the loan term.[3] However, as discussed in Chapter 16, borrowers have the option to prepay residential mortgages, at par, any time over the term of the mortgage. Moreover, borrowers are increasingly likely to exercise this option to prepay when mortgage rates fall below the contract rate on the existing mortgage. Although the dominant cause of prepayments on fixed-rate mortgages is interest rate declines, most borrowers also are forced to prepay an existing mortgage if they sell the home that is pledged as collateral for the loan. Thus, relocation-induced (or mobility-induced) prepayments are also common.[4] In addition, mortgage defaults (also discussed in Chapter 15 and Chapter 16) typically accelerate the prepayment of principal. As a result of interest rate–driven prepayments, mobility-driven prepayments, and defaults, originating lenders and secondary market investors do not usually expect that mortgages will remain outstanding for the entire loan term.

The expectation that residential mortgages will be repaid, at par, prior to maturity has significant ramifications for valuation. Consider again the $100,000, 8.75 percent mortgages discussed above. If the market yield immediately after origination is 9 percent, the present value of the monthly payments, if held to maturity, is $97,772.54. What happens if secondary market investors assume the mortgage will be prepaid, for whatever reason, at the end of eight years? The present value of the expected monthly payments is equal to $98,620.60. The calculator keystrokes are

$N = 96$	$I = 9.0\%/12$	$PV = ?$	$PMT = 786.70$	$FV = 92,041$

The future value of $92,041 is the remaining mortgage balance after eight years.

Why is the discount equal to $1,379.40 ($100,000 − $98,620.60) instead of $2,227, the discount under the assumption that the mortgage will be outstanding the entire 30 years? Because the discount required by investors is a function of the amount by which the contract rate is less than the market yield *and* the length of time investors expect they will earn the below-market rate. The shorter the expected holding period, the smaller is the required discount from par.[5]

---

[3] The yield-to-maturity also implicitly assumes that the periodic mortgage payments can be reinvested at an interest rate equal to the yield-to-maturity.

[4] The provision that requires the remaining mortgage balance to be paid by the borrower is the due-on-sale clause. For more detail, see Chapter 15.

[5] Consider an extreme case: If you purchased a below-market-rate mortgage, but expected the mortgage to prepay next month, you would not require much of a discount because your capital gain would come quickly.

What is the effect of expected prepayments on the value of premium mortgages? Recall that the example mortgage would have a present value of $102,313 if the market yield immediately after origination was 8.5 percent and prepayment before 30 years was not expected. However, if secondary market investors expect the mortgage to be prepaid after eight years, the present value of the mortgage is reduced to $101,403, which is calculated with the following keystrokes:

$N = 96$	$I = 8.5\%/12$	$PV = ?$	$PMT = 786.70$	$FV = 92,041$

Why has the premium declined from $2,313 (assuming no prepayment) to $1,403 ($101,403 − $100,000), assuming prepayment after eight years? The premium reflects the value to investors of owning an 8.75 percent mortgage when current market rates equal 8.5 percent. The shorter the time period over which investors expect to earn the 0.25 percent differential, the lower is the value they place on the differential. Put differently, the size of the premium increases (decreases) as the expected holding period increases (decreases).

What is the relationship between the expected yield on a mortgage and its yield-to-maturity? The answer depends on whether the mortgage is being purchased at a premium or a discount. If purchased at a premium, the expected yield on a prepayable mortgage is *less* than the yield-to-maturity, if purchased at a discount, the expected yield will *exceed* the yield-to-maturity.

REALIZED YIELD

The realized—or actual—yield on a mortgage investment cannot be determined until the mortgage is terminated. Consider again the newly originated 8.75 percent, $100,000 example mortgage when the current market yield is 9 percent. If the consensus opinion of mortgage investors is that this mortgage, and others like it, will prepay at the end of eight years, the mortgage will be discounted $1,379 to $98,621. An investor who purchases the mortgage at a price of $98,621 therefore expects to earn a 9 percent return if the mortgage also is expected to be outstanding for eight years. That is, the mortgage is "priced to yield" 9 percent, assuming an eight-year holding period. What happens if an investor purchases the mortgage for $98,621, but the borrower prepays after four years? The realized yield will increase to 9.17 percent, relative to the expected (required) yield of 9 percent. Thus, prepayment that occurs sooner than expected *increases* the realized yield on mortgages purchased at a discount.

If the current market yield is 8.5 percent, and the consensus opinion is that the mortgage will be outstanding for eight years, the mortgage will be priced at $101,403. If the investor purchases at this price but the borrower prepays after four years, the yield will decrease to 8.33 percent;[6] below the expected yield of 8.5 percent. The associated keystrokes are

$N = 48$	$I = ?$	$PV = -101,403$	$PMT = 786.70$	$FV = 96,708$

---

[6]The annualized yield of 8.33 percent is equal to the monthly yield times 12.

EXHIBIT 19-1

CONTRACT INTEREST RATES, YIELDS-TO-MATURITY,
EXPECTED YIELDS, AND REALIZED YIELDS

Mortgage Purchased at a	Yield-to-Maturity	Expected Yield	Realized Yield
Discount	Greater than contract interest rate	Greater than yield-to-maturity	Greater than expected yield if prepayment occurs sooner than expected; less if prepayment occurs later than expected.
Premium	Less than contract interest rate	Less than yield-to-maturity	Less than expected yield if prepayment occurs sooner than expected; greater if prepayment occurs later than expected.

Thus, prepayment that occurs sooner than expected *decreases* the realized yield on mortgages purchased at a premium.

The above discussion illustrates the sensitivity of both expected and realized yields to the prepayment behavior of borrowers. What adds to the complexity is that the effect of prepayments on realized yields critically depends on whether the mortgage security is purchased at a premium or at a discount. The relationships between contract interest rates, yields to maturity, expected yields, and realized yields are summarized in Exhibit 19–1.

HOW ARE MORTGAGE INVESTMENT DECISIONS MADE?

One thing should now be clear: both the expected and realized returns on residential mortgage securities depend critically on the prepayment behavior of borrowers. The convention in mortgage markets is to measure the mortgage yield against the yield on a "comparable" Treasury security. For example, the required yield on mortgage securities—determined using some assumption about prepayments—if often compared to the yield currently available on a Treasury bond with a comparable maturity, typically 7 to 10 years. The Treasury security used as a benchmark for valuing the mortgage is not subject to default risk because the Federal government can always issue new securities to pay off existing bondholders. In addition, investing in the benchmark Treasury security does not expose the investor to prepayment risk because the Federal government is not allowed to prepay the obligation prior to maturity.[7] Because standard fixed-rate mortgages are subject to both default and prepayment risk, they must be priced to yield an expected return enough in excess of the yield on the comparable Treasury security to induce investors to purchase mortgages instead of the Treasury security. The difference between the expected yield on the mortgage security and the yield on the comparable Treasury security is called the yield **spread.** If the spread over Treasuries on a particular mortgage investment is, for the moment, not sufficient to compensate potential investors for the increased risk, then the demand for this mortgage security, and therefore its price, will decline relative to the price of the Treasury security. This price decline will continue until the

---

[7]The U.S. Treasury has, occasionally, issued bonds that are prepayable.

expected mortgage yield, and therefore the spread, is sufficient to make the typical investor at least indifferent between purchasing the mortgage security and purchasing the riskless benchmark Treasury security.[8]

The spread over Treasuries on standard fixed-rate mortgages changes frequently, as the risk of mortgages change relative to nondefaultable and nonprepayable Treasury securities. In 1993, the average difference between the contract rate on conventional mortgages and the yield on a seven-year Treasury security was 1.83 percentage points (or 183 basis points). In 1994 and 1995, the spread averaged 1.76 and 1.55 percentage points, respectively.[9]

In addition to providing compensation for default and prepayment risk, the yield spread on mortgages also must provide compensation for the relative illiquidity of mortgages. Although many mortgage securities are actively traded in the secondary mortgage market, all mortgage securities are less liquid than the benchmark Treasury security. Investors must be compensated for this in the form of an increased expected return. Finally, because owning a Treasury security entails no servicing on the part of the investor, the yield spread on mortgage securities also must compensate investors for servicing costs.[10]

In summary, mortgage securities are "priced off the yield curve." That is, the required return on a mortgage security is equal to the yield on a Treasury security of comparable maturity, plus a spread. The spread must be sufficient to compensate mortgage investors for the prepayment and default risk associated with mortgages, as well as the cost of servicing and the relatively illiquidity of mortgages. Investors should purchase a mortgage security when the expected yield (spread) exceeds their required yield (spread).

PASSTHROUGH SECURITIES

Prior to the late 1960s, home mortgage loans, originated primarily by savings and loan associations, were extremely illiquid, although large life insurance companies and S&Ls did purchase some mortgages. Why were residential mortgages so difficult for originators to sell in the secondary market? Many potential capital market investors—other life insur-

---

[8]Treasury bonds that pay periodic (that is, coupon) interest are not technically, riskless. First, such bonds are subject to "reinvestment risk," which is the risk that interest rates will fall and the periodic payments will have to be reinvested at lower rates. Second, the real return on a Treasury security is risky because it will depend on the rate of general inflation in the economy over the investment holding period.

[9]The average contract rates are from the U.S. Department of Housing and Urban Development and are based on commitment rates for conventional first mortgages. The average yields on seven-year Treasury securities are adjusted to constant maturities. Both data series come from the *Federal Reserve Bulletin,* Tables A23 and A34.

[10]As discussed in Chapter 16, loan servicing includes collecting the monthly payment from the borrower and insuring that the borrower's monthly escrow payments for hazard insurance and property taxes are sufficient to allow the servicer to pay in full the annual insurance premium and property taxes on behalf of the borrower when they are due. Servicers also are responsible for sending out notifications if the borrower is delinquent with his or her payment. Mortgage bankers and other servicers receive a monthly fee for servicing the loan that amounts to 0.25 to 0.50 percent (annual) of the outstanding loan balance.

ance companies, pension funds, mutual funds, and the like—avoided residential mortgages because they were not homogeneous. Mortgage loans could vary greatly by size, by the income and assets of the borrower, by loan-to-value ratio, by the strength of the local market in which the housing collateral was located, and by other factors. This variability made it difficult to evaluate the risk/return characteristics of individual mortgages. Many investors were more familiar and comfortable with other bond market alternatives, such as corporate and government bonds. These more traditional fixed-income investments were largely viewed as commodities; that is, investments with many close substitutes, all of which were relatively standard and easy to evaluate compared to individual home mortgages. In particular, potential investors across the nation (and the world) found it difficult to evaluate the default and prepayment risks associated with pools of nonstandard mortgages originated in diverse local housing markets.

Although FHA-insured and VA-guaranteed mortgages protected investors against default, for several reasons this protection was not sufficient to entice many nontraditional mortgage investors to acquire mortgages. First, FHA and VA mortgages accounted for less than 20 percent of residential originations. Conventional (nongovernment sponsored) mortgages provided investors no protection against default, as private mortgage insurance did not yet exist. Second, even though FHA-insured mortgages could be purchased, investors often experienced delays in payments when borrowers defaulted. This delay occurred because, in the event of default, owners of FHA mortgages would have to submit a claim to FHA for the remaining loan balance plus any past-due payments. Resolving these claims required time and effort on the part of investors. Moreover, this waiting period reduced yields and made mortgage cash flows less predictable, and therefore less valuable. To understand the dampening effect of these shortcomings on mortgage purchases, consider again the Treasury bond of comparable maturity that is always available as an alternative investment. Treasury bonds provide investors with safety of principal and delays in interest payments do not occur.

Investors in FHA and VA mortgages also found it difficult to diversify away prepayment risk, which has both a systematic and nonsystematic component. Systematic prepayment risk is caused primarily by changes in interest rates that affect, to varying degrees, all fixed-income securities. Unsystematic prepayment risk is caused by the substantial variability across households in their sensitivity to interest rate declines, and by the variability in the propensity of households to move and, therefore, prepay the mortgage. Household mobility has been shown to vary significantly by local market, and by age, income, and other household characteristics. It was difficult for investors to diversify away this unsystematic risk by purchasing individual mortgages from various originators across the country.

Passthrough securities solved many of the problems associated with investing in individual mortgages. Although the specific characteristics of passthroughs vary depending on the issuers, they all have similar features. First, with a passthrough, the investor is said to have an undivided ownership interest, or participation, in a pool of mortgages. The issuer of the passthrough services the underlying mortgages, collecting payments, and then passing through in bulk (1) any principal payments, both scheduled and unscheduled, and (2) interest on any outstanding principal that issuers have not returned to the investors. The issuer of the passthrough keeps the difference, or spread, between the interest rate paid on the underlying mortgages and the interest rate paid to the passthrough investors.

Passthrough mortgage securities largely eliminate the need for investors to evaluate the default risk of the underlying mortgages because issuers of passthroughs typically guarantee the payment of principal and interest on the passthroughs, as discussed below. Issuers also tend to pool mortgages that are diversified across originating lenders and across local housing markets. This diversification tends to eliminate unsystematic prepayment risk. In addition, although passthroughs protect investors against loss of capital from borrower defaults, when default does occur, the remaining mortgage balance on the loan is distributed to investors as principal payments. Thus, to a passthrough investor with guaranteed payments, defaults have the same effect on yields as prepayments. The diversified pool of mortgages used as collateral for a passthrough therefore protects investors from the unsystematic risk of default-induced prepayments.

PASSTHROUGH EXAMPLE

Assume a mortgage banker originates 100 fixed-rate mortgages. Each mortgage has a face value of $100,000, a contract rate of 8.25 percent, and a loan term of 30 years. For simplicity, assume payments will be made annually. These mortgages have been pooled together and used as collateral for the issuance of a passthrough security. The issuing mortgage banker has promised to pay investors in the passthrough an interest rate of 7.75 percent on their investment, with interest paid annually. The difference between the 8.25 percent rate on the underlying mortgages and the 7.75 rate promised to the passthrough investors will be retained by the mortgage banker as compensation for structuring the passthrough security and for servicing the underlying mortgages.

What cash flows will be distributed to the passthrough investors each year? Total payments will equal 7.75 percent of the previous year's outstanding balance on the passthrough investor's investment, plus any principal payments. Exhibit 19–2 displays a partial amortization schedule for one of the underlying mortgages. The fixed payment due at the end of each year is equal to $9,093. In year 1, $843 of this is scheduled principal amortization and the remaining $8,250 is interest. Thus, each mortgage in the pool will have a remaining balance of $99,157 at the end of year 1, and $89,361 after 9 years, assuming the mortgage is not prepaid prior to that time.

Exhibit 19–3 displays the cash flows on the mortgage pool assuming 10 of the underlying mortgages are prepaid at the end of both year 3 and year 4, 20 mortgages are prepaid at the end of year 5, 30 are terminated in year 6, 20 in year 7, and the remaining 10 in year 8. No prepayments are expected to occur during the first two years. Thus, payments on the pool in the first year consist of $825,000 in interest ($8,250 × 100) and $84,309 in scheduled amortization ($843 × 100).[11] Ten mortgages are expected to prepay at the end of year 3, which produces $972,563 in *unscheduled* principal payments ($97,256 × 10). At the beginning of year 4, 90 mortgages are left in the pool, which

---

[11]Differences are due to rounding.

EXHIBIT 19-2

**PARTIAL AMORTIZATION SCHEDULE
FOR $100,000, 8.25%, 30-YEAR MORTGAGE**

Year	Beginning Mortgage Balance	Ending Mortgage Balance	Scheduled Principal Payment	Annual Interest Payment
1	$100,000	$99,157	$ 843	$8,250
2	99,157	98,244	913	8,180
3	98,244	97,256	988	8,105
4	97,256	96,187	1,069	8,024
5	96,187	95,029	1,158	7,935
6	95,029	93,776	1,253	7,840
7	93,776	92,419	1,357	7,737
8	92,419	90,951	1,468	7,625
9	90,951	89,361	1,590	7,503

EXHIBIT 19-3

TOTAL PRINCIPAL AND INTEREST ON UNDERLYING MORTGAGES

Year	Number of Mortgages Prepaid	Number of Mortgages Left	Principal Payments Scheduled	Unscheduled	Total Principal Payments	Total Interest
1	0	100	$84,309	$ 0	$ 84,309	$825,000
2	0	100	91,265	0	91,265	818,045
3	10	90	98,794	972,563	1,071,357	810,515
4	10	80	96,250	961,869	1,058,119	722,128
5	20	60	92,614	1,900,584	1,993,198	634,833
6	30	30	75,191	2,813,281	2,888,472	470,395
7	20	10	40,697	1,848,389	1,889,086	232,096
8	10	0	14,685	909,510	924,195	76,246
9	0	0	0	0	0	0

reduces both scheduled amortization and interest. The $909,510 in unscheduled principal in year 8 reflects the prepayment of the final 10 mortgages that each have a remaining balance of $90,951 at the end of year 8.

The total cash flows distributed to investors are contained in Exhibit 19–4. As discussed, the principal payments on the underlying mortgages are not restructured—they are simply "passed through" directly to the investors. Moreover, there is only one class or type of investor in a passthrough, and each investor purchases a pro rata share of the cash flows from the underlying mortgages. That is, the percentage of the total cash flows each investor receives is equal to the percentage of the passthrough security purchased. In our example, if an investor purchased 1/10, or $1 million of the $10 million passthrough, he or she would receive 10 percent of the interest and principal distributed to investors.

Interest paid to investors in year 1 is equal to the $10 million par value of the security times the coupon interest rate of 7.75 percent. The mortgage banker retains $50,000 in interest: $825,000 total interest minus the $775,000 that is distributed to investors.

E X H I B I T   1 9 - 4

C A S H   F L O W S   O N   P A S S T H R O U G H   S E C U R I T Y

Year	Beginning Balance	Interest	Total Principal Payments	Total Cash Flow	Principal Repaid to Date to Investors
1	$10,000,000	$775,000	$ 84,309	$ 859,309	$ 84,309
2	9,915,691	768,466	91,265	859,731	175,574
3	9,824,426	761,393	1,071,357	1,832,750	1,246,931
4	8,753,069	678,363	1,058,119	1,736,482	2,305,050
5	7,694,950	596,359	1,993,198	2,589,557	4,298,248
6	5,701,752	441,886	2,888,472	3,330,358	7,186,719
7	2,813,281	218,029	1,889,086	2,107,115	9,075,805
8	924,195	71,625	924,195	995,820	10,000,000
9	0	0	0	0	0

Unless potential investors require *exactly* a 7.75 percent yield, the passthrough security will sell at a premium or discount to its $10 million par value. For example, if investors require an 8.2 percent yield, the passthrough price will be discounted to $9,807,812, given the prepayment schedule assumed in Exhibit 19–3. If investors purchase the passthrough at this price, their realized gain will depend on the actual pattern of mortgage terminations. If the underlying mortgages prepay faster than expected, the realized yield will exceed the 8.2 percent yield they required at purchase; if prepayments are slower than expected, the realized yield will be less than 8.2 percent.[12]

AGENCY PASSTHROUGHS

There are three major issuers, or guarantors, of passthroughs: Ginnie Mae, Fannie Mae, and Freddie Mac. The passthroughs guaranteed by these organizations are called **agency passthroughs.** Although the features of agency passthroughs vary by agency and by program, Fabozzi and Modigliani list the following general features:[13] (1) the type of guarantee, (2) the number of originators with loans that are permitted in the pool, (3) the design and characteristics of the underlying mortgages, (4) the method for distributing payments to investors, and (5) the minimum size of the pool used as collateral. Variation in these features can have a significant effect on the risk/return characteristics of a passthrough, especially its prepayment characteristics.

Ginnie Mae MBSs.   The Ginnie Mae program was introduced in 1968 and led to a virtual explosion in the secondary market. Ginnie Mae passthroughs, generally referred to

---

[12]Prices of passthrough securities are actually quoted in the same manner as Treasury coupon securities. For example, a price quote of 98–05 means the price is 98 and 5/32nds of par value, or 98.15625 percent of par value. For more institutional detail on the trading of MBSs, see William W. Bartlett, *Mortgage-Backed Securities: Products, Analysis, and Trading* (Englewood Cliffs, NJ: Prentice Hall, 1989).

[13]Frank J. Fabozzi and Franco Modigliani, *Mortgage and Mortgage-Backed Securities Markets* (Boston: Harvard Business School Press, 1992).

REAL ESTATE FOCUS 19-1

GNMA Mutual Funds

Numerous mutual funds specializing in investments in GNMA mortgage-backed securities have appeared in recent years. These funds allow institutions and individuals to buy shares in portfolios of GNMA without incurring the high minimum cost of investing directly in the securities ($25,000). Such funds have substantially increased the demand for GNMAs and therefore the flow of money to housing.

The prior three-year annualized performance of select GNMA funds as of 7/1/96 is summarized below:

Fund	Annualized Yield	Net Assets (millions)
Lexington GNMA	5.6%	$ 121.8
Vanguard F/I GNMA	5.5	6,940.2
Benhem GNMA Income	5.1	1,088.2
T. Rowe Price GNMA	5.0	917.5
Fidelity Ginnie Mae	5.0	778.4
USAA GNMA	4.9	301.9
Dreyfus GNMA	4.7	1,353.5
Federated GNMA Inst.	4.6	1,278.0
Stagecoach Ginnie Mae A	4.6	163.1
Premier GNMA A	4.5	121.8
Scudder GNMA	4.3	408.4
Safeco GNMA	3.8	40.4

SOURCE: *Money Magazine,* August 1996

as "Ginnie Maes," provide investors with a guarantee of *timely* principal and interest payments. A distinguishing feature of Ginnie Maes is that the agency does not purchase mortgages in the secondary market and does not itself issue MBSs. Rather, Ginnie Mae guarantees the MBSs issued by approved, private entities that use pools of FHA and VA mortgages with similar interest rates and maturities as collateral for the passthrough. When borrowers default or are late with payments, the issuer of the Ginnie Mae passthrough, often a mortgage banker, is still required to make timely payments to the investors. The issuer must then seek reimbursement from the agency that has insured or guaranteed the problem mortgages, the FHA or VA. If the issuer cannot make timely payments on the passthrough, Ginnie Mae will. Ginnie Mae's guarantee is backed by the "full faith and credit" of the U.S. government—making the creditworthiness of the issuer unimportant.

As a result of the guarantee, Ginnie Mae passthroughs are considered free of default risk and the risk of delayed payments. In fact, investors view Ginnie Mae passthroughs as very similar to investments in government securities with respect to default risk. The difference (spread) between the Ginnie Mae coupon rate and the rate on the underlying mortgages is ½ of a percentage point, or 50 basis points. The passthrough issuer retains 44 basis points and passes the remaining 6 basis points on to Ginnie Mae as a fee for providing the guarantee. The guarantee allows the issuer to sell the passthroughs at a lower yield than if the issuer's private guarantee were the only protection offered against default and untimely payments. Lower required yields translate into higher prices for the issuers.

To be approved as a Ginnie Mae issuer, lenders must meet certain minimum capital requirements set by Ginnie Mae. After gathering a pool of mortgage collateral, the issuer

EXHIBIT 19-5

THE GNMA PROCESS (CREDIT ENHANCEMENT)

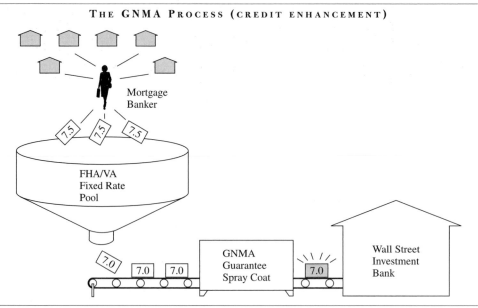

SOURCE: Wayne Archer, University of Florida

seeks a guarantee certificate from Ginnie Mae. When Ginnie Mae agrees to issue the guarantee, the mortgage documents are sent to a custodian, who holds them for the benefit of Ginnie Mae and the investors. With the guarantee certificate in hand, the lender-issuer then sells the Ginnie Maes to a dealer, typically a Wall Street investment banking firm. The investment bank then sells the securities to investors.

This process is summarized in Exhibit 19–5. Pools of, say, 7.5 percent FHA or VA mortgages or both, written against numerous homes, are originated by the mortgage banker and dropped into a mortgage pool. From this pool, a number of 7.0 percent Ginnie Mae certificates are created. These certificates are then sent to Ginnie Mae for a "fresh coat of paint," that is, for credit enhancement. Once Ginnie Mae issues the guarantee, the issuer sells the "enhanced" certificates to a Wall Street investment bank, which, in turn, sells them to investors.

Freddie Mac PCs. The second largest type of agency passthrough, first introduced in 1971, is the participation certificate (PC) issued by Freddie Mac. Whereas the mortgage pool underlying a Ginnie Mae passthrough consists of FHA or VA mortgages, most of the pools underlying Freddie Mac PCs consist of conventional mortgages. Unlike Ginnie Mae, Freddie Mac actually purchases the mortgage pools used as collateral for their PCs. Freddie Mac guarantees the payment of principal and interest; however, this guarantee is not explicitly backed by the full faith and credit of the U.S. government. Nevertheless, most investors view the creditworthiness of PCs as being very similar, if not quite identi-

EXHIBIT 19-6

GINNIE MAE/FREDDIE MAC SECURITIZATION

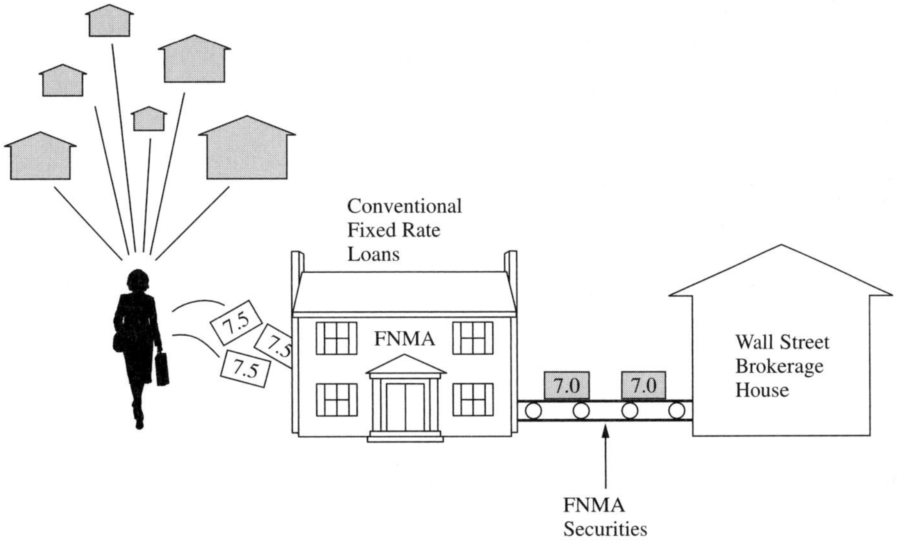

cal, to Ginnie Mae passthroughs. By helping to provide an active secondary market in conventional mortgages, the various PC programs offered by Freddie Mac provide the capital that conventional loan originators need to make additional loans.

Fannie Mae MBSs. The passthroughs, or MBSs, issued by Fannie Mae include Fannie Mae's guarantee of timely payments. Fannie Mae's MBSs are similar in credit-worthiness to Freddie Mac PCs because Fannie Mae MBSs are not, strictly speaking, obligations of the U.S. government. Two of Fannie Mae's standard MBS programs are backed by conventional mortgages; another is backed by FHA or VA mortgages.

The process Fannie Mae and Freddie Mac use to issue passthroughs is summarized in Exhibit 19–6. Various lenders originate and sell, for example, 7.5 percent fixed-rate mortgages to, say, Fannie Mae. (Note that the homes are larger than the typical home used as collateral for a FHA or VA loan!) Fannie Mae or Freddie Mac, not the mortgage originator, then pools the 7.5 percent mortgages, issues 7.0 percent passthrough securities against this pool, and then applies its own guarantee. The enhanced 7.0 percent securities are then sold to a Wall Street investment bank for distribution to investors.

CONVENTIONAL PASSTHROUGHS

Conventional, or "private label," passthroughs are issued by S&Ls, commercial banks, life insurance companies, and private conduits, such as G.E. Capital, Merrill Lynch, and Salomon Brothers. Private conduits securitize pools of nonconforming mortgages—

mortgages that do not meet the underwriting standards required for purchase in the secondary market by Fannie Mae or Freddie Mac. Midway through 1995, the outstanding amount of private conventional passthroughs was $205 billion, or 6 percent of the value of all outstanding residential mortgages. Conventional passthroughs are similar in design to agency passthroughs. However, the payment of principal and interest do not benefit from an explicit (Ginnie Mae) or implicit (Freddie and Fannie) U. S. government guarantee.

The default risks of many conventional passthroughs are rated by commercial rating agencies such as Standard & Poor's and Moody's. To receive an **investment-grade rating,** the creditworthiness of the passthroughs must be enhanced. An investment grade rating is important because it allows the issuers to lower the yield on a passthrough offering by 20 to 40 basis points. The lower the required yield, the higher the price the issuer can receive from the sale of the passthrough.

A widely used form of **credit enhancement** on conventional passthroughs is the **senior/subordinate structure.** In this structure, the passthrough issuer creates two classes of security holders form the underlying pool: a senior class and a subordinate class. The senior bond holders have a claim on the underlying principal and interest payments that is superior to the claim of the subordinate class. For example, the $10 million mortgage pool of 8.25 percent mortgages could be divided into a senior passthrough security, with a par value of $9 million, and a subordinate security, with a par value of $1 million. The credit quality of the senior passthrough is enhanced because the cash flows from $10 million in mortgages are available to meet the issuer's payment obligations on only $9 million in senior passthroughs. Because the subordinated class absorbs all of the default risk, passthroughs in this class are difficult to sell to institutional investors and are therefore typically retained by the issuer. The senior class is rated by the commercial rating agencies and sold to investors as a conventional passthrough, with the credit rating determined by the size of the subordinate class relative to the senior class. At a minimum, issuers will allocate enough of the pool to the subordinate class to insure that the senior passthrough receives an investment-grade rating.

SEQUENTIAL PAY STRUCTURES

Passthrough securities have been extremely popular with investors because of their liquidity, protection against default risk, and relatively high yields. As a result, these securities have attracted a large number of nontraditional mortgage investors. This has resulted in more investment funds flowing to the mortgage market, relative to stock and other fixed-income security markets. Passthrough investors, however, are still exposed to the total prepayment risk associated with the underlying mortgage pool. Thus, the timing of passthrough cash flows, and therefore yields, is uncertain. In addition, the 7- to 11-year average maturity of a passthrough does not fit the portfolio needs of many investors who require investments with shorter maturities. As a result, a large segment of traditional fixed-income investors remain reluctant to invest in passthroughs.

Sequential pay securities were introduced to address the prepayment concerns of many potential investors. Instead of distributing the cash flows from the underlying mortgages on a pro rata (proportional) basis, the principal payments on the underlying collateral are distributed on a priority basis; that is, one class of security holders begins to receive principal payments from the underlying collateral only after the principal on any previous classes with a higher priority has been completely retired. Thus, all principal payments, scheduled and unscheduled, are first directed to the first sequential class (A) until it is retired. This continues until the last sequential pay class is retired. While class A principal is being paid down, lower sequential pay classes (B, C, etc.) receive monthly interest payments on their principal.

The mortgage-backed security that is created by this priority pay structure is commonly called a sequential pay **collateralized mortgage obligation,** or sequential pay CMO. This structure does more than simply pass through principal and interest in a timely fashion. It rearranges the cash flows from the underlying collateral into several different bond-like securities—each with a different expected maturity. A typical sequential pay CMO will have three or four sequential pay classes, which are also called **tranches.** Each sequential pay class (tranche) carries a different coupon interest rate. In addition, the structure may contain a residual class into which all cash flows from the collateral not paid out to other investors will flow. This residual class is often retained by the issuer of the CMO. The collateral for a sequential pay CMO is either a pool of loans or, alternatively, one or more passthrough securities. In the latter case, the underlying mortgages are said to have been "resecuritized." In either case, the sequential pay CMO must be structured to ensure that the underlying cash flows will be sufficient to meet the obligations on all classes—regardless of the rate at which the underlying mortgages prepay. If not, a high quality rating will not be obtained from the commercial rating agencies.

The principal objective of the sequential pay structure is to redistribute the prepayment and interest rate risk associated with standard passthrough securities. By absorbing all principal payments first, the class A security will have a significantly shorter maturity than lower priority classes, and therefore it will be less sensitive to changes in interest rates after the CMO is issued. Financial institutions with primarily short-term liabilities (e.g., S&Ls and commercial banks) have been active purchasers of the class A securities. Recall that these institutions raise funds primarily by issuing short-term liabilities (money market obligations and certificates of deposit). Therefore, holding as assets passthrough securities with expected maturities of approximately 8 to 12 years creates a maturity mismatch between their assets and liabilities. However, the class A piece of a sequential pay CMO has a typical expected maturity of two to three years. Life insurance companies, with relatively long-term liabilities, have been frequent investors in the lower priority sequential pay classes with longer maturities and higher coupon rates.

In short, the redirecting (or reengineering) of the cash flows from the underlying collateral creates bondlike securities with more predictable maturities that better match the asset/liability objectives of many institutional investors than a passthrough. It is important to understand, however, that the *total* prepayment risk associated with the underlying collateral is unchanged. However, the prepayment risk is more efficiently distributed among investors. In essence, a situation is created where the value of the individual securitized parts (the sequential classes) is greater than the value of the underlying collateral.

SEQUENTIAL PAY EXAMPLE

Consider again the pool of 8.25 percent, 30-year, fixed-rate mortgages. Assume that a multiple-class, sequential pay security is issued against this $10 million of mortgage collateral. The first class, or tranche, has a par value of $4 million and carries a coupon rate of 7.75 percent. All principal payments will flow to the class A investors until the $4 million in principal is completely retired. The second class of security holders purchase an ownership interest in a security with a par value of $5½ million and a coupon rate of 8 percent. These class B investors receive regular interest payments, but do not receive any principal payments until the $4 million in class A principal has been retired. The third class is issued with a par value of $500,000. Coupon payments at a predetermined rate are not promised to this residual class of security holders. Rather, these investors receive whatever interest is not paid to the class A and B investors. Moreover, no portion of their $500,000 principal is returned until both class A and B are completely retired.

The distribution of principal payments, both scheduled and unscheduled, is displayed in Exhibit 19–7. Both show that the class A investors receive all principal payments through year 4. In year 5, the $1,993,198 in total principal payments on the underlying mortgages is sufficient to satisfy the $1,694,950 balance due class A investors, as well as to return $298,248 in principal to class B investors. Class B investors then receive all principal payments until year 8, at which time the principal payments on the remaining mortgages in the pool are sufficient to satisfy the balance owed to both class B investors and the residual class. The $310,000 in interest paid to class A investors in year 1 is equal to the $4 million initial balance, times the class A coupon rate of 7.75 percent. The $303,466 in year 2 interest is equal to the $3,915,691 balance at the beginning of year 2, times the 7.75 percent coupon rate. The $440,000 in interest paid to class B investors is equal to $5.5 million times the 8 percent coupon rate. Notice that interest paid to the class B investors is constant over the first five years because their balance is not reduced until they begin to receive principal payments at the end of year 5. Finally, the $75,000 in residual class interest is equal to total first-year interest on the underlying mortgages of $825,000, minus the first-year interest paid to class A and B investors. Given the assumed prepayment schedule, the residual class receives no principal until year 8.

OTHER RESPONSES TO PREPAYMENT RISK

Although sequential pay classes create mortgage securities with more predictable maturities, numerous innovations in the structuring of CMOs have addressed investors' desires for (1) even greater predictability of cash flows, (2) classes with adjustable or "floating" rates to better match their floating-rate liabilities, and (3) classes that can be used to hedge mortgage origination and servicing activities, as well as to hedge long-term investment strategies.

For example, in addition to sequential pay classes, most CMO structures also have an **accrual class** (bond), commonly referred to as the class Z tranche. The class Z bond holders do *not* receive interest payments until the other classes are retired. Instead, their unpaid interest accrues; that is, it is added to the principal balance of the Z class. Because

EXHIBIT 19-7

CASH FLOWS TO THREE INVESTOR CLASSES ON A SEQUENTIAL PAY CMO

Class A Investors

Year	Beginning Balance	Interest	Principal Payments	Total Payments
1	$4,000,000	$310,000	$84,309	$394,309
2	3,915,691	303,466	91,265	394,731
3	3,824,426	296,393	1,071,357	1,367,570
4	2,753,069	213,363	1,058,119	1,271,482
5	1,694,950	131,359	1,694,950	1,826,309
6	0	0	0	0

Class B Investors

Year	Beginning Balance	Interest	Principal Payments	Total Payments
1	$5,500,000	$440,000	$0	$440,000
2	5,500,000	440,000	0	440,000
3	5,500,000	440,000	0	440,000
4	5,500,000	440,000	0	440,000
5	5,500,000	440,000	298,248	738,248
6	5,201,752	416,140	2,888,472	3,304,612
7	2,313,281	185,062	1,889,086	2,074,149
8	424,195	33,936	424,195	458,130

Residual Class Investors

Year	Beginning Balance	Interest	Principal Payments	Total Payments
1	$500,000	$75,000	$0	$75,000
2	500,000	74,578	0	74,578
3	500,000	74,122	0	74,122
4	500,000	68,765	0	68,765
5	500,000	63,475	0	63,475
6	500,000	54,254	0	54,254
7	500,000	47,033	0	47,033
8	500,000	42,310	500,000	542,310

the accrual class is last to be paid off in a sequential pay CMO, this class appeals to investors seeking bonds with long-term maturities. However, the longer maturity also makes the market value of the class Z bonds much more sensitive to changes in market interest rates and prepayments.

In order to increase further the stability of cash flows for some CMO investors, **planned amortization classes** (PACs) are often included along with the sequential pay and accrual classes. The most important characteristic of a PAC is that the cash flow pattern, and therefore the yield and maturity, is known with certainty—as long as the rate of prepayment on the underlying collateral remains in a prespecified range.

Alternative CMO structures contain classes that receive only principal payments from the underlying collateral (POs) or only interest (IOs). Both POs and IOs are purchased at a price deeply discounted from par value, and the market value of both is extremely sensitive to changes in prepayment rates, and therefore in interest rates. A **floating-rate class** (floater) pays a coupon rate that is tied to a benchmark index such as the London Interbank Offered Rate (LIBOR). Floaters are attractive to investors who pay variable rates on some (or all) of their liabilities and are therefore seeking to match their variable rate obligations with variable rate assets.

VALUING MORTGAGE-BACKED SECURITIES

Our discussions of passthrough MBSs and the various types of classes found within a CMO structure have emphasized that changes in prepayment rates on the underlying collateral can significantly affect the market value and realized yield of these securities. Moreover, the reaction of mortgage values to changes in market interest rates is complicated because borrowers do not exercise their options to prepay in a predictable fashion. In fact, some borrowers never exercise their options to prepay no matter how far interest rates decline. Thus, although interest and *scheduled* principal amortization on the collateral are fairly predictable, unscheduled principal payments are difficult to forecast.

Nevertheless, estimating the cash flows from an MBS requires the investor to make an assumption about prepayment rates. When current market rates are below (above) the coupon rate on the MBS, the MBS will sell at a premium (discount). However, the magnitude of the premium or discount depends critically upon the future prepayment rates assumed by market participants. Faster expected rates of prepayment reduce the magnitude of premiums and discounts; slower prepayment rate assumptions increase the magnitudes.

In our example using the $10 million pool of 8.25 percent mortgages, we assumed, for simplicity, that a certain *number* of mortgages would prepay (at the end of) each year. In practice, investors estimate the *rate* at which unscheduled principal payments will reduce the balance on the underlying pool. The most widely used models or techniques for estimating prepayment rates on a mortgage pool are the **constant prepayment rate** assumption, the **Public Securities Association** benchmark model, and the statistical prepayment models developed by many secondary market agencies and Wall Street firms.

When using the constant prepayment rate (CPR) method, the investor assumes the unscheduled principal payments will occur at a constant rate over time. For example, consider our $10 million pool of 8.25 percent mortgages. Under the assumption that none of the mortgages will prepay in years 1 and 2, the projected rate of unscheduled principal payments is zero for both years. The projected third year rate of unscheduled payments, in which 10 mortgages prepay, is $972,563/$9,824,426, or 9.9 percent, where $9,824,426 is the remaining balance on the pool at the beginning of year 3.

If instead, we assumed a constant (annual) prepayment rate of 6 percent, the principal reduction and remaining balances in years 1 through 3 would equal the amounts shown in Exhibit 19–8.

The scheduled principal payments in years 2 and 3 of $85,789 and $86,939 equal 94 percent and 88 percent, respectively, of what they would be if there were no prepay-

EXHIBIT 19-8

Year	Beginning Principal Balance (1)	Scheduled Principal Payments (2)	Scheduled Principal Balance (3) = (1) − (2)	Total Prepayments @ 6% of Scheduled Balance (4) = 0.06 × (3)	Projected Principal Balance (5) = (3) − (4)
1	$10,000,000	$84,309	$9,915,691	$594,941	$9,320,750
2	9,320,758	85,789	9,234,960	554,098	8,680,862
3	8,078,288	86,939	8,593,923	515,635	8,078,288

ments. The CPR assumed by investors should be based on the characteristics of the mortgage pool, the current mortgage interest rate and economic conditions, and expected future interest rates and economic conditions.

The Public Securities Association (PSA) model assumes, based on an analysis of historical prepayment rates, that 0.0167 percent (0.2 percent annually) of the pool balance will be paid off in the first month. This rate increases 0.0167 percent per month for the next 30 months, at which time the monthly rate is 0.50 percent (or 6 percent annually). The monthly prepayment rate is then assumed to remain at approximately 0.50 percent. This benchmark rate of prepayment is referred to as *100% PSA*. Slower or faster expected prepayment speeds are expressed as some percentage of PSA. For example, 50 percent PSA means that the prepayment rate in any month is expected to be ½ the benchmark PSA rate.[14]

Once the total cash flows on an MBS, including unscheduled principal, are estimated, the value or yield is determined by using standard discounted cash flow techniques. Potential MBS investors are often quoted a yield, as well as a price, by sellers and dealers. It should be clear that the quoted yield is based upon some assumed rate of prepayment. If investors do not perform their own expected yield calculation, they should make sure they know what prepayment rate assumption was used by the seller in calculating the quoted yield. Sellers of premium securities, for example, may be tempted to assume a slow rate of prepayments when quoting yields because expected yields on premium securities are higher the slower the assumed rate of prepayment. The Public Securities Association encourages market participants to use the PSA model when quoting yields. An investor can then compare is the assumed PSA rate—say, 150 percent PSA—to their assumed prepayment speed. If an investor feels the mortgages will prepay faster than 150 percent PSA, the quoted yield on a premium security will overstate the investor's expected yield.

---

[14]Statistical, or regression-based, models of prepayment are constructed by first quantifying the historical relationship between prepayment rates and a number of variables associated with prepayment. Typical explanatory variables include the age of the mortgages in the pool, the difference between the contract rate on the mortgages and the current mortgage rate, the season of the year (for example, more people move and prepay their mortgages in the summer), the geographical location of the properties serving as collateral, and, in some cases, borrower characteristics. The calculated historical relationships between these explanatory variables and prepayment rates are then used to forecast future prepayment rates. This exercise requires estimates of the future values of the explanatory variables and the assumption that past relationships between prepayment rates and the explanatory variables is predictive of future relationships. The accuracy of these models therefore decreases for more distant periods.

THE COMMERCIAL MORTGAGE-BACKED SECURITIES MARKET

The development of a secondary market in commercial or income-property mortgages has proceeded more slowly than the development of the secondary market for single-family residential mortgages. Because of the perceived importance of home ownership in our society, the U.S. government has concentrated its efforts on developing a secondary market in residential mortgages. Commercial mortgage-backed securities (CMBS) carry no explicit or implicit government guarantees as do most residential MBSs. The CMBS market has developed slowly primarily for this reason. Since 1991, however, the pace of commercial mortgage securitization has accelerated rapidly. The lack of government guarantees continues to impede active trading of outstanding commercial mortgage-backed securities, but it has not impeded growth in the number of public offerings of commercial mortgages since 1991. Investors in CMBS remain willing to accept illiquidity in exchange for the attractive yields they offer.

SOURCES OF PUBLIC DEBT FOR COMMERCIAL-PROPERTY INVESTMENT

Public debt to finance commercial-property investment comes from three sources: corporate bond issues, REIT unsecured debt issues, and CMBS issues. Corporations with sizable real estate holdings, such as Host Marriott and Wal-Mart, regularly enter the corporate bond market to finance real estate development and acquisitions. The resurgence and growth of REITs as a form of real estate ownership since the early 1990s has created opportunities for these firms to issue unsecured debt claims against their real estate portfolios. These nonmortgage, corporate bondlike issues rose to $3.7 billion in 1995.

The most significant growth in debt financing of real estate has come in the private CMBS market. During the entire decade of the 1980s, only $13.7 billion was raised for real estate investment in the CMBS market. In 1995 and 1996, real estate investors raised $18.7 billion and $30.4 billion, respectively. However, despite the rapid increase in CMBS activity, less than 15 percent of the commercial property mortgages in the United States serve as collateral for CMBS. If the current pace of commercial mortgage securitization continues, this percentage will soon compare to the roughly 50 percent securitization of U.S. residential mortgages.

BRIEF HISTORY OF CMBSs

As early as 1980, Freddie Mac began buying apartment (multifamily housing) mortgages from lenders and issuing securities backed by these mortgages. Also during the early 1980s, the now-defunct real estate development and investment company Olympia and York, with the help of Salomon Brothers, issued various types of mortgage securities backed by single, albeit very large, properties. Later in the decade Goldman Sachs assisted a small number of mortgage companies in securitizing their portfolios of commercial property mortgages.

EXHIBIT 19-9

COMMERCIAL MORTGAGE-BACKED SECURITY VOLUME
FROM 1990 THROUGH 1996

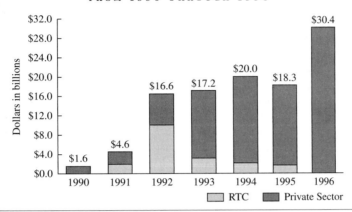

SOURCE: E&Y Kenneth Leventhal Real Estate Group, *1995/1996 Commercial Mortgage-Backed Securitization Survey.*

The significant breakthrough in the development of the CMBSs came as the result of the disposition of mortgages by the Resolution Trust Corporation (RTC). The RTC was formed by the U.S. Congress to collect assets from failed savings and loan institutions (financially insolvent institutions taken over by the federal government) and return the ownership of these assets to the private markets in an orderly manner. The RTC assembled mortgage pools and, with the aid of investment bankers, created tranches in ways that made CMBS investment easier for investors to evaluate and understand than in the past. Through its M-series and C-series issues of CMBSs, the RTC and Wall Street converted $12.5 billion of multifamily and nonresidential, commercial mortgages to mortgage-backed securities during the early 1990s. Because of attractive yields, many pension funds and mutual funds purchased the securities despite the lack of explicit government guarantees. In addition, investment banking firms issued over $75 billion of private-label CMBSs from 1990 through 1996, as shown in Exhibit 19–9.

DIFFERENCES BETWEEN RESIDENTIAL MBSs AND CMBSs

Many of the innovations in security design and structure that occurred during the evolutionary period of residential mortgage securitization, such as sequential payment, transfer directly to CMBSs. In fact, the typical CMBS issue today closely resembles a residential MBS issue. The major differences between the two types of securities involve dissimilarities in their default risk and prepayment risk.

Borrower default constitutes the greatest risk to CMBS investors because of the potential for severe losses. Not only do the payments from the borrower stop coming to investors, but defaults can result in capital losses. However, most residential MBS investors gain complete protection from capital losses due to defaults by virtue of the explicit or implicit government guarantees that come with agency securities. Ginnie Mae or one of the GSEs absorbs all losses from defaults and assures investors they will not experience delays. Investors in CMBSs must rely on credit rating agencies, as discussed later in this chapter, for assessments of default risk because these investors acquire securities without government backing of any kind.

Borrower prepayment represents the biggest concern of residential MBS investors. Prepayments typically produce losses for MBS investors because most occur when borrowers refinance their mortgages at lower rates. Residential mortgage borrowers in the United States prepay their mortgages without restriction or penalty. Therefore, most investors in residential MBSs must carefully evaluate the prepayment risks associated with residential mortgage investment.

Investors in CMBSs have exactly the opposite problem. As discussed earlier, CMBSs can carry substantial risk of loss due to default. However, mortgage contract design can remove most of the prepayment risk. As discussed in Chapter 18, the commercial property mortgages that collateralize CMBS issues frequently contain lock-out and yield maintenance provisions.

HOW COMMERCIAL MORTGAGE SECURITIZATION OCCURS

Commercial property owners and investors face two basic mortgage financing options: loans from conventional lenders, such as commercial banks and life insurance companies, and loans from lenders who intend for the mortgages to become part of a CMBS issue soon. The clauses in the mortgages with each option usually differ. Conventional lenders take more relaxed stances on prepayment provisions, especially lock-outs, whereas CMBS lenders must offer CMBS investors substantial prepayment protection to help sell the securities.

What about the relative costs of these two options? Jun Han found that conventional lenders are more competitive (that is, they offer a lower combined interest rate and fees) in providing mortgage financing for "ordinary" commercial properties.[15] However, he also found that conventional lenders have refused to participate in several segments of the market. Owners and investors of lower-quality properties or certain property types (such as hotels), and those attempting to refinance have been forced to deal with CMBS lenders during the 1990s because of the lack of interest in these mortgages by conventional lenders. In addition, CMBS lenders are more competitive than conventional lenders, according to this study, in financing jumbo properties and mortgage portfolios.

---

[15]Jun Han, "To Securitize or Not To Securitize? The Future of Commercial Real Estate Debt Markets," *Real Estate Finance* (Summer 1996), pp. 71–80.

EXHIBIT 19-10

COMMERCIAL MORTGAGE SECURITIZATION THROUGH PORTFOLIO REFINANCING

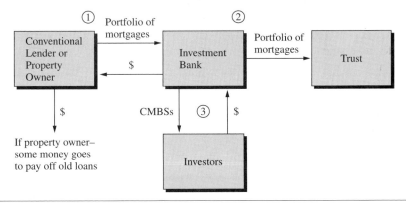

Conventional lenders suffered substantial losses as the result of commercial property lending during the 1980s and therefore faced intense pressure from bank and insurance regulators to avoid all but the least risky commercial mortgage loans. As the commercial property markets improved, Wall Street moved in to fill the void in mortgage lending with programs to serve the entire market and facilitate securitization of the loans. These programs, discussed below, include portfolio refinancing, conduit arrangements, and direct lending.

These recent experiences raise the following questions about the future of borrower and lender relationships in commercial property lending:

1. Will investors in CMBSs suffer large losses from defaults because the loans collateralizing the issues were too low in quality? And will these losses cause a reduction in CMBS investing?
2. Will changes in regulations that make it easier for conventional lenders to invest in CMBSs give them less incentive to originate commercial mortgage loans?
3. Who will provide mortgage money for commercial property development?

PORTFOLIO REFINANCING

A large share of the CMBS activity after 1992 involved conventional lenders selling their portfolios to Wall Street investment banks, which then issued and sold securities backed by these mortgages. These actions became necessary as regulatory pressure intensified. Similarly, borrowers with numerous mortgages saw opportunities to refinance their portfolios jointly with investment bankers. As shown in Exhibit 19–10, portfolio refinancing

E X H I B I T   1 9 - 1 1

C O M M E R C I A L   M O R T G A G E   S E C U R I T I Z A T I O N
T H R O U G H   C O N D U I T   A R R A N G E M E N T S

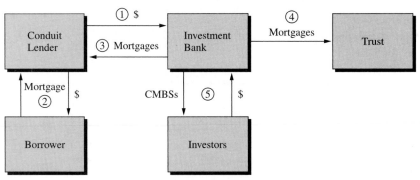

involves a simple exchange of mortgages for money between the conventional lender or property owner and the investment bank. Once the investment banking firm obtains the mortgages, they are placed in a trust, legal rules are followed leading to securitization, and the CMBSs are sold to investors who then own the rights to receive payments from the mortgages. Usually, the investment banking firm hires a servicer (not shown in the exhibit) to collect payments from the borrowers and to make payments to the CMBS investors.

C O N D U I T   A R R A N G E M E N T S

Conduit lending represents another important source of commercial property mortgages for CMBS issues. Exhibit 19–11 indicates that the conduit lending process begins with the investment bank loaning money to the conduit lender. Conduit lenders are mortgage companies that specialize in originating mortgage loans, such as mortgage bankers. This relationship between mortgage companies and investment banks requires the mortgage company to originate loans for borrowers under a prescribed set of standards and then transfer the mortgages to the investment bank. After receiving the mortgages, the investment bank follows the same procedures to securitize and sell CMBSs as in the case of portfolio refinancing.

D I R E C T   L E N D I N G   B Y   I N V E S T M E N T   B A N K S

Investment banks entered into conduit relationships with mortgage companies because they lacked the experience and expertise to underwrite and originate commercial property mortgage loans. Some large investment banks realized that they could generate a flow of mortgage loans to securitize and sell by hiring their own underwriting and originating

E X H I B I T   1 9 - 1 2

COMMERCIAL MORTGAGE SECURITIZATION THROUGH DIRECT LENDING

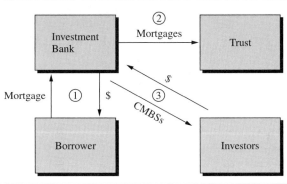

staff, thereby cutting out the additional costs associated with the conduit arrangement. As shown in Exhibit 19–12, direct lending essentially puts the investment banking firm in the same position as conventional portfolio lenders. The primary difference is that the investment bank makes no pretense about holding mortgages in a portfolio and collecting the mortgage payments. The main business of investment banking firms involves selling securities (see Real Estate Focus 19–2).

THE ROLE OF THE RATING AGENCIES

Issuers of CMBS seek ratings from independent rating agencies for all or a significant share of the tranches in each issue. Ratings for CMBS issues provide investors with much-needed information about default risk. Because of government protection against losses, these ratings have less value to residential MBS investors, and the issuer therefore does not obtain them.

Ratings inform CMBS investors about the likelihood of timely payment of interest and principal. By examining the ratings for an issue, investors understand which securities place them in **first-loss,** second-loss, and subsequent-loss **positions.** Investors who buy the lowest-rated securities may begin to lose the capital they invested with the *first* default of any mortgage in the pool that collateralizes the security issue. Investors in the second-loss position only begin to experience reductions in their capital balances if investors in the lowest rated security have lost all of their invested capital. Investors who purchase the highest rated securities seldom suffer any capital losses, but the highest rated securities pay their holders the lowest rate of interest. Conversely, investors in the first-loss position receive the highest contract rate of interest in exchange for bearing the risk associated with that position.

REAL ESTATE FOCUS 19-2

Need a Commercial Property Mortgage? Call Nomura Securities Directly?

By 1994, Nomura Securities had established itself as a leader on Wall Street in issuing CMBSs through portfolio refinancing and conduit relationships with mortgage companies. With a growing staff of knowledgeable commercial property finance people, it was a small step to establish a telephone-based system for originating uncomplicated mortgages directly with borrowers. The following procedures for obtaining a mortgage using the *Nomura Direct* program come from the program brochure:

THE WAY IT WORKS

When you call NOMURA DIRECT here's what you can expect. Our four-step process for obtaining financing that is quick and easy.

Stage 1. Call 1-800-GET-DIRECT to talk with one of our loan officers. Provide us with key information about your property. Within 48 hours of receiving this information, Nomura reviews the property's operating history and characteristics and calls you with our quote.

Two days after you accept this quote, you receive an application letter.

Stage 2. The underwriting typically takes 2½ weeks to complete. We inspect the site and review the information you supplied. Upon completion of underwriting, our commitment letter, which outlines the terms we agree upon, is delivered to you. The financing will depend upon satisfactory third-party reports, fulfillment of any conditions, and settling any open items.

If the underwriting is unsuccessful, we return your application fee in full, less any out-of-pocket expenses.

Stage 3. Once you return the commitment letter along with the commitment fee, Nomura starts the loan documentation and orders the third-party reports. Generating these reports takes two to three weeks, during which time we resolve open items and complete the legal formalities.

Stage 4. We contact you and lock in the loan rate. Funding and closing take place one to two days later.

AGENCIES THAT RATE CMBS ISSUES

Standard & Poor's became the first of the commercial rating agencies to develop standards for rating CMBSs. Later, Duff & Phelps, Fitch Investor Services, and Moody's Investor Services entered the business. These firms operate in much the same way when rating CMBSs as they do when rating stock and bond issues. Using a predetermined set of qualitative and quantitative standards and stress tests, the rating agencies separately grade each class or tranche of the issue. The issuer, usually an investment banking firm, pays to secure the rating early in the securitization process to assist in the sale of the securities. Typically, only a few tranches of a CMBS issue go unrated or receive a rating below investment grade.

Exhibit 19–13 shows the rating system used by Duff & Phelps. This firm grades securities along a 17-level scale on which ratings 1 through 7 match up to generic A-rated securities, ratings 8 through 16 match up to generic B-rated securities, and rating 17 identifies unrated securities. The various tranches of a CMBS issue typically carry the informal labels "A pieces" and "B pieces."

EXHIBIT 19-13

DUFF & PHELPS RATING SCALE

D&P Rating	Generic Category	Category
1	Triple A	Highest credit quality. The risk factors are only slightly more than for risk-free U.S. Treasury debt.
2 3 4	Double A High Middle Low	High credit quality. Protection factors are strong. Risk is modest but varies slightly from time to time because of economic conditions.
5 6 7	Single A High Middle Low	Good quality investment grade securities. Protection factors are average but adequate. However, risk factors are more variable and greater in periods of economic stress.
8 9 10	Triple B High Middle Low	Below-average protection factors but still considered sufficient for institutional investment. Considerable variability in risk during economic cycles.
11 12 13	Double B High Middle Low	Below investment grade but deemed likely to meet obligations when due. Protection factors fluctuate according to economic conditions. Overall quality may move up or down frequently within this category.
14 15 16	Single B High Middle Low	Below investment grade and possessing risk that obligations will not be met when due. Protection factors will fluctuate widely according to economic cycles. Potential exists for frequent changes in rating within this category or into a higher- or lower-quality rating grade.
17	Substantial Risk	Well below investment grade with considerable uncertainty as to timely payment of interest. Protection factors are narrow. Risk can be substantial with unfavorable economic conditions.

SOURCE: Duff & Phelps.

The rating agencies have different grading scales and follow different theories when assigning grades, but each performs qualitative and quantitative reviews of the properties and mortgages underlying the securities to estimate expected losses from defaults. The equation below defines expected losses.

$$Expected\ Losses = Probability\ of\ Default \times Loss\ Severity$$

Loss severity is the percentage of principal *not* returned to investors. Thus, a loss severity of 0.25 indicates that 25 percent of the investors' capital would not be returned if default occurs. The expected loss severity is primarily a function of how far property values are expected to fall below the remaining principal balances of the underlying mortgages. The qualitative and quantitative reviews yield information on the likelihood of borrowers defaulting on their *mortgages,* and then, given default, the losses that will likely occur with the sale of the foreclosed *property.*

QUALITATIVE REVIEW

The qualitative review focuses mainly on the property, although borrower quality also receives attention. Loss severity ultimately depends on what happens to property values during periods of economic distress when most defaults occur. Some property types, such as hotels, are more sensitive to economic decline than others, for example, apartments. Similarly, some geographic areas and site locations are more sensitive than others to changing economic conditions. Other key factors considered during the qualitative review include tenant quality, lease terms, property management, property seasoning, construction quality, and environmental liability.

QUANTITATIVE REVIEW

Default probability estimation is the primary focus of the quantitative review. Two financial ratios used in mortgage underwriting, the debt coverage ratio and the loan-to-value ratio, have more influence on the rating of CMBSs than any other considerations. The debt coverage is fundamental to estimating future default because borrower delinquency generally precedes default. A property with a low DCR makes the mortgage more susceptible to delinquency when NOI falls, relative to a property in which NOI substantially exceeds the debt service payment. Not all delinquent mortgages go into default and foreclosure, but few borrowers default before first becoming delinquent.

In nearly every empirical study of mortgage default, the relationship between the loan balance and property value emerges as the most important determinant of borrowers' decisions to default. The **equity theory of default** says that borrowers will become delinquent on their mortgages when income shortfall makes it difficult for them to make payments, but they will not typically consider default unless their equity in the property becomes negative (that is, the loan balance exceeds the property value). Therefore, the lower the loan amount relative to the value of the property when the loan is originated, the less likely the probability of negative equity and default.

Exhibit 19–14 presents the quantitative rating scale used by Duff & Phelps for hotel property loan analysis by hotel industry segment. The grading relies on combinations of debt coverage ratios and loan-to-value ratios. To receive a triple-A rating, a loan for a resort property, for example, must be underwritten at a 2.25 DCR and a 30 percent LTV.[16]

CREDIT ENHANCEMENT

In addition to passing qualitative and quantitative tests, issuers of CMBSs must enhance the credit of mortgage pools to achieve the desired ratings. Credit enhancements include overcollateralization; reserve funds; guarantees; letters of credit; and cross-

---

[16]Because of their risk, hotel properties warrant the strictest DCR and LTV at any rating level.

EXHIBIT 19-14

DUFF & PHELPS QUANTITATIVE RATING SCALE FOR HOTEL LOANS

D&P has established minimum standards for debt coverage ratios (DCR) and loan-to-value ratios (LTV) for hospitality properties. Hotels that do not enjoy the competitive advantage of an affiliation with a regional or national chain must support more conservative ratios. These guidelines reflect the impact of the type of hospitality property: (1) luxury and upper market, (2) middle market, (3) economy, and (4) destination resorts.

D&P Rating	Destination Resort		Economy Motels		Middle Market		Upper Luxury	
	DCR	LTV	DCR	LTV	DCR	LTV	DCR	LTV
1	2.25	.30	2.20	.30	2.10	.35	2.05	.40
2	1.85	.45	1.80	.45	1.75	.50	1.70	.50
3	1.75	.45	1.70	.45	1.65	.50	1.60	.50
4	1.75	.45	1.70	.45	1.65	.50	1.60	.50
5	1.65	.50	1.60	.50	1.55	.55	1.50	.55
6	1.65	.50	1.60	.50	1.55	.55	1.50	.55
7	1.65	.50	1.60	.50	1.55	.55	1.50	.55
8	1.55	.55	1.50	.55	1.45	.60	1.40	.60
9	1.55	.55	1.50	.55	1.45	.60	1.40	.60
10	1.55	.55	1.50	.55	1.45	.60	1.40	.60
11	1.45	.60	1.40	.60	1.35	.65	1.30	.65
12	1.45	.60	1.40	.60	1.35	.65	1.30	.65
13	1.45	.60	1.40	.60	1.35	.65	1.30	.65
14	1.35	.70	1.30	.70	1.25	.75	1.20	.75
15	1.35	.70	1.30	.70	1.25	.75	1.20	.75
16	1.35	.70	1.30	.70	1.25	.75	1.20	.75
17	1.30	.75	1.25	.75	1.20	.80	1.15	.80

SOURCE: Duff & Phelps

collateralization, cross-defaulting. *Overcollateralization* means that the issuer contributes more mortgages or other assets to the issue than the amount securitized, thus lowering the overall loan-to-value ratio of the issue. Issuers usually must establish *reserve funds* for debt service shortfalls and capital improvements. *Guarantees and letters of credit* represent promises by third parties, such as corporations and banks, to pay for the losses incurred by CMBS investors in case of defaults—these third parties take the first-loss position. Finally, *cross-collateralization, cross-defaulting* arrangements enhance the credit of issues in which only one borrower with many properties is involved. These arrangements allow investors to raid the cash flows to any and all properties in the issue to make up debt service shortages from one property and to raid refinancing and sale proceeds from any property to make up losses due to a default of one property loan.

THE SECURITIES

Who purchases CMBSs? Most of these securities become part of the massive portfolios of pension funds. Mutual funds managers and foreign investors also participate in this market. Investors are attracted to the high yields offered by CMBSs, but must accept

EXHIBIT 19-15

STRUCTURING A CMBS ISSUE

Face Amount	Rating	Coupon	Zero Loss Yield
$105.5 million	AAA	6.68%	6.66%
$ 8.4 million	AA	6.68	7.06
$ 10.1 million	A	6.68	7.46
$ 10.0 million	BBB	6.68	8.01
$ 10.1 million	BB	6.68	10.61
$ 8.3 million	B	6.68	11.50
$ 15.1 million	Nonrated	6.68	22.33

SOURCE: David P. Jacob and Kimbell R. Duncan, *Commercial Mortgage-Backed Securities: An Emerging Market,* Mortgage Securities Research, Nomura Securities International, Inc., January 1994.

illiquidity and default risk. The CMBS market has not yet matured to the point where these securities trade on exchanges. Investors seeking to sell CMBSs must work with security brokerage firms that locate buyers.

STRUCTURING CMBS ISSUES

Investment bankers structure CMBS issues to meet the demands of investors. Structuring means dividing the cash flows from the mortgages in the pool into tranches that will attract investors, subject to the limitations imposed by the rating agencies. Nomura Securities used the structure shown in Exhibit 19–15 during the mid-1990s for a CMBS issue. The collateral consisted of 33 fixed-rate loans with an aggregate balance of $167.5 million.

Because of a favorable rating, most of the issue ($105.5 million) was sold as AAA-rated securities. These securities have the lowest yield because the investors occupy the last-loss position, they have the shortest maturity, and they are the easiest for the issuer to sell. The coupon rate of 6.68 percent represents the periodic return all investors receive from the mortgages after the payment of fees to the servicer that collects the payments for investors, for the trustee who holds the mortgages, and for the investment banker who securitized the mortgages and sold the CMBSs. The zero loss yield represents the IRR based on the purchase price of each tranche and the assumption that all of the investors' capital is returned. The zero loss yield (expected return) exceeds the coupon rate when the tranche is sold at a discount.

VALUATION: THE PRICE AND YIELD RELATIONSHIP

Investors in CMBSs must consider three factors when deciding what prices to pay for the securities. First, they observe the coupon rate and the purchase price of each tranche. Second, they consider the timing of return of their investment. As discussed earlier in this chapter, most MBSs today have sequential pay arrangements, whereby the first class of

EXHIBIT 19-16

PRICE AND YIELD RELATIONSHIPS FOR CMBS INVESTOR CLASSES

Class A Investors

	$349,309	$394,731	$1,367,750	$1,271,482	$1,826,309	$0	$0	$0
0	1	2	3	4	5	6	7	8

$4 million – 7.46%

Class B Investors

	$440,000	$440,000	$440,000	$440,000	$738,248	$3,304,612	$2,074,149	$458,130
0	1	2	3	4	5	6	7	8

$5.5 million – 8%

$4,552,825 – 12%

Residual Class Investors

	$75,000	$74,578	$74,122	$68,765	$63,475	$54,254	$47,033	$542,310
0	1	2	3	4	5	6	7	8

$500,000 – 13.12%

$373,276 – 20%

investors receives all principal from the mortgages during the earliest years of the life of the security issue, then the second class of investors begins receiving principal once the first class is paid off. Third, they evaluate the loss potential given their loss position in the issue and the probability of the mortgages in the issue generating losses through default.

Suppose a CMBS issue has a structure identical to the structure of the CMO defined in Exhibit 19–7. Exhibit 19–16 restates the cash flows to each investor class on a time line. If the issuer of these classes of securities can sell out each class at its par amounts, then the yields to Class A, Class B, and the Residual Class are 7.46 percent, 8.00 percent, and 13.12 percent, respectively. Note that these yields result from straightforward IRR calculations in which the par amount becomes the cash outflow in period 0 and the total payments represent cash inflows during subsequent periods. Unfortunately for the issuer, the Residual Class investors recognize that they stand in the precarious first-loss position, and given the strong likelihood of some defaults in this issue, they require a higher yield than 13.11 percent. Similarly, the Class B investors consider the 8 percent return too low for the second-loss position they occupy. Prepayment risk does not factor into the decisions of these investors assuming the underlying mortgages contain lock-out and yield maintenance clauses. If the Residual Class investors need 20 percent to compensate for their risk and the Class B investors need 12 percent, the issuer must reduce the prices of these securities to $373,276 for the Residual Class and $4,552,825 for Class B.[17] As this example demonstrates, structuring and pricing of CMBS issues depend on two major forces: the rating agencies and the investors, who have specific yield requirements in response to the risk of loss due to defaults.

SUMMARY

As discussed in previous chapters, mortgage originations create streams of cash flows consisting of interest, scheduled principal amortization, and unscheduled amortization. Traditionally, these cash flows came to the lenders who originated the loans and held them in their portfolios. During the 1970s, residential lenders began selling the rights to the cash flows from mortgages to investors in MBSs. Commercial property lenders have slowly followed a similar path. The development of secondary mortgage markets, in which investors can buy rights to cash flows from mortgages, provides numerous advantages including these:

1. In many local markets, the demand for mortgage money exceeds the capital of the local lending institutions. An active secondary market allows these lenders to sell their originations, thereby replenishing the funds they need to make new originations. Lending institutions in slow-growing areas can continue to add mortgage investments to their portfolios by taking the opposite side of the transaction; that is, by purchasing mortgages and MBSs.

2. Many major participants in the mortgage market, such as government agencies and pension funds, do not have local offices and therefore benefit from their ability to invest in mortgage securities in the secondary market.

3. Most mortgage investors prefer to hold diversified portfolios of mortgages and mortgage-backed securities to protect themselves against local eco-

nomic downturns and defaults. Thus, the ability to construct a portfolio that is geographically diversified is important.

4. The secondary market reduces the costs of holding and marketing loans. This increased efficiency and liquidity ultimately benefits the mortgage borrower in the form of lower mortgage rates.

5. By eliminating or reducing default risk, by increasing liquidity, and by repackaging prepayment risk, a large variety of mortgage-backed securities are able to attract a large number of investors who would otherwise avoid the mortgage market.

Before mortgages can actively trade in secondary markets, they must undergo securitization. This step involves the review and approval of plans to offer pools of mortgages to the public as MBSs by the Securities and Exchange Commission and marketing efforts by the MBS issuer or by investment banking firms. Special arrangements to secure government guarantees or the introduction of clauses in mortgage documents to protect investors also occur at this stage.

The secondary market in CMBSs has reached the stage in its brief history where large numbers of commercial mortgages are converted into securities each year, but active secondary markets for these securities have not yet developed. Unlike the residential mortgages collateralizing MBSs, the commercial mortgages backing CMBSs usually include lock-out and yield-maintenance clauses to protect investors against prepayment risk. However, CMBS investors do not receive the same level of protection from default risk

---

[17]These prices come from present value calculations using 20 percent and 12 percent.

available to residential MBS investors through implicit and explicit government guarantees. Investors in CMBSs must rely on the assessments of default loss potential from independent rating agencies, such as Standard & Poor's.

The structuring of CMBS issues closely resembles the structures invented for residential MBS issues. Most CMBS issues have sequential payment arrangements. Tranching, however, also depends on credit.

The unrated classes, for example, usually receive principal payments last and therefore occupy first-loss positions. This means that actual losses of invested capital from defaults of mortgages in the pool collateralizing the CMBS issue are charged first against the principal balance of the unrated class. Only after all of the principal of the unrated class is used do investors in the next lowest class begin to suffer losses of capital.

KEY TERMS

Accrual class 590
Agency passthroughs 584
Collateralized mortgage obligation (CMO) 589
Conduit lending 598
Constant prepayment rate 592
Credit enhancement 588
Discount 576
Equity theory of default 602

Financial intermediation 574
First-loss position 599
Floating-rate class 592
Investment-grade rating 588
Market yield 576
Par value 576
Passthrough security 581
Planned amortization class 589
Premium 576

Public Securities Association (PSA) 592
Securitization 573
Senior/subordinate structure 588
Sequential pay securities 588
Spread 579
Tranches 589

TEST YOURSELF

Answer the following multiple choice questions:

1. The issuer of MBSs (e.g., Freddie Mac or an investment banker) must
   a. Make sure all loans in the pool have the same interest rate.
   b. Make sure that all loans in the pool were originated by the same lender.
   c. Make sure that no single loan constitutes more than 30 percent of the issue.
   d. Secure approval to sell securities from the Securities and Exchange Commission.
   e. Do both *b* and *d*.

2. Ginnie Mae's most important activity is to
   a. Package and issue passthrough MBSs backed with Ginnie Mae's guarantee.
   b. Package and issue passthrough MBSs backed with the guarantee of approved issuers.

   c. Guarantee passthrough MBSs issued by approved issuers.
   d. Guarantee CMBSs issued by approved issuers.

3. The majority of residential mortgages purchased by Freddie Mac and Fannie Mae in the secondary mortgage market are
   a. Combined into mortgage pools that are used as collateral for the issuance of MBSs by Freddie Mac and Fannie Mae.
   b. Held as long-term investments by Freddie Mac and Fannie Mae.
   c. Sold to pension funds and life insurance companies.
   d. Sold to savings and loan associations and commercial banks.

4. If a mortgage is purchased in the secondary

mortgage market at a discount, the expected yield will be
a. Less than the contract interest rate.
b. Greater than the yield-to-maturity.
c. Less than the yield-to-maturity.
d. Equal to the contract interest rate if the borrower does not prepay.

5. If a mortgage is purchased in the secondary market at a premium, and actual prepayment occurs sooner than expected, the realized yield will be
a. Less than the expected yield.
b. Greater than the expected yield.
c. Greater than the yield-to-maturity.
d. Equal to the yield-to-maturity.

6. The MBS participation certificates (PCs) issued by Freddie Mac
a. Are viewed to be of slightly higher credit quality than Ginnie Mae passthroughs.
b. Have a guarantee that is explicitly backed by the full faith and credit of the U.S. government.
c. Have a guarantee that is not explicitly backed by the full faith and credit of the U.S. government.
d. Are viewed to be of much higher credit quality than Fannie Mae MBSs.

7. If two identical pools of residential mortgages are used as collateral for the issuance of a passthrough MBS and a sequential pay structure, the maturities of the sequential pay classes
a. Are more uncertain than the maturity of the passthrough.
b. Are less uncertain than the maturity of the passthrough.
c. Can be predicted with certainty.
d. Do not depend on the rate at which the underlying mortgages are prepaid.

8. Relative to residential MBSs, CMBSs normally have
a. Greater prepayment risk.
b. More government guarantees.
c. Greater default risk
d. More classes of investors.
e. All of the above.

9. In rating a CMBS issue, a rating agency, such as Duff & Phelps, relies most heavily on
a. The physical condition of the property.
b. The relationship between the mortgage loan amounts and the values of the properties.
c. The relationships between the NOIs of the properties and the debt service payments on the mortgages.
d. The financial strength of the borrowers.
e. Both *b* and *c*.

10. In a sequential pay structure, until tranche A is paid off, tranche B receives
a. Interest.
b. Principal.
c. Both *a* and *b*.
d. Neither *a* nor *b*.
e. It depends on the other tranches in the structure.

PROBLEMS FOR THOUGHT AND SOLUTION

1. Mortgage securities are "priced off the yield curve." Explain this expression.

2. What is the effect of an investment-grade rating on the required yield of a mortgage-backed security?

3. How do securitization and the secondary mortgage market increase the flows of funds to mortgages?

4. Explain the advantages of investing in passthrough mortgage-backed securities relative to investing in individual mortgage loans.

5. Explain the advantages to investors of having sequential pay collateralized mortgage obligations available instead of only passthrough mortgage-backed securities.

6. Explain why the secondary market in commercial mortgages was slow to develop.

7. Discuss how investment risks differ between residential and commercial mortgage-backed securities and how contract terms and the securities rating agencies affect these risks.

8. Explain what it means to be in the first-loss position of a CMBS issue and how being in this position influences the price and yield relationship for that class of investors.

CASE PROBLEMS

1. Consider an $80,000 fixed-rate mortgage with an 8.25 percent annual interest rate, monthly payments, and an original loan term of 15 years. Assume the mortgage was originated yesterday.

  a. What is the monthly payment?

  b. What is the (present) *value* of the mortgage in the secondary mortgage market if investors are currently requiring an 8.0 percent return on similar investments—assuming the mortgage is not prepaid prior to maturity?

  c. What is the (present) *value* of the mortgage in the secondary mortgage market if investors are currently requiring an 8.0 percent return on similar investments—assuming the mortgage is prepaid at the end of eight years?

  d. If the mortgage is purchased today by an investor in the secondary mortgage market for $83,000, what is the investor's *expected* yield—assuming the mortgage is not prepaid prior to maturity?

  e. If the mortgage is purchased today by an investor in the secondary mortgage market for $83,000, what is the investor's *expected* yield—assuming the mortgage is prepaid at the end of eight years?

  f. If the mortgage is purchased for $83,000, what

is the investors *realized* yield if the loan is actually prepaid at the end of the fourth year?

2. Assume a mortgage banker has originated 300 fixed-rate mortgages, each with a face value of $90,000, a contract rate of 9.0 percent, and a loan term of 30 years. For simplicity, assume payments will be made annually. This mortgage pool is to be used as the collateral for the issuance of a pass-through MBS that has a coupon rate of 8.5 percent. It is assumed that unscheduled principal repayments reduce the scheduled principal balance by 6 percent at the end of each year. That is, a constant (annual) prepayment rate of 6 percent is assumed.

  a. What are the scheduled principal payments on the underlying mortgages in years 1, 2, and 3 (assuming no unscheduled prepayments)?

  b. What will be the scheduled principal payments in year 2, assuming the remaining principal balance is paid down by 6 percent at the end of year 1?

  c. What will be the scheduled principal payments in year 3, assuming the remaining principal balance is paid down by an additional 6 percent at the end of year 2?

  d. Fill in the following table of principal payments and loan balances.

Year	Beginning Principal Balance (1)	Scheduled Principal Payments (2)	Scheduled Principal Balance (3) = (1) − (2)	Total Prepayments @ 6% of Scheduled Balance (4) = 0.06 × (3)	Projected Principal Balance (5) = (3) − (4)
1	$27,000,000				
2					
3					

e. Fill in the following table, which summarizes the total cash flows to the investors on the pass-through MBS.

Year	Beginning Balance	Interest	Total Principal Payments	Total Cash Flow	Principal Repaid to Date to Investors
1	$27,000,000				
2					
3					

3. The Wall Street investment banking firm of Dingle and Dangle plans to securitize a pool of apartment loans it obtained through a conduit relationship with Dimple and Dample Mortgage Company. The mortgage pool has a principal balance of $100 million, an average loan-to-value ratio of 75 percent, and an average debt coverage of 1.25. The rating agency and Dingle and Dangle agree that the probability of default for this pool should be 6 percent. However, Dingle and Dangle does not agree with the rating agency's expectation that losses from default and foreclosure will amount to $2.7 million. They recently acquired data from Freddie Mac indicating that loan loss severity for similar apartment mortgages averages 35 percent. What is the difference between the rating agency's estimate of expected losses and the estimate developed by Dingle and Dangle? Do you think this amount is substantial enough to influence ratings and pricing of the issue?

ADDITIONAL READINGS

Substantial portions of the following books are devoted to the secondary market for residential mortgages and residential mortgage-backed securities:

Brueggeman, William B., and Jeffrey D. Fisher. *Real Estate Finance and Investment,* 10th ed. Burr Ridge, IL: Richard D. Irwin, 1997.

Maisel, Sherman J. *Real Estate Finance,* 2nd ed. Hinsdale IL: Dryden Press, 1992.

Clauretie, Terrence M., and G. Stacy Sirmans. *Real Estate Finance,* 2nd ed. Upper Saddle River, NJ: Prentice Hall, 1996.

The following books are completely devoted to mortgage markets and mortgage-backed securities:

Fabozzi, Frank J., and Franco Modigliani. *Mortgage and Mortgage-Backed Securities Markets.* Boston: Harvard Business School Press, 1992.

Bartlett, William W. *The Valuation of Mortgage-Backed Securities.* Burr Ridge, IL: Irwin Professional, 1994.

Davidson, Andrew S., and Michael D. Herskovitz. *Mortgage-Backed Securities: Investment Analysis and Advanced Valuation Techniques.* Chicago: Probus Publishing, 1994.

Two publications from Wall Street firms listed below provide details about CMBSs:

Jacob, David P., and Kimbell R. Duncan. *Commercial Mortgage-Backed Securities: An Emerging Market.* New York: Mortgage Securities Research, Nomura Securities International, Inc., January 1994.

Quigg, Laura. *Commercial Mortgage-Backed Securities.* New York: Fixed Income Research–Mortgage Securities, Lehman Brothers, December 1993.

P A R T

IV

LEGAL
PERSPECTIVE

20
Real Property Rights

21
Real Property Taxation

22
Transfer of Real Property Rights

23
Real Estate Brokerage and Listing Contracts

24
Contracts for Sale and Closing

This part of *Real Estate Perspectives* views real estate from a legal perspective. The importance of legal systems in establishing rules to protect the institution of private property throughout the world—an institution that is vital to the conduct of business in a free market economy—cannot be overstated. Without legal rights to acquire, earn income from, and dispose of property, individuals and firms will not invest in real estate or provide real estate services. An understanding of real property rights and the mechanisms for transferring rights within the legal system, therefore, is fundamental for anyone who participates in the real estate markets.

The Legal Perspective begins with Chapter 20, which contains many of the essential concepts, terms, and definitions found in property law, albeit presented in layperson's language. This material includes limitations on property ownership, such as the right to foreclose on property owners who do not pay their property taxes. We devote Chapter 21 to the further study of the property tax. Chapter 22 presents the legal fundamentals for transferring real estate ownership. The transfer of real estate involves various contracts to assist the process. The mortgage contract discussed in Chapter 15 is one of these contracts. The others are the listing contract between the seller of property and the real estate broker, presented in Chapter 23, and the contract for sale between the seller and the buyer of property presented in Chapter 24. Also presented in the final chapter is coverage of how the closing of real estate transactions occur, which is a fitting way to end the book.

20
C H A P T E R

REAL PROPERTY RIGHTS

INTRODUCTION TO REAL PROPERTY RIGHTS
Physical Property Rights to Real Estate
Real Versus Personal Property Rights: The Problem of Fixtures
Legal Property Rights of Real Estate Ownership
Property Rights: A Value Perspective

ESTATES IN REAL ESTATE
Freehold Estates
Nonfreehold Estates

PROPERTY RIGHTS AMONG CO-OWNERS: CONCURRENT ESTATES
Direct Co-Ownership Forms
Indirect Co-Ownership Forms

PUBLIC AND PRIVATE LIMITS ON PROPERTY RIGHTS
Government's Role in Determining Property Rights
Private Contracts and Other Methods of Limiting Property Rights

SUMMARY

KEY TERMS

TEST YOURSELF

PROBLEMS FOR THOUGHT AND SOLUTION

CASE PROBLEMS

ADDITIONAL READINGS

After reading this chapter, students will be able to:

1. Distinguish between the legal rights of real estate ownership and the physical rights.

2. Define the various types of estates in land.

3. Distinguish among tenancy in common, joint tenancy, and other forms of co-ownership of real estate.

4. Explain the government's role in limiting private property rights.

5. Explain how real property rights can be limited by private contracts.

INTRODUCTION TO REAL PROPERTY RIGHTS

The United States uses the *private* ownership system for control of the use of land. Not all countries permit such relatively unrestricted ownership and free exchange of land within their boundaries. In the remaining communist countries, state-controlled *communal* ownership systems allow only the state or communes to own the land used by citizens. These systems provide limited opportunities for private ownership (e.g., an apartment may be purchased through government-assisted financing). *Tribal* ownership systems prevail in parts of Africa. *Religious* land ownership systems exist in the Middle East. The ownership rights of those who use land within a country therefore result from the *land tenure system* under which the country operates. Our concern in this chapter lies with rights under the private land tenure system.

For most purposes, the terms *real estate* and **real property** are synonymous.[1] This is not to say these terms mean exactly the same thing—they don't. However, making a formal distinction in meaning serves no useful purpose for most real estate practitioners. The important point to understand is that one acquires a set of distinct and separable real **property rights** when one purchases real estate. Consequently, these real property rights include rights to the physical characteristics of real estate and rights of legal ownership of real estate. This means that with the purchase of real estate, owners receive a **bundle of rights**, which includes rights to the physical characteristics of the real estate and legal rights of ownership. In the following sections we define these different rights of real estate ownership. We also look at how rights become restricted and how they become separated from the main bundle of rights. The information contained in this chapter provides a critical foundation to the business and valuation of real estate. To use real estate successfully, businesspeople and owners must *know* the concepts and terminology of real property rights.

---

[1] *Black's Law Dictionary* defines real estate as "Land and anything permanently affixed to the land, such as buildings, fences, and those things attached to the buildings, such as light fixtures, plumbing and heating fixtures, or other such items which would be personal property if not attached. The term is generally synonymous with *real property*."

EXHIBIT 20-1

PHYSICAL RIGHTS TO REAL ESTATE

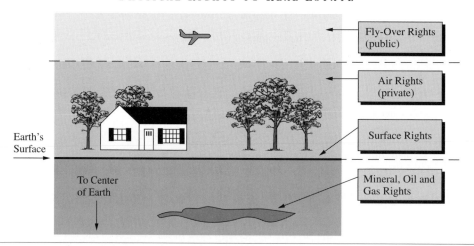

Fly-Over Rights
(public)

Air Rights
(private)

Surface Rights

Mineral, Oil and
Gas Rights

Earth's
Surface

To Center
of Earth

PHYSICAL PROPERTY RIGHTS TO REAL ESTATE

Normally, when individuals purchase real estate, such as a single-family home, they receive a complete set of physical rights. As shown in Exhibit 20–1, a complete set of physical rights includes surface rights; above-surface rights or air rights; and subsurface rights, including mineral, oil, and gas rights. Rights to water differ widely among the states (see Real Estate Focus 20–1). The surface rights of land encompass the legal rights of ownership to the surface of the land and anything permanently affixed to the land. These attachments include *improvements on land,* such as a single-family structure and garage, and *improvements to land,* such as streets, gutters, sewer and water lines, landscaping, grading, and retaining walls.

The air rights of real estate owners generally extend above the earth's surface to the height of the tallest man-made improvements.[2] Currently, this height is approximately 1,500 feet. The space above this zone of private air rights constitutes the public airspace, which provides fly-over rights to accommodate air transportation.

The physical rights of real estate owners also extend below the earth's surface—theoretically to the center of the earth in the shape of an inverted pyramid. As a practical matter, however, these subsurface rights, including the rights to all minerals, oil, and water, extend only to the physical limits of human ability to explore below the surface of the earth (currently to a depth of about 50,000 feet).

This set of physical property rights provides opportunities for subdivision in a variety of interesting and unusual ways. In urban areas, air rights freely trade to facilitate

---

[2]Property in the vicinity of airports is an exception to this rule. Also, this is a general rule. It does not mean, for example, that a developer would be prohibited from putting up a building that is one story higher than the tallest existing building.

REAL ESTATE FOCUS 20-1

Water Rights

Riparian land describes land adjacent to nonnavigable* bodies of water, and the landowners' rights to use the water constitute their **riparian rights**. In the eastern half of the United States, the abundance of water means that adjustments to the level of water on streams and lakes by one party do not usually affect the ability of others to use the water. So, a *reasonable-use* theory applies in most of the eastern United States. Riparian landowners may use all the water they need as long as their use remains reasonable.

Many states in the western United States reject the reasonable-use concept of riparian rights and instead apply the *prior appropriation* concept. This concept, first adopted in Colorado, relies on the idea that not enough water exists to satisfy everyone's needs; thus the first party to use the body of water for some *beneficial economic purpose* obtains superior rights to the water.

Rights to water usage remain one of the fundamental differences in real estate law (and perhaps life in general) between the states in eastern and western parts of the United States.

———

*Navigability generally depends on whether the body of water can carry transporting boats loaded with freight in the regular course of trade.

---

development, as shown in Exhibit 20–2. Sale of rights to cut timber from raw land offers another example of subdivision, an arrangement that can yield excellent returns and defers carrying costs (such as property taxes) while holding land for possible future development. The states follow different legal concepts with respect to ownership of oil and gas rights. States following the traditional *ownership-in-place* concept recognize ownership of oil and gas as part of land ownership. Thus, the physical rights of oil and gas trade independently from the rest of the land. Other states (e.g., California, Louisiana, and Oklahoma) reject this concept in favor of a nonownership concept in which no actual ownership in subsurface oil and gas exists in conjunction with land ownership. Instead, rights exist to *search and bring oil and gas to the surface into possession*. Landowners control access to these natural resources through easements, license, and servitude but cannot sell oil and gas rights they do not own.[3]

REAL VERSUS PERSONAL PROPERTY RIGHTS: THE PROBLEM OF FIXTURES

The law recognizes only two basic types of property: personal property (personalty) and real property (realty). *Realty* refers to land and anything permanently affixed to land, while *personalty* includes all other tangible property. Distinguishing between personalty and realty often has important implications during the transfer of real property rights for determination of property taxes, determination of tax depreciation deductions, and pledging real estate as security for mortgage loans.

———

[3]See Richard W. Hemingway, *Law of Oil and Gas* (St. Paul, MN: West, 1983).

EXHIBIT 20-2

AIR RIGHTS

Photo by Jack Corgel

L'Enfant Plaza, Washington, D.C., is constructed over highway and railroad rights of way.

Assume, for example, you recently sold a home purchased several years ago. In the living room of your home, a giant-screen television was built into a bookcase. When removing your furniture, clothing, and other personal property, you detach the television set from the bookcase and take it with you. The day after the closing, you receive a telephone call from the buyer's attorney who says you violated the terms of the contract for the sale of the house because you removed an item, the television, that was permanently affixed to the realty. The attorney claims the television rightfully belongs to the buyer.

This dispute over rights to the television set typifies the type of problem buyers and sellers encounter with **fixtures**. The term *fixture* refers to something that was once personalty, but by reason of its purpose or attachment to real property became part of the realty. In addition to cases involving buyers and sellers, fixtures often present difficulties for landlords and tenants in residential and commercial lease agreements, for tax assessors and taxpayers in the valuation of real estate for property-tax purposes, and for lenders and borrowers in determining the nature of property pledged as security for loans.

In resolving disputes about fixtures, the courts rely on the following tests:

1. *Intent test.* The intention of the parties or what stands as customary in a particular situation emerges as the most crucial factor for determining whether to declare an item a fixture. Builders of new homes, for example, regularly install built-in refrigerators. If the property later sells, the refrigerators would become part of the realty as fixtures. Customarily, the room furnishings accompany the real property when hotels sell.
2. *Annexation test.* If removal of an item causes physical damage to the adjacent property, then the item may be deemed a fixture. Yet annexation occurs in relation to other factors, including intent, adaptation, and relationship of the parties.
3. *Adaptation test.* The everyday use of an item in relation to the real property may help determine a fixture. Storm doors and windows specially designed to fit doors and windows of a particular house would qualify as fixtures under the adaptation test. Also, specially designed industrial equipment in particular buildings often qualifies as fixtures.
4. *Relationship-of-the-parties test.* The courts in recent years have favored purchasers, tenants, and mortgagees (lenders) in disputes involving fixtures. This "test of last resort" becomes primary when all other tests fail to help the courts resolve these disputes.

No universal standard has emerged from the case law on fixtures. Usually, the factual evidence of each case and an application of some combination of the four tests govern court decisions. All contracts for the sale of real property should spell out specifically the nature of all physical real property rights involved in the transaction.

So who gets the television set? Most likely the buyer because the intention of the seller remains difficult to determine, some damage resulted from removal of the television set from the bookcase, this particular television set fits into this particular space, and the courts tend to favor buyers over sellers.

Fixtures, such as the one just described, differ from property referred to in commercial leases as *trade fixtures*. Trade fixtures consist of items such as display counters, mobile partitions, and cabinets used by tenants in shopping centers, office buildings, and other income properties. Unlike ordinary fixtures, this personal property stays with the tenants before, during, and after the lease term. Commercial lease contracts should specify clearly those items provided by the landlord and those items provided by the tenant—the trade fixtures.

LEGAL PROPERTY RIGHTS OF REAL ESTATE OWNERSHIP

The idea of the bundle of rights acquired with the purchase of real estate, including a set of physical rights and a set of legal rights of ownership, equates conceptually to a bundle of sticks containing two types of sticks: a thick and sturdy type and some thin, fragile, and more difficult-to-grasp sticks. The intangible legal rights of real estate ownership resemble the second variety of sticks in the bundle: the thin, fragile, and somewhat difficult to grasp sticks.

REAL ESTATE FOCUS 20-2

Restrictions on the Right of Disposition:
The Special Case of Real Estate Ownership by Aliens

Laws in more than one-half of the states restrict rights of voluntary disposition of land in transactions involving transfers to nonresident aliens. Nonresident aliens include persons, partnerships, and corporations located outside of U.S. boundaries. Resident aliens are foreign-born residents of the United States who have not become naturalized citizens. The laws in most states exempt resident aliens from ownership restrictions.

Some states, for example, limit ownership of land by nonresident aliens within the vicinity of cities and villages. Other states restrict foreign ownership of rural farmland. Certain states also allow nonresident aliens to own real estate anywhere within state boundaries when they come from particular countries. For example, one state allows nonresident citizens of France to freely own real estate.

Income tax treaties, negotiated between the federal government and foreign governments, may alter state laws governing ownership of land by nonresident aliens. Some treaties, for example those with the Netherlands and Germany, allow foreign investors specific rights to lease property. Many treaties modify certain restrictions in state laws regarding inheritance of property by nonresident aliens.

The outright ownership of real estate in a free economy carries with it three fundamental legal rights. First, owners of real estate have the *right of exclusive possession and control*. This means owners have the legal right to control entry to real property, to collect damages in case of trespass, and to use real property as collateral for loans. Second, owners have the legal *right of quiet enjoyment*. This right refers to the legal claim of owners to hold possession without unfounded disturbances from those claiming defects in the title—it has nothing to do with noise! This right entitles owners to receive rent from real property and receive sale proceeds without the continued aggravation of fending off others who make grandstand legal maneuvers to grab these flows of funds. Finally, owners have rights of disposition that allow them to transfer ownership to others in the way they see fit (e.g., sale, gift, or will), provided that no violations occur in the federal and state laws against discrimination and foreign ownership of land.

PROPERTY RIGHTS: A VALUE PERSPECTIVE

Societies create legal rights in property and in doing so create property values. Suppose the members of a society decide to support the idea of private real estate ownership but vote against owners living on privately owned land or developing the land for any commercial purpose. The market value of the real estate in this society would barely exceed zero. Further, the often-told story of the farmer who plants corn but, under the rules of society cannot prevent neighbors from entering the land and sharing in the harvest, points to the importance of the exclusivity component of legal rights to property. The farmer may plant corn one year and experience a harvest in which the farmer benefits little from this use of land. The next year, the farmer will either defend against trespassers with physical violence (if permitted in the society) or will abandon the land and the idea of farming. This example demonstrates that legal protection of property rights, particularly the right of exclusive possession, provides incentives to use real estate efficiently. *The opportunity to make efficient use of real estate makes real estate valuable.*

ESTATES IN REAL ESTATE

In most instances, real estate owners have a complete set of fundamental legal rights. Like physical real property rights, however, private contracts can create separated legal rights. This section of the chapter considers ways in which legal rights of real estate ownership become subdivided and altered.

The term *estate* refers to the degree of legal interest a party has in real estate. The degree of interest follows from the extent of the legal rights contained in the main bundle of rights. Thus, each estate defined below, when mentioned in writing or conversation, conveys a mental image of the set of legal rights held in real estate. These estates, known as *estates in severalty,* occur when only *one* party owns real estate—that owner's interest becomes *severed* from other owners' interests. Concurrent estates, discussed later in this chapter, involve ownership by more than one owner in the same property.

The tree diagram in Exhibit 20–3 presents some of the more common estates. In most instances, these estates involve only current interests (legal rights that begin at acquisition), but in some cases, parties to estates have future interests (legal rights that may begin at some future time).

The initial separation of the branches on the tree diagram divides the estates in land into freehold and nonfreehold categories. **Freehold estates** have *indefinite* duration. The parties to these estates do not know when their rights to properties will expire. *Nonfreehold estates* have a duration set by private contract. The contracts that create these estates define definite points when property rights terminate. The freehold estates branch divides into freehold estates of, and not of, inheritance. The term *inheritance* refers to the ability of parties to pass their interests to heirs.

The following sections discuss each estate on the branches of the tree diagram, beginning with the freehold estates of inheritance, and specifically, with the fee simple absolute estate.

FREEHOLD ESTATES

Fee simple absolute.   The **fee simple absolute** estate or *fee simple* estate represents the most complete estate.[4] Regardless of the physical rights involved, fee simple ownership entitles owners to the three fundamental legal rights: the right of exclusive possession, the right of quiet enjoyment, and the right of disposition. In a fee simple estate, these legal rights are unabridged and unaltered.

Most owners of land hold fee simple estates. Yet many situations arise in which one or more of the parties involved in transfers of physical property rights wish to limit in

---

[4]The word *fee* refers to ownership of land, and the word *simple* suggests that title is held without restrictions.

EXHIBIT 20-3

ESTATES IN SEVERALTY: CURRENT AND FUTURE ESTATES
(FUTURE INTERESTS IN PARENTHESES)

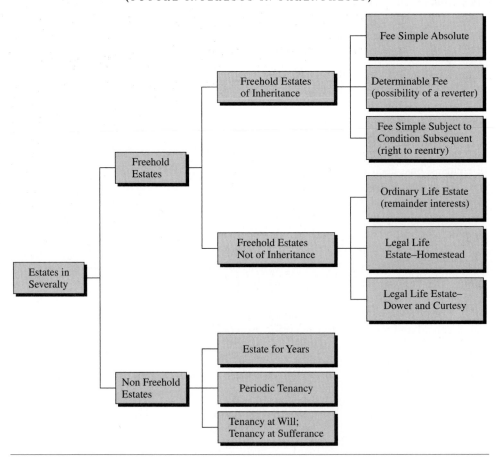

some way the set of legal rights. Therefore, the other freehold estates shown on the tree diagram describe altered and incomplete sets of legal rights.

Determinable fee. A party with a determinable fee estate receives, for example, through sale, gift, or will, an interest in real property that lasts *for as long as* some stipulation remains satisfied. The legal interest equals that of the fee simple estate except all rights terminate on the occurrence of the event specified by the party making the grant (grantor). The party receiving the gift, the grantee, has a current interest known as the *determinable fee*, while the grantor has a future interest termed the *possibility of a reverter*. If the specified event occurs, all physical and legal rights to the property revert *immediately* to the grantor.

Assume a wealthy alumnus and ex-football player of a major university makes a gift to his alma mater of an office building near campus for as long as the university's football team wins at least one game during the season. The university has a determinable fee estate in the building, and the alumnus has a possibility of a reverter estate. Within five years of the gift, croquet replaces football as the nation's premier college spectator and participation sport. After a series of student riots, university officials drop football to allow the university's croquet team to compete in the stadium Saturday afternoons. At the end of the football season, when the football team has not had the opportunity to win one game, the alumnus immediately regains all rights (a fee simple estate) to the office building.

Fee simple subject to condition subsequent. Suppose the wealthy alumnus in the previous example had given the office building with the condition that the football team "fails to win" one game instead of the language "as long as" the team wins one game. In this case the estate held by the university becomes a fee simple subject to condition subsequent, and the estate of the alumnus becomes a *right of reentry* estate. The only difference between this and the previous arrangement is that reversion to the grantor does *not* occur immediately on the occurrence of the event, but instead only after the grantor takes *specific action* to recover the property. Thus, the university has use of the office building until the alumnus takes action to recover the property should the school's football team fail to win a game during the season. This action may only involve a simple letter or telephone call notifying the grantee to vacate the premises.

Ordinary life estate. The ordinary **life estate** provides the most common example of a freehold estates not of inheritance. This type of estate has an uncertain duration and cannot be passed to heirs. The ordinary, or conventional, life estate contains provisions imposed by the parties to the contract creating the estate. By contrast, legal life estates contain provisions imposed by state law.

Suppose two old friends, Mr. I and Mr. Spry, who are both in their 70s, enter into an ordinary life estate. Mr. Spry recently married a woman in her 50s, and Mr. I, who owns an exclusive oceanside condominium in Florida, wants Mr. Spry and his wife to have exclusive use of the premises. Mr. I therefore grants the condominium to Mr. Spry until Mr. Spry dies. On the death of Mr. Spry, the property reverts back to Mr. I. If Mr. I predeceases Mr. Spry, then the property goes to Mr. I's son, Mr. i.

In this case, Mr. Spry has an ordinary life estate (current interest) that terminates on his death. The property cannot be passed on in a will to his wife. Mr. I has a future interest called a *remainder* that vests in the grantor. If the grantor predeceases the grantee, then the contingent remainder interest (that interest vested to Mr. I's son) ripens. Thus, with ordinary life estates, legal rights of ownership equal those of fee simple estates, except for limits on the right of disposition. Owners cannot ignore the rights of those holding remainder interests by, for example, allowing properties to run down to save money for themselves by not paying operating expenses.

Legal life estate—homestead. Most states exempt family homes, under homestead laws, from the actions of those to whom families owe money. The magnitude of the homestead exemption (dollar amount or acreage) differs among the states, yet the social policy that supports homestead laws does not differ. States have an interest in protecting the security and financial independence of families. Family homes and farms receive protection against the actions of all creditors except taxing authorities, mortgage lenders, and mechanics (those who are entitled to payment because of work done or materials purchased for properties).

Homesteads represent interests created in specified properties by state law and may not be passed to heirs.[5] Thus they fall into the category of freehold estates not of inheritance called legal life estates. Many issues surround homestead protection, such as the definition of *family*, that extend beyond the scope of this text. The following definition of *homestead* under Texas law typifies how homestead laws read across the United States:

a. *If used for purpose of an urban home or as a place to exercise a calling or business in the same urban area, the homestead of a family or a single, adult person, not otherwise entitled to a homestead, shall consist of not more than one acre of land which may be in one or more lots, together with any improvements thereon.*

b. *If used for the purposes of a rural home, the homestead shall consist of:*
   (1) *For a family, not more than 200 acres, which may be in one or more parcels, with the improvements thereon; or*
   (2) *For a single, adult person, not otherwise entitled to a homestead, not more than 100 acres, which may be in one or more parcels, with the improvements thereon.*

c. *The definition of a homestead as provided in this section applies to all homesteads in this state whenever created.*

Legal life estate—dower and curtesy. In common law property states, as opposed to community property states discussed later in the section on concurrent estates in land, *dower* refers to the property rights that ripen for wives on the death of their husbands. Thus, if a valid marriage exists during which the husband predeceases the wife, and if real estate was acquired during the marriage that becomes subject to dower, the wife typically obtains an automatic one-third interest in the real estate.

Even if husbands acquire real property on their own, wives may be entitled to an inactive dower right that ripens at the time of the husband's death. These rights of wives supersede unsecured claims of creditors of the estate of the husband. They do not supersede the claims of mortgage lenders, taxing authorities, and mechanics.

Dower rights constitute an important factor to consider in real estate transactions. Assume, for example, Mr. Peabody sells property to Mr. Quebody acquired during Peabody's marriage. Without proper care to release the dower rights of Mrs. Peabody on or following the sale, she may exercise her dower rights and lay claim to one third of Mr. Quebody's property on the death of Mr. Peabody.

Curtesy refers to the property rights of the husbands in the properties of their wives. State laws today involving curtesy rights vary widely. Certain states abolished curtesy

---

[5]Often, homestead protection terminates when the surviving family head dies and the minor children attain the age of majority.

while other states merged dower and curtesy under dower or a new title. These actions attempt to promote sexual equality in state law. For example, Florida refers to the merged and equal dower and curtesy rights as elective share.

Like homestead, dower and curtesy interests exist in specific property in accordance with state law and may not pass to heirs. Thus, these freehold estates not of inheritance fall into the category of legal life estates.

NONFREEHOLD ESTATES

Nonfreehold estates have a definite or certain duration. These include the estate for years, periodic tenancy, tenancy at will, and tenancy at sufferance.

Estate for years. The **estate for years** describes the typical set of property rights possessed by tenants in lease agreements. Another term for tenants' interest is *leasehold estate*, while landlords' interest is a *leased fee estate* (fee simple subject to a lease). The estate for years falls into the category of a nonfreehold estate (certain duration) because the contract limits the period over which tenants maintain use and possession of the properties. Agreements of this type may extend as long as 99 years, as in the case of some land leases.

The property rights transferred to tenants by landlords have severe restrictions. Leasehold interests of retailers in shopping malls, for example, give tenants rights of exclusive possession but do not give tenants full rights of disposition of the real estate. Leasehold interests involve only rights to use and possession and, in the case of the estate for years, only over a defined period. Chapter 8 contains considerable detail about the provisions of the contracts creating these leasehold estates.

Periodic tenancy. The **periodic tenancy** constitutes another type of leasehold interest. These agreements establish periods over which tenants have rights of use and possession, but at the end of these periods, rights automatically renew, usually for another period of equal length. Periodic tenancies end when one party gives advance notice according to the agreement of intent to terminate.

Tenancy at will; tenancy at sufferance. **Tenancies at will** exist when rights of possession transfer with oral instead of written agreements. The rights of tenants can terminate at any time without notice by either landlords or tenants. This type of estate occurs most often when tenants retain rights of possession with the consent of landlords *after* the terms of their leases have expired. For example, a student may wish to continue occupancy of an apartment for two weeks at the end of the school year and the end of the periodic tenancy.

A **tenant at sufferance** is essentially a trespasser. This type of tenancy occurs without written or oral consent of landlords. Tenants at sufferance have few or no legal rights. Courts often must determine in cases involving tenant and landlord disputes whether tenants became tenants at will or tenants at sufferance. State laws vary widely on the definition and treatment of tenants at will and tenants at sufferance.

E X H I B I T   2 0 - 4

EXHIBIT 20-4

CONCURRENT ESTATES IN LAND

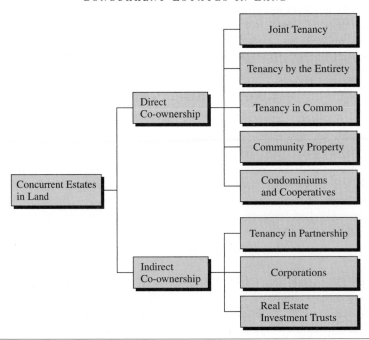

PROPERTY RIGHTS AMONG CO-OWNERS: CONCURRENT ESTATES

Preceding sections discussed the separation of the bundle of rights along physical and legal lines and the separation of legal rights to create various estates. This section considers alternative ways to divide real property rights among *co-owners*. Specific strategies, such as limiting personal liability and maximizing tax benefits through the selection of ownership form, appear in Chapter 5.

The tree diagram in Exhibit 20–4 presents various concurrent estates in land. The branches show estates divided into direct and indirect co-ownership interests. Direct concurrent estates allow owners to become closely involved in the day-to-day operations of the real estate, usually through their actual use and possession of property. Indirect co-ownership means limited or passive involvement. These estates often exist for investment in real estate rather than for personal or business use and possession.

DIRECT CO-OWNERSHIP FORMS

Joint tenancy. In a **joint tenancy** two or more parties own property together and each co-owner possesses exactly the same property rights as any other co-owner. For a joint tenancy to exist, the ownership rights of all co-owners must begin at the same time (known as *unity of time*), have transferred to all co-owners under the same title (the *unity of title*), remain equal among all co-owners (the *unity of interest*), and establish equal ability for each co-owner to possess or use the property (the *unity of possession*). If one of these four unities does not exist, the courts will likely rule in disputes over property rights that no joint tenancy exists.

Legal disputes over the existence of joint tenancies are usually the result of conflicts involving the **right of survivorship** inherent in joint tenancies. The right of survivorship means that if one co-owner dies, that owner's rights become divided among the surviving partners. These rights cannot pass to the heirs of the deceased co-owner.

Assume, for example, that Mr. Evad and Mr. Lah purchase a parcel of land together and decide to own the property as joint tenants. On the death of Mr. Evad, his son discovers that all rights to the parcel of land go to Mr. Lah under the right of survivorship. Thus, the son and the only heir of Mr. Evad has a strong economic incentive to show that a joint tenancy did not exist between his father and Mr. Lah. His challenge stems from the argument that one of the unities never entered the agreement.

The creation of joint tenancies normally occurs between a few close business partners or between family members.

Tenancy by the entireties.   Tenancies by the entireties exist in some states as a form of concurrent ownership for husbands and wives. The characteristics of tenancy by the entirety ownership resemble those of joint tenancy, including survivorship rights and unity of title. The difference lies in the fact that creditors of the individual spouses cannot proceed against the entirety interest; hence, tenancy by the entirety ownership shields real property from the individual obligations of each spouse.

Tenancy in common.   Under a **tenancy in common** agreement, co-owners may have unequal interest, they may have separate titles to property, and their rights may begin at different periods. However, each co-owner must have equal rights of use and possession. Perhaps more important, *no* rights of survivorship exist among tenants in common. If Mr. Evad and Mr. Lah created a tenancy in common instead of the joint tenancy, Mr. Lah retains no claims to Mr. Evad's share and Mr. Evad's son would likely inherit those rights.

Community property.   Several states, mainly in the western and southwestern sections of the United States, enforce laws establishing **community property** rights between spouses.[6] In contrast to common law property states, which operate with dower, curtesy, or some variation thereof, community property states recognize the husband and wife as *equal* partners in certain community property. Community property means any property not considered separate property. Separate property means property of either spouse that

---

[6]Community property states are Arizona, California, Idaho, Louisiana, Nevada, New Mexico, Texas, Washington, and Wisconsin. Mississippi is a title state in which title alone controls ownership rights. For a discussion of property distribution arrangements across the states in cases of divorce, see Doris Jonas Freed and Timothy B. Walker, "Family Law in the Fifty States: An Overview," *Family Law Quarterly* 21 (Winter 1988), p. 417.

was owned at the time of the marriage or that was acquired by a spouse during the marriage by gift, will, or inheritance.

Condominiums and cooperatives. The term **condominium**, while almost unheard of 50 years ago, frequently appears today in conversation. Some people mistakenly think *condominium* refers to a multiunit residential development in which people own their units rather than renting them. Actually, *condominium* refers to a form of co-ownership of real estate with fee simple ownership of units, and ownership as tenants in common for the common grounds (e.g., elevators, halls, and swimming pool).

The definition of *unit* determines the extent of physical property rights of fee simple ownership in condominiums. Many state statutes contain definitions of unit boundaries that apply if, in the unlikely event, the condominium declaration does not address this issue. Typically, the laws and declarations define units as the areas enclosed by the unexposed faces of the inside drywall that divides each unit from other units to the sides and the area between the underside of the finished floor and the unexposed face of the drywall ceiling. Tenant in common ownership prevails for all other physical property rights, including air rights and subsurface rights.

Almost any style of building (e.g., high-rise or garden) and use (e.g., residential, office, retail, industrial) lends itself to condominium ownership provided that the units have physical separation. Residential condominiums have been constructed or converted from apartments in most areas of the country. In recent years, hotel and office condominiums became a popular option, particularly for smaller offices, such as doctors' offices. Condominium ownership also may occur in periods of time as described in Real Estate Focus 20–3. The owners of units carry responsibility for repairs and maintenance of their units; however, owners' associations typically handle repairs and maintenance of common areas. To finance these outlays, owners' associations assess monthly fees to owners.

Specific co-ownership rights under the condominium form appear within the contents of the following documents:

1. *Declaration.* The condominium declaration commits the property to condominium ownership. It defines the rights and responsibilities of individual owners with respect to maintenance and financial liabilities.
2. *Bylaws.* Similar to corporate bylaws, condominium bylaws outline the structure for administering the association (e.g., composition of the board of directors) and property (e.g., rules and regulations that must be followed by owners).
3. *Management agreements.* Before the sale of all the units, the developer performs all management duties. Sometime thereafter, the owners' associations usually negotiate outside contracts for property management services.

In most physical respects, cooperative ownership resembles condominium ownership, but legally major differences appear. Mainly, cooperative ownership has occurred for co-ownership of multiunit residential property in a few major metropolitan areas in

REAL ESTATE FOCUS 20-3

Time-Sharing in Condominium Ownership

Time-sharing of residential condominiums remains popular, especially in resort areas. It represents an interesting and unique way to view the separation of co-ownership rights in real estate. Suppose, for example, that Leah Sherwood desires a place to stay in Colorado for two weeks every year during ski season. She has three options. First, she can face the uncertainties of renting every year. Second, she can buy a condominium in the area with the problem of renting the unit for most of the year. Third, she can purchase the two weeks she desires in a time-share condominium near the ski area.

In a time-share condominium, the fee simple interest is *restricted* each year to the time period purchased. If this ski enthusiast purchases the first two weeks in February in a one-bedroom unit for $20,000, then each year she has the rights of use, possession, and quiet enjoyment for those two weeks. She also has the right to sell her period of ownership at any time, to lease the unit for that period, or to trade her weeks in Colorado for, say, two weeks in Miami Beach through a time-share exchange.

The purchase of a time-share unit represents the acquisition of physical and legal property rights for only the desired period of *time* and thus avoids uncertainties of renting and the costs of purchasing a traditional fee simple interest. Yet one must follow caution when considering a time-share unit because of several potential pitfalls. For example, mismanagement by time-share developers sometimes causes owners to lose their total investment.

---

the United States. New York City, for example, has many cooperative buildings. In this type of ownership, a nonprofit corporation, the **cooperative**, purchases or develops an apartment house. Prospective residents purchase shares in the nonprofit corporation in proportion to the value of the unit in which they will reside. Purchasers receive proprietary leases from the corporation that entitle shareholders to use and occupy the units.

Cooperatives are inferior to condominiums for residential ownership in two respects. First, the financing of cooperatives under a single mortgage allows shareholders to share in the payments and interest deductibility of the mortgage, but a narrower range of mortgage financing options may exist for cooperative owners compared to condominium owners who make their own deals with lenders. Second, condominium unit owners face unrestricted rights of disposition, whereas shareholders of cooperatives often face limitations, such as a requirement to sell back shares to the corporation at the original purchase price. In New York City, cooperative sellers sometimes pay a percentage of profits on sales to the corporation.

INDIRECT CO-OWNERSHIP FORMS

Tenancy in partnership. Under common law, partnerships exist by agreement between two or more parties desiring to conduct business together. However, common law partnerships do not constitute legal entities. Thus, the partners must own the real estate used in a partnership business as either tenants in common (the usual case) or in joint tenancy.

With the adoption of the Uniform Partnership Act in almost every state, partnerships may hold title to real estate in an estate called the **tenancy in partnership**. In this arrangement, partners share partnership properties equally, partnership interests may not transfer without the consent of the other partners, partnership properties have an exemption from rights of dower and curtesy, and, unlike a tenancy in common, partners may not divide properties among themselves until the claims of partnership creditors are satisfied. Moreover, when partnerships dissolve, the real estate must be sold. Although the Uniform Partnership Act defines the co-ownership rights in real estate under tenancy in partnership, specific rights and responsibilities of partners, such as the rights to cash flows and tax losses, management responsibilities, and personal liability for partnership debts, appear in partnership agreements.

The two most common types of partnership forms include general partnerships, created among two or more parties to own real estate in which each partner has personal liability for partnership debts, and limited partnerships. In the latter type of partnership, two classes of partners exist: general partners and limited partners. General partners take on the role of the business managers, while limited partners provide most of the money, have *no* active involvement in the operation of the real estate, and do *not* incur personal liability for partnership debts.[7]

Corporations.[8] Real estate corporations, like other corporations, are chartered under state law and, for federal income tax purposes, must follow the Internal Revenue Code. The traditional corporate form, the C-corporation, offers stockholders limited liability (there is no personal liability for debts of the corporation) but has some disadvantageous tax features for stockholders, primarily double taxation. An alternative corporate form, the S-corporation, limits shareholders' liability and has more tax advantages, but applies only to smaller firms with fewer than 35 shareholders. Another alternative form, the limited liability corporation, offers investors limited liability and single taxation without burdensome restrictions.

As legal entities, corporations own and operate real estate independently of their shareholders. The shareholders retain indirect co-ownership in proportion to the number of shares they own.

Real estate investment trusts (REITs). As discussed in Chapter 5, these trusts function as mutual funds for investment in real estate or mortgages. Technically, a trust is an arrangement in which one party holds property for the benefit of others. REITs borrow funds to acquire real estate or make mortgage loans and then sell shares of the real estate or mortgage portfolio, thus holding real property or mortgages in trust for shareholders. The indirect ownership rights to real estate or mortgages of REIT shareholders resemble those of shareholders in corporations.

---

[7]This means that if the liabilities of the partnership exceed its assets, creditors cannot collect by placing liens on the assets (e.g., automobile or stereo) of limited partners.

[8]Chapter 5 contains a detailed discussion of the advantages and disadvantages of these ownership forms for investment purposes.

EXHIBIT 20-5

PUBLIC AND PRIVATE LIMITATIONS ON PROPERTY RIGHTS

Public Limitations	Definition of Right
Police power	The inherent right (power) of government(s) to limit the activities of private entities to protect the general public's health, safety, and welfare.
Eminent domain	The right of government (Fifth Amendment) to take private real property for a public purpose after paying just compensation to the owners.
Taxation	The right of government to raise revenue through assessments against private property according to constitutional and statutory law.
Escheat	The right of government to take title to the property of a person who dies without a will or legal heirs.
Private Limitations	
Easement	A right transferred by private contract that gives an entity other than the owner of property the ability to make specific use of some part of that property.
Restrictive covenant (deed restrictions)	A limitation on the use of real property created by language in the deed at the time ownership is transferred.
Lien	A legal claim against the property by an entity other than the owner that if not satisfied can be enforced in the courts to force sale of the property (e.g., tax lien, mortgage lien, mechanic's lien).

PUBLIC AND PRIVATE LIMITS ON PROPERTY RIGHTS

Thus far, this chapter has concentrated on the ways of assembling and dividing physical, legal, and co-ownership rights to real estate. Now the focus shifts to the creation of limits to legal and physical rights of real estate ownership. Two sources limit the rights of real estate owners. First, governments impose limitations on property rights, specifically on the use of property. Second, private contracts, such as easements and deeds, may limit the rights of real estate owners. Because many of the limitations emanating from governments and private contracts involve rights of use and possession of real estate, they may significantly affect real estate values. Therefore, the set of public and private limitations discussed next is an integral part of the analysis of each real estate transaction. A summary of the public and private limitations that may affect the rights of real estate owners appears in Exhibit 20–5.

GOVERNMENT'S ROLE IN DEFINING REAL PROPERTY RIGHTS

Government power to impose limitations on the rights of private property owners comes from the United States Constitution and state constitutions. Many of these powers pass to local governments. These powers exist to protect the public welfare, raise revenues, and provide public facilities. Resolutions of disputes between private property owners and public agencies in the courts play a significant role in defining real property rights.

Police power.   **Police power** represents the inherent right of government to control the activities of people and companies to protect the health, safety, moral character, and general welfare. For example, a city government may have an ordinance outlawing the discharge of firearms within city limits.

The police power extends to real estate in several interrelated ways. Land-use planning and zoning systems found in the majority of communities represent the most direct applications of the police power. These systems, discussed in Chapter 10, regulate matters such as the height of buildings, the density of development (units per acre), the location of shopping areas, and the types of business activities conducted in single-family homes. Land-use and zoning regulations exist to protect the public by eliminating the opportunities of owners to use land and improvements in ways that might harm others. Placing shopping areas along major highways and away from residential areas, for example, represents an attempt to keep traffic volumes low in residential areas, minimizing potential hazards to children.

Local government housing codes restrict the number of persons that can inhabit housing units, require that housing units be kept in good repair, and establish minimum lighting and ventilation requirements. The authority for these codes comes under the police power of protecting the general public from the nuisances and problems of overcrowding and protecting the health and safety of the residents. Similarly, local building codes set construction standards for the community's buildings and subdivisions. These codes also fall under the police power to prevent harm to the general public as a result of builder or developer negligence.

Economists refer to the actions of one member of society that inflict physical, psychological, or economic harm on others as an *external cost* or *negative externality*. In this context, the police power provisions, especially land-use and zoning controls, seek to prevent or control negative externalities.

Taxation.   Another power of the states that passes to local governments involves the power to levy taxes on real property. The proceeds from the *ad valorem* ("toward value") real property tax and personal property tax go toward financing local government operations such as schools, libraries, and street improvements. The power of taxation represents a limitation on real estate ownership rights because if property owners fail to pay the property taxes, local governments may exercise their powers to have property sold at tax foreclosure sales. Chapter 21 focuses on the subject of real property taxation.

Eminent domain.   Under the power of **eminent domain**, governments and their agencies have the right to force private property owners to sell their properties for just compensation if these properties are needed for a public purpose (e.g., a highway or recreation area). Usually, the implementing public agency offers the property owner what it considers just compensation for the property being taken. The property owner has two options: either to accept the initial offer or to go through formal condemnation proceedings in which just compensation will be decided in court, usually with the aid of two or more real estate appraisals.

Escheat.   The system of land tenure in the United States requires that each parcel of property be owned by either a private or public entity. If a property owner dies without a will or any known heirs, after attempts are made to locate all legal heirs, the property goes to the owner of last resort, the state, via the power of escheat. When this unusual series of events occurs, the property returns to private ownership via public sale.

PRIVATE CONTRACTS AND OTHER LIMITATIONS ON PROPERTY RIGHTS

In addition to the set of publicly imposed limitations on the rights of real estate ownership, the actions of property owners and other parties may create limits. Even the actions of previous owners can impose restrictions on the rights of current owners. The main sources of privately created limitations on property rights include easements, restrictive covenants, and liens.

Easements.   When owners of real estate give or sell easements to others, they give up rights to use all or part of properties for specific purposes. Easements, therefore, generally involve rights of use and are granted for specific purposes. In some instances, holders of easements possess the right to convey or transfer their easement as well.

The most common form of easement, the **easement in gross** (also known as *commercial easement,* creates a set of personal rights that "run" with the *user* because the party granted the right must use land for a specific purpose. An example of an easement in gross appears in Exhibit 20–6. The Joneses recently purchased a residence on a one-acre lot. Subsequently, they discovered that the previous owners, the Martins, negotiated an easement in gross with the electric utility company so that wires could be installed along the road. The easement of the utility company involves a right to use a particular part of the Joneses' property in a specific manner.

Conventional practice establishes that easements with utility companies renew automatically with any new owner of the fee simple estate (in our example, the Joneses) and easily transfers, say to another utility company, as long as the purpose for which the property is used remains the same. Had the Martins sold an easement to an advertising firm to maintain a billboard on the edge of the property, for example, the easement in gross would have to be renegotiated by the advertising firm with the Joneses. In addition, the advertising firm could not sell or otherwise convey its right to use the property for a billboard to any other entity.

The second type of easement, the **easement appurtenant**, involves nonpersonal rights that "run" with the *land.* Exhibit 20–7 shows the Jones homestead and the Smiths' parcel, immediately to the rear and located on a lake. While examining the property for purchase from the Martins, the Joneses discovered the Martins had negotiated a 30-foot easement through the property that allows the Smiths to use this strip of land for access to the public road. This arrangement established an easement appurtenant in which the Joneses have the servient estate and the Smiths have the **dominant estate**. When the Joneses purchased the fee simple estate from the Martins, this servient estate transferred with the title to the land. This easement indefinitely remains a limitation on the property

EXHIBIT 20 - 6

ILLUSTRATION OF EASEMENT IN GROSS

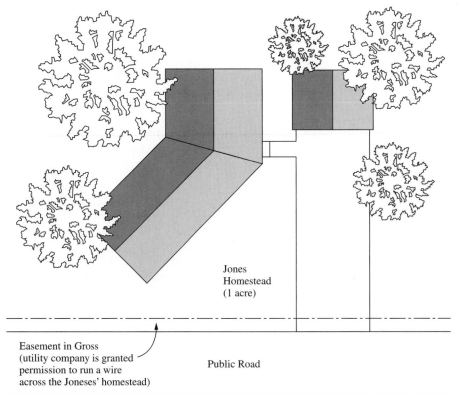

Jones
Homestead
(1 acre)

Easement in Gross
(utility company is granted
permission to run a wire
across the Joneses' homestead)

Public Road

rights of owners of the parcel unless legal action occurs to remove the easement, the Smiths abandon the easement, or the two properties become merged under one title.

Easements and related nonpossessory property rights take on other forms. These forms, which appear in Exhibit 20–8, include license, **easement by implication**, **easement by necessity**, and **easement by prescription**.

Restrictive covenants. Deeds, as discussed in Chapter 22, are legal instruments used to convey title to property. Recording of deeds in the county courthouse provides evidence of the transfers of title. Sometimes owners of real property desire to impose limitations on the use of the property by future owners. They do so at the time of sale of the property by including **restrictive covenants** in deeds to property (also known as *deed restrictions*). Legally enforceable restrictions must pass the test of reasonability; a covenant cannot state, for example, that only a nuclear bomb factory can operate on the land being deeded. Also, they must not violate public policy; for example, a covenant cannot state that certain minority groups can never own the land being deeded.

EXHIBIT 20-7

ILLUSTRATION OF AN EASEMENT APPURTENANT

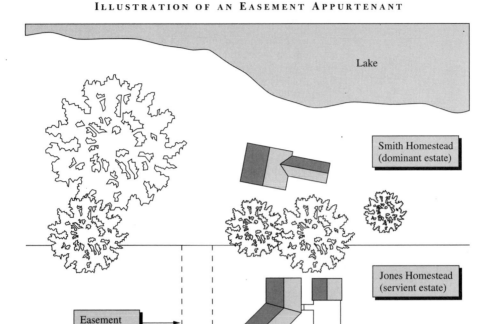

Although deed restrictions occur in a wide variety of situations, they most commonly arise in two instances. First, adjacent property restrictions often appear in deeds. Suppose Farmer Brown suddenly finds that the family farm has become quite valuable for commercial development. He divides the farm into two parcels, as shown in Exhibit 20–9, and sells the parcel nearest the city to real estate developers. He plans to retire with his family on the other parcel. To maintain a view of the city and a tranquil atmosphere for his retirement, Farmer Brown includes a set of restrictive covenants in the deed to the parcel being sold. The most important covenant states, "Use of this land is restricted to single-family residences on no less than one-acre lots and of no more than one story in height." These restrictions lower the price developers will pay for the land, but they ensure that the land will not be developed for any use that might disturb Farmer Brown's retirement.

E X H I B I T 2 0 - 8

A D D I T I O N A L N O N P O S S E S S I O N A R Y P R O P E R T Y R I G H T S

Right	Example in Use
License	X gives Y the right to fish in X's pond. This right can be given verbally and can be revoked at any time.
Easement by implication	X and Y own adjoining lots. A drain located on Y's property carries water away from X's property. If Y conveys her property to Z, there is no need to include specified statements about the drain in the transfer of title. The easement is implied.
Easement by necessity	X buys a landlocked parcel from Y who had divided a larger parcel into two parts. One part includes all frontage to the road, and the back parcel, purchased by X, has no frontage. X, therefore, is entitled to an easement by necessity through the front parcel.
Easement by prescription	For years, X used Y's land for a trail to a lake nearby instead of walking around Y's land. X goes to court and is granted an easement by prescription. X was using the trail privately, the usage was adverse to Y, and a long period of usage had been established (the number of years varies from state to state).

E X H I B I T 2 0 - 9

R E S T R I C T I V E C O V E N A N T O N A N A D J A C E N T P A R C E L

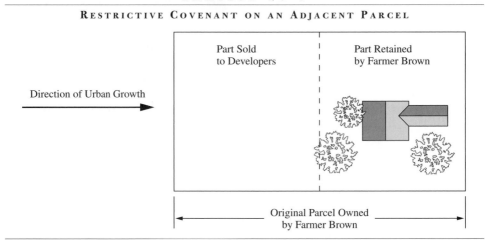

The second situation involving the use of restrictive covenants occurs in conjunction with the development of new residential subdivisions. General plan restrictions attempt to create quality residential atmospheres. They extend beyond the existing zoning requirements. For example, a developer may deed lots in a subdivision with a covenant stating, "Trucks or any large vehicles must be parked in a garage and cannot be parked on the street or in the driveway." Once the subdivision has sold out, these covenants become enforced through court actions taken by residents seeking relief through injunctions against violators.

Lien.   This restriction involves the right of a creditor to petition the court to force repayment of a debt through foreclosure and sale of real or other property. Specific **liens** are the rights of creditors against specific real property; general liens are rights of creditors against all assets of the party. Examples of specific liens include (1) tax liens against property (actually part of the power of taxation, a public limitation), (2) mortgage liens borrowers give to lenders on real property, and (3) mechanic's and materialman's liens, the rights of those who provide labor and materials for real property improvements (e.g., carpenters, plumbers, and landscape architects).

Purchasers of real property should make certain of the removal of all prior liens prior to making a commitment to purchase because liens represent rights to foreclosure against the property. In essence, liens limit real property rights because they represent property rights given up by the owner.

SUMMARY

This chapter analyzes the rights of real estate owners in four ways. First, the market divides and facilitates the exchange of real property rights along physical lines. This means, for example, the rights to use the airspace above the land trade separately from the land itself. Second, the market may carve out one or more of the three fundamental and inherent legal rights of real estate ownership—the right of use and possession, the right of quiet enjoyment, and the right of disposition—into different estates in land The fee simple estate provides an ownership position in which all three of the basic rights remain undisturbed. Other estates have less complete bundles of legal rights.

Third, co-owners may share real property rights. In most instances, co-owners create special sets of rights to facilitate the joint ownership of real estate. Perhaps the best example of such a right involves the right of survivorship in the joint tenancy form.

Finally, the public, through governments, imposes limitations on real property rights to protect the public welfare, raise taxes, and provide public facilities. Limitations also occur as the result of past and current private contracts. An examination of these limitations represents a crucial part of evaluating any real estate deal because public and private restrictions affect the values of real estate.

KEY TERMS

Bundle of rights 615
Community property 627
Condominium 628
Cooperative 629
Easement appurtenant 633
Easement by implication 634
Easement by necessity 634
Easement by prescription 634
Easement in gross 633
Eminent domain 632

Estate for years 625
Fee simple absolute 621
Fixtures 618
Freehold estates 621
Joint tenancy 626
Liens 637
Life estates 623
Periodic tenancy 625
Police power 632
Property rights 615

Real property 615
Restrictive covenants 634
Right of survivorship 627
Riparian rights 617
Tenancy at sufferance, 625
Tenancy at will 625
Tenancy in common 627
Tenancy in partnership 629

TEST YOURSELF

Answer the following multiple choice questions.

1. An easement in gross is said to
   a. Follow a riverbed.
   b. Carry no legal rights.
   c. "Run with" the party granted the easement.
   d. "Run with" the land.
   e. "Run with" the wrong crowd.

2. Which of the following is *not* a public limitation on the rights of owners of real estate?
   a. Easement.
   b. Police power.
   c. Eminent domain.
   d. Taxation.
   e. Escheat.

3. Which of the following tests used by the courts to determine the existence of a fixture is the most important?
   a. Annexation test.
   b. Relation-of-the-parties test.
   c. Intent test.
   d. Adaptation test.
   e. Smoking-gun test.

4. Restrictions against ownership of land by non-resident aliens
   a. Are so burdensome that foreigners are prohibited from owning land in the United States.
   b. Are largely determined by state laws, which vary widely from state to state.
   c. Are practically nonexistent.
   d. Have changed only slightly during the past 10 years in most states.
   e. Are largely determined by federal laws rather than state laws.

5. In most states, family homes are exempt from the actions of creditors under
   a. Dower rights.
   b. Tenancy at sufferance estates.
   c. Curtesy rights.
   d. Joint tenancy estates.
   e. Homestead laws.

6. In disputes over property, courts look for the following "unities" to establish the existence of joint tenancy:
   a. Unities of merit, title, interest, and possession.
   b. Unities of time, title, interest, and possession.
   c. Unities of time, structure, title, and interest.
   d. Unities of possession, title, time, and financing.
   e. Unities of financing, time, title, and interest.

7. A legal claim against property by a party other than the owner who can force the sale of property if the claim is not satisfied is
   a. An easement.
   b. Eminent domain.
   c. A joint tenancy.
   d. A lien.
   e. A tenancy in common.

8. Some states follow an "ownership-in-place" concept that allows landowners to sell the physical rights to oil and gas separate from other physical rights. Other states
   a. Have laws controlling the amounts of oil and gas that can be sold.
   b. Have laws allowing only certain parties to purchase oil and gas rights.
   c. Have laws granting landowners rights only to control access to oil and gas through easement license.
   d. Have laws giving all citizens rights to freely explore for oil and gas.
   e. Allow no exploration for oil and gas.

9. Mr. Evad owns real estate under a fee simple estate. His legal rights in the real estate are
   a. Not subject to public controls.
   b. Not subject to private controls.
   c. Reduced by the extent of his physical rights.
   d. Complete to the extent that the fundamental legal rights are unaltered.
   e. Severely restricted by the conditions imposed under this estate.

10. Rights of survivorship inherent in joint tenancies
   a. Mean that when one owner dies, the legal heirs of that owner are entitled to the property.
   b. Mean that when one owner dies, co-owners are entitled to the deceased's property.
   c. Mean that the state is the legal heir to the property.
   d. Are also inherent in tenancies in common.
   e. Are also inherent in condominiums.

PROBLEMS FOR THOUGHT AND SOLUTION

1. Explain why real estate ownership is often described as a bundle of rights.

2. Distinguish between condominium and cooperative ownership by defining each in terms of their underlying estates and ownership forms.

3. What property rights are created and limited by easements?

4. In nonfreehold or leasehold estates, tenants can become tenants at will and tenants at sufferance. Why is it important to landlords to have an unwanted tenant declared by the court to be a tenant at sufferance?

5. What is the relationship between property rights in land granted by society and the value of the land?

CASE PROBLEMS

1. Two years ago you purchased a wonderful parcel of land for development as luxury condominiums. While allowing the market to ripen for this development, the county passed a zoning ordinance designating your parcel for community open space. What are the conflicting principles of public limitations on property rights that this situation raises?

2. You grant your roommate title to land you own in fee simple for as long as your roommate remains enrolled in college. Once your roommate is no longer enrolled, you regain title without taking any action. What estate in this land do you hold? What estate does your roommate hold?

ADDITIONAL READINGS

These books contain chapters with detailed discussion of real property rights:

French, William B., and Harold F. Lusk. *Law of the Real Estate Business.* Homewood, IL: Richard D. Irwin, 1984, Chapters 2–4 and 6–8.

Gibson, Frank, James Karp, and Elliot Klayman. *Real Estate Law.* Chicago: Dearborn Financial Publishing, 1992, Chapters 2–7.

Werner, Raymond J., and Robert Kratovil, *Real Estate Law.* Englewood Cliffs, NJ: Prentice Hall, 1993, Chapters 2–4.

An excellent book about legal systems in the world, including different ways of viewing real property rights, is

David, René, and John E. C. Brierley. *Major Legal Systems in the World Today.* London: Stevens and Sons, 1985.

The following periodicals regularly contain useful articles on real property rights:

Journal of Real Estate Law
Real Estate Law Journal

21
CHAPTER

REAL PROPERTY TAXATION

NATURE OF THE TAX ON REAL PROPERTY

A BRIEF HISTORY OF THE PROPERTY TAX IN THE UNITED STATES

MECHANICS OF THE PROPERTY TAX
Determining a Jurisdiction's Budget and Tax Rate
Tax-Exempt Properties
Homestead and Other Exemptions
Calculating Tax Liability
The Effective Tax Rate
Evaluating the Tax on an Individual Property
Special Assessments
Nonpayment of Taxes

CRITERIA FOR EVALUATING THE PROPERTY TAX
Efficiency of the Property Tax
Potential Disadvantages of the Property Tax
Fairness, or Equity, of the Property Tax

SUMMARY

KEY TERMS

TEST YOURSELF

PROBLEMS FOR THOUGHT AND SOLUTION

INTERNET EXERCISES

CASE PROBLEMS

ADDITIONAL READINGS

After reading this chapter, students will be able to:

1. Calculate a community's tax rate, given budgeted expenditures, other income, total assessed value, and the value of exempt properties.

2. Explain why the property tax cannot be used by the federal government to raise revenue.

3. Calculate an individual property owner's tax liability and effective tax rate, given the tax rate, the assessed value, the amount of any exemption, and any applicable percentage.

4. Give at least four reasons why the property tax is considered an efficient tax.

5. Give at least three criteria for evaluating the fairness of the property tax.

6. Calculate the average tax burden, given the tax bills and recent sale prices of several properties.

NATURE OF THE TAX ON REAL PROPERTY

The largest single source of revenue for most local governments is the tax on real estate. Cities, counties, school districts, and other special taxing jurisdictions, such as urban service districts and water management districts, levy real property taxes. These taxes are levied on the owners of real estate in the jurisdiction based on the assessed value of the property owned. Thus, this is called **ad valorem** taxation.

Although the tax liability imposed on owners of real estate may seem burdensome, the revenue raised by the tax generally provides important benefits to the owners. The revenue pays for police and fire protection, schools, streets, curbs, sewers, street lighting, parks, and a number of social services. Without these services, the properties would be worth much less; thus, we may view the property tax as the price of higher property values. Nevertheless, the property tax, like other taxes, may be levied unfairly or unwisely, which tends to lower property values.

The property tax is popular with local governments because it can raise large amounts of revenue and may not be used by the federal government. The United States Constitution (Section 9) effectively prohibits a federal property tax by the following provision: "No capitation or other direct tax shall be laid, unless in proportion to the census or enumeration herein before directed to be taken."

In other words, the federal government may not levy a tax that is not borne *equally* by every person. Although taxes on incomes were specifically exempted from this requirement by the 16th Amendment, ratified in 1913, the requirement applies to all other taxes. The property tax does not meet this criterion because property owners pay different amounts based on the different values of their properties.

REAL ESTATE FOCUS 21-1, INTERNATIONAL

Property Taxation in Other Countries

Almost every country has a property tax. For most countries, however, the property tax is a relatively less important source of revenue than in the United States, averaging from 1 to 3 percent of the total tax revenue from all sources, while in the United States and other English-speaking countries, the percentage is around 9 percent. Property tax administration varies greatly from country to country, with some countries (such as Denmark, South Africa, and Argentina) taxing land only. Most countries, like the United States, tax both land and improvements, but the taxable value may be determined by a criterion other than market value. In the Netherlands, for example, municipalities can elect to use either area or market value as the criterion, although the trend is toward market value.

In many countries the property tax is based on a combination of factors that may have some relationship to the property's market value (such as size and type of property), although the criterion is not market value. Even in western European countries with market-based economies, the property tax is typically determined by broad categories of factors that may not relate closely to value differences among specific properties.

In Italy, for example, which has a property tax system similar to several other European countries (such as France, Spain, and Great Britain), each property is registered in a "cadastre," an official register of the quantity, value, and ownership of real estate. Values of properties are determined by an imputed, or hypothetical, amount of income the property *would* or *should* produce, whether it is rented or not. This income is then multiplied by a coefficient specified in the national law for each property type. After the tax value is established, a municipality may tax the property for three purposes:

1. A general municipal tax. This tax can vary by law between 4 percent and 6 percent of the cadastral value. It is levied on both residential and income-producing properties.

2. A tax on properties used in businesses, arts, and professions (nonresidential properties). This tax depends on the size and characteristics of the property and the type of enterprise, art, or profession using the property. The tax must also be paid on property that is rented for these activities.

3. A tax for the elimination of solid wastes. This tax is based on the average quantity and quality of waste and rubbish produced on the property, the use to which the real estate is put, and the cost of rubbish disposal.

SOURCES: International Association of Assessing Officers, *Property Appraisal and Assessment Administration* (Chicago: IAAO, 1990), Chapter 1; Giovanni Rolle, *Lo Schema del Sistema delle Tasse Italiane (An Overview of the Italian Tax System)*, unpublished paper, 1995.

In contrast, the national governments of most other countries determine the property tax rate, although local governments may actually levy and collect the tax (see Real Estate Focus 21–1). The property tax in these countries is counted as an important component of national fiscal and economic policy, just as the federal income tax in the United States. A good example of the role of the property tax in national economic policy making is described in Real Estate Focus 21–2.

REAL ESTATE FOCUS 21-2, INTERNATIONAL

The Property Tax as a Tool of Economic Policy in Japan

In late 1995 Japan's ruling coalition parties agreed on a tax policy for 1996 that would cut in half a key property tax. Although the government expected the plan to reduce government revenues by almost $100 billion, the step was regarded as crucial to revival of the real estate market and the national economy.

The tax that was cut was introduced in 1992 to end the speculative frenzy in Japan's property market. This tax apparently worked well; over the next two to three years property values plummeted by 60 percent or more, hampering economic expansion and wreaking havoc on bank balance sheets. It was hoped that the cut in the tax would have effects of a similar magnitude on the positive side.

SOURCE: *The Wall Street Journal,* December 18, 1995, p. A11.

A BRIEF HISTORY OF THE PROPERTY TAX IN THE UNITED STATES

The U.S. property tax system was derived from the English system, which existed in various forms long before the European settlement of North America. In the British colonies of North America five types of taxes were in common use.[1]

1. Poll (capitation or head) taxes were flat-rate taxes levied on all adult males and sometimes on slaves of either sex.
2. Property taxes were levied on specific items (such as land, farm animals, and even slaves) enumerated in the law, usually at an arbitrary rate specified in the law that typically was not related to market value.
3. Faculty taxes were imposed on the potential earning capacity (faculty) of persons in certain trades or having certain skills. Note that the tax was levied on a person's estimated *ability* to earn, not on actual earnings.
4. Import taxes were levied on goods exported from or imported to the colony.
5. Excise taxes were applied to specified items for consumption, particularly liquor.

As revenue needs increased during the Revolutionary War the tax burden increased, particularly on the politically weak; the classes owning land were generally favored. The inequities grew to the point of rebellion in some jurisdictions, and gradually the idea that taxes should be levied and paid on the basis of the value of one's possessions became accepted. The ownership of property was seen as an indication of one's ability to pay.

---

[1]Glenn W. Fisher, *The Worst Tax? A History of the Property Tax in America*, (Lawrence, KS: University Press of Kansas, 1996), p. 13.

All forms of property were included in the early property taxes, intangibles (paper assets) and other types of personal property as well as real property. Problems began early, however, for the taxation of intangibles and other personal property. They could be hidden or moved from place to place in order to escape enumeration on the specified tax day. Additionally, the taxation of some types of intangibles produced double taxation of wealth. For example, a mortgage on real property has value because it represents an interest in the property; however, its value is based on the property's value, which is already taxed. Thus, the property was, in effect, being taxed twice.

Because of these types of conceptual problems and the administrative problems of finding and valuing intangibles and other types of personal property, most states no longer tax *residential* personal property. However, many states continue to tax personal property (furniture and equipment) used in businesses, professions, or other income-producing ventures. Some states have a separate tax on intangibles such as publicly traded securities that are purchased and held by a third party, for example, a brokerage company. The third party pays the tax and then passes it on to the owner-client.

The property tax today is controlled and regulated by the states, with the administrative responsibility delegated or reserved by state constitution to local jurisdictions, in most cases counties. An elected official called the County Tax Assessor or County Property Appraiser is the administrative officer for the property tax in each county, and it is his or her responsibility to estimate the taxable values of all nonexempt real properties (the tax base) in the county. As discussed in the following section, the tax rate to be applied to the tax base is determined by the elected officials of the jurisdictions in the county that have the power to levy taxes.

MECHANICS OF THE PROPERTY TAX

Several jurisdictions within which a property is located may levy property taxes simultaneously. A property owner, for example, may pay property taxes to support the budget of a city, a county, a school district, and a special taxing district (*e.g.*, a downtown redevelopment area). Determining a property owner's tax liability requires a general understanding of property-tax mechanics such as tax rates, exemptions, and special assessments, as well as the requirements for each jurisdiction.

DETERMINING A JURISDICTION'S BUDGET AND TAX RATE

A jurisdiction's **tax rate** is established by the percentage of budgeted expenditures to the jurisdiction's **tax base**. The budget for expenditures is determined by accumulating the proposed expenditures of each unit within the jurisdiction—for example, the police department, the utilities department, the planning and zoning office, the cultural affairs office, the street maintenance department, and the social services department. As each department estimates its needed expenditures for the coming fiscal year, it considers the level of services provided in previous years, the level of services it believes is needed for the coming year, new or replacement equipment needed, and additional employees that may be needed. The departments may also be under guideline constraints, such as a directive not to increase budgets more than a specified percentage (*e.g.*, 5 percent).

The jurisdiction's overall administrative staff (usually supervised by an elected mayor or a professional city or county manager) reviews the individual units' budgets and may revise them for consistency with general objectives and priorities. The staff also estimates revenues to be obtained from *nontax* sources such as license fees, inspection fees, garbage removal fees, fines, intergovernmental transfers (*e.g.*, when a city sells fire protection services to the county), and profits from subsidiary operations (*e.g.*, when a city owns a utility company that earns a profit).

The proposed budget, including projected expenditures and nontax revenue sources, is then presented to the elected governing board of the jurisdiction (*e.g.*, a city council or a city or county commission) for approval. Since the tax base (which consists of all the jurisdiction's taxable properties) is known, approval of the budget requires approval of the tax rate. Thus, presentation of the budget in public hearings often provokes political debate over budget items and tax rates. The governing board may then approve, modify, or reject the proposed budget. Usually the budget is approved, possibly with some modifications, and it serves as the financial plan for the coming fiscal year.

Given a jurisdiction's budget, the basic formula for determining the tax rate is

$$R_T = (E_B - I_O)/(V_T - V_X)$$

where

R_T = Tax rate
E_B = Budgeted expenditures
I_O = Income from sources other than the property tax
V_T = Total assessed value of all properties
V_X = Value of exempt properties

As an example, consider a community's budget, which forecasts expenditures for the coming year of $50 million. Nonproperty-tax income is forecast to be $10 million, and the community contains properties with a total value of $2.5 billion. The total taxable value of properties exempt from the property tax is $500 million. The tax rate would be established by the following calculation:

$$R_T = (\$50{,}000{,}000 - \$10{,}000{,}000)/(\$2{,}500{,}000{,}000 - \$500{,}000{,}000)$$
$$R_T = 0.020 \text{ or } 2.0 \text{ percent}$$

In other words, 2 percent of the value of all taxable properties in the community is required in taxes to pay for the community's expenditures during the coming year. Instead of percentages, however, tax rates are usually stated in **mills**, or dollars per $1,000 of value. Converted to mills, the tax rate, or **millage rate**, for the above community would be 20 mills. (To obtain mills, the decimal point is moved one place to the right to convert from percentage or three places to the right to convert from decimals.)

TAX-EXEMPT PROPERTIES

Most communities contain a number of **tax-exempt** properties. Such properties include government-owned properties and others exempted by state law or the state constitution. This category typically includes universities, schools, hospitals, and places of worship.

Exempt properties lower the tax base of the community, thus raising the taxes of other property owners. Tax-exempt properties require public services, such as police and fire protection, and sometimes house families that use schools, roads, sewers, and all other public services. When military bases affect a local community, the federal government makes payments in lieu of taxes to the community to defray the costs of such services. Similarly, housing agencies may make such payments for public housing projects.

While public opinion generally favors tax exemption for churches and synagogues, their related enterprises sometimes create controversy over a claimed tax exemption. How much business activity should a church or synagogue be allowed before losing its tax exemption? Ongoing profit-making ventures will probably subject a religious organization to demands that its property be taxed.

HOMESTEAD AND OTHER EXEMPTIONS

Some states allow homeowners to deduct a specified amount from their assessed valuations before calculating their property tax bills. The largest of these is the **homestead exemption**. In these states, if the property owner occupies a home as the family's principal residence and has lived in the state for a required period (usually one year), the property is regarded as the family's homestead. For example, in Florida, homeowners who have lived in the state for at least one year may apply for the homestead tax exemption for their principal residences. If they qualify, $25,000 will be deducted from the assessed valuation before their taxes are calculated.

Many states also allow property tax exemptions for disabled persons, veterans, widows, and blind persons. The value of all such exemptions must be subtracted from the total value of properties in calculating a community's tax base. Obviously, homestead and other types of exemptions result in higher taxes for those who are not eligible for the exemptions. They represent subsidies by some property-owning taxpayers to other property owners. Clearly the homestead exemption is a subsidy to encourage and reward home ownership.

Since these exemptions are available to homeowners but not to renters, the question of their fairness may be raised. If the owners of apartment units charge higher rents to cover the taxes (as they must do ultimately to remain in business), tenants must pay higher rents than they would if the apartment owners received the same tax reduction that homeowners received and competitive market pressures forced them to pass the savings along to the tenants. The inequity is compounded by the fact that most renters have lower incomes than most homeowners; thus, many lower-income renters may pay proportionately higher property taxes than higher income homeowners.

Another issue regarding the homestead exemption is that some homeowners with low assessed property values (particularly in rural areas) pay little or no property tax.

Since these homeowners often require city or county services to the same (and sometimes greater) extent as taxpaying homeowners, the tax rate must be higher than it would be if all homeowners paid some tax.

CALCULATING TAX LIABILITY

The **tax assessor** (or county property appraiser) appraises all taxable properties in a jurisdiction for property tax assessment. The value for taxation, or **assessed value**, is always related to market value, with some states specifying that the assessed value must be calculated as some percentage less than 100 percent of market value, such as 50 percent or 80 percent. Many states today, however, require that assessed values be 100 percent of market values as defined in the law or as interpreted by a state agency, such as the Department of Revenue. For example, assessed value may be defined or interpreted as market value less the costs of making a property ready for sale and less a normal real estate commission. Thus, the assessed value, while nominally representing 100 percent of market value, is really perhaps 90 to 94 percent of market value, assuming that the market value is estimated accurately by the property tax assessor (or property appraiser). After the property value for tax purposes is determined, the tax rate is multiplied times the value, less any applicable exemptions, to determine the amount of tax owed.

As an example, consider a property appraised for $100,000 in a state that requires tax assessments to be 80 percent of market value. Thus, the assessed value for tax purposes is $80,000. The owner qualifies for a $5,000 homestead exemption. The principal taxing jurisdictions where the property is located have established tax rates as follows:

County	0.0075 (7.5 mills)
City	0.0080 (8.0 mills)
School district	0.0064 (6.4 mills)
Total	0.0219 (21.9 mills)

The property owner's tax bill would be

$$(\$80,000 - 5,000) \times 0.0219 = \$1,642.50$$

If the property owner did not qualify for the homestead exemption, the tax liability would be

$$\$80,000 \times 0.0219 = \$1,752.00$$

Thus, the value of the homestead exemption in terms of property taxes saved is $1,752.00 - \$1,642.50 = \$109.50$, or $0.0219 \times \$5,000 = \$109.50$.

THE EFFECTIVE TAX RATE

A property owner's **effective tax rate** is an important calculation for comparison purposes. It is defined as the amount of tax paid (or owed) divided by the market value of the property. The effective tax rate for this property is 1.64 percent ($1,642.50/$100,000).

EXHIBIT 21-1

TAX BURDEN ANALYSIS

	Property				
	A	**B**	**C**	**D**	**Subject**
Tax liability, 1997	$ 1,000	$ 1,150	$ 975	$ 1,050	$ 1,200
Recent sale price or value	92,500	112,000	98,000	105,000	100,000
Effective tax rate	1.08%	1.03%	0.99%	1.00%	1.20%

$\bar{x}$ (mean) = 1.06%

Generally, taxes among properties and among taxing jurisdictions are compared on an effective rate basis.

EVALUATING THE TAX ON AN INDIVIDUAL PROPERTY

In evaluating tax consistency among properties, a **tax burden analysis** is often useful. This study compares the effective tax rates of similar properties. Suppose Joe Takhomasak is thinking about purchasing a house for $100,000. He finds several similar properties in the same neighborhood that sold recently, and he calculates their tax burdens to compare them with the tax burden of the property he is considering purchasing (the subject property). The tax liability, sale price or value, and effective tax rates for the subject and comparable properties are shown in Exhibit 21–1.

This analysis shows that the tax burden for the subject property is higher than the average for similar properties, which is 1.06 percent. Thus, Joe might decide to offer less for the property and would attempt to have the tax reduced if he is successful in purchasing the property. It appears that he would have a good chance of getting the tax reduced to about $1,060.

Taxpayers who wish to contest their tax assessments should first appeal to the county tax assessor or property appraiser. If they are not satisfied with the decision of the assessor, they may appeal to a *tax* or *property-appraisal appeals board* (sometimes called a *board of equalization*). Finally, appeals can be carried to the court system if the taxpayer is not satisfied with the decisions by the administrative agencies (see Real Estate Focus 21–3 and Real Estate Focus 21–5).

SPECIAL ASSESSMENTS

Another form of the property tax is sometimes levied to finance public improvements. Properties adjacent to the improvements may be charged a portion of the total cost (*e.g.*, 50 or 75 percent), with the community paying the remainder of the cost. Such taxes are termed **special assessments** and are typically used to finance streets, gutters, sewers, and sidewalks.

Special assessments will not be upheld by the courts if the improvements do not increase the value of the properties. For example, homeowners cannot be required to pay for widening a street when it results in increased traffic and decreases the properties'

REAL ESTATE FOCUS 21-3

A Successful Tax Appeal

In tendering his decision to reduce the property tax assessment of a nearly vacant 33-story office building in Manhattan's financial district, State Supreme Court Justice Stanley Parness agreed that the market values of buildings in lower Manhattan were in a "free fall" since 1987. "The building that is the subject of the lawsuit, as well as other similar Class B buildings downtown, suffers not only from poor economics, but is functionally obsolete. Tenants, therefore, can find other, more modern buildings for lesser rent."

Although the city's tax assessor conceded that there was little or no sale or leasing market for such buildings, Judge Parness concluded that "rather than recognizing these developing financial problems, the city continued to raise taxes by inflating values."

SOURCE: *Real Estate Forum* 50, no. 2 (February 1995), p. 14.

---

desirability for residential purposes. The same special assessment would probably be legal for commercial properties where increased traffic would be desirable.

Another form of special assessment occurs when a property is located in a special taxing jurisdiction. Suppose a city decides to redevelop its downtown area through substantial investment of public funds for street improvements and parks. Since the property owners in the downtown area will benefit directly from such investments, city administrators establish a special taxing district in the downtown area. Property owners within this district are assessed additional taxes to help pay for these improvements.

NONPAYMENT OF TAXES

Foreclosure for nonpayment of property taxes takes several forms among various states. Typically, lists of delinquent taxpayers are published in a newspaper of general circulation, and the delinquents are given a grace period to pay the taxes plus interest and penalties. This right to pay unpaid taxes plus interest and penalties before public sale and to reclaim full title to the property, like overdue mortgage payments (see Chapter 15), is known as the *equity of redemption*. If the taxes are not paid, the properties may be sold at public auction, with the proceeds first used to pay back taxes. In some states, the original owner has a period of time (up to two years) after the sale to pay all back taxes, interest, and penalties and to reclaim the property. This right is known as *statutory redemption*. In some states, the purchaser obtains title without this liability at time of the public sale.

In certain states (*e.g.*, Florida) taxing jurisdictions sell **tax certificates** for unpaid taxes. The certificates carry a rate of interest determined by public bidding. To avoid losing the property, the owner must pay back the owner of the tax certificate the amounts advanced to pay both the tax and the interest. If the owner does not pay the certificate holder within a certain period (usually two years), the certificate holder may force a public sale of the property. The sale proceeds must be used first to pay off the certificate holder. Of course, the certificate holder may bid for the property, the amount of the certificate plus interest constituting part of the purchase price. Real Estate Focus 21–4 gives the steps

REAL ESTATE FOCUS 21-4

Buying Properties for Delinquent Taxes

The state laws governing tax delinquencies vary a great deal. If you wish to purchase a property for delinquent taxes, you should check the precise requirements for obtaining a tax lien or title in the state where the property is located. In general, however, the steps listed below are representative of the requirements that should be followed:

1. Check the list of properties that have delinquent taxes in the local newspaper. (You can call the county tax collector's office to find out when the list is published.)

2. Decide on a property you would like to buy. (You should check its assessed value, location, condition, and other liens against it.)

3. Appear at the auction where the properties or tax certificates are to be sold. Be prepared to pay the amount of the delinquent taxes or the price of the property, plus interest and expenses. The bidder who pays the highest price in states where the properties are sold, or the bidder who will accept the lowest interest rate in states where tax certificates are sold, will obtain either a tax deed to the property, a lien on the property, or the tax certificate.

4. In states selling tax certificates and in states having statutory redemption, the delinquent taxpayer can redeem the property by paying back the price of the property, the amount of the lien, or the amount of the tax certificate—plus all interest and expenses. This period of redemption runs for one or two years.

5. After the required period of time (one or two years), you (the tax lien or certificate holder) can ask for a tax deed or a public sale. In states that give a tax deed at this time, the property is yours.

6. In states that hold a public sale at this time, you can bid for the property. Any bid superior to yours must be sufficient to pay back the full amount of the tax lien or certificate plus all accrued interest and expenses.

7. If you are the successful bidder, you will receive title to the property by means of a tax deed. If there are no other bidders, of course, you will obtain title for the amount of the unpaid taxes, interest, and expenses.

8. Once title to the property is transferred by tax deed, all other liens against the property—including mortgages—are wiped out with the exception of government liens.

that someone must follow in order to buy a property for which the taxes have not been paid.

CRITERIA FOR EVALUATING THE PROPERTY TAX

As with all taxes, we may evaluate the property tax on the basis of two criteria—*efficiency* and *equity (fairness)*. *Efficiency* pertains to the ability to raise large amounts of revenue quickly and at relatively low cost through a tax. *Equity* refers to the equal taxation of property owners who are in comparable ownership positions.

Efficiency of the Property Tax

Several characteristics of the property tax contribute to its efficiency as a source of revenue for local governments:

- The property tax is capable of raising large amounts of revenue because the tax base is large.
- The object of the tax is fixed in location; it cannot be moved or hidden to avoid taxation.
- Owners of private property can be identified relatively easily; if the owners of a parcel of real estate cannot be found, title to the property reverts to the state.
- The value of properties for tax purposes can be established relatively easily by common appraisal procedures.
- The property tax discourages land hoarding. Unused land produces no income, but is subject to property taxes; therefore, landowners are not likely to leave valuable land unused.
- The federal government is effectively precluded from levying a property tax, and state governments rely primarily on other taxes such as sales and income taxes.
- The amount of revenue raised tends to keep up with inflation, since property values generally increase with inflation.

Potential Disadvantages of the Property Tax

The efficiency criterion also can be applied to analyze the *effect* of the tax on the property tax base—property values. From this standpoint, four main disadvantages of the property tax have been cited.

Increases in property taxes decrease property values. Property tax increases may reduce property values, individually and in total for a community. This process is called **tax capitalization**—the conversion of a higher stream of future taxes into an immediate reduction in property values. Tax capitalization does not result in a dollar-for-dollar reduction in the market value of affected properties, of course, because the higher taxes will occur in the future, and these amounts must be discounted to a present value, just as future income must be discounted. Furthermore, it may be reasoned that the higher taxes will result in more or better government services, a belief that would serve to offset the extent to which the property value would be reduced.

A study of property tax capitalization in Massachusetts showed the degree of tax capitalization to be approximately 20 percent.[2] The study was conducted after the Massachusetts Supreme Court ordered cities and towns to assess all houses at full market value. The resulting reassessments produced large changes in assessed values and tax

---

[2]John Yinger, *Property Taxes and Housing* (Boston: Academic Press, 1988), Chapter 1.

payments. The researchers studied values for properties that sold twice—once before and once after the revaluations.

The degree of tax capitalization (20 percent) means that about 20 percent of the value of the capitalized tax results in property value reductions. For example, if the property tax increases by $300 per year and the appropriate capitalization rate is 0.10 (10 percent), the value of the property tax is $300/.10 = $3,000. The property value reduction would be .20 × $3,000 = $600. The researchers found that the degree of capitalization varied greatly among cities in the study, ranging from 9 percent to 79 percent, although the cities having the most reliable data showed a range of 16 to 33 percent. The activity level of the market (that is, whether the market tends to be a strong sellers' market or a strong buyers' market) determines the degree of tax capitalization.

Property taxation of improvements inhibits new construction. Perhaps if owners did not have to pay taxes on newly constructed buildings and other improvements, they would construct more improvements. To raise needed revenue in adequate amounts, much of the tax burden would presumably be shifted to the land portion of real estate.

Studies generally have concluded that a single property tax on land could not raise enough revenue to provide the current level of local governmental services. One tax economist, however, has suggested that a relatively larger share of the tax should be levied against the land portion of real estate,[3] while another tax economist has suggested combining a land tax with user charges, especially for congestion and pollution.[4] Given the entrenched practice of taxing both improvements and land at the same percentage of value, it seems unlikely that a major shift away from the taxation of improvements will occur in the foreseeable future.

Property taxation inhibits maintenance and rehabilitation of existing improvements and may lead to abandonment. This criticism is similar to the previous argument against the taxation of improvements: If owners did not anticipate higher taxes resulting from more valuable improvements, they would tend to maintain them in better condition and to rehabilitate them earlier in their economic lives. In some situations, particularly when real estate values are declining (such as the period from 1988 to 1994), the necessity to pay property taxes may lead the owners to abandon some properties. Abandonment usually results when rents and values are declining and property tax assessments are not reduced commensurately. As illustrated in Real Estate Focus 21–3, tax assessors (property appraisers) typically resist lowering assessments when values decline.

It is doubtful that this contention applies to the vast majority of commercial, industrial, office, and middle-to-upper-class residential properties, at least in "normal" eco-

---

[3]James Heilbrun, *The Real Estate Tax and Urban Housing* (New York: Columbia University Press, 1966), p. 169.

[4]Dick Netzer, "Is There Too Much Reliance on the Local Property Tax?" in *Property Tax Reform*, ed. George E. Peterson (Washington, D.C.: John C. Lincoln Institute and Urban Institute, 1973), p. 23.

nomic periods. To the owners of such properties, the tax incidence is a relatively minor consideration,[5] and the value lost by inadequate maintenance or rehabilitation more than offsets increases in property taxes incurred with adequate maintenance and timely rehabilitation.

For the owners of low-income residential properties, however, the property tax is usually a relatively more important annual expense. Rental rates usually cannot be increased to cover increased tax rates, and owner-occupants cannot usually afford any increased housing expenses. Programs of tax abatement on the *additional* values created by rehabilitation of low-income housing might alleviate a significant part of the problem of providing adequate housing for low-income households. Such programs require owners to spend the tax dollars saved on upgraded maintenance or rehabilitation. While additional revenue to the local community would not be obtained, the original tax base would be maintained and revenue would not be lost, as it has been under the existing system.

The property tax may induce premature development of land. This is the opposite point of view to the argument that the property tax discourages the hoarding of land that is ripe for development. This point of view recognizes that it is desirable to keep some unused land in reserve in order to keep urban development flexible. If all land is developed according to a plan, and the plan mistakenly leaves something out, vacant land can be developed to fill the need.

Given the advantages of the property tax for raising revenue for local jurisdictions and the limited disadvantages, we may conclude that the property tax is a relatively *efficient* tax. Although some economic disincentives for new construction, adequate maintenance, and timely rehabilitation are created, they are probably not sufficient to produce serious calls for abandonment of the property tax.

FAIRNESS, OR EQUITY, OF THE PROPERTY TAX

In general, two equity standards can be analyzed to judge the fairness of any tax. **Horizontal equity** requires that members of society in the same economic circumstances pay the same costs and receive the same benefits. **Vertical equity** requires that members of society in different economic circumstances pay different costs and receive different levels of benefits. According to these standards of equity, the property tax burden should be higher for those who can afford to pay more and lower for those who can afford to pay less. The benefits, or services received, should also vary according to the contributions of each taxpayer. Several major criticisms of the property tax have been based on horizontal and vertical equity.

---

[5]A study by Helene A. Cameron showed property tax levels have relatively little impact on locational choices for new industrial plants. Other factors such as labor costs and nearness to raw materials and product markets were shown to be much more important. See "The Effects of the Property Tax on Location of Industrial Plants," *Bulletin of Business Research,* Center for Business and Economic Research, Ohio State University (April 1969).

Property taxation is regressive. This criticism holds that lower-income households pay higher property taxes than higher-income households *relative to their incomes.* Higher-income households do not tend to occupy housing that is proportionately more valuable than lower-income households. For example, households with $500,000 annual incomes might own houses averaging $1 million in value (twice the size of their incomes), whereas $50,000 households might have houses averaging $200,000 in value (four times their incomes). Since the property tax is based on property values, the lower-income households would be paying substantially more property taxes per dollar of income than the higher-income households.

In his landmark study, Netzer concluded that property tax payments tend to be regressive.[6] However, he also found that lower-income taxpayers use locally provided services to a greater extent than higher-income households. Relative to the taxes paid, lower-income households required more police and fire protection and used more school facilities, public health benefits, and public welfare benefits. Netzer concluded that the net result of the property tax, when benefits received are taken into account, is that it is not regressive.

Property taxes are not related to ability to pay. This criticism suggests that the criterion of vertical equity is violated. High-income households may elect to live in modest housing, escaping high levels of the property tax. Other forms of wealth such as securities, savings accounts, and personal property are typically taxed at lower rates than real estate. Lower-income households, on the other hand, may be required by their large families or personal desires to live in larger, relatively more valuable housing. To the extent that real estate is taxed at a higher rate than other forms of property, these lower-income owners are placed at a disadvantage.

The other side of this issue is that homeowners enjoy various tax advantages. Although the earnings of most assets are taxed by the federal government, homeowner-occupants are not required to pay income taxes on "rent" saved. They may also deduct mortgage interest and real estate taxes in calculating their federal income tax liability.

Although it may occur in some individual cases, overall the property tax does not appear to represent a major violation of vertical equity. Higher-income households tend to live in higher-value housing and pay higher taxes. Although the relationship between the tax and ability to pay may be indirect, it exists nevertheless.

Property taxes vary among geographic areas. Because of the local nature of the property tax and its administration, the incidence of the tax may vary from property to property, county to county, and state to state. Within a taxing jurisdiction, tax appraisers usually attempt to appraise properties consistently; still, inconsistencies can often be found.

Since each county has a different tax assessor or property-tax appraiser, wide differences often occur among counties. For example, a study conducted several years ago in one state showed that tax appraisals in the counties varied from an average of about

---

[6]Netzer, "Is There Too Much Reliance?" pp. 45–62.

REAL ESTATE FOCUS 21-5

How to Appeal Property Taxes

Many owners complain about their property taxes, but few appeal. There is a relatively simple process in every county for appealing assessments, but it requires that property owners first do some homework. Of those who do appeal, a high percentage (over 50 percent in some areas) receive an adjustment. The details of the appeal process vary from state to state, but in general the following stages must be followed:

1. If you believe your assessment is too high, find the amount of taxes and prices of similar properties that have sold recently in your neighborhood. This information can be obtained from the county assessor's (property appraiser's) office.

2. Estimate the current market value of your property. (You may need to have an appraisal of your property.)

3. Calculate the effective tax rates, as shown in Exhibit 21–1, of your property and the comparable properties.

4. If your effective tax rate is higher than that of the comparable properties, present this evidence to the county assessor (property appraiser), who may adjust your assessment.

5. If you do not obtain satisfaction from the assessor, take your case to the county assessment appeals board (sometimes called by other names such as property appraisal appeals board or board of equalization).

6. If you do not obtain satisfaction from the appeals board and you still believe your assessment is too high, consult an attorney or one of the many firms that specialize in property tax appeals (you can find many on the World Wide Web or in your local telephone book), and consider appealing to the appropriate court.

7. If you do not want to do the research and make the presentations to the assessor and appeals board, or if your case is large and complicated, you may prefer to employ a property tax appeals company from the beginning.

---

55 percent to about 75 percent of market value. Because of such variations, criticisms have been raised about the property tax as the major source of school funding. Schools in counties appraised at lower percentages of market value could be less well-funded than schools in counties where tax property appraisals are at a higher percentage of market value. Also, schools in poorer counties could be less well-funded than schools in wealthier counties, even if the properties in all counties are appraised at the same percentage of market value.

To counter these criticisms, most states have supplemental funding formulas to even out school funding among counties. And most states have undertaken programs to equalize the percentage of tax appraisals to market value among their counties. In these states the tax rolls for each county must be submitted to a state agency (such as a Department of Revenue) for testing and approval. Counties that have properties appraised below a targeted percentage are required to adjust their tax appraisals to reach the specified percentage of market value.

While states may attempt to *equalize tax burdens* among counties, no such attempts have been made among states. Thus, similar properties in different states may bear highly different tax liabilities. While the typical annual tax burden ranges between 1 and 2 percent of market value, properties in some states have been taxed at considerably higher rates. Therefore, a number of states have enacted constitutional provisions or laws to limit property taxes. The most famous of these (because it was the first and started the trend) was Proposition 13, enacted in 1978 in California, which limited the property tax rate to 1 percent of property values.

Benson, Benson, McClelland, and Thompson suggest that the property tax should be administered on a *regional* basis.[7] This would combine groups of states into a large region for tax assessment, with the country divided into six to eight such regions. Regional administration would enable assessment officials to strive for uniformity in tax burdens within these large areas. The goals of vertical and horizontal equity presumably would be advanced. The prospect that states would or should give up their authority over the property tax, however, seems very unlikely. Variations among states reflect the different characters of the states and the political and economic choices made by their residents.

The property tax is poorly administered. In many states, county tax assessors or appraisers are elected officials. Special qualifications are not required; they need no special knowledge about appraisal procedures or other matters related to taxation. Given this lack of required qualifications and the large number of assessing officials, the *quality* and *uniformity* of assessing procedures are likely to be less than ideal. While the assessors in most large counties are usually quite competent, assessors in small counties may have little education or background in property appraisal.

Assessors are also often subject to *political pressures*. Political supporters and large financial contributors may be able to exert considerable influence for favorable appraisals. City or county officials may want favorable treatment for a local industry. Friends and associates may seek special treatment. While most assessors will not consider direct requests for favorable treatment, their general desire not to alienate large groups of voters, financial supporters, government officials, or friends may lead to subtle, but noticeable, efforts to maintain assessments at acceptable levels.

To promote education and competence in tax assessing, the International Association of Assessing Officials (IAAO) sponsors courses and other educational programs for members. Many assessors also take courses and seminars sponsored by the leading professional appraisal organizations. And state departments of revenue require that assessors follow prescribed procedures and adhere to minimum appraisal standards.

---

[7]George C. S. Benson, Sumner Benson, Harold McClelland, and Procter Thompson, *The American Property Tax: Its History, Administration, and Economic Impact* (Claremont, CA: Claremont Men's College, Institute for Studies in Federalism and the Lincoln School of Public Finance, 1965).

SUMMARY

The property tax is the principal source of revenue for local governments and taxing jurisdictions, such as school districts. The tax is levied on the value of all property in the taxing jurisdiction, less exempt property. Additionally, taxpayers may qualify for exemptions such as homestead, disability, and military service. A property's value for tax purposes is usually equal to or a direct function of market value. Comparative analyses of property taxes among properties in a given area, or among taxing jurisdictions, are made on the basis of effective tax rates. Special assessments are a form of property taxation for financing public improvements adjacent to private properties.

The property tax, like other taxes, can be evaluated in terms of efficiency and equity. The taxation of real property is an efficient means of raising revenue because large amounts can be generated at a relatively low cost. Some disincentive for new construction, maintenance, and rehabilitation is created by the property tax—a cost that is ultimately borne by all users of real estate. Also, increases in property taxes tend to decrease property values.

In terms of equity, the property tax is potentially undesirable. Without exemptions for certain classes of taxpayers, equalization of burdens among tax jurisdictions, and professional administration, the tax is more burdensome to some property owners than to others. Efforts to improve the fairness of the property tax have been undertaken in most states. Also, since low-income taxpayers benefit more than high-income taxpayers from the services funded by the property tax, the tax tends to be more fair than would be indicated by considering only the incidence of the tax without considering the incidence of benefits.

KEY TERMS

Ad valorem 641
Assessed value 647
Effective tax rate 647
Homestead exemption 646
Horizontal equity 653
Millage rate 645

Mills 645
Special assessments 648
Tax assessor 647
Tax base 644
Tax burden analysis 648
Tax capitalization 651

Tax certificates 649
Tax exempt 646
Tax rate 644
Vertical equity 653

TEST YOURSELF

Answer the following multiple choice questions:

1. Property taxes are the principal source of revenue for
   a. The federal government.
   b. School districts.
   c. Local governments.
   d. State governments.
   e. Local governments and school districts.

2. County assessors (or property appraisers) determine
   a. The tax rate.
   b. The tax amount.
   c. Property value for taxation.
   d. Homestead and other exemptions.
   e. All or none of the above.

3. A regressive tax is one in which

a. Lower-income households pay more taxes relative to their incomes than higher-income households.

b. Lower-income households pay less taxes relative to their incomes than higher-income households.

c. Higher-income households pay more taxes relative to their incomes than lower-income households.

d. Higher-income households pay the same ratio of taxes to income as lower-income households.

e. None of the above.

4. The property tax generally is regarded as an efficient tax because

a. It is capable of raising large amounts of revenue.

b. The object of the tax is fixed in location.

c. Owners of property can be identified easily.

d. The amount of revenue tends to keep up with inflation.

e. All of the above.

5. The best evidence about the regressivity of the property tax is that it is

a. Regressive.

b. Not regressive.

c. Based on ability to pay.

d. Regressive, but when benefits are considered, the net result is not regressive.

e. Variable among geographic areas.

6. A property's assessed value should be a function of (based on) its

a. Cadastral value.

b. Cost.

c. Insurance value.

d. Market value

e. All of the above.

7. Examples of properties exempt from property taxation are

a. Churches, service stations, and grain elevators.

b. Office buildings, schools, and abattoirs.

c. Restaurants, synagogues, and courthouses.

d. Farms, food processing plants, and stockyards.

e. Schools, churches and synagogues, and government buildings.

8. Before appealing one's property taxes, what type of study should be conducted?

a. Market analysis.

b. Feasibility study.

c. Tax burden analysis.

d. Highest and best use study.

e. Appraisal.

9. Usually the largest variance between the property tax liabilities of two properties in the same county is caused by

a. Incompetent tax assessors (property appraisers).

b. A difference in property values.

c. A difference in tax rates.

d. Timing of the assessments.

e. Faulty appraisal methods.

10. The federal government may not levy a direct tax on property because

a. The U.S. Constitution prohibits the levying of unequal taxes, except on incomes.

b. State laws forbid it.

c. The U.S. Constitution specifically prohibits the federal government from levying a property tax.

d. It would be regarded as double taxation.

e. The tax would be uncollectible.

PROBLEMS FOR THOUGHT AND SOLUTION

1. A property owner who owes 8 mills in school taxes, 10 mills in city taxes, and 5 mills in county taxes and who qualifies for a $25,000 homestead exemption would owe how much tax on a property assessed at $80,000?

2. A street is to be paved and gutters installed in front of your property. The city assesses property owners 75 percent of the cost of such improvements, which is estimated to be $60 per running foot. Your property has 100 feet of frontage on one side of the street. How much will be your special assessment?

3. Calculate the average tax burden for the following four properties:

	Property			
	A	**B**	**C**	**D**
Tax liability	$ 4,250	$ 5,000	$ 4,750	$ 4,500
Recent sale price	$240,000	$300,000	$280,000	$262,000

4. Calculate the tax rate for a city, based on the following estimates.

Forecast expenditures	$ 70,000,000
Nonproperty tax income	15,000,000
Total property values	3,000,000,000
Value of tax-exempt properties	100,000,000

5. What is the value of a homestead exemption of $10,000 for a property appraised at $100,000 for tax assessment? The total tax rate is 18 mills (.018).

INTERNET EXERCISES

1. On the World Wide Web go to

   <http://www.propappr.co.hillsborough.fl.us>

   Select the relevant links and answer the following questions:
   a. What are the *categories* of taxing authorities in Hillsborough County?
   b. To what does "Save Our Homes" refer? List its principal provisions.
   c. In the database of county properties, select a property and list the types of information about properties that can be obtained from the county property appraiser's office.

2. On the World Wide Web go to

   <http://.iaao.org>

   a. What is the mission of this organization?
   b. List a few of its principal activities.
   c. Where is its headquarters?

CASE PROBLEMS

1. Some states provide a substantial homestead exemption from property taxes for properties up to a specified assessed value. (In Florida, for example, the amount is $25,000.) The basic idea behind such an exemption is to encourage home ownership, to provide a tax break for low-income property owners, and to protect families. The exemption has been criticized, however, for removing large numbers of properties from the tax rolls, particularly in rural counties where property values are generally low. It is argued that many people are able to avoid the responsibility of paying taxes that finance schools, roads, police and fire protection, and many social services. These people use local services as much as those who own higher-valued properties, and they should pay some reasonable amount for them.

a. What do you think about the advantages and disadvantages of a homestead exemption for property taxes?

b. How might a homestead exemption be structured more fairly?

2. The property tax has been criticized as an unfair base for financing public schools. Areas that have high property values are able to pay for better schools than areas having lower property values. Thus, there is inequality of educational opportunities that tends to perpetuate educational and social disadvantages for those who live in low-income areas.

a. Do you agree or disagree?

b. How could the school financing arrangement be modified to provide more equal funding among all regions of a state?

ADDITIONAL READINGS

This article reports on the use of multiple regression analysis (MRA) to test for consistency in the assessment of properties in one jurisdiction. The article concludes that MRA should be used for assessment purposes:

Donnelly, William A. "The Methodology of Housing Value Assessment: An Analysis." *Journal of Real Estate Research* 4, no. 2 (Summer 1989), pp. 1–12.

Would you like to know more about the history of the property tax? If so, check out the following book:

Fisher, Glenn W. *The Worst Tax? A History of the Property Tax in America*. Lawrence, KS: University Press of Kansas, 1996.

This book is a landmark study on the property tax:

Netzer, Dick. *Economics of the Property Tax*. Washington, D.C.: Brookings Institution, 1966.

The author of this article emphasizes that the concepts of property and value are used differently in certain aspects of the law of real property and the taxation of real property. He compares and contrasts several of these differences to show how the concept in one field can be instructive in the other.

Korngold, Gerald. "Comparing the Concepts of 'Property' and 'Value' in Real Estate Law and Real Property Taxation," *Real Estate Law Journal* 25, no. 1 (Summer 1996), pp. 7–27.

The following book is an excellent reference for information about legal issues involved in assessment valuation and taxation. It includes text and cases:

Youngman, Joan. *Legal Issues in Property Valuation and Taxation: Cases and Materials*. Chicago: International Association of Assessing Officers, 1994.

22
C H A P T E R

TRANSFER OF REAL PROPERTY RIGHTS

THE IMPORTANCE OF REAL PROPERTY TRANSFER

EVIDENCE AND CONVEYANCE OF OWNERSHIP
Titles
Evidence of Good Title
Deeds in Private Grants of Title
Public Grants of Title to Real Estate
Devise and Descent
Foreclosure
Adverse Possession and Prescription
Title from Nature

CONTRACTS FOR TRANSFER OF REAL PROPERTY RIGHTS
Validity and Enforceability of Contracts
General Categories of Contracts
Contract Law: A Value Perspective
The Four Basic Contracts

PROPER DESCRIPTIONS OF REAL PROPERTY
Surveys
Metes and Bounds
Recorded Plat Map
Government Survey System

SUMMARY

KEY TERMS

TEST YOURSELF

PROBLEMS FOR THOUGHT AND SOLUTION

CASE PROBLEMS

ADDITIONAL READINGS

After reading this chapter, students will be able to:

1. Describe the ways title to real estate is evidenced.

2. Compare and contrast the ways in which rights to real estate may be transferred from one party to another.

3. Define and discuss the functions of the various types of deeds used in real estate transactions.

4. Discuss the market implications of strong contract laws.

5. Distinguish among the contracts used in real estate.

6. Use recorded plat maps, metes and bounds, and the government survey system to describe property.

THE IMPORTANCE OF REAL PROPERTY TRANSFER

Applying the concepts of real property rights presented in Chapter 20 represents the first of two necessary skills for creating successful legal arrangements for real estate ownership. The second skill involves the use of legal and institutional concepts necessary for *transferring* real property rights. The importance of understanding these concepts stems from the fact that so much of the real estate business revolves around transfers of property rights. The real estate brokerage industry, which includes hundreds of thousands of real estate salespeople and brokers, offers an obvious example. The private and public mortgage lending business exists primarily to provide financing for real property rights transfers. Most real estate appraisals supply information on property value for real estate transactions. Real estate developers are in the business of selling and leasing their products.

This chapter discusses the various methods for transferring title to real estate and the methods for physically describing real estate. The ability to freely transfer real estate is essential to maintaining real estate values in a market economy. Physical descriptions of property represent an important component of real estate title transfers and real estate appraisal. This chapter also discusses the basic contractual arrangements used to transfer real property rights. The final two chapters in this section focus on the contracts involved in the sale of real estate, culminating in the closing.

EVIDENCE AND CONVEYANCE OF OWNERSHIP

The transfer of interests in real estate among owners occurs in several ways. **Public grant** means that a government component conveyed real estate to private owners whereas voluntary transfers of property between private entities (e.g., via a sale, gift, or exchange) are

private grants. Private entities also obtain real estate through foreclosure actions, inheritance, legal possession, and even as the result of acts of nature. This section begins with a discussion of what provides evidences of title to real estate and concludes with discussion of the ways in which rights change hands in real estate markets.

TITLES

Most people become familiar with titles through their experiences with buying and selling automobiles. To transfer ownership of cars, sellers simply sign title certificates over to buyers. Buyers then record title transfers with state motor vehicle departments. Titles to real estate differ from titles to personal property, such as automobiles, in that the evidence of ownership occurs in ways that do not involve the use of actual title certificates.[1]

Public records.   Recording laws in every state require that local governments maintain records of all legal instruments affecting title to real estate. The common law registration systems used to maintain these records fall into two categories: legal and fiscal. The following legal records exist in most city, county, or equivalent halls of records (e.g., courthouse):

- Grantor-grantee or tract books.
- Mortgagor-mortgagee books.
- Plat and plan books.
- Secured personal property books.

Local governments also maintain records for fiscal and regulatory purposes. These include tax and special assessment books usually kept in tax assessors' offices and land-use and zoning maps usually kept in the local planning department offices. Real estate brokers, appraisers, developers, investors, and other market participants rely heavily on the legal and fiscal registration systems in local real estate markets (see Real Estate Focus 22–1).

Historical perspective.[2]   During the early days of business activity in the United States, the legalities of real estate title transfers were handled informally. To protect their clients from those who might have superior claims to title, lawyers for buyers would go to local courthouses and tax collectors' offices and casually discuss prior ownership and tax payment records on subject parcels with the appropriate designated public officials (usually friends and neighbors of the lawyers). If these discussions yielded no problems with titles, such as outstanding tax liens or dower rights of previous owners, then the lawyers would simply prepare opinions of title, which served as evidence of titles.

Informality gave way to more formal procedures as the number and complexity of real estate transactions increased. Abstract companies began appearing to assist lawyers

---

[1] The terms *title* and *estate* should not be confused. Recall from Chapter 18 that the term *estate* describes the nature or extent of interests owned in real property.

[2] From Robert Kratovil and Raymond J. Werner, *Real Estate Law* (Upper Saddle River, N.J.: Prentice Hall, 1993), pp. 231–38.

REAL ESTATE FOCUS 22-1

Databases Compiled from the Public Records: REDI or Not!

Market data are vital for successful real estate brokerage, appraisal, research, and planning. Since 1958, Real Estate Data Incorporated (REDI)* has compiled and indexed public record information providing the real estate community with real property data. Today, REDI is available in 250 markets in 35 states and the Virgin Islands. The firm provides parcel-specific information such as owner details, property characteristics, structural characteristics, neighborhood demographics, property taxes, assessed values, and sales data including financing details. In select areas, REDI provides products, such as a building and property atlas, that give subscribers detailed information about the footprint of every structure in, for example, Chicago's office building market and Atlanta's shopping center market (including computer aerial photos). REDI is only one example of the many firms throughout the nation that collect and sell data obtained from public records.

*1700 Northwest 66th Avenue, Fort Lauderdale, FL 33313. (800) 345–7334, ext.1302 or (954) 321–7667.

and buyers. Abstractors followed the daily activities of the local recorders of real estate transfers and tax collectors to maintain current records or books on each property. If investors wanted a list of transactions and tax payments for a given property, they would simply examine (for a fee) the appropriate pages in the abstract company's books. Such lists became known as **abstracts of title**.

Innovations in developing abstracts of title resulted in increasingly more efficient processes for examining and evidencing title. Abstracts, however, become ineffective for evidencing title when mistakes occur. Abstract companies, therefore, began to guarantee their work by issuing insurance policies against losses of title, in which buyers were named as beneficiaries. These companies are the forerunners of the **title insurance** companies of today (see Real Estate Focus 22–2).

EVIDENCE OF GOOD TITLE

Establishing the chain of title through public records represents an important first step for evidencing title to real estate. This activity begins the title search, which includes an investigation of whether previous liens against the property (e.g., mortgage liens, tax liens) exist. Evidence of no superior claim to title or outstanding liens means the title is good. The title search plays an integral role in each of the three commonly accepted methods for evidencing good title to real estate in use today. These methods include

1. *Abstract and attorney's opinion.* This conventional method of evidencing good title relies on the development or continuation (that is, updating) of the property abstract. An attorney prepares or updates the abstract of the property, and once the attorney becomes satisfied that no prior liens exist or that no prior owner or owner's spouse has an outstanding claim, the

REAL ESTATE FOCUS 22-2, INTERNATIONAL

*Land and Title Registration around the World**

Generally, the more economically developed the country, the more sophisticated the land and title registration system, and thus the more efficient the real estate transfers within the country. These registration systems, or **cadastres**, have three forms: legal, fiscal, and multipurpose. The legal system identifies in the public record the owners of real estate, parcel boundaries, and claims against the real estate (e.g., liens). The fiscal system identifies the location, ownership, size, and improvements for the purpose of assessing property taxes. Multipurpose systems, which provide data to serve both legal and property-tax assessment purposes, are less commonly found around the world. Iceland, for example, has operated with a land register for legal and property tax purposes since the 1600s. Australia has adopted a computerized system that includes real estate transactions dating back to the 1600s. This system functions as a multipurpose land registration system.

Adequate legal and fiscal registration systems appear in most economically developed places, including the United States, Canada, Hong Kong, Singapore, Western Europe, Scandinavia, Japan, and England. The People's Republic of China recently initiated its first comprehensive land survey. The land registration systems in most other places in the world, however, lack efficiency and reliablity.

---

*See Mary Alice Hines, *Guide to International Real Estate Investment* (New York: Quorum Books, 1988), pp. 28–30; and Dudley S. Hinds and Nicholas Ordway, *International Real Estate Investment* (Chicago: Real Estate Education Co., 1983), p. 130.

---

attorney issues a letter of opinion regarding the title. Therefore, an updated abstract and **letter of opinion** constitute evidence of good title.

2. *Title insurance*. The most common method for evidencing good title in residential transactions involves the purchase of a title insurance policy by the buyers of properties. With this method, the title insurance company that issues the policy guarantees to pay any losses the grantee suffers resulting from the loss of title. Before issuing the policy, the title insurance company performs a title search. Buyers pay the policy premium in full at the closing. Mortgage lenders usually require buyers to purchase title insurance only for losses up to loan amounts. These policies protect lenders against losses. Buyers often purchase coverage for the entire value of properties to protect the value of buyers' interests as well as lenders' interests. The title insurance policy provides evidence of good title.

3. *Torrens system*. The **Torrens system** represents the most unusual method for evidencing good title to real estate. While this system is authorized under the laws of 19 states, only a few locations use the system.[3] From the property abstract, a lawyer develops a list of all persons and prior lien holders who might have an interest in the subject property. The lawyer submits the list to the local registrar of Torrens certificates (often the county clerk) with an application for a Torrens certificate on the property.

---

[3]Mainly in parts of Minnesota, Illinois, Massachusetts, and Hawaii.

The application results in a lawsuit filed against all persons on the list requiring them to come forward and make their claims against the property. If no claims appear, the registrar issues a certificate that serves as a defense against any claims that might be brought in the future. Thus, a Torrens certificate provides evidence of good title to real estate. In essence, these certificates constitute title certificates to real estate.

DEEDS IN PRIVATE GRANTS OF TITLE

The transfer of title to real estate, unlike the transfer of titles to other property (e.g., automobiles), occurs through the use of a separate legal instrument called a deed. The existence of a valid deed evidences the transfer of title to real estate. People commonly refer to a real estate transfer of ownership by saying, for example, "Smith deeded property to Corgel." Deeds underlie transfers involving private grants, public grants, and most other types of real estate title transfers.

Historically, ownership of land provides a measure of political and economic power. In the past, societies have even limited voting rights to landowners. The transfer of real estate ownership among members of society, therefore, has great historical interest to society. The deed, which becomes recorded in the name of both the seller and buyer in a deed book (usually located in the county courthouse), provides a convenient means to determine past and current ownership of land. The existence of such records facilitates title searches and the construction of computerized databases of real estate ownership and transfer.

Requirements of a valid deed. Legal transfers of ownership of real estate follow from the issuance of valid deeds. The following list includes the minimum requirements for valid deeds:

- The names of the grantor and grantee must appear on the deed. Both parties must be competent to act, and there must be no barriers to mutual assent.[4]
- A proper description of the property must be included.[5]
- Words of conveyance (e.g., "I, Laina S. Corgel, hereby transfer all my rights in the subject property to Leah S. Corgel . . .") must be included.
- A statement of consideration must be included.[6]
- The grantor must sign the deed and, in some states, a seal must be affixed. The grantee usually is not required to sign the deed.
- The deed must be delivered by the grantor to the grantee. Proper delivery occurs when there is a *meeting of the minds*. Delivery of the deed often

---

[4]*Mutual assent* refers to a meeting of the minds between the parties. An example of a barrier to mutual assent is if one of the parties were under duress when executing the deed.

[5]This topic is covered in the last section of this chapter.

[6]*Consideration* refers to giving up something of value and receipt of a benefit.

occurs at the closing with both parties typically present so the meeting-of-the-minds requirement becomes easily satisfied. Delivery of deeds can be actual, as during closings, or in escrow by agents of the parties.

States often impose other requirements for deeds (e.g., witnessing and dating), but in most cases, satisfaction of the above requirements creates legally valid instruments. Recording of deeds also should occur; however, unrecorded deeds remain valid as long as proper delivery occurred. The validity of unrecorded deeds in disputes about property ownership becomes more difficult to prove, however.

Sales, gifts, inheritances, and exchanges between private parties constitute the majority of real estate title transfers. Each private grant occurs using one of the several types of deeds. The most commonly used deeds include the general warranty deed, the special warranty deed, the quitclaim deed, and the bargain-and-sale deed.

General warranty deed. From the perspective of buyers, the **general warranty deed** has the most desirable features. In issuing general warranty deeds, sellers of property make several guarantees to buyers. These guarantees, known as *covenants of title*, include the

- *Covenant of seisin*. With this covenant, sellers guarantee that they possess legal (good) title to the properties conveyed.
- *Covenant against encumbrances*. Sellers guarantee that no encumbrances (e.g., liens) against the title exist other than those disclosed to buyers.
- *Covenant for quiet enjoyment*. This covenant means sellers will protect buyers against any parties claiming a superior title to the properties.
- *Covenant of further assurances*. Sellers promise to take any action necessary to perfect titles delivered to buyers should defects appear in titles following delivery.
- *Covenant of warranty forever*. This covenant represents a culmination of the guarantees made by sellers imbedded in a general warranty deed. Sellers guarantee that buyers will enjoy ownership and possession forever because no one has superior title.

These covenants provide the grounds for legal action against sellers should buyers encounter problems related to titles in the future. When title insurance has been purchased, these covenants merely provide added security for buyers.

Special warranty deed. The general warranty deed includes guarantees from sellers that date back to the period before they owned the properties. The **special warranty deed** contains guarantees that pertain *only to events that have occurred during the sellers' period of ownership*. The same basic covenants apply, though they become limited to the specific period of seller ownership. Sellers prefer to issue this type of deed in situations in which potential title problems may result from events occurring before they purchased the property. For example, the property may have gone through foreclosure proceedings sometime before the seller owned the property.

Quitclaim deed. A **quitclaim deed** does not convey actual rights to real estate, nor does it contain any warranties on the part of grantors. This instrument simply *transfers rights that a specific party has in the property, not rights in the property itself.* If grantors have no rights, then no rights can transfer by issuing a the quitclaim deed. The quitclaim deed becomes useful for correcting defects in titles and in a variety of other related situations. For example, if some uncertainty arises about the legality of a title because a previous owner's spouse did not sign the general warranty deed and therefore did not release dower rights, the issuance of a quitclaim deed releases those rights. The previous owner's spouse must be found and persuaded to sign the quitclaim deed.

Bargain-and-sale deed. **Bargain-and-sale deeds**, like quitclaim deeds, contain no warranties from grantors. But unlike quitclaim deeds, bargain and sale deeds do convey actual rights to real estate. Thus, this type of deed does not afford grantees any protection. Corporations commonly use bargain-and-sale deeds in real property transfers as a means of limiting their liability to grantees.

PUBLIC GRANTS OF TITLE TO REAL ESTATE

Because most of the land in the United States was initially owned by the government, the original grants of real estate to private owners were public grants.[7] In old western movies, the settlers lined up in wagons loaded with possessions to stake their claims in a *land rush.* A public grant such as the one that settlers received occurs with a specific type of deed known as a **patent.** Many existing abstracts of title contain references to the patent that originally conveyed title to land to a private entity. In current real estate practice, public grants rarely occur.

DEVISE AND DESCENT

Holders of real property rights who die leaving wills indicating who obtains title to their real estate have conveyed title by devise. Wills serve as legal instruments that convey title from the grantors (the deceased persons or devisors) to the grantees (the devisees). When real estate owners die without valid wills, called *intestate*, the rights to real property transfer to others according to the probate laws of the state. State probate laws describe the line of succession for inheriting real property from persons who die intestate, usually beginning with spouses and children. In such instances, real property rights transfer by descent. Special types of deeds, known as **officer's deeds, executor's deeds**, and **sheriff's deeds**, which contain no warranties, come into usage in these cases. Generally, these deeds carry warrants that the court has done nothing to encumber the title.

---

[7]This also applies to land granted from state governments, the king of Spain, or American Indian nations.

REAL ESTATE FOCUS 22-3

Acquiring Title by Adverse Possession

The requirements for acquiring title to land by adverse possession are not easily met. But in a 1982 Texas case, the court ruled in favor of a farmer who purchased land from an adverse possessor. In 1941, the plaintiff in this case, Mr. A, leased a farm he owned as an absentee landlord to Mr. B for zero rent simply to maintain the farm. Mr. B sold the lease to Mr. C who, in 1955, transferred the lease to Mr. D. Mr. D made several improvements to the land including fencing, root plowing, and digging a pond during the 14 years he used the land. In 1969, he sold the land to Mr. E, and in 1977, Mr. A, the original owner of the land, filed suit against Mr. E for trespassing.

Mr. E called several witnesses during the hearing to show that, in the late 1950s, Mr. D claimed the land against the world and threatened to shoot anyone crossing the farm. The court was convinced that Mr. D had given notice of a constructive nature of his adverse possession of the land and ruled that Mr. D had acquired title as an adverse possessor. Mr. A no longer had any claim to the farm and therefore could not remove Mr. E as a trespasser.

SOURCE: *Dalo* v. *Laughlin*, 636 S.W. 2nd 585 (Ct. App. 1982).

FORECLOSURE

Those holding valid liens (e.g., mortgage lenders with mortgage liens and roofers with mechanic's liens) can force public sale of real estate to receive overdue payments through foreclosure. Deeds transferring ownership resulting from foreclosure sales contain no warranties and have the names *referee's deeds, sheriff's deeds*, and *officer's deeds,* depending on where the foreclosure occurs.

ADVERSE POSSESSION AND PRESCRIPTION

Ownership of real property rights may change from one owner to another by certain legal means designed to ensure that land becomes used rather than left idle, as in the case of adverse possession; or to ensure that parties are not denied rightful access to their properties, as in the case of prescription. Although state laws vary, someone may gain ownership of real estate owned by another through adverse possession by using the property in a way defined as actual, continuous, hostile (to the owner), visible, and exclusive for a period of usually no less than 10 years. In other words, owners who fail to use their property or take action against adverse possessors for the prescribed period stand to lose their property rights, assuming the adverse possessors make profitable use of the property (see Real Estate Focus 22–3).

Similarly, the courts sometimes issue prescriptive easements (rights of use) to those who establish patterns of actual, continuous, hostile, and visible (not exclusive) use of another's property, usually for no less than three to seven years, to gain access to another parcel (e.g., a roadway through a neighbor's land). Instances of acquiring real property rights through adverse possession and prescription, while not common, occasionally occur.

TITLE FROM NATURE

Recorded deeds include physical descriptions of the property, often by describing the natural boundaries (such as a river, lake, and rock formation). When natural landscape features change, transfers of ownership may occur. For example, if land becomes deposited in a given area from a body of water, ownership rights to that land occur through **accretion**. Where boundary water recedes leaving dry land, ownership rights transfer through **reliction**. When bodies of water, such as rivers or streams, change course, no rights transfer between adjacent property owners because the dry beds remain as the boundaries.

CONTRACTS FOR TRANSFER OF REAL PROPERTY RIGHTS

Contract law exists as the dominant rule of social order governing the transfer of real property rights. Because buyers and sellers of real estate rely heavily on contract law, an understanding of basic definitions and concepts of contracts emerges as the first step in using real estate contracts. The law of real estate contracts comes from general contract law, so first we examine certain general provisions of contract law and then examine the specific contracts used in real estate transactions.

VALIDITY AND ENFORCEABILITY OF CONTRACTS

A valid contract refers to an instrument that satisfies all legal requirements. Specifically, it must contain all five of the following elements:

1. Parties must be competent to act.
2. Parties must have lawful intent.
3. There must be an offer and an acceptance.
4. There must be a statement of consideration.
5. There must be no defects to mutual assent.

And, for most real estate contracts,

6. The contract must be in writing.
7. The property must be properly described.

A void contract does not exist in the eyes of the law because it does not include one or more of the essential elements of a valid contract. Because such contracts do not exist in the eyes of the law, they are unenforceable.

A voidable contract begins as a valid contract and becomes unenforceable against one of the parties because of special circumstances. The most common example of a voidable contract involves a contract with a minor (a person under the legally specified age) or an insane person. Because these persons do not possess the legal capability to act for themselves, contract provisions cannot be enforced against them.

A valid and enforceable contract has all the essential elements of a legal contract and does not include provisions that violate public policy, such as provisions promoting racial discrimination. Contracts for the transfer of real property rights have an additional requirement beyond the essential elements: writing. Usually, oral contracts for the transfer of real property rights lack enforceability.[8]

GENERAL CATEGORIES OF CONTRACTS

Contracts may take unilateral or bilateral forms. A **unilateral contract** results from a promise exchanged for an act; a **bilateral contract** results from a promise exchanged for a promise. Real estate contracts for sale possess the characteristics of bilateral contracts. Sellers promise to deliver the deeds and thus titles to properties, and buyers promise to pay money or other property according to the agreed-on terms. Both parties must fulfill their promises, and their respective promises presumably lie within their power. In general, all contracts involving real property rights are bilateral contracts.

Most contracts are expressed, but sometimes contracts and parts of contracts originate by implication. An **expressed contract**, either oral or written, reflects explicitly the intentions, terms, and conditions of the parties; an **implied contract** (known as a contract implied-in-fact) involves an agreement evidenced by acts or conduct.

Suppose, for example, you own an apartment complex and hire a resident manager to collect rents and show units for rent, but no explicit statement exists in your agreement with the resident manager about making repairs. One day, as you drive through the complex, you observe the resident manager fixing a broken window for one of the tenants. You slow down, honk your horn, and wave to the resident manager. The next day, the resident manager asks for reimbursement for the additional time it took to replace the window. You refuse on the ground that such acts fall outside this particular resident manager's realm of responsibilities. The case eventually goes to court. The court rules in favor of the resident manager because an implied contract was created when you acknowledged, and implicitly approved, the actions of the manager while you were driving through the complex.

CONTRACT LAW: A VALUE PERSPECTIVE

Economic analyses find that contracts and contract laws have three essential roles in free market economies. First, enforceable contracts provide incentives for contracting parties to do exactly what they say they will do in contracts. Second, contract laws, with their many standard terms, reduce the costs of exchange to contracting parties by allowing them to focus on the unique aspects of their exchanges. Finally, contracts force contracting parties to think about future risks of exchanges and plan for those risks by introducing provisions that describe contingency arrangements.

All of these important economic consequences of contracts and contract laws apply to real estate transactions. In addition, enforceable contracts facilitate the exchange of

---

[8]Exceptions exist in some states (e.g., Colorado) in which oral real estate contracts can be enforced.

EXHIBIT 22-1

BASIC CONTRACTS FOR TRANSFERRING REAL PROPERTY RIGHTS

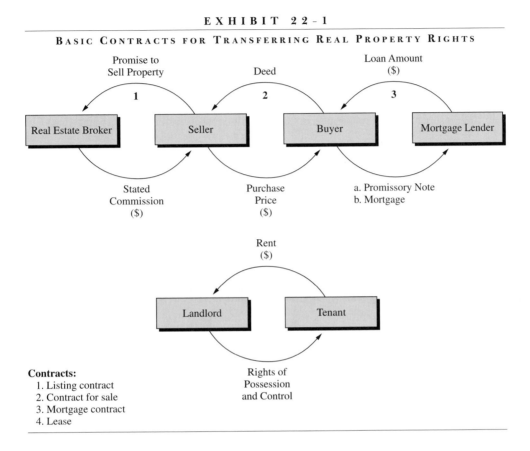

Contracts:
1. Listing contract
2. Contract for sale
3. Mortgage contract
4. Lease

property to those who value it the most. In other words, real estate would not evolve to the highest and best use if it were not for enforceable contracts. Consequently, real estate values would not move near their highest possible levels because those levels only occur in the highest and best use.

Two essential legal pillars support the prices of real estate observed in markets throughout the world: property laws and the property rights they define and contract laws and the integrity of the contracts they protect. With strong property and contract laws, real estate tends to be put to its highest and best use and prices reflect its underlying values.

THE FOUR BASIC CONTRACTS

Although transfers of real property rights occur as the result of a number of different agreements, the following general types of contracts appear most often in practice: (1) listing contracts, (2) contracts for sale, (3) mortgage contracts, and (4) leases. Exhibit 22–1 shows the relationships between the parties in each of these four basic contracts. The first three contracts usually apply in situations in which all or most legal rights are being transferred through sales of property, including the transfer of complete or partial rights (e.g., air rights or subsurface rights). Lease agreements transfer the legal rights of use and possession for limited periods.

Listing contract. Listing contracts occur between real estate owners who wish to sell their properties and real estate brokers who maintain businesses of selling property. Not all transactions involve listing contracts with brokers because some owners prefer to sell properties themselves. Nevertheless, because of the somewhat complex legal arrangements in real estate transactions and the unique characteristics of real estate markets that make matching buyers with sellers difficult, most transactions involve contracts with brokers. In such contracts, sellers agree to pay brokerage fees (usually a percentage of the sale price), if brokers find willing and able buyers. The details about listing contracts appear in Chapter 23.

Contract for sale. Contracts for sale involve agreements between buyers and sellers to transfer real property rights. In these contracts, sellers receive money or its equivalent (notes or other property), and buyers receive deeds to properties. Chapter 24 contains a thorough discussion of contracts for sale.

Mortgage contract. As discussed in Chapter 15, most, but not all, transactions involve the use of funds borrowed by buyers to finance the purchase of real property. In mortgage contracts, borrowers receive money and mortgage lenders receive two legal instruments. The first is the promissory note representing borrowers' promises to repay the loans. Second, the mortgage (in most states) gives lenders legal rights to foreclose on the properties if necessary to obtain reimbursement.

Leases. In leasing arrangements, landlords give up rights of use and possession of property for set periods to tenants in exchange for rent. Along with sales agreements, leases represent the most common type of contract found in real estate practice. Leases are described in Chapter 8.

PROPER DESCRIPTIONS OF REAL PROPERTY

A proper description of real estate appears in listing contracts, contracts for sale, deeds, mortgage contracts, leases, and other legal instruments or documents that affect the transfer of title to real estate. Property descriptions also appear regularly in real estate business practice for appraisal, investment analysis, and mortgage loan review. Such descriptions set boundaries of parcels to distinguish them from all other parcels. A *proper description* of land, therefore, identifies the parcel and distinguishes it from all other parcels. A legal description of property will hold up in a court of law if it provides an exact delineation of the property boundaries.

Describing a property as 101 Oak Street (its street address), for example, may satisfy the definition of a proper description, but will not enter legal documents because of the lack of precision it provides in defining boundaries. The following three ways of describing real estate qualify as both proper and sufficiently precise for legal documents: metes and bounds, recorded plat map, and the Government Rectangular Survey System.

SURVEYS

To ensure the accuracy of the legal descriptions, property surveys by licensed (or registered) surveyors accompany most real estate transactions. The most common example is the case of a mortgage contract for a single-family residence in which the mortgage lender, as a condition for making a loan, requires a survey of the property. Exhibit 22–2 shows an example of such a survey. This survey defines the physical features of a typical residential lot. The dimensions of the lot are stated and the placement of all improvements such as house and driveway appear on the survey. The letter *D* refers to the block and the number 14 is the lot number. These designations relate to the recorded plat description discussed below.

Although the survey serves to verify the accuracy of the legal description, it also serves to uncover any **encroachments**. Exhibit 22–3 indicates an encroachment. The owner of the adjacent parcel constructed a driveway that extends into (encroaches on) the subject parcel. An encroachment represents an encumbrance on the title. The owner has the right to force the removal of the encroachment. However, owners of these two parcels will likely reach a settlement to adjust the boundary lines. If the owner of the encroached-on parcel takes no action, the owner of the adjacent parcel ultimately may claim legal title to the affected portion of land through adverse possession or prescriptive easement.

METES AND BOUNDS

The oldest of the methods for describing real estate is the **metes-and-bounds** (distances-and-boundaries) description. The success of this method rests on the ability to identify naturally occurring landmarks, such as a rock formation, and man-made landmarks, such as a road intersection, and then define the boundaries of the property by measuring the distances and directions between these landmarks.[9] In essence, the reader of a metes-and-bounds description takes a tour around the perimeter of the property. This tour begins at a particular landmark known as the *point of beginning*. The following is an example of a metes-and-bounds description that might be found in a deed:

Beginning at a point 50 feet east of the intersection of Abbey Road and Penny Lane, South 80 degrees, 200 feet to an iron pin (part of the description omitted) . . . returning to the point of beginning.

---

[9]Landmarks are sometimes referred to as *monuments*. A related method for describing real estate is also known as the *monuments method*.

EXHIBIT 22-2

SURVEY OF A TYPICAL RESIDENTIAL LOT

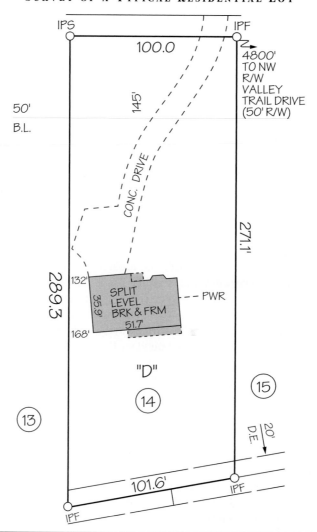

Before developers began using iron pins and concrete markers, naturally occurring landmarks, such as an old oak tree, were commonly used in metes-and-bounds descriptions. Reliance on natural objects presents a problem when the object disappears due to the actions of human beings or nature; thus, the need arises to check such descriptions carefully. Metes-and-bounds descriptions become more common when dealing with rural property. Parcels in urban and suburban areas are typically described by recorded plat maps.

EXHIBIT 22-3

SURVEY SHOWING AN ENCROACHMENT

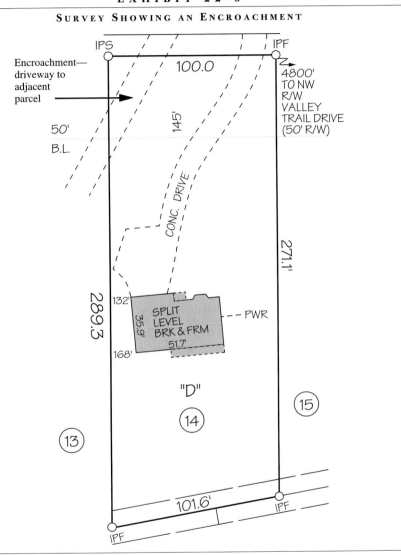

RECORDED PLAT MAP

In most cities and counties in the United States, developers seeking to subdivide land must file detailed maps of subdivisions showing the exact locations and configurations of the lots, streets, sewers, utility easements, park land, and other physical features. These maps, known as **recorded plat maps**, receive consideration, along with other relevant information, from the appropriate city or county government officials to determine whether the

EXHIBIT 22-4

HEAVENLY ACRES SUBDIVISION PLAT MAP

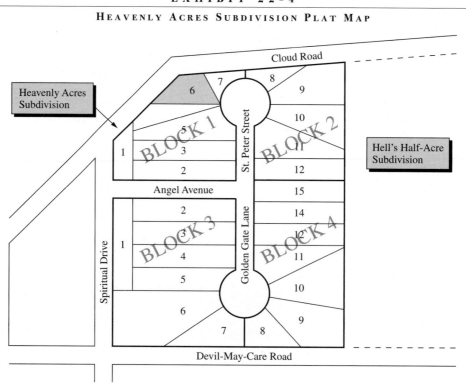

development conforms to local zoning and subdivision regulations. If approved, maps become part of the public record by being included in **plat books** at the county courthouse or city hall. Because plat maps contain sufficient detail about the boundaries of each lot, the description of lots as part of "platted" parcels constitutes proper and legal description of real estate.

Exhibit 22–4 shows a plat map of Heavenly Acres Subdivision. All of the lots in the subdivision have numbers and all streets have names. In addition, details on easements, sewer lines, and measurements usually would appear. The subdivision consists of four blocks. A block is a set of lots, all of which can be reached without crossing a street. Also, a metes-and-bounds description for the entire subdivided parcel, by referencing the intersections of the surrounding roads, could serve as a proper description.

The recorded plat map description for the lot shaded on the map would be as follows:

Lot 6, Block 1 of Heavenly Acres Subdivision according to the plat recorded March 16, 1998, as plat number 5000, page 3000, book number 1, Almost Heavenly County, State of West Virginia.

GOVERNMENT SURVEY SYSTEM

The government survey system, formally known as the **Government Rectangular Survey System (GRSS),** was initiated by Congress under the Land Ordinance of 1785. This ordinance created a system for describing lands the United States acquired following the American Revolution. Thus, GRSS, as it exists today, is in effect in 30 states, mostly in the midwestern and western United States.[10]

A description of real estate using the government survey system begins with the identification of a point that can be located on a general map of the United States and may end with a parcel as small as one-quarter acre. This system involves continually subdividing larger areas into smaller areas, using a hierarchy of lines on a map. The process begins with the identification of a principal meridian and **baseline**, then, with the aid of **township lines** and **range lines**, locates one-square-mile **sections**. Identification and description of smaller areas occurs by subdividing the appropriate section. To help explain the government survey system, a description of a 10-acre parcel near Orlando, Florida is developed later in this chapter along with discussion of each component of the GRSS.

Principal meridians and base lines. The first step in using the GRSS involves identifying the appropriate principal meridian and baseline. *Principal meridians* mean survey lines that run north and south throughout the portions of the United States affected by GRSS. *Baselines* mean lines running east and west associated with principal meridians. Each principal meridian has a corresponding baseline. The intersection of a principal meridian and baseline, known as the *initial point*, marks the point for beginning the description of a particular parcel.

Exhibit 22–5 presents a map showing all of the principal meridians and accompanying baselines in the United States. The different shadings indicate association with different meridians and baselines. The initial point indicates which areas (states and parts of states) are associated with which meridians and baselines. The initial point in describing the parcel near Orlando, Florida, appears at the intersection of the Tallahassee principal meridian and its baseline, as shown in Exhibit 22–6.

Township and range lines. Township lines run east and west at six-mile intervals parallel to a base line. Range lines run north and south, also at six-mile intervals, parallel to a principal meridian. Thus, township and range lines create a grid on the map consisting of squares called *townships* of six miles by six miles. A square area consisting of 16 townships (that is, four townships by four townships) is known as a *check*.

Exhibit 22–6 presents a map of Florida with selected range and township lines superimposed. These lines have numbers and are referenced by direction beginning at the principal meridian and baseline. For example, the first township line below the baseline is

---

[10]The 30 states are Alabama, Alaska, Arizona, Arkansas, California, Colorado, Florida, Idaho, Illinois, Indiana, Iowa, Kansas, Louisiana, Michigan, Minnesota, Mississippi, Missouri, Montana, Nebraska, Nevada, New Mexico, North Dakota, Ohio, Oklahoma, Oregon, South Dakota, Utah, Washington, Wisconsin, and Wyoming.

EXHIBIT 22-5

MAP OF THE UNITED STATES SHOWING PRINCIPAL MERIDIANS AND BASELINES

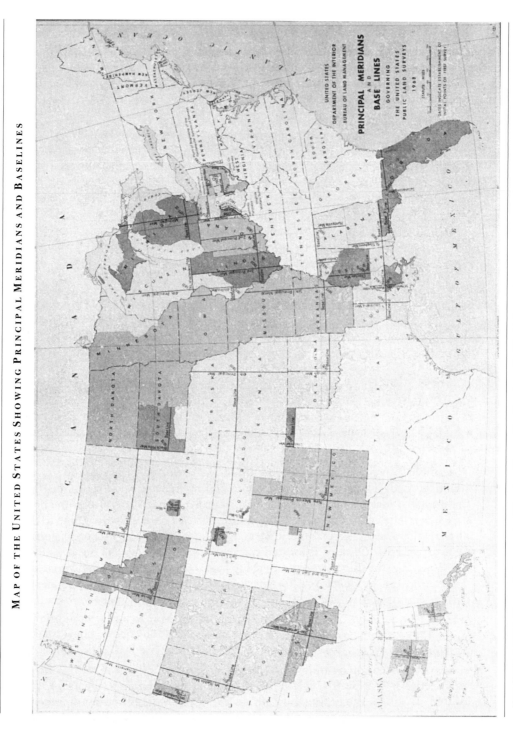

Note: Shadings distinguish areas that come under different meridians and baselines (e.g. all of Florida is associated with the Tallahassee principal meridian, whereas Alabama and Louisiana have different shadings, meaning they are associated with different meridians).

SOURCE: Bureau of Land Management, U.S. Department of Interior.

MAP OF FLORIDA SHOWING SELECTED GRSS INDICATORS

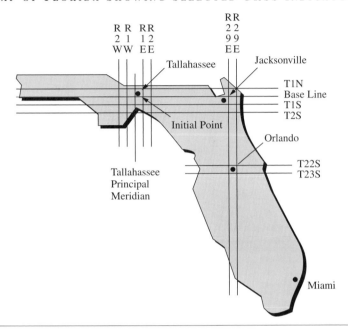

labeled T (township) 1 S (south). Similarly, the first range line to the right of the Talla-hassee principal meridian is R (range) 1 E (east). Proceeding south and east, we find the location of Orlando between T22S and T23S and between R28E and R29E. Using the furthermost township and range line from the initial point, a description results for the appropriate township in Orlando. The correct description becomes—T23S, R29E of the Tallahassee Principal Meridian and Base Line.

Sections. A township consists of 36 square miles in area, and within each township appear 36 one-square-mile sections. Exhibit 22–7 represents the township for Orlando. It shows the 36 sections within the township and the numbering system used to designate each section. Section 1 is in the upper right corner, then sections are numbered consecu-tively in a right-to-left, left-to-right fashion until section 36 is reached in the lower right corner. The GRSS description of a parcel in Section 1 becomes "Section One, T23S, R29E of the Tallahassee Principal Meridian and Baseline."

Finer detail in describing parcels under the GRSS comes as a result of subdividing the appropriate section. Exhibit 22–8 shows Section 1 with subdivision to the 10-acre level. The specific 10-acre parcel targeted for description consists of the shaded area. To begin, in what part of the square, designated as (a), is the shaded parcel located? It is in the NE? Moving out one dimension, in what part of the square designated as (b) is the

EXHIBIT 22-7

SECTIONS WITHIN A PARTICULAR TOWNSHIP

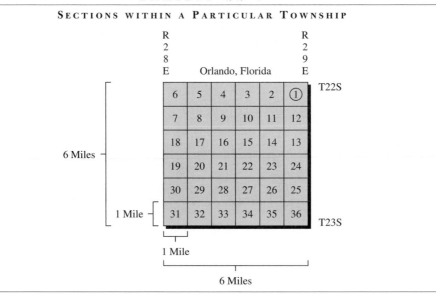

EXHIBIT 22-8

SUBDIVIDED SECTION (SECTION 1)

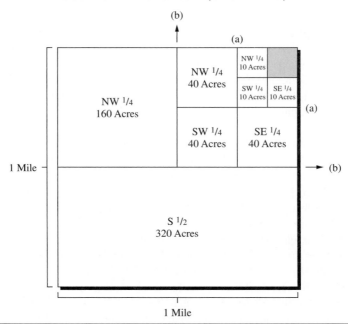

shaded area located? Again, it is the NE. Now moving out to consider the entire section, in what part of the section is the shaded parcel located? Again, the answer is NE. Thus, the complete GRSS description of the Orlando parcel becomes "The NE quarter of the NE quarter of the NE quarter of Section 1, T23S, R29E of the Tallahassee Principal Meridian and Baseline."

The key to assigning GRSS descriptions is to begin with the subject parcel and then work outward through the successive subdivisions to the section, to the township and range, and finally, to the principal meridian and baseline.

Correction lines. Description by the GRSS does not involve as straightforward an application as illustrated above because the earth's curvature does not allow the placement of a flat and featureless grid without distortions. To correct for the earth's curvature, correction lines appear every 24 miles beginning from each principal meridian and baseline. This means that sections along the borders of townships affected by correction lines will not measure exactly 640 acres.

SUMMARY

Appreciation of the legal perspective of real estate requires a thorough understanding of both the system of property rights in real estate and the methods for transferring property rights. This chapter presented the basic concepts and terminology underlying these methods for transferring real property rights. We emphasized that the value of real estate depends, along with property rights created by property laws, on contracts made enforceable by strong contract laws. Without such laws, property will not achieve its highest and best use and potential value.

Deeds are the legal instruments that evidence the transfer of real property rights. Evidence of good title to real estate occurs in several ways, including an updated abstract and title insurance. Transfer of title to real estate involves either public grant, private grant (usually sales), devise and descent, foreclosure, adverse possession and prescription, or as the result of acts of nature.

Some basic legal fundamentals of contracts also appear in this chapter, including the elements of valid and enforceable contracts. The four types of contracts most commonly found in real estate transactions include listing contracts, contracts for sale, mortgage contracts, and leases. The legal and institutional structure for transferring real property rights depends on the enforceability of these contracts. Other chapters in this text contain detailed discussions of each of these four common contracts.

The final section of the chapter presents the ways to properly and legally describe property real estate contracts and practice. They include metes-and-bounds descriptions, which rely on natural and manmade physical features of the land; recorded plat descriptions used for describing parcels in urban areas; and the Government Survey System, which applies in most of the United States except the original 13 states and a few others.

KEY TERMS

Abstracts of title 665
Accretion 671
Bargain-and-sale deed 669
Bilateral contract 672
Cadastres 666
Encroachments 675
Executor's deeds 669
Expressed contract 672
General warranty deed 668

Government Rectangular Survey
  System 679
Implied contract 672
Letter of opinion 666
Metes and bounds 675
Officer's deeds 669
Patent 669
Plat books 678
Private grants 664

Public grants 663
Quitclaim deed 669
Recorded plat map 677
Reliction 671
Sheriff's deeds 669
Special warranty deed 668
Title insurance 665
Torrens system 666
Unilateral contract 672

TEST YOURSELF

Answer the following multiple choice questions:

1. Special warranty deeds are used if
   a. Title is not sufficiently secure to qualify for a warranty deed.
   b. Sellers wish to restrict their liability to title defects occurring after they acquired title.
   c. Sellers wish to transfer only an interest in real estate.
   d. No title insurance is available.
   e. Sellers warrant special property rights.

2. Which of the following statements describes a voidable contract?
   a. An instrument that satisfies all legal requirements but lacks one essential element required by law.
   b. Parties to the contract have no legal agreement.
   c. A contract that may be enforced or rejected at the option of one of the parties.
   d. An oral contract conveying interest in real estate.
   e. A contract implied-in-fact.

3. Title is not conveyed until the deed is
   a. Recorded.
   b. Executed by the seller.
   c. Stamped by the county clerk.
   d. Physically handed by the grantee to the grantor.
   e. Delivered by the grantor to the grantee and accepted by the grantee.

4.

a		b	
c		d	e

Identify the north one half of the NW quarter of the NW quarter of the section shown above.
   a.
   b.
   c.
   d.
   e.

5. A deed that describes the consideration (property) given and conveys title to real property without giving any warranties of title is a
   a. Quitclaim deed.
   b. General warranty deed.
   c. Special warranty deed.

  d. Bargain and sale deed.

  e. Private grant deed.

6. The purpose of fiscal systems of land registration in countries around the world is to

  a. Identify parcels of land to facilitate title transfers.

  b. Identify parcels of land to facilitate payment of property taxes.

  c. Identify parcels of land to promote international investment.

  d. Determine voting rights (in many countries).

  e. Promote local government land-use control and planning.

7. A form of insurance that protects real estate owners from loss of ownership because of the existence of prior liens against properties is

  a. Hazard insurance.

  b. Mortgage insurance.

  c. Property life insurance.

  d. FHA insurance.

  e. Title insurance.

8. The main purpose of describing parcels of land is to

  a. Facilitate property tax assessment.

  b. Help lawyers prepare contracts.

  c. Avoid mistakes involving boundary lines in real estate transfers.

  d. Satisfy legal requirements of deeds.

  e. Provide evidence of good title.

9. Which of the following is *not* one of the generally accepted methods of legally describing real estate?

  a. Metes and bounds.

  b. Government Survey System.

  c. Recorded plat map.

  d. Street address.

  e. All of the above are generally acceptable for real estate contracts.

10. A Torrens certificate

  a. Evidences good title to real estate.

  b. Is obtainable in most states as a substitute for a deed.

  c. Only applies to titles for residential real estate.

  d. Is a type of deed to real estate.

  e. Gives owners of real estate discounts on their property taxes.

PROBLEMS FOR THOUGHT AND SOLUTION

1. Give a brief historical account of how abstracts of title evolved to title insurance.

2. What relationship exists between strong contract laws that promote the development of enforceable contracts and the prices of real estate observed in the market?

3. What importance should be placed on obtaining a general warranty deed as the buyer of real estate when the lender requires title insurance?

4. Can an implied contract be used to transfer real property rights?

5. Is there anything wrong with using the property street address in a contract for sale?

CASE PROBLEMS

1. The Greens sold their house several years ago to the White family. Now, the Whites are attempting to sell the same house to the Silvers, but a problem has surfaced. It seems that when the Greens sold to the Whites, Mr. and Mrs. Green were obtaining a divorce. Thus, there is some question about

whether or not Mrs. Green has remaining dower rights in the property.

As the broker for the Whites, what is your next step (the fee is in jeopardy!)? Explain the nature of any legal instruments that may come into play in this situation.

2.

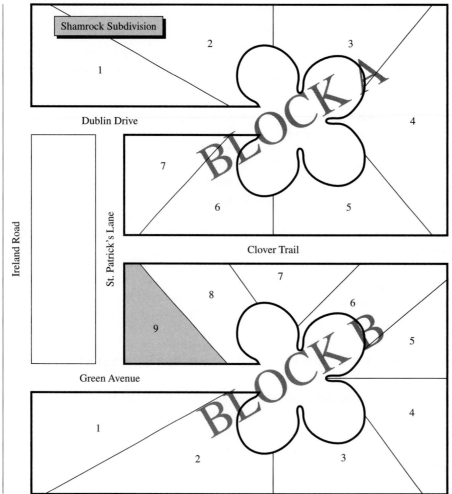

Provide a complete plat description of the shaded parcel in this map. Other information you need is given below:

Plat book number 1, page 17, plat number 500

County: Blarney

State: Vermont

Date recorded: March 17, 1998

ADDITIONAL READINGS

These books contain chapters with detailed discussions of deeds, titles, contracts, and property descriptions:

Gibson, Frank, James Karp, and Elliot Klayman. *Real Estate Law*. Chicago: Dearborn Financial Publishing, 1992, Chapters 8–10.

Werner, Raymond J., and Robert Kratovil. *Real Estate Law*. Englewood Cliffs, N.J.: Prentice Hall, 1993, Chapters 6, 7, 9, and 15.

An excellent book about the Torrens system for evidencing title to real estate is:

Mapp, Thomas W. *Torrens' Elusive Title*. Alberta, Canada: The Alberta Institute for Law Research, 1978.

The following periodicals regularly contain useful articles on real property rights:

Journal of Real Estate Law
Real Estate Law Journal

23
CHAPTER

REAL ESTATE BROKERAGE AND LISTING CONTRACTS

BROKERAGE: THE BEST-KNOWN TYPE OF REAL ESTATE BUSINESS
Real Estate Brokers as Market Facilitators
Economic Rationale for Employing a Broker

LAW OF AGENCY
Types of Agents
Fiduciary Responsibilities
Real Estate Agents
Transaction Brokers
Salespersons as Subagents

LICENSING OF REAL ESTATE BROKERS AND SALESPERSONS
Brokerage Licensing Administration
How to Obtain a Real Estate License
License Law Infractions

CERTIFICATION OF REAL ESTATE OCCUPATIONS

THE MARKETING FUNCTION
Market Segmentation and Specialization
Service
Commercial Brokerage
Residential Brokerage
International Aspects of Brokerage

LISTING CONTRACTS

TYPES OF LISTING CONTRACTS
Open Listing
Net Listing
Exclusive Agency Listing
Exclusive Right of Sale Listing

LISTING CONTRACT PROVISIONS
Protective Provisions for Property Owners
Protective Provisions for the Broker
Termination
Splitting the Commission

CHOOSING A REAL ESTATE BROKER

LISTING SITUATION— EXAMPLE

SUMMARY

KEY TERMS

TEST YOURSELF

PROBLEMS FOR THOUGHT AND SOLUTION

CASE PROBLEMS

INTERNET EXERCISES

ADDITIONAL READINGS

After reading this chapter, students will be able to:

1. Describe the brokerage function.

2. State three reasons sellers use brokers.

3. Explain the real estate licensing process.

4. Explain the difference between licensing and certification.

5. Explain how commission rates are determined.

6. List and describe four types of listing contracts.

7. Describe three types of agency relationships in real estate brokerage.

8. List at least three protective provisions each for a property owner and broker that should be included in a listing contract.

9. List the ways in which a listing contract can be terminated.

BROKERAGE: THE BEST-KNOWN TYPE OF REAL ESTATE BUSINESS

Many people think of real estate brokerage as *the* real estate business. While we take a much broader view of real estate, we agree that brokerage is one of the largest and most visible parts of the real estate business. Also, most people are more apt to come in contact with real estate brokers or salespeople than other real estate professionals.

Real estate brokerage also tends to be better known than other real estate businesses because it is easier to enter than other types of businesses. Educational requirements are not extensive, and capital requirements are not as high as in other businesses; a small office, a telephone, and a car may be the only requirements. Although many people enter the business, many also leave it; turnover is high.

Yet, real estate brokerage is a professionally demanding occupation for those who succeed. It requires a great deal of knowledge, skill, and hard work. It can also be quite rewarding, both monetarily and psychologically. But, as with any other business or profession, the price of success is educational preparation, dedication to the welfare of customers, and hard work.

REAL ESTATE BROKERS AS MARKET FACILITATORS

Real estate brokers serve as intermediaries. They are the catalysts of real estate transactions; they help make markets work by bringing buyers and sellers together physically and emotionally to create sales and purchases. For this reason they may be regarded as *facilitators of market value*. Without their services, it would be more difficult and costly

EXHIBIT 23-1

THE BROKERAGE FUNCTION

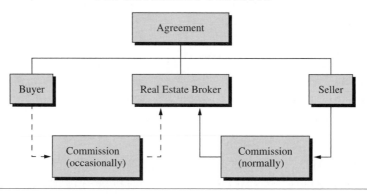

to buy and sell properties, and values of real estate—at least in some markets—would undoubtedly be lower.

For this service, brokers are paid a fee, usually called a **commission**. Commissions are typically paid by sellers, but they may be paid by buyers or—in some unusual situations—by both sellers and buyers. Exhibit 23–1 shows the nature of the brokerage function.

ECONOMIC RATIONALE FOR EMPLOYING A BROKER

Brokers are employed to sell properties because they perform a useful service. Brokers have specialized knowledge of the market for properties and have developed expertise in selling such properties. Furthermore, they spend time and effort in finding buyers for listed properties. Brokers have knowledge and expertise in the following areas:

- Prices and terms of recent market transactions for similar properties.
- Marketing procedures that have been successful in the past.
- Legal obligations of buyers and sellers.
- Similar properties, prices, and terms currently listed for sale.
- Needs of prospective buyers who seek out brokerage firms as sources of properties.
- Procedures that buyers and sellers should follow in consummating a transaction (*e.g.*, how to obtain a title search, financing, insurance, utility services, and the like).

While some property owners attempt to sell their properties themselves to avoid the cost of a broker, such owners often find they are ill-equipped for this task, and they may end up with less cash than if they had employed a broker. Consider the two alternative transactions in Exhibit 23–2 for the same property—one without and the other with a

E X H I B I T   2 3 - 2

**ALTERNATIVE TRANSACTIONS
WITH AND WITHOUT A REAL ESTATE BROKER**

		Without Broker	With Broker
Price		$95,000	$100,000
Marketing costs	$1,000	—	
Time of owner (60 hrs. @ $50/hr.)	3,000	4,000	—
Commission (6½%)		—	6,500
Proceeds to owner		$91,000	$ 93,500

broker. The gain to the owner by using a broker is the result of a number of factors. While some owners may believe otherwise, buyers tend to negotiate prices downward by at least a portion of the commission when they know a broker is not involved. Furthermore, the offering price may be lower to begin with because a seller who does not employ a broker does not have access to the number of prospective buyers that a broker usually has. And sellers may waste time with unqualified buyers. In other words, an owner-seller must usually rely on a "thinner" market than a broker, and the selling time may be longer.

Astute readers of Exhibit 23–2 may agree with these points but may also realize that by not including the owner's time in the calculation he or she would be ahead not to use a broker. Also, the time of the owner does not represent a cash outlay. Nevertheless, the owner's time should normally be counted, since he or she must typically take time off from a job or give up other valuable or pleasurable activities. Owners also subject themselves to greater legal and financial risks because they are less aware of the pitfalls of selling property than brokers who specialize in this activity.

The net result is that sellers who employ brokers often end up better off economically than sellers who do not employ brokers. In reality, brokerage commissions are quite low in relation to the service provided and to the costs borne by brokerage firms (see Real Estate Focus 23–1). If this were not so, most owners would not use brokers, and the number of brokerage firms would decline dramatically.

LAW OF AGENCY

Real estate brokers and salespersons operate under the **law of agency**. It is the applicable law in every state that gives a broker or salesperson the right to act for a **principal** in trying to buy or sell a property. In acting for another person brokers automatically fall into the category of agents (except when the category of *transaction broker* is created, as explained in the section, "Transaction Broker"), which means that the broker must "stand in the shoes" of the principal. Thus, a broker must look out for the best interests of the principal and can do nothing to compromise a principal's interests, position, or bargaining power.

REAL ESTATE FOCUS 23-1

The Effect of Competitive Market Forces on Commission Rates

Brokerage commissions are, by practice, a certain percentage of the sale price of property. Usually, the salesperson must split with the broker (e.g., 50 percent each) any commission earned from the sale of a property the salesperson listed or from the sale of a property by the salesperson. This is because the broker provides training, office space, telephones, and secretarial support so the salesperson can produce listings and sales.

By law, brokerage commissions must be established by negotiations between the broker and clients. Many brokers in the same area are members of a multiple listing service and charge similar commission rates, which has led some observers to suspect price fixing. This pattern, however, apparently results from competitive market forces that drive rates to their lowest possible levels, rather than from collusion among brokers.

TYPES OF AGENTS

In general, three types of agents can be created by the scope of the relationship between a principal and an agent. The broadest scope of authority is the **universal agent,** to whom a principal delegates the power to act in *all* matters that can be delegated in place of the principal. A **general agent** is delegated by the principal to act within the confines of a business or employment relationship. An insurance agent, for example, may be a general agent of the insurance company if the agent can sign contracts that bind the company, supervise employees of the company, and in other ways carry out the business of the company. Similarly, a property manager is a general agent if he or she can rent apartments, collect rents, handle tenant relations, supervise maintenance, and perform accounting functions. Keep in mind that such agents are not employees of the companies. A **special agent** is authorized by the principal to handle only a specific business transaction or to perform only a specific function. In most cases a real estate broker acts in the capacity of a special agent in representing the buyer or seller to purchase or dispose of a single property or set of properties.

FIDUCIARY RESPONSIBILITIES

The significance of an agency relationship is that agents have a **fiduciary relationship** with their principals, and this relationship carries special responsibilities, particularly on the part of the agents, but also on the part of the principals. Fiduciaries must be completely open and honest with their principals, and they must not betray confidential information about their principals, their financial status, or their motivations. In effect they must represent the interests of their principals to the best of their ability—in the same way they would represent themselves, and according to any instructions given to them by their principals. A fiduciary's duties include confidentiality, loyalty, obedience, disclosure, accounting, care, skill, and due diligence.

A principal's duties are to be open, honest, and fair with the agent. This implies also that the principal will cooperate with the agent in providing information about the property (such as repair and expense records) when requested by the agent. When the agent has successfully completed the task assigned (the sale of the property), the agent is entitled to prompt payment for services rendered.

REAL ESTATE AGENTS

An **agency** relationship is created between a seller and a broker when both parties agree to a **listing contract**. Such a contract may be written or oral, and it establishes the rights and duties of each party. In most listing contracts the sellers agree to make the properties available for purchase at a specified price for a specified period of time (such as four months). They also agree to pay the broker a specified fee or a certain percentage of the selling price when the broker finds a buyer who is "ready, willing, and able" to purchase the property, or upon closing of the transaction. Brokers usually agree to use their best efforts to try to sell the property on the terms acceptable to the sellers. Listing contracts are covered in detail later in this chapter.

An agency relationship is created between a buyer and a broker by a contract (which also may be written or oral) usually called a *buyer agency agreement.* In such a contract brokers usually agree to use their best efforts to find properties meeting the requirements of the buyer. The buyer agrees to pay the broker a commission or a fee upon consummating a purchase or to permit the broker to share a commission paid to the seller's broker.

Another agency relationship that can be created under the laws of most states is **dual agency**. In these situations the broker is an agent of both a seller and a buyer, and the broker owes equal loyalty to both. A duel agency must be disclosed to all parties in the transaction, and both principals must give their informed written consent. While the broker owes equal loyalty to both parties, it cannot be *undivided* loyalty. For example, a dual agency broker cannot inform the seller that the buyer will pay a price higher than the price stated in the written offer or that the seller or buyer will accept financing terms other than those offered. Similarly, the broker cannot reveal to the buyer that the seller will accept a price lower than the listing price, unless instructed in writing to do otherwise. While dual agency has been widely used in the past, the current trend is to replace it with the role of transaction broker.

TRANSACTION BROKERS

Another type of relationship has come to be recognized between brokers and clients in many states—a *nonagency* type of relationship. This type of relationship is represented by the term **transaction *(or facilitating)* broker.** In this relationship a broker assists with a brokerage transaction between a buyer and seller, but the broker does not represent either party. Transaction brokers are required to exercise skill, care, and diligence in dealing with the parties, and they must deal honestly and fairly with both parties. In other words, they owe both parties the standard business characteristics of competence and fair dealing, but they are not bound by the fiduciary requirements of agents. A transaction broker's status must also be disclosed in writing to all relevant parties.

EXHIBIT 23-3

AGENCY RELATIONSHIPS IN REAL ESTATE BROKERAGE

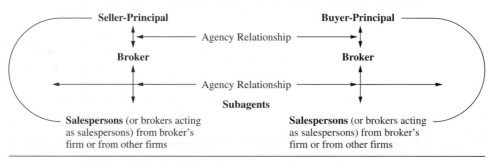

DISCLOSED DUAL AGENT

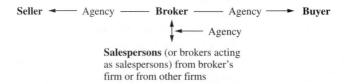

TRANSACTION BROKER
(Not an Agency Relationship)

SALESPERSONS AS SUBAGENTS

As shown in Exhibit 23–3, salespersons or other brokers who work for or through a broker have a fiduciary relationship with both the broker and the broker's principal(s). This relationship is known as **subagency**, and it requires the same level of loyalty, confidentiality, and trust as between the broker and principal. In other words, a real estate salesperson, or a broker acting in the capacity of a salesperson, with respect to both the broker (whether the salesperson is an employee or independent contractor for tax purposes) and the broker's principal(s) is required to abide by the duties of confidentiality, loyalty, obedience, disclosure, accounting, care, skill, and due diligence.

LICENSING OF REAL ESTATE BROKERS AND SALESPERSONS

All the states and the District of Columbia have **licensing laws** that regulate persons and companies that engage in the brokerage business. In all of these jurisdictions, a license is required to conduct real estate brokerage activities, which include the purchase, sale, renting, leasing, auctioning, and managing of real estate for others.

State licensing laws generally prescribe two levels of real estate brokerage licensing—the broker license and the salesperson license. The most complete license is the **broker license,** because only a broker is permitted to own and operate a real estate brokerage business. Brokers are responsible for the completion of documents used in sales and leases negotiated by people in their business, for handling money held in trust for clients (*e.g.*, earnest-money deposits or rent collected), and for the actions of their employees. Each real estate sales office, therefore, must have at least one licensed broker.

To enter the brokerage business, one must first obtain a **salesperson license.** The salesperson may be an employee of a broker or an independent contractor who conducts brokerage activities in one or more firms. The salesperson may perform business activities, such as negotiating listing contracts or contracts for sale, but must perform them in the name of the broker. Also, laws and regulations usually strictly forbid salespersons from holding client monies in trust; these funds must be delivered to the broker or the broker's trust account shortly after receiving them.

BROKERAGE LICENSING ADMINISTRATION

As shown in Exhibit 23–4, the line of authority for real estate brokerage licensing begins with the legislative branch of state government, which originates licensing laws and amendments. Interpretations of state licensing laws take the form of rules and regulations set by the state's **real estate commission**. The commission is usually comprised of prominent brokers and nonbroker (public interest) members. In some states, the commission is part of the department of state government that is responsible for licensing many occupations (*e.g.*, appraisers, barbers, contractors, and morticians).

The real estate commission has several functions. First, it specifies educational requirements for applicants and licensees. It may also prescribe courses and determine whether other courses, usually offered outside the state, are equivalent to those prescribed. The second function is to provide examinations. Passing the state license examination is the determining factor in obtaining a real estate license. Finally, the commission enforces the license law and regulations implementing the law. The commission must hold hearings for licensees accused of violating state licensing laws and has the right to reprimand licensees and to suspend or revoke their licenses.

The commission staff carries out the day-to-day business of administering the license law. The chief administrative officer is responsible to the commission for developing educational materials, record keeping, collecting license fees, and researching complaints against licensees.

EXHIBIT 23-4

ORGANIZATIONAL STRUCTURE FOR ADMINISTERING REAL ESTATE LICENSING LAWS

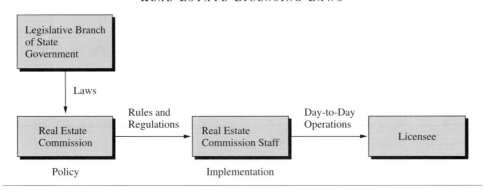

HOW TO OBTAIN A REAL ESTATE LICENSE

Unlike a driver's license, a real estate license obtained in one state does not necessarily qualify one to practice real estate brokerage in another state. The requirements for obtaining brokerage licenses, however, generally have become more uniform among the states in recent years. A greater degree of reciprocity exists today than in the past, especially with respect to education and examination requirements. To answer the question of how to obtain a broker license, we examine the various licensing requirements, which include exemptions, general requirements, education, examinations, and experience.

Exemptions. Some persons who buy, sell, rent, or lease real estate for others are exempt from licensing laws. Usually attorneys, because of their extensive legal training, are exempt. Other exempt categories may include resident managers, government employees (*e.g.*, state transportation department employees), trustees, executors, and those with power of attorney. These exemptions either involve public employees or persons who have a special relationship with the parties for whom they perform brokerage services.

General requirements. Anyone interested in obtaining a salesperson license must apply to take the salesperson license examination. On the application, individuals must demonstrate that they have completed specified educational requirements and have satisfied a set of general requirements, such as minimum age (usually 18 years old for a salesperson license and 21 years old for a broker license), general education (usually a high school diploma), and a good reputation. Some states require references.

Once applicants satisfy these general and educational requirements and pay a fee, they may sit for the state examination. If they earn a passing grade, applicants may receive or apply for a license from the state real estate commission. Another fee may be required then. Applicants for a license usually must choose a broker (sponsor) with whom the license will be placed.

Traditionally, applicants for brokerage licenses had to demonstrate their financial capacity to cover damage judgments brought against them by clients. Some states now, however, have established a **recovery fund** with moneys from license fees. Payments from this fund can be used to pay some types of judgments against licensees. Other states require licensees to purchase **errors and omission insurance** to cover damages arising from professional mistakes.

Experience requirements.   Generally, states do not impose a brokerage experience requirement (that is, an apprenticeship) for obtaining salesperson licenses. For a brokerage license, however, an applicant must have actual experience as a salesperson in addition to taking further course work in real estate. This experience requirement involves at least one year and does not exceed five years.

LICENSE LAW INFRACTIONS

State licensing laws prescribe behavioral requirements with which licensees must comply to keep their licenses. Most laws specify that licensees must not behave in an unethical, fraudulent, or dishonest manner toward their clients and prospective buyers. License laws generally regulate the following activities:

- *Mishandling trust money*, including practices such as commingling trust money with personal funds and accepting noncash payments in trust.
- *Improper handling of fees*, including paying commissions to licensees not in the broker's employ and paying commissions to unlicensed persons.
- *Failure to provide required information,* including failure to provide copies of contracts to all relevant parties and failure to inform buyers of closing costs.
- *Misrepresentation and fraud*, including taking kickbacks without the employer's knowledge, false advertising, and intentionally misleading clients or prospective buyers.
- *Improper business practices*, including offering property at terms other than those specified by clients or failure to submit all offers to clients.

An additional control over the business practices of salespersons and brokers is federal legislation to guarantee equal, or fair, housing opportunities. Title VIII of the Civil Rights Act of 1968 and subsequent amendments make it illegal to discriminate against persons in housing transactions when transactions occur with the aid of a third party (that is, a salesperson or broker).

Specifically, under the provisions of this law, salespersons and brokers cannot refuse to sell or rent to anyone on the basis of sex, creed, race, color, or national origin. They may not discriminate on terms or conditions in sales or rentals, advertise preferences or discrimination, or falsely claim that properties are unavailable. Also, salespersons and brokers cannot practice "steering," which is showing buyers properties only in certain areas, or "blockbusting," which involves spreading rumors to homeowners about a change in the racial or socioeconomic composition of neighborhoods to secure listings.

CERTIFICATION OF REAL ESTATE OCCUPATIONS

There are a number of certification or designation programs in real estate brokerage. Practitioners voluntarily seek designations and certificates from trade or professional organizations because they want to differentiate themselves from less competent, undesignated practitioners. These credentials signal to buyers the holder's competence and honesty; in return, designated practitioners expect to obtain more customers or to be able to charge higher fees. When licensed practitioners seek certification in a specialty (*e.g.*, industrial property brokerage) they seek to signal buyers that they have expertise beyond other licensed brokers in a particular segment of the market.

Brokerage and salesperson licensees may choose to become affiliated with a local Board of Realtors, which is associated with the **National Association of REALTORS (NAR)**[1] as a REALTOR (broker) or REALTOR-Associate (salesperson).[2] Salespersons working under a broker member of a Board of Realtors are also required to belong to the Board. Typically the Board charges the broker for all of the firm's members, who in turn usually charges the salespersons for their memberships. Such affiliations are secondary signals to the public that licensees abide by the NAR code of ethics, in addition to the primary signaling device of state licensing.

Various institutes, societies, and councils affiliated with NAR offer specialized designations in various aspects of the real estate brokerage business. Some of these designations are primary signaling devices within a particular segment of the real estate business (such as property management, industrial and office properties, and real estate counseling).[3]

THE MARKETING FUNCTION

MARKET SEGMENTATION AND SPECIALIZATION

Real estate brokerage firms, like most firms that have a marketing function, practice **market segmentation**; that is, they attempt to identify **submarkets** in which they can specialize and concentrate. The focus of such specialization should be on the needs of

---

[1]The headquarters of NAR are located at 430 North Michigan Avenue, Chicago, Illinois 60611.

[2]The term Realtor® is a federally registered collective trademark. Only active brokers who are members of local and state Boards of Realtors affiliated with NAR are permitted to use this trademark.

[3]The on-line exercise at the end of the chapter will provide you with a list of NAR affiliates, including their purpose, the designations offered, and some general requirements for earning the designations.

potential clients. Therefore, some brokers specialize by property type—they serve sellers and buyers of commercial, industrial, residential, agricultural, office, or recreational properties. Sometimes brokers limit their activities to a particular section of a city, such as the southeast or northwest areas. Brokers who specialize in large commercial or industrial properties may operate over a wide geographic area, sometimes even nationally or internationally.

In all cases, however, successful brokers are able to relate to the needs of buyers and sellers and help them solve their problems. Obviously, sellers want to sell properties quickly for as high a price as they can obtain. Buyers want to find properties that will best serve their needs quickly for as low a price as possible. Thus, the broker's role is to explain the selling and buying processes to both types of clients and guide them through the steps necessary to complete a transaction. Successful brokers also understand that clients must be pleased with their service and continue to be satisfied after the transaction is closed.

SERVICE

As marketing specialists, real estate brokers have only one thing to sell—their service. We have already seen that buyers can buy and sellers can sell properties without the help of real estate brokers. Thus, they would not employ brokers unless they believe brokers provide a valuable service. Brokers usually need an inventory of properties, but even this is not a requirement for some brokerage companies. Buyers can specify the types of property needed, and brokers can search for them.

COMMERCIAL BROKERAGE

While the function of commercial brokerage is the same as that of residential brokerage—facilitating transactions between buyers and sellers—the activities of commercial brokers usually differ considerably from those of residential brokers. Almost all types of properties except one- to four-family residential properties, public properties (schools, municipal buildings, court houses, and the like), and churches can be included in the catch-all commercial category. In reality it includes almost all income-producing properties.

Since the category is so large, many commercial brokers specialize in a particular property type such as apartments, motels and hotels, shopping centers, recreational properties, office buildings, and industrial properties. Typically transactions are larger, and the parties are more knowledgeable. Thus, brokers often seek to match potential buyers with the owners of specific properties and then "get out of the way." Even in these cases, however, potential buyers will want important information about the property and perhaps competing properties. They will want a multiyear record of income and expenses; information on major repairs, additions, or renovations; and certifications of inspections compliance with all relevant laws and regulations. They also may want inspections to detect the presence of any hazardous wastes on the property. The broker often must work with the seller in obtaining and providing all requested information.

Commercial brokers also must negotiate compromises between buyers and sellers when they reach an impasse over a particular issue. Often a major impasse arises over the price to be paid, and the brokers find it in their best interest to suggest a compromise. For example, if a buyer and seller are $50,000 apart on the sale of a grain elevator, the broker may suggest that the seller include some equipment or items of personal property, such as one or two trucks or some office equipment, that were not originally in the deal. Not infrequently the broker is required to lower the commission in order to bring the offer and bid prices into line.

RESIDENTIAL BROKERAGE

Most residential brokers obtain an inventory of properties by belonging to a local **multiple listing service** (MLS). In an MLS, all members submit their listings (properties they have for sale) to the service. From this inventory, any member broker can attempt to sell any property. The commission is split between the listing broker and the selling broker, unless the listing broker also finds the buyer. Members of the MLS also must pay fees to the MLS for its operation.

Almost all brokers in a community have the same inventory (the list of MLS properties), and buyers could learn about at least some of these properties by reading classified advertising. Therefore, a broker's property inventory is not the main reason buyers and sellers use brokers or choose one brokerage firm over others. Rather, it is the service the firm is expected to provide.

Potential customers usually choose a brokerage firm on the basis of reputation in the community, personal acquaintance with the broker or a salesperson, or recommendation by a satisfied customer. Some customers may also rely on the reputation or general image of a brokerage franchise operation such as REMAX, ERA, Better Homes and Gardens, Century 21, Prudential Preferred Properties, or Coldwell Banker.

To attract customers, successful brokerage firms attempt to provide good service and to develop a favorable image in the community or within a professional specialty (such as office buildings, commercial properties, or midpriced residential properties). For example, one residential firm may try to create the image of a young, fast-growing, dynamic firm, whereas another firm may try to promote the image of an old, reliable, stable firm that will continue to serve customers over many years.

The service provided by the brokerage firm must be to help clients make a decision and then to help them implement that decision. For example, buyers will usually need information about alternative choices of properties in the market, their prices, and how they may meet the buyer's needs. The broker or salesperson can obtain information about such matters as utility expenses, taxes, maintenance, and legal issues regarding alternative properties. The broker or salesperson can also suggest ways of modifying or using the property in particular ways needed by the buyer. Finally, the broker or salesperson can help the buyer find and compare financing alternatives. Overall, the broker's or salesperson's objective should be to help the client (whether it be a buyer or seller) to analyze the proposed purchase or sale and to guide the client to a decision with which he or she is comfortable.

REAL ESTATE FOCUS 23-2

Some Major U.S. Companies and Properties Currently or Formerly Owned by Foreign Investors

Company or Property	Owner (total or major interest)	Country
Intercontinental Hotels (including Mark Hopkins, San Francisco)	Seibu/Saison	Japan
Citicorp Headquarters, New York City	Daiiehi Seinei	Japan
Holiday Inns	Bass PLC	Great Britain
Bel Air Hotel and Country Club, Los Angeles	Sekitei	Japan
Ravines Resort and Country Club, Jacksonville, Florida	Kondo Sangyo	Japan
Ramada Inns	New World Development Prime Motor Inns	Hong Kong and United States
Nikko Hotels, New York, Chicago, San Francisco, Beverly Hills, Waikiki, Mexico City	Japan Air Lines and Prudential	Japan and United States
Rockefeller Center, New York City	Mitsubishi (ownership ended in bankruptcy in 1995)	Japan
Columbia Pictures, Hollywood	Sony	Japan
Firestone Tire and Rubber, Akron, Ohio	Bridgestone	Japan
Paine Webber Groups	Yasuda Mutual Life Insurance	Japan
MGM/UA, Hollywood	Qintex Group	Australia

INTERNATIONAL ASPECTS OF BROKERAGE

World economies have become increasingly intertwined, and real estate markets, as parts of these economies, have also become internationalized. This trend has been labeled the *globalization* of real estate markets. Many U.S. companies and investors have purchased real estate in foreign countries, and many foreign companies and investors have purchased U.S. real estate. In the early 1990s Japanese companies purchased a number of prominent buildings in the downtowns of major U.S. cities for relatively high prices, attracting media attention. Since that time, however, Japanese investors have sold some of these properties, and foreign ownership of some properties (such as Rockefeller Center in New York City) has ended in bankruptcy. The Japanese, however, were never the largest foreign investors in U.S. real estate. Canadian, British, and West German investors outpace the Japanese in this category. Real Estate Focus 23–2 lists some major U.S. properties that are (or were) owned by foreign investors.

A number of large firms, both in the United States and abroad, find foreign investment to be a lucrative part of their business. While some of the largest purchases of U.S. real estate have been made without the aid of brokerage firms, most deals have involved brokers. The commission on a typical transaction can be several million dollars, and the brokerage firms are expected to earn these large commissions by being of real service to buyers and sellers. To serve sellers of large U.S. properties, brokers must attempt to know as much about the properties as they possibly can. They often must provide computerized analyses of leases, showing when their terms will end, their significant provisions, and how much rents may be increased. They also may have to provide estimates of modernization or rehabilitation costs and show how such costs will affect income and rate of return on investment.

Although most foreign investors speak English or have English-speaking staffs, most U.S. brokers must work through cooperative arrangements with brokers in non-English speaking countries. Brokers who deal with foreigners must be sensitive to the cultures, customs, and mores of other countries. Speaking a foreign language can facilitate communication with a client and also increase a person's sensitivity to other cultures. To deal in international real estate, U.S. brokers increasingly must think in terms of a global market and be prepared to deal with foreign investors on their own terms.

LISTING CONTRACTS

A **listing contract** provides the authority for a broker to try to sell an owner's property. As shown in Exhibit 23–5, it is an agreement between the owner of real estate and a real estate broker or brokerage firm that requires the broker to attempt to sell the property of the owner. If the broker is successful in finding a buyer for the property, the agreement requires the owner to pay the broker a fee or commission. The broker's fee or commission is usually calculated as a percentage of the selling price (*e.g.*, a commission of 6 percent on a selling price of $100,000 is $6,000). If the broker is unsuccessful, the agreement lapses after a specified time period (or reasonable time period, if the time period is not specifically stated), and neither party has any further obligation.

As discussed previously in this chapter, the broker, as an agent, has a fiduciary relationship with the principal and therefore cannot do anything that would not be in the best interests of the principal. For example, the broker may not purchase the property for himself or herself secretly through a third party. The broker could, of course, purchase the property openly and directly from the principal (owner), provided the complete identity of the broker and his or her relationship to the principal is known by the principal. Furthermore, the broker-agent cannot withhold information from the principal. The broker must present every offer to purchase the property to the principal, even if the agent considers an offer too low, since it may be in the principal's best interest to sell the property quickly, no matter how low the offer.

Additionally, the broker-agent may not attempt to frighten the principal into accepting a low offer or suggest to a prospective buyer that the seller will accept a price lower

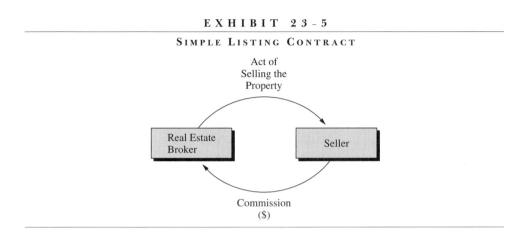

E X H I B I T   2 3 - 5

SIMPLE LISTING CONTRACT

Act of
Selling the
Property

Real Estate
Broker

Seller

Commission
($)

than the listed price, unless the principal has specifically instructed him to convey such information to a prospective buyer. (A broker can, of course, state the obvious fact that the seller *might* accept a lower price and that he or she is obligated to present every offer to the seller.)

In signing a listing contract, an owner agrees to sell the property at a specified price and under specified terms. If the broker finds a purchaser who is *ready, willing* and *able* to purchase the property at the *specified price* and *terms*, the broker is usually entitled to the agreed-upon fee or commission. If the owner then refuses to sell the property, the broker is still entitled to the commission and may sue the owner if the owner does not pay. The prospective buyer may also have legal recourse against the seller by asking a court to compel the seller to complete the transaction, or by suing for damages.

TYPES OF LISTING CONTRACTS

There are four basic types of listing contracts, although only two—the **open listing** and the **exclusive right of sale listing**—are used with much frequency. Another term, *multiple listing,* is sometimes confused as a type of listing; however, multiple listing is actually a cooperative arrangement among brokerages to share their listings. It is not a basic type of listing contract between a seller and a broker.

OPEN LISTING

The open listing is a contract between a property owner and a broker that gives the broker the right to market the property. As with any listing contract, if the broker finds a buyer who is *ready, willing, and able* to purchase the property at the price and terms specified in the contract, the broker will be due a fee or commission. The distinguishing characteristic of the open listing is its lack of exclusivity. The property owners are not precluded from listing the property with other brokers. If they do list the property with two or more brokers, only the broker who procures a buyer will be owed a commission. If the owners sell the property themselves, none of the brokers will be owed a commission.

The open listing is sometimes used with large, special-purpose, or otherwise difficult-to-sell properties. The owners may not be willing to tie up the property with one broker. A single brokerage firm may not operate in a wide enough geographic area or have sufficient expertise, so the owners may list with several brokers to obtain a wider market for their property. A broker may be willing to accept such a listing because he or she believes (1) there is a good chance of selling the property, and the owner will not accept an exclusive agency or exclusive right of sale listing or (2) there is not a good chance of selling the property, but there is little to lose in accepting the listing (there is *some* chance the property will sell, and it would yield a large commission).

NET LISTING

The distinguishing feature of a **net listing** is the commission arrangement. The broker's commission is the difference between the property's sale price and a specified net amount required by the seller. For example, the contract might state that the sellers require a minimum net amount of $100,000 and the broker may keep as commission the difference between any higher price obtained and $100,000. Thus, if the broker sells the property for $110,000, the commission would be $10,000. A net listing can be an open listing or one of the types of listings discussed below—an exclusive agency or exclusive right of sale listing.

The net listing is not used very often. Brokers normally do not like it because it may not produce adequate compensation for a sale. Additionally, the net listing produces a disincentive for brokers to live up to their fiduciary responsibilities. For example, if a broker knows a highway is going to be built or expanded, he or she might attempt to obtain net listings of properties from owners who are not aware of the highway plans. This could produce a higher sale price than the owner expects, which would result in a large commission to the broker and lower net proceeds to the owner than another type of listing arrangement would bring. This situation is not in the owner's best interest. For this reason, the laws of certain states (e.g., New York) prohibit the use of net listings, and professional standards discourage their use in other states.

EXCLUSIVE AGENCY LISTING

This type of listing contract requires the sellers to pay a commission to the broker if the property is sold by anyone, including brokers, other than the owners. The owners, however, retain the right to sell the property without incurring liability for a commission. In effect, the sellers agree not to list their property with other brokers but reserve the right to sell the property themselves without owing a commission.

Like the net listing, this type of listing is used infrequently. Since the owner can sell the property and avoid paying a commission, the **exclusive agency listing** provides far less protection to the broker than the next type of listing discussed below. Thus, brokers are usually less willing to spend time and effort to market properties listed under this arrangement.

EXCLUSIVE RIGHT OF SALE LISTING

For the exclusive right of sale listing contract, the sellers list their property with one broker and agree to pay the broker a commission if the property is sold within a specified time, or, if not specified, within a reasonable time. Thus, the broker will be owed a commission if any other brokers, *or even the owner,* sells the property during the contract period. A typical exclusive right of sale listing contract form is shown in Exhibit 23–6. Note the operative words, "I . . . authorize and give to Broker the exclusive right and power . . . to sell . . . the real property herein described" (line 2 of Exhibit 23–6).

The exclusive right of sale feature is included in the vast majority of brokerage arrangements. Although one might think at first that such a feature would create an unfair burden on sellers, the exclusivity provision has produced faster sales. Brokers are more willing to commit their firms to engage in thorough marketing programs for properties and to spend whatever time is necessary to sell them. Under this arrangement, brokers usually advertise in public media, prepare photographs and brochures about listed properties, and work long hours to obtain buyers. Brokers are protected no matter how or by whom the properties are sold. Without this protection, brokers may not spend enough time, effort, and money to sell the properties.

Second, brokers have realized that to justify their best efforts, they must have the protection provided by the exclusive right of sale provision. Thus, most brokers require sellers to accept this feature. Owners may, of course, refuse and attempt to find a broker who will accept an open or exclusive agency listing. But most do not, because most brokers will not accept other types of listings for residential properties.

Finally, multiple listing services (MLS) accept only exclusive right of sale listings. Other types of listings would undermine the workings of an MLS. For example, if an MLS property were sold by an owner or a broker who was not an MLS member, the MLS broker would probably lose the commission. It would not take many such sales to put the MLS out of business. Thus, to obtain the advantages of having their properties listed by an MLS, owners must agree to an exclusive right of sale listing contract with their broker.

LISTING CONTRACT PROVISIONS

While most brokers use standard, preprinted listing contract forms (see Exhibit 23–6) and most property owners are willing to sign such forms, both parties to such a contract should be certain their interests are protected.

E X H I B I T   2 3 - 6

S A M P L E   L I S T I N G   F O R M

EXCLUSIVE LISTING CONTRACT
For Filing Property With

FIRST MULTIPLE LISTING SERVICE, INC.
ATLANTA, GEORGIA

LISTING COMPANY

NAME _____

BRANCH _____

Dated _____

In consideration of the Undersigned Broker's agreement to to use its best efforts to sell the property within the terms of this contract, I, the undersigned Owner or Legal Agent, do hereby authorize and give to Broker the Exclusive right and power from this date and until 12 o'clock midnight the _____ day of _____, 19 _____, to sell at a price of $ _____ □ All Cash at Closing
□ To Be Refinanced □ To be Sold on Loan Assumption □ Other _____
or any other lesser price acceptable to Owner, the real property herein described.

Broker is a member of FIRST MULTIPLE LISTING SERVICE, INC., of Atlanta and Broker binds himself that he will file this listing with said service within 48 hours after owner signs same. Owner agrees that members of FMLS may act in association with Broker in procuring or attempting to procure a purchaser. Owner agrees to pay to Broker a sales commission of_____ of the sales price, in the event that during the terms of this contract: (1) Broker or any member of said FMLS procures a person ready, willing and able to purchase said property at the price and on terms stated above; or (2) Owner enters into an enforceable contract for the sale or exchange of said property with any purchaser, whether by or through the efforts of Broker or any other person, including Owner. Owner agrees to pay to Broker such commission as stated above, if, within 90 days after the termination of this agreement, said property be sold, exchanged or conveyed to any person to whom the property had been submitted during the life of this agreement, unless the property is sold to such purchaser during said 90 day period by or through another licensed real estate broker with whom Owner has made an exclusive listing contract. Owner agrees to refer all inquiries concerning the sale of the property to Broker during the term hereof.

This agreement shall be binding upon, and shall inure to the benefit of the parties hereto, their heirs, successors, legal representatives, administrators, executors and assigns.

Owner hereby grants permission for the property to be photographed and for said photograph to be used in promoting the sale. Broker is also hereby authorized to place his "For Sale" sign upon said property.

If a sales contract on this property is accepted by Seller and Buyer and if this sales contract later becomes void or impossible to consummate, then the terms of this listing contract shall be automatically extended for a period of time, not to exceed 60 days, equal to the length of time that the sales contract was in effect.

Owner hereby releases and discharges FMLS and Broker and its employees and salespersons, from all claims, suits, or causes of action, whenever asserted, for any and all bodily and personal injuries, damages to or loss of property, and the consequences thereof, which result from any acts of persons who are not employees or salespersons of Broker, or which result from any negligent acts of persons who are employees or salespersons of Broker, whenever said acts occur during the period of this agreement (or any extension thereof).

Owner warrants that it has title to the property described herein, and/or has full authority to enter into this agreement.

Owner warrants that the information with respect to the property as set out in this agreement is true and correct, that there are no defects in the house adversely affecting its value, that all appliances, if any, remaining with the dwelling, heating and air conditioning systems, septic tank (if applicable) and all plumbing and electrical systems are in normal operating condition (except _____),
that Owner has fully revealed to Broker all pertinent information with respect to the house, including defects therein, if any, and that Broker is authorized to convey all such information to prospective purchasers.

Owner acknowledges that Broker intends to rely upon the accuracy of the information furnished by Seller and Owner agrees to hold Broker harmless from any cost, expense of damage incurred by Broker as a result of Owner's withholding any information from Broker or as a result of Owner's giving Broker any information which is incorrect.

LEGAL DESCRIPTION

All that tract or parcel of land lying and being in LAND LOT _____ of the _____ DISTRICT, _____

COUNTY, and being known as LOT _____ , BLOCK _____ of the _____ SUBDIVISION,

according to plat recorded in PLAT BOOK _____ , PAGE _____ , _____ COUNTY RECORDS, and
                                                                              (county)
being improved property known as _____ STREET, _____ ,
                                              (number & name)   (city)
GEORGIA, _____ . The full legal description of said property is the same as is recorded with the Clerk of the Superior
              (zip code)
Court of the County in which the property is located and is made a part of this agreement by reference.

Owner hereby acknowledges receipt of a copy of this contract.

Profile Sheet is attached to and made a part of this agreement by reference.

In witness whereof, the parties have this _____ day of _____ , 19 _____ , duly executed and sealed this Contract.

OWNER (DOES/DOES NOT) REQUEST BROKER TO FURNISH FREE RELOCATION INFORMATION ABOUT _____

_____ (CITY) _____ (STATE).

Rev: 7/15/83   Broker _____   Agent _____   Owner _____

PROTECTIVE PROVISIONS FOR PROPERTY OWNERS

When signing a listing contract, property owners may want to assure themselves about the following matters:

- The brokerage firm will put forth its best efforts to find prospective buyers. The firm should be willing to advertise frequently in local newspapers and perhaps in other publications or on television. It should take photographs of the property, prepare a brochure about the property, conduct group inspections by other brokers and sales personnel, and hold open houses.
- The brokerage firm should indicate its intention to place the listing in a multiple listing service. As discussed above, this will require the property owner to sign an exclusive right of sale listing contract.
- The real estate broker should agree to report every offer promptly. This procedure is a legal and ethical requirement of all brokers.
- The owners and broker should reach understanding and agreement about access to the property. If the property is vacant is the broker allowed to place a lockbox on the door, allowing all brokers and sales personnel access to the property at all times? Will access be limited to specified times? Or must any broker or salesperson call for an appointment to show the property?
- The listing agreement should be limited to a reasonable period. A reasonable period may vary from a month to a year, depending on the type of property, the circumstances, and the conditions of the market. A typical listing period for a residential property is approximately three months; for an industrial property, it may be six months to one year. If the owner must make a business or personal decision within a month that depends on selling the property, the listing might be limited to one month. If no period is specified in the contract and the issue becomes the subject of a lawsuit, courts will specify a reasonable and typical period that is consistent with local practice.
- The broker should agree to provide periodic reports about the marketing program and specific steps taken to attract prospective buyers. Such reports should be made at least monthly.

PROTECTIVE PROVISIONS FOR THE BROKER

Since the brokerage firm usually prepares the contract or decides which standard form to use, its interests are usually adequately protected. Thus, the following matters are usually covered in a listing contract:

- The property owner agrees to pay a commission or fee to the broker on the broker's finding a buyer who is ready, willing, and able to buy the property at the specified price and terms, or at whatever price and terms are acceptable to the property owner.

  While the brokerage commission is usually payable at the time of closing, the broker may be due a commission even if the transaction is not

REAL ESTATE FOCUS 23-3

A Ready, Willing, and Able Buyer

Lloyd and Edna Evans desired to sell their property. They employed the services of Fleming Realty and Insurance, Inc., a corporation engaged in providing real estate brokerage services. These parties entered into an exclusive right of sale listing agreement, which contained a procurement clause that required the Evanses to pay a commission if Fleming obtained a ready, willing, and able purchaser. The broker located Neal Hasselbach, who signed a standardized purchase agreement offering to buy the Evanses property on the terms specified in the listing agreement. In essence, in this document Mr. Hasselbach offered to pay the asking price to the Evanses. Based on their fears that Mr. Hasselbach was not financially able to purchase their property, Mr. and Mrs. Evans refused to sign a sales contract with this buyer.

Issue:

Did Fleming Realty and Insurance procure a ready, willing, and able buyer, and was it therefore entitled to the agreed-on commission?

Decision:

Yes.

Reasons:

The evidence at the trial court showed that Hasselbach had a net worth, in cash and property, in excess of $250,000. The proposed contract for the Evanses' land totaled $155,840, to be paid by a down payment of $35,000 and 10 annual installments of $12,184 each. The jury's conclusion that Hasselbach was financially able to perform this sale contract was reasonable. Since the buyer fulfilled the requirements of the listing agreement's procuring clause, the broker was entitled to collect the commission established even though the sale was not closed.

SOURCE: *Fleming Realty and Insurance Inc.* v. *Evans,* 259 NW 2d 604 (Neb. 1977).

closed. The sellers, for example, might decide not to go through with the sale. The broker would still be owed the commission because he or she procured a ready, willing, and able buyer (see Real Estate Focus 23–3). Occasionally, sellers insist that the commission-due clause be stated so that the broker is not owed a commission until the transaction is closed. Obviously, this provision is less favorable to the broker than the ready, willing, and able buyer provision. The commission or fee is usually (but not necessarily) based on a percentage of the selling price. While this percentage must be negotiable between sellers and broker, there is a tendency for commission rates to converge around a common number, such as 6 or 7 percent, in most communities. Below these rates, brokers cannot earn a reasonable profit and tend to go out of business. Strong competition usually limits commission rates above these levels for single-family homes. Commission rates on commercial, industrial, and unimproved properties are more varied, usually ranging between 3 and 15 percent.

- The broker attempts to obtain a listing agreement for a sufficient period of time to allow a reasonable chance to sell the property. Short periods are not in the broker's interest (and not necessarily in the seller's interest, either) because a broker's time, effort, and expenditures can easily be wasted. For single-family residences, brokers usually like to obtain listings for at least three months. For larger, more specialized properties, longer listing periods—up to six months or a year—are not uncommon.

- The broker wants adequate access to the property to allow brokers and sales personnel to show the property without undue limitations and hassle. A lockbox arrangement provides the greatest access, and many listing contracts give the broker the right to place a lockbox on the property. The house key is placed inside the box, which is a heavy metal container usually attached to the front doorknob. MLS brokers have a key for the lockbox, so brokers and sales agents can show the house to prospective buyers even when the owners are not home or the house is unoccupied. If the owners do not want the device placed on the property, they should strike out that clause.

- Brokers usually insist on a provision protecting their right to a commission after the listing period expires if the property is sold to someone who learned about the property from the broker. Such a provision reduces the opportunity for a seller and buyer to conspire to wait until after the listing expires to complete a transaction and avoid liability for a commission. In most standard listing contracts this provision has a time period equal to the specified listing period. Thus, if the listing period is three months, the broker's protection period is for an additional three months; if the listing period is one year, the protection period typically is for one year. There is no reason, however, that this period cannot be longer or shorter, depending upon the negotiations between seller and broker.

TERMINATION

A listing contract terminates under any of three circumstances: the specified period expires, the property is sold, or one of the parties abrogates the terms of the contract. The first two courses of termination are straightforward, and there is usually little question about the result.

Abrogation of terms is less clear and usually more difficult to prove. On the owners' part, the most clear-cut abrogation would be their unwillingness to sign a sale contract with a ready, willing, and able purchaser. While such a refusal happens rarely, it may result in legal action against the owners by both the broker and the buyers. The owners may be legally compelled to pay the broker's commission, since the broker fulfilled his or her part of the contract. In cases in which the owners abrogate the terms by refusing to show the property or by otherwise discouraging prospective buyers, the broker usually refuses to make any further efforts to sell the property.

The broker may abrogate the terms of the contract by failing to market the property effectively. The broker may not advertise sufficiently or make enough effort to sell the property. While in some cases owners may have good legal grounds for terminating the contract, their usual remedy is to wait for the listing to expire. Such contentions are both difficult to prove and costly to pursue legally.

SPLITTING THE COMMISSION

The commission paid by a principal upon consummation of a transaction can be divided between the listing and selling broker in any way they agree. In most communities, however, members of the Board of Realtors® agree to a specified percentage of the total commission that the listing brokerage firm and the selling brokerage firm receive. In many communities this percentage is 50 percent to each, but occasionally it is 60 percent to 40 percent (in either direction).

Within each firm the policy differs as to what percentage the salesman who actually obtained the listing and the salesman who actually found the buyer receive, but, again, 50 percent each is typical. For some salespersons in certain firms, however, the percentage may go as high as 90, if the salesperson has been with the firm many years, is a high producer, or has officer or other responsibilities in the firm. If both the listing salesperson and selling salesperson work in the same firm, the typical arrangement would be for each of them to share 50–50 in one-half of the total commission, that is, each would receive 25 percent of the total commission. A buyer's broker is usually treated the same as a selling broker. Exhibit 23–7 shows a typical commission split in a transaction involving different listing and selling brokerage firms.

CHOOSING A REAL ESTATE BROKER

Most owners are mainly concerned with selling their property. However, the listing contract form does not guarantee that the broker will take specific steps or actions to sell the property; it only promises that the broker will use his or her "best efforts." For this reason, owners often must rely on a broker's reputation and track record. Thus, owners wishing to sell their properties should inquire about brokerage firms before signing a listing contract. How has the firm marketed similar properties? What specific procedures has the firm followed and with what degree of success? How much advertising has the firm done for each property?

An owner should talk to other sellers to find out how various firms have performed. What marketing and advertising efforts do the firms make? How often and what types of reports do they make to owners? What is their reputation in the community? Would the sellers use the firms again?

Choosing a real estate brokerage firm is much like choosing any other professional service. How does one choose a doctor, lawyer, or accountant? Reputation, track record, and personal integrity are the hallmarks of quality and reliability. A property owner should be no less careful in choosing a real estate broker than in selecting other professionals.

EXHIBIT 23-7

TYPICAL COMMISSION SPLIT

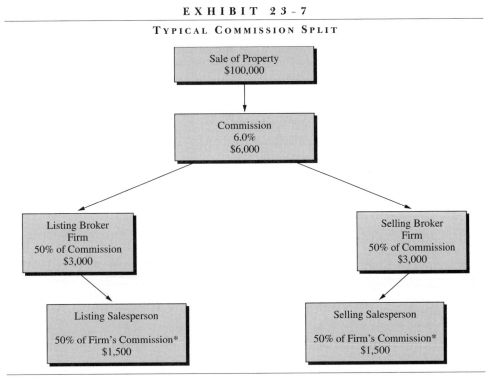

*These percentages can vary from 50 percent to 90 percent depending on such factors as the length of time the salesperson has been with the firm and whether he or she is an officer of the firm.

LISTING SITUATION—EXAMPLE

Fred and Louise Johnson decide to sell their home in Gainesville, Florida, because Fred's job has been transferred to Fort Myers. They contact Carol Locascio, a realtor with Bosshardt Realty Service, Inc., who sold them the house five years ago. They like Carol— she was courteous and efficient when she helped them find a home, and she has stayed in touch with them since.

On May 1, 1998, Carol comes to the Johnsons' house, which is located at 1822 NW 40th Avenue. The Johnsons remind Carol that they paid $72,500 for the house five years ago, and since prices have risen considerably in the meantime, they believe the house should be worth around $90,000. Carol points out some recent sales of similar houses in the neighborhood ranging from $80,000 to $90,000, and she tells them that realistically she believes the house will not sell for more than $85,000. (She really believes this is high and that it will ultimately sell for between $80,000 and $85,000.) After some discussion,

EXHIBIT 23-8

GAINESVILLE MULTIPLE LISTING, INC.
EXCLUSIVE RIGHT OF SALE LISTING AGREEMENT

In consideration of the agreement contained here, the sufficiency of which is hereby acknowledged by

Bosshardt Realty, Inc.
_____ hereinafter called BROKER, and

Fred and Louise Johnson
_____ hereinafter called SELLER,
we hereby jointly agree to the following:

1. AUTHORITY TO SELL PROPERTY: SELLER gives BROKER the EXCLUSIVE RIGHT TO SELL the real and personal property (collectively "Property") described below, at the price and terms described below, beginning the 1st day of May , 19 98 , and terminating at 11:59 p.m. the 31st day of October , 19 98 ("Termination Date"). Upon full execution of a contract for sale and purchase of the Property, all rights and obligations of this Contract will automatically extend through the date of the actual closing of the contract for sale and purchase. SELLER certifies and represents that he/she/it is legally entitled to convey the Property and all improvements.

Price $85,000 _____ Terms Cash to owner _____

Legal Description Parcel No. 3, Block 2 of Spring Meadow Estates, Gainesville, _____

____ Alachua County, Florida. Tax Parcel No. 0123-444-555 _____

All taxes for the current year, rentals, monthly insurance premiums, hazard insurance premiums and interest on existing mortgages (if any) shall be prorated as of the date of closing. Personal property to be included in the purchase price: All fixed equipment including drapery hardware, light fixtures, carpeting and plants and shrubbery now installed on said property, and such additional personal property as may be listed on the attached profile sheet.

2. SELLER further certifies and represents that the property has no known latent defects and SELLER knows of no facts materially affecting the value or desirability of the property which are not readily observable, except the following none _____ (See Attachment). SELLER agrees to indemnify and save BROKER harmless of and from any and all loss, damage, suits and claims, including attorney's fees and costs of defense incurred by BROKER on account of any representation made by BROKER in reliance on SELLER'S representation herein. There is attached to this Agreement a GAINESVILLE MULTIPLE LISTING, INC. Profile Sheet and Feature Sheet which are by reference included in and made a part of this exclusive right of sale listing agreement.

3. If a lockbox is to be used, the BROKER agrees to use due care in the installation, use, maintenance, and operation of the lockbox. The SELLER agrees to hold the BROKER harmless of and from all claims, demands, costs, judgments and liability which SELLER may suffer as a result of losses or damages arising out of the use, maintenance or operation of the lockbox during the term of this agreement. Gross negligence on the part of the BROKER or agents acting through him are expressly excluded from this covenant.

SELLER is to initial one of the following:

a. SELLER agrees to permit use of lockbox. _FJ_LJ_ b. SELLER does not agree to permit use of lockbox. _____

4. The SELLER agrees, at his expense, to provide for: (a) preparation of and delivery to the BUYER of a good and sufficient warranty deed (unless otherwise required) conveying an insurable title free and clear of all liens, except encumbrances of record, to be assumed by the BUYER as part of the purchase price and taxes for the year of sale; (b) binder and policy for fee title insurance or abstract from earliest records; (c) state documentary stamps on the deed; (d) SELLER'S attorney fee; (e) recording fees for satisfactions of the liens of record, if same are paid off; (f) certificate of a locally licensed entomologist dated within thirty days prior to closing, showing any improvements on the premises, exclusive of fences, to be apparently free from active infestation (other than infestation by wood destroying fungi) or visible damage (including that caused by wood destroying fungi) by termites or other wood destroying organisms as required to be disclosed by Florida Law.

5. The SELLER agrees that BROKER has the right, at the BROKER'S discretion, to order and obtain on behalf of the SELLER all items necessary to consummate a closing on subject property, such as, but not limited to, pest control report, title insurance, and survey, as may be agreed to in a subsequent purchase and sales agreement and to obtain information relating to the present mortgage(s) on the property. SELLER agrees to reimburse BROKER for any cost incurred in ordering and obtaining such information.

6. (a) For finding a BUYER ready, willing and able to purchase the above described property, SELLER agrees to pay BROKER a compensation of six (6.0)% of the total purchase price, on the terms herein mentioned, or at any price and upon terms acceptable to SELLER, whether the BUYER be secured by BROKER or SELLER, or by ANY OTHER PERSON, or if the property is afterwards sold within ___3___ months from the termination of this agreement, or any written extension thereof signed by the BROKER and the SELLER ("The Protection Period") to any person to whom the Property has been shown by the BROKER or his representatives or by cooperating BROKERS, or by the SELLER, or by ANY OTHER PERSON; provided, nevertheless, that the BROKER shall not receive a commission on such a subsequent sale if the SELLER has relisted the property with another Licensed Real Estate Broker. At SELLER'S request, BROKER may agree to conditionally terminate this Contract as of a date prior to the Termination Date. If BROKER agrees to conditional termination, SELLER must sign a withdrawal agreement and pay a cancellation fee of $ 1,000.00 _____ plus applicable sales tax. BROKER may void the conditional termination and SELLER shall pay the cancellation fee in the event SELLER transfers or contracts to transfer the Property during the time period from the date of conditional termination to Termination Date and Protection Period, if applicable.

(b) In the event the property is rented or leased by the SELLER in lieu of sale or in connection with a lease/option agreement, the SELLER will pay the listing BROKER a rental or leasing fee equal to 10.0 % of the rent to be received, except in cases of occupancy agreements between the SELLER and the BUYER to accommodate the surrender and delivery of possession in connection with closing. Upon exercise of the option to purchase, the owner will pay BROKER compensation in accordance with paragraph 6 (a) hereof.

(c) **SELLER DEFAULT:** In the event a transaction fails to close because of a refusal or failure of SELLER to perform, or Seller refuses to sign a contract for sale and purchase at the price and terms stated in this Contract, SELLER shall pay to BROKER on demand the fee stated in Paragraph 6 (a) hereof.

7. **BROKER OBLIGATIONS AND AUTHORITY:** BROKER agrees to make diligent and continued efforts to sell the Property until a contract for sale is pending on the Property. SELLER authorizes BROKER to: (SELLER to initial if applicable).

_____ Advertise Property as BROKER deems advisable.

_____ Place For Sale signs on the Property and Sale Pending and or Sold signs upon full execution of a contract to sell.

_____ Place the Property in a Multiple listing service ("MLS"). SELLER authorizes BROKER to cooperate with and compensate subagents, and/or buyer/tenant agents and transaction brokers as specified in paragraph 9. SELLER further authorizes BROKER to report to the multiple listing service, in accordance with its rules and regulations, this listing information and price, terms, and financing information on any resulting sale for publication, dissemination and use by authorized Board/Association members, MLS participants and Subscribers.

_____ Utilize SELLER'S name in connection with marketing or advertising the Property, either before or after the sale.

_____ Withhold verbal offers.

_____ Obtain any information relating to the present mortgage(s) on the Property including, but not limited to, existing balance, interest rate, monthly payment, balance in escrow account and payoff amount.

E X H I B I T   2 3 - 8   (c o n c l u d e d)

8. **SELLER OBLIGATIONS:** In consideration of the obligations of BROKER, SELLER agrees:

(a) To cooperate with BROKER in carrying out the purpose of this Contract
(b) To refer immediately to BROKER all inquiries regarding the purchase or property lease.
(c) To provide BROKER with keys to the Property and make the Property available to BROKER to show during reasonable times.
(d) To inform BROKER prior to leasing, mortgaging or otherwise encumbering the Property.
(e) To indemnify BROKER and hold BROKER harmless from losses, damages, costs, and expenses of any nature including attorney's fees, and from liability to any person, which BROKER incurs because of SELLER'S negligence, representations, actions, or inactions, or which arise because of use of a lockbox.
(f) To perform any act reasonably necessary to comply with FIRPTA (Internal Revenue Code Section 1445).

9. **COOPERATION WITH OTHER BROKERS:** Broker's office policy is to cooperate with other brokers (check as many as apply):
[X] Buyer's agents (who represent the interest of the buyer and not the interest of **Seller** in a transaction, even if compensated by **Seller** or **Broker**)
[X] Sub Agents   [X] Dual Agents   [X] Transaction brokers.   ☐ None of the above (if this box is checked, the Property cannot be placed in MLS).

10. **COMPENSATION WITH OTHER BROKERS:** Broker's office policy is to offer compensation to other brokers (check as many as apply):
[X] Buyer's agents (who represent the interest of the buyer and not the interest of **Seller** in a transaction, even if compensated by **Seller** or **Broker**)
[X] Sub Agents   [X] Dual Agents   [X] Transaction brokers.   ☐ None of the above (if this box is checked, the Property cannot be placed in MLS).

11. **POTENTIAL FOR DUAL AGENCY:** By signing this Contract, BROKER agrees to represent and act as agent for SELLER within the scope of the contract. However, in any of the following situations, a potential conflict of interest arises which could result in BROKER representing both SELLER and Buyer/Tenant:

(a) BROKER represents a Buyer/Tenant who expresses interest in SELLER'S property.
(b) BROKER or an agent in the listing office wishes to buy the Property.
(c) REALTOR has dealt with Buyer/Tenant as a Former Client, or is a close personal friend **of the Buyer/Tenant.**

In the event one of these situations arise, BROKER will, prior to taking a position in conflict with SELLER'S interests, disclose to SELLER all facts pertaining to the potential dual agency and will not undertake dual representation without SELLER'S Buyer's/Tenant's written consent.

12. SELLER authorizes BROKER or cooperating BROKER to accept in escrow and hold all money paid or deposited as a binder on the subject property and if such deposit is later forfeited by the BUYER to disperse the deposit as follows: (1) all loan application fees, and other costs incurred on behalf of either the BUYER or the SELLER shall be reimbursed to the BROKER; (2) one-half of the remaining net deposit or the total commission the BROKER would have received, whichever is less, shall be disbursed to the BROKER as compensation for his services and marketing expenses; (3) the remainder of the deposit, if any, shall be disbursed to the SELLER as liquidated damages. In the disbursement of any escrowed funds, the BROKER shall be governed and shall comply with the provisions of Chapter 475, Florida Statutes.

13. SELLER and BROKER acknowledge that this Agreement does not guarantee a sale and that there are no other agreements, promises or understandings either expressed or implied between them other than specifically set forth herein and that there can be no alterations or changes to this contract except in writing and signed by each of them. They also agree that this agreement supersedes any prior agreement regarding the marketing of this property.

14. **ATTORNEY'S FEES AND COSTS:** In the event any litigation arises out of the Contract, the prevailing party shall be entitled to recover reasonable attorney's fees and costs.

15. THIS IS A LEGAL AND BINDING CONTRACT ON ALL PARTIES HERETO, INCLUDING THEIR HEIRS, LEGAL REPRESENTATIVES, SUCCESSORS AND ASSIGNS. IF NOT FULLY UNDERSTOOD SELLER SHOULD SEEK COMPETENT LEGAL ADVICE.

16. THE SELLER AND BROKER ACKNOWLEDGE THAT THIS LISTING SHALL BE WITHDRAWN FROM THE GAINESVILLE MULTIPLE LISTING UPON THE BROKER'S WITHDRAWAL, SUSPENSION OR TERMINATION FROM MLS.

BROKER Bosshardt Realty, Inc.

By: _Carol Locascio_

Date: _____May 1, 1998_____

SELLER _Fred Johnson_

SELLER _Tonie Johnson_

SELLERS' Address 1822 N.W. 40th Avenue

_____ Gainesville Florida 32605

PLEASE DO NOT ASK OR EXPECT TO RESTRICT THE SALE OF YOUR PROPERTY ACCORDING TO RACE, COLOR, RELIGION, SEX, HANDICAP, FAMILIAL STATUS, OR NATIONAL ORIGIN. REALTOR POLICY AS WELL AS FEDERAL LAW PROHIBITS REALTORS FROM PLACING ANY SUCH RESTRICTIONS ON SHOWING OR INFORMATION ABOUT THE AVAILABILITY OF HOMES FOR SALE OR RENT.

about the advantages and disadvantages of their house relative to other houses in the neighborhood, the Johnsons agree the listing price should be $85,000, which will include the kitchen stove and refrigerator, two window air conditioners, and one picnic table as well as the real estate.

The property is free of encumbrances except for an existing mortgage with a remaining balance of $45,000. The Johnsons prefer not to give a second mortgage or other financing terms. The existing mortgage has a "due on sale" clause (that is, it cannot be *assumed*—taken over—by the buyer).

The house has four bedrooms, two baths, a living room, a dining room, a screened porch, a double carport, and an outside storage room. It has central heating, but not central air-conditioning. It was built in 1966 with concrete block and stucco (CBS)-on-slab construction. The entire house, except for the kitchen, was carpeted about eight years ago. The house is in reasonably good condition, although the interior and exterior paint is beginning to look dull and the carpet is becoming worn in heavy traffic areas. The lot is approximately one-half acre and is nicely landscaped. The neighborhood contains similar modest but generally well-maintained houses, and property values have increased about 2 percent per year over the past 10 years. According to the Johnsons' deed in the Alachua County Courthouse, the property description is "Parcel No. 3, Block 2 of Spring Meadow Estates, recorded in Plat Book 12, page 28." Carol and the Johnsons agree on a commission rate of 6 percent. Exhibit 23–8 shows the completed listing form for the Johnsons' property.

SUMMARY

Real estate brokerage is an important type of real estate business dealing with marketing. Brokers provide a service for sellers and buyers of properties that involves finding available properties, finding potential buyers, helping buyers identify needs and set priorities, negotiating between buyers and sellers, providing advice about other needs and specialists (*e.g.*, financing, attorneys, architects), making certain all relevant federal and state laws are followed (*e.g.*, those regarding discrimination and disclosure), and arranging for the closing of the transaction. Probably the most important of these functions is helping buyers and sellers determine their needs and enabling them to meet those needs in the best possible manner.

Listing contracts create an agency relationship between a real estate broker and the owners of real estate. Such a relationship requires honesty, trust, and openness between the broker and the owner. An owner lists a property with a broker to obtain the convenience and expertise of the broker in selling the property.

There are four types of listing contracts: open, exclusive agency, exclusive right of sale, or net. The exclusive right of sale listing is the predominant type of contract used, especially for residential properties. This type of contract is required when the property is to be filed with a multiple listing service. A multiple listing service is a cooperative arrangement among brokerage firms in which all member firms pool their listings. All sales personnel of the members can then attempt to sell the listed property. On sale of the property, the commission is split between the listing and selling firms according to a predetermined schedule.

In signing a listing contract, both broker and owner obtain rights and responsibilities. The brokerage firm has the right to collect a commission if the property is sold within a specified or reasonable period and agrees to exert its best efforts to sell the property. The owner can expect the firm to try to sell the property through a marketing program. The owner can also expect an MLS member firm to file the listing with the MLS and for other member firms' sales personnel to work on the sale. The owner is obligated not to impede the selling effort and to pay a commission if the property is sold.

Real estate businesses are regulated by the various states. In every state, brokers and salespersons must be licensed. To obtain a license, one must meet prescribed prelicensing education requirements, pass a state exam, and (in many states) meet postlicensing and continuing education requirements. State real estate commissions can discipline licensees for infractions of laws and rules governing real estate activity.

Many brokers also belong to trade and professional organizations, such as the National Association of REALTORS. These organizations promote education and ethical standards. They also may award professional designations that provide secondary signaling about competence in the area of general brokerage or primary signaling in a specialty area.

KEY TERMS

Agency 693
Broker license 695
Commission 690
Errors and omission insurance 697
Exclusive agency listing 705
Exclusive right of sale listing 703
Fiduciary relationship 692
General agent 692
Law of agency 691

Licensing laws 695
Listing contract 693
Market segmentation 698
Multiple listing service 700
National Association of
  REALTORS 698
Net listing 704
Open listing 703
Principal 691

Real estate commission 695
Recovery fund 697
Salesperson license 695
Special agent 692
Submarket 698
Transaction broker 693
Universal agent 692

TEST YOURSELF

Answer the following multiple choice questions:

1. A salesperson who collects a down payment deposit from a potential buyer must place the funds in
   a. The seller's bank account.
   b. His own bank account.
   c. His broker's bank account.
   d. Long-term government bonds.
   e. The hands of his broker.

2. Which of the following is considered a secondary signaling device to the purchasers of real estate services?
   a. A construction contractor's license.
   b. An MAI designation.

   c. A salesperson license.
   d. A broker license.
   e. None of the above.

3. A broker, who is the agent of a seller, must deal honestly and fairly with whom?
   a. Only the seller.
   b. The seller and the buyer.
   c. The seller and a lender.
   d. The seller and a title insurance company.
   e. Everyone involved in the transaction.

4. Real estate salespersons can lose their licenses for
   a. Using aggressive sales techniques.
   b. Not showing buyers all available properties in an area.

c. Commingling escrow (trust) money with personal funds.

d. Not using modern sales methods.

e. All of the above.

5. The state real estate commission is responsible for
   a. Setting fees for brokerage services.
   b. Marketing data on real estate transactions.
   c. Establishing education requirements for licensees.
   d. Overseeing the activities of mortgage lenders.
   e. Setting up multiple listing systems.

6. Real estate brokers are paid commissions primarily for
   a. Having an inventory of properties.
   b. Having many contacts.
   c. Providing a service.
   d. Knowing how to close a transaction.
   e. Having specialized education.

7. A real estate broker is what type of agent for his or her principal?
   a. General agent.
   b. Special agent.
   c. Limited agent.
   d. Designated agent.
   e. All of the above.

8. If a seller refuses to complete a transaction after a broker has obtained a buyer who is ready, will-

ing, and able to purchase the property on the terms specified by the seller, the seller may be liable to the broker for
   a. The commission.
   b. The market value of the property.
   c. The broker's expenses.
   d. Damages.
   e. The commission plus the broker's expenses.

9. How are commission rates charged by real estate brokers determined?
   a. By agreement among local Realtors.
   b. By rule of the local Board of Realtors.
   c. By state real estate commissions.
   d. By agreement between broker and principal.
   e. By state law.

10. According to most listing contracts, a broker has earned a commission when
   a. A contract for sale is signed by the buyer.
   b. The transaction closes.
   c. The broker finds a buyer who is ready, willing, and able to buy on the terms specified in the listing contract.
   d. The seller signs a listing contract.
   e. The broker sends a bill for services rendered to the principal (usually the seller).

PROBLEMS FOR THOUGHT AND SOLUTION

1. Mr. Ted Richardson owns a large industrial building in your city that he wishes to sell. As a real estate broker, you would be delighted to obtain the listing on this property. You have worked with Richardson on two other transactions in which he was the buyer; therefore, you approach Richardson to request that he consider listing his property with you.

   Richardson agrees to do so, but indicates that he will not give you an exclusive right of sale listing, because he wants to retain the right to sell the property himself without owing a real estate com-

mission. He will, however, give you an exclusive agency listing.

   What should you do? Should you accept such a listing from Richardson? Are there any provisions that you would propose including in the listing contract to give yourself some protection? If so, what?

2. You are a real estate salesperson working for Good Earth, Realtors, Inc. You receive 50 percent of all commissions received by the firm (net of MLS fees) for which you were either the listing agent or the selling agent. The firm receives 40 percent of

commissions for sales of properties it lists and 45 percent of commissions for sales of properties it sells in cooperation with other firms. Fifteen percent of all commissions for properties sold through the multiple listing service must be paid to the MLS. If you are both the listing and selling agent in a transaction, you receive 60 percent of the firm's proceeds. If you are either the listing agent or the selling agent for a transaction in which another member of Good Earth is the selling agent or the listing agent, your split remains the same as when another firm cooperates in the transaction.

Recently, you were the selling agent for a property that sold for $127,250. Another salesperson associated with Good Earth had listed the property two months previously for $135,000. The property was in the MLS, and the commission rate was 6.0 percent.

a. How much in total commission, net of the MLS fee, will your firm receive?

b. What will be your split of the commission?

3. If you owned your own real estate brokerage firm, how could you establish a niche in the market for your firm? In other words, how could you set your firm apart from other brokerage firms, and how could you create a unique image for your firm?

4. How do you think the real estate marketing function will change in the future? Do you believe that real estate brokers will play a more important or a less important role in the selling-buying process? Why?

INTERNET EXERCISES

1. On the World Wide Web go to

/http://www.realtor/.com/

Click on the link "REALTOR Associations."

a. How many societies, institutes and councils are affiliated with NAR?

b. Identify each affiliate, and briefly describe its area of specialization.

c. List the designations offered by each affiliate. What do these designations indicate?

2. On the Realtors' home page, click again on "REALTOR Associations." Then click on "State and Local Real Estate Associations." Obtain information about your state association of Realtors and write a short report on your findings.

3. One of the best set of links is found on the home page of the Society of Industrial and Office Realtors. Go to **www.sior.com** and click on "links". Then click on "National Professional Real Estate Associations" and discover more about the various associations listed there. Write a brief report on your findings.

4. Note the other links on the SIOR home page and peruse any that may be of interest to you.

CASE PROBLEMS

1. A friend of yours, Cindy Heather Malvern, is moving to your town. She graduated from college a few years ago and has since been working in another city. Recently, however, she was offered a job at a higher salary in the regional office of a national insurance company located in the city where you attend college. Cindy has decided to buy a condominium, and because you are taking a real estate course, she asks you how to proceed.

You first look at the classified ads in the local

newspaper and notice that a number of existing condominiums are for sale. Most of them are advertised by brokers, but some are advertised by the owners. You also notice ads by some local builders for new condominiums. You ask Cindy whether she prefers to buy a previously owned condominium or a new one. She says she doesn't know; it depends on the condominium, the location, the price, and so on.

Next you look in the Yellow Pages of the phone book and find several pages of ads for real estate brokers. You have heard of three or four of the firms, but you have had no direct contact or dealings with any of them.

a. How would you advise Cindy to proceed? Should she call a real estate brokerage firm? Why or why not?

b. If Cindy decides to call a real estate broker, how should she select the broker? What criteria should she use?

c. If Cindy decides to work through a real estate broker, can she look at new condominiums for sale by builders? If she buys a new condominium while working with a broker, would she or the builder have to pay a commission to the broker?

2. You decide to open a real estate office in your community, but you know the competition with established firms would be difficult. You believe that one method of drawing attention to your firm and obtaining clients that would otherwise go to other brokers is to advertise that you will sell any house in town and charge a commission of only $1,000.

Do you believe such a marketing tactic would be successful? Why or why not?

ADDITIONAL READINGS

The following periodical is the monthly journal of the National Association of Realtors®. It contains articles on both residential and commercial brokerage and runs several special features:

Today's Realtor (monthly), National Association of Realtors®, 430 North Michigan Avenue, Chicago, Illinois 60611-4049.

Additionally, several of the affiliates of NAR publish professional journals in more specialized areas of brokerage, and many state boards of REALTORS publish monthly magazines containing articles and news features about brokerage issues in those states. You may find information about the publications of the NAR affiliates by using the links on the home page of NAR at <**http://www.realtor.com/**>.

The following book contains statistics and other information about real estate firms:

National Association of Realtors®. *Profile of Real Estate Firms* (Chicago: NAR, 1992).

The following article is a research study on residential brokerage firms. It analyzes marketing strategy concepts of brokerage firms and reports on the effectiveness of several strategy variables.

Richins, Marsha L., William C. Black, and C. F. Sirmans. "Strategic Orientation and Marketing Strategy: An Analysis of Residential Real Estate Brokerage Firms." *Journal of Real Estate Research* 2, no. 2 (Winter 1987), pp. 41–54.

The following article reports on research about the renegotiation of listing contracts between brokers and sellers when listing contracts are about to expire. It concludes that courts should enforce such renegotiations, given that transaction costs between brokers and sellers are ordinarily low:

Micelli, Thomas J. "Renegotiation of Listing Contracts, Seller Opportunism and Efficiency: An Economic Analysis." *Real Estate Economics* 23, no. 3 (Fall 1995), pp. 369–83.

This article describes theoretical and empirical research on the impact of listing price on the optimal tradeoff between time on the market (TOM) and selling price. The authors conclude that for midprice houses an increase in the listing price increases TOM; for low-price and high-price houses, however, listing price has no significant effect on TOM:

Yavas, Abdullah, and Shiawee Yang. "The Strategic Role of Listing Price in Marketing Real Estate: Theory and Evidence." *Real Estate Economics* 23, no. 3 (Fall 1995), pp 347–68.

24
CHAPTER

CONTRACTS FOR
SALE AND CLOSING

THE MOST IMPORTANT DOCUMENT IN REAL ESTATE

RIGHTS AND OBLIGATIONS OF SELLERS AND BUYERS
Rights and Obligations of Sellers
Rights and Obligations of Buyers

REQUIREMENTS OF A CONTRACT FOR SALE
The Parties Must Be Competent to Act
The Parties Must Have Lawful Intent
There Must Be an Offer and an Acceptance
There Must Be Consideration
There Must Be No Defects to Mutual Assent
The Contract for Sale of Real Estate Must Be in Writing
The Property Must Be Properly Described

TITLE
Legal Title
Equitable Title

THE FORM OF THE CONTRACT FOR SALE
Simple Contract
Standard Form Contracts
Components of a Form Contract
Estimated Closing Expense Statements

CONTINUING SAGA OF A SALE

CONTRACTS WITH CONTINGENCIES

ASSIGNMENT

REMEDIES FOR NONPERFORMANCE
Remedies for a Seller
Remedies for a Buyer
Escrow

CLOSING
Steps before Closing
Steps at Closing
Prorations
Buyers' Expenses
Sellers' Expenses

CLOSING AND CLOSING STATEMENTS
Role of the Brokers
Role of the Lenders
Real Estate Settlement Procedures Act
Preparation of Closing Statements

SUMMARY

KEY TERMS

TEST YOURSELF

PROBLEMS FOR THOUGHT AND SOLUTION

CASE PROBLEMS

ADDITIONAL READINGS

After reading this chapter, students will be able to:

1. List the seven requirements for a valid contract for the sale of real estate.

2. Write a simple contract that contains the seven requirements.

3. Complete a standard form contract, given the facts of a property transaction.

4. Identify five expenses typically paid by the seller and five expenses typically paid by the buyer.

5. List three remedies for nonperformance by a buyer and three remedies for nonperformance by a seller.

6. List the steps that must be taken before closing a real estate transaction.

7. Describe the activities that occur at closing.

8. Explain the principal provisions of the Real Estate Settlement Procedures Act (RESPA).

9. Explain why a binder deposit is a credit to the buyer.

10. Complete a closing statement and reconciliation statement for Case Problem 3.

THE MOST IMPORTANT DOCUMENT IN REAL ESTATE

The value of real estate depends on the rights that a buyer obtains at closing, as conveyed by the deed. The rights and type of deed, in turn are determined by the **contract for sale**, which is the written agreement in which buyers and sellers of real estate specify the details of the agreement. The principal provisions of a contract for sale, as shown in Exhibit 24–1, require the seller to deliver a deed to the property to the buyer in exchange for payment of the purchase price by the buyer. The contract is signed when a buyer and seller decide to commit themselves to the transaction under terms and conditions worked out between them. **Terms** refers to the arrangements agreed to by the parties, such as price and date of closing, whereas **conditions** refers to the circumstances that must prevail, such as mechanical equipment being in good condition and title being unencumbered. Thus, real estate transactions differ from personal property transactions in that realty sales almost always involve a two-step process. The parties reach agreement first; sometime later (for example, one month) they complete the sale at a meeting called the **closing**. In a personal property transaction, the parties usually close the transaction at the same time they reach agreement.

EXHIBIT 24-1

CONTRACT FOR SALE

A contract for sale of real estate, like any contract, is a legal, enforceable document. If its provisions are not carried out, financial penalties (damages) may be imposed on the party unwilling or unable to fulfill the contract. Thus, a contract for sale is the *most important document* in a real estate transaction. Whereas most contracts are legal and enforceable whether they are written or oral, the laws of every state (called statutes of frauds) require that contracts for the sale and purchase of real estate be *in writing* to be enforceable.[1] The many provisions in such a contract leave too much room for both legitimate misunderstandings and purposeful disagreements (fraud) when the agreements are oral. Although disagreements may arise with written contracts as well, they contain definite language that the courts can interpret and enforce.

RIGHTS AND OBLIGATIONS OF SELLERS AND BUYERS

A contract for the sale of real estate creates certain rights and obligations for both sellers and buyers.

RIGHTS AND OBLIGATIONS OF SELLERS

Rights of Sellers.

1. To receive the sale price specified in the contract at the specified date.
2. To obtain the specified terms of the sale price, such as all cash or part secondary financing.
3. To obtain reimbursement for any property expenses that have been paid for the period during which the property will be occupied by the buyers.

---

[1]This rule of law is known as the *parol evidence rule*.

Obligations of Sellers.
1. To deliver clear title to the buyers on the specified date by the specified type of instrument, such as a warranty deed.
2. To maintain the property in good repair until title is conveyed to the buyers.
3. To maintain major appliances and systems, such as heating, cooling, and electrical, in good condition and to turn them over to the buyers in a condition no worse than when the contract was signed.
4. To allow the buyers or their representative to inspect the property just before closing to determine its condition.
5. To provide the type of evidence of title specified in the contract (*e.g.*, abstract or title insurance).
6. To pay operating expenses of the property until closing and to reimburse the buyers for property expenses, such as property taxes, they may pay for the period during which the property is occupied by the sellers.
7. To pay the agreed-on brokerage commission at closing.

RIGHTS AND OBLIGATIONS OF BUYERS

Rights of Buyers.
1. To obtain clear legal title to the property on the date specified in the contract for sale.
2. To obtain the property in the same condition as when the contract was signed.
3. To obtain the appliances and subsystems in the same condition as when the contract was signed.
4. To have title conveyed by the type of instrument specified in the contract.
5. To back out of the transaction if the property is substantially damaged or destroyed by fire, earthquake, or other hazard.
6. To obtain reimbursement for any property expenses paid for the period during which the property was occupied by the sellers (e.g., property taxes).

Obligations of Buyers.
1. To pay the specified price on the terms in the contract on the date of closing.
2. To reimburse the sellers for property operating expenses they have paid that cover the period of occupancy by the buyers.

REQUIREMENTS OF A CONTRACT FOR SALE

A legally binding contract for sale can take many forms. It can be a short handwritten note, a preprinted form containing several standard paragraphs, or a lengthy document prepared by attorneys to cover many points in a complex transaction. Whatever the form, any contract, whether it be for the sale of real estate or for some other purpose, must contain the following elements:

1. Competent parties.
2. Legal objective.
3. Offer and acceptance.
4. Consideration.
5. No defects to mutual assent.

Two additional requirements must be part of any contract for the sale of real estate:

1. Written form.
2. Proper description of the property.

The Parties Must Be Competent to Act

The principal parties to a transaction must be legally *competent*. In the case of individuals, such parties must have reached a minimum age (18 years in most states) and be of sound mind. Although minors may be legally competent to participate in real estate transactions, a contract with a minor is *voidable*: the minor may legally declare the contract invalid and refuse to carry out its provisions.

In the case of corporations, a party acting on behalf of the corporation must be legally empowered to do so. For example, if a corporation sells property, its president or some other officer must be authorized by a board of directors resolution or bylaw to act in this capacity. Similarly, personal representatives (*e.g.*, executors, administrators, agents, and attorneys-in-fact) and trustees must be authorized to act on behalf of their principals by a legal instrument or order, such as a *power of attorney*. Their powers are defined and limited by the instrument. Real estate purchasers or professionals should always assure themselves that personal representatives and trustees have legal authority to sell properties.

The Parties Must Have Lawful Intent

The objective of a contract must not be illegal or against public policy. For example, a contract to commit a crime for payment is not enforceable in the courts. Similarly, a contract to sell property for the purpose of growing marijuana or for storing illegal weapons is legally invalid. A contract to sell property to members of a certain race, or to exclude members of a certain race, would be counter to public policy against racial discrimination and would be void.

There Must Be an Offer and an Acceptance

An offer and acceptance indicate that the parties to a contract have a meeting of the minds, or *mutual assent*. The contract binds the parties to specified actions in the future: for the seller to deliver *marketable* legal title to the buyer and for the buyer to pay the stipulated price for a property. In a real estate contract for sale, the buyer normally offers a specified

CHAPTER 24 CONTRACTS FOR SALE AND CLOSING

price under specific terms for specific property rights. The seller has three options: to *reject* the offer outright, to *accept* the offer outright, or, as frequently occurs, to reject the offer and present a *counteroffer*. A series of offers and counteroffers often will ensue until an agreement is reached—there is a successful offer and acceptance—or one party rejects an offer outright.

The basic agreement ultimately reached between buyer and seller may be simple and straightforward. However, it usually creates many other issues on which agreement must be reached, including the closing date, prorating of expenses, type of title evidence, liability for property damage, and condition of the property. The purpose of a contract for sale is to specify these agreements and to make them legally binding.

THERE MUST BE CONSIDERATION

The value given up, or promise made, by each party to a contract is the **consideration**. Both parties to a valid and enforceable contract must provide consideration. In a contract for the sale and purchase of real estate, the seller's consideration is the property to be given up. The buyer's consideration is the money or other goods that constitute the purchase price. Mere promise of consideration by one party does not constitute a contract and cannot be enforced. For example, I. M. Rich promises to deed a property to his friend, B. Weiser, and even writes this promise on a piece of paper. Such a promise cannot be enforced because Mr. Weiser did not promise anything in return. Mutual obligations of the parties are necessary to create a legally binding contract.

THERE MUST BE NO DEFECTS TO MUTUAL ASSENT

In certain circumstances, mutual assent—the meeting of the minds—between the contracting parties may be broken, thus invalidating the contract. The following constitute defects to mutual assent:

1. One party attempts to perpetrate a fraud on the other party or makes a misrepresentation.[2]
2. A substantial error is made (*e.g.*, the name of one of the parties to a written contract is incorrect).
3. One of the parties is under duress, undue influence, or menace.[3]

In addition to the elements described above for any contract, an enforceable *contract for the sale of real estate* must fulfill two additional requirements.

---

[2]Fraud is intentional misrepresentation, whereas a misrepresentation *per se* is unintentional. However, both have the same effect.

[3]Undue influence involves an abuse of the influence that one person (often a relative) has over another. Duress involves compelling a person to act by the use of force, and menace is the use of the threat of force to compel a person to act.

THE CONTRACT FOR SALE OF REAL ESTATE MUST BE IN WRITING

The statute of frauds, the Old English law that serves as the basis for contract law in most states, imposed the requirement of writing on some types of contracts in order for them to be enforceable.[4] Many agreements involving real estate are subject to this requirement, including contracts for sale, installment sales contracts, option contracts, exchange contracts, and in many states, leases, listing contracts, and mortgage contracts.[5] In most states, the *parol evidence rule* is in effect, which prohibits the admission of oral evidence in disputes involving written contracts.

As noted, most real estate contracts contain many technicalities and points of agreement. Legitimate misunderstandings could easily arise over any of these points in an oral contract. Even more important, unscrupulous parties to an oral contract could gain an unfair advantage by later claiming they did not agree to protective provisions. For example, most written contracts contain a provision that allows a buyer to back out of a transaction if the building is destroyed by fire or other hazard before the closing. A seller could easily claim such a provision was not part of an oral contract; it would be his or her word against the buyer's.

To satisfy the writing requirement, the contract usually must include adequate identification of the parties, the subject matter, and the terms of agreement, as well as the signatures of the parties or their legally empowered agents. It is essential that both principal parties to a transaction—buyers and sellers—sign the contract. The signatures are legal evidence that the parties understand and agree to the provisions in the contract. They cannot later claim they did not agree to a provision in the contract or did not understand its meaning.

In addition to the principals' signatures, the statute of frauds may require a spouse's signature to release his or her marital rights such as homestead rights, dower rights, or community property rights. Technically, a spouse's signature on a contract indicates his or her agreement to sign the deed, where these rights are actually waived. Also, as noted, legal written authorization must accompany a contract that is signed by an agent, personal representative, or trustee.

THE PROPERTY MUST BE PROPERLY DESCRIBED

Satisfying the written-form requirement is fairly straightforward. But the second requirement—identification of the contract's subject matter—means that the legal rights being sold must be identified, and the physical boundaries of the property must be delineated precisely and unambiguously. The importance of proper description of the physical assets and the accompanying property rights in a real estate contract cannot be overstated. The specific purpose of the property description is to ensure that buyer and seller understand

---

[4]The statute of frauds was intended to prevent fraudulent practices in contracting; thus, the writing requirement was imposed for situations where substantial sums of money would normally be involved.

[5]Leases for less than one year normally are not required to be in writing to be enforceable.

exactly what real estate is being transferred. Boundary lines, easements, air rights, mineral rights, and other types of partial interests create a situation, unlike that for personal property, in which it is essential the sale contract contain a proper and adequate description.

The term *proper and adequate description* means that the description in a contract must enable a knowledgeable person to determine the boundaries or limits of the property. Chapter 22 explained several popular forms of description, including the recorded plat description and the government survey system. Each form is acceptable for contracts for sale. However, some forms are preferable to others because they provide more precise identification. The recorded plat description, for example, is generally preferred to the metes and bounds description or the government survey system in urban areas. Also, recorded plat descriptions are generally preferred over street addresses. The government survey and metes and bounds systems are used in rural areas.

TITLE

LEGAL TITLE

As discussed in Chapter 22, **legal title** means the ownership of an estate (a bundle of rights) in real estate. Legal title passes from seller to buyer at the time of closing, when the deed is delivered by the seller and accepted by the buyer. Legal title gives the owner all of the rights and obligations of the estate. For example, the owners of a fee simple estate can occupy and use the property in any legal manner. They also can convey title to someone else, and by their wills, they can designate to whom title will transfer at the time of their deaths. The owners of a life estate generally have the same rights as the owners of a fee simple estate, except their rights of occupancy and use are for a specified period. Legal title is neither created nor conveyed by the contract for sale.

EQUITABLE TITLE

Equitable title is a legal concept that gives buyers the right to obtain legal title to real estate. It is created and conveyed by the contract for sale. With equitable title, buyers can be assured they will obtain full legal title at the time of closing if they perform their obligations under the contract.

Equitable title places a limitation on sellers: they may not sell their property to another buyer, no matter how attractive the other offer may be. This limitation is more severe than the normal penalty for breach of contract, which is liability for damages. Thus, if it were not for equitable title, sellers could sell to someone else and let the buyers sue for damages.

Sellers may negotiate with other potential buyers so long as the buyers' equitable title is not violated. For example, another buyer may agree to purchase the property if the original buyers fail to close the transaction. The original buyers' equitable title is not disturbed, since the second contract is contingent on default by the original buyers.

THE FORM OF THE CONTRACT FOR SALE

While the contract for sale may take a variety of forms, the important question to be answered is whether all essential ingredients of a valid and enforceable contract for sale are present. Most transactions today, especially residential transactions, are completed with the use of standard forms, which force the parties to consider all of the necessary elements.

SIMPLE CONTRACT

The following statement constitutes a simple real estate contract:

I, Ben Byer, agree to buy and pay $20,000, and I, Cecil Celler, agree to sell the parcel of real estate at 1013 NE Seventh Road in North Platte, Nebraska.
        Signed: Ben Byer   Signed: Cecil Celler

For most transactions, such a brief contract would not be sufficient; however, it contains the seven essential elements, and therefore it would be legal. Mr. Byer and Mr. Celler are competent. Mr. Byer offers $20,000, and Mr. Celler accepts by agreeing to sell. Consideration is stated for both: $20,000 for the buyer and the property for the seller. The objective is legal, the property is identified, and there are no defects to mutual assent. The contract is written and is signed by both parties.

But several important points are omitted. These could be subject to disagreement later, and they could cause the transaction to be delayed or even aborted. The missing points are:

- Date of the contract.
- Date and place of closing.
- The parties' marital status.
- Financing terms, if any.
- Prorating of costs and expenses.
- Condition of any buildings.
- Condition of subsystems and appliances.
- Right of occupancy (or rents) until closing.
- Liability for major damage to buildings before closing.
- Remedies by each party for breach of contract by the other party.
- Exact dimensions and location of the property.
- Brokerage commission, if any.
- Earnest-money deposit.

Since these points are not covered in the contract, misunderstandings and severe losses for both parties can result. For example, the seller may need the money and count on closing within two weeks. The buyer, however, may be in no hurry and not want to close for three months. Since the contract does not specify the date of closing, the courts

REAL ESTATE FOCUS 24-1

A Contract Dispute

A new marketing professor, Dr. David Dennis, was hired by a large midwestern university. After looking at a number of houses, he and his wife, Marie, decided to purchase a large, older home in a pleasant section of town. When they looked at the house, Marie noted that the master bedroom was carpeted, with the carpet fastened to the floor. After the transaction was closed and they began moving in, however, they discovered the carpet in the master bedroom had been removed.

The Dennises immediately protested to the broker who had sold them the house, Ms. Jan Dancy. She contacted the former owners, Mr. and Mrs. Jim Rockledge, who had moved several hundred miles to another city, to inquire why they had removed the carpet. They told Jan they had every right to remove the carpet. It was not part of the house, since it was not tacked to the floor.

When told that Marie had noticed the carpet was fastened to the floor, Mrs. Rockledge replied that the carpet had been tacked down only at the doorway to prevent its being kicked up. It was not fastened down in other places and was not permanently installed. The contract did not mention the carpet, and it was not intended to be sold as part of the house.

The Dennises were deprived of carpet they believed should have belonged to them; the Rockledges refused to pay; and the broker suffered customer dissatisfaction.

Note: To keep their goodwill, Jan bought the Dennises new bedroom carpet.

---

will interpret the time between contract and closing as a reasonable time—which could easily be three months. As another example, consider the buyer's problem if the building burns down before closing. Without the contract specifying otherwise, the buyer must complete the transaction even if the building is destroyed. For these reasons, a longer contract form is usually used.

STANDARD FORM CONTRACTS

Since the issues in many transactions are similar, brokers often use standard preprinted forms. In such forms, all or most of the normal issues requiring agreement are addressed in a way that protects both buyers and sellers. For small residential properties in straightforward transactions, a standard form contract is usually adequate to protect the interests of both parties. Even so, buyers and sellers should read such contracts carefully; once they sign such a contract, they can be held to its provisions, no matter how deleterious to their interests.

Both parties can achieve maximum protection by having a competent attorney examine the document *before* signing. Having an attorney examine a contract after it has been signed is like locking the barn door after the horse has run away. While many buyers and sellers of single-family homes do not hire an attorney to draft or examine the contract and do not suffer severe financial losses, small disagreements and losses are relatively common (see Real Estate Focus 24–1).

Contracts for the purchase and sale of larger, more complex, income-producing properties are usually drafted by attorneys. Typically, the sellers or buyers will have their attorneys draft the instrument, sign it, and then submit it to the other parties and their attorneys. The instrument tends to protect the parties that have drafted the instrument, to the detriment of the other side. Thus, acceptance of the first draft of a contract drawn by the other parties' attorneys is rare. Usually, objections will be raised, new drafts will be prepared, and a bargaining process will occur before a contract is acceptable to both sides.

For most straightforward transactions, standard contract forms usually are prepared and approved by boards of Realtors® in various communities or states. Use of these forms has some advantages. First, they usually contain provisions that address common issues such as prorations, closing, financing terms, liability for property damage, easements, condition of fixtures and appliances, real estate commission, and so on. Second, such forms tend to treat both parties fairly. They are not inherently biased toward one party or the other, as tends to be the case with contracts drawn by one of the parties to a transaction.

The main disadvantage in using standard form contracts is that such forms cannot fit every situation. For example, most standard contract forms state that the buyer agrees to take the property subject to any easements of record. Since easements do not affect most properties' usefulness, many buyers, especially of single-family residential properties, do not check the public records for easements. Sometimes, however, an easement that could cause severe damage to the property is accepted by a buyer who is unaware of its existence. A house, for example, could be constructed over a utility easement that gives the utility company the right to service the utility line—by destroying part or all of the house, if necessary. If buyers did not check the public records showing the platting of the property and utility easements, they would be unaware of the utility easement.

A standard form contract for the purchase and sale of real estate is presented in Exhibit 24–2 showing the purchase and sale agreement between the Johnsons and the Joneses. This form, developed by a board of Realtors®, is relatively comprehensive and fair to both parties. It contains 16 paragraphs or sections covering common issues to be agreed on in most transactions. Furthermore, the contract is accompanied by 19 "Standards for Real Estate Transactions." The standards explain and interpret the provisions of the contract and are explicitly included in it.

COMPONENTS OF A FORM CONTRACT

Notice that the form contract in Exhibit 24–2 contains the elements of any valid contract. The parties to the transaction are identified at the top of the form. There is an offer and acceptance, stated as an agreement that the seller shall sell and the buyer shall buy. Consideration is stated as the purchase price for the buyer and the property for the seller. The conveyance of title to the property is the legal objective, and the property is identified adequately. The contract is in writing, and the buyers and sellers sign in the spaces provided.

In addition to the elements, the contract form also covers other matters. It explicitly incorporates the Standards for Real Estate Transactions, which provide further explanation and interpretation of the contract provisions and are thereby agreed to by the parties.

E X H I B I T 2 4 - 2

GAINESVILLE-ALACHUA COUNTY ASSOCIATION OF REALTORS®, INC.
DEPOSIT RECEIPT AND
PURCHASE AND SALE AGREEMENT
CONVENTIONAL FINANCING

Date __May 15_____, 19 __98__

Receipt is hereby acknowledged by __Bosshardt Realty Services, Inc._____, hereinafter called REALTOR®, of
the sum of __one thousand dollars_____ (__$1000.00_____) (by check) from
_____, hereinafter called BUYER as a deposit and as a part of the purchase
price on account of an offer to purchase the property of __Fred and Louise Johnson_____
_____, hereinafter called the SELLER, said property being in __Alachua_____ County, Florida, and described as
follows:

    Parcel No. 3, Block 2 of Spring Meadow Estates, Gainesville, Alachua County, Florida
    Tax Parcel No. 0123-444-555

also known as: __1822 N.W. 40th Avenue, Gainesville, Florida 32605_____ together with
the following personal property:

    1 Kenmore Range, 1 Hotpoint refrigerator, 2 Fedders window air conditioners,
    and 1 picnic table

The SELLER hereby agrees to sell said property to the BUYER and the BUYER hereby agrees to purchase said property from the SELLER upon the following
terms and conditions: *83,000.00* *65.65.*

1. PURCHASE AND SALES PRICE: $ ~~80,000.00~~

    Payable as follows:

    (a) Deposit paid herewith $1,000.00

    (b) Additional Deposit within ____ days after Effective Date ....

    (c) Cash at Closing (U.S. cash, certified or cashiers check) ....*15,600*...... $~~15,000.00~~

    (d) Balance payable ....

    (e) New first mortgage _____ *66,400* ~~64,000.00~~   *83,000.00* ~~$80,000.00~~

    TOTAL PURCHASE AND SALES PRICE

2. ADDITIONAL TERMS AND CONDITIONS:

    a. Contingent upon buyers' obtaining a commitment of an ARM loan with initial interest
        rate not to exceed 8.5 percent, with a 30-year term in the amount of $64,000.00.
        Buyers must apply for loan within 5 working days.

    b. Contingent upon a satisfactory radon and building inspection to be made within 10
        days of final acceptance of contract, to be paid for by buyers. Failure to notify
        sellers in writing of nonacceptance within this time period will automatically
        remove this contingency.

3. RIDERS: (check if applicable) ☐
Additional riders are attached to this agreement and are made a part thereof.

4. CLOSING DATE: This transaction shall be closed and the deed and other closing papers delivered on __July 1, 1998_____ or such
earlier date as may be mutually agreed upon, unless extended by other provisions of this Contract.

Revised 9/93 — © Gainesville-Alachua County Association of REALTORS, Inc. All Rights Reserved.

EXHIBIT 24-2 (continued)

5. A. NEW FINANCING: If the purchase price or any part thereof is to be financed by a third party loan, this contract is conditioned upon the BUYER obtaining a firm commitment for said loan within __30__ days from the effective date at an interest rate not to exceed __nine__ percent (9.0 %), if a fixed rate mortgage, or _eight and one half_ percent (8.5 %) for the initial period of an adjustable rate mortgage; term of __thirty__ (30) years; and in the principal amount of not less than __sixty four thousand__ Dollars ($_64,000.00_). BUYER shall make application within __five__ (5) days from the effective date, and use reasonable diligence to obtain said loan, including furnishing all documents and information required by the Lender, and failure to do so shall constitute a breach hereunder. If BUYER fails to obtain same or to waive BUYER'S right hereunder within said time, either party may cancel this contract and all deposit(s) paid by BUYER shall be refunded to BUYER.

B. EXISTING FINANCING: If the purchase price or any part thereof is to be paid by assumption of existing financing, this contract is contingent upon such loan being assumable without qualifying or BUYER qualifying to assume same within _____ days of the effective date if required by the mortgagee. The existing Mortgage has (Check One): ☐ 1) a variable interest rate of _____ or ☐ (2) a fixed interest rate of _____% per annum. At the time of title transfer some interest rates are subject to increase. If increased, the rate shall not exceed _____% per annum. SELLER shall, within ten (10) days from effective date, furnish a copy of the existing note and mortgage to the BUYER. If BUYER has agreed to assume a Mortgage which requires approval of BUYER by the Mortgagee for assumption, the BUYER shall promptly obtain all required applications and will diligently complete and return them to the Mortgagee, and failure to do so shall constitute a breach hereunder. If the BUYER is not accepted by the Mortgagee, or the requirements for assumption are not in accordance with the terms of this Contract, BUYER may rescind this Contract by prompt written notice to the other party or his/her Agent. Any charges connected with assuming the existing mortgage shall not exceed $_____ and shall be paid by _____. Should such charges exceed this amount, the party responsible to pay the charge may rescind the contract unless the other party elects to pay the excess.

C. PURCHASE MONEY NOTE AND MORTGAGE TO SELLER: The purchase money note and mortgage, if any, shall provide for a thirty (30) day grace period in the event of default if it is a first mortgage and a fifteen (15) day grace period if it is a second mortgage, shall provide for right of prepayment in whole or in part without penalty, and shall be otherwise in form and content in accordance with covenants established by the Eighth Judicial Circuit Bar Association. Said note and mortgage shall provide that in the event any installment is more than fifteen (15) days delinquent, the holder may assess a late charge of five percent (5%) of the late installment payment, or Ten Dollars ($10.00) whichever is greater, which late payment shall be due with the late installment payment, and in any event, shall be due no later than the due date of the next installment payment. Failure to pay the late charge when due shall constitute a default under the promissory note and mortgage. Said mortgage shall require all prior liens and encumbrances to be kept in good standing and shall forbid modifications of or future advances under prior mortgage(s).

The purchase money mortgage and note: (check one)
☐ shall be fully assumable.
☐ shall not be assumable, directly or indirectly, and shall include a standard due on sale clause prohibiting sale or transfer other than by descent and distribution in case of death or for a lease of three years or less not containing an option to purchase.
☐ shall be assumable on these conditions:_____

6. EVIDENCE OF TITLE: The SELLER shall furnish to the buyer or his ATTORNEY or agent whose name is_____
(Check One)
☐ An abstract from earliest public records, brought current, showing title to be marketable or insurable.
☒ ALTA Owner's Title Insurance Commitment in the amount of the purchase price. If BUYER is required to furnish a mortgagee title insurance policy, SELLER agrees to select a title agent approved by BUYER'S lender who can provide a simultaneous issue mortgagee policy.
Title Evidence to be furnished within (Check One)
☐ _____ ( ) days from the effective date of this contract or
☒ _five_ (5) days from _date of loan approval_

7. EXAMINATION OF TITLE: The BUYER or his attorney shall have __ten__ (10) days within which to examine the abstract of title or title insurance commitment and to signify willingness to accept the same, whereupon the transaction shall be concluded on the closing date specified above. If title is not acceptable, BUYER shall furnish SELLER a written statement specifying title defects to be cured. If the title is unmarketable, the SELLER shall have __ten__ (10) days or a reasonable period of time within which to cure the designated defects in the title that render same unmarketable or uninsurable in the opinion of the BUYER or his said Agent, and the SELLER hereby agrees to use reasonable diligence in curing said defects. Upon the defects being cured and notice of that fact being given to BUYER or his said Agent, this transaction shall then be closed within __ten__ (10) days of the delivery of the notice. At the option of the BUYER, upon SELLER'S failure or inability to correct the marketability of the title within the time limit or a reasonable period of time, the SELLER shall deliver the title in its existing condition, otherwise the deposit(s) shall be returned to the BUYER upon demand therefor, and all rights and liabilities on the part of the BUYER arising hereunder shall terminate. Provided, however, that in the event of disagreement between the SELLER and the BUYER or his said Agent, as to the marketability of the title, the SELLER may offer a commitment for an ALTA Owner's Title policy issued by a recognized title insurance company doing business in this area, agreeing to insure said title against all exceptions other than those mentioned in this Agreement and the standard printed exceptions, which commitment shall be conclusive evidence that said title is marketable. The commitment and Owner's Title policies pursuant thereto shall be paid for by the BUYER.

8. TERMITES OR OTHER INFESTATION: SELLER shall furnish to BUYER or his attorney or his agent at least five (5) days prior to closing a certificate of a locally licensed entomologist dated within thirty (30) days prior to closing, showing any improvements on the premises, exclusive of fences and __wood deck__ to be apparently free from active infestation (other than infestation by wood-destroying fungi) or damage (including that caused by wood-destroying fungi) by termites or other wood-destroying organisms as required to be disclosed by Florida Law. If active infestation or damage is found to be present, the SELLER shall bear the total costs of remedying such active infestation and damage, except BUYER shall be responsible for damage caused by wood-destroying fungi where the cost of repair is less than One Hundred Dollars ($100.00). Should the cost of such treatment and repair exceed __five hundred__ Dollars ($ _500.00_), the SELLER may elect to terminate this agreement and all rights and liabilities of all parties shall be at an end and the deposit shall be returned to BUYER, unless the BUYER elects to proceed with the transaction, having the above amount as a credit at closing.

9. ASSIGNABILITY: This Contract (Check One) ☐ is assignable ☒ is not assignable.

10. RESTRICTIONS, EASEMENTS AND LIMITATIONS: The BUYER shall take title subject to: zoning, restrictions, prohibitions and other requirements imposed by governmental authority, restrictions and matters appearing on the plat or otherwise common to the subdivision, public utility easements of record, taxes for year of closing and subsequent years, assumed mortgage(s) and purchase money mortgages, if any, other: __none__ _____ provided, however, that there exists at closing no violation of the foregoing and that the foregoing do not affect the marketability of title, and they do not prevent the use of the property for __single-family__ purpose(s)

11. UTILITIES: SELLER represents subject property is served by (check if applicable):
☒ Central water system
☐ Well
☒ Central wastewater system
☐ Septic tank
☐ None of the above

Revised 9/93 — © Gainesville-Alachua County Association of REALTORS® , Inc. All Rights Reserved.

EXHIBIT 24-2 (continued)

12. EXPENSES: SELLER shall pay for the following expenses:

a. Real estate compensation.

b. State documentary stamps to be affixed to deed.

c. Preparation of instruments required of SELLER.

d. Abstract or title insurance.

e. Termite inspection fee.

f. SELLER'S attorney fee

g. _____

h. _____

BUYER shall pay for the following expenses:

a. Title examination and title opinion, if any.

b. Recording of deed.

c. All expenses relative to all notes and mortgages, or a contract for deed, including preparation, recording, documentary stamps, intangible tax, and mortgagee title insurance.

d. Transfer costs of any existing mortgage(s).

e. Survey, if any.

f. BUYER'S attorney fee.

g. _____

h. _____

13. INSPECTION, REPAIR AND MAINTENANCE: Unless otherwise stated in this Agreement, SELLER warrants that: (a) the ceiling, roof (including fascia and soffit), and exterior and interior walls do not have any visible evidence of leaks, water damage or structural damage. In the event repairs or replacements are required, SELLER shall pay up to ___five hundred___ dollars ($_500.00___) for such repairs or replacements; (b) SELLER further warrants that the septic tank, pool, all major appliances, heating, cooling, electrical, plumbing systems and machinery are in good working condition. In the event repairs or replacements are required, SELLER shall pay up to ___five hundred___ dollars ($_500.00___) for such repairs or replacements. However, if the cost for such repairs or replacements for either (a) or (b) above exceeds the stated amount, BUYER or SELLER may elect to pay such excess, failing which either party may cancel this Agreement. BUYER may, at BUYER'S expense, have inspections made of the roof and said items and shall report in writing to SELLER such items that do not meet the above warranty **prior to possession or not less than ten (10) calendar days prior to closing,** whichever date first occurs. Unless BUYER reports such deficiencies within said period, BUYER shall be deemed to have waived SELLER'S warranties as to deficiencies not reported. All such inspections shall be at BUYER'S expense, including any utility turn-on charges and costs of electricity and gas if these utilities are not currently on at the property. Notwithstanding the provisions hereof, between the effective date of the Agreement and the closing, SELLER shall maintain the real and personal property in the condition herein warranted, reasonable wear and tear excepted, and shall maintain the lawn and shrubbery in substantially the same condition as exists on the effective date of this Agreement. BUYER'S designee shall be permitted reasonable access for inspection prior to closing in order to confirm the compliance with the maintenance requirements. For the purpose of this provision, all inspections, repairs and replacements shall be made by an appropriately licensed firm or individual, or by a firm or individual specializing in home inspections and holding an appropriate license if required, or other mutually acceptable person. **The items listed above are the only repair items covered by this Agreement unless otherwise specifically provided for in the Agreement.** SELLER makes no warranties as to conformity with current, applicable code requirements.

14. CONVEYANCE: SELLER shall convey title to the property by statutory warranty, trustee, personal representative or guardian deed, as appropriate to the status of SELLER, free and clear of all encumbrances and liens of whatsoever nature, except taxes for the current year, and except as herein otherwise provided. The SELLER shall also deliver to the BUYER a lien and possession affidavit at closing, sufficient to remove lien and possession exceptions from title insurance coverage. Conveyance of title shall be to ___George and Helen Jones___ .

15. DATE OF POSSESSION: BUYER shall be given possession ___upon closing___

16. TIME FOR ACCEPTANCE-FACSIMILE: If this Agreement is not executed by all parties hereto, or FACT OF EXECUTION communicated in writing between the parties, on or before ___May 18___ , 19 _98_, the aforesaid deposit(s) shall, at the option of the BUYER, be returned to BUYER and this Agreement shall be null and void. A facsimile copy of this Agreement and any signatures hereon shall be considered for all purposes as originals.

17. FLOOD ZONE REPRESENTATION: Flood Zone "A" is the designation for property that may be subject to more than a minimal risk of flooding. SELLER represents that the improvements (or the effective buildable area of unimproved property) are: (CHECK ONE OF THE FOLLOWING)

☐ within flood zone "A"

☒ not within flood zone "A"

☐ flood zone status is unknown to SELLER

If the SELLER has not represented the improvements (or effective buildable area) to be within Flood Zone "A", and the BUYER produces evidence prior to closing of title that Flood Zone "A" is in fact applicable, the BUYER shall have the option to declare the contract terminated and shall thereupon be entitled to a refund of all deposits. Should the BUYER close title without obtaining evidence of flood zone status, the BUYER shall be deemed to have waived all objections as to flood zone regardless of the representation set forth in this paragraph.

18. DISCLOSURES: Buyer ☒ acknowledges or ☐ does not acknowledge receipt of agency and estimated closing costs disclosures.

BUYER'S INITIALS _GJ_ _HJr_

STANDARDS FOR REAL ESTATE TRANSACTIONS

A. EFFECTIVE DATE: The Effective Date as referred to in this Contract shall be the date when the last one of the SELLER and BUYER has signed this Contract.

B. VARIANCE IN AMOUNT OF FINANCING TO BE ASSUMED: Any variance in any amount of financing to be assumed from the amount stated herein shall be added to or deducted from purchase money financing if such is contemplated by this Contract otherwise said variance shall be added to or deducted from the cash at closing, provided that if such procedure results in an increase in cash due at closing in excess of Five Hundred Dollars ($500.00), the BUYER shall not be obligated to perform unless SELLER reduces the purchase price by the amount of the excess over said specified sum.

C. SURVEY: If the BUYER desires a survey of the property, he may have the property surveyed at his expense at least five (5) days prior to the closing date. If the survey shows any encroachments on the land herein described, or that the improvements located on the land herein described encroach on other lands, or any shortage, written notice to that effect along with a copy of the survey shall be given to the SELLER and the same shall be treated as defects in title to be eliminated by SELLER. SELLER agrees to provide BUYER with copies of existing surveys he has, if any, within five (5) days from the effective date.

D. PRORATIONS: All taxes for the current year, rentals, insurance premiums, association assessments and interest on existing mortgages (if any) shall be prorated as of the date of closing with BUYER paying for the day of closing. If part of the purchase price is to be evidenced by the assumption of a mortgage requiring deposit of funds in escrow for payment of taxes, insurance or other charges, the BUYER agrees to reimburse the SELLER for escrowed funds assigned to BUYER at closing. All mortgage payments shall be current at the time of closing.

E. WARRANTIES: SELLER warrants that there are no facts or defects known to SELLER materially affecting the value of the real property which are not readily observable by BUYER or which have not been disclosed to BUYER in writing.

F. DESTRUCTION OF PREMISES: If any improvements located on the above described premises at the time of execution of this Contract are damaged by fire or other casualty prior to closing and can be substantially restored within a period not to exceed 45 days after the anticipated closing date, SELLER shall so restore the improvements and the closing date shall be extended accordingly. If such restoration cannot be completed within said period of time, this Contract, at the option of the BUYER, shall terminate and all deposit(s) shall be returned to BUYER. All risk of loss prior to closing shall be borne by the SELLER.

Revised 9/93 — © Gainesville-Alachua County Association of REALTORS', Inc. All Rights Reserved.

E X H I B I T   2 4 - 2   (c o n c l u d e d)

G. ESCROW: Any escrow agent ("Agent") receiving funds or equivalent is authorized and agrees by acceptance of them to deposit them promptly, hold same in escrow and, subject to clearance, disburse them in accordance with the terms and conditions of this Contract. At SELLER'S option, failure of clearance of funds shall be considered a default. If in doubt as to Agent's duties or liabilities under the provisions of this Contract, Agent may, at Agent's option, continue to hold the subject matter of the escrow until the parties mutually agree to its disbursement or until a judgment of a court of competent jurisdiction shall determine the rights of the parties, or Agent may deposit said escrowed funds with the clerk of the circuit court having jurisdiction of the dispute. Upon notifying all parties concerned of such action, all liability on the part of Agent shall terminate, except to the extent of accounting for any items previously delivered out of escrow. If escrow agent is a licensed real estate broker, Agent will comply with provisions of Chapter 475, F.S. (1987), as amended. Any suit between BUYER and SELLER where Agent is made a party because of acting as Agent hereunder, or in any suit wherein Agent interpleads the subject matter of the escrow, Agent shall recover reasonable attorney's fees and costs incurred, with the fees and costs to be charged and assessed as court costs in favor of the prevailing party. Parties agree that Agent shall not be liable to any party or person for misdelivery to BUYER or SELLER of items subject to this escrow, unless such misdelivery is due to willful breach of Contract or gross negligence of Agent.

H. DISBURSEMENT OF CLOSING PROCEEDS: Disbursement of closing proceeds shall be made as soon after closing as final title certification and examination have been made, but which shall be no later than five (5) business days after closing.

I. FAILURE OF PERFORMANCE: If BUYER fails to perform this Contract within the time specified (including payment of all deposits hereunder), the deposit(s) paid by BUYER may be retained by or for the account of SELLER as agreed upon liquidated damages, consideration for the execution of this Contract and in full settlement of any claims; whereupon BUYER and SELLER shall be relieved of all obligations under this Contract; or SELLER, at SELLER'S option, may proceed in equity to enforce SELLER'S rights under this Contract. If, for any reason other than failure of SELLER to make SELLER'S title marketable after diligent effort, SELLER fails, neglects or refuses to perform this Contract, the BUYER may seek specific performance or elect to receive the return of BUYER'S deposit(s) without thereby waiving any action for damages resulting from SELLER'S breach.

J. OTHER AGREEMENTS: This Contract constitutes the entire agreement between the parties, and any changes, amendments or modifications hereof shall be null and void unless same are reduced to writing and signed by the parties hereto.

K. PERSONS BOUND: The covenants herein contained shall bind, and the benefits and advantages shall pass to, the respective heirs, administrators, successors and assigns of the parties hereto. Whenever used, the singular number shall include the plural, and the use of any gender shall include all genders.

L. ATTORNEY'S FEES AND COSTS: In any litigation arising out of this Agreement, the prevailing party in such litigation which, for the purposes of this Standard, shall include SELLER, BUYER, listing broker, BUYER'S broker and any subagents to the listing broker or BUYER'S broker, shall be entitled to recover reasonable attorneys fees and costs, including reasonable attorney's fees and costs incurred in any appeal.

M. PROVISIONS: Typewritten or handwritten provisions inserted in this form shall control all printed provisions in conflict therewith.

N. INSULATION RIDER: If this Contract is utilized for the sale of a new residence, an Insulation Rider or equivalent shall be attached hereto and become a part hereof.

O. FOREIGN INVESTMENT IN REAL PROPERTY TAX ACT ("FIRPTA") RIDER: The parties shall comply with the provisions of FIRPTA and applicable regulations which could require SELLER to provide additional cash at closing to meet withholding requirements, and a FIRPTA Rider or equivalent may be attached to this Contract.

P. INGRESS AND EGRESS: SELLER warrants and represents that there is ingress and egress to the Real Property sufficient for the intended use as described herein.

Q. TIME: Time periods herein of less than six (6) days shall, in the computation, exclude Saturdays, Sundays and state or national legal holidays, and any time period provided for herein which shall end on a Saturday, Sunday, or legal holiday shall extend to 5:00 p.m. of the next business day. Failure of any party to perform any covenant of this contract within the time limits set forth for performance of such covenant shall not be considered a material breach excusing performance unless such failure results in a material loss to the aggrieved party.

R. LEASES: SELLER shall, not less than 15 days before closing, furnish to BUYER copies of all written leases and estoppel letters from each tenant specifying the nature and duration of the tenant's occupancy, rental rates; and advanced rent and security deposits paid by tenant. If SELLER is unable to obtain such letter from each tenant, the same information shall be furnished by SELLER to BUYER within that time period in the form of a SELLER'S affidavit and BUYER may thereafter contact tenants to confirm such information. SELLER shall, at closing, deliver and assign all original leases to BUYER.

S. SPECIAL ASSESSMENTS:

1. UNIMPROVED PROPERTY: SELLER shall be responsible for payment of all special assessments for improvements whether in place or under construction as of the effective date of this agreement. BUYER agrees to be responsible for all water and wastewater flow base and connection charges, if any, associated with placing any improvements upon the property.

2. IMPROVED PROPERTY: SELLER shall be responsible for payment of all special assessments for improvements whether in place or under construction as of the effective date of this agreement. SELLER shall pay (or has paid) all water and wastewater flow base and connection charges.

T. ADDITIONAL INFORMATION:

RADON: Radon is a naturally occurring radioactive gas that, when it has accumulated in a building in sufficient quantities, may present health risks to persons who are exposed to it over time. Levels of radon that exceed federal and state guidelines have been found in buildings in Florida. Additional information regarding radon and radon testing may be obtained from your county public health unit.

THIS IS A LEGALLY BINDING CONTRACT AND SHALL NOT BE RECORDED UNLESS OTHERWISE AGREED TO BETWEEN THE PARTIES. IF NOT FULLY UNDERSTOOD, SEEK COMPETENT LEGAL ADVICE. DO NOT SIGN UNTIL ALL BLANKS ARE COMPLETED. YOUR REALTOR® RECOMMENDS THAT YOU OBTAIN TITLE INSURANCE OR A TITLE OPINION FROM YOUR ATTORNEY.

George Jones   May 15, 1998 Date   _Fred Johnson_   May 16, 1998 Date
(BUYER)   (SELLER)

Social Security or Tax I.D.# _122-21-2221_   Social Security or Tax I.D.# _211-12-1112_

Helen Jones   May 15, 1998 Date   _Susie Johnson_   May 16, 1998 Date
(BUYER)   (SELLER)

Social Security or Tax I.D.# _322-32-2223_   Social Security or Tax I.D.# _233-23-3332_

Deposit(s) if other than cash, then subject to clearance. ___Bosshardt Realty Service, Inc._____
                                                              Escrow Agent (REALTOR®)

                                                         By: _Carol Locascio_____

BROKER'S FEE: (CHECK & COMPLETE THE ONE APPLICABLE)

[X] IF A LISTING AGREEMENT IS CURRENTLY IN EFFECT:
     SELLER agrees to pay the Broker, according to the terms of an existing, separate listing agreement;

OR

[ ] IF NO LISTING AGREEMENT IS CURRENTLY IN EFFECT:
     SELLER agrees to pay the Broker named below, at time of closing, from the disbursements of the proceeds of the sale, compensation in the amount of

(COMPLETE ONLY ONE) _____% of gross purchase price OR $_____, for Broker's services in effecting the sale by finding a BUYER ready, willing and able to purchase pursuant to the foregoing Contract. If BUYER fails to perform and deposit(s) is retained, 50% thereof, but not exceeding the Broker's fee above provided, shall be paid to the Broker, as full consideration for Broker's services including costs expended by Broker, and the balance shall be paid to SELLER. If the transaction shall not be closed because of refusal or failure of SELLER to perform, the SELLER shall pay said fees in full to Broker on demand. In any litigation arising out of this Contract, concerning the Broker's fee, the prevailing party shall be entitled to recover reasonable attorney fees and costs.

_____   _____
(firm name of Broker)   (SELLER)

By: _____
(authorized signatory)   _____
                                                                              (SELLER)

_____
Firm (name of cooperating agent)

_____   Revised 9/93 — © Gainesville-Alachua County
(Address of cooperating agent)   Association of REALTORS®, Inc. All Rights Reserved.

The contract also includes a space to specify items of personal property and questionable items (such as the carpet described in Real Estate Focus 24–1) as property to which title is being conveyed. The purchase price and form of payment are listed in paragraph 1, and a financing contingency clause is provided in 4. Buyers normally pay a deposit (known as escrow money, earnest money, or a binder) at the time they make an offer to show they are serious and to indemnify the sellers in the event they (the buyers) fail to perform. The broker holds the deposit in a segregated account called an **escrow account** until closing or until other arrangements are made for its disposition.

The contract form also covers type of title evidence, time for acceptance by the parties, closing date, restrictions, easements, limitations, occupancy, assignability, liens, assessments, front footage charges, expenses, inspections, repair, maintenance, and flood zone representation. Spaces are provided for signatures of the principals and the representative of the real estate firm.

A section is provided for a separate agreement between the sellers and the broker if no listing agreement is in effect. The sellers agree to pay the broker a commission at time of closing from the disbursement of proceeds. If the buyers fail to perform, the broker and sellers agree to split any deposits, with the broker's share not to exceed the amount of the commission. If the sellers fail to perform, they agree to pay the full commission to the broker.

ESTIMATED CLOSING EXPENSE STATEMENTS

The laws of some states require that real estate brokers provide buyers and sellers with a list of **estimated closing costs** before signing a contract for sale. Also, the federal Real Estate Settlement Procedures Act (RESPA) requires lenders to provide borrowers with an estimate of the settlement expenses that are likely to occur. Such estimates must be provided when the borrower applies for a loan or within three business days. Exhibits 24–3 and 24–4 show the estimated closing expenses in the sale of the Johnson property. The various costs and expenses should closely approximate the final amounts on the closing statement (Exhibit 24–5).

CONTINUING SAGA OF A SALE

Recall from Chapter 23 that Fred and Louise Johnson have listed their house with Bosshardt Realty, Inc., through Carol Locascio, a Realtor with the firm. The listing price is $85,000. Another salesperson, Linda Lavin, shows the Johnson home to George and Helen Jones, who are moving to Gainesville from Ohio. They like the house and believe it would suit their needs, but they note several maintenance and replacement items. They believe they would have to paint the interior and exterior, install new carpeting, and purchase drapes. Thus, they decide to make the following offer:

Price: $80,000

Financing: New ARM loan of $64,000 from a local lending institution at 8.50 percent (adjusted annually)

Closing: July 1, 1998

Binder deposit: $1,000

EXHIBIT 24-3

BUYER'S ESTIMATED CLOSING COSTS

BOSSHARDT REALTY
BOSSHARDT REALTY SERVICES INC.

BUYER'S ESTIMATED CLOSING COSTS

SELLER: Fred and Louise Johnson   BUYER: George and Helen Jones
PROPERTY ADDRESS: 1822 N.W. 40th Avenue
ASSOCIATE: Carol Locascio   DATE: May 15, 1998

Purchase/Sales Price		
		$ 83,000.00
Binder Deposit	$1,000.00	
Additional Deposit	$ –	
Remaining Down Payment	$ –	
New Base Mortgage	$66,400.00	
__ VA Funding Fee __ FHA Mtg. Ins. Premium	$	
Total Mortgage		$ 66,400.00

Estimated Closing Costs		
Documentary Stamps on Note ($.35 per $100)	$ 332.40	
Intangible Tax on Note (.002)	$ 132.80	
Recording Deed and Mortgage	$ 34.00	
Origination Fee (Base loan-FHA/VA)	$ –	
Discount Points (____ points)	$1,328.00	
Appraisal Fee	$ 150.00	
Credit Report	$ 55.00	
Mortgage Title Insurance	$ 200.00	
Owners Title Insurance	$ 150.00	
Mortgage Insurance (on loan amount)	$ –	
Survey/Flood Certification	$ 10.00	
Attorney's Fee	$ 150.00	
Transfer Fee	$ –	
Home Warranty Plan	$ –	
Courier/Express Fee	$ –	
Underwriting Fee	$ –	
Preparation of Documents	$ 50.00	
	$	
Total Estimated Closing Cost		$ 2,592.20

Escrow (prepaid insurance and taxes)		
14 Months Hazard Insurance:	$ 329.00	
3 Months Real Estate Taxes @ 166.33	$ 490.00	
2 Months FHA Mortgage Ins. @ ____	$ –	
____ MIP ___ VA Funding Fee	$ –	
Total Escrow		$

Monthly Payment Estimate		
Principal and Interest (8.5 % 30 years)	$ 510.56	
Taxes	$ 166.33	
Hazard Insurance	$ 27.42	
FHA Mortgage Insurance	$ –	
Association Fee (if any)	$ –	
Total Estimated Monthly Payment		$ 704.31

Summary		
Down Payment (___ including ___ excluding)	$ 16,600.00	
Total Estimated Closing Costs	$ 2,592.20	
Total Escrow or Prepaids	$ 819.00	
Estimated Interest in Advance	$ 470.33	
TOTAL		$ 20,481.53
Less Deposit		$ 1,000.00
Estimated Cash at Closing		$ 19,481.53

It is understood that the above cost figures are an estimate only and prorations will be determined by the closing agent at closing. Buyer acknowledges that this instrument has been read and signed before any Contract for Sale and Purchase of the real estate in question has been signed.

May 15, 1998
DATE
George Jones
George Jones
BUYER

Helen Jones
Helen Jones
BUYER

5542 N.W. 43RD STREET, GAINESVILLE, FLORIDA (904) 371-6100

EXHIBIT 24-4

SELLER'S ESTIMATED CLOSING COSTS

BOSSHARDT REALTY SERVICES INC.

SELLER'S ESTIMATED CLOSING COSTS

SELLER: Fred and Louise Johnson   BUYER: George and Helen Jones

PROPERTY ADDRESS: 1822 N.W. 40th Avenue

ASSOCIATE: Carol Locascio   DATE: May 15, 1998

Purchase/Sales Price   (A) $ 83,000.00

Estimated Closing Costs:

Documentary Stamps on Deed ($.70 per $100)	$ 581.00
Recording Satisfaction of Mortgage	$ 10.00
Preparation of Deed	$ 75.00
Abstract/Abstract Re-certification/Title Ins.	$ 800.00
Attorney's Fee	$
Termite Clearance	$ 50.00
Mortgage Prepayment Penalty	$ –
Title Insurance Endorsements	$ –
Tax Service Fee (FHA/VA)	$ –
Underwriting Fee	$ –
Preparation of Documents (FHA/VA)	$ –
Courier/Express fees (FHA/VA)	$ –
Loan Processing/Assignment Fee	$ –
Buyer's Costs Paid by Seller	$ –
Lender's Discount	$ –
Buyer's Protection Plan	$
Brokerage Fee (6.0 %)	$4,980.00
_____	$_____
_____	$_____
_____	$_____

Total Estimated Closing Costs	(B) $ 6,496.00
Adjusted Sales Price (A minus B)	(C) $ 76,504.00

Other Charges:

Mortgage Payoffs	$ 45,000.00
Taxes	$ 997.98
Interest (in arrears)	$ –
Association Fees (if any)	$ –

Total Other Charges:	(D) $ 45,997.98
Net to Seller (C minus D)	$ 30,506.02
Less Mortgage Held by Seller	$ –

Cash to Seller at Closing	$ 30,506.02
Less any repairs (as per contract) up to	$ 1,000.00

I understand the above closing costs are estimated only and the final costs and tax and interest prorations will be determined by the closing agent. I further understand the discount points on loans are subject to daily fluctuation and may change until locked in. If the interest rate changes during this time, the discount point lock-in may be invalidated. I further understand that Bosshardt Realty Services, Inc. in no way warrants or guarantees any of the above estimated figures.

Seller acknowledges this instrument has been read and signed before any contract for sale of real estate has been signed.

This ___15th_ day of __May_____, 19 98 .

BY: Carol Locascio   SELLER: Fred Johnson
      REALTOR
                                      SELLER: Louise Johnson

5542 N.W. 43RD STREET, GAINESVILLE, FLORIDA (904) 371-6100

Carol and Linda present the offer to the Johnsons, who reject it and counter with a price of $83,000. The counteroffer is then presented to the Joneses. They accept this offer contingent on their obtaining a 30-year, 80 percent ARM loan commitment at an initial rate not to exceed 8.5 percent for 30 years. They also want the sellers to furnish a title insurance policy and a termite inspection report, and they want to have the right to have radon and building inspections made at their own expense. This offer/counteroffer process is reflected in the sale contract form shown in Exhibit 24–2.

CONTRACTS WITH CONTINGENCIES

Contracts for sale may contain clauses that cause implementation of the contract to depend on the successful completion of some prior action or condition. These are known as **contracts with contingencies.** Examples are financing contingencies in which the buyer can back out of the transaction if financing cannot be obtained on specified terms, and engineering contingencies in which the buyer can back out if an inspection shows the property is physically deficient. Contingencies appear most often in contracts for properties that are difficult to sell.

ASSIGNMENT

In general, most contracts—including real estate contracts—can be assigned. **Assignment** means that one party's contractual rights and obligations are transferred to someone else. If buyers of real estate assign the contract, new buyers, in effect, take their place. The new buyers may pay the agreed-upon price and obtain title to the property.

But any type of **personal performance** contracted by one party cannot be assigned without that party's permission. For example, if the seller has agreed to take a purchase money mortgage as part of the payment for the property, the buyer cannot assign this right to someone else unless he or she remains personally liable to the seller for payment of the loan. Similarly, land (installment sale) contracts are not assignable without the owner's permission. In these situations, the seller relies on the buyer's qualifications, and the assignee may not be as well qualified.

Although buyers may assign their rights to someone else, they do not escape liability under the contract. They are still obligated to the seller and, should the assignees not fulfill the contract's requirements, the seller can look to the assignors for satisfaction. In effect, assignment is an agreement by the assignee to carry out the obligations of the assignor; the assignor's contract with the other party is not affected.

Of course, the other party can agree to an assignment and relieve the assignor of all obligations. When this occurs, a contract is created between the third party and the assignee that absolves the assignor of further responsibility under the contract.

A contract can also prohibit assignment. Such a prohibition would be contained in an *assignment clause.*

REAL ESTATE FOCUS 24-2

Cases on Real Estate Contracts

Case No. 1

Lach paid a deposit of $1,000 to Cahill for the purchase of a house. The sales contract recited that, "This agreement is contingent upon buyer (Lach) being able to obtain a mortgage . . . on the premises." Lach applied to a bank for a mortgage, but his application was denied. Thereafter, his application was denied by five other lending institutions. Cahill was unwilling to finance the house himself, and Lach notified Cahill that he was unable to secure a mortgage and that he wanted his deposit returned. When Cahill refused to return the $1,000 deposit, Lach brought legal action to recover the deposit.

Issue: Was Lach entitled to the return of his deposit?

Decision: Yes. Lach had no duty to buy Cahill's house.

Reasons: To recover his deposit, Lach was required to show that (1) his ability to secure a mortgage was a *condition precedent* to his duty to perform under the terms of the sales contract; and (2) he had made a reasonable effort to secure financing. A condition precedent is a factor or event the parties intend must exist or take place before the duty of performance arises. If the condition is not fulfilled, the right to enforce the contract does not come into existence. The language of the contract clearly showed that Lach's ability to secure a mortgage was a condition precedent to his performance. The condition, in addition, implies a promise by Lach that he would make reasonable efforts to secure a suitable mortgage. His attempts to find financing were reasonable under the circumstances, and Lach should accordingly recover his deposit.

Lach v. *Cahill,* 85 A.2d 481 (Conn. 1951).

Case No. 2

This is an appeal from a trial court decision denying a motion for specific performance of a purported real estate sales contract. The complaint alleged that on February 16, 1978, a purchaser, William Jones, presented the sellers with an unsigned form contract in writing for the purchase of certain real estate. The complaint also alleged that the purchaser delivered a $12,000 check to the sellers, Paul and Catherine Cooper, the check stating it was earnest money for the purchase of 029 Lakeview, Mundelein. Sellers endorsed the check and deposited it on February 25, 1978. However, they never signed the sales contract form.

The transaction was not closed, the $12,000 was not returned, and the buyers brought suit for specific performance of the contract. Although the contract was not signed and the names of the purchaser and the sellers did not appear on the contract, it did include the address 029 Lakeview, Mundelein, with a lot size of "150 × 150." It further provided for $12,000 earnest money in the form of a check, payable to sellers, to be deposited by sellers on acceptance of the contract. The contract form stated it was to be void if not accepted by February 28, 1978, and it contained the purchase price, method of payment, terms, and conditions of sale.

Issue: Did the contract violate the statute of frauds, which requires the signatures of both parties to a contract?

Decisions:

1. The trial court dismissed the motion for specific performance, stating that the contract violated the statute of frauds for lack of signatures. The court also held that the check did not satisfy the signature requirement because it did not express the terms and conditions of sale.

2. The appellate court reversed the trial court's decision.

Reasons: The appellate court held that the form contract and the check were sufficiently connected to allow them to be read together. Both documents refer to the same common address and the same amount as the earnest money specified in the contract. Also, the check and the contract have the same date, and the check was deposited before February 28, 1978, as required by the contract.

The case was sent back to the trial court, where the motion for specific performance was granted.

Jones v. *Olsen*, 400 NE 2d 665 (Ill. App. 1980).

REMEDIES FOR NONPERFORMANCE

Buyers and sellers sometimes fail to live up to a contract's provisions. They may change their minds for a number of reasons. For example, if one spouse dies, the other may not want to move. Or, if their financial circumstances change, they may decide they cannot afford a new home.

When a party fails to perform (breach of contract, nonperformance, or default), the other party may have one or more remedies (see Real Estate Focus 24–2).

REMEDIES FOR A SELLER

If a buyer defaults, a seller may take one of the following actions:

1. *Rescind the contract.* The contract is canceled, and any deposits are returned to the buyer.
2. *Sue for specific performance.* The seller asks a court to require the buyer to complete the transaction and to live up to all other provisions of the contract.
3. *Sue for damages.* The seller may sue the buyer for any loss of financial advantage. Damages are measured as the difference between the purchase price and the market value of the property. If no difference can be shown, the seller is not able to collect.
4. *Retain all or a portion of earnest-money deposits as liquidated damages.* Most form contracts contain a provision awarding all or a portion of earnest-money deposits to the seller if the buyer defaults. Retention of a deposit is known as liquidating the damages. This is the remedy most often followed by sellers because suits for damages and specific performance are costly and time consuming.

REMEDIES FOR A BUYER

If a seller defaults, the buyer may:

1. *Rescind the contract.* The contract is canceled, and any earnest-money deposits are returned to the buyer.
2. *Sue for specific performance.* The buyer asks a court to require the seller to convey title to the property to him or her and to live up to all other provisions of the contract.
3. *Sue for damages.* The buyer may sue the seller for any loss of financial advantage. Damages are measured as the difference between the market value of the property and the purchase price. If no difference can be shown, the buyer is not able to collect.

Contracts can also provide for *liquidated damages* of a specified amount in the event of seller nonperformance. Under such a provision, the sellers would have to put a specified amount of cash in escrow that would be given to the buyers if the sellers back out of the sale. However, sellers are usually unwilling to put up earnest money for this purpose. They have, in effect, put up their property, and a suit for specific performance would be effective in most cases.

E S C R O W

To lessen the chances for nonperformance, real estate contracts are often placed in **escrow**. An **escrow agent** is a third party who is instructed to carry out the provisions of the contract by means of a separate escrow agreement. The escrow agent must be impartial and may not benefit from the provisions of the purchase and sale contract. The escrow agent is allowed, of course, to collect a fee for services rendered.

Escrow agents are usually attorneys, financial institutions, or title companies, although in some states they may be separate individuals or companies. They hold the documents and funds relevant to a transaction and distribute them according to the written instructions at time of closing.

For example, a buyer would give a deposit or full purchase price to the escrow agent, while the seller would deliver a deed and evidence of title (such as an abstract or a title insurance policy) to the escrow agent. Insurance policies, mortgage financing information, and any other documents would also be provided. When all the documents have been assembled, title has been searched, funds have been obtained, and all other conditions met, the escrow agent delivers the deed to the buyer and the funds to the seller.

When escrow agents are not used, attorneys or financial institutions usually provide closing services. Although they assemble the necessary documents and arrange for the title search and evidence of title, the real estate broker may hold the earnest-money deposit until closing. The broker, however, must hold the deposit for the benefit of the principal, cannot commingle deposits with personal funds, and must not disburse deposits except as provided in the contract.

C L O S I N G

The saga of the sale of Fred and Louise Johnson's house to George and Helen Jones continues. Recall that the contract for sale signed by the Johnsons and Joneses specifies, "The transaction shall be concluded on July 1, 1998, or such earlier date as may be mutually agreeable." (See item 3 in Exhibit 24–2.) It is now July 1, 1998. The Johnsons; the Joneses; the Joneses' attorney, James Henry; and Carol Locascio, the Realtor® arrive at the offices of DownTrust Bank, where closing is to take place. The Joneses' application for a 8.50 percent, 30-year, adjustable rate mortgage (ARM) was approved by DownTrust. DownTrust's attorney, Joe Jenkins, is there to handle the closing.

S T E P S   B E F O R E   C L O S I N G

After signing the contract for sale on May 15, 1998, and before arriving for closing July 1, 1998, the Joneses and their attorney took the following steps:

1. Had the property surveyed for possible encroachments. (Paid for directly by the Joneses; therefore, this charge does not appear on the closing statement.)
2. Reviewed an abstract of documents in the public records to make certain there are no violations of private restrictions.
3. Reviewed the zoning ordinance to make certain the property is used as legally permitted.
4. Examined the list of estimated closing costs to make certain they are correct and reasonable.
5. Ordered a mortgagee's title insurance policy from the same company the sellers asked to issue an owners' title policy. When a title company issues a policy to both an owner and a mortgagee, it is termed a *simultaneous issue*.
6. Inspected the property to verify condition and vacancy for possession. (Many buyers hire a professional property inspector for this.)
7. Reviewed the contract to make certain other terms of the contract have been met by the sellers, such as having the property inspected for termites.
8. Made arrangements to have hazard insurance coverage, utilities, telephone, and other services begin on the date of closing.

Note: If the Joneses were assuming any mortgages, the attorney would obtain an *estoppel certificate* (or letter) from the mortgagee that would show the amount being assumed, interest rate, length of debt period, periodic payments, and frequency of amortization.

The Johnsons also took some steps between the signing of the contract and the closing. They

1. Ordered an owners' title insurance policy. (Although not stated in the contract, the Joneses subsequently agreed to pay $150 of the $950 title insurance premium.)

   Note: If the contract for sale had specified that an abstract and attorney's opinion serve as the evidence of title, they would have
   a. Ordered the abstract brought up to date.
   b. Had the abstract delivered to the buyers' attorney, Mr. Henry, for examination.
2. Ordered a termite inspection and had the certificate showing the improvements to be free of active infestation or visible damage delivered to the Joneses' attorney.
3. Ordered their hazard insurance coverage, utilities, and other services to be stopped on the closing date.

As closing agent and representative of DownTrust Bank, Mr. Jenkins has obtained or prepared the following documents and legal instruments:

1. General warranty deed in proper form, to be signed by the Johnsons at closing.

2. Mortgage and note, to be signed by the Joneses at closing.
3. Check from the lender made payable to the seller.
4. Closing statement showing the expenses and obligations incurred by both parties. Real estate taxes for 1998, as specified in the contract for sale, are prorated between buyers and sellers as of the date of closing.
5. A *satisfaction of mortgage* from the previous lender.

Note: If there had been any leases or assignments of interests being transferred to the buyers, copies of these documents would also have been obtained.

STEPS AT CLOSING

The Johnsons, the Joneses, Ms. Locascio, Mr. Henry, and Mr. Jenkins go to a small conference room for the closing. They take seats around a rectangular table, with Mr. Jenkins sitting at the head of the table. He informs everyone that he is closing the transaction on behalf of DownTrust Bank and is also serving as the Johnsons' attorney. He introduces Mr. Henry as the Joneses' attorney. Mr. Jenkins states he has prepared all documents in accordance with the terms of the contract for sale, the loan application and approval, and applicable state and federal laws. He also states that he has coordinated title matters, inspections, and documents with Mr. Henry and Ms. Locascio.

Mr. Jenkins presents copies of the composite **closing statement** shown in Exhibit 24–5 to the Johnsons and Joneses and explains it as follows: Debits are charges, or amounts due from each party. In this transaction the sellers are owed, or credited, the total purchase price of $83,000, and the buyers are debited this amount. The buyers are credited the binder deposit (or escrow or earnest money), since it has already been paid. There is no corresponding entry on the seller's statement because it is included in the total purchase price. The buyers are also credited with the amount of the new mortgage they are obtaining from DownTrust Bank. In effect, they are responsible for bringing these funds into the transaction and are committed to paying off the loan with interest, over the next 30 years.

PRORATIONS

Property taxes are the only item *prorated* in this transaction. **Proration** means dividing an expense between buyers and sellers proportionally on the basis of the time the property is occupied by each party. Since property taxes are usually paid in arrears (after the period for which they are incurred), the *buyers* will have to pay the tax bill for the entire year of 1998 in November or December of 1998. Therefore, they are given credit for the amount of time the property was occupied by the sellers—181 out of 365 days. Item D in the Standards for Real Estate Transactions (see Exhibit 24–2) indicates that the buyer pays for the day of closing. Since the total tax bill for 1998 was estimated to be $2,012.50 the credit of $997.98 to the buyers (and debit of the same amount to the sellers) is calculated as follows:

$$(181/365) \times \$2,012.50 = \$997.98$$

EXHIBIT 24-5

COMPOSITE CLOSING STATEMENT FOR JOHNSON SALE TO THE JONESES

Sellers' Statement			Buyers' Statement	
Debit	**Credit**	**Item**	**Debit**	**Credit**
	$83,000.00	Purchase price	$83,000.00	
$45,000		Existing mortgage repaid		
		Binder deposit		$ 1,000.00
		New mortgage		66,400.00
997.98		Prorated taxes		997.98
		EXPENSES—BUYER		
		Discount points (2)	1,328.00	
		Appraisal fee	150.00	
		Credit report	55.00	
		Attorney's fee	150.00	
		Preparation of documents	50.00	
		Flood certification	10.00	
		Preparation of note and mortgage	50.00	
		PREPAYMENTS		
		Hazard insurance	329.00	
		Real estate taxes (3 mos.)	490.00	
		Mortgage payment (1 mo.)	510.56	
		TITLE INSURANCE		
800.00		Owners'	150.00	
		Mortgagee's	200.00	
		DOCUMENTARY STAMPS		
581.00		Deed		
		Mortgage note	332.40	
		Intangible tax—Note	132.80	
		RECORDING		
10.00		Mortgage satisfaction		
		Mortgage and deed	34.00	
4,980.00		Broker's commission (6.0%)		
75.00		Deed preparation		
50.00		Termite clearance		
52,493.98	83,000.00	COLUMN TOTALS	86,971.76	68,397.98
		Amount Due		
30,506.02		To sellers		
		from buyers		18,573.78
$83,000.00	$83,000.00	GRAND TOTALS	$86,971.76	$86,971.76

BUYERS' EXPENSES

The buyers are charged for various expenses incurred to obtain the loan and to purchase the property. The lender charged a discount of 2 points (2 percent of the loan amount), an appraisal fee of $150, a credit report fee of $55, and a flood zone certification fee of $10. The lender also requires the borrowers (buyers) to pay a 14-month hazard insurance premium and three months real estate taxes in advance, and to provide a mortgagee's title policy. Mr. Henry is charging $150 for his services.

Documentary stamp taxes are required on the loan documents in the amounts shown, and the lender requires borrowers to pay these amounts. The calculation of these items is discussed further in the section on preparation of closing statements. It should be noted, however, that such taxes vary from state to state.

The borrowers must also pay to have the mortgage and note prepared and to have both the mortgage and the deed **recorded**. Recording documents in the public records provides *constructive notice* of an interest in real property. It informs anyone who may have a potential interest in the property of both the owner's and the lender's interests.

The sellers' first deduction is for paying off the balance on their existing loan of $45,000. The sellers must also provide an owners' title insurance policy for the new owners (buyers). They purchase a policy from a title company that researches the public records to assure that the Joneses will obtain legal title. The mortgagee's policy purchased by the buyers is issued simultaneously.

The sellers are also responsible for paying the attorney's fee charged by Mr. Jenkins; the brokerage commission of 6 percent of the sale price; and the costs of preparing the deed, having their mortgage satisfaction recorded, and obtaining a termite inspection. These amounts, together with the debit for prorated taxes, are deducted from the sale price of $83,000. The sellers will thus receive a check for $30,506.02. The buyers must write a personal check for $18,573.78, which together with the binder deposit, borrowed funds, and prorated tax credit will cover all the amounts owed.

To assure that the amounts received fully cover amounts owed, a **cash reconciliation** statement (Exhibit 24–6) has been prepared. All of the cash inflows and outflows are listed and tested for balance. The prorated property tax credit is not included since it is not a cash item. After explaining the various items on the closing statement, Mr. Jenkins asks the Joneses to write a check to DownTrust Bank in the amount of $18,573.78 and to sign the note and mortgage. He asks the Johnsons to sign the deed and to hand it to the Joneses. He then hands a check for $30,506.02 to the Johnsons and states that all of the expenses have either been paid or will be paid immediately. He gives a check for $4,980 payable to Bosshardt Realty, Inc., to Ms. Locascio. The closing is now completed, and all parties in the room rise, shake hands, and leave.

CLOSING AND CLOSING STATEMENTS

The Johnson-Jones closing was relatively simple and straightforward. Closings for large commercial properties can be very complex and lengthy. Particularly burdensome are closings for properties subject to many leases having a variety of terms and durations,

---

EXHIBIT 24-6

CASH RECONCILIATION STATEMENT

	Receipts	Disbursements
Binder deposit	$ 1,000.00	
Check from buyer	18,573.78	
Check from lender	66,400.00	
Brokerage fee		$ 4,980.00
Check to seller		30,506.02
Sellers' expenses (less commission and prorated tax)		46,516,00
Buyers' expenses		3,971.76
TOTALS	$85,973.78	$85,973.78

---

properties being purchased by trusts and partnerships, and properties in probate or litigation. Such transactions can take days or even weeks to close.

ROLE OF THE BROKERS

The selling broker's role usually is finished when the contract for sale is signed (if the selling broker is different from the listing broker). Recall from Chapter 23 that the selling broker is the agent who brings the buyers to the property and works with them during the buying process. The selling broker is normally not an agent of the buyer but, rather, a subagent of the listing broker. Once the contract is signed, therefore, the selling broker has no further *legal* responsibility to the buyers or the listing broker. The selling broker should, however, as a good marketing practice, continue to counsel the buyers about how to proceed to closing and help to allay post-purchase feelings of unease or regret.

The listing broker's role at closing can vary widely from state to state and community to community. Because real estate brokers are not permitted to give legal advice, in many parts of the country their role is largely finished when the contract for sale is signed. Nevertheless, like the selling broker, the listing broker should continue to counsel the sellers about steps to take before closing and may take care of details such as arranging for title evidence, surveys, termite inspections, and agreed-upon repairs. It is in the listing broker's best interest to make certain closing actually occurs at the time specified in the contract for sale.

Although attorneys, lending institutions, and title companies normally take over a transaction after the contract for sale is signed, the listing broker continues to have *legal* responsibility to the sellers through the closing. In some transactions not financed by a financial institution, the listing broker might actually conduct the closing. Although someone else may prepare the closing statement, the broker is also responsible to the sellers for its accuracy. Thus, real estate brokers must know what happens at closings, as well as all other aspects of a transaction.

ROLE OF THE LENDER

Lenders must protect their security interest in a property involved in a transaction. They want to be certain the buyer is obtaining marketable title to the property and the tax and insurance payments are continued. These checks assure there are no liens of higher priority than the mortgage and that insurance proceeds will cover the property if it is damaged or destroyed. Lenders normally participate in the closing of a real estate transaction by having an attorney present, often conducting the proceedings. The lender normally requires the buyers to have a fire and hazard insurance policy and a title insurance policy, with the lender as the beneficiary. The lender also usually wants a survey, a termite inspection, a certificate of occupancy (for a new building), and establishment of an escrow account for payment of insurance and taxes.

REAL ESTATE SETTLEMENT PROCEDURES ACT

The Real Estate Settlement Procedures Act (RESPA) is a federal law that requires federally chartered or insured lenders (banks, savings institutions, and credit unions) to provide buyers and sellers of one- to four-family homes, cooperatives, and condominiums with information on all settlement costs. Whenever a buyer obtains a *new* first mortgage loan from one of these lenders, the loan is insured by the FHA or guaranteed by the VA, or the loan will be sold to one of the federally related secondary mortgage market agencies (Fannie Mae or Freddie Mac) the following RESPA requirements must be met:

1. *Special information booklet.* A booklet titled "Settlement Costs and You," written by the U.S. Department of Housing and Urban Development, must be given to every loan applicant. The booklet contains general information about settlement costs and explains the various RESPA provisions. It also includes a line-by-line explanation of the Uniform Settlement Statement (item 3 below).
2. *Good faith estimate of settlement costs.* Within three business days of the loan application, the lender must provide the applicant with a good faith estimate of the settlement costs the borrower is likely to incur. The estimates may be specific figures or a range for each cost, based on recent comparable transactions in the area. Also, if the lender requires the closing to be conducted by a particular attorney or title insurance company, the lender must reveal any business relationship with the attorney or title company and estimate the charges for the service.
3. *Uniform Settlement Statement (HUD Form 1).* Loan closing information must be prepared on a special HUD form, the *Uniform Settlement Statement.* All charges imposed by the lender must be listed; charges incurred by the buyer and seller separately and outside of the closing are not re-

quired to be disclosed. The borrower must be permitted to inspect the statement one business day before the closing to the extent that figures are available. Final figures must be available at time of closing.

4. *Prohibition against kickbacks.* Before 1974 when RESPA was enacted, kickbacks were prevalent in real estate transactions and closings. Borrowers, for example, would be charged for title insurance, but part of the title insurance premium would be rebated to the attorney or lender who recommended or required the title insurance. Thus, buyers were faced with hidden costs and were not free to bargain for services on a competitive basis. RESPA explicitly prohibits all such kickbacks or unearned fees. Note, however, that fee splitting between cooperating real estate brokers, members of multiple listing services, or brokers and their salespersons is not prohibited.

PREPARATION OF CLOSING STATEMENTS

Normally, when a buyer signs an offer to purchase, the broker receives a **binder** (or escrow deposit or earnest money) from the purchaser amounting to 5 or 10 percent of the purchase price. This amount should immediately be placed in an account with a title company or financial institution. Most states have laws requiring brokers to maintain a separate account for earnest-money deposits (an escrow account) and to be able to account for all such monies at any time. Failure to do so may result in a broker's license being suspended or revoked.

The seller must sign the offer to signify acceptance. The accepted offer is then a contract for sale (and purchase). Expenses incurred by the closing agent for the buyer and seller must be strictly accounted for and accurately disclosed in separate statements prepared for the buyer and seller at closing. The broker must also keep a copy of the closing statement and a summary of receipts and disbursements of all monies involved in the transaction.

A closing statement is comprised of three parts:

1. Buyer's statement.
2. Seller's statement.
3. Cash reconciliation statement.

These three statements may be presented in a composite form, as in the Johnson-Jones transaction (Exhibits 24–5 and 24–6). Whether shown in composite form or separately, each statement must be accurate. Buyers, sellers, their attorneys, and their real estate brokers should check the accuracy of the statements and their consistency with the contract for sale.

Listed in Exhibit 24–7 are the typical expenses that are paid in full at time of closing or prorated between buyer and seller. These latter expenses have been paid by the seller for the time during which the buyer will occupy the property or will be paid by the buyer for the time during which the seller occupied the property. All expenses must be accounted for on the closing statement. Each item is shown as either a debit (charge) or

E X H I B I T   2 4 - 7

C L O S I N G   E X P E N S E S   A N D   A L L O C A T I O N S

Item	**Debit**	**Credit**
1. Purchase price	Buyer	Seller
2. Binder deposit	—	Buyer
3. First mortgage balance (when assumed by buyer)	Seller	Buyer
4. Second mortgage (to seller)	Seller	Buyer
Prorations and prepayments:		
5. Rent (when paid in advance)	Seller	Buyer
6. Interest on mortgage (when existing mortgage is assumed by buyer)	Seller	Buyer
7. Prepayment on mortgage (when existing mortgage is assumed by buyer)	Buyer	Seller
8. Insurance (for unexpired term)	Buyer	Seller
9. Property taxes	Seller	Buyer
Expenses:		
10. Title insurance		
a. Owner's policy	Seller	—
b. Mortgagee's policy	Buyer	—
11. Attorney's fee (buyer)	Buyer	—
12. Attorney's fee (seller)	Seller	—
13. State documentary stamp tax on new mortgage and note	Buyer	—
14. State documentary stamp tax on deed	Seller	—
15. State intangible tax on new mortgage and note	Buyer	—
16. Recording of new mortgage	Buyer	—
17. Recording of deed	Buyer	—
18. Brokerage commission	Seller	—

credit to each party. Payment of closing expenses should be governed by the contract for sale; if they are not covered by the contract, local custom should be followed in charging and crediting each expense.

Buyers and sellers can (and often do) negotiate as to which party will pay various closing expenses. In soft markets, buyers can often insist sellers pay all or part of the expenses that would normally be the buyers' responsibility. Substantial amounts can be saved through such negotiations. The logic leading to the allocations in Exhibit 24–7 is as follows:

1. The purchase price is the principal charge to the buyer. It is the ultimate closing cost, for without its payment there would be no closing. The seller is credited for receiving it, and the buyer is debited for owing it.
2. The binder has already been paid by the buyer before the closing. Thus, the buyer is not charged for this amount. It is contained in the purchase price already credited to the seller in 1; however, the seller has not yet received it.
3, 4. An assumed first mortgage and a purchase money second mortgage are long-term obligations taken on by the buyer that reduce the amount of cash the buyer must pay the seller at closing. The buyer is thus cred-

ited for assuming these obligations, and the seller is debited for being relieved of them.

5. When rent is paid to the seller in advance by the lessee (renter), the seller owes the buyer the amount proportionate to the time the buyer will own the property for the rental period. Thus, the seller is debited this amount, and the buyer receives an offsetting credit.

6. Interest on a mortgage is paid at the end of the period. Thus, the buyer will make a payment on an assumed mortgage, part of which represents the seller's ownership period and part of which represents the new owner's period. The seller will therefore be debited the amount representing his or her ownership period, and the buyer will be credited.

7. A prepayment by the seller on an assumed mortgage is for at least a portion of the buyer's ownership period. Thus, the buyer must "pay" the proportionate amount by being debited. The seller will receive a credit for this amount.

8. When a buyer takes over the seller's insurance policy, the seller will already have paid for the entire period. The seller is credited the amount proportionate to the time the buyer will use the insurance, and the buyer is debited this amount.

9. Property taxes are paid in arrears (after the tax year) by the buyer. Thus, the estimated tax bill must be allocated between the time the property is owned by the respective parties. The seller is debited for the amount the buyer will pay on behalf of the seller's ownership period. The buyer receives a credit for this amount.

10. It is logical for the seller to provide assurance of good title to the new owner. Also, mortgagees demand assurance of good title and indemnification in the event title is not good.

11. Buyers should hire an attorney to examine the seller's evidence of title and to represent them at the closing. The seller is not involved.

12. Sellers usually hire an attorney to prepare the deed and represent their interests at closing. Most states levy taxes on deeds, mortgages, notes, and contracts. They are discussed in items 13–15.

13. A state documentary stamp tax on mortgages, notes, and contracts may be required on any new loans used to finance the transaction.

14. A state documentary stamp tax on deeds also may be required. It is considered an expense of delivering title to the buyer and is therefore paid by the seller, unless there is an agreement to the contrary.

15. A state intangible tax on mortgages and notes may be imposed. Since the buyers are obtaining such mortgages to finance the purchase, the tax is usually charged to them.

16, 17. Recording of both the mortgage and the deed is usually the buyer's burden. Recording of the deed is necessary to protect the buyer's interest, whereas the lender requires the borrower (buyer) to pay the mortgage recording charges.

18. Usually the seller has hired the broker and therefore owes the commission.

The procedures for prorating should reflect the actual number of days in the period, the number of days during the period the property was owned by the seller, and the number of days it will be owned by the buyer. The date for dividing the financial responsibilities of buyers and sellers is subject to agreement between the parties. Often the day of closing is counted as a day of seller ownership, although many transactions specify the day of closing as "belonging" to the buyer. If the contract does not cover this matter, local custom will prevail.

For example, if a transaction is scheduled to close on May 14 of a 365-day year, taxes for the year would be allocated between buyers and sellers as shown below (day of closing belongs to buyer):

Jan.1		May 14		Dec. 31
	Sellers		Buyers	
	133 days		232 days	

If the estimated tax for the year is $500, the sellers would be debited $182.19, thus:

$$(133/365) \times \$500 = \$182.19$$

The buyers would be credited with this amount, since they will pay the tax for the present calendar year.

As another example, consider the insurance proration for a transaction scheduled to close on March 16 of a 365-day year. The premium in the amount of $250 was paid by the sellers for the policy commencing December 15 of the previous year and ending December 14 at midnight of the current year. The premium is prorated between buyers and sellers as shown below, with day of closing belonging to buyers:

Dec. 15		March 16		Dec. 14
	Sellers		Buyers	
	91 days		274 days	

Since the sellers have already paid the premium, they are credited with the portion of the policy period the buyers will own the property, thus:

$$(274/365) \times \$250 = \$187.67$$

The buyers would be debited this amount.

SUMMARY

The contract for sale is the most important document in real estate. It contains the rights and obligations to which the principals in a transaction—buyers and sellers—commit themselves. The contract governs all elements of a transaction; a court can enforce its provisions.

Contracts for sale can be simple or complex. They may be typed, handwritten, or prepared on preprinted forms. No matter what the form, however, an agreement is valid and enforceable if it contains the seven elements required of real estate contracts: (1) competent parties, (2) offer and acceptance, (3) consideration, (4) legal objective, (5) no defects to mutual assent, (6) written form, and (7) a proper description of the property.

Since a contract is a legally binding document, buyers and sellers can protect themselves by having a competent attorney examine the contract before signing; after the contract has been signed is too late and any changes would have to be agreed to by both parties.

When one party breaks the provisions of a contract, the other party may have one or more remedies. Either buyer or seller may (1) rescind the contract, (2) sue for specific performance, or (3) sue for damages. Additionally, some contracts may specify actions that can be taken by one party in the event of default by the other party. For example, the seller may be able to retain all or a portion of any deposits if the buyer fails to complete the transaction. Escrow agents often assist in carrying out the provisions of a contract and lessen the chances of default by either party.

Closing is the consummation of a real estate transaction. At closing, title is conveyed and the purchase price is paid. Expenses are paid by each party, and prorations between the parties are made. A document summarizing the financial flows that occur at closing is known as the closing statement. It comprises three statements: the buyer's statement, the seller's statement, and the cash reconciliation statement. Various money flows are debited or credited to the buyer or seller reflecting the charges and credits to each party. Each party incurs expenses in connection with the closing, and these are debited to the appropriate party, with no corresponding credit to the other party.

Prorating is required when an expense has been prepaid by the seller, or will be paid subsequently by the buyer, and covers a time period during which both buyer and seller own the property. The procedure involves crediting the party that pays the expense with the proportionate amount covering the period during which the other party owns the property. Typical items to be prorated are prepaid rent, insurance, real estate taxes, mortgage interest (either prepaid or paid in arrears), and prepaid mortgage principal.

KEY TERMS

Assignment 738
Binder 748
Cash reconciliation 745
Closing 721
Closing costs 735
Closing statement 743
Conditions 721

Consideration 725
Contract for sale 721
Contracts with contingencies 738
Equitable title 727
Escrow 741
Escrow account 735
Escrow agent 741

Estimated closing costs 735
Legal title 727
Proration 743
Recorded 745
Terms 721

TEST YOURSELF

Answer the following multiple choice questions:

1. If a buyer defaults on a contract to purchase real property, which of the following is *not* a remedy the seller can pursue?
   a. Rescind the contract.
   b. Sue for damages.
   c. Sue for assignment.
   d. Return all or part of the binder deposit.
   e. Sue for specific performance.

2. When contracts for the sale of real property are placed with a disinterested third party for executing and closing, they are said to be placed in
   a. Safe keeping.
   b. A title company or financial institution.
   c. Option.
   d. Escrow.
   e. Assignment.

3. Which of the following conditions would be a defect to mutual assent in a contract for the sale of real property?
   a. One party attempts to perpetrate fraud on the other.
   b. The contract is in written form.
   c. The contract contains an inadequate description of the property.
   d. One of the parties is legally incompetent.
   e. The contract does not specify a time for closing.

4. Oral evidence in contract disputes is prohibited by
   a. A parol contract.
   b. An executory contract.
   c. An inferred contract.
   d. An unspecified contract.
   e. The parol evidence rule.

5. Which of the following is one of the *terms* of a real estate contract?
   a. Mechanical equipment must be in good condition.
   b. Title must be marketable.
   c. Price to be paid.
   d. Property must be free of termites.

   e. All of the above items are terms.

6. Real estate transactions do not close when the contract for sale is signed by both parties because
   a. An inspection must be made.
   b. Financing must be arranged.
   c. Title must be checked.
   d. Documents must be prepared.
   e. All of the above.

7. A binder-deposit is a(n)
   a. Preliminary contract.
   b. Provision in a contract for sale.
   c. Payment of money by a buyer to evidence good faith.
   d. Escrow provision.
   e. Conveyance.

8. In most straightforward transactions involving houses or other relatively small properties, the contract is
   a. Prepared by the seller's attorney.
   b. Prepared by the buyer's attorney.
   c. Prepared by the broker.
   d. A form, with blanks filled in by the broker.
   e. A form, with blanks filled in by buyer and seller.

9. Equitable title to real estate is
   a. Legal ownership of property.
   b. Legal title obtained in a court of equity.
   c. Title obtained by adverse possession.
   d. A legal interest in a property conveyed by a listing contract to a broker.
   e. The right to obtain legal title conveyed by the contract for sale.

10. The purpose of a closing statement is to
    a. Determine who pays the brokerage commission.
    b. Allocate expenses and receipts of buyer and seller.
    c. Prorate expenses between buyer and seller.
    d. Account for monies in a transaction.
    e. All but *a* above.

PROBLEMS FOR THOUGHT AND SOLUTION

1. If a closing occurs on September 1 of a 365-day year, how will the year's property tax of $900 be prorated? (Note: the taxes will be due on January 2 of the following year and the day of closing "belongs" to the buyer.)

Use the following information to answer questions 2-5. Rosie Malone sold her house to Bud Wiser. The contract was signed June 1, 1998, and closing was set for June 25, 1998. Rosie had prepaid her three-year hazard insurance policy in the amount of $425.00 on April 1, 1997, and Bud agreed to assume it at closing. Water and sewer are paid the first of each month for the previous month. They are estimated to total

$100 for June. Bud also agrees to assume Rosie's mortgage, which will have a balance of $85,385 on date of closing. Monthly payments are $817.83 payable on the first of the month for the previous month. The seller is responsible for day of closing.

2. How would the hazard insurance premium be prorated?

3. How would the water and sewer charges be prorated?

4. How will the mortgage assumption be entered?

5. How will the monthly mortgage payment be prorated?

CASE PROBLEMS

1. The owner of a parcel of land containing approximately 25 acres contracted a debilitating disease and decided to sell his real estate as quickly as possible. Within a week, he received an offer of $12,250. The owner accepted this offer by signing a standard form contract that had been obtained and prepared by the buyer. Soon after, when the owner's family discovered the situation, they convinced him he had sold the land at much too low a price and he should not complete the transaction.

The owner commissioned an appraisal that showed the land to be worth $16,000, a difference of $150 per acre between the contract price and the property value. He then refused to attend the closing and to deliver title to the buyer. The buyer sued the owner for damages in the amount of the difference between the property value and the contract price ($3,750). The buyer contended he had a valid contract and he was damaged by the owner's unwillingness to complete the transaction. The seller contended he was not of sound mind when he signed the contract and the price was so ridiculously low, the contract should not be enforced.

Identify the issues the court probably would consider in deciding whether or not to enforce the contract.

2. A couple decided to sell their house in Washington, D.C., without the aid of a real estate broker. Their asking price was $225,000, which they believed was about $15,000 less than the price they would need to list the property with a broker. They realized they would probably have to accept an offer as low as $220,000. Another couple looked at the house, liked it, and offered to buy it for $223,500. The sellers were delighted and suggested that they would fill in the blanks on a form sales contract used by many of the local real estate brokerage firms, and both parties could sign it. The buyers, however, objected, saying they preferred to write their own contract. The wife was an attorney who worked for the U.S. State Department, specializing in international law.

What advice would you have given the sellers?

3. Given the following situation and facts, complete a composite closing statement and reconciliation statement in a form similar to that shown in Exhibits 24–5 and 24–6.

On May 15, 1998, Eric Martin signed a contract to purchase a rental house for $95,000. Closing is to occur June 8, 1998, with the day of closing to be counted as a day of ownership by the buyer. Eric can assume the seller's first mortgage, which will have a balance of $49,000 on June 8. The seller, Reuben Smith, has agreed to take a second mortgage of $30,000 as part of the payment at closing. Eric paid a binder deposit of $5,000 when he signed the purchase contract. Other pertinent facts include these:

a. The monthly interest on the first mortgage is $347.08, which must be paid by the 20th of the month.

b. Reuben paid a hazard insurance policy for the calendar year 1998. The premium was $550, and Eric has agreed to purchase Reuben's interest in the policy.

c. The monthly rental of $850 has been collected by Reuben for June.

d. The total amount of property tax for 1998 is estimated to be $1,200. The tax will be paid by Eric at the end of the year.

e. The broker will pay the following expenses for Reuben and will be reimbursed at the closing:

Abstract continuation	$ 85.00
Attorney's fee	200.00
Deed stamps (tax)	522.50
Brokerage commission (6%)	5,700.00

f. The broker will also pay the following expenses for Eric and will be reimbursed at the closing:

Attorney's fee	$150.00
Deed recording fee	6.00
Mortgage recording fee	10.00
Mortgage note stamps (tax)	45.00
Intangible tax on mortgage	60.00

ADDITIONAL READINGS

The following real estate law text contains chapters on real estate contracts and closing:

Werner, Raymond J. *Real Estate Law*, 10th ed. Englewood Cliffs, N.J.: Prentice Hall, 1993.

This quarterly publication contains articles on a wide variety of legal issues in real estate, including contracts and closings:

Real Estate Law Journal, Boston, MA: Warren, Gorham & Lamont.

This monograph presents the fundamentals and many important considerations for attorneys and others (real estate practitioners) who are regularly involved in the writing of real estate contracts:

Holtzschue, Karl B. *Holtzschue on Real Estate Contracts*, 2nd ed. New York: Practicing Law Institute, 1994.

This pamphlet presents a step-by-step analysis of closing procedures and the costs that home buyers must pay:

U.S. Department of Housing and Urban Development. *Settlement Costs: A HUD Guide.*

APPENDIX A

Answers to Test Yourself Questions

CHAPTER 2
1. *d*   6. *c*
2. *b*   7. *e*
3. *a*   8. *e*
4. *b*   9. *b*
5. *a*   10. *d*

CHAPTER 3
1. *a*   6. *b*
2. *a*   7. *b*
3. *c*   8. *b*
4. *a*   9. *d*
5. *b*   10. *a*

CHAPTER 4
1. *b*   7. *b*
2. *a*   8. *a*
3. *e*   9. *c*
4. *a*   10. *b*
5. *c*   11. *a*
6. *b*   12. *c*

CHAPTER 5
1. *b*   6. *c*
2. *c*   7. *d*
3. *b*   8. *c*
4. *c*   9. *c*
5. *c*   10. *c*

CHAPTER 6
1. *a*   6. *c*
2. *c*   7. *b*
3. *d*   8. *b*
4. *b*   9. *b*
5. *a*   10. *d*

CHAPTER 7
1. *a*   5. *d*
2. *b*   6. *e*
3. *b*   7. *b*
4. *a*   8. *a*

CHAPTER 8
1. *b*   6. *e*
2. *a*   7. *b*
3. *c*   8. *c*
4. *a*   9. *a*
5. *d*   10. *c*

CHAPTER 9
1. *c*   3. *b*
2. *d*   4. *b*

CHAPTER 10
1. *c*   6. *a*
2. *e*   7. *a*
3. *e*   8. *d*
4. *c*   9. *e*
5. *b*   10. *e*

CHAPTER 11
1. *d*   6. *d*
2. *e*   7. *b*
3. *a*   8. *d*
4. *b*   9. *c*
5. *a*   10. *e*

CHAPTER 12
1. *c*   6. *d*
2. *d*   7. *c*
3. *b*   8. *e*
4. *c*   9. *d*
5. *c*   10. *d*

CHAPTER 13
1. *b*   6. *d*
2. *d*   7. *b*
3. *a*   8. *c*
4. *d*   9. *d*
5. *b*   10. *a*

CHAPTER 14
1. *d*   6. *c*
2. *b*   7. *a*
3. *a*   8. *c*
4. *e*   9. *c*
5. *d*   10. *d*

CHAPTER 15
1. *e*   6. *e*
2. *d*   7. *a*
3. *e*   8. *b*
4. *b*   9. *b*
5. *e*

CHAPTER 16
1. *b*   7. *a*
2. *b*   8. *d*
3. *e*   9. *e*
4. *d*   10. *b*
5. *a*   11. *a*
6. *d*

CHAPTER 17
1. *d*   6. *b*
2. *c*   7. *b*
3. *b*   8. *b*
4. *a*   9. *d*
5. *c*   10. *b*

CHAPTER 18
1. *d*   7. *d*
2. *c*   8. *e*
3. *c*   9. *d*
4. *c*   10. *c*
5. *e*   11. *c*
6. *b*   12. *b*

CHAPTER 19
1. *d*   6. *c*
2. *c*   7. *b*
3. *a*   8. *c*
4. *b*   9. *e*
5. *a*   10. *a*

CHAPTER 20
1. *c*   6. *b*
2. *a*   7. *d*
3. *e*   8. *c*
4. *b*   9. *d*
5. *e*   10. *b*

CHAPTER 21
1. *e*   6. *d*
2. *c*   7. *e*
3. *a*   8. *c*
4. *e*   9. *b*
5. *d*   10. *a*

CHAPTER 22
1. *b*   6. *b*
2. *c*   7. *e*
3. *e*   8. *c*
4. *a*   9. *d*
5. *d*   10. *a*

CHAPTER 23
1. *e*   6. *c*
2. *b*   7. *b*
3. *e*   8. *d*
4. *c*   9. *d*
5. *c*   10. *c*

CHAPTER 24
1. *c*   6. *e*
2. *d*   7. *a*
3. *a*   8. *d*
4. *e*   9. *e*
5. *c*   10. *e*

APPENDIX B

Real Estate–Related Internet Information Sources (Chapter Listing)

CHAPTER 1: REAL ESTATE PERSPECTIVES
Bureau of the Census: www.census.gov
Bureau of Economic Analysis: www.bea.gov
International Real Estate Directory: www.ired.com
National Association of Realtors: www.realtor.com
STAT-USA: www.stat-usa.gov
Teleres: www.teleres.com
U.S. Department of Commerce: www.doc.gov
U.S. Department of Housing and Urban Development: www.hud.gov

INVESTMENT PERSPECTIVE
CHAPTER 2: BASIC VALUATION CONCEPTS
GNN personal finance: www.gnn.com
Good Neighbor Reinvestment Mortgage Assistance Loan Program: www.gingermae.com
National Center for Financial Education: www.ncfe.org

CHAPTER 3: INVESTMENT DECISION MAKING
Barron's Online: www.barrons.com
Bloomberg: www.bloomberg.com
Business Week Online: www.businesweek.com
CNN Financial Network: www.cnnfn.com
Federal Reserve Board: www.bog.frb.fed.us
Financenet: www.financenet.gov
Financial Times Online: www.ft.com
Kiplinger: kiplinger.com
Money Online: pathfinder.com/money/
Morningstar.net: www.morningstar.net
National Real Estate Investor: www.internetreview.com/pubs/nrei/nrei.htm
Networth: networth.galt.com
New York Stock Exchange: www.nyse.com
Teleres: www.teleres.com
USA Today (Money Section): www.usatoday.com
Wall Street Journal Interactive Edition: wsj.com

CHAPTER 4: INCOME TAXATION
Internal Revenue Service: www.irs.ustreas.gov
U.S. Tax Code On-Line: www.fourmilab.ch

CHAPTER 5: FORMS OF OWNERSHIP
National Association of Real Estate Investment Trusts: www.nareit.com
National Council of Real Estate Investment Fiduciaries: www.ncreif.com
Pension Real Estate Association: www.prea.org

CHAPTER 6: PROPERTY TYPES
American Industrial Real Estate Association: www.csz.com
International Council of Shopping Centers: www.icsc.org
International Hotel Association: www.ih-ra.com
Internet Review Online: www.internetreview.com

National Association of Industrial and Office Parks: www.naiop.org
Property Digest and Economic Development: www.barryinc.com
Realtors Land Institute: www.rliland.com
Shopping Center World Online: www.internetreview.com/pubs/scw/scw.htm
Society of Industrial and Office Realtors: www.sior.com

CHAPTER 7: RISK AND REAL ESTATE INVESTMENT
International Real Estate Clearinghouse: www.irec.org
Internet Review Online: www.internetreview.com
National Association of Real Estate Investment Trusts: www.nareit.com
National Council of Real Estate Investment Fiduciaries: www.ncreif.com
National Real Estate Investor: www.internetreview.com/pubs/nrei/nrei.htm
Pension Real Estate Association:

www.prea.org
Teleres: www.teleres.com

CHAPTER 8: MANAGEMENT OF THE SPACE ASSETS
Building Owners and Managers Association International: www.boma.org
FacilitiesNet: www.facilitiesnet.com
Institute of Real Estate Management: www.irem.org
International Development Research Council: www.irdc.org
International Facility Management Association: www.ifma.org
National Association of Corporate Real Estate Executives: www.nacore.org
National Association of Residential Property Managers: www.naprm.org

MARKET PERSPECTIVE
CHAPTER 9: REAL ESTATE MARKETS
American Real Estate Exchange Network: www.amrex.com

Association of American Geographers: www.aag.org

Bureau of the Census: www.census.gov

National Association of Homebuilders: www.nahb.com

National Real Estate Investor: www. internetreview.com/ pubs/nrei/nrei.htm

PikeNet: www.pike.net

Teleres: www.teleres.com

U.S. Department of Housing and Urban Development: www.hud.gov

CHAPTER 10: LAND USE, PLANNING, ZONING, AND ENVIRONMENTAL HAZARDS

American Institute of Urban and Regional Affairs: www. intr.net/susdev/

American Planning Association: www.planning.org

Lincoln Institute on Land Policy: www.igc.apc.org/ lincoln/

National Association of Regional Planning Councils: narc.org/narc/

The Brookings Institution: www.brook.edu

The Urban Institute: www.urban.org

U.S. Environmental Protection Agency: www.epa.gov

CHAPTER 11: MARKET AND FEASIBILITY ANALYSIS

American Demographics: www. demographics.com

American Real Estate Exchange Network: www.amrex.com

Bureau of Economic Analysis: www.bea.gov

Bureau of Labor Statistics: stats.bls.gov

Bureau of the Census: www.census.gov

Dow Jones and Company: www.dowjones.com

Economic History Services: cs.muohio.edu

Land Value Analysis: www.hollybar.com

National Real Estate Investor: www. internetreview.com/ pubs/nrei/nrei.htm

PikeNet: www.pike.net

STAT-USA: www.stat-usa.gov

The Urban Land Institute: www.uli.org

USA CityLink: www.usacitylink.com

CHAPTER 12: INTRODUCTION TO DEVELOPMENT

American Institute of Architects: www.aia.org

Builder Online: www.builderonline.com

FW Dodge Construction Information Group: www.fwdodge.com

National Association of Home Builders: www.nahb.org

National Real Estate Investor: www. internetreview.com/ pubs/nrei/nrei.htm

PikeNet: www.pike.net

The Urban Land Institute: www.uli.org

CHAPTER 13: VALUATION BY THE SALES COMPARISON AND COST APPROACHES

American Society of Appraisers: www.apo.com

Appraisal Institute: www. appraisalinstitute.org

Marshall and Swift: www. marshallswift.com

National Association of Independent Fee Appraisers: www.naifa.com

RS Means Company: www.rsmeans.com

The Online Appraiser: www.ola.net

CHAPTER 14: VALUATION BY INCOME CAPITALIZATION

American Society of Appraisers: www.apo.com

Appraisal Institute: www. appraisalinstitute.org

Argus Financial Software: www. argussoftware.com

National Association of Independent Fee Appraisers: www.naifa.com

The Online Appraiser: www.ola.net

MORTGAGE FINANCE PERSPECTIVE
CHAPTER 15: CREATION OF MORTGAGES

AllRegs: Home Lending Regulations: www.allregs.com

International Real Estate Directory: www.ired.com

Mortgage Mag: www. mortgagemag.com

CHAPTER 16: RESIDENTIAL MORTGAGE TYPES AND BORROWER DECISIONS

AllRegs: Home Lending Regulations: www.allregs.com

Bank Rate Monitor: www.bankrate.com

Federal Home Loan Mortgage Corporation: www.freddiemac.com

Federal Housing Administration: www.hud.gov/fha/ fhahome.html

Federal National Mortgage Association: www.fanniemae.com

Good Neighbor Reinvestment Mortgage Assistance Loan Program: www.gingermae.com

Government National Mortgage Association: www.ginniemae.com

Homebuyer's Fair: www.homebuyers.com

Mortgage Bankers Association: www.mbaa.org

Mortgage-Net: www.mortgage-net.com

CHAPTER 17: SOURCES OF FUNDS FOR RESIDENTIAL MORTGAGES

Federal Home Loan Mortgage Corporation: www.freddiemac.com

Federal Housing Administration: www.hud.gov/fha/ fhahome.html

Federal National Mortgage Association: www.fanniemae.com

Government National Mortgage Association: www.ginniemae.com

Mortgage Bankers Association: www.mbaa.org

U.S. Department of Housing and Urban Development: www.hud.gov

Veterans' Administration: www.va.gov/vas/ lgyinfo.htm

CHAPTER 18: COMMERCIAL PROPERTY FINANCING

American Real Estate Exchange Network: www.amrex.com

Bank Rate Monitor: www.bankrate.com

DataMerge, Inc.: www.datamerge.com

Mortgage Bankers Association: www.mbaa.org

Teleres: www.teleres.com

CHAPTER 19: MORTGAGE-BACKED SECURITIES

Federal Home Loan Mortgage Corporation: www.freddiemac.com
Federal National Mortgage Association: www.fanniemae.com
Government National Mortgage Association: www.ginniemae.com

LEGAL PERSPECTIVE CHAPTER 20: REAL PROPERTY RIGHTS

American Bar Association: www.abanet.org
House of Representatives Internet Law Library: law.house.gov
Law Journal Extra:

www.ljx.com
Legal Information Institute: www.law.cornell.edu
Tenant Net: tenant.net
The Law Office: www.thelawoffice.com
The WWW Virtual Library: www.law.indiana.edu
Thomas Legislative Information: thomas.loc.gov
U.S. Environmental Protection Agency: www.epa.gov

CHAPTER 21: REAL PROPERTY TAXATION

Institute of Property Taxation: www.ipt.org
International Association of Assessing Officers: www.iaao.org

CHAPTER 22: TRANSFER OF REAL PROPERTY RIGHTS

American Bar Association: www.abanet.org
Homebuyer's Fair: www.homefair.com
House of Representatives Internet Law Library: law.house.gov
Law Journal Extra: www.ljx.com
Legal Information Institute: www.law.cornell.edu

CHAPTER 23: REAL ESTATE BROKERAGE AND LISTING CONTRACTS

American Bar Association: www.abanet.org

Commercial Investment Real Estate Institute: www.ccim.com
Counselors of Real Estate: www.cre.org
Law Journal Extra: www.ljx.com
Legal Information Institute: www.law.cornell.edu
National Association of Realtors: www.realtor.com
PikeNet: www.pike.net
Realty Mall: www.realtymall.com
RealtyTrac Information Systems: www.realtytrac.com
Residential Sales Council: www.rscouncil.com

CHAPTER 24: CONTRACTS FOR SALE AND CLOSING

AllRegs: Home Lending Regulations: www.allregs.com
American Bar Association: www.abanet.org
American Land Title Association: www.alta.org
Federal Housing Administration: www.hud.gov/fha/fhahome.html
House of Representatives Internet Law Library: law.house.gov
Law Journal Extra: www.ljx.com
Legal Information Institute: www.law.cornell.edu

Real Estate–Related Information Sources on the Internet (Topic Listing)

FEDERAL GOVERNMENT SOURCES
Bureau of Economic Analysis: www.bea.gov
Bureau of Labor Statistics: stats.bls.gov
Bureau of the Census: www.census.gov
Federal Housing Administration: www.hud.gov/fha/fhahome.html
Internal Revenue Service: www.irs.ustreas.gov
STAT-USA: www.stat-usa.gov
U.S. Department of Commerce: www.doc.gov
U.S. Department of Housing and Urban Development: www.hud.gov
U.S. Environmental Protection Agency: www.epa.gov
Veterans' Administration: www.va.gov

GENERAL INVESTMENT INFORMATION
Dow Jones and Company: www.dowjones.com
Economic History Services: cs.muohio.edu
GNN personal finance: www.gnn.com
Morningstar.net: www.morningstar.net
National Center for

Financial Education: www.ncfe.org
Networth: networth.galt.com
New York Stock Exchange: www.nyse.com

NEWS AND INFORMATION SERVICES
Barron's Online: www.barrons.com
Bloomberg: www.bloomberg.com
Business Week Online: www.businessweek.com
CNN Financial Network: www.cnnfn.com
Financial Times Online: www.ft.com
Kiplinger: kiplinger.com
Money Online: pathfinder.com/money/
National Real Estate Investor: www.internetreview.com/pubs/nrei/nrei.htm
USA Today (Money Section): www.usatoday.com
Wall Street Journal Interactive Edition: wsj.com

PLANNING, POLICY, AND DEVELOPMENT SOURCES
American Institute of Urban and Regional Affairs: www.intr.net/susdev/

Lincoln Institute on Land Policy: www.igc.apc.org/lincoln/
Property Digest and Economic Development: www.barryinc.com
The Brookings Institution: www.brook.edu
The Urban Institute: www.urban.org

PROFESSIONAL ASSOCIATIONS
American Industrial Real Estate Association: www.csz.com
American Institute of Architects: www.aia.org
American Land Title Association: www.alta.org
American Planning Association: www.planning.org
American Society of Appraisers: www.apo.com
Appraisal Institute: www.appraisalinstitute.org
Association of American Geographers: www.aag.org
Building Owners and Managers Association International: www.boma.org
Commercial Investment Real Estate Institute: www.ccim.com

Counselors of Real Estate: www.cre.org
Institute of Property Taxation: www.ipt.org
Institute of Real Estate Management: www.irem.org
International Association of Assessing Officers: www.iaao.org
International Council of Shopping Centers: www.icsc.org
International Development Research Council: www.irdc.org
International Facility Management Association: www.ifma.org
International Hotel Association: www.ih-ra.com
National Association of Corporate Real Estate Executives: www.nacore.org
National Association of Home Builders: www.nahb.com
National Association of Independent Fee Appraisers: www.naifa.com
National Association of Industrial and Office Parks: www.naiop.org
National Association of Real Estate Investment Trusts: www.nareit.com
National Association of Realtors: www.realtor.com

National Association of Regional Planning Councils: narc.org/narc/
National Association of Residential Property Managers: www.naprm.org
National Council of Real Estate Investment Fiduciaries: www.ncreif.com
Pension Real Estate Association: www.prea.org
Realtors Land Institute: www.rliland.com
Residential Sales Council: www.rscouncil.com
Society of Industrial and Office Realtors: www.sior.com
The Urban Land Institute: www.uli.org

MORTGAGE MARKET AND INTEREST RATE INFORMATION
Interest Rate Information
Federal Reserve Board: www.bog.frb.fed.us

Primary Mortgage Market Information
Bank Rate Monitor: www.bankrate.com
DataMerge, Inc.: www.datamerge.com
Financenet: www.financenet.gov

Good Neighbor Reinvestment Mortgage Assistance Loan Program: www.gingermae.com

Homebuyer's Fair: www.homebuyers.com

Mortgage Mag: www.mortgagemag.com

Mortgage-Net: www.mortgage-net.com

Secondary Mortgage Market Information

Federal Home Loan Mortgage Corporation: www.freddiemac.com

Federal National Mortgage Association: www.fanniemae.com

Government National Mortgage Association: www.ginniemae.com

REAL ESTATE SERVICES CONSTRUCTION INFORMATION

Builder Online: www.builderonline.com

FW Dodge Construction Information Group: www.fwdodge.com

Marshall and Swift: www.marshallswift.com

RS Means Company: www.rsmeans.com

LEGAL INFORMATION

AllRegs: Home Lending Regulations: www.allregs.com

American Bar Association: www.abanet.org

House of Representatives Internet Law Library: law.house.gov

Law Journal Extra: www.ljx.com

Legal Information Institute: www.law.cornell.edu

Tenant Net: tenant.net

The Law Office: www.thelawoffice.com

The WWW Virtual Library: www.law.indiana.edu

Thomas Legislative Information: thomas.loc.gov

MARKET INFORMATION

American Demographics: www.demographics.com

USA CityLink: www.usacitylink.com

OTHER REAL ESTATE SERVICE INFORMATION

American Real Estate Exchange Network: www.amrex.com

Argus Financial Software: www.argussoftware.com

FacilitiesNet: www.facilitiesnet.com

International Real Estate Clearinghouse: www.irec.org

International Real Estate Directory: www.ired.com

Internet Review Online: www.internetreview.com

Land Value Analysis: www.hollybar.com

PikeNet: www.pike.net

Realty Mall: www.realtymall.com

RealtyTrac Information Systems: www.realtytrac.com

Shopping Center World Online: www.internetreview.com/pubs/scw/scw.htm

Teleres: www.teleres.com

The Online Appraiser: www.ola.net

TAX INFORMATION

U.S. Tax Code On-Line www.fourmilab.ch

GLOSSARY

Absorption rate   the number of units that are (or are expected to be) sold or leased over a given time period, such as one month or one year

Abstract of title   historical summary of legal documents affecting real property

Acceleration clause   makes all future payments due upon a single default of a loan

Accretion   growth in size by addition or accumulation of soil to land by gradual, natural deposits

Accrual class   a class or tranche in most CMO structures that does not receive principal or interest payments from the underlying mortgages until all other classes are retired

Active income   income earned from salaries wages, commissions, fees, and bonuses

Adjustable rate mortgage   alternative mortgage form where the interest rate is tied to an indexed rate over the life of the loan, allowing interest rate risk to be shared by borrowers and lenders

Adjustment rate caps   limits on the amount the contract interest rate can increase or decrease at each payment adjustment date

Adjustments   additions or subtractions from a price or cost in order to cause a comparable property to reflect the value represented by the characteristics of a subject property

Ad valorem   according to value. Property taxes are based on the value of the property

Affordable housing allocation   a reasonable and fair component of affordable housing required by state law to be included in the comprehensive plans of local governments

After-tax cash flow   the residual claim on the property's cash flow after the federal government has collected its share

Agency   law governing the relationship between employers (principals) and the professionals they employ (agents)

Agency passthroughs   passthrough securities on which the timely payment of principal and interest is guaranteed by Fannie Mae, Freddie Mac, or Ginnie Mae

Amortization   a partial repayment of principal

Annual debt service   the yearly sum of the payment of interest and repayment of principal on a loan

Annual percentage rate   an approximation of the loan's effective borrowing cost

Appraisal Foundation   the organization that supervises the regulation of the appraisal profession

Arbitrage   buying an asset at one price and simultaneously selling at a higher price without taking on additional risk

Arm's-length bargaining   negotiations between two parties that have no relationship with each other and who are negotiating in behalf of their own best interests

Assessed value   the value determined as the basis on which a property owner's tax is calculated, usually a percentage of market value

Asset manager   the representative of property owners responsible for overseeing property managers and advising owners on important decisions involving properties

Assignment   transfer of lessees' right to another tenant. The lessee and the new tenant may be co-liable if rent payments are not made

Assumption subject to the mortgage   when buyers take over payments of mortgages of sellers but do not become personally liable for the debt, or become co-liable with the seller

Balloon mortgage   a mortgage loan with an amortization schedule length longer than the maturity

Balloon payment   the large payment required at maturity to retire partially amortizing and interest-only loans

Bargain-and-sale deed   deed that conveys the land itself rather than ownership interests through warranties

Base rent   amount paid by tenants in percentage leases regardless of the level of tenant business sales

Basic employment   the workers or employees of a city or community, or the number of such workers or employees, that are involved in the production of goods or services that will be sold outside of the city or community

Bilateral contract   contract that involves the exchange of one promise for another promise

Binder   (1) a deposit or escrow money or earnest money; (2) an agreement between a potential buyer and seller that commits both parties to sign a contract for sale and purchase after certain details are decided

Break-even ratio   a measure of the ability of an income property to cover its obligations, defined as operating expenses plus debt service, divided by effective gross income

Breaks in transportation   locations where it is necessary to change transportation modes to continue to move factors of production or goods through space

Broker license   authority granted by a state for one to own and operate a real estate brokerage business; the most complete type of real estate license

Builder   a company or individual involved in construction of improvements on land

Bundle of rights   the collection of physical and legal rights that come with real estate ownership

Buydowns   payments made by home builders to lenders, prevalent during periods of high interest rates, to entice them to offer lower-rate mortgages to purchasers of homes in the new development

***C* corporation**   corporate ownership structure that provides limited liability, but suffers from double taxation and does not enable losses to flow through to investors for current use

Cadastres   generic term that refers to various types of land registration systems around the world

Capital asset   an asset held for investment purposes

Capitalization rate   calculated as expected net operating income in year 1 divided by the property's value or initial acquisition price, it is a measure of the current relationship between a property's income stream and price

Capture rate   the percentage of total new units in a community that a given development can sell or lease; the portion of the market that a particular development can "capture"

Cash flow before debt service and income taxes   net operating income minus leasing and capital costs

Cash reconciliation   statement showing all closing cash inflows and outflows as a test of balance of the closing agent's cash receipts and disbursements

Certificate of occupancy   issued by the local building inspector to allow the public to safely occupy completed properties

Certified appraiser   a person approved by a state to appraise properties. There are two types of certification: residential and general. A certified general appraiser may appraise all types of properties whereas a certified residential appraiser may appraise one- to four-family residential properties

Closed-end REITs   real estate investment trusts that do not offer shares of stock to the public after the initial stock is sold and the assets are purchased

Closing   event at which title to real estate is transferred from one party to another

Closing costs   sometimes called settlement costs, costs in addition to the price of a property, usually including mortgage origination fee, title insurance, attorney's fee, and prepayable items such as taxes and insurance payments collected in advance and held in an escrow account

Closing statement   a document showing the financial accounting of the receipts and disbursements in a real estate transaction

Coefficient   the calculated relationship between an independent variable and a dependent variable in a regression equation. The coefficient also takes into account the influence of other independent variables and represents the marginal contribution of its variable to the predicted value

Coefficient of variation   a measure of risk per unit of return, defined as the standard deviation of the return divided by the expected return

Collaterialized mortgage obligations (CMOs)   a popular name for MBSs that do not distribute cash flows from the underlying mortgages on a proportional basis, for example, sequential pay structures

Commercial banks   depository institutions primarily engaged in the business of making short-term loans to businesses for inventory financing and other working capital needs

Commingled real estate funds   a collection of resources from various pension funds that are pooled to purchase properties

Commission   payment a broker receives for services rendered, usually expressed as a percentage of the property sale price

Community center   a larger version of a neighborhood shopping center, often anchored by a discount department store, and containing outlets such as clothing stores, banks, furniture stores, video rental store, and professional services

Community property   some states recognize equal ownership by married persons in all property acquired during the marriage

Community Reinvestment Act of 1977   a congressional act that encourages mortgage originators to actively lend in their communities and that requires financial institutions to evaluate their lending practices

Comprehensive plan   a local government's general guide to a community's growth and development based on the community's goals and objectives

Concentric marketing   promotional activities to tenants in neighboring buildings because these tenants have the same location needs as tenants in the subject building

Conditions   the circumstances that must prevail for a closing to occur, such as mechanical equipment being in good condition and title being unencumbered

Condominium   an ownership form that combines a fee simple estate for ownership of individual units and tenancy in common for ownership of common areas

Condominium complexes   residential units with adjoining walls but with separate entrances and patios for each unit and ample parking

Conduit lending   arrangements between mortgage companies and investment banking firms in which mortgage companies originate loans that investment banks later securitize

Conduits   agencies and private companies that pool mortgages and sell mortgage-backed securities

Conforming conventional loan   a conventional loan that meets the standards required for purchase in the secondary market by Fannie Mae or Freddie Mac

Consideration   anything of value given to induce another party to enter into a contract

Constant   the a term in a regression equation. The constant is the base value that represents all positive and negative factors not explained by the equation, and to which the coefficients, or adjustment factors, are added

Constant prepayment rate   this method for estimating mortgage prepayments assumes unscheduled principal payments will occur at a constant rate over time

Construction loans   loans used to finance the costs associated with erecting the building or buildings

Construction manager   hired by developers to oversee day-to-day construction activities

Contingent interest   additional payments, in excess of principal and interest, that the lender receives as a result of lending to the borrower

Contract for sale   legal document between a buyer and seller that states the purchase price and the manner in which ownership rights are to be transferred

Contract for sale with contingencies   a contract for sale of property that makes the sale conditional on specific events, such as developers obtaining financing

Contract rent   the rent specified in the lease contract

Contract with contingencies   agreement for sale that makes the sale conditional on the buyer's obtaining something such as financing or a favorable engineering report

Conventional mortgages   mortgage loans that do not enjoy government backing in the form of FHA insurance or a Veterans Administration (VA) guarantee

Convertible mortgage   debt obligation that gives the lender an option to convert the mortgage debt to equity after a specified number of years

Cooperative   an ownership form based on a corporation structure

Correlated   returns that move together when market conditions change

Correlation coefficient   a relative measure of the tendency of an asset's return to vary with that of another asset over time

Correspondent relationship   a business relationship in which a large lender agrees to purchase loans or to consider loan requests from a mortgage banker

Cost approach   one of the three principal methods of appraisal in which accrued depreciation is subtracted from a property's reproduction cost, and the land value (estimated separately) is added to the result

Cost recovery period   the period of time over which an asset is depreciated for tax purposes

Covariance   an absolute measure of the tendency of an asset's return to vary with that of another asset over time

Covered construction loan   a forward commitment has been obtained to repay the construction loan

Credit enhancement   steps that are taken to reduce the probability that investors in a security will suffer losses of capital (principal), including supplying letters of credit and cross-collateratizations, that provide additional security for mortgage loans over and above the pledge of the property

Credit unions   depository institutions that are restricted by their charters to serving a group of people who can show a common bond such as employees of a corporation, government unit, labor union, or trade association

Dealer property   real estate held for sale to others

Debt service   loan payments made to satisfy outstanding debt (mortgage) obligations

Debt service coverage ratio   a measure of the extent to which NOI can decline before it is insufficient to service the debt, defined as net operating income over debt service

Deeds-in-lieu of foreclosure   a legal instrument issued by defaulting borrowers that transfers all rights they have in properties

Deeds-of-trust   legal documents used in certain states that grant a trustee the power of sale to initiate foreclosure actions

Deep tax shelter   negative taxable income from operations

Default   the consequence of prolonged delinquency

Deferral benefits   the gain from delaying the payment of taxes until the property is sold

Deficiency judgment   the legal right of lenders to file suit against borrowers when the proceeds from foreclosure sales do not pay off loans

Delinquency   when mortgage payments are overdue

Dependent variable   the variable being "explained" in a regression equation

Depreciable basis   generally, the value of the acquired property less the value of the land

Depreciation   in appraisal, the loss of value for any reason

Derived demand   recognition that market forces of demand result from more basic physical and psychological needs of people. For example, the demand for housing is derived from people's needs for shelter and for ego-gratifying prestige characteristics of the housing. Similarly, the demand for automobiles results from the basic need of people to transfer themselves from place to place

Developer   a company or individual involved in activities necessary to take undeveloped or previously developed land to a state of operations for residential or commercial purposes

Development team   a collection of professionals such as contractors, lawyers, architects, and engineers associated with developers for the purpose of completing development projects

Direct capitalization   the process of dividing a property's net operating income by an overall capitalization rate

Discount   the amount by which the market value of a security is less than par value

Discount rate   the yield, or expected yield, on a property or investment

Discounted cash flow analysis   the process and procedures for estimating net operating incomes and net selling prices, and the discount rate, and then using these inputs to generate meaningful summary information for investors

Diversifiable   unsystematic risk that can be eliminated from a portfolio by holding securities and other investments with less than perfectly correlated returns

Diversification   allocating portfolio resources among alternative investments to reduce risk

Due-on-sale clause   the sentence or words in a mortgage document that require the borrower to pay off the loan if the property serving as security for the loan is sold

***E*arly payment mortgages**   loans where the borrower makes additional payments to reduce principal more quickly than scheduled

Earned income   labor income

Easement   right that the owners of another property may have to use one's land

Easement appurtenant   a right of use that continues from owner to owner until it becomes legally removed

Easement by implication   a right of use that continues because of its obvious nature although it is not found in the public record

Easement by necessity   a right of use granted by courts to assist owners of landlocked parcels

Easement by prescription   a right of use obtained by continuous trespass

Easement in gross   a right of use negotiated between a property owner and a commercial firm that may end with the sale of the property

Economic and environmental impact statements studies of the effect that a new development will have on the economy or the environment of the region

Economic base analysis   the method of analyzing a local economy and forecasting population based on the number of employees in industries and businesses that export goods, products, and services beyond the community's boundaries

Economic feasibility   a condition that occurs when the market value of a completed and stabilized development project exceeds the cost of bringing the property to a completed and stabilized state

Effective cost   the true borrowing cost, including the effect of up-front financing costs

Effective gross income   the total annual income the property produces after vacancy losses and miscellaneous income

Effective tax rate   tax liability divided by the property's market value or sale price

Effective yield   the yield actually earned by the investor

Efficient markets   markets in which all available information is incorporated into prices so quickly that money cannot be made by having that information

Eminent domain   the power of government in the United States to take private property for a public purpose by paying the owner just compensation

Encroachments   unauthorized intrusion of a building or other improvement onto property owned by another

Equitable title   right of someone to obtain full, legal title to real estate, provided the terms and conditions of the document creating equitable title (usually a contract for sale) are fulfilled

Equity   money invested by the property owner

Equity dividend rate   the capitalization rate for equity. It is derived by dividing the before-tax cash flow by the value of the equity

Equity joint venture   a relationship between developers and others who supply all or most of the cash to develop properties that will be used in their business or enter their portfolios

Equity kickers   enticements offered to lenders that call for splitting the proceeds from the sale of the property between borrower and lender

Equity of redemption   a period of time allowed by courts in every state that grants delinquent borrowers the opportunity to make overdue payments before foreclosure begins

Equity REITs   real estate investment trusts that invest in and operate income producing properties

Equity theory of default   theory that borrowers will default when the outstanding loan amount on their mortgages exceeds the value of the property regardless of what happens to their ability to make payments on the mortgage

Errors and omission insurance   type of insurance that indemnifies professionals if they make an error in their profession or if they omit something important from their analyses

Escrow   the status of real estate transactions that are closed through the help and intercession of a third party, called an escrow agent. The deed is delivered to the escrow agent for delivery to the buyer on performance of a condition (payment of the purchase price)

Escrow account   a segregated account held by brokers for the deposit of earnest money (deposit) funds

Escrow agent   person or company that performs the closing function for a fee; escrow agents collect all needed documents and funds for disbursement at the closing

Escrowing   a provision inserted in mortgages by lenders requiring that borrowers pay into separate accounts amounts that will accumulate to pay annual insurance premiums and property taxes

Estate for years   a leasehold estate with a set term

Exclusive agency listing   agreement between a seller of property and a broker in which the seller agrees to pay a commission to the broker if the seller's property is sold by anyone other than the owner, during the period of the agreement

Exclusive right of sale listing   agreement between a seller of property and a broker in which the broker is assured of receiving a commission if the property is sold by the broker or anyone else, including the owner, during the period of the agreement

Executor's deeds   documents that transfer property from a public official to an auction purchaser without warranties from the public

Expected value   the weighted average of a series of potential outcomes and their associated probabilities

Expense stop   a clause in leases that requires landlords to pay property expenses up to a specified amount and tenants to pay the expenses beyond that amount

Expressed contract   oral or written contract that explicitly states the intentions, terms, and conditions of the parties

External obsolescence   losses of property value caused by forces or conditions beyond the borders of the property. The losses are deducted from a building's reproduction cost in the cost approach

Extraterritorial jurisdiction   control by a community of an area larger than the community or jurisdiction for planning and zoning purposes, granted by the state legislature

*F*actor substitution   exchanging an expensive factor of production for a cheaper factor of production

Feasibility study   a study of the constraints on and the potential profitability of a proposed project. Included in the profitability analysis is consideration of the financing arrangements that will be required

Federal Home Loan Mortgage Corporation   government-sponsored enterprise commonly known as "Freddie Mac"; one of the largest purchasers of residential mortgages in the secondary market

Federal National Mortgage Association   government-sponsored enterprise commonly known as "Fannie Mae"; one of the largest purchasers of residential mortgages in the secondary market

Fee developer   a developer that has little or no equity investment, but instead, is hired to perform development services

Fee simple absolute   an estate in land that provides the owner with a complete set of legal rights

FHA mortgage insurance   government-sponsored mortgage insurance that protects lenders from any loss after foreclosure and conveyance of title to the property to the U.S. Department of Housing and Urban Development (HUD)

Fiduciary relationship   the special duties and obligations to a principal required of an agent, including complete loyalty, confidentiality, obedience, disclosure, accounting, care, skill, and due diligence

15-year mortgage   increasingly popular, short-term fixed-rate mortgage alternative that allows borrowers to pay substantially less interest over the life of the loan when compared to a 30-year loan

Final adjusted sale price   the price paid for a comparable property in the sales comparison approach adjusted for all conditions and characteristics to reflect the subject property and the current date

Financial assets   claims to the incomes generated from the use of real assets

Financial intermediaries   institutions that collect money in the form of deposits, insurance premiums, and pension contributions and then invests or loans the money

Financial intermediation   the process whereby a financial institution, such as a commercial bank, collects small deposits from investors in order to originate larger mortgage loans

Financial leverage   the use of borrowed money to fund investment projects

Financial risk   the risk NOI will be less than debt service

Finite-life REITs   real estate investment trusts that are established to purchase and operate properties for a prespecified number of years

First mortgage   the mortgage contract that gives the lender the highest priority among lenders for repayment from the sale of the property upon default

First-loss position   investors in the CMBS class that begins to suffer reductions in the initial investments with the first losses due to a mortgage default

Fixed-payment mortgages   fully amortizing loans that call for equal periodic payments

Fixtures   personal property that becomes real property by virtue of permanent attachment

Floating rate class   this class pays investors a coupon rate that is tied to a short-term benchmark index of interest rates

Floating-rate mortgage   a debt instrument whose interest rate changes over the life of the loan based on a market index such as the prime rate or LIBOR

Floor-to-ceiling commitment   financing arrangement where if occupancy falls short of the specified rate when the building is completed, the permanent lender will not disburse the full amount of the loan proceeds (the ceiling), but instead will advance a lower loan amount (the floor)

Foreclosure   a process to force the public sale of property to satisfy the financial obligations of a delinquent borrower to a lender. The sale forecloses the borrower's equity of redemption

Forward commitment   a legal document binding on the long-term mortgage lender to provide a loan upon the completion of construction and fulfillment of other conditions

Freehold estates   interests in real estate for which the duration is not set

F statistic   provides the measure of the predictive ability of the regression model. It should equal at least 3.0.

Functional obsolescence   losses in value of a building relative to its reproduction cost that reflect the fact that the building is not consistent with modern standards or with tastes of the market

Fundamentals   the demand and supply characteristics that determine prices and rents assuming rational economic behavior by all market participants

Gap loan   a short-term loan that is often employed as a buffer or intermediate financing device between construction loans and long-term permanent financing

Garden apartments   low-density residential developments common in suburban and nonurban areas

General agent   a professional who is empowered to represent a principal, often a business firm, in its business relationships. A general agent can contract and bind the principal within the confines of the business or employment relationship

General contractor   usually a construction company that has responsibility for seeing that all aspects of construction are completed on time and within budget

General market studies   studies that analyze the general real estate needs in a community or jurisdiction, for example, studies that forecast the number of new housing units that will be needed in a community over the next two years and in what price ranges, and studies that forecast the number and types of industrial, retail, and office units that will be needed over a specified time period

General partnership   an ownership form characterized by multiple owners, unlimited liability for each equity holder, and flow-through taxation of both income and losses

General warranty deed   highest form of deed in that grantees become liable for any title defects created during their period and all previous periods of ownership

Geographic information systems   computerized methods for analyzing data about communities using various maps and combinations or layers of maps

Government National Mortgage Association   a federal government agency that promotes affordable housing by buying subsidized mortgages in the secondary market. This agency also insures mortgage-backed securities issued by other lenders

Government Rectangular Survey System   land ordinance of 1785 that created a rectangular grid system for legal description of land acquired by the United States following the American Revolution

Government-sponsored enterprises   a term that refers to the Federal National Mortgage Association and the Federal Home Loan Mortgage Corporation, which are entities created by acts of Congress to promote an active secondary market for home mortgages

Graduated payment mortgage   a mortgage loan, designed to reduce affordability problems, where the monthly payment is low during the initial years and gradually increases over time

Gross income multiplier   the number of times that sale prices exceed the annual gross incomes of nonresidential, income-producing properties

Gross lease   lease in which the landlord pays all operating expenses of the property

Gross rent multiplier   the number of times that the gross rents of residential properties are reflected in sale prices. That is, sale price / monthly gross rent

Ground (land) lease   lease on vacant land or the land under improvements

Growth limits   an area beyond which urban growth densities will not be permitted by zoning or infrastructure

Growth moratorium   a temporary prohibition of further development in a community or jurisdiction

Growth rate   the annual percentage at which the net operating income and value of a property are expected to increase in current terms, that is, including expected inflation, in the forecast growth rate

Hard costs   amounts committed in development projects to materials, labor, and other tangible or nonservice inputs

High-rise apartment buildings   residential facilities, popular in major cities, with at least 10 to 15 stories

Highest and best use of a property as improved   the type of occupancy that will yield the greatest return, and thus the highest value, for an existing property with a building or other improvement

Highest and best use of a vacant site   the type of improvement that will result in the highest value of a vacant site, or an improved site under the assumption that the site could be made vacant, that is, that the existing building could be demolished

Home equity loan   a type of second mortgage, traditionally used to finance home improvement loans, where a homeowner can borrow against the equity invested in the property

Home Mortgage Disclosure Act of 1975   an act of Congress that discourages lenders from avoiding, or redlining, certain neighborhoods

Homestead exemption   a provision in some states that allows specified taxpayers (usually owners of their principal, full-time residences) to apply for a deduction of a certain amount from the property's assessed value in calculating the property tax liability

Horizontal equity   the economic principle that persons in similar conditions and situations should be taxed or otherwise treated the same

Hoteling   having salespersons, the auditing staff of accounting firms, and other personnel who are frequently out of the office share the use of unreserved space when they need to be in the office

Hybrid REITs   real estate investment trusts that invest in both properties and mortgages

*I*mplied contract   contract created by the actions of the parties involved

Improvements on land   buildings

Improvements to land   items such as streets, parking areas, and landscaping

Income kickers   enticements offered to lenders where borrowers pay the lender a specified percentage of the property's gross of net income

Independent variable   one of the variables in a regression equation that is believed partially to explain variations in the dependent variable

Indicated value   the final number resulting from application of one of the major approaches in the appraisal process

Industrial parks   subdivisions offering a controlled environment with buildings designed to accommodate a wide variety of light-industrial and research and development tenant needs

Infinite-life REITs   real estate investment trusts that operate as a going concern

Information costs   payments in terms of actual outlays and time to acquire information for making decisions

Infrastructure   any improvement on or off site that is used by the public, especially occupants and visitors to properties, including roads and schools

Input linkages   the spatial relationship between a property and the locations of factors of production needed to generate income at that property

Installment sale   financing arrangement, commonly used to defer taxes due on the sale of commercial property, where the seller allows the buyer to pay the purchase price over a number of years

Interest   the adjustment required to equate the value of money received at two different points in time

Interest-only loans   loan alternative in which borrowers pay only interest over the life of the loan, and then completely repay the principal in one installment at maturity

Internal rate of return   the rate of interest that equates the present value of the cash inflows to the present value of the cash outflows

Inverse condemnation   loss of property rights by government action, such as downzoning

Investment activity   actions taken to maximize the production of future income

Investment objectives   general guidelines for choosing specific properties consistent with the investment philosophy

Investment philosophy   an outline of the relationship investors would like to have with their real estate investments, mainly whether they will be active or passive investors

Investment policies   financial criteria and other special considerations that are used to create a profile of investments that satisfy investor objectives and are consistent with the investor's philosophy

Investment property   real estate held as an investment for the production of income

Investment value   the value of the property to a particular investor

Investment-grade rating   a rating issued by one of the commercial rating agencies that, if obtained, signals to investors that the security has minimum credit risk. Allows the security to be sold at a higher price/lower yield

*J*oint tenancy   an estate for co-ownership in which the surviving partners divide the interests of a deceased partner

Joint venture   a business partnership formed between a lender and a developer or investor to develop or purchase a specific property or properties

Judicial foreclosure   process of bringing the property of delinquent borrowers to public sale that involves court action—followed in lien theory states

Jumbo loans   nonconforming loans that exceed the maximum value established by Fannie Mae or Freddie Mac

Junior mortgage   any second, third, and greater mortgage

*L***and acquisition loans**   loans to finance the purchase of the raw land

Land contract   a seller financing agreement that falls outside mortgage law and in which the title passes when the loan is repaid

Land developer   a company or individual that takes land from an undeveloped condition to a state in which the land may be sold as subdivided lots

Land development loans   loans to finance the installation of the on-site and off-site improvements to the land that are necessary to ready the land for construction

Land purchase option   a contract that gives the developer the right, but not the obligation, to purchase the land before the expiration date of the option at a predetermined price

Landlord-tenant laws   state laws governing the relationships between residential landlords and tenants

Law of agency   see *Agency*

Leased fee estate   the bundle of rights possessed by the landlord in a lease agreement

Leasehold estate   the bundle of rights possessed by the tenant in a lease agreement

Leasehold mortgage   a debt obligation in which the collateral is the security of the payment stream created by a lease

Legal title   ownership of property

Letter of intent   a document prepared by a potential buyer of property expressing interest but without making an offer for the property of the owner

Letter of opinion   statement from an attorney declaring that title to real estate is clear of prior ownership interests, liens, and other legal encumbrances

Licensing laws   state laws that authorize persons who meet specified qualifications to engage in a business or profession

Lien   a right to bring foreclosure action against a property for payment of a debt, taxes, goods, or services

Lien theory   the mortgage represents a lien against mortgaged property that must be exercised upon default

Life estates   interests in real estate that terminate at the end of the life of the holder of the property

Life-of-loan caps   a ceiling that the contract rate may never exceed

Limited partnership   a partnership in which one party assumes unlimited liability in exchange for control of all material decision making, while all parties benefit from flow-through income and taxation

Listing contract   agreement between an owner of real estate and a real estate broker that obligates the broker to attempt to sell the property under specified conditions and terms. It obligates the property owner to pay a commission to the broker if the broker is successful in selling the property on terms specified or on terms acceptable to the seller

Loan amortization schedule   a table showing the breakdown of a fixed mortgage payment between interest and the return of principal

Loan servicing   all actions and activities associated with administering a mortgage loan, including collection of payments, monitoring insurance and tax obligations, and notification of delinquent borrowers

Loan underwriting process   the process by which a prospective borrower submits a formal loan application and the lender analyzes all relevant information and decides whether or not to fund the loan

Loan-to-value ratio   a measure of the percentage of the property's value that is encumbered by debt, defined as the outstanding mortgage amount divided by the value of the property

Location monopoly   the fact that each property's time-distance relationships with other properties is unique

Location quotient   the ratio between the percentage of employees in a certain type of work or job classification in a community and the percentage of employees in that same type of work or job classification nationally

Lock-out provision   a provision prohibiting prepayment of the mortgage for a specified period of time after origination

*M***argin**   the premium, typically two to three percentage points, over and above the indexed rate, which is charged on adjustable rate mortgages

Market area   the geographic confines within which most of a store's or shopping center's customers will reside or originate

Market conditions   the relationship between supply and demand for a particular type of real estate in a local market at a specified point in time

Market rent   the rent that could be obtained by renting the property on the open market

Market segmentation   identification and delineation of submarkets

Market value   the price a property should sell for in a competitive market when there has been a normal offering time, no coercion, arm's-length bargaining, typical financing, and informed buyers and sellers

Market yield   the holding period (internal) rate of return that investors in a particular security are currently requiring

Market-adjusted normal sale price   "normal sale price" adjusted for changes in market conditions between the date of sale and the date of appraisal of the subject property

Marketability study   an analysis of how best to bring a product or service to the market. It considers characteristics of the product or service in relation to the needs of potential customers and which marketing channels are most likely to produce the desired results

Materially participate   involvement on a regular, continuous, and substantial basis in the operation of the activity

Maturity imbalance problem   situation faced by mortgage lenders in which long-term assets are funded with short-term liabilities

Mean-variance   an analysis of the trade-off between expected return and the expected variability of that return

Metes and bounds   method of describing real estate in which a *mete* is a unit of measure (foot, mile) and a *bound* is a boundary marker

Mid-rise apartments   residential facilities, frequently found in cities and suburbs, with between four and nine stories

Millage rate   the dollars of tax per $1,000 of property value. For example, a millage rate of 20 means that a person owning a property having an assessed value of $100,000 would pay 20 × 100 = $2,000 in tax

Mills   the number of dollars per $1,000. Twenty mills means $20 per each $1,000

Mini-perm loan   a loan from an interim lender that provides financing for the construction period, the lease-up period, and for several years beyond the lease-up stage

Mixed-asset portfolio   a portfolio that contains a variety of types of assets

Mortgage   a loan contract or legal document in which real estate serves as collateral

Mortgage assumption   when buyers take over payments of mortgages of sellers and become personally liable by creating a note in their name

Mortgage bankers   full-service mortgage companies that process, close, provide funding, and sell the loans they originate in the secondary mortgage market

Mortgage brokers   an intermediary between those who demand mortgage funds and those who supply the funds

Mortgage joint venture   a relationship between developers and others who supply all or most of the funds in the form of loans to develop properties that will be used in their business or enter their portfolios

Mortgage menu   the many types of residential loans offered by originating lenders to residential borrowers. The menu includes the cost of the various mortgage items, including the contract interest rate and number of up-front discount points and origination fees

Mortgage pipeline   An originating lender's approved, but currently unfunded, loan commitments

Mortgage REITs   real estate investment trusts that purchase mortgage obligations and effectively become real estate lenders

Mortgage-equity analysis   estimation of an overall capitalization rate by calculating a weighted average of the capitalization rate for debt (mortgage constant) and the capitalization rate for equity (equity dividend rate). The weight is determined by the percentage that each component (debt and equity) is of the total investment

Multiple listing service sharing of property sales listings by a number of real estate brokers with an agreement as to how costs and commissions are to be shared

Multiple regression analysis the process of simultaneously relating the variations of two or more independent variables to the variation in a dependent variable, in order to "explain" movements in the dependent variable

Mutual Mortgage Insurance Fund the depository for FHA insurance premiums and the source of reimbursement for lenders in the case of foreclosure losses on FHA-insured properties

NAREIT index a value-weighted index that tracks the total return pattern of all exchange-listed REITs on a monthly basis

National Association of Realtors® trade or professional organization of real estate brokers who agree to abide by a code of ethics

Natural vacancy the relationship between unoccupied space and total available space over a complete business cycle

NCREIF Classic Property Index a measure of the historical performance of income properties held by (or for) pension funds and profit-sharing plans

Negative amortization the increase in the outstanding loan balance during the early years of a graduated payment mortgage

Neighborhood or "strip" center a set of retail establishments offering mostly convenience goods and services, typically anchored by a large chain grocery store or drugstore, and catering to a close-by resident population

Net contract rent payment for space stated in a net lease contract

Net effective rent payment for space in a net lease contract time-value adjusted for rental concessions granted in the contract

Net lease lease in which the tenant pays some or all of the operating expenses of the property in addition to rent

Net listing type of contract in which sellers specify the amount they will accept from the sale, with brokers keeping all proceeds in excess of that amount

Net operating income the type of income to a property used in direct capitalization, calculated by deducting from potential gross income vacancy and collection losses and adding other income to obtain effective gross income. From this amount all operating expenses are subtracted, including management expense and a reserve for replacements and other nonrecurring expenses

Net present value the difference between the present value of the cash inflows and the present value of the cash outflows

"Noisy" prices prices that exhibit extreme volatility

Non judicial foreclosure process of bringing the property of delinquent borrowers to public sale that involves a series of public notices of the sale—followed in title theory states

Nonbasic employment jobs that are not involved in the production of goods or services that will be exported outside of a community. These are usually jobs involved in serving local residents. Examples are barbers, beauticians, real estate and insurance salespersons, and local bankers

Nonconforming conventional loan a conventional loan that does not satisfy one or more underwriting standard established by Fannie Mae or Freddie Mac

Nondiversifiable systematic risk that cannot be eliminated from a portfolio, regardless of how many securities are included, and regardless of how they co-vary

Nonrealty items items of personal property

Nonrecourse financing when a note is used and borrowers do not have personal liability for the debt obligation

Normal sale price the transaction price of a comparable property adjusted for nonmarket financing and non-arm's-length bargaining (conditions of sale)

Note the document used to create a debt when a loan is made to finance real estate

Off-price centers retailers that offer large discounts on name-brand merchandise that consists of factory overruns, seconds and discontinued items, and overstocks from other stores

Officer's deeds same as definition of executor's deed

Open listing agreement between the seller of property and a broker that provides for the broker to receive a commission if he or she sells the property. No exclusive protection is provided to the broker

Open-end construction loan a forward commitment has not been obtained to repay the construction loan

Open-end REITs real estate investment trusts that are able to sell new shares to raise capital for the acquisition of additional assets or other uses

Operating expense ratio a measure of annual operating costs, defined as operating expenses divided by effective gross income

Operating expenses the expenses owners incur in operating their property

Option contract sets a time over which developers may buy property at a specified price

Outlet centers establishments that sell name-brand goods at lower prices by eliminating the wholesale distributor

Output linkages the spatial relationship between a property and the locations of the markets in which the products and services produced at the property are sold

Overall capitalization rate the type of capitalization rate used in direct capitalization, calculated by dividing comparable properties' net operating incomes by their selling prices

Package mortgage mortgage loans that include funds for home-related items of personal property such as a range, dishwasher, refrigerator, and furnishings

Par value the remaining balance of the mortgage or security, also referred to as *book value* and *face value*

Partial tax shelter taxable income from operations that is less than before-tax cash flow

Partially amortized mortgages loan alternative in which the outstanding principal is partially repaid over the life of the loan, then fully retired with a larger lump sum payment at maturity

Pass-through clause a clause in leases that requires tenants to pay increases in property expenses above an initial amount

Passive activity loss restrictions IRS rules that, in general, allow losses on passive activities to be used only to offset gains on other passive investments

Passive income income generated from trade and business activities in which the taxpayer does not materially participate and income generated from certain rental activities such as rental real estate

Passthrough security a mortgage security that provides the investor with an undivided ownership interest, or participation, in a pool of mortgages

Patent special type of deed that conveys title to real property owned by the federal government to a private party

Pension funds retirement savings accounts that now represent a major source of equity capital in commercial real estate markets

Percentage lease a lease often used for retail properties in which the tenant pays a base rent plus a percentage of revenues for the business

Periodic tenancy a leasehold estate in which the term ends when one party gives notice of intent to terminate

Permanent loan long-term mortgage financing

Personal property items such as furniture and tenants fixtures that are often purchased in conjunction with real property acquisitions

Personal residence an owner-occupied housing unit

Physical deterioration loss of value of a building from its reproduction cost resulting from wear and tear over time

Planned amortization class often included along with sequential pay and accrual classes, this class provides investors with a cash flow pattern, and therefore yield and maturity, that is known with certainty so long as the underlying mortgages prepay at rates that fall into a prespecified range

Planned unit development (PUD) a development project, often involving a mixture of land uses and densities not permitted by normal zoning. It is allowed because the entire development is viewed as an integrated whole

Plat books register of recorded plat maps which show boundaries, shapes, and sizes of land parcels maintained by a city or county

Plottage value   value added to land by assembling small parcels into larger tracts

Point system   a process of grading the desirability of a proposed development based on the number of points assigned to various aspects of the proposal

Police power   right of government in the United States to regulate the use of property to protect the health, welfare, and safety of the population

Polychlorinated biphenyls (PCBs)   cancer-causing chemicals formerly used in the manufacture of electrical connectors and equipment

Portfolio income   income from a group of investments in securities

Portfolio lenders   financial institutions that fund long-term home mortgage loans and hold the whole loans as investments

Portfolio management   responsibility for a collection of assets (properties) with special consideration for how the assets are mixed to lower investor risk

Potential gross income   the total annual income the property would produce if it were fully rented and had no collection losses

Power centers   large retail centers having gross leasable areas ranging from 250,000 to 750,000 square feet, characterized by a high ratio of anchors to ancillary tenants

Power of sale clause   mortgage provision that grants the authority to initiate the foreclosure process to either the lender or a trustee

Premium   the market value of a security in excess of par value

Prepayment clause   provision stating the compensation to lenders if borrowers prepay loans

Prepayment penalties   charges, designed to discourage prepayment, incurred when a mortgage is retired before maturity

Price discovery   learning beforehand about prices by studying prices in a related market

Primary data   bits of information gathered by the analyst personally from surveys, personal interviews, or other methods of observing events and phenomena

Primary mortgage market   the loan origination market where borrowers and lenders negotiate mortgage terms

Principal   in brokerage, the person giving authority to an agent; in finance, the amount borrowed and owed on a loan

Private grants   conveyance of property from one private owner to another

Private markets   market where assets are offered for sale to only a specially selected customer base

Private mortgage insurance   insurance offered by private companies that reimburses the lender in the event of default by the borrower

Probability distributions   the distribution of all potential outcomes and their associated likelihood

Promissory note   a legal document evidencing a personal pledge by a borrower to repay a loan

Property characteristics   the physical and locational nature of a property, as contrasted with transactional characteristics, which reflect the nature and condition of a sale-purchase

Property management   direction of the day-to-day operations of properties

Property rights   the ability granted by society to do certain things with property. The foundation of value

Proration   allocation of costs and revenues between buyer and seller of real property at closing, based on the time of ownership by each party

Public grants   conveyance of property from government to a private owner

Public markets   market where assets are sold to any and all buyers, usually on an organized exchange

Public Securities Association (PSA)   an industry organization that publishes standard monthly rates of prepayment on mortgage pools based on historical prepayment rates

Purchase money mortgage   a mortgage loan where the seller lends all or part of the purchase price of a property to the purchaser, and the loan is secured by a mortgage on the property

Quitclaim deed   deed that passes an individual's property rights without guarantees

q   the ratio of prices or market values of assets to their replacement costs

Radon   naturally occurring radioactive gas found in soils in most parts of the country. In large concentrations, the gas may contribute to or cause cancer

Real asset   tangible things that have value because they are useful

Real estate   the collection of rights associated with real actions involving land

Real estate commission   state agency empowered to grant, revoke, suspend, and otherwise discipline real estate brokers operating in the state

Real Estate Settlement and Procedures Act   a federal law requiring lenders to provide information on all costs associated with closing a residential loan within three business days of the loan application

Real property   rights associated with ownership of land and all permanent attachments to land

Reconciliation   the process of forming a single point estimate from two or more numbers. It is used widely in the appraisal process, for example, in the sales comparison approach to develop a single indicated value from several final adjusted sale prices of comparables, and in final reconciliation to develop a final estimate of value from two or more indicated values

Reconstructed operating statement   a table reporting basic measures of income and expense items in terms of current market conditions

Recorded plat map   see plat book

Recording   filing of a document with the appropriate public official or office in order to provide constructive notice to the public

Recourse financing   mortgage documents that include a note containing a personal promise to repay the loan

Recovery fund   reserve of funds collected from real estate license fees to pay for losses to clients legally judged to have been caused by a licensed salesperson or broker. The existence of such funds varies from state to state

Regional and super-regional centers   major shopping outlets with at least two department store anchor tenants and at least 200,000 square feet of gross leasable area devoted to nonanchor tenants

Reinvestment risk   the risk that lenders will have to reinvest the remaining loan balance at a lower rate when borrowers prepay mortgages with above-market rates

Reliction   receding water line that leaves dry land to be added to the title holder's property

Remainder   recipient of interests in a life estate after the estate has ended

Rent   price paid for the use of space

Replacement cost   the cost to build a new building of equal utility to an existing building that is not a physical replica of the existing building

Replacement reserves   money set aside each year to accumulate a fund for the eventual replacement of personal property

Reproduction cost   the cost to build a new building that is exactly like an existing building in physical detail

Reservation price   maximum price or rent a buyer or tenant will pay; minimum price or rent a seller or landlord will accept

Reserve for replacements and other nonrecurring expenses   an allowance in a reconstructed operating statement to reflect an annual allocation for building part replacements, releasing expenses, and tenant improvements. These types of costs and expenses occur only at intervals of several years, but they must be accounted for in the estimate of annual income that is capitalized into an estimate of market value

Restrictive covenant   a limitation on the use of real property created by a clause in the deed at the time a property is conveyed from one owner to another; also called a deed restriction

Reverse annuity mortgage   an arrangement where the lender agrees to pay the homeowner a monthly payment, or annuity, and to be repaid from the homeowner's equity when he or she sells the home or obtains other financing

Reversion   the rights of lessors to properties at the end of leases

Right of survivorship   the rights of surviving partners in a joint tenancy to divide the interests of a deceased partner

Riparian rights   interests in water

Risk-weighted assets   the sum of an institution's portfolio assets weighted by their appropriate risk classification, used to determine regulatory capital requirements

R^2 coefficient of multiple determination. Its value is the extent to which the variation in a dependent variable is "explained" by the regression equation

S corporation   corporate ownership structure that provides limited liability. It is not, however, a separate taxable entity; hence, income and losses flow through to stockholders and are reported on their individual tax returns

Sale price   payment in the asset market for rights of ownership of space

Sale-and leaseback   an agreement in which a property owner simultaneously sells the property to a buyer and leases the property from the buyer

Salesperson license   authority granted by a state to engage in the real estate brokerage business as an employee or agent of a real estate broker

Sandwich lease   a sublet arrangement in which the initial lessee collects rent from the new lessee and pays rent to the landlord under the original lease agreement

Savings and loan associations   today, a general financial institution, but historically, a highly specialized home mortgage lending institution

Savings banks   historically empowered with wider investment powers than S&Ls, the two institutional forms are virtually indistinguishable today

Secondary data   bits of information obtained from sources other than one's efforts, for example, data obtained from books, data banks, and federal documents

Secondary mortgage market   the market where mortgage originators can divest their holdings

Section 1231 assets   trade or business property held for more than one year

Section 203 loans   the most widely used FHA program, covering single-family home mortgages insured by the FHA under Title II, section 203 of the National Housing Act

Securitization   the process of creating securities from single assets or, more commonly, from multiple assets. The process involves reviews and approvals of plans to publicly sell securities by the U.S. Securities and Exchange Commission

Selling expenses   costs associated with the disposition of a property

Senior/subordinate structure   an MBS structure that creates two classes of security holders: a senior class and a subordinate class. The senior bond holder's claim on the underlying principal and interest payments is superior to the claim of the subordinate class

Sequential pay structures   with this structure, the principal payments on the underlying mortgage collateral, both scheduled and unscheduled, are distributed on a priority basis instead of in proportion to each investor's equity contribution

Sheriff's deed   same as definition of executor's deed

Single-factor model   a model that classifies investment risk into only two categories, systematic (or macroeconomic) and property-specific (or microeconomic)

Sinking fund factor   the amount that must be deposited periodically at a specified interest rate, for a specified time period, to accumulate to $1.00

Site plan   map of a project on its site

Sludge   another term for toxic wastes

Soft costs   amounts paid to those who provide services, such as legal services, during the course of development

Sole proprietorship   ownership structure where all cash flow and income tax consequences flow through directly to the individual's income tax return, thereby avoiding taxation at the entity level

Special agent   a person to whom a principal has granted authority to handle a specific business transaction or to perform a specific function

Special assessments   taxes levied to finance special improvements to benefit property owners. For example, property owners in a subdivision could receive a special assessment to install sanitary sewers

Special warranty deed   deed in which grantors covenant only against claims arising from the time they owned the property

Specialty shopping centers niche retailers characterized by a dominant theme or image

Speculative bubble extraordinary increase in price caused by irrational human behavior

Spread the difference between the expected yield on a security and the yield on a riskless Treasury security with a comparable maturity

Standard deduction the amount of deductible expenses, specified by Congress, that a taxpayer may claim in lieu of itemizing allowable personal expenditures

Standard deviation an alternative measure of the dispersion of a distribution around its expected value, defined as the square root of the variance

Standard error the degree of variation in a dependent variable that is not explained by a regression equation containing one or more independent variables. Thus, it is the likely amount of error in an estimate derived from the model. It can be used to establish a confidence interval around the estimate

Standby forward commitment forward commitments where the mortgage banker has the right, but not the obligation, to sell a prespecified dollar amount of a certain loan type

Statutory redemption law in some states that provides time to borrowers of foreclosed properties to regain title after the sale

Subcontractors companies or individuals who provide specialized construction activities, such as painting and carpet installation

Subjective probability distributions an opinion or guess as to the likelihood of particular events occurring

Sublet transfer of lessees' rights to another tenant, although the lessee continues to be obligated for payments

Submarket segment or portion of a market in which all of the properties are considered to be close substitutes by a relatively homogeneous group of potential buyers; similar properties that provide equal utility or satisfaction

Substantial improvements major alterations to a property made in the years after purchase. These improvements are treated as a separate building for tax purposes

Survey process of accurately establishing the boundaries of a parcel of real estate

Syndicate a group of persons or legal entities who come together to carry out a particular activity

***T*ake-out commitment** agreements, issued by long-term lenders, to disburse the permanent loan proceeds when the project has been completed according to specifications

Tax assessor local public official in charge of determining the taxable value of property in the jurisdiction as the basis for property taxation. In some states this official is called the county property appraiser

Tax base all of the taxable properties in a jurisdiction

Tax burden analysis analysis of the taxes levied against one property in comparison with the taxes levied against other similar properties

Tax capitalization discounting to present value of an increase in the property tax

Tax certificates obligations for unpaid taxes sold by taxing jurisdictions in order to collect the amount of unpaid taxes. The property owner, in order to redeem (take back) the property, or any future purchaser of the property, must pay off the tax certificates to obtain title to the property

Tax depreciation the reduction in taxable income intended to reflect the wear and tear that income properties experience over time

Tax exempt properties against which local jurisdictions may not levy taxes, usually including churches, synagogues, public schools, and government buildings

Tax rate the number of dollars of property tax divided by the assessed value of the properties. The percentage that, when multiplied by a property's assessed value, will yield the tax liability

Teaser rate the initial interest rate on an adjustable rate instrument if it is less than the index rate plus the margin at the time of origination

Tenancy in common a co-ownership estate without survivorship rights

Tenancy in partnership a form of ownership in which rights of partners are defined by the agreement they file with the state

Tenancy-at-sufferance   an illegal tenancy in which tenants claim they are tenants-at-will

Tenancy-at-will   an estate granted by landlords to tenants allowing them to remain in possession without written agreement

Terms   arrangements of a sale agreed to by the parties, for example, the transaction price, the date of closing, and condition of the property upon closing

Thematic image   common theme for logos and other promotional devices that capitalize on the property's name and unique features (e.g., architectural style)

Title insurance   insurance paying monetary damages for loss of property from unexpected superior legal claims

Title theory   lender receives title to the mortgaged property that ripens upon default

Torrens system   method of providing evidence of ownership of real estate by means of a legal process leading to a certificate

Toxic waste   hazardous materials such as asbestos, fiberglass, lead paint, radon, PCBs, leaking underground storage tanks, and the like

Trade or business property   real estate held for use in a trade or business, including most income-producing property

Tranches   the different classes of security owners in a sequential pay MBS, each of which provides a different expected yield and maturity

Transaction broker   one who facilitates a real estate transaction but who is not an agent of either buyer or seller. A transaction broker is required to deal honestly and fairly with both parties and to exercise skill, care, and diligence in carrying out his or her duties

Transferable development rights   rights to develop that cannot be used at one site but can be sold and used at another site

Truth-in-Lending Act   a federal law requiring lenders to provide residential borrowers with estimates of the total finance charges and the annual percentage rate (APR)

Unearned income   nonlabor income, often resulting from investments

Uniform Standards of Professional Appraisal Practice   Rules governing the appraisal process and reporting of appraisals that are developed by the Appraisal Standards Board of the Appraisal Foundation. Appraisers are obligated by law to follow these rules and guidelines

Unilateral contract   agreement in which one party agrees to act in return for a promise from the other party

Universal agent   one to whom a principal delegates the power to act in all matters that can be delegated in place of the principal

Unsystematic risk   the variation in portfolio returns that can be eliminated by holding securities and other investments with less than perfectly correlated returns

Urban service area   an area delineated around a community within which the local government plans to provide public services and facilities and beyond which urban development is discouraged or prohibited

Urban sprawl   the decentralization of the urban landscape

Use   the type of improvement on a site, or the type of occupancy of a building

VA-guaranteed loans   government loan guarantees designed to help veterans obtain home mortgage loans for which they might not otherwise qualify

Variance   a permitted deviation for a particular property from the zoning category for that property

Vertical equity   the economic principle that persons in different economic conditions and situations should be taxed and otherwise treated proportionately to their different circumstances

Warehouse   a structure that provides space for the temporary storage of goods

Warehousing   the provision of short-term funds to mortgage banking companies to enable them to originate mortgage loans and sell them in the secondary mortgage market

Wrap-around mortgage   financing, usually from the seller, in which a new loan is created around an existing loan that the seller keeps in place

Yield spread   difference between rates on capital market investments

Yield-maintenance agreements   an agreement in which the prepayment penalty borrowers pay depends on how far interest rates have declined since origination

Yield-to-maturity   the yield (return) on an investment project if held until maturity

Zoning   regulation of land use, population density, and building size by district. May be viewed as a phase of comprehensive planning in which the plan's implementation is enforced through the police power

INDEX

Absolutely net lease, 246
Absorption rate, 335
Abstracts of title, 665
Accelerated methods, of depreciating
   real estate, 126–128
Acceleration clause, of mortgages, 457
Accredited Appraiser Canadian Insti-
   tute (AACI), 431
Accretion, ownership rights through,
   671
Accrual class, 590–591
Accrued depreciation, 388, 389–393,
   406
   elements of, 390
   external obsolescence, 392–393
   functional obsolescence, 391–392
   physical deterioration, 390–391
Acquisition, development, and con-
   struction (ADC) loans, 560–566
Acquisition price, 97
Active income, 111
Active investors, 72
Adaptation test, for fixtures, 619
Adjustable rate mortgages (ARMs),
   476–480, 505, 738
   borrowing cost of, 494
   interest rates and payments, 480
   mechanics, 477–479
   options, 479–480
   rate caps, 479–480
Adjusted basis (AB), 132, 133, 134
Adjusted gross income (AGI), 115,
   137
Adjustment clause, of mortgage con-
   tracts, 458
Adjustment rate caps; See Rate caps
Adjustments, 376–384
   market analysis for, 400–403
   sequence of, 382–384
   types of, 382
Ad valorem taxation, 641
Advance rent, 245
Adverse possession, 670
Aetna Life Insurance Co., 549

Affordability ratios, 525–527
Affordable housing allocation, 313
After-tax cash flows (ATCF), 107,
   122, 130, 131, 135, 219
After-tax equity reversion (ATER),
   133, 135, 219
Agency passthroughs, 584–587
   Fannie Mae MSBs, 587
   participation certificates (PCs),
      586–587
Agency problems, reducing, 238–240
Agency relationships, 237–238, 693
   in real estate brokerage, 694
Air rights, to real estate, 616
Aldrich, Eastman and Waltch, 164,
   228
Alexander, Alan A., 259
All-inclusive deed of trust, 451
Alonso, William, 267
Alternative financing structures,
   choosing, 551–553
Ambler Realty Company, 305
American ownership
   equity ownership, 15
   mortgage value, 15
American Society of Appraisers, 431
American Society of Farm Managers
   and Rural Appraisers, 431
American University, 7
Ameritech, 555
Amortization, 26
Amortized financing costs (AFC),
   122, 123, 130, 131
Amsterdam, University of, 7
Anderson, Paul E., 145, 149, 152, 171
Andreoli, Tom, 549
Annexation test, for fixtures, 619
Annual effective gross income, 427
Annual percentage rate (APR), 493
Annuity
   future value of, 58
   present value of, 60
Annuity payment, 37–38, 41

Apartment management, and drug
   testing, 243
Apartment properties, 12
Apartment rent, 278
Applied demand analysis, 339–340
Appraisal foundation, Appraisal Stan-
   dards Board of, 430
Appraisal Institute, 431, 432
Appraisal Institute of Canada, 431
The Appraisal of Real Estate (Bab-
   cock), 6
Appraisal profession, 429–432
   careers, 432
   organizations and destinations,
      431–432
   regulation of, 430–431
Appraisal reports, and loan applica-
   tion, 556–557
Appreciation, 415
Approvals, for development process,
   362–363
Arbitrage, 265
Architect, 363
ARGUS, 98
Arm's-length bargain, 377
Asbestos, 315
Assessed value, 647
Asset management, 227–228
Asset managers, 226, 227
Asset market, 272, 278–289
   and economic fundamentals, 279
   and government influences,
      279–281
   and individuals, 281–282
   noisy prices, 287–288
   participants, 285
   prices and values, 286–287
   replacement cost and values, 287
   and securitized market, 288–289
Asset-pricing model, required risk pre-
   miums, 217–218
Assignment, 244
   of contracts, 738
Assignment clause, 738

Assumption of the mortgage, 451
Assumption transactions, and mortgage contracts, 463
AT&T, 555
AT&T Capital, 515
Auctioning, and prices, 285
Average tax rates, versus marginal tax rates, 113–115
Axiom Real Estate Mgt., Inc., 229

Babcock, Fredrick, 6
Bach, Robert, 178
The Balcor Co., 230
Balloon mortgages, 539–540
Balloon payment, 475
Banerjee, Neela, 443
Bargain-and-sale deeds, 669
Barkham, Richard, 289
Barovick, Barry, 149
Barrett, Vincent G., 334
Barron, David W., 249
Barron's/John B. Levy & Co. National Mortgage Survey, 539
Bartlett, William W., 584, 610
Base case solution, 219
Baseline, 679
Base rent, 247
Bass PLC, 701
Beachfront Management Act, 307
Beaton, William, 282
Bedrock Partners, 164
Before-tax cash flow from annual operations (BTCF), 89, 96, 97, 116, 120, 122, 131, 134, 543, 549
Before-tax equity reversion (BTER), 90, 96, 133, 549
Bel Air Hotel and Country Club, 701
Belloit, Jerry D., 352, 385, 399, 436
Below-line costs, 80
Benjamin, John D., 214, 278
Benson, George C. S., 656
Benson, Sumner, 656
Berens, Gayle, 373
Better Homes & Gardens, 700
Betts, Richard M., 292
Bid-rent curve, 267
Bigelow, Glen, 157
Bilateral contract, 672
Binders, 361, 748
Black, William C., 718
Blind fund; *See* Unspecified fund
Board of equalization, 648
Board of Realtors , 698

Bodie, Zvi, 215, 218, 223
Boeing Company, 341
Bohannan, Art, 327
Bond, 446
Bonus maximum, of zoning, 310
Bookout, Lloyd W., Jr., 373
Borrower quality, and commercial property financing, 558
Boston Financial, 228
Boyle, Glenn W., 278
Break-even ratio (BER), 95, 97, 560
Breaks in transportation, 271
Brealey, Richard A., 10, 20
Bridge loan; *See* Gap loan
Bridgestone, 701
Brierley, John E. C., 639
British Columbia, University of, 7, 8
Brokerage, 689–691, 695–698
    brokers as market facilitators, 689–690
    choosing a broker, 710
    commercial, 699–700
    international aspects, 701–702
    licensing of brokers and salespersons, 695–698
    marketing function, 698–702
    rationale for employing brokers, 690–691
    residential, 700–701
Brokerage licensing administration, 695–696
Broker license, 695
Brokers, 285
    role in closing, 746–747
Brookings Institute, 277
Brueggeman, William B., 145, 171, 223, 232, 467, 503, 532, 570, 610
Bruno, Carl, 14
Budget of jurisdiction, determining, 644–645
Builders, 355
Building permit process, 301
Building quality, and commercial property financing, 558
Building valuation, 422–427
Building value, 392
Bundle of rights, 615
Burger King Corporation, 148
Business property, 108–110
Buy down, interest rate, 483–484, 492
Buyer default, 740
Buyers, rights and obligations, 723
Buyers expenses, in closing, 744–745
Buyer's statement, 748

Cadastres, 666
California at Berkeley, University of, 7, 8, 9
California at Los Angeles, University of, 7, 8
California State University, Sacramento, 7
Cameron, Helene A., 653
Capacity, and underwriting, 526
Capital asset, definition, 137
Capital asset market; *See* Asset market
Capital flow matrix, for real estate, 448
Capital gain income, versus ordinary income, 136–137
Capital improvements, versus operating expenses, 123
Capitalization rate, 52–53, 60–61, 87, 92–93, 411, 414–421; *See also* Equity dividend rate
    overall, 415–420
    type of, 415
Capitalization rates, and discount rates, 88
Capital markets, 448
    integration with mortgage markets, 449
Capital substitution, 267–268
Capture rate, 345
Carn, Neil, 276, 352
Casazza, John, 373
Case, Karl E., 283
Cash calculation, versus tax calculation, 123
Cash flow
    creating, 229–232
    maintaining, 232–235
Cash flow before debt service and income tax, 80
Cash flow estimates, and loan application, 556
Cash flow forecasting, 76–81
    cash flow estimates, 81
    effective gross income, 78–79
    net operating income, 79–80
    nonrecurring expenses, 80
    operating expenses, 79
    potential gross income, 76–78
Cash flow risk, 235–236
Cash flows, effect of debt on, 88–90
Cash inflows, 47
Cash reconciliation statement, 745, 746, 748

Catanese, Anthony J., 322
CB Commercial Real Estate Group, Inc., 229
C corporation, 148–149, 153, 630
Ceiling, 456
Central business district (CBD), 176
Century 21, 700
Certificate of occupancy (CO), 365
Certified appraiser, 430
Check, 679
Chesterton Binswanger International, 229
Chevron Corporation, 149
Chevy Chase Federal Savings Bank, 528
Chicago Mercantile Exchange, 549
Churchill, Winston, 3
Cincinnati, University of, 7
Cititcorp, 701
Civil Rights Act of 1968, 697
Clapp, John M., 352
Clark, Dave, 352
Classical land economics, 5–9
Clauretie, Terrence M., 503, 532, 570, 610
Clean Air Act, 314
Clean Water Act, 314
Cleveland State University, 7, 8
Closed-end loans, 487
Closed-end REITs, 159
Closing, 721, 741–751
    buyers' expenses, 744–745
    preparation of statements, 748–751
    prorations, 743–744
    Real Estate Settlement Procedures Act (RESPA), 747–748
    role of the brokers, 746–747
    role of the lender, 747
    sellers' expenses, 745
    steps at, 743
    steps before, 741–743
Closing costs, estimating, 493
Closing expense statements, 735–737
    buyers, 736
    sellers, 737
Closing statement, 743
CME Finance NV, 549
Coefficient of variation, 199–200
    coefficients, 387
Coleman, David S., 57
Collateral, and underwriting, 526
Collateral assessment, 386
Collateralized mortgage obligation (CMO), 589

Columbia Pictures, 701
Columbia University, 7, 8
Colwell, Peter F., 16
Commercial appraisers, 386
Commercial banks (CBs), 509–510
    and conventional passthroughs, 587–588
Commercial brokerage, 699–700
Commercial easements, 297–300, 633
Commercial mortgage-backed securities (CMBSs), 537, 594–596
    difference from residential MSBs, 595–596
    history of, 594–595
    occurrence of, 596–599
    sources of public debt, 594
    structuring issues, 604
Commercial property financing, 535–566
    acquisition, development and construction, 560–566
    borrower's decision-making process, 546–554
    common loan provisions, 540–541
    floating rate loans, 541
    installment sale financing, 541–542
    lender's decision process, 557–560
    loan documents and provisions, 538–539
    requesting a permanent loan, 554–557
    sources of, 536–538
Commercial property leases, 246–252
    basis for rent payment and timing, 247
    lease economics, 250–252
    lessee considerations, 248
    lessor considerations, 248
    specific lease contracts, 249–250
    term of leases, 247–248
Commercial real estate, 15, 161–165
    private, 161–165
    sources of equity capital, 162
Commingled fund, 161
Commingled real estate funds, 163–165
    public real estate markets, 165
Commissions, 690
    effect of market forces on, 692
    splitting between brokers, 710, 711
Common areas maintenance (CAM), 183
Communal ownership, 615

Community center, 182
Community property, 627
Community Reinvestment Act (CRA) of 1977, 527, 528
Competitive area, 338
Competitive market survey, 344
Compounding, interest, 30
Comprehensive Environmental Response Compensation and Liability Act, 314
Comprehensive plans, 300–304, 305
    alternative approaches, 302–303
    conditions of, 302
    implementation and review, 304
    innovation and flexibility in, 303–304
    objectives of, 301–302
    political process, 303
Comptroller of the Currency, 510
Concentric marketing, 232
Concurrency requirement, for development, 313
Concurrent estates, 621, 626–631
    direct co-ownership forms, 626–629
    indirect co-ownership forms, 629–631
Conditions of sale, 383
Condominium, 628–629
Condominium complexes, 174
Conduits, 444, 471
    lending, 598
Conforming conventional loan, 472
Congestion, 310
Conley, Chip, 253
Connecticut, University of, 7, 8
Consideration, 242, 667, 725
Constant, 387
Constant prepayment rate (CPR) model, 592, 593
Construction businesses, 355–356
    financial capital suppliers, 357–358
Construction financing, 562–564, 565
    and income property mortgages, 456
    and single-family residential mortgages, 454–455
Construction Industry Association of Sonoma County, 302
Construction loans, 454, 560
Construction manager, 359–360, 363
Contingent interest, 544–545
Continuing care facilities, 187

Contract for sale, 674, 721–727
  closing, 741–751
  conditions, 721
  default on, 740–741
  form of, 728–735
  requirements of, 723–727
  terms, 721
Contracting, 236
Contract nonperformance, 740–741
  escrow, 741
  remedies for sellers, 740
Contract rent, 75
Contracts, 9, 236–252
  assignment of, 738
  cases on real estate, 739
  categories of, 672
  closing, 741–751
  components of form, 730–735
  with contingencies, 738
  default, 740–741
  for development process, 362–363
  dispute, 729
  four basic contracts, 673–674
  management, 239–242
  oral, 726
  in real estate management, 237
  simple, 728–729
  standard form, 729–730
  validity and enforceability, 671–672
  value perspective, 672–673
  written, 726
Contracts for sale with contingencies, 361
Contracts with contingencies, 738
Conventional loans, ratios for, 525–526
Conventional mortgages, 471–476
  alternative amortization schedules, 474–476
  fixed-payment, fully amortized, 472–474
Convertible mortgages, 546
Cooper, James R., 189
Cooperatives, 629
Coral Gables Federal Savings and Loan, 477
Corcoran, Patrick J., 280
Corgel, John B., 175, 238, 282, 287, 377
Cornell University, 8
Corporations, 630
Correlation coefficient, 205–207
Correspondent relationship, 557

Corsmithling Companies, 254, 255
Cost approach, 388–393, 395, 405–408, 427, 428
  accrued depreciation, 389–393, 406
  cost, 389
  locational adjustments, 406–408
  market conditions adjustment, 406
  reproduction cost, 405–406
  site valuation, 406
Cost estimation, of development, 367–368
Cost recovery period, 125–126
Counteroffer, 725
Covariance, 205–207
Covenant against encumbrances, 668
Covenant for quiet enjoyment, 668
Covenant of seisin, 668
Covenant of warranty forever, 668
Covenants of title, 668
Covered construction loans, 455
Credit enhancement, 588
  and rating agencies, 602–603
Credit reputation, and underwriting, 526
Credit unions, 508
Creditworthiness, 234
Cross-collateralization, 603
Cross-defaulting arrangements, 603
Crowe, Robert M., 57
Csar, Micheal F., 236
Curable functional obsolescence (CFO), 391–392
Curtesy, 624–625
Cushman & Wakefield, 178, 229
Custom home building, 454
Cycles, in real estate markets, 283–284

Daiiehi Seinei, 701
Dallman, Robert E., 145, 171
Davidson, Andrew S., 610
Davidson, Lance S., 251
Davis, Jerry C., 561
Dealer property, 108–110
Debt, private, 448
Debt service coverage ratio (DSCR), 96, 97, 559, 602
Debt service (DS), 97, 131
Deeds-in-lieu of foreclosure, 463
Deeds-of-trust, 447–448
  states, 451
Deep tax shelter, 130

Default
  decision of, 497–498
  in mortgage contracts, 461
  on a sales contract, 740–741
Default decisions, and commercial property financing, 554
Default ratio; *See* Break-even ratio
Defects, 245
Deferral benefits, 135
Deferred maintenance problem, in the mortgage contract, 463
Deficiency judgment, 446
Delaney, Charles J., 323
Delinquency, 461
  in mortgage contracts, 461
Demand, 5–6
  density, 270
Demand and supply
  factors for property types, 276
  in the space market, 274–275
Demand and supply scissors, 6
Demonstration appraisal report, 432
Dennis, Marshall W., 467
Denver, University of, 7
DePaul University, 7
Dependent variable, and multiple regression analysis (MRA), 385
Deposits, 245
Depreciable basis, 124–125
Depreciation, 415
Depreciation deductions, 124–128
Depreciation (DEP), 122, 123, 130, 131
Depreciation rate, estimating a building, 423–425
Derived demand, 208, 338
deRoos, Jan A., 282
Desktop underwriter, 386
Determinable fee, 622–623
Developer rate of return, 368
Developers, 355
Development businesses, 355–356
  financial capital suppliers, 357–358
Development rights
  acquisition rights, 361
  contracts for acquiring, 362
Development team
  formation of, 357–360
  relationships, 357
Diaz, Julian III, 20
DiPasquale, Denise, 292
Direct capitalization, 414, 417
Direct costs; *See* Hard costs

Direct equity investments, 162
Direct equity investors, 164
Direct market extraction, 417
The Directory of Real Estate Development and Related Education Programs, 7
Discount, 576
Discounted cash flow (DCF) analysis, 82–87, 107, 215, 219, 220, 414
Discounting, interest, 30
Discount rates, 82, 415, 421–422
    abstracting from market, 216–217
    determining capitalization rates, 88
Discrete probability distribution, 193
Diversifiable portfolio risk, 203–205
    examples of, 207
Diversification, 152
    and risk management, 202
Dividend, 89
Doctorate of Business Administration, 7
Doctor of Philosophy, 8
Dolan v. City of Tigard, 307
Dole Foods Company, 149
Dominant estate, 633
Donnelly, William A., 660
Dower, 624
Downs, Anthony, 277
Downzoning, 306
Drug testing, and apartment management, 243
Dual agency, 693
    disclosed, 694
Due-on-sale clause, of mortgage contracts, 458
Due-on-sale clauses, 377
Duff & Phelps, 599, 600, 601, 602
Duffy, Stephen, 149
Duncan, Cymbal R., 558
Duncan, David, 163
Duncan, Kimbell R., 610
Durham, James Geoffrey, 467
DYNALEASE, 98

Early payment mortgages, 474, 475–476
Earned income, 111
Easement appurtenant, 633, 635
Easement by implication, 634
Easement by necessity, 634
Easement by prescription, 634
Easement in gross, 633

Easements, 297–300, 633–634
Economic feasibility, 365–369
    definition, 366
    market disequilibrium, 365–366
    market equilibrium, 365–366
    of office building development, 366–369
Economic fundamentals, 279
Economic impact statements, 313
Economic life, 391
Economic lives, of income properties, 424
Economic Recovery Tax Act of 1981 (ERTA), 125, 156
Economic zoning, 296
Effective age, 391
    of a building, 423
Effective borrowing cost (EBC), 480, 492, 543, 551
    calculation, 493
Effective cost; *See* Internal rate of return (IRR)
Effective cost of borrowing, 50–52
Effective gross income (EGI), 78–79, 94, 97, 131, 238
Effective tax rate, 647–648
Effective yield; *See* Internal rate of return (IRR)
Efficiency, and property tax, 650, 651
Efficient portfolio, 210
Elayan, Fayez A., 282
Elements of Land Economics (Ely and Morehouse), 6
Ely, Richard, 6
Eminent domain, 632
Eminent domain takings, 306
Employment, estimating future, 340
Encroachments, 675
Engineer, 363
Environmental concerns, and commercial property financing, 558
Environmental hazards, 314–318
    governmental regulation, 314
    and real estate investors, 317–318
    types of hazardous material, 315–317
Environmental impact statements, 313
Environmental Protection Agencies (EPAs), state, 314
Environmental value assessments, three types of, 318
Epstein, Paul C., 322
Equal utility, 389

Equitable Real Estate Investment Mgt. Inc., 228
Equitable title, 727
Equity
    horizontal, 653
    private, 448
    and property tax, 650
    vertical, 653
Equity capitalization rate, 418
Equity dividend rate (EDR), 93, 97, 421; *See also* Capitalization rate
Equity financing, 442
Equity joint ventures, 358
Equity kickers, 542; *See also* Equity participation
Equity of redemption, 649
    in mortgage contracts, 461
Equity participation, 553; *See also* Equity kickers
Equity REITs, 159, 282, 448, 574
Equity returns
    magnification of, 548
    variability from leverage, 548–551
Equity theory of default, 602
Equity-to-value ratio, 418
ERA, 700
Errors and omission insurance, for real estate brokers, 697
Escalator clauses, 247
Escheat, 633
Escrow, 741
Escrow account, 735
Escrow agent, 741
Escrowing, 458
Estate for years, 625
Estates in severalty, 621, 622
Estimated closing costs, 735–737
    buyers, 736
    sellers, 737
Euro Disney, 326
European Business School, 8
Evans, Michael L., 165
Eviction, 234, 241
Exce l, 35, 61–68, 98
Exclusive agency listing, 704–705
Exclusive right of sale listing, 703, 705
Executor's deeds, 669
Existing mortgage, assumption of, 451
Existing properties
    and income property mortgages, 455–456
    and single-family residential mortgages, 453–455

Expected rate of return, 193
Expected return, 92
Expected value, 193, 194
Expected yield, 577–578, 579
Expense stop clauses, 247
Export industries, 340
Expressed contract, 672
Externalities, 297
External obsolescence (EO), 390,
    392–393
Extraterritorial jurisdiction, 313
Exxon Corporation, 149

*F*abozzi, Frank J., 503, 532, 584, 610
Facilitating broker; *See* Transaction
    brokers
Factor substitution, 268
Faggen, Ivan, 145, 171
Fair Housing Laws, 243
Fannie Mae, 384, 385, 386, 444, 470,
    472, 486, 514, 527, 747
   agency passthroughs, 584, 587, 588
   creation of, 519–520
   importance of, 521–522
   MSBs, 587
Farm Credit System, 515, 523
Farmers Home Administration
    (FmHA), 515–516, 523
Farrell, Michael D., 109
Fass, Peter M., 152
Feasibility, and development process,
    361–362
Feasibility studies, 325–328, 335–337
   definition of, 327
   and loan application, 557
   types of, 328
Federal Agriculture Mortgage Corpo-
    ration (Farmer Mac), 523
Federal Deposit Insurance Corporation
    (FDIC), 508, 510
Federal Financial Institutions Exami-
    nation Council (FFIEC), 430
Federal Financing Bank (FFB), 523
Federal Home Loan Mortgage Corpo-
    ration; *See* Freddie Mac
Federal Housing Administration
    (FHA), 463, 471, 493, 516
   and agency passthroughs, 585–587
   default insurance program, 516
   insured loans, 516–517, 522–523
   loan programs, 453, 526, 581, 747
   Reverse Mortgage Program, 486

Federal Housing Enterprise Financial
    Safety and Soundness Act, 522
Federal income taxation, 107–139
   classes of real property, 108–110
   deferring taxes on disposition,
    138–139
   forms of ownership, 110–111
   income subject to taxation, 111–112
   income tax calculation, 115–116
   law, 109
   taxable income from sale, 132–137
   tax law, 108
   tax rates, 112–115
   using federal tax forms, 116–120
Federal Mortgage Association, 318
Federal National Mortgage Associa-
    tion; *See* Fannie Mae
Federal programs and regulations, ef-
    fects on mortgage lending,
    527–528
Federal Reserve System (Fed), 510
Federal Savings and Loan Insurance
    Corporation, 507
Fee developers, 358
Fees, 245
Fee simple absolute estate, 621–622
Fee simple interest, 250
Ferguson, Jerry T., 306
FHA mortgage insurance, 516
Fiberglass, 315
Fiduciary responsibilities, 237–238
   in agency relationship, 692–693
Fifteen-year mortgages, 472–474
Final adjusted sales prices, 376
Financial asset market; *See* Asset
    market
Financial assets, 11
Financial economics, 9–10
Financial Institutions Recovery, Re-
    form, and Enforcement Act
    (FIRREA), 508, 527
Financial intermediaries, 443,
    506–510
Financial intermediation, 574
Financial leverage, 90
Financial ratios, 92, 94–96
Financial risk, 548
Financing, sequence of, 564–566
Financing Corporation (FICO), 523
Financing costs, 490–493
Financing terms, 377–378, 383
Finite-life REITs, 159
Firestone Tire and Rubber, 701

First-loss position, rating, 599
First mortgage, 450
Fisher, Ernest, 6
Fisher, Glenn W., 643, 660
Fisher, Jeffrey D., 145, 166, 167, 171,
    213, 223, 232, 436, 467, 503,
    532, 570, 610
Fitch Investor Services, 599
Fixed expenses, 79
Fixed-payment mortgages (FPMs),
    472, 483, 490, 505, 512, 513
   borrowing cost of, 494
Fixed rental, 247
Fixtures, 618
   resolving disputes over, 619
Floating-rate class, 592
Floating rate mortgage, 541
Floor, 456
Floor-to-ceiling commitment, 563
Florida, University of, 7, 8
Follain, James R., 157
Forbes, 14
Ford, Deborah Ann, 171
Forecast, 342
Foreclosure, 446, 670
Forward commitment, 455, 512
Fraud, 725
Freddie Mac, 317–318, 384, 385, 386,
    444, 470, 472, 474, 514, 519,
    527, 594, 747
   agency passthroughs, 584, 586–587,
    588
   creation of, 521
   importance of, 521–522
   participation certificates (PCs),
    586–587
Freed, Doris Jonas, 627
Freehold estates, 621–625
Free markets, 263
Free-rider problem, 296
French, William B., 639
Frey, Dale, 334
Friedman, Avery, 243
Fully specified fund, 155
Functional obsolescence, 390,
    391–392
Future value (FV), 30, 39
   of an annuity, 58
   of a lump sum, 57–58, 63–64
   of a series of level payments, 64–65
Future values (FV), calculating, 35–37
F value, 386–387

*G*abriel, Stuart A., 275
Gaines, George, Jr., 57
Galbreath Co., 334
The Galreath Co., 229
Gap analysis, 329
Gap loan, 564, 565
Garden apartments, 174
Garn-St Germain Depository Act of 1982, 458
Gatzlaff, Dean H., 266
Gau, George, 285
Geddes, John, 477
Geltner, David M., 166, 167, 213, 289
General agent, 692
General contractor, 358–359, 363
General Electric Capital, 587
General Electric Investments (GEI), 334
General market studies, 327, 328–331
General Motors Acceptance Corporation, 515
General Motors Corporation, 148, 178
General partners, 150, 151, 154, 155, 158; *See also* Syndicators
General partnerships, 150, 153, 630
General warranty deed, 668
Geographic diversification, 208
Geographic information systems (GIS), 346–347
  definition, 346
Geographic scope, of investment markets, 75
The George Washington University, 7
Georgia, University of, 7, 8
Georgia Institute of Technology, 364
Georgia State University, 7, 8
Gibson, Frank, 467, 639, 687
Giliberto, S. Michael, 167, 213
Ginnie Mae, 519, 522–523
  agency passthroughs, 584–586, 588
  mutual funds, 585
Ginnie Mae MBSs, 514, 523
Giudice, Don, 259
Glasscock, John L., 278
Goebel, Paul R., 57, 449
Gold, Richard B., 416
Goldman, Sachs & Co., 456, 594
Government
  and real estate markets, 279–281
  role in real property rights, 631–633
Government National Mortgage Association; *See* Ginnie Mae

Government Rectangular Survey System (GRSS), 679–683
  correction lines, 683
  identifying principal meridians and baselines, 679
  sections, 681–683
  township and range lines, 679–683
Government regulation, of land uses, 314
Government sponsored enterprises (GSEs), 471, 472, 521, 522
Government survey system; *See* Government Rectangular Survey System (GRSS)
Graduate degree, in real estate, 7
Graduate Diploma in Real Estate, 7
Graduate Diploma in Valuation, 7
Graduated payment mortgages (GPMs), 487
Greenberg, Michael, 342
Greer, Gaylon E., 109, 145, 171, 199, 223
Grenadier, Steven R., 283
Grissom, Terry V., 399, 436
Gross Domestic Product (GDP), 13
Gross income multipliers (GIM), 93, 97, 427–428
Gross leasable area (GLA), 182
Gross lease, 246
Gross rent multiplier (GRM), 392, 393–394, 395
  analysis, 403–405
Gross sales price, 132, 134
Ground leases, 249–250
Growth limits, 313–314
Growth management, 313–314
Growth moratorium, 314
Growth rates, 219, 415
  for a building, 422–423
  for a site, 425
Grub & Ellis Company, 178
Guarantees, 603
Guidry, Krisandra A., 278
Guttentag, Jack M., 478
Guy, Donald C., 307
Gyourko, Joseph, 213

*H*all, Robert W., 315
Haly, Jack, 163
Hamilton, Bruce W., 6, 20, 293
Han, Jun, 596
Haney, Richard L., 373

Hard costs, 367–368
Harrison, Henry S., 373
Hartley, Robert F., 326
Hartzell, David J., 209
Harvard University, 7
Heilbrun, James, 652
Heitman/JMB Advisory Corp., 228
Hemingway, Richard W., 617
Hendershott, Patric H., 157
Heriot-Watt University, 8
Herskovitz, Michael D., 610
High density of demand, 270
Highest and best use of a property as improved, 332–333
Highest and best use of a vacant site, 331–332
High-rise apartment building, 173–174
Hinds, Dudley S., 666
Hines, Mary Alice, 666
Hines Interest, 184
Hirsch, Warner Z., 241, 293
Historical returns, 167–168
  and real estate, 212–214
Historical securitized returns, REIT-based index of, 166–167
Historical unsecuritized returns, appraisal-based index of, 165–166
Holiday Inns, 701
Holliday Fenoglio Dockery & Gibson, Inc., 456
Holloway, James E., 307
Holmes, Oliver Wendell, 306
Holtzschue, Karl B., 755
Home Depot, 182
Home equity loans, 487–489
  borrowed amount, 488
  closing costs, 489
  guidelines, 489
  interest rates, 488–489
  tax advantages, 489
  types of, 487–488
Home Mortgage Disclosure Act (HMDA) of 1975, 527
Homestead exemption, 646–647
Homestead laws, 623–624
Hoover, Kevin A., 436
Hopkins, Robert, 15
Horizontal equity, 653
Horvitz, Paul M., 528
Hospitality properties, 185
Host Marriott, 594
Hoteling, 179

Housing and Community Development and Government Service Enterprise Act, 527
Housing element market study, 329, 330, 331
Howarth, Robin A., 352
Hudson-Wilson, Susan, 227, 259
Hunter College, 8
Hybrid Index, 167
Hybrid REITs, 159
Hylton, Richard D., 555

*I*bbotson Associates, 11–12
IBM, 253
Illinois at Urbana-Champaign, University of, 8
Implied contract, 672
Improvement allowance, 80
Improvements on land
    concerns with, 363–365
    and property rights, 616
Improvements to land, 355
    concerns with, 363–365
    and property rights, 616
Income, 412–414
    and taxation, 111–112
    types of, 111–112
Income capitalization, 87
Income capitalization equation, 412
Income kickers, 542; *See also* Income participation
Income participation, 553; *See also* Income kickers
Income-producing property
    appraising, 428
    financing, 553
    types of, 74
Income property mortgages, 455–456
    and construction financing, 456
    existing properties, 455
    important clauses in, 460
Incurable functional obsolescence (IFO), 392
Independent variables, and multiple regression analysis (MRA), 385
Indexed rental, 247
Indiana University, 7
Indicated value, 376
Indirect costs; *See* Soft costs
Individuals, and property transactions, 281–282
Industrial parks, 181
Industrial properties, 180–181

Industrial warehouse design, 180
Infinite-life REITs, 159
Inflows of money, 30
Information costs, 265
Information standard, for real estate markets, 163
Information technology, and real estate markets, 277
Infrastructure, 356–357
Inheritance, 621
Input linkage, 269
Installment sale, 138, 541
Institute of Real Estate Management (IREM), 177
Institutions, 10–11
    definition, 10
Insurance clause, of mortgage contracts, 458
Intent test, for fixtures, 619
Intercontinental Hotels, 701
Interest, 28–29, 30–35, 36
Interest escalation, of mortgage contracts, 458
Interest expense (INT), 122, 130, 131
Interest on interest, 37
Interest-only loans, 44, 474
Interest-only mortgages, 475
Interest rate buydowns, 483–484, 492
    inflated prices of, 484
    payment shock of, 484
Interest rates, and adjustable rate mortgages (ARMs), 480
Internal mobility, 344
Internal rate of return (IRR), 49–52, 53, 84, 96, 135, 219, 220, 336, 548, 549, 550, 551, 560; *See also* Yield-to-maturity
    analysis, 215
    compared to net present value (NPV), 86–87
    effect of debt and taxes on, 136
    effect of debt on, 90–92
    method, 84–86
    sensitivity of, 219
Internal Revenue Code, 108, 630
    Section 1031, 138–139
International Association of Assessing Officers, 431
International Association of Assessing Officials (IAAO), 656
Inverse condemnation, 306
Invesco Realty Advisors, 228
Investment activity, 109

Investment analysis, 46–52
    present-value measures, 46–48
    yield measures, 48–52
Investment banks, lending by, 598–599
Investment decisions, 71–98
    cash flow forecasting, 76–81
    cash proceeds from sale, 81–82
    income property investments, 74–75
    measuring value and returns, 82–87
    mortgage financing, 88–92
    other criteria, 92–98
    purchasers as investors, 75
    real estate analysis, 72–74
    varying the assumptions, 98
Investment-grade rating, 588
Investment perspective, 17–18
    framework, 18
Investment philosophy, 72–73
Investment policies, 73–74
Investment property, 108–110
Investment specific dealer, 109
Investment strategy, 72–74
    investment objectives, 73
    investment philosophy, 72–73
    investment policies, 73–74
Investment value, 26
Investor objectives, 73
Investors, and borrowing, 90–92

*J*acob, David P., 558, 610
Jaffe, Austin J., 27, 145, 223, 238
Jahanian, Shirin, 278
Japan Air Lines, 701
Jefferies, Spencer, 157
Johns Hopkins University, 8
Joint tenancy, 626–627
Joint ventures, 164, 545, 553
Jordan, Bradford D., 237
Judicial foreclosure rules, 461–462
Jumbo loans, 472
Junior mortgage, 450

*K*ane, Alex, 215, 218, 223
Kane, Edward J., 157
Kapplin, Steven D., 189
Karp, James, 467, 639, 687
Keim, Donald B., 213
Kelley, Edward N., 259
Kelly, Hugh F., 436
Key Trends in the External Environment of Commercial Real Properties, 277
Kickbacks, 748

Kim, Kyung-Hwan, 283
Kincheloe, Stephen C., 399
Klayman, Elliot, 467, 639, 687
Koll, 229
Kondo Sangyo, 701
Korngold, Gerald, 660
Kramer, John L., 137, 145, 150, 489
Kratovil, Robert, 639, 664, 687
Kroll, Mark, 369
Krueckeberg, Donald A., 342

*L*and
  investments to improve, 12–13
  new uses, 273
  proper description of, 674–683
  purchase and development financing, 561–562
Land acquisition loans, 560
Land contracts, and purchase money mortgage, 452
Land development, 355
  conceptual scheme for, 334
Land development loans, 560
Land leases; *See* Ground leases
Landlord-tenant laws, 240, 244–246
  types of, 245–246
Landmarks, 675
The Landmarks Group, 233
Land purchase option, 562
Land substitution, 267–268
Land tenure system, 615
Land use, 295–309
  categories, 295–296
  and externalities, 297
  local controls, 302
  the market solution, 296
  private restrictions, 297–300
  public planning for, 300–304
  zoning administration, 308–309
  zoning legality, 305–306
  zoning purposes, 304–305
Lapides, Paul D., 189
LaSalle Partners, Ltd., 229
Lawful intent, in contracts, 724
Laws of Agency, 238
Laws of agency, 691–694
  fiduciary responsibilities, 692–693
  real estate agents, 693
  salespersons as subagents, 694
  transaction brokers, 693–694
  types of agents, 692
Lead paint, 315, 316

Leaking underground storage tanks
    (LUSTs), 315, 316
Lease contract, 240
Leased fee estate, 240, 625
Leased fee interests, 250–251
Lease economics, 250–252
Leasehold estate, 240, 626
Leasehold interests, 250–251
Leasehold mortgages, 251
Leases, 11, 674
  nature of, 240–242
  residential, 242–246
  valid and enforceable, 241–242
Lease terms, and commercial property
    financing, 558
Lease-up period, 565, 566
Leasing, versus owning, 254–256
Leasing and capital costs, 80
Legal aspects, of loan application, 556
Legal characteristics, adjustment for,
    381
Legality of objective, 242
Legal perspective, 19
Legal title, 727
Lehman Brothers G/C Index, 167, 213
Lender, role in closing, 747
Lender frenzy, 156
Lender yield, 50–52
Lessees, 241
  considerations for, 248
  right to assign and sublet, 244
Lessors, 241
  considerations for, 248
  payment of expenses, 246–252
  right of entry, 244, 246
Letter of opinion, 666
Letters of credit, 603
Letters of intent, 361
Levy, David E., 311
Licensed appraiser, 430
Licensing laws
  for brokerage business, 695–698
  infractions, 697–698
Lien, 637
Lien theories, 446–447
Lien-theory states, 447, 450
Life estates, 623–624
  legal, 623–625
  ordinary, 623
Life insurance companies (LICS), 523
  and conventional passthroughs,
    587–588
Life-of-loan caps, 479

Like-kind exchanges, 138–139
Limited liability company, 152–153
Limited liability corporation, 161
Limited partner, 151, 154
Limited partnerships, 111, 151, 153,
    154, 161, 181
Lincoln Properties Co., 229
Ling, David C., 157, 470
Linkage, and location decisions, 269
Linkages, 379–380
Lintner, John, 218
Liou, Thomas, 323
Liquidated damages, 740
Liquidity, 152
Listing contracts, 674, 693, 702–710
  provisions, 705–710
  types of, 703–705
L.J. Melody & Co., 228
Loan, maximum amount, 559–560
Loan amortization, 43–46
  schedule, 43
Loan application, evaluating, 558
Loan balance, calculating, 45–46
Loan prospector, 386
Loan provisions, common, 540–541
Loan servicing, 511–512
Loan size, 494–495, 548
Loan submission package, 325,
    554–557
  appraisal report, 556–557
  cash flow estimates, 556
  channels, 557
  feasibility study, 557
  legal aspects, 556
  loan application, 555–557
  property description, 556
Loan-to-value ratio (LTVR), 95–96,
    97, 418, 470, 481, 490, 517, 539,
    545, 549, 551
  and default probability estimation,
    602
  lender's maximum allowable, 559
  maximum, 546–547
Loan underwriting process, 554
Loan underwriting standards, 524–525
Location, 263–272, 379–380
  commercial and industrial, 269–272
  and commercial property financing,
    558
  residential decisions, 268–269
  theory, 266–268
Locational adjustments, 406–408
Location monopoly, 263

Location quotients, 340–342
Location theory, 266–268
Lochmoeller, Donald C., 373
Lockout provisions, 540
    of income property mortgages, 458
London Interbank Offered Rate (LI-
    BOR), 592
Long-lived physical deterioration, 391
Long-term capital gain (LTCG), 136,
    137
Long-term capital loss (LTCL), 137
Lotus 1–2–3 , 61–68, 98
Low density of demand, 270
Low-income housing, tax incentives
    of, 129
Lump sum, 30
    future value of, 57–58, 63–64
    present value of, 59–60, 66
Lusht, Kenneth L., 285, 399, 436
Lusk, Harold F., 639

*M*a, Christopher K., 449
Machi, Donna, 15
Mahoney, Peter E., 526
Maintenance, 245–246
    four types of activities, 237
Maisel, Sherman J., 610
Malizia, Emil E., 352
Management contracts, 237–240
Maniscalco, Robert A., 238
Manning, Christopher A., 254
Manolakas, Thomas G., 145, 149, 152,
    171
Mapp, Thomas W., 687
Marcus, Alan J., 215, 218, 223
Margin, and adjustable rate mortgages
    (ARMs), 478
Marginal tax rate, versus average tax
    rate, 113–115
Marino, Vivian, 488
Maris, Brian A., 282
Marketability studies, 335
Market-adjusted normal sale price,
    378–379, 382, 383
Market analysis, 337–346
    case study, 399–409
    correlating supply and demand,
      345–346
    defining the problem, 337
    delineating the market area, 338
    establishing supply conditions,
      344–345
    estimating the demand, 338–344

Market analysis—Cont.
    evaluating constraints, 337–338
    ignoring the findings, 327
    major errors of, 326
Market area, 338
Market conditions, 383
    and appraisers, 378
Market conditions adjustment, 406
Market disequilibrium, 365–366
Market equilibrium, 365–366
Marketing, and development process,
    364–365
Market perspective, 18–19
Market rent, 75
Market risk premium (MRP), 218
Market segmentation, for real estate
    brokers, 698–699
Market studies, 325–335
    general, 328–331
    site-specific, 327, 331–335
    types of, 327, 328
Market transactions, analysis of, 379
Market value, 26, 375
Market value estimation, 368
Market yield, 576
Markowitz, Harry, 210
Marshall, Alfred, 5
Martin, Robert S., 436
Massachusetts Institute of Technology,
    8
Master in Design Studies, 7
Master of Arts, 7
Master of Arts in Urban and Regional
    Planning, 7
Master of Business Administration/Ju-
    rum Doctor, 7
Master of Management, 7
Master of Philosophy, 7
Master of Planning, 7
Master of Professional Studies, 8
Master of Real Estate, 7
Master of Real Estate and Construc-
    tion Management, 7
Master of Real Estate Development, 7
Master of Regional Planning, 8
Master of Science, 8
Master of Science in Business, 8
Master of Science in Land Develop-
    ment, 8
Master of Science in Land Manage-
    ment, 8
Master of Science in Real Estate, 8

Master of Science in Real Estate De-
    velopment, 8
Master of Science in Urban Land Ap-
    praisal, 8
Master of Science/Master of Architec-
    ture, 8
Master of Urban and Regional Plan-
    ning, 8
Master of Urban Planning, 8
Master of Urban Planning, Design,
    and Development, 8
Maturity imbalance problem, 476
Maximum debt service, 559
McClelland, Harold, 656
McCrory, Don, 184
McDonald, John F., 278
McGill, Gary A., 470
McKenzie, Dennis J., 292
McKenzie, Martha, 486
McLoughlin, Daniel P., 467
McMahan, John, 189, 338
Mean; *See* Expected value
Mean-variance analysis, 203
Mechanic's lien, 450
Mellon Bank Corp., 561
Meltzer, Allan, 515
Merrill Lynch, 587
Merton, Robert, 10
Metes-and-bounds, 675–677
Metropolitan Life, 555
MGM/UA, 701
Micelli, Thomas J., 719
Michaelson, Connie, 342
Michigan, University of, 7
Michigan State University, 8
Microsoft Corporation, 148
Mid-rise apartment, 174
Miglin-Beitler Developments, 561
Miles, Mike E., 15, 373
Millage rate, 645
Miller, Norman G., 57, 104
Mills, 645
Mills, Edwin S., 6, 20, 293
Mini-perm loan, 564, 565
Miniwarehouses, 181
Mitsubishi, 701
Mixed-asset portfolio, 212
Modigliano, Franco, 503, 532, 584,
    610
Monuments; *See* Landmarks
Monuments method; *See* Metes-and-
    bounds
Moody's Investor Services, 588, 599

Morey, Scott, 259
Morrill, William K., Jr., 162, 209
Mortgage-backed securities (MBSs), 163, 444, 448, 471, 472, 494, 514, 518, 519, 520, 521, 522, 547, 573–606
  commercial, 285, 537
  commercial market, 594–596
  and commercial mortgage securitization, 596–599
  guaranteed by Ginnie Mae, 523
  mortgage securitization, 573–575
  and passthrough securities, 580–588
  role of rating agencies, 599–603
  and the secondary market, 575–580
  securities, 603–606
  sequential pay structures, 588–592
  valuing, 592–593
  valuing individual mortgages, 575–580
Mortgage bankers, 510, 511–514
  loan commitment and funding, 511
  regulation, 514
  sales of mortgage loans, 512
  servicing, 511–512
  sources of revenue, 514
Mortgage Bankers Association, 495
Mortgage brokers, 510, 514–515
  as intermediaries, 514
  nongovernment-sponsored lenders, 515
Mortgage capitalization rate, 418
Mortgage constant, 60–61, 418
Mortgage contract, 674
  extension, 450–452
Mortgage documentation, 456–460
  common clauses, 457–458
  requirements of, 457
  residential, 458–460
Mortgage equity analysis, 417–419
Mortgage finance perspective, 19
Mortgage financing, costs of, 123–124
Mortgage Index, 167
Mortgage insurance premium (MIP), 516
Mortgage joint ventures, 358
Mortgage lending, and bias, 528
Mortgage markets, integration with capital markets, 449
Mortgage menu, 470
Mortgage options, comparing, 493–494

Mortgage payments
  calculating, 42–43
  calculating with spreadsheets, 67–68
Mortgage pipe-line, 512
Mortgage rates, versus T–bond rates, 449
Mortgage ratio; *See* Loan-to-value ratio
Mortgage REITs, 159, 448
Mortgages, 11, 441–464, 469–498, 505–528
  and adjustable rate mortgages (ARMs), 476–480
  borrower and lender relationships, 449–456, 461–464
  borrower's loan decisions, 489–498
  capital flow to, 448–449
  clauses found in documents, 456–460
  common loan provisions, 540–541
  contract with deed of trust, 447
  conventional fixed-payment, 471–476
  convertible, 546
  definition, 441
  depository lenders, 506–510
  with equity participation, 542–546
  government-sponsored programs, 515–518
  income property, 539
  international perspectives, 442–444
  lender's decisions, 524–528
  life, 445
  nondepository lenders, 510–515
  other types, 482–489
  primary versus secondary market, 470–471
  private mortgage insurance (PMI), 481–482
  recasting, 463
  residential financing, 506
  sale of, 463–464
  secondary market for residential, 518–524
  securitization, 573–575
  story of, 444–445
  theory, 445–448
  types of permanent, 539–540
Mossin, Jan, 218
Mueller, Glenn R., 162, 209, 352
Muhlebach, Richard F., 259
Multifactor asset-pricing model, 218

Multiple listing service (MLS), 700, 705
Multiple regression analysis (MRA), 384–388, 395
  for apartment rents, 387
  application of model, 388
  equation for, 385
Multipliers, 92, 93–94
Muth, Richard F., 268, 271
Mutual assent, 667
  in contracts, 724
  defects to, 725
Mutual funds, Ginnie Mae, 585
Mutual Mortgage Insurance Fund, 516
Myers, Stewart C., 10, 20

*N*aive diversification, 210
National Association of Homebuilders, 355
National Association of Independent Fee Appraisers, 431
National Association of Master Appraisers, 431
National Association of Real Estate Appraisers, 431
National Association of Real Estate Investment Managers (NAREIM), 163
National Association of Real Estate Investment Trusts (NAREIT), 212, 213
National Association of Real Estate Investment Trusts (NAREIT) Index, 165
National Association of Realtors (NAR), 698
National Association of Review Appraisers, 431
National Council of Real Estate Investment Fiduciaries (NCREIF), 163, 165, 175, 191, 212
  Classic Property Index (NCPI), 165, 166, 213
National Credit Union Administration Board, 508
National Credit Union Share Insurance Fund, 508
National Housing Act, 516, 522
National Register of Historic Places, 129
Natural price, 5
Natural vacancy, 274–275
Nebraska at Omaha, University of, 7

Negative amortization, 487
Negative externalities, 297
Negative taxable income, 114
Negotiated posted-offer transactions, 285
Neighborhood center, 181
Neoclassical economics, 5–10
Neoclassical location theory, 267–268
Net, 246
Net contract rent, 275–278
Net effective rent, 275–278
Net income multiplier (NIM), 93, 96, 97
Net lease, 177, 246
Net listing, 704
Net-net lease, 246
Net-net-net lease, 246
Net operating income (NOI), 79–80, 82, 89, 92, 96, 97, 122, 123, 130, 131, 229, 230, 238, 332, 412–414, 415, 416, 547, 548, 550, 559, 602
    allocating between building and site, 426–427
    growth rate, 422–423
Net present value (NPV), 47, 49, 53, 96, 135, 219, 220, 336
    to analyze refinancing, 496–497
    compared to internal rate of return (IRR), 86–87
    effect of debt and taxes on, 136
    effect of debt on, 90–92
    method, 83–84
Net sale proceeds, 132, 133, 134
Net selling price (NSP), 82
Netzer, Dick, 652, 654, 660
Newcastle Upon Tyne, University of, 7
Newman and Associates, Inc., 456
New South Wales, University of, 7
New World Development, 701
New York City Landmarks Preservation Commission, 311
New York Life, 555
New York Stock Exchange (NYSE), 10, 167, 429, 520
New York University, 8
Nikko Hotels, 701
Nippon Credit Bank Ltd., 164
No-equity home loan, 488
Noisy prices, 287–288
Nomura Securities International, 456, 600
Nonconforming conventional loan, 472

Nondiversifiable portfolio risk, 203, 209
Nonfreehold estates, 621, 625–626
Nonjudicial foreclosure rules, 461–462
Nonlabor income; *See* Unearned income
Nonrealty items, 381
Nonrecourse financing, 446, 538–539
Normal sale price, 382, 383
Norman, Emily J., 214
North Carolina at Chapel Hill, University of, 7, 8
North Texas, University of, 7, 8
Northwestern University, 7
Note, and commercial property financing, 538–539
Nothaft, Frank E., 275
Nourse, Hugh O., 20

Occupancies, 332
Occupational Safety and Health Act, 314
Offer, 725
Offer and acceptance, 242
Office buildings, 176–180
    classes of, 176–177
    supply and demand factors, 179
Office of Secondary Market Examination and Oversight (OSMEO), 522
Office rent, 278
Officer's deeds, 669, 670
Off-price centers, 182
Ohio State University, 7, 8
O'Mara, W. Paul, 373
Open-ended loans, 455, 564, 565
Open-end lines of credit, 487–488
Open-end REITs, 159
Open listing, 703–704
Operating expense ratio (OER), 94–95, 97
Operating expenses (OE), 79, 94, 131, 219
    versus capital improvements, 123
Operating income (OI), 97
Options contracts, 361
Oral contracts, 726
Ordinary annuity (OA), 30
Ordinary income, versus capital gain income, 136–137
Ordway, Nicholas, 666
Outflows of money, 30, 36
Outhred, David R., 436
Outlet centers, 182

Output linkage, 269
Outright sale, 132–133
Overage rent, 247
Overall capitalization rate, 415–420
    direct market extraction, 417
    methods, 420–421
    mortgage equity analysis, 417–419
    single-factor asset pricing model, 419–420
Overall cap rate (R), 97
Overall yield, 421
Overcollateralization, 603
Owner-occupied homes, 15
Owners, rights and obligations, 241
Ownership forms
    comparing, 153–154
    comparison summary, 153
Ownership-in-place, and land ownership, 617
Owning, versus leasing, 254–256

Pacetti, Eileen, 259
Pacific Gas & Electric Company, 149
Pacific Telesis Group, 149
Package mortgages, 484
Pagliari, Joseph L., Jr., 227, 259
Paine Webber Groups, 701
Paired sales analysis, 380
Parness, Stanley, 649
Parole evidence rule, 722, 726
Partially amortized mortgages, 474
Partially amortizing mortgages, 475
Partially specified fund, 156
Partial tax shelter, 130
Participation certificates (PCs), 586–587
Participation mortgages, 542–545
Partnership, types of, 629–630
Partnership Profiles Inc., 157
Par value, 576
Passive active income, 112
Passive activity loss (PAL), 114, 120–122
Passive activity loss restrictions, 112
Passive investors, 72
Pass-through clauses, 247
Passthrough securities, 580–588
    agency passthroughs, 584–587
    conventional, 587–588
Patchin, Peter J., 323
Patent, 669
Pauley, Keith R., 162, 209
Payment in full, of mortgage contracts, 461

Peiser, Richard B., 373
Penn Central Transportation Co, Inc., 311
Penn State University, 7, 8
Pennsylvania, University of, 7
Pennsylvania Coal Company v. Mahon, 306
Pension funds, 162–163
Pension Real Estate Association (PREA), 163
Percentage leases, 183–184
Percentage rent, 247
Percentage rental, 247
Perfect, Steven B., 287
Performance standards, of comprehensive plans, 303–304
Periodic tenancy, 625
Perk extraction, 238
Permanence potential, 234
Permanent loan, 454
Personal performance, assignment of, 738
Personal property, 128
Personal residence, 108–110
Personalty, 617
Phase I EVA, 318
Phase III EVA, 318
Phase II EVA, 318
Philip Morris Corporation, 311
Phillips, Lawrence C., 137, 145, 150, 171, 489
Phyrr, Stephen, 145, 189, 223
Physical characteristics, and paired sales analysis, 380–381
Physical deterioration, 390–391
long-lived, 391
Physical rights, to real estate, 616
Pineiro, John de Clef, 249
PITI, 458
Planned amortization classes (PACs), 591
Planned unit developments (PUDs), 303, 312
Planning, and property values, 310
Planning organization, 301
Plat books, 678
Plattner, Robert H., 306
PM Realty Group, 229
Pogodzinski, J. M., 281
Point of beginning, 675
Point system, 303, 314
Police power, in real estate, 632
Polychlorinated bephenyls (PCBs), 315, 316, 317

Pooled equity investments, 162
Pooled investments, 165
Population, estimating future, 340
Population composition, and real estate markets, 277
Population growth, and real estate markets, 277
Portfolio, choosing optimal, 209–212
Portfolio income, 111–112
Portfolio lenders, 510
Portfolio management, 235–236
Portfolio managers, 226, 227
Portfolio refinancing, 597–598
Portman, John, 364
Positive externalities, 297
Positive financial leverage, 469
Posner, Kenneth A., 249
Potential gross income (PGI), 76, 131
Power centers, 182
Power of attorney, 724
Power-of-sale clauses, 447
and mortgage contracts, 462
Predetermined use studies, 333–335
PREEF Funds, 230
Premium, 576
Prepayment, and commercial property financing, 554
Prepayment clause, of mortgages, 457–458
Prepayment penalties, 541
Prescriptive easements, 670
Present value factor (PVF), 84
Present value (PV), 30, 35, 36, 38, 39, 40–42, 85
of an annuity, 60
of a lump sum, 59–60, 66
measures, 46–48
of a series of level payments, 66–67
Price, and multiple regression analysis (MRA), 385
Price discovery, 289
Price/yield relationship, 604–606
Primary data, 339–340
Primary mortgage market, 444, 470–471
depository lenders in, 506–510
Principal, 691
Principal amortization (PA), 122, 123
Principles of Real Estate (Fisher), 6
Private debt, 448
Private equity, 448
Private grants, 664
Private mortgage insurance (PMI), 481–482

Private offerings, 155
Private real estate markets, return performance of, 165–168
Private REITs, 161, 162
Probability distribution, 192, 194
continuous, 194
discrete, 193, 194
Product homogeneity, 263
Production, factors of, 275
Profitability ratios, 92–94
PRO-JECT, 98
Projection, 342
Project-specific risk, 197–201
coefficient of variation, 199–200
and standard deviation, 198–199
use of subjective probabilities, 200–201
and variance, 197–199
Promissory note, 446
Property, renovating and repositioning, 231–232
Property-appraisal appeals board, 648
Property characteristics, 377, 379–381
Property description, 556
Property growth rate, 422–423
estimating for building, 422–423
Property management, 228
and commercial property financing, 558
Property managers, 110, 226
administration, 234–235
and cash flow, 229–232
and cash flow risk, 235–236
Property rights, 3, 9, 25, 26, 615
cases in, 307
Property tax liens, 450
Property type
demand and supply for, 276
and investment, 74
Property type diversification, 208
Property values, 310, 392
Proration, 743–744
Prospectuses, 155
The Prudential Insurance Co. of America, 149, 456, 549, 701
Prudential Preferred Properties, 700
Prudential Property Investment Separate Account (PRISA), 73
Public grant, 663
Public limited partnerships, 154, 165
Public offerings, 155
Public real estate markets, return performance of, 165–168
Public real estate syndication, 156

Public record databases, 665
Public Securities Association (PSA)
    model, 592, 593
Purchase money mortgages (PMMs),
    451–452, 482–483, 484
    and land contract, 452
Purchasers, as investors, 75

*Q*intex Group, 701
Qualitative review, and rating agen-
    cies, 602
Quan, Daniel C., 281, 285
Quantitative review, and rating agen-
    cies, 602
Quantity survey method, 389
Quebec, University of, 7
Quigg, Laura, 610
Quigley, John M., 281
Quitclaim deed, 669

*R*abianski, Joseph S., 259, 344, 352
Rabin, Sol L., 352
Racster, Ronald, 352
Radon, 315, 316–317
Ramada Inns, 701
Range lines, 679
Ratcliff, Richard U., 293
Rate caps, 479–480
Rating agencies, 599–603
    for CMBS issues, 599–602
    credit enhancement, 602–603
    qualitative review of, 602
    quantitative review of, 602
Ratio analysis, limitations of, 96–98
Ravines Resort and Country Club, 701
Reading, University of, 7, 8
Real assets, 11
Real estate
    definition of, 16
    importance of value, 16
Real estate agents, 693
Real estate careers, 14
Real estate commission, 695
Real estate corporations, 448
Real estate creation, 355–360
    development and construction busi-
        nesses, 355–356
    development process, 360–365
    development team formation,
        357–360
    relationships with consumers,
        356–357

Real Estate Data Incorporated (REDI),
    665
Real estate developer, becoming, 369
Real estate diversification risk, strate-
    gies, 208–209
Real estate finance, four quadrants of,
    448
Real estate investments, decisions in,
    27–28
Real Estate Investment Trust (REIT),
    17, 72, 110, 111, 112, 147, 151–
    152, 153, 159–161, 212, 213,
    218, 284, 288, 357, 419, 420,
    594, 630
    equity, 282
    exchange-traded, 162
    initial public offering (IPO) market,
        160
    publicly traded, 165
    purchases with equity capital, 285
Real Estate Investment Trust (REIT)
    Act of 1960, 151, 159–160
Real estate management, 8, 225–256
    contracts, 236–252
    corporate asset management,
        252–256
    importance of, 225–228
    value perspective of, 228–236
Real estate markets
    in China, 280
    and location, 263–272
    psychology of, 283–284
    trends affecting, 277
Real estate occupations, certification,
    698
Real estate operating companies
    (REOCs), 165
Real estate partnerships, comeback of,
    157
Real estate prices, default and, 549
Real Estate Report, 216
Real Estate Research Corporation
    (RERC), 216
Real estate risk, 212–214
Real Estate Settlement and Procedures
    Act (RESPA), 493, 735, 747–748
Real estate syndicate, 154–159
    business environment of, 156–158
    role of syndicator, 158–159
    types, 155–156
Real estate valuation, 26–27
Realized return, 92
Realized yield, 578–579

Real property, 18, 128
    classes of, 108–110
    proper descriptions of, 674–683
Real property rights, 615–637
    definition, 615
    estates in, 621–626
    legal property rights, 619–620
    nonpossessionary property rights,
        636
    versus personal property rights,
        617–619
    physical rights to real estate,
        616–617
    property values, 620–621
    public and private limits, 631–637
    rights among co-owners, 626–631
Real property taxation, 641–656
    appealing taxation, 655
    criteria for evaluating, 650–656
    disadvantages of, 651–653
    fairness of, 653–656
    mechanics of, 644–650
    in other countries, 642, 643
    United States history of, 643–644
Real property transfer, 663–683
    contracts for, 671–674
    descriptions of property, 674–683
    evidence and conveyance of owner-
        ship, 663–671
    importance of, 663
Realty, 617
Receiving area, of development rights,
    310
Reconciliation, and estimating value,
    428–429
Reconstructed operating statement, 76
Recorded plat map, 677–678
Recording documents, in contract clos-
    ing, 745
Recourse financing, 446, 538–539
Recovery fund, 697
Referee's deeds, 670
Refinancing, decision, 495–497
Regional centers, 182
Reid, Paul, 495
Reid, Tanis, 238
Reinvestment risk, 541
REIT IPOs, 160
Relationship-of-the-parties test, for
    fixtures, 619
Reliction, ownership rights through,
    671
Religious ownership, 615

Remaining economic life (REL), 422

Remaining mortgage balance (RMB), 90, 133

REMAX, 700

René, David, 639

Renegotiation rental, 247

Rent, 5, 75, 273, 275–278
advance, 245
definition, 9
and multiple regression analysis (MRA), 385
withholding, 240

Rental income, 75

Rent loss, 392

Rent roll, 77

Repairs, 245–246

Replacement cost, 287, 389

Replacement reserves, 123

Reproduction cost, 388, 389, 405–406
of building, 391

Reservation prices, 282

Reserve for replacements and other nonrecurring expenses, 413–414

Reserve funds, 603

Residential appraisers, 386

Residential brokerage, 700–701

Residential Cost Handbook, 405, 406

Residential leases, 242–246
landlord-tenant laws, 244–246
maintenance and repairs, 243, 245–246
possession and use of property, 242–243

Residential property, linkages for, 379

Residential rental property, 173–176
definitions, 173–174
demand for, 174–175
investment prospects, 175–176

Resolution Trust Corporation (RTC), 282, 285, 595

Resource Conservation and Recovery Act, 314

Restrictions, on land use, 297–300

Restrictive covenants, 297–300, 634–636
on adjacent parcel, 636

Resyndication, 159

Retail establishments, 181–184
attracting shoppers, 184
characteristics of shopping centers, 183

Retail rent, 278

Return, in real estate investment, 27

Return on investment (ROI), 421; *See also* Yield

Reverse annuity mortgages (RAMs), 484–486

Reversions, 81, 241

Ricardo, David, 266

Richins, Marsha L., 718

Right of entry, 244, 246

Right of exclusive possession and control, 620

Right of quiet enjoyment, 620

Right of reentry estate, 623

Right of survivorship, 627

Rights of disposition, 620

Riparian rights, for landowners, 617

Risk, 191–220, 192
attitudes toward, 195
choosing an optimal portfolio, 209–212
of development, 369
management, 201–202
portfolio concept of, 203–209
project-specific, 197–201
and real estate, 212–214
in real estate investment, 27
specification of preferences, 195–197
and valuation decisions, 215–220

Risk-adjusted discount rate, 215–217

Risk-averse investor, 195

Risk-free rate, 83, 218

Risk-loving investor, 195

Risk management, 201–202, 236
avoiding risky projects, 201–202
and diversification, 202
hedging, 201–202
insurance, 201–202

Risk-neutral investor, 195

Risk-weighted assets, 508

Robert A. Stranger & Co., 156

Roberts, John, 15

Rockefeller Center, 701

Root, Linda Crawford, 352, 385, 399, 436

Rosenberg, Sidney B., 238

Ross, Stephen A., 87, 223, 237

Roulac, Stephen E., 239, 323

The RREEF Funds, 228

*S*afe Drinking Water Control Act, 314

Safe permanent loan, 565

Safeway Developers, 327

Saint Cloud State University, 7

Sale, conditions of, 377

Sale-leasebacks, 545–546
deals, 253–254
land, 546

Sale prices, 279

Sales comparison approach, 376–384, 400–403
adjustment grid, 383
adjustments, 376–384
indicated value, 385
market analysis for adjustments, 400–403
reconciliation, 384

Salesperson license, 695

Salomon Brothers, 277, 514, 587, 594

Sandburg Property Management, 227, 228

San Diego State University, 7, 8

Sandwich leasehold, 244, 245

Sass, Tim R., 281

Satisfaction of mortgage, 743

Savings and loan associations (S&Ls), 507–509, 521, 580
and conventional passthroughs, 587–588
debacle, 507
failure of, 476

Savings Association Insurance Fund (SAIF), 508

Savings banks (SBs), 508

Schallheim, James S., 252

Schottlekotte, Suzie, 486

Schwab, Stephen M., 252

Schwanke, Dean, 373

S corporation, 149–150, 153, 154, 161

Sears Roebuck, 149

Secondary data, 340

Secondary market mortgages, 444, 470–471, 518–524
and life insurance companies, 523
other purchasers, 523–524
valuing individual mortgages in, 575–580

Section 1231 assets, tax treatment for, 137

Sections, in surveys, 679, 681–683

Section 203 loans, 516

Securities, 603–606
structuring CMBS issues, 604
valuation, 604–606

Securitization, 573–575
importance of, 574
and secondary markets, 574–575

Securitized market, 284
  and asset market, 288–289
Seibu/Saison, 701
Sekitei, 701
Seller default, 740–741
Sellers, rights and obligations of, 722–723
Sellers' expenses, in closing, 745
Seller's statement, 748
Selling expenses (SE), 82, 132, 134
Selling price (SP), 52, 82
Sending area, of development rights, 310
Senior Housing, 187
Senior/subordinate structure, 588
Sensitivity analysis, 218–220
Sequential pay securities, 588–592
  collateralized mortgage obligation, 589
  responses to prepayment risk, 590–592
Service industries, 340
Servient estate, 633
Shaff, Michael E., 152
Sharpe, William E., 218
Shearer, Kenneth A., 239
Shell, Jeffrey, 178
Sheriff's deeds, 669, 670
Shiller, Robert J., 283
Shilling, James D., 175
Shimizu Construction Co., 164
Shirking, 238
Shopping centers
  characteristics of, 183
  leases, 249
Short-lived items, 391
Short-term capital gain (STCG), 137
Short-term capital loss (STCL), 137
Sign ordinances, 308
Simon, David, 184
Simon Property Group, 184
Simple income capitalization, 87–88
Simple linear projection technique, 341–342
Single-factor model, 217
Single-family homes, 12, 13
Single-family residential mortgages, 453–455
  and existing properties, 453
Sinking fund factor, 37, 58–59, 65–66
Sirmans, C. F., 27, 145, 175, 223, 278, 282, 718
Sirmans, G. Stacy, 214, 278, 503, 532, 570, 610

Site analysis, 361
Site plan, 308
Site selection, 361
Site-specific market studies, 327, 331–335
Site valuation, 406, 422–427
Site value, 388
Sludge, 315
Smart diversification, 210
Smith, Adam, 5
Smith, Charles, 369
Smith, David A., 315, 323
Smith, Halbert C., 352, 377, 385, 399, 436
Smith, Marc T., 323
Snyder, James C., 322
Soft costs, 367–368
Sole ownership, 153
Sole proprietorships, 111, 147–148
Sony Corporation, 701
South Carolina Supreme Court, 307
Southern California, University of, 7, 8
Southern Methodist University, 7
Space, value of, 3–4
Space market, 272–284
  functions, 272–273
  natural vacancy, 274–275
  in an office market, 275
  rents, 275–278
  supply and demand, 274–275
Spec homes, 454
Special agent, 692
Special assessments, 648–649
Specialty shopping centers, 182
Special warranty deed, 668–669
Speculative bubble, 283
Spink, Frank H., Jr., 373
Spread, 579–580
Standard deduction, 116
Standard deviation, 198–199, 212, 213
Standard error (SE), 386, 387
Standard & Poor's, 445, 588, 599
Standard & Poor's 500 Index, 167, 213, 419
Standards for Real Estate Transactions, 730
Standby forward commitments, 513
State-certified appraisers, 430
Statutory redemption, 649
  and mortgage contracts, 462
Step leases, 247
Stiglitz, Joseph E., 283
Stone, Charles A., 491

Straight-line method, of depreciating real estate, 126–128
Straight-term mortgages; *See* Interest-only mortgages
Strategic real estate plans, 149
Strip center; *See* Neighborhood center
Subagency, 694
Subcontractors, 359
Subdivision ordinance, 308
Subjective probabilities, 200–201
Subjective probability distribution, 192
Subject property, 200
Subject to the mortgage, 451
Subject to transactions, and mortgage contracts, 463
Sublet, 244
Submarkets, identifying, 698
Substantial improvements, 128
Suchman, Diane R., 373
Suh, Seoung Hwan, 283
Sumitomo Bank Ltd., 164
Sun Oil, 149
Superfund legislation, 314
Superior liens, 450
Super-regional centers, 182
Supply, 5–6, 9
Supply and demand
  factors for property types, 276
  in the space market, 274–275
Surveys, 675
Syndicate, 154–155
Syndication process, 158–159
Syndicators; *See also* General partners
  role of, 158–159

*T*able factor (TF), 35, 36, 37, 39, 41
Take-out commitment, 563, 565
Takings Clause, 307
Taxable gain (TG), 132, 134, 135
Taxable income (TI), 122, 130, 131, 134
Tax-appraisal appeals board, 648
Tax assessor, 647
Taxation, 632
  on income, 111–112
Tax base, 644
Tax burden analysis, 648
Tax calculation, 123
Tax capitalization, 651–652
Tax certificates, 649
Tax credits, 128–129
Tax delinquencies, buying property for, 650

Tax depreciation, 109
net benefits of, 134–135
Tax due on sales (TDS), 132, 133, 134, 135
Taxes
effect on values and returns, 135–136
evaluating property tax, 650–656
nonpayment of, 649–650
Tax-exempt properties, 646
Tax liability (TAX), 122, 130, 131
calculating, 647
Tax rate (TR), 112–115, 122, 130, 131, 132, 133, 134
determining, 644–645
Tax Reform Act of 1986, 154, 156, 159
Tax shelter, 120, 130–132
TCW Realty Advisors, 228
Teaser rate, 479
Tenancies at will, 625
Tenancy at sufferance, 625
Tenancy by the entireties, 627
Tenancy in common, 627
Tenancy in partnership, 629
Tenant compatibility, 234
Tenant finish allowance, 276
Tenant quality, and commercial property financing, 558
Tenants, 242, 273
rights and obligations, 241
Teodorescu, Gabreila, 443
Terminal costs, 271–272
Texas A&M University, 7, 8
Texas at Austin, University of, 7, 8
Texas Eastern, 317
Thematic image, 232
Thomas, Ben, 327
Thompson, Procter, 656
Time line, in value of money, 29–30
Time-sharing, condominiums, 629
Time value of money, 28–46
applying to real estate, 57–61
calculators, 30–35
definitions, 28–30
equations, 30–35
loan amortization, 43–46
problem solving with spreadsheets, 61–68
six operations, 35–43
spreadsheets, 30–35
tables, 30–35
time line, 29–30
Tirtiroglu, Dogan, 266

Title insurance, 665
Titles, 664–669
acquiring by adverse possession, 670
deeds in private grants, 667–669
devise and descent, 669–670
equitable, 727
evidence of good, 665–667
historical perspective, 664–665
legal, 727
from nature, 671
public grants, 669
public records, 664
Title theories, 446–447
Title-theory states, 446
Tobin, James, 287
Torrens system, 666
Torto, Raymond G., 278
Township lines, 679
Townships, 679
Toxic Substances Control Act, 314
Toxic waste, 315
Trade property, 108–110
Trammell Crow Co., 229
Tranches, 589
Transactional characteristics, 376, 377
Transaction brokers, 693–694
Transaction costs, and land use decisions, 296
Transaction price, 382
Transferable development rights (TDRs), 310–312
from Grand Central Station, 310–311
Transportation, and city location, 271–272
Transportation costs, 271–272
Trefzger, Joseph W., 16
Tribal ownership, 615
Triple-net lease, 246
Trump, Donald, 3, 17, 265, 334, 356
Trust deeds; *See* Deeds-of-trust
Truth-in-Lending Act, 493

*U*mbrella partnership REIT, 161
Uncovered construction loans, 455
Underwriting, automated, 526
Undeveloped land, 185–187
Undue influence, 725
Unearned income, 111
Uniform clauses, of mortgage contracts, 459–460
Uniform Partnership Act, 629

Uniform Settlement Statement, 747
Uniform Standards of Professional Appraisal Practice (USPAP), 430
Unilateral contract, 672
United States Census Bureau, 340
United States Congress, 486, 508, 519, 521, 574, 595
United States Constitution, 631, 641
United States Court of Appeals, 302
United States Department of Housing and Urban Development (HUD), 314, 516, 747
United States Department of Interior, 129
United States Environmental Protection Agency (EPA), 314, 315, 316, 317
United States Federal District Court, 302
United States Federal Housing Finance Board (FHFB), 508
United States Internal Revenue Service (IRS), 108, 110, 127, 128, 133, 150, 151
United States Justice Department, 528
United States real estate, and the Japanese, 164
United States Securities and Exchange Commission (SEC), 445, 575
United States Supreme Court, 302, 305, 306, 307
United States Treasury Department, 107, 114, 125, 478, 508, 522
bond rates versus mortgage rates, 449
bonds, 419
Office of Thrift Supervision, 508
securities, 479, 579–580
Unity of interest, 627
Unity of possession, 627
Unity of time, 627
Universal agent, 692
Unsecuritized markets, 284
Unspecified fund, 156
Unsystematic risk; *See* Diversifiable portfolio risk
Urban Land Institute, 7
Urban service areas, 313
Urban spatial economy, 267
Urban sprawl, 176, 310
Use, 383
adjustments for, 381
US West, 149
Utility easements, 299

*V*acancy, 219
supply and demand model, 274–275
Vacancy and collection losses, 78
Valuation, of CMBSs, 604–606
Value, 16, 25–53
capitalization rate, 52–53
investment analysis, 46–52
making investment decisions, 27–28
real estate valuation, 26–27
reconciliation of, 408–409
return and risk, 27
time value of money, 28–46
Value perspective, of real estate, 16
Value-weighted real estate returns, 165
Variability, 192–195
Variable expenses, 79
Variance, 197–199, 308
Vernor, James D., 344
Vertical equity, 653
Veterans Administration (VA), 463, 471, 493
and agency passthroughs, 585–587
guaranteed loans, 518, 522–523
loan guarantees, 516
loan programs, 453, 526, 581, 747
Village of Euclid v. Ambler Realty Co., 305
Virginia, University of, 7
Virginia Commonwealth University, 7, 8
von Thunen, 267

*W*aldorf-Astoria Hotel, 186
Walker, Timothy B., 627
The Wall Street Journal, 200, 284, 488
Wal-Mart, 182, 594
Warehouse, 180
Warehousing, and commercial banks (CBs), 509–510

Water rights, and real estate, 617
Watkins, David E., 209
The Wealth of Nations (Smith), 5
Webb, R. Brian, 166, 168, 213
Weiss, Robert M., 145, 171
Werner, Raymond J., 639, 664, 687, 755
Westerfield, Randolph W., 87, 223, 237
Westinghouse Electric Corporation, 149
Wheaton, William C., 278, 292
Wiedemer, John P., 503, 532
Wiles, Kenneth W., 287
Williams, Bob, 442
Willis, Eugene, 145, 171
Wilson, Albert R., 318
Wincott, Richard D., 352, 436
Wisconsin, University of, 6
Wisconsin at Madison, University of, 8
Wofford, Larry E., 189
World economy, 11–17
investments improving land, 12–13
ownership of America, 13–16
wealth of real estate, 11–12
Wrap-around mortgage, 450–451
Written contracts, 726
Wurtzebach, Charles H., 209, 227, 259
Wynn, Shirley, 477

*Y*ang, Shiawee, 719
The Yarmouth Group, Inc., 228
Yasuda Mutual Life Insurance, 701
Yavas, Abdullah, 719
Yield, 421; *See also* Return on investment (ROI)
expected, 577–578, 579
realized, 578–579
relationship with price, 604–606

Yield maintenance, 458
agreement, 541
Yield measures, 48–52
internal rate of return (IRR), 49–52
Yield on a leasehold, 421
Yield on a mortgage, 421
Yield on building, 421
Yield on equity, 421
Yield on land, 421
Yield on leased fee, 421
Yield spread, 579–580
Yield-to-maturity, 575–577, 579; *See also* Internal rate of return (IRR)
Yinger, John, 651
York University, 7
Youngman, Joan, 660
Yuan, Lim Lan, 280

*Z*ankel, Martin I., 248
Zero-lot-line layouts, 303
Ziff, Donald B., 152
Zissu, Anne-Marie, 491
Zoning, 295, 296
administration, 308–309
bonus maximum, 310
and comprehensive plans, 304
definition of, 304
legality of, 305–306
and property values, 310
public land use, 300
purpose of, 304–305
and transferable development rights (TDRs), 310–312
Zoning laws, 306
Zorn, Peter M., 526